A WORLD HISTORY
OF PHOTOGRAPHY

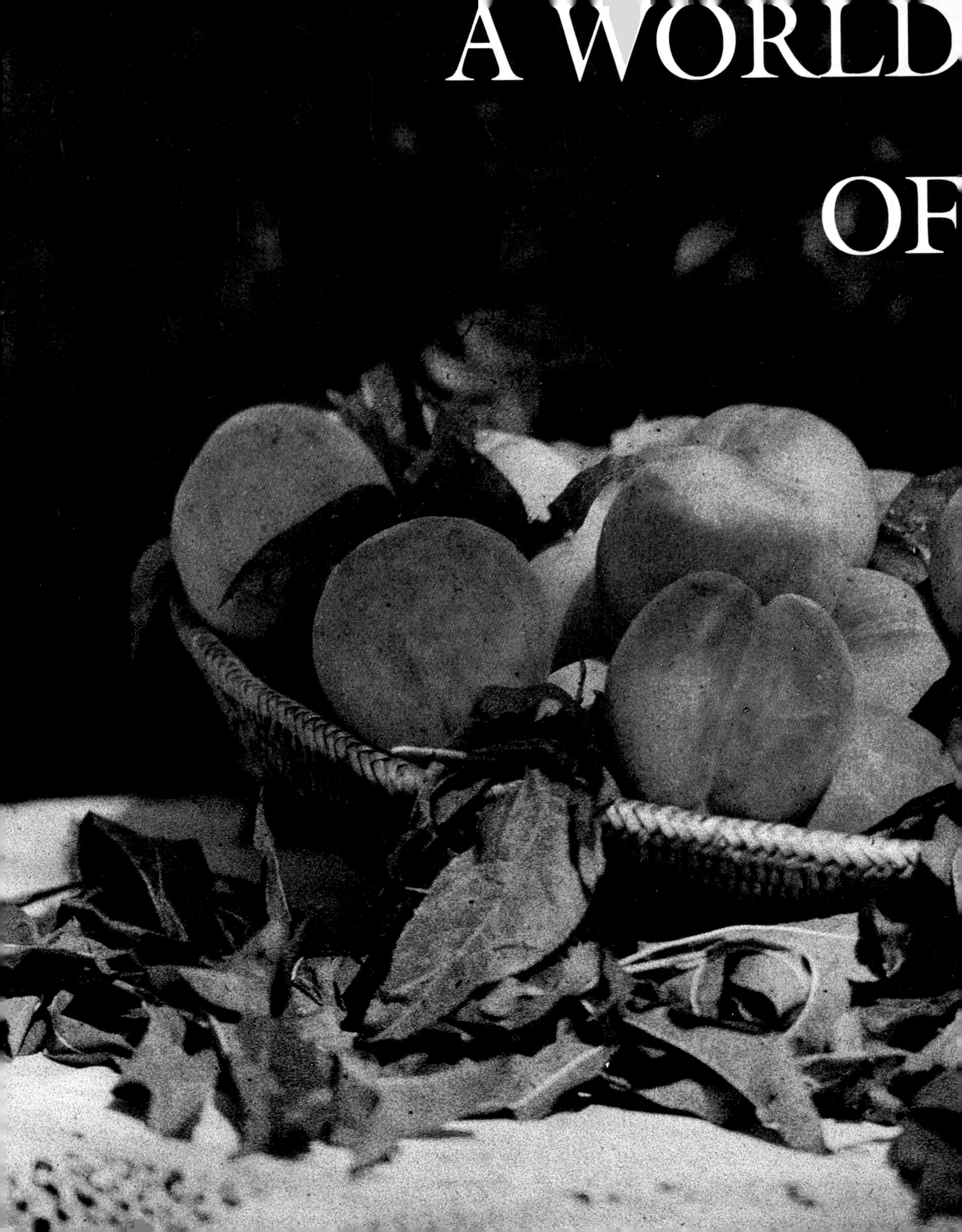
A WORLD
OF

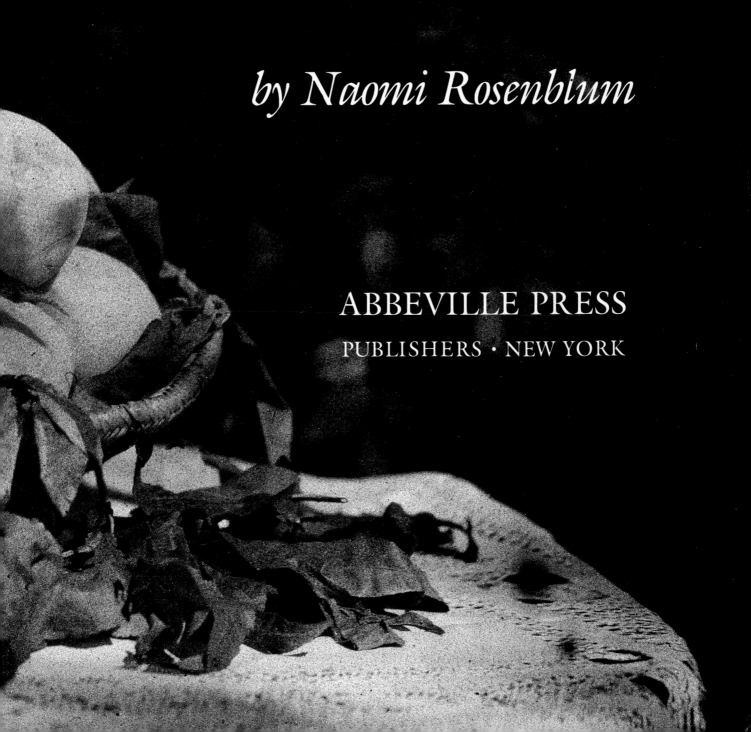

HISTORY PHOTOGRAPHY

by Naomi Rosenblum

ABBEVILLE PRESS

PUBLISHERS · NEW YORK

The background illustration for the title-page spread is a detail of
Still Life by Laura Gilpin, 1912, which appears on page 295.
© 1981 Laura Gilpin Collection, Amon Carter Museum, Fort Worth, Texas.

Editor: WALTON RAWLS
Designer: PHILIP GRUSHKIN
Picture Researcher: JAIN KELLY
Production Manager: DANA COLE
Production Editor: ROBIN JAMES

Library of Congress Cataloging in Publication Data

Rosenblum, Naomi.
  A world history of photography.

  Bibliography: p.
  Includes index.
  1. Photography—History.   1. Title.
TR15.R67   1984   770'.9   83-73417
ISBN 0-89659-438-6

Contents

Preface

AS A WAY OF MAKING IMAGES, photography has flourished in unprecedented fashion ever since its origins 150 years ago. From Paris to Peking, from New York to Novgorod, from London to Lima, camera images have emerged as the least expensive and most persuasive means to record, instruct, publicize, and give pleasure. Not only are photographs the common currency of visual communication in the industrialized nations, they have become the paradigm democratic art form in that more people than ever before use cameras to record familial events or to express personal responses to real and imagined experiences. Because of their ubiquity, photographs (actual or reproduced in print media) have been paramount in transforming our ideas about ourselves, our institutions, and our relationship to the natural world. That the camera has altered the way we see has become accepted wisdom; that it has confirmed that no single view of reality can be considered imperishably true also has become evident.

Used in a multitude of ways and with varying intentions photographs have served to confuse and to clarify, to lull and to energize. Interposed between people and their direct experiences, they often seem to glorify appearance over substance. They have endowed objects, ideologies, and personalities with seductive allure, or clothed them with opprobrium. They have made the extraordinary commonplace and the banal exotic. At the same time, photographs have enlarged parochial perspectives and have impelled action to preserve unique natural phenomena and cherished cultural artifacts. On their evidence, people have been convinced of the inequity of social conditions and the need for reform.

The photograph has affected the other visual arts to a profound degree. Now accepted for itself as a visual statement with its own aesthetic character, photography's earlier role in replicating and popularizing artistic expression in other media had an incalculable effect on the taste of vast numbers of people in urbanized societies. Photography has made possible an international style in architecture and interior design. It has inspired new ways of organizing and representing experience in the graphic arts and sculpture. How and why the medium has attained the position it occupies in contemporary life are questions that this history seeks to explore.

Throughout the 19th century, expanding interest in photography provoked curiosity about its origins and stimulated investigations into its invention, developments, and the contributions of individual photographers. The first histories, which began to appear soon after 1839 and became exhaustive toward the end of the century, were oriented toward technological developments. They imposed a chronology on discoveries in chemistry, physics, and applied mechanics as these disciplines related (at times tenuously) to photography. Exemplified by Josef Maria Eder's *Geschichte der Photographie (History of Photography)*, first published under a different title in 1891, revised several times, and issued in English in 1945, these histories were not at all concerned with the aesthetic and social dimensions of the medium, which they barely acknowledged.

Soon after 1900, as the art movement in photography gained adherents, histories of the medium began to reflect the idea that camera images might be considered aesthetically pleasing artifacts as well as useful technological products. The concept that photographs serve the needs of both art and science and that, in fact, the medium owes its existence to developments in both these spheres of activity is basic to the best-known general history that has appeared in the 20th century: *The History of Photography, from 1839 to the Present*, by Beaumont Newhall, first published as an exhibition catalog in 1937, rewritten in 1949, and revised in 1964 and 1982. Another redoubtable work, *The History of Photography, from the Camera Obscura to the Beginning of the Modern Era* by Helmut and Alison Gernsheim, 1955, revised by both in 1969 and by Helmut Gernsheim in 1983, also includes a discussion of the emergence of artistic photography and situates scientific developments within a social framework. Besides acknowledging the aesthetic nature of camera images, these works reflect the influence of the socially oriented temper of the mid-20th century in that they concede the relationship of photography to social forces. To an even more marked degree, a conception of photography as a socio-cultural phenomenon informs *Photography and the American Scene* by Robert Taft, 1938, and *Photographie et Société* by Gisèle Freund—the latter based on investigations begun in the 1930s but not published until 1974 in France and until 1980 in English translation. "The Work of Art in the Age of Mechanical Reproduction," by Walter Benjamin, originally published in 1931 as a three-part article entitled *"Kleine Geschichte der Photographie"* is an early seminal discussion of the social and aesthetic consequences of mass-produced camera images, which has engendered many later works. A recent survey that places photographic imagery within an aesthetic and social context is Ian Jeffrey's *Photography: A Concise History*, 1981.

The obvious impress of camera images on the painting style of the 1960s, combined with the affirmation at about the same time of the photographic print as an artistic commodity, may account for the appearance of histories concerned primarily with the effects of photography on graphic art. *The Painter and the Photographer* by Van Deren Coke, 1964, and *Painting and Photography* by Aaron Scharf, 1968, are two such books that examine the role played by the medium in developments in the traditional visual arts. More recently, *Photographie als Kunst* by Volker Kahmens, published in English in 1974 as *Art History of Photography*, and *Photography: History of an Art* by Jean Luc Duval, the English-language version of *Histoire d'un Art: La Photographie*, 1982, have examined photographic expression in the light of its intrinsic nature and its relationship to graphic art.

Within the past two decades, topical histories that survey the origins of documentation, photojournalism, and fashion photography have appeared. Monographs on historical figures and compendiums that offer a selection of images from the past without being historical have enriched our knowledge of the medium's contributions. Our understanding of developments in all spheres—technological, aesthetic, and social—has been amplified through articles appearing in periodicals, notably *History of Photography*, a scholarly journal initiated in 1977 by Professor Heinz Henisch of Pennsylvania State University to expand the horizons of historical research in photography. All these inquiries into specific aesthetic, scientific, and social facets of photography have made it possible to fill in a historical outline with concrete facts and subtle shadings.

In view of this storehouse of material, this book, *A World History of Photography*, is designed to distill and incorporate the exciting findings turned up by recent scholarship in a field whose history is being discovered daily. It summarizes developments in photography throughout the world and not just in the areas of Europe and the Americas that in the past received almost exclusive attention. It presents the broad applications that photography has had and it articulates the relationship of the medium to urban and industrial developments, to commerce, to ideas of progress, and to transformations in the visual arts. And while the discussion of developments deals with social and contextual matters, it also attempts to examine the role of photography as a distinctive means of personal expression. In sum, this book is intended to present a historical view that weaves together the various components that have affected the course of photography, revealing an overall design and pattern without obscuring individual threads.

To do justice to these objectives, the material in this book has been structured in a somewhat unusual way. The chapters have been organized chronologically around themes that have been of special significance in the history of the medium—portraiture, documentation, advertising and photojournalism, and the camera as a medium of personal artistic expression. This organization seemed to be appropriate also as a way to suggest both the similarity of ideas and images as they recurred in widely separated localities and the transformations that sometimes characterized the work of individual photographers over a period of time. Admittedly, this treatment makes for a degree of overlap in that the work of an individual may be discussed in more than one chapter. Edward Steichen, for example, began his career around 1900 as a Pictorialist, was then in charge of aerial documentation during World War I (again in World War II), later became a highly regarded magazine photographer, and finally was director of a museum department of photography; his contributions are examined both in the chapter on Pictorialism and in the one devoted to advertising and photojournalism. While this organization of the chapters emphasizes the subject matter and context within which photographers work, in select instances short biographies called profiles have been included at the end of the appropriate chapter in order to underscore the contribution of those whose work epitomizes a style or has proved a germinal force.

Photography is, of course, the result of scientific and technical procedures as well as social and aesthetic ideas. Nevertheless, in consideration of the fact that large amounts of technical detail inserted into a narrative tend to be confusing rather than enlightening, summaries outlining developments in equipment, materials, and processes during three separate time periods have been isolated from the descriptive history and placed at the end of each relevant time period. While not exhaustive, these short technical histories are meant to provide a framework for the social and aesthetic developments discussed in the preceding chapters.

A great aid in the task of weaving everything together is the generous number of illustrations, which will permit the reader to relate facts and ideas within a general historical structure not only to familiar images but to lesser-known works. In addition to the photographs reproduced in the text, the book includes albums of prints designed to highlight a few of the many themes that photographers have found compelling. They comprise outstanding examples in portraiture, landscape, social and scientific documentation, and photojournalism.

The complex relationships between photography and

other aspects of human thought and activity that have emerged as a consequence of greater investigation into the medium's past are a challenge to the historian who wishes to provide an overview and, at the same time, communicate a sense of the excitement and variety of expression that have characterized the evolution of photography. It is my hope that this richly illustrated survey will satisfy many of the needs of the general reader and of students of the history of photography, and will inspire them to further investigation and study.

That this work is so well provided with visual images is owed to my publisher Robert Abrams, whose personal interest in producing an abundantly illustrated history of photography is herewith gratefully acknowledged. In all respects, my association with Abbeville Press has been pleasurable; I am indebted to my editor Walton Rawls for his unfailing kindness and respect for my ideas; to the book's designer Philip Grushkin for his sensitivity and meticulousness in dealing with text and image; to Jain Kelly whose grace and dexterity in pursuing pictures for reproduction turned an involved chore into a pleasant undertaking.

In writing this survey I had the help of many individuals who collected information, corrected misapprehensions, pointed out omissions, and suggested sources for pictures. I thank them all. In particular, I am grateful to Gail Buckland, Cornell Capa, Alan Fern, William I. Homer, Anne Hoy, William Johnson, Estelle Jussim, and Larry Schaaf for helpful suggestions regarding portions of the text. My thanks also to James Enyeart and Terrence Pitts of the Center for Creative Photography; to Tom Beck of the Edward L. Bafford Photography Collection, University of Maryland, Baltimore County Library; to Mary Fanette, Susan Kismaric, and John Pultz of the Museum of Modern Art; to Gretchen Van Ness and David Wooters of the International Museum of Photography at George Eastman House; to Sharon Frost, Richard Hill, and Julia Van Haaften of The New York Public Library; and to Miles Barth and Anna Winand of the International Center of Photography for expediting my researches.

I am indebted also to Mark Albert, Jaroslav Andel, Ellen Bearn, Margaret Betts, Franca Donda, Karen Eisenstadt, Helen Gee, Arthur T. Gill, Andy Grundberg, Jon Goodman, Scott Hyde, Rune Hassner, Ann Kennedy, Hildegarde Kron, Alexander Lavrientiev, Eugene Prakapas, Sandra Phillips, William Robinson, Olga Suslova, and David Travis for information and leads to photographs and collections. In particular, I must thank those who helped with the material on China: Judith Luk and H. Kuan Lau in New York and Elsie Fairfax-Cholmeley and Zang Suicheng in China. My French connection,

Madeleine Fidell-Beaufort, was especially efficient with regard to the photographs in French collections. My assistant Georgeen Comerford brought her technical expertise and orderly nature to the problem of providing a visual record of hundreds of images, and to keeping books and files in serviceable order. My typist, Ann Goldstein, was proficient and helpful.

The support of Professor Milton W. Brown, formerly executive officer of the Art History Program at the Graduate Center, City University of New York, and of Professor Sam Hunter of the Art History Department of Princeton University on an earlier project helped make my involvement in this one a reality. The belief in my work evinced by Martica Sawin, Chair of the Art History Department at the Parsons School of Design, where I currently teach, has been a sustaining factor.

I could not have embarked on this project without the support of my family. I am grateful for the enthusiasm of my daughters Nina and Lisa and deeply appreciative for the constant and loving understanding offered by my husband Walter.

About the Illustrations

Few readers mistake the reproduction of a painting for the original work, but with illustrations of photographs distinctions between the two sometimes become clouded and the viewer assumes that the original print and its image in printers ink are interchangeable. It is important to realize that in the photographic medium, as in other forms of visual expression, size, coloration, and surface appearance may be significant aspects of the photographic statement, and that these attributes are affected by being translated from their original form into mechanically printed media.

The question of size can be especially confusing. Positive prints of varying sizes can be obtained by making enlargements from glass plates or negatives of a specific dimension, and the size of the images may change again when the work is transferred to gravure or lithographic context. This is especially true in the era since the invention of the 35mm camera, since negatives made with apparatus of this size were meant to be seen in enlarged format rather than in their original size. As a consequence, for modern viewers, the exact size of an original negative, even in works produced before the advent of 35mm cameras, has assumed a less significant role. Photographic prints also are easily cropped—either by photographer or user—and the print may represent only a portion of the original negative. Furthermore, the images in this book have been found in hundreds of archives, libraries, museums, and private collections, some of which were unable to provide information about original size. In view of the reasons outlined above, and in the interest of consistency, the dimensions of both negative and positive images have been omitted in the captions. Care has been taken, whenever possible, to reproduce the entire image on the print even when, as is sometimes the case, the edges are damaged.

A more significant problem in reproducing photographs concerns the coloration of the image. With the exception of the color plates, in which the colored dyes of the original print or transparency have been translated with reasonable accuracy into pigmented ink, nearly all the monochromatic images have been printed in the same color ink. It is obvious that the silver and gold tonalities of the metal daguerreotype plates have not been duplicated and must be imagined by the viewer; this is true also for many of the monochromatic prints on paper included in the book. From the inception of photography, paper prints were produced in a range of colors that include the reddish-orange tones of salt prints, the siennas and brown-blacks of carbon prints, the mulberry and yellow-brown hues of albumen prints, and the warm silvery tones of platinum paper. In numerous instances, colored pigments were added by hand to metal plate or paper to enhance the image. The coloration that became possible with the flowering of the manipulative processes favored around the turn of the century also will, in general, have to be seen in the mind's eye. However, in order to provide the reader with some indication of the variety and richness of coloration in photography, an album of images entitled "The Origins of Color" has been included as one of a group of special sections. In it are reproduced the actual colors found in hand-painted daguerreotypes, paper prints, carbon prints, and bichromate prints as well as in several of the earliest color-process prints.

In addition to distinctive colors, photographic prints sometimes display significant differences in surface appearance and texture, the result of using different processes and printing on different papers; these, too, do not translate easily in reproduction. In all cases, the reader should keep in mind that in addition to the variety of theme and the broad range of aesthetic treatment visible in the illustrations, photographs may exhibit a distinctiveness of color and texture that can be appreciated only in the original.

Owing to the fact that photographs are fragile and that for a long time many were not thought important enough to merit special handling, some images selected for illustration contain extraneous marks caused by the deterioration of the emulsion on the negative. In other cases, scratches and discoloration on the metal daguerreotype plates or cracks and tears in the paper on which the print was made also are visible. No effort has been made to doctor such works so that they look new, or to add pieces of the image that might be missing in the original photograph.

About the Captions

Caption information is structured as follows: name of photographer, where known; title of the work, with foreign titles other than place names translated into English; medium in terms of the positive print from which the reproduction was made; and the source of the print. In the case of 19th-century paper prints, the word calotype has been used to denote all prints on salted paper, made either from paper negatives produced by Talbot's calotype process or a variation thereof. Salt print is used when the negative medium is not known. Dimensions of the original negatives are not given, but *carte-de-visite* and stereograph formats are indicated.

I.

THE EARLY YEARS: TECHNOLOGY, VISION, USERS

1839–1875

What is the secret of the invention? What is the substance endowed with such astonishing sensibility to the rays of light, that it not only penetrates itself with them, but preserves their impression; performs at once the function of the eye and the optic nerve—the material instrument of sensation and sensation itself?

—*"Photogenic Drawing," 1839*[1]

IN THE YEAR 1839, two remarkable processes that would revolutionize man's perceptions of reality were announced separately in London and Paris; both represented responses to the challenge of permanently capturing the fleeting images reflected into the *camera obscura*. The two systems involved the application of long-recognized optical and chemical principles, but aside from this they were only superficially related. The outcome of one process was a unique, unduplicatable, laterally reversed monochrome picture on a metal plate that was called a daguerreotype after one of its inventors, Louis Jacques Mandé Daguerre *(pl. no. 1) (see Profile)*. The other system produced an image on paper that was also monochromatic and tonally as well as laterally reversed—a negative. When placed in contact with another chemically treated surface and exposed to sunlight, the negative image was transferred in reverse, resulting in a picture with normal spatial and tonal values. The result of this procedure was called photogenic drawing and evolved into the calotype, or Talbotype, named after its inventor, William Henry Fox Talbot *(pl. no. 2) (see Profile)*. For reasons to be examined later in the chapter, Talbot's negative–positive process initially was less popular than Daguerre's unique picture on metal, but it was Talbot's system that provided the basis for all substantive developments in photography.

By the time it was announced in 1839, Western industrialized society was ready for photography. The camera's images appeared and remained viable because they filled cultural and sociological needs that were not being met by pictures created by hand. The photograph was the ultimate response to a social and cultural appetite for a more accurate and real-looking representation of reality, a need that had its origins in the Renaissance. When the idealized representations of the spiritual universe that inspired the medieval mind no longer served the purposes of increasingly secular societies, their places were taken by paintings and graphic works that portrayed actuality with greater verisimilitude. To render buildings, topography, and figures accurately and in correct proportion, and to suggest objects and figures in spatial relationships as seen by the eye rather than the mind, 15th-century painters devised a system of perspective drawing as well as an optical device called the *camera obscura* that projected distant scenes onto a flat surface *(see A Short Technical History, Part I)*—both

means remained in use until well into the 19th century.

Realistic depiction in the visual arts was stimulated and assisted also by the climate of scientific inquiry that had emerged in the 16th century and was supported by the middle class during the Enlightenment and the Industrial Revolution of the late 18th century. Investigations into plant and animal life on the part of anatomists, botanists, and physiologists resulted in a body of knowledge concerning the internal structure as well as superficial appearance of living things, improving artists' capacity to portray organisms credibly. As physical scientists explored aspects of heat, light, and the solar spectrum, painters became increasingly aware of the visual effects of weather condi-

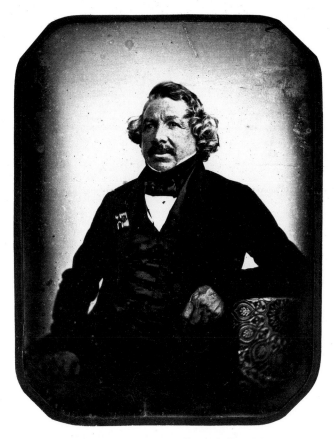

1. JEAN BAPTISTE SABATIER-BLOT. *Portrait of Louis Jacques Mandé Daguerre*, 1844. Daguerreotype. International Museum of Photography at George Eastman House, Rochester, N.Y.

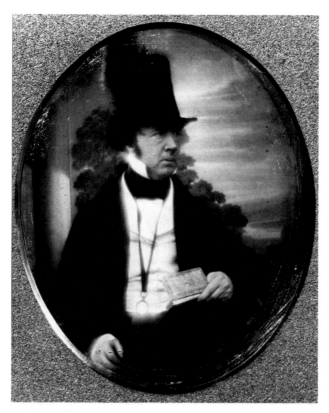

2. ANTOINE CLAUDET. *Portrait of William Henry Fox Talbot*, c. 1844. Daguerreotype. Fox Talbot Museum, Lacock, England.

artists rejected the old historical themes for new subjects dealing with mundane events in contemporary life. In addition to renouncing traditional subject matter, they also sought new ways to depict figures in natural and lifelike poses, to capture ephemeral facial and gestural expression, and to represent effects of actual conditions of illumination—information that the camera image was able to record for them soon after the middle of the century.

Another circumstance that prepared the way for photography's acceptance was the change in art patronage and the emergence of a large new audience for pictorial images. As the church and noble families diminished in power and influence, their place as patrons of the arts was taken by the growing middle class. Less schooled in aesthetic matters than the aristocrats, this group preferred immediately comprehensible images of a variety of diverting subjects. To supply the popular demand for such works, engravings and (after 1820) lithographs portraying anecdotal scenes, landscapes, familiar structures, and exotic monuments were published as illustrations in inexpensive periodicals and made available in portfolios and individually without texts. When the photograph arrived on the scene, it slipped comfortably into place, both literally and figuratively, among these graphic images designed to satisfy middle-class cravings for instructive and entertaining pictures.

Though the birth of photography was accompanied by incertitude about scientific and technical matters and was plagued by political and social rivalries between the French and the British, the new pictorial technology appealed enormously to the public imagination from the first. As photographs increasingly came to depict the same kinds of imagery as engravings and lithographs, they superseded the handmade product because they were more accurate in the transcription of detail and less expensive to produce and therefore to purchase. The eagerness with which photography was accepted and the recognition of its importance in providing factual information insured unremitting efforts during the remainder of the century to improve its procedures and expand its functions.

The Daguerreotype

The invention of the daguerreotype was revealed in an announcement published in January, 1839, in the official bulletin of the French Academy of Sciences, after Daguerre had succeeded in interesting several scientist-politicians, among them François Arago, in the new process of making pictures. Arago was an eminent astronomer, concerned with the scientific aspects of light, who also was a member of the French Chamber of Deputies. As spokesman for an enlightened group convinced that researches in physics and chemistry were steppingstones to national economic

tions, sunlight and moonlight, atmosphere, and, eventually, the nature of color itself.

This evolution toward naturalism in representation can be seen clearly in artists' treatment of landscape. Considered a necessary but not very important element in the painting of religious and classical themes in the 16th and 17th centuries, landscape had become valued for itself by the beginning of the 19th. This interest derived initially from a romantic view of the wonders of the universe and became more scientific as painters began to regard clouds, trees, rocks, and topography as worthy of close study, as exemplified in a pencil drawing of tree growth by Daguerre himself *(pl. no. 3)*. When the English landscapist John Constable observed that "Painting is a science and should be pursued as an inquiry into the laws of nature,"[2] he voiced a respect for truth that brought into conjunction the aims of art and science and helped prepare the way for photography. For if nature was to be studied dispassionately, if it was to be presented truthfully, what better means than the accurate and disinterested "eye" of the camera?

The aims of graphic art and the need for photography converged in yet another respect in the 19th century. In accord with the charge of French Realist painter Gustave Courbet that it was necessary "to be of one's time," many supremacy, Arago engineered the purchase by France of the process that Daguerre had perfected on his own after the death of his original partner, Joseph Nicéphore Niépce *(pl. no. 4) (see A Short Technical History, Part I)*. Then on August 19, 1839, with the inventor at his side, Arago presented the invention to a joint meeting of the Academies of Sciences and of Fine Arts *(pl. no. 5)*; the process was later demonstrated to gatherings of artists, intellectuals, and politicians at weekly meetings at the *Conservatoire des Arts et Métiers*.

The marvel being unveiled was the result of years of experimentation that had begun in the 1820s[3] when Niépce had endeavored to produce an image by exposing to light a treated metal plate that he subsequently hoped to etch and print on a press. He succeeded in making an image of a dovecote *(pl. no. 6)* in an exposure that took more than eight hours, which accounts for the strange disposition of shadows on this now barely discernible first extant photograph. When his researches into heliography, as he called it, reached a standstill, he formed a partnership with the painter Daguerre, who, independently, had become obsessed with the idea of making the image seen in the *camera*

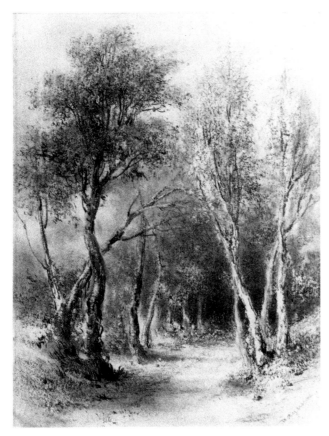

3. LOUIS JACQUES MANDÉ DAGUERRE. *Woodland Scene*, n.d. Pencil on paper. International Museum of Photography at George Eastman House, Rochester, N.Y.

obscura permanent. Daguerre's fascination with this problem, and with the effects of light in general, is understandable in view of his activities as a painter of stage sets and illusionistic scenery for The Diorama, a popular visual entertainment in Paris. Evolved from the panorama, a circular painted scene surrounding the viewers, The Diorama contrived to suggest three-dimensionality and atmospheric effects through the action of light on a series of realistically painted flat scrims. The everyday world was effectively transcended as the public, seated in a darkened room, focused on a painted scene that genuinely appeared to be animated by storms and sunsets.

In promoting The Diorama into one of Europe's most popular entertainments, Daguerre had shown himself to be a shrewd entrepreneur, able to gauge public taste and balance technical, financial, and artistic considerations, and he continued this role with respect to the new invention. He understood, as his partner Niépce had not, that its progress and acceptance would be influenced as much by promotional skill as by intrinsic merit. After the death of Niépce in 1833, Daguerre continued working on the technical problems of creating images with light, finally achieving a practicable process that he offered to sell in 1838, first for a lump sum and then by subscription. When these attempts failed, he altered his course to a more politically inspired one, a move that culminated in the acquisition of the process by the French government[4] and led to the painter's presence beside Arago at the gathering of notables in the Palace of the Institute in August, 1839.

In an electric atmosphere, Arago outlined Daguerre's methods of obtaining pictures (basically, by "exposing" a silver-coated copper plate sensitized in iodine vapor and "developing" its latent image by fuming in mercury vapor), enumerated potential uses, and prophetically emphasized unforeseen developments to be expected. The making of inexpensive portraits was one possibility keenly desired, but in 1839 the length of time required to obtain a daguerreotype image ranged from five to 60 minutes, depending on the coloring of the subject and the strength of the light—a factor making it impossible to capture true human appearance, expression, or movement. For instance, in one of two views from his window of the Boulevard du Temple *(pl. no. 7)* that Daguerre made in 1838, the only human visible is the immobile figure of a man having his boots polished, all other figures having departed the scene too quickly to have left an imprint during the relatively long exposure. Therefore, efforts to make the process practicable for portraiture were undertaken immediately *(see Chapter 2)*.

Shortly after the public announcement, Daguerre published a manual on daguerreotyping, which proved to many of his readers that the process was more easily written about than executed. Nevertheless, despite the additional difficulty of transporting unwieldly cameras and equipment to suitable locales—not to mention the expenditure of considerable time and money—the process immediately attracted devotees among the well-to-do, who rushed to purchase newly invented cameras, plates, chemicals, and especially the manual—about 9,000 of which were sold within the first three months. Interest was so keen that within two years a variety of cameras, in addition to the model designed by Daguerre and produced by Alphonse Giroux in Paris, were manufactured in France, Germany, Austria, and the United States. Several knowledgeable opticians quickly designed achromatic (non-distorting) lenses for the new cameras, including the Chevalier brothers in Paris and Andrew Ross in London, all of whom had been providing optical glass for a wide range of other needs, as well as the Austrian scientist Josef Max Petzval, a newcomer. Focusing on monuments and scenery, daguerreotype enthusiasts were soon to be seen in such numbers in Paris, the countryside, and abroad that by December, 1839, the French press already characterized the phenomenon as a craze or "*daguerréotypomanie*" (*pl. no. 8*).

One of the more accomplished of the gentlemen ama-

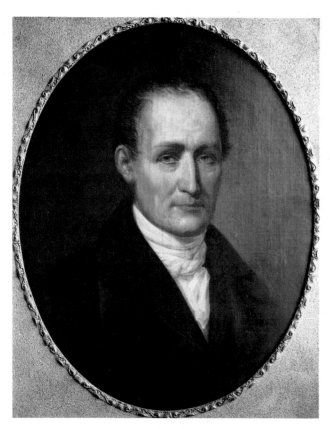

4. LÉONARD-FRANÇOIS BERGER. *Portrait of Joseph Nicéphore Niépce*, 1854. Oil on Canvas. Musée Nicéphore Niépce, Ville de Chalon-sur-Saône, France.

teurs who were intrigued by daguerreotyping was Baron Jean Baptiste Louis Gros, who made the first daguerreotype images of the Parthenon while on a diplomatic mission to Greece in 1840. After returning to Paris, he was fascinated by his realization that, unlike hand-drawn pictures, camera images on close inspection yielded minute details of which the observer may not have been aware when the exposure was made; far removed from the Acropolis, he found that he could identify sculptural elements from the Parthenon by examining his daguerreotypes with a magnifying glass. The surpassing clarity of detail, which in fact still is the daguerreotype's most appealing feature, led Gros to concentrate on interior views and landscapes whose special distinction lies in their exquisite attention to details (*pl. no. 9*).

At the August meeting of the Academies, Arago had announced that the new process would be donated to the world—the seemingly generous gift of the government of Louis Philippe, the Citizen King. However, it soon became apparent that before British subjects could use the process they would have to purchase a franchise from Daguerre's agent. Much has been written about the chauvinism of Daguerre and the French in making this stipulation, but it should be seen in the context of the unrelenting competition between the French and British ruling-classes for scientific and economic supremacy. The licensing provision reflected, also, an awareness among the French that across the Channel the eminent scientist Talbot had come up with another method of producing pictures by the interaction of light and chemicals.

Regularly scheduled demonstrations of Daguerre's process and an exhibition of his plates took place in London in October, 1839, at the Adelaide Gallery and the Royal Institution, the two forums devoted to popularizing new discoveries in science. Daguerre's manual, which had appeared in translation in September (one of 40 versions published within the first year), was in great demand, but other than portraitists, whose activities will be discussed in the next chapter, few individuals in England and Scotland clamored to make daguerreotypes for amusement. Talbot, aware since January of Daguerre's invention from reports in the French and British press and from correspondence, visited the exhibition at the Adelaide Gallery and purchased the equipment necessary for making daguerreotypes; however, even though he praised it as a "splendid" discovery, he does not appear to have tried out the process.

Reaction to the daguerreotype in German-speaking cities was both official and affirmative, with decided interest expressed by the ruling monarchs of Austria and Prussia.[5] Returning from a visit to Paris in April, 1839, Louis Sachse, owner of a lithographic firm, arranged for French cameras, plates, and daguerreotype images to be sent to Berlin by

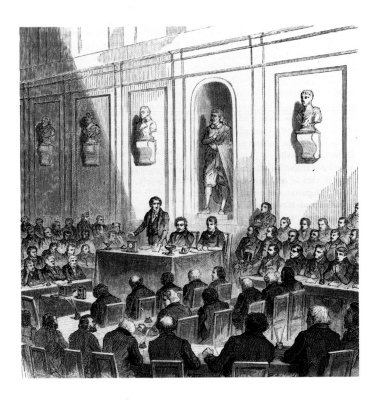

5. UNKNOWN. *Joint Meeting of the Academies of Sciences and Fine Arts in the Institute of France, Paris*, August 19, 1839. Engraving. Gernsheim Collection, Humanities Research Center, University of Texas, Austin.

6. JOSEPH NICÉPHORE NIÉPCE. *View from His Window at Le Gras*, c. 1827. Heliograph. Gernsheim Collection, Humanities Research Center, University of Texas, Austin.

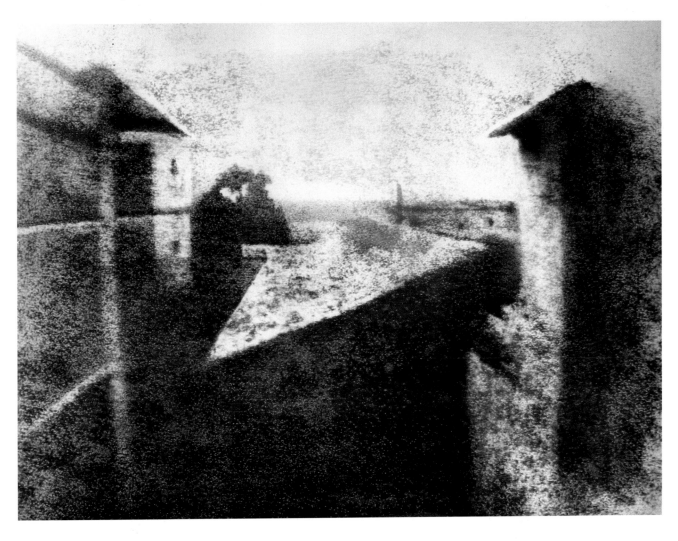

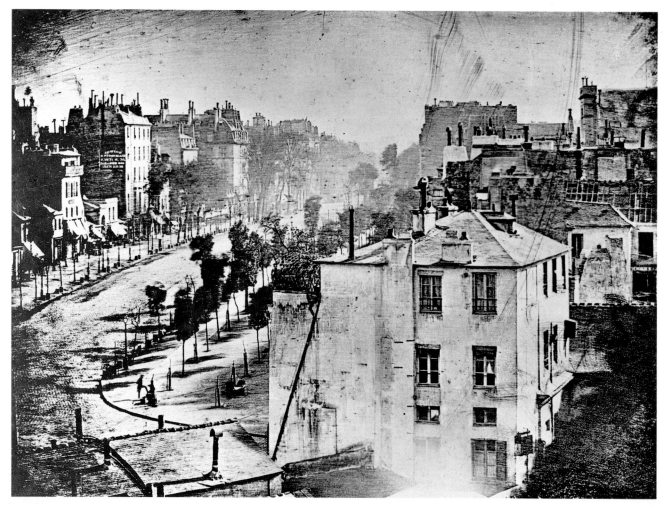

7. Louis Jacques Mandé Daguerre. *Boulevard du Temple, Paris*, c. 1838. Daguerreotype. Bayerisches Nationalmuseum, Munich.

mid-year; a few months later, views taken with locally constructed apparatus also were being shown. However, even though urban scenes in a number of cities were recorded quite early, among them an 1851 view of Berlin by Wilhelm Halffter *(pl. no. 10)*, daguerreotyping for personal enjoyment was less prevalent in Central Europe because the *bourgeoisie* were neither as affluent nor as industrially advanced as their French counterparts. As in all countries, German interest in the daguerreotype centered on expectations for a simple way to make portraits.

Avid interest in the new picture-making process, a description of which had appeared in scientific journals following the January announcement in Paris, motivated Anton Martin, librarian of the Vienna Polytechnic Institute, to attempt daguerreotype images in the summer of 1839, even before Daguerre had fully disclosed his procedures or had his plates exhibited in Vienna that fall. *Winter Landscape (pl. no. 11)*, a view made two years later by Martin, is mundane in subject matter and artlessly organ-

ized. But by the 1830s this kind of scene already had begun to appeal to artists, and it is possible that the documentary camera image, exemplified by this work, hastened the renunciation of romantic themes and bravura treatment of topographical scenes in the graphic arts.

One of the earliest Europeans to embrace and extend the possibilities of the daguerreotype was the Swiss engraver Johann Baptist Isenring who, between 1840 and 1843, exhibited plates of native scenery, colored by hand, in Augsburg, Munich, Stuttgart, and Vienna. He also was among the first to publish aquatint views *(pl. no. 12)* based on daguerreotypes, signaling the form in which the unique image would begin to reach a larger public. His subject matter, too, anticipated the attraction that Continental landscape was to have for a great many photographers working between 1850 and 1880, many of whom continued the tradition begun in the late 18th century of publishing landscape views.

Curiosity about the new picture processes was pro-

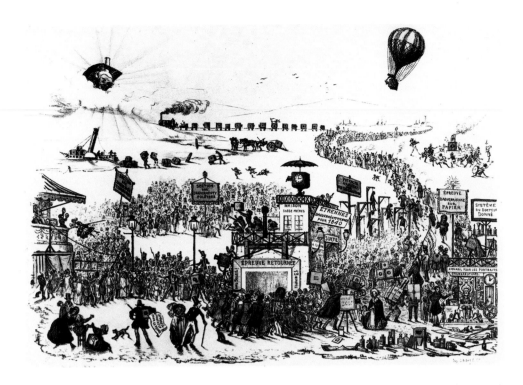

8. THÉODORE MAURISSET. *La Daguerréotypomanie*, December, 1839. Lithograph. Gernsheim Collection, Humanities Research Center, University of Texas, Austin.

9. JEAN BAPTISTE LOUIS GROS. *Bridge and Boats on the Thames*, 1851. Daguerreotype. Bibliothèque Nationale, Paris.

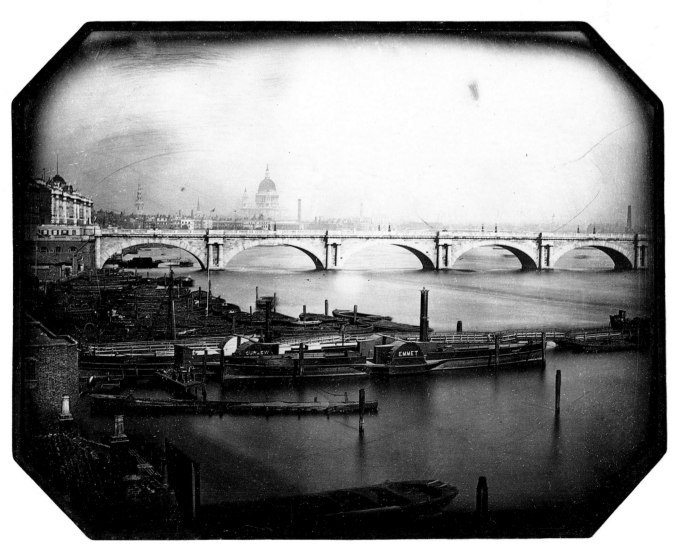

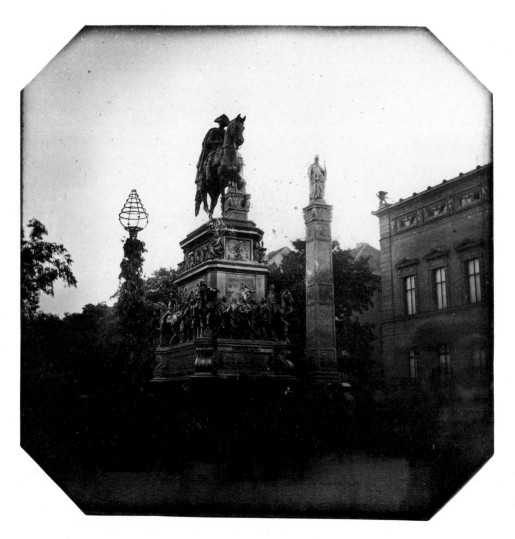

10. WILHELM HALFFTER.
*Statue of Frederick the Great,
Berlin*, May 31, 1851.
Daguerreotype. Agfa-Gevaert
Foto-Historama,
Leverkusen, Germany.

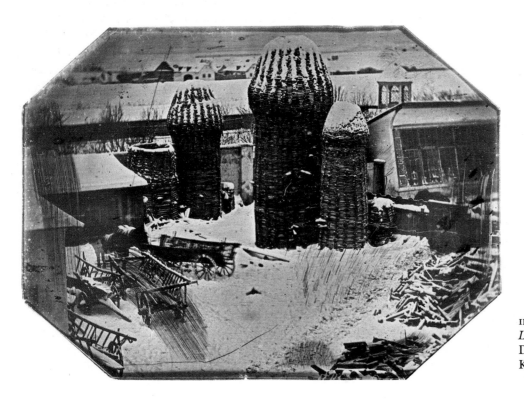

11. ANTON MARTIN. *Winter
Landscape, Vienna*, C. 1841.
Daguerreotype. Museum für
Kunst und Gewerbe, Hamburg.

nounced among scientists, artists, and travelers in Italy. In addition to translations of French manuals, which started to appear in 1840, visitors from the north brought along their own equipment for both the daguerreotype and Talbot's negative–positive process. Among the early Italian daguerreotypists, Lorenzo Suscipj was commissioned to make views of the Roman ruins for English philologist Alexander John Ellis. Indeed, the presence of classical ruins and the interesting mix of French, British, German, and American nationals living and traveling in Rome and Florence during mid-century gave Italian photography in all processes a unique character in that the rapid commercialization of scenic views and genre subjects became possible. For example, within ten years of the introduction of photography, camera images had taken the place of the etchings, engravings, and lithographs of ruins that tourists traditionally had purchased.

As one moved farther east and north from Paris, daguerreotyping activity became less common. News of the discovery, reprinted from the January notices in the French press, reached Croatia, Hungary, Lithuania, and Serbia in February, 1839, and Denmark, Estonia, Finland, and Poland during the summer, with the result that a number of scientific papers on the process began to appear in these localities. In Russia experimentation succeeded in producing a less expensive method of obtaining images on copper and brass rather than silver, and by 1845 a Russian daguerreotypist felt confident enough to exhibit landscape views of the Caucasus Mountains in a Paris show. Nevertheless, early photography in all these distant realms suffered from the absence of a large and stable middle class. Only in the three primary industrial powers—England, France, and the United States—was this group able to sustain the investment of time and energy necessary to develop the medium technically and in terms of significant use.

The Daguerreotype in America

As had been the case with other technologies originating in Europe, Americans not only embraced the daguerreotype, but quickly proceeded to turn it to commercial advantage. The view that "the soft finish and delicate definition of a Daguerreotype has never yet been equalled by any other style of picture produced by actinic agency,"[6] which appeared in the photographic magazine *Humphrey's Journal* in 1859, was only one expression of an opinion held especially by the first generation of American photographers. Daguerreotyping remained the process of choice for 20 years—long beyond the time that Europeans had turned to the more flexible negative–positive technology. The reasons for this loyalty are not entirely clear, but a contributing factor must have been the excellent quality attained by

American daguerreotypists. The sparkling North American light, envied by fog-enshrouded Londoners, was said to have been partly responsible, but social and cultural factors undoubtedly were more significant. Considered a mirror of reality, the crisp, realistic detail of the daguerreotype accorded with the taste of a society that distrusted handmade art as hinting of luxuriousness and was enamored of almost everything related to practical science. With its mixture of mechanical tinkering and chemical cookery, the daguerreotype posed an appealing challenge to a populace that was upwardly and spatially mobile despite periods of economic depression. As a means of livelihood, it combined easily with other manual occupations such as case- or watchmaking, and those who wished to follow a western star were to find it a practicable occupation while on the move.

Some Americans had higher aspirations for the daguerreotype. As an image produced by light, it appeared in their minds to conjoin the Emersonian concept of the "divine hand of nature" with the practicality of scientific positivism. Some hoped that the new medium might help define the unique aspects of American history and experience as expressed in the faces of the citizenry. Others believed that because it was a picture made by machine it would avoid too great artifice and, at the same time, would not demonstrate the obvious provinciality of outlook and training that often characterized native graphic art at mid-century.

The daguerreotype reached America after it had been seen and praised by Samuel F. B. Morse *(pl. no. 13)*, a skillful painter who also invented the electro-magnetic telegraph. His enthusiastic advocacy in letters to his brother in the spring of 1839 helped spur interest in the first manuals and descriptions that arrived in New York late in September by packet ship from England. By early October, details were available in the press, enabling Morse and others to attempt daguerreotyping, but although he worked with esteemed scientist John William Draper and taught others, including Mathew Brady, few images produced by Morse himself have survived.

Another factor that contributed to the rapid improvement of the daguerreotype in the United States was the arrival in November, 1839, of the French agent François Gouraud, with franchises for the sale of equipment. His demonstrations, along with exhibitions of Daguerre's images, evoked interest in the many cities where they were held, even though Americans did not consider it necessary to purchase rights or use authorized equipment in order to make daguerreotypes. As in Europe, technical progress was associated with portraiture, but improvement also was apparent in images of historical and contemporary monuments and structures. Owing to the primitive nature of his

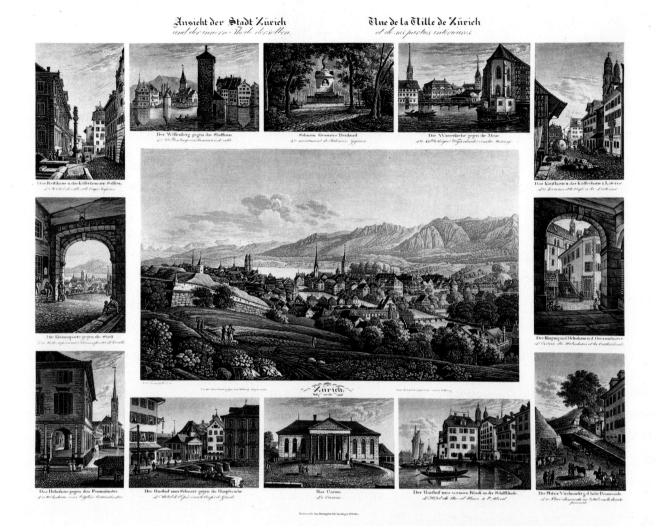

12. JOHANN BAPTIST ISENRING. *View of Zurich*, n.d. Aquatint. Burgerbibliotek Bern, Switzerland.

equipment and the experimental state of the technique, engraver Joseph Saxton's very early view of the Arsenal and Cupola of the Philadelphia Central High School *(pl. no. 14)*, made in October, 1839, is not nearly as crisply defined as John Plumbe's *Capitol Building (pl. no. 15)* of 1845/46 and William and Frederick Langenheim's 1844 view of the Girard Bank, occupied by the Philadelphia Militia *(pl. no. 16)*.

Plumbe, a visionary businessman who built and then lost a small daguerreotyping empire, was interested mainly in portraits, but the Langenheim brothers, of German extraction, hoped to improve American photographic technology by introducing German daguerreotype cameras, the calotype, and photography on glass. John Adams Whipple, of Boston, was similarly concerned with expanding the frontiers of the medium. In addition to a partnership in a fine portrait practice, Whipple attempted to make

daguerreotypes by artificial light and to experiment with images on albumen-coated glass. His special interest was astrophotography; in March, 1851, after three years of experimentation, he produced successful daguerreotypes of the moon *(pl. no. 17)*. The Langenheims and Whipple were among the small group of Americans who realized the drawbacks of the daguerreotype; the populace, however, was too engrossed by the seeming fidelity of "the mirror with a memory"[7] to deplore its limitations.

The Calotype

For much of its existence, photography has been understood by most to be a process resulting in a negative image that can be replicated almost endlessly to produce positives in which tonal and spatial values are in normal relationship.[8] Using the same matrix, the picture can be made

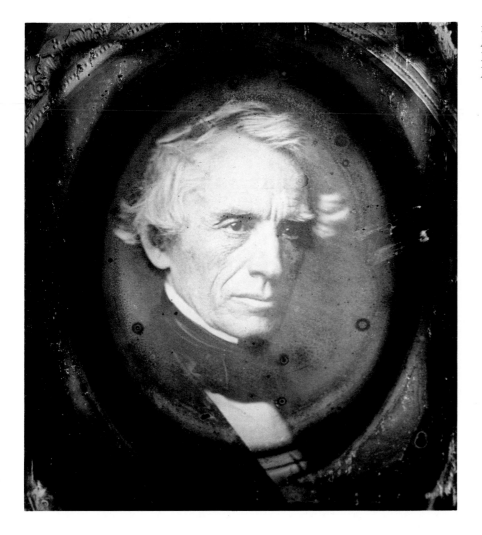

13. PHOTOGRAPHER UNKNOWN.
Portrait of Samuel F. B. Morse, c. 1845.
Daguerreotype. Collection Mrs.
Joseph Carson, Philadelphia.

14. JOSEPH SAXTON. *Arsenal and
Cupola, Philadelphia Central High
School*, October 16, 1839.
Daguerreotype. Historical Society of
Pennsylvania, Philadelphia.

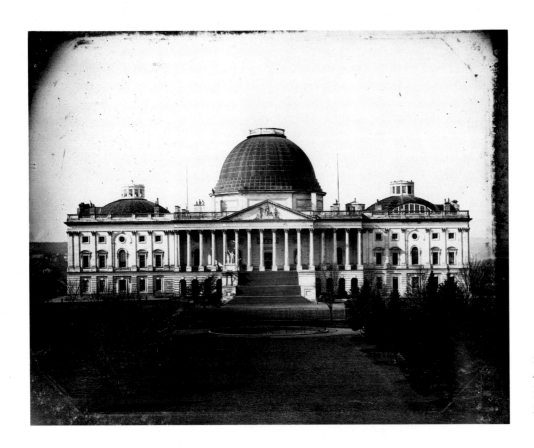

15. JOHN PLUMBE. *Capitol Building, Washington, D.C.,* 1845–46. Daguerreotype. Library of Congress, Washington, D.C.

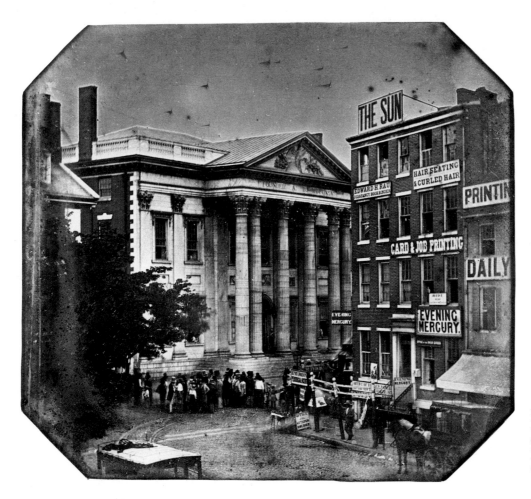

16. WILLIAM and FREDERICK LANGENHEIM. *Girard Bank*, May, 1844. Daguerreotype. Library Company of Philadelphia.

larger and, because of the light weight of the support (paper, fabric, plastic), it can be inserted into books and albums, attached to documents, and sent through the mails, as well as framed and hung on the wall. The photograph's physical and utilitarian advantages over the daguerreotype are so obvious that it may seem incredible that when first announced the negative–positive process took a most definite second place in the public mind.

The reasons are complex, involving timing, technique of production, aesthetic standards, and social factors. Photogenic drawing, as Talbot first called the paper image, was made public by the inventor in London in February, 1839, only after the news of Daguerre's discovery had been relayed from across the Channel. For most people, the potential value of replication may have seemed too abstract an idea at the time, while the actual process of turning negative into positive was perceived as rather complicated. Most important, however, was the fact that—even to Talbot's most ardent supporters—the fuzziness of his earliest results was demonstrably less pleasing than the finely detailed daguerreotype image.[9] Furthermore, the French invention, sponsored by scientist-politicians, had received official government sanction while Talbot had to steer his discovery himself through the quicksands of the British scientific and patenting establishments, at the same time pursuing improvements and attempting to realize a commercial return.

A patrician background and university training had enabled Talbot to become involved with the most advanced thinking of his time. This resourceful scientist was drawn more to astronomy, mathematics, and optics than to chemistry (which in any case was barely a discipline at the time), and his interests also embraced linguistics and literature. For a man of science he was a somewhat romantic and antisocial figure who traveled incessantly; it was while sketching on a honeymoon trip to Italy in 1833 *(pl. no. 18)* that he conceived the notion of making permanent the image visible on the translucent ground-glass surface of the *camera obscura*. Taking up this idea on his return to England, Talbot managed first to expose and thereby transfer leaf forms directly onto chemically sensitized paper *(pl. no. 21)*. Then, in the summer of 1835, with treated paper inserted in small specially constructed cameras, he succeeded in producing a number of negatives of his ancestral home, Lacock Abbey, including a tiny postage-stamp-size image of a latticed window *(pl. no. 20)* with diamond panes initially distinct enough to count.

In common with Daguerre, Talbot first used a solution of ordinary table salt to stop the continuing action of light on the silver deposits, but it was not until both inventors had switched to hyposulphite of soda (hypo, as it is still called even though its scientific name is now sodium thio-

sulphate) that the unexposed silver salts were completely removed and the image satisfactorily stabilized. This characteristic of hypo had been discovered in 1819 by John Herschel (later knighted), a prominent astronomer, physical scientist, and friend of Talbot, who informed both inventors of this fact. Herschel's contributions to the chemistry of photography reveal both scientific brilliance and disinterested generosity. Returning in 1838 after several years as an independent researcher in South Africa where he had himself made drawings with optical devices *(pl. no. 19)*, Herschel learned of the experiments in England and France to produce images by the action of light. He proceeded to conduct his own intensive researches to discover the effectiveness of different silver halides and other chemicals, among them ferric salts from which cyanotypes, or blueprints, are made.

Herschel's suggestions with regard to terminology were especially effective in that he convinced Talbot to consider, instead of photogenic drawing, the broader term photography—light writing—a term believed to have been first used by both the Brazilian Hercules Florence and the German astronomer Johann H. von Maedler.[10] Herschel also coined the terms negative and positive to refer to the

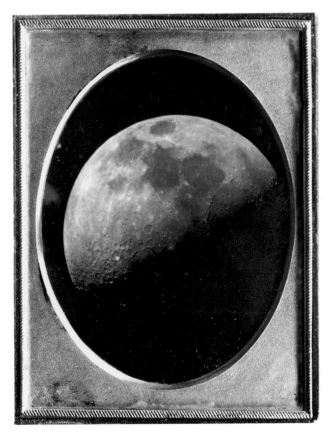

17. JOHN ADAMS WHIPPLE. *Moon*, 1851. Daguerreotype. Science Museum, London.

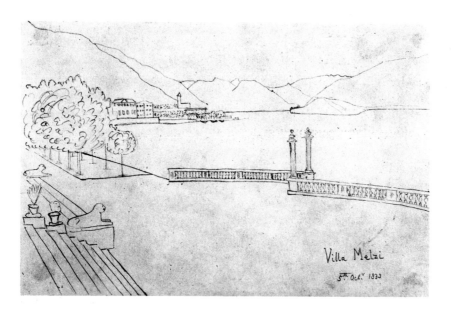

18. WILLIAM HENRY FOX TALBOT. *Villa Melzi*, October 5, 1833. Camera lucida sketch on paper. Fox Talbot Collection, Science Museum, London.

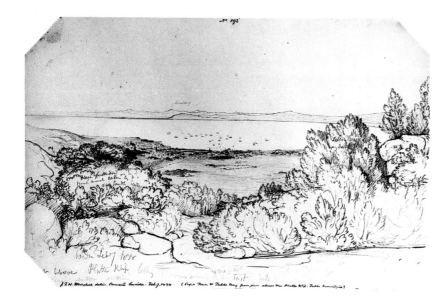

19. JOHN HERSCHEL. *Cape Town and Table Bay from Just Above Platte Klip Gorge, Table Mountain*, February 7, 1838. Camera lucida sketch on paper. Special Collections, South African Library, Capetown.

20. WILLIAM HENRY FOX TALBOT. *Latticed Window at Lacock Abbey*, 1835. Photogenic drawing. Fox Talbot Collection, Science Museum, London.

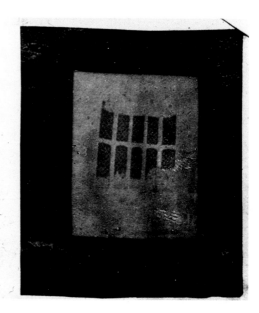

inverse and reverted images that were basic to the system. Had he wished, he probably could have arrived at a patentable process at the same time as Talbot, but his interests lay elsewhere. His intellectual openness has been contrasted with Talbot's more secretive attitudes, but the two were mutual admirers, with Herschel refreshingly liberal about sharing the experimental results of his genius.

The report in January, 1839, of Daguerre's discovery forced Talbot to make public his process even though he had done little work on it since 1837. His initial announcements, made to the Royal Society, the Royal Institution, and the French Academy of Sciences at the end of January and in February were received with interest and evoked a small flurry of excitement among a few individuals in the scientific community and in Talbot's circle of family and friends. However, in comparison with the verisimilitude of the finely detailed daguerreotype, this image, incorporating the texture intrinsic to its paper support, was too broad and indistinct to have wide appeal despite Talbot's description of the effect as "Rembrandtish."

Another disadvantage at first was the length of time required to make an exposure. Talbot had not then discovered the possibility of latent development, a procedure Daguerre had stumbled on, whereby the image, invisible on the exposed plate or paper, was made to appear by treatment with a chemical solution (developer). When he did discover this in the fall of 1840, his exposure time was decreased from about half an hour to as little as 30 seconds on a very bright day, making possible portraiture and a much broader selection of subjects and atmospheric effects, as seen in one of the inventor's early views of London (*pl. no. 22*).

In 1841 Talbot took out the first of his patents,[11] using the word calotype to describe the resulting image, which he also referred to as a Talbotype. This action initiated a ten-year period during which English scientific and artistic endeavor in photography became entangled in problems of commercial exploitation. Both during his lifetime and long afterward, Talbot was accused of obstructing the development of photography because of his intransigence with regard to the four patents he held on the calotyping process. Critics have suggested that he regarded them as covering all advances in photographic technology occurring between 1841 and 1851 and that he included as his own the contributions of others, in particular Herschel's suggestion of hyposulphite of soda as a fixer. However, Talbot's biographer, H. J. P. Arnold, notes that a close reading of the language indicates that the patents protected methods of utilizing substances rather than the chemical agents themselves.[12]

Talbot himself was caught up in a controversy over the moral and practical effects of patenting inventions, a di-

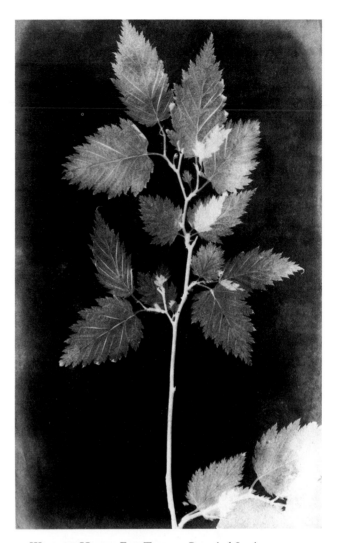

21. WILLIAM HENRY FOX TALBOT. *Botanical Specimen*, 1839. Photogenic drawing. Royal Photographic Society, Bath, England.

lemma that occupied the British from mid-century on. While some individuals maintained that patent fees were too high and rules too lax for protection, others argued that patents were indefensible because inventions "depended less on any individual than on progress in society."[13] Talbot may have agreed, but he patented his processes because, like countless others in Britain, France, and the United States at the time, he considered that those who had invested considerable effort should reap the material rewards of their genius and industry. That he did not benefit financially was because he was an indifferent businessman with a more compelling interest in intellectual matters—an attitude bolstered by the fact that he could count on income from his landed estate. Neither the surge of amateurs photographing in calotype for their own pleasure nor the utilization of the process for commercial portraiture materialized. Among the well-to-do who did take

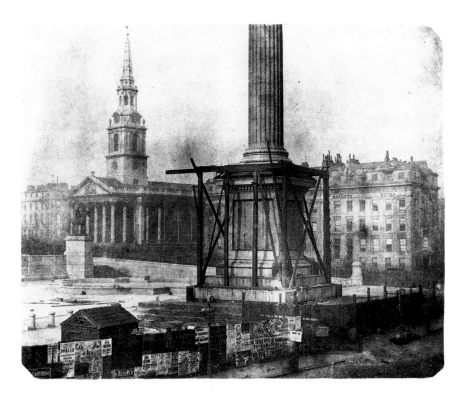

22. WILLIAM HENRY FOX TALBOT.
The Nelson Column, Trafalgar Square,
London, under Construction, c. 1843.
Salted paper print from a calotype
negative. Fox Talbot Collection,
Science Museum, London.

23. WILLIAM HENRY FOX TALBOT.
The Open Door, 1843. Salted paper
print from a calotype negative. (Plate
VI, *The Pencil of Nature,* 1844–46.)
Fox Talbot Collection, Science
Museum, London.

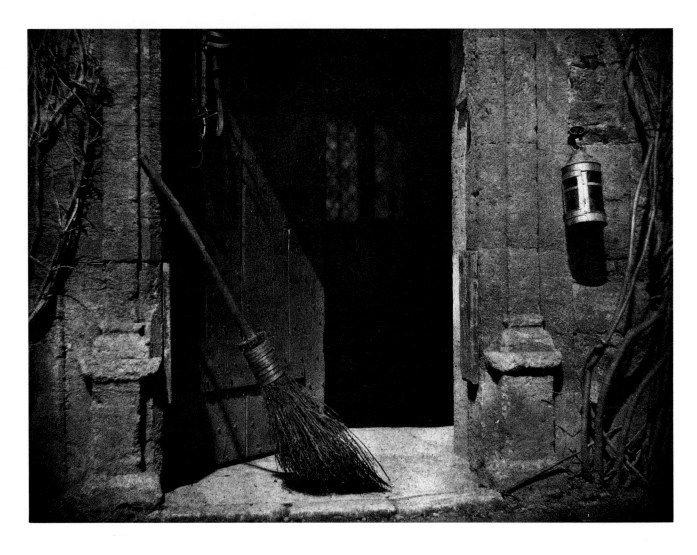

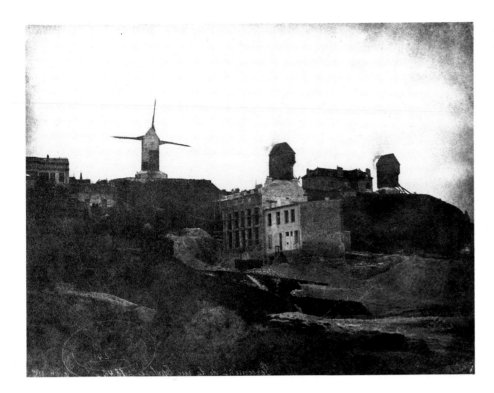

24. HIPPOLYTE BAYARD.
Excavation for rue Tholozé, 1842.
Paper negative. Société
Française de Photographie,
Paris.

up calotyping were Talbot's wife Constance, his Welsh relatives Emma and John Dillwyn Llewelyn, and two friends, the Reverends Calvert Richard Jones and George W. Bridges, both of whom conceived the idea of making a calotype record of their travels abroad *(see Chapter 3)*.

Paper photography occasioned a more significant response in Scotland where no licensing arrangements were necessary. With the help of Sir David Brewster, an eminent scientist who corresponded frequently with Talbot, Robert Adamson, a young Scottish chemist, was able to perfect the calotype technique and open a studio in Edinburgh in 1841. Two years later, he and painter-lithographer David Octavius Hill began to produce calotypes; these images, mainly portraits *(see Chapter 2)*, still are considered among the most expressive works in the medium.

Talbot, though disinclined to pursue the commercial exploitation of his discovery actively, was keenly concerned with the potential uses of the medium. In setting up a publishing establishment at Reading under the supervision of Nicolaas Henneman, an assistant he personally had trained, Talbot promoted the use of the photographic print itself in book and magazine illustration. The *Pencil of Nature*, issued serially between 1844 and 1846 with text and pictorial material supplied by Talbot, was the first publication to explain and illustrate the scientific and practical applications of photography. One of the plates, *The Open Door (pl. no. 23)* was singled out in the British press for its exceptional tonal range and textural fidelity, its "micro-

scopic execution that sets at nought the work of human hands."[14]

Talbot regarded photography as important primarily for its role in supplying visual evidence of facts, but this "soliloquy of the broom," as Talbot's mother called *The Open Door*, reveals a telling interest in the artistic treatment of the mundane. Along with the theme, the careful attention to the way light and shadow imbue a humble scene with picturesque dimension suggests the inventor's familiarity with examples of Dutch genre painting of the 17th century—works that enjoyed considerable esteem in Victorian England and, in fact, were specifically mentioned in the *Pencil of Nature*. Several other calotype images in the same style bear witness to Talbot's conviction that photography might offer an outlet for artistic expression to those without the talent to draw or paint.

Other publications by Talbot included *Sun Pictures of Scotland*, for which he made 23 photographs in 1844, and *Annals of Artists in Spain*, the first book to utilize the photograph for reproducing works of art. However, he disposed of the Reading firm in 1848 because of managerial and technical problems in running a large-scale photographic printing enterprise, not the least of which was the fact that calotypes were subject to fading. This instability was to trouble photographers who worked with paper prints throughout the next 25 years.

In France, where the daguerreotype held the general populace enthralled, artists were greatly interested in the calotype. In their view, the paper process offered a greater range of choices within which one might fashion an affective image. In addition to view, pose, and lighting—the sole aesthetic decisions for the daguerreotypist—the calotypist could exercise interpretive judgment in the production of subsequent prints from the same negative. Aesthetic decisions concerning tonality and coloration could be made by adjustments in the toning and sensitizing baths and by the choice of paper itself, while retouching on the negative (or print) could alter forms. In this respect, the paper process called to mind traditional procedures in etching and engraving, lending the calotype greater esteem among those interested in photography as a creative pursuit.

Other Developments in Paper Photography

Actually, a paper process had been discovered independently in France. Early in 1839, Hippolyte Bayard, a civil servant in the Ministry of Finance, had made and exhibited both photogenic drawings and direct positive paper images exposed in a camera (*see A Short Technical History, Part I*), among them a view of a rural enclave in Paris in the process of being urbanized (*pl. no. 24*). These works were produced soon after the first reports of Talbot's process reached France but before the official announcement in August of Daguerre's process. However, political pressure, especially from Arago, who had committed himself to the promotion of the daguerreotype, kept the discovery from the public. Bayard expressed his indignation at this shabby treatment by the French establishment[15] by creating an image of himself as a suicide victim (*pl. no. 25*); nevertheless, he soon went on to become a prominent member of the photographic community in Paris.

Aware of Bayard's discoveries and concerned that this other paper process might achieve precedence on the Continent, Talbot sought to promote the calotype in France. Although he signed a contract for its promotion with Joseph Hugues Maret (known as the Marquis de Bassano), and traveled to Paris in 1843 to demonstrate the procedure, his associates in France turned out to be incompetent and the project a fiasco. Loath to purchase franchises directly from Talbot in England, French artists and photographers preferred to wait until 1847 when Louis Désiré Blanquart-Evrard, a photographer in Lille who was to become an influential figure in book publication, announced a modified paper process based on Talbot's discoveries. One of the most ardent champions of paper photography in France was the painter Gustave Le Gray, who in 1851 described a method of waxing the negative before exposure to improve definition and tonal sensitivity. The calotype, employed by

Le Gray and other French photographers in an 1851 project to document historic monuments (*see Chapter 3*), enjoyed spirited acclaim by French critics before it was made obsolete by the new collodion technology discussed below.

Early in 1839, two Munich scientists, Carl August von Steinheil and Franz von Kobell, had experimented with paper negatives as a result of a report on Talbot's discoveries given at the Bavarian Royal Academy of Sciences, but even though successful results were exhibited in July, on hearing of the wonderful detail possible with the daguerreotype Von Steinheil switched to metal plates. In the United States as in England, the soft forms of the calotype appealed mainly to a small group of intellectual lights (many of whom lived in Boston), but on the whole reaction to paper photography was cool. Following an unproductive business arrangement with Edward Anthony, a prominent figure in the photographic supply business in New York, Talbot sold the patent rights to the Langenheims who, in turn, expected to sell licenses for the process throughout the United States. The calotypes made by the Langenheims were admired in the press, but the firm soon was forced into bankruptcy as the American public continued its allegiance to the daguerreotype.

Introduction of the Glass Plate and Collodion

Lack of definition and fading were considered the two most pressing problems in paper photography, especially by portraitists and publishers with commercial interests. To improve sharpness, efforts to replace the grainy paper negative with glass—a support that both Niépce and Herschel had already used—gained ground. The first practicable process, using albumen, or egg white, as a binder for the silver salts, was published in France in 1847, while in the United States Whipple and the Langenheims also had succeeded in making finely detailed glass negatives with these substances, from which they made prints called crystalotypes and hyalotypes, respectively. Glass also provided a suitable material for experimentation undertaken by the Langenheims to produce stereographic images (see below) and positive slides for projection. But while albumen on glass resulted in negatives without grain, the procedures were complicated and the exposure time was longer than that required for the daguerreotype.

An effective alternative materialized in 1850 when Frederick Scott Archer, an English engraver turned sculptor, published a method of sensitizing a newly discovered colorless and grainless substance, collodion, to be used on a glass support (*see A Short Technical History, Part I*). Because exposure time decreased dramatically when the plate was used in a moist state, the process became known as the wet

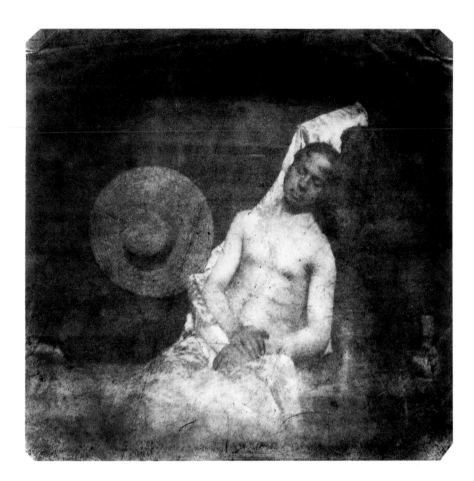

25. HIPPOLYTE BAYARD. *Self-Portrait as a Drowned Man*, 1840. Direct paper positive. Société Française de Photographie, Paris.

plate or wet collodion method. Today one can scarcely imagine the awkwardness of a procedure that required the user to carry a portable darkroom about in order to sensitize each plate before using it and to develop it immediately afterward. Still, the crisp definition and strong contrast afforded by sensitized collodion on glass proved to be just what many in the photographic profession had hoped for in a duplicatable process. Its discovery initiated an era of expanded activity in professional portraiture, in the publication of views, in amateur photographic activity around the globe, and led to numerous collateral photographic enterprises. The introduction of collodion also signaled the end of Talbot's exasperating efforts to litigate his patent rights against those who had taken up calotyping for commerce without purchasing a franchise. The gift of the collodion process to the public by Archer (who was to die impoverished in 1857) was in noticeable contrast to Talbot's attempts to cover all his inventions. When he claimed in 1854 that collodion, too, was protected by his 1843 calotype patent, the outrage expressed in the press made a favorable decision on his pending infringement cases impossible.[16] Talbot gave up his photography patents in 1855, but by then the calotype had faded from sight, in many cases quite literally.

Developments in the Paper Print

Besides the soft definition, the other problem that plagued calotypists involved the quality of the print. Uneven and blotchy tonalities and, of greater concern, the tendency for rich-looking prints to fade and discolor were nightmares, especially for those in commercial enterprises. In addition, satisfactory salt prints—positives produced by exposing sensitized paper in contact with a negative until the image appeared—were thought to look lifeless by a public enticed by superior contrast and clarity. Because the problems were perceived as intrinsic to paper manufacture, an emulsion consisting of albumen and light sensitive silver salts was proposed as a surface coating to keep the image from penetrating into the paper structure itself.

Coming into use at about the same time as the collodion negative, the albumen print rapidly became part of a new photographic technology. Lasting some 30 years, it promoted a style that featured sharp definition, glossy surface, and strong contrasts. In response to this preference, Blanquart-Evrard established his *Imprimerie Photographique* (Photographic Printing Works) at Lille, the first successful photographic printing plant to employ a substantial labor force of men and women to process prints for the dozen different publications issued during the 11 years of its existence. Similar firms soon appeared in Alsace, Germany, England, and Italy, as photographically illustrated books and portfolios became popular.

However, despite the optimistic scenario for the future of the albumen print, problems with stability continued to haunt photographers, making large-scale production a demanding undertaking. At times the unappealing yellow-brown tonality of faded albumen prints was likened to that of stale cheese. Again, sizings were blamed, and it was determined that impurities in the water used in paper manufacture also left a residue that caused the discoloration; only two mills in northeastern France were thought capable of producing paper free from such mineral contamination. Stock from these mills was shipped to nearby Dresden to be albumenized, establishing this German city as the main production center for photographic paper throughout the collodion era.

Other causes of fading, among them imperfect washing, inadequate fixing with hypo baths, interaction with mounting adhesives and air pollution, were confirmed by individuals and by committees set up to study the situation by the two most prominent photographic organizations of the era—the Photographic Society of London and the *Société Française de Photographie*. A two-part prize offered in 1856 by an eminent French archeologist, Honoré d'Albert, Duc de Luynes, testified to the fact that the solution would be found in two spheres of activity related to photography. In offering a larger sum for photomechanical procedures and a smaller one for the discovery of a truly permanent method of chemical printing, De Luynes and other French industrialists recognized the importance of mechanical over hand methods for reproducing photographs. Alphonse Louis Poitevin, a noted French chemist who was recipient of both parts of the prize, worked out a photolithographic process called the collotype *(see A Short Technical History, Part II)* and a non-silver procedure for printing collodion negatives. Based on researches undertaken in 1839 by the Scottish scientist Mungo Ponton that established the light-sensitivity of potassium bichromate, this process, called carbon printing, used a mixture of bichromated gelatin and powdered carbon instead of silver salts to effect a positive image.

During the 1860s, the results obtained by printing with carbon were greatly admired for their deep, rich tonalities as well as their resistance to fading. The technique was actively promoted in Europe, especially after Joseph Wilson Swan, the holder of numerous British patents in the photochemical field (and the inventor of the incandescent light bulb), simplified manipulation by manufacturing carbon tissues in various grades and tonalities. Called Autotype in England, the Swan carbon process was franchised to the

Annan brothers in Scotland, Hanfstaengl in Germany, and Braun in France, rendering these large-scale photographic publishing firms more productive than formerly. However, despite a campaign to promote the carbon method by a leading American publication, *The Philadelphia Photographer*, no great interest developed in the United States, perhaps because efforts already were underway to find a method of printing photographs on mechanical presses through the creation of a metal matrix. Another process that utilized similar chemical substances—the Woodburytype, named after its English creator Walter Woodbury—began to supplant carbon production printing in the early 1870s. It, too, produced a richly pigmented permanent image, but because it incorporated elements of mechanical printing technology it was more productive. Despite these improvements in positive printing materials, albumen paper continued in use for portraits and scenic views until the 1880s when significant new developments in both negative and printing materials made it obsolete. The pigmented carbon process was used less frequently in commercial photographic printing after the 1880s; however, it then became a means of individualized artistic expression for pictorialist photographers.

The Stereograph and Stereoscope

One final element in this inaugural period of photography helped assure the medium's incredible popularity. This was the invention of the stereograph and stereoscope—an image and a device that fused photographic technology with entertainment. Stereographs—two almost identical images of the same scene mounted side by side on a stiff support and viewed through a binocular device to create an illusion of depth—held late-19th-century viewers in thrall. Early examples, which had used daguerreotypes to create this effect, were not entirely successful because reflections from the metal surfaces interfered with the illusion; but after collodion/albumen preempted other technologies, stereograph views became more convincing and immensely salable. Produced in large editions by steam-driven machinery and mounted on cards using assembly-line methods, they reached a substantial clientele, especially in the United States, through mail-order and door-to-door sales. Stereograph publishers offered an unparalleled selection of pictorial material; besides the landscapes, views of monuments, and scenes of contemporary events that often were available in regular format photographs also, there were educational images of occupations and work situations around the globe, reproductions of works of art, especially sculpture, and illustrations of popular songs and anecdotes—all of which provided middle-class viewers with unprecedented materials for entertainment.

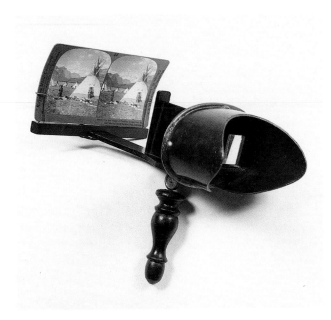

26. Holmes-Bates Stereoscope with stereograph. Keystone-Mast Collection, California Museum of Photography, University of California, Riverside.

Histories of the medium have acknowledged this popular appeal, but the stereograph should be seen as more than a faddish toy. After Queen Victoria had expressed her approval at the Crystal Palace Exhibition of 1851, where stereographs were on public display for the first time, the purchase, exchange, and viewing of stereographs became a veritable mania. It was promoted in the United States as a significant educational tool by Oliver Wendell Holmes in two long articles in the *Atlantic Monthly*, in 1859 and 1862. Besides envisioning "a comprehensive and systematic library . . . where all . . . can find the special forms they desire to see as artists . . . as scholars, . . . as mechanics or in any other capacity,"[17] Holmes suggested that in the future the image would become more important than the object itself and would in fact make the object disposable. He also designed an inexpensive basic viewer *(pl. no. 26)* to enable ordinary people of little means to enjoy these educational benefits. In the latter part of the 19th century, stereography filled the same role as television does in the 20th, providing entertainment, education, propaganda, spiritual uplift, and aesthetic sustenance. Like television, it was a spectator activity, nourishing passive familiarity rather than informed understanding. Long viewed as a pleasant household pastime, its effect on attitudes and outlook in the 19th century only recently has become the subject of serious study.[18]

Looking back at the evolution of the medium during the first half of the 19th century, it is obvious that photography's time had come. Industrialization and the spread of education mandated a need for greater amounts of comprehensible pictorial material encompassing a broader range of subjects—a necessity to which only the camera image was able to respond. Besides the figures mentioned in this chapter, other all-but-forgotten individuals were attempting to produce images by the means of light. And as soon as the glimmers of success were hinted at in London and Paris, people in outlying areas of Europe and the Americas began to embrace the new technology, hoping to expand its possibilities and, in the process, to make or improve their own fortunes.

Within 25 years of Niépce's first successful image, enough of the major technical difficulties had been worked out to insure that both daguerreotype and photograph could be exploited commercially. This activity, which centered on two areas—portraiture and the publication of scenic views—created a photographic profession with its own organizations and publications. Amateurs employed the medium for documentation and for personal expression, while graphic artists came to rely on photography as an indispensable tool for providing a record of appearances and, eventually, for suggesting different ways of viewing actuality. As will become apparent in the chapters that follow, the traditional divisions separating amateur from professional, art from commerce, document from personal expression were indistinct from the earliest days of the medium, and any boundaries that did exist became even more indefinite as camera images increased their authority and scope.

Profile: Louis Jacques Mandé Daguerre

Nothing in Daguerre's early career as a successful scenic designer hinted that eventually he would become transfixed by the problems of producing permanent images by using light. He was born in 1787 into a *petit bourgeois* family in Cormeilles-en-Parisis; when his natural artistic gifts became apparent he was apprenticed to a local architect. Paris beckoned in 1804, the year of Napoleon's coronation, so Daguerre served another apprenticeship in the studio of the stage designer Ignace Eugène Marie Degotti. His intuitive sensitivity to decorative effect enabled him to rise quickly, and in 1807 he became an assistant to Pierre Prévost, who was renowned for his realistically painted panoramas. During the nine years that Daguerre worked for Prévost, he occasionally submitted oils to the Paris Salon and made sketches and topographical views for the 20-volume *Voyages pittoresques et romantiques en l'ancienne France (Picturesque and Romantic Travels in Old France)*, a work to which the painters Géricault, Ingres, and Vernet also contributed.

In 1816, Daguerre's exceptional skill and imagination

were recognized by his appointment as stage designer to one of the best-known small theaters in Paris; three years later he also was designer for the *Opéra*. The audience for these entertainments was drawn from the new urban middle class, whose taste ran to verisimilitude in execution and romanticism in content. When, in 1821, Daguerre undertook to promote a new entertainment, The Diorama, he was convinced that the public would pay for illusionistic deception on a grand scale. The Diorama, which opened in July, 1822, with his own deceptively real-looking representation of "The Valley of the Sarnen" (and one of "The Interior of Trinity Chapel, Canterbury Cathedral," painted by his partner Charles Marie Bouton) achieved its striking effects by the manipulation of light that transformed the scene from a serene day to one of tempestuous storminess, underscoring the desolation of the painted landscape. Despite a temporary setback during the political troubles of 1830, The Diorama continued to offer romantic subjects until 1839, when it was entirely destroyed by fire.

To achieve the perspective effects on the large scrims, and on the easel paintings that he sometimes painted of the same subjects, Daguerre used the conventional tool of his trade—the *camera obscura*. At what point he began to consider how to make the view on the translucent glass surface permanent is not known, but in 1824 he started to frequent the shop of the Chevalier brothers, well-known Parisian makers of optical instruments. The result was an association with Niépce, through the Chevaliers, that led first to an agreement to perfect Niépce's process and finally to the daguerreotype.

After the French government had acquired the process, Daguerre occasionally demonstrated its methods and entered into arrangements to supply cameras and manuals of instruction, but he was considerably less active than others in perfecting his discovery. He preferred creating scenic effects on his estate in Bry-sur-Marne and in the local church where he painted a large *trompe l'oeil* perspective scene behind the altar. Although at Bry he made a small

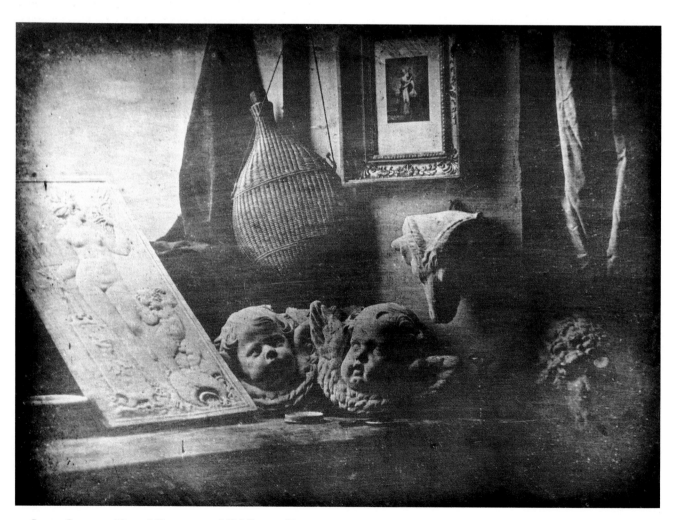

27. LOUIS JACQUES MANDÉ DAGUERRE. *Still Life*, 1837. Daguerreotype. Société Française de Photographie, Paris.

number of daguerreotypes of family and scenery, no further discoveries issued from his workshop nor did he develop artistically between 1839 and his death in 1851.

On the whole, Daguerre's output in the new medium reveals the influence of his artistic training and experience as the creator of picturesque yet convincing-looking scenes. His earliest surviving metal-plate image, an 1837 still life of plaster casts *(pl. no. 27)*, discloses a subject dear to Romantic artists, one to which he returned on a number of occasions. These works, and views made in Paris and Bry, demonstrate sensitivity to tonal balance, feeling for textural contrast, and a knowledge of compositional devices such as diagonal framing elements to lead the eye into the picture, but from Daguerre's complete output—some three dozen plates according to Helmut and Alison Gernsheim[19]—it is difficult to credit him with exceptional perception regarding the stylistic or thematic possibilities of the new pictorial medium.

Profile: William Henry Fox Talbot

As an heir of the Enlightenment, Talbot was concerned with practical application as well as with scientific theory, with combining intellectual interests and commercial endeavor. A patrician background, close and supportive family relationships, and the ownership of a lucrative estate, Lacock Abbey, made it possible for him to pursue his multifarious interests to successful conclusions. Besides inventing the first duplicatable image system generated by light, he envisaged the many uses to which photography has since been put, prophesying that "an alliance of science with art will prove conducive to the improvement of both."[20]

Born in 1800, shortly after the death of his father, Talbot was educated at Harrow and Cambridge and became learned in several fields of science. Despite the paltriness of scientific instruction in English universities of the time, he received satisfactory grounding in mathematics and optics, two areas that remained fundamental to his interests throughout his lifetime. Talbot augmented his formal training by closely following the work of British and foreign scientists, including Brewster, Herschel, Arago, Joseph von Fraunhofer, and Augustin Jean Fresnel, and during the 1830s and '40s he traveled abroad almost yearly on scholarly pursuits.

In 1839, events forced Talbot's hand with reference to the researches in photography that he had commenced in 1834—efforts to make images appear on light-sensitive materials—which he then had put aside to continue studies in optics and spectrology. In order to establish the priority of his discovery, Talbot exhibited at the Royal Society the photogenic drawings he had made in 1835 both by direct contact and in the camera, although he apparently had not considered them especially significant prior to the French announcement. His pictures' unflattering comparison with the daguerreotype's greater detail and shorter exposure time, coupled with the realization that his system possessed greater potential, caused Talbot to resume experimentation and resulted shortly in his perfection of the negative/positive process that he called calotype (a name derived from the Greek *kalos*: beautiful), which he patented in 1841. Unlike Daguerre, Talbot continued to improve the discovery, to envision its possibilities, and to devise practical methods of reproducing photographic images by photomechanical means, at the same time producing some 600 photographs, among them genre subjects, landscapes, urban views, and portraits.

In the 1850s, following unsuccessful legal battles to secure his patent rights, he turned again to studies in theoretical mathematics and etymology, and to a new interest, Assyriology, contributing substantially to the decipherment of Assyrian cuneiform. After his death in 1877, the achievements of this fine, if somewhat unfocused scholar were obscured for a long period despite the fact that he had written seven books and more than 50 papers on a variety of scientific topics, held 12 significant patents, and made at least eight comprehensive translations from Assyrian literature, besides discovering the system of photographic image-making that continues in use today.

2.

A PLENITUDE
OF PORTRAITS

1839–1890

*From that moment onwards, our loathsome society rushed, like Narcissus,
to contemplate its trivial image on a metallic plate. A form of lunacy,
an extraordinary fanaticism took hold of these new sun-worshippers.*

—*Charles Baudelaire, 1859*[1]

*. . . it is required of and should be the aim of the artist photographer to
produce in the likeness the best possible character and finest expression
of which that face and figure could ever have been capable. But in the result
there is to be no departure from truth in the delineation and
representation of beauty, and expression, and character.*

—*Albert Sands Southworth, 1870*[2]

VIRTUALLY FROM ITS INCEPTION, photography has been involved with portraiture, continuing in a new medium the impulse to represent human form that goes back to the dawn of art. The daguerreotype and negative–positive technologies provided the basis for flourishing commercial enterprises that satisfied the needs for public and private likenesses, while individuals who wished to express themselves personally through portraiture were able to do so using the calotype and collodion processes. Approaches to camera likenesses, whether made for amateur or commercial purposes, ranged from documentary to artistic, from "materialistic" to "atmospheric," but whatever their underlying aesthetic mode, photographic portraits reflected from their origin the conviction that an individual's personality, intellect, and character can be revealed through the depiction of facial configuration and expression.

Indeed, from the Renaissance on, portraits have been most esteemed when they portrayed not only the sitter's physical appearance but inner character as well. Toward the end of the 18th century, the concept that pose, gesture, and expression should reveal the inner person became codified in a number of treatises that exhorted the portraitist to rise above merely mechanical graphic representation of the human features. The most significant expression of this idea was contained in the 1789 publication *Essays on Physiognomy* by Johann Kaspar Lavater, a work that proposed that painters develop the "talent of discovering the interior of Man by his exterior—of perceiving by certain natural signs, what does not immediately attract the senses."[3] These ideas still were current when the early promoters of photography were endeavoring to provide quickly made and inexpensive likenesses, and they have continued to inform serious portrait photography on into the 20th century.

Before photography was invented, however, artists already had devised methods to respond to the demand for portraits from a new clientele emerging as a result of the rise of bourgeois societies in England, France, Holland, and America from the 17th century on. Earlier, the painted portrait had been largely the privilege of aristocrats and the very wealthy, but simplifications in terms of what was included in the painting, and transformations in size and materials enabled merchants and farming gentry in the 18th and early 19th centuries to contemplate having portraits made of themselves and their families. By the mid-19th century, in addition to the large, officially sanctioned portraits of royalty and public figures that still were being commissioned, the miniature, the silhouette, the physionotrace, the *camera lucida* drawing, and finally the photograph had arrived to accommodate the needs of new patrons for likenesses. Of these, the miniature was most like the traditional large-scale portrait. Although small, it was painted in full color, often on an ivory surface, and required imaginative skill and a delicate touch to evoke the character of the sitter. Regarded as precious keepsakes, miniatures such as the American example shown—a portrait of Eben Farley by Edward Greene Malbone (*pl. no. 28*)—usually were enclosed in elegant cases or inserted in lockets, the manner in which the daguerreotype portrait would be pre-

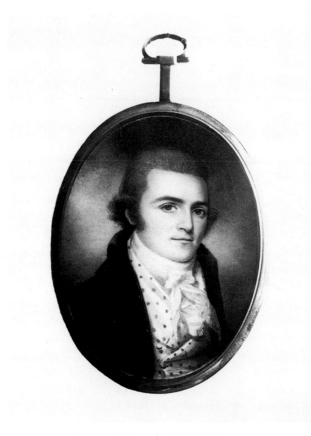

28. EDWARD GREENE MALBONE. *Eben Farley*, 1807. Miniature on ivory. Worcester Art Museum, Worcester, Mass.

sented also. The silhouette, on the other hand, might be considered the poor man's miniature, though it was not always small and often it appealed to those who could also afford a painted likeness. Traced from a cast shadow and inked in, or cut freehand from black paper, which then was mounted on a lighter ground, the silhouette showed only the profile, which would seem to leave little room for disclosing expression. Nevertheless, the conviction that profiles were as strong a key to character as other views impelled Lavater to include an illustration of a silhouetting device *(pl. no. 29)* in his work on physiognomy.

Both miniature and silhouette were unique objects— one-of-a-kind images. For duplicates of the same likeness, whether for personal use or in conjunction with a printed text, different systems were required—among them one made possible by a device called the physionotrace. Invented in France in 1786 by Gilles Louis Chrétien, it consisted of a pointer attached by a series of levers to a pencil, by means of which the operator could trace on paper a profile cast onto glass. A pantograph reduced and transferred the image to a copper plate, which, when engraved and inked, would permit the printing of an edition.[4] From Paris, the physionotrace was introduced to other cities in Europe and taken to the United States by a French émigré, Charles Fevret de Saint-Memin, who practiced the technique in the major New World centers between 1793 and 1844. Numerous figures in the arts, sciences, and public life, among them Thomas Jefferson *(pl. no. 30)*, sat for the four minutes required to make a portrait tracing by physionotrace.

Daguerreotype Portraits

That the photograph might provide a more efficient method than either physionotrace or silhouette to produce faithful likenesses seems obvious today, but when first announced, neither Daguerre's nor Talbot's process was capable of being used to make portraits. In 1839, sittings would have required about 15 minutes of rigid stillness in blazing sunshine owing to the primitive nature of the lenses used and the insufficient sensitivity to light of the chemically treated plates and paper. Because the highly detailed daguerreotype was considered by many the more attractive of the two processes and, in addition, was unrestricted in many localities, individuals in Europe and the United States scrambled to find the improvements that would make commercial daguerreotype portraits possible. They were aided in their purpose by the general efforts in progress to improve the process for all kinds of documentation.

Among the means used to accomplish this goal were the reduction of plate size, the improvement of lenses, the use of mirrors to reverse the plate's laterally inverted image back to normal, the shortening of exposure times by the addition of chemical accelerants in the sensitizing process, and the toning of the plate. Experimentation along these lines took place wherever daguerreotypes were made—in France, the German-speaking countries, and the United States—even in England where there was less commercial daguerreotyping activity owing to patent restrictions.

The earliest improvements were made to cameras and lenses. Daguerre's cumbersome experimental camera was redesigned, and lighter models, accommodating smaller plates, were manufactured in France by both amateurs and optical-instrument makers, among them Alphonse Giroux, a relative of Daguerre's wife who became the first commercial producer of the daguerreotype camera. These changes made it possible to carry the equipment to the countryside or abroad and even to make likenesses, provided the sitter did not object to holding absolutely still for two minutes. But commercial portraiture could not be contemplated until after chemical procedures were improved and a faster portrait lens, designed by Viennese scientist Josef Max Petzval to admit more than 20 times as much light, was

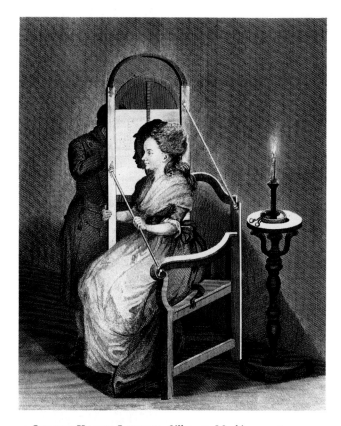

29. JOHANN KASPAR LAVATER. *Silhouette Machine*, c. 1780. Engraving from *Essays on Physiognomy*. Gernsheim Collection, Humanities Research Center, University of Texas, Austin.

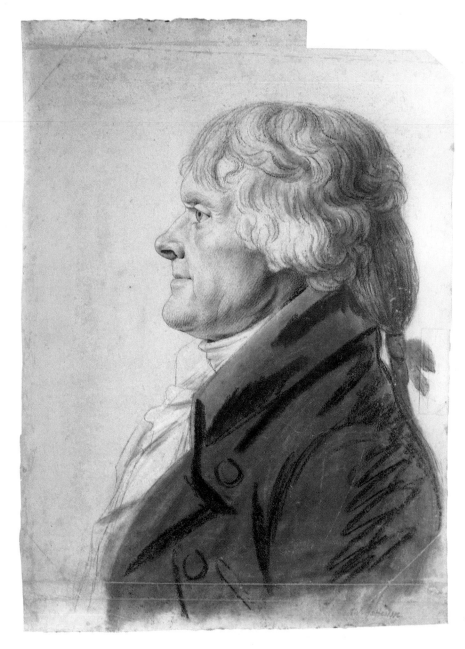

30. CHARLES FEVRET DE SAINT-MEMIN. *Thomas Jefferson*, 1804. Pastel, charcoal and chalk on paper. Worcester Art Museum, Worcester, Mass.

introduced in 1840 by his compatriot Peter Friedrich Voigtländer.

The first efforts to make the silver surface more receptive to light resulted from experiments conducted late in 1840 by English science lecturer John Frederick Goddard. By fuming the plate in other chemicals in addition to mercury vapor, he decreased exposure time considerably; plates sensitized in this manner and used in conjunction with the Petzval lens required exposures of only five to eight seconds. Alongside these developments, a method of gilding the exposed and developed plate in a solution of gold chloride—the invention of Hippolyte Fizeau in 1840—made the image more visible and less susceptible to destruction, and prepared the daguerreotype for its first paying customers.

With the stage set for the business of making portraits by camera, one might ask where the photographers would be found. As is often true when older professions seem on the verge of being overtaken by new technologies, members drift (or hurry) from allied fields into the new one. A large number of miniature and landscape painters, in France especially, realized during the 1840s that their experiences as craftsmen might fit them for making camera portraits (and other documents). French author Charles Baudelaire's contention that the photographic industry had become "the refuge of failed painters with too little talent"[5] may have been too harsh, but it is true that unemployed and poorly paid miniaturists, engravers, and draftsmen turned to portrait photography for the livelihood it seemed to promise. Watchmakers, opticians, tinkers, and

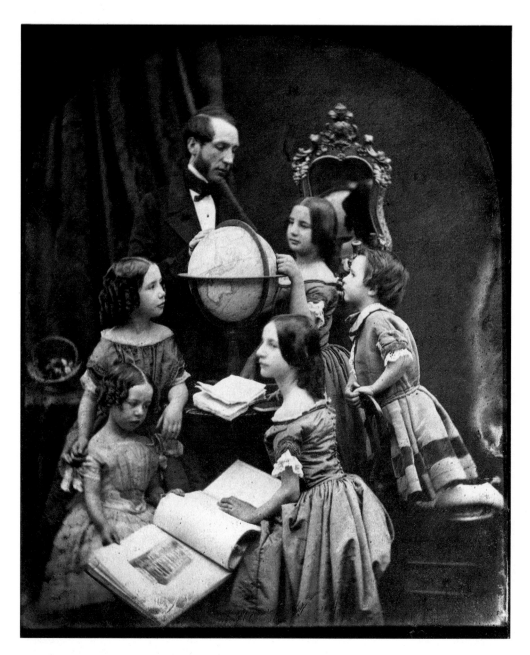

31. Antoine François
Claudet. *The Geography
Lesson*, c. 1850.
Daguerreotype. Gernsheim
Collection, Humanities
Research Center,
University of Texas,
Austin.

other artisans also were intrigued by the new technology and the chance it offered to improve their material well-being.

In England and the United States, portraiture sometimes attracted businessmen who hired artists and others to make exposures and process plates. Antoine François Claudet, a French émigré residing in London, had been in the sheet glass business before opening a daguerreotype studio. Eminently successful as a portraitist, Claudet also demonstrated a broad interest in photography in general—in technical problems, paper processes, and aesthetic matters. In spite of his belief that the process was so difficult that "failure was the rule and success the exception,"[6] the

portraits made in his studio are exceptional in their fine craftsmanship and in the taste with which groups of figures were posed, arranged, and lighted *(pl. no. 31)*.

Richard Beard, partner in a coal firm who had bought a patent from Daguerre's agent in 1841 to sell the rights in England, Wales, and the colonies, started his portrait studio with the idea that the new American Wolcott camera, in which he held an interest, would insure the financial prospects of daguerreotype portraiture. In addition to selling licenses to others, Beard eventually owned three establishments in London, with daguerreotypists hired to operate the cameras, as seen in the image of Jabez Hogg *(pl. no. 32)* making an exposure in Beard's studio (Hogg, however, is believed to have been an associate rather than a paid employee).

Since this image may be the earliest representation of the interior of a portrait studio showing a photographer at work, it affords an opportunity to examine the equipment and facilities in use in the opening years of portraiture. A tripod—actually a stand with a rotating plate—supports a simple camera without bellows. It is positioned in front of a backdrop painted in rococo style, against which female figures probably were posed. The stiffly upright sitter—in this case a Mr. Johnson[7]—is clamped into a head-brace, which universally was used to insure steadiness. He clutches the arm of the chair with one hand and makes a fist with the other so that his fingers will not flutter. After being posed, the sitter remains in the same position for longer than just the time it takes to make an exposure, because the operator must first obtain the sensitized plate from the darkroom (or if working alone, prepare it), remove the focusing glass of the camera, and insert the plate into the frame before beginning the exposure. Hogg is shown timing the exposure with a pocket watch by experience while holding the cap he has removed from the lens, but in the course of regular business this operation was ordinarily left to lowly helpers. In all, the posing process was nerve-wracking and lengthy, and if the sitter wished to have more than one portrait made the operator had to repeat the entire procedure, unless two cameras were in use simultaneously—a rare occurrence except in the most fashionable studios. No wonder so many of the sitters in daguerreotype portraits seem inordinately solemn and unbending.

Following the exposure, the plate, with no image yet visible, would have been removed from the camera and taken to the darkroom to develop by fuming in mercury vapor. By 1842/43, when this image was made, darkroom

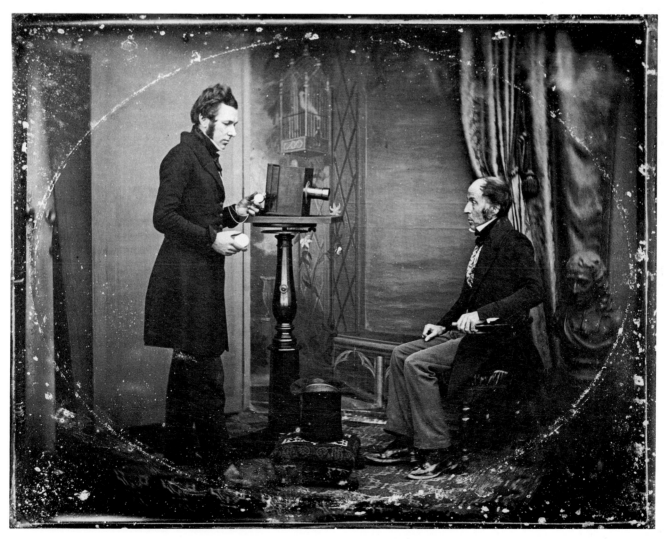

32. UNKNOWN PHOTOGRAPHER. *Jabez Hogg Making a Portrait in Richard Beard's Studio*, 1843. Daguerreotype. Collection Bokelberg, Hamburg.

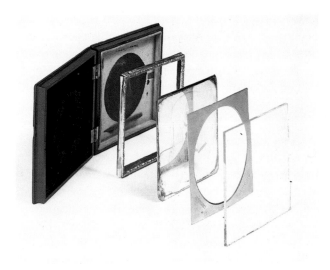

33. Daguerreotype case, frame, and matte. International Museum of Photography at George Eastman House, Rochester, N.Y.

operations already were performed under red safelight, an invention Claudet devised to facilitate development. The plate then would have been fixed in hypo and washed in chloride of gold. Because the daguerreotype's principal drawback was thought to be its "ghastly appearance . . . like a person seen by moonlight, or reflected in water,"[8] the portrait would have been hand-colored by a method Beard patented in 1842, but such coloring was practiced almost universally in all the better studios. Although gold toning had made the daguerreotype less susceptible to oxidation, its delicate pigmented surface required protection and was sheathed in a metal mat, covered with glass, and enclosed in a case (pl. no. 33), lending the final assemblage the appearance of the more expensive painted miniatures. Daguerreotype portraits were made in a variety of sizes, all derived from the standard "whole plate," which measured 6½ x 8½ inches. The most common portrait sizes were "quarter plate," 3¼ x 4¼ inches—the size of the Hogg image—and "sixth plate," 2¾ x 3¼ inches.

Unfortunately, the interior shown in the Hogg portrait does not reveal the method of lighting the subject, for illumination was a most important factor in the success of the portrait. Early studios usually were situated on the roofs of buildings where sunlight was unobstructed. On clear days, exposures might be made out-of-doors, although not ordinarily in direct sunlight because of the strongly cast shadows, while interior rooms somewhat resembled greenhouses with banks of windows, adjustable shades, and, occasionally, arrangements of blue glass to soften the light and keep the sitter from squinting in the glare.

With the introduction of the Petzval portrait lens and

the knowledge of the accelerating action of a combination of chemicals in sensitizing the plate, portrait daguerreotyping began to expand throughout Europe. Its popularity in France was immediate. In 1847 some thousand portraits were exhibited in Paris alone, and daguerreotypists were active in many provincial cities as well. A hand-tinted daguerreotype of a family group, made in Paris in the 1850s, is typical of the general level and style of commercial portraiture in that it conveys the manner in which the figures were disposed in the space and the handling of lighting directed to focus the eye both on the familial relationship and on material facts (pl. no. 34).

In the German-speaking cities of Berlin, Hamburg, Dresden, Vienna, and Bern, the volume of daguerreotype portraiture was smaller than that produced in France but seems otherwise comparable in style and craftsmanship. Although artists who took up daguerreotyping occasionally were denounced as "paint-sputterers" who had turned themselves into artistic geniuses with the help of sunlight,[9] they produced skillfully realized and authoritative images, among them Alexander von Humboldt (pl. no. 35) by Hermann Gunther Biow and Mother Albers (pl. no. 36) by Carl Ferdinand Stelzner, a miniature painter of repute who for a brief period was associated with Biow in a Hamburg daguerreotype studio. Another example, an 1845 portrait of three young girls (pl. no. 37) by Berlin daguerreotypist Gustav Oehme, displays a feeling for grace and symmetry in the grouping of the figures and an unusual sense of presence in the direct level gaze of the three youngsters. The Dresden photographer Hermann Krone was acclaimed not only for excellent portrait daguerreotypes but for his topographical views, nude studies, and still lifes (see Chapters 3 and 5); like a number of serious daguerreotypists of this era, he was interested in the widest application of the medium and in its potential for both art and documentation.

The taking of likenesses by daguerreotype spread more slowly through the rest of Europe during the 1840s and '50s. Investigations have turned up a greater amount of activity than once was thought to exist, but, other than in the larger cities, portrait work in Central Europe was done mainly by itinerants. However, much of that was lost in the nationalistic and revolutionary turmoils of the 19th century. In a number of countries, the daguerreotype and, later, photography on paper and glass came to be considered apt tools for ethnic self-realization. One example entitled A Magyar Föld és Népei (The Land of Hungary and Its People), published in 1846/47, was illustrated with lithographs based on daguerreotypes thought to have been made by János Varsányi, and included ethnographic portraits as well as the expected images of landscape and monuments.

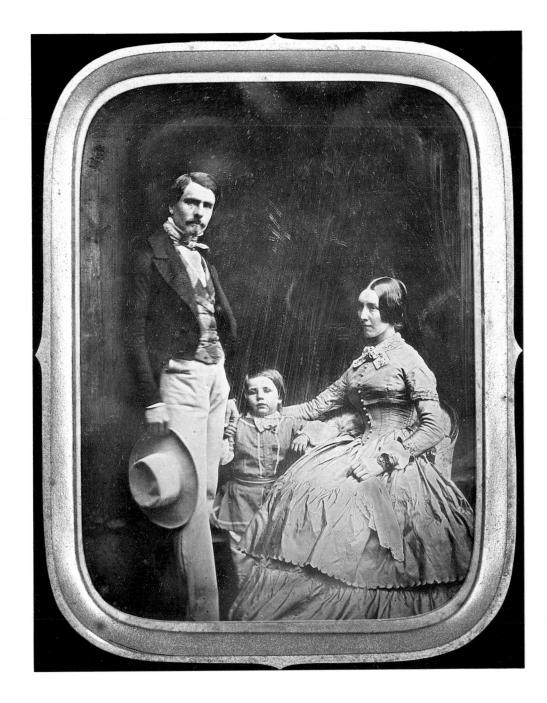

34. D. F. MILLET. *Couple and Child*, 1854–59. Daguerreotype. Bibliothèque Nationale, Paris.

Farther east, the progress of both daguerreotype and calotype in France and England was monitored in Russia by the Petersburg Academy of Sciences, and in 1840 Aleksei Grevkov, who tried to work with the less costly metals of copper and brass for the sensitized plate, opened the first daguerreotype studio in Moscow. Sergei Levitskii, who started a portrait studio in Petersburg in 1849 following a period of practice in Italy and study in Paris, experimented with the electroplating of daguerreotypes and with calotype procedures before turning to collodion photography; he sought also to combine electric and natural light in order to shorten the lengthy exposure times made necessary by the long Russian winters. In general, however, the profession of portrait photography in all of these localities, whether practiced for commercial or artistic purposes, was not able to expand until about 40 years after its debut, an understandable state of affairs when one realizes that in the 1840s in Belgrade, for instance, a daguerreotype cost as much as a month of daily dinners in the finest restaurant.[10]

Daguerreotype Portraiture in America

Daguerreotype portraiture was made to order for the United States, where it reached a pinnacle of success dur-

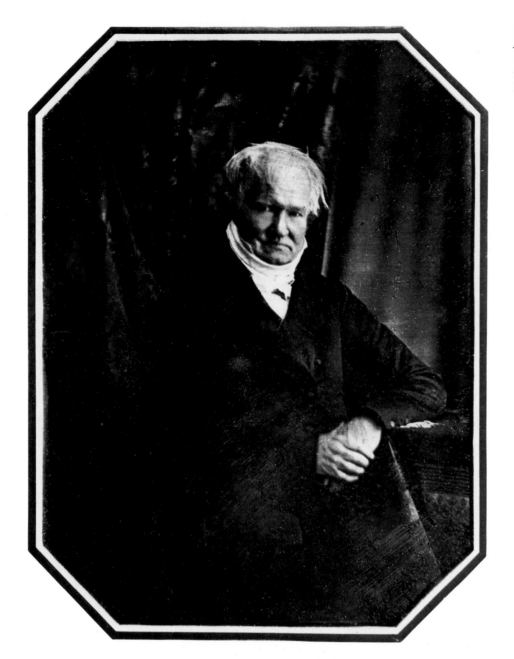

35. HERMANN GUNTHER BIOW. *Alexander von Humboldt, Berlin*, 1847. Daguerreotype. Museum für Kunst und Gewerbe, Hamburg.

ing the 20 years that followed its introduction into the country. In the conjunction of uncanny detail, artless yet intense expression, and naive pose, Americans recognized a mirror of the national ethos that esteemed unvarnished truth and distrusted elegance and ostentation. The power of "heaven's broad and simple sunshine" to bring out "the secret character with a truth that no painter would ever venture upon," which Nathaniel Hawthorne praised in *The House of the Seven Gables*,[11] helped propel the silver camera likeness into an instrument through which the nation might recognize its best instincts. Furthermore, the cohesive bodies of work produced to distill this message were the products of commercial studios, a fact that accorded with the native respect for entrepreneurial initiative.

Attempts to make daguerreotype portraits preoccupied Americans from the start. Shortly after instruction manuals arrived from England in September, 1839, Samuel F. B. Morse, his colleague John William Draper, Professor of Chemistry at New York University, Henry Fitz in Boston, and Robert Cornelius in Philadelphia managed to overcome the estimated 10-20 minute exposure time and produce likenesses—some with eyes closed against the glaring sunlight—by reducing the size of the plate and whitening the sitter's face. The exposure time for Draper's well-known 1840 portrait of his sister, Dorothy Catherine *(pl. no. 38)* (sent by the chemist to John Herschel as a token of esteem for the English scientist's contributions to photography), was 65 seconds, still too long for commercial portraiture, and an image produced around the same time by Henry Fitz, Jr., a telescope maker, showed the face with eyes closed on a plate the size of a large postage stamp.

Europeans had to wait until 1841 to sit before the studio daguerreotype camera, but in America the first commercial enterprises were opened in New York City by Alexander S. Wolcott and John Johnson and in Philadelphia by Cornelius in the spring of 1840. Working with Fitz, Wolcott and Johnson patented a camera of their own design (mentioned previously in connection with Beard) and installed an ingenious plate glass mirror arrangement in their studio window that increased illumination on the sitter, softening the glare with a baffle of glass bottles filled with a blue liquid. Although their mirror camera was eventually discarded, improvements in daguerreotype technology in the United States were rapid. The finest lenses and

plates continued to be imported, but, during the 1840s, optical systems and cameras as well as plates and chemicals also were manufactured locally, resulting in less expensive products and in the setting-up of photographic supply houses, the forerunners of the giant companies of today. Techniques for harnessing the buffing and polishing machinery to steam power and for creating a rational assembly line—the so-called German system—in manufacturing and studio processing procedures soon followed.

The absolute frontality in Draper's portrait of Catherine, the result of his scientific intent, is nevertheless emblematic of the approach taken by a great many early daguerreotypists in America. The work of John Plumbe, an enterprising businessman out to make a success of selling equipment, supplies, and lessons as well as inexpensive likenesses, who opened a studio in Boston in 1841 and by the mid-'40s was the owner of a chain of portrait estab-

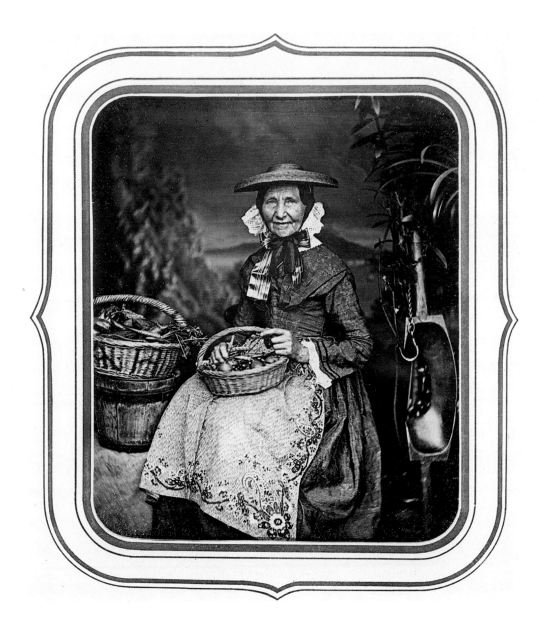

36. CARL FERDINAND STELZNER. *Mother Albers, The Family Vegetable Woman*, 1840s. Daguerreotype. Museum für Kunst und Gewerbe, Hamburg; Staatliche Landesbildstelle, Hamburg.

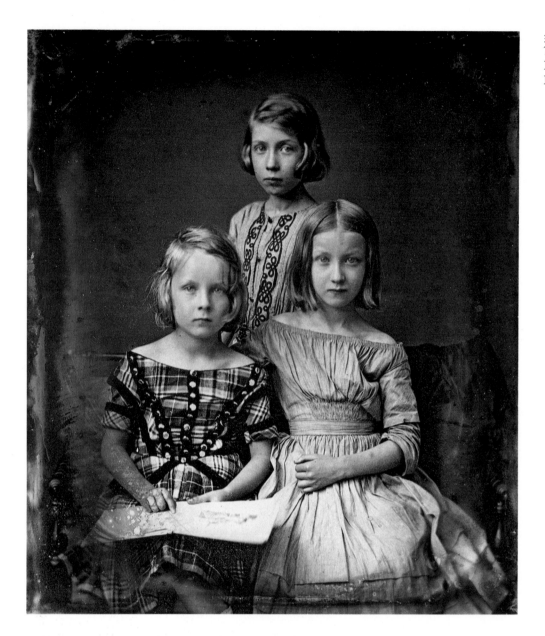

lishments in 14 cities, is typical of this style. As in the Draper image, the portrait of Mrs. Francis Luqueer *(pl. no. 39)*, taken in one of the Plumbe studios, fills the space frontally and centrally, with no attempt at artistic pose, dramatic lighting, or grandiloquent props such as the drapery swags and statuary found in European daguerreotype portraits. This style must have appealed to Americans in part because of its similarity to the solemn portraits by native limners, exemplified in the likeness of Mrs. John Vincent Storm *(pl. no. 40)* by Ammi Phillips, made just a few years earlier. Nor was the sober approach limited to ordinary folk; the same directness and lack of artifice is seen in an 1847 daguerreotype, by an unknown maker, of the future abolitionist leader Frederick Douglass *(pl. no. 41)*. In this work, the absence of artistic pretension is mod-

erated by the sense of powerful psychological projection, by the suggestion of a distinctive presence.

The successes of the portrait establishments in New York and Washington started by Mathew Brady *(see Profile, Chapter 4)* are now legendary *(pl. no. 42)*. After taking lessons in the daguerreotype process from Morse, this former manufacturer of cases for jewelry and daguerreotypes opened his first "Daguerrean Miniature Gallery" on lower Broadway in 1844. His stated aim, "to vindicate true art" by producing better portraits at higher prices than the numerous competitors who were to be found in the same part of the city, was realized in part as a result of the patronage of Tammany Hall politicians and entertainment entrepreneur P. T. Barnum, and in part because Brady seems to have recognized the value of public relations.[12] By

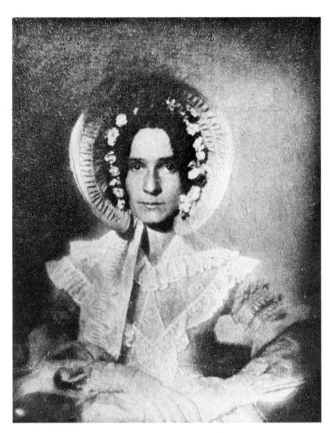

38. JOHN WILLIAM DRAPER. *Dorothy Catherine Draper*,
1840. Original destroyed. Collotype from a daguerreotype.
Chandler Chemical Museum, Columbia University, New York.

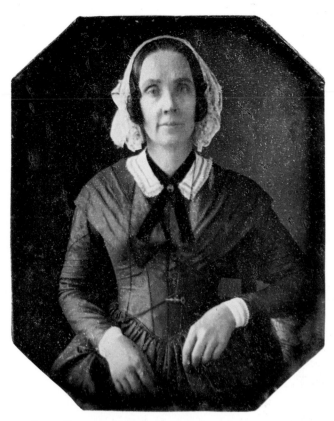

39. JOHN PLUMBE. *Mrs. Francis Luqueer*, n.d.
Daguerreotype. New-York Historical Society, New York.

sending portraits of celebrities and views of the gallery
interior to the newly launched picture journals, *Frank
Leslie's* and *Harper's Weekly*, for translation into wood-
engraved illustrations *(pl. no. 43)*, he was able to focus
attention on his own enterprise and on the role the daguerreotype might play in urban communication despite the
fact that it was a one-of-a kind image.

This limitation had prompted the enterprising Plumbe
to circumvent the unduplicatable nature of the daguerreotype by issuing in 1846 a series of engravings entitled *The
National Plumbeotype Gallery*, based on his camera portraits
of national figures. Brady followed with his *Gallery of Illustrious Americans*. Issued in 1850, it comprised 12 lithographs
by François D'Avignon based on Brady studio daguerreotypes of famous Americans, among them the artist John
James Audubon *(pl. no. 44)*. In both publications, the
implicit assumption that the character of an individual's
contribution to public life can be seen in physical features
and stance is testament to the continuing vigor of Lavater's
ideas about physiognomy.

An even stronger belief in the conjunction of appearance and moral character is evident in the fine daguerreotype portraiture that issued from the Boston studio of

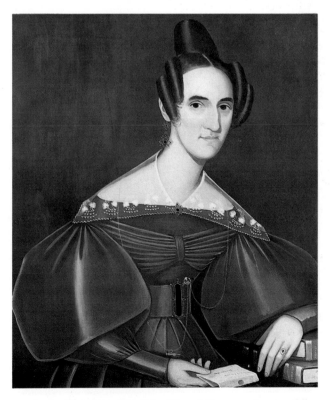

40. AMMI PHILLIPS. *Mrs. John Vincent Storm*, c. 1835–40. Oil
on canvas. Brooklyn Museum; gift of Mrs. Waldo Hutchins, Jr.

Albert Sands Southworth and Josiah Hawes. In business for almost 20 years—1843 to 1862—during the ascendancy of transcendentalist thought in that city, the partners approached portraiture with a profound respect for both spirit and fact. Convinced that "nature is not at all to be represented as it is, but as it ought to be and might possibly have been," they sought to capture "the best possible character and finest expression"[13] of which their sitters were capable without departing from the truth. Southworth and Hawes made more than 1,500 likenesses, a great many of which exhibit the exceptional authority apparent in an 1856 image of Charles Sumner (*pl. no. 45*). A medallion portrait of an unknown sitter (*pl. no. 46*), made with a sliding plateholder patented by Southworth in 1855, is un-

usually fine. The varied positions of the head, the split dark and light backgrounds, and the arrangement of ovals to suggest a lunar cycle convey the sense that camera images can ensnare time as well as depict physical substances.

It would be a mistake to think that most American daguerreotype portraiture attained the level of the work produced by Southworth and Hawes or even Brady. Most likenesses were simply records, whether made in fashionable studios or by small-town or itinerant daguerreotypists who charged little enough—from 25 cents to one dollar—to enable a broad sector of the populace to afford a portrait. On occasion, such images are appealing because of unusual pose or piquant expression or because of boldness and singular subject matter, as in a portrait of the Sauk chief

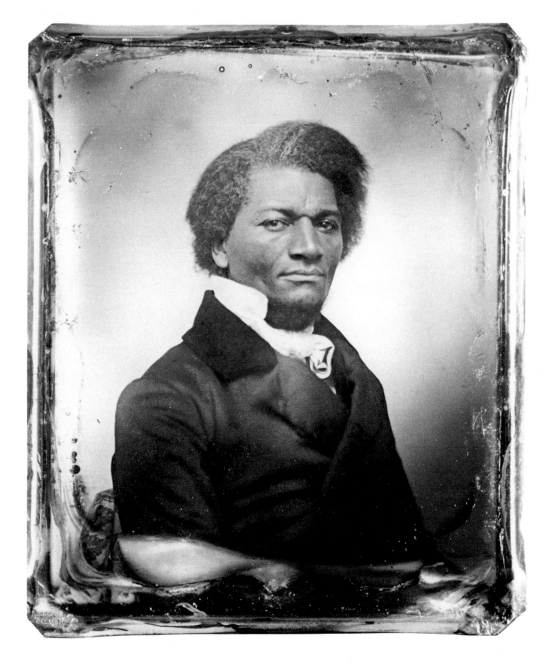

41. UNKNOWN PHOTOGRAPHER. *Frederick Douglass*, 1847. Daguerreotype. Collection William Rubel; National Portrait Gallery, Smithsonian Institution, Washington, D.C.

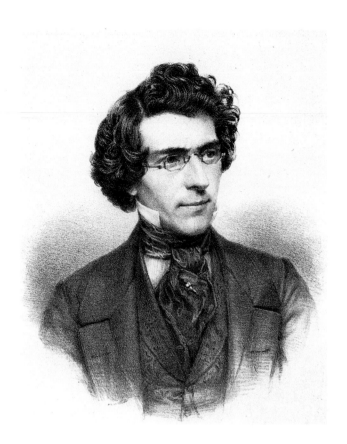

Keokuk (*pl. no. 47*) made by Thomas Easterly, working in Missouri in 1847. On the whole, however, daguerreotype likenesses were remarkably similar to each other in their unrelieved straightforwardness and the solemn, almost frozen demeanor of the sitters. As a writer for *Gleason's Pictorial and Drawing Room Companion* of 1853 observed of a daguerreotype display: "If you have seen one of these cases you have seen them all. There is the militia officer in full regimentals . . . there is the family group, frozen into wax statuary attitudes and looking . . . as if . . . assembled for a funeral. . . . the fast young man, taken with his hat on and a cigar in his mouth; the belle of the locality with a vast quantity of plaited hair and plated jewelry . . . the best baby . . . the intellectual . . . and the young poet. . . . There is something interesting in the very worst of these daguerreotypes because there must be something of nature in all of them."[14]

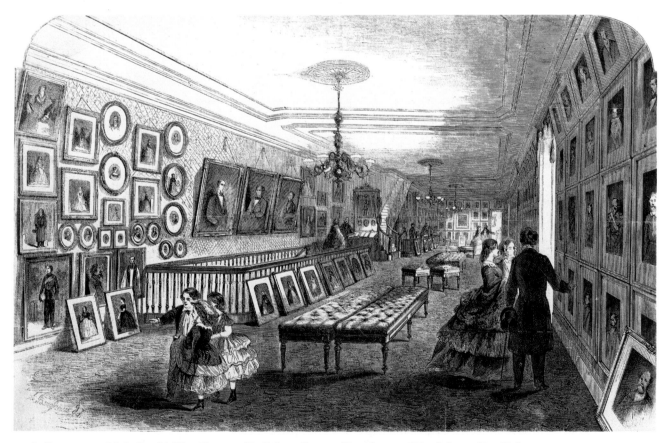

43. A. BERGHAUS. *M. B. Brady's New Photographic Gallery, Corner of Broadway and Tenth Street, New York* from *Frank Leslie's Illustrated Newspaper*, Jan. 5, 1861. Engraving. Library of Congress, Washington, D.C.

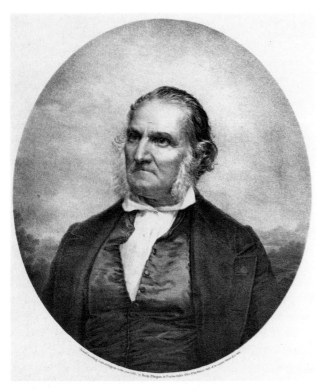

44. FRANÇOIS D'AVIGNON. *John James Audubon* from *Gallery of Illustrious Americans*, 1850. Lithograph after a photograph by Brady. Print Collection, New York Public Library, Astor, Lenox, and Tilden Foundations.

Of course, the unrelieved seriousness of expression in daguerreotype portraiture was in part the result of the lengthy process of arranging the sitter, head in clamp and hand firmly anchored, and then making the exposure, but spontaneity not only was technically difficult to achieve, it also was considered inappropriate to the ceremonial nature of an undertaking that for most sitters required proper deportment and correct attire. Even more joyless were the images of the dead *(pl. no. 48)* made as keepsakes for bereaved families for whom they possessed "the sublime power to transmit the almost living image of . . . loved ones."[15] Nevertheless, this "Phantom concourse . . . mute as a grave,"[16] evoked a singular response in the United States. As Richard Rudisill has pointed out in a provocative study, "the daguerreotypists employed their mirror images for the definition and recording of their time and their society. . . . They confronted Americans with themselves and sought to help them recognize their own significance."[17]

In the rest of the Americas, both north and south, portraiture followed a course similar to that in eastern Europe, with the exception that the first portraits in Canada and Latin America often were made by itinerants from the United States and Europe seeking a lucrative employ-

ment. By the 1850s permanent studios had been established in the major cities of Canada and South America, where despite the provincial character of urban life in those regions, both metal and paper portraits were seen as symbols of economic well-being and national self-realization.

Among the itinerant photographers traveling to Canada, mention is made of a female daguerreotypist who spent a month making likenesses in Montreal in 1841. The names of other women crop up in notices and reports on photography's early years to suggest that in spite of the medium's association with chemicals and smelly manipulations, it was not in itself regarded as an unsuitable pastime for women. Anna Atkins, Julia Margaret Cameron, Geneviève Elizabeth Disdéri, Lady Clementina Hawarden, Mrs. John Dillwyn Llewelyn, and Constance Talbot in Europe and Mary Ann Meade in the United States are only the best known of the women drawn to photography either in association with other members of the family or on their own. Women also were active behind the scenes in daguerreotype and paper printing establishments where they worked on assembly lines; later they were employed in

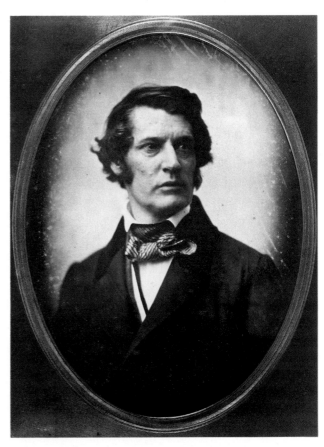

45. ALBERT SANDS SOUTHWORTH and JOSIAH JOHNSON HAWES. *Charles Sumner*, 1856. Daguerreotype. Bostonian Society, Boston.

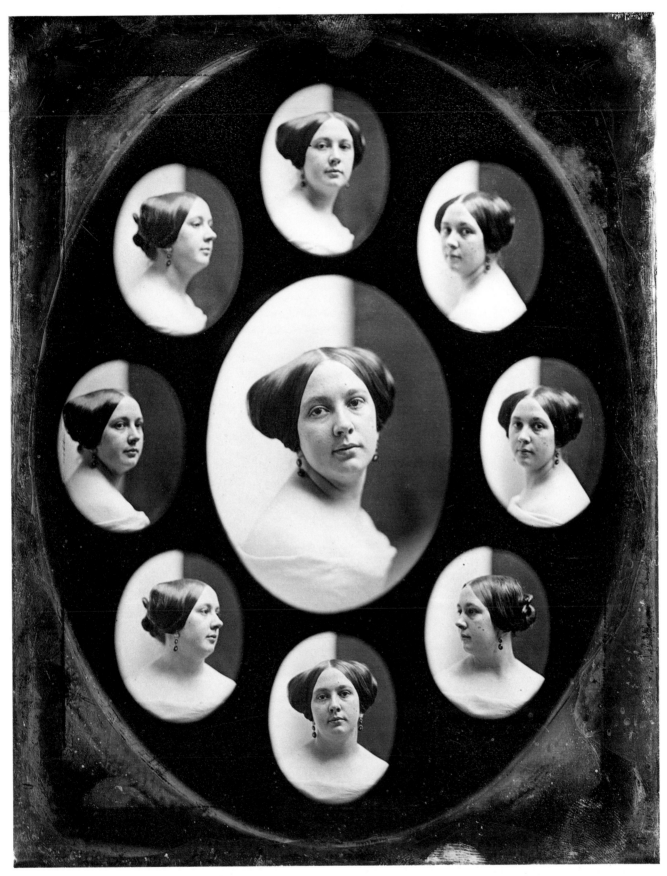

46. ALBERT SANDS SOUTHWORTH and JOSIAH JOHNSON HAWES. *Unknown Lady*, n.d. Medallion daguerreotype.
Museum of Fine Arts, Boston; gift of Edward Southworth Hawes in Memory of his Father, Josiah Johnson Hawes.

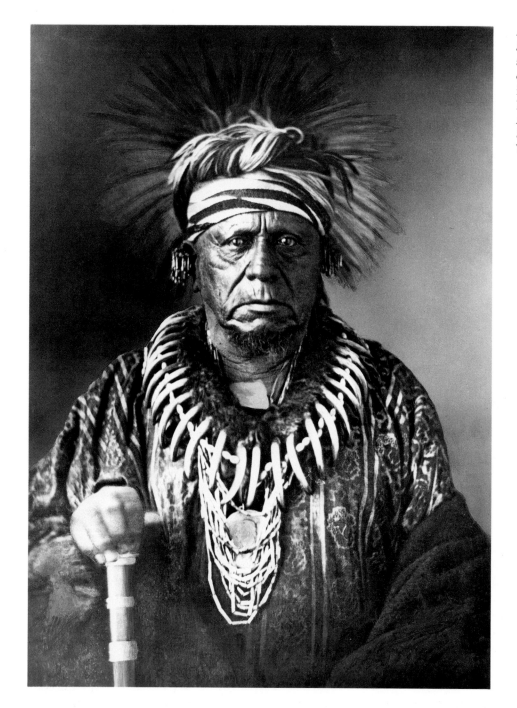

47. THOMAS EASTERLY. *Keokuk, Sauk Chief,* 1847. Modern gelatin silver print from a copy negative of the original daguerreotype in the collection of the Missouri Historical Society. National Anthropological Archives, Smithsonian Institution, Washington, D.C.

firms that produced and processed photographic materials, among them those owned by George Eastman and the Lumière brothers.

Portraits on Paper: The Calotype

Calotype portraiture never achieved the commercial popularity of the daguerreotype. Talbot's first successes in portraying the human face occurred in October, 1840, when he made a number of close-ups of his wife Constance, among them a three-quarter view of exceptional vitality requiring a 30 second exposure *(pl. no. 50)*. Convinced that paper portraiture was as commercially feasible as the daguerreotype, Talbot entered into an arrangement with a painter of miniatures, Henry Collen, to make calotype likenesses, but the resulting portraits, including one of Queen Victoria and the Princess Royal *(pl. no. 49)*, often were so indistinct that considerable retouching—at which Collen excelled—was necessary. Since neither Collen nor Talbot's next partner in portraiture, Claudet, were able to convince the public that the duplicatable paper image with its broad chiaroscuro style was preferable to the fine detail

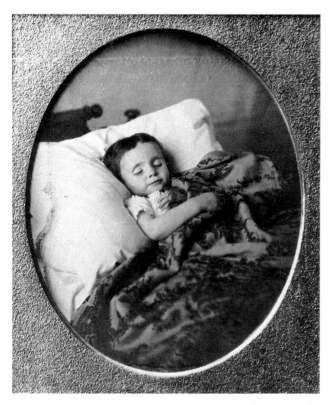

48. UNKNOWN PHOTOGRAPHER (American). *Dead Child*, c. 1850. Daguerreotype. Collection Richard Rudisill, Santa Fe, N.M.

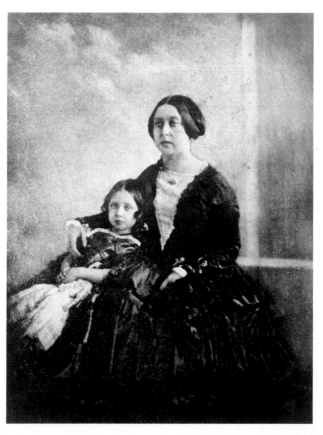

49. HENRY COLLEN. *Queen Victoria with Her Daughter, Victoria, Princess Royal*, 1844–45. Calotype. Royal Library, Windsor Castle. Reproduced by Gracious Permission of Her Majesty Queen Elizabeth II.

of the daguerreotype, commercial paper portraiture in England languished until the era of the glass negative.

The situation was different in Scotland, where, as noted in Chapter 1, Talbot's associate Sir David Brewster was instrumental in introducing the calotype to David Octavius Hill and Robert Adamson *(see Profile)*. In an endeavor to record the 400 or so likenesses to be included in a painting that Hill decided to make in 1843 commemorating the separation of the Church of Scotland from the Church of England, the two became so caught up in photography that they also produced hundreds of commanding portraits of individuals who had no relationship to the religious issues that were the subject of the painting. Aware that the power of the calotype lay in the fact that it looked like the "imperfect work of man . . . and not the perfect work of God,"[18] Hill and Adamson used the rough texture of the paper negative to create images with broad chiaroscuro effects that were likened by contemporaries to the paintings of Sir Joshua Reynolds and Rembrandt.

Among the sitters, who posed for one to two minutes either in an out-of-doors studio in Edinburgh, with a minimum of furnishings arranged to simulate an interior, or on location, were artists, intellectuals, the upper-class gentry of Scotland, and working fisherfolk in the nearby town of Newhaven. Simplicity of pose and dramatic yet untheatrical lighting emphasize the solid strength of the sitter James Linton *(pl. no. 51)*, a working fisherman. On the other hand, the genteel character of well-bred Victorian women is brought out in the poses, softer lighting, and gracefully intertwined arrangement of the three figures in *The Misses Binny and Miss Monro (pl. no. 52)*. Such Hill and Adamson images recall the idealized depictions of women in paintings by Daniel McClise and Alfred Chalons, popularized in the publication *Book of Beauty*, but as photographs they gain an added dimension because the camera reveals a degree of particularity entirely lacking in the paintings.

In artistic and literary circles in Britain and France, these photographs were considered the paradigm of portrait photography in that they made use of traditional artistic concepts regarding arrangement and employed atmospheric effects to reveal character. During the 1850s, a

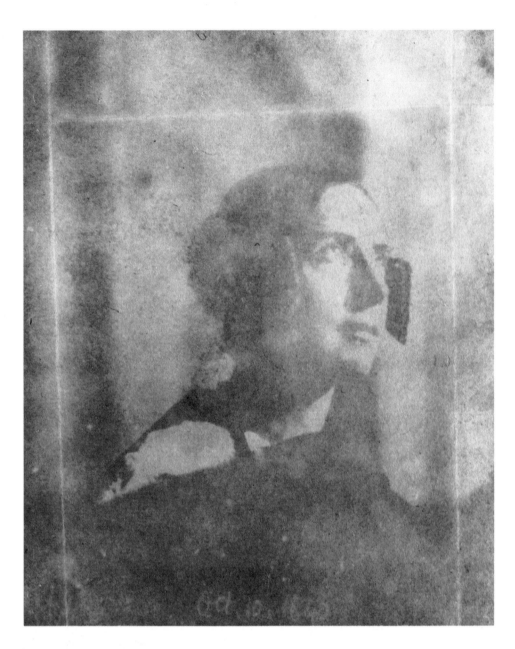

50. WILLIAM HENRY FOX
TALBOT. *"C's Portrait"*
(Constance Talbot), Oct. 10,
1840. Calotype. Royal
Photographic Society, Bath,
England.

group that included William Collie in the British Isles and
Louis Désiré Blanquart-Evrard, Charles Hugo, Gustave
Le Gray, Charles Nègre, and Victor Regnault on the Continent followed a similar path, using themselves, members
of their families, and friends to make calotype portraits
that emphasize light and tonal masses and suppress fussy
detail.

Portraits on Paper: Collodion/Albumen

For commercial portraitists, Frederick Scott Archer's
invention of the collodion negative seemed at first to solve
all problems. The glass plate made possible both sharp
definition and easy duplication of numbers of prints on
paper from one negative, while the awkward chemical procedures that the wet-plate process entailed were minimized
in a studio setting. Collodion opened up an era of commercial expansion, attracting to the profession many photographers who resorted to all manner of inducements to
entice sitters—among them elegantly appointed studios;
likenesses to be printed on porcelain, fabric, and other
unusual substances, as well as on paper; or set into jewelry;
photosculpture; and the most popular caprice of them
all—the *carte-de-visite*.

But before public acceptance of paper portraiture was
established, photographers were occupied for a number of
years with a half-way process, in which the collodion glass
negative was used to create a one-of-a-kind image that was
less costly than the daguerreotype. While both Talbot and
Archer had been aware that a bleached or underexposed

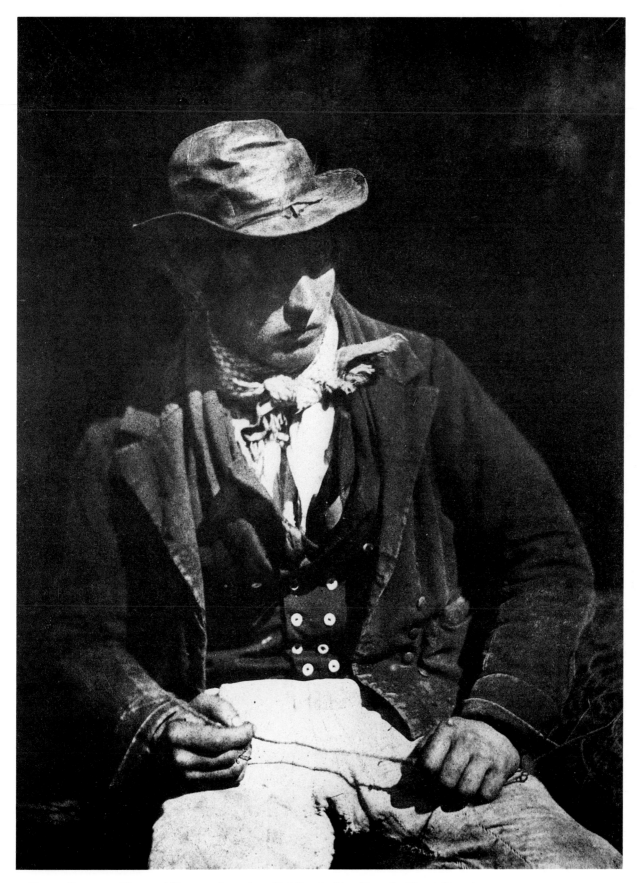

51. DAVID OCTAVIUS HILL and ROBERT ADAMSON. *Redding the Line (Portrait of James Linton)*, c. 1846. Calotype. Scottish National Portrait Gallery, Edinburgh.

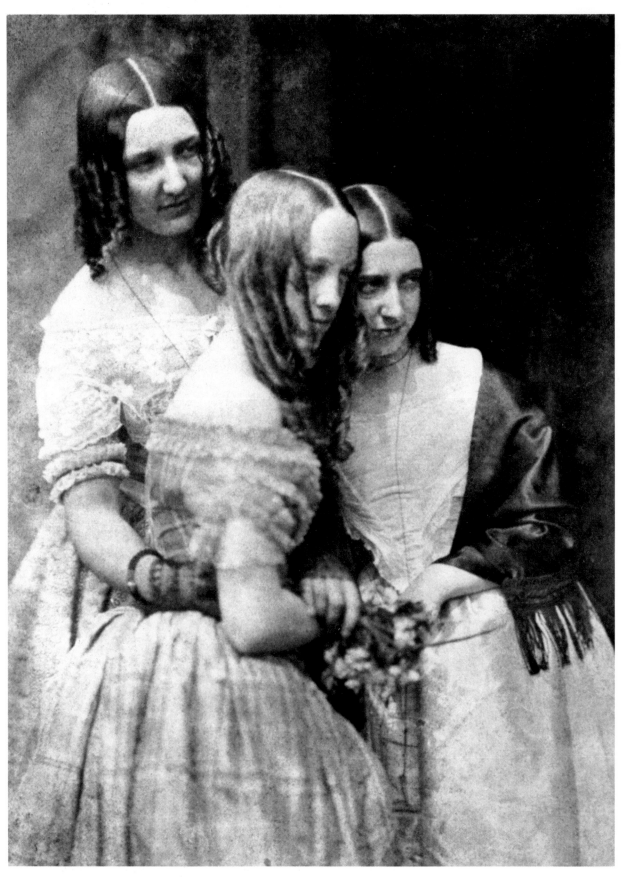

52. DAVID OCTAVIUS HILL and ROBERT ADAMSON. *The Misses Binny and Miss Monro*, c. 1845.
Calotype. Metropolitan Museum of Art, New York; Harris Brisbane Dick Fund, 1939.

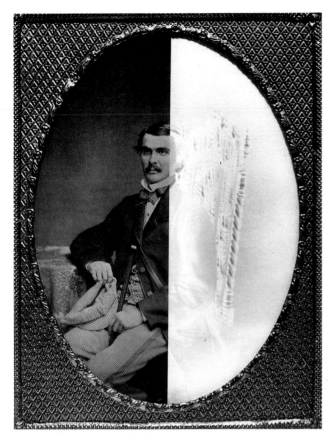

53. UNKNOWN PHOTOGRAPHER (American). *Untitled Portrait*, c. 1858. Ambrotype with backing partially removed to show positive and negative effect. Gernsheim Collection, Humanities Research Center, University of Texas, Austin.

The tintype, even less expensive than the ambrotype (to which it was technically similar), was patented in 1856 by an American professor at Kenyon College in Ohio.[19] Like the daguerreotype, it was a one-of-a-kind image on a metal plate (iron instead of silvered copper) that had been coated with black varnish and treated with sensitized collodion. Dull gray in tone without the sheen of the mirrorlike daguerreotype, the tintype was both lightweight and cheap, making it an ideal form for travelers and Civil War soldiers, many of whom were pictured in their encampments by roving photographers with wagon darkrooms. Not memorable for either insight or artistry, tintypes were being made in provincial areas until recently.

The combination of a negative on glass coated with sensitized collodion and a print on paper coated with sensitized albumen—the collodion/albumen process—made commercial portraiture possible on an undreamed of scale despite the fact that the prints themselves were subject to fading and discoloration. From the 1850s until the 1880s, studios in the major capitals of the world invested in ever-more elegant and unusual furnishings in order to attract a well-paying clientele. As the displays of status through attire and props grew more prominent, the goal of revealing character became secondary and portraits often seemed merely to be topographies of face and body, "dull, dead, unfeeling, inauspicious,"[20] as expressed in the words of the time.

The skillful handling of pose, lighting, props, and decor visible in the work of the highly regarded European portraitists Franz Hanfstaengl, Antoine Samuel Adam-Salomon, and Camille Silvy became models for emulation. Hanfstaengl, already renowned as a lithographer of artworks and portraits, opened a photographic art studio in Munich in 1853; his work soon won acclaim internationally for the tasteful poses, well-modulated lighting, and the exceptional richness of his prints on toned albumen paper, as exemplified by *Man With Hat (pl. no. 54)*. Hanfstaengl's earlier work, exhibited at the 1855 *Exposition Universelle* in Paris where it was both praised and criticized for extensive retouching (on the negative), is believed to have inspired Adam-Salomon to change his profession from sculptor to photographer. The poses preferred by Adam-Salomon—modeled on antique sculpture—and his penchant for luxurious fabrics and props, appealed to the materialistic concerns of the French bourgeoisie during the Second Empire. The photographer's heavy hand with the retouching brush—the only thing about his work that was considered disagreeable—is apparent in the lighter tonality behind the figure in this image of his daughter *(pl. no. 55)*.

Besides attesting to the sitter's status, props and poses might offer clues to personality, enriching the image psychologically and visually. The oval picture frame used

glass negative could be converted to a positive by backing the glass with opaque material (paper or fabric) or varnish *(pl. no. 53)*, the patent for this anomaly was taken out by an American, James Ambrose Cutting, in 1854. Called ambrotypes in the United States and collodion glass positives in Europe, these glass images were made in the same sizes as daguerreotypes and were similarly treated—hand-colored, framed behind glass, and housed in a slim case.

By the mid-'50s, when this portrait process was supplanting the metal image in Europe, although not yet in the United States, the case-making industry, which accommodated both types of portrait, was expanding. The earliest daguerreotypes had been enclosed in cases of *papier mâché* or wood covered with embossed paper or leather and usually were lined with silk in Europe and velvet in the United States, when they were not encased in lockets, brooches, and watchcases. In 1854, the "union" case was introduced. Made in the United States of a mixture of sawdust and shellac, these early thermoplastic holders were exported globally, eventually becoming available in a choice of about 800 different molded designs.

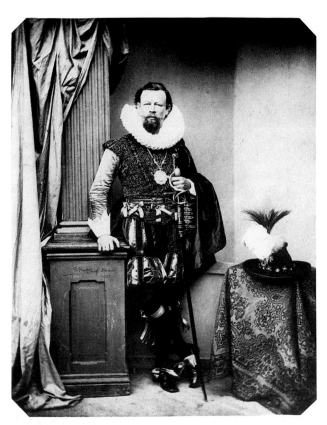

54. FRANZ HANFSTAENGL. *Man with Hat*, 1857. Salt print. Agfa-Gevaert Foto-Historama, Leverkusen, Germany.

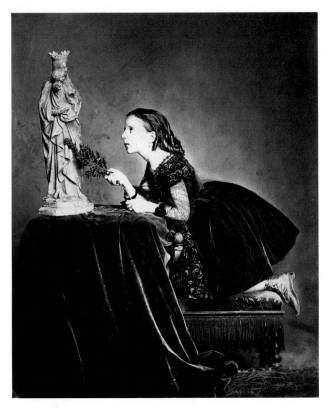

55. ANTOINE SAMUEL ADAM-SALOMON. *Portrait of a Girl*, c. 1862. Albumen print. Daniel Wolf, Inc., New York.

coyly as a lorgnette and the revealing drapery in the portrait of the Countess Castiglione *(pl. no. 56)* by Louis Pierson,[21] a partner in the Paris studio of Mayer Brothers and Pierson, suggest the seductive personality of Napoleon III's mistress, who was thought also to be an Italian spy. Oscar Gustave Rejlander's portrait of Lewis Carroll (Reverend Charles L. Dodgson—*pl. no. 57*) depicts the author of *Alice in Wonderland* holding a lens and polishing cloth and suggests through facial expression and demeanor the sense of propriety that Carroll brought to his photography. This work is part of Rejlander's substantial number of portraits that include images of friends, amusing views of himself and his female companion, and of the children who figured in the genre scenes *(see Chapter 5)* for which he is better known.

As studio photography preempted the role of the portrait painter, the aesthetic standards of handmade likenesses were embraced by the photographic portraitists. Manuals appeared early in the daguerreotype era, and continued through the collodion period (and into the 20th century), giving directions for appropriate dress and the correct colors to be worn to take advantage of the limited sensitivity of daguerreotype and glass plates. Included also were instructions for the proper attitudes in which sitters should be posed. Because the public still believed hand-painted portraits were more prestigious than photographs, likenesses often were painted over in watercolors, oils, or pastels, without entirely obliterating the underlying trace of the camera image, as in a typical example *(pl. no. 332)* from the studio of T. Z. Vogel and C. Reichardt, in Venice.

Meanwhile, the professional portrait painter, aware of the public appetite for exactitude, found the photograph a convenient crutch, not just for copying the features but actually for painting upon. Projection from glass positives to canvas was possible as early as 1853; shortly afterward several versions of solar projection enlargers, including one patented in 1857 by David Woodward, a professor of fine arts in Baltimore, simplified enlargement onto sensitized paper and canvas. When partially developed, the image could be completely covered with paint, as recent X-rays of a life-size painted portrait of Lincoln *(pl. no. 58)* by Alexander François have disclosed. This practice, common in the last half of the 19th century, was not considered reprehensible because in the view of many painters the role of photography was as the artist's "helpmate" in creative handwork. Although the photographic "underpainting" was rarely acknowledged, the desire for verisimilitude on the part of painter and public, and the hope for artistic status on the part of the photographer, resulted in a hybrid form of portraiture—part photochemical and part handwork.

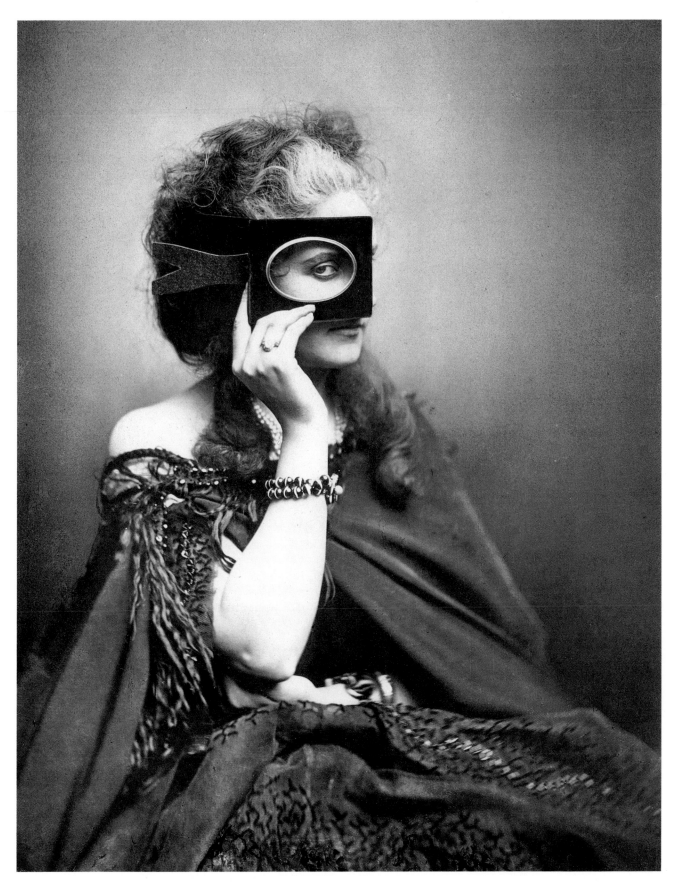

56. LOUIS PIERSON. *Countess Castiglione*, c. 1860. Albumen print (previously attributed to Adolphe Braun).
Metropolitan Museum of Art, New York; David Hunter McAlpin Fund, 1947.

Carte-de-visite and Celebrity Portraits

With the possibility of endless replication from the collodion negative, it was only a matter of time before a pocket-size paper portrait was devised. Suggestions along this line, made by several photographers in Europe and the United States, included the substitution of a likeness for the name and address on a calling card—the traditional manner of introducing oneself among middle- and upper-class gentry—and the affixing of small portraits to licenses, passports, entry tickets, and other documents of a social nature. However, André Adolphe Disdéri, a photographer of both portraits and genre scenes who also was active in improving processes and formulating aesthetic standards, patented the *carte-de-visite* portrait in 1854. This small image—3½ x 2½ inches, mounted on a slightly larger card—was produced by taking eight exposures during one

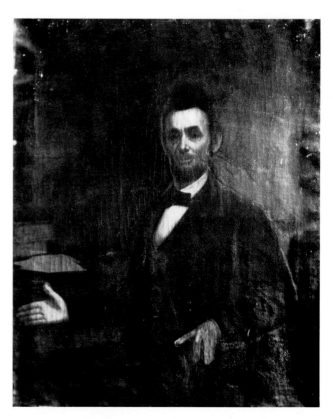

58. ALEXANDER FRANÇOIS. *Abraham Lincoln*, n.d. Oil on canvas. Collection George R. Rinhart, Colebrook, Conn.

sitting, using an ingenious sliding plate holder in a camera equipped with four lenses and a vertical and horizontal septum *(pl. no. 226)*. A full-length view of the figure in more natural and relaxed positions became possible, and it was not necessary for each pose to be exactly the same, as can be seen in an uncut sheet of *carte-de-visite* portraits taken by Disdéri of Princess Gabrielli *(pl. no. 59)*.

The reasons why the *carte* portraits became so enormously popular after 1859 are not entirely clear, but for a considerable part of the next decade this inexpensive format captured the public imagination in much the same way the stereograph view had. Portrait studios everywhere—in major cities and provincial villages—turned out millions of full- and bust-length images of working and trades people as well as of members of the bourgeoisie and aristocracy. These could be sold inexpensively because unskilled labor cut the images apart after processing and pasted them on mounts on which trademarks or logos of the maker appeared either on the front of the card, discreetly placed below the image, or on the reverse. Frequently, elaborate displays of type and graphic art suggested the connections between photography and painting. Backgrounds still included painted gardens, balustrades, drapery swags, and furniture, but sitters also were posed against undecorated walls, and vignetting—in which the

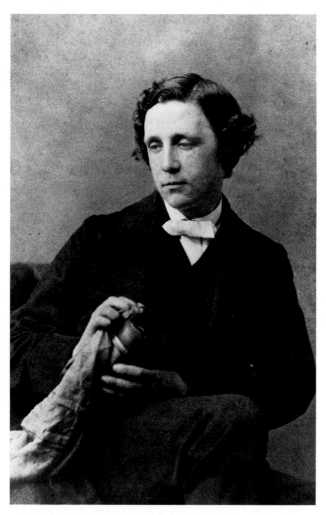

57. OSCAR GUSTAVE REJLANDER. *Lewis Carroll (Rev. Charles L. Dodgson)*, March 28, 1863. Albumen print. Gernsheim Collection, Humanities Research Center, University of Texas, Austin.

background was removed—was not uncommon. Adults displayed the tools of their trade, the marks of their profession, and the emblems of their rank; children were shown with toys; and attention was paid to women's attire and hair arrangements. Nevertheless, apart from the informality of pose that imbues some of these images with a degree of freshness, *carte* portraits offered little compass for an imaginative approach to pose and lighting as a means of evoking character.

As their popularity continued, famous works of art, well-known monuments, portraits of celebrities and of fashionably attired women (at times pirated and reproduced from other *cartes* rather than from the original collodion negative) appeared on the market. That the wide dispersal of celebrity images had consequences beyond that of a pleasant pastime can be seen in the fact that already in the 1860s such images influenced the course of a public career. Both the moderately gifted Jenny Lind and the unexceptional Lola Montez became cult figures in the United States largely owing to their promotion through *carte* portraits. Lincoln is said to have ascribed his election to the Presidency at least in part to Brady's *carte* of him when he still was an unknown, and both the French and British Royal families permitted the sales of *carte* portraits of themselves; on the death of Prince Albert, for example, 70,000 likenesses of Queen Victoria's consort were sold. *Cartes* also took over the function formerly performed by lithographs and engravings in popularizing types of female

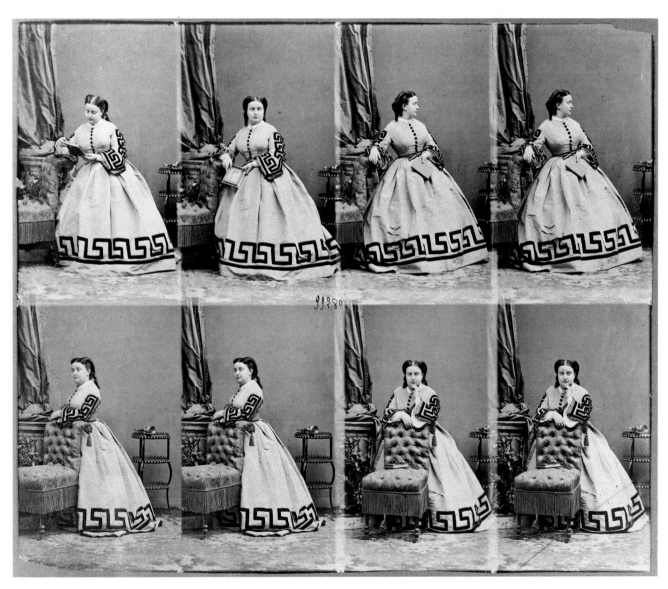

59. ANDRÉ ADOLPHE EUGENE DISDÉRI. *Princess Gabrielli* (born Augusta Amelia Maximilienne Jacqueline Bonaparte), c. 1862. Uncut albumen print from a *carte-de-visite* negative. Gernsheim Collection, Humanities Research Center, University of Texas, Austin.

beauty and fashionable attire. Silvy, a French photographer of artistic taste who in 1859 opened a studio in his lavishly decorated London residence, specialized in posing his upper-class sitters in front of mirrors so that the softly modulated lighting not only called attention to attire and hairstyle—fore and aft, so to speak—but surrounded them also with an aura of luxuriousness.

Cartes were avidly collected and exchanged, with ornate albums and special holders manufactured to satisfy the demand for gimmickry connected with the fad. This activity received a boost from the enthusiasm of Queen Victoria, who accumulated more than one hundred albums of portraits of European royalty and distinguished personages. Indeed, the British royal family was so taken with photography that they not only commissioned numberless portraits but purchased genre images, sent photographs as state gifts, underwrote photographic ventures, and were patrons of The Photographic Society; in addition they installed a darkroom for their own use in Windsor Castle. British and French monarchs staunchly supported photography in general because it represented progress in the chemical sciences, which was emblematic of the prosperity brought to their respective nations, and also because the easily comprehended imagery accorded with the taste for

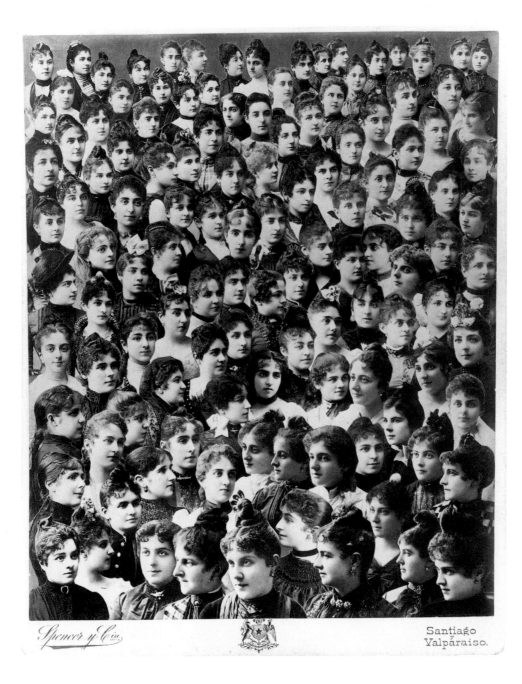

60. SPENCER Y CIA.
Chilean Ladies, n.d.
Albumen print. Neikrug
Photographica, Ltd., New
York.

Spencer y Cia.   Santiago
Valparaiso.

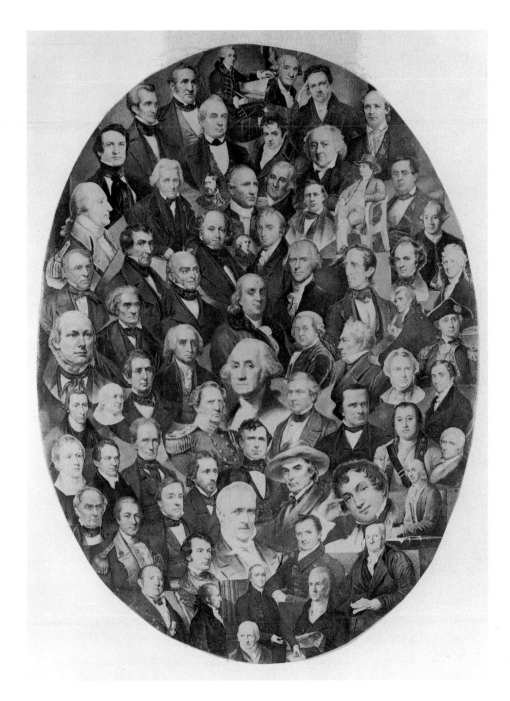

61. UNKNOWN PHOTOGRAPHER (American). *Seventy Celebrated Americans Including All the Presidents*, c. 1865. Albumen print. Library Company of Philadelphia.

verisimilitude evinced by the middle class and their royal leaders.

During the 1860s, portrait studios began to assemble a selection of individual likenesses on a single print. Produced by pasting together and rephotographing heads and portions of the torso from individual *carte* portraits, these composites paid scant attention to congruences of size and lighting, or to the representation of real-looking space. Designed as advertising publicity to acquaint the public with the range and quality of a particular studio's work, as in this example from the studio of a portrait photographer

in Valparaiso and Santiago, Chile *(pl. no. 60)*, the format was taken over as a means of producing thematic composites of political *(pl. no. 61)* or theatrical figures that might be sold or given away as souvenirs.

One form of commercial exploitation of portrait photography in Europe that did not fare as well as *cartes* was called photosculpture. Invented by François Willême in France in 1860, this three-dimensional image was produced by a company whose English branch briefly included the usually prudent Claudet as artistic director. The procedure necessitated a large circular studio in which 24

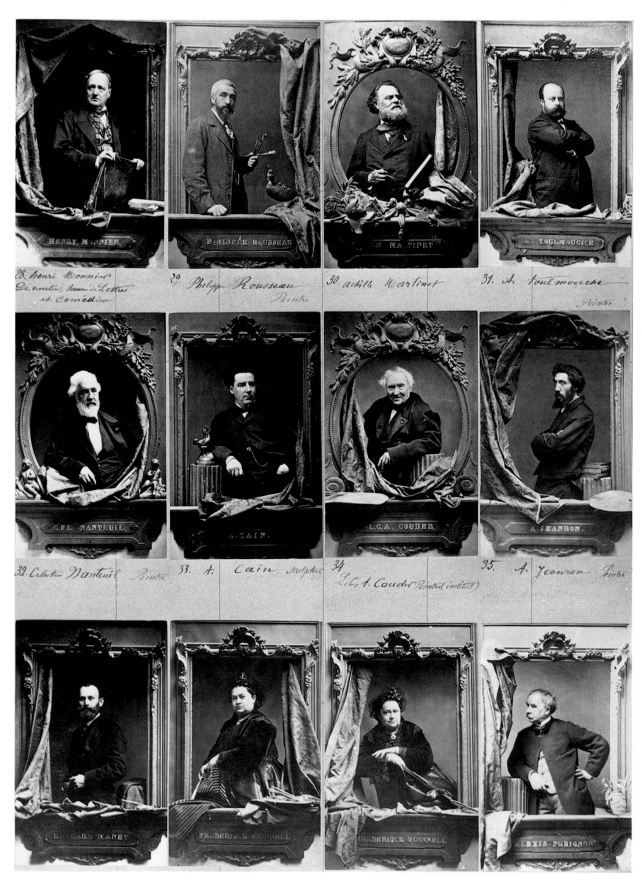

62. ADOLPHE JEAN FRANÇOIS MARIN DALLEMAGNE. *Artists' Portraits*, c. 1866. Albumen prints assembled into *Galerie des artistes contemporaines*. Bibliothèque Nationale, Paris.

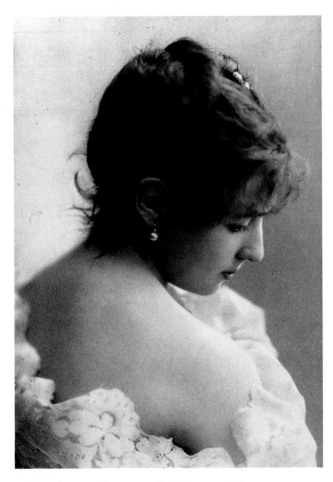

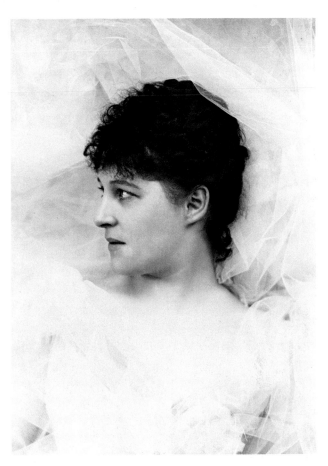

63. REUTLINGER STUDIO. *Mlle. Elven*, 1883. Albumen or gelatin silver print. Bibliothèque Nationale, Paris.

64. PAUL NADAR. *Lillie Langtry*, n.d. Gelatin silver print. Bibliothèque Nationale, Paris.

cameras were positioned to take simultaneous exposures of a centrally placed sitter. These were processed into lantern slides, projected, and traced in clay (or wood in one adaptation) with a pantograph, theoretically insuring a head start on exactitude for the sculptor. Despite royal patronage, photosculpture had a short life, although every once in a while this gimmick crops up again as an idea whose time has come.

Editions of prints on paper in sizes and formats other than *cartes* also were popular from the 1860s on. Because the problems with albumen prints mentioned in Chapter 1 never were completely solved, carbon printing—often referred to as "permanent"—and Woodburytype reproduction were favored for the production of celebrity likenesses that appeared in the "galleries" and albums issued by photographers and publishers in western Europe and the United States. Well-known examples are Hanfstaengl's *Album der Zeitgnossen* (*Album of Contemporary Figures*), portraits of German scientists, writers, and artists; the British *Gallery of Photographic Portraits*, undertaken by the studio of Joseph John Elliot and Clarence Edmund Fry

(who encountered refusals from politicians who found their likenesses too realistic); and the *Galerie des contemporaines* (*Gallery of Contemporaries*)—initiated in 1859 in Paris by Pierre Petit. This project was a precursor of the highly regarded French series, *Galerie contemporaine, litteraire, artistique* (*Contemporary Gallery of Writers and Artists*), published intermittently by Goupil and Company between 1876 and 1884, to which all the major portraitists of the period contributed. Less concerned than most studio portraiture with fashionable decor and dress, this collection was "physiognomic" in intent—to evoke the character of the giants of French literary and artistic life through pose and expression, as in the commanding presence projected in Etienne Carjat's portrait of Victor Hugo *(pl. no. 94)*. Other such publications catered to the taste for elaborate decor, as in Adolphe Jean François Marin Dallemagne's *Galerie des artistes contemporaines* (*Gallery of Contemporary Artists*) of 1866 *(pl. no. 62)*, a group of 50 portraits of artists shown posing in *trompe l' oeil* frames that are suggestive of the conceits of baroque portrait painting.

The best-known photographer of French intellectual,

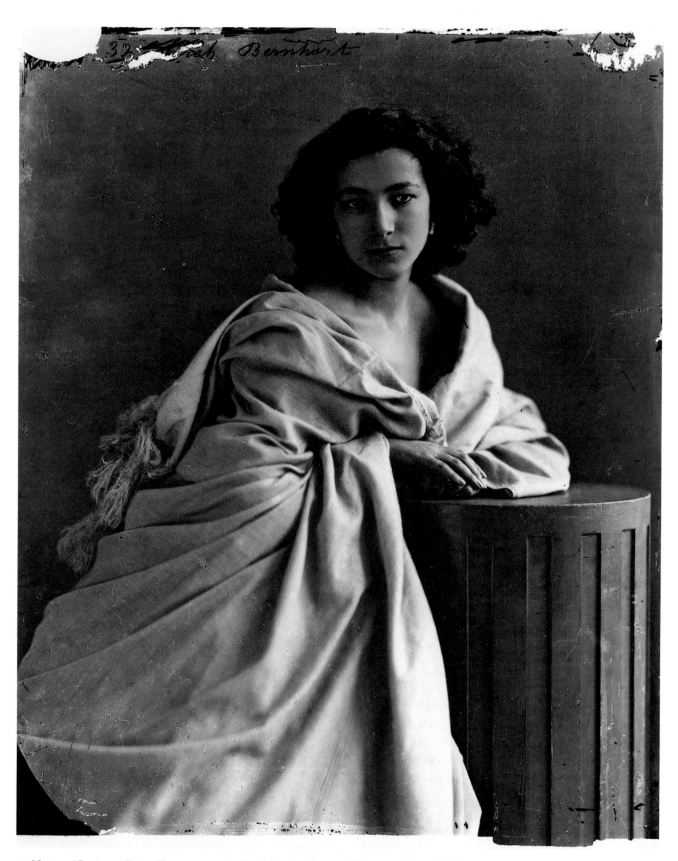

65. NADAR (GASPARD FÉLIX TOURNACHON). *Sarah Bernhardt*, 1865. Albumen print. Bibliothèque Nationale, Paris.

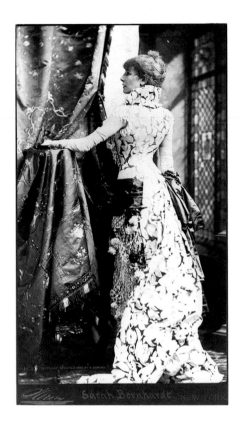

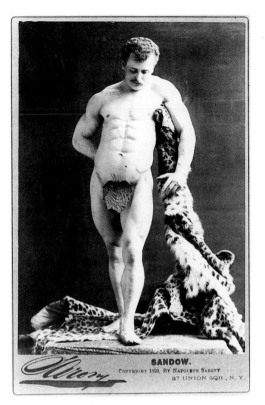

literary, and artistic figures during the collodion era is Gaspard Félix Tournachon, known as Nadar *(see Profile)*. His aim in portraiture was to seek, as he wrote, "that instant of understanding that puts you in touch with the model—helps you sum him up, guides you to his habits, his ideas, and character and enables you to produce . . . a really convincing and sympathetic likeness, an intimate portrait."²² One example—a portrait of the young Sarah Bernhardt in 1865 *(pl. no. 65)*—typifies Nadar's ability to organize the baroque forms of drapery, a truncated classical column, and the dramatic contrasts of hair and skin and still suggest character—in this case both the theatricality and vulnerability of a young actress who had just achieved her first stage success. As French art critic Philippe Burty wrote of Nadar's entries exhibited at the *Société Française de Photographie* exhibition in 1859, "his portraits are works of art in every accepted sense of the word," adding that "if photography is by no means a complete art, the photographer always has the right to be an artist."²³ Nadar's later output included many unexceptional portraits of entertainers and modishly dressed women, a direction necessitated by the demands of the middle class for glamorous images that became even more marked when his son Paul took control of the studio in the late 1880s. The style of Paul Nadar's portrait of the royal mistress Lillie Langtry *(pl. no. 64)*, like that of contemporaries such as Charles and Émile Reutlinger *(pl. no. 63)* whose firm began to specialize

in fashion photography in the same years, was oriented toward evoking glamour by seductive pose, bland expression, and attention to elegant attire.

By the time collodion/albumen photographs had begun to displace daguerreotypes and ambrotypes in the United States, the Civil War had erupted, relegating portraiture to a secondary place in the minds of many photographers. Brady, whose Washington studio had been opened in 1858 to take advantage of the concentration of political figures in the Capital, turned his attention to war reportage (to be discussed in Chapter 4), but continued to make portraits. In addition, Lincoln, his family, the Cabinet members and the Army generals all sat for other well-known portraitists, among them Alexander Gardner, a former manager of Brady's Washington gallery who took what may be the last likeness of the President in April, 1865, shortly before his assassination *(pl. no. 68)*.²⁴

In the period after the Civil War, besides *cartes* and cabinet-size images (approximately 4 x 5½ inches, mounted on a slightly bigger card), larger formats called Promenade, Boudoir, and Imperial Panel were introduced to appeal to the newly rich bourgeoisie that had emerged. Fashionable portrait studios in large cities, among them Fredericks, Gurney, Falk and Kurtz in New York, Gutekunst in Philadelphia, and Bachrach in Baltimore, served as pacesetters in terms of pose, decor, lighting, and the manner of presenting the finished image. As in Europe, there was a

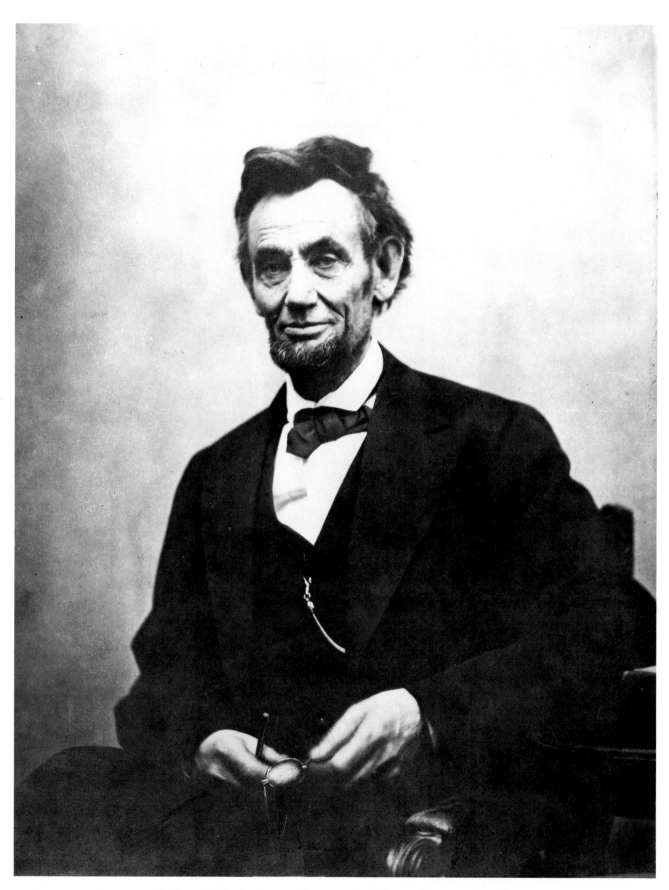

68. ALEXANDER GARDNER. *Abraham Lincoln*, April, 1865. Albumen print. Library of Congress, Washington, D.C.

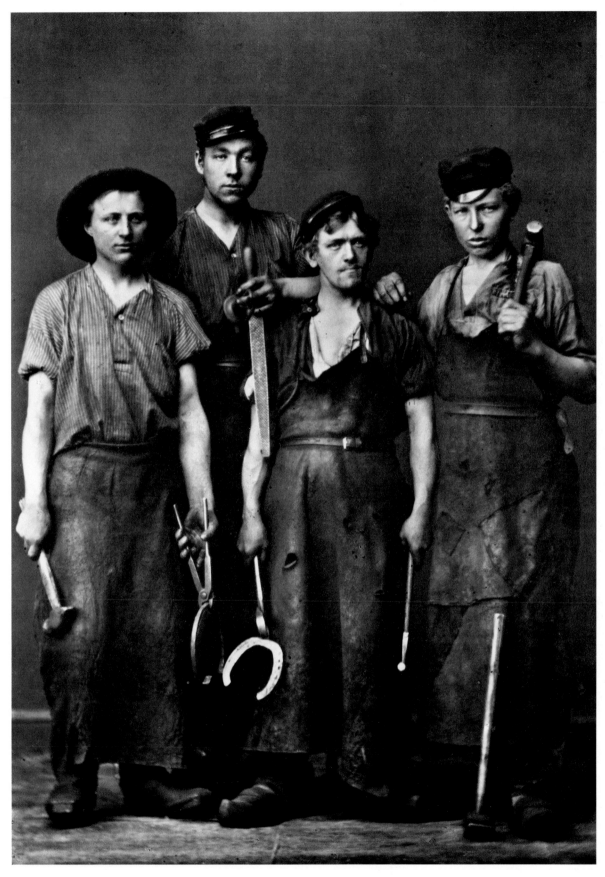

69. HEINRICH TÖNNIES. *Four Young Blacksmiths*, c. 1881. Modern gelatin silver print from original negative. Collection and © 1978 Alexander Alland, North Salem, N.Y.

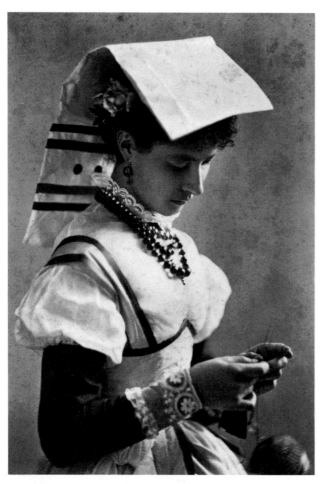

70. AWIT SZUBERT. *Amelia Szubert*, c. 1875.
Albumen print. Collection Konrad Pollesch, Cracow;
International Center of Photography, New York.

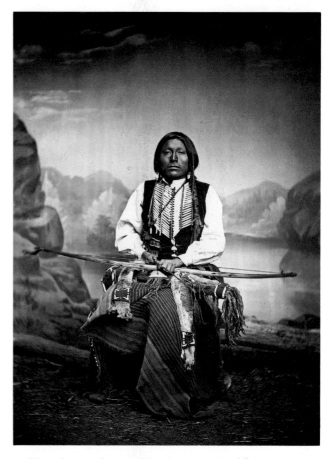

71. WILL SOULE. *Brave in War Dress*, c. 1868. Albumen
print. Western History Collection, Natural History
Museum of Los Angeles County, Los Angeles.

demand for images of theatrical and entertainment personalities that was satisfied in the main by the New York studios of Napoleon Sarony and his competitor José Mora. A prominent lithographer before the War, Sarony made over 40,000 negatives of celebrities, some of whom were paid extravagantly for the sitting. The eclectic decor visible in his images of Sarah Bernhardt (*pl. no. 66*) and strongman Eugene Sandow (*pl. no. 67*) necessitated a large collection of fusty props and led to a reference to his studio as a "dumping ground . . . for unsaleable idols, tattered tapestry and indigent crocodiles."[25]

During the last 40 years of the 19th century, portraiture expanded more rapidly in the less-industrialized portions of Europe, and in Australia, India, China, Japan, Mexico, and South America. Owing to the fact that owners of commercial studios in provincial towns frequently served a clientele drawn from all classes, they sometimes produced extensive documentations not only of physiognomies but of social and psychological attitudes. One such example is the large output of portraits by Danish photographer

Heinrich Tönnies, working in Aalborg from the 1860s into the 1900s, which includes some 750 portraits of working people attired in the garments and displaying the tools of their occupations. Despite the formality of the poses in studio settings (*pl. no. 69*), these images are not merely descriptive but suggest prevailing attitudes toward work on the part of both photographer and sitters. In some localities, patriots saw the camera as a means of emphasizing ethnic or national origin. A fine line may separate the portrait taken by Polish photographer Awit Szubert of his wife in native dress (*pl. no. 70*) from many similar images of locally costumed figures that were made and sold in *carte* and cabinet size for the tourist trade, but even in some of these images a sense of national pride is discernible.

Besides playing a role in the development of cultural nationalism in Europe, portraits also reflected the rising interest in anthropology. In the western hemisphere, early manifestations of the interest in native types included portraits of individual members of the Indian tribes indigenous to the West, made in the course of the land surveys and explorations *(see Chapter 3)* that followed the end of the Civil War. In the wake of these expeditions, several frontier studios opened their doors to Native American sitters, among them that of Will Soule, in Fort Sill, Oklahoma, which specialized in commercial portrayals of individuals posed formally in front of painted backdrops, as in an 1868 photograph titled simply *Brave in War Dress (pl. no. 71)*. In South America, Marc Ferrez, the best-known Brazilian photographer of the 19th century, photographed Indians of the Amazon region while on expeditions to the interior in the mid-1870s; in the same years strong interest in images of indigenous peoples prompted studios in Australia to photograph the Aborigines of the region.

Camera Portraits in Asia

The introduction of portrait photography in the Far East coincided with changes from insular traditionalism to the acceptance of modern ideas in science, symbolized by the 1854 American diplomatic ultimatum that Japan be opened to the West; indeed, the ideographs used to denote photograph in Japanese *(shashin)* literally mean "copy truth." The first portrait daguerreotypes made in that country appear to be those by Eliphalet Brown, Jr., American artist and photographer attached to Commodore Matthew Perry's expedition to Japan, but experimentation with the daguerreotype process had been going on since 1848 when a Nagasaki merchant imported the first camera.[26] However, successful daguerreotypes by Japanese photographers were not made until 1857, only a year before the first collodion portraits by a Japanese photographer. As shown in a woodblock print of 1861, *French Couple with a Camera (pl. no. 72)*, photographers working in Japan during the early period were foreigners who not only provided views and portraits but taught the process to the Japanese. Apparently by the mid- to late-'70s they were so successful that professional studios were opened in all the major cities of Japan, with more than 100 in the Tokyo area alone; even the unapproachable royal family permitted members to sit for camera likenesses.

Although China remained isolated from Western ideas of progress longer than Japan, photographers from the West began to make portraits there, too, during the 1860s. Among the succession of foreigners, Milton Miller, a Californian who ran a studio in Hong Kong in the early 1860s, made formally posed yet sensitive portraits of Cantonese merchants, Mandarins, and their families, while the Scottish photographer John Thomson photographed workers and peasants as well, including their portraits in his ambitious four-volume work *Illustrations of China and Its People*, published in England in 1873/74. It is thought that native Chinese photographers were introduced to photography

when they were employed during the 1850s as copyists and colorists in the Hong Kong studios run by foreigners, but while some 20 native studios with Chinese names are known, little else has been discovered about these portraitists. The studio of Afong Lai appears to have been the most stable of the native-owned commercial enterprises, lasting from 1859 on into the 20th century and with the artistry of its work acclaimed by Thomson.

On the Indian subcontinent, however, photography in all its varieties, including portraiture, was promoted by the British occupying forces and eagerly taken up by Indian businessmen and members of the ruling families. Commercial firms owned by Indian photographers, individuals appointed by the courts, and those working in bazaars began to appear in large cities after the 1860s in order to supply the British and Indian ruling class with images of themselves. The most renowned enterprise was that started

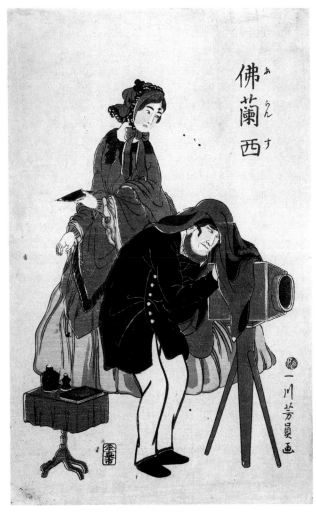

72. YOSHIKAZU ISSAN. *French Couple with a Camera*, 1861. Color woodblock print. Agfa-Gevaert Foto-Historama, Leverkusen, Germany.

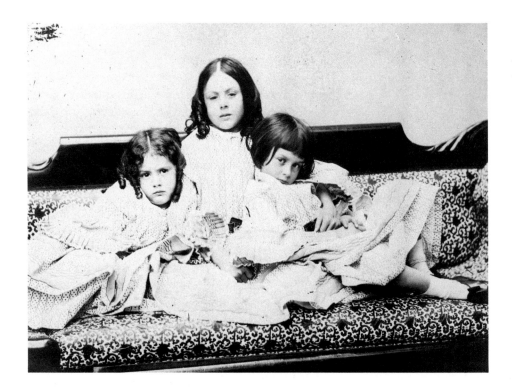

by Lala Deen Dayal, owner of studios in Indore, Bombay, and Hyderabad from the 1880s on, who became court photographer to the nizam of Hyderabad. Many portraits made in India during this period were painted over in the traditional decorative style of Indian miniatures just as in the West painted camera portraits were treated naturalistically. This attitude toward the photographic portrait in India has led to the suggestion that the camera itself was used in a different fashion from the West, that Indian photographers were somehow able to avoid the representation of space and dimensionality even before the paint was added.[27] However, allowing for obvious differences in pose, dress, and studio decor, Indian photographic portraits that were not painted over do not seem remarkably different from the general run of commercial portraiture everywhere.

The Portrait as Personal Expression

Alongside the likenesses produced by commercial studios, a more intimate style of portraiture developed in the work of amateurs—men and women in mostly comfortable circumstances who regarded photography as an agreeable pastime but did not make their living from it. During the 1860s and '70s this group, which included Olympe Count Aguado and Paul Gaillard on the Continent and Julia Margaret Cameron, Lewis Carroll, Lady Clementina Hawarden, and Cosmo Innes in Britain, used the collodion process to portray family and associates, at times in elabo-

rately casual poses, in actual domestic interiors and real gardens. When Carroll photographed his artistic and intellectual friends and their children, he favored the discreet and harmonious arrangements seen in the grouping of the Lidell sisters—Alice, Lorina, and Edith *(pl. no. 73)*. At the same time, his stress on the virgin beauty of these young sitters (and those taken in the nude, *see Chapter 5*) reflects a deep commitment to the ideals of feminine innocence that were central to the Pre-Raphaelite movement.

Cameron, the most widely known Victorian portraitist (usually considered an amateur even though she sold and exhibited her work), also used the camera to idealize her subjects. She sought out men and women whose individuality or impressive artistic and literary contributions appeared to her to redeem the materialism of the time, and importuned them to pose so that she might record, in her words, "faithfully, the greatness of the inner as well as the features of the outer man."[28] Avoiding sharp focus, she concentrated on the evocative handling of light, seen at its most effective in portraits of Sir John Herschel—a family friend of many years *(pl. no. 74)*—and of her niece Julia Jackson, who had just wed Herbert Duckworth and was to be the mother of novelist Virginia Woolf *(pl. no. 75)*.

Cameron's work, like that of Carroll, can be related to the Pre-Raphaelite search for ideal types, but her portrait style especially seems to have been inspired by the paintings of her artistic mentor George Frederick Watts, which in turn reflected the taste among the British intelligentsia for Rembrandt-like chiaroscuro effects in the treatment of

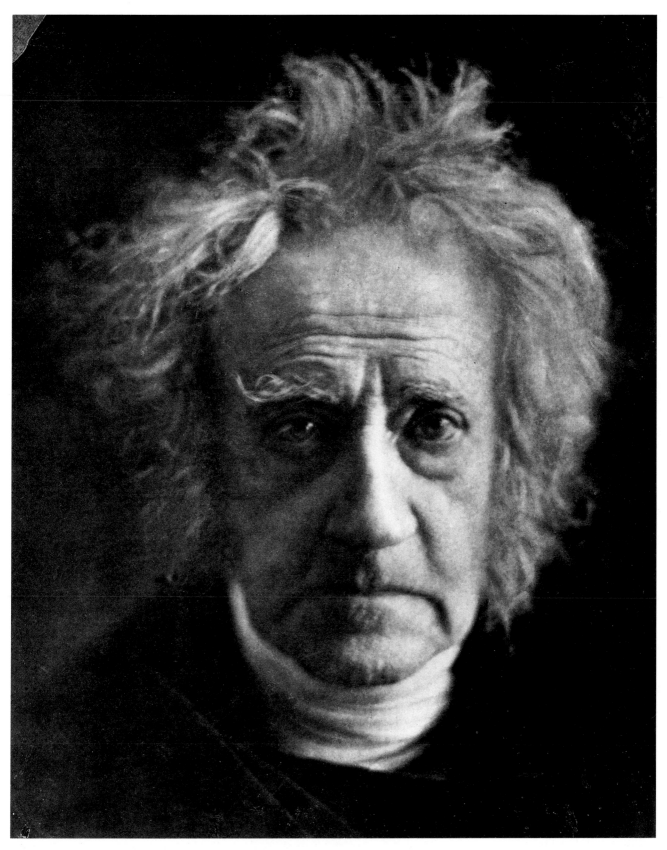

74. JULIA MARGARET CAMERON. *Sir John Herschel*, April, 1867. Albumen print.
Museum of Fine Arts, Boston; Gift of Mrs. J. D. Cameron Bradley.

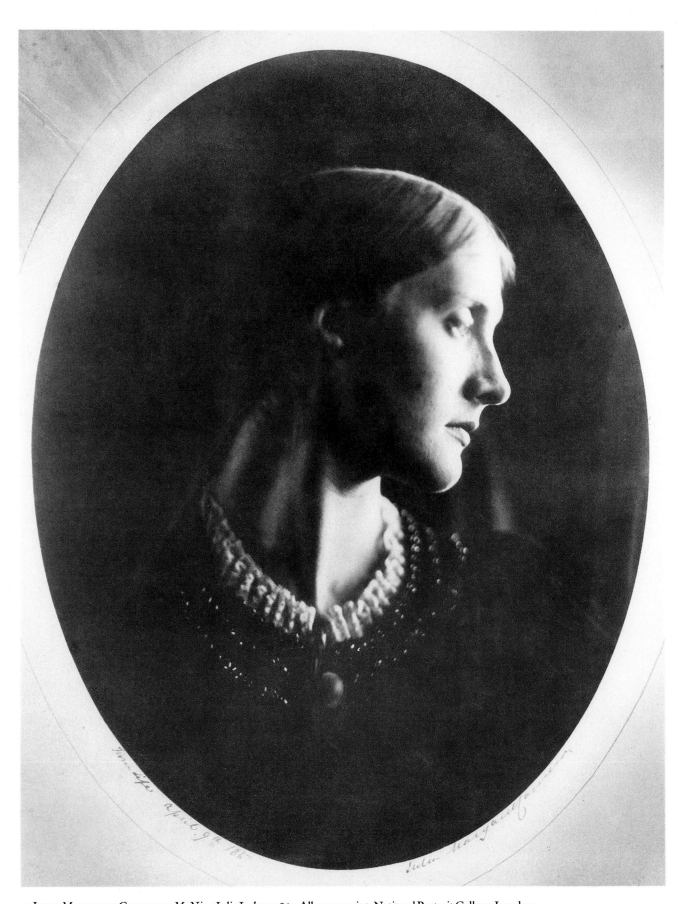

75. JULIA MARGARET CAMERON. *My Niece Julia Jackson*, 1867. Albumen print. National Portrait Gallery, London.

form. Critical reaction from Cameron's contemporaries was divided; while art critics for the general press and a number of photographers in England and abroad approved of her approach, the medium's most vocal proponents of art photography criticized the "slovenly manipulation" and regarded her work as "altogether repulsive."[29]

Newly emerging scientific ideas provided still other uses for the photographic portrait during the collodion era. Aside from the documentation of strictly medical problems (skin lesions, hydrocephalism, etc.), the camera was called upon to document psychological reactions and mental aberrations. Dr. Hugh Welch Diamond, who became interested in the calotype shortly after the announcement of Talbot's discovery, was one of the first to advocate such scientific documentation. After he was introduced to collodion by Archer—a former patient—he used the new technology to photograph female inmates in the Surrey County Asylum *(pl. nos. 76–77)*, where he was superintendent. In a paper read to the Royal Society in 1856, Dr. Diamond outlined the relationship of photography to psychiatry, suggesting that portraits were useful in diagnosis, as treatment, and for administrative identification of the patients. In *The Physiognomy of Insanity*, illustrated with engravings based on Dr. Diamond's likenesses, physiognomic theories that had related photography to the depiction of normal character were extended to embrace the mentally abnormal.

Fleeting facial expressions were photographed in 1853 by Adrien Tournachon (brother of Félix) for a work on human physiognomy by the noted Dr. Guillaume Benjamin Duchenne de Boulogne, the founder of electrotherapy, and in 1872 Charles Darwin chose to use photographs to illustrate *The Expression of the Emotions in Man and Animals*, for which he approached Rejlander. In addition to images supplied by Duchenne, and by two lesser-known figures, the book included a series showing emotional states, and for five of them Rejlander himself posed as model *(pl. nos. 78–79)*. Despite the theatricality of a number of the expressions depicted in these portraits, the use of the camera image in this capacity relegated to a minor role the traditional graphic conventions for portraying the human passions.

In the 30 years following the discovery of photography, the camera portrait occupied center stage. Images on metal, glass, and paper provided likenesses for large numbers of people—the newly affluent as well as many who formerly could not have imagined commissioning a painted portrait. Many of these images can be regarded today as no more than "archeological relics," but in their time they served to make generations of sitters more aware of their position in society and of themselves as individuals, even when they glossed over physiological and psychological

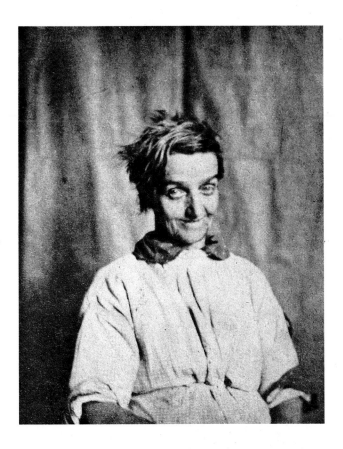

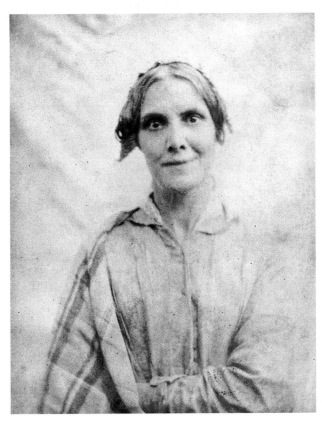

76–77. Dr. Hugh Welch Diamond. *Inmates of Surrey County Asylum*, 1852. Albumen prints. Royal Photographic Society, Bath, England.

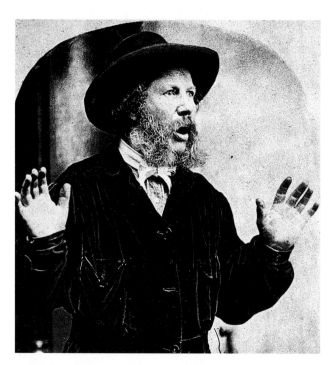 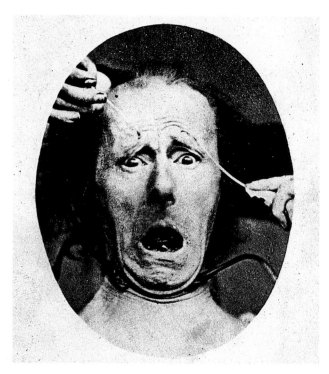

78–79. OSCAR GUSTAVE REJLANDER. Illustrations for *The Expression of the Emotions in Man and Animals*, by Charles Darwin, 1872. Heliotypes. Photography Collection, The New York Public Library, Astor, Lenox, and Tilden Foundations.

frailties. In addition, photographs taken at various stages of life—youth, middle age, and elderly—made people more conscious of mortality and their relationship to ephemeral time. The cult of individualism also was promoted by the practice of publishing and selling likenesses of famous persons. With the image as a surrogate, more people were made to feel closer to political and cultural figures, even while the likenesses themselves emphasized distinctiveness. On the whole, the general run of commercial camera portraiture is quickly exhausted in terms of insight or aesthetic interest, yet in the hands of creative individuals (both amateur and professional), among them Southworth and Hawes, Hill and Adamson, Cameron, Carroll, and Nadar, portraits seemed to distill an artistic ideal while still probing individual personality. The importance of studio portraiture was diminished by the invention of new cameras and technologies that permitted people to make likenesses of family and friends at home, but the portrait itself—as a mirror of personality, as an artistic artifact, and as an item of cultural communication—has remained an intriguing challenge to photographers.

Profile: David Octavius Hill and Robert Adamson

At his death in 1870, David Octavius Hill was mourned for being a deeply religious but blithe spirit who had devoted his life to improving the arts in Scotland. An unexceptional though competent painter of the Scottish countryside (*pl. no. 80*), Hill played an important role in the cultural life of Edinburgh. He was born into a family of booksellers and publishers in Perth and learned lithography early in his career, publishing, in 1821, the first lithographic views of Scotland in *Sketches of Scenery in Perthshire*. In association with other artists who were dissatisfied with the leadership of the Royal Institution, Hill established the Scottish Academy in 1829, and remained connected with it in unpaid and, later, official capacity until his death. By the 1830s, Hill's interest turned to narrative illustration; among his works were lithographs for *The Glasgow and Garnkirk Railway Prospectus*, The Waverly Novels, and *The Works of Robert Burns*.

Involvement in the Scottish Disruption Movement, which led to the establishment of the Free Church of Scotland and independence from the Church of England, inspired in Hill a wish to commemorate this event in a painting of the clergymen who took part in the dispute. Introduced by Sir David Brewster to Robert Adamson (*pl. no. 81*), through whom he became aware of Talbot's process, Hill planned to use photography as an aid in painting the likenesses of the 400 members of the Disruption Movement. In 1843 he entered into a partnership with Adamson, about whom relatively little is known, to produce calotypes in a studio at Rock House, Calton Hill, Edinburgh, and

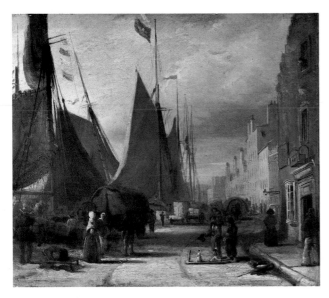

80. DAVID OCTAVIUS HILL. *On the Quay at Leith*, 1826.
Oil on wood. Scottish National Portrait Gallery, Edinburgh.

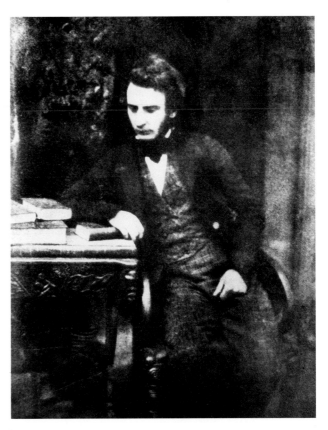

81. DAVID OCTAVIUS HILL. *Robert Adamson*, c. 1843.
Calotype. Gernsheim Collection, Humanities Research
Center, University of Texas, Austin.

sometimes on location. In their joint work, each man provided an element missing in the other. Before 1843, Adamson's work was wanting in composition and lighting, while, on the evidence of work done with another collaborator some 14 years after Adamson's premature death, Hill lacked sensitivity and skill in handling the camera. During the partnership, Hill energetically organized the sittings for his proposed painting, but as the two partners became more deeply involved with the medium, they calotyped subjects, persons, and landscape views that had no relation to the Disruption painting, producing between 1843 and 1848 about 2,500 separate calotypes. Unfortunately, Hill discovered that many of the negatives tended to fade, a circumstance that along with Adamson's death seemed to make further involvement in photography unattractive.

After 1848, Hill continued to use photographs as studies for his paintings and to sell individual calotypes from his brother's print shop, while devoting time to the affairs of the Scottish Academy and other local art associations. Following a second marriage in 1862 and the unsuccessful attempt to photograph in collodion with another partner, Hill returned to the Disruption painting, completing it in 1866. Compared with the vitality and expressiveness of the calotype studies, the painted figures are unconvincing and seem to exist without air or space; the picture, however, was greeted with kindness, and Hill's last photographic project involved an endeavor to make photographic facsimiles of this work. Had he not become involved with photography, it is unlikely that Hill would have merited more than a footnote in the history of the arts of the 19th century.

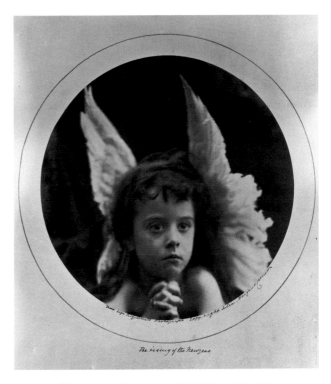

82. JULIA MARGARET CAMERON. *The Rising of the New Year*, 1872. Albumen print. Private Collection.

Profile: Julia Margaret Cameron

One of seven daughters of a prosperous British family stationed in India, Julia Margaret Pattle was regarded by friends as generous, impulsive, enthusiastic, and imperious—"a unique figure, baffling beyond description."[30] Educated in England and France after the death of her parents, she returned to India and in 1838 married Charles Hay Cameron, an eminent jurist and classical scholar, who invested his fortune in coffee plantations in Ceylon. In the ten years prior to their return to England, Mrs. Cameron assumed the social leadership of the Anglo-Indian colony, raised money for victims of the Irish Famine, and translated the well-known German ballad, *Lenore*, but her boundless energy craved greater challenges.

After settling in Freshwater on the Isle of Wight, Cameron, using a camera given her by her daughter in 1863, embarked on a career in photography, concentrating on portraits and allegorical subjects. Models, at times paid but mainly importuned, were drawn from among her family, the household staff at the Cameron residence, *Dimbola*, and from the households and visitors to the homes of Tennyson and Sara Prinsep, Mrs. Cameron's sister. These embraced many of the most famous figures in British artistic and literary circles, including Tennyson, Carlyle, Darwin, Herschel, Marie Spartali, Ellen Terry, and Watts, but the photographer also was interested in portraying the unrenowned as long as she found them beautiful or full of character. Besides hundreds of idealized portraits, she created allegorical subject groups *(pl. no. 82)* that led eventually to a series commissioned by Tennyson for *Idylls of the King*. Because of her disappointment with the poor quality of the woodcut transcriptions that appeared in the 1874 edition of this work, Cameron raised money to issue two editions that were photographically illustrated.

Cameron's attitude toward photography was that of a typical upper-class "amateur" of the time. She refused to consider herself a professional although the high cost of practicing the medium led her to accept payment on occasion for portraits and to market photographic prints through P. and D. Colnaghi, London printsellers. They often bore the legend: "From Life. Copyright Registered Photograph. Julia Margaret Cameron," to which she sometimes added that they were unretouched and not enlarged. Her work was shown at annual exhibitions of the Photographic Society of London and in Edinburgh, Dublin, London, Paris, and Berlin; at the latter it was acclaimed by Hermann Wilhelm Vogel and awarded a gold medal in 1866. In 1875, the Camerons returned to Ceylon, where for the three years before her death she continued to photograph, using native workers on the plantations and foreign visitors as models.

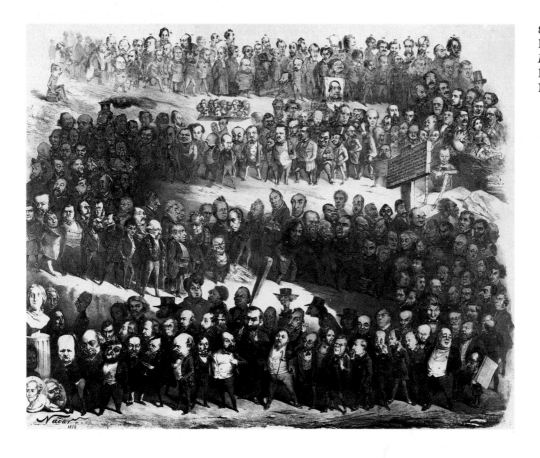

83. Nadar (GASPARD FÉLIX TOURNACHON). *Panthéon Nadar*, 1854. Lithograph. Bibliothèque Nationale, Paris.

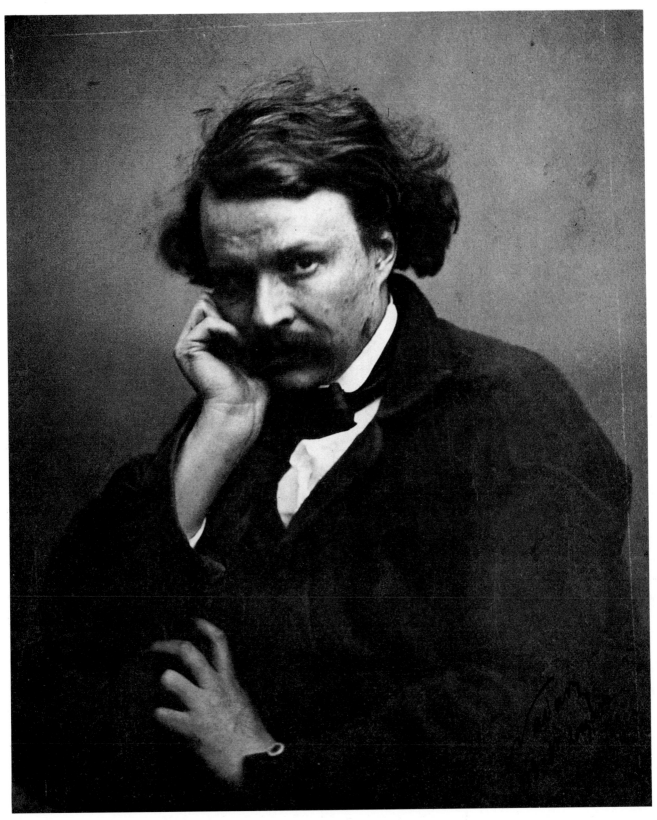

84. NADAR (GASPARD FÉLIX TOURNACHON). *Self-Portrait*, c. 1855. Salt print. Collection Sam Wagstaff, New York.

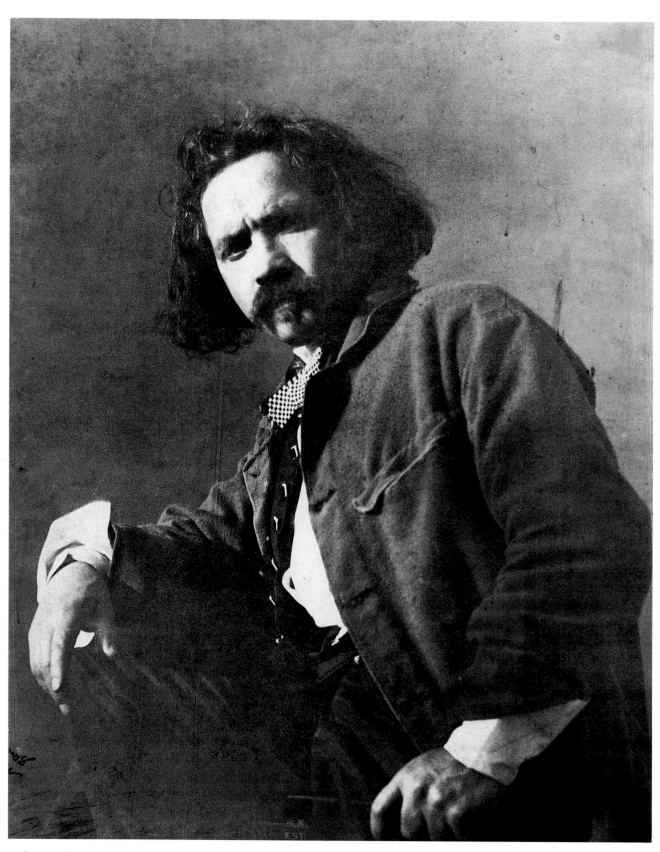

85. ADRIEN TOURNACHON. *Emile Blavier*, c. 1853. Albumen print. Bibliothèque Nationale, Paris.

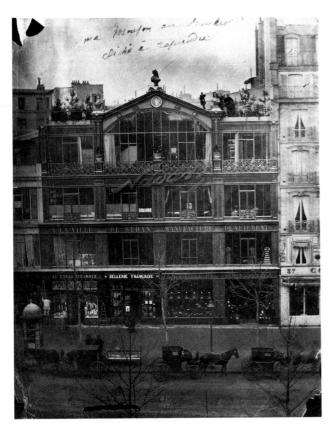

86. UNKNOWN PHOTOGRAPHER (French). *Façade of Nadar's Studio at 35 Boulevard des Capucines, Paris*, after 1880. Albumen print. Bibliothèque Nationale, Paris.

Profile: Nadar

In many ways Nadar (Gaspard Félix Tournachon) *(pl. no. 84)* typifies the best qualities of the bohemian circle of writers and artists that settled in Paris during the Second Empire. Born into a family of printer tradespeople of radical leanings, young Nadar became interested in many of the era's most daring ideas in politics, literature, and science. After an ordinary middle-class education and a brief stab at medical school, he turned to journalism, first writing theater reviews and then literary pieces. Although a career in literature seemed assured, he gave up writing in 1848 to enlist in a movement to free Poland from foreign oppressors, an adventure that ended suddenly when he was captured and returned to Paris. There followed a period of involvement with graphic journalism, during which he created cartoons and caricatures of well-known political and cultural figures for the satirical press. This culminated in the *Panthéon Nadar (pl. no. 83)*, a litho-

graphic depiction of some 300 members of the French intelligentsia. Only mildly successful financially, it made Nadar an immediate celebrity; more important, it introduced him to photography, from which he had drawn some of the portraits.

In 1853, Nadar set up his brother Adrien as a photographer and took lessons himself, apparently with the intention of joining him in the enterprise. However, despite the evident sensitivity of Adrien's portrait of the sculptor Emile Blavier *(pl. no. 85)*, his lack of discipline is believed to have caused Nadar to open a studio on his own, moving eventually to the Boulevard des Capucines *(pl. no. 86)*, the center of the entertainment district. He continued his bohemian life, filling the studio with curiosities and *objets d'art* and entertaining personalities in the arts and literature, but despite this flamboyant personal style he remained a serious artist, intent on creating images that were both life-enhancing and discerning.

Ever open to new ideas and discoveries, Nadar was the first in France to make photographs underground with artificial light and the first to photograph Paris from the basket of an ascendant balloon. Even though a proponent of heavier-than-air traveling devices, he financed the construction of *Le Géant*, a balloon that met with an unfortunate accident on its second trip. Nonetheless, he was instrumental in setting up the balloon postal service that made it possible for the French government to communicate with those in Paris during the German blockade in the Franco-Prussian War of 1870.

Ruined financially by this brief but devastating conflict, Nadar continued to write and photograph, running an establishment with his son Paul that turned out slick commercial work. Always a rebel, at one point he lent the photo studio to a group of painters who wished to bypass the Salon in order to exhibit their work, thus making possible the first exhibition of the Impressionists in April, 1874. Although he was to operate still another studio in Marseilles during the 1880s and '90s, Nadar's last photographic idea of significance was a series of exposures made by his son in 1886 as he interviewed chemist Eugène Chevreul on his 100th birthday, thus foreshadowing the direction that picture journalism was to take. During his last years he continued to think of himself as "a daredevil, always on the lookout for currents to swim against."[31] At his death, just before the age of ninety, he had outlived all those he had satirized in the famous *Panthéon*, which had started him in photography.

The Galerie Contemporaine— *Appearance and Character in 19th-Century Portraiture*

The *Galerie Contemporaine*, a series of 241 portraits of celebrated artistic, literary, and political figures in France during the Second Empire and Third French Republic, was issued in Paris between the years 1876 and 1894. A different portrait, accompanied by biographical text, appeared each week from 1876 to 1880; after that the album became an annual devoted almost exclusively to those in the mainstream pictorial arts. The images were the work of some 28 photographers who operated studios in Paris during this period; they were published in different sizes, depending on the dimensions of the original negative or plate, and usually were presented within a decorative border. Because in some cases they were taken long before they were used in the *Galerie*, the individual portraits are difficult to date. Whether these photographs were produced by carbon process or Woodburytype has not been definitively established, but the fact that the publisher, Goupil et Cie., had purchased a franchise for the Woodburytype process in France some years earlier suggests that the images were made by this method.

In this selection, portraits by noted photographers Etienne Carjat and Nadar exemplify the pictorial excellence possible through adroit manipulation of pose, demeanor, and lighting, while the image by Tourtin indicates that the work of little-known portraitists included in this ambitious publication also achieved a high level of excellence.

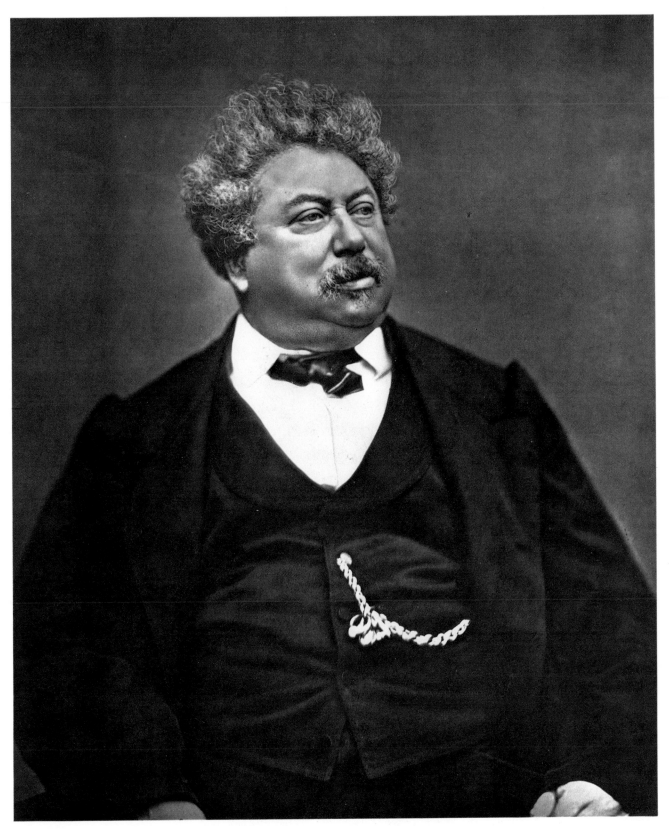

87. ETIENNE CARJAT. *Alexandre Dumas*, from *Galerie Contemporaine*, 1878. Woodburytype.
International Museum of Photography at George Eastman House, Rochester, N.Y.

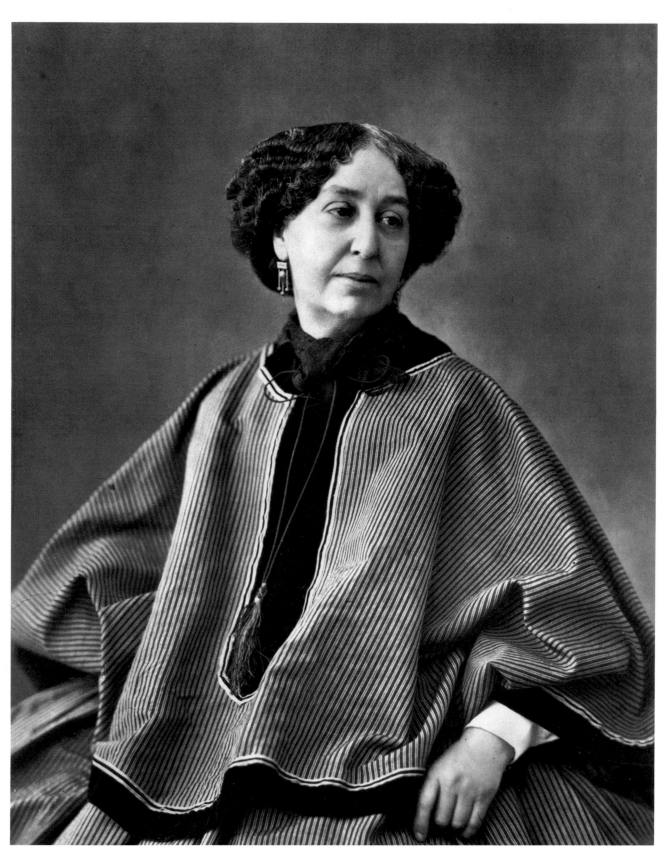

88. NADAR (GASPARD FÉLIX TOURNACHON). *Georges Sand*, from *Galerie Contemporaine*, 1877.
Woodburytype. International Museum of Photography at George Eastman House, Rochester, N.Y.

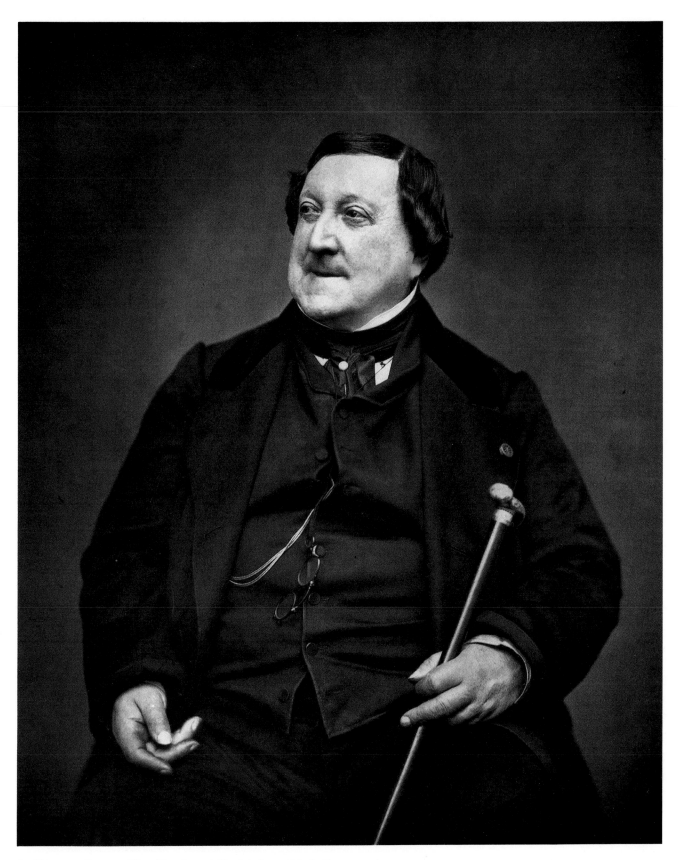

89. ETIENNE CARJAT. *Gioacchino Antonio Rossini*, from *Galerie Contemporaine*, 1877.
Woodburytype. International Museum of Photography at George Eastman House, Rochester, N.Y.

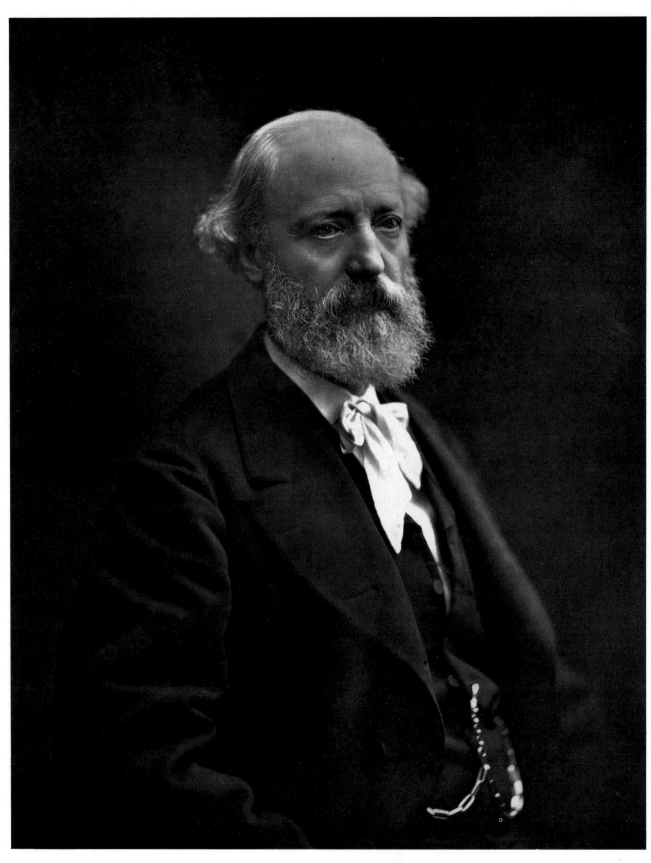

90. NADAR (GASPARD FÉLIX TOURNACHON). *Eugène Emmanuel Viollet-le-Duc*, from *Galerie Contemporaine*, 1878. Woodburytype. International Museum of Photography at George Eastman House, Rochester, N.Y.

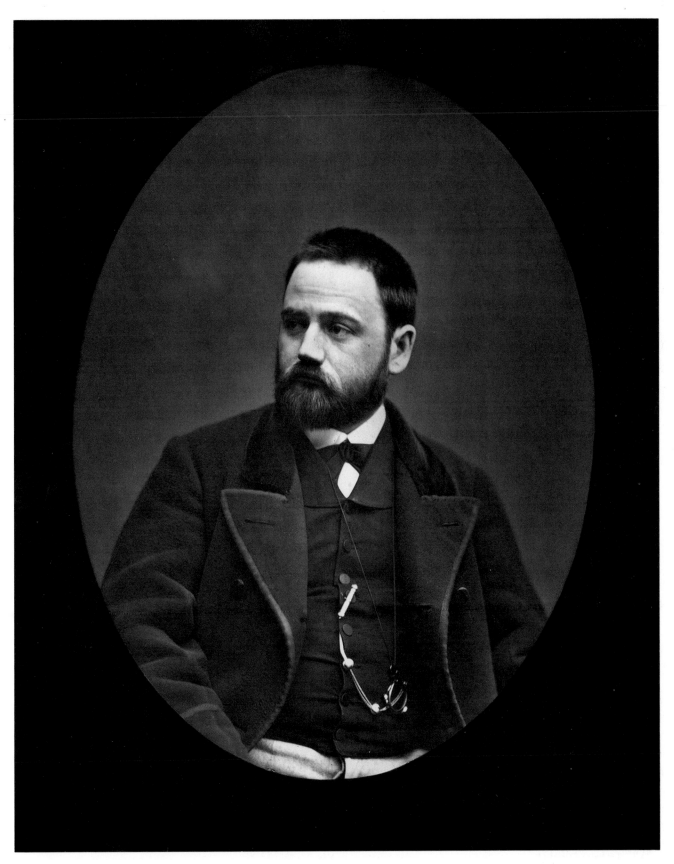

91. ETIENNE CARJAT. *Emile Zola*, from *Galerie Contemporaine*, 1877.
Woodburytype. Private Collection.

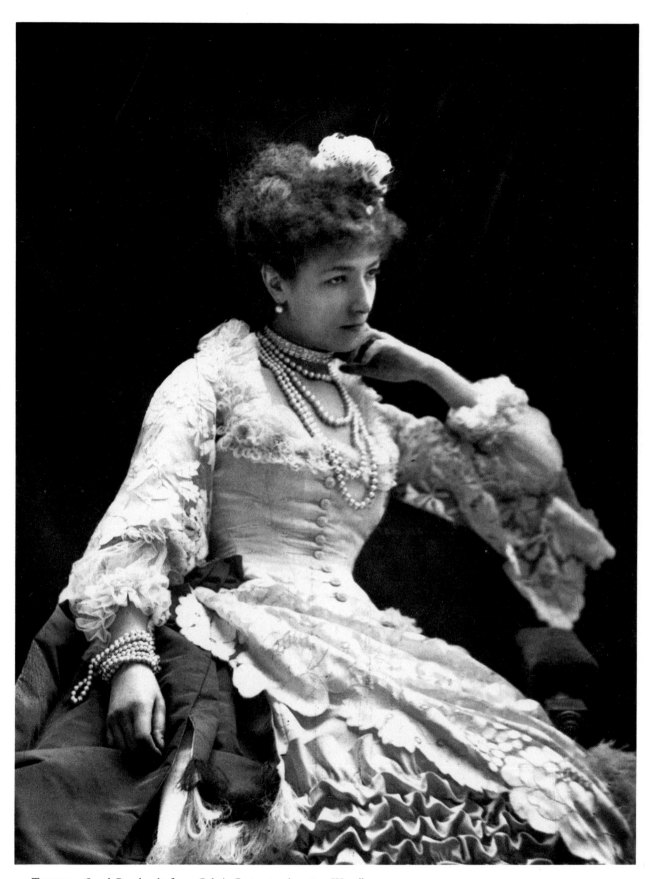

92. TOURTIN. *Sarah Bernhardt*, from *Galerie Contemporaine*, 1877. Woodburytype.
International Museum of Photography at George Eastman House, Rochester, N.Y.

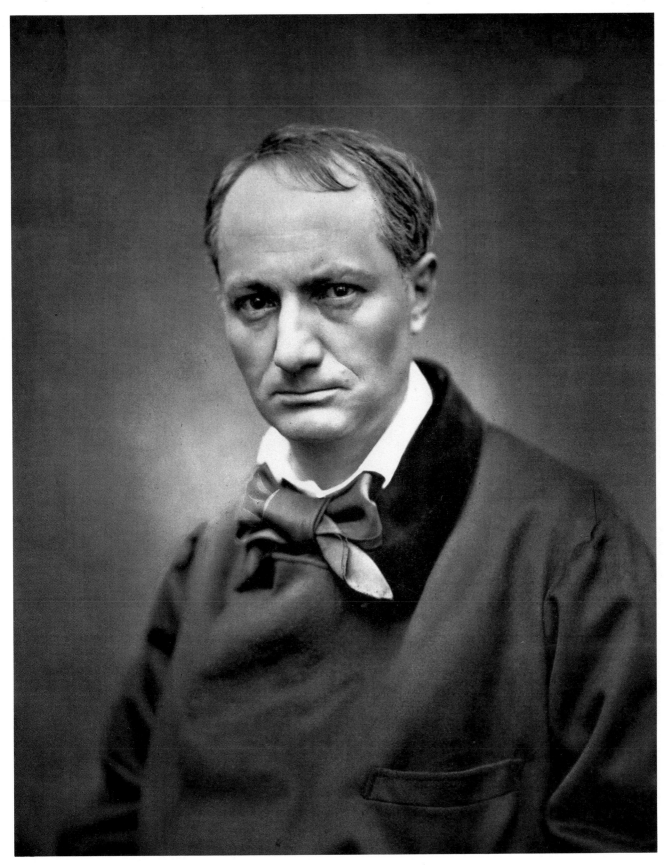

93. ETIENNE CARJAT. *Charles Baudelaire*, from *Galerie Contemporaine*, 1878. Woodburytype.
International Museum of Photography at George Eastman House, Rochester, N.Y.

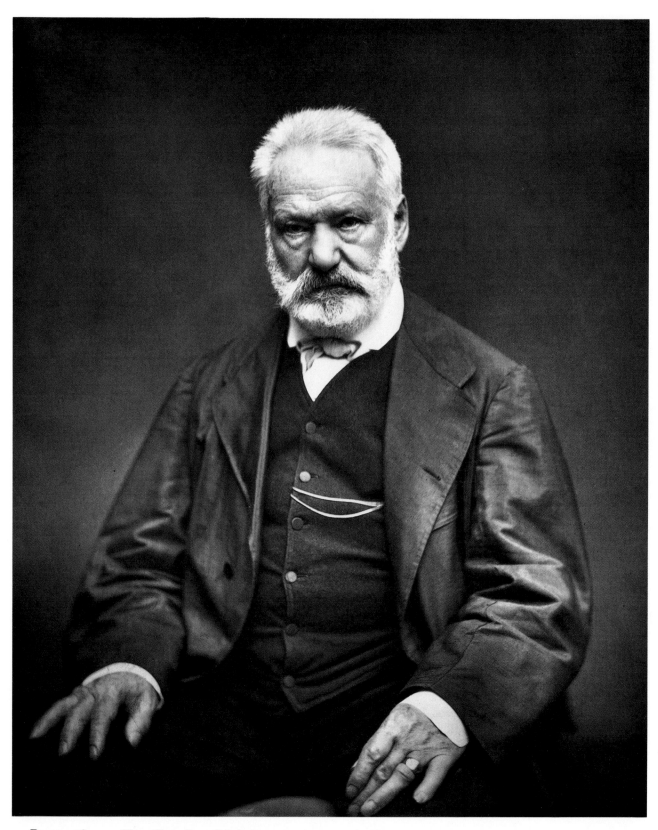

94. ETIENNE CARJAT. *Victor Hugo*, from *Galerie Contemporaine*, 1876. Woodburytype. Private Collection.

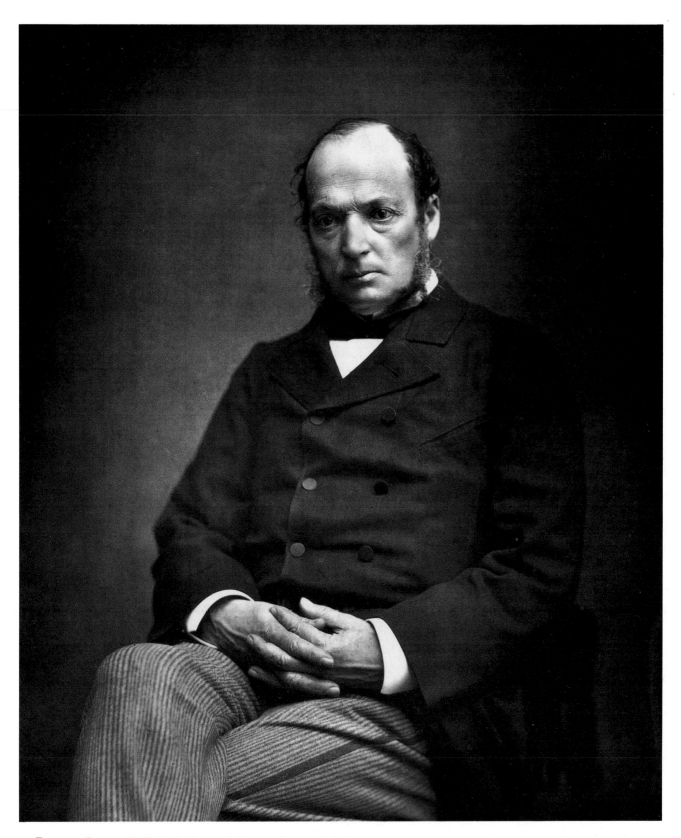

95. ETIENNE CARJAT. *Emile Louis Gustave de Marcère*, from *Galerie Contemporaine*, 1878. Woodburytype. Private Collection.

3.

DOCUMENTATION: LANDSCAPE AND ARCHITECTURE

1839–1890

To represent . . . the beautiful and the sublime in nature . . . demands qualities alike of head and of heart, in rapt accordance with the Infinite Creative Spirit.

—*Marcus Aurelius Root, 1864*[1]

There is only one Coliseum or Pantheon; but how many millions of potential negatives have they shed,—representatives of billions of pictures,—since they were erected! Matter in large masses must always be fixed and dear; form is cheap and transportable. . . . Every conceivable object of Nature and Art will soon scale off its surface for us.

—*Oliver Wendell Holmes, 1859*[2]

EASY OF ACCESS, generally immobile, and of acknowledged artistic appeal, landscape, nature, and architecture provided congenial subjects for the first photographers. The desire for accurate graphic transcription of scenery of all kinds—natural and constructed—had led to the perfection of the *camera obscura* in the first place, and it was precisely because exactness was so difficult even with the aid of this device that Talbot and others felt the need to experiment with the chemical fixation of reflected images. Beginning with the daguerreotype and the calotype, 19th-century scenic views evolved along several directions. They provided souvenirs for the new middle-class traveler, and brought the world into the homes of those unable to make such voyages. Photographs of natural phenomena provided botanists, explorers, geologists, and naturalists with the opportunity to study previously undocumented specimens and locations. And as scientific knowledge increased, as changing conditions of life in urban centers promoted new concepts of how to understand and represent the material world, the camera image itself became part of the shifting relationship between traditional and modern perceptions of nature and the built environment.

From the Renaissance up until the middle of the 18th century, painted landscape, with few exceptions, had been considered important mainly as a background for historical and religious events; landscape as such occupied a low position in the hierarchy of artistic subjects. With the relaxation of academic art strictures and the introduction during the Romantic era of a more sensuous depiction of nature, artists turned to a wider range of motifs from the material world. These extended from pastoral landscapes, seen from afar, to depictions of singular formations—water, skies, trees, rocks, and fruits of the field. As heirs to these evolving attitudes toward nature, photographers, armed with a device they believed would faithfully record actuality, approached the landscape with the conviction that the camera might perform a dual function—that photographs might reveal form and structure accurately and at the same time present the information in an artistically appealing fashion.

The public appetite for scenic views had a significant effect on early landscape photographs also. Through most of the 18th century, oil paintings, watercolors, engravings, and (after 1820) lithographs of topographical views (often

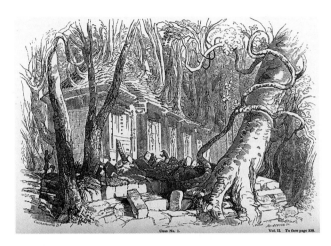

96. FREDERICK CATHERWOOD. *The Ruins of Palenqué, Casa No. 1,* 1841. Lithograph from *Incidents of Travel in Central America, Chiapas, and Yucatan,* Vol. II, 1841, by John Lloyd Stephens. Collection George R. Rinhart, Colebrook, Conn.

based on drawings made with the *camera obscura* or *camera lucida, see A Short Technical History, Part I*) had become increasingly popular. The landscape or view photograph was welcomed not only because it was a logical extension of this genre, but also for its supposedly more faithful representation of topography, historic monuments, and exotic terrain. As an example of the overlap that came about in the wake of changing technologies, drawings made by the American explorers Frederick Catherwood and John L. Stephens of their findings on expeditions to the Yucatan peninsula *(pl. no. 96)* in 1839 and 1841 were based on unaided observation, on the use of a *camera lucida*, and on daguerreotypes the two had made. Since many views, including these, were made with publication in mind, the camera image promoted a more accurate translation from drawing to mechanically reproduced print, supplying the engraver or lithographer with detailed information at a time when inexpensive methods of transferring the photograph directly to the plate had not yet been developed.

Landscape Daguerreotypes

Truthful representation of the real world without sentimentality presented itself as an important objective to many

19th-century scientists and intellectuals, including French novelist Gustave Flaubert, who held that the artist should be "omnipotent and invisible."[3] This position reflected one aspect of the positivist ideas of social philosopher Auguste Comte and others who were convinced that a scientific understanding of material reality was the key to economic and social progress. The camera image was regarded as a fitting visual means for just such an impersonal representation of nature. Nevertheless, it is difficult to determine the full extent of daguerreotyping activities with reference to views of nature, architecture, and monuments. Many plates have been lost or destroyed; others, hidden away in archives or in historical and private collections, have been surfacing in recent years, but no overall catalogs of such images exist. From the works most often seen, it seems apparent that the finely detailed daguerreotype was supremely suited to recording architectural features while somewhat less useful for pure nature. The influential British art critic John Ruskin, who in 1845 began to make his own daguerreotypes as well as to use those of others in preparing the drawings for his books on architecture, praised the verisimilitude of the daguerreotype image as "very nearly the same thing as carrying off the palace itself."[4]

Daguerreotype scenic views made on both sides of the Atlantic reveal attitudes about nature and art of which neither the photographer nor the viewer may have been aware at the time. The stark mountains and graceless buildings in an 1840 image by Samuel Bemis of a farm scene in New Hampshire *(pl. no. 97)* seem to suggest the solitary and obdurate quality of the New England countryside. Admittedly, this Boston dentist, who acquired his photographic equipment from Daguerre's agent Gouraud, was working at the very dawn of photography, when materials and processes were in a state of flux. In contrast, the harmonious landscape *(pl. no. 98)* by Alexandre Clausel, probably made near Troyes, France, in 1855, attests to not only a firmer grasp of technique but also to a greater sensitivity to the manner in which the traditional canons of landscape composition were handled.

Landscape photography evolved as a commercial enterprise with the taking of views of well-known or extraordinary natural formations for the benefit of travelers. A favorite site in the United States, Niagara Falls was daguerreotyped by Southworth and Hawes in 1845, ambrotyped as well as daguerreotyped by George Platt Babbitt in 1848, and photographed on stereographic glass plates by the Langenheim brothers in 1855. Albumen prints from collodion negatives of the Falls were made by English commercial photographers John Werge and William England in 1853 and 1859 respectively, and from dry plates by George Barker. In the Midwest, daguerreotypes of similar scenic wonders were made by Alexander Hesler and others in

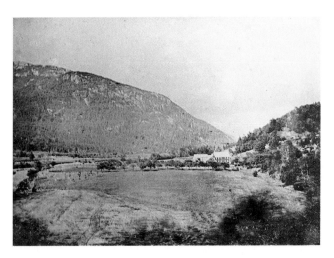

97. SAMUEL BEMIS. *New Hampshire Landscape*, 1840. Daguerreotype. Collection Ken Heyman, New York.

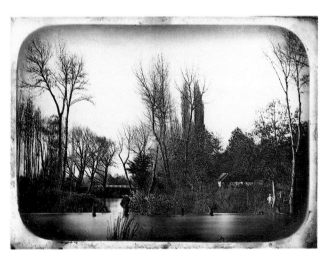

98. ALEXANDRE CLAUSEL. *Landscape, Probably Near Troyes, France*, c. 1855. Daguerreotype. International Museum of Photography at George Eastman House, Rochester, N.Y.

larger numbers than is generally appreciated today.

The urban scene also was considered appropriate for the daguerreotypist. *Bridge and Boats on the Thames (pl. no. 9)* of 1851 by Baron Jean Baptiste Louis Gros typifies the incredible amount of detail made visible by this process, and indicates the way bodies of water might be used to unify sky and foreground, a solution that virtually became a formula for many landscape photographers. The drama of dark silhouette against a lighter sky, seen in Wilhelm Halffter's image of Berlin *(pl. no. 10)* demonstrates another method of treating the problem of visually unrelated rectangles of light and dark areas that the actual land- or cityscape frequently presented; this, too, became a commonplace of view photography.

Most landscape imagery was designed for a broad market—the buyers of engraved and lithographed scenes—so the problem of the nonduplicatable metal plate was solved by employing artists to translate the daguerreotype into engravings, aquatints, and lithographs. One of the first publishers of an extensive work based on daguerreotypes, Noël Marie Paymal Lerebours, an optical-instrument maker who had been associated with Daguerre's endeavors, made use of daguerreotyped scenes in Europe, the Near East, and the United States, both commissioned and purchased outright as material for the engravings, with figures and fillips often added by artists. Among the daguerreotypists whose work appeared in Lerebours's *Excursions Daguerriennes: Vues et Monuments les plus remarquables du globe (Daguerrian Excursions: The World's Most Remarkable Scenes and Monuments)*, issued between 1840 and 1843, were Frederic Goupil-Fesquet, Hector Horeau *(pl. no. 99)*, Joly de Lotebinière, and Horace Vernet, all of whom supplied views of Egypt where it seemed the daguerreotype had become the indispensable companion of those who could not draw and artists who did not have the time to make drawings.

Interest in unusual scenery and structures was so strong that even though daguerreotyping in the field was not easy, a number of other similar projects were initiated in the early 1840s, generally by affluent individuals who hired guides and followed safe routes. Dr. Alexander John Ellis, a noted English philologist, was inspired by *Excursions Daguerriennes* to conceive of *Italy Daguerreotyped*, comprising views of architecture engraved from full-plate daguerreotypes that he had supervised or made himself in 1840/41; the project was abandoned although the plates still exist. The British physician Dr. George Skene Keith and a well-to-do French amateur, Joseph Philibert Girault de Prangey, took daguerreotypes hoping to publish works on Near Eastern architecture that might show details and structure in close-ups, and suggest connections between architecture and biblical history. In Switzerland, Johann Baptist Isenring, the painter and engraver turned daguerreotypist, who traveled by caravan throughout the country in order to make portraits, also took views of scenery to be engraved and published.

Panoramic Views

Before giving way to the more practicable negative–positive process, the daguerreotype achieved a measure of additional popularity with respect to panoramic views—images that are much wider than they are high. It will be recalled that panoramas (and in Paris, The Diorama), with minutely rendered landscape detail, were among the most popular entertainments of the early 1800s in Europe and the United States.[5] Soon after the announcement of the daguerreotype, photographers attempted to capitalize on the appetite for this kind of encompassing yet accurate visual experience. At first, series of individual daguerreotypes arranged in contiguous order to depict a wider prospect were popular, especially in the United States where the urge to document urban development occupied photographers in virtually all major cities, as exemplified by *Fairmount Waterworks (pl. no. 100)*, a series by William Southgate Porter consisting of eight plates made in Philadelphia in 1848. While photographers throughout the nation made panoramic views of the cities in an attempt to encompass the urban growth taking place before their eyes, a 360 degree panorama of Chicago made by Alexander Hesler in 1858 was possibly the first such effort. Wilderness landscape was treated similarly by San Francisco daguerreotypist Robert Vance and by John Wesley Jones, early American daguerreotypists of western scenery. Jones took 1,500 views in the Rockies and the Sierra Nevada mountains (none of which has survived) on which to base a painted panorama entitled *The Great Pantoscope*.[6]

Panoramic views also were made on single plates of extended width, achieved either by using a wide-angle lens, or by racking the camera to turn slowly in an arc

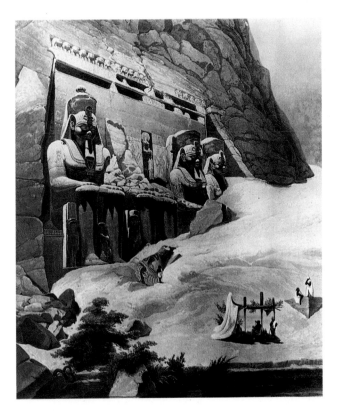

99. HECTOR HOREAU. *Abu Simbel*, 1840. Aquatint. Collection Gérard-Lévy, Paris.

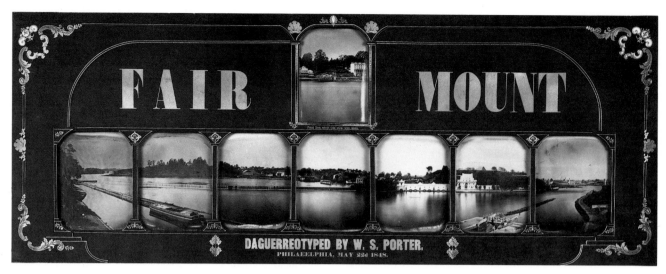

100. WILLIAM SOUTHGATE PORTER. *Fairmount Waterworks*, 1848. Daguerreotype panorama in eight plates. International Museum of Photography at George Eastman House, Rochester, N.Y.

while the plate moved laterally in the opposite direction. In 1845, Fredrich von Martens, a German printmaker living in Paris, was the first to work out the optical and mechanical adjustments necessary to make single panoramic daguerreotypes of his adopted city, then he turned to a similar format in collodion for Alpine landscapes. Indeed with the advent of the wet plate, the panorama came into its own, even though panoramas on paper had been made by the calotype process. While exposure time for the glass negative often remained long, the resulting sharply detailed segments of a scene, printed and glued together to form an encompassing view, were taken as embracing reality even though the human eye could not possibly have seen the landscape in that fashion. However, these panoramas were more realistic than the lithographed bird's-eye views that were so popular. By using panoramic cameras that rotated in an arc of approximately 120 degrees, photographers might avoid the exacting calculations needed to assure that the panels of the panorama would join properly without overlaps or missing segments, but these devices could not encompass as wide an angle as the segmented panoramas and consequently seemed less dramatic. Panoramas were produced by photographers everywhere, by the Bisson brothers, Adolphe Braun, Samuel Bourne, and many now-unknown figures in Europe, Asia, and India, and by American photographers of both urban development and western wilderness. George Robinson Fardon, William Henry Jackson, Carleton E. Watkins, and especially Eadweard Muybridge, who devoted himself to making panoramic views of San Francisco on three different occasions, were among the more successful panoramists in the United States during the collodion/albumen era *(pl. no. 165)*.

Landscape Calotypes

Despite unparalleled clarity of detail in landscape daguerreotypes, the difficulties in making and processing exposures in the field and the problems of viewing an image subject to reflections and of replicating the image for publication made it an inefficient technology with respect to views. From the start, the duplicatable calotype was accepted by many as a more congenial means of capturing scenery, and it achieved greater sensitivity and flexibility for this purpose after improvements had been made by Louis Désiré Blanquart-Evrard and Gustave Le Gray. Between 1841 and about 1855, when collodion on glass supplanted paper negatives entirely, calotypists documented cityscape, historic and exotic monuments, rural scenery, and the wilder, less-accessible terrains that were beginning to appeal to Europeans who had wearied of the more familiar settings. Because of their broad delineation, calotype views more nearly resembled graphic works such as aquatints, and this tended to increase their appeal to both artists and elitists in the intellectual community who preferred aesthetic objects to informational documents. Nevertheless, the calotype still had enough detail to recommend it as a basis for copying, as the British publication *The Art Union* pointed out in 1846 when it noted that painters, not being as enterprising as photographers, could depend on "sun-pictures" (calotypes) of places such as "the ruins of Babylon or the wilds of Australia"[7] for accurate views from which they could make topographical paintings.

Somewhat easier to deal with than daguerreotyping in the field, the chemistry of the early calotype still was complicated enough to make its use in travel a problem. Nevertheless, a number of British amateurs (often aided by servants and local help) transported paper, chemicals, and cameras to the Continent and the Near East soon after Talbot's announcement. Three members of his circle, Calvert Jones, George W. Bridges, and Christopher Rice Mansel Talbot were the first hardy souls to journey from Great Britain to Italy, Greece, and North Africa with calotype equipment. Through its high vantage point and pattern of light and shade, a view of the *Porta della Ripetta* in Rome *(pl. no. 101)* suggests that Jones (who photographed in Italy and Malta) was interested in atmospheric and artistic qualities as much as in description. Bridges, who traveled in the region for seven years, made some 1,700 pictures, which he found were subject to serious fading; a small group was published in 1858 and 1859 in an album entitled *Palestine as it is: In a Series of Photographic Views . . . Illustrating the Bible*. Another group of calotypes of the area by Dr. Claudius Galen Wheelhouse was gathered together in an album entitled *Photographic Sketches from the Shores of the Mediterranean*. Ernest De Caranza in Anatolia, Maxime du Camp in Egypt *(see Chapter 4)*, and Pierre Trémaux in the Sudan were others among the early figures who attempted, with varying degrees of success, to use the calotype process to photograph in North Africa and the Near East. These works were forerunners of the numerous views on paper whose appeal to the Victorian public may

have been in part because they afforded a contrast between the progress visible at home and the undeveloped landscape of the region, and in part because they recalled to viewers their biblical and classical heritage.

In spite of these efforts, however, and even though Talbot placed no restrictions on the noncommercial use of the calotype process, viewmaking did not exactly flourish in England its first ten years of existence. Instead, images of landscape and architecture achieved a pinnacle of excellence in France during the 1850s, as a result of interest by a small group of painter-photographers in an improved paper process that had evolved from experiments by Blanquart-Evrard and Le Gray. By waxing the paper negative before exposure, Le Gray achieved a transparency akin to glass, making the paper more receptive to fine detail. The spread of this improved technique in France during the early 1850s gave the calotype a new lease and resulted in images of extraordinary quality. This flowering coincided with the concern among Barbizon landscape painters for capturing the quality of light and revealing the value of unspoiled nature in human experience.

The improved calotype also made it conceivable to launch the photographic campaign—that is, government or privately sponsored commissions to produce camera images of a specific nature and theme. One of the most renowned, the *Missions héliographiques*, was organized in

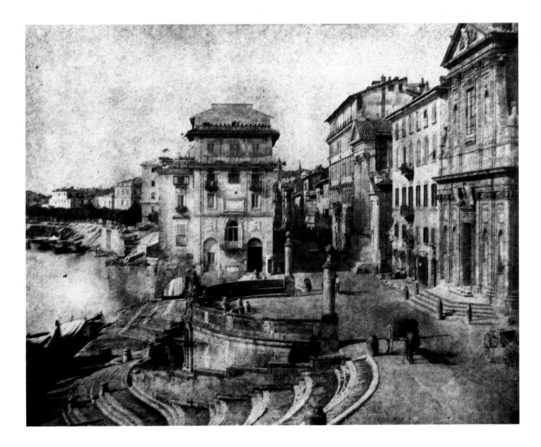

101. REV. CALVERT JONES. *Porta della Ripetta, Rome,* 1846. Calotype. Science Museum, London.

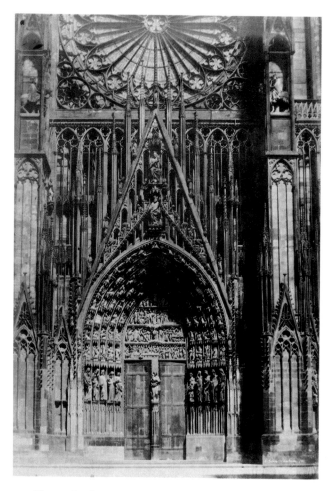

102. HENRI LE SECQ. *Strasbourg Cathedral*, 1851.
Calotype. International Museum of Photography at
George Eastman House, Rochester, N.Y.

1851 by the *Commission des Monuments historiques* (Commission on Historical Monuments) in order to provide a pictorial census of France's architectural patrimony. Undertaken initially during the period of the Second Republic, and in accord with continuing efforts by Napoleon III to preserve and modernize France, it involved the documentation of aged and crumbling churches, fortresses, bridges, and castles that were slated for restoration under the guidance of architect Eugène Emmanuel Viollet-le-Duc.

The five photographers engaged in this innovative documentation were Edouard Denis Baldus, Hippolyte Bayard, Le Gray, Henri Le Secq, and O. Mestral. Photographers received itineraries and instructions, quite exact at times, detailing the localities to be photographed. Among the most accomplished of the group were Le Gray and Le Secq, both of whom had been trained as painters in the studio of Paul Delaroche (along with British photographer Roger Fenton). Le Secq's *Strasbourg Cathedral*, 1851 *(pl. no. 102)*, one of a series of architectural monuments, is an exhila-

rating organization of masses of sculptural detail. Le Gray *(see Profile)*, in whose studio many calotypists first learned the process, was a demanding technician who also was involved in making collodion negatives; his images will be discussed shortly in the context of developments in that material. Little is known of Mestral, a former daguerreotypist and an associate of Le Gray, other than that he photographed in Brittany and Normandy on his own and from the Dordogne southward in company with Le Gray. The image of the bridge *Pont Valentre (pl. no. 103)* in Cahors, included because of impending plans to restore what was then considered the finest example of medieval military architecture in France, suggests a distinctive feeling for volume and silhouette.

Unhappily, the *Missions* project never reached full fruition. Negatives—some 300—and prints were filed away without being reproduced or published, either because the project's sole aim was to establish an archive or because the photographers depicted these ancient structures in too favorable a light for the images to serve as propaganda for restoration efforts.[8] Individually, they were used by architects and masons working under Viollet-le-Duc's guidance in matching and fabricating decorative elements that had been destroyed. Nevertheless, the government of France under Napoleon III continued to regard photography— whether calotype or collodion/albumen—as a tool integral to its expansive domestic and foreign programs, commissioning documentations of the countryside, the railroad lines, and of natural disasters as evidences of its concern for national programs and problems. Baldus produced about 30 large-format negatives of the flooding of the Rhone River in 1856 *(pl. no. 104)*. It is apparent from the amplitude of his vision and the sense of structure in this example that no dichotomy existed in the photographer's mind between landscape art and documentation. These images were exhibited in the major international expositions in Paris, London, and Brussels, gaining medals and the praise of the photographic critics of the time.

Not all French landscape calotypists were trained artists nor was their work invariably commissioned. Indeed, one of the intriguing aspects of the epoch is that scientists as well as painters found the paper negative a congenial process for representing nature. Victor Regnault, director of the Sèvres porcelain factory (after 1852) and president of both the French Academy of Sciences and the *Société Française de Photographie*, had first become curious about paper photography when Talbot disclosed the process, but only pursued this interest in 1851 after improvements had been made by Blanquart-Evrard. Using the waxed-paper process, he experimented with exposure and produced a number of idyllic, mist-shrouded views of the countryside around the factory, among them *The Banks of the Seine at*

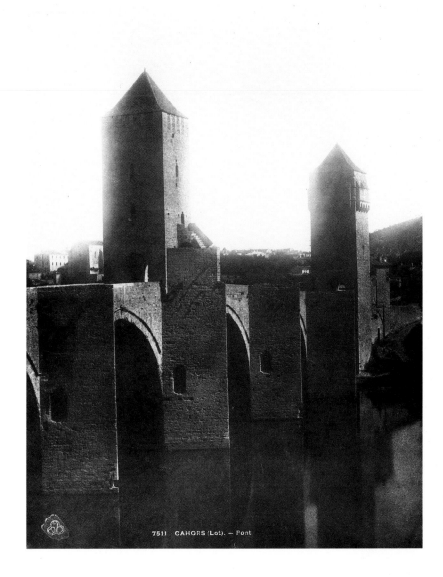

7511 CAHORS (Lot). — Pont

103. O. MESTRAL. *Cahors: Pont Valentre*, c. 1851.
Calotype. Caisse Nationale des Monuments
Historiques et des Sites, Paris. © Arch. Phot.
Paris/SPADEM.

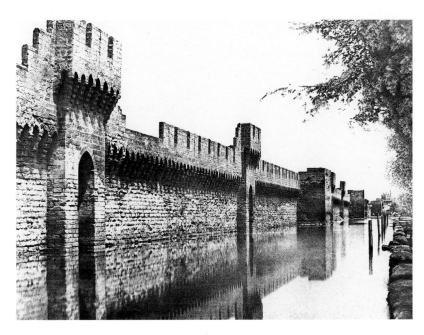

104. EDOUARD DENIS BALDUS. *The Flooding of
the Rhône at Avignon*, 1856. Calotype. Caisse
Nationale des Monuments Historiques et des
Sites, Paris. © Arch. Phot. Paris/SPADEM.

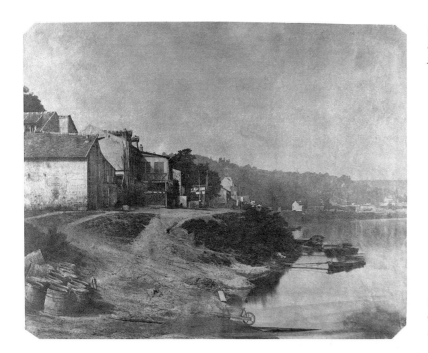

105. VICTOR REGNAULT. *The Banks of the Seine at Sèvres*, 1851–52. Collection André Jammes, Paris. Art Institute of Chicago.

106. LOUIS ROBERT. *Versailles, Neptune Basin*, c. 1853. Calotype. Collection André Jammes, Paris. Art Institute of Chicago.

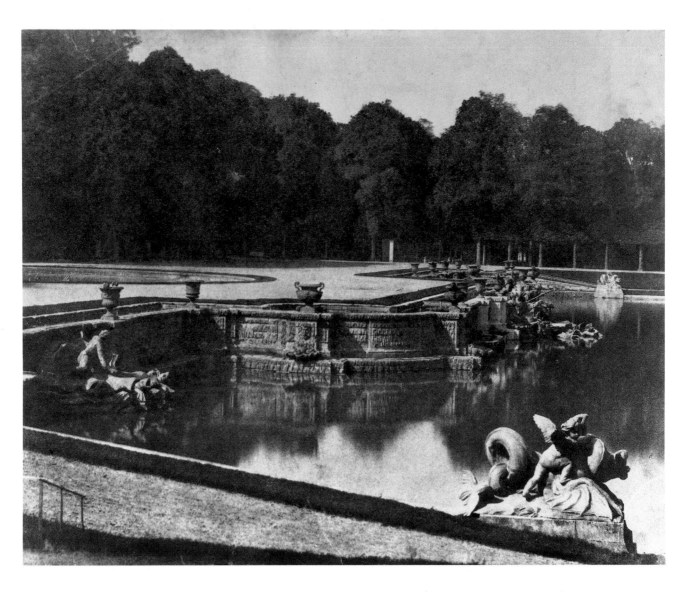

Sèvres (pl. no. 105), in which he included the everyday objects of rural existence such as casks and barrow. Louis Robert, chief of the painters and gilders at the porcelain factory, worked both at Sèvres and Versailles, using the calotype process before turning to albumen on glass; a number of his calotypes were included in Blanquart-Evrard's 1853 publication *Souvenirs de Versailles (pl. no. 106)*. These images display a sensibility that is similar to that of Barbizon painters in their lyrical approach to the homely and simple aspects and objects of nature and rural life.

British amateur photographers welcomed the improved calotype for its greater sensitivity and definition. As heirs to picturesque and topographical traditions in landscape imagery, they sought to maintain a delicate balance between affective expression and the descriptive clarity that the improved process made possible. At times, English camera images of buildings and their surroundings seem to reflect the notion put forth by contemporary writers that architectural structures have expressive physiognomies much like those of humans. For example, *Guy's Cliffe, Warwickshire (pl. no. 107)* by the English amateur Robert Henry Cheney brings to mind a melancholy spirit, a phrase used by Ruskin to describe the character of certain kinds of buildings. The most celebrated English photographer of this period, Roger Fenton (to be discussed shortly), was extravagantly praised in the British press for the marked "character" of his architectural images.

Benjamin Brecknell Turner, an English businessman who made pure landscape calotypes *(pl. no. 108)* as well as portraits and architectural views, found the paper negative so sympathetic to his vision of untrammeled nature that he continued to work with the material until 1862, long after most photographers had switched to glass plates. On the other hand, Thomas Keith, a Scottish physician, practiced the calotype for only a very few years, and then only on occasions when the quality of light enabled him to make negatives of great tonal range. Keith's interest in the expressive nature of light, inspired perhaps by his acquaintance with Hill and Adamson, is apparent in images made in 1856 on the island of Iona, among them *Doorway, St. Oran's Chapel (pl. no. 109)*, where the factual record of ancient church architecture is given unusual force by strongly accentuated illumination.

Calotyping also appealed to Englishmen who made their homes outside the British Isles, among them Maxwell Lyte and John Stewart, who lived in Pau in the Pyrenees in the 1850s. Stewart's views of the rugged terrain of this region *(pl. no. 110)*, published by Blanquart-Evrard and exhibited in England, were praised by his father-in-law Sir John Herschel for the artistic effects of their "superb combination of rock, mountain, forest and water."[9] Both Lyte and Stewart were members of the *Société Française de Photo-*

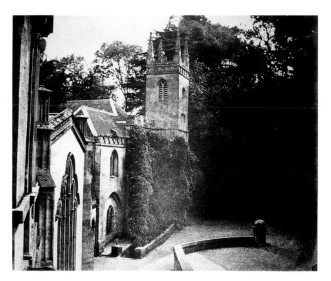

107. ROBERT HENRY CHENEY. *Guy's Cliffe, Warwickshire*, 1850s. Albumen print. Collection Centre Canadien d'Architecture/Canadian Centre for Architecture, Montréal.

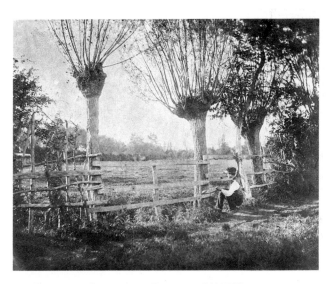

108. BENJAMIN BRECKNELL TURNER. *Old Willows*, c. 1856. Waxed paper negative. Collection André Jammes, Paris. Art Institute of Chicago.

graphie. Along with Thomas Sutton, the first in Britain to use Blanquart-Evrard's process in a publishing venture, they kept open the channels of communication between the French and British regarding the latest in photochemical technology.

French and British imperial interest in the countries of the Near East, Egypt in particular, continued to lure photographers using paper (and later glass) negatives into these regions. In 1849, the wealthy French journalist

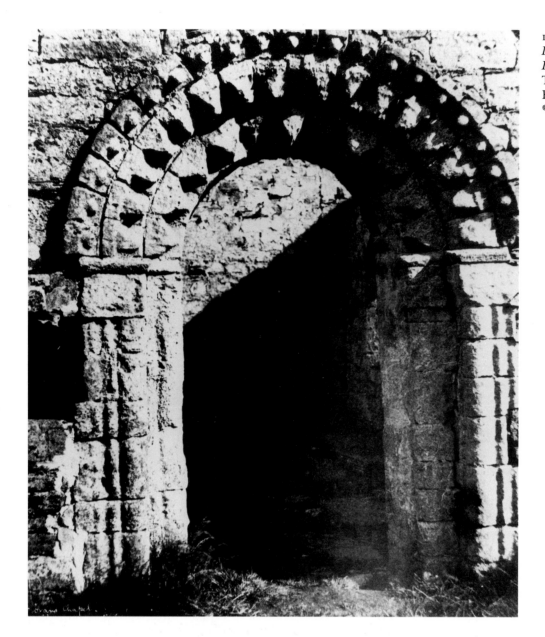

Maxime du Camp, accompanied by the young Flaubert, was sent on an official photographic mission to Egypt. Trained by Le Gray and equipped with calotyping apparatus "for the purpose of securing, along the way, and with the aid of this marvelous means of reproduction, views of monuments and copies of inscriptions," Du Camp also was expected to make facsimile casts of hieroglyphic inscriptions.[10] The calotypes, printed in 1852 by Blanquart-Evrard for his first publication *Egypte, Nubie, Palestine et Syrie*,[11] display a concern for establishing accurate scale, as seen in the human yardstick provided by a native assistant in *The Colossus of Abu Simbel (pl. no. III)*, but they also demonstrate the definition and clarity that the improved calotype made possible.

Five years later, the amateur French archeologist Auguste Salzmann briefly used the calotype with similar authority to make documents of architectural ruins in Jerusalem in order to "render a service to science"[12] and to help solve a controversy about the antiquity of the monuments. Working with an assistant, Salzmann was able to produce about 150 paper negatives under difficult circumstances; these, too, were printed at the Blanquart-Evrard establishment at Lille. In addition to an avowed scientific aim, images such as *Jerusalem, Islamic Fountain (pl. no. 112)* indicate the photographer's mastery of composition and sensitivity to the effects of light. The work of both Du Camp and Salzmann indicate that in the hands of imaginative individuals the camera image might develop a unique aesthetic, an ability to handle volume and light in an evocative manner while also documenting actuality.

Landscapes in Collodion/Albumen

The new collodion technology, discovered and publicized by Archer in 1850 and 1851, forced landscape photographers and documentarians operating in the field to transport an entire darkroom—tent, trays, scales, chemicals, and even distilled water—besides cameras and glass plates *(pl. nos. 113 and 114)*. It may seem astonishing today that, under such circumstances, this technique should have been considered an improvement over the calotype, which also was somewhat more sensitive to natural tonalities and had greater range. But paper negatives required time-consuming skills for complete realization. With the promise of sharper and more predictable results in less time, the glass negative with its coating of collodion and silver-iodide preempted all other processes for the next 30 years. Together with the albumen print, which retained the sharpness of the image because the printing paper was also coated with an emulsion, collodion made the mechanization of the landscape view possible, turning the scenic landscape into an item of consumption, and landscape photography into photo-business.

Limitations in the sensitivity of the collodion material itself were responsible for evoking contradictory aesthetic attitudes about images made from glass plates. Because of the limited responsiveness of silver-iodide to the colors of spectral light other than blue (and ultraviolet radiation), landscape images that displayed blank white skies and dark, relatively undifferentiated foregrounds were not uncommon. While commercial publishers seem not to have been unduly disturbed, this characteristic was decried by Lady Elizabeth Eastlake, one of the first serious English critics of photography. Writing in the *Quarterly Review* in 1857, she observed, "If the sky be given, therefore, the landscape remains black and underdone; if the landscape be rendered, the impatient action of light has burnt out all cloud form in one blaze of white."[13] She added that the collodion landscape photograph was unable to represent the tonal gradations that the eye accepts as denoting spatial recession, and that by its combined lack of atmosphere and too great precision, the image showed both too little and too much. Among others who objected to the lack of realism in the extreme contrast between dark and light areas in landscape photographs was Hermann Wilhelm Vogel, an influential German photographer, critic, and photo-chemical researcher, whose opinions appeared frequently in American periodicals during the 1860s and '70s, and who was successful in his efforts to improve the sensitivity of the silver halides to the various colors of light.

Photographers concerned with artistic landscapes avoided these problems with what was called "artifice." This involved using masks and combining two negatives on the same print—one for the sky and one for the ground—or employing hand-manipulations to remove unattractive mottled and gray areas. *Valley of the Huisne (pl. no. 115)* by Camille Silvy, praised as a "gem" when exhibited in 1858, exemplifies the possibilities of this technique for creating scenes that a contemporary critic characterized as "rich in exquisite and varied detail, with broad shadows stealing over the whole."[14] Le Gray, whose role in paper photography has been noted, used double printing in a number of collodion seascapes made at Sète (Cette) *(pl. no. 116)* around 1856—works similar in theme and style to seascapes painted by French artists Eugène Delacroix and Gustave Courbet at about the same time. Less traditionally picturesque than Silvy's scene, Le Gray transformed clouds, sea, and rocks into an evocative arrangement of volume and light, into an "abstraction called art," in today's language.[15] That composite landscapes of this period could be and often were unconvincingly pieced together is apparent from contemporary criticism that complained of pictures with clouds that were not reflected in the water or of foregrounds taken in early morning joined to skies taken at noon.

In Europe, where landscape views were considered souvenirs for travelers and restoratives for businessmen

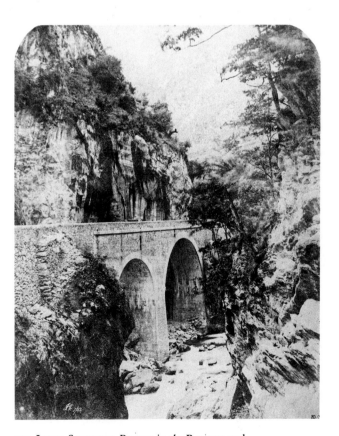

110. JOHN STEWART. *Passage in the Pyrenees*, n.d. Calotype. Royal Scottish Academy, Edinburgh.

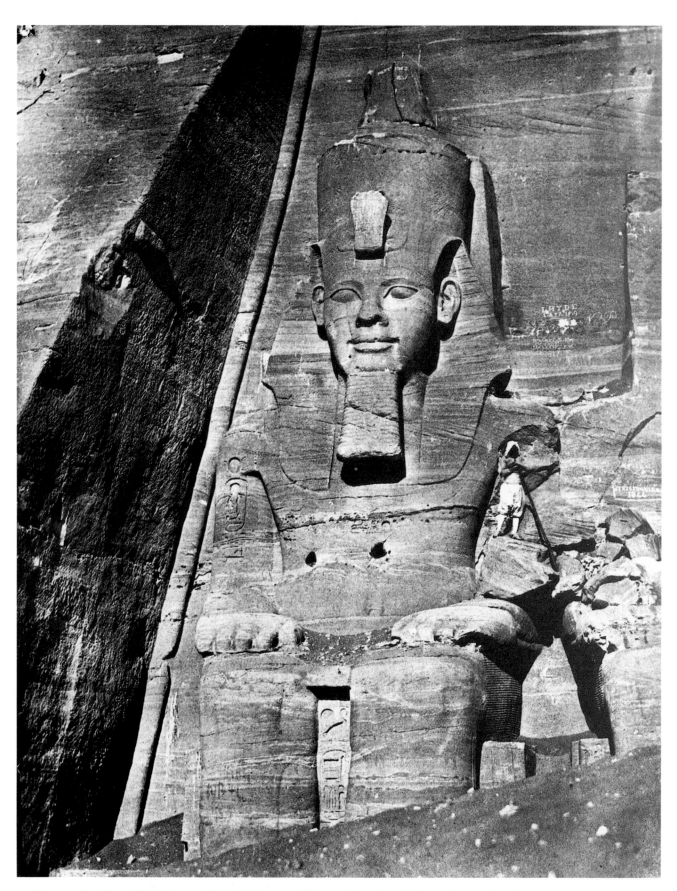

III. MAXIME DU CAMP. *The Colossus of Abu Simbel*, c. 1850. Calotype. Victoria and Albert Museum, London.

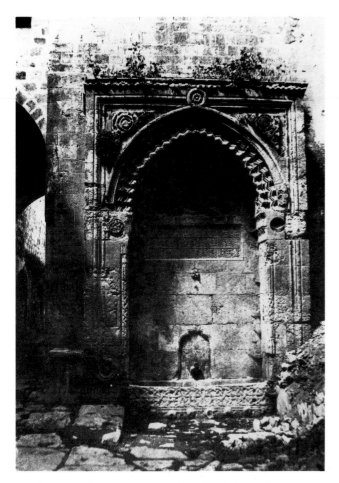

112. AUGUSTE SALZMANN. *Jerusalem, Islamic Fountain*, 1854. Calotype. National Gallery of Canada, Ottawa.

tied to the city, hundreds of thousands of scenes on albumen paper were turned out to be sold and pasted into albums or used in stereograph viewers. To satisfy this market, freelance photographers were dispatched around the globe by enterprising publishers, or they set up their own view-making businesses. Others photographed for privately or publicly funded expeditions. As a consequence, artistic landscape effects were not usually considered of primary import in images whose aim was to present information palatably. For example, Francis Frith and George Washington Wilson, to name two prominent mass publishers of landscape views, embraced artistic considerations in so far as they contributed to producing agreeable compositions. They aimed for the best vantage point and most harmonious tonalities, but avoided expressive or dramatic effects of light and shadow such as had greatly delighted Keith, Salzmann, Baldus, or Le Gray. As Wilson noted, he had to "study the popular taste . . . and not only to get a pleasing picture of a place, but one also that can be recognized by the public."[16] Besides promoting a style that might be called "straight," this mass consumption of images had a profound if not always determinable effect on the viewing public in that photographic evidence was considered synonymous with truth and the image as a substitute for firsthand experience.[17]

The government of Napoleon III, which had promoted the calotype as a means of documenting both scientific progress and royal patronage, continued to regard collodion images in the same light. What at first glance may

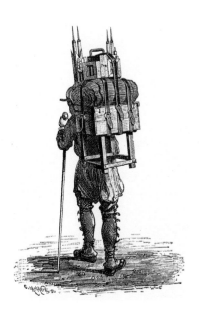

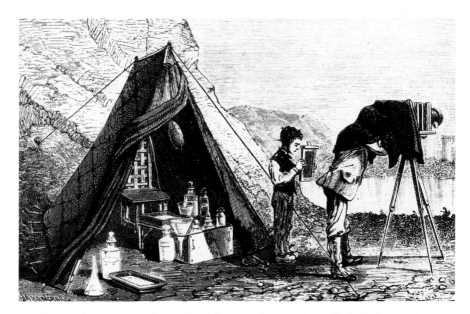

113–114. UNKNOWN. *European-style Portable Darkroom Tent*, 1877. Wood engravings from *A History and Handbook of Photography*, edited by J. Thompson, 1877. Metropolitan Museum of Art, New York; gift of Spencer Bickerton, 1938.

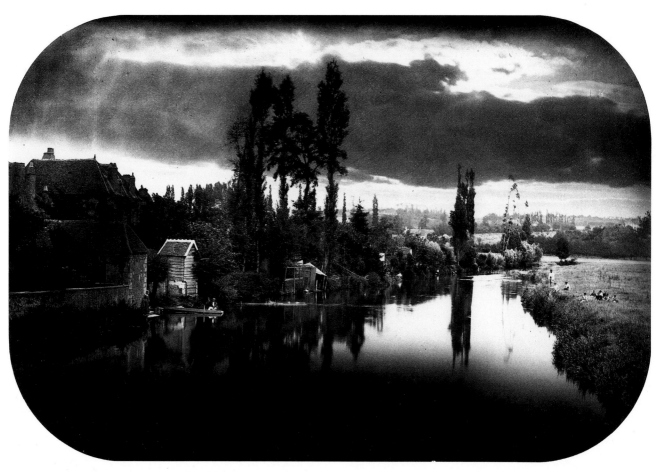

115. CAMILLE SILVY. *Valley of the Huisne, France*, 1858. Albumen print. Victoria and Albert Museum, London.

seem to be landscape pure and simple, such as views taken in the Alps by the Bisson brothers, was motivated by the Imperial desire to celebrate territorial acquisition—in this case the ceding to France of Nice and Savoy by the Kingdom of Sardinia. During the collodion era, the Bissons had rapidly extended their range of subjects to embrace art reproductions, architecture, and landscapes, often in very large format. *Passage des Echelles (pl. no. 117)*, one of the six views made by Auguste-Rosalie as a participant in the second scaling of Mont Blanc in 1862, integrates the description of distinctive geological formations with a classical approach to composition, achieving in its balance of forms and tonalities a work of unusually expressive power. A similar evocation of solitary nature unaltered by human effort can be seen in *Gorge of the Tamine (pl. no. 118)* by Charles Soulier, a professional view-maker who is better known for his urbane Paris scenes than for Alpine landscapes. In view of steadily encroaching urbanization, these images suggest a public nostalgia for virgin nature that will be encountered again, more forcefully, in camera images of the American wilderness during the 1860s and '70s.

Scenic views found an avid entrepreneur as well as photographer in Adolphe Braun. With studios in both Paris and Alsace, he was not only a prolific view-maker, but a large-scale publisher who supplied prints in a variety of formats—stereoscope to panoramic—to subscribers in England, France, Germany, and the United States. Responding to the imperial desire to make Alsatians aware of their French heritage, Braun first photographed the landscape and monuments of this province and then went on to make more than 4,000 images of Alpine, Black Forest, and Vosges mountain scenery, eventually printing in carbon instead of albumen in order to insure print stability. Braun's views, of which *Lake Steamers at Winter Mooring, Switzerland (pl. no. 119)* is an outstanding example, display a skillful blend of information and artistry but also present the landscape as accessible by the inclusion of human figures or structures.

England, too, had landscapists with an authentic respect for what the collodion process could accomplish, but government patronage was limited to royal acclaim and, at times, purchase of individual images by members of the royal family, with documentations of the countryside and historical monuments initiated by photographers themselves or by private publishers rather than by the state. Fenton, the commanding figure in English photography before his retirement in 1862, had made calotypes of architectural monuments in Russia in 1852. He changed to collodion in 1853, and after his return from the Crimean War *(see Chapter 4)*, he had another traveling darkroom constructed to facilitate making views of rugged rocks, mountain gorges, waterfalls, and ruins—romantic themes to which the British turned as industrialization advanced. Contemporary critics on both sides of the Channel considered his landscapes to have reached the heights to which camera images could aspire, especially with respect to capturing atmosphere and a sense of aerial perspective. However, because Fenton refused to combine negatives or do handwork, images with strong geometric pattern, such as *The Terrace and Park, Harewood House (pl. no. 120)*, were criticized as offensive.[18] A number of Fenton's landscapes were

published as stereographs in *The Stereoscopic Magazine (see below)*, as photoengravings in *Photographic Art Treasures*, and as albumen prints in albums and books devoted to native landscape—these being the forms in which scenic images found an audience in the 1850s and '60s.

Albumen prints became popular as book illustration between 1855 and 1885 when, it is believed, more than a thousand albums and books, sponsored by private organizations and public personalities, were published, mainly in England, Scotland, France, India, and the United States.[19] Original photographs provided artistic, biographical, historical, and scientific illustration as well as topographical images to supplement and enhance texts on a wide variety of subjects. Even the small, relatively undetailed stereograph view was considered appropriate to illustrate scientific and travel books; one of the first to use the double image in this manner was C. Piazzi Smyth's *Teneriffe*,

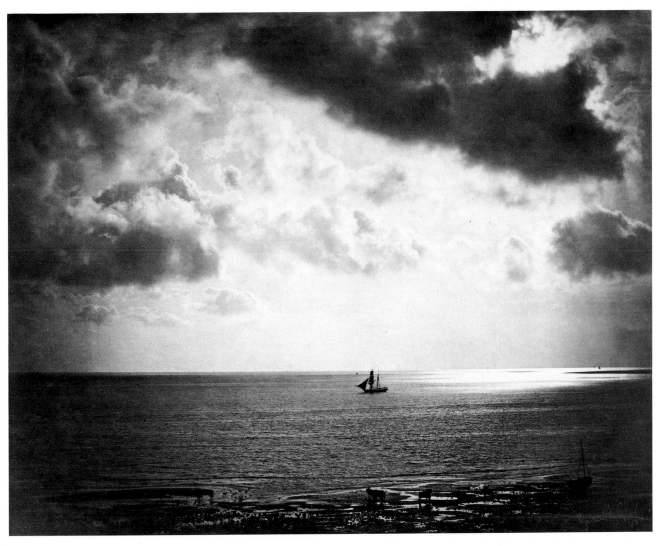

116. GUSTAVE LE GRAY. *Brig Upon the Water*, 1856. Albumen. Albumen print. Victoria and Albert Museum, London.

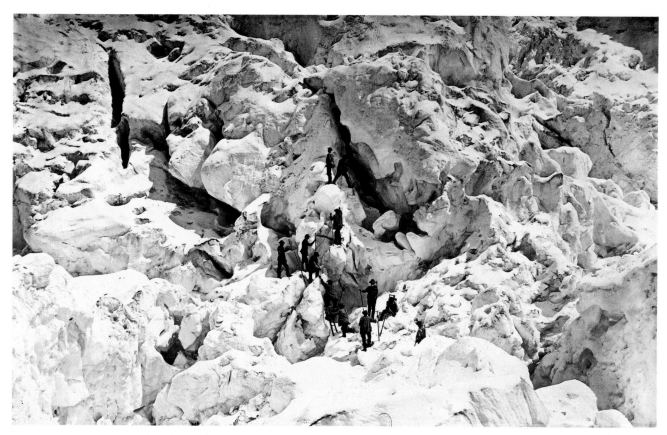

117. LOUIS-AUGUSTE and AUGUSTE-ROSALIE BISSON. *Passage des Echelles (Ascent of Mt. Blanc)*, 1862. Albumen print. Bibliothèque Nationale, Paris.

which appeared in 1858 with 18 stereograph views of the barren island landscape where Smyth and his party conducted astronomical experiments. It was soon followed by *The Stereoscopic Magazine*, a monthly publication that lasted five years and included still lifes and land- and cityscape stereographs. The success of illustration with photographic prints of any kind may be ascribed to their fidelity and cheapness and to the relative rapidity with which paper prints could be glued into the publication, while the decline of this practice was the result of even more efficient photomechanical methods that made possible the printing of text and image at the same time.

Wales and Scotland provided other English photographers besides Fenton with localities for wilderness images, among them Francis Bedford who made *Glas Pwil Cascade (pl. no. 122)* in 1865. In common with many landscapists of the period, Bedford issued stereographs as well as larger-format views because they were inexpensive and in popular demand. However, it was the Scottish photographer Wilson, probably the most successful of the view publishers, who is believed to have had the world's largest stock of scenic images in the 1880s *(pl. no. 121)*. Interested also in instantaneous pictures *(see Chapter 6)*, Wilson

noted that "considerable watching and waiting is necessary before the effect turns up which is both capable and worthy of being taken."[20] Using a tent darkroom in the field to prepare the exposures, this meticulous former portrait painter employed over 30 assistants in his Aberdeen printing establishment to carefully wash and gold-tone the prints in order to remove all chemical residue. As a consequence, Wilson albumen prints are of greater richness and stability than was usual for the era. Other British landscapists of the collodion era included Frith *(see below)*, William England, and James Valentine whose successful enterprise in Dundee, Scotland, turned out views similar to those by Wilson. While competently composed and well-produced, the absence of atmosphere and feeling in commercial views were contributing factors in the endeavors that began in the 1870s to fashion a new aesthetic for landscape photography.

Similar ideas about landscape motivated German viewmakers of the 1850s and '60s. Outstanding calotype views had been made in the early 1850s by Franz Hanfstaengl and Hermann Krone, before these individuals changed to collodion. Krone, the more versatile of the two, who advertised his *Photographisches Institut* in Dresden as a source for

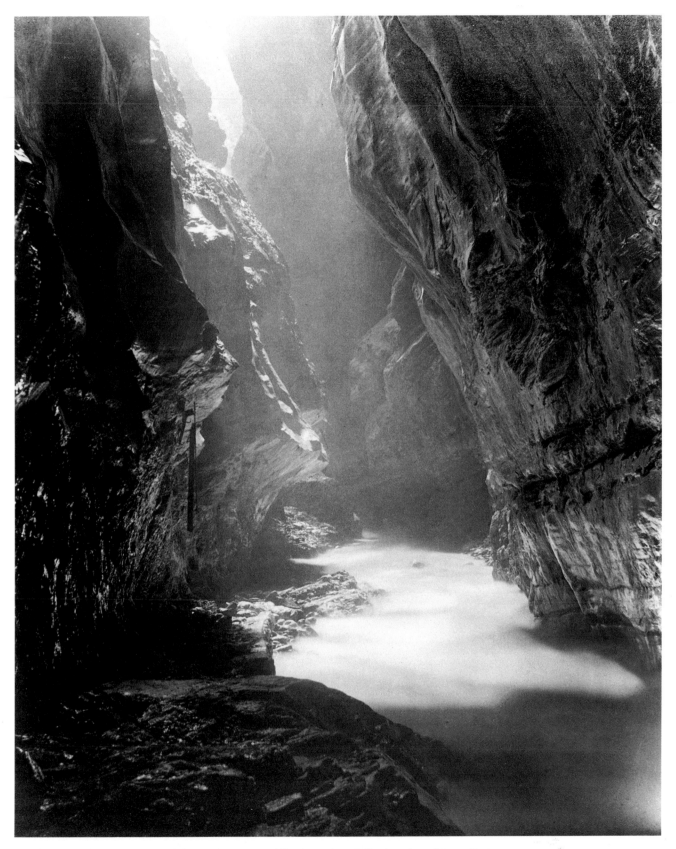

118. CHARLES SOULIER. *Gorge of the Tamine*, c. 1865. Albumen print. Collection Gérard-Lévy, Paris.

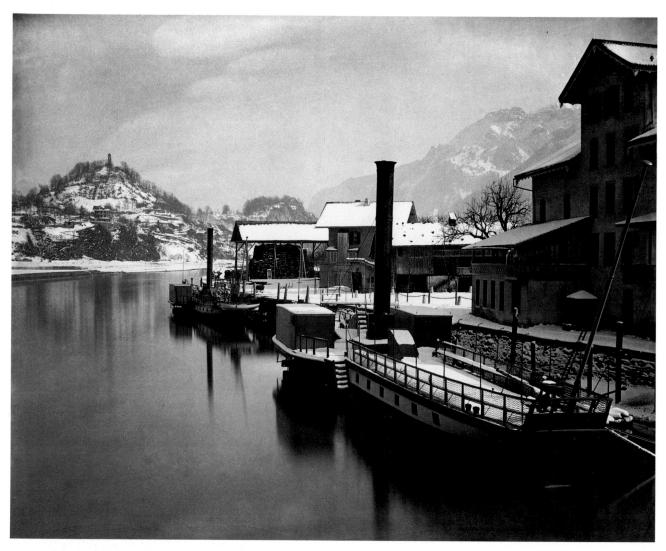

119. ADOLPHE BRAUN. *Lake Steamers at Winter Mooring, Switzerland*, c. 1865.
Carbon print. Collection Sam Wagstaff, New York.

scenic views and stereographs as well as portraits, was commissioned by the crown to produce views of the countryside and cityscape throughout Saxony, which resulted in the appearance in 1872 of his *Koenigs-Album der Stadte Sachsens (King's Album of Saxon Cities)* to celebrate the golden wedding anniversary of the rulers of Saxony. Though less idealized than some, these views of Dresden and its natural environs, exemplified by *Waterfall in Saxon Switzerland (pl. no. 123)*, still reflect the romantic attitude of the view painters of the early 19th century. Romanticism also suffuses *Bridge Near King's Monument (pl. no. 124)*, an 1866 image by Vogel, but the focus of this work is light and not locality. In a still different vein, studies of forest foliage and trees *(pl. no. 125)* made in the mid- to late-1860s and typified by the work of Gerd Volkerling suggest the influence of the Barbizon style of naturalism.

Landscape photography developed in the Scandinavian countries in the 1860s and '70s in response to the tourism that brought affluent British and German travelers to the rocky coasts of this region in search of untamed nature. Photographers Marcus Selmer of Denmark, Axel Lindahl and Per Adolf Thören of Sweden, and the Norwegians Hans Abel, Knud Knudsen, and Martin Skøien, all supplied good souvenir images to voyagers who, there as elsewhere, wished to individualize their recollections with picturesque travel images. The most dramatic of these views—the mist-shrouded mountains and tormented ice and rock formations *(pl. no. 126)* captured by Knudsen during his 35 or so years as an outstanding scenic photographer—reflect the prominent influence of the German Romantic style of landscape painting in that they not only serve as remembrances of places visited but encapsulate a sense of the sublime.

Landscape photographs of Italy were made almost

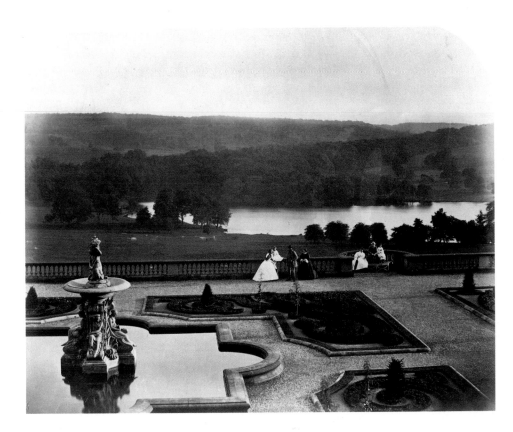

120. ROGER FENTON. *The Terrace and Park, Harewood House*, 1861. Albumen print. Royal Photographic Society, Bath, England.

121. GEORGE WASHINGTON WILSON. *The Silver Strand, Loch Katrine*, c. 1875–80. Albumen print. George Washington Wilson Collection, Aberdeen University Library.

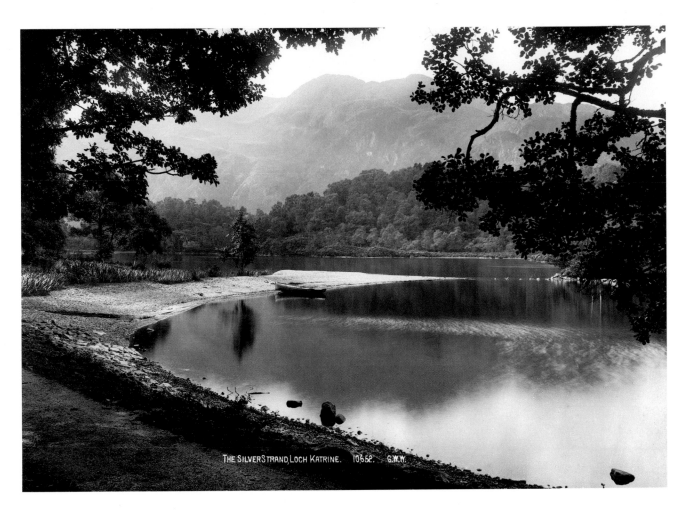

THE SILVER STRAND, LOCH KATRINE. 10652. G.W.W.

exclusively as tourist souvenirs. A continuing stream of travelers from northern Europe and the United States ensured an income for a group of excellent foreign and Italian photographers. Here, especially, the romantic taste for ruins was easily indulged, with most images including at least a piece of ancient sculpture, building, or garden. As photography historian Robert Sobieszek has pointed out, because Italy was seen as the home of civilization, early photographers were able to infuse their views with a sense of the romantic past at almost every turn.[21] In *Grotto of Neptune, Tivoli (pl. no. 127)*, taken in the early 1860s, Robert

MacPherson, a Scottish physician who set himself up as an art dealer in Rome, captured the strong shadows that suggest unfathomable and ancient mysteries while fashioning an almost abstract pattern of tonalities and textures. Interest in romantic effects is apparent also in *Night View of the Roman Forum (pl. no. 128)* by Gioacchino Altobelli, a native Roman who at times collaborated with his countryman Pompeo Molins on scenic views. Altobelli, later employed by the Italian Railroad Company, was considered by contemporaries to be especially adept at combining negatives to recreate the sense of moonlight on the ruins—a popular

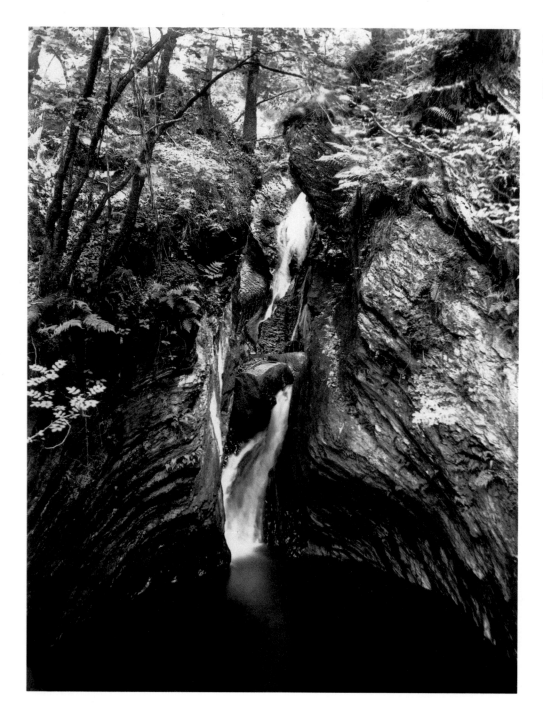

122. FRANCIS BEDFORD. *Glas Pwil Cascade (Lifnant Valley)*, 1865. Albumen print. National Gallery of Canada, Ottawa.

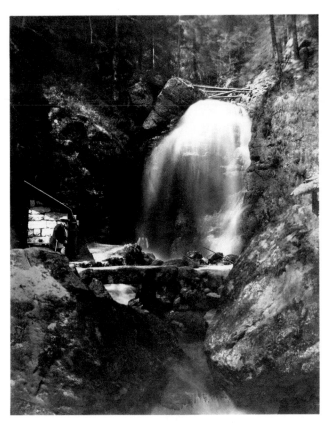

123. HERMANN KRONE. *Waterfall in Saxon Switzerland,*
1857. Albumen print. Deutsches Museum, Munich.

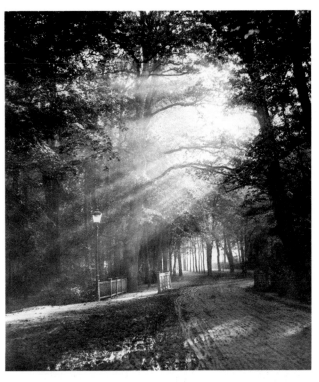

124. HERMANN VOGEL. *Bridge Near King's Monument,*
1866. Albumen print. Agfa-Gevaert Foto-Historama,
Leverkusen, Germany.

image because of the touristic tradition of visiting Roman
ruins by night.

The best known by far of the Italian view-makers were
the Brogi family and the Alinari brothers; the latter established a studio in Florence that is still in existence. Like
Braun in France, the Alinari ran a mass-production photographic publishing business specializing in art reproductions, but their stock also included images of fruit and
flowers and views of famous monuments and structures in
Rome and Florence. In the south, Giorgio Sommer, of
German origin, began a similar but smaller operation in
Naples in 1857, providing genre scenes as well as landscapes. In Venice, tourist views were supplied by Carlo
Ponti, an optical-instrument maker of fine artistic sensitivity that is apparent in *San Giorgio Maggiore Seen from the
Ducal Palace (pl. no. 129)*, made in the early 1870s. Given the
long tradition in Italy of *vedute*—small-scale topographical
scenes—it is not surprising that camera views of such subject matter should so easily have become accomplished and
accepted.

Other European nations on the Mediterranean such as
Spain and Greece, while renowned for scenic beauty and

ruins, were not documented with nearly the same enterprise as Italy, probably because they were outside the
itineraries of many 19th-century travelers. The best-known
photographs of Spain were made by Charles Clifford, an
expatriate Englishman living in Madrid, who was court
photographer to Queen Isabella II. Working also in other
cities than the capital, Clifford photographed art treasures
as well as landscapes and architectural subjects; his view
The Court of the Alhambra in Granada (pl. no. 130) suggests
a sense of sunlit quietude while still capturing the extraordinary richness of the interior carving. As one might anti-
cipate, views of Greece, particularly the Acropolis, were
somewhat more common than of Spain and also more
commonplace. Photographed by native and foreign photographers, the most evocative are by James Robertson,
Jean Walther, and William Stillman, an American associated with the British Pre-Raphaelites who had turned to
photography as a result of disappointment with his painting. Stillman's images, published in 1870 as *The Acropolis of
Athens Illustrated Picturesquely and Architecturally (pl. no.
131)*, were printed by the carbon process, which in England
was called Autotype.

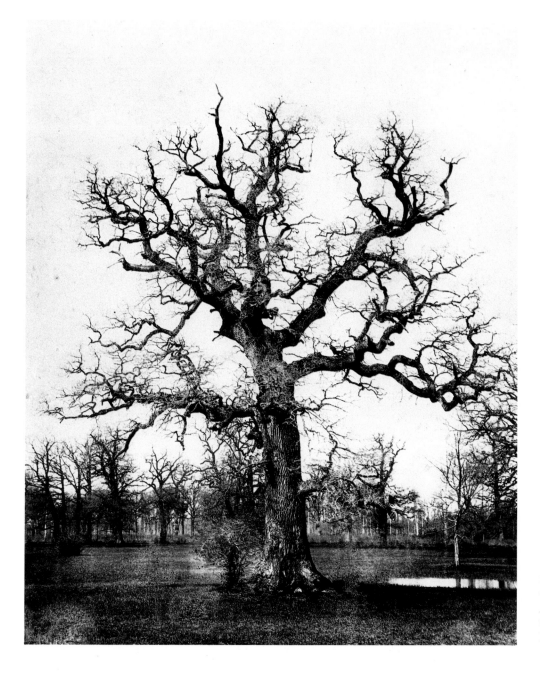

125. GERD VOLKERLING.
Oak Trees in Dessau, 1867.
Albumen print. Agfa-
Gevaert Foto-Historama,
Leverkusen, Germany.

Landscape Photography in the Near East and the Orient

Tourists were the main consumers of the views of Italy, but armchair travelers bought scenes from other parts of the world in the hope of obtaining a true record, "far beyond anything that is in the power of the most accomplished artist to transfer to his canvas."[22] These words express the ambitious goal that Frith set for himself when he departed on his first trip to the Nile Valley in 1856. Before 1860, he made two further journeys, extending his picture-taking to Palestine and Syria and up the Nile beyond the fifth cata-

ract *(pl. no. 132)*. In addition to photographing, he wrote voluminously on the difficulties of the project, especially owing to the climate, commenting on the "smothering little tent" and the collodion fizzing—boiling up over the glass—as well as on the sights in which he delighted—temples, sphinxes, pyramids, tombs, and rock carvings.

Frith's discussion of the compositional problems of view photography throws light on an aspect of 19th-century landscape practice often ignored. This was "the difficulty of getting a view satisfactorily in the camera: foregrounds are especially perverse; distance too near or too far; the falling away of the ground; the intervention of some brick

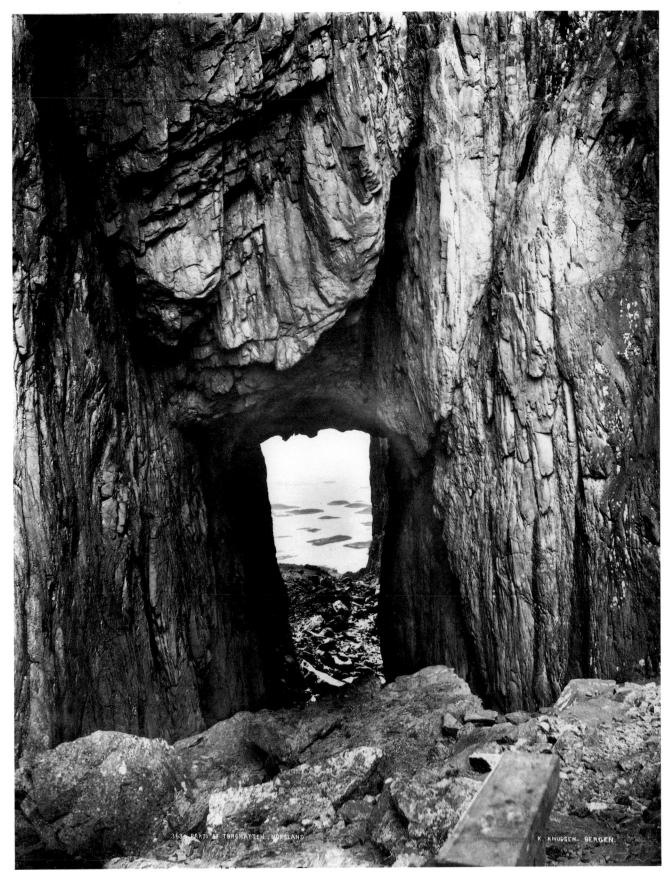

126. Knud Knudsen. *Torghattan, Nordlund*, c. 1885. Albumen print. Picture Collection, Bergen University Library, Bergen, Norway.

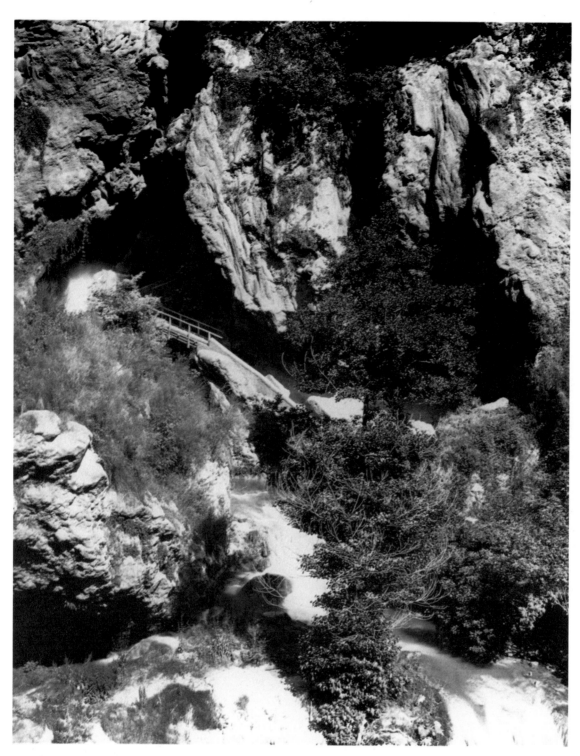

127. ROBERT MACPHERSON. *Grotto of Neptune, Tivoli*, 1861. Albumen print. Collection Sam Wagstaff, New York.

OPPOSITE ABOVE:

128. GIOACCHINO ALTOBELLI. *Night View of the Roman Forum*, 1865–75. Albumen print.
International Museum of Photography at George Eastman House, Rochester, N.Y.

OPPOSITE BELOW:

129. CARLO PONTI. *San Giorgio Maggiore Seen from the Ducal Palace*, 1870s.
Smith College Museum of Art, Northampton, Mass.

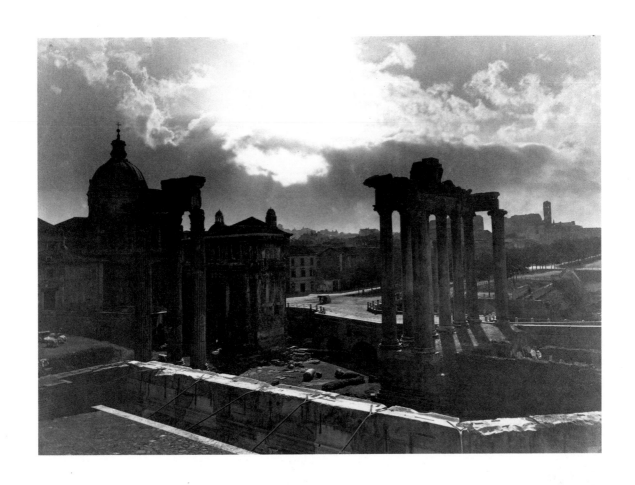

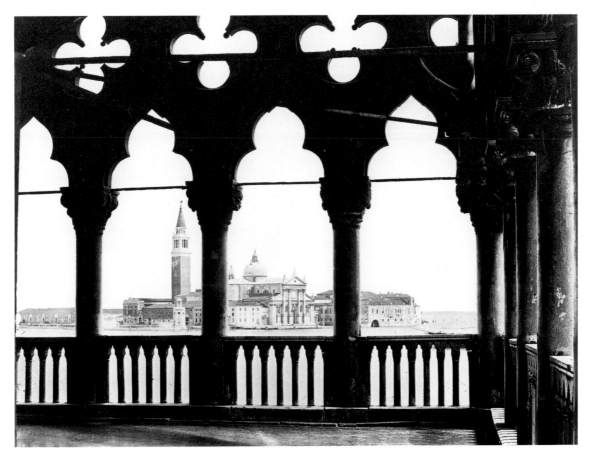

wall or other common object. . . . Oh what pictures we would make if we could command our points of view."[23] While Frith undoubtedly had traditional painting concepts in mind when he wrote this, images such as *Approach to Philae (pl. no. 133)* show that he was capable of finding refreshing photographic solutions to these problems. The Egyptian and Near Eastern views were published by Frith himself and by others in a variety of sizes, formats, and in a number of different volumes, some in large editions. The most ambitious, *Egypt and Palestine Photographed and Described*,[24] had a significant effect on British perceptions of Egypt, as Frith had hoped it would, because the photographer, in addition to sensing the money-making possibilities of the locality, had voiced the belief that British policy-makers should wake up to the pronounced French influence in North Africa.

Some 40 photographers, male and female, from European countries and the United States, are known to have been attracted to the Near East before 1880, among them Bedford, who accompanied the Prince of Wales in 1862, the Vicomte of Banville, Antonio Beato, Félice Beato, Felix and Marie Bonfils, Wilhelm Von Herford, and James Robertson. Studios owned by local photographers also sprang up. Due to the superficial similarities of subject and identical surnames, for many years the two Beatos, Antonio and Félice, were thought to be the same individual, com-

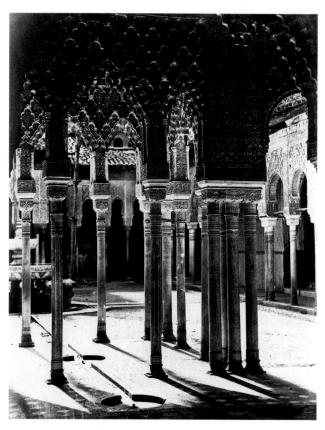

130. CHARLES CLIFFORD. *The Court of the Alhambra in Grenada,* c. 1856. Albumen print. Collection Sam Wagstaff, New York.

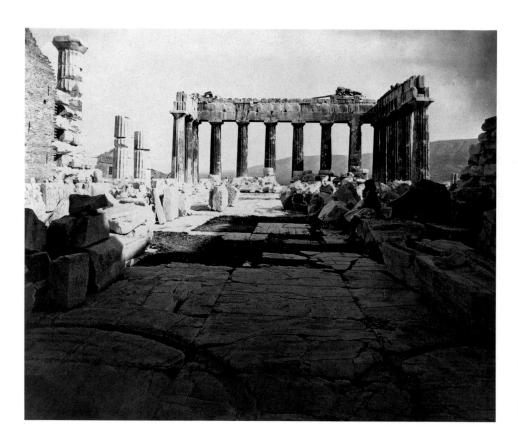

131. WILLIAM STILLMAN. *Interior of the Parthenon from the Western Gate,* 1869. Carbon print. Photograph Collection, New York Public Library, Astor, Lenox, and Tilden Foundations.

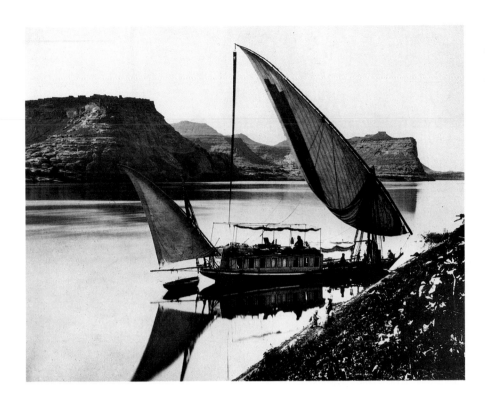

132. FRANCIS FRITH (?). *Traveller's Boat at Ibrim*, c. 1859. Albumen print. Francis Frith Collection, Andover, England.

133. FRANCIS FRITH. *Approach to Philae*, c. 1858. Albumen print. Stuart Collection, New York Public Library, Astor, Lenox, and Tilden Foundations.

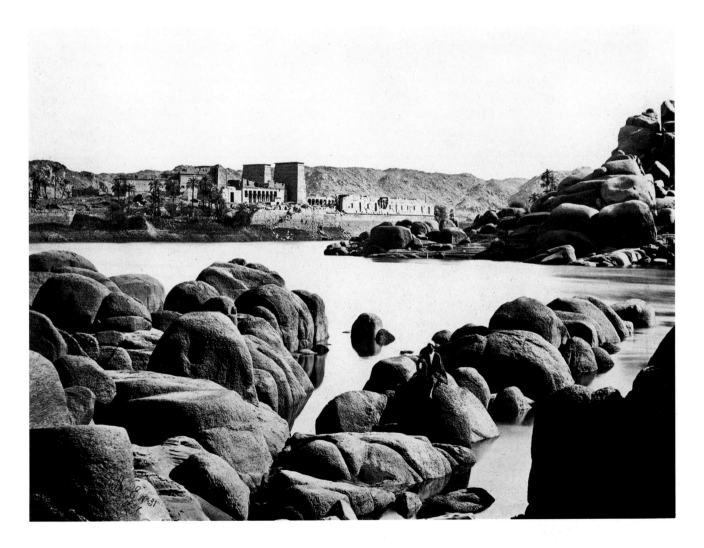

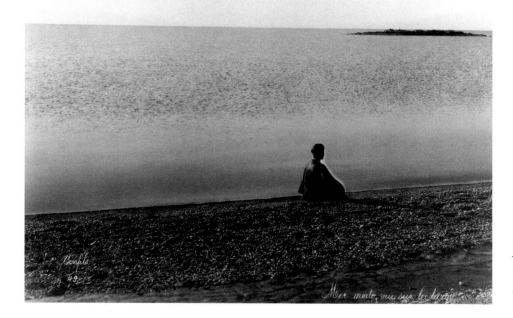

134. FELIX BONFILS, or family. *Dead Sea, A View of the Expanse*, 1860–90. Albumen print. Semitic Museum, Harvard University, Cambridge, Mass.

muting heroically between the Near and Far East, but now it is believed that Antonio was the proprietor of an Egyptian firm based in Luxor that produced thousands of tourist images after 1862, among them this view of the interior of the Temple of Horus at Edfu *(pl. no. 135)*, while Félice, after a brief visit to Egypt with Robertson, was responsible for photographic activities in India and the Orient.

The Bonfils family enterprise, operating from Beirut where they had moved from France in 1867, is typical of the second generation of Near East photographers. In a letter to the *Société Française de Photographie* in 1871, Bonfils reported that he had a stock of 591 negatives, 15,000 prints, and 9,000 stereographic views, all intended for an augmented tourist trade. Because the business was handed down from generation to generation, and stocks of photographs were acquired from one firm by another, there is no way of deciding exactly from whose hand images such as *Dead Sea, A View of the Expanse (pl. no. 134)* actually comes. Furthermore, by the 1880s, scenic views of the region and its monuments had lost the freshness and vitality that had informed earlier images, resulting in the trivialization of the genre even though a great number of photographers continued to work in the area.

Photographers working with paper and collodion began to penetrate into India and the Far East toward the end of the 1850s, but providing images for tourists was not their only goal. In India, photography was considered a documentary tool with which to describe to the mother country the exotic and mysterious landscape, customs, and people of a subject land; as such it was supported by the British military and ruling establishment. Dr. John McCosh and Captain Linnaeus Tripe were the first to calotype monuments and scenery, the latter producing prize-winning views that were considered "very Indian in their character and picturesquely selected."[25] As a consequence of imperialistic interest, a spate of photographically illustrated books and albums issued from both commercial and military photographers during the 1860s and '70s, with illustrations by Félice Beato, P. A. Johnston, and W. H. Pigou. Samuel Bourne, the most prominent landscapist working in collodion in India, was a partner with Charles Shepherd in the commercial firm of Bourne and Shepherd, and traveled at times with 650 glass plates, two cameras, a ten-foot-high tent, and two crates of chemicals. He required the assistance of 42 porters, without whom, it was noted in the British press, photography in India would not have been possible for Europeans.[26] As part of an endeavor to produce *A Permanent Record of India*, Bourne explored remote areas in the high Himalaya mountains and in Kashmir during his seven-year stay. A perfectionist who had left a career in banking to photograph, he claimed that he waited several days for the favorable circumstances that might allow him to achieve the tonal qualities seen in, for example, *Boulders on the Road to Muddan Mahal (pl. no. 136)*.[27] Colin Murray, who took over Bourne's large-format camera when the latter returned to England, apparently

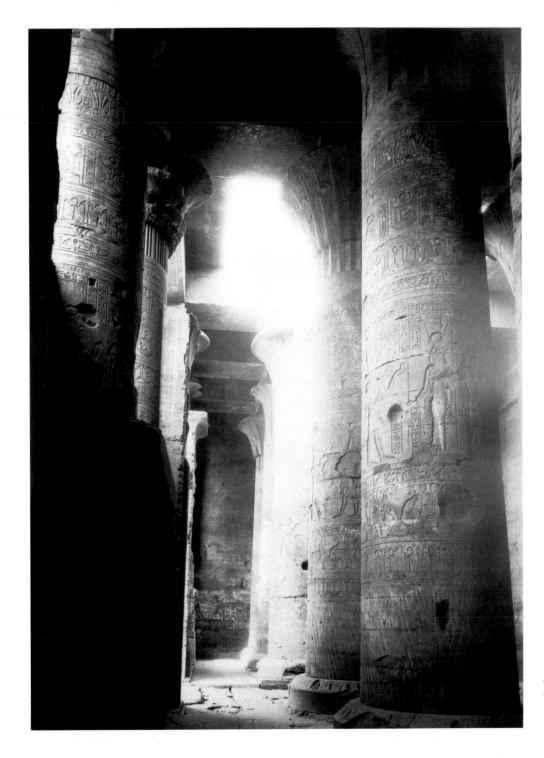

135. ANTONIO BEATO.
*Interior of Temple of Horus,
Edfu*, after 1862. Albumen
print. National Gallery of
Canada, Ottawa.

also inherited his approach to landscape composition; both believed that a body of water almost inevitably improved the image. The lyrical *Water Palace at Udaipur (pl. no. 137)* is one of a group of landscapes that Murray made for a publication entitled *Photographs of Architecture and Scenery in Gujerat and Rajputana*, which appeared in 1874.

Lala Deen Dayal, the most accomplished Indian photographer of the 19th century, and Darogha Ubbas Alli, an engineer by profession, appear to have been the only Indian photographers to publish landscape views. Deen Dayal of Indore began to photograph around 1870, becoming official photographer to the viceroy and soon afterward to the nizam (ruler) of Hyderabad; his studios in Hyderabad and Bombay, known as Raja Deen Dayal and Sons, turned out portraits, architectural views, and special documentary projects commissioned by his patron *(see Chapter 8)*. Architectural images by Ubbas Alli of his native city Lucknow, issued in 1874, are similar in style to those produced by the Europeans who were responsible for the majority of Indian scenic views.

As on the Indian subcontinent, scenic views in China and Japan were made first by visiting Europeans who brought with them, in the wake of the rebellions and wars that opened China to Western imperialism, equipment, fortitude, and traditional Western concepts of pictorial organization. The earliest daguerreotypists of the Orient included Eliphalet Brown, Jr., who arrived with Commodore Perry's expedition, and Hugh McKay, who operated a daguerreotype studio in Hong Kong in the late 1840s; they were followed by other Westerners who arrived in China hoping to use wet-plate technology to record scenery and events in commercially successful ventures. Sev-

eral of these photographers purchased the negatives of forerunners, amassing a large inventory of views that were turned out under the new firm name. Among the outsiders who were active in China during this period were M. Rossier, sent by the London firm of Negretti and Zambra (large-scale commercial publishers of stereographic views), and Félice Beato, who in addition to recording episodes in the conquests by the Anglo-French North China Expeditionary Force in 1860 *(see Chapter 4)* photographed landscapes and daily activities. Between 1861 and 1864, the American photographer Milton Miller, apparently taught by Beato and recipient of many of his negatives, worked in Hong Kong, specializing in portraiture and street scenes.

The most energetic outsider to photograph in China

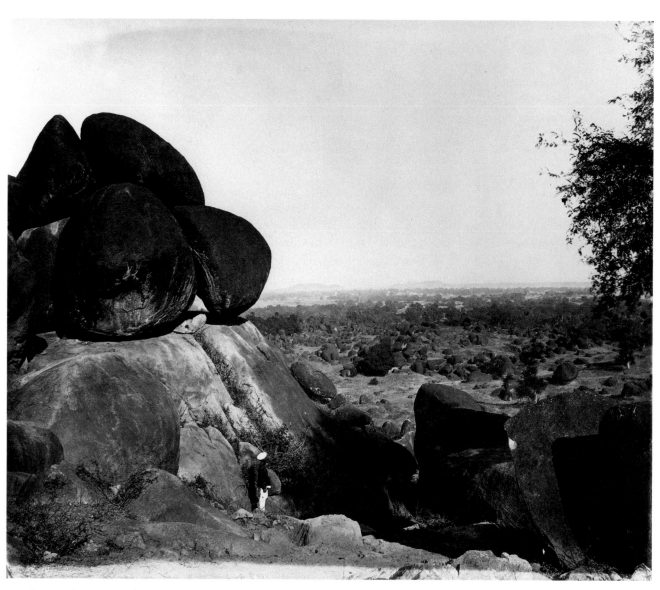

136. SAMUEL BOURNE. *Boulders on the Road to Muddun Mahal*, c. 1867. Albumen print.
Royal Photographic Society, Bath, England.

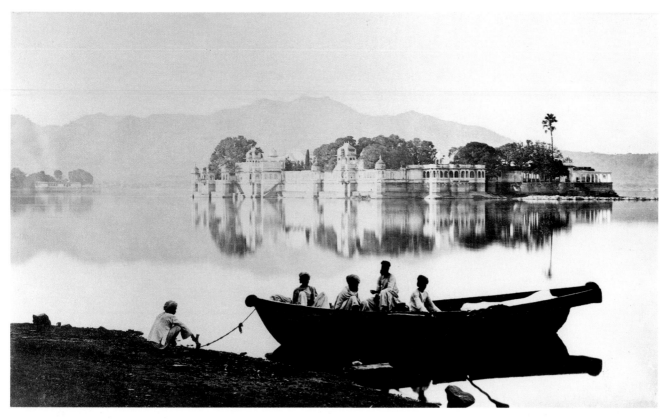

137. COLIN MURRAY. *The Water Palace at Udaipur*, c. 1873. Albumen print. Collection Paul F. Walter, New York.

was John Thomson, originally from Scotland. Using Hong Kong as home base and traveling some 5,000 miles throughout the interior and along the coast—usually accompanied by eight to ten native bearers—Thomson worked in China between 1868 and 1872 before returning to England to publish a four-volume work on Chinese life. His images display a genuine interest in Chinese customs and seem influenced by traditional Chinese painting, as exemplified by his treatment of the landscape in *Wu-Shan Gorge, Szechuan (pl. no. 138)*.

Commercial view-making by native photographers began very slowly, but in 1859 a studio was opened in Hong Kong by Afong Lai, who was to remain preeminent in this area throughout the remainder of the century. Highly regarded by Thomson as "a man of cultivated taste" whose work was "extremely well executed,"[28] Afong Lai's images, such as a view of Hong Kong Island *(pl. no. 139)*, also reveal an approach similar to that seen in traditional Chinese landscape painting. Although Afong Lai was virtually alone when he began his commercial enterprise, by 1884 it was estimated that several thousand native photographers were in business in China, although not all made scenic views.

Amateur photography also appears to have begun slowly, with neither foreign residents nor native Chinese mer-

chants expressing much interest in this form of expression before the turn of the century. One exception was Thomas Child, a British engineer working in Peking in the 1870s, who produced (and also sold) nearly 200 views he had taken of that city and its environs, including an image of a ceremonial gate *(pl. no. 140)*. After 1900, Ernest Henry Wilson, a British botanist, made ethnographic views, while Donald Mennie, also British and the director of a well-established firm of merchants, approached Chinese landscape with the vision and techniques of the Pictorialist, issuing the soft-focus romantic-looking portfolio *The Pageant of Peking* in gravure prints in 1920.

Social and political transformations in Japan during the 1860s—the decade when the Meiji Restoration signaled the change from feudalism to capitalism—created an atmosphere in which both foreign and native photographers found it possible to function, but besides Beato, who appears to have come to Japan in 1864, few photographers were interested at first in pure landscape views. In general, a truly native landscape tradition did not evolve in India or the Far East during the collodion era, and, in the period that followed, the gelatin dry plate and the small-format snapshot camera combined with the influence of imported Western ideas to make the establishment of an identifiable national landscape style difficult.

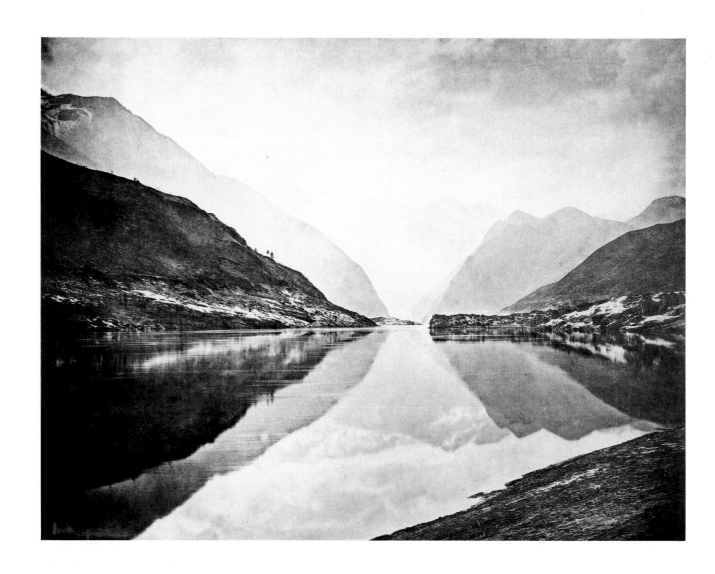

138. John Thompson. *Wu-Shan Gorge, Szechuan*, 1868. Albumen print. Philadelphia Museum of Art.

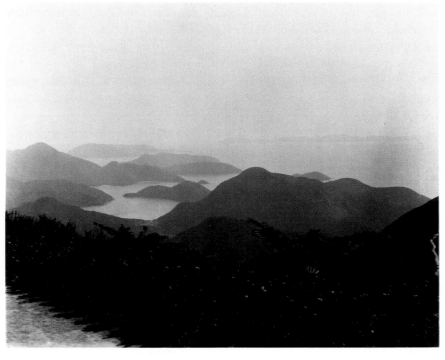

139. Afong Lai. *Hong Kong Island*, late 1860s. Albumen print. Collection H. Kwan Lau, New York.

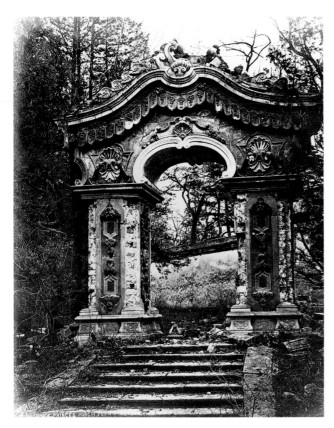

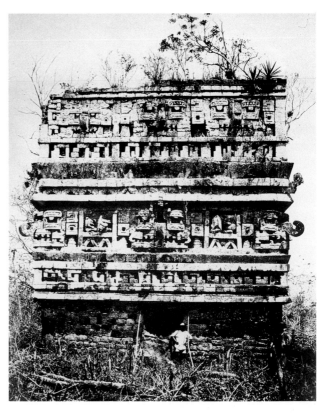

140. THOMAS CHILD. *Damaged Portal of Yuen-Ming-Yuan, Summer Palace, Peking, after the Fire of 1860, set by English and French Allied Forces*, 1872. Albumen print. Collection H. Kwan Lau, New York.

141. DÉSIRÉ CHARNAY. *Chichén Itzá, Yucatan*, c. 1858. Albumen print. Collection Centre Canadien d'Architecture/Canadian Centre for Architecture, Montréal.

Landscape in the Americas

On the opposite side of the Pacific, Mexico was seen by some sectors of the French government as a possible area of colonialist expansion and therefore came under the scrutiny of the camera lens. Désiré Charnay, a former teacher with an itch for adventure and a belief in France's destiny in the Americas, explored and photographed in the ancient ruined cities of Chichén-Itzá, Uxmal, and Palenque between 1858 and 1861 (and was again in Mexico from 1880 to 1882). The first in this part of the world to successfully use the camera as a research tool in archeological exploration, Charney published the views in an expensive two-volume edition of photographs with text by himself and French architect Viollet-le-Duc, and he made images available for translation into wood engraving to accompany articles in the popular press.[29] Despite the fantasy of ideas put forth by the authors concerning the origins of the ancient cities of the new world, the photographs themselves, in particular those of the ornately carved facades of the structures at Chichén-Itzá *(pl. no. 141)*, reveal a mysterious power that most certainly served to promote popular and scientific interest in the cultures that had created these edifices. Though Charney later worked on expeditions to Madagascar, Java, and Australia, this first group of images appears to be the most completely realized.

Urban topographical views—harbors, public buildings, and town squares—comprise a large portion of the photographic landscape documentation made in South America after mid-century. Supported in some cases by the avid interest of the ruling family, as in Brazil under Emperor Dom Pedro II—himself an amateur camera enthusiast—and in other countries by the scientifically minded European-oriented middle class, professional view-makers turned out images that sought to present topography and urban development in a favorable if not especially exalted light. The most renowned South American photographer of the time, Marc Ferrez, a Brazilian who opened his own studio in Rio de Janeiro after spending part of his youth in Paris, advertised the firm as specializing in Brazilian views. Introducing figures to establish scale in his 1870 *Rocks at Itapuco (pl. no. 142)*, Ferrez's image balances geological descriptiveness with sensitivity to light to create a serene yet visually arresting image.

North American attitudes about scenery reflected the unique situation of a nation without classical history or fabled ruins that shared a near religious exaltation of virgin nature. Many Americans were convinced that the extensive rivers and forests were signs of the munificent hand of God in favoring the new nation with plenty; others recognized the economic value of westward expansion and found photography to be the ideal tool to enshrine ideas of "manifest destiny." Painters of the Hudson River School and photographers of the American West recorded landscape as though it were a fresh and unique creation, but while the optimism of many East Coast artists had vanished in the aftermath of the Civil War, photographers (and painters) facing untrammeled western scenery continued to express buoyant reverence for nature's promise.

In a literal sense, a photographic "Hudson River School" did not exist. Eastern landscapists working in the Hudson Valley and the Adirondack and White mountains regions,

among them James Wallace Black, the Bierstadt and Kilburn brothers, John Soule, and Seneca Ray Stoddard, were concerned largely, though not exclusively, with a commerce in stereograph views, a format in which it was difficult to express feelings of sublimity. On occasion, a sense of the transcendent found its way into images such as Black's mountain scene *(pl. no. 143)*; Stoddard's *Hudson River Landscape (pl. no.* 144*)*, in which the horizontal format, luminous river, and small figure suggest the insignificance of man in relation to nature, is another such example. Although American view photographers were urged to avoid "mere mechanism" by familiarizing themselves with works by painters such as Claude, Turner, and Ruisdael, as well as by contemporary American landscape painters, artistic landscapes in the European style were of concern only to a small group working out of Philadelphia in the early 1860s. These photographers responded to a plea by a newly established journal, *Philadelphia Photographer*, to

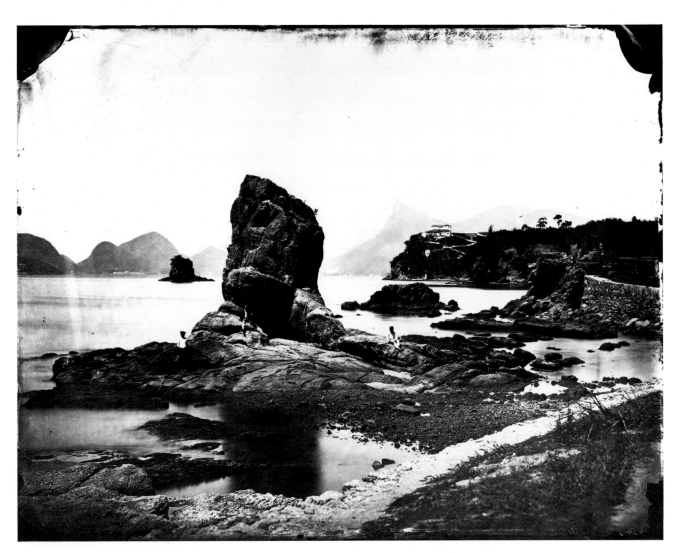

142. MARC FERREZ. *Rocks at Itapuco*, 1870. Albumen print. Collection H. L. Hoffenberg, New York.

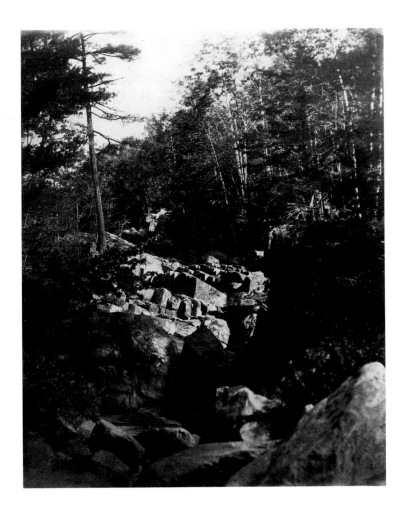

143. James Wallace Black. *In the White Mountain Notch*, 1854. Albumen print. Art Museum, Princeton University, Princeton, N.J.; Robert O. Dougan Collection.

144. Seneca Ray Stoddard. *Hudson River Landscape*, n.d. Albumen print. Chapman Historical Museum of the Glens Falls-Queensbury Association, Glens Falls, N.Y.

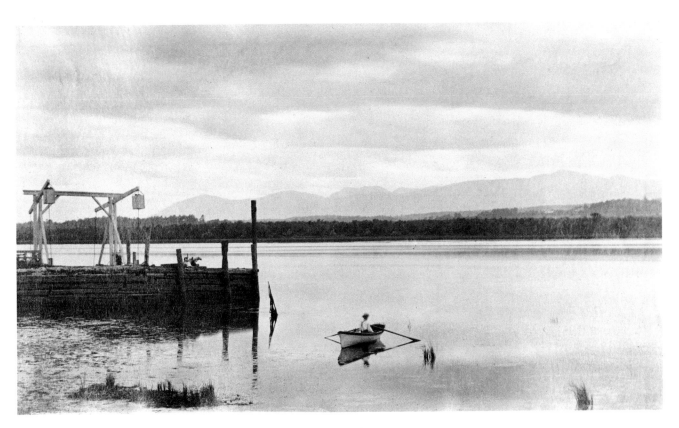

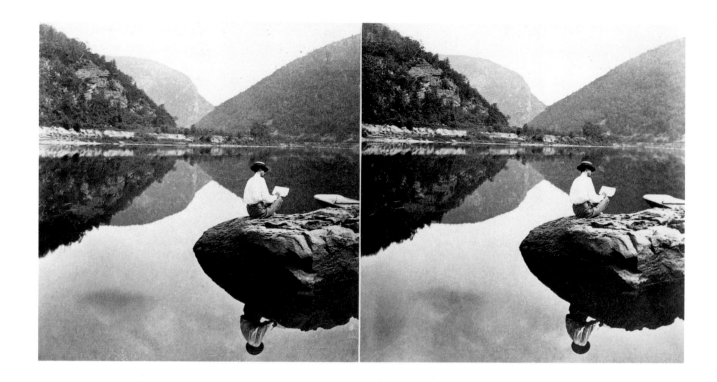

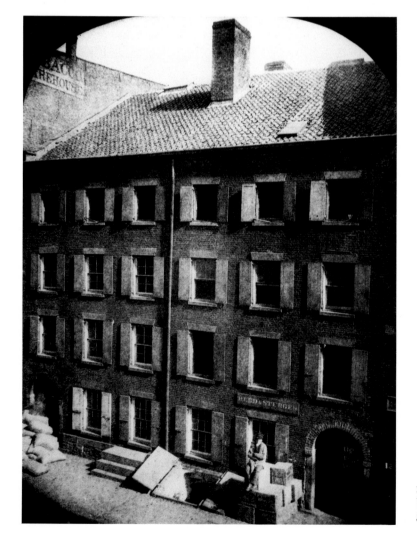

145. JOHN MORAN. *Scenery in the Region of the Delaware Water Gap*, c. 1864. Albumen stereograph. Library Company of Philadelphia.

146. VICTOR PRÉVOST. *Reed and Sturges Warehouse*, c. 1855. Calotype. New-York Historical Society, New York.

create a native landscape school to do "really first class work," that is, to imbue landscape with a distinctive aura. *Scenery in the Region of the Delaware Water Gap (pl. no. 145)* by John Moran, who had been trained as a painter along with his more famous brother Thomas, is representative of the work of an individual whose photographic activities were strongly colored by a conscious regard for artistic values. Farther west, the Chicago-based, Canadian-born Alexander Hesler had switched to making collodion negatives of the natural wonders of the upper Mississippi Valley with similar objectives in mind. Nevertheless, despite the promotion of native landscape expression in art and photography periodicals, this genre only flowered when photographers became involved in the western explorations.

At the same time, it is also apparent from early camera documentations of buildings and the cityscape that most photographers made little effort to do more than produce a prosaic record of architectural structures. Images of buildings by George Robinson Fardon in San Francisco, James McClees, Frederick Debourg Richards, and even John Moran, working in Philadelphia, or by the anonymous recorders of architecture in Boston and New York, are largely unnuanced depictions of cornices, lintels, and brick and stone work. With the exception of the photographs of Victor Prévost, a calotypist from France whose views of Central Park and New York buildings, made around 1855, are informed by a fine sense of composition and lighting and, in the *Reed and Sturges Warehouse (pl. no. 146)*, by a respect for the solid power of the masonry, camera pictures of cities often appear to be a record of urban expansion—a kind of adjunct to boosterism.

Western Views

Photographs of western scenery were conceived as documentation also, but they project a surpassing spirit, a sense of buoyant wonder at the grandeur of the wilderness. These images embody the romanticism of mid-century painting and literature—an ideological attitude which held that nature in general and mountains in particular are tangible evidence of the role of the Supreme Deity in the Creation. Though necessarily different in scale and subject from paintings that depicted the discovery and exploration of the North American continent, these photographs reflect the same confidence in the promise of territorial expansion that had moved painters of the 1840s and '50s.

Photography became a significant tool during the 1860s, when railroad companies and government bodies recognized that it should be included as part of the overall efforts of survey teams to document unknown terrain in the far west. Scientists, mapmakers, illustrators, and pho-

tographers were hired to record examples of topography, specimens of botanical and geological interest, and to make portraits of Native Americans as an aid in determining areas for future mineral exploitation and civilian settlements. In addition to being paid for their time, and/or supplied with equipment, individual photographers made their own arrangements with expedition leaders regarding the sale of images. Views were issued in several sizes and formats, from the stereograph to the mammoth print—about 20 by 24 inches—which necessitated a specially constructed camera. For the first time, landscape documentation emerged as a viable means of livelihood for a small group of American photographers.

Whether working in the river valleys of New York, New England, and Pennsylvania, or the mountains of the West, American wet-plate photographers transported all their materials and processing equipment without the large numbers of porters who attended those working in Europe and the Orient, although assistance was available from the packers included on survey teams. Besides the cameras (at times three in number), photographers carried glass plates in various sizes, appropriate lenses, and chemicals in special vans and by pack animals, while tents and developing boxes, among them a model patented by photographer John Carbutt in 1865 *(pl. no. 147)*, enabled individuals to venture where vehicles could not be taken. Constant unpacking and repacking, the lack of pure water, the tendency of dust to adhere to the sticky collodion—problems about which all survey photographers complained—make the serene clarity of many of these images especially striking.

Following unsuccessful efforts to daguerreotype topography on Colonel John C. Frémont's explorations west of the Mississippi, the American painter Albert Bierstadt, ac-

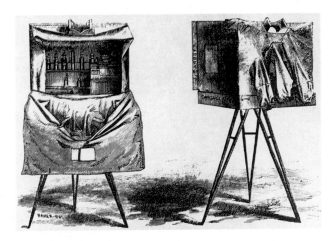

147. *Carbutt's Portable Developing Box*. Wood engraving from *The Philadelphia Photographer*, January, 1865. Private Collection.

companying an expedition to the Rocky Mountains in 1859, was among the first to attempt to publicize the grandeur of western scenery. His wet-plate stereographs are visually weak, but they (and articles written on the subject for *The Crayon*, a periodical devoted to the support of a native landscape art) exemplify the interest in the West on the part of scientists and writers as well as artists. California, especially, became the focus of early documentation, including that of photographers Charles L. Weed and Carleton E. Watkins, who began to portray the scenery around the Yosemite Valley in the early 1860s. Both had worked in the San Jose gallery of daguerreotypist Robert Vance, who stocked a large inventory of scenic views from around the world. By 1868, Watkins, who had made his first views of Yosemite five years earlier and had worked on the Whitney Survey of the region in 1866, where he took *Cathedral Rock, Yosemite (pl. no. 148)*, had become internationally re-

cognized in photographic circles for establishing the mountain landscape as a symbol of transcendent idealism. Impelled perhaps by the then-current controversies among naturalists, including expedition leader Clarence King, regarding the relationships among religion, geology, and evolution, Watkins's images of rocks seem to emphasize the animate qualities in these formations.

Eadweard Muybridge, Watkins's closest competitor, produced views of Yosemite in 1868 and 1872 that likewise enshrined the wilderness landscape as emblematic of the American dream of unsullied nature. Muybridge sought to imprint his own style on the subject by the selection of unusual viewpoints and the disposition of figures in the landscape. Sensitive to the requirements of artistic landscape style, he at times printed in the clouds from separate negatives to satisfy critics who found the contrast between foreground and sky too great, but he also devised a more

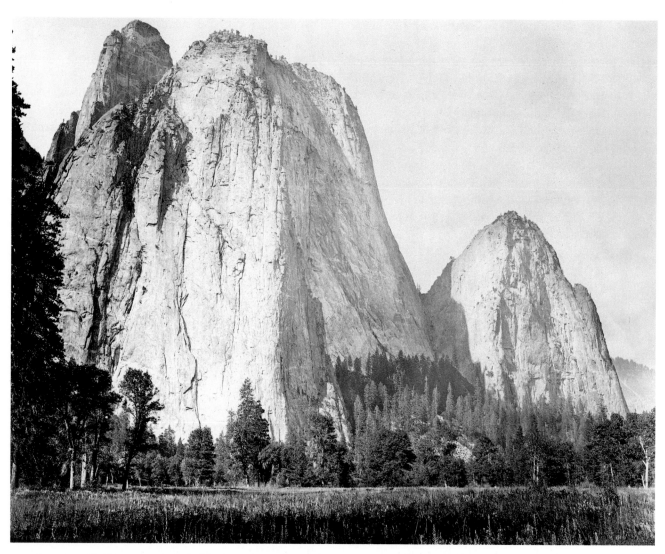

148. CARLETON E. WATKINS. *Cathedral Rock, 2,600 Feet, Yosemite, No. 21*, published by I. Taber, c. 1866. Albumen print. Metropolitan Museum of Art, New York; Elisha Whittelsey Collection, Elisha Whittelsey Fund, 1922.

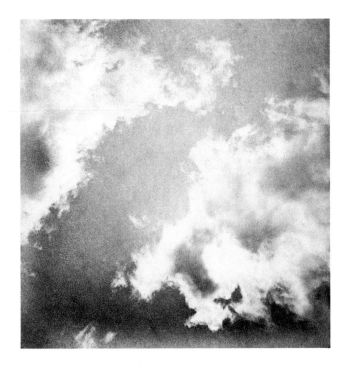
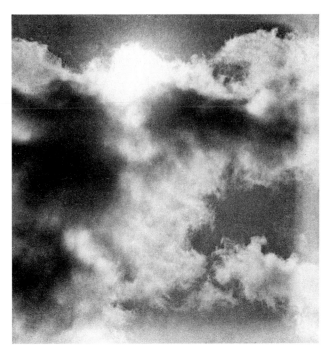
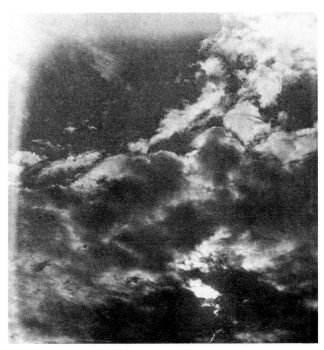
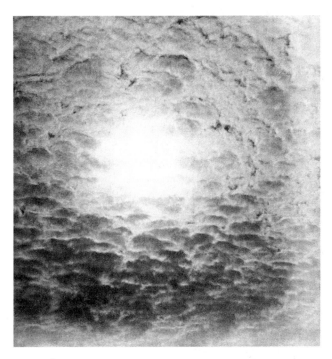

149. EADWEARD MUYBRIDGE. *A Study of Clouds*, c. 1869. Albumen stereographs.
Bancroft Library, University of California, Berkeley, Cal.

authentically photographic method—the sky shade—a shutterlike device that blocked the amount of blue light reaching the plate. As has been noted, cloud studies, similar to this group by Muybridge *(pl. no. 149)*, were made by photographers everywhere during this period, in part to redress the problem of an empty upper portion of the image and in part because of the photographers' fascina-

tion with the ever-changing formations observable in the atmosphere. Muybridge, whose deep interest in ephemeral atmospheric effects was perhaps inspired by association with Bierstadt in 1872, also made a number of remarkable pictures in 1875 of smoke and mist-filled latent volcanoes in Guatemala *(pl. no. 150)*.

Timothy O'Sullivan, a former Civil War photographer

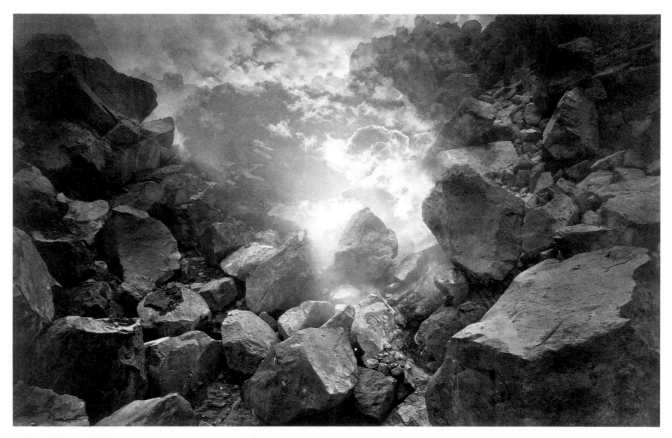

150. EADWEARD MUYBRIDGE. *Volcano Quetzeltenango, Guatemala*, 1875. Albumen print.
Department of Special Collections, Stanford University Library, Palo Alto, Cal.

who became part of Clarence King's 40th Parallel Survey in 1867 *(see Profile)*, was exceptionally fitted by nature and experience on the battlefield for the organizational and expressive demands of expedition photography. O'Sullivan photographed the volcanic formations of desolate areas, among them Pyramid Lake *(pl. no. 151)*, with an accuracy—the rocks were photographed in varying light conditions—that reflected King's absorption with geological theory. His images surpass scientific documentation, however, and create an unworldly sense of the primeval, of an untamed landscape of extraordinary beauty. Furthermore, by his choice of vantage point he was able to evoke the vastness and silence of this remote area in intrinsically photographic terms without resorting to the conventions of landscape painting. The work of William Bell, O'Sullivan's replacement on the Wheeler Survey of 1871–72, reveals a sensitivity to the dramatic qualities inherent in inanimate substances; his *Hieroglyphic Pass, Opposite Parowan (pl. no. 152)* is also unusual in its absence of atmosphere or sense of scale.

In 1871, an expedition down the Colorado River, headed by John Wesley Powell, included E. O. Beaman, an eastern landscape photographer, whose image of a magnificent and lonely mountain pass, *The Heart of Lodore, Green River*

(pl. no. 154), is given scale and a touch of humanity by the inclusion of a small seated figure. John K. Hillers learned photographic techniques from Beaman, whom he eventually replaced; his view of *Marble Canyon, Shinumo Altar (pl. no. 153)*, a place that he characterized as "the gloomiest I have ever been in—not a bird in it,"[30] displays imaginative as well as technical skill. A similar capacity to both document and infuse life into obdurate substances can be seen in *Hanging Rock, Foot of Echo Canyon, Utah (pl. no. 168)*, taken by Andrew Joseph Russell, a former painter and Civil War photographer, while he was documenting the construction of the Union Pacific Railroad.

William Henry Jackson, employed for eight years on the western survey headed by geologist Ferdinand V. Hayden, was in a privileged position to evolve from journeyman photographer to camera artist of stature. That survey *(pl. no. 155)*, begun in 1870 in the Uintas Mountains and expanded in the following years to embrace the Grand Canyon and the Yellowstone River, included artists Sanford R. Gifford and Thomas Moran, whose landscape paintings helped shape Hayden's and Jackson's pictorial expectations. The close relationship that developed between Jackson and Moran enabled the photographer to refine his vision, even to the point of setting up his camera in positions scouted by Moran, who is seen in Jackson's view of *Hot Springs on the Gardiner River, Upper Basin (pl. no. 156)*.

Unlike the fate of the photographs made for France's *Missions héliographiques*, American survey images were seen by a large public. In addition to satisfying the voracious appetite of publishers for marketable landscape stereographs, they also were presented in albums and as lantern slides to members of Congress and other influential people to drum up support for funding civilian scientific expeditions and creating national parklands. For example, besides the sketches that Moran made available to *Scribner's Magazine (pl. no. 157)* in support of Hayden's campaign for a Yellowstone National Park, Jackson printed up albums of *Yellowstone Scenic Wonders* to convince the United States Congress of the distinctive grandeur of the scenery.[31] In later years, Jackson established a successful commercial

enterprise in western images, but it is his work of the mid-'70s, inspired by the land itself and by the artistic example of Moran, that is most compelling.

At about the same time that western survey photography was getting under way, photographers were also included on expeditions to Greenland, organized by Isaac Hayes, and to Labrador, sponsored by the painter William Bradford. John L. Dunmore and George Critcherson, of Black's Boston studio, worked with the painter to photograph icebergs and glacial seas, providing plates for Bradford's publication *The Arctic Regions* as well as material for his intensely colored Romantic seascapes. Besides recording the forms of icebergs, the incisive reflections and sharp contours of *Sailing Ships in an Ice Field (pl. no. 158)*, for example, suggest the sparkling sharpness of the polar climate. Photography of the polar regions continued into what has been called the heroic period of Polar exploration, with expeditions led by Amundsen, Mawson, Peary, and

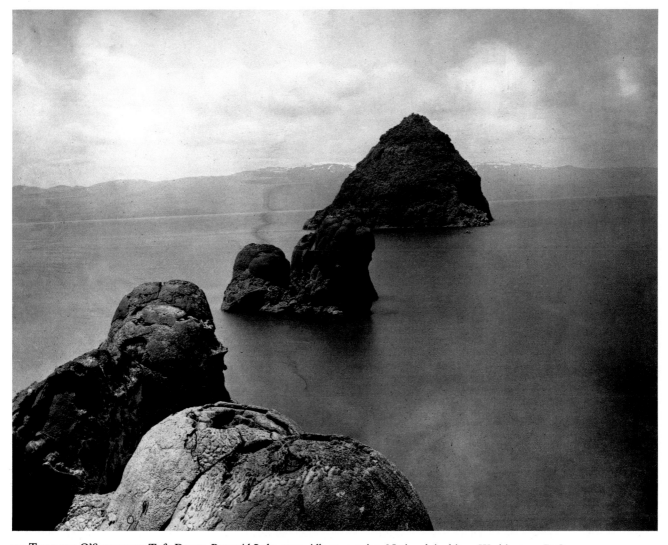

151. TIMOTHY O'SULLIVAN. *Tufa Domes, Pyramid Lake*, 1867. Albumen print. National Archives, Washington, D.C.

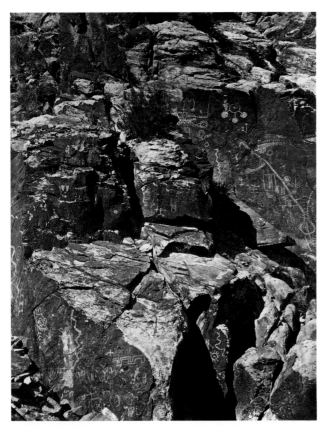

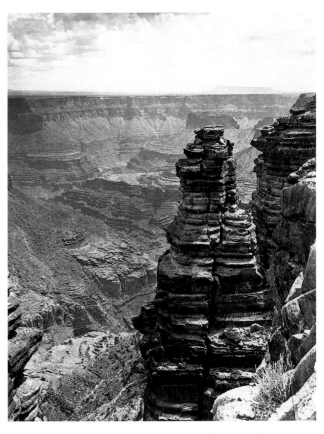

152. WILLIAM BELL. *Utah Series No. 10, Hieroglyphic Pass, Opposite Parowan, Utah*, 1872. Albumen print. Art, Prints and Photograph Division, New York Public Library, Astor, Lenox, and Tilden Foundations.

153. JOHN K. HILLERS. *Marble Canyon, Shinumo Altar*, 1872. Albumen print. National Archives, Washington, D.C.

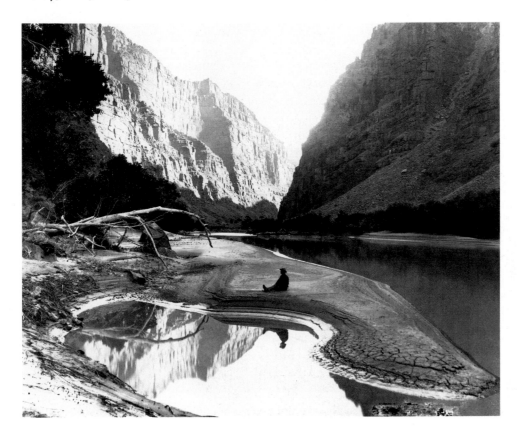

154. E. O. BEAMAN. *The Heart of Lodore, Green River*, 1871. Albumen print. National Archives, Washington, D.C.

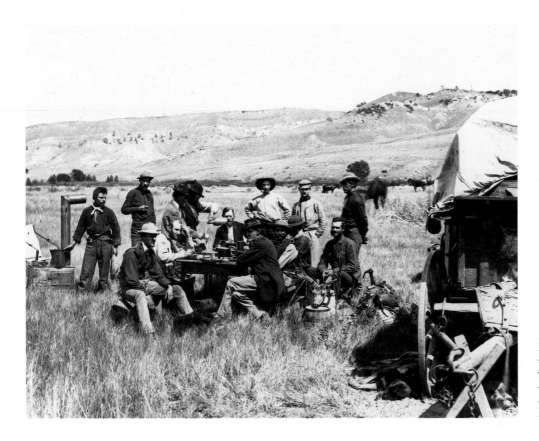

155. WILLIAM HENRY
JACKSON. *Members of the
Hayden Survey*, 1870.
Albumen print. National
Archives, Washington,
D.C.

Scott in the early years of the 20th century, and it is not surprising that some of these later images, among them *An Iceberg in Midsummer, Antarctica (pl. no. 159)* by British photographer Herbert Ponting, made between 1910 and 1913 while accompanying Scott to Antarctica, should recall the freshness of vision that characterized the first views of the western wilderness.

Influenced by westward movements in the United States and by the discovery of gold in British Columbia, the Province of Canada funded an expedition in 1858 to what is now Manitoba; although images made by staff photographer Humphrey Lloyd Hime, a partner in a Toronto engineering firm, were concerned mainly with inhabitants of the region, the few rather poor landscapes indicate the nature of the problems of expedition photography at this early date. Hime noted that to make adequate topographical pictures he required better equipment, pure water, and, most important, more time for taking and processing than expedition leaders were willing to spend.[32] Other Canadian surveys made in connection with railroad routes or border disputes also employed photographers, most of whom produced documents that are more interesting as sociological information than as evocations of the landscape.

Among the few Canadians to imbue scenic images with a sense of atmosphere were Alexander Henderson and

William Notman, the best-known commercial photographer in Canada. Henderson, a latecomer to photography and a well-to-do amateur, may have been influenced by English landscape photography with which he was familiar through his membership in the Stereoscope Exchange Club. But *Spring Flood on the St. Lawrence (pl. no. 160)* of 1865 also seems close in spirit to the idyllic outlook of the American Hudson River artists.

Surveys had provided an effective structure for the documentation of the West, but during the 1880s their functions, including photography, were taken over by the newly established United States Geological Survey and the Bureau of Ethnology. While areas of the West continued to attract individual photographers, most of the images made in frontier studios or in the field during the last quarter of the century consisted of documentation of new settlers or of native tribespeople and their customs, with landscape a by-product of these concerns. Furthermore, as the nation moved into high gear industrially, the natural landscape no longer was seen as a symbol of transcendent national purpose.

Scenic views made during the 1880s, after the gelatin dry plate had begun to supplant collodion, embodied varied attitudes toward nature. Many landscapists on both sides of the Atlantic were influenced by the ideas of Naturalism, an attitude that celebrated the ordinary and un-

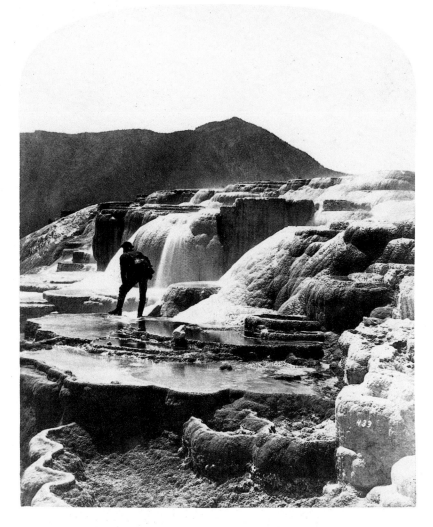

156. WILLIAM HENRY JACKSON. *Hot Springs on the Gardiner River, Upper Basin (Thomas Moran Standing)*, 1871. One-half of an albumen stereograph. International Museum of Photography at George Eastman House, Rochester, N.Y.

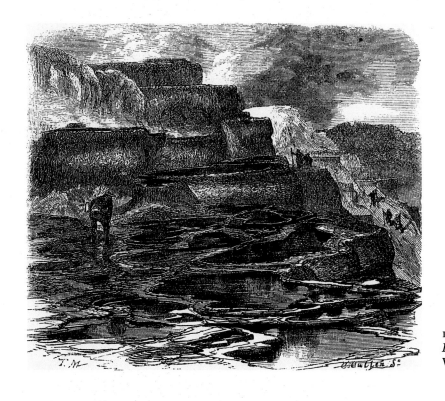

157. THOMAS MORAN. *Bathing Pools, Diana's Baths*, 1872. Engraving. Library of Congress, Washington, D.C.

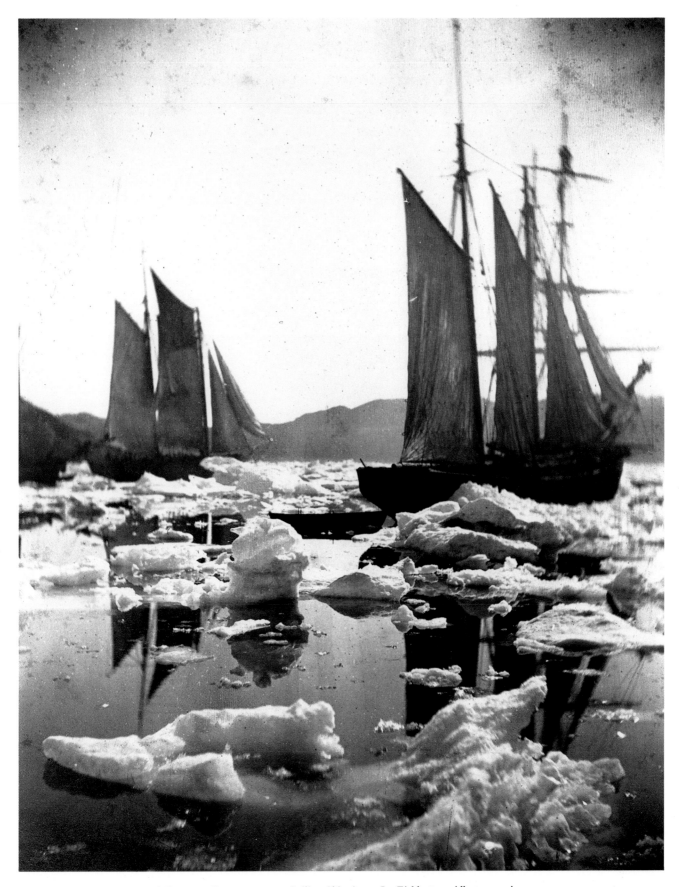

158. JOHN L. DUNMORE and GEORGE CRITCHERSON. *Sailing Ships in an Ice Field*, 1869. Albumen print.
International Museum of Photography at George Eastman House, Rochester, N.Y.

spectacular both in landscape and social activity *(see Chapter 5)*. Some Americans, among them George Barker, continued their romance with the magnificence of native scenery, but a different sensibility is apparent in images such as Barker's *Moonlight on the St. Johns River (pl. no. 161)*—one suggestive of the end of an era rather than the onset of a period of promise. Barker was nationally renowned for views of Niagara Falls, in which rock and water spray are invested with spectacular drama rather than with the noble clarity that had characterized earlier images. Another landscapist of the period, Henry Hamilton Bennett, proprietor of a commercial studio in Kilbourn, Wisconsin, domesticated the wilderness photograph in his views of picnicking and boating parties on the Wisconsin Dells *(pl. no. 162)*, an area that formerly had been famed for its wilderness of glorious valleys and lofty perpendicular rocks.

The flowering of landscape and scenic views during the eras of the calotype and collodion was partly the result of the general urge in all industrialized societies to measure, describe, and picture the physical substances of all things on earth and in the heavens. It was partly a reaction to urbanization—an attempt to preserve nature's beauty. The compelling power of many of these images also flows in a measure from the difficulty of the enterprise. Whether in the Alps, Himalayas, or Rockies, on the Colorado, Nile, or Yangtze, the photographer had to be profoundly committed to the quest for scenic images before embarking on an arduous journey, with the result that many images embody

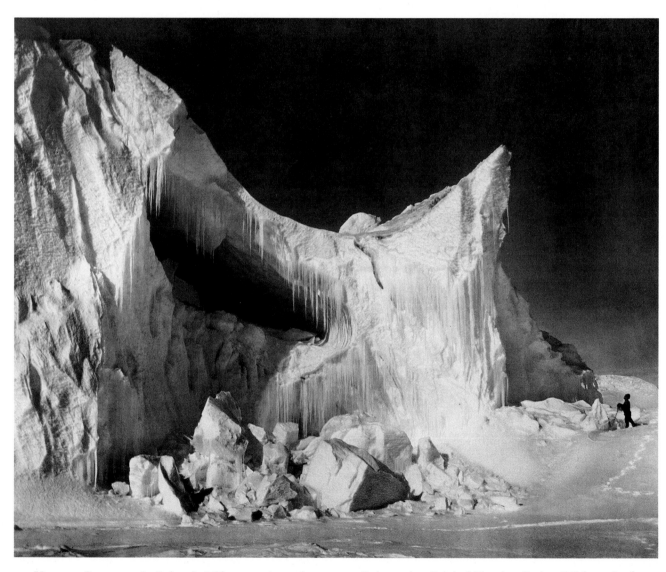

159. HERBERT PONTING. *An Iceberg in Midsummer, Antarctica*, 1910–13. Carbon print. Original Fine Arts Society Edition print from the Antarctic Divisions Historical Print Collection, University of Melbourne, Parkville, Australia.

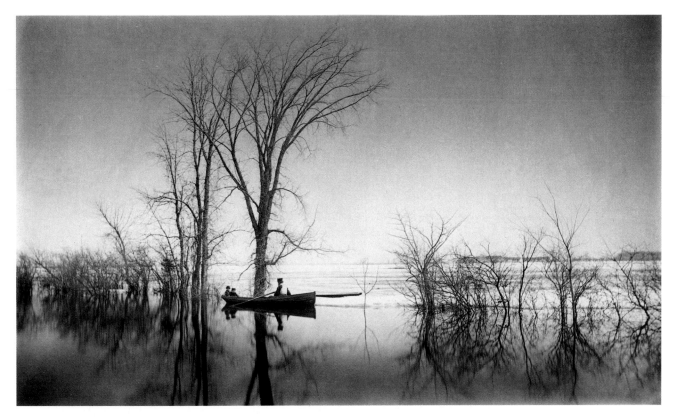

160. ALEXANDER HENDERSON. *Spring Flood on the St. Lawrence*, 1865. Albumen print.
National Gallery of Canada, Ottawa, Ralph Greenhill Collection.

this passion and resolve. After 1880, the ease and convenience first of the gelatin dry plate, and then of the roll-film
camera, made landscape photographers out of all who
could afford film and camera, and led to an inundation of
banal scenic images that often were, in Bourne's words,
"little bits, pasted in a scrapbook."[33]

Profile: Gustave Le Gray

Gustave Le Gray combined the imaginative curiosity
and skill of both artist and scientist. While still a student in
the studio of the academic salon painter Paul Delaroche, he
became aware of photography but did not involve himself
in the new medium until the end of the 1840s. His inability
to survive as a painter in the overcrowded art field of Second
Empire France kindled an enthusiasm for working with
the paper negative. A strong interest in the chemistry of
paint, applied now to the problems of the calotype, led
him to perfect in 1849 the dry waxed-paper process that
came to be utilized, at least briefly, by most of the major
figures in mid-19th-century French photography. Although
Le Gray also had worked out a collodion process at the
same time, he was uninterested in glass at first and did not

publish either discovery until 1851, when they appeared in
his publication *Nouveau Traité théorique et pratique de
photographie sur papier et sur verre (New Treatise on the Theory and Practice of Photography on Paper and Glass)*, by which
time Archer already had made the first public disclosure of
a collodion method.

The instructor of many artists and intellectuals eager to
learn photography, including Du Camp, Fenton, Le Secq,
Marville, and Nègre, Le Gray was held in uniformly high
esteem by his contemporaries for his ability to use light
suggestively. He was invited to participate in important
photographic projects, among them the *Missions héliographiques*, where he photographed by himself as well as with O.
Mestral, and in 1856 he was asked to provide a reportage on
the newly established Imperial Army camp at Châlons *(pl.
no. 199)*. Enshrouded in mist and surrounded by silent,
empty terrain, the groups of soldiers in these images suggest an unworldly convocation, a vision that accorded with
the emperor's almost religious regard for this military
encampment. On his own, Le Gray made artistic calotype photographs in the Barbizon tradition at Fontainbleau
forest in 1849 and five years later, in collodion, of the
movement of clouds and sea at Sète (Cette) *(pl. no. 18)*, and

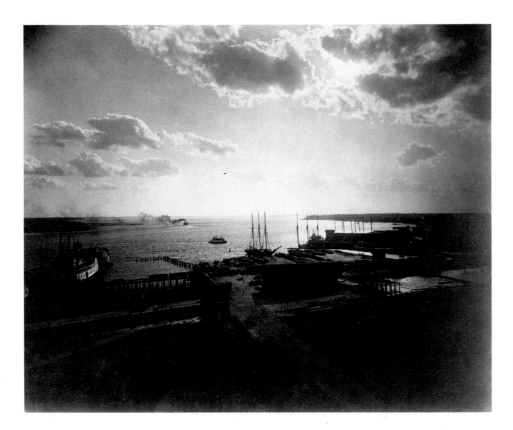

161. GEORGE BARKER. *Moonlight on the St. Johns River*, 1886. Albumen print. Library of Congress, Washington, D.C.

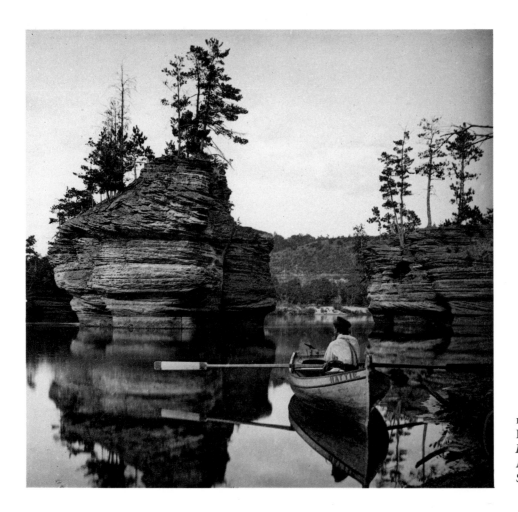

162. HENRY HAMILTON BENNETT. *Sugar Bowl with Rowboat, Wisconsin Dells*, 1868. Albumen print. © H.H. Bennett Studio, Wisconsin Dells, Wis.

at Dieppe where he recorded Napoleon III's naval fleet. These images, exhibited repeatedly, were highly acclaimed, inviting a first prize at the 1855 *Exposition Universelle*.

In view of these successes, Le Gray's withdrawal from the photographic scene after 1858 may seem difficult to understand, but his situation reveals some of the problems confronting photographers in France in the 19th century. Lacking independent means, Le Gray was able to support himself by commercial photography—portraiture, technical illustration, reproductions of artwork—and indulge his high standards through the generosity of a patron, the Comte de Briges. However, as the medium itself became more competitive and commercial, and the count's patronage ended, Le Gray found himself more interested in problems of light and pictorial organization than in making salable views that "were got up in a style that renders them a fit ornament for any drawing room."[34] What his friend Nadar characterized as poor business sense was more probably Le Gray's reluctance to accept prevailing marketplace standards; in any event, he left family and associates and traveled to Italy, Malta, and finally Egypt, where he finished his career as professor of design in a polytechnic institute.

The acclaim accorded Le Gray was for the exceptional quality of his salt and albumen prints as well as for his innovative vision. His technical mastery of gold-chloride toning, which permitted the revelation of details buried in the deepest shadows, derived from a conception of printing as an integral aspect of an entire process by which the photographer transforms nature into art.

Profile: Timothy O'Sullivan

Timothy O'Sullivan came to landscape photography after four years of experience photographing behind the lines and on the battlefields of the Civil War. A former assistant in Mathew Brady's New York studio, in 1861 he had joined the group known as "Brady's Photographic Corps," working with Alexander Gardner. Because Brady refused to credit the work of individual photographers, Gardner, taking O'Sullivan along, established his own Washington firm to publish war views. War images taken by O'Sullivan are wide-ranging in subject and direct in their message, including among them the weariness of inaction and continual waiting, and the horror of fields of the dead *(pl. no. 209)*.

After the war, O'Sullivan, faced with the dullness of commercial studio work, discovered an optimum use for his energies and experience as a photographer on the survey teams that were being organized under civilian or military leadership to document wilderness areas west of the Mississippi. Departing from Nevada City with 9 x 12 inch and stereograph cameras, 125 glass plates, darkroom equipment, and chemicals, for more than two years he explored the strange and inhospitable regions along the 40th Parallel with a group headed by the eminent geologist Clarence King. Following a brief period with the Darien Survey to the Isthmus of Panama, where both the humid atmosphere and the densely foliated terrain made photography difficult, he found another position on a western survey. As Weston Naef has pointed out,[35] photography on the Geological Surveys West of the 100th Meridian, as the expedition commanded by Lieutenant George M. Wheeler of the Army Corps of Engineers was called, "was not so much a scientific tool as it was a means of publicizing the Survey's accomplishments in the hopes of persuading Congress to fund military rather than civilian expeditions in the future."

O'Sullivan's purpose in joining this team was more likely personal than political in that he was allowed by Wheeler to be his own master, in charge of portions of the expedition, and thus did not have to take orders from geologists. Involved in the dramatic if not scientifically defensible exploit of attempting to ascend the Colorado River through the Grand Canyon, Wheeler noted O'Sullivan's professionalism in producing negatives in the face of all obstacles, including a near drowning. Following another brief period with King, O'Sullivan joined a Wheeler-led survey to the Southwest where he documented not only geological formations but members of the pueblo and rock-dwelling tribes in the region of the Canyon de Chelle *(pl. no. 163)*. After 1875, O'Sullivan's problematical health and the winding down of survey photography put an end to further involvement with the western landscape. Following a brief period in 1879 as photographer in the newly established United States Geological Survey, of which King was first director, and a position with the Treasury Department in Washington, O'Sullivan was forced by his tubercular condition to resign; he died a year later in Staten Island at age forty-two.

O'Sullivan approached western landscape with the documentarian's respect for the integrity of visible evidence and the camera artist's understanding of how to isolate and frame decisive forms and structures in nature. Beyond this, he had the capacity to invest inert matter with a sense of mysterious silence and timelessness; these qualities may be even more arresting to the modern eye than they were to his contemporaries, who regarded his images as accurate records rather than evocative statements.

The Western Landscape— Natural and Fabricated

This selection of early views of the American West suggests the dual role that the photograph played after the Civil War in the exploration and development of this relatively unknown part of the continent. Taken between the years 1867 and 1878, these pictures are the work of five among the numerous photographers who either accompanied geological survey teams, were employed by railroad companies, or were professionals with established studios in West Coast cities. Beyond their roles as documenters, all were inspired by the spectacular scale and breadth of the pristine wilderness landscape, by its strange rock formations, its steamy geysers, and its sparkling waterfalls. Using the cumbersome wet-plate process, they sought out the vantage points that might make it possible to recreate for Easterners a sense of the immensity and primordial silence of the region.

A number of the same photographers were called upon to document the building of rail lines, bridges, water sluices, and urban centers. Eadweard Muybridge produced a panorama of the young and growing metropolis of San Francisco, from which four of the thirteen mammoth (18 x 24 inch) plates are reproduced, showing cable cars, churches, and public and commercial buildings as well as dwellings laid out in a well-defined street system. As the frontier moved westward and industrialization began to change the character of the landscape, Americans increasingly turned to the photograph as a means of both celebrating technology and of expressing reverence for the landscape being threatened by its advance.

163. TIMOTHY H. O'SULLIVAN. *Ancient Ruins in the Canyon de Chelle, New Mexico*, 1873. Albumen print. International Museum of Photography at George Eastman House, Rochester, N.Y.

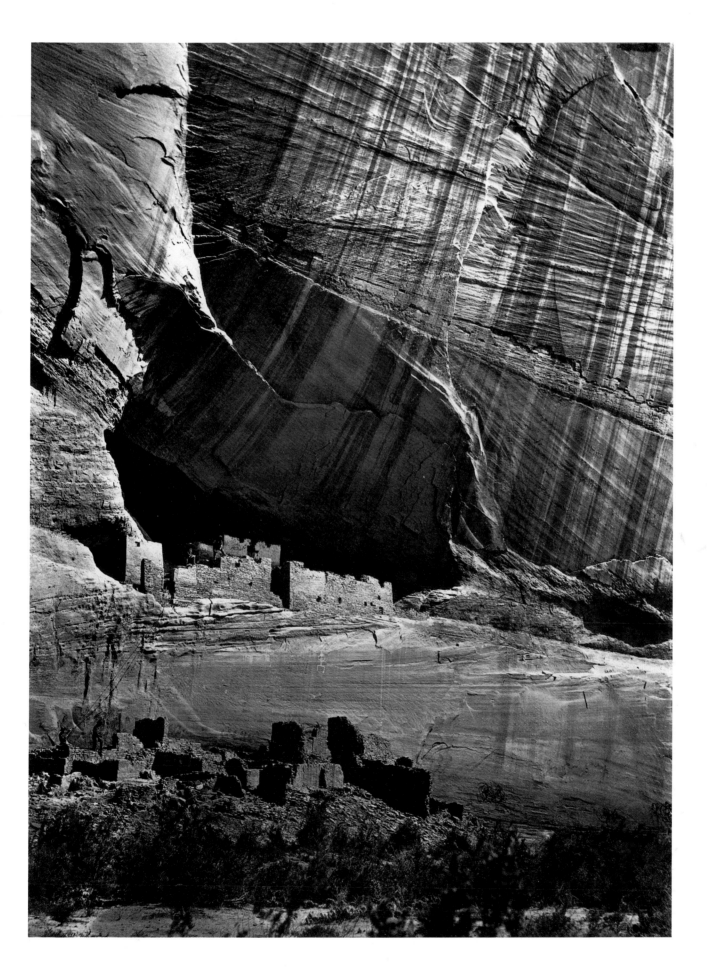

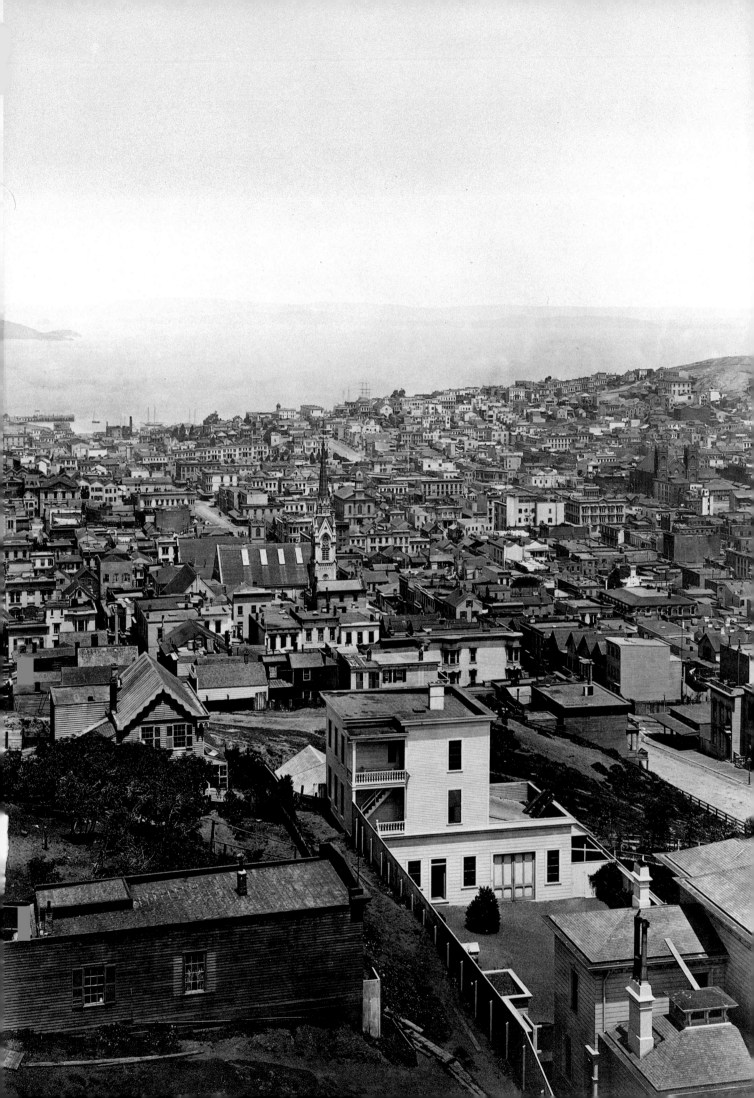

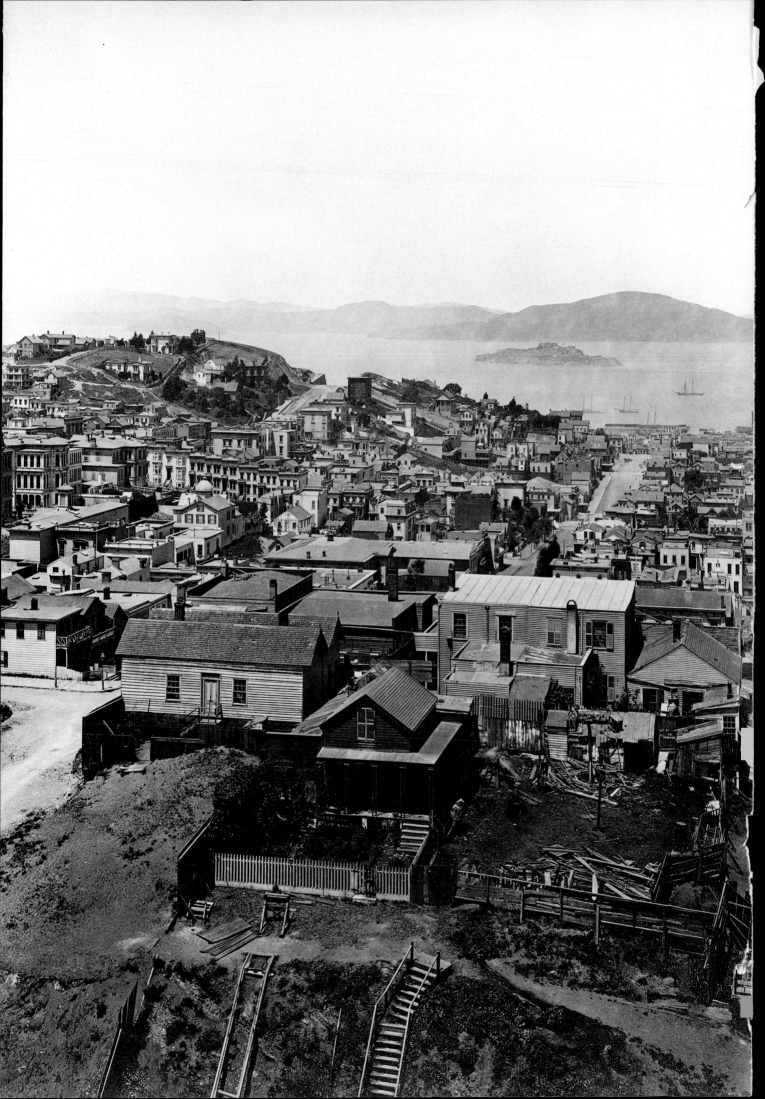

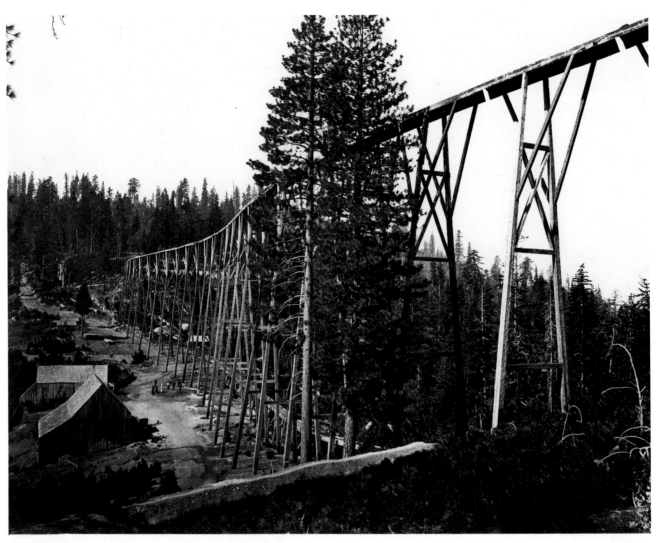

164. CARLETON E. WATKINS. *Magenta Flume Nevada Co., California*, c. 1870.
Albumen print. Collection George H. Dalsheimer, Baltimore.

OPEN FOR FOLDOUT:

165. EADWEARD MUYBRIDGE. *Panorama of San Francisco from California Street Hill*, 1878.
Panorama in 13 plates (four plates reprinted here). Albumen prints. Bancroft Library, University of California, Berkeley, Cal.

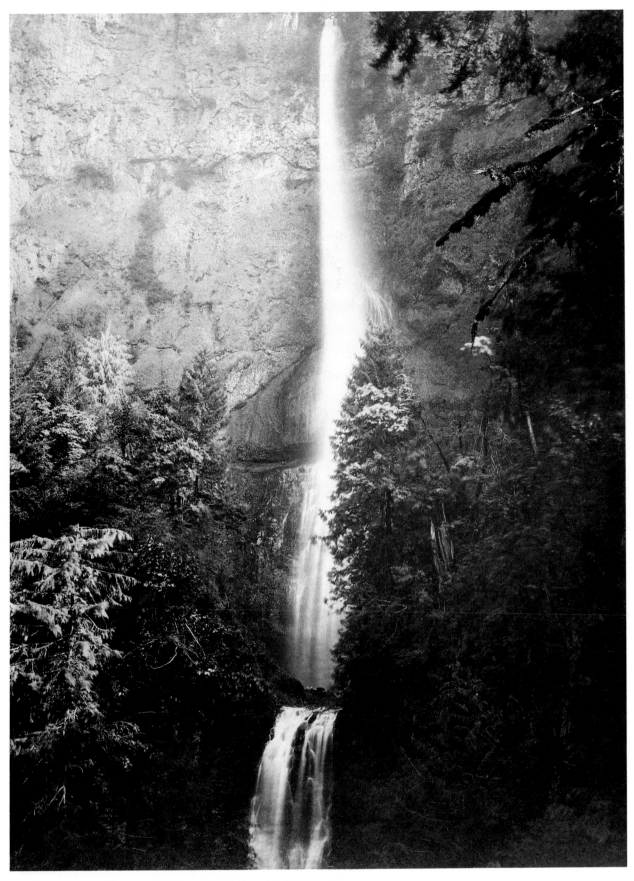

166. CARLETON E. WATKINS. *Multnomah Fall Cascade, Columbia River*, 1867.
Albumen print. Gilman Paper Company, New York.

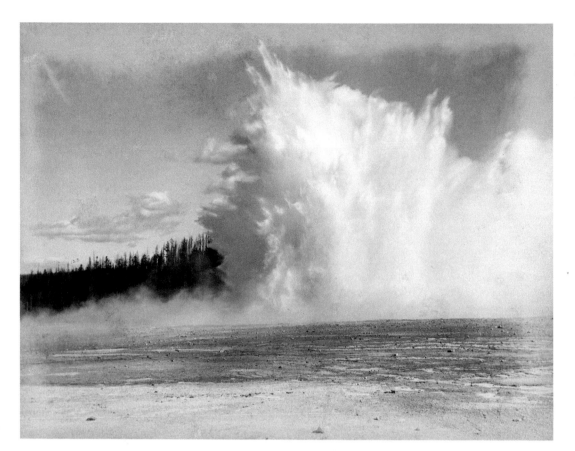

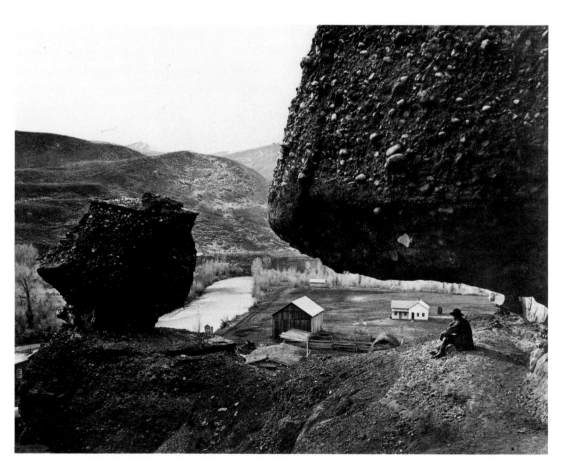

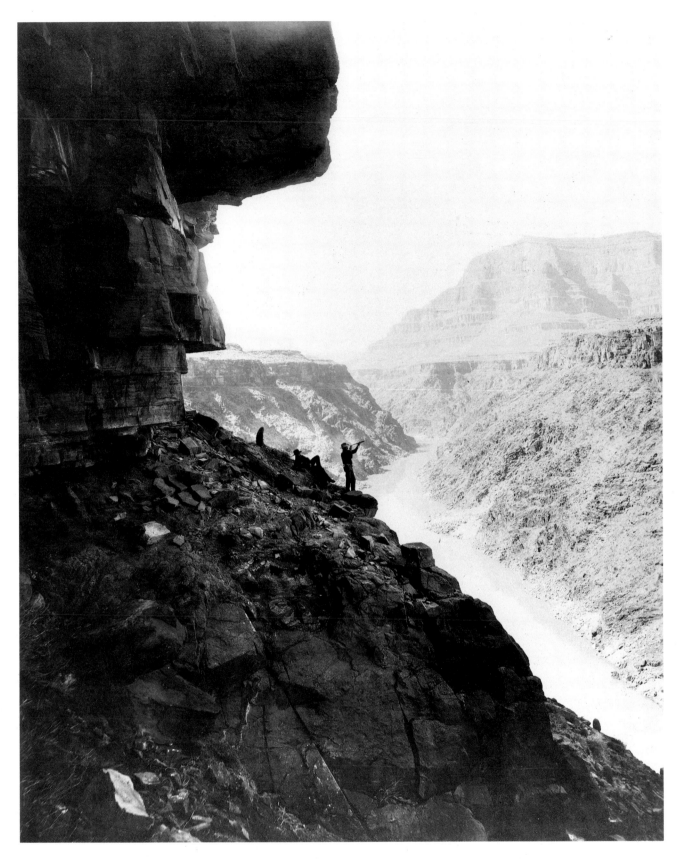

169. WILLIAM HENRY JACKSON. *Grand Canyon of the Colorado*, 1870s–80s.
Albumen print. Collection Lee D. Witkin, New York.

4.

DOCUMENTATION: OBJECTS AND EVENTS

1839–1890

Let him who wishes to know what war is look at this series of illustrations.

—Oliver Wendell Holmes, 1863[1]

NEARLY ALL CAMERA IMAGES that deal with what exists in the world may be considered documents in some sense, but the term documentation has come to refer to pictures taken with an intent to inform rather than to inspire or express personal feelings (though, of course, such images may answer these needs, also). The materialistic outlook of the industrialized peoples of the 19th century, their emphasis on the study of natural forces and social relationships, and their quest for empire promoted the photographic document as a relatively unproblematical means of expanding knowledge of the visible world. Depictions of topography and architecture (treated separately in the previous chapter), of the physical transformation of city and countryside, of wars, uprisings, revolutions, and natural disasters, of sociological and medical conditions and oddities—all were considered by intellectuals, scientists, artists, and the general public to be eminently suitable themes for camera images.

The photograph was regarded as an exemplary record because it was thought to provide an objective—that is, unaltered—view of solid fact and achievement. This faith in the capacity of light to inscribe truth on a sensitized plate, which lay behind the acceptance of camera documentation, was given its most persuasive verbal argument by the American Oliver Wendell Holmes, whose contributions to the popularization of stereography have been mentioned earlier. Suggesting that the "perfect photograph is absolutely inexhaustible,"[2] because in theory everything that exists in nature will be present in the camera image (in itself a dubious statement), Holmes also felt that incidental truths, missed by participants in the actual event, would be comprehended in the photograph and, in fact, might turn out to be of greater significance. As "form divorced from matter" but mirroring truth, documentary photographs were conceived as catalogs of related facts—surrogates of reality. Specific temporal meanings might be obscure, contextual relationships unexplained, but these images, which by a miracle of technolgy had found their way into stereoscopes and picture albums far removed in time and place from the actual object or event, increasingly became the data to which the public turned for knowledge of complex structures and occurrences. According to American art historian William M. Ivins, "the nineteenth century began by believing that what was reasonable was true, and it wound

up by believing that what it saw a photograph of, was true."[3]

The need for pictorial documentation had been recognized even before the invention of photography, however. In the 1830s and '40s, publishers of periodicals in Europe sought to enliven informational texts with graphic illustrations directed to a diversified mass audience. The *Penny Magazine*, an early starter in London, was followed by the *Illustrated London News*, *L'Illustration* in Paris, *Illustrierte Zeitung* in Leipzieg, and, in the United States, *Harper's Weekly* and *Frank Leslie's Illustrated Newspaper*. To make good their promise to present a living and moving panorama of the world's activities and events, these journals began in the 1850s to use the photographic document as a basis for graphic imagery. The need to translate photographs quickly into wood engravings to meet publication deadlines led to the practice of dividing up an illustration into sections and farming out the parts to a number of woodblock engravers, after which the pieces were reassembled into a unified block for printing. Just before 1860, a more sophisticated procedure enabled the collodion negative to be printed directly onto the block, bypassing the artist's drawing and incidentally substituting a more realistic facture that the engraver then endeavored to represent. Until the 1890s, when the printing industry began to use the process halftone plate, documentation based on photographs reached the public in several forms—as original albumen, carbon or Woodburytype prints (stereograph and other formats), as lantern slides, or transformed by engravers and lithographers into graphic illustrations for the publishing industry.

Photographic documentation might be commissioned by the government (primarily in France and the United States), by private companies and individuals, or by publishers. Albumen prints, more sharply defined and easier to produce in large numbers than calotypes, were organized into presentation albums made up for selected individuals and governing bodies, while thousands upon thousands of stereographs reached mass audiences through the sale and distribution activities of companies such as T. & E. Anthony in New York, the Langenheim brothers' American Stereoscopic Company in Philadelphia, the London Stereoscopic and Photographic Company, Gaudin in Paris, and Loescher and Petsch in Germany.

Camera Documentation: Industrial Development

"Objective" documentation by camera coincided with the physical transformation of industrialized countries during the mid-19th century. The role played by photography in the campaign to restore the architectural patrimony of France has been mentioned, but, in addition, images were commissioned to show the demolition and reconstruction of urban areas, the erection of bridges and monuments, and the building of transportation facilities and roads. The industrial expositions and fairs that were mounted every several years in Britain, France, and the United States during this period both symbolized and displayed the physical changes made possible by new technologies and new materials, which were contrasted with the exotic products of underdeveloped nations. The directors of the first important exposition, at the Crystal Palace in London in 1851—the Great Exposition—were eager to document the event as well as to display camera equipment and pictures, but the insufficiencies of Talbot's calotype process limited the effort to a visual catalog of the exhibits, which was included in *Report by the Juries*.[+] However, shortly after the decision was made to rebuild the Crystal Palace at Sydenham, collodion technique made it possible to document the entire reconstruction. Photographing weekly for about three years—1851 to 1854—the noted painter-photographer Philip Henry Delamotte recorded the rebirth of the glass hall in its new location *(pl. no. 170)* and the installation of the exhibits. In itself, the iron structure of Sir Joseph Paxton's huge pavilion provided interesting shapes and forms, but Delamotte's obvious delight in the building's airy geome-

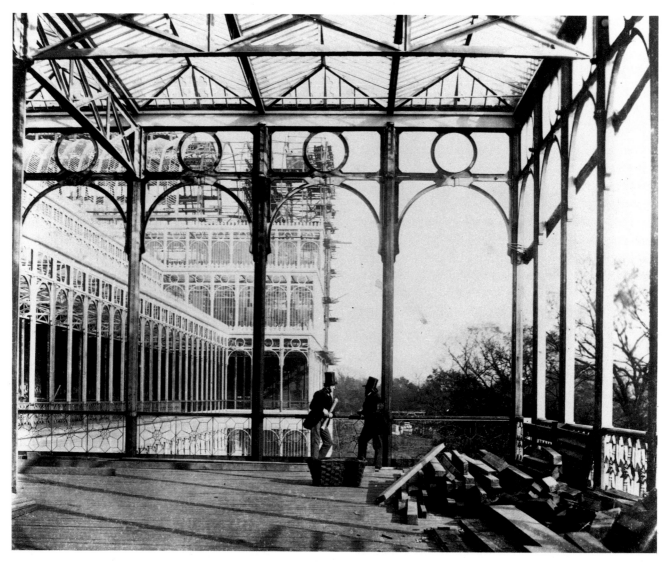

170. PHILIP HENRY DELAMOTTE. *The Open Colonnade, Garden Front*, c. 1853. Albumen print. Greater London History Library, London.

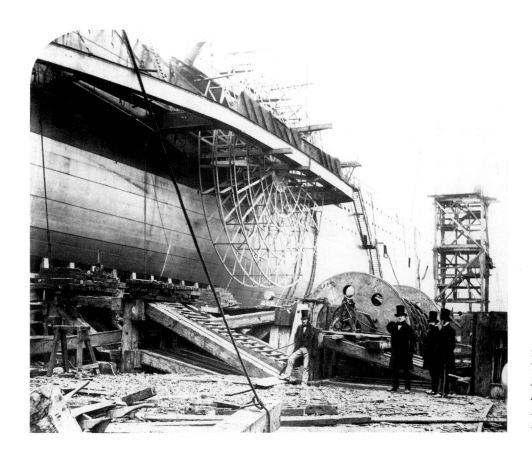

171. ROBERT HOWLETT (?).
The "Great Eastern" Being Built in the Docks at Millwall, Nov. 30, 1857. Albumen print. Collection Sam Wagstaff, New York.

try contributes to the pleasurable satisfaction these images still afford, and indeed this first record is among the more interesting documentations of the many that were made of the industrial fairs that followed.

From the 1850s on, the mechanical-image maker frequently was called upon to record other feats served up by the age of mechanization. The usefulness of such records was demonstrated by the documentation *(pl. no. 171)* of Isambard Kingdom Brunel's British steamship *Great Eastern*, an enormous coal-driven liner capable of carrying 4,000 passengers. The vivid handling of light, form, and volume seen in views by Robert Howlett and Joseph Cundall of this "leviathan"—made for the *Illustrated Times* of London and the London Stereoscope Company—was praised because it embraced real rather than synthetic situations. Contrasting these works with artistically conceived and reenacted studio compositions that were being turned out at about the same time *(see Chapter 5)*, critics suggested that the true measure of camera art was in the sensitive treatment of actuality.

Soon after mid-century, photographers were called upon to record the building of rail routes in France and the United States, both latecomers in this endeavor compared with Britain. One such commission, initiated by the French rail magnate Baron James de Rothschild, went to Edouard Denis Baldus, who in 1855 and 1859 followed the

building of the north–south line from Boulogne to Paris, Lyons, and eventually to the Mediterranean ports. These large-format prints, exemplified by *Pont de la Mulatière (pl. no. 172)*, were made up into "presentation albums," one of which was given to Queen Victoria; they also were exhibited at the major industrial expositions where they were acclaimed for elegant clarity of vision and superb tonal range. Gallic respect for order and precision also characterizes an image of engines in the roundhouse at Nevers *(pl. no. 173)*, taken between 1860 and 1863 by the little-known French photographer A. Collard, whose work for the *Departement de Ponts et Chausées* (Department of Bridges and Roads) resulted in impressive views that emphasized the geometric rationality of these structures.

Baldus, whose other commissions included the previously mentioned reportage on the Rhone floods and a documentation of the building of the new Louvre Museum was entirely committed to the documentary mode. His images established the paradigm documentary style of the era in that he brought to the need for informative visual material a sure grasp of pictorial organization and a feeling for the subtleties of light, producing works that transcend immediate function to afford pleasure in their formal resolution. When increasing commercialization—the need to mass-produce albumen prints for indiscriminate buyers of stereographs and tourist images—made this approach to

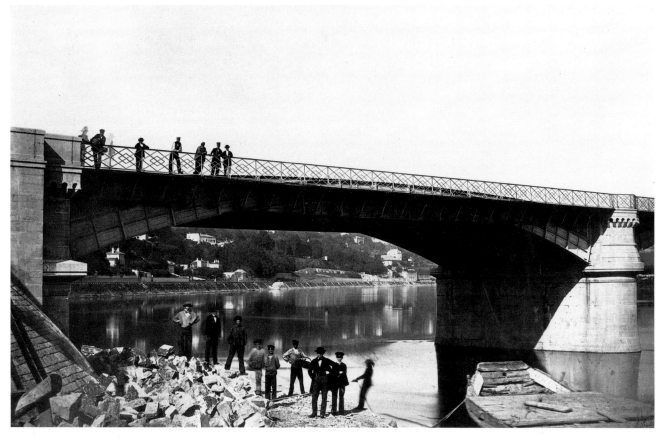

172. EDOUARD DENIS BALDUS. *Pont de la Mulatière*, c. 1855. Albumen print.
International Museum of Photography at George Eastman House, Rochester, N.Y.

documentation financially untenable, Baldus turned to re-printing his negatives and reproducing his work in gravure rather than alter the high standards he had set for himself. His attitude may be compared with that of William England, a highly competent British photographer who traveled widely to provide his publisher with images for stereoscopes and albums. As John Szarkowski has pointed out,[5] England's view of the Niagara Suspension Bridge *(pl. no. 174)* has something for everyone—scenery, human interest, an engineering marvel, and the contrast between old and new means of transportation. Nevertheless, though well-composed and satisfying as a document, it lacks the inspired tension that put Baldus's work onto another plane of visual experience, perhaps because its aim was simply to provide the kinds of information the public wanted in the clearest fashion.

The character of new engineering materials and con-struction methods that were altering the appearance of Europe at mid-century seems to have had a special appeal to photographers called upon to document bridges and railway construction. To select only one example, *Two Bridges (pl. no. 175)*, a work by Louis Auguste Bisson whose portrait firm sought to expand with such documentary

commissions, explores the geometries of arc and rectangles to enhance the contrast between the traditional stone of the past and the modern metal span. At times, fascination with the design properties of construction materials became so pronounced as to almost obscure the utilitarian purpose of the structure; in an 1884 image of the building of the Forth Bridge in Scotland by an unknown photographer *(pl. no. 176)*, the angled beams take on an animated life of their own, swallowing up the small figures in the foreground.

Photographs of industrial activity that included the work force also were made, although often they were less formally conceived. Taken for a variety of purposes—as a record of engineering progress, as material for illustrators —many such records were not deemed important, with the result that in time the names of the makers or the particulars of their careers became lost. Yet these images, too, can exert a spell through a formal structure that con-verts mundane activity, such as work, into evocative expe-rience. Few images in either Europe or the Americas were concerned with the actual conditions of work, an interest that did not manifest itself photographically until late in the century *(see Chapter 8)*.

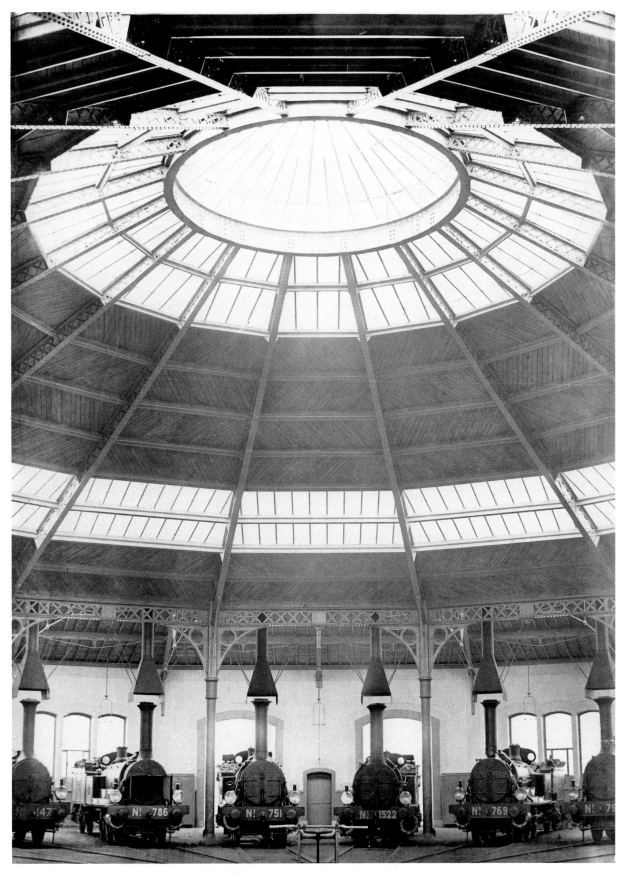

173. A. COLLARD. *Roundhouse on the Bourbonnais Railway, Nevers*, 1860–63. Albumen print.
International Museum of Photography at George Eastman House, Rochester, N.Y.

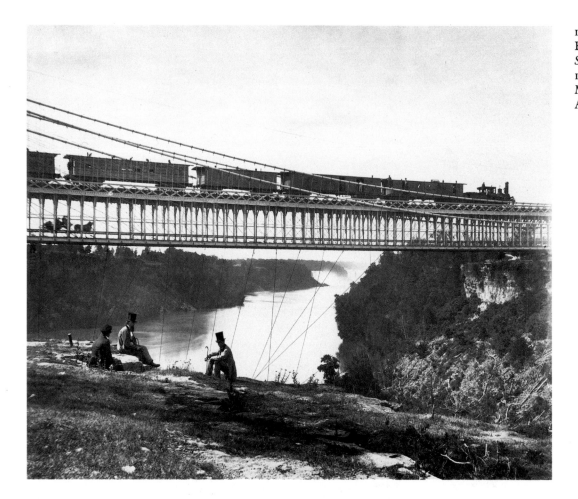

174. WILLIAM
ENGLAND. *Niagara
Suspension Bridge*,
1859. Albumen print.
Museum of Modern
Art, New York.

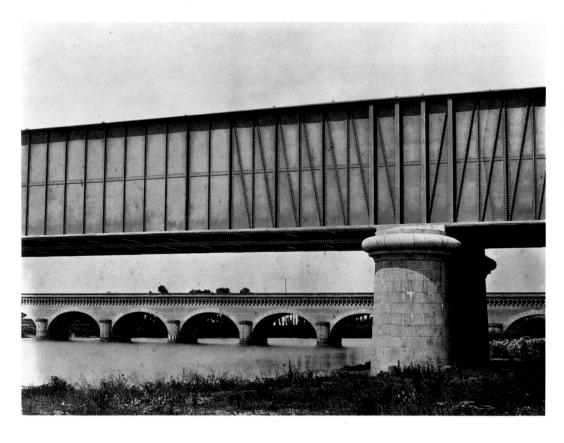

175. AUGUST
ROSALIE and LOUIS
AUGUSTE BISSON.
Two Bridges, n.d.
Albumen print.
Bibliothèque
Nationale, Paris.

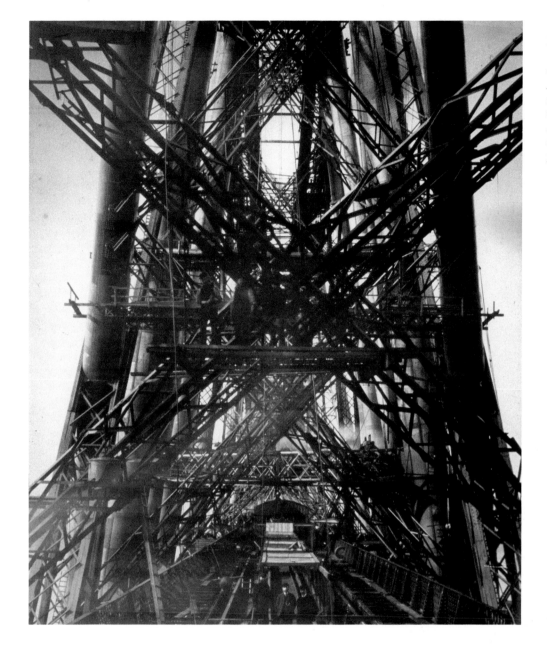

The transformation of Paris from a medieval to a modern city, ordered by Prefect of the Seine Baron Haussmann (who took office in 1853), provided an exceptional opportunity for urban camera documentation. Old buildings and neighborhoods scheduled for demolition were photographed in collodion in the 1860s by Charles Marville *(pl. no. 177)*, a former illustrator, whose early work in the waxed-paper process appeared in many of Blanquart-Evrard's publications. These images display a poignant regard for the character and texture of vanishing ways, indicating again that documentary records might be invested with poetic dimension. Working on his own (after recovering from the disappointing events of 1839, in which his own paper process was suppressed), Hippolyte Bayard made

decorous views of the streets and buildings of Paris *(pl. no. 24)*. In all major cities, the urban milieu offered photographers a chance to capture the contrast of old and new and also to document aspects of anonymous street life, producing views that after 1859 were much in demand by the buyers of stereographs *(see below)*.

Another aspect of Victorian photographic activity concerned the appropriation of the physical remains of the past. Popular interest in archeology, initiated in the 18th century with the finds at Troy, Pompeii, and Herculaneum, was further stimulated by the acquisition of works unearthed by 19th-century European scholars and diplomats investigating ancient cultures in Egypt, Greece, and the Near East, often while pursuing imperialistic interests.

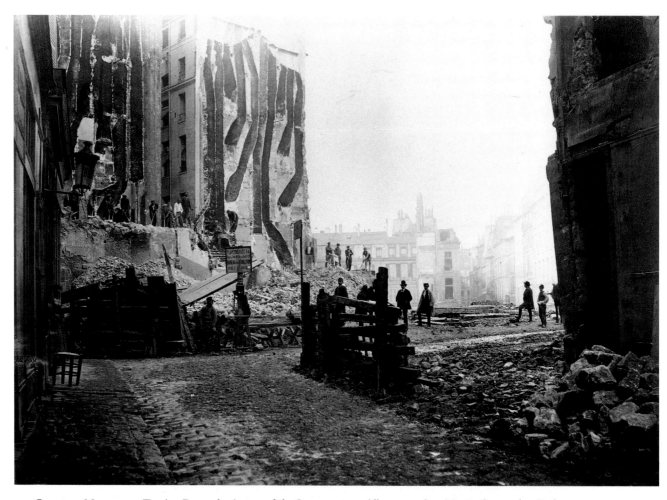

177. CHARLES MARVILLE. *Tearing Down the Avenue of the Opera*, c. 1865. Albumen print. Musée Carnavelet, Paris.

Fortunately, Europeans did not heed Holmes's quintessentially American view that the artifacts themselves might be dispensed with as long as their images remained; instead, their goal was to disinter and relocate actual objects. Though frequently wrenched from historical context and incorrectly restored, these works confirmed a sense of continuous history for Europeans experiencing the unsettling advance of industrialization. The excavation, transportation, and restoration of this cultural booty produced some visually stimulating camera images. Almost every aspect of industrial Europe's romance with the past, from the pilgrimage to ancient lands *(pl. no. 178)*, to the installation of the object in a modern setting *(pl. no. 179)* was captured by the camera. And while by mid-century European museums already had become the repositories of statuary and decorative objects from all over the ancient world, the growing popular interest in archeology and its finds must be attributed in some measure to the camera.

Monumental contemporary works of statuary also provided subjects for photographers intrigued by the contrast in scale afforded by such pieces. The documentation of the production of the Statue of Liberty in France, by Albert Fernique *(pl. no. 180)*, and its installation in the United States was just one of a number of such picturizations of an activity that was going on in other industrial countries, too. One suspects that the amusing contrast between the lively figures of the real workmen and the grandiose inertia of the idealized effigy, seen in this work and also in Aloïs Löcherer's record of the construction and transport of the mammoth statue *Bavaria (pl. no. 181)*, constituted at least part of the appeal of such images.

Camera Documentation: United States

Camera documentation of industrial progress in North America differed significantly from that of Europe, primarily because of America's lack of historical monuments and its attitude to photography in general. Drawn largely from the ranks of graphic artists, mid-century European photographers were influenced by attitudes instilled in them about art in general, but in the "new world" sound academic training in the arts was limited. With few exceptions, Americans regarded photography as a business and the camera as a tool with which to record information. Neither poets nor reformers, many photographers in the United States were unconcerned with subtleties, endeavoring instead to present material objects in a clear-cut and competent fashion without involvement in the artistic effects of light and shade or unusual compositional angles.

This said, it still is curious that in a country so con-

sumed by interest in mechanical devices, few images that take advantage of the forceful geometry of engineering structures were made. From the daguerreotype era to the end of the century, when Americans photographed bridges, railways, machinery, and buildings—emblems of the growing industrialization of the nation—their major concern was to be informative rather than inspirational. The choice of camera position in *Brooklyn Bridge Under Construction* (by an unknown photographer) *(pl. no. 182)* diminishes the scale and beauty of the pylons in order to direct attention

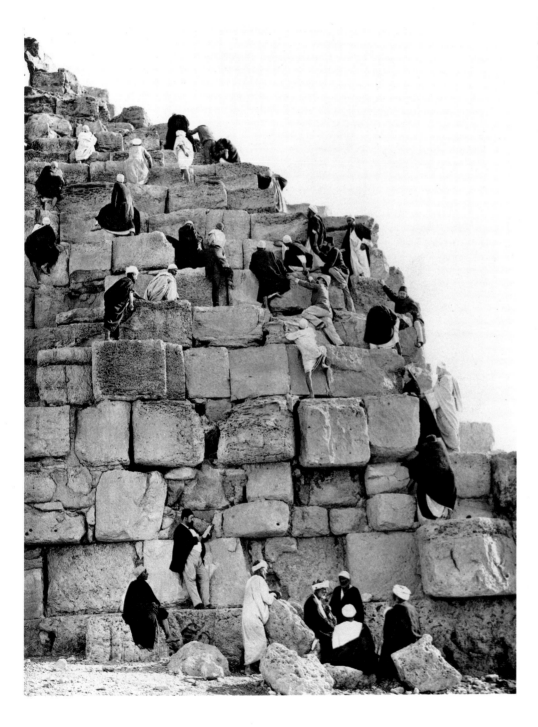

178. HENRI BÉCHARD. *Ascending the Great Pyramid*, c. 1878. Phototype from *L'Egypte et la Nubie*, 1888. Charles Edwin Wilbour Library of Egyptology, Brooklyn Museum.

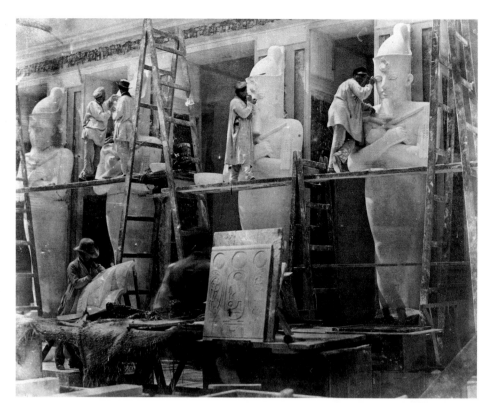

179. PHILIP HENRY
DELAMOTTE. *Setting up the
Colossi of Rameses the Great*, 1853.
Albumen print. Greater
London History Library.

180. ALBERT FERNIQUE (?).
*Construction of the Statue of
Liberty, Workshop View, Paris*,
c. 1880. Albumen print. Rare
Books and Manuscripts
Division, New York Public
Library, Astor, Lenox, and
Tilden Foundations.

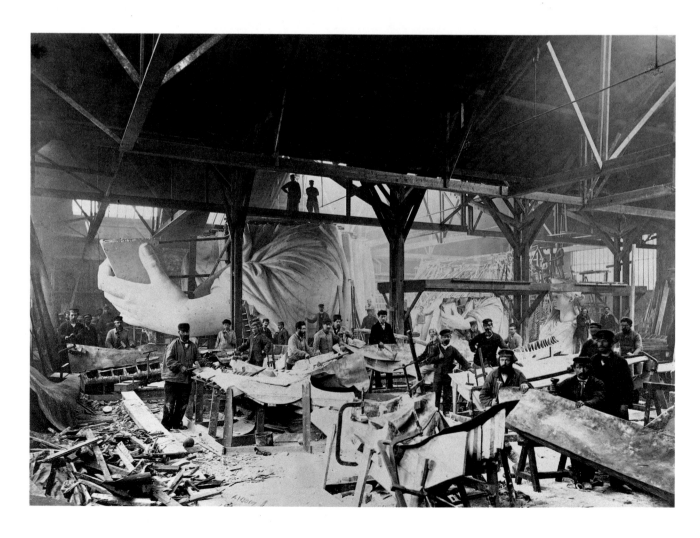

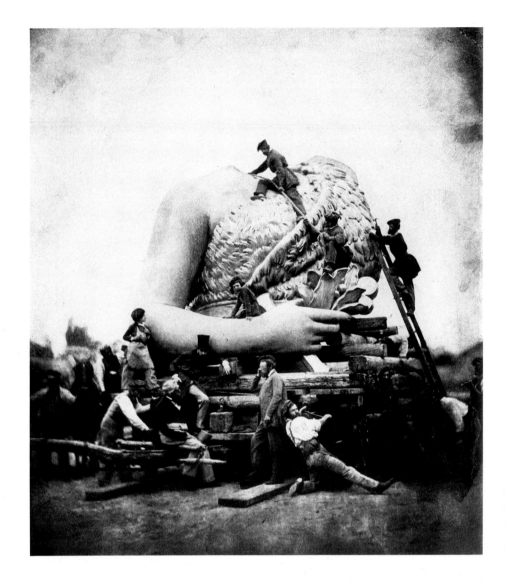

181. ALOÏS LÖCHERER. *Transport of the Bavaria (Torso)*, 1850. Albumen print. Agfa Gevaert Foto-Historama, Leverkusen, Germany.

to the small group of top-hatted figures. Typical of the many views of this project, the image falls short of embodying the daring energy which the bridge itself still symbolizes. In comparison, Canadian William Notman's 1859 photograph of the framework and tubing of the Victoria Bridge *(pl. no. 183)* creates an arresting visual pattern that also is suggestive of the thrust and power of the structure. As F. Jack Hurley points out, 19th-century photographs of American industry concentrate on depicting the individuals responsible for "taming, dominating and bending to their wills . . . the vast virginity of the continent"[6] rather than on the expressive possibilities inherent in structural and mechanical forms.

However, there are exceptions: in the years following the Civil War, photographic documentation of the western rail routes—in particular the construction of track-beds and spans and the laying of rails—resulted in images of decided visual impact. Inspired by the grandeur of the wilderness, the photographers, among them Alexander

Gardner, Alfred A. Hart, William Henry Jackson, Andrew Joseph Russell, and Charles R. Savage, recorded not only actual construction but settlements along the way, unusual vegetation, geological formations, and Indian tribal life. The best-known of these images—a work by Russell of the joining of the cross-continental tracks at Promontory Point, Utah Territory, in 1869 *(pl. no. 184)*—is in the mainstream tradition of American documentation, with workers and dignitaries the focus of the celebratory occasion, but in other works, typified by Russell's *The Construction of the Railroad at Citadel Rock (pl. no. 185)*, landscape predominates—the understandable effect of an attitude that regarded the western wilderness with near-religious awe. Many of Russell's images emphasize curving rails and intricately constructed bridge spans, foreshadowing the handling of similar themes by William Rau, official photographer of the Pennsylvania and Lehigh Valley railroads at the end of the century. The clean, formal organization of track-beds and rails in Rau's images *(pl. no. 186)* suggests that indus-

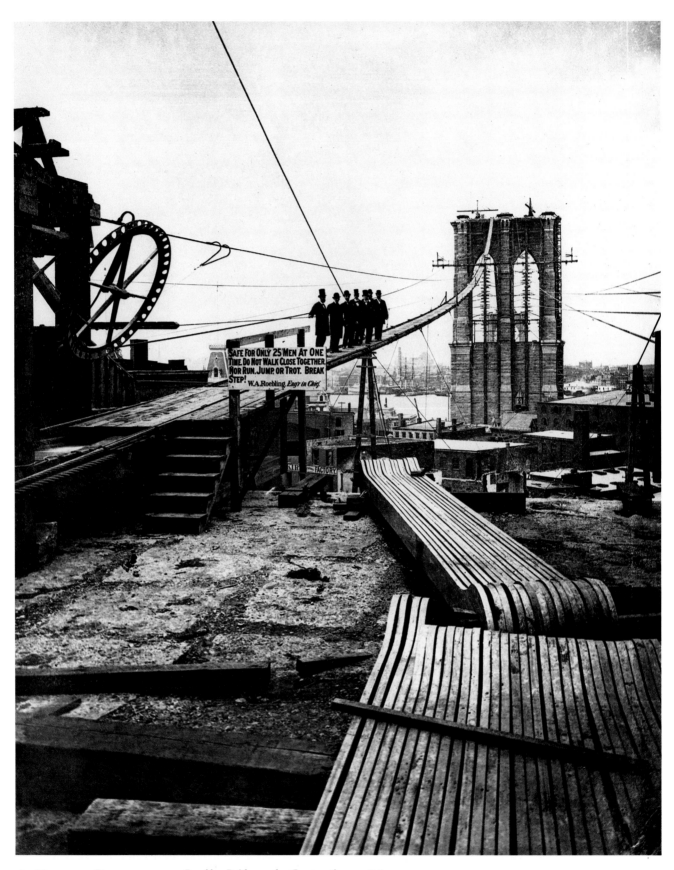

182. UNKNOWN PHOTOGRAPHER. *Brooklyn Bridge under Construction*, C. 1878.
Albumen print. New-York Historical Society, New York.

trial might had emerged without trauma or exertion—a view that was to gain ascendancy in visual expressions of machine culture in the 1920s. As was true of western scenic photographs, railroad images were sold in stereograph and large-format, used to make up presentation albums, shown in photographic exhibitions, and copied by engravers for the illustrated press.

Newsworthy Events and Instantaneous Views

Large-format documentary images required that human figures, when included, remain still during exposure, as can be seen in the posed stance of the workers in the Russell photograph. Recording events that were in a state of flux on this size plate would have resulted in blurring sections of the image, an effect that 19th-century viewers regarded as a sign of imperfection. In fact, during the 1840s and '50s, in order to present occurrences in which there was continuous, if not very rapid, action, it was necessary to restage the scene, as was done for the daguerreotypes by Southworth and Hawes taken in the operating room of Massachusetts General Hospital in 1848 (*pl. no. 187*). Nonetheless, the inadequacy of the earliest technology

had not prevented daguerreotypists from attempting to capture images of fires, floods, and storms—catastrophes over which people have little control but show strong interest in. George N. Barnard was able to make a daguerreotype during an actual conflagration that took place in Oswego, New York, in 1851 (*pl. no. 188*). Even after glass plates took over, however, on-the-spot news photography was difficult because the photographer had to arrive on the scene armed with chemicals and equipment to sensitize the plates before they could be exposed in the camera. Luck obviously played a great role in mid-19th-century documentation of such events, which frequently were translated into engravings in the illustrated press.

With the perfection during the 1850s of shorter focal-length (4½ to 5 inches) stereographic cameras, accompanied by the publication in 1856 of Sir David Brewster's manual on stereography, photography became capable of freezing certain kinds of action. "Instantaneous" views made in stereograph format began to appear around 1858; among the earliest in America was a series taken of long stretches of lower Broadway, commissioned by the E. and H. T. Anthony Company, of which this street scene (*pl. no. 189*) is a typical example. In Great Britain, William England and George Washington Wilson began to market

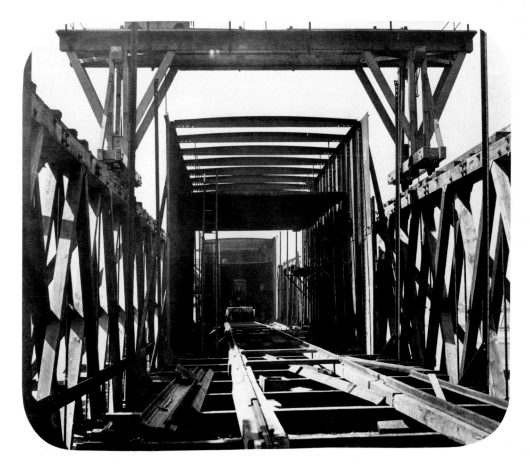

183. WILLIAM NOTMAN. *Victoria Bridge, Framework of Tube and Staging, Looking in,* May, 1859. Albumen print. Notman Photographic Archives, McCord Museum, McGill University, Montréal.

"instantaneous" images of crowded street scenes while Adolphe Braun and Hippolyte Jouvin *(pl. no. 190)* were involved with the same kind of imagery in France. In addition to the stereograph cameras produced in all three countries, small single-lens apparatuses designed to arrest action began to appear *(see A Short Technical History, Part I)*, but despite these refinements, collodion technology still was burdensome, preventing action photography of the sophistication and speed to which modern viewers are accustomed.

Documentation: Daily Life and Ethnic Customs

Curiosity about the everyday lives of the world's peoples predates the invention of photography, but as industrial nations involved themselves in imperialist adventures around the globe, the camera emerged as a most apt tool for satisfying the thirst for sociological information that emerged. Between 1855 and about 1880, collodion/albumen technology made it possible for resolute photographers, both amateur and professional, to follow their countrymen to Africa, the Americas, Asia, and the Near East in order to record, besides scenery, aspects of daily life and ethnic customs. Though under the impression that these documentations were "objective"—that is, truthful records of what exists—those behind the cameras were guided in their selection and treatment of material both by a sense of being emissaries of a "higher civilization,"[7] as John Thomson called it, and by the desire for commercial success. Nevertheless, despite assumptions of superiority, the close observation of indigenous customs altered ethnocen-

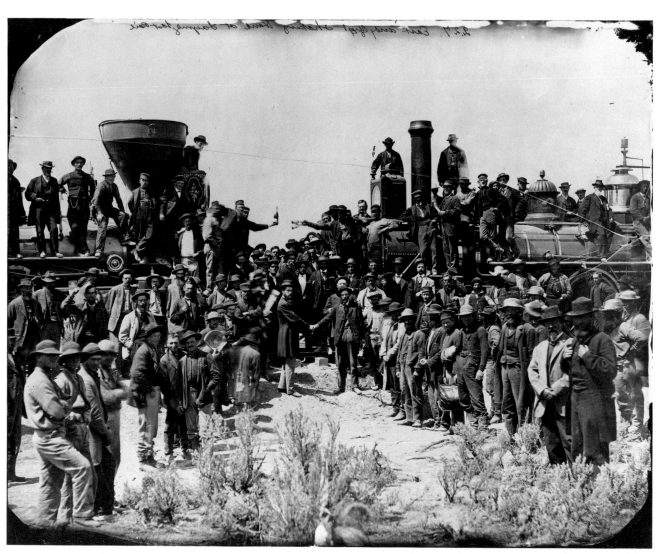

184. ANDREW J. RUSSELL. *Meeting of the Rails, Promontory Point, Utah*, 1869. Albumen print. Union Pacific Historical Museum, Omaha, Neb.

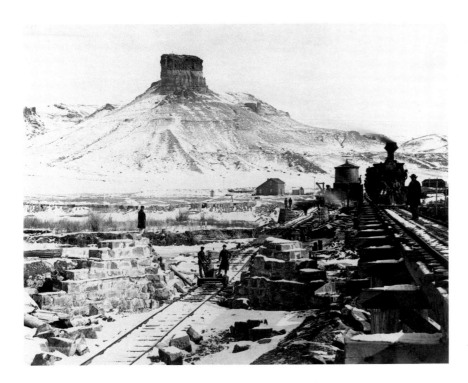

185. ANDREW J. RUSSELL. *The Construction of the Railroad at Citadel Rock, Green River, Wyoming*, 1867–68. Albumen print. Western Americana Collection, Beinecke Rare Book and Manuscript Library, Yale University, New Haven, Conn.

186. WILLIAM RAU. *New Main Line at Duncannon*, 1906. Gelatin silver print. Collection Sam Wagstaff, New York.

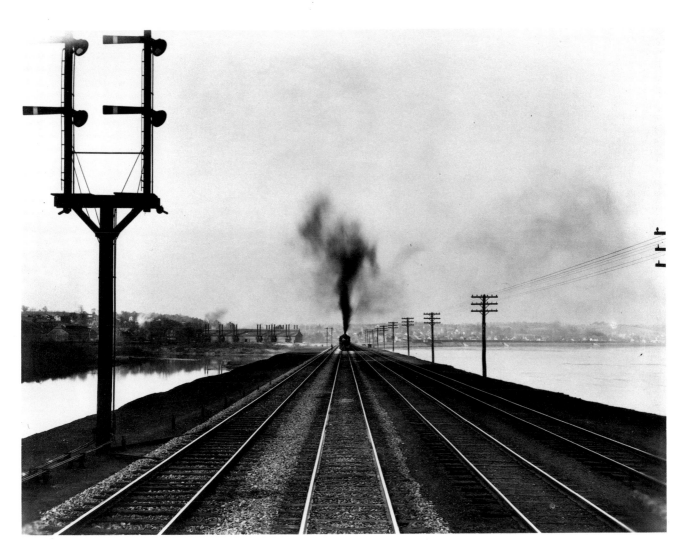

tric attitudes and in some cases even evoked admiration for elements of so-called "backward" cultures among photographers.

Understandably, India under British rule provided the greatest opportunity to satisfy the desire on the part of occupying residents and folks back home for this kind of imagery. Among those portraying native life in the areas where Britons maintained interests in the jute, tea, and teak industries were Félice Beato (a naturalized British subject of Italian birth about whom little has been written), Samuel Bourne (whose catalog listings included "Groups of Native Characters"), and John Burke, who worked in the Punjab and in Kashmir before recording the course of the Second Afghan War. The now little-known William Johnson, a founder of the Bombay Photographic Society, published his views of Indian teachers, vendors, and workers periodically in 1857 in the *Indian Amateurs Photographic Album* and then in a single volume

containing 61 photographs; *Group of Cotton Carders (pl. no. 191)* has a mannered quality common to many such staged indoor scenes of the time, whereas the out-of-doors settings that served as the locales for Captain Willoughby Wallace Hooper gave his images of lower-caste Hindu life and famine victims a more natural-looking aspect.

Known or unknown, British photographers sent to oversee or to document colonial activities in other parts of the empire on which "the sun never set" sent home views of the native peoples of South Africa, Australia, and New Zealand, as well as of India. The effects on Western viewers of scores of camera pictures of scantily clad, sometimes tatooed or painted humans of color from unindustrialized parts of the world are difficult to determine. No doubt as a group these images stimulated 19th-century positivists in their quest for anthropological information, but whether they reinforced dominant stereotypes against nonwhites or made viewers more conscious of individual differences

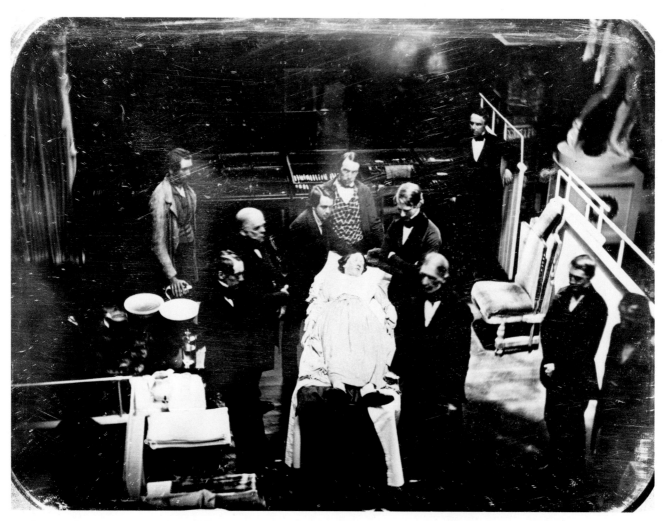

187. ALBERT SANDS SOUTHWORTH and JOSIAH JOHNSON HAWES. *Operating Room, Massachusetts General Hospital, Woman Patient*, 1846–48. Daguerreotype. Massachusetts General Hospital News Office, Boston.

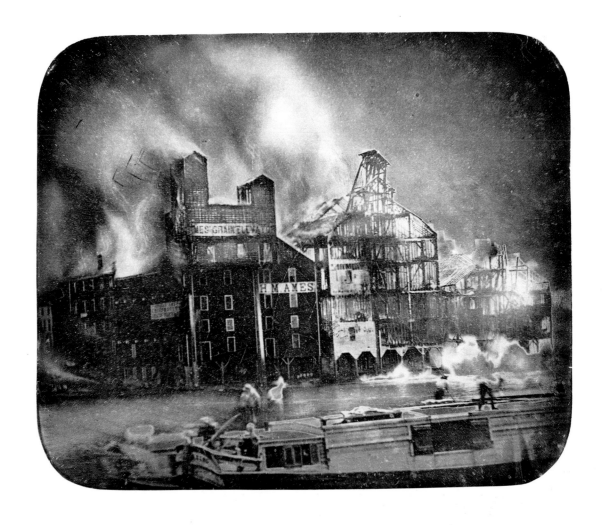

188. GEORGE N. BARNARD. *Burning Mills,
Oswego, New York*, 1851. Daguerreotype.
International Museum of Photography at George
Eastman House, Rochester, N.Y.

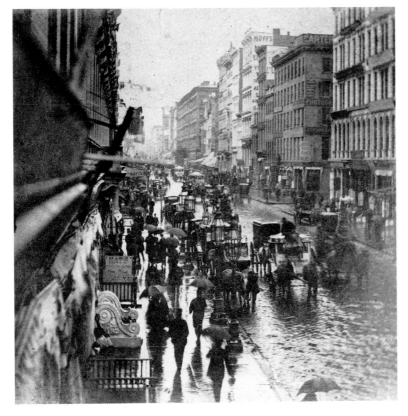

189. EDWARD ANTHONY. *New York Street Scene*,
1859. One-half of an albumen stereograph.
Collection George R. Rinhart, Colebrook, Conn.

among subjected peoples depended in part on the individual photographer's attitude and treatment, and on the context in which they were seen.

In China, posed studio photographs simulating typical occupations appeared on *cartes-de-visite* made in the port cities during the 1850s, but actual views of street life did not reach the West until Thomson issued *Illustrations of China and Its People* in 1873–74. The 200 photographs reproduced in heliotype with descriptive letterpress texts—the result of nearly five years spent in Hong Kong, Formosa, and on the mainland—include, besides portraits and scenery, images of people engaged in mundane activities, among them *Itinerant Tradesmen, Kiu Kiang Kiangsi (pl. no. 192)*. To eyes accustomed to the blurs of modern street photography, this image may suggest a staged view, but the overall sharpness and inclusive detail were meant to convince 19th-century viewers of the reality of a scene happened upon by accident.

Views of everyday life in Japan (based on photographs) appeared in the *Illustrated London News* soon after the country was opened to Western exploitation by Commodore Matthew C. Perry; after the establishment of an official British Mission, native customs began to receive extensive photographic documentation. The peripatetic Félice Beato arrived in Japan about 1863, and five years later his *Photographic Views of Japan with Historical and Descriptive Notes* appeared—one of its two volumes devoted to "Native Types." Though similar in intent to Thomson's views of China, many of Beato's portrayals depicted aristocrats, military men, laborers, vendors, and geisha *(pl. no. 333)* posed in the studio holding emblems of their rank or trade. Gracefully composed against simple backgrounds and delicately hand-colored by Japanese artists, these works suggest the influence of the decorative *ukiyo-e* woodblock depictions of daily life. Similar amalgams of sociological information and artistic effect designed to attract travelers characterize the work of Baron Reteniz von Stillfried, an Austrian who settled in Yokohama in 1871, bought Beato's studio, and produced, with a partner and Japanese assistants, an album entitled *Views and Costumes of Japan (pl. no. 193)*; the genre was further refined by the Japanese photographer Kusakabe Kimbei, an assistant to Von Stillfried who took over the latter's studio around 1885 *(pl. no. 194)*.

Tribespeople fulfilled similar roles for those intrigued by exotic customs in the western hemisphere. In the United States, railroad, survey, and frontier photographers, among them Gardner, Jackson, and John K. Hillers (first official photographer for the Bureau of Ethnology), documented aspects of Indian life in the course of other work, while, to the north, Humphrey Lloyd Hime included "native races" in his portfolio on the Assiniboine and Saskatchewan expe-

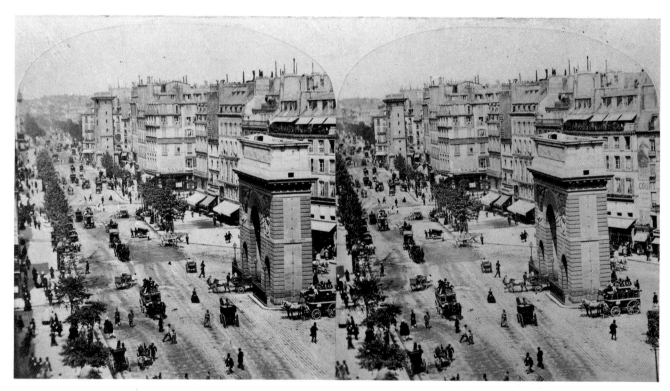

190. Hippolyte Jouvin. *Pont St. Denis, Paris*, c. 1860. Albumen stereograph. Collection Yvan Christ, Paris.

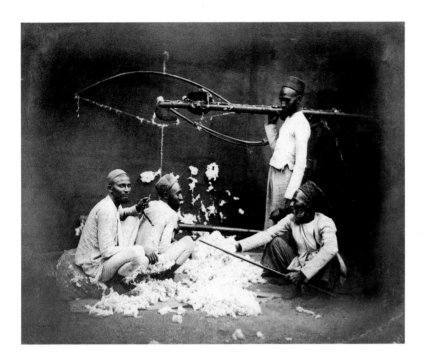

191. WILLIAM JOHNSON. *Group of Cotton Carders* from *The Indian Amateur's Photographic Album*, 1856. Albumen print. India Office Library and Records Department, British Library, London.

192. JOHN THOMSON. *Itinerant Tradesman, Kiu Kiang Kiangsi*, c. 1868. Albumen print. Philadelphia Museum of Art; Purchase of Stieglitz Restricted Fund.

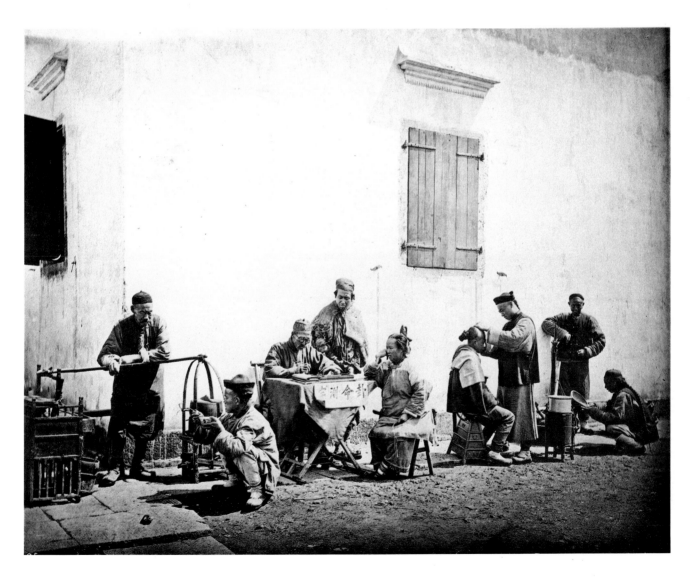

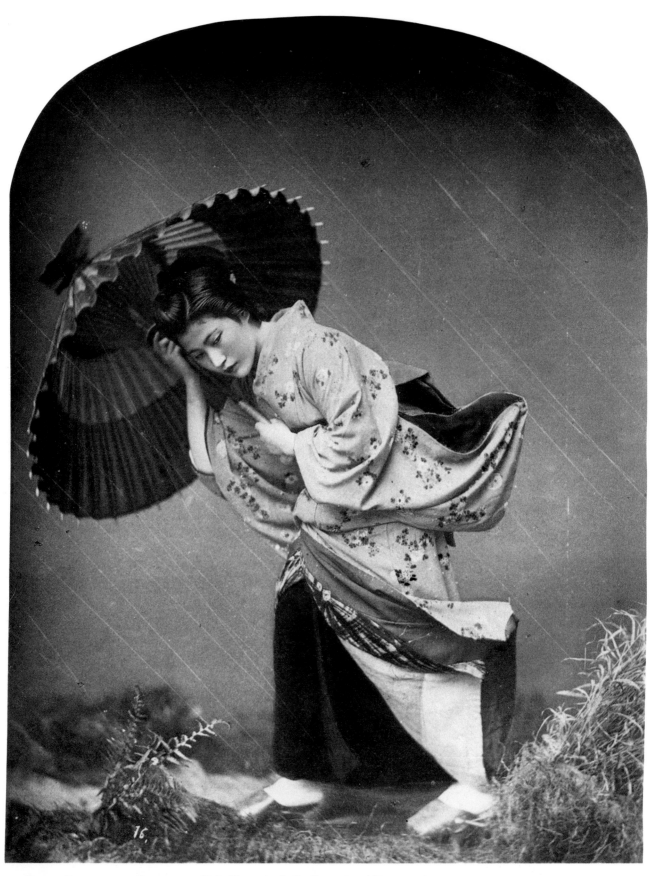

193. Baron Reteniz von Stillfried. *Rain Shower in the Studio*, c. 1875. Albumen print.
International Museum of Photography at George Eastman House, Rochester, N.Y.

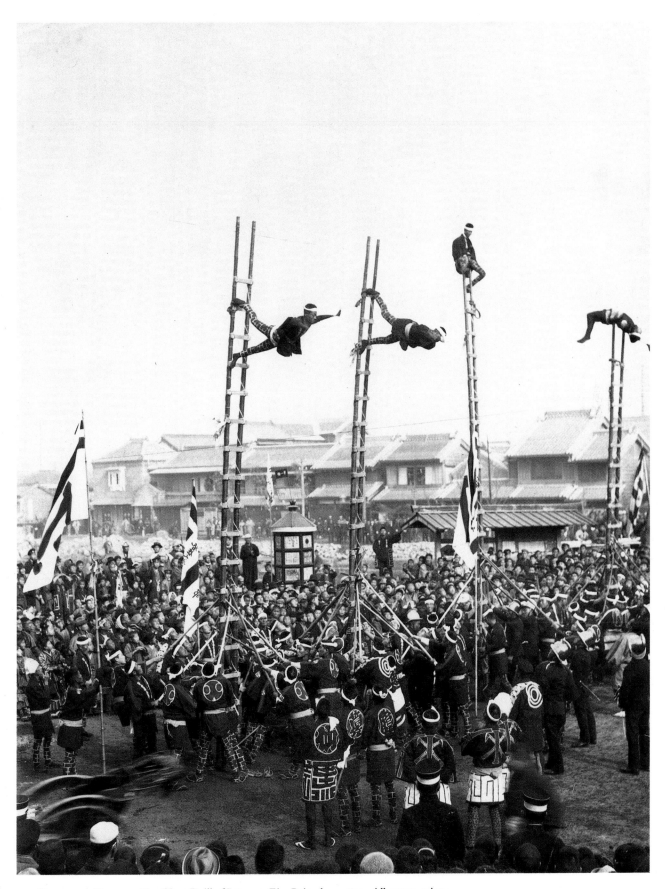

194. KUSAKABE KIMBEI. *New Year Drill of Japanese Fire Brigade*, c. 1890. Albumen print.
International Museum of Photography at George Eastman House, Rochester, N.Y.

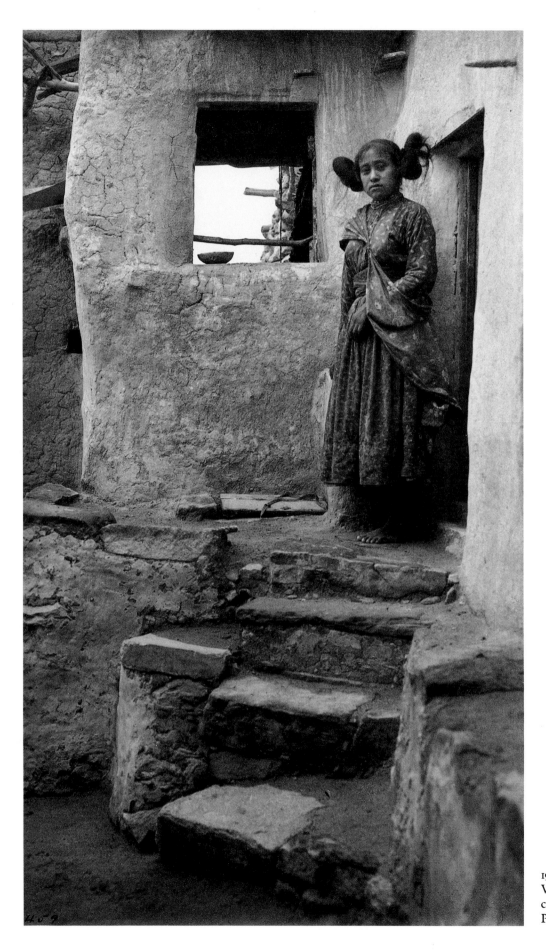

195. Adam Clark
Vroman. *Hopi Maiden*,
c. 1902. Platinum print.
Private Collection.

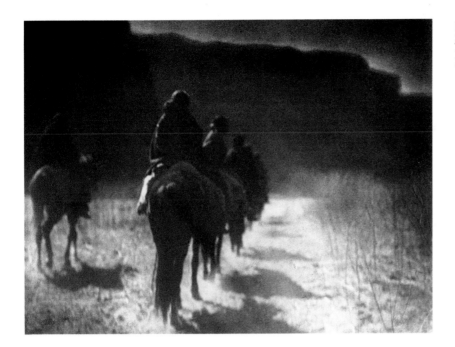

196. EDWARD S. CURTIS. *The Vanishing Race*, c. 1904. Platinum print. San Francisco Museum of Modern Art; extended loan of Van Deren Coke.

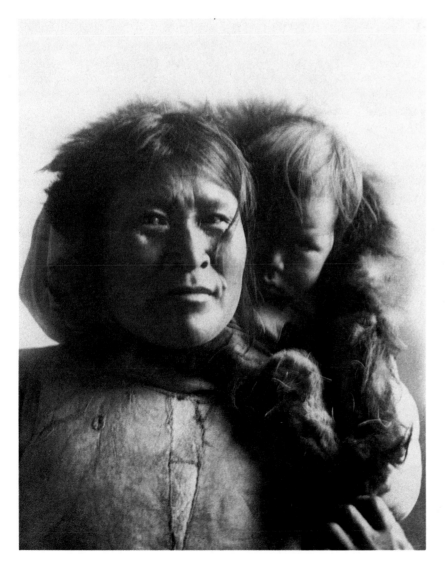

197. ROBERT FLAHERTY. *Portrait of Mother and Child, Ungava Peninsula*, 1910–12. Gelatin silver print. Public Archives of Canada, Ottawa.

ditions in 1858. As the open lands and simple life of the west began to attract escapees from densely settled industrialized sections (and nations), straightforward documentations of Indian life became tinged with idealizing intentions. Individuals such as Adam Clark Vroman, a California bookseller who first accompanied a party of ethnologists to the southwest in 1895, used the camera to emphasize the dignity, industriousness, and charm of the Hopi and Zuni *(pl. no. 195)* as well as to depict customs and ceremonies. Besides donating images to the Bureau of Ethnology archives, Vroman employed them in slide lectures and publications that he hoped would awaken others to the indignities of reservation life.

In the same era, Edward S. Curtis, an ambitious commercial photographer in Seattle, felt moved to record vestiges of the culture of what he conceived as a "vanishing race,"[8] eventually creating a 20-volume survey of the customs, habitations, and dress of the Indians of North America. Supported initially by financial help from investment banker J. P. Morgan, Curtis saw tribal life through a veil of cultural preconceptions that at times led him to introduce false costumes and artifacts into the so-called documentations. The mythic "Indians" that issued from these interventions were further removed from reality by an aesthetic treatment that made use of soft-focus lenses and retouching to add highlights or remove attributes considered un-Indian by Curtis. Often haunting in character *(pl. no. 196)*, these images of Native American life might also be considered within the framework of pictorialism rather than of documentation *(see Chapter 7)*. In a similar vein, *Mother and Child (pl. no. 197)*, 1910, one of some 1,500 still photographs by filmmakers Robert and Frances Flaherty, combines sociological information with a heroicizing vision that seeks to celebrate the unspoiled essence of Eskimo life.

Scientific and Medical Documentation

The second half of the 19th century was an era of expanding use of photography in connection with scientific documentation, also. The first daguerreotype microphotographs were by John Benjamin Dancer, who reduced a 20-inch document to ⅛ of an inch using a camera with a microscope lens; other early experiments in both calotype and daguerreotype produced micrographs of bones, teeth, butterfly wings, and seed pods that were harbingers of the contributions anticipated when the camera was harnessed to the microscope. However, the daguerreotype was too unwieldy and the calotype too indistinct to be of great service to science, even though a textbook and atlas based on micro-daguerreotypes taken by Jean Bernard Foucault was issued by Alfred Donné, the chief clinical physician of

a Paris hospital, in 1845. With the development of the glass-plate negative, along with the refinement of microscopes, lenses, and shutters, ever-more-minute analyses of unseen and barely seen forms and structures became possible. An important contribution in this advance was *Human Physiology* by Professor John William Draper, whose portrait experiments were discussed in Chapter 2. Published in 1856 with woodcuts based on photographs, it was, according to *Harper's New Monthly Magazine*, the first "attempt . . . on an extensive scale to illustrate a book on exact science with the aid of photography."[9] Not long afterward, the first text on the use of photography in microscopic research was written by a German physiologist, Joseph Gerlach, according to Alison Gernsheim, one of the first writers to investigate the historic uses of the camera in medicine. A *Photographic Atlas of the Nervous System of the Human Frame* was projected for publication in Munich in 1861.[10]

Collodion photography made great contributions to medical knowledge in the area of straight documentation of external conditions also. Used at first in England and Germany to provide before-and-after records, camera images soon began to illustrate medical texts on a wide variety of problems, from skin lesions to glandular and skeletal aberrations. In 1858, the London *Photographic Journal* prophesied that every medical school soon would be furnished with a library of photographic illustrations of disease, and by 1870 the medical profession acknowledged that stereographs and the stereoscope had become "important adjuncts to the microscope for representing the appearance of different phases of disease."[11]

In the area of the study of mental instability, photography assumed administrative, diagnostic, and therapeutic functions. Dr. Hugh Welch Diamond's 1852 portraits taken in a mental asylum have been mentioned, but a year earlier photography already had been used as a component of a concept known as "moral treatment";[12] it was an intervention that sought to provide confined mental patients with antidotes to boredom and nonconstructive activity by showing them lantern slides. In what may have been the first use of photographic rather than hand-painted slides, the Langenheim brothers collaborated with the chief physician of the Philadelphia Hospital for the Insane in this magic-lantern therapy.

The Documentation of Wars and Conflicts

War coverage did not really become feasible until the collodion era. It was obvious from the first that the slow one-of-a-kind daguerreotype was ill-suited for war coverage, although portraits of army personnel occasionally were made by this method. The involved procedures of the

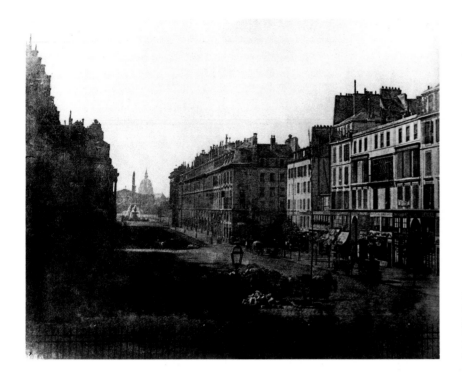

198. Hippolyte Bayard. *Remains of the Barricades of the Revolution of 1848, rue Royale, Paris*, 1849. Albumen print. Société Française de Photographie, Paris.

199. Gustave Le Gray. *Souvenir of the Camp de Châlons, Addressed to General Decaën*, 1857. Albumen print. Collection Paul F. Walter, New York; Museum of Modern Art, New York.

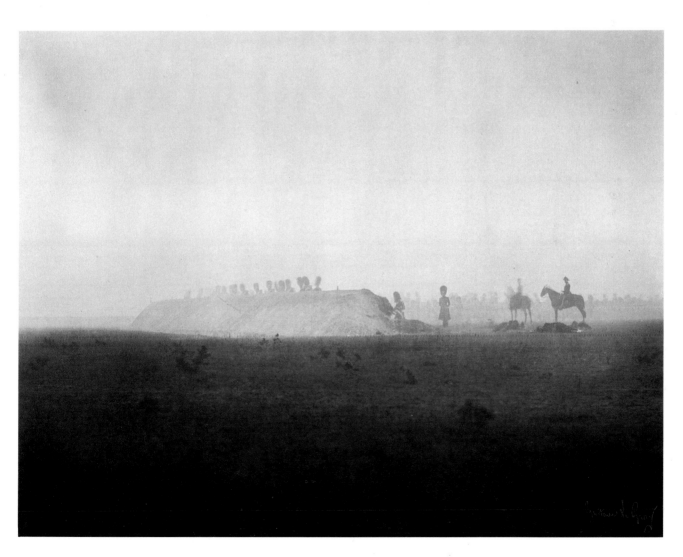

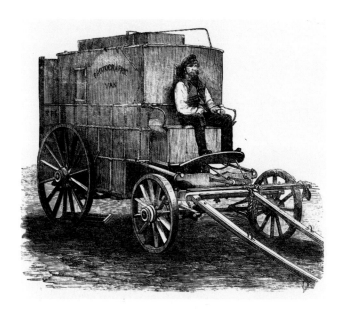

200. UNKNOWN. *Roger Fenton's Photographic Van with Aide Sparling*. Woodcut from *The Illustrated London News*, Nov. 10, 1855. Gernsheim Collection, Humanities Research Center, University of Texas, Austin.

calotype process, although used by Bayard to depict the barricades set up in Paris during the revolution of 1848 *(pl. no. 198)* and by British Army surgeon John McCosh to record episodes in the wars between British and native troops in India and Burma in the mid-19th century, made it, also, a difficult technique for successful battlefield photography. Collodion glass-plate photographers showed themselves capable of exceptional documentation of actuality in relation to military conflicts, perhaps because they recognized that such events were of unusual historical significance. Though somewhat static by modern standards, compelling images of imperialistic adventures, civil disorders, and revolutionary uprisings often go beyond the description of surface appearance to express in visual terms the psychological and physical trauma that such conflicts occasion.

The awkwardness for the photographer of transporting an entire darkroom and of processing the plates on the battlefield is hard to imagine. This incumbrance was balanced, however, by the wet plate's capacity for sharply defined images that could be easily duplicated—factors that made the commercialization of such photographs possible. Still, those working in collodion concentrated on portraying war-related activities rather than action under fire, in part for logistical reasons but also because documentary images were expected to be in sharp focus, a virtual impossibility for photographers using the collodion process in the midst of battle. The documentation of army life by Le Gray made at an encampment of soldiers during peace-

time reflects the near religious exultation with which Napoleon III regarded his army camp at Chalons *(pl. no. 199)*.

Photography entered the arena of war on the wings of politics. Ironically, the first large group of sustained images that have survived[13] was commissioned because the British Establishment wished to present evidence to controvert written reports by William Russell, correspondent for *The Times* of London, detailing the gross inefficiency of military leaders during the Crimean War. The images were made by Roger Fenton, a founder of the elitist Photographic Society of London, during four months spent with the British Army at Sebastopol on the shores of the Black Sea. Bankrolled by a Manchester publishing firm and blessed by Prince Albert, Fenton arrived at Balaclava Harbor in March, 1855, with two assistants, five cameras, 700 glass plates, and a horse-drawn van (formerly that of a wine merchant) converted into a darkroom *(pl. no. 200)*. Working at times in insufferable heat, with plates constantly being ruined by dust and insects, and besieged by the curious crowds of soldiers that flocked around begging for portraits, he complained of getting little done, but by the time he arrived back in England he had produced some 360 photographs.[14]

To modern eyes, these images, especially the portraits, may seem static and contrived. This was partly the result of

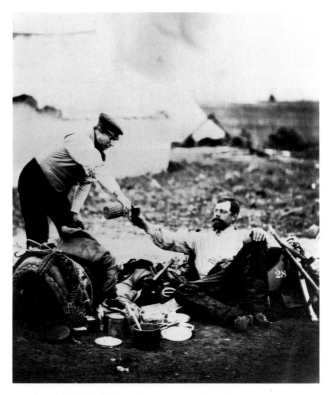

201. ROGER FENTON. *Lt. Col. Hallewell—28th Regiment—His Day's Work Over*, 1855. Albumen print. National Army Museum, London.

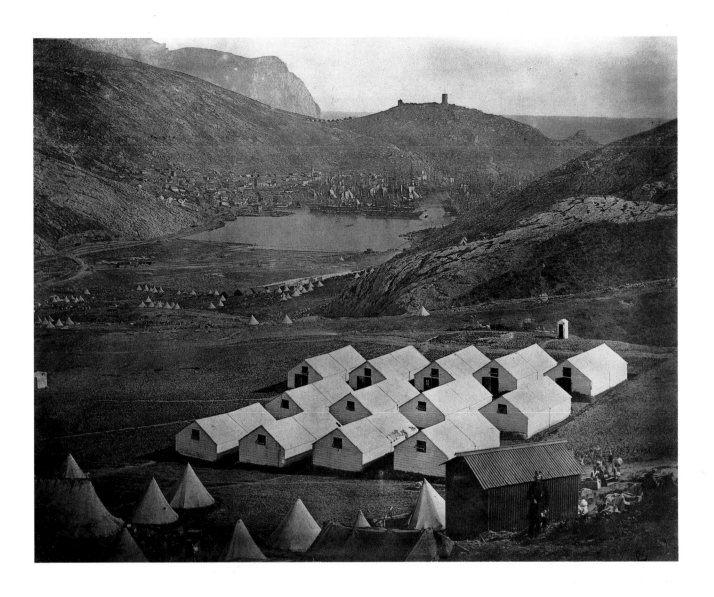

202. JAMES ROBERTSON.
Balaclava Harbor, Crimean War,
1855. Albumen print. Victoria and
Albert Museum, London.

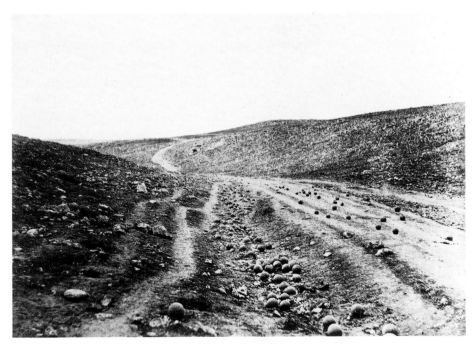

203. ROGER FENTON. *Valley of the
Shadow of Death*, 1855. Albumen
print. Science Museum, London.

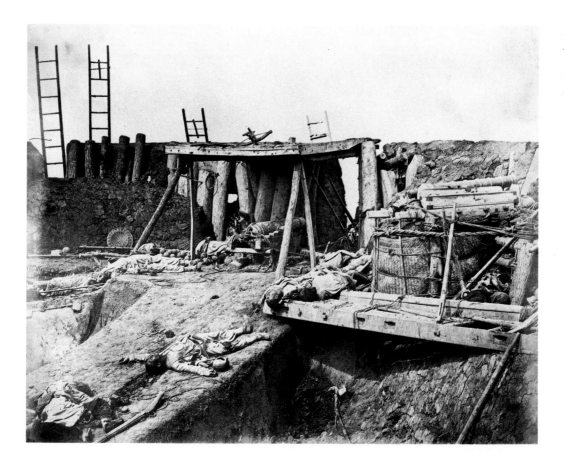

204. FÉLICE BEATO. *Embrasure, Taiku Fort,* 1860. Albumen print. National Army Museum, London.

the limitations of collodion—exposures required from about 3 to 20 seconds—but their character also reflects Fenton's commission to present British Army personnel and ordnance in the best light. *Lt. Col. Hallewell—28th Regiment—His Day's Work Over (pl. no. 201)*, an almost bucolic scene despite the embattled surroundings in which class hierarchies are still—incredibly—observed, is typical of many of the portraits. At the same time, Fenton acknowledged a broader mission. Noting that despite the arduousness of the project he could not leave until he had "secured pictures and subjects most likely to be historically interesting,"[15] he made views of the harbor and deserted battlefields that are visual expressions of the suffering and destruction, of the longing for home, of which he wrote so movingly.

James Robertson, the British Superintendent of the Mint at Constantinople, who for 15 years had been making occasional scenic photographs of the Near East, took over in the Crimea after Fenton returned to England. The 60 or so images he produced after the British had conquered Sebastopol are well-composed but far less artful documents of ruins, docks, left-over ammunition piles, and hospital facilities. Among the evidences of the disastrous incursions wrought by foreign forces on the landscape is a view by Robertson of Balaclava Harbor *(pl. no. 202)* show-

ing an army encampment in what formerly had been a magnificent wooded wilderness. Both Fenton and Robertson's photographs were assembled into presentation albums for British and French royalty, were exhibited in London and Paris, and sold individually in these cities and New York; in addition, they provided material for engraved illustrations in the London press.

Photographs of desolation and destruction, among them Fenton's own *Valley of the Shadow of Death (pl. no. 203)*, had a profound effect on viewers used to artistic depictions of wartime heroics. They were completely unlike drawings made by artists sent to the Crimea, which Fenton criticized for their "total want of likeness to reality."[16] The absence of uplifting tone in camera documentations was especially shocking because the images were unhesitatingly accepted as real and truthful; indeed, discussing Fenton's Crimean pictures in a review of 1855, an *Art Journal* critic held that the "palpable reality" of which the camera was capable could be matched by no other descriptive means.[17] Robertson's photographs received fewer accolades, and one wonders if the warmer reception of Fenton's work was a consequence of his friendships among the British upper class. However, by the time Robertson's images were exhibited, the war was about over, and public sentiment in Britain had turned from concern to indifference, with

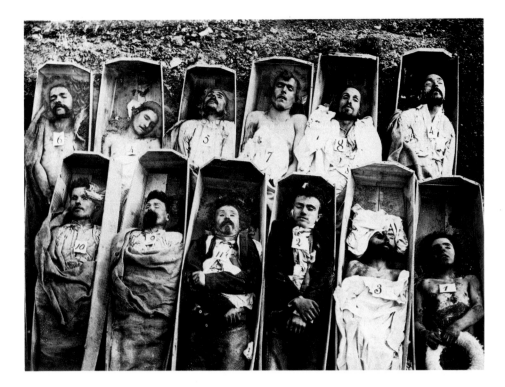

205. UNKNOWN
PHOTOGRAPHER. *Communards
in Their Coffins*, May, 1871.
Albumen print. Gernsheim
Collection, Humanities
Research Center, University
of Texas, Austin.

206. EUGÈNE APPERT. *The
Massacre of the Argueil Dominicans*,
May 25, 1871. Albumen print.
Bibliothèque Nationale, Paris.

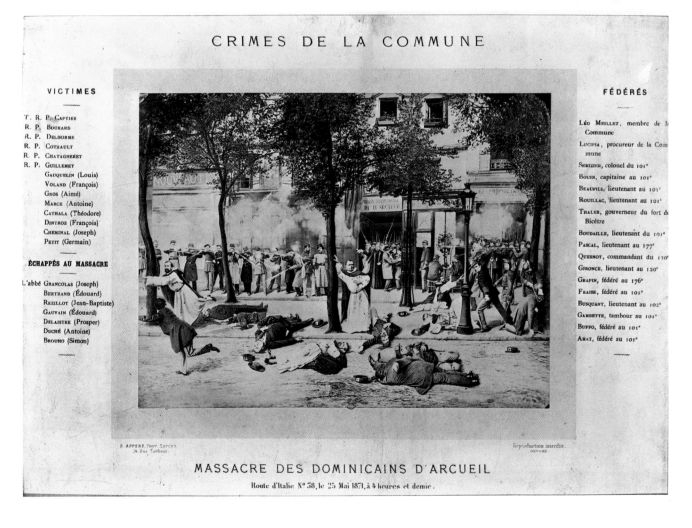

the result that even Fenton's work did not sell to the extent anticipated by its publisher.

No full-scale wars occupied Europeans for the remainder of the century, but uprisings, mutinies, and imperialist adventures were fairly continuous on the Continent, and in Africa, the Far East, and Latin America. Returning from the Crimea to Constantinople, Robertson and his former partner, Félice Beato, traveled east to record the aftermath of the Indian Mutiny of 1857, in which the Indian Sepoy regiments rebelled (unsuccessfully) against the British garrisons and, ultimately, against British rule in India. In addition to an interest in architecture, social customs, and landscape, Beato apparently was fascinated by scenes of devastation. In China in 1860 he documented the destruction of the Taiku forts near Tientsin (Tianjin) during the Second Opium War *(pl. no. 204)*, then, in Japan, the fighting at Simonaki Straits, and, during the 1880s, he turned up on the battlefields of the Sudan. Carefully composed and printed, his photographs present the aftermath of battles somewhat in the manner of ghoulish still lifes, an approach that has been characterized as "distant and detached."[18] However, considering the state of photographic technology, the fact that Beato was an outsider representing an oppressor nation in both China and Japan, and that the public was as yet unused to such photodocumentation, the reproach may be irrelevant; these images must have evoked a powerful response that current jaded perceptions can no longer imagine. Others whose approach to war documentation was also that of a "distant witness," but whose work has less visual interest, were John Burke, working in India and Afghanistan in the 1870s, and Sergeant Harrold, photographing for the British Royal Engineers in Abyssinia between 1868 and 1870.

Between 1855 and 1870, camera images of wars and insurrections generally were accepted as truthful, if painful, mirrors of reality, but after the Paris Commune of 1871, other issues emerged in connection with documentations of politically controversial events. One involved the uses to which such photographs might be put, a problem that arose when portraits of the Communard leaders, made during the brief two-and-one-half months of their ascendancy, were used afterward by political opponents to identify and round up participants for trial and execution *(pl. no. 205)*. The other problem concerned authenticity; documents purported to be of Communard atrocities were later shown to be fakes *(pl. no. 206)* issued by the Thiers government that took power after the fall of the Commune.[19] Though not the first time that photographs had been doctored, the acknowledgment that *documentary* images could be altered marked the end of an era that had believed that such photographs might be pardoned anything because of their redeeming merit—truth.

Documenting the Civil War in the United States

The American Civil War was the first conflict to be thoroughly photographed, with cameramen on hand from the early Union defeat at Bull Run in 1861 to the final surrender of the Confederate forces at Appomattox in 1865. The thousands of photographs that issued from this enterprise were considered by William Hoppin, a prominent member of the New-York Historical Society at the time, to be "by far the most important additions to the pictorial history of the war."[20] Hoppin went on to suggest that because successful views of action were not possible under battle conditions, most of the images were of the dead or dying, but, in fact, photographers documented a broad range of behind-the-lines activities. In today's terms, the frontal poses and clearly defined detail in the majority of images have a static quality that has been ascribed, generally, to the limitations of collodion technology. However, ideological factors also were significant; in order to accept the photograph "as an unmediated medium of picture-making," viewers expected the image to appear technically unflawed, to be clear, inclusive, and finely detailed—indeed, to present itself as reality itself.[21]

There can be little disagreement that the extensive coverage and excellent quality of Civil War photography stemmed largely from Mathew Brady's visionary belief in the role of the camera as historian, even though it is now acknowledged that he actually made few of the images that bore his name. Convinced, as were most people at the time that the conflict would be of short duration, Brady claimed to have obeyed an inner "spirit" that commanded him to leave his lucrative portrait business to demonstrate the role that photography might play in the conflict. In truth, his connections with influential Northern politicians made it possible for him to outfit a wagon darkroom and participate in the First Battle of Bull Run in July, 1861.[22] From then on, Brady regarded himself as an "impresario" —organizer, supplier, and publisher—for a corps of about 20 men, among them the former employees of the Brady portrait studios, Gardner and Timothy O'Sullivan. Using 16 x 20 inch, 8 x 10 inch, and stereograph cameras, these men photographed bridges, supply lines *(pl. no. 207)*, bivouacs, camps, the weary, the bored, the wounded, and the dead—just about everything except actual battles, which would not have been sharp because exposure time was still counted in seconds. Published as *Incidents of the War*, and sold by Brady and the Anthonys, the images appeared with the Brady imprint only. This angered Gardner (and others) and led to the establishment in 1863 of an independent corps and publishing enterprise that credited the images to the individual photographers. Although most cameramen working during the Civil War were attached to units of the U.S. Army, George Cook, a daguerreotypist in Charleston who had managed Brady's New York studio in 1851, photographed for the Confederate forces *(pl. no. 208)*.

Much scholarship has gone into separating the work of the various Brady field operatives, with the result that our knowledge and appreciation of individual contributions have increased, but the effect of the enormous body of work—some seven to eight thousand images—is and was independent of considerations of attribution. The extensive coverage also reflected the increased need by the contemporary media—the weekly illustrated journals, *Harper's* and *Frank Leslie's*—for images of catastrophic events. By reproducing on-the-spot graphic illustrations, and hiring artists to transform photographs into wood engravings, these magazines brought the battlegrounds into comfortable drawing rooms for the first time. As the documentation proceeded, readers of the illustrated press and purchasers of stereograph views were made acutely aware of what the *New York Times* called "the terrible reality." *A Harvest of Death (pl. no. 209)*, taken by O'Sullivan at Gettysburg (printed by Gardner) and later included in *Gardner's Photographic Sketchbook of the War*, is a pictorial evocation rather than merely an illustration in that it encapsulates the tone of Lincoln's sorrowful words commemorating the battle.

It brought home the anonymity of modern warfare, in which it was realized that shoeless soldiers, their pockets turned out, "will surely be buried unknown by strangers, and in a strange land."[23] The haunting stillness of *Ruins of Richmond (pl. no. 210)*, made toward the end of the war and frequently attributed to Gardner, is a quintessential evocation of the desolation occasioned by four years of death and destruction.

Civil War reportage owed its successes also to the readiness of the military to accept photography as a new visual tool, hiring photographers other than "Brady's Men" to work with various units. Barnard, the well-respected former daguerreotypist, worked with Brady briefly and then was attached to the Military Division of the Mississippi, where he documented the aftermath of General Sherman's march across Georgia in 1863; three years later he published a selection of images as *Photographic Views of Sherman's Campaigns*. The surpassing "delicacy of execution . . . scope of treatment and . . . fidelity of impression,"[24] noted by a reviewer for *Harper's Weekly*, are evidences of Barnard's commitment to a style that included the printing in of sky negatives when he believed they might enhance the truthfulness of the image. One such photograph *(pl. no. 211)*, a view of the deserted rebel works occupied by Sherman's forces following the battle that

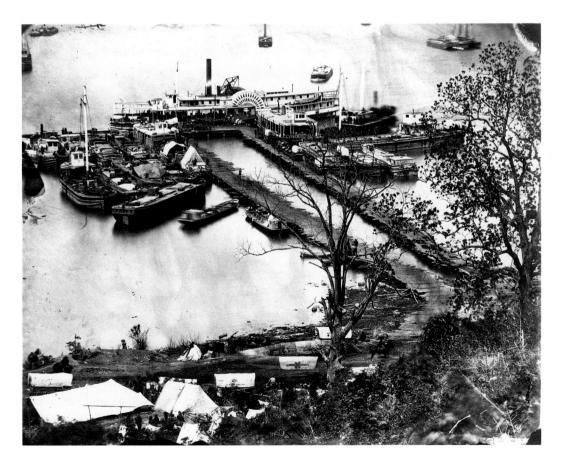

207. MATHEW BRADY OR ASSISTANT. *Landing Supplies on the James River*, c. 1861. Albumen print. Library of Congress, Washington, D.C.

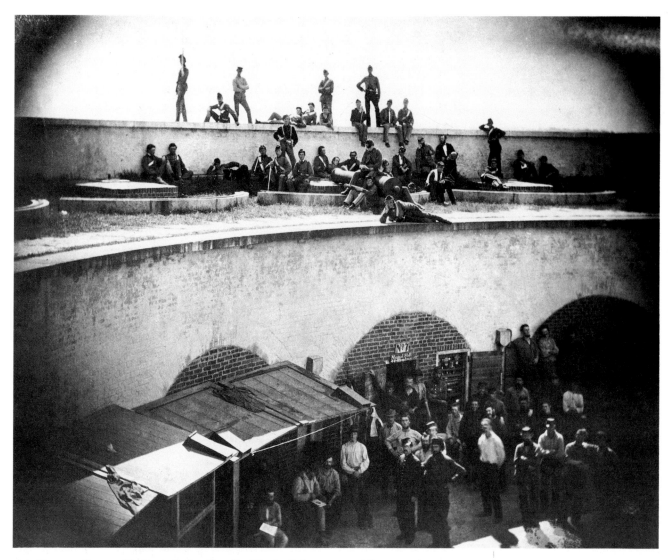

208. GEORGE COOK. *Charleston Cadets Guarding Yankee Prisoners*, 1861. Albumen print.
Cook Collection, Valentine Museum, Richmond, Va.

delivered Atlanta to the Union Army, is especially moving as an emblem of the nation's psychological and physical exhaustion.

Sometime around the surrender of the Confederate Army at Appomattox, April 10, 1865, Gardner took what would be the last portrait of Lincoln *(pl. no. 68)*.[25] Following the assassination, he photographed the President's corpse four days later, and arranged to make portraits of those involved in the plot. Gardner was on hand July 7, 1865, with camera set up on a balcony overlooking the Arsenal Penitentiary courtyard, and from this position he made a sequence of exposures of the hangings of the conspirators—one of the earliest photographic essays on a specific event of political or social significance. The views that issued from this seminal documentation constitute a bleakly powerful story.

War photographers of the collodion period were in-terested in objectivity and craftsmanship. Through choice of subject, position, and exposure, they attempted to present accurate information about the localities, events, and methods of war, in the light of what they conceived to be the national interest. While close-ups, blurring, and distortion—the modern stylistic devices used by contemporary photographers in conflict situations—would have been antithetical to both the goals of the photographers and the desire by the public for clear pictorial records, there still was a need to invest the images with dramatic qualities consistent with their objectives but transcending temporal limitations. One frequently used approach was to incorporate silhouetted forms and figures within the frame; the stark *Ruins of Richmond (pl. no. 210)* and Gardner's *Hanging at the Washington Arsenal (pl. no. 234)* illustrate how this stylistic device serves to isolate and emphasize certain forms while investing the image with a sense of timelessness.

Photographic Documentation and Graphic Art

Pictorial documentation of the Crimean and Civil wars was commissioned also of graphic artists by periodical publications on both sides of the Atlantic. In fact, the illustrator Alfred Waud, a competent if uninspired drafts-man, accompanied Brady on his first foray. Today, the most renowned of the Civil War "sketch artists" is Winslow Homer, at the time a young unknown sent by *Harper's Weekly* to cover front-line action in 1861. Besides turning out on-the-spot drawings that engravers converted into magazine illustrations, Homer collected material that he developed into paintings to create the only body of work of consistently high caliber with the Civil War as theme. His unconventional realism and his preference for mundane scenes that express the human side of army experience

imbue these oils with a nonheroic modernity similar to that found in many camera images of the war. Although there is no evidence that Homer used actual photographs in his compositions of camp-life, his painting, *A Trooper Meditating Beside a Grave (pl. no. 212)*, evokes the same sense of direct experience visible in *Three Soldiers (pl. no. 213)*, a stereograph by an unknown maker.

Homer aside, there is no question that soon after their appearance, photographic documentations, with their keen sense of being an on-the-spot witness to reality, affected the course of the graphic arts in terms of theme and treatment. Though the camera lens might seem to be a more efficient tool than the brush for excising discrete moments of reality, the urge to recreate the daily dramas of ordinary people and the political events of the time on canvas also moved painters—especially the group in France known as Realists. That these artists consciously sought to

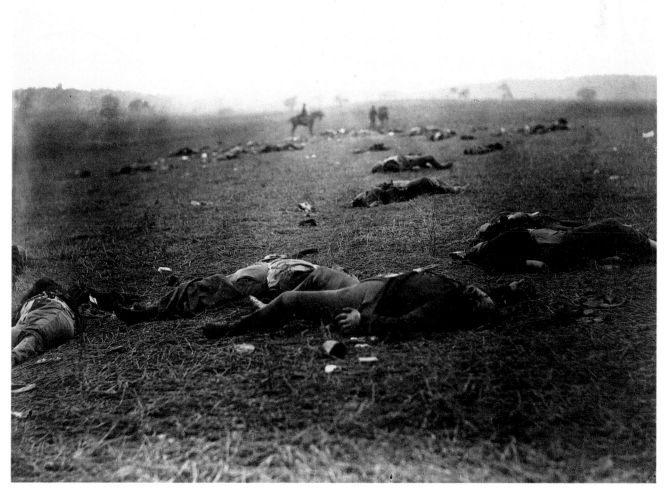

209. TIMOTHY H. O'SULLIVAN (originally printed by Alexander Gardner). *A Harvest of Death, Gettysburg, Pennsylvania*, July, 1863. Albumen print. Rare Books and Manuscript Division, New York Public Library, Astor, Lenox, and Tilden Foundations.

emulate photography, to capture "the temporal fragment as the basic unit of perceived experience," as American art historian Linda Nochlin has observed,[26] can be seen in the *Execution of Maximilian*, an 1867 work by Edouard Manet. Availing himself of news reports and using actual photographs of the shooting by firing squad as a basis for this work, the painter endeavored to de-heroicize and de-mythicize a political occurrence that artists had classically treated with reverence. By emphasizing what the eye sees rather than invoking timeless moral or religious truths, both Realist painters and documentary photographers provided the public with alternative concepts about valor on the battlefield, triumph in death, and the sanctity of life.

It is a paradox nevertheless that documentary photographs are most memorable when they transcend the specifics of time, place, and purpose, when they invest ordinary events and objects with enduring resonance. Sensitivity to the transforming character of light, to the way it structures, reveals, and dramatizes, enabled 19th-century photographers to infuse gesture, expression, and, especially, portions of the built and natural world with feeling. In transmuting bits and pieces of an uninflected, seamless reality into formally structured entities, these pioneers of the medium demonstrated the unique potential of the camera to illuminate as well as record.

Profile: Roger Fenton

"Gentlemen photographer" might be an apt description of Roger Fenton, although his images are neither effete nor languid. His outlook, associations, and activities were reflections of his firmly established position in the comfortable reaches of British society in the mid-1800s. For about 15 years, starting in the late 1840s, he was in the forefront of activity in the medium, producing art photographs and documentation, traveling widely, and organizing activities to promote photography. In 1862, without explanation he suddenly renounced all interest, sold his equipment and negatives, and returned his mind to the legal interests that had occupied him before photography.

From his youth, Fenton's interest was in art rather than in his family's textile and banking businesses. After graduating from college, he pursued training in Paris in common with other aspiring painters, studying with the French salon artist Paul Delaroche in 1841. This fortunate choice led to an acquaintanceship with photography and with several other young artists who were interested in the new field, including Le Gray. Eventually, Fenton returned to England and trained also for a more practical career in law, but he retained an interest in painting, exhibiting at the Royal Academy, and in photography, dabbling in the calotype.

In 1847, he joined with Frederick Archer, Hugh Welch Diamond, Robert Hunt, and William Newton to form the Photographic Club of London (also called the Calotype Club). Three years later, he proposed the establishment of a formal society, modeled on the French *Société héliographique*, that would meet regularly, publish a journal, and maintain a library and exhibition rooms. This entity, The Photographic Society of London (later the Royal Pho-

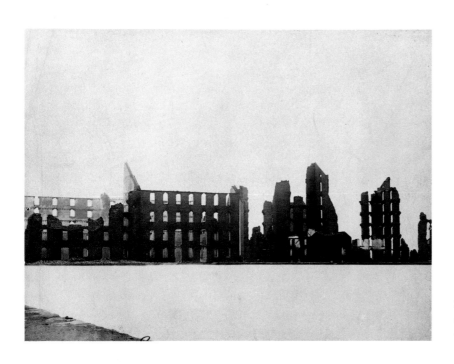

210. UNKNOWN PHOTOGRAPHER.
Ruins of Richmond, 1865. Albumen print.
Museum of Modern Art, New York.

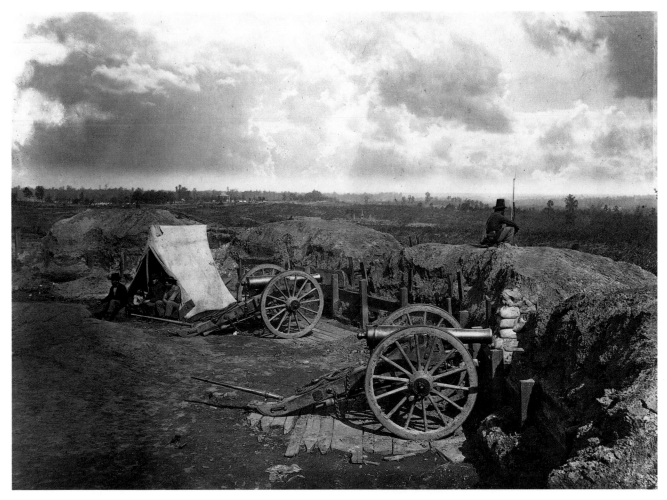

211. GEORGE N. BARNARD. *Rebel Works in Front of Atlanta, Georgia,* 1864. Albumen print.
Stuart Collection, Rare Books Division, New York Public Library, Astor, Lenox, and Tilden Foundations.

tographic Society), was finally inaugurated in 1853, after the relaxation of a part of Talbot's patent, with Sir Charles Eastlake as president and Fenton as honorary secretary. Fenton's influential associations brought about the patronage of Queen Victoria and Prince Albert for the new society. In addition, he was a member of the Photographic Association, a professional body, and sat on committees to consider problems related to the fading of paper and copyright laws.

Fenton also photographed. In 1853 he made a number of portraits of the royal family; a year later he traveled to Russia to document the building of a bridge in Kiev, stopping to make calotypes in St. Petersburg and Moscow, as well. On his return, he was employed by the British Museum to document collections of classical art and drawings. For a good part of 1855, he was involved with the Crimean War project, presenting his pictures and experiences to the crowned heads of Britain and France and trying to regain his health after a bout with cholera. The next year, he

returned to his post at the museum. From this time until 1862, he was involved with art photography, with landscape documentation, with a publication devoted to engravings made from photographs, and with stereography. After providing 21 images for a work entitled *Stereoscopic Views of Northern Wales,* he contributed regularly to *Stereoscopic Magazine,* a publication founded by Lovell Reeves that lasted for about five years. Aside from the documentations and landscapes already mentioned, he turned out images of models posed in exotic costumes and mannered still lifes, some replete with the overdecorated crockery dear to Victorians.

Fenton did not explain or justify his abrupt renunciation of photography, but a number of factors probably were involved. On the technical side, the instability of paper images continued to present problems; an album of his photographs done for the British Museum faded for no apparent reason. Perhaps of greater importance, in view of his own excellent craftsmanship that has kept most of his

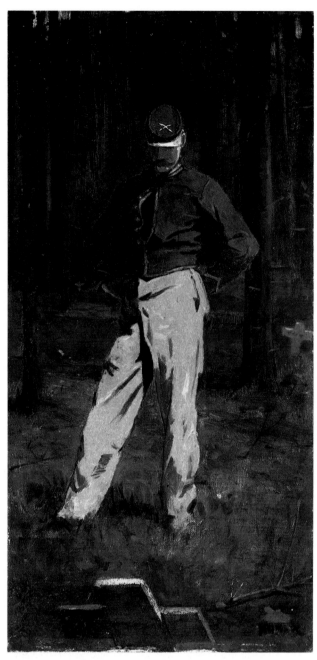

212. WINSLOW HOMER. *A Trooper Meditating Beside a Grave*, c. 1865. Oil on canvas. Joslyn Art Museum, Omaha, Neb.; gift of Dr. Harold Gifford and Sister Ann Gifford Forbes.

spirited campaign in the photographic press to consider them as art. Like contemporaries in France who also withdrew (Le Gray, Baldus), Fenton may have found these events too discouraging.[27]

In some ways, Fenton's activities are of as great interest as his images. While he made fine landscapes and still lifes, and some compelling views of the Crimean conflict, his campaigns to promote photography are indicative of the concern displayed by many young camera artists about the rapid commercialization of the field. In organizing photographic societies, they were attempting to control and maintain standards that would prevent the medium from being used as a purely mechanical picture-maker. This elitism was only partially successful, as first collodion, then the dry plate, and finally the snapshot camera pushed photographic practice in the opposite direction, making the battle for standards a recurring feature in the history of the medium.

Profile: Mathew Brady

As unlikely as it may at first seem, Mathew Brady was in some ways the New World counterpart of Roger Fenton. Differing in background, class position, training, and range of subjects, Brady nevertheless shared with Fenton a sense of mission as well as high critical esteem. Son of poor Irish farmers, Brady arrived in New York City from upstate, probably in the mid-1830s. He was introduced by the painter William Page to Samuel F. B. Morse, from whom he may have learned daguerreotyping, although there is no mention in Morse's papers of Brady as a student. His early years in the city are scantily documented, but sometime in 1844 he opened a portrait studio in what was the busiest commercial section of lower Broadway. By the late 1850s, after one failure in Washington and several moves in New York, he was the owner of fashionable portrait establishments in both cities. Friend to politicians and showmen, he was known to all as the foremost portraitist of the era.

Brady's success was based on high standards of craftsmanship and an unerring feeling for public relations. To this end his luxuriously appointed studios turned out a well-made but not exceptional product that cost more than the average daguerreotype or, later, albumen portrait. In Brady's establishments, the line between a painted and a camera portrait was dim: daguerreotypes could be copied life-size on albumen paper, inked or painted in by well-trained artists, while collodion glass negatives often were enlarged for the same purpose. In addition to displays of portraits of celebrities, his studios contained stereoscope apparatus with which customers could view the latest cards by a variety of makers. It is little wonder that the well-to-do and influential were attracted to Brady's studios.

work remarkably well preserved, was the changing attitudes toward the medium that became apparent as collodion technology turned photography into business. His arrangements with the British Museum reflected the fact that the photographer was considered by many to be an artisan with little to say over the sales of images. Furthermore, photographs hung in the 1862 International Exhibition had been relegated to the machinery section, despite a

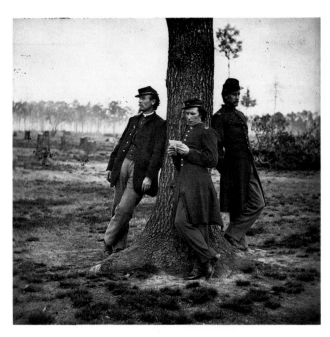

213. UNKNOWN PHOTOGRAPHER. *Three Soldiers*, 1860s. One-half of an albumen stereograph. Library of Congress, Washington, D.C.

Brady was an entrepreneur, setting up the studios, cajoling famous sitters, and arranging for reproductions of his work in the illustrated press, but the actual exposures were made by "operators," among them James Brown, George Cook, O'Sullivan, and, Gardner. In addition, a line of assembly workers that included many women saw to it that the firm's daguerreotypes and, later, its albumen prints were properly finished and presented. Nevertheless, at the time it was taken for granted that honors for excellence in portraiture, starting with a silver medal at the 1844 American Institute Exhibition and extending into the collodion era, should go to Brady himself. His greatest critical triumph was at the Crystal Palace Exhibition of 1851, where the Americans swept the field. It was on the trip to Europe for this event that Brady first investigated collodion and made the acquaintance of Gardner, who was to be influential in the success of his Washington portrait gallery.

Had Brady contented himself with commercial portraiture, it is doubtful that his role in the history of the medium would have been prominent, but he seems always to have been aware that photography could be more than just a successful commercial enterprise. In 1845, he proposed the publication of a series of portraits of famous American personalities in all professions. Issued in only one edition, *A Gallery of Illustrious Americans*, with lithographs by François D'Avignon based on Brady daguerreotypes, was premature and did not sell. However, a portrait of Lincoln, the first of many, became so well-known that the President ascribed his election to this likeness. Taken just before the famous Cooper Union campaign address, this work showed a beardless Lincoln with softened features to make him appear more agreeable.

When the Civil War broke out, Brady's sense of photography's destiny finally could be tested. He was able to demonstrate not only that war reportage was possible but also his own personal courage in continuing the mission after his photographic wagon was caught in shell-fire at Bull Run. In the spring of 1862, Brady trained crews of photographers, assigned them to various territories, had wagons especially constructed in order to transport the photographic gear securely, and arranged for materials and equipment to be supplied from the New York house of T. and E. Anthony. Brady had expected to make back the expenses of his ambitious undertaking by selling photographs, mainly in stereograph format, but after the war the demand for such images ceased as Americans, engulfed in an economic recession, tried to forget the conflict and deal with current realities. Debts incurred by the project, the slow trade in portrait studios generally, and the downfall of Brady's New York political patrons—coupled with the panic of 1873—resulted in the eventual loss of both his enterprises. At the same time, Brady's efforts to interest the War Department in his collection of Civil War images were unavailing. One set of negatives was acquired by the Anthony company as payment for the supplies, and another remained in storage, slowly deteriorating. When this collection of more than 5,000 negatives came up at auction in 1871, it was bought by the government for the storage charges of $2,840; somewhat later the sick and by-now impoverished Brady was awarded $25,000 in recognition of the historic services he had performed. At the time, it was impossible for most bureaucrats to realize the significance of the Civil War project. This vast enterprise not only had made it possible for photographers to gain the kinds of experience needed for the documentation of the West, but it had, for the first time in the United States, given shape to photography's greater promise—that of transforming momentary life experiences into lucid visual expression.

A Short Technical History: Part I

PRE-PHOTOGRAPHIC OPTICAL AND CHEMICAL OBSERVATIONS AND EARLY EXPERIMENTS IN PHOTOGRAPHY

Before Photography

Observations that the reflected light rays of an illuminated object passing through a pinhole into a darkened enclosure resulted in an inverted but otherwise exact image of the object were recorded by Mo Ti in China in the 5th century BC. In the following century in the West Aristotle described seeing, during an eclipse, a crescent-shaped image of the sun on the ground beneath a tree that was projected by rays of light passing through the interstices of foliage onto a darkened surface. In the 10th century, Arabian scholar Ibn Al-Haitham (Alhazen) added the observation that the image thus formed was sharply defined when the aperture through which it was projected was small and became diffuse as the hole was enlarged to admit more light. Similar optical phenomena were noted by Roger Bacon in the 13th century and Reinerius Gemma-Frisius in the 16th.

During the Renaissance, efforts to control and direct this phenomenon resulted in the concept of a *camera obscura*—literally a dark room—that enabled light to enter through a hole in a wall facing another wall or plane on

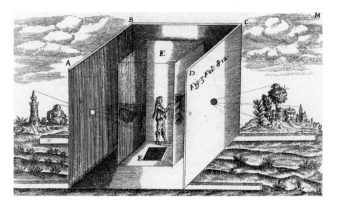

215. ATHANASIUS KIRCHER. *Large Portable Camera Obscura*, 1646. Engraving. Gernsheim Collection, Humanities Research Center, University of Texas, Austin.

which the projected image appeared in natural colors. Sixteenth-century descriptions by Leonardo da Vinci, Vitruvius, and Girolamo Cardano in Italy and by Erasmus Reinhold and Gemma-Frisius in Northern Europe make it difficult to assign exact dates or authorship to the construction of the first *camera obscura*, but references in Giovanni Battista della Porta's *Magiae naturalis* of 1558 indicate that by then the device had become familiar to scientists, magicians, and artists. By the 17th century the *camera obscura* had emerged as a necessary tool for the working out of new concepts of pictorial representation, in which artists and draftsmen depicted objects and space as if seen from one position and one point in time *(pl. no. 214)*.

From the 17th to the 19th century, the *camera obscura* underwent continual improvement. Lenses were added to sharpen the image, and mirrors corrected the inversion and projected the picture onto a more convenient surface for drawing. Portable models were popular among European geographers as well as artists, including a tentlike demountable version by Athanasius Kircher *(pl. no. 215)* illustrated in his 1646 treatise on light as a suitable instrument for drawing the landscape. That scientists and artists regarded it as both a device for aiding graphic representation and a means of ascertaining basic truths about nature is apparent from Dutch philosopher Constantijns Huygen's descrip-

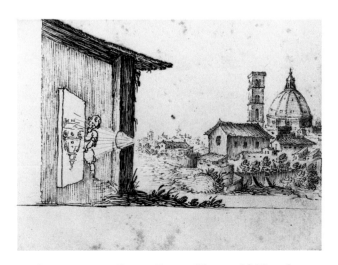

214. STEFANO DELLA BELLA. *Camera Obscura with View of Florence*, n.d. Ink drawing. Library of Congress, Washington, D.C.; Lessing J. Rosenwald Collection.

tion of the *camera obscura* image as "life itself, something so refined that words can't say," while others of the 17th century remarked on its ability to produce a "picture of inexpressible force and brightness . . . of a vivacity and richness nothing can excell."[1]

During the 18th century, fantastic literary and graphic explanations about phenomena caused by light rays appeared, among them an allusion in Tiphaigne de la Roche's fictional work *Giphantie* to a canvas as a mirror that retains images that light transmits, and a visual representation of this concept is seen in an anonymous engraving, *The Miraculous Mirror (pl. no. 216)*. Actual *camera obscurae*, used by artists to improve the accuracy of their depictions, were shown on occasion in portrait paintings *(pl. no. 217)*, as though suggesting that the portrait was a truthful image of the pictured individual. Interest in faithfully transcribing the visible world from the point of view of the individual led to the invention of other devices besides the *camera obscura*. For example, the *camera lucida*, invented by William Hyde Wollaston in 1807, is an arrangement of a prism and lens on a stand that enables the draftsman to see a distant object superimposed on the drawing paper, theoretically making transcription easier.

The chemical components necessary for photography were not recognized until some 200 years after the *camera obscura* was first conceived. From antiquity to the Renaissance, the mystery surrounding organic and mineral substances and their reactions to light and heat made chemical experimentation an inexact exercise practiced mainly by alchemists. In the 17th century, more accurate observation led to the identification of silver nitrate, silver chloride, and ferrous salts, the first chemical substances used in the experiments that led to photography. The accidental discovery in 1725 by Johann Heinrich Schulze, Professor of Medicine at the University of Altdorf, that silver nitrate

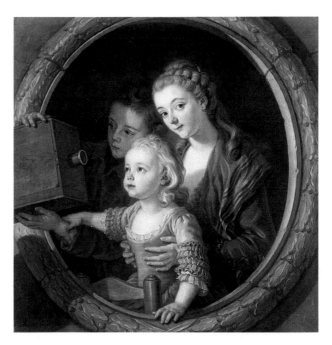

217. CHARLES AMÉDÉE PHILIPPE VAN LOO. *The Magic Lantern*, 18th century. Oil on canvas, National Gallery of Art, Washington, D.C.; Gift of Mrs. Robert W. Schuette, 1945.

darkened when exposed to sunlight and that this change was the result of exposure to light and not heat was crucial to photography. The light sensitivity of silver chloride was the subject of experiments by Swedish Chemist Carl Wilhelm Scheele who published his results in 1777, unaware that at mid-century an Italian, Giacomo Battista Beccaria, had discovered the same phenomenon. Scheele also established that the violet end of the solar spectrum was actinically[2] more active in producing this effect and that the darkened material consisted of particles of metallic silver that could be precipitated by ammonia. Silver chloride was one of the many elements tested in 1782 by Jean Senebier, the Chief Librarian of Geneva, in order to determine the time required for various degrees of light to darken the chemical salts. He also studied the reaction of the chloride to different portions of the spectrum, foreshadowing later experiments that demonstrated that the spectrum reproduced itself in natural colors on the chloride surface.

Two 18th-century English scientists, Dr. William Lewis and Joseph Priestley, formed the link between these early chemical experiments and later efforts to find a way to retain an image produced by the darkening of silver halides by light. The notebooks of Dr. Lewis, who had repeated Schulze's experiments by painting designs in silver nitrate on white bone that he exposed to sunlight, were acquired by Josiah Wedgwood, the British commercial potter, who may have become interested in finding a photochemical process when he was commissioned by Catherine the Great

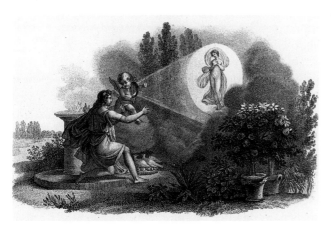

216. UNKNOWN. *The Miraculous Mirror*, 18th century. Engraving. International Museum of Photography at George Eastman House, Rochester, N.Y.

of Russia to provide a table service with 1,282 views of country mansions and gardens, many of which were made with the aid of the *camera obscura*.[3] As a member of Wedgwood's Lunar Society discussion group, Priestley imparted information about the photochemical properties of silver halides that he gathered from his association with prominent figures in the European scientific community. In 1802, young Thomas Wedgwood attempted to transfer paintings on glass to white leather and paper moistened with a solution of nitrate of silver, describing the resulting negative image as follows: "where the light is unaltered, the color of the nitrate is deepest."[4] Neither Wedgwood nor his associate in the experiments, chemist Humphry Davy, were able to find a way to arrest the action of light on the silver salts; unless kept in the dark the picture eventually was completely obliterated. Their early experiments demonstrated, however, that it was possible to chemically transfer by means of light not only pictures but objects in profile such as leaves and fabrics.

First Successful Experiments

Interest in the practical uses of new scientific discoveries developed among both the enlightened British and French bourgeoisie during the early years of the 19th century and led the brothers Joseph Nicéphore Niépce (*pl. no. 4*) and Claude Niépce, who returned to the family estates at Chalon-sur-Saône after the Napoleonic Wars, to become involved with a series of inventions, including a motor-driven rivercraft (the *pyréolophore*), a method of making indigo dye, a device for printing lithographs, and a process for obtaining images by the action of light. In 1816, Nicéphore and Claude produced an image in the *camera obscura* using paper sensitized with silver chloride,[5] but because the tones were inverted and efforts to make positive prints were unsuccessful, Nicéphore eventually turned to using bitumen, an ingredient in resist varnish that hardens and becomes insoluble when exposed to light. Between 1822 and 1827, while his brother was abroad, Nicéphore produced transfers of engravings, first on glass and then on pewter, by coating the plates with bitumen, placing them against engravings made translucent by oiling or varnishing, and exposing the sandwich to sunlight. The bitumen hardened on the portions not covered by the lines of the print and remained soluble on the rest of the plate; after washing, an image appeared with the bare pewter forming the lines. It was Niépce's plan to etch these plates, thus creating an intaglio matrix from which inked prints might be pulled. Heliography, as he called this process, was the forerunner of photomechanical printing processes.

In the summer of 1827, Niépce exposed a pewter plate coated with bitumen in the *camera obscura*, achieving after some eight hours an image of a dovecote on his estate at Le Gras (*pl. no. 6*). Although he changed from pewter to silver and silver-coated copper plates, and introduced iodine to increase the sensitivity of the silver surface to light, he was unable to decrease substantially the exposure time needed to obtain an image. In his search for improved optical elements for his work, Niépce had contacted the Parisian optical-instrument maker Vincent Chevalier, who in turn acquainted scenic designer and Diorama owner Jacques Louis Mandé Daguerre with the nature of the experimentation at Le Gras. Daguerre's parallel interest in obtaining a permanent image in the *camera obscura* led to contacts with Niépce and resulted in a meeting in 1827 and the signing of a deed of partnership in 1829 to pursue the process together.

Following Niépce's death in 1833, activity shifted to Paris as Daguerre continued to work with iodized silver plates, discarding bitumen altogether. However, he, too, was not notably successful in reducing the time needed for the image to appear until 1835, when he hit upon a phenomenon known as latent development, which means that the photographer does not have to wait to see the image appear on the plate during exposure, but can bring it out by chemical development—in this case, mercury vapor—making possible a radical reduction in exposure time. A problem that remained unsolved was how to stop the continued action of light on the silver halides, which caused the image to darken until it was no longer visible, but in 1837 Daguerre found a way to arrest the action of light with a bath of sodium chloride (common table salt), a method he used until March, 1839, when he learned about the property of hypo (hyposulphite of soda now called sodium thiosulphite) to wash away unexposed silver salts indirectly from its discoverer, the English scientist John Herschel. The daguerreotype, as he called his product, was delicate—easily damaged by fingerprints and atmospheric conditions—and therefore needed the protection of being enclosed in a case under glass (*pl. no. 33*).

In 1833, at about the same time as Daguerre's early experiments, English scientist and mathematician William Henry Fox Talbot conceived of making a permanent image of what could be seen in the *camera obscura*; within two years he had succeeded in obtaining pictures by the action of light on paper treated with alternate washes of sodium chloride and silver nitrate. His first pictures were of flat objects, made by placing leaves, lace, or translucent engravings against the sensitized paper and exposing both to sunlight to produce a tonally and spatially inverted image in monochrome on the paper. Also in 1835, Talbot carried this discovery a step forward when he produced a one-inch-square negative image of his ancestral home, Lacock

Abbey *(pl. no. 20)*, made by inserting sensitized paper in a very small camera with a short focal length (distance between lens and film) for about ten minutes in bright sunshine. To stabilize these early images, Talbot employed either potassium iodide or salt, but early in 1839 he changed to hypo on the advice of Herschel. Calling these images "photogenic drawings," Talbot proposed to correct their tonal and spatial inversions by placing another sheet of silver-sensitized paper against the negative image (waxed to make it translucent) and exposing both to light, but it is doubtful if he actually made such positive prints at this time.[6]

Apart from the profoundly ingenious concept of a negative from which multiple positives might be made, Talbot's most significant discovery was latent development, which he arrived at independently in 1840. He sensitized paper with a combination of chemical solutions that he called gallo-nitrate of silver, exposed it in the camera, removed the seemingly blank paper after a time and bathed it in the same chemical solution, during which time the image gradually appeared. With exposure time reduced by chemical development to as little as 30 seconds on a bright day, Talbot took out his first patent in February, 1841, for a negative/positive process he called the calotype.

Other Experiments

Widespread interest during the early 19th century in light-related phenomena led to similar experiments by others; among them, Hercules Florence, a French-born artist who had joined a Russian expedition to the interior of Brazil in 1828, successfully produced direct positive

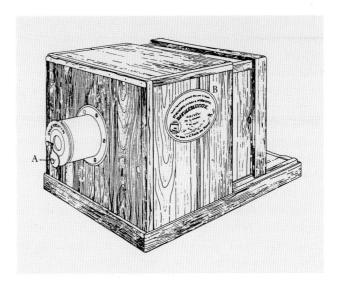

219. *Daguerre-Giroux Camera.* Giroux's camera of 1839, based on Daguerre's patent, was the first camera to be sold in any numbers to the public. The lens was fitted with a pivoted cover plate (A), which acted as a shutter. A plaque (B) bore Daguerre's signature and Giroux's seal.

prints. In 1833, Florence began to work with paper sensitized with silver salts (the exact nature of which are unknown) in an effort to produce images of drawings by a process he actually called photography (from the Greek *phos*—light—and *graphos*—writing), apparently the first recorded use of the word that came into general usage in Europe in 1839. However, because he was isolated from the mainstream of scientific invention and was unable to find an effective fixing agent, Florence and his work were forgotten until 1973 when his journals and examples of his work came to light in Brazil.[7]

In May, 1839, Hippolyte Bayard, a French civil servant, announced a direct positive process for obtaining photographic images on paper, which he achieved by darkening a sheet of paper with silver chloride and potassium iodide, upon which light acted as a bleach when the plate was exposed in the camera. Bayard's contribution was largely ignored at the time owing to the official support for the daguerreotype,[8] but since some photographers in France evinced strong interest in a paper process in preference to the daguerreotype, experimentation along this line continued.

By 1847, Louis Désiré Blanquart-Evrard, a leading figure in the improvement of the calotype in France, had developed a method of bathing the paper in solutions of potassium iodide and silver nitrate rather than brushing these chemical baths on the surface as Talbot had done. Exposed in a damp state (as Talbot's had been), the resulting negative showed improved tonal range because the paper fibers were more evenly saturated.

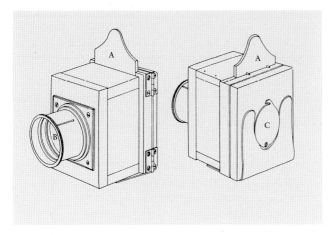

218. *Talbot's Mousetrap Camera.* In 1839 Talbot made cameras with removable paper-holders (A). The image produced by the lens (B) on the thin, sensitive paper could be inspected from behind through a hole, which normally was covered by a pivoted brass plate (C).

Further improvements in definition followed when French painter Gustave Le Gray developed the wax paper negative—a method of using white wax on the paper negative before it was sensitized. After immersion in a solution of rice water, sugar of milk, potassium or ammonium iodide, and potassium bromide, and sensitizing in silver nitrate and acetic acid, the paper was ready to use in either damp or dry state. Le Gray's attentiveness to the aesthetics of photography led him to experiment with the timing of various chemical baths in an effort to produce different colorations in his prints.

In 1839 Herschel had suggested glass as a support for negatives, but it was not until 1847 that a procedure for making albumen negatives on glass plates evolved. Claude Félix Abel Niepce de Saint-Victor (a relative of the Niépce brothers) proposed a mixture of egg white with potassium iodide and sodium chloride to form a transparent coating on glass, which then was immersed in silver nitrate solution and after exposure developed in gallic and pyrogallic acid. Though this process produced a negative without texture, the material reacted too slowly to light to be of use to commercial portraitists; however, it did serve as an excellent means of making glass lantern slides.

Those working with glass then turned to collodion, a derivative of guncotton that became liquid, transparent, and sticky when dissolved in alcohol.[9] Experiments with this substance were undertaken by Le Gray and Robert Bingham in France in 1850, but the first practicable directions for using collodion as a binder for light-sensitive silver salts appeared in 1850 and 1851 in a two-part article in *The Chemist* written by Frederick Archer, an English sculptor. By pouring the viscous collodion liquid containing potassium iodide (later potassium bromide was added) evenly onto a glass plate, then immersing the plate in a silver nitrate bath to form silver iodide, exposure time was shortened considerably, but only if the plate was used immediately in its wet state. Furthermore, because it had to be developed—usually in ferrous sulphate—while still moist, the "wet plate," as it came to be called, made portable darkrooms for out-of-doors work a necessity.

Before the collodion process became exclusively used for negatives, it enjoyed a period of popularity in the form of the glass positive, or Ambrotype as its American version, patented in 1854 by James Ambrose Cutting of Boston, was called. By adding chemicals to the developer and backing the glass negative either with black cloth or black varnish, the image was reversed visually from a negative into a one-of-a-kind positive *(pl. no. 53)* that usually was presented to the client encased in the same fashion as a daguerreotype. Sensitized collodion also figured in the production of direct positive images on sheet iron. Known generally as tintype, but also called Ferrotype and Melainotype, the

process was discovered in 1853 in France and in 1856 in both England and the United States; a dry tintype process was introduced in 1891. Since tintypes were quickly made (requiring just over a minute from start to finish), inexpensive to produce, and easy to send through the mails, they were popular with soldiers during the American Civil War and have continued to be made of and for working-class people on into the 20th century.

To prevent silver salts from penetrating the irregular fiber structures or affecting the chemical sizings used in paper manufacture, the same albumen or egg white suggested by Niepce de Saint-Victor as a binder for glass negatives was advanced as a filler to close the pores of photographic printing papers. The first practicable process for making albumen paper, announced in 1850 by Blanquart-Evrard, required coating the paper with a mixture of egg white and either salt or ammonium chloride, after which it was dried and kept until needed. Before exposure, the paper was sensitized by floating it albumen-side down in a strong solution of silver nitrate; after drying it was exposed in contact with a negative for so long as was needed to achieve a visible image—that is, no chemical developer was used. Blanquart-Evrard also contrived a paper that was chemically developed in gallic acid after exposure with the negative—a procedure that enabled his printing plant at Lille to turn out from 300 to 400 prints a day from a single negative. Fine prints resulted when, after exposure of both negative and sensitized paper in a

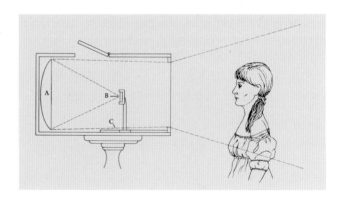

220. *Wolcott Camera.* In Wolcott's camera, as patented in 1840, a large, concave mirror (A) was placed at the back of an oblong box. A small, sensitized daguerreotype plate (B) was fitted into a wire frame and was held in place by a spring clip. A surviving example of the camera has, however, a more elaborate holder. The frame could be moved backward and forward on a track (C) to focus the image on the sensitive surface of the plate, which faced the mirror. The exposure was made by opening a door on the camera front. Other doors gave access to the mirror and the plate frame and allowed the focus to be checked. The camera took plates measuring about 2 x 2.5 inches (51 x 64 mm).

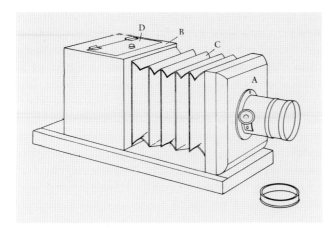

221. *Lewis Folding Camera*. The Lewis daguerreotype camera of 1851 had a fixed, chamfered front panel (A), connected to a sliding box (B) at the rear by bellows (C), which gave extra extension. A door (D) gave access to the plate-holder and focusing screen.

dampened state in the camera, the print was developed in gallic acid, left for a longer period of time in the fixing bath, and exposed to sunlight afterward in order to change its color from russet to a deep, rich, almost-black tonality. During the mid-1850s, albumen papers with a glossy surface became popular. The combination of collodion glass negative and albumen paper made large-scale commercial printing feasible, but because "no preparation made for photography caused so many complaints as albumen paper,"[10] the search for a stable printing medium continued.

The carbon process, based on researches into the light sensitivity of dichromate (then called bichromate) of potassium by Scottish scientist Mungo Ponton in 1839 (continued in France by Edmond Becquerel in 1840 and Alphonse Poitevin in 1855, and in England by John Pouncy in 1858), substituted chromated gelatin mixed with pigment for silver salts as a light-sensitive agent for positive prints. When exposed against a negative, a sheet of paper coated with a mixture of gelatin, coloring matter—which initially was carbon black, hence the name—and potassium dichromate received the image in proportion to the amount of light passing through the negative; where thin, the gelatin hardened, where dense—the light areas of the scene—it remained soluble and was washed away with warm water after exposure. In its early applications, the light areas in the carbon print tended to become completely washed out, but this problem was solved in 1864 when British inventor Joseph Wilson Swan discovered that by using carbon tissue coated with pigmented gelatin in conjunction with a transfer tissue of clear gelatin, the lightest tonalities were retained. This material became commercially available in 1866, and Swan shortly thereafter sold franchises for the mass production of carbon prints to the Autotype Company in England, Adolphe Braun in Dornach, and Franz Hanfstaengl in Munich.

Another nonsilver process, the cyanotype or blueprint (first described by Sir John Herschel in 1842) is based on the photosensitivity of ferric (iron) salts, which are reduced by light to a ferrous state so it can thereby combine with other salts to produce an image. For his experiments, Herschel used either ferric chloride or ferric ammonium citrate, and potassium ferricyanide. In the mid-1840s, this simple and inexpensive system was used to reproduce botanical specimens *(pl. no. 329)*, and around 1890 it attracted amateur photographers, but its use during the 20th century has been mainly for duplicating industrial drawings. While in the past, aesthetic photographers found the brilliant blue color intrusive, cyanotype is one of the processes currently being employed by contemporary artistic photographers.

A somewhat different system of obtaining permanent nonsilver positive prints, patented in 1865 as the Woodburytype after its inventor Walter Woodbury, involved making a relief image from a negative in dichromated gelatin from which a thin lead mold was formed in a hydraulic press. Filled with warm, pigmented gelatinous ink, the mold was brought into contact with the paper in a hand press, thereby transferring the pigmented image from mold

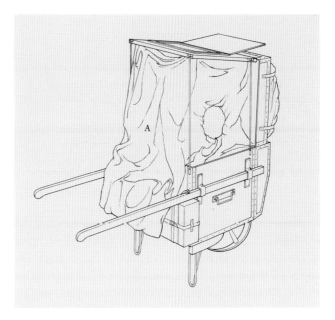

222. *Edwards' Dark-Tent*. The "perambulator" or "wheelbarrow" form of dark-tent devised by Ernest Edwards was popular with wet-collodion photographers. When packed up, the handcart was easily taken along. All the apparatus and chemicals required were stowed in compartments under the lid, which formed the back of the tent (A) when it was all rigged.

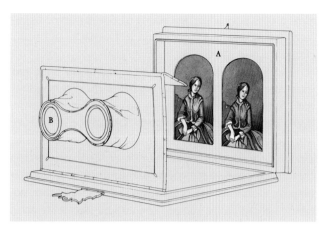

223. *Claudet Stereoscope*. The top opened up to form the back, into which the stereoscopic daguerreotypes (A) were fitted; the lenses (B) were set in telescoping mounts.

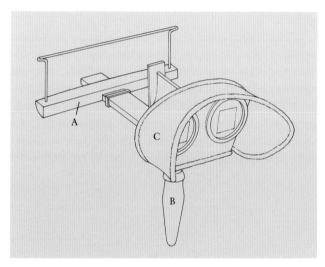

224. *Holmes-Bates Stereoscope*. Joseph Bates manufactured an inexpensive viewer invented in 1861 by Oliver Wendell Holmes; it was sold in this improved form from the mid-1860s until 1939. The stereograph was held on the cross-piece (A), which could be slid up and down the central strip for focusing. A folding handle (B) and a curved eyeshade (C) were fitted.

to paper surface under pressure and necessitating, after the hardening of the gelatin in an alum bath, the trimming of its borders to remove the colored ink that had overrun the edges of the image. A photomechanical, rather than a strictly photochemical procedure, Woodburytype (confusingly called *photoglyptie* in France) produced rich-looking prints without grain structure of any kind.

Early Equipment

The earliest cameras used by Niépce, Daguerre, and Talbot were modeled on *camera obscurae* in use since the

17th century. Those of Niépce and Daguerre consisted of two rectangular boxes, one sliding into the other, with an aperture to receive the lens and a place to position the plate. Talbot's first small instruments, referred to as "mousetraps" *(pl. no. 218)*, were crude wooden boxes; later British and French makers provided him with better-crafted instruments that incorporated besides the lens a hole fitted with a cork or brass cover through which one could check focus and exposure. The first commercial photographic camera was designed by Daguerre and was manufactured by Alphonse Giroux (a relative by marriage) from 1839 on *(pl. no. 219)*. A unique design was made by Alexander S. Wolcott, an American who in 1840 substituted for the lens a concave mirror that produced a brighter image by concentrating the light rays and reflecting them onto the surface of the daguerreotype plate *(pl. no. 220)*. Conical and metal cameras appeared in Austria and Germany in 1841, the same year that a cylindrical instrument enclosed in a wooden box was manufactured in Paris, but these did not catch on. A bellows focusing system for a camera was first suggested in 1839, but did not come into use until 1851 when it was incorporated into a rectangular camera made by the firm of W. and W. H. Lewis in New York *(pl. no. 221)*. A number of folding cameras, on view first at the Great Exhibition in 1851, with either rectangular or tapered bellows, were manufactured during the 1850s mainly by British firms. By the 1860s many bellows cameras included rising fronts, and swing fronts and backs.

The first arc-pivoted camera, devised in 1844 by Friederich von Martens, was capable of taking a panoramic view of about 150 degrees on a curved daguerreotype plate measuring approximately 4½ by 15 inches. Curved glass plates were required for the similar apparatus in use during the collodion era. A Pantascope camera, patented in England in 1862 by John R. Johnson and John A. Harrison, rotated on a circular base, as a holder containing a wet collodion plate was moved by a string and pulley arrangement past an exposing slot.

Photographic accessories such as buffing tools and sensitizing boxes had been necessary for daguerreotyping; during the collodion or wet plate era, photographers in the field were required to carry even greater amounts of additional equipment besides camera and tripod. Portable handcarts and perambulator tents were devised to stow chemicals and apparatus and to allow the photographer to erect a light-tight tent virtually anywhere in order to sensitize plates before exposure and to develop them immediately afterward. The most popular design in England, that of Ernest Edwards, was a type of suitcase mounted on a wheelbarrow or tripod that opened to form a darkroom within a cloth tent *(pl. no. 222)*.

The stereoscope, conceived by Charles Wheatstone in

1832 before the invention of photography, originally was a device that permitted a view by means of mirrors of a pair of superimposed pictures that had been drawn as if seen by each eye individually, but appeared to the viewer to be a single three-dimensional image. In 1849, Scottish scientist David Brewster adapted the stereoscopic principle to lenticular viewing, devising a viewer with two lenses placed about 2½ inches apart laterally for viewing the stereograph —an image consisting of two views appearing side by side either on a daguerreotype plate, a glass plate, or on paper mounted on cardboard. Stereographic calotypes were made for viewing by Talbot, Henry Collen, and Thomas Malone after photography was invented. Stereographs and stereoscopes manufactured by the French optical firm of Duboscq and shown at the Great Exposition in 1851 became exceedingly popular and were produced for all tastes and pocketbooks. The viewers ranged from the simple devices invented by Antoine Claudet *(pl. no. 223)* and Oliver Wendell Holmes *(pl. no. 224)* to elaborately decorated models for the very wealthy to large stationary floor viewers that housed hundreds of cards that could be rotated past the eyepieces.

Stereographic views could be made by moving a single camera laterally, a few inches, but care was needed to make sure that the two images were properly correlated. In 1853,

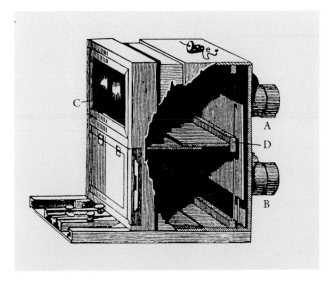

226. *Disdéri Camera.* André Adolphe Eugène Disdéri's stereoscopic camera of c. 1864: the upper compartment was equipped with a pair of lenses (A), which were matched to the taking lenses (B) and were focused on a ground-glass screen (C), fitted in the back of the compartment in the same plane as the plate-holder below. A vertical, sliding shutter (D) was opened by pulling a string (E).

a means of moving the camera laterally along a track was devised. Another method, first described by John A. Spencer in England in 1854, involved moving a plateholder in a stationary camera equipped with an internal septum so that the images did not overlap. During the 1850s, a binocular camera with two lenses was patented in France by Achille Quinet, and a twin-lens stereoscopic camera designed by John Benjamin Dancer *(pl. no. 225)* was offered for general sale in 1856. A number of other designs appeared during the 1860s, including a folding bellows binocular camera made by George Hare and a stereoscopic sliding box camera divided into an upper and lower compartment, each with a pair of lenses, designed by André Eugène Disdéri *(pl. no. 226)*.

In 1857, David A. Woodward, an American artist, patented a device he called a "solar microscope or magic lantern" [11] for the enlargement of photographic negatives. A mirror fixed at a 45-degree angle to receive the rays of the sun reflected them onto a condensing lens inside a box into which a negative on paper or glass could be fitted, throwing an enlargement of the image onto a sensitized support placed at a suitable distance away. Woodward actively promoted this device in the United States and Europe. Along with a similar apparatus developed by the Belgian scientist Desiré von Monckhoven, this forerunner of the enlarger proved to be a significant tool in graphic as well as photographic portraiture.

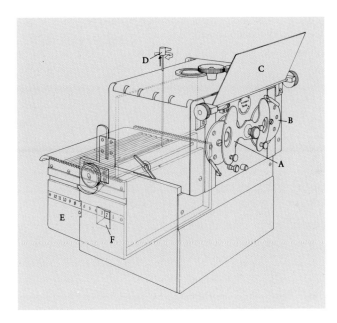

225. *Dancer Camera.* Dancer's stereoscopic camera of 1856 had two lenses, which were fitted with a pivoted shutter (A) and with aperture wheels (B). In addition, some models had a lens shade (C) in the form of a pivoted flap. Dry plates could be drawn up, one by one, by means of a screwed rod (D), from a plate-changing box (E). The number on the exposed plate could be read through a window (F).

A 19th-Century Forerunner of Photojournalism— The Execution of the Lincoln Conspirators

The events that followed the assassination of Abraham Lincoln in the Presidential Box at the Ford Theater on the night of April 14, 1865, provided sensational pictorial material for graphic artists and photographers. Sketch artists for the weekly magazines turned out drawings of the theater interior, the death scene, the funeral cortege, and the capture of those involved, but it is the photographs of the individual conspirators, and above all of the hanging of four of them on July 7th, that remain by far the most vivid representations of this tragedy. The portraits, other than that of Booth, who perished in an ambush during his capture, were made by Alexander Gardner, presumably aboard the ironclad monitors *Montauk* and *Saugus*, where the conspirators were held while awaiting trial by a military tribunal. For the views of the actual execution, Gardner set up his camera on a roof overlooking the gallows erected in the courtyard of the Arsenal (or Old) Penitentiary and made a sequence of seven exposures of the preparations for and the hanging of George Atzerodt, David E. Herold, Lewis Payne, and Mary E. Surratt. This series appears to be the first photographic picture story of an event as it happened, and was all the more remarkable because of the secrecy surrounding the affair. While it was not possible at the time to reproduce these images by halftone in the popular press, this group of photographs signaled the important role that sequential images would play in news reporting in the future.

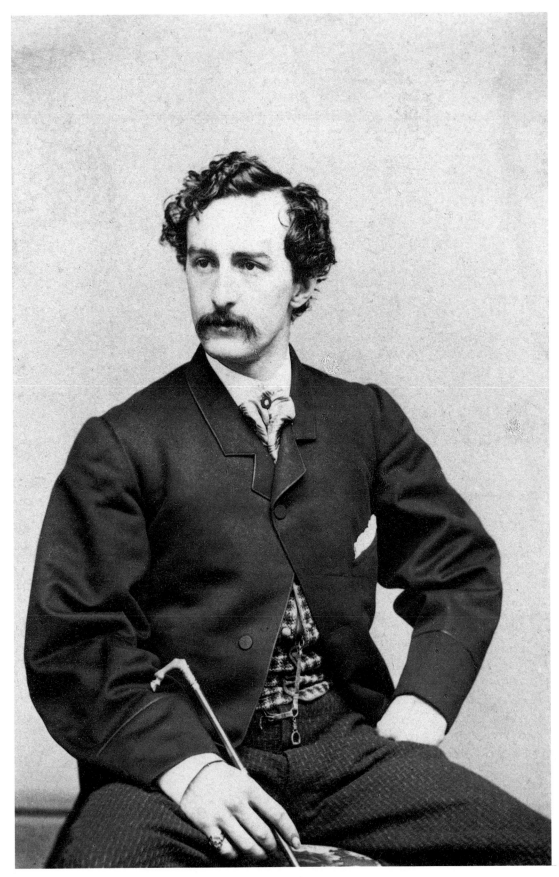

227. UNKNOWN PHOTOGRAPHER. *John Wilkes Booth*, n.d. Albumen *carte-de-visite*.
International Museum of Photography at George Eastman House, Rochester, N.Y.

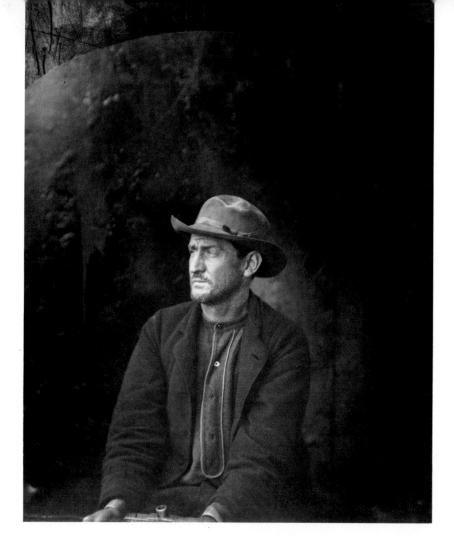

228. ALEXANDER GARDNER. *Edward Spangler, a Conspirator*, April, 1865. Albumen print. Library of Congress, Washington, D.C.

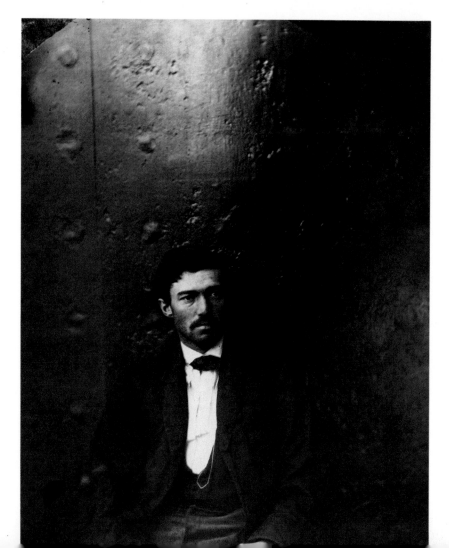

229. ALEXANDER GARDNER. *Samuel Arnold, a Conspirator*, April, 1865. Albumen print. Library of Congress, Washington, D.C.

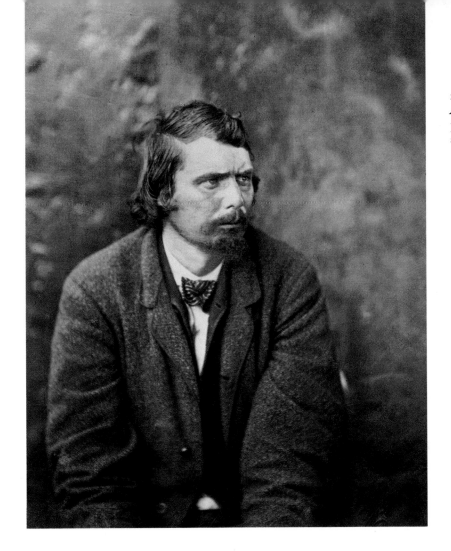

230. ALEXANDER GARDNER. *George A. Atzerodt, a Conspirator*, April, 1865. Albumen print. International Museum of Photography at George Eastman House, Rochester, N.Y.

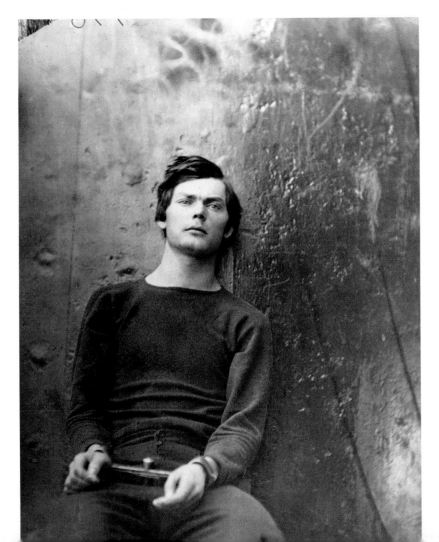

231. ALEXANDER GARDNER. *Lewis Payne, a Conspirator, in Sweater, Seated and Manacled*, April, 1865. Albumen print. Library of Congress, Washington, D.C.

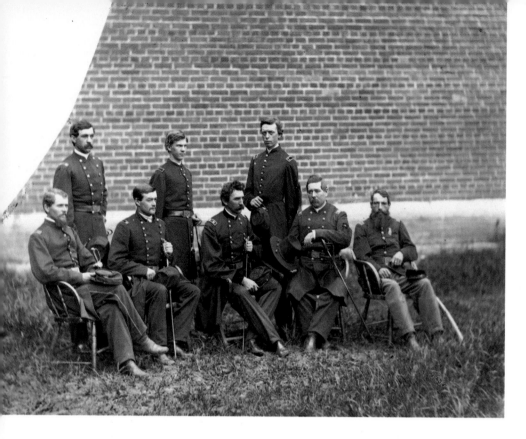

232. ALEXANDER GARDNER. *General John F. Hartranft and Staff, Responsible for Securing the Conspirators at the Arsenal. Left to Right: Capt. R. A. Watts, Lt. Col. George W. Frederick, Lt. Col. William H. H. McCall, Lt. D. H. Geissinger, Gen. Hartranft, unknown, Col. L. A. Dodd, Capt. Christian Rath*, 1865. (Cracked Plate). Albumen print. Library of Congress, Washington, D.C.

233. ALEXANDER GARDNER. *Execution of the Conspirators: Scaffold Ready for Use and Crowd in Yard, Seen from the Roof of the Arsenal, Washington, D.C.*, July 7, 1865. Albumen print. Library of Congress, Washington, D.C.

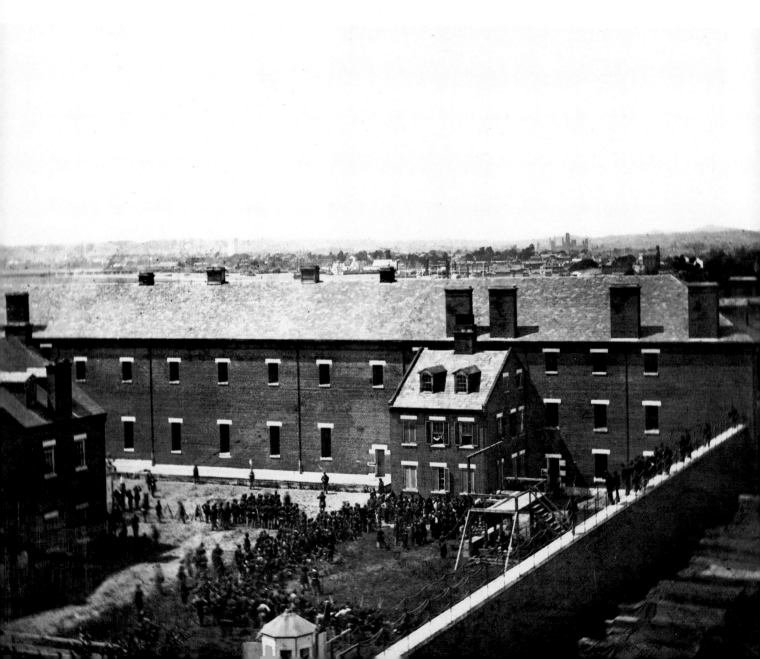

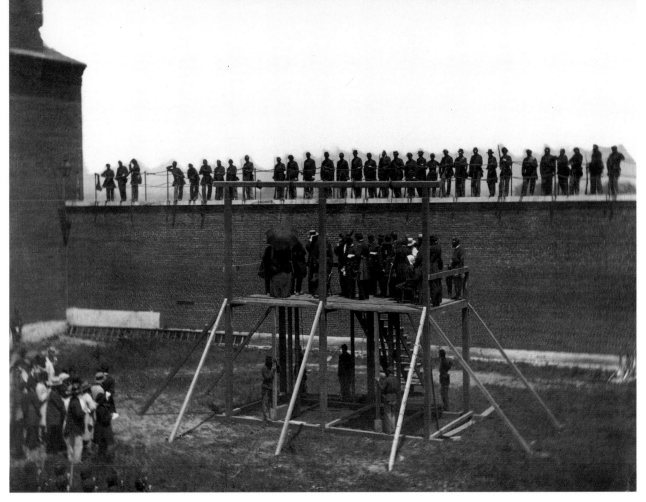

234. ALEXANDER GARDNER. *The Four Condemned Conspirators (Mrs. Surratt, Payne, Herold, Atzerodt), with Officers and Others on the Scaffold; Guards on the Wall, Washington, D.C.*, July 7, 1865. Albumen print. Library of Congress, Washington, D.C.

235. ALEXANDER GARDNER. *General John F. Hartranft Reading the Death Warrant to the Conspirators on the Scaffold, Washington, D.C.*, July 7, 1865. Albumen print. Library of Congress, Washington, D.C.

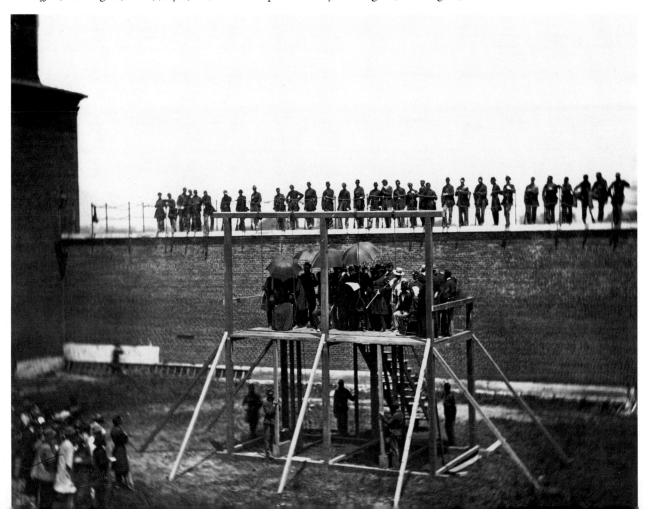

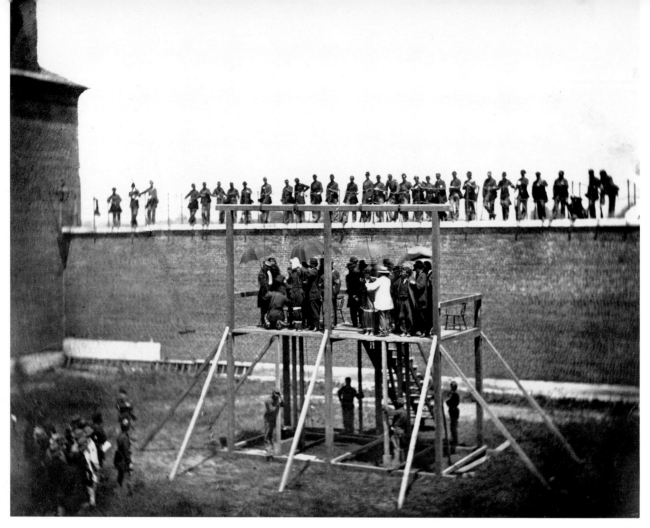

236. ALEXANDER GARDNER. *Adjusting the Ropes for Hanging the Conspirators, Washington, D.C.*,
July 7, 1865. Albumen print. Library of Congress, Washington, D.C.

237. ALEXANDER GARDNER. *Hanging at Washington Arsenal; Hooded Bodies of the Four Conspirators; Crowd Departing,*
Washington, D.C., July 7, 1865. Albumen print. International Museum of Photography at George Eastman House, Rochester, N.Y.

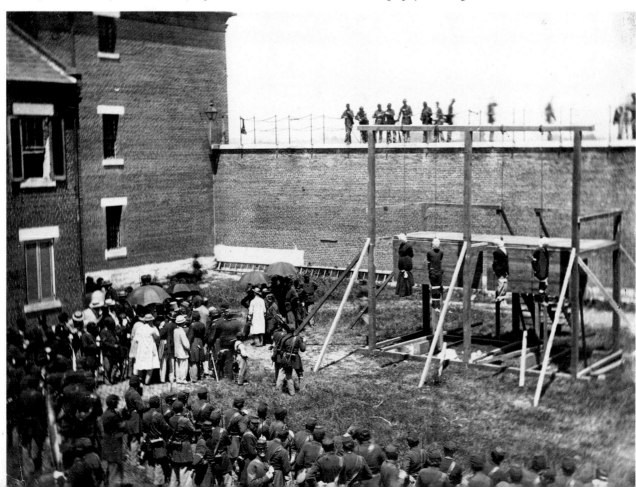

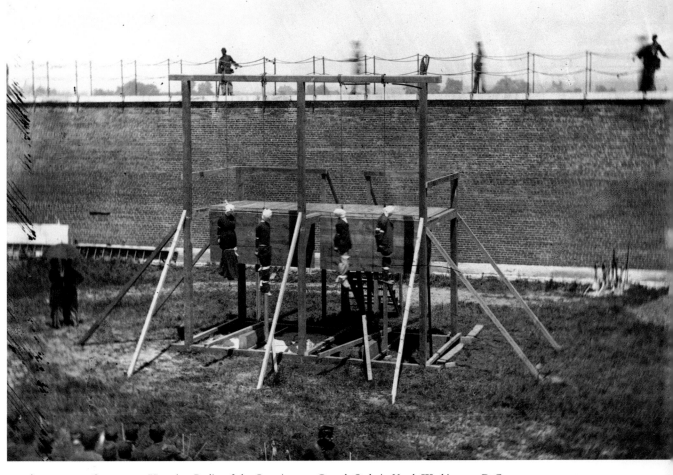

238. ALEXANDER GARDNER. *Hanging Bodies of the Conspirators; Guards Only in Yard, Washington, D.C.,* July 7, 1865. Albumen print. Library of Congress, Washington, D.C.

239. ALEXANDER GARDNER. *Coffins and Open Graves Ready for the Conspirators' Bodies at Right of Scaffold, Washington, D.C.,* July 7, 1865. Albumen print. Library of Congress, Washington, D.C.

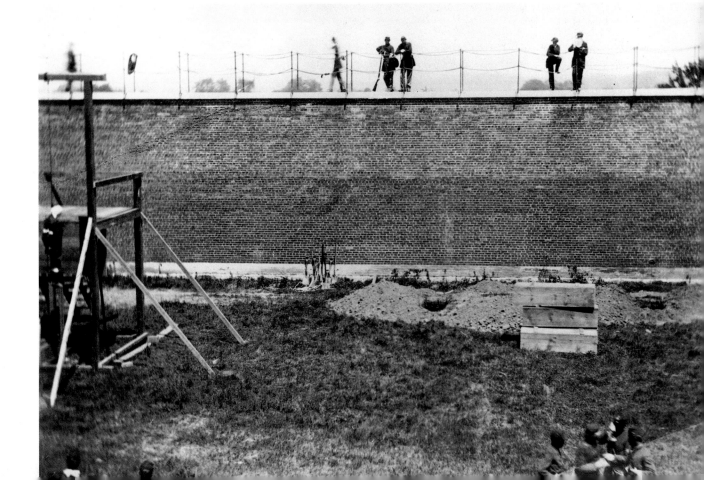

5.

PHOTOGRAPHY AND ART: THE FIRST PHASE

1839–1890

. . . of all the delusions that possess the human breast, few are so intractable as those about art.

—*Lady Elizabeth Eastlake, 1857*[1]

When photography was invented artists thought that it would bring ruin to art but it is shown that photography has been an ally of art, an educator of taste more powerful than a hundred academies of Design would have been. . . .

—*"Photography and Chromo-lithography," 1868*[2]

"IS PHOTOGRAPHY ART?" may seem a pointless question today. Surrounded as we are by thousands of photographs of every description, most of us take for granted that in addition to supplying information and seducing customers, camera images also serve as decoration, afford spiritual enrichment, and provide significant insights into the passing scene. But in the decades following the discovery of photography, this question reflected the search for ways to fit the mechanical medium into the traditional schemes of artistic expression. Responses by photographers, which included the selection of appropriate themes and the creation of synthetic works, established directions that continue to animate photography today. And while some photographers used the camera to emulate the subjects and styles of "high" art, graphic artists turned to photographs for information and ideas. The intriguing interplay that ensued also has remained a significant issue in the visual arts. Photographs that reproduce art objects also have had a profound effect on the democratization of public taste and knowledge, changing public perceptions of visual culture and making possible the establishment of art history as a serious discipline.

The much-publicized pronouncement by painter Paul Delaroche that the daguerreotype signaled the end of painting is perplexing because this clever artist also forecast the usefulness of the medium for graphic artists in a letter to François Arago in 1839.[3] Nevertheless, it is symptomatic of the swing between the outright rejection and qualified acceptance of the medium that was fairly typical of the artistic establishment. It was satirized in a group of cartoons by Nadar (*pl. nos. 240–241*) depicting an artistic community that denied photography's claims while using the medium to improve its own product. Discussion of the role of photography in art was especially spirited in France, where the internal policies of the Second Empire had created a large pool of artists, but it also was taken up by important voices in England. In both countries, public interest in this topic was a reflection of the belief that national stature and achievement in the arts were related. In central and southern Europe and the United States, where the arts played a lesser role, these matters were less frequently addressed.

From the maze of conflicting statements and heated articles on the subject, three main positions about the potential of camera art emerged. The simplest, entertained by many painters and a section of the public, was that photographs should not be considered "art" because they were made with a mechanical device and by physical and chemical phenomena instead of by human hand and spirit; to some, camera images seemed to have more in common with fabric produced by machinery in a mill than with handmade creations fired by inspiration. The second widely held view, shared by painters, some photographers, and some critics, was that photographs would be useful to art but should not be considered equal in creativeness to drawing and painting. Lastly, by assuming that the process was comparable to other replicatable techniques such as etching and lithography, a fair number of individuals realized that camera images were or could be as significant as handmade works of art and that they might have a beneficial influence on the arts and on culture in general.

Artists reacted to photography in various ways. Many portrait painters—miniaturists in particular—who realized that photography represented the "handwriting on the wall" became involved with daguerreotyping or paper photography; some incorporated it with painting, as in the case of Queen Victoria's painter Henry Collen, while others renounced painting altogether. Still other painters, the most prominent among them Ingres, began almost immediately to use photography to make a record of their own output and also to provide themselves with source material for poses and backgrounds, vigorously denying at the same time its influence on their vision or its claims as art. While there is no direct evidence to indicate that Ingres painted from daguerreotypes, it has been pointed out that in pose, cropping, and tonal range, the portraits made by the painter after Daguerre's invention virtually can be characterized as "enlarged daguerreotypes."[4] Yet, this politically and artistically conservative artist was outspoken in contesting photography's claims as art as well as the rights of photographers to legal protection when their images were used without permission. The irony of the situation was not lost on French journalist Ernest Lacan, who observed that "photography is like a mistress whom one cherishes and hides, about whom one speaks with joy but does not want others to mention."[5]

The view that photographs might be worthwhile to artists—acceptable for collecting facts, eliminating the drudgery of study from the live model, and expanding the possibilities of verisimilitude—was enunciated in considerable detail by Lacan and Francis Wey. The latter, a philologist as well as an art and literary critic, who eventually recognized that camera images could be inspired as well as informative, suggested that they would lead to greater naturalness in the graphic depiction of anatomy, clothing, likeness, expression, and landscape configuration. By studying photographs, true artists, he claimed, would be relieved of menial tasks and become free to devote themselves to the more important spiritual aspects of their work, while inept hacks would be driven from the field of graphic art.[6]

Wey left unstated what the incompetent artist might do as an alternative, but according to the influential French critic and poet Baudelaire, writing in response to an exhibition of photography at the Salon of 1859, lazy and "unendowed" painters would become photographers. Fired by a belief in art as an imaginative embodiment of cultivated ideas and dreams, Baudelaire regarded photography as "a very humble servant of art and science, like printing and stenography"—a medium largely unable to transcend "external reality."[7] For this critic as well as for other idealists, symbolists, and aesthetes, photography was linked with "the great industrial madness" of the time, which in their eyes exercised disastrous consequences on the spiritual qualities of life and art. Somewhat later, the noted art critic Charles Blanc made the same point when he observed that because "photography copies everything and explains nothing, it is blind to the realm of the spirit."[8]

Eugène Delacroix was the most prominent of the French artists who welcomed photography as helpmate but recognized its limitations. Regretting that "such a wonderful invention" had arrived so late in his lifetime, he still took lessons in daguerreotyping, made *cliché verre* prints *(see below)*, joined the recently established *Société héliographique*, and both commissioned and collected photographs. These included studies of the nude made by the amateur Eugène Durieu *(pl. no. 242)*, with whom the artist collaborated on arranging the poses. Delacroix's enthusiasm for the medium can be sensed in a journal entry noting that if photographs were used as they should be, an artist might "raise himself to heights that we do not yet know."[9]

The question of whether the photograph was document or art aroused interest in England also. *A Popular Treatise on the Art of Photography*, an 1841 work by Robert Hunt, emphasized processes rather than aesthetic matters, but noted that "an improvement of public taste," which had devolved from the fact that "nature in her rudest forms is more beautiful than any human production," already was discernible because of photography.[10] The most important statement on this matter was the previously mentioned

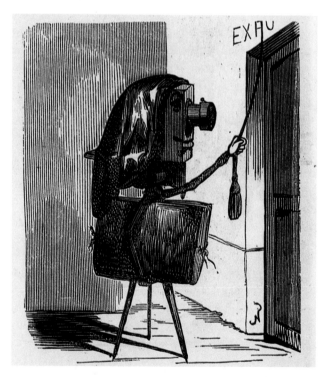 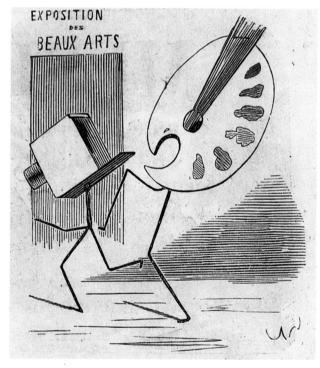

240–241. NADAR (GASPARD FÉLIX TOURNACHON). Two cartoons. "Photography asking for just a little place in the exhibition of fine arts." Engraving from *Petit journal pour rire*, 1855. "The ingratitude of painting refusing the smallest place in its exhibition to photography to whom it owes so much." Engravings from *Le journal amusant*, 1857. Bibliothèque Nationale, Paris.

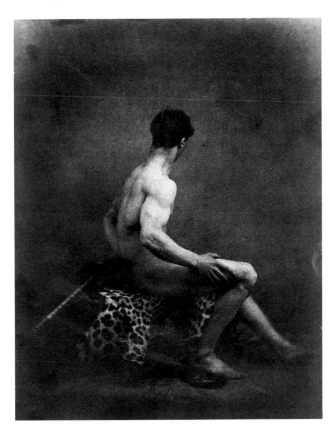

242. EUGÈNE DURIEU. *Figure Study No. 6*, c. 1853.
Albumen print. Bibliothèque Nationale, Paris.

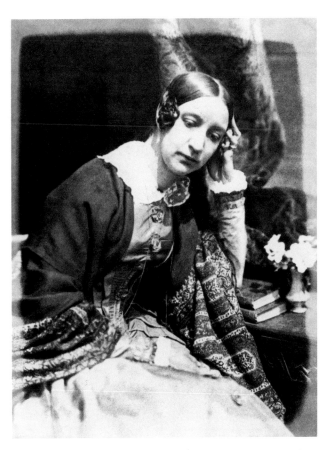

243. DAVID OCTAVIUS HILL and ROBERT ADAMSON.
Portrait of Elizabeth Rigby, Later Lady Eastlake, c. 1845.
Calotype. National Portrait Gallery, London.

unsigned article by Lady Eastlake, "Photography" *(pl. no. 243)*. Concerned with the relationship of "truth" and "reality" to "beauty," she contended that while depictions of the first two qualities were acceptable functions of the camera image, art expression was expected to be beautiful also. And beauty was a result of refinement, taste, spirituality, genius, or intellect—qualities not found in minutely detailed super-realistic visual descriptions made by machine. This formulation was addressed to collodion–albumen technology and enabled her to exempt the "Rembrandt-like" calotypes of Hill and Adamson from her condemnation. In addition to the broadly handled treatment seen in her own portrait or in *The Misses Binny and Miss Monro (pl. no. 52)*, for example, Hill's and Adamson's images expressed the refinement of sentiment that Lady Eastlake considered an artistic necessity. She concluded that while photography had a role to play, it should not be "constrained" into "competition" with art; a more stringent viewpoint led critic Philip Gilbert Hamerton to dismiss camera images as "narrow in range, emphatic in assertion, telling one truth for ten falsehoods."[11]

These writers reflected the opposition of a section of the cultural elite in England and France to the "cheapening of art," which the growing acceptance and purchase of camera pictures by the middle class represented. Collodion technology made photographic images a common sight in the shop windows of Regent Street and Piccadilly in London and the commercial boulevards of Paris. In London, for example, there were at the time some 130 commercial establishments (besides well-known individual photographers like Fenton and Rejlander) where portraits, landscapes, genre scenes, and photographic reproductions of works of art could be bought in regular and stereograph formats. This appeal to the middle class convinced the elite that photographs would foster a taste for verisimilitude instead of ideality, even though some critics recognized that the work of individual photographers might display an uplifting style and substance that was consonant with art.

John Ruskin, the most eminent figure in both English and American art at mid-century, first welcomed photography as the only 19th-century mechanical invention of value, and then reversed himself completely and denounced it as trivial.[12] He made and collected daguerreotypes as well

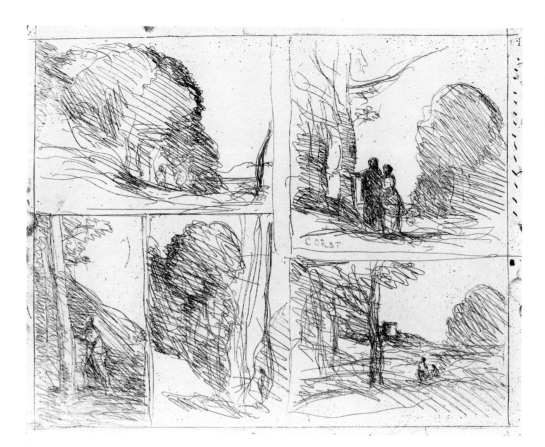

as paper prints of architectural and landscape subjects, and counseled their use to students and readers of his *Elements of Drawing*. Both academic and Pre-Raphaelite painters, among them William Frith, John Millais, Ford Madox Brown, Dante Gabriel Rossetti, and the American Pre-Raphaelite William Stillman, employed photographs of costumes, interiors, models, and landscapes taken from various vantage points as study materials. While they insisted that their canvases were painted strictly from nature, some of their productions seem close enough in vision to extant photographs to suggest "that the camera has insinuated itself" into the work.[13] English painters may have been even more reticent than the French about acknowledging their use of photographs because of the frequent insistence in the British press that art must be made by hand to display a high order of feeling and inspiration.

The 20 years following the introduction of collodion in 1851 was a period of increased activity by the photographic community to advance the medium's claims as art. Societies and publications were founded in England, France, Germany, Italy, and the United States, with the Photographic Society of London (now the Royal Photographic Society) and the *Société Française de Photographie*, established in 1853 and 1854 respectively, still in existence. Professional publications, including *La Lumière* in Paris, the *Photographic Journal* in London, and others in Italy, Germany, and the

United States, were in the vanguard of discussions about photographic art, devoting space to reviews of exhibitions of painting as well as photography.

Between 1851 and 1862, individual photographers, among them Antoine Claudet, André Adolphe Disdéri, and numbers of the now-forgotten, joined artistic photographers Rejlander, Henry Peach Robinson, and William Lake Price in publishing articles and letters to the professional journals that attempted to analyze the aesthetic similarities and differences between graphic works and photographs and to decide if photography was or was not Art. Notwithstanding their long-winded, often repetitious contentions, the photographers and their allies evolved a point of view about the medium that still forms the basis of photographic aesthetics today. Summed up in a piece by an unknown author that appeared in the *Photographic Journal* at the beginning of 1862, ostensibly it addressed the immediate question of whether photography should be hung in the Fine Arts or Industrial Section of the forthcoming International Exposition. The author observed that "the question is not whether photography is fine art per se—neither painting nor sculpture can make that claim—but whether it is capable of artistic expression; whether in the hands of a true artist its productions become works of art."[14] A similar idea, more succinctly stated, had illuminated the introduction by the French naturalist Louis

Figuier to the *Catalogue of the 1859 Salon of Photography* (the exhibition that apparently inspired Baudelaire's diatribe). Figuier was one of a number of scientists of the era who were convinced that artistic expression and mass taste would be improved by photography, just as the general quality of human life would benefit from applied science. He observed that "Until now, the artist has had the brush, the pencil and the burin; now, in addition, he has the photographic lens. The lens is an instrument like the pencil and the brush, and photography is a process like engraving and drawing, for what makes an artist is not the process but the feeling."[15]

The leading French painters of landscapes and humble peasant scenes—known as the Barbizon group—as well as the Realists and Impressionists who concerned themselves with the depiction of mundane reality, accepted photographs more generously than Ingres and the Salon painters, in part because of their scientific interest in light and in the accurate depiction of tonal values. A number of them, including Camille Corot, Gustave Courbet, and Jean François Millet, collected calotypes and albumen prints, apparently agreeing with Antoine Claudet that when a painter desires to imitate nature, there could be nothing

better than to consult the "exacting mirror" of a photograph. These artists considered the camera a "wonderfully obedient slave," and while not all of them painted from photographs directly, such camera "notes" had an important effect on their handling of light and tonality.

Frequenting the forests around Arras and Fontainebleau, the haunt also of a number of photographers, Barbizon painters became acquainted with *cliché verre (see A Short Technical History, Part I)*, a hybrid form—part drawing, part photographic print.[16] Known since the early days of photography and included in both Hunt's treatise and a French work on graphic art processes, it was taught to many artists visiting the region by Adalbert and Eugène Cuvelier.[17] It could be used as a sketching technique, as in a set of *Five Landscapes (pl. no. 244)* by Corot, or to yield a more finely detailed print, exemplified by *Woman Emptying a Bucket (pl. no. 245)*, an 1862 work by Millet. *Cliché verre* seems to have been exceptionally congenial to painters working in and around Barbizon, but an American artist, John W. Ehninger, supervised an album of poetry illustrated by this technique. Entitled *Autograph Etchings by American Artists*, it included the work of Asher B. Durand *(pl. no. 246)*, one of the nation's most prominent mid-century landscapists. In England, its primary use was as a method of reproduction (called electrography) rather than as an expressive medium.

The effect of photography on the handmade arts became irreversible with the spread of collodion technology. Besides using camera images as studies of models and draperies and for portraits that were to be enlarged and printed on canvas, painters began to incorporate in their work documentary information and unconventional points of view gleaned from familiarity with all sorts of photographs. The high horizons, blurred figures, and asymmetrical croppings visible in many Impressionist and post-Impressionist paintings, which seem to establish a relationship between these works and camera vision have been discussed by Scharf, Van Deren Coke, and others.[18] To cite only one of numerous examples of the complex fashion in which painters incorporated camera vision into their work, an 1870 collaborative painting by the Americans Frederic E. Church, G. P. A. Healy, and Jervis McEntee, entitled *The Arch of Titus (pl. no. 247)*, makes use of a studio portrait of the American poet Henry Wadsworth Longfellow and his daughter Edith *(pl. no. 248)* as a focal point. But in addition to this obvious usage, the extreme contrast between monochromatic sky and the dark under portion of the arch, the transparency of the shadow areas, and the pronounced perspective of the view through the arch all suggest the close study of photographs. Artists using photographs in this way usually did not obtain permission or give credit to photographers, and it is not surprising that a

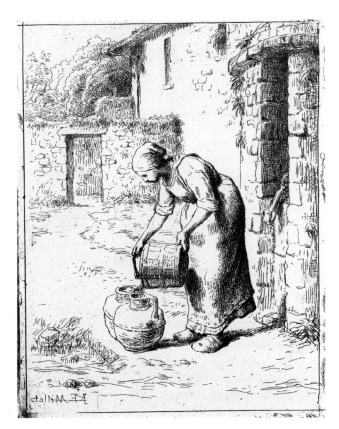

245. JEAN FRANÇOIS MILLET. *Woman Emptying A Bucket*, 1862. *Cliché verre.* © 1983 Founders Society, Detroit Institute of the Arts; John S. Newberry, Jr., Fund.

not only emulated the conventional subject matter of paintings but manipulated their photographs to produce "picturesque" images.

Starting in the early 1850s, photographic prints were shown in exhibition rooms and galleries and selected for inclusion in expositions where problems of classification sometimes resulted. For instance, nine Le Gray calotypes, submitted to the 1859 Salon, were first displayed among the lithographs and then, when their technique became known, were removed to the science section. For the remainder of the century, photographers attempted to have camera images included in the fine arts sections of the expositions, but indecision on the part of selection committees continued. On the other hand, exhibitions organized by the photographic societies in the 1850s at times included many hundreds of images that were displayed according to the conventions of the academic painting salons, eliciting criticism in the press and eventual repudiation in the late 1880s. "How is it possible," wrote an English reviewer in 1856,

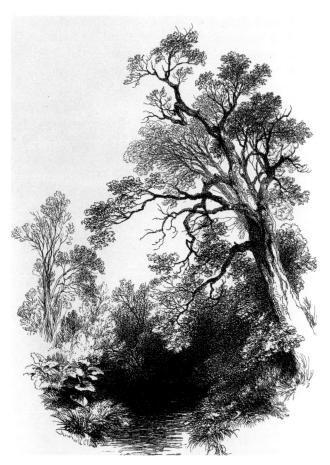

246. ASHER B. DURAND. *The Pool*, No. 1, 1859. *Cliché verre* albumen print from *Autograph Etchings by American Artists*, supervised by John W. Ehninger, 1859. Stuart Collection, Rare Books and Manuscripts Division, The New York Public Library, Astor, Lenox, and Tilden Foundations.

number of court cases occurred involving better-known photographers who contested the right of painters to use their images without permission, a situation that has continued to bedevil photographers up to the present.[19]

While painters were using photographs and critics were arguing the merits of this practice, how did the photographers themselves feel about the medium's status as art? Coming from a spectrum of occupations and class positions, and approaching the medium with differing expectations, they displayed a range of attitudes. Several, among them Sir William Newton, a painter–photographer who helped found the Photographic Society of London, and the fashionable society portraitist Camille Silvy, were outspoken in claiming that the medium was valuable only for its documentary veracity. Others, including Fenton, Edouard Denis Baldus, and Charles Nègre, endeavored to infuse photographic documentation with aesthetic character in the belief that camera images were capable of expression, while still others, notably Rejlander and Robinson,

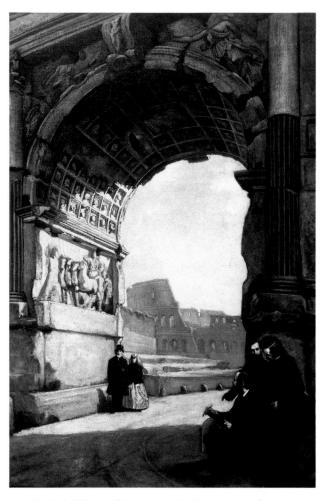

247. G. P. A. HEALY, FREDERICK E. CHURCH, and JERVIS McENTEE. *The Arch of Titus*, 1871. Oil on canvas. Newark Museum, Newark, N.J.; Bequest of J. Ackerman Coles.

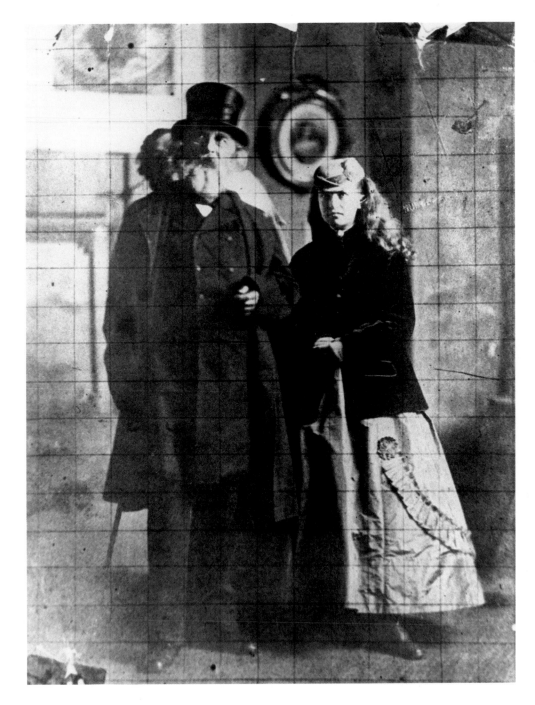

248. UNKNOWN
PHOTOGRAPHER.
*Longfellow and Daughter in
the Healy Studio in Rome*,
1868–69. Albumen print.
Marie de Mare Papers,
Archives of American Art,
Smithsonian Institution,
Washington, D.C.

"for photographs, whose merit consists in their accuracy and minuteness of detail, to be seen to advantage when piled, tier upon tier, on the crowded walls of an exhibition room?"[20] As if in answer to this criticism, photographers turned to the album as a format for viewing original photographs.

Photography and the Nude

That camera studies of both nudes and costumed figures would be useful to artists had been recognized by daguerreotypists since the 1840s; Hermann Krone's *Nude Study (pl. no. 249)* is typical of the conventional Academy poses produced for this trade. A calotype of a woman with a pitcher, by former French painter Julien Vallou de Villeneuve *(pl. no. 251)*, exemplifies the numerous studies on paper of models costumed as domestic servants—designed to serve the same clientele—that probably were inspired by the work of French painters like François Bonvin; these simply posed and dramatically lighted figure studies continued a tradition of painted genre imagery with which photography—on the occasions when it was judged to be

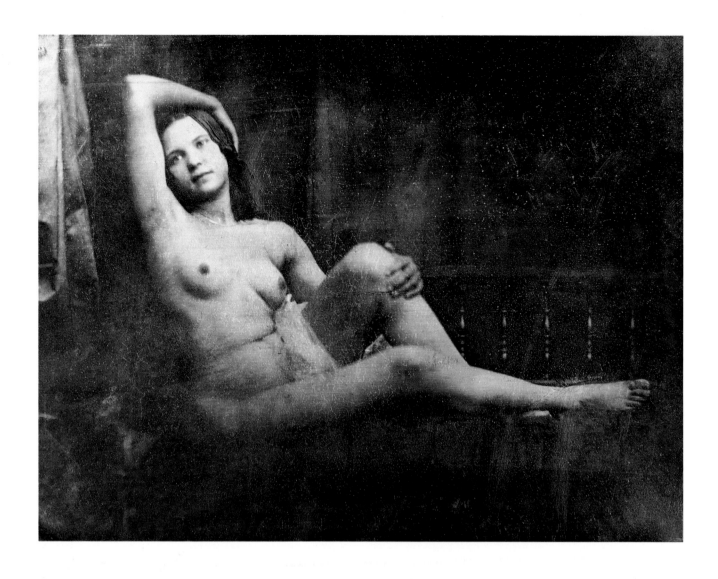

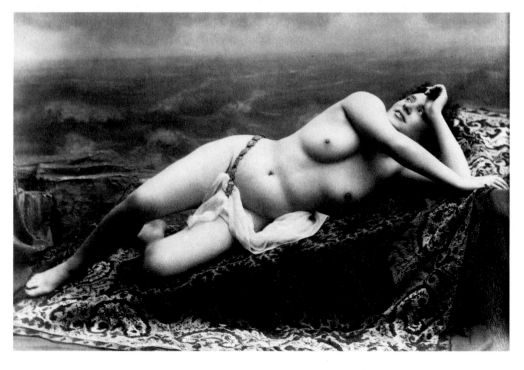

249. HERMANN KRONE.
Nude Study, c. 1850.
Daguerreotype.
Deutsches Museum,
Munich.

250. UNKNOWN
PHOTOGRAPHER.
Nude, 1870s.
Albumen print.
Private Collection.

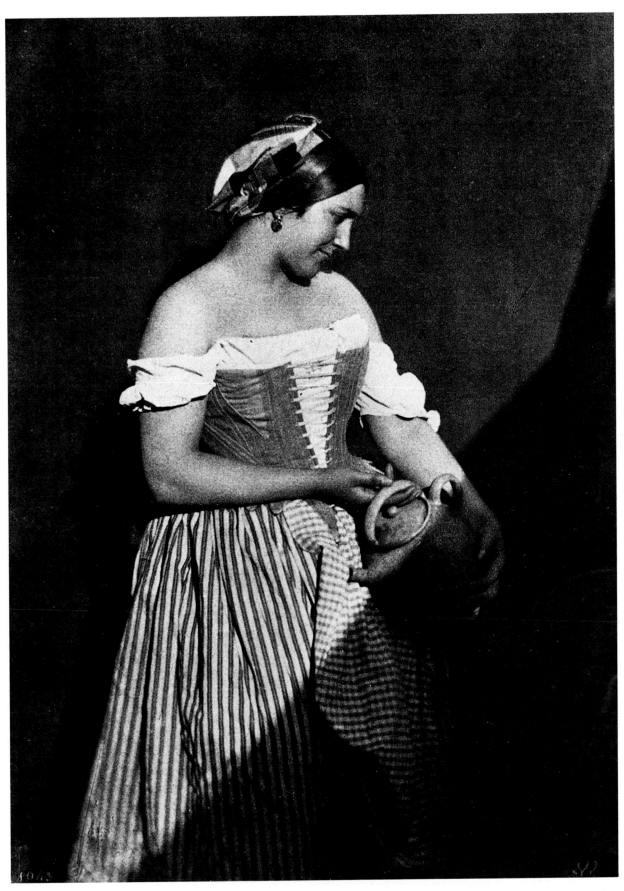

251. Julien Vallou de Villeneuve. *Woman with Pitcher*, c. 1855. Calotype. Bibliothèque Nationale, Paris.

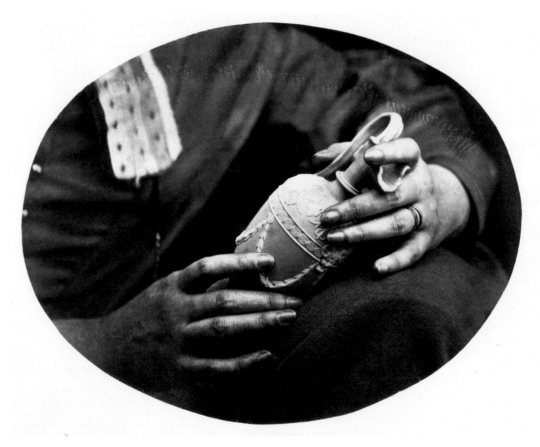

252. OSCAR GUSTAVE REJLANDER. *Study of Hands*, c. 1854. Albumen print.
Gernsheim Collection, Humanities Research Center, University of Texas, Austin.

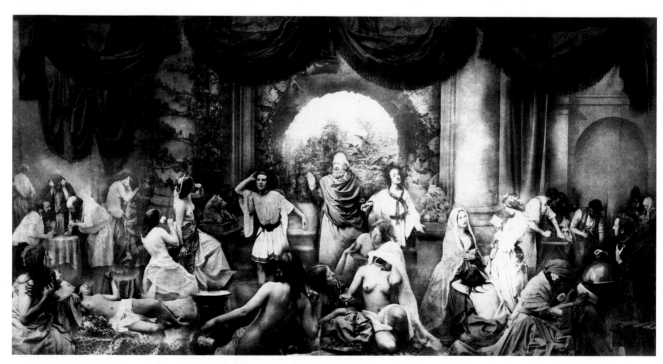

253. OSCAR GUSTAVE REJLANDER. *Two Ways of Life*, 1857. Albumen print.
International Museum of Photography at George Eastman House, Rochester, N.Y.

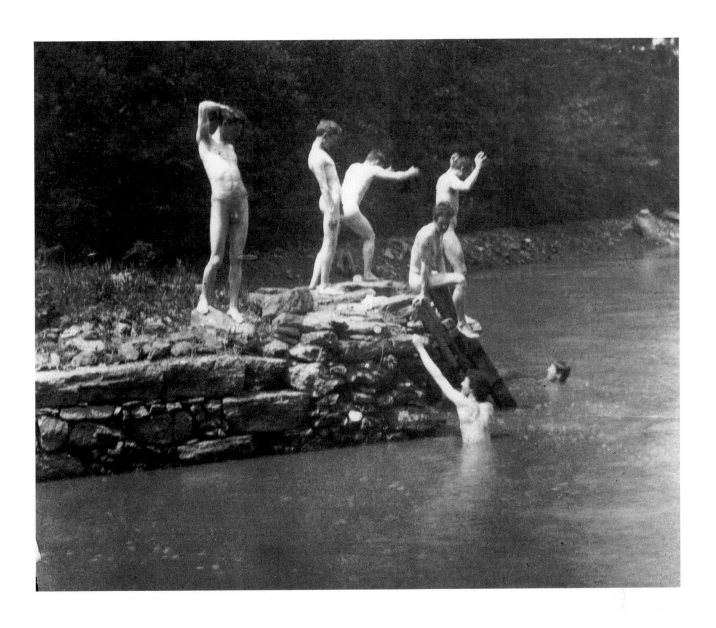

254. THOMAS EAKINS. *Eakins's Students at the Site of "The Swimming Hole,"* 1883. Gelatin silver print. Hirshhorn Museum and Sculpture Garden, Smithsonian Institution, Washington, D.C.

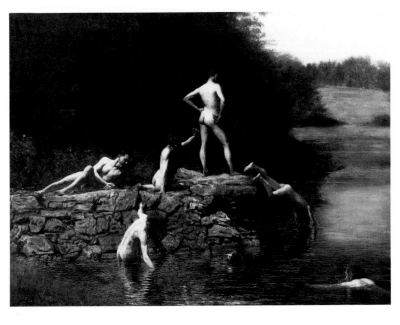

255. THOMAS EAKINS. *The Swimming Hole,* 1883. Oil on canvas. Permanent Collection, Fort Worth Art Museum, Fort Worth, Tex.

art—was invariably associated. Even well-known photographers provided studies of all aspects of the human figure for artists, as can be seen in Rejlander's *Study of Hands* *(pl. no. 252)*.[21]

Predictably, photographs of nudes appealed to others besides graphic artists. Indeed, soon after the invention of the medium, daguerreotypes, followed by ambrotypes, albumen prints, and stereographs, often hand-colored to increase the appearance of naturalness, were made expressly for salacious purposes *(pl. no. 250)*. Photographic journals inveighed against this abuse of the camera, and studios were raided at times as a result of court findings in Britain and the United States that photographs of nudes were obscene, but erotic and pornographic images continued to find an interested market. More to the point is the fact that to many Victorians no clear distinctions existed between studies of the nude made for artists, or as personal expression, or as commercial images meant to titillate. In a *milieu* where people were scandalized by realistic paintings of unclothed figures other than in mythological or historical contexts, where Ruskin was allowed to destroy J. M. W. Turner's erotic works, it would have been too much to expect that the even more naturalistic camera depiction of nudity be accepted, no matter what purpose the images were designed to serve.

This was true even when such images were conceived with high artistic principles in mind, as was the case with Rejlander's *Two Ways of Life (pl. no. 253)*, to be discussed shortly. The same Victorian moral code no doubt accounts for the decision by Lewis Carroll to destroy the negatives of his own artistically conceived images of young nude girls that he realized "so utterly defied convention," and to have the photographs of the daughters of his friends, including *Beatrice Hatch (pl. no. 334)*, painted in by a colorist who supplied the fanciful outdoor decor. In this context, a comparison between the painted and photographed nudes by the American painter Eakins is instructive. Camera studies of a group of swimmers *(pl. no. 254)*—made by Eakins or a student—for the painting *The Swimming Hole (pl. no. 255)*, captured movement and anatomical details with lively accuracy. Nevertheless, the painter, apparently concerned with avoiding anything that his Philadelphia patrons and critics might find offensive, discreetly rearranged the poses of the nude boys in the final work.[22]

Artistic Photography

With works of art in all media attracting the interest of the urban bourgeoisie during the second half of the 19th century, critics became more vocal in their exhortations to photographers as well as painters to select themes and treatments that not only would delineate situations nat-

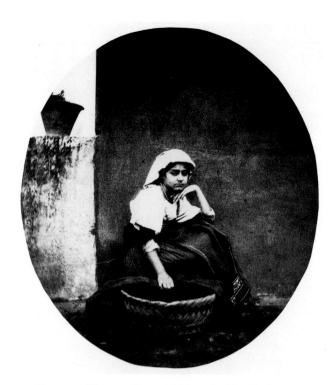

256. CHARLES NÈGRE. *Young Girl Seated with a Basket*, 1852. Salt print. Collection André Jammes, Paris; National Gallery of Canada, Ottawa.

uralistically but would also embody uplifting sentiments. Everywhere, but especially in England, articles and papers read before the professional photographic societies as well as reviews of annual and special exhibitions translated traditional precepts of art into huffy "do's and don'ts" for photographers. At the same time, painting exhibitions were reviewed in photography publications to establish the relationship between the media. Solutions to the demand that photographs be at once truthful, beautiful, and inspirational encompassed making still lifes, genre scenes, portraits of models in allegorical costume and, finally, composite images that aimed at being competitive with the productions of "high-art." To overcome the sharp definition decried by some as too literal for art, photographers were urged to use slower collodion, inferior optical elements, to smear the lens or kick the tripod during exposure or blur the print during processing.

Efforts to transcend the literalness of the lens without aping too closely the conventions of graphic art were most successful in France. As a consequence of their art training, the several painters associated with Delaroche who became adept at the calotype process around 1850 understood the importance of "effect"—a treatment that involved the suppression of excess detail. For example, in *Young Girl Seated With a Basket (pl. no. 256)*, Nègre *(see Profile below)* concentrates the light on the head, hands, and basket rim, purposefully leaving the texture of wall and background indistinct. His choice of subject—an Italian peasant in France—derived from the painting tradition that counted Murillo and Bonvin among its advocates and conformed to the idea that lower-class themes were acceptable in art as long as they were treated picturesquely. This concept also had inspired Hill and Adamson in their photographs of the fisherfolk of Newhaven *(see Chapters 2 and 8)* and William Collie in his calotypes of rural folk on the Isle of Jersey.

While a variant of this theme appealed to Baron Humbert de Molard, a founding member of the *Société* *Française de Photographie* who posed gamekeepers, hunters *(pl. no. 257)*, milkmaids, and shepherds against real or reconstituted rural backgrounds, genre scenes generally were made less frequently in France than in England and the United States, where a taste for narrative content was explicit. Still another variety of posed imagery involving humble pursuits used more sophisticated settings and pastimes, as in an 1850 calotype, *Chess Game (pl. no. 258)* by Aloïs Löcherer; later German examples of the same type in collodion were called *Lebende Bilder (Living Pictures)* because they portrayed costumed models, often artists and students, posing as knights, literary figures, or as well-

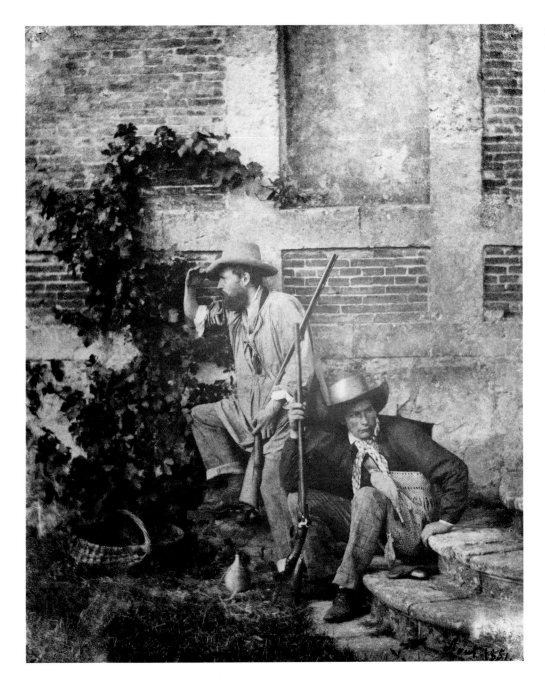

257. HUMBERT DE MOLARD. *The Hunters*, 1851. Calotype. Société Française de Photographie, Paris.

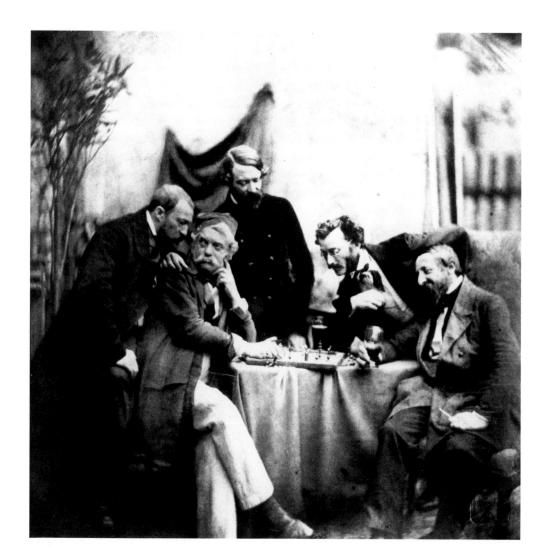

258. ALOÏS LÖCHERER. *Chess Game*, c. 1850. Calotype. Gernsheim Collection, Humanities Research Center, University of Texas, Austin.

known painting subjects. These genre images with their artistic intent should not be confused with the posed portraits of men and women in ethnic costume meant as souvenirs for tourists or as reflections of nationalistic aspirations among middle-Europeans who had not yet established political identities.

Before discussing the irruption of storytelling imagery that characterized English photography during the collodion era, the photographic still life as an acceptable artistic theme should be mentioned. Tabletop arrangements of traditional materials—fruit, crockery, statuary, subjects that had appealed to Daguerre and Talbot as well as to conventional painters—continued to attract photographers on the continent during the calotype and collodion eras. While these arrangements also made it possible for photographers to study the effects of light on form, the conventions of still life painting appear at times to have been transferred to silver with little change in style and iconography *(pl. no. 260)*; other works, exemplified by Krone's *Still Life of the Washerwoman (pl. no. 259)*, are captivating because they embrace less conventional objects.

Arrangements of flowers, which at first might seem to be singularly unsuited to a monochromatic medium, were successfully photographed perhaps because in some cases the images were regarded as documents rather than purely as artistic expressions. In the early 1850s, close-up studies of leaves, blossoms, and foliage arranged by Adolphe Braun in formal and casual compositions were highly praised for their intrinsic artistry as well as their usefulness *(pl. no. 261)*; these prints may have inspired Eugène Chauvigne and Charles Aubry, among others, to attempt similar themes. In the dedication to *Studies of Leaves (pl. no. 262)*, Aubry wrote that they were made to "facilitate the study of nature" in order to "increase . . . productivity in the industrial arts."[23] Nevertheless, other flower still lifes by the same artist included skulls and props, suggesting that he also wished them to be comparable to painted counterparts, although the simple arrangements and crisp detailing of

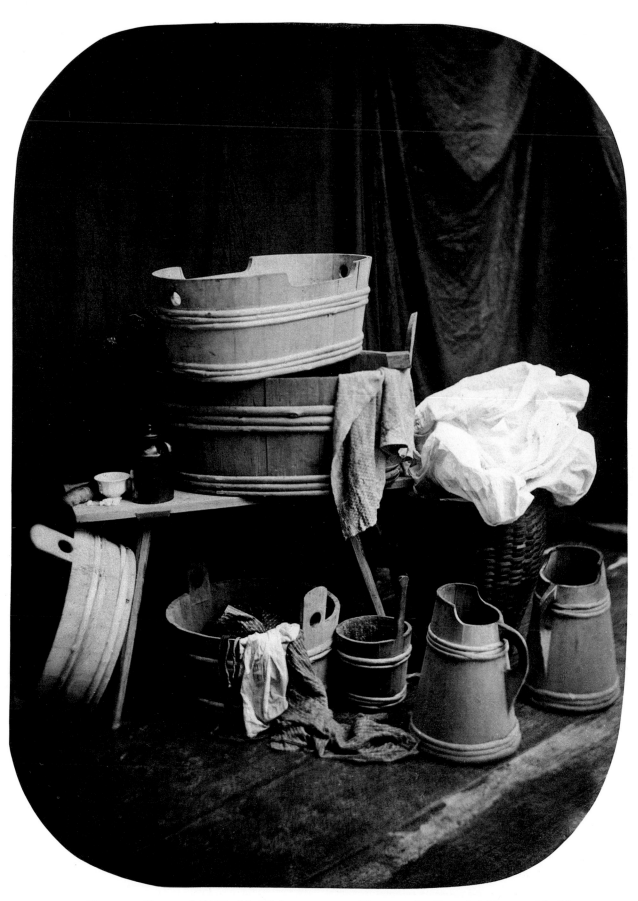

259. HERMANN KRONE. *Still Life of the Washerwoman*, 1853. Albumen print. Deutsches Museum, Munich.

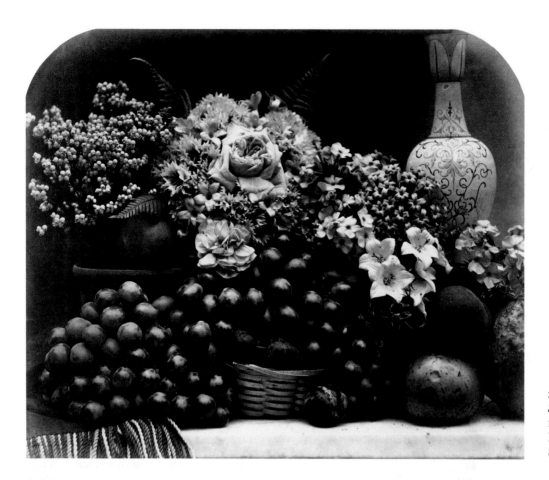

260. ROGER FENTON. *Still Life of Fruit*, c. 1860. Albumen print. Royal Photographic Society, Bath, England.

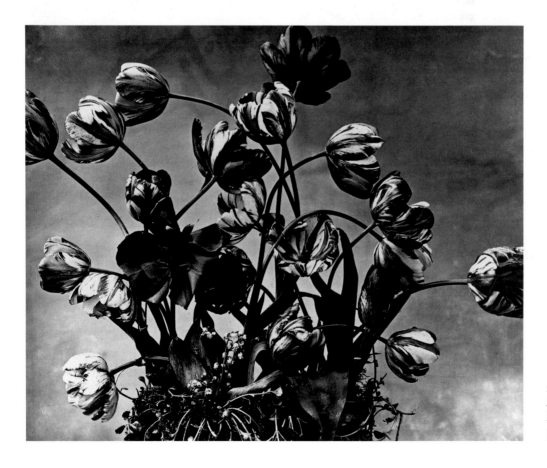

261. ADOLPHE BRAUN. *Flower Study*, c. 1855. Modern gelatin silver print. Private collection.

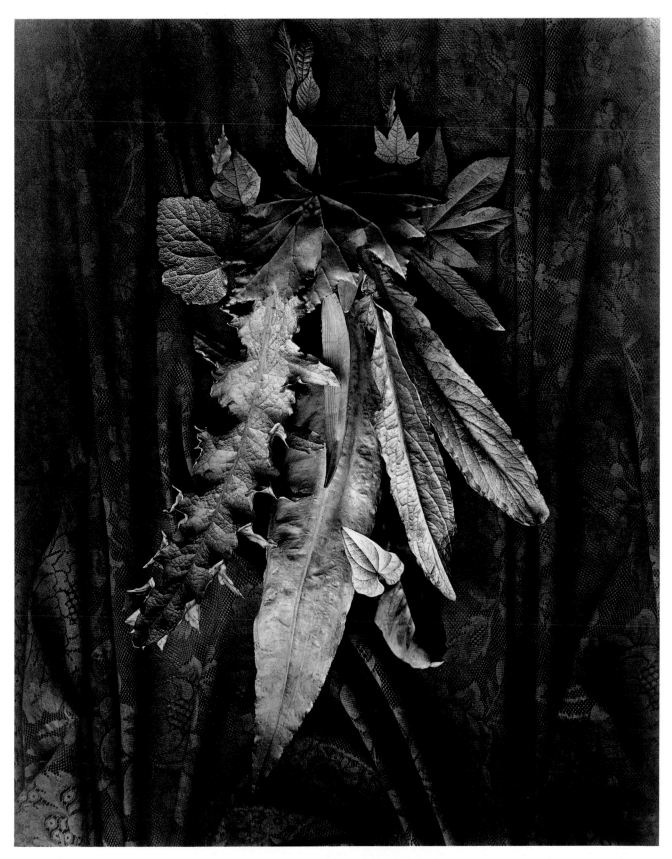

262. CHARLES AUBRY. *Leaves*, 1864. Albumen print. Collection André Jammes, Paris;
purchased with funds from the American Museum of Photography, Philadelphia Museum of Art.

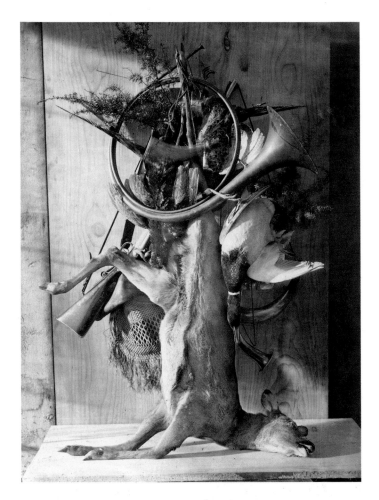

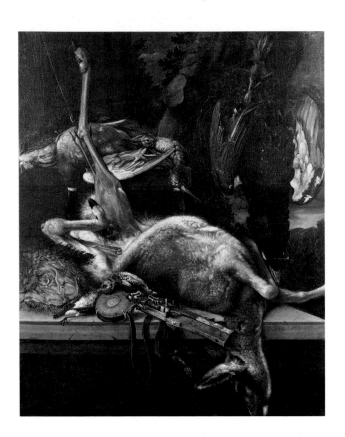

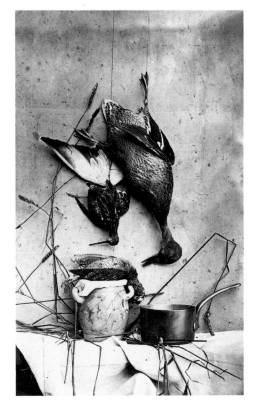

foliage in the studies suggest that his work was most original when not competing with paintings of similar themes.

But, as always, there are exceptions. A group of large-format "after-the-hunt" still lifes by Braun *(pl. no. 263)*, portraying arrangements of hung game, waterfowl, and hunting paraphernalia, successfully emulated works of graphic art that had been popular with painters of Northern Europe for two centuries. That painters and photographers both drew upon a common tradition can be seen in an oil painting *(pl. no. 264)* of the same theme by Valentin Gottfried, who worked near Strasbourg in the late 17th and early 18th centuries.[24] For his images, Braun printed collodion negatives of approximately 23 x 30 inches on thin tissue, using the carbon process to achieve a broad range of delicate tones *(see A Short Technical History, Part I)*. "After-the-hunt" scenes similar in size and generally less complex in arrangement were made also by Dr. Hugh Welch Diamond, Fenton, William Lake Price, Louise Laffon, Charles Carey *(pl. no. 265)*, and others, but the difficulties of tran-

scribing this theme from painting to photography is apparent in the many cluttered compositions and lack of saving gracefulness.

Composite Photography

Convinced that visual art should uplift and instruct, some English photographers specialized in producing reenacted narratives synthesized in the darkroom, an enterprise known as combination printing. By staging *tableaux* and then piecing together separate images to form a composition, photographers were able to choose agreeable models and control the narrative content of the work. The technique was adopted briefly—with unfortunate results to be discussed shortly—by Rejlander, but its high esteem during the 1860s was the result of the tireless efforts of Robinson, who saw himself both as a theoretician with a mission to elevate photography, and as a practitioner. He wrote numerous articles and eleven books on aesthetics

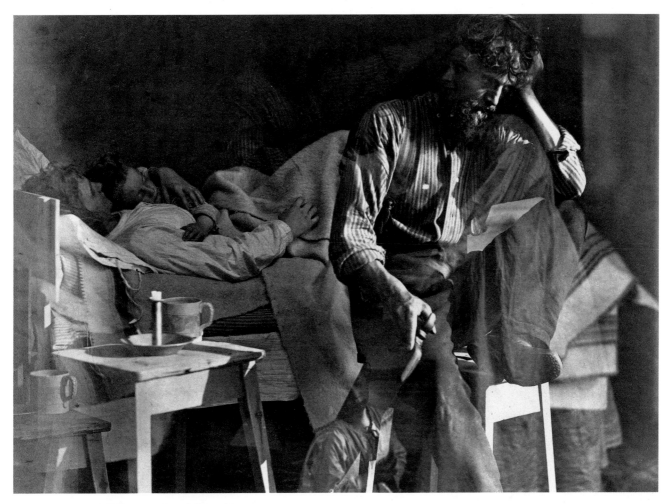

266. OSCAR GUSTAVE REJLANDER. *Hard Times*, 1860. Albumen print. International Museum of Photography at George Eastman House, Rochester, N.Y.

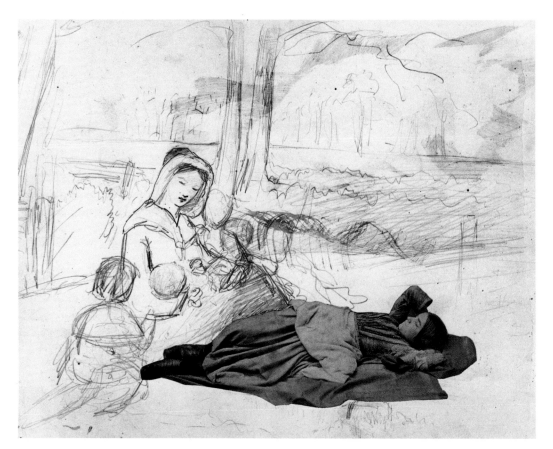

267. HENRY PEACH ROBINSON. *Preliminary Sketch with Photo Inserted,* c. 1860. Albumen print and pastel collage on paper. Gernsheim Collection, Humanities Research Center, University of Texas, Austin.

268. HENRY PEACH ROBINSON. *Fading Away,* 1858. Albumen composite print. Royal Photographic Society, Bath, England.

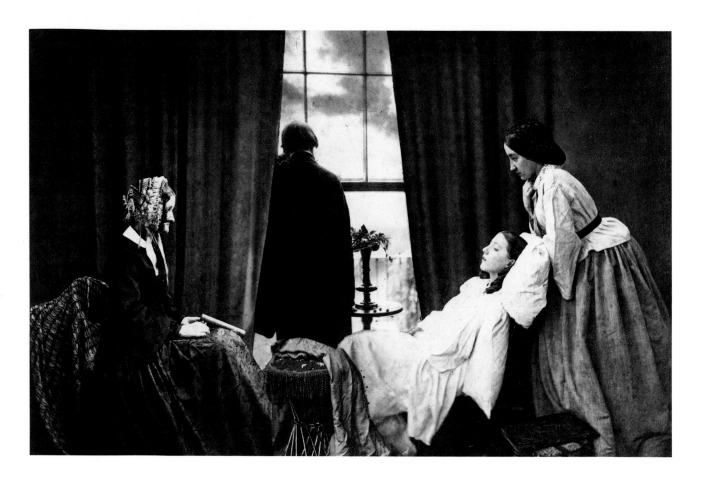

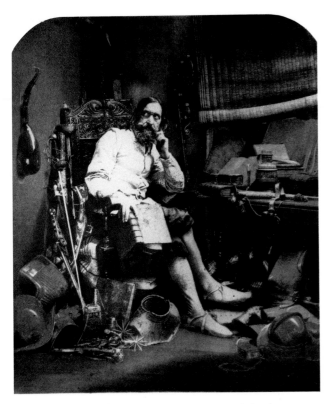

269. WILLIAM LAKE PRICE. *Don Quixote in His Study*,
c. 1890. Albumen print. Gernsheim Collection,
Humanities Research Center, University of Texas, Austin.

and techniques, several of which were translated into French and German. His first and most widely read work, *Pictorial Effect in Photography, Being Hints on Composition and Chiaroscuro for Photographers*, of 1869, emphasized traditional artistic principles of pictorial unity and concluded with a chapter on combination printing.

However, Rejlander was the first to make imaginative use of combination printing despite what some may consider the flawed judgment that led him in 1857—two years after his first attempt—to work on a major opus entitled *Two Ways of Life (pl. no. 253)*. At least five versions existed of this large bathetic composition (31 x 16 inches) formed from some 30-odd separate negatives posed for by 16 professional and other models. Loosely based on Raphael's *School of Athens* fresco, it represents an allegory of the choice between good and evil (also between work and idleness) that was meant to compete thematically and stylistically with the paintings and photographs entered in the Manchester Art Treasures Exhibition of 1857, and, incidentally, to serve as a sampler of photographic figure studies for artists.[25] With such vaunting, if disparate ambitions, it is little wonder that despite the seal of approval from Queen Victoria and Prince Albert, who purchased a version, critics termed it unsuccessful as allegory; works of "high art,"

they claimed, should not be executed by "mechanical contrivances."[26] When exhibited in Edinburgh in 1858, the partially nude figures were covered over while a discussion ensued as to whether or not the work was lascivious. Reacting to the criticism, Rejlander deplored "the sneering and overbearing manner in which . . . [critics] assign limits to our power,"[27] but he refrained from further grandiose compositions. Though sentimental at times, Rejlander's less ambitious combination prints—*Hard Times (pl. no. 266)* with its social and surreal overtones is one example—and his many posed figure pieces, including studies of workers, are among the thematically and visually more interesting works of this nature.

After seeing Rejlander's work, Robinson, a fellow painter-turned-photographer who had started as a portraitist but had set his sights on a higher purpose, adopted combination printing. Claiming that "a method that will not admit of modifications of the artist cannot be art,"[28] he first worked out preliminary sketches *(pl. no. 267)* into which the photographic parts were fitted in the manner of a puzzle or patchwork quilt. *Fading Away (pl. no. 268)*, his inaugural effort created from five different negatives—also acquired by the royal couple—was praised for "exquisite sentiment" by some and criticized as morbid by others. Though Robinson avoided such emotion-laden subjects again, for 30 or so years he continued to mix the "real with the artificial," as he described it, using models "trained to strict obedience"[29] in order to produce scenes agreeable to a public that esteemed engravings after the genre paintings of Sir David Wilkie and Thomas Faed.

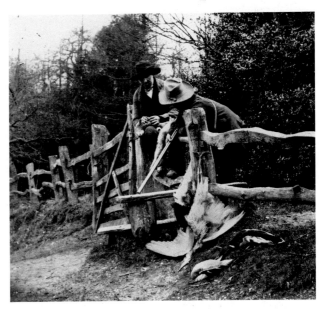

270. WILLIAM GRUNDY. *A Day's Shooting*, c. 1857.
Albumen print. BBC Hulton Picture Library/Bettmann
Archive.

Narrative, Allegorical, and Genre Images

The precepts that photographic art should deal with suitable themes, that the image be judiciously composed and sharply defined, dominated the theoretical ideas of a generation of amateur photographers in England. Among them, William Grundy specialized in what the French publication *La Lumière* called "a peculiar type of rustic humor" *(pl. no. 270)* while Price, a watercolorist and author of a popular manual on artistic photography, produced besides landscapes and still lifes, literary figure pieces of which *Don Quixote (pl. no. 269)* is an example. Though some critics denounced this kind of photography as inadequate for conveying moral messages, theatrically contrived literary and allegorical subjects continued to appeal, as can be seen in Silvy's portraits of a middle-class sitter, Mrs. Leslie, garbed in the mantle of truth *(pl. no. 271)*. In its concentration on narrative, its avoidance of sensuous and atmospheric effects, its preference for sharp definition, the work

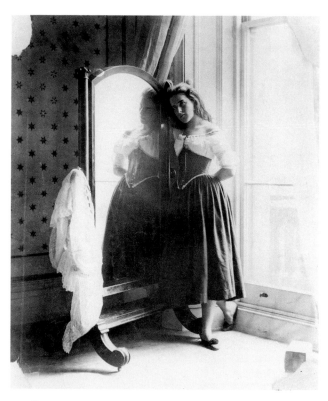

272. CLEMENTINA HAWARDEN. *Young Girl with Mirror Reflection*, 1860s. Albumen print. Victoria and Albert Museum, London.

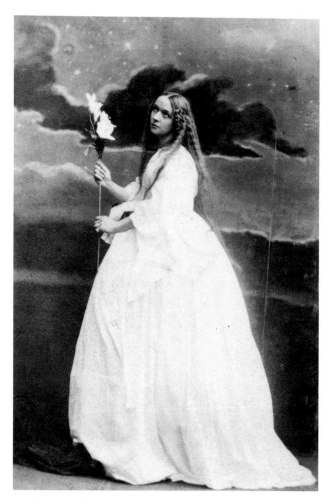

271. CAMILLE SILVY. *Mrs. John Leslie as Truth*, March 16, 1861. Albumen print. National Portrait Gallery, London.

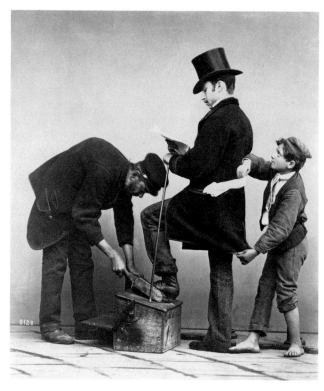

273. GIORGIO SOMMER. *Shoeshine and Pickpocket*, 1865–70. Albumen print. Museum of Fine Arts, Boston; Abbott Lawrence Fund.

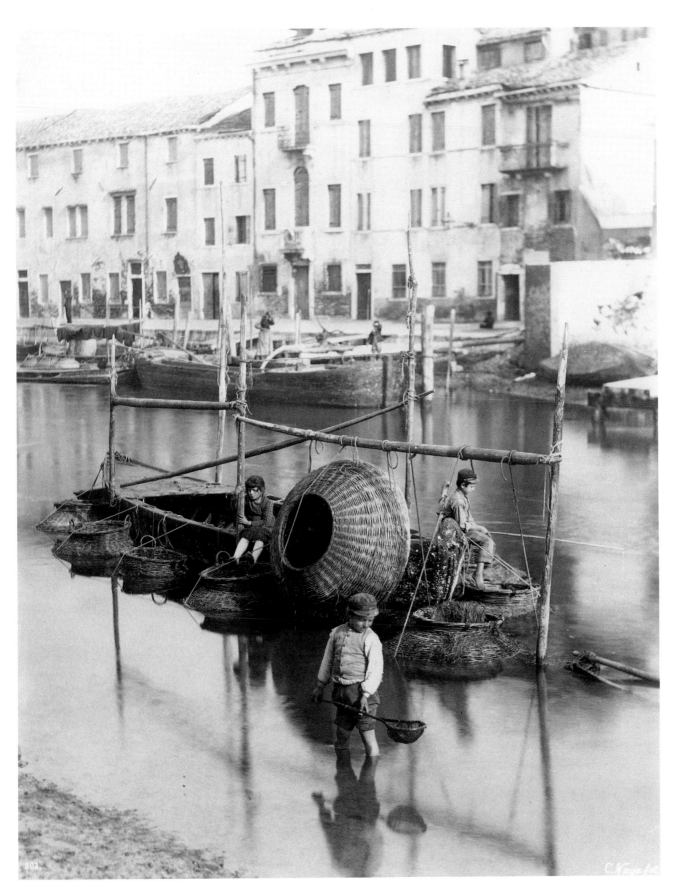

274. CARLO NAYA. *Children on a Fish Weir, Venice*, c. 1870s.
Albumen print. Museum of Fine Arts, Boston; Abbott Lawrence Fund.

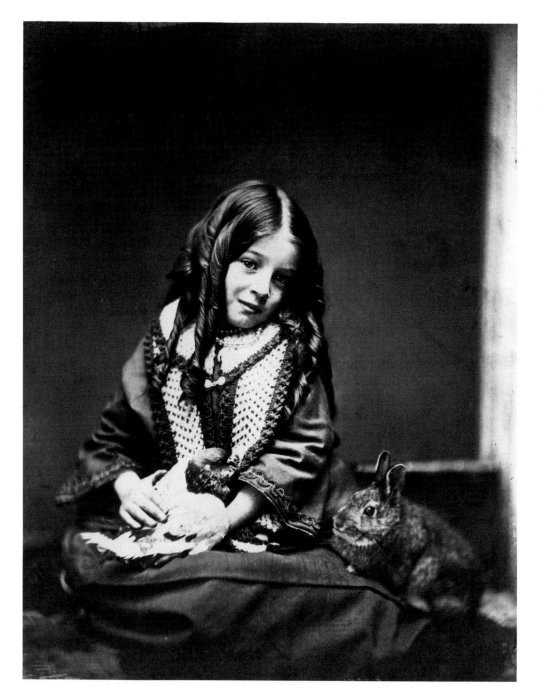

275. ALEXANDER HESLER.
Three Pets, c. 1851.
Crystalotype from original
daguerreotype in
*Photographic and Fine Arts
Journal*, April, 1854.
International Museum of
Photography at George
Eastman House,
Rochester, N.Y.

of the English pictorial photographers of the 1860s and '70s mimics effects and themes found in both Pre-Raphaelite and Academic paintings.

A different concept of photographic aesthetics informed literary and allegorical images by Julia Margaret Cameron *(see Profile, Chapter 2)*, whose purposefully out-of-focus technique was derided by Robinson as inexcusable. Cameron drew upon an extensive knowledge of the Bible and English literature for her themes, using the same props, draperies, and models time and again. *The New Year Rising (pl. no. 82)*, one of many images using the children

of her friends and servants, reflects the ideas of her artistic mentor, the painter George Frederic Watts, whose great admiration for the themes of Renaissance art communicated itself to the photographer through his canvases, writings, and close personal friendship. Cameron's intuitive understanding that light can mystify as well as illuminate invests a number of these allegorical *tableaux* with more interest than their derivative subject matter deserves. Imaginative handling of tonal contrast characterizes the small body of work produced by Lady Clementina Hawarden also, but these posed and costumed figure pieces

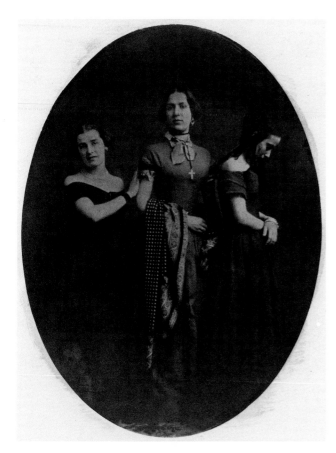

276. GABRIEL HARRISON. *Past, Present, Future*, c. 1854.
Crystalotype. International Museum of Photography at
George Eastman House, Rochester, N.Y.

(pl. no. 272) reveal an ardent sensuality lacking in Cameron's
sentimental narrative works.

Picturesque genre images were made in Italy for the
tourist trade rather than as examples of high art. Most
were contrived reenactments, similar in theme and treatment to the theatrical vignettes staged in the Naples studio
of Giorgio Sommer. Given titles like *The Spaghetti Eaters*
or *Shoeshine and Pickpocket (pl. no. 273)*, they were supposedly
humorous reminders of what travelers from the north
might expect to find in Italian cities. Staged and unstaged
images of bucolic peasant and street life, produced by the
Alinari brothers in Florence and by Carlo Naya in Venice,
were intended for tourists who wished to point out to the
folks back home both the simple pleasures and sharp practices one might expect when visiting Italy. Naya, a well-
educated dilettante who at first regarded photography as a
curiosity rather than a means of livelihood, eventually was
considered by his contemporaries to have "transformed
this art into an important industry while retaining its aesthetic character."[30] In effect, by posing the beadworkers,
beggars, and street vendors of Venice against real and stu-

dio backgrounds *(pl. no. 274)*, he transformed social reality
into mementos for tourists.

Artistic Photography in the United States

"The sharp contest going on abroad between advocates
of painting and photography,"[31] was less engaging to
most Americans. A number of photographers, among them
George N. Barnard, Gabriel Harrison, Alexander Hesler,
and John Moran, were convinced that both media spoke
the same language and addressed the same sentiments; but
although they were concerned with photography as art,
the prevailing climate was one of indifference to theoretical issues. This probably was due to the low esteem for the
arts in general, to the continued success of commercial
daguerreotyping long after its eclipse in Europe, and to
the upheaval caused by the Civil War. The situation began
to change toward the end of the 1860s, largely through the
urging of publications such as the *Philadelphia Photographer*
that photographers give greater consideration to photographic aesthetics.

On the other hand, painters in the United States were
not in the least hesitant about using photographs in their
work. Agreeing with Samuel F. B. Morse's judgment of
the medium as a utilitarian tool that would supply "rich
materials . . . an exhaustive store for the imagination to
feed upon . . . [and] would bring about a new standard in
art,"[32] portrait and genre painters began to copy from
photographs soon after the daguerreotype was introduced.
The lucrative business of enlarging and transferring photographic portraits to canvas, mentioned in Chapter 2, continued, but, even before the Civil War, landscape painters—
among them Albert Bierstadt, Thomas Cole, and Church—
also welcomed the photograph as an ally. It served landscapists particularly well in their endeavors to represent
scientific fact animated by heavenly inspiration—a visual
concept reflective of Emerson's new-world philosophy of
the divinity of the native landscape. In terms of style, the
stereograph was especially important. Contemporary critics noted the combination of minutely detailed foregrounds, misty panoramic backgrounds, and a powerful
illusion of depth in the work of Church and Bierstadt, the
two most renowned painters of their era. These effects are
exactly those of the stereograph image seen on a much
reduced scale through the viewing device.[33] Furthermore,
references in Church's diaries and the evidence of a large
collection of photographs found in his studio reinforce the
suspicion that this painter, along with many others, collected stereographs and regular-format photographs for
information and at times, to paint over. Also, between 1850
and 1880, artists explored the mountain regions of the west
and northeast in the company of photographers, resulting

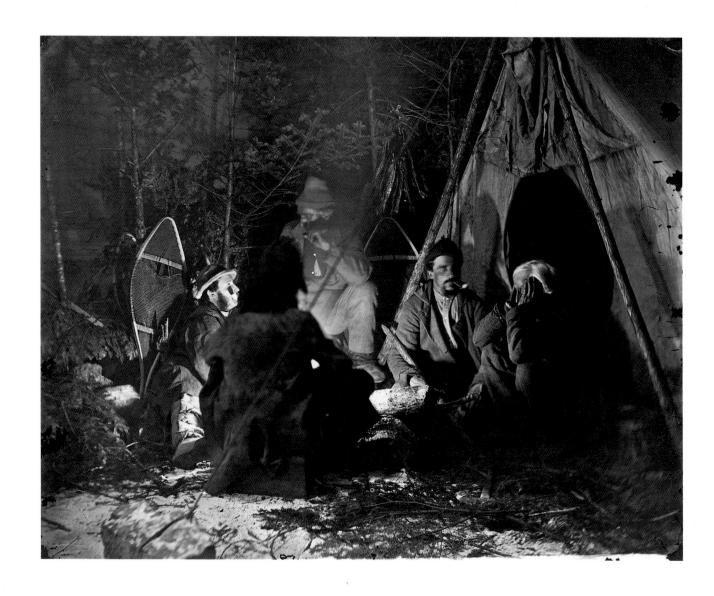

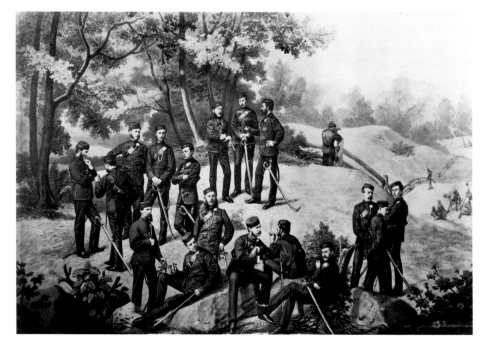

277. WILLIAM NOTMAN.
*Caribou Hunting: The Return of
the Party*, 1866. Albumen print.
Notman Photographic
Archives, McCord Museum,
McGill University, Montréal.

278. JAMES INGLIS. *Victorian
Rifles*, 1870. Composite albumen
print; painting by W. Lorenz.
Notman Photographic
Archives, McCord Museum,
McGill University, Montréal.

in an opportunity for interchange of ideas and images that affected both media.

Curiously, American photographers did not at first manifest the widespread interest in genre themes apparent in painting at mid-century. Individual daguerreotypists who were determined to rescue the medium from what they called "Broadway operators" arranged mundane, sentimental, and allegorical subjects. *Three Pets (pl. no. 275)*, a daguerreotype by Hesler, which was awarded a gold medal at the 1851 London Great Exhibition and then reproduced as a crystallotype in *American Photography and Fine Art Journal*, is an example of the sentimental subjects chosen by this individual to demonstrate the artistic possibilities of the medium. In concert with Marcus Aurelius Root and Henry Hunt Snelling (early critics and historians of the medium), Hesler urged photographers to interest themselves in something more than paltry gain.

A similar motive prompted Harrison, a prominent New York daguerreotypist, to improve his compositions by studying the works of European and American painters. In selecting allegorical subjects such as *Past, Present and Future (pl. no. 276)*, this friend of Walt Whitman, who furnished the portrait of the poet for the frontispiece of *Leaves of Grass*, hoped to show that photographs could reflect "merit, taste and a little genius," that they might embody the unifying thread of human experience that he perceived in the poetry. According to the *Photographic Art Journal*, Harrison's images on metal were eagerly collected by contemporary painters in New York, but even this recognition was insufficient to sustain him in his pursuit of art photography.[34]

Aside from these examples, posed genre compositions and combination printing were not widely favored in the United States at this time owing to both the general dis-

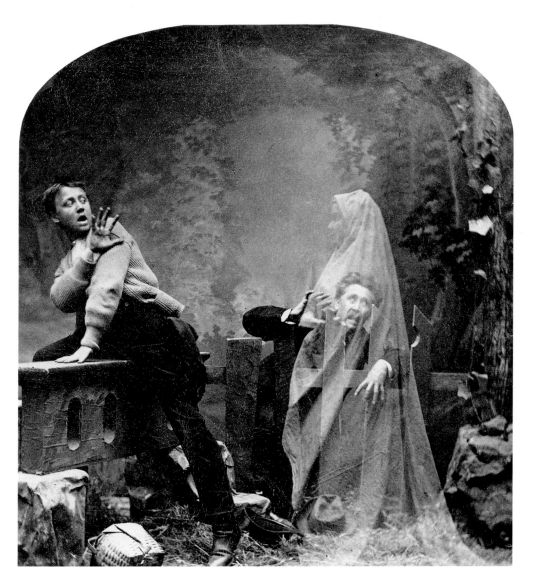

279. L. M. MELENDER and BROTHER. *The Haunted Lane*, c. 1880. One-half of an albumen stereograph. Library of Congress, Washington, D.C.

trust of mannerism in the arts and the firm conviction that the camera should not tamper with reality. *The Philadelphia Photographer* may have believed that such practices would improve the quality of photographic expression, but the more common view, enunciated by Holmes, was that composite images were "detestable—vulgar repetitions of vulgar models, shamming grace, gentility and emotion by the aid of costumes, attitudes, expressions and accessories."[35] Indeed, this enthusiastic realist was scornful of any kind of hand manipulation on photographs; his preference for the stereograph to other formats was in part because it was too small for retouching.

Genre photographs became more acceptable after the Civil War, but the most proficient producer was the Canadian William Notman. His Montreal studio was claimed to be "all alone in this branch of photography on our side of the water," and was outfitted with a full complement of properties and a wind machine for creating the illusion of snowy outdoor climate and landscape, as in *Caribou Hunting: The Return of the Party (pl. no. 277).*[36] Both Notman and James Inglis, also of Montreal, were among the very few who made composite images using methods akin to those of Rejlander and Robinson in that they pasted prints into place and retouched and rephotographed them to form compositions such as Inglis's *Victorian Rifles (pl. no. 278)* of 1870, truly a pastiche of handwork and photochemical processes.

Holmes's repudiation notwithstanding, stereograph format and genre themes were made for each other. By the 1860s, when many painters were turning away from narrative and sentimental subjects, publishers of stereographs were discovering the public taste for pictures of love, death, domestic tribulation, and rustic humor—a taste that formerly had been satisfied by lithographic prints as well as works in oil. Since these images were considered popular entertainment rather than "high art"—in effect, forerunners of the situation comedies and dramas of television—viewers did not fault the stiff postures, exaggerated perspective, or absence of atmosphere. Made in Europe also, most notably by the London Stereograph Company and the German firm of Loescher and Petsch, their chief appeal was in the United States where it was said that no parlor was without a stereoscope.

Large-scale manufacturers, notably the Weller and Melender companies, produced a considerable portion of the genre subjects in the United States before 1890, but local photographers turned out a variety of such images, often stressing regional characteristics. An exceptionally popular subject—one that figured also in regular-format photographs of the time, was the "spirit" image. Dealing with some aspect of the supernatural, as in *The Haunted Lane (pl. no. 279)* published in 1880 by L. M. Melender and Brother, these pictures were made by allowing the model for the "spirit" to leave the scene before exposure was

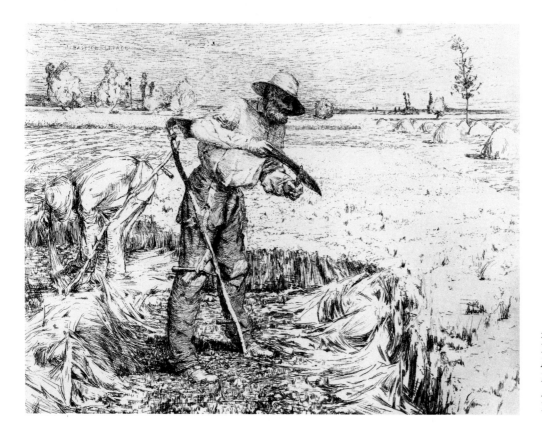

280. JULES BASTIEN-LEPAGE. *Reapers at Damville*, 1879. Etching. Metropolitan Museum of Art, New York; Harrison Brisbane Dick Fund, 1927.

completed and by resorting to complicated techniques. They were taken seriously by many photographers and appealed to the same broad audience for whom seances, Ouija boards, and spiritualism seemed to provide a release from the pressures caused by urbanization and industrialization.

Naturalism

Reaction was inevitable to the mannered contrivance of combination images and to the trivialization of photography by mass-production genre images. The former subverted an inherently direct process with a superabundance of handwork while the latter submerged photographic expression in a wash of banal literalism. And toward the end of the 1880s, a further lowering of standards appeared certain with the invention and marketing of new equipment and processes designed to make photographers out of just about everyone *(see Chapter 6)*.

The most irresistible protest against these developments was embodied in the theory of "naturalism" pro-

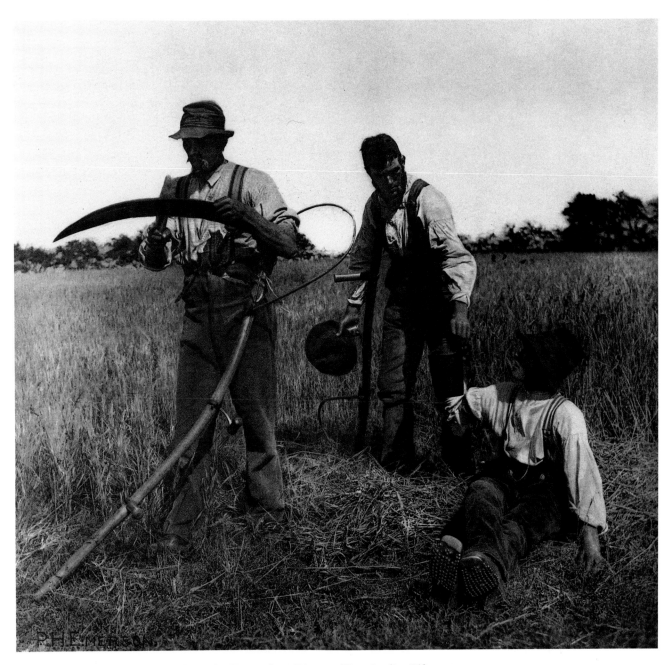

281. PETER HENRY EMERSON. *In the Barley Harvest* from *Pictures of East Anglian Life*, 1888. Gravure print. Royal Photographic Society, Bath, England.

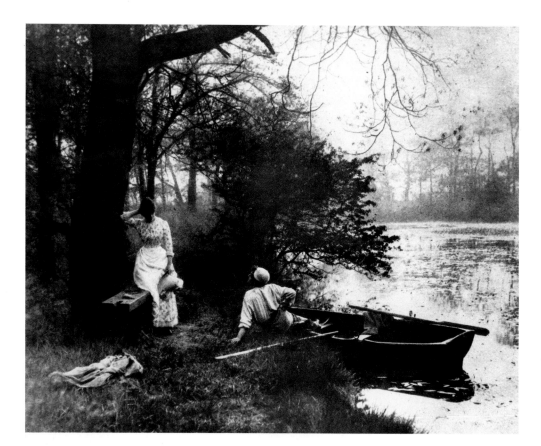

282. LIDELL SAWYER.
In the Twilight, 1888.
Gravure print.
Gernsheim Collection,
Humanities Research
Center, University of
Texas, Austin.

claimed by the English photographer Peter Henry Emerson *(see Profile below)*. Set forth in an 1889 publication entitled *Naturalistic Photography*, Emerson held that camera images (and all visual art) ought to reflect nature with "truth of sentiment, illusion of truth . . . and decoration,"[37] that only by following this path would photographs achieve an aesthetic status independent of and equal to the graphic arts without resorting to handwork on print or negative.

In Emerson's lexicon, "naturalism" was a substitute for impressionism, a word he felt was limited in connotation and too closely associated with controversial artists such as his friend James McNeill Whistler. Asserting that the role of the photographer was to be sensitive to external impressions, he observed that "nature is so full of surprises that, all things considered, she is best painted (or photographed) as she is." At the same time, his emphasis on the importance of selection and feeling made his ideas congenial to the aesthetic artists of the late 19th century. In a field already confused by inaccurate terminology, Emerson further compounded the issue by stating that realism was "false to nature" because it was descriptive, while "naturalism" was both "analytical and true."[38]

For eight years beginning with 1882, Emerson photographed in the tidal areas of East Anglia. A careful ob-

server, he probed beyond the surface to expose in both word and image the difficult existence of the English rural poor while also documenting their fast-disappearing customs and traditions. In exalting the sturdy folk and revealing the quiet beauty of the countryside, he showed himself part of a growing movement of English artists and intellectuals that sought to make a statement about the incivility of modern life. Despite his insistence on a distinctive aesthetic for photography, however, these images reflect the heroicizing attitudes of painters such as Jean François Millet, Jules Breton, and Jules Bastien-Lepage, who had idealized French peasant life a few decades earlier. *Reapers at Damville (pl. no. 280)*, an etching of 1879 by Bastien-Lepage, is both visually and ideologically a forerunner of *In the Barley Harvest (pl. no. 281)*, a plate from Emerson's *Pictures of East Anglian Life* of 1888.

The concepts and techniques of Naturalism challenged the Pictorialist dictates of Robinson, initiating an acrimonious dispute in the leading photographic journals where the two principals were joined by other photographers and editors. In addition, the Naturalist approach began to influence the work of other established English camera artists. *In the Twilight*, 1888, *(pl. no. 282)* by Lidell Sawyer, a Pictorialist "born, nursed and soaked" in photography who deplored the fragmentation of the medium into schools, incorporates a sense of atmosphere into a carefully composed genre scene in an effort to balance contrivance and naturalness. One of the most renowned Pictorialist photographers in England, Frank M. Sutcliffe worked in Whitby, a fishing village that was at the time a mecca for painters and amateur photographers. Interested in the hand camera as well as in portraiture, landscapes, and genre scenes made with a stand camera, Sutcliffe's work displays a sensitive application of the Naturalistic precept of spontaneity. The conscious selection of an expressive vantage point, along with carefully controlled printing techniques enabled him to invest *Water Rats (pl. no. 283)* with both the immediacy of real life and a transcendent lyricism.

Emerson renounced his great expectations for artistic photography in 1890, convinced that the pioneering studies in sensitometry—the scientific relation of tonality to exposure—published in the same year by Frederick Hurter and Vero Driffield *(see A Short Technical History, Part II)*, proved that photographers could not truly control the

tonal quality of the print, and therefore the medium was at best a secondary art. Despite this turnabout, however, Naturalism—refined and reinterpreted—continued to find adherents, providing a foundation for the photographic art movements that developed throughout Europe and North America after 1890. This "second coming" of pictorial or art photography will be the subject of Chapter 7.

Art Works in Photographic Reproduction

While the struggle for the acceptance of camera pictures as art was being carried on by a small group of aesthetically minded photographers, a development of much greater consequence for the general population was underway. Realizing that the accurate reproduction of works of art could be both commercially and culturally beneficial, a number of professional photographers throughout Europe started in the 1850s to publish photographic prints of the masterworks of Western art. There is little question that

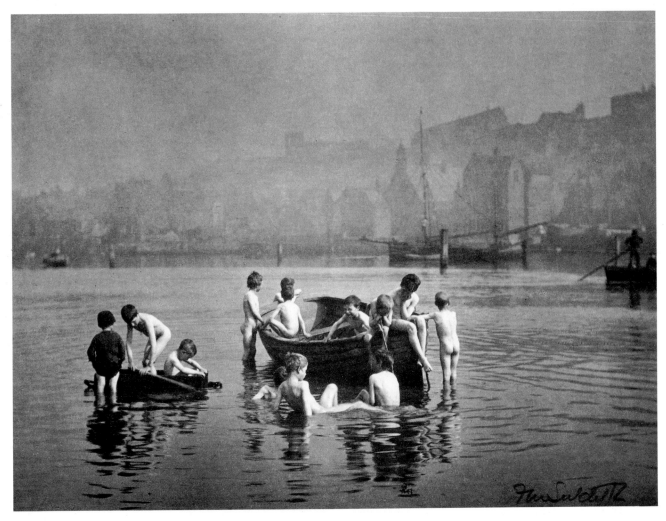

283. FRANK M. SUTCLIFFE. *Water Rats*, 1866. Albumen print. Private Collection.

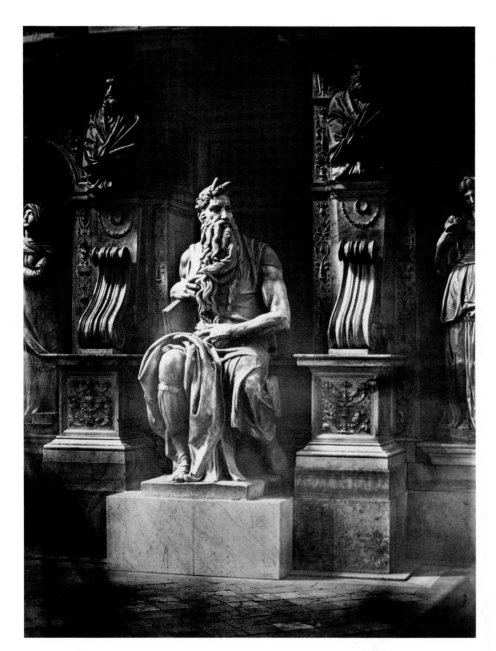

284. JAMES ANDERSON. *Michelangelo's Moses from the Tomb of Julius II*, early 1850s. Albumen print. Collection Centre Canadien d'Architecture/ Canadian Centre for Architecture, Montréal.

since that time the camera image has been the most significant purveyor of visual artifacts, revolutionizing public access to the visual art heritage of the world. The same verisimilitude denounced by elitists as too real when applied to recording actuality was welcomed when used for reproducing art objects, because it was believed that familiarity with masterful works of art through facsimiles would not only uplift the spirit but would improve taste and enable people to make better selections of decor and dress in their daily lives.

It will be recalled that photographs of engravings and casts were among the earliest themes in daguerreotypes and calotypes, in part because these objects provided unmoving subjects but also because they established the possi-

bility of making graphic art available to a wide audience. With the inclusion of the *Bust of Patroclus* and a drawing of *Hagar in the Desert* in *The Pencil of Nature*, and a publication on Spanish painting, Talbot specifically pointed to this important application of photography. Instructions for photographing works of art, notably by Blanquart-Evrard and Disdéri, appeared during the 1850s, at the same time that photographers in Italy were including such works in views made for tourists. James Anderson (born Isaac Atkinson), an English watercolorist, was one of the first to make photographic reproductions of paintings and sculpture along with the better-known architectural monuments of Rome. Considering the dimness of the interior of the Church of San Pietro in Vincoli, Anderson's achievement

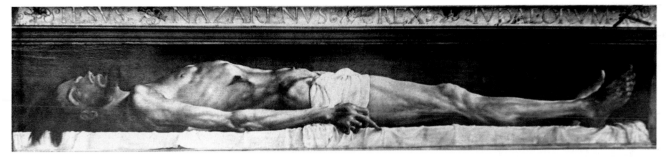

285. ADOLPHE BRAUN. *Holbein's Dead Christ*, 1865. Albumen print. Société Française de Photographie, Paris.

in conveying both the sculptural form and expressive drama of *Michelangelo's Moses from the Tomb of Julius II (pl. no. 284)* is remarkable.

During the 1850s, a considerable number of photographers outside of Italy, among them Antoine Samuel Adam-Salomon, Baldus, Diamond, Disdéri, Fenton, and Franz Hanfstaengl in Europe and John Moran in the United States, began to photograph art objects ranging from those in royal and renowned collections to obscure artifacts in antiquarian societies. As a result of the favorable response by prestigious art critics to the photographic reproductions at the *Exposition Universelle* of 1855, a more programmatic approach ensued. Between 1853 and 1860, Fenton worked for the British Museum, providing them with negatives and selling prints to the public, from which he garnered a not inconsiderable income; besides sculpture and inscribed tablets, he photographed stuffed animals and skeletons. The Alinari brothers of Florence, Braun in Dornach, Hanfstaengl in Munich, and, later, Goupil in Paris—to name the most famous companies—organized large enterprises for the publication and sale of art reproductions. In spite of objections from painters in Italy who regarded photographs as a threat to their livelihood as copyists, these projects all prospered.

Braun, who was said to have higher ambitions than mere commercial success and who might be considered the exemplar of this activity, began modestly by photographing rarely seen Holbein drawings *(pl. no. 285)* in the museum at Basel, not far from his studio at Dornach; when access to other collections became possible through favorable publicity in the press and a bit of lobbying in the proper circles, the company he established photographed some forty collections of drawings, frescoes, paintings, and sculpture in Paris, Rome, Florence, Milan, Dresden, and Vienna.[39] During the mid-1860s, the firm changed from albumen to carbon printing in order to produce permanent images, but the change also made possible exact facsimiles because the photographs incorporated earth pigments similar to those used in the original drawings in the carbon tissues. Widely acclaimed for the improvement in taste engendered by the excellence of his work, Braun kept abreast of changing technologies in both photography and printing, and at the time of his death in 1877 had begun to solve the problem of reproducing oil paintings in color.

The effect of this large-scale activity on the part of Braun and others was to increase the accuracy of representation, making low-cost reproductions of artworks available not only to individuals but to art schools in Europe and the United States. One English enthusiast even suggested that both the expenses and cultural risks of sending English students to study in France and Italy might be avoided because such excellent reproductions had become obtainable! While students thoughtfully continued to insist on contact with real works, photographic reproductions did have a profound effect on the discipline of art history. For the first time, identically replicated visual records enabled scholars in widely separated localities to establish chronologies, trace developments, and render aesthetic judgments. Besides familiarizing people with the acknowledged masterpieces of Western art, photographs made lesser works visible and awakened interest in artifacts and ceremonial objects from ancient cultures and little-known tribal societies. As a substitute for actual visual and tactile experiences, especially in the case of multifunctional three-dimensional structures (architecture), camera images clearly present problems,[40] but it is all but impossible to imagine how the study of visual artifacts would have fared without photography.

In its early struggles to show itself capable of artistic expression, photography wandered down some uneasy byways, and its practitioners initiated some enduring arguments about camera art. These developments were due in part to the hesitation by critics and painters to acknowledge the camera's expressive potential and in part to confusion among photographers themselves as to what constituted artistic images. From a historical perspective, it seems possible to conclude that the medium was at its best when

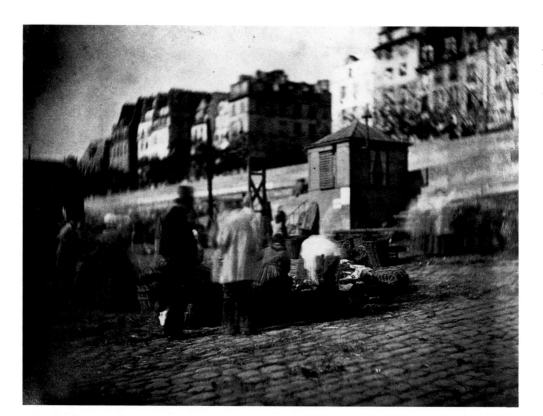

286. CHARLES NÈGRE.
*Market Scene at the Port de
L'Hotel de Ville, Paris*, 1851.
Salt print. Collection
André Jammes, Paris;
National Gallery of
Canada, Ottawa.

illuminating aspects of the real world, and least inspiring when emulating the sentimental conventions of genre (or other) painting. Sensitivity to the disposition of form, to the varieties of textural experience, to the nuances and contrasts of light rather than emphasis on narrative content, gave photographs their expressive power whether their makers called their images documents or art.

During the same period, painters faced with the threat presented by a potentially rival visual medium, found a variety of ways to use the photograph, whether or not they admitted doing so. Of even greater significance was the transformation that occurred in the handmade arts as camera images began to suggest to artists new ways to delineate form and new areas of experience worthy of depiction. Tenuous at first, these interconnections between graphic and photographic representation have gained strength over the years and continue in the present to invigorate both media.

Profile: Charles Nègre

Charles Nègre was an established painter of some repute who became interested in photography for its expressive and technical capabilities as well as its possible commercial exploitation. Born in Grasse in 1820, the nineteen-year-old Nègre arrived in Paris determined to become an artist in the classical tradition. He enrolled first in the

studio of Delaroche, with Fenton, Le Gray, and Le Secq as classmates, and later studied with Ingres. A canvas was accepted for exhibition in the Paris Fine Arts Salon of 1843, and for the next ten years Nègre regularly exhibited under this prestigious sponsorship.

In common with other Delaroche students, Nègre experimented with daguerreotyping, producing a number of landscapes, and around 1849/50 began to make calotypes as an aid in painting. In the following years, Nègre began to photograph actively, drawing upon the picturesque tradition made popular in France by François Bonvin. In his portrayal of beggars, shepherds, and peasants, and the working-class poor of the city, he subordinated detail to overall effect by the careful manipulation of light and shade exemplified by *A Young Girl Seated with a Basket (pl. no. 256)*. The delicate pencil shadings that Nègre applied to the paper negatives in order to adjust values and subdue sharpness were all but invisible on the rough-textured paper surface of the calotype print.

Attracted by spontaneous street activity, the photographer invented a combination of fast lenses to capture aspects of passing life such as market scenes *(pl. no. 286)*, one of which he translated almost directly into a small oil in 1852. He also undertook an ambitious architectural documentation in the south of France, culminating in a portfolio of some 200 prints of buildings, ruins, and landscapes of the Midi, which he endeavored to publish but without much success. Eventually, the project led to a government commission for a series of photographs of Chartres Cathedral. The rich architectural textures and clear details revealed in these images suggest that Nègre had found an inherently photographic aesthetic that was not dependent on painted antecedents.

Besides perfecting calotyping techniques, Nègre displayed an interest in the craft aspect of photography that led to an involvement with printing processes. Convinced that gravure printing would solve the problems of permanence and make possible the inexpensive distribution of photographs, he improved on the process developed by Niepce de Saint Victor, receiving his own patent in 1856. Two years earlier, his gravure prints had been commended for "subtlety of detail, tonal vigor and transparency of middle tones,"[41] but to his great disappointment and the surprise of many, the Duc de Luynes prize for a photographic printing technology went in 1867 to Alphonse Louis Poitevin. Nègre, by then a drawing master in Nice, continued to work for several years on a gravure project but seems to have lost interest in photography. At their best, his calotypes demonstrate a respect for the integrity of the medium informed by exceptional sensitivity to light and form.

Profile: Peter Henry Emerson

Peter Henry Emerson, a gifted but contentious individual who only briefly practiced the medical profession for which he was trained, was involved with photography for some 30 years, but all his important contributions were made between 1885 and 1893. During this period, as he developed, refined, and then denounced a theory of aesthetics, he also documented aspects of rural life in England with the stated aim of "producing truthful pictures."[42]

Born in Cuba of a family distantly related to Ralph Waldo Emerson, Peter Henry arrived in England in 1869 to begin a disciplined education that eventually was crowned with degrees in medicine and surgery. In 1882 he began to photograph, and three years later, on gaining his last medical title, embarked on a documentation of the marshy region of East Anglia inhabited mainly by poor farm laborers, fishermen, hunters, and basket-makers. Hiring a boat to cruise through the inland waterways and fens, Emerson met the landscape painter T. F. Goodall, with whom he collaborated on a book of images of this area,

Life and Landscape of the Norfolk Broads—40 platinum prints with text, issued in 1886. Over the next five years, despite his avowedly aesthetic outlook, Emerson continued to work in this region and to publish images in book form—that is, as sequential statements rather than as individual works of art.

In considering techniques for capturing the "truth" of the real world on photographic plates, Emerson was motivated both by his revulsion against what he considered the meretricious art of the past and by his scientific outlook. A trip to Italy in 1881 had convinced him that the renowned masterpieces of church art, from the mosaics at Ravenna to Michelangelo's frescoes in the Sistine Chapel, were unnatural and mannered—that one might learn more from a walk "in the fields of Italy" than from visits to museums and churches to see "some middle-age monstrosity."[43] His scientific background led him to examine physiological factors in human vision, and on the basis of the optical theories of Hermann Ludwig Ferdinand von Helmholtz, he argued that during a momentary glance human vision is sharp only at the point of focus, whereas the camera lens produces an image that is equally sharp over the entire field; therefore, photographers should use long-focal-length soft lenses to approximate natural vision—that is, to replicate instantaneous perception. He ignored the fact that the human eye does not fix itself on one point but travels rapidly over the visual scene communicating as it does so a sharply defined picture to the brain. It is ironic, also, that his call for softer delineation came at the very moment that the sharpest lenses developed were being introduced into Europe.

That Emerson sought a scientific basis for truthfully depicting actuality while concluding that the goals of art and science are incongruous is one of the paradoxes of his career. It also is puzzling that he could so deftly renounce his great expectations for photography when presented with a means for controlling the relationship of exposure and development. Apart from these inconsistencies, his contributions include the promotion of platinum printing paper for its subtle gradations and permanence, of hand-gravure for reproduction, and of sensible rules for the submission and display of photographs in competitions and exhibitions. As a means of avoiding the fictive and the false in art, his theory of Naturalism inspired a generation of photographers to seek both truth and beauty in actuality.

6.

NEW TECHNOLOGY, NEW VISION, NEW USERS

1875–1925

. . . photography, from being merely another way of procuring or making images of things already seen by our eyes, has become a means of ocular awareness of things that our eyes can never see directly. . . . it has effected a very complete revolution in the ways we use our eyes and . . . in the kinds of things our minds permit our eyes to tell us.

—*William M. Ivins, Jr., 1953*[1]

IN THE FIFTY YEARS that followed the announcement that pictures could be made with sunlight, processes and ideas were continuously tried and discarded as people involved with the medium sought answers to the technical problems created by the expanding aesthetic, commercial, and scientific demands upon photography. As these needs unfolded it became apparent that professional photographers were looking for more sensitive film and for stable, standardized products to document an ever-widening range of subjects; that the scientific community required refined and specialized equipment; that artistic photographers were seeking materials of long tonal range and permanence. Still another constituency was added to those who made and used camera images when at the end of the 1880s simplified apparatus and processing methods—"push button" photography—turned potentially everyone into a photographer. During the same period, the persistent struggle to produce images in color in the camera was won, even though the solution turned out to be one of limited application. This explosion of products, techniques, and processes *(detailed in A Short Technical History, Part II)* produced significant changes in the kinds of images made and how they were used, and as a consequence established new audiences for photographic images. In turn, the increasing numbers of images provided information that altered public attitudes and perceptions of reality.

By 1890, photographic technology had taken wing. Wet collodion, in use for some 25 years before going the way of the daguerreotype, was supplanted by the dry plate—a silver-bromide gelatin emulsion available first on glass plates and later on lightweight, flexible celluloid film. This material was not only easier to use; it was more sensitive to light, thus shortening exposure time, and eventually it became orthochromatic—corrected for all colors of the spectrum except red (and blue, to which it was oversensitive). Camera design also flourished; during the final decades of the 19th century, photographers could choose from among a variety of instruments designed for different purposes. For professional work in the field there were view cameras in several sizes with extension bellows, swings, and tilts; for the serious amateur, hand-held reflex cameras. Stereographic and panoramic apparatus was available, as were tiny detective cameras—so named because they might be concealed in clothing or in other artifacts to make picture-taking unobtrusive. Concurrently, manufacturers began to produce faster lenses, shutters, exposure meters, flash equipment—all of which gave the photographer greater control over capturing on the negative what was occurring in actuality. At the same time, printing papers that satisfied both artistic and commercial purposes appeared on the market.

Standardization—the rational production of photographic materials and processes—accelerated toward the end of the 19th century for a number of reasons. Basic among them was the continuing trend in Western capitalist countries toward the regularization of all manufactured goods and many services, with photography considered an intrinsic part of industrial capacity. Another stimulus was the growth of the chemical and dye industries, especially in Germany after its unification in 1871, which led to competition (in other countries, too) in the manufacture of new sensitizing materials and more refined apparatus. Possibly the most important stimulus was the realization that photography had shown itself to be more than a craft that reproduced what the eye could see, that its potential as a tool for revealing scientific, sociological, and physical phenomena never actually seen had transformed it into the most significant pictorial means in modern industrial society. And as printing technology progressed to make possible the direct transcription of photographic illustration in news and informational media *(see Chapter 10)*, the pressure for more accurate equipment and flexible materials increased.

Photography from the Air

The expanded roles that the medium would presently assume had been hinted at soon after mid-century as photographers attempted to depict the physical universe from unusual vantage points or under abnormal conditions using the unwieldy collodion wet plate. For example, in connection with the growing interest in "flying machines," efforts were begun in the late 1850s to photograph from the sky, to reaffirm scientifically the vision of artists who from the Renaissance on had imagined a "bird's-eye view" of the earth. In 1858, Nadar became the first to succeed, producing a somewhat murky image of Paris while stripped to the skin (for lightness) and concealed behind a dark curtain in

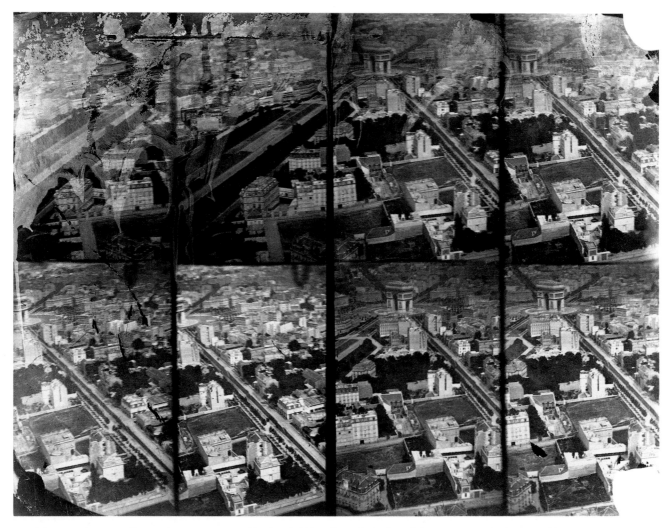

287. NADAR (GASPARD FÉLIX TOURNACHON). *The Arc de Triomphe and the Grand Boulevards, Paris, from a Balloon, 1868.*
Modern gelatin silver print from the original negative. Caisse Nationale des Monuments Historiques et des Sites, Paris.

the basket of a captive balloon manned by the famous Goddard brothers. He spent the next two years promoting his own lighter-than-air creation *(see Profile)*, but his greatest success in aerial photography stemmed from the views of the *Arc de Triomphe (pl. no. 287)* taken in 1868 with a multilens camera from the basket of another balloon, the Hippodrome.

Aside from the romance associated with the balloon—called the "ultimate engine of democracy" by the French—the practical nature of balloon transport was demonstrated when it turned out to be one of the two ways that mail could be delivered to and from the besieged city of Paris during the Franco-Prussian War (1870–71). The other way, by carrier pigeon, involved photography in that the written messages were reduced microphotographically and later enlarged for reading in a projection enlarger, foreshadowing the V-mail of the second World War.

At about the same time as Nadar's experiments—1860—the Boston photographer James Wallace Black, a partner in the astrophotographic research conducted at Harvard by John Adams Whipple *(see Chapter 1)*, ascended 1,200 feet in a balloon tethered over the Boston Common. Black used a Voigtländer camera and a shutter of his own contrivance to make the first aerial photographs in America, six of which are extant. Although the extraordinary feat of viewing the city "as the eagle and the wild goose saw it" *(pl. no. 288)* was praised by Oliver Wendell Holmes,[2] and the photographer himself suggested that reconnaissance photography by balloon be tried during the Civil War, no action was taken. Despite attempts by several other photographers to make topographical views from the air, at times with balloon and kite cameras, the airborne camera seems not to have evoked further interest until the 20th century.[3]

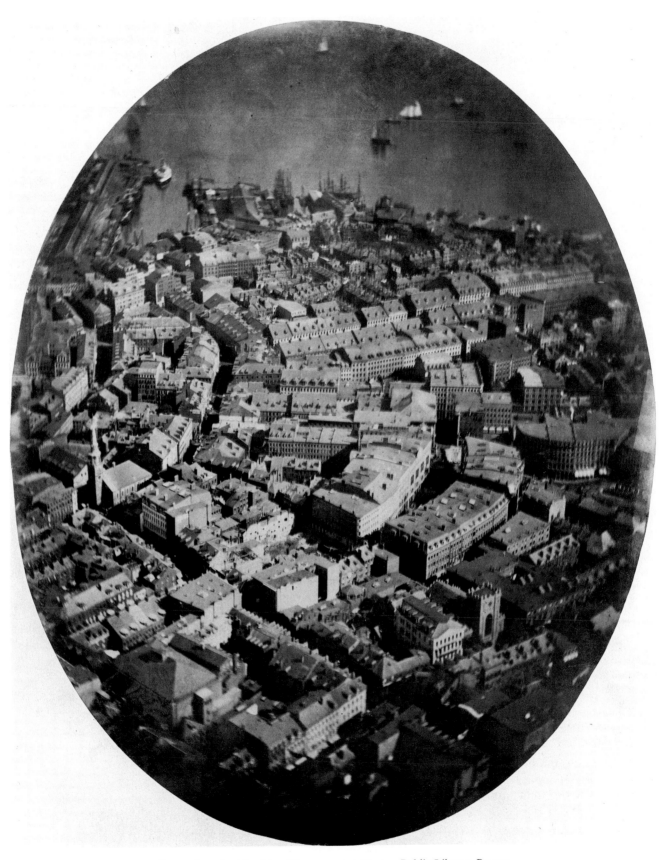

288. James Wallace Black. *Boston from the Air*, 1860. Albumen print. Boston Public Library, Boston.

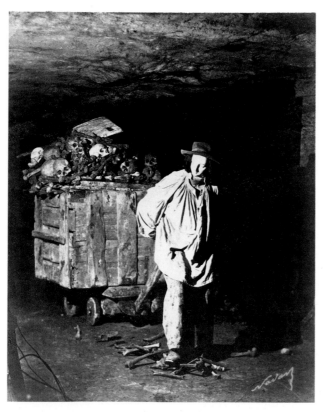

289. NADAR (GASPARD FÉLIX TOURNACHON). *Workmen in the Paris Catacombs*, 1861. Albumen print. Bibliothèque Nationale, Paris.

Photography by Artificial Light

Another group of experiments undertaken to extend the scope of the medium soon after its invention involved artificial illumination. Electric batteries made it possible for Talbot in 1851 to produce a legible image of a swiftly revolving piece of newsprint *(see below)* and also provided artificial light for Nadar's experiments in this realm. Using Bunsen batteries[+] and reflectors, Nadar first made portraits and then, in 1861, took the complicated apparatus below the streets to photograph in the sewers and catacombs (ancient burial grounds) of Paris. Some of the exposures took as long as 18 minutes, necessitating the substitution of manikins for humans *(pl. no. 289)*, but despite having to cart lights, reflectors, rolls of wire, and camera and collodion equipment through narrow and humid corridors, Nadar produced about 100 underground scenes. Views of the pipes and drains, the walls of bones, and the tomb markers that constitute the nether regions of the city demonstrated the medium's potential to disclose visual information about a wide range of physical facts.

Commercial portraiture by electric light using Bunsen cells was attempted by Adolphe Ost in Vienna in 1864, but it was not until the end of the following decade that the quality of portraits made by electric light became almost indistinguishable from those made with natural lighting. Because electric batteries initially were both weak and costly, photographers experimented with other chemical agents, including oxyhydrogen flame directed against lime (limelight) and magnesium wire. The latter substance was first put to the test in attempts to picture mine interiors in England in 1864; soon afterward it made possible images taken inside the Great Pyramid, and in 1866 the American Charles Waldack employed it for a series inside Mammoth Cave in Kentucky *(pl. no. 290)*. This substance was also used for indoor portraiture; a group portrait, one of a series of early experiments with magnesium light made by John C. Browne in 1865, includes the editor of the *Philadelphia Photographer*, the journal most eager to promote new photographic technologies in the United States. In its most common form—flash-powder (used from the 1880s on)—magnesium emitted a cloud of acrid white smoke when ignited, and its intense light created harsh tonal contrasts, but until the flash bulb was invented in Germany in 1925 there was no practical alternative portable lighting agent.

Urban nighttime views presented another intriguing problem for photographers, but during most of the 19th century the gaslight used in street lamps was so weak in its illuminating power that exposures of from three to four hours were required to represent the tonalities of the night scene. In an early experiment by Whipple in 1863, photographs of the Boston Common, where the illumination had been boosted with the aid of electric light, still required exposures about 180 times as long as those taken in sunlight. Following the gradual electrification of cities from the 1880s on, there were more frequent attempts to capture people, carriages, and especially the street lighting itself at night. Works by Paul Martin in London and Alfred Stieglitz in New York in the 1890s are among the numbers of images testifying to the fact that both documentary and pictorialist photographers were fascinated by night scenery, especially the reflections of electric lights on glistening pavements and the tonal contrasts between virgin snow and velvety night sky.

The keen interest shown by Talbot and other photographers in objects and phenomena not ordinarily visible to the human eye *(see Chapter 1)*, in conjunction with the increasing need on the part of the scientific community for precise information about microorganisms, prompted improvements in the design of equipment and methods that enabled scientists to study such matter as the structure of crystals and the forms of cells. At the same time, astrophotography gained ground with the capability of photographing, besides sun and moon, planetary bodies; by 1877 it was possible to contemplate a complete photographic mapping of the fixed star firmament. In the following decade,

Austrian and German photographers succeeded in making clear images of the phases of lightning in the night sky. Toward the end of the century, X-rays—spectral rays that penetrate opaque structures—were discovered by Conrad Wilhelm Roentgen (recipient of a Nobel prize in 1901) at the University of Würzberg, stimulating their immediate use in camera images for medical diagnoses; within a year more than a thousand publications about X-rays appeared.

The Photography of Movement

The most dramatic developments in terms of popular acclaim occurred in the realm of motion study as the camera began to provide artists, scientists, and the lay person with visual evidence about ordinary matters that the unaided eye could not see, such as walking and running. Talbot's success in stopping action with the aid of an electric flash (mentioned earlier) was acclaimed because it pointed the way to photographing "with all the animation of full life . . . the most agile dancer during her rapid movements . . . the bird of swiftest flight during its passage,"[5] but these experiments were not followed up until the 1880s when Austrian scientist Ernst Mach, working in Prague, made exposures of flying projectiles, sound waves, and air streams using electric flash as a lighting source. Incidentally, al-

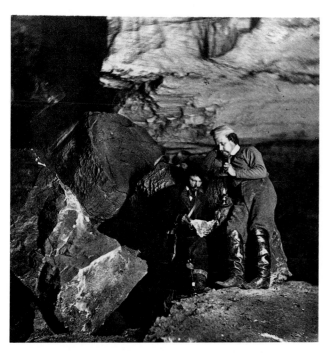

290. CHARLES WALDACK. *Beyond the "Bridge of Sighs"* from *Mammoth Cave Views*, 1866. Albumen print. New-York Historical Society; George T. Bagoe Collection, gift of Mrs. Elihu Spicer.

though concerned with providing scientific information, Mach also wished these images to be visually pleasing, arguing that aesthetic quality in no way detracts from usefulness. Simultaneously, experimentation in stop-action photography took off in other directions also—one based on the capacity of the short-focal-length lens used on stereograph cameras to freeze motion in street photography *(see below)* and the other on the ability of successive exposures to record the intrinsic elements of movement.

Throughout the 19th century, the need to institute proper training programs for horses and the desire by painters of history pictures for greater accuracy in the depiction of battle scenes had led to efforts by scientists to graphically analyze motion; after its invention photography became the favored instrument for this endeavor. Beginning in 1872, the analysis of motion by the camera was carried on for some 20 years by Eadweard Muybridge and Thomas Eakins in the United States, by Etienne Jules Marey in France, and by Ottomar Anschütz in Germany.

Muybridge's prominent role in this adventure was the result, as he noted, of an "exceptionally felicitous alliance" with Leland Stanford, ex-governor of California, president of the Central Pacific Railroad, and owner of the Great Palo Alto Breeding Ranch, who nevertheless eventually disavowed the collaboration.[6] Curiosity among racing enthusiasts about the positions of the legs of a horse running at full gallop prompted Stanford to call upon Muybridge— by 1872 the most renowned cameraman in the American West—to photograph his trotter Occident in motion. While not remarkably clear, the first images from Muybridge's camera established to Stanford's satisfaction that at one point all four of the animal's hooves left the ground —although not, it should be added, in the position usually chosen for painted representations *(pl. no. 291)*.[7]

This experiment initiated a collaboration beginning in 1878 between Stanford and Muybridge with the goal of providing visual information about animal movements useful in the training of horses and human athletes. This time, the animals were photographed as they moved in front of a calibrated backdrop, tripping specially designed electrically operated shutters of 12 cameras equipped with Dallmeyer stereographic lenses at one-thousandth of a second. News of the sensational photographs that resulted—photographs that documented what the human eye had never registered —appeared in the California press in 1877, in the prestigious *Scientific American* the following year *(pl. no. 292)*, and in journals in London, Paris, Berlin, and Vienna soon afterward. Having become an international celebrity, Muybridge lectured in the United States and Europe, where his work was acknowledged by the French physiologist Marey.

Late in 1883, as a result of the withdrawal of Stanford's patronage, Muybridge accepted an invitation to continue

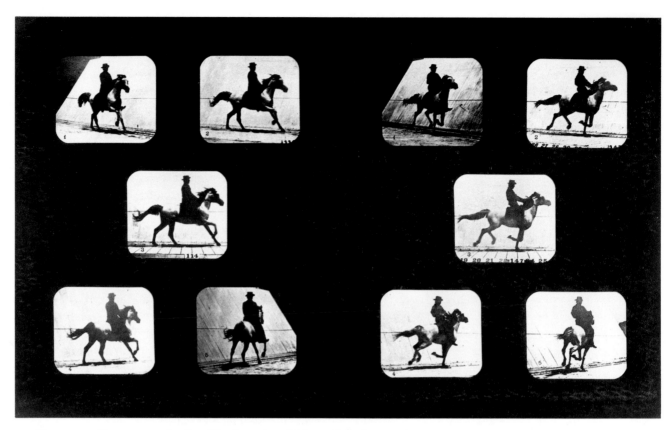

291. EADWEARD MUYBRIDGE. *Studies of Foreshortenings; Mahomet Running*, 1879.
Modern print from a wet-plate glass collodion negative. Stanford University Art Museum, Stanford, Cal.

his work at the University of Pennsylvania where he boldly extended the cast of characters and the range of movements. His human subjects were drawn from the teaching staff at the university, from professional models for the female nudes (about whose lack of grace he complained!), and from friends in the arts, among them Eakins, whose hand he photographed in various positions *(pl. no. 293)*. In an elaboration of the California experiments, the movements generally were performed in front of a backdrop marked with a grid of vertical and horizontal lines and before a battery of 24 cameras about six inches apart in a line parallel with the grid, while smaller groups of cameras were maneuvered into position to capture frontal, rear, and foreshortened views, as in *Woman Emptying a Bucket on a Seated Companion (pl. no. 294)*. By the time the Pennsylvania project began in 1884, advances in technology enabled Muybridge to use more sensitive dry plates instead of collodion, and to afix a roller shutter in front of each camera lens. These were operated by an electromagnetic system (designed by the photographer) that tripped the shutters in succession and at the same time operated a chronograph or timing device. In a year-and-a-half of work, Muybridge produced some 100,000 images analyzing the movements involved in walking, running, playing ball, pirouetting, curtseying, and laying bricks, among other activities. The university selected 781 plates for *Animal Locomotion*, an expensive publication, after which Muybridge issued smaller editions entitled *Animals in Motion* and *The Human Figure in Motion*.[8]

Eakins, the American painter whose long-standing interest in the accurate graphic representation of movement had prompted him to correspond with Muybridge and to purchase a set of studies of the horse in motion,[9] applied the knowledge he gained to the depiction of the horse's legs in his first Philadelphia commission—the oil painting, *The Fairman Rogers' Four in Hand (pl. no. 295)*, in which ironically the carriage wheels are blurred as if moving while the horses' hooves are frozen in one phase of their movement. In his own studies of motion, Eakins, who started to make photographs as soon as dry plates became available *(see Chapter 5) (pl. no. 297)*, preferred to work with apparatus that registered the successive phases of action on one plate, as can be seen in *History of a Jump (pl. no. 298)*, a frequently reproduced work.

Marey's contribution to the photographic documentation of movement was made in conjunction with his primary vocation of physiology, for which he initially had devised graphic methods of recording skeletal and muscle

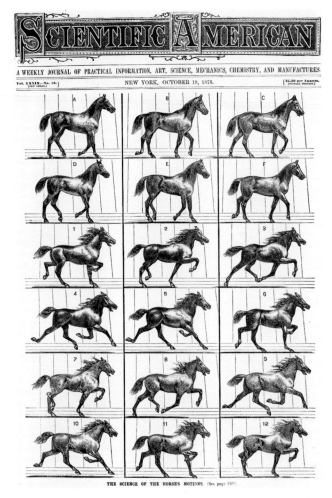

SCIENTIFIC AMERICAN

A WEEKLY JOURNAL OF PRACTICAL INFORMATION, ART, SCIENCE, MECHANICS, CHEMISTRY, AND MANUFACTURES.

Vol. XXXIX.—No. 16.]   NEW YORK, OCTOBER 19, 1878.   [$3.20 per Annum.]

THE SCIENCE OF THE HORSE'S MOTIONS. (See page 241)

292. UNKNOWN. *Cover of Scientific American with Muybridge's Series of Horses*, Oct. 19, 1878. Engraving. New York Public Library, Astor, Lenox, and Tilden Foundations.

movements. After reading about Muybridge's experiments in *La Nature* in 1878 (and later through personal contact), Marey turned to the camera as a more accurate tool for such documentation. Because he was more interested in schematic diagrams of muscle movements than in random, if timed, depictions of moving figures, he adapted for his own use the *fusil photographique* (photographic gun)—a camera inspired by the rotating bullet chamber of a revolver —which Eakins also used. Originally, he produced a sequence of separate images with this apparatus but soon realized that more precise information could be gained if the sequential movements appeared on the same plate. For these timed images—chronophotographs—Marey employed a rotating slit shutter and experimented with a variety of black and white garments on models who moved against similarly colored backdrops; eventually he settled on a figure clothed entirely in black with bright metal bands attached to the sides of the arms and legs, photographed against a black background *(pl. no. 299)*. This yielded a "working geometric drawing"—a linear graph of 60 skeletal movements per second.[10] As was true of other kinds of instantaneous studies, these images were to have a telling effect on concepts and styles in art as well as on the scientific understanding of movement.

Similar experiments in arresting motion were made by Anschütz, who had studied photography in Berlin, in Munich with Franz Hanfstaengl, and in Vienna, before returning to his native Prussia. Growing out of a series of stills of horses in motion that Anschütz had made with a shutter mounted in front of the plate, he embarked on a project to produce instantaneous photographs of animals

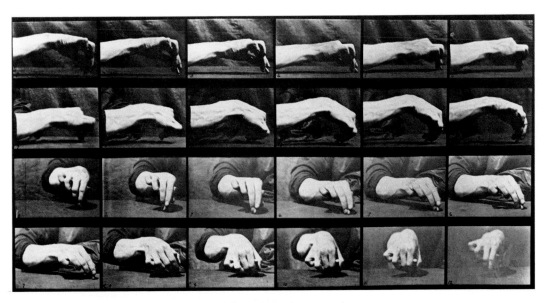

293. EADWEARD MUYBRIDGE. *Eakin's Hand* from Animal Locomotion, 1887. Collotype. Museum of the Philadelphia Civic Center.

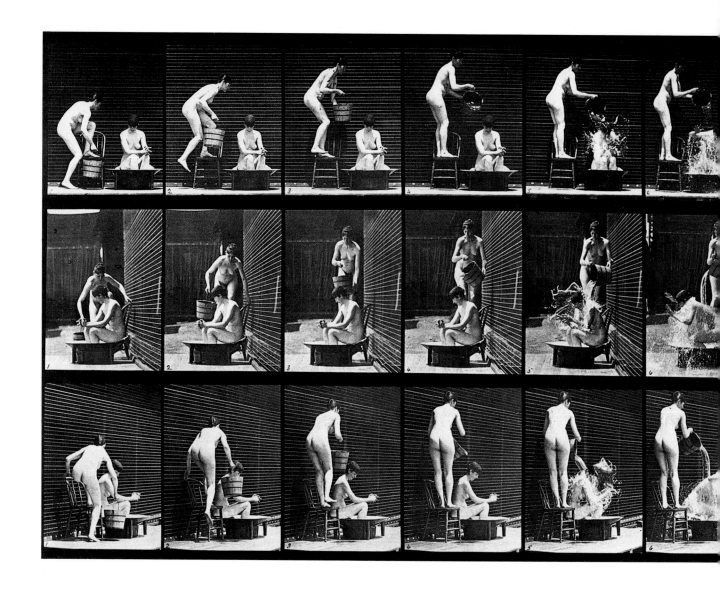

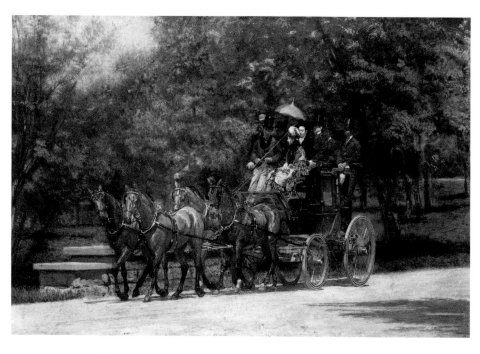

294. EADWEARD MUYBRIDGE. *Plate 408* from *Animal Locomotion*, 1887. Collotype. Photograph Collection, New York Public Library, Astor, Lenox, and Tilden Foundations.

295. THOMAS EAKINS. *The Fairman Rogers' Four-in-Hand*, 1879. Oil on canvas. Philadelphia Museum of Art; gift of William Alexander Dick.

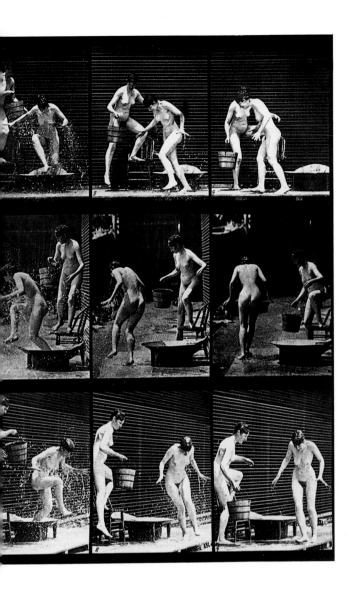

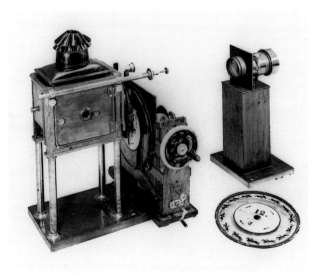

296. EADWEARD MUYBRIDGE. *Zoöpraxiscope*, c. 1870.
Eadweard Muybridge Collection, Kingston Upon
Thames Museum, England.

in the Breslau Zoo. Widely publicized, the most famous among these images are 120 exposures of the activities of a family of storks *(pl. no. 300)*. By 1886 Anschütz had adapted Muybridge's system of using multiple cameras to the very small instruments with which he worked, and with the aid of the Prussian ministries of war and education he continued to photograph both animal movements and army maneuvers, using a specially designed "Anschütz" lens manufactured by the Goerz Company.

Three of the photographers involved in stop-motion experimentation envisaged the next logical step—the reconstitution of the appearance of movement by viewing the separate analytical images in rapid sequence. For this purpose Marey and Muybridge turned to a range of so-called philosophical toys, among them the Phenakistoscope (or zoetrope) and the Praxinoscope, both of which involved rotating cylinders or disks with a sequence of images on one moving element viewed through either counter-rotating or stationary slots on the other. This reconstitution of motion, suggested first by Sir John Herschel in 1867[11] and later by Marey in 1873, struck Stanford as a means to test the correctness of the photographic evidence seen in the stills; therefore Muybridge worked out the Zoöpraxiscope *(pl. no. 296)*, a device consisting of a glass disk on which images were arranged equidistantly in consecutive order, with a slotted counter-rotating viewer; its function, as stated by its designer, was "for synthetically demonstrating movements analytically photographed from life."[12] These first "motion pictures" were seen by the Stanford family in Palo Alto in 1879, and two years later during Muybridge's trip abroad they were projected for audiences of influential European artists and intellectuals. Anschütz's endeavor in 1887 to reconstruct movement employing an Electro-Tachyscope, a device in which enlarged diapositives (slides), illuminated by a spark, revolved in sequence on a disk, was limited in effect because the small-format images were not projected but had to be viewed directly.

Science and art became more profoundly intertwined when the camera began to supply evidence of animal movement beyond what even the most naturalistically inclined artist was capable of seeing. Stop-motion photography and the various publications attracted a wide spectrum of artists working in a variety of styles, among them the salon painters Adolphe William Bouguereau and Franz von Lenbach, the realist Edgar Degas, the Pre-Raphaelite John Everett Millais, the expressionist Auguste Rodin, and the symbolist James Abbott McNeill Whistler. As in the past, many painters used the newly revealed information to correct inaccurate representation and to make their work appear more naturalistic, as was true of Jean-Louis Meissonier, a French painter of prestigious historical battle

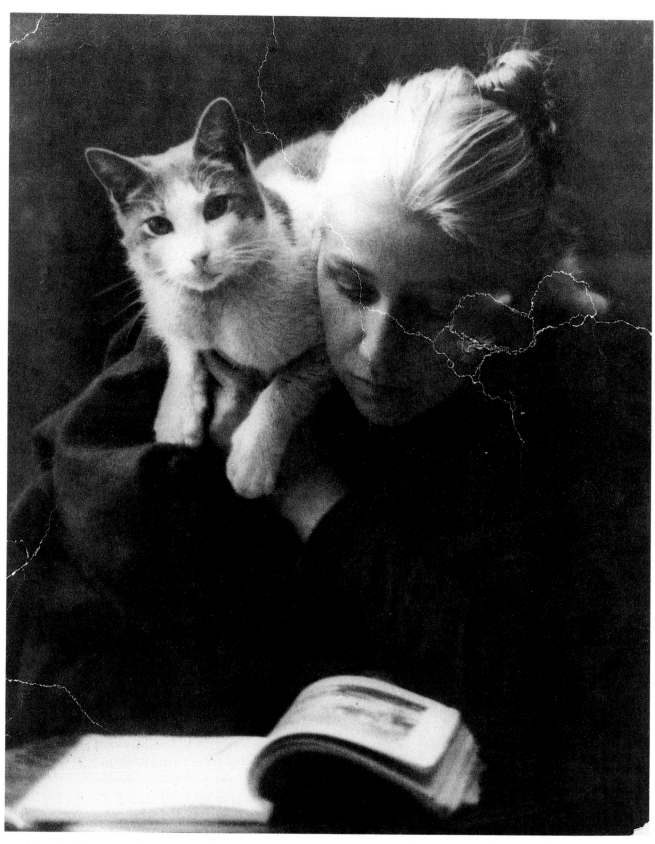

297. THOMAS EAKINS. *Amelia Van Buren with a Cat*, c. 1891. Platinum print.
Metropolitan Museum of Art, New York; David Hunter McAlpin Fund, 1947.

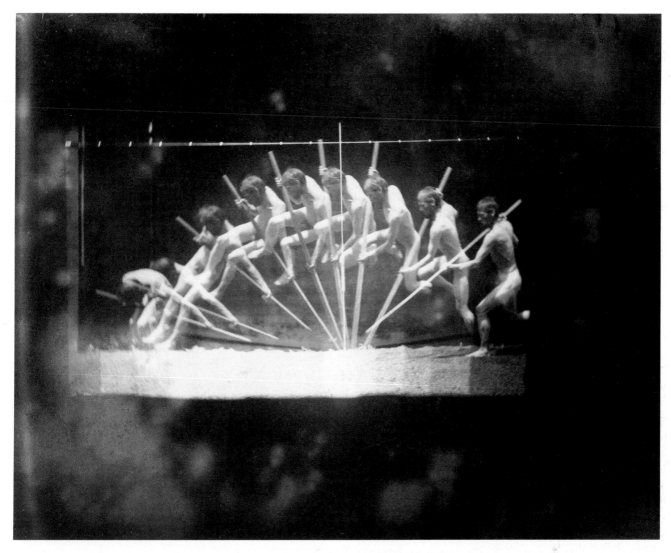

298. THOMAS EAKINS. *History of a Jump*, 1884–85. Gelatin silver print. Philadelphia Museum of Art; gift of George Bregler.

scenes, some of which he altered to conform to the new knowledge. Other artists became engrossed with the idea of movement and time, integrating various views of the same object seen in several positions as the theme of their paintings and creating images suggestive of the fluidity of situations and events. For example, Degas, an enthusiast who was himself a sensitive photographer, conveyed lively animation by painting on a single canvas the same seated dancer in a variety of positions *(pl. no. 301)*.

Time, movement, and change exerted an even greater fascination on the early-20th-century European painters who sought a new language to express the shifting realities of their own era. Photography may have been blamed by a small group of these avant-garde artists for a "disgraceful alteration" in seeing, but, as Aaron Scharf has pointed out, "stop-motion camera imagery, in particular the geometric diagrams of Marey, with their emphasis on pattern and movement, offered Cubist, Vorticist, and Futurist painters a fresh vocabulary."[13] In the most famous of a number of such examples, *Nude Descending a Staircase (pl. no. 302)*, French artist Marcel Duchamp adapted Marey's schema to transform the posed female nude—conventionally an expression of immobility—into a supremely energetic statement that proclaims its modernism while maintaining a tie to hallowed tradition. Of all those seeking to embody the vitality of their time in the painted image, Duchamp most clearly recognized that photography in all its ramifications had subverted the long-standing relationship between the artists and the conventions of painting. Interest in the graphic depiction of movement based on Marey's studies reached a climax among European artists of the Cubist and Futurist movements between 1911 and 1914, but other kinds of stop-motion photographs have continued to inspire artists everywhere up to the present.

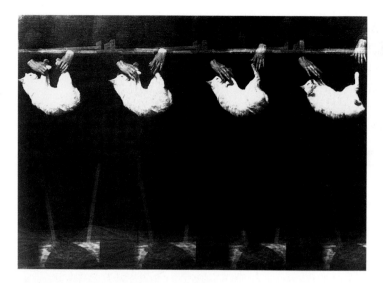

299. ETIENNE JULES MAREY. *Falling Cat Sequence*, c. 1880s. Gelatin silver prints. National Museum of American History, Smithsonian Institution, Washington, D.C.

FACING PAGE:

300. OTTOMAR ANSCHÜTZ. *Series of Storks in Flight*, 1884. Gelatin silver prints. Agfa-Gevaert Foto-Historama, Leverkusen, Germany.

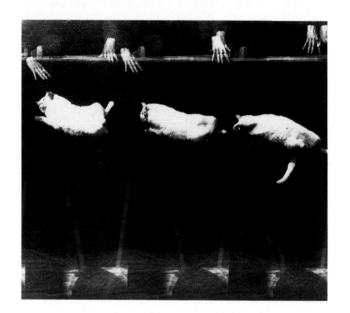

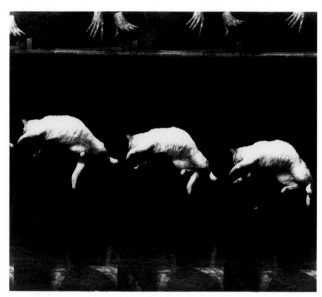

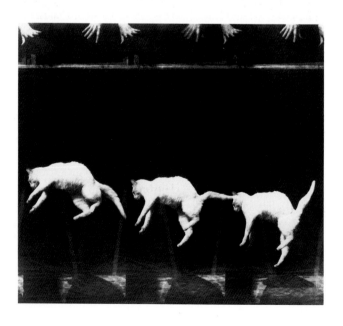

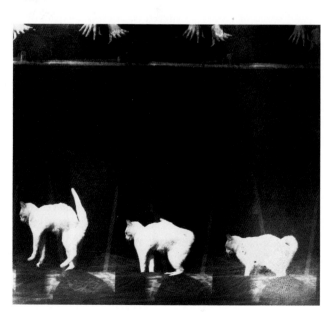

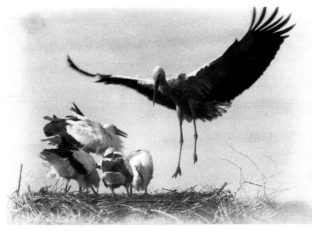 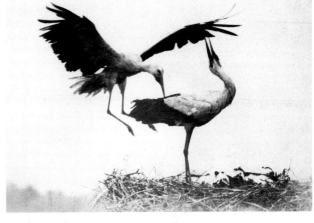

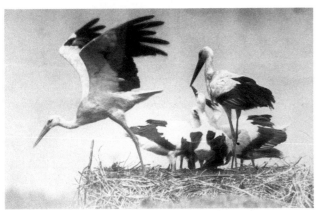 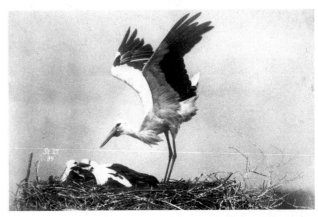

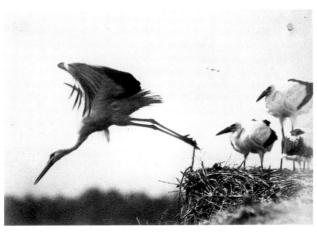 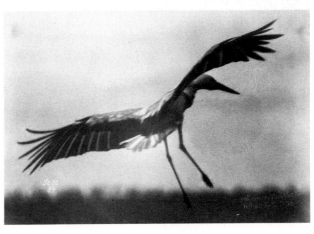

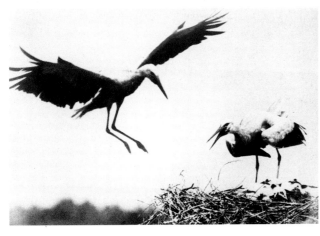 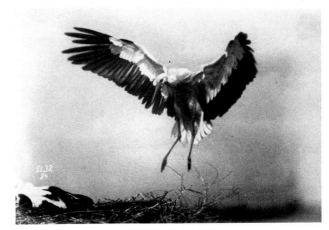

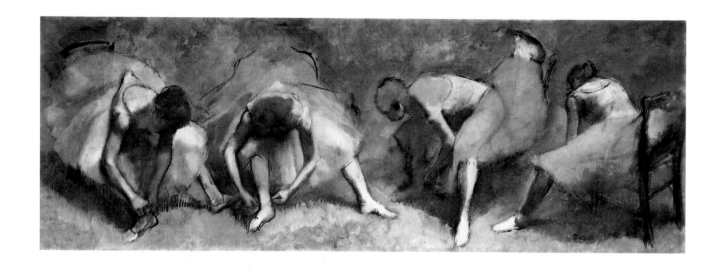

301. EDGAR DEGAS. *Frieze of Dancers*, c. 1883. Oil on canvas. Cleveland Museum of Art; gift of the Hanna Fund.

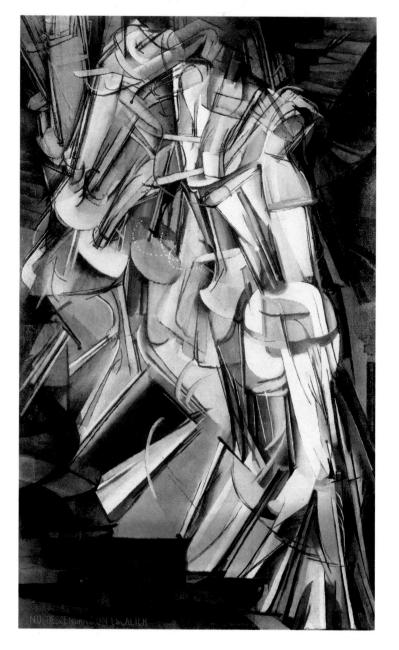

302. MARCEL DUCHAMP. *Nude Descending a Staircase #2*, 1912. Oil on canvas, Philadelphia Museum of Art; Louise and Walter Arensberg Collection.

Instantaneous Photographs of Everyday Life

Whether facing the natural landscape or the urban scene, many photographers other than those investigating motion for scientific reasons found that they, too, were eager to arrest the continuous flux of life, to scrutinize and savor discrete segments of time and to capture them on glass plates and, later, film. This first became possible with the short-focal-length lenses on stereograph cameras. Roger Fenton, for example, was able to capture the forms of flowing water and fleeting clouds on the stereograph plate. By 1859, Edward Anthony in New York *(pl. no. 189)*, George Washington Wilson in Edinburgh, and Adolphe Braun and Hippolyte Jouvin in Paris *(pl. no. 190)*—among others—began to make and publish stereograph views of the "fleeting effects" of crowds and traffic on the principal streets of urban centers and, in Jouvin's case, in market-places, public gardens, and at festive events. Acclaimed because they seemed to embody "all . . . life and motion,"[14] these views also disclose the distinctiveness of different cultural environments; stereographs of city streets reveal at a glance the profound dissimilarities between the tone of public life in New York and Paris, for example, while others make visible the contrast between social conditions in the industrialized countries and in areas being opened to colonization and exploitation *(see Chapter 8)*.

That this interest in the flux of urban life engaged painters of the time as well as photographers is apparent in the canvases of the French Impressionists that seem to "capture" as if by camera the moving forms of people and traffic in the streets and parks of Paris. Besides a preference for high horizons and blurred figures, similar to that seen in numbers of stereographs of city streets, and exemplified in Claude Monet's *Boulevard des Capucines (pl. no. 303)*—a view actually painted from Nadar's studio—the Impressionists broke with tradition in their preference for accidental-looking arrangements of figures that appear to be sliced through by the edges of the canvas in the manner of the photographic plate. Certain canvases by these painters also mimic the optical distortions of figure and space visible in stereographs, suggesting that, as Scharf observed, "photography must be accorded consideration in any discussion of the character of Impressionist painting."[15]

The appeal of the spontaneous and informal continued unabated during the last decade of the 19th century and resulted in the extraordinary popular interest in small, hand-held single-lens cameras that would simplify the taking of informal pictures *(see A Short Technical History, Part II)*. Of all the apparatus developed to fulfill this need, the most sensational was the Kodak camera, first marketed in 1888 by its inventor George Eastman. However, this fixed-

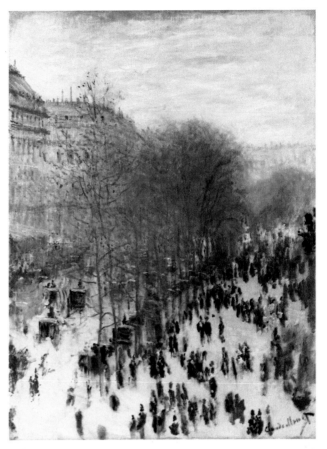

303. CLAUDE MONET. *Boulevard des Capucines, Paris (Les Grands Boulevards)*, 1873–74. Oil on canvas. Nelson-Atkins Museum of Art, Kansas City, Mo.; Kenneth A. and Helen F. Spencer Foundation Acquisitions Fund.

focus box did more than make it easy for people to take pictures of everyday events; by making developing and printing independent of exposure it encouraged a new constituency to make photographs and inaugurated the photo-processing industry.

The Kodak and the snapshot (Herschel's term to describe a series of instantaneous exposures) were promoted through astute advertising campaigns that appealed to animal lovers, bicyclists, campers, parents, sportsmen, travelers, and tourists. Freed from the tedium of darkroom work, large numbers of middle-class folk in Europe and the United States used the Kodak during leisure hours to depict family and friends at home and at recreation, to record the ordinary rather than the spectacular. Besides serving as sentimental mementos, these unpretentious images provided later cultural historians with descriptive information about everyday buildings, artifacts, and clothing—indisputable evidence of the popular taste of an era.

The convenience of merely pressing the button resulted in a deluge of largely unexceptional pictures. Despite the

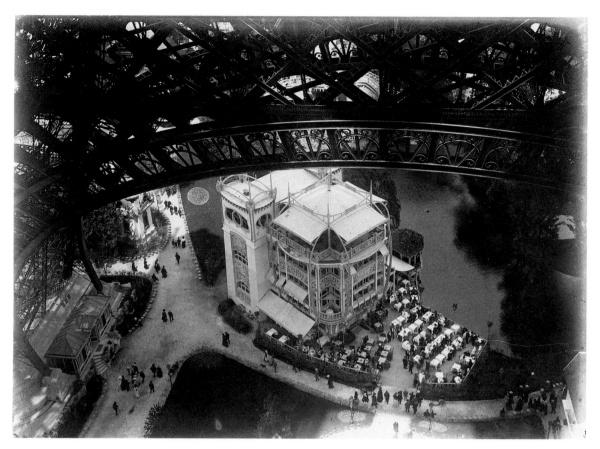

304. EMILE ZOLA. *A Restaurant, Taken from the First Floor or Staircase of the Eiffel Tower, Paris,* 1900. Gelatin silver print. Collection Dr. François Emile Zola, Gif-sur-Yvette, France.

suggestion today that the "aesthetic quality of the snapshot has received less attention than it deserves,"[16] most were made solely as personal records by individuals of modest visual ambitions. Untutored in either art or science, they tended to regard the image in terms of its subject rather than as a visual statement that required decisions about where to stand, what to include, how best to use the light. Further, since they were untroubled by questions of print size or quality, they mostly ignored the craft elements of photographic expression. This attitude, coupled with the fact that "every Tom, Dick and Harry could get something or other onto a sensitive plate,"[17] contributed to the emerging polarity between documentary images—assumed to be entirely artless—and artistic photographs conceived by their makers (and others) to embody aesthetic ideas and feelings.

Nevertheless, whether by accident or design, snapshots do on occasion portray with satisfying formal vigor moments that seem excised from the seamless flow of life. For one thing, the portability of the instrument enabled the user to view actuality from excitingly different vantage points, as in a 1900 image made by French novelist Émile

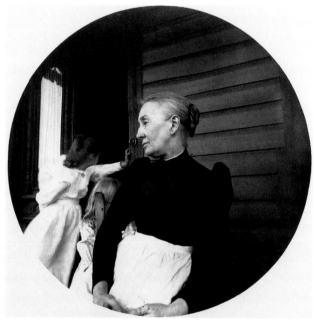

305. HORACE ENGLE. *Unknown Subject, Roanoke, Virginia,* c. 1901. Gelatin silver print from the original negative. Pennsylvania State University Press, University Park; courtesy Edward Leos.

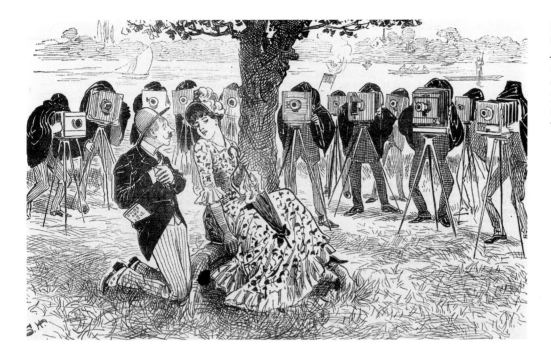

306. UNKNOWN. "What an Exposure!" from *The Amateur Photographer*, Sept. 23, 1887. Engraving. Gernsheim Collection, Humanities Research Center, University of Texas, Austin.

Zola from the Eiffel Tower looking down *(pl. no. 304)*. In its organization of space it presented an intriguing pattern of architectural members and human figures, foreshadowing the fascination with spatial enigmas that would be explored more fully by photographers in the 1910s and '20s. In a different vein, the small camera made possible the refreshing directness visible in images of small-town life by Horace Engle *(pl. no. 305)*, an American engineer who used a Gray Stirn Concealed Vest camera before turning to the Kodak. Because the camera was so easy to use, a photographer stationed behind a window or door, as Engle sometimes was, might intuitively manage light and form to explore private gestures and expressions that almost certainly would be withheld were his presence known. This urge to ensnare ephemeral time, so to speak, also foreshadowed developments of the late 1920s when the sophisticated small Leica camera made "candid" street photography a serious pursuit among photojournalists. Viewed in sequence rather than singly, snapshots sometimes suggest an underlying theme or the emotional texture of an event in the manner of later photojournalistic picture stories and might be considered forerunners in this sense, too.

However, despite the claim that "the man with a box-camera has as many chances of preserving pleasure as those blessed (?) *[sic]* with the more expensive instruments,"[18] the Kodak in itself was limited in scope. But the spontaneity it emblematized appealed to many serious photographers, who armed themselves with a more sensitive apparatus of a similar nature—the hand camera. Individuals of both sexes, from varying backgrounds and classes, of differing aesthetic persuasions, who usually processed their own work, produced the kind of imagery that for want of a better term has come to be called documentation. Turning to the quotidian life of cities and villages for inspiration, artists used the hand camera as a sketchbook, pictorialists tried to evoke the urban tempo, and still others found it a disarming device with which to conquer the anonymity of modern life. Serious workers rather than snapshooters, this new breed of image-maker sought to express a personal vision that embraced the special qualities of the time and place in which they lived.

The invasion of personal privacy that the small camera user could effect with ease became an issue in the late 19th century—one that still elicits discussion today. The question of propriety was raised when individuals and groups of amateurs, often organized into camera and bicycle clubs, began to photograph unwitting people in the streets and at play. Reaction ran the gamut from the gentle satire of an 1887 cartoon in Britain's *Amateur Photographer (pl. no. 306)* to more strident denunciations in which "hand-camera fiends" were admonished to refrain from photographing "ladies as they emerge from their morning dip, loving couples, private picnicking parties" under threat of having their cameras "forcibly emptied."[19] Indeed, it has been suggested that the many images of working-class people in the streets around the turn of the century may reflect the fact that they were less likely than middle-class folk to protest when they saw strangers approaching with a camera.[20]

Street life began to attract hand-camera enthusiasts

(and some using larger equipment, as well) partly because it offered an uncommon panorama of picturesque subjects. Previously, photographers in search of visual antidotes for the depressing uniformity of life in industrialized societies had ventured abroad either to exotic lands or had searched out quaint pastoral villages as yet untouched by industrial activity. They also had photographed the city's poor and ethnic minorities for their picturesqueness. As urbanization advanced, documentarians, pictorialists, hand-camera enthusiasts, and even some who worked with large-format cameras were drawn by the animated and vigorous street life in the city to depict the varieties of peoples and experiences to be found in urban slum and working-class neighborhoods with less artifice.

To some extent, the experiences of Paul Martin, working in London from about 1884 on, typify the changes that occurred in the practice, usage, and character of photography everywhere. When Martin began an apprenticeship as an engraver he came in contact with photography as a useful resource—a boon to the illustrator. He taught himself the craft from magazines that, along with amateur photography clubs, provided technical assistance and aesthetic guidelines to growing numbers of hand camera enthusiasts. Like Martin, some were working people from moderate backgrounds who were unable to afford expensive camera equipment or time-consuming processes that used the platinum and carbon materials favored by aesthetic photographers. Martin became an accomplished craftsman nevertheless, adept at making composites, vignetting, and solving technical problems connected with photographing out-of-doors at night; during the 1890s, a number of his straight silver prints were awarded prizes in competitions despite being judged at times as lacking in atmosphere, as too "map-like."

Able to photograph only after a full-day's work or on holidays, Martin roamed the grimy neighborhoods of London's poor, and the resorts where working people spent their holidays, with a Facile hand camera, seeking out

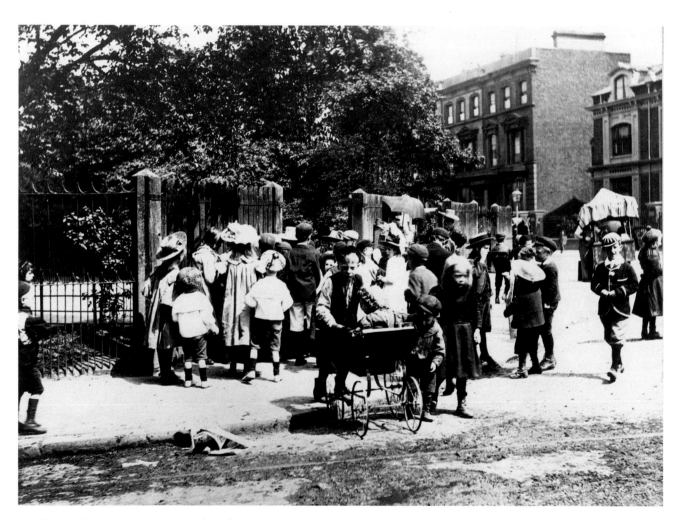

307. PAUL MARTIN. *Entrance to Victoria Park*, c. 1893. Gelatin silver print.
Gernsheim Collection, Humanities Research Center, University of Texas, Austin.

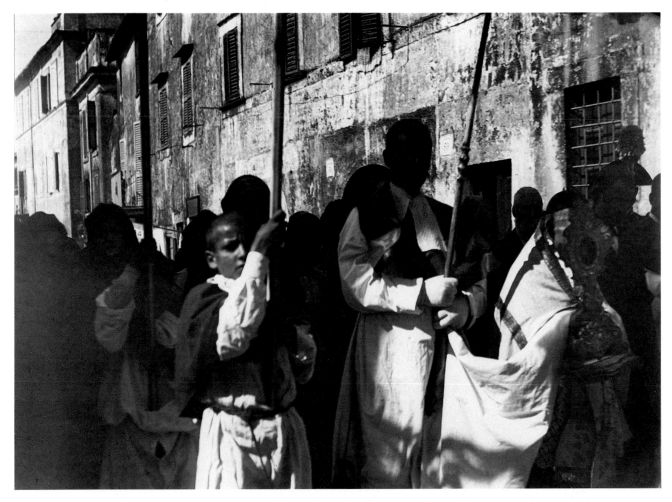

308. GIUSEPPE PRIMOLI. *Procession, Ariccia*, c. 1895. Gelatin silver print. Fondazione Primoli, Rome.

animated scenes of individuals or groups engaged in ordinary activities *(pl. no. 307)*. At first glance, his work may suggest images made by John Thomson in similar London localities or by Jacob Riis in New York—social photographers to be discussed in Chapter 8—but the emotional texture of Martin's vision is lighthearted and the scenes are casually composed. His are social documents in the sense that they reveal facets of the street life of the poor—formerly an undocumented portion of the populace—but Martin did not have the missionary zeal and commitment to change that informed the work of all the early social documentarians.

Martin claimed that he became a street photographer because he lacked the financial means to become a pictorialist,[21] but not only those with limited incomes were drawn to photographing the passing scene. In fact, enthusiasm for "real life" cut across class lines, appealing to a broad sector of the population that included wealthy and leisured individuals typified by Guiseppe Primoli and Jacques Henri Lartigue. Primoli, a Bonaparte descendant who

numbered among his circle the intellectual and cultural elite of Italy and France, worked between 1889 and 1905 (at first with a brother) using a variety of hand cameras to document the doings of beggars, laborers, street vendors and performers, as well as the carefree pursuits of his own social class. Even though they were not intended as social indictments, as a group these images reveal the extremes of life in Italy during the *belle époque*. Mostly amiable in tone, with open space surrounding the figures that are the focus of attention, Primoli's vision also could be intense, as evidenced by the strong contrasts and spatial compression in a view of a religious procession in Ariccia in 1895 *(pl. no. 308)*.

The search for the unexpected in the tedium of daily occurrence was another aspect of hand-camera street photography of the time. As urbanization advanced, it swept away the distinctive physical and social characteristics of the culture of the past, substituting undifferentiated built environments and standardized patterns of dress and behavior. Hand-camera users endeavored to reaffirm individ-

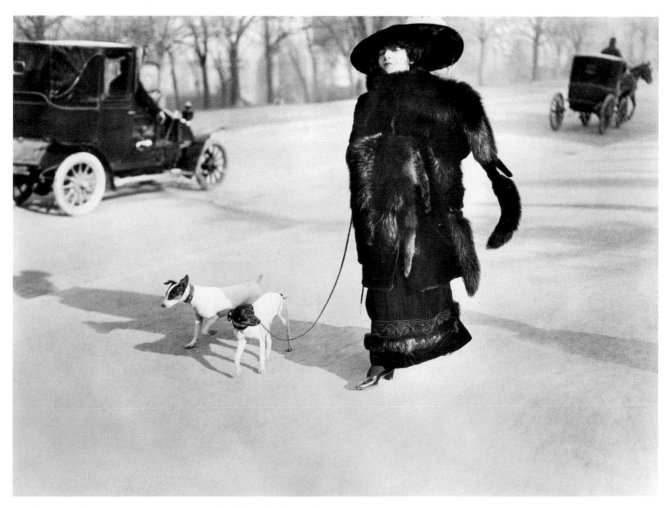

309. JACQUES HENRI LARTIGUE. *Avenue du Bois de Boulogne*, January 15, 1911.
Gelatin silver print. © Association Lartigue/SPADEM/VAGA

uality and arrest time in the face of the encroaching depersonalization of existence. The French photographer Lartigue was exceptional in that he was given a hand camera in 1901 at the age of seven and continued to use it throughout his lifetime to chronicle the unexpected. His early work portrayed the idiosyncratic behavior of his zany upper-class family whose wealth and quest for modernity impelled them to try out all the latest inventions and devices of the time, from electric razors to automobiles to flying machines. The young Lartigue's intuitive sensitivity to line, strong contrast, and spatial ambiguity, as seen in a view made in the Bois de Boulogne in 1911 *(pl. no. 309)*, evokes the insouciance of affluent Europeans before the first World War, a quality that is visible also in many images by unnamed photographers who worked for the illustrated press at the time.

Other photographers sought out moments of extreme contrast of class and dress, as in *Fortune Teller (pl. no. 310)* by Horace W. Nicholls, a professional photojournalist who recorded the self-indulgent behavior of the British upper class before World War I. Others celebrated moments of uncommon exhilaration, a mood that informs *Handstands (pl. no. 311)* by Heinrich Zille, a graphic artist who used photography in his portrayal of working-class life in Berlin around 1900. Still others, Stieglitz among them, looked for intimations of tenderness and compassion to contrast with the coldness and impersonality of the city, exemplified in *The Terminal (pl. no. 312)* and other works made soon after Stieglitz returned to New York from Germany in 1890.

Indeed, in the United States at the turn of the century, photographers were specifically urged to open their eyes to the "picturesqueness" of the city, to depict its bridges and structures, to leave the "main thoroughfares" and descend to the slums where an animated street life might be seen.[22] In part, this plea reflected the conviction held by Realist painters, illustrators, pictorial and documentary photographers, joined by social reformers, educators, and novelists, that the social life of the nation was nurtured in the cities, that cities held a promise of excitement in their free-

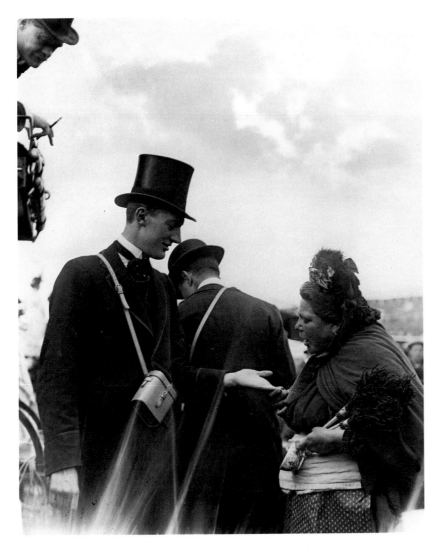

310. HORACE W. NICHOLLS. *The Fortune Teller*, 1910. Gelatin silver print. Royal Photographic Society, Bath, England.

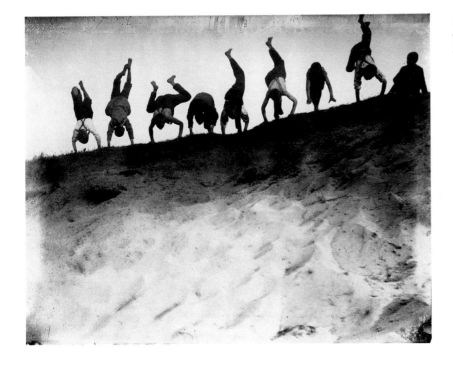

311. HEINRICH ZILLE. *Handstands*, c. 1900. Gelatin silver print. Schirmer/Mosel, Munich.

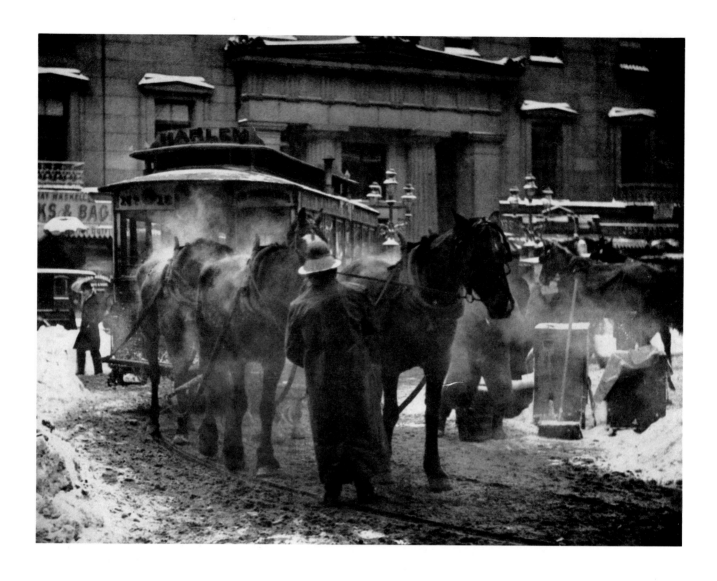

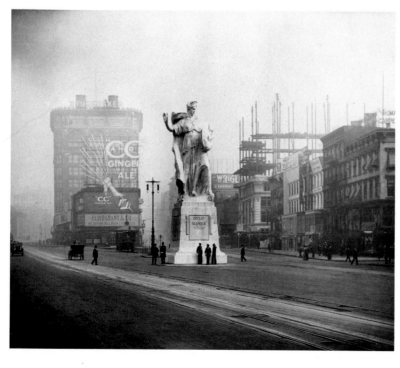

312. ALFRED STIEGLITZ. *The Terminal, New York*, 1892. Gravure print. From *Camera Work*, 1911, No. 36. Museum of Modern Art, New York; gift of Georgia O'Keeffe.

313. ROBERT L. BRACKLOW. *Statue of Virtue*, New York, after 1909. Gelatin silver print from the original negative. New-York Historical Society; Alexander Alland Collection.

dom from conformity and ignorance. Stieglitz, in whose magazine the article appeared, confessed in 1897 that after opposing the hand camera for years, he (and other Pictorialist photographers) had come to regard it as an important means of evoking the character of contemporary life. His suggestion that those using the hand camera study their surroundings and "await the moment when everything is in balance," seems to have forecast a way of seeing that 30 years later became known as the "decisive moment."[23] Whether undertaken consciously or not, the endeavor to assert the prodigal human spirit by capturing the fortuitous moment has continued to be one of the leitmotifs of 20th century small-camera photography.

Nor was this development limited to New York. Soon after arriving in California from Germany in 1895, the young Arnold Genthe obeyed his "vagabond streak," as he called it,[24] to photograph with a concealed hand camera in the reputedly inhospitable Chinese quarter of San Francisco. Over the next ten years, he returned continually to the "Canton of the West" in search of tantalizing glimpses of an unusual culture. The images range from the pictorial to the reportorial *(pl. no. 314)*, a dichotomy that continued to characterize his work. As owner of a professional studio in San Francisco at the time of the 1906 earthquake, Genthe documented the aftermath of the disaster with fine dramatic clarity, but after relocating in New York he specialized in polished soft-focus portraits of dancers and theatrical figures.

Ethnic enclaves were not the only source nor was the small camera the only instrument for capturing the kinds of subjects now considered picturesque. Countless photographers began to document aspects of the life around them using large-plate view cameras to penetrate beyond appearances. That one might approach the city as a subject using a large-format camera, and photograph it with reserved grace rather than subjective urgency, can be seen in the images made by Robert L. Bracklow, an amateur photographer of means, to document the physical structures, architectural details, and street activity of New York at the turn of the century *(pl. no. 313)*. With a flair for well-organized composition, Bracklow's photographs of slums, shanties, and skyscrapers suggest that by the end of the 19th century both hand and view cameras had become a significant recreational resource. For instance, E. J. Bellocq, a little-known commercial photographer working in New Orleans during the 1910s, was able to pierce the facade of life in a Storyville brothel. Whether commissioned or, as is more likely, made for his own pleasure, these arrangements of figure and decor *(pl. no. 315)* project a melancholy languor that seems to emanate from both real compassion and a voyeuristic curiosity assuaged by the camera lens.[25]

The new photographic technologies had a signal effect

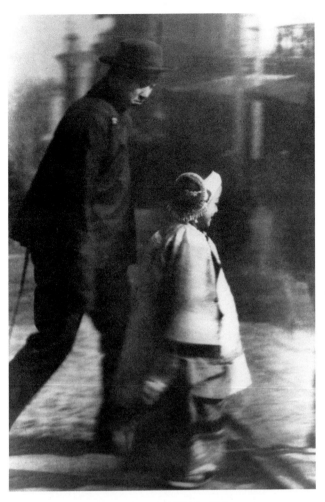

314. ARNOLD GENTHE. *Man and Girl in Chinatown*, c. 1896. Gelatin silver print. Sheldon Memorial Art Gallery, University of Nebraska, Lincoln; F.M. Hall Collection.

on the role of American women in photography.[26] Simplified processing enabled greater numbers of "genteel" women to consider photography a serious avocation and even a profession, because by the late 1880s they were able to take advantage also of the availability of domestic help and store-bought food, both of which provided some relief from household routines. At about the same time, writers in the popular and photographic press, suggesting that the medium was particularly suited to "the gentler sex," urged women to consider "an accomplishment which henceforth may combine the maximum of grace and fascination."[27] Encouragement came also from The Federation of Women Photographers and from competitions designed especially for female photographers. Unlike the older arts, photography did not require training in male-dominated academies or long periods of apprenticeship, or large commitments of time in practice, although impressive work usually was the result of greater involvement in the medium.

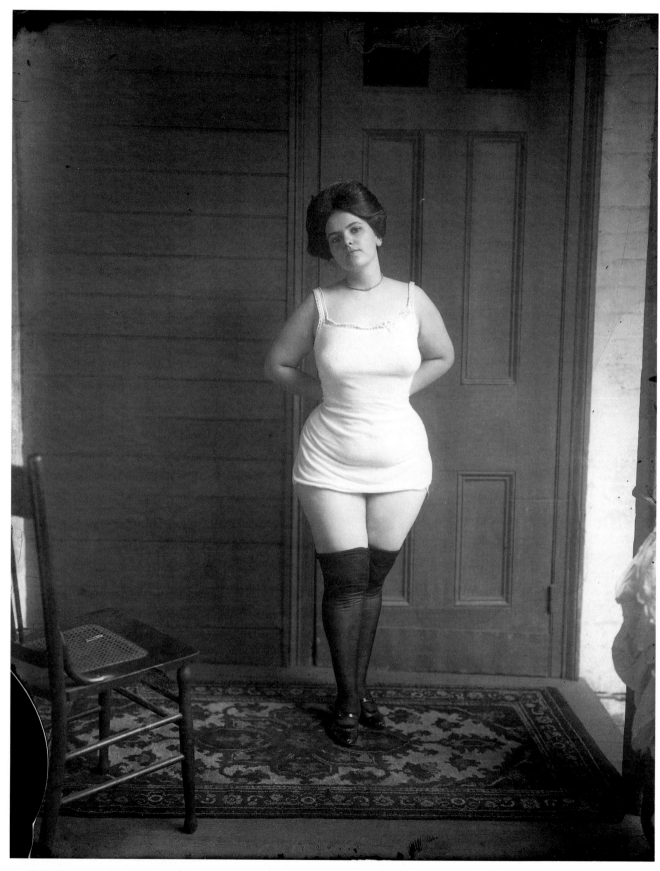

315. E. J. BELLOCQ. From *Storyville Portraits*, c. 1913. Silver print on printing-out paper, made by Lee Friedlander from the original plate. © Lee Friedlander, New City, N.Y.

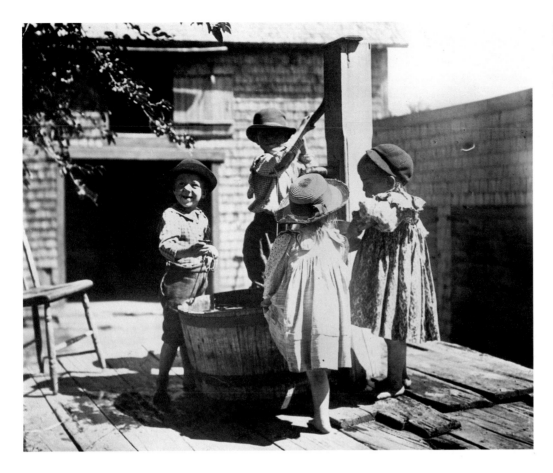

316. CHANSONETTA STANLEY EMMONS. *Children at Well*, 1900. Gelatin silver print. Culver Pictures, New York.

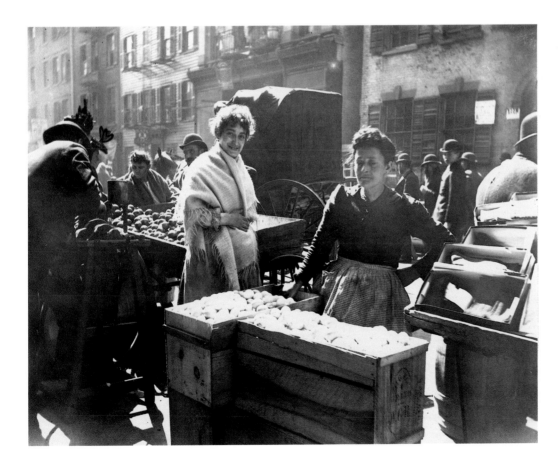

317. ALICE AUSTEN. *Hester Street, Egg Stand*, 1895. Gelatin silver print. Staten Island Historical Society, Staten Island, N.Y.; Alice Austen Collection.

Aside from those who became prominent in photojournalism and pictorial work *(see Chapters 8 and 9)*, numbers of women worked with both hand and view cameras to document family life and domestic customs, recreational and street activities. Chansonetta Stanley Emmons and Alice Austen are two such women. Images of small-town life, typified by a scene in the village of Marlborough, New Hampshire *(pl. no. 316)*, were made in 1900 by the recently widowed Emmons, who had turned to photography as a solace and a means of augmenting a meager income. Nurtured on genre imagery, Emmons's domestic scenes often were sentimental and derivative, but she could also capture evanescent moments of childhood play with refreshing directness. Austen, originally from a well-to-do Staten Island family, was less typical in that she had not only devoted some 25 years to a visual exploration of her own social *milieu*, she investigated the vibrant working-class neighborhoods of lower Manhattan *(pl. no. 317)* with an eye for expressive lighting and gesture. In Austen's case, as was undoubtedly true of other women, the camera provided a means to overcome psychological and social barriers, enabling a shy and conventionally reared Victorian "lady" to participate in the excitement of urban street life.

In the decade before 1900, the possibility that camera views of the city might be a salable commodity began to interest individuals and commercial studios. Using view cameras and tripods as well as hand cameras, photographers working on their own or for photographic enterprises undertook to provide images for post cards and magazine reproduction, for antiquarian societies and libraries, for artists and decorators, creating in the process a formidable number of such visual documentations. For instance, in New York, between 1890 and 1910, Joseph Byron, descendant of a family of English photographers, was involved in a business with his wife and five children, including the well-known Percy, that exposed and processed almost 30,000 large-format views both on commission and for speculation. A similar pictorial record of Paris, from the studio of the Seeberger brothers—Jules, Henri, and Louis—includes scenes of urban labors *(pl. no. 318)* as well as the

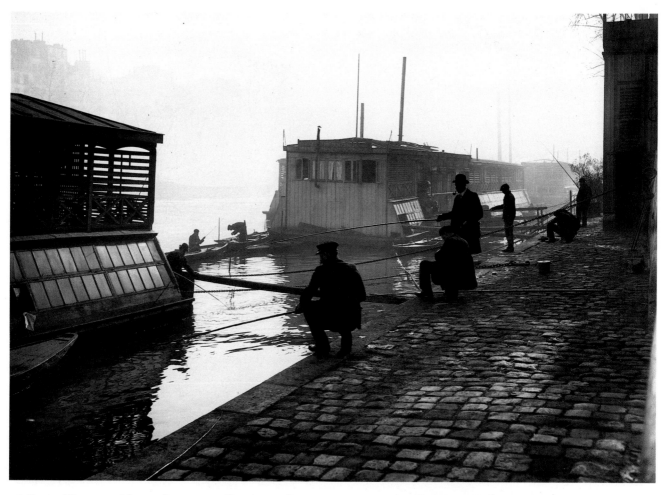

318. Jules, Henri, and Louis Seeberger (Seeberger Frères). *Fishermen near Washerwoman's Boats,* c. 1905–10. Gelatin silver print. Caisse Nationale des Monuments Historiques et des Sites, Paris. © Arch. Phot. Paris/SPADEM.

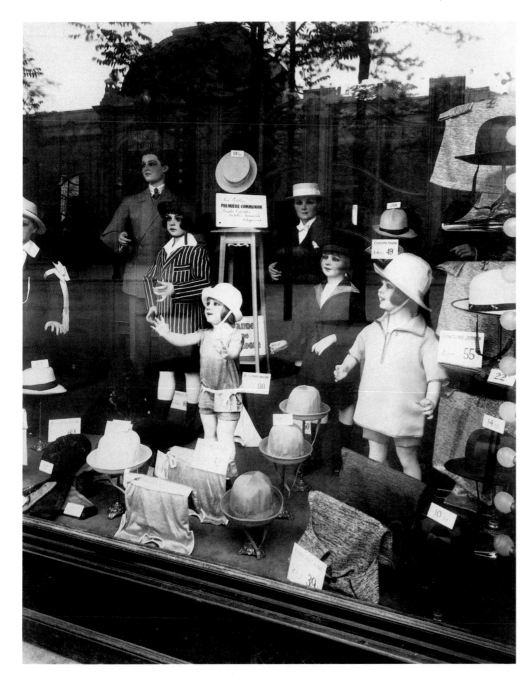

319. EUGÈNE ATGET.
Avenue des Gobelins, 1925.
Gold-toned printing-out
paper. Museum of Modern
Art, New York; Abbott-
Levy Collection; partial
gift of Shirley C. Burden.

activities of the bourgeoisie on their daily rounds. With exceptions, these competent if detached records of buildings, neighborhoods, sporting and theatrical events, people at play and at work are interesting mainly for their rich fund of sociological information.

The most extensive and in some judgments the most visually expressive document of the urban experience—also of Paris—was begun just before 1900 by Eugène Atget *(pl. no. 326) (see Profile)*. Using a simple 18 x 24 centimeter camera mounted on a tripod, this former actor began to document the city and its environs for a varied clientele that included architects, decorators, painters, publishers, and sculptors. Aside from their value and use as descriptive records of buildings, decor, statuary, storefronts *(pl. no. 319)*, costumes, and gardens, these beautifully composed images resonate with an intense though not easily defined passion. Rich in detail but not fussy, affecting but not sentimental, this great body of work represents Atget's yearning to possess all of old Paris and in so doing to embrace the authentic culture of France that modern technology was destroying.

Other large-scale commercial documents often exhibited a patriotic character, reflecting the growing movements for national self-determination taking place in various parts of Europe. Forty thousand views of Irish life,

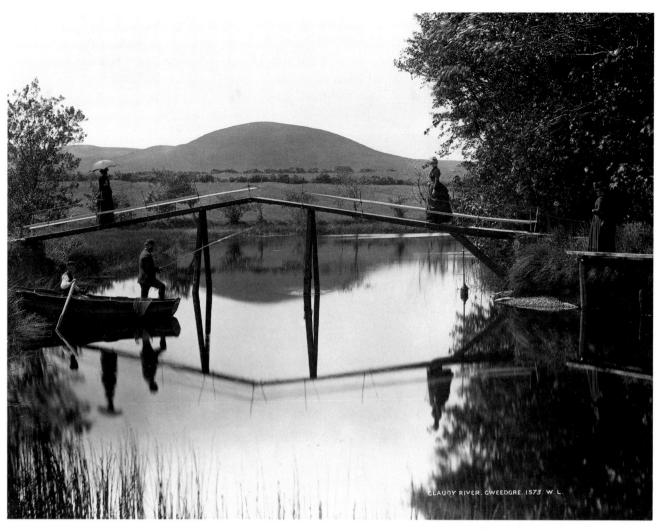

320. ROBERT FRENCH. *Claudy River, Gweedore, County Donegal*, c. 1890.
Gelatin silver print. National Library of Ireland, Dublin.

which include scenes of work and play, of city thorough-fares and serene country landscape *(pl. no. 320)*, were made by Robert French for the firm of William Lawrence in Dublin. And in view of the political agitation for independence among groups inhabiting the vast reaches of Russia, it is not surprising to find the tradition of ethnographic images, mentioned earlier, continuing into the dry-plate era, with photographers from many sections documenting places and customs in order to bolster feelings of national identity. Just as ethnographers in Eastern Europe were determined to collect evidence of a distinctive literature and folk music, photographers in Latvia, Bulgaria, Croatia, and Poland contributed to this surge of nationalism with images of national costume, typical environments, and regional customs. Since in these less industrialized regions the medium received less financial support from the urban populace than in Western Europe and the United States, distinctions between professional and amateur, between

documentary and artistic were not as codified; the same individual might fulfill all these roles, might at the same time make commercial post cards and other documentations and submit works to the local camera club exhibitions.

A similar ethnic consciousness emerged among black photographers in the United States in the early 20th century. The demand for portraits and other kinds of pictorial records, coupled with easier access to equipment, materials, and processing resulted in an increase in the number of commercially successful studios run by black entrepreneurs in their own communities. From the early days of the medium, daguerreotypes and other camera portraits had been made by unheralded black photographers, but these later enterprises produced images that depicted, in addition, the social activities of upwardly mobile urban dwellers and life in rural communities, made both for commerce and as expressions of black pride. Addison N. Scurlock started a portrait studio in Washington in 1904 and soon began

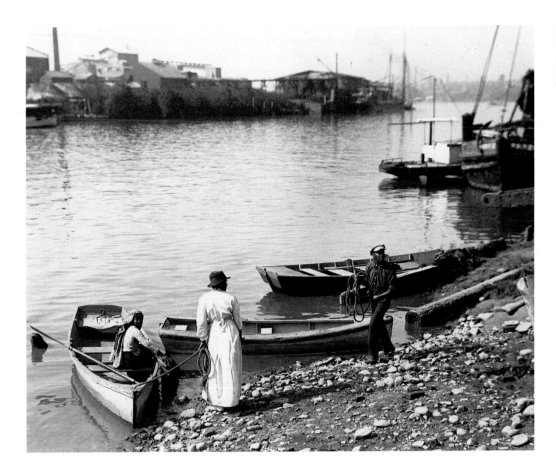

321. ADDISON N. SCURLOCK. *Waterfront*, 1915. Gelatin silver print. © Scurlock Studio, Washington, D.C.

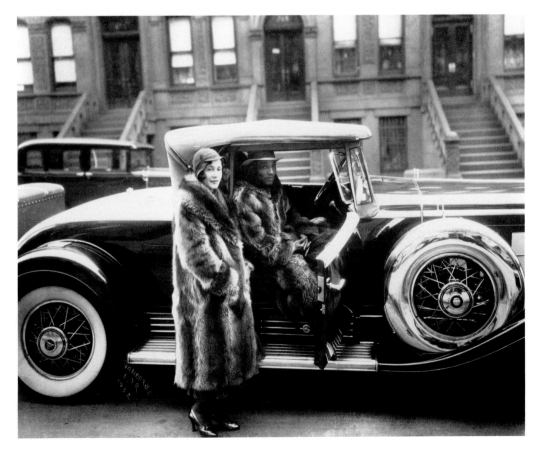

322. JAMES VAN DER ZEE. *Couple in Raccoon Coats*, 1929. Gelatin silver print. James Van Der Zee Estate, New York; © 1969 James Van Der Zee.

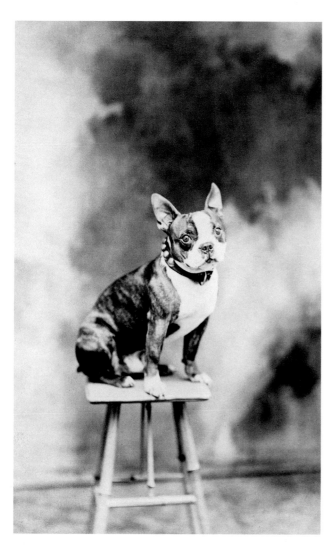

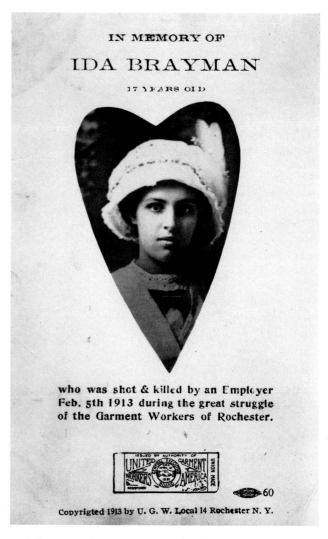

323. Unknown Photographer (American). *Untitled*, c. 1900–10. Gelatin silver post card. Private Collection.

324. Unknown Photographer (American). *In Memory of Ida Brayman*, 1913. Gelatin silver post card. Gotham Book Mart, New York.

to document activities at Howard University where he was official photographer; *Waterfront*, 1915, *(pl. no. 321)* is suggestive of his feeling for mood and texture when not confined to portraiture or straight documentation. James Van Der Zee, probably the best-known black studio photographer in the United States, began a professional career in 1915, opening an establishment in Harlem a year later to which the well-to-do and famous came for portraits *(pl. no. 322)*. He also documented social activities for the community and made genre images for his own pleasure. Had these photographers not faced the necessity of earning a living in studio work, both might have produced such images more frequently, a situation that obviously was true also for the majority of commercial photographers everywhere who were able to make affecting documents of their social milieu only in the time spared from studio work. Unlike white Americans, however, black photographers

could not afford the leisure and financial freedom to indulge in personal expression nor were they able to find a niche in photojournalism, advertising photography, or social documentation until after the second World War.

Anyone who has poked around attics, antique shops, and secondhand bookstores is aware of the formidable quantities of photographic post cards that have accumulated since camera techniques were simplified in the late 19th century. The post card format—approximately 3¼ x 5½ inches—appeared in Europe in 1869 and shortly after in the United States, but it was not until after the happy conjunction of new rural postal regulations, hand cameras, and special printing papers that occurred shortly after the turn of the century that the picture card became immensely popular with Americans—individuals and commercial studios alike. Artless yet captivating, post card images (even when turned out in studios) display a kind of irreverent good humor in their depictions of work, play, children, and pets *(pl. no. 323)*, although they also could deal with grimmer realities *(pl. no. 324)*. In the absence of telephones, glossy picture magazines, and television, the photographic post card was not merely a way to keep in touch, but a form of education and entertainment as well.

Photographs in Color

Of all the technological innovations occurring in photography between 1870 and 1920, none was more tantalizing or possessed greater potential for commercial exploitation than the discovery of how to make images in color. This search, which had begun with the daguerreotype, entailed much dead-end experimentation before a practicable if temporary solution was found in the positive glass Autochrome plate, marketed in 1907 by its inventors the Lumière brothers *(pl. no. 325)* *(see A Short Technical History, Part II)*. Though easy to use, the process required long exposures, was expensive, and while the colors were subtle they were not faultless. Because a simple, efficient method of turning the transparencies into satisfactory photographic color

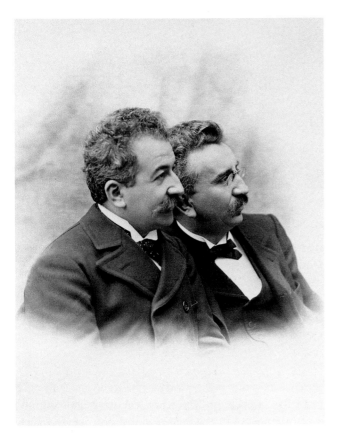

325. UNKNOWN PHOTOGRAPHER (French). *Lumière Brothers*, n.d. Gelatin silver print. La Fondation Nationale de la Photographie, Lyon, France.

prints was not available, the images had to be viewed in a diascope (single) or stereograph viewer; as late as the 1920s commercial portraitists still were being advised to send black-and-white work out to be hand-painted when a color image was desired. Nevertheless, Autochrome from the start attracted amateurs with leisure and money, photographers of flowers and nature, and in the United States, especially, individuals and studios involved in producing commercial images for publication. It also appealed briefly to aesthetic photographers who recognized at the time that rather than augmenting reality, color was best treated as another facet of artistic expressiveness *(see Chapter 7)*.

Despite the long exposures needed to make color images, a group of French "*autochromistes*" followed the example of the Lumières *(pl. nos. 342, 343, and 344)* in documenting family activities at home, at play, and in their professions. Among them, views of military life in the barracks of Part-Dieu in Lyon *(pl. no. 345)* by Jean Tournassoud (later director of photography for the French Army) are unusual in terms of subject. Autochrome appealed to Lartigue; convinced that "life and color cannot be separated from each other,"[28] he took elegant if somewhat mannered snapshots exemplified by *Bibi in Nice*, 1920, *(pl. no. 351)*, and this color material was used in a similar fashion throughout Europe for a brief while.

Not surprisingly, amateurs who liked to photograph flowers were delighted by Autochrome, but it also attracted a serious nature photographer, Henry Irving, who was quick to recognize the value of even a flawed system for botanical studies *(pl. no. 348)*. While less frequently employed by documentary photographers, Autochrome was used by William Rau, the Philadelphia commercial photographer of railroad images who by the turn of the century had become interested in artistic camera expression; *Produce (pl. no. 347)*, 1910, is an example of a subject and treatment unusual in the color work of the time.

While Autochrome plates (and its commercial variants) were based on the theory of adding primary colors together on one plate to effect the full range of spectral hues, experiments that led to the production of three different color negatives that subsequently were superimposed and either projected or made into color prints were in progress *(see A Short Technical History, Part II)*. Around 1904, this procedure was used for an extensive documentation of Russian life conceived by Sergei Milhailovich Prokudin-Gorskii, a well-educated member of the Russian Imperial Technological Society. An educational and ethnographic project made with the tsar's patronage, it involved the production of three color-separation negatives on each plate by using a camera with a spring-operated mechanism that changed filters and repeated the exposures three times. After development, these were projected in an apparatus

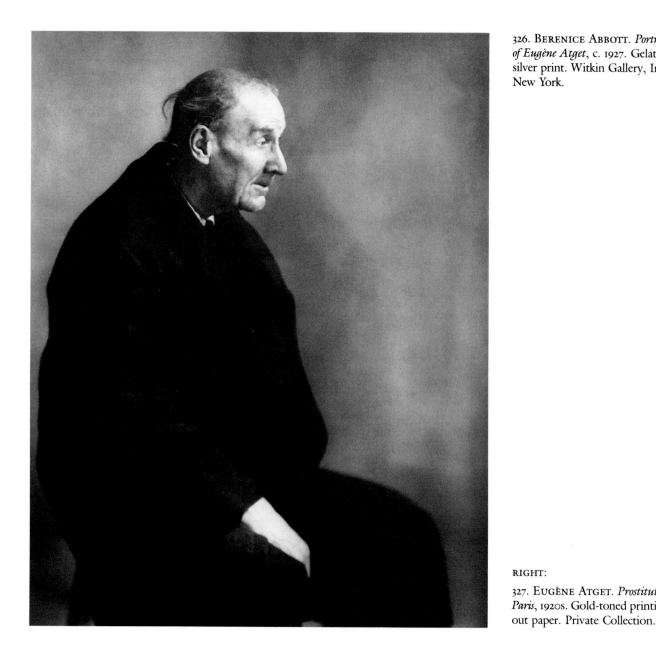

326. BERENICE ABBOTT. *Portrait of Eugène Atget*, c. 1927. Gelatin silver print. Witkin Gallery, Inc., New York.

RIGHT:

327. EUGÈNE ATGET. *Prostitute, Paris*, 1920s. Gold-toned printing-out paper. Private Collection.

that used a prism to bring the three color plates into one sharply focused image. Because of the cumbersomeness of tripling the exposure, the subjects, taken throughout Russia, had to be more or less immobile, but despite the technical and logistical difficulties of this complicated undertaking, Prokudin-Gorskii produced what surely must be the most ambitious color documentation of the time.

In its early stages, it was hoped that color would add an element of naturalness to the image—the missing ingredient in verisimilitude—since actuality obviously was many-hued rather than monochromatic as shown in photographs. However, as photographers began to work with the materials they realized that rather than making camera images more real, color dyes comprised another element

that had to be considered in terms of its expressive potential. The recognition that the seductiveness of color—its capacity to make ordinary objects singularly attractive—would have a powerful effect on the fields of advertising and publicity was the paramount stimulus in efforts that led to another breakthrough in color technology in the 1930s.

By 1890, photography no longer was an arcane craft practiced by initiates for whom artistic, informational, and social purposes were conjoined in the same image. Transformed and compartmentalized as a result of changes in materials, processes, techniques, and equipment, photographs became at once highly specialized and everybody's

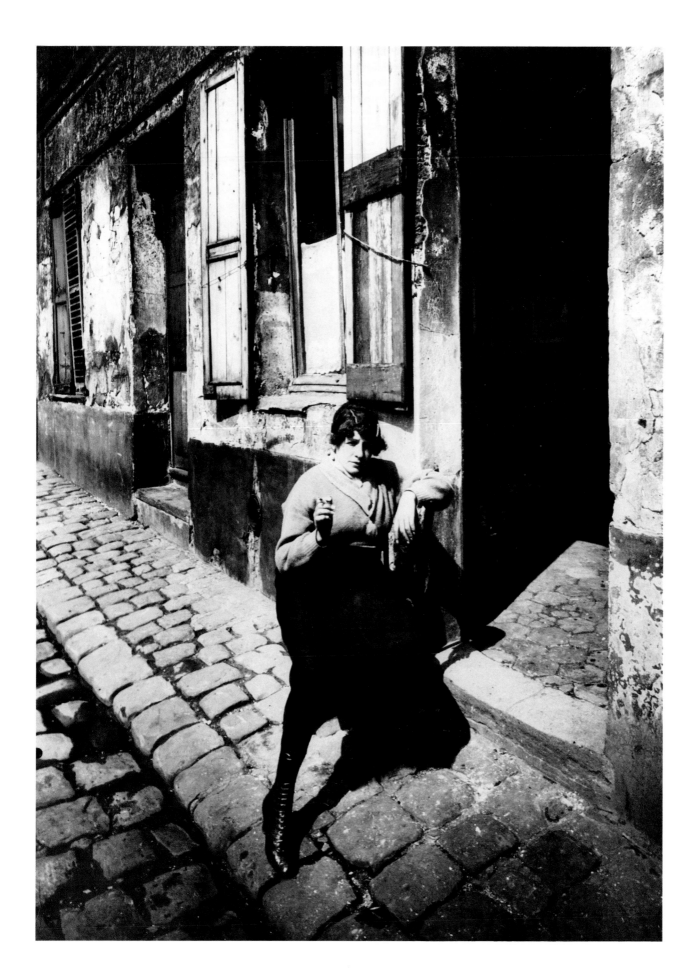

business (and for some, big business). In the face of the medium's capacity to provide information and entertainment on such a broad scale, a small group of photographers struggled to assert the medium's artistic potential, to lend weight to an observation made some 40 years earlier that photography had "two distinct paths"—art or science—"to choose from."[29]

Profile: Eugène Atget

Few facts are known of the early life of Eugène Atget (*pl. no. 326*), the photographer whose extraordinary documentation of Paris in the first quarter of the 20th century was for many years uncelebrated. Born in Libourne, near Bordeaux, in 1857 and orphaned at an early age, he was employed as cabin boy and seaman after completing his schooling. During the 1880s, Atget took up acting, playing in provincial theaters, but settling permanently in Paris in 1890 he realized the impossibility of a stage career in the capital. Instead, he turned to the visual arts, deciding on photography in view of his limited art training and also because he expected that it was a profession that might yield income from the sale of camera images to artist neighbors in Montparnasse.

Between 1898 and 1914, Atget received commissions from and sold photographs to various city bureaus, including the archive of the national registry, *Les Monuments historiques*, and the recently established Carnavalet Museum that had been set up to preserve a record of the history of Paris. He also supplied documents to a clientele of archi-

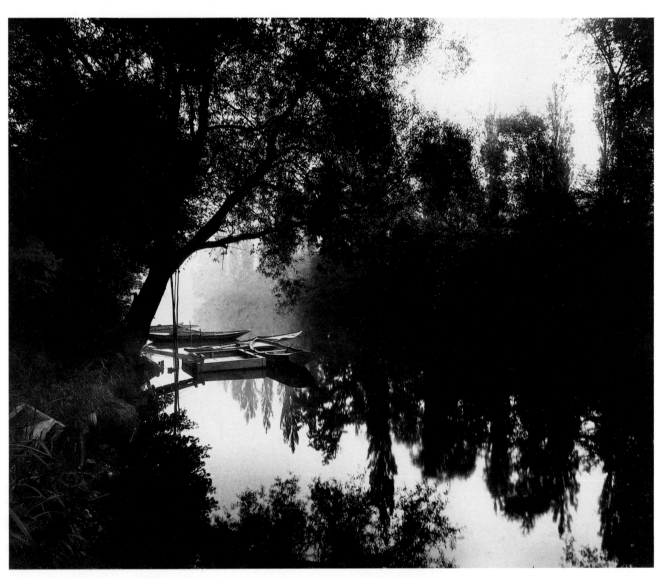

328. EUGÈNE ATGET. *La Marne à la Varenne*, 1925–27. Gold-toned printing-out paper.
Museum of Modern Art, New York; Abbott-Levy Collection; partial gift of Shirley C. Burden.

tects, decorators, and publishers, as well as artists, keeping records of both subjects and patrons. One project, for a book on brothels, planned but never realized by André Dignimont in 1921, is said to have annoyed the photographer, but the images for this work *(pl. no. 327)* have the same sense of immutable presence as those of other working people photographed by Atget in the streets or shops of Paris. Often self-motivated rather than directly commissioned, Atget nevertheless followed in the tradition marked out by the photographers of the 1850s *Monuments historiques* project and by Charles Marville, who had photographed the neighborhoods about to be replaced by Baron Haussmann's urban renewal projects. In common with these photographers, Atget did not find documentation and art antithetical, but attempted to invest all images with intrinsically photographic form. He showed no interest in the art photography movement that already was well established when he began to work in the medium, seeking instead to make the expressive power of light and shadow as defined by the silver salts evoke resonances beyond the merely descriptive.

Beyond supplying images to clients, Atget seems to have had an allover design or intention for many of his projects. A voracious reader of 19th-century French literature, he sought to recreate the Paris of the past, photographing buildings and areas marked for demolition in the hope of preserving the ineffable imprint of time and usage on stone, iron, and vegetation. A series of tree and park images *(pl. no. 328)*, made in the outlying sections to the south of Paris, suggest a compulsion to preserve natural environments from the destruction already visible in the industrialized northern districts of the city, and, in the same way, images of working individuals may have been made to record distinctive trades before the changes in social and economic relationships already taking place swept them away.

In the manner of a cinematic director, Atget made close-ups, long shots, details, views from different angles, in different lights, at different times, almost as though in his mind he were challenging time by creating an immutable world in two dimensions. The vast number of images— perhaps 10,000—of storefronts *(pl. no. 319)*, doorways, arcades, vistas, public spaces, and private gardens, of crowds in the street and workers pursuing daily activities—of just about everything but upper-class life—evoke a Paris that appears as part legend, part dream, yet profoundly real.

During the 1920s, the extent and expressive qualities of Atget's work were unknown to all but a small group of friends and avant-garde artists, among them Man Ray, who arranged for several works to be reproduced in *La Révolution Surréaliste* in 1926. Atget's final year, made especially difficult by the death of a longtime companion as well as by his insecure financial situation, brought him into contact with Berenice Abbott, at the time Man Ray's technical assistant. After Atget's death in August, 1927, Abbott was able to raise funds to purchase the photographer's negatives and prints and thus bring his work to the attention of American photographers and collectors when she returned to the United States in 1929. In 1968 this vast but still uncataloged collection was acquired by the Museum of Modern Art, which has since started to display and publish Atget's exceptional images.[30]

The Origins of Color in Camera Images

The images reproduced in this section constitute a brief pictorial survey of the ways in which color was made part of the photographic image from the inception of the medium up through the invention of the first viable additive color process. It opens with an example of a cyanotype, an early discovery whose brilliant blue was thought to be too unrealistic, and follows with a selection of daguerreotypes and paper prints that were hand-colored by tinting or painting to make them more lifelike or artistic. This group also includes works in carbon and gum bichromate—the manipulative processes that permitted photographers working from about the 1860s through the turn of the century to introduce colored pigments into their positive prints. These are succeeded by examples of the early efforts to produce color images by using colored filters or incorporating dyes into the light-sensitive film emulsions. The first such color experiment—an image of a tartan ribbon— is the work of James Clerk Maxwell, a theoretical physicist who used the additive system to demonstrate color vision by projecting three black and white images through colored filters to achieve a surprising full-color image. The experiments of Ducos du Hauron, John Joly, and Auguste and Louis Lumière—the inventors of Autochrome—are shown, as are examples of work in Autochrome by enthusiasts in Europe and the United States who in the early years of the 20th century recorded family and friends, documented nature, and made aesthetic statements using its mellow hues.

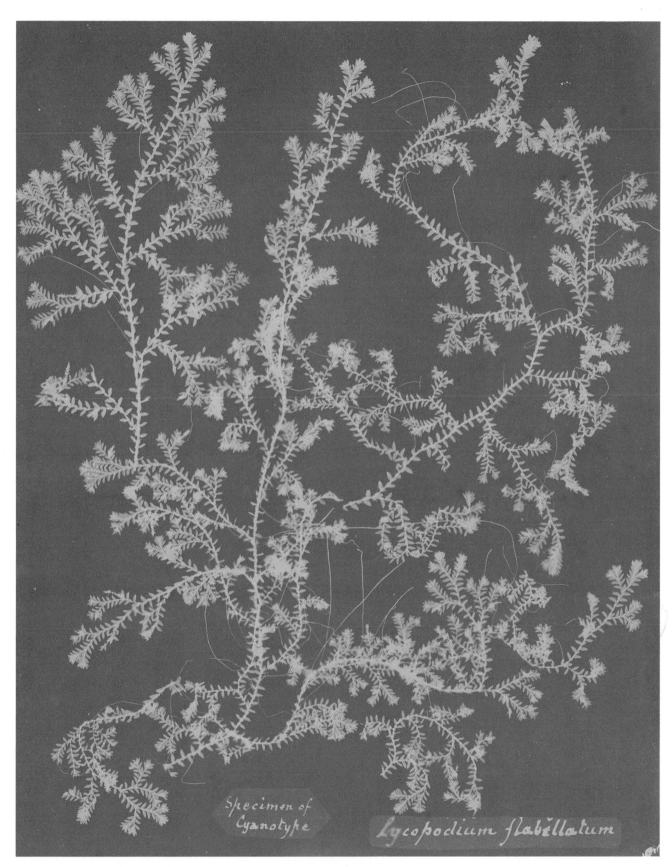

329. ANNA ATKINS. *Lycopodium Flagellatum (Algae)*, 1840s–50s. Cyanotype.
Gernsheim Collection, Humanities Research Center, University of Texas, Austin.

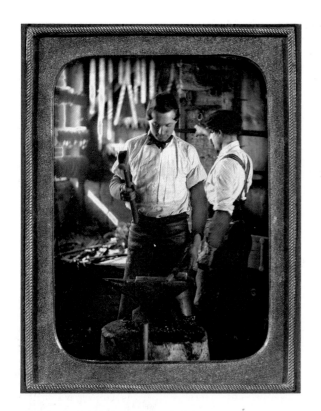

LEFT:

330. UNKNOWN PHOTOGRAPHER (American). *Blacksmiths*, 1850s. Daguerreotype with applied color. Collection Leonard A. Walle, Northville, Mich.

BELOW:

331. W. E. KILBURN. *The Great Chartist Meeting on Kennington Common*, April 10, 1848. Daguerreotype with applied color. Royal Library, Windsor Castle, England. Reproduced by Gracious Permission of Her Majesty Queen Elizabeth II.

RIGHT:

332. T. Z. VOGEL and C. REICHARDT. *Seated Girl*, c. 1860. Albumen print with applied color. Agfa-Gevaert Foto-Historama, Leverkusen, Germany.

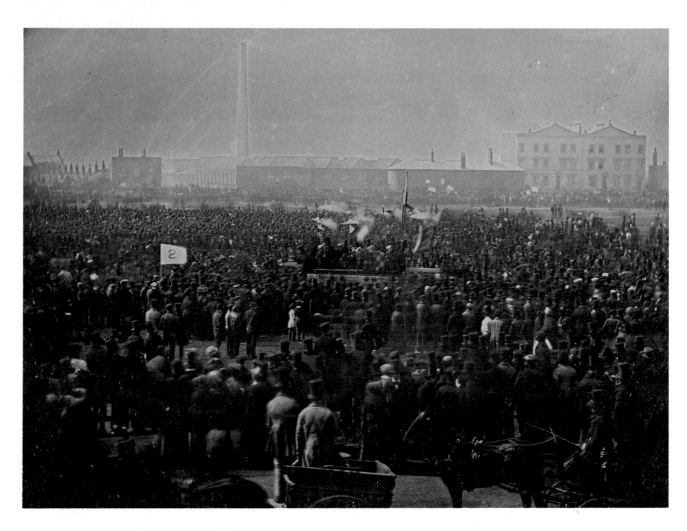

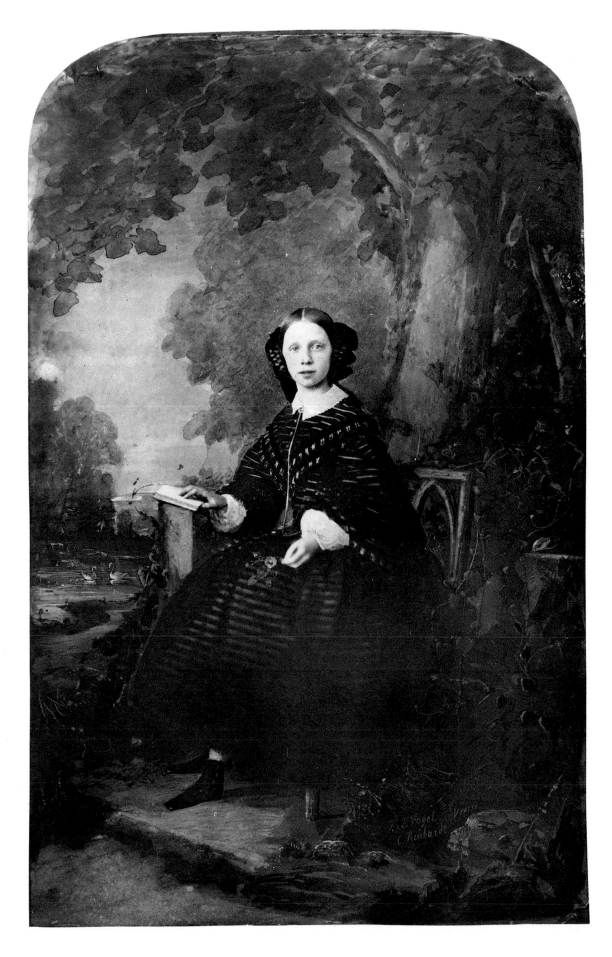

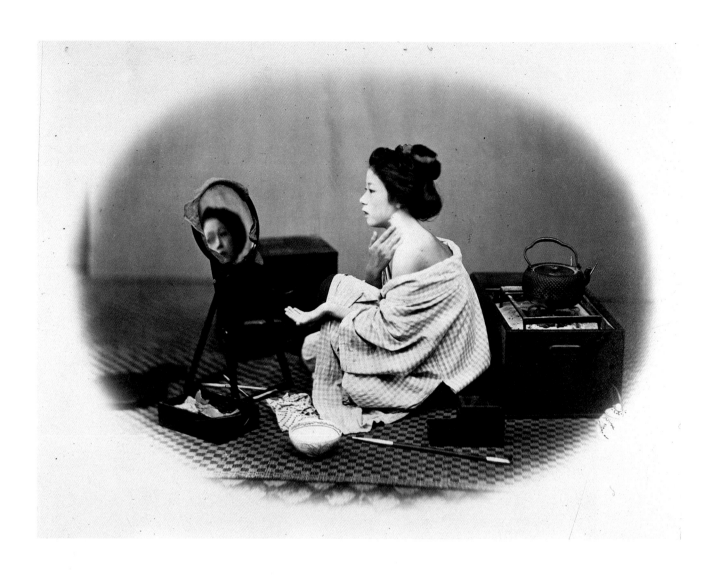

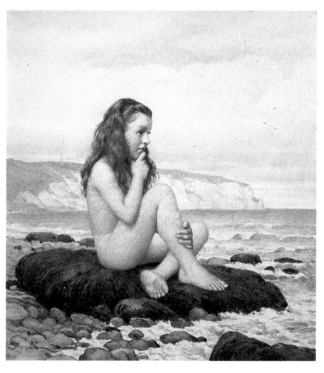

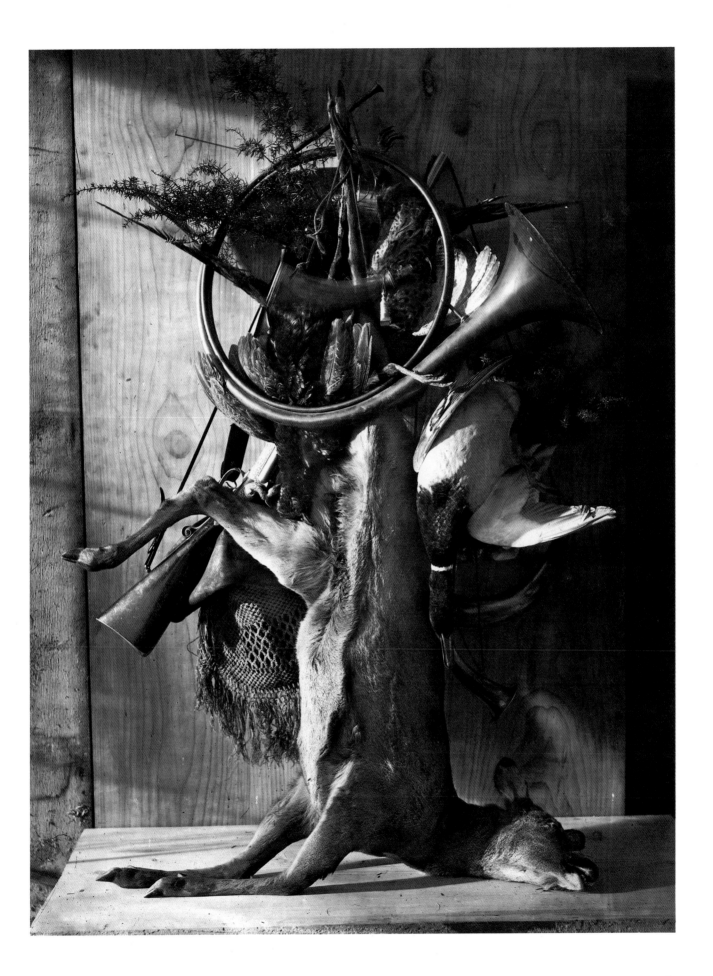

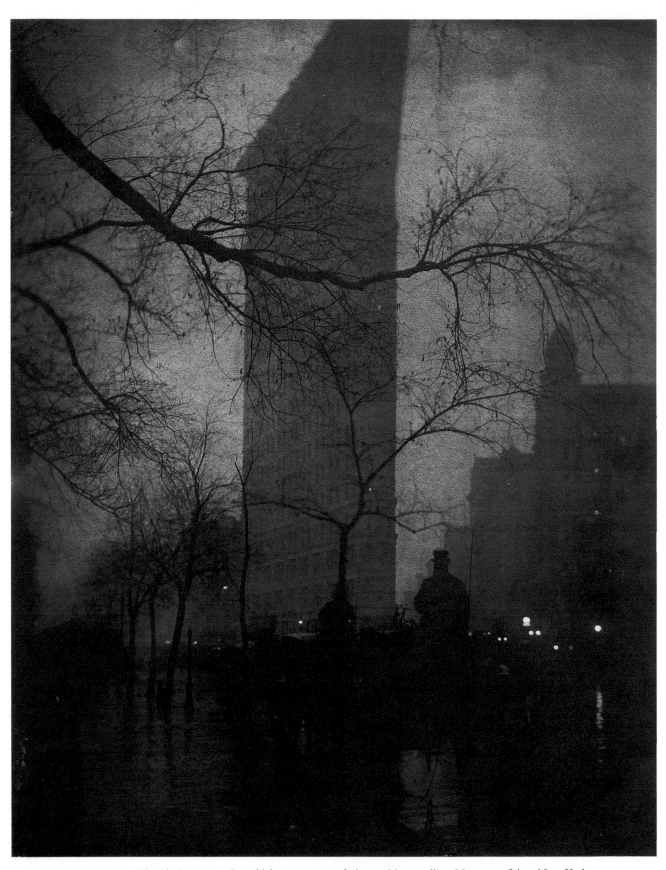

336. EDWARD STEICHEN. *The Flatiron*, 1905. Gum-bichromate over platinum. Metropolitan Museum of Art, New York.

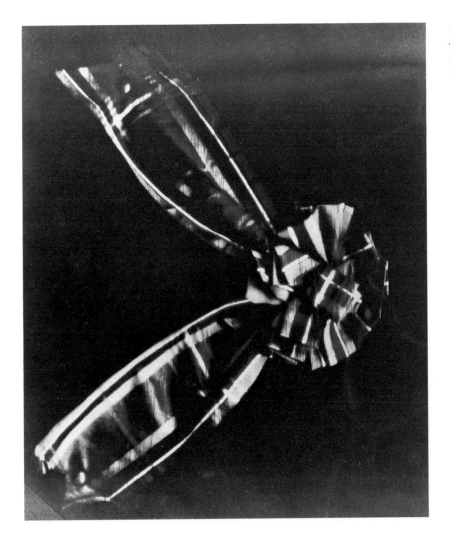

337. JAMES CLERK MAXWELL. *Tartan Ribbon*, 1861. Reproduction print from a photographic projection. Science Museum, London.

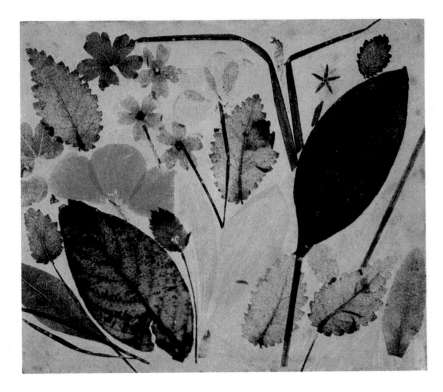

338. LOUIS DUCOS DU HAURON. *Diaphanie (Leaves)*, 1869. Three-color carbon assembly print. Société Française de Photographie, Paris.

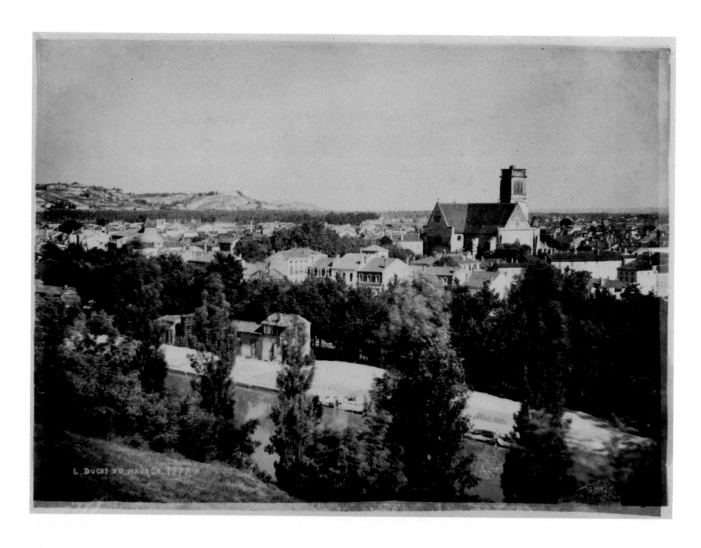

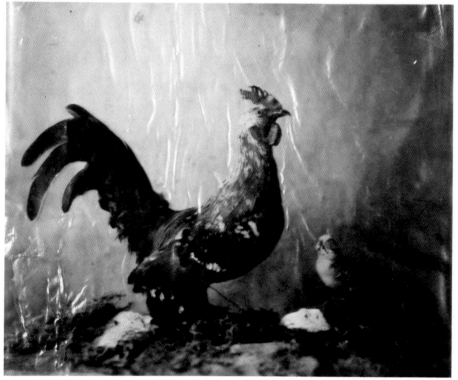

339. LOUIS DUCOS DU HAURON.
View of Angoulême, France (Agen),
1877. Heliochrome (assembly)
print. International Museum of
Photography at George Eastman
House, Rochester, N.Y.

340. LOUIS DUCOS DU HAURON.
Rooster and Parrot, 1879.
Heliochrome (assembly) print.
International Museum of
Photography at George Eastman
House, Rochester, N.Y.

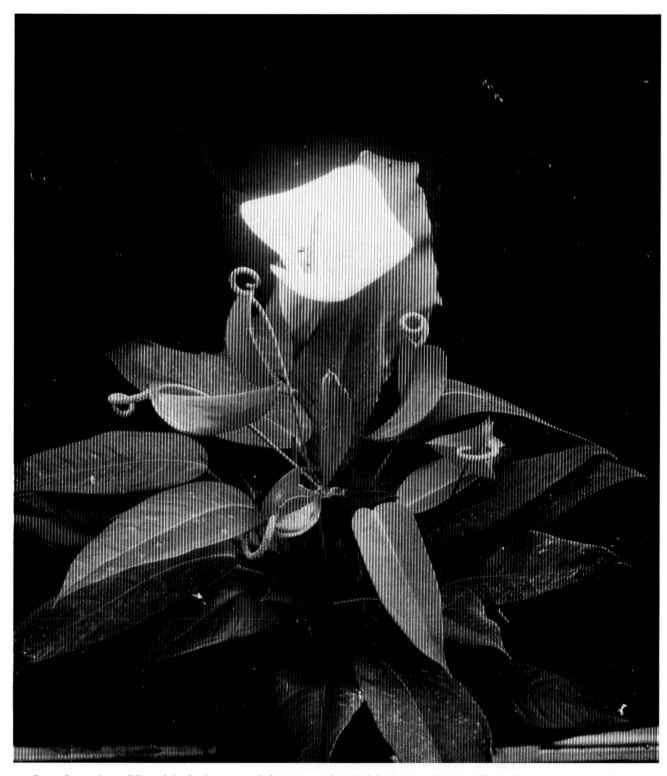

341. JOHN JOLY. *Arum Lily and Anthuriums*, 1898. Joly process print. Kodak Museum, Harrow, England.

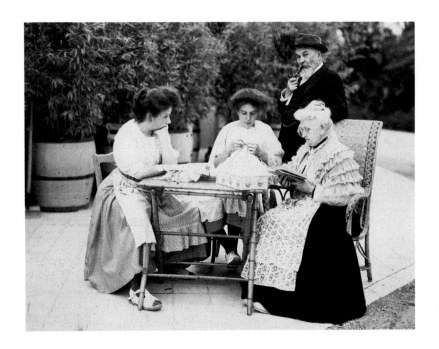

342. LUMIÈRE BROTHERS. *Lumière Family in the Garden at La Ciotât*, c. 1907–15. Autochrome. Ilford S.A., France.

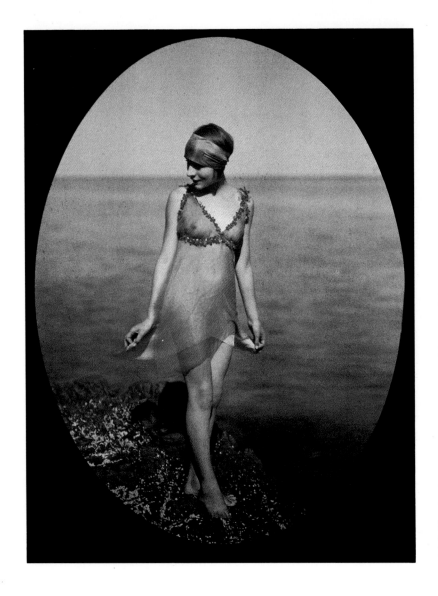

343. LUMIÈRE BROTHERS. *Untitled*, c. 1907–1915. Autochrome. Fondation Nationale de la Photographie, Lyons, France.

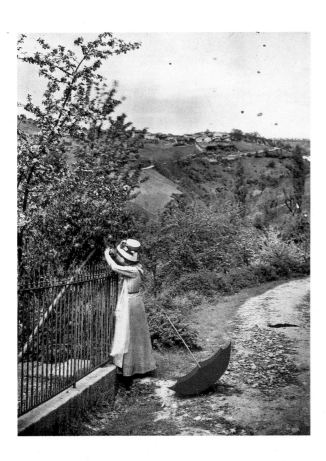

344. LUMIÈRE BROTHERS. *Untitled*, c. 1907–1915. Autochrome. Fondation Nationale de la Photographie, Lyons, France.

345. JEAN TOURNASSOUD. *Army Scene*, c. 1914. Autochrome. Fondation Nationale de la Photographie, Lyons, France.

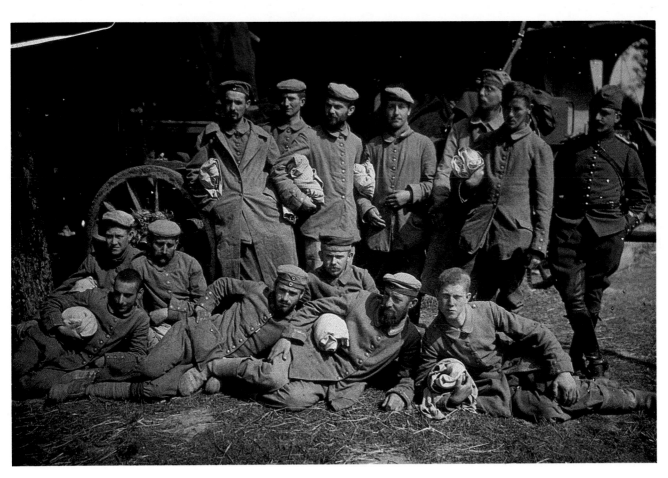

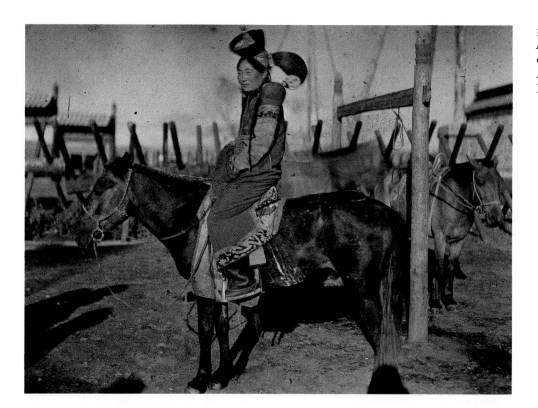

346. STÉPHANIE PASSET.
Mongolian Horsewoman,
c. 1913. Autochrome.
Albert Kahn Collection,
Hauts-de-Seine, France.

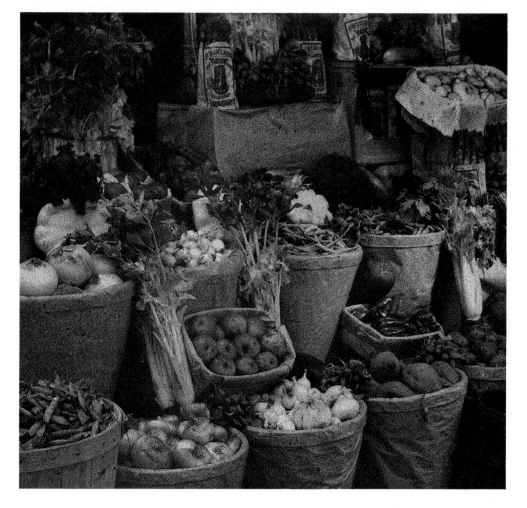

347. WILLIAM RAU.
Produce, c. 1910.
Autochrome. Library
Company of
Philadelphia,
Pennsylvania.

RIGHT:

348. HENRY IRVING.
*Cornflowers, Poppies, Oat,
Wheat, Corncockle*,
c. 1907. Autochrome.
British Museum (Natural
History), London.

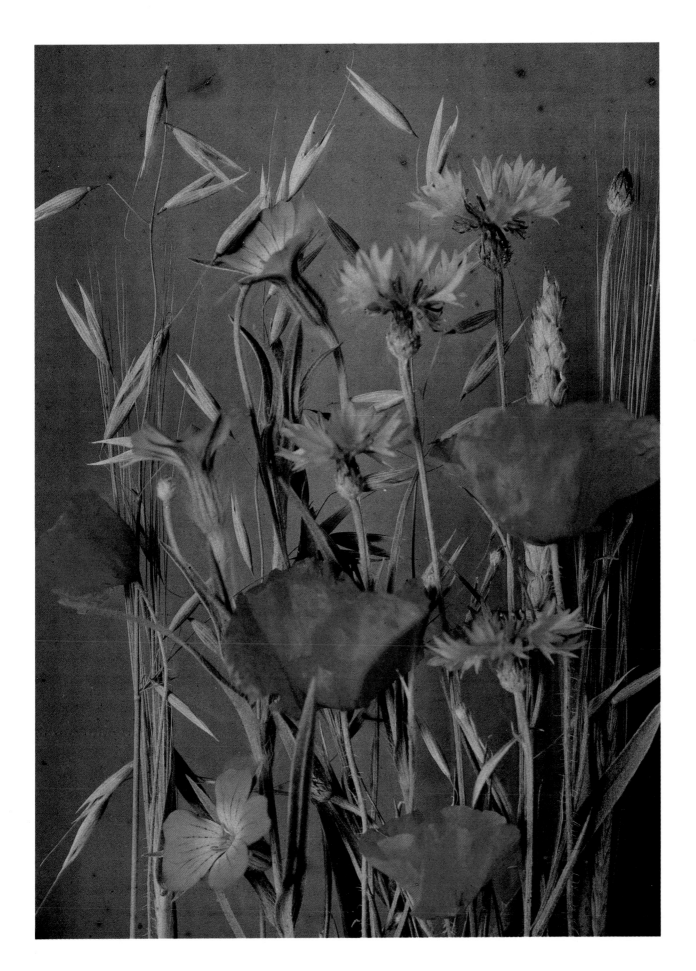

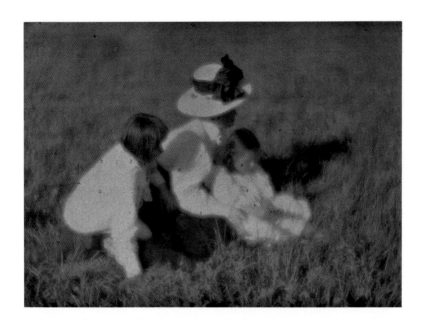

349. HEINRICH KUEHN. *Mother and Children on the Hillside*, 1905. Autochrome. Robert Miller Gallery, New York.

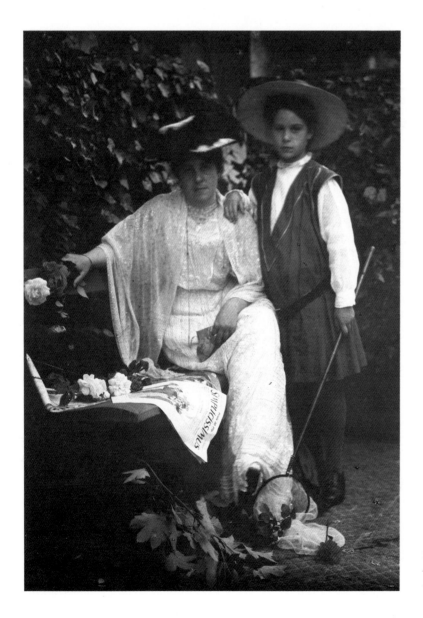

350. FRANK EUGENE. *Emmy and Kitty, Tutzing, Bavaria*, 1907. Autochrome. Metropolitan Museum of Art, New York.

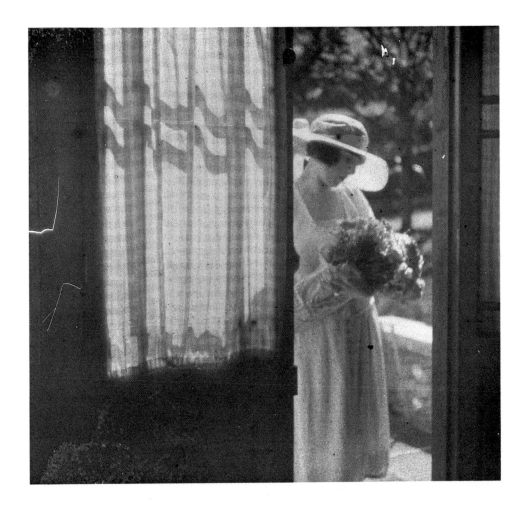

351. JACQUES HENRI LARTIGUE. *Bibi in Nice*, 1920. Autochrome. © Assocation Lartigue/SPADEM/VAGA.

352. LAURA GILPIN. *Still Life*, 1912. Autochrome. © 1981 Laura Gilpin Collection, Amon Carter Museum, Fort Worth, Texas.

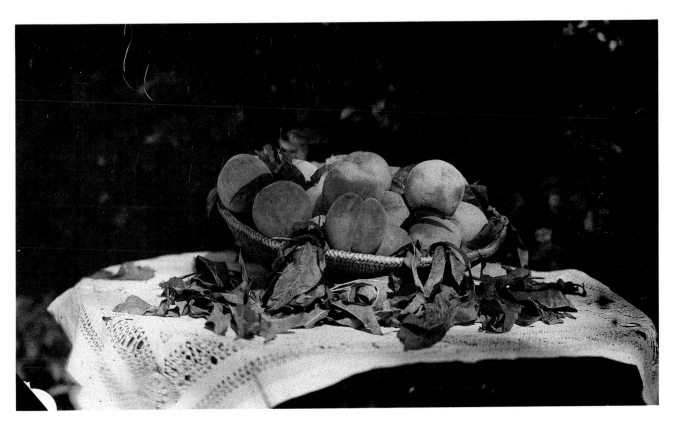

7.

ART PHOTOGRAPHY: ANOTHER ASPECT

1890–1920

Art is not so much a matter of methods and processes as it is an affair of temperament, of taste and of sentiment. . . . In the hands of the artist, the photograph becomes a work of art. . . . In a word, photography is what the photographer makes it—an art or a trade.

—William Howe Downes, 1900[1]

THE PROMOTION OF THE PHOTOGRAPH to the status of an art object was the goal of a movement known as Pictorialism. Based on the belief that camera images might engage the feelings and senses, and nourished initially by the concept of Naturalism articulated by Peter Henry Emerson, Pictorialism flourished between 1889 and the onset of the first World War as a celebration of the artistic camera image. The aesthetic photographers who were its advocates held that photographs should be concerned with beauty rather than fact. They regarded the optical sharpness and exact replicative aspects of the medium as limitations inhibiting the expression of individuality and therefore accepted manipulation of the photographic print as an emblem of self-expression. Animated by the same concern with taste and feeling as other visual artists, Pictorialists maintained that artistic photographs should be regarded as equivalents of work in other media and treated accordingly by the artistic establishment. Many of the images made under the banner of Pictorialism now seem little more than misdirected imitations of graphic art, as uninspired as the dull documentary images to which they were a reaction, but a number have retained a refreshing vitality. More significantly, the ideas and assumptions that sparked the movement have continued to inspire photographers, even though as style Pictorialism became outmoded around 1912.

Why the growing interest in artistic camera images in the last decade of the 19th century? It followed from the simplification of processes and procedures discussed in Chapter 6, and reflected the divergent uses to which the medium was being put as industrialization and urbanization proceeded. The dramatic expansion in the number of photographers (owing to the introduction of dry film and hand cameras) permitted many individuals to regard the photograph simply as a visual record, but it encouraged others to approach the medium as a pastime with expressive potential. Simultaneous with the publication of photographs of daily events, social conditions, and scientific phenomena in reading matter for the increasingly literate public, the wide dissemination of accurate reproductions of masterworks of visual art—also made possible by photographic and printing technologies—made the public more aware of visual culture in general. Furthermore, the emphasis on craft and artistry in journals and societies devoted to amateur photography was specifically aimed at fostering an aesthetic attitude toward the medium on the part of photographers.

This multiform expansion in photography took place against a background of stylistic transition in all the arts. As a consequence of greater familiarity with the arts of the world through reproductions, art collections, and increased travel, artists were able to expand their horizons, confront new kinds of subject matter, and embrace new concepts and ideologies. Within the diversity of styles that emerged, an art of nuance, mystery, and evocation, an art "essentially concerned with personal vision" held a special attraction.[2] Realism, the ascendant motif in the visual arts during much of photography's early existence, was challenged by Symbolists and Tonalists who proclaimed new goals for the arts. Less involved with the appearances of actuality, or with the scientific analysis of light that had engaged artists from Courbet to Monet, Symbolists maintained that while science might answer the demand for truthful information, art must respond to the need for entertainment and stimulation of the senses. However, in photography the situation was complicated by the fact that while some aesthetic photographers held truth and beauty to be antithetical aims, others viewed the medium as a means of combining the aims of art and science and imbuing them with personal feeling.

Pictorialism: Ideas and Practice

During the 1890s, serious amateurs as well as professionals deplored the "fatal facility"[3] that made possible millions upon millions of camera images of little artistic merit. In seeking to distinguish their own work from this mass of utilitarian photographs, Pictorialists articulated a dual role for the medium in which images would provide an unnuanced record on the one hand, and, on the other, provoke thought and feeling. Aesthetic photographers were convinced that in the past "the mechanical nature" of photography had "asserted itself so far beyond the artistic, that the latter might . . . be described as latent,"[4] and they sought to redress this perceived imbalance by selecting subjects traditional to the graphic arts, by emphasizing individualistic treatment and by insisting on the artistic presentation of camera images. Photographs, they held,

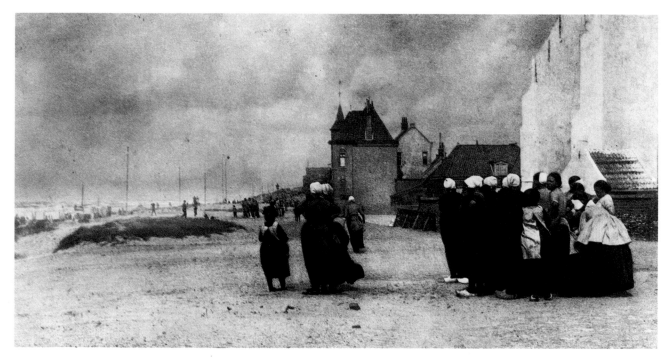

353. ALFRED STIEGLITZ. *Waiting for the Return*, c. 1895. Gravure print. Royal Photographic Society, Bath, England.

should be regarded as "pictures" in the same sense as images made entirely by hand; that is, they should be judged for their artistry and ability to evoke feeling rather than for their powers of description. In their insistence that photographs show the capacity to handle "composition, chiaroscuro, truth, harmony, sentiment and suggestion,"[5] Pictorialists hoped to countervail the still prevalent attitude among graphic artists and the public in general that the camera could not duplicate "the certain something . . . personal, human, emotional . . . in work done by the unaided union of brain, hand and eye."[6] They hoped also to appeal to collectors of visual art for whom aesthetic quality and individuality were important considerations.

Individuality of style was expressed through the unique print, considered by many at the time to be the hallmark of artistic photography. Using non-silver substances such as bichromated[7] gelatin and carbon *(see A Short Technical History, Part II)*—materials originally perfected to assure permanence—photographers found that they were able to control tonalities, introduce highlights, and obscure or remove details that seemed too descriptive. Many of these effects were accomplished by using fingers, stumps, pencils, brushes, and etching tools to alter the forms in the soft gum, oil, and pigment substances before they hardened, or by printing on a variety of art papers, from heavily textured to relatively smooth Japanese tissues. In that no positive print emerged as an exact version of the negative, or an identical duplicate of itself, these manipulations and materials, in addition to serving the expressive needs of the photographer, also satisfied collectors who preferred rare or singular artifacts. Gum printing, which involves a combination of gum arabic, potassium bichromate, and colored pigment, became popular after 1897 when photographers Robert Demachy in France and Alfred Maskell in England together published *Photo-Aquatint, or the Gum-Bichromate Process*. In 1904 a method of printing in oil pigments evolved, resulting in a greater range of colors available to the photographer. These procedures could be used only if the print were the same size as the negative, but in 1907, the Bromoil process made it possible to work with enlargements as well as contact prints.

These procedures, sometimes called "ennobling processes"[8] because they permitted the exploration of creative ideas by hand manipulation directly on the print, provoked a lively controversy among aesthetic photographers themselves as well as among critics. Excessive handwork produced photographs that at times were indistinguishable from lithographs, etchings, and drawings and led some Pictorialists to deplore the eradication of the unique qualities of the photograph; others cautioned discretion, observing that gum printing "is only safe in exceptionally competent hands,"[9] which regrettably were not numerous. During the early 1900s, the viewpoint that initially had held that the artistic quality of the final work would justify whatever choice of printing materials and techniques had been made gave way, as prestigious figures in artistic photography joined with less sympathetic critics to decry murky, ill-defined photographs as "fuzzygraphics."

Pictorialist advocates of straight printing did not usually intervene directly in the chemical substances of the print, although on occasion they might dodge or hold back portions of the negative. In the main, they followed the course marked out by Emerson, finding in carbon- and platinum-coated paper (Platinotype) the luminous tonalities and long scale of values they believed were unique to the expressive character of the medium. Again like Emerson, many preferred to make multiple images by the hand-gravure process—a method of transferring the photograph to a copper plate that was etched, inked, and printed on fine paper on a flatbed press to produce a limited edition of nearly identical prints.

Pictorialism: Styles and Themes

In looking to painting for inspiration, late-19th-century aesthetic photographers were confronted by a confusing array of outmoded and emerging artistic ideologies and stylistic tendencies, from Barbizon naturalism to Impressionism, Tonalism, and Symbolism. Not surprisingly, many were attracted by motifs that already had been found acceptable by art critics and the public, among which the idealization of peasant life, first explored by Barbizon painters at mid-century, ranked high. This concept in the work of Emerson and Frank Sutcliffe is expressed with down-to-earth robustness, while other aesthetic photographers turned such scenes into embodiments of the picturesque and artful. In one example, *Waiting for the Return (pl. no. 353)*[10]—a photograph of the wives of fishermen waiting on the beach at Katwyck, Holland, for the boats to come in—Alfred Stieglitz selects a vantage point from which he can create an uncluttered arrangement; he controls the tonalities to suggest an atmospheric haze that softens the forms and at the same time endows the women with larger-than-life stature. The horizontal format, the flat tonalities of the figural groups, and the treatment of recessional space also suggest the influence of Japanese woodblock prints.

A theme that attracted both aesthetic photographers and painters was the pure natural landscape. In common with the Symbolist and Tonalist painters who viewed nature as the only force "undisturbed by the vicissitudes of man,"[11] aesthetic photographers in Europe and America regarded landscape with a sense of elegiac melancholy. Taking their cues from the Nocturnes of Whistler, the mystic reveries of the Swiss painter Arnold Boecklin, or the poetic impressions of the Americans George Inness and Henry Ward Ranger, they regarded suggestiveness as more evocative than fact, and preferred the crepuscular moment to sun-drenched daylight, the quiet, intimate pond to dramatic mountain wilderness. Instead of the crisply de-fined forms and strong contrasts of earlier topographical imagery, they offered the vague shapes and subdued tonalities visible in *Woods Interior (pl. no. 354)* by Edward Steichen, a work obviously related in its organization, treatment, and mood to Ranger's scene, *Bradbury's Mill Pond, No. 2 (pl. no. 355)*.

The female figure, both as a study in beauty and a symbol of motherhood was another subject of common interest to painters and aesthetic photographers. Softly focused portraits of elegantly attired enigmatic women—favored by Pictorialists everywhere—stressed stylishness and charm rather than individual strength of character. A related theme, women and children engaged in leisurely domestic activity or at play in home and garden, appealed to both men and women photographers, who produced idealized visions of intimate family life, transforming what formerly had been a prosaic genre subject into a comforting visual idyll of middle-class gentility. With its seemingly random arrangement, curvilinear forms, and delicate tonalities, *The Picture Book* (also called *Instruction, pl. no. 356*) by the renowned American portraitist Gertrude Käsebier isolates its two intertwined figures in a peaceable terrain untroubled by domestic or social friction.

Few motifs better illustrate the gulf that developed between aesthetic camera "pictures" and straight camera documents than the nude figure. Around the turn of the century, Pictorialists on both sides of the Atlantic approached the unclothed body with great diffidence, picking their way timidly through the "canons of good taste." Camera studies of the nude by artists, among them those made by Czechoslovak painter Alphonse Marie Mucha for various decorative commissions in his native land, France *(pl. no. 357)*, and the United States, or the numerous studies of the undraped figure taken by Thomas Eakins (or his students) as study materials for paintings, or for anatomy classes as celebrations of the human form *(pl. no. 254)* were not intended for exhibition or public delectation. Convinced that "ART alone"[12] might sanction this troublesome yet attractive subject, photographers avoided ordinary or coarse-looking models and selected ideally proportioned females whose bodies, it was believed, would suggest beauty rather than sensuality *(pl. no. 358)*. Combining classical poses in landscape settings, to which props suggestive of the "Antique" were sometimes added, with artistic lighting and handwork (at times, extensive) to obliterate telling details, aesthetic photographers hoped to prove that in photography "nude and lewd" need not necessarily be "synonymous terms."[13]

Other than those engaged in a commerce in erotic images, early photographers of the nude had been constrained by the realistic nature of the medium and by Victorian attitudes toward the unclothed human body to

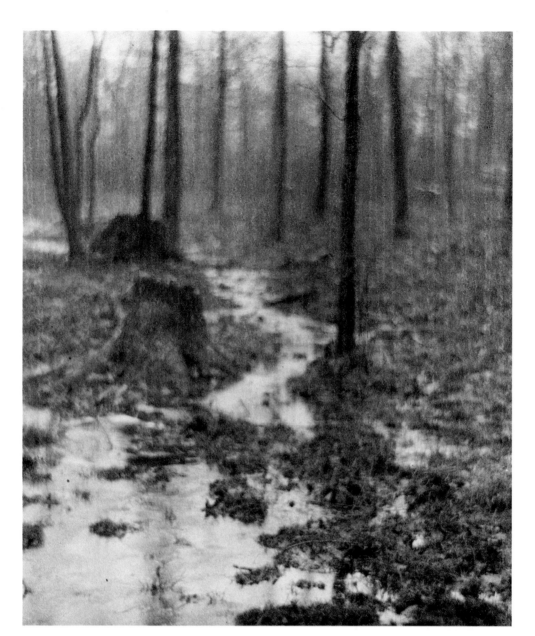

354. Edward Steichen.
Woods Interior, 1898.
Platinum print.
Metropolitan Museum of
Art, New York; Alfred
Stieglitz Collection, 1933.

FACING PAGE ABOVE:

355. Henry Ward
Ranger. *Bradbury's Mill
Pond, No. 2*, 1903. Oil on
Canvas. National Museum
of American Art,
Smithsonian Institution,
Washington, D.C.; gift of
William T. Evans.

FACING PAGE BELOW:

356. Gertrude Käsebier.
The Picture Book, 1899–1902.
Gravure print. Library of
Congress, Washington,
D.C.

endow their images with allegorical dimension (when they did not direct them to the needs of graphic artists, *see Chapter 5)*. Attitudes began to change shortly before the turn of the century, and as the nude in painting and graphic art emerged from a long history of masquerading as goddess or captive slave (or as in Edouard Manet's *Olympia* as prostitute), the female nude figure became a motif in and for itself in both painting and aesthetic photography. Some photographers still cast their nude figures as sprites and nymphs, but others no longer felt the need to obscure their attraction to the intrinsically graceful and sensuous forms of the unclothed female. Indeed, the very absence of allegory or narrative in this treatment served to emphasize the new role of the photograph as a strictly aesthetic artifact.

While Pictorialists everywhere photographed the nude, aesthetic photographers working in France and the United States most enthusiastically explored the expressive possibilities of this motif. Conventional academic poses and extensive manipulation of the print, typified by the works of French photographers Demachy and René LeBègue *(pl. no. 359)* and the American Frank Eugene *(pl. no. 360)*, rendered some photographs of the nude almost indistinguishable from etchings and lithographs, while a group portrait of nude youngsters by American Pictorialist Alice Boughton *(pl. no. 361)* exemplifies the less derivative arrangement and more direct treatment of light and form that also was possible.

The great majority of aesthetic images of the nude were of adult females, the undraped male body being con-

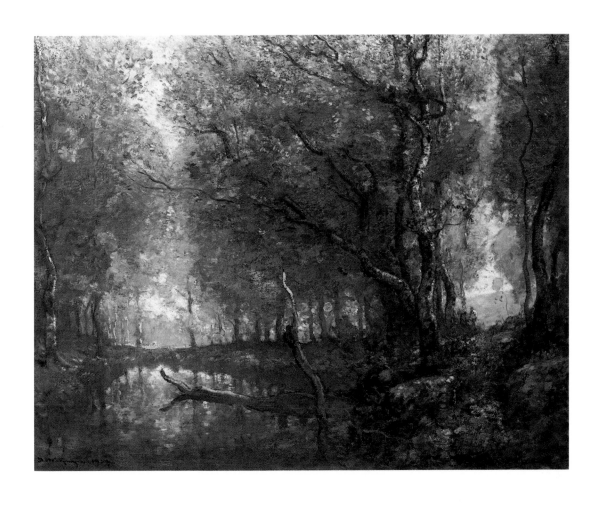

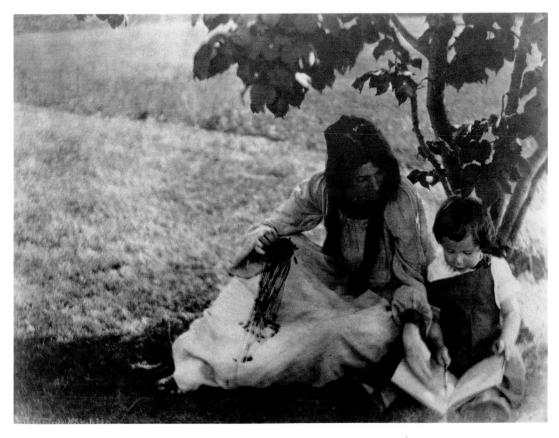

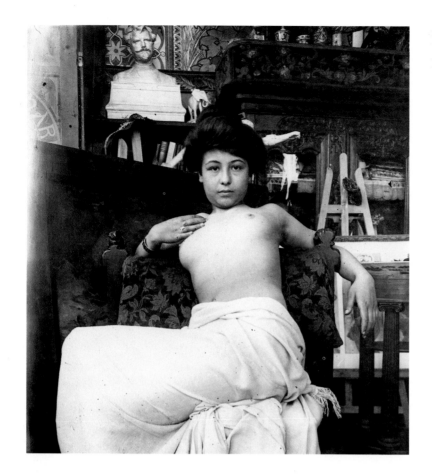

357. ALPHONSE MARIE MUCHA. *A Study for "Figures Décoratifs," No. 39*, 1903. Gelatin silver print. Collection Jiri Mucha, Prague.

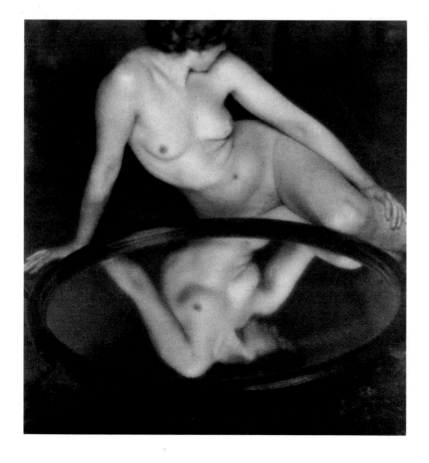

358. CLARENCE WHITE. *Nude*, c. 1909. Platinum print. Private collection.

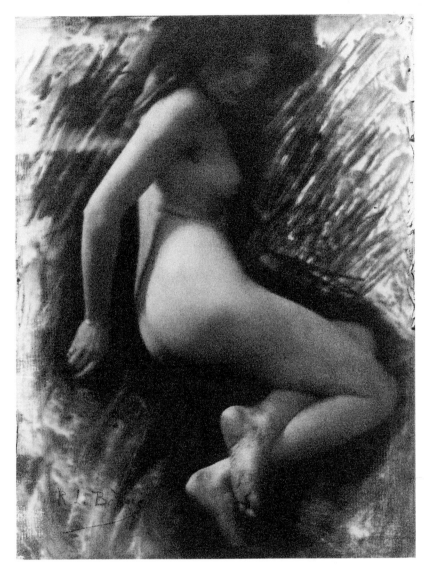

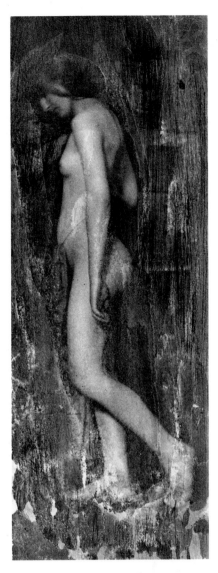

359. RENÉ LE BÈGUE. *Academie*, 1902. Gum bichromate print.
Metropolitan Museum of Art, New York; Alfred Stieglitz Collection, 1933.

360. FRANK EUGENE. *Study*, 1899 or
before. Platinum print. Metropolitan
Museum of Art, New York; Alfred
Stieglitz Collection, 1949.

sidered by nearly everyone as too flagrantly sexual for depiction in any visual art intended for viewers of mixed sexes. However, articles on nudity in photography (written largely by men), which had begun to appear in camera journals after 1890, suggested that young boys would make especially appropriate models because their bodies were less sensually provocative than those of women.[14] Wilhelm von Gloeden and F. Holland Day were two significant figures of the period who chose to photograph not only adolescent boys but older males, too. Von Gloeden, a trained painter who preferred the mellow culture of the Mediterranean to that of his native Germany, worked in Taormina, Sicily, between 1898 and 1913 *(pl. no. 362)*, while Day, an early admirer of Symbolist art and literature, was

an "improper" Bostonian of means working in Massachusetts and Maine during the same period. Their images display a partiality to the trappings of classical antiquity, perhaps because they realized that to be artistically palatable the male nude—youthful or otherwise—needed a quasi-allegorical guise. However, although the head wreaths, draperies, and pottery that abound in Von Gloeden's works may have suggested elevated aesthetic aims, and the images were in fact proposed as "valuable for designers and others,"[15] his young Sicilians often seem unabashedly athletic and sexual to modern eyes. On the other hand, Day handled the poses and lighting of the nude male presented in the guise of pastoral figures with such discretion that a contemporary critic observed that "his nude studies

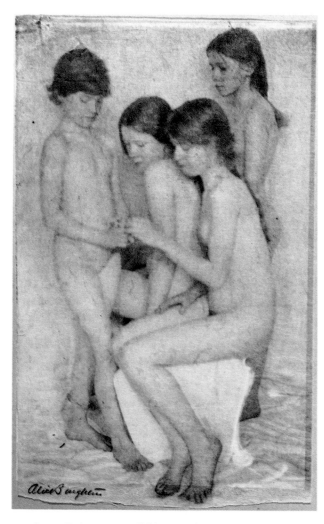

361. ALICE BOUGHTON. *Children-Nude*, 1902. Platinum print. Metropolitan Museum of Art, New York; Alfred Stieglitz Collection, 1933.

are free of the look that makes most photographs of this sort merely indecent."[16]

Some Pictorialist photographers embraced allegorical or literary themes, posing costumed figures amid props in the manner of the Pre-Raphaelites and Julia Margaret Cameron, with results that ranged from merely unsuccessful to what some consider ridiculous. Among the more controversial examples of this penchant for historical legend were reconstituted "sacred" images by Day, by French Pictorialist Pierre Dubreuil, by Lejaren à Hiller—the latter an American photographer who eventually turned this interest into a success in commercial advertising—and by Federico Maria Poppi, an Italian Pictorialist. The obvious fact that Day's series of religious images were staged with the photographer himself posing for the Christ figure *(pl. no. 363)* prompted critic Charles Caffin to call "such a divagation from good taste intolerably silly."[17] Possibly even

more misguided because of a complete absence of originality, subtlety, or psychological nuance were camera images that aimed to emulate high art by appropriating actual compositions painted by Renaissance masters or Dutch genre painters. Guido Rey and Richard Polack *(pl. no. 364)*, from Italy and the Netherlands respectively, photographed costumed models arranged in settings in which props, decor, and lighting mimicked well-known paintings. In view of the lack of conviction or genuine emotion in all of these works, one may conclude that the orchestration necessary to recreate religious or historical events or painted scenes is inimical to the nature of the photographic medium. As a critic noted about Day's tableaux, "In looking at a photograph, you cannot forget that it is a representation of something that existed when it was taken."[18]

A strong interest in light and color, which for some Pictorialists had found an outlet in pigment printing processes prompted others to experiment with Lumière Autochrome plates when this color material reached the market in 1907. In general, European Pictorialists who favored gum and oil pigment processes for working in color regarded Autochrome as too precise a tool for artistic control.[19] An exception was Heinrich Kuehn, who joined with the Americans Alvin Langdon Coburn, Frank Eugene *(pl. no. 350)*, Steichen, and Stieglitz to investigate the range and possibilities of the material. Kuehn was highly successful in harmonizing the dyes—cool, airy blues and greens—to achieve a sense of spontaneous intimacy in views of family life *(pl. no. 349)* despite the long exposures required. Works in Autochrome by members of the American Photo-Secession *(see below)*, several of which also pictured family members and their activities, are somewhat more static in organization and more mellow in color, reflecting the somber harmonies of some *fin-de-siècle* painting in Europe and the United States. The fact that Autochrome transparencies were difficult to exhibit and reproduce may account for their relatively brief popularity among the leading Photo-Secessionists, but other (later) American Pictorialists, including Arnold Genthe and Laura Gilpin *(pl. no. 352)*, continued to use the material into the following decade.

Pictorialist Societies: Goals and Achievements

By the early 1890s, established photographic societies, set up in an era when objectives in photography were largely undifferentiated, no longer served the needs of all photographers. Unconcerned with, and indeed often contemptuous of the commercial and scientific aspects of photography that the older societies accommodated, partisans of aesthetic photographs began to form groups whose sole

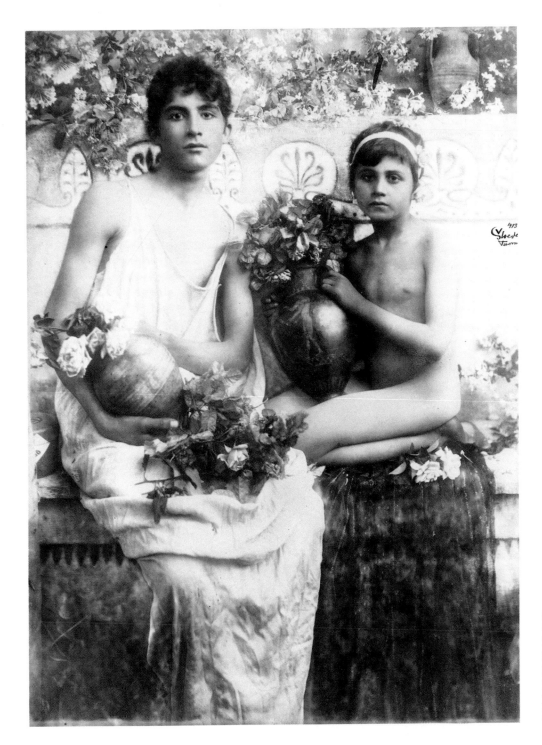

362. WILHELM VON
GLOEDEN. *Study,
Taormina, Sicily*, 1913.
Gelatin silver print.
International Museum of
Photography at George
Eastman House,
Rochester, N.Y.

aim was to promote camera art. The Secession movement led to the formation of the Wiener Kamera Klub in 1891, The Linked Ring in 1892, the Photo-Club de Paris in 1894, and the Photo-Secession in New York in 1902. In the same years, amateur photographic societies in Germany, Italy, the Hapsburg domains, Russia, and the smaller cities of the United States made available forums for the exchange of information about aesthetic concepts and processes, and provided exhibition space for the work of local Pictorialists

and that of the better-known figures of the Secession movement.

Exhibiting aesthetic photographs in an appropriate context was a paramount goal of the movement. Besides sponsoring their own gallery spaces, the most famous of which was the Little Galleries of the Photo-Secession in New York (known as "291"), photographers attempted to interest galleries, museums, and fine arts academies in displaying camera images either alone or in conjunction

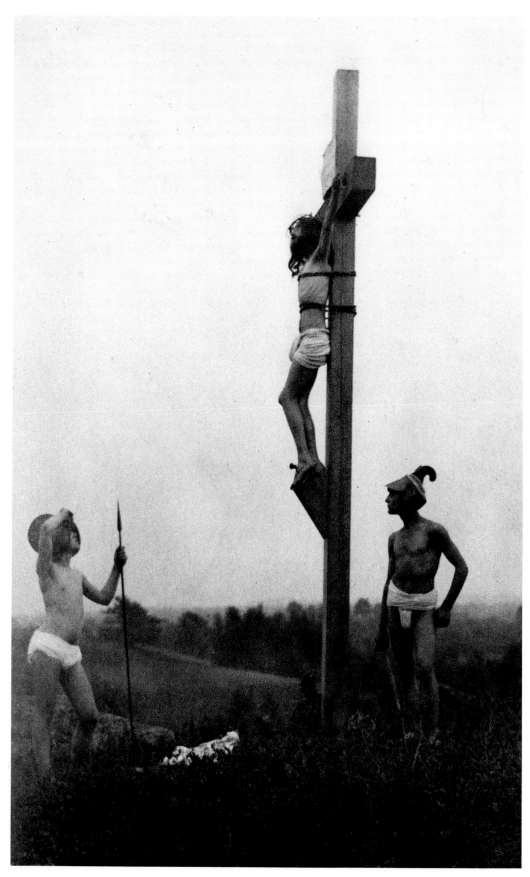

363. F. HOLLAND DAY. *Untitled (Crucifix with Roman Soldiers)*, c. 1898.
Platinum print. Library of Congress, Washington, D.C.

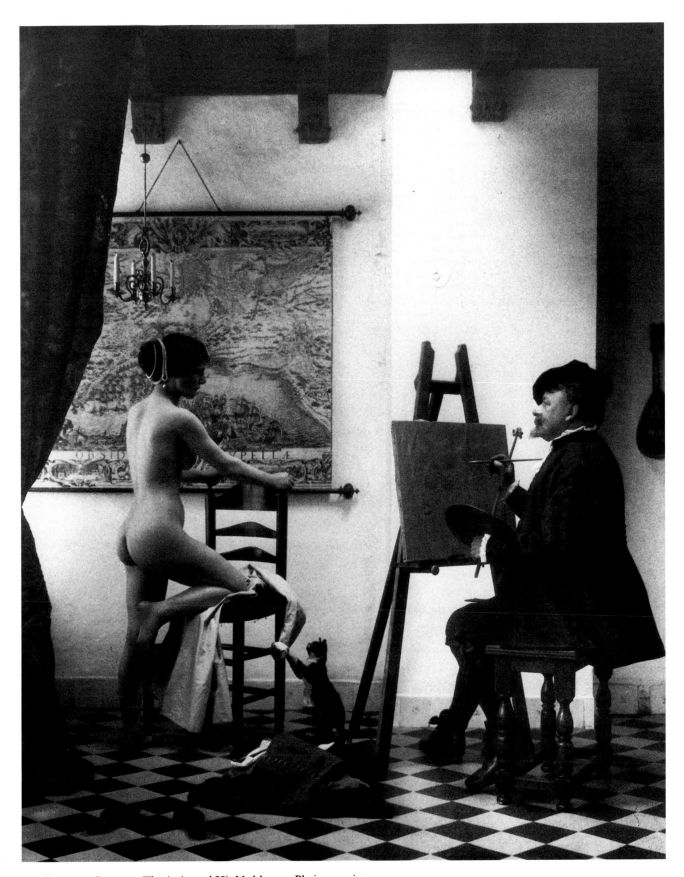

364. RICHARD POLACK. *The Artist and His Model*, 1914. Platinum print.
Royal Photographic Society, Bath, England.

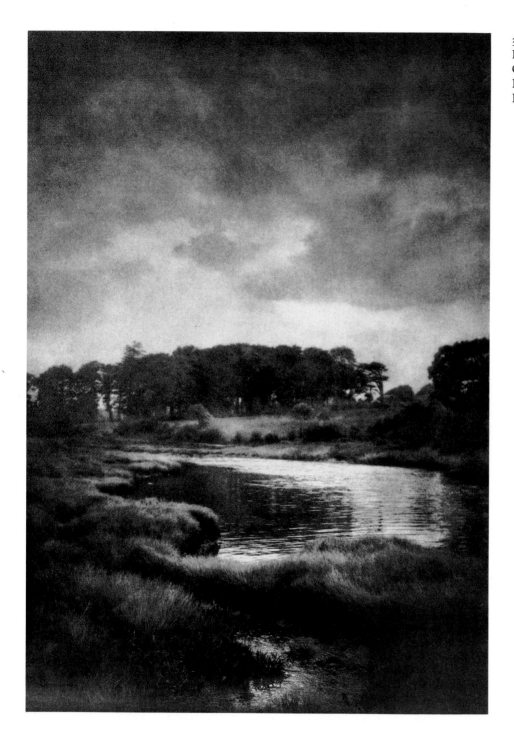

with examples of graphic art. They urged also that photographers be represented on the juries of selection for photographic shows, since they alone would have the experience to separate imaginative and tasteful from uninspired works. Starting in 1893, and continuing into the 20th century, a number of prestigious institutions in Germany and the United States began to exhibit camera images, among them the Royal Academy in Berlin, the Hamburg Künsthalle, and the Albright, Carnegie, and Corcoran galleries in the United States. Artistic photographs were exhibited

at several of the large fine and decorative art exhibitions, including one sponsored by the Munich Secession in 1898, and the international shows at Glasgow in 1901 and in Turin in 1904. An exhibition devoted entirely to artistic photography held in 1891 under the auspices of the *Club der Amateur-Photographien* of Vienna became a model for annual exhibitions or Salons that were started in London and Hamburg in 1893, in Paris in 1894, and in Brussels, Vienna, and The Hague in the following years.

Art photography attracted articulate support in periodicals and books. Before 1890, photographic, literary, and general interest journals in Europe and the United States had devoted space to a discussion of the artistic merits of the medium, and while they continued to do so, after 1890 a literature whose sole purpose was to promote the movement flowered not only in the cosmopolitan centers of the west but in Russia, Italy, and Eastern Europe. *Camera Work*, launched in New York in 1903 by members of the Photo-Secession, and praised for the exceptional level of design and gravure reproduction it maintained throughout its 14 years of existence, was one of a number of periodicals that included *Photogram*, *La Révue Photographique*, and *Photographische Kunst* in which similar aesthetic positions were as lucidly (if not as tastefully) embraced. Magazines with a popular readership also included articles on artistic photography. Between 1898 and 1918, for example, American art critic Sadakichi Hartmann, who was eulogized "as the first art critic who realized the possibility of photography being developed into a fine art,"[20] placed some 500 articles on artistic photography in a variety of American and European journals. Around 1900, full-length works conceived in the tradition of earlier tracts on photographic art by Emerson or Henry Peach Robinson formulated the theoretical arguments for aesthetic photography. To cite but two, *La Photographie est elle une art?* by French critic Robert de la Sizeranne—a work exceptionally influential in Eastern Europe as well as in France—and *Photography as a Fine Art*, by the American critic Charles Caffin, attempted to convince the cultivated viewer that since the same expressive concerns animated all artists no matter what medium they used, the same criteria should be applied to images made by camera and by hand.

The Linked Ring—the first major organization to institutionalize the new aesthetic attitudes—was formed by a number of English amateurs whose disenchantment with The Photographic Society of London (renamed the Royal Photographic Society in 1894) prompted them to secede from that body in 1891 and 1892. This group, which included George Davison, Alfred Horsley Hinton (editor after 1893 of *Amateur Photography*), Maskell, Lydell Sawyer, and Henry Peach Robinson, modeled their organization on a contemporary art group—the New English Art Club—and encouraged members, accepted by invitation only, to pursue "the development of the highest form of Art of which Photography is capable."[21] Though Emerson himself was not a member, the Ring followed his precept that "a work of art ends with itself; there should be no ulterior motive beyond the giving of aesthetic pleasure. . . ."[22] They established relationships with Pictorialist photographers in other countries, some of whom were honored with invitations to become "Links" and to submit work to the yearly exhibitions at the annual Salon of Picto-

rial Photography, known as the London Salon. British members seem to have been inspired primarily by landscape; their work is marked by the unusually somber moods visible in gum prints by Hinton (*pl. no. 365*) or in Davison's *The Onion Field* (also called *An Old Farmstead, pl. no. 366*), made using a camera with a pinhole instead of a lens. Combining the rural subject matter of Naturalistic photography with an impressionistic treatment that makes all substances—fields, buildings, sky, and clouds—appear to be made of the same stuff, this work was exceptionally influential among photographers of the time. For example, it prompted Alexander Keighley, a photographer of somewhat derivative genre scenes, to turn to romantic soft-focus treatments of landscape (*pl. no. 367*). A similar use of atmospheric haze and broad shapes and tonalities in dealing with city themes can be seen in John Dudley Johnston's *Liverpool—An Impression (pl. no. 368)*, a pensive view with subtle Whistler-like nuances achieved by consummate handling of the gum process.

James Craig Annan, Frederick H. Evans, and Frank M. Sutcliffe represent members of the Ring who favored straight printing and chose to evoke poetic feelings through means other than the manipulation of printing materials. Annan, an accomplished gravure printer,[23] produced artistic effects by the subtle handling of light and shadow seen in the linear patterns in the water in *A Black Canal (pl. no. 369)*. Sutcliffe suggests the ethereal quality of fog-enshrouded places in *View of the Harbor (pl. no. 370)* by his control of the relationship of foreground to background tonalities. In *Kelmscott Manor: In the Attics, (pl. no. 371)* Evans, the Ring's most esteemed architectural photographer, summons up a serene sense of peacefulness and of humane order in the arrangement of architectonic elements and delicate tonalities.

The *Photo-Club de Paris* was organized in 1894 by Maurice Bucquet to provide an alternative to the professionally oriented *Société Française de Photographie*; in the same year it inaugurated an annual Salon. Members included Demachy, LeBègue, and E. J. Constant Puyo, all ardent enthusiasts of handwork. Up until 1914, when he gave up the medium, Demachy used his considerable means and leisure to promote artistic photography and its processes, collaborating, as has been noted, with Maskell in 1897 and with Puyo in 1906 on a manual of artistic processes in photography.[24] In his own work, he favored nudes, bucolic landscapes, and dancers, and frequently printed in red, brown, and gray pigments using the gum process. The images of ballet dancers (*pl. no. 372*) were considered "delightful" by his contemporaries, but when compared with paintings and drawings on this theme by Edgar Degas, they seem derivative and lacking in vitality. Puyo, a former commandant in the French army, at times favored impressionistic effects in landscape and genre scenes (*pl.*

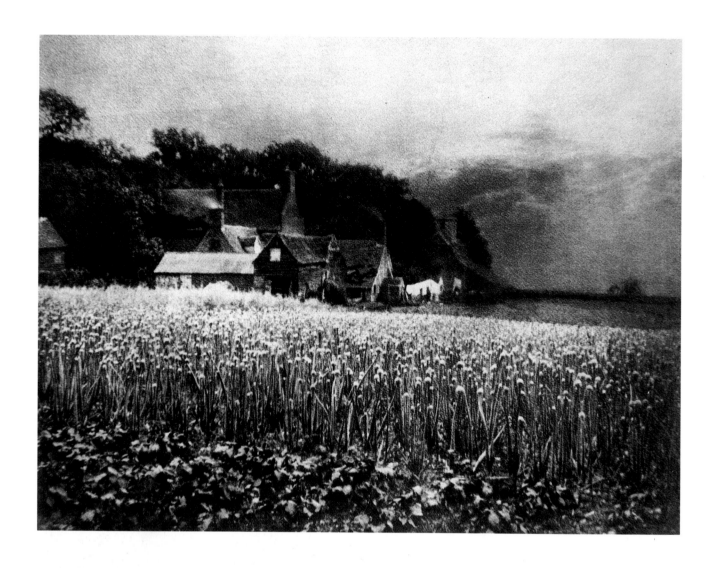

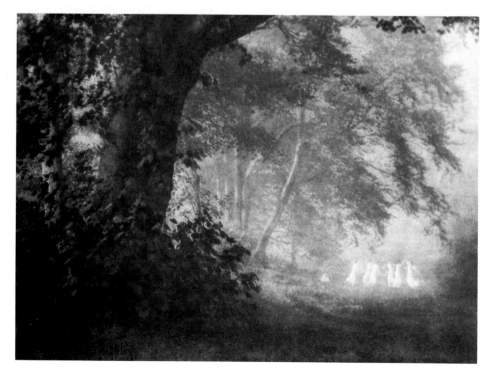

366. GEORGE DAVISON.
The Onion Field, 1890.
Gravure print. Kodak
Museum, Harrow, England.

LEFT:

367. ALEXANDER
KEIGHLEY. *Fantasy*, 1913.
Carbon print. Royal
Photographic Society, Bath,
England.

RIGHT:

368. JOHN DUDLEY
JOHNSTON. *Liverpool—An
Impression*, 1906. Gum
bichromate print. Royal
Photographic Society, Bath,
England.

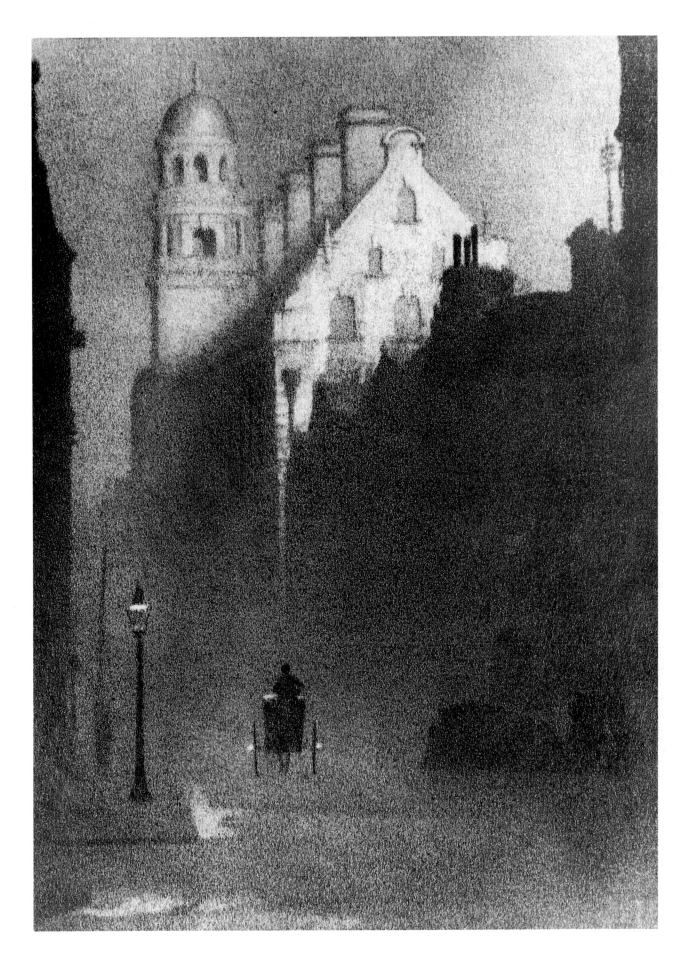

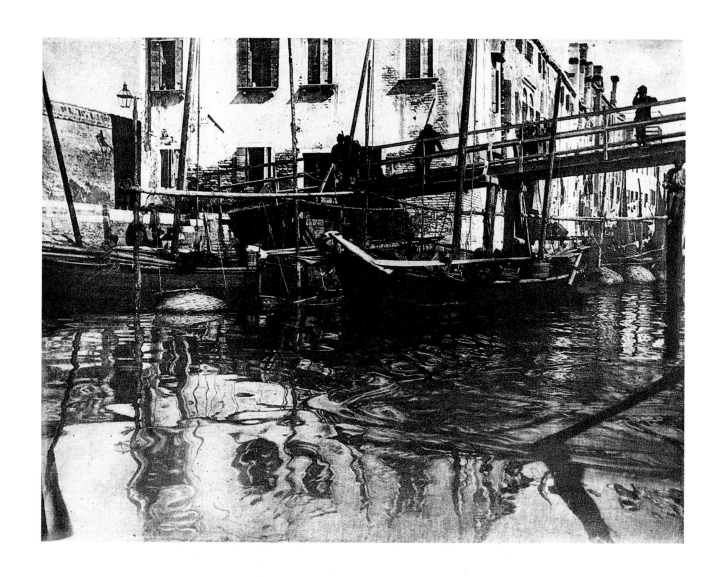

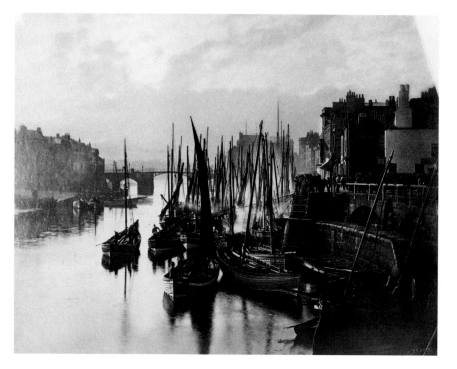

369. JAMES CRAIG ANNAN. *A Black Canal (probably Venice)*, 1894. Gravure print. Metropolitan Museum of Art, New York; Alfred Stieglitz Collection, 1949.

LEFT:

370. FRANK MEADOW SUTCLIFFE. *View of the Harbor*, 1880s. Carbon print. Photograph Collection, New York Public Library, Astor, Lenox, and Tilden Foundations.

RIGHT:

371. FREDERICK H. EVANS. *Kelmscott Manor: In the Attics*, 1896. Platinum print. Collection Sam Wagstaff, New York.

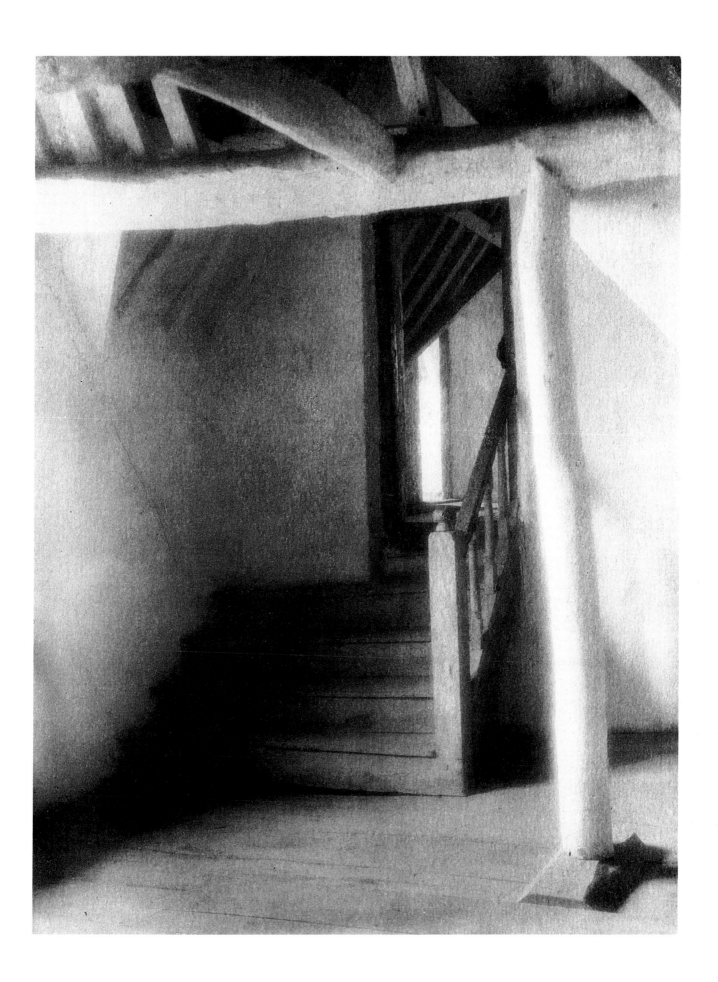

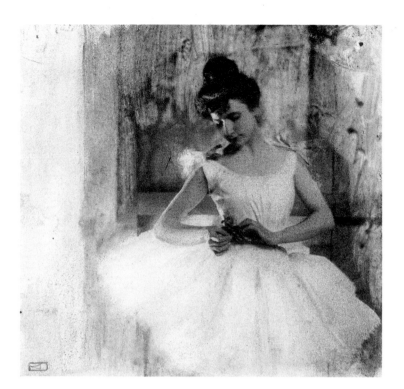

372. ROBERT DEMACHY. *A Ballerina*, 1900. Gum bichromate print. Metropolitan Museum of Art, New York; Alfred Stieglitz Collection, 1949.

373. E. J. CONSTANT PUYO. *Summer*, 1903. Green pigment ozotype. Metropolitan Museum of Art, New York; Alfred Stieglitz Collection, 1933.

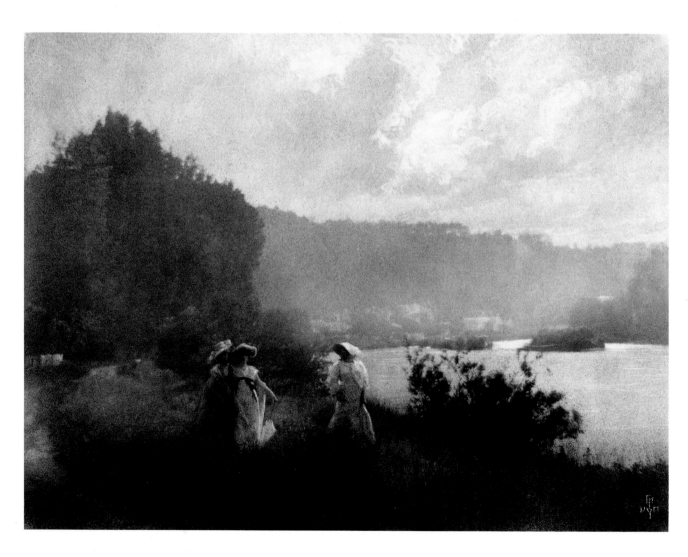

no. 373) and at other times sharply defined Art Nouveau decorative patterns, especially in portraits of fashionable women. He designed and used special lenses to create these effects, but also condoned extensive manipulation as a way of vanquishing what he called "automatism"—that is, the sense that the image was produced by a machine without feeling. Other members included Leonard Misonne, a Belgian photographer of city and rural scenes, and Dubreuil, who portrayed pastoral landscape around Lille in the manner of French painter Constant Troyon *(pl. no. 374)*.

The earliest international exhibition of Pictorialist works in German-speaking countries took place in Vienna in 1891 under the auspices of the *Wiener Kamera Klub.* It was seen by the Austrian Kuehn *(see Profile),* and the Germans Hugo Henneberg *(pl. no. 375)* and Hans Watzek *(pl. no. 376)*; three years later all three emerged as the most prominent figures in art photography in central Europe, exhibiting together as the *Trifolium* or *Kleeblatt.* In Germany itself, the exhibitions held at Berlin, Hamburg, and especially Munich toward the end of the 19th century had made it clear that the camera was more than a practical tool, and that the photograph might be a source of aesthetic pleasure as well as information. Portraiture was one of the first motifs to be affected by the new sensibility, with inspiration coming from an exhibition of portraits by David Octavius Hill and Robert Adamson included in the Hamburg International Exhibition in 1899 and again in a later exhibition in Dresden in 1904. Portrait photographers began to realize that artistic discrimination in lighting, combined with attention to expressive contour might create more evocative works than was possible with the unmodulated studio illumination that played evenly over conventionally posed sitters. This awareness prompted a new approach on the part of the well-known portrait team of Rudolph Dührkoop and his daughter Minya-Diez Dührkoop *(pl. no. 377)* of Hamburg, and of Hugo Erfurth in Dresden. The strong tonal contrast and attention to contour in Erfurth's portrait of Professor Dorsch *(pl. no. 378)* continued to mark the persuasive portraits made by this photographer into the 1920s. Other portraitists of the time whose work reflected an interest in artistic lighting and treatment were Nicola Perscheid, working in Berlin and Leipzig, and the partners Arthur Benda and Dora Kallmus —better known as Madame d'Ora—who maintained a studio in Vienna from 1907 through 1925. Besides printing in silver and gum, all three were interested in a straight color printing process known as Pinatype, a forerunner of dye-transfer printing invented in France in 1903 *(see A Short Technical History, Part II)*.

Landscapes, still life, and figural compositions, many of which were subject to extensive manipulation, absorbed

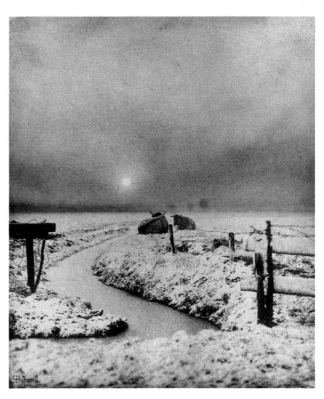

374. PIERRE DUBREUIL. *Dusk on the Marsh in the Snow,* 1898. Silver bromide print. Museum für Kunst und Gewerbe, Hamburg.

both professional and amateur photographers in Germany. Large works in gum in strong colors, produced jointly by the Hamburg amateurs Oskar and Theodor Hofmeister *(pl. no. 379)*, were exhibited at the London Salon and 291, and collected by Stieglitz, but other German Pictorialists were equally adept and turned out images similar in style and quality; *The Reaper (pl. no. 380)*, a gum print in blue pigment, by Perscheid, is typical of the genre. Heinrich Beck, a minor government official was awarded a silver medal at the 1903 Hamburg exhibition of Art Photography *(pl. no. 381)*; Georg Einbeck, a former painter, combined graphic and photographic techniques to create exhibition posters; and Gustav E. B. Trinks, an employee of an import-export company, exhibited silver bromide and gum prints at all the important Pictorialist exhibitions. Otto Scharf, in his time one of the most respected art photographers in Germany, was extravagantly praised for the brilliance with which he handled silver, platinum, and colored gum materials to evoke mood and feeling in scenes typified by *Rhine Street, Krefeld (pl. no. 382)*, a green gum print of 1901.

Artistic photography made headway elsewhere in Europe, too, with individuals in Holland, Belgium, and the Scandinavian countries drawing inspiration from Pictorialist activity in France and Germany. The work of

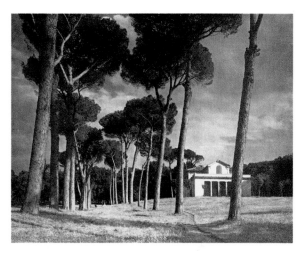

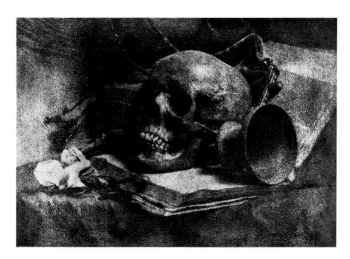

375. HUGO HENNEBERG. *Italian Landscape and Villa*, 1902. Pigment gum print. Metropolitan Museum of Art, New York; Alfred Stieglitz Collection, 1933.

376. HANS WATZEK. *Still Life* (from the portfolio *Gummidrucke*), c. 1901. Gravure print. Art Museum, Princeton University, Princeton, N.J.

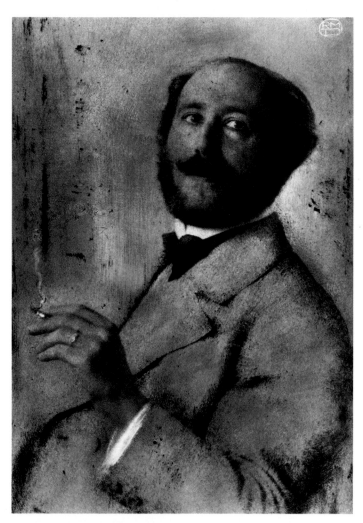

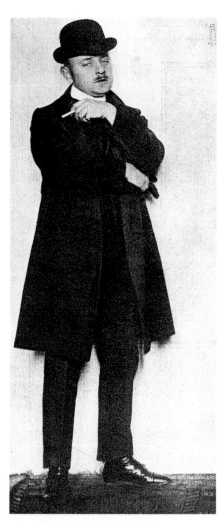

377. RUDOLPH and MINYA DÜHRKOOP. *Alfred Kerr*, 1904. Oil pigment print. Royal Photographic Society, Bath, England.

378. HUGO ERFURTH. *Professor Dorsch*, 1903. Gum bichromate print. Staatliche Landesbildstelle, Hamburg; Museum für Kunst und Gewerbe, Hamburg.

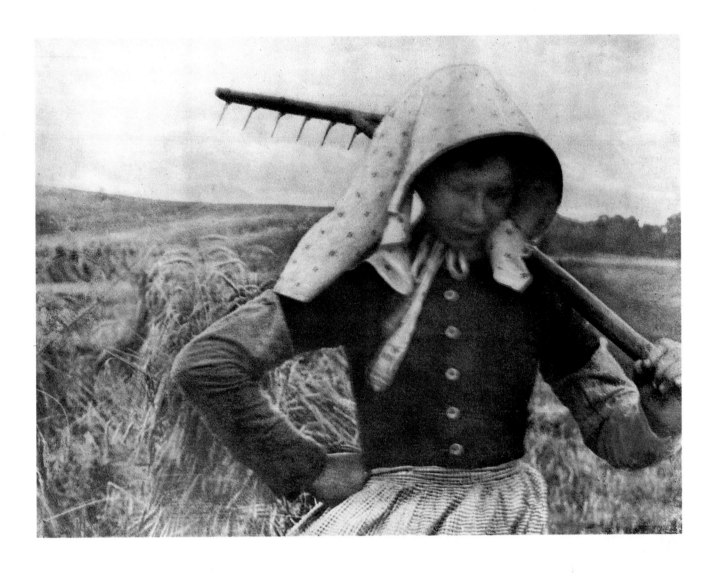

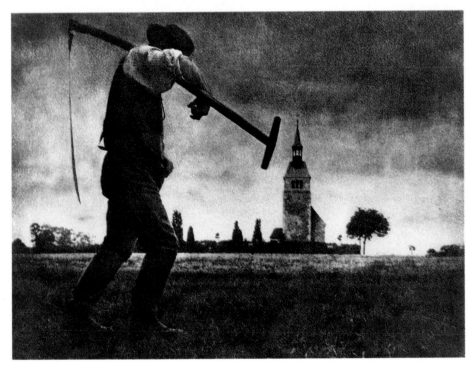

379. Oskar and Theodor Hofmeister. *The Haymaker*, c. 1904. Gum bichromate print. Royal Photographic Society, Bath, England.

380. Nicolas Perscheid. *The Reaper*, 1901. Gravure print. Museum für Kunst und Gewerbe, Hamburg.

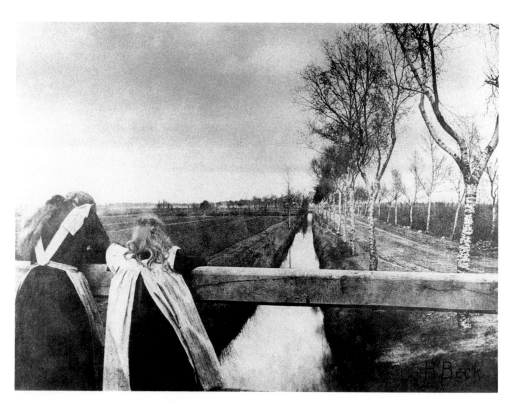

381. HEINRICH BECK.
Childhood Dreams, 1903.
Gum bichromate print.
Museum für Kunst und
Gewerbe, Hamburg.

382. OTTO SCHARF.
Rhine Street, Krefeld,
1898. Gum bichromate
print. Museum für
Kunst und Gewerbe,
Hamburg.

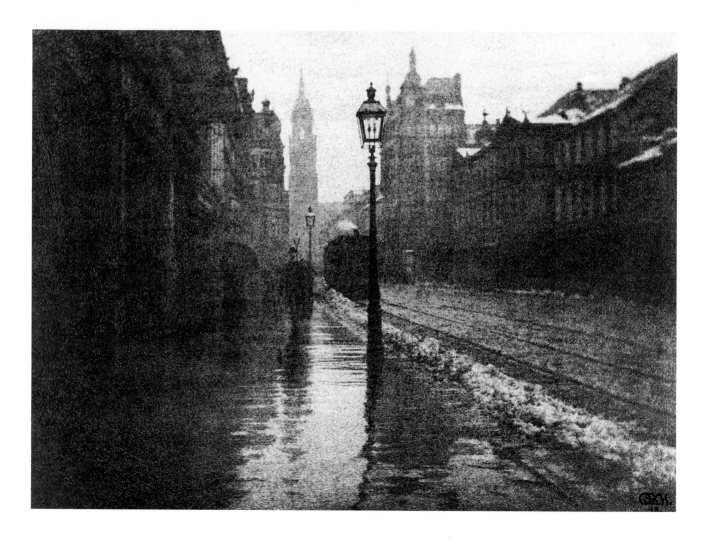

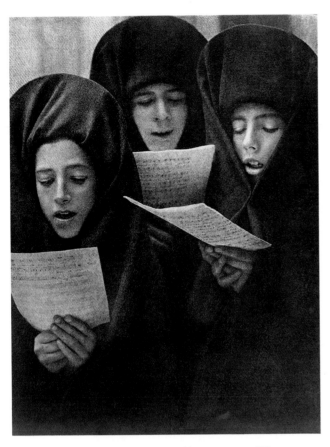

383. JOSÉ ORTÍZ ECHAGÜE. *Young Singers*, c. 1934. Direct carbon print. San Diego Museum of Art; purchased by the Fine Arts Society, 1934.

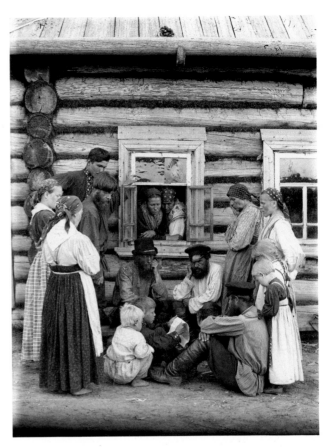

384. SERGEI LOBOVIKOV. *Peasant Scene*, probably late 1890s. Gelatin silver print. *Sovfoto Magazine* and VAAP, Moscow.

Finnish photographers Konrad Inha (born Nyström) and Wladimir Schohin suggests the range of artistic camera work outside the better-known cosmopolitan centers of Europe. Inha, a journalist, made romantic images of rural landscape and peasant life in the Naturalist mode, which he published in 1896 as *Pictorial Finland*, while Schohin, owner of a retail business in Helsinki, used carbon, gum, and bromoil processes, and experimented with Autochrome, in his depictions of the middle-class life of his milieu.

To the south, the city of Turin, Italy, played host to the International Exposition of Modern Decorative Art in 1903, thereby providing Italians with an opportunity to see a collection of American works selected by Stieglitz. A year later, *La Fotografica Artistica*, an Italian review of international pictorial photography was founded, and a small group began to make artistic works in the medium. Their work ran a gamut from the previously mentioned reconstructed religious scenes to genre studies of provincial life to atmospheric landscapes. The Spanish amateur photographer José Ortíz Echagüe began to work in the Pictorialist style around 1906, continuing in this tradition until long

after the style had become outmoded; his artfully posed and lighted genre images *(pl. no. 383)*, reproduced in several publications on Spanish life that appeared during the 1930s, tend toward picturesqueness.[25]

Despite the political instability and economic changes taking place in eastern Europe and the continued emphasis in many localities on ethnographic photographs to advance the cause of nationalism, a strong interest in photography as self-expression led to the formation of amateur Pictorialist societies in the major cities of an area that now includes Czechoslovakia, Rumania, and Hungary, with the movement especially vital in Poland. The Club of Photographic Art Lovers and the journal *Photographic Review*, established in Lvov in 1891 and followed by similar groups in other Polish cities, provided an opportunity for the exhibition and reproduction of the works of important Pictorialists, including Demachy, Kuehn, and Steichen. The president of the Lvov group, Henryk Mikolasch, observed that artistic photographs might "reflect thought, soul, and word," in place of "tasteless and pedantic . . . exactness,"[26] a concept that led him to idealize peasant life in his own images, which he printed in gum. In common

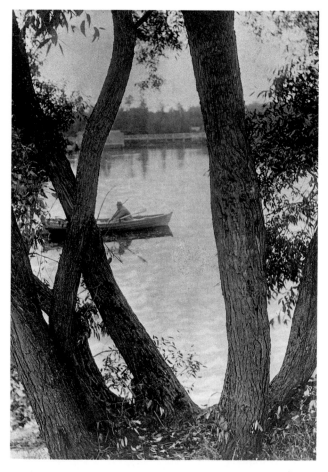

385. ALEXIS MAZOURINE. *River Landscape with Rowboat*,
n.d. Platinum print. Staatliche Landesbildstelle,
Hamburg; Museum für Kunst und Gewerbe, Hamburg.

with much Pictorialist photography outside of London, Paris, and New York, artistic camera work in Poland was firmly tied to Naturalism and the Barbizon tradition, to which the so-called ennobling processes added a sense of atmosphere; eventually these means were integrated into the modernist style that emerged in Poland in the 1920s *(see Chapter 9)*.

Around 1900, the concept of art photography attracted a number of Russian photographers of landscape and genre, who heeded the call by Nikolai Petrov, later artistic director of the Pictorialist journal *Vestnik Fotografi (Herald of Photography)*, to go beyond the unfeeling representation of nature. Employing gum and pigment processes, they, too, adopted a creative approach to subjects taken from Russian village life. This work, exemplified in photographs by Sergei Lobovikov *(pl. no. 384)* that were exhibited in Dresden, Hamburg, and Paris as well as in Russia, also evolved from the concept of the nobility of peasant life, but in their subtle balance of art documentation and compassion they exhibit a distinctive character that avoids

sentimentality. In contrast, Alexis Mazourine, descendant of an esteemed Moscow family, sought inspiration in the more cosmopolitan centers of Hamburg and Vienna where, according to contemporary sources, his small-format platinum landscapes and figure compositions, an example of which is *River Landscape with Rowboat (pl. no. 385)*, were as well known as in his own country.

Pictorialism in the United States

American photographs shown at the London Salon in 1899 were singled out for the "virtues" of "concentration, strength, massing of light and shade and breadth of effect,"[27] qualities exemplified in Day's unusual portrait of a young black man entitled *An Ethiopian Chief (pl. no. 386)*. Several factors made American work appear so vigorous in European eyes. For one, the Pictorialist movement was exceptionally broad-based, with activities in small towns and major cities, and it attracted people from varied economic, social, and regional backgrounds. Unlike their European counterparts, who were mainly men of means or in the arts, Americans of both sexes, active in commercial photography, in the arts, in business, in the professions, and as housewifes, joined photographic societies, giving the movement a varied and democratic complexion.

Women were especially prominent in Pictorialism, just as they were more active in all aspects of photography in the United States. For example, Gertrude Käsebier, the most illustrious of the female portraitists, was praised for having done more for artistic portraiture *(pl. no. 387)* than any other of her time—painter or photographer—by her discerning sense of "what to leave out."[28] Many women, among them Boughton, Mary Deven, Emma Farnsworth, Zaida ben-Yusuf, Clara Sipprell, Eva Watson-Schutze, Mathilde Weil, and Louise Deshong Woodbridge, specialized in portraiture and refined themes, exemplified by *The Rose (pl. no. 388)*—a somewhat mannered portrait in Pre-Raphaelite style—by Watson-Schutze. The nude, sometimes conceived in allegorical terms, attracted Anne W. Brigman, Adelaide Hanscom Leeson, and Janet Reece; Brigman's 1905 work, *The Bubble (pl. no. 389)*, is typical of the idyllic treatment accorded this subject by both men and women at a time when such camera images were just becoming accepted by sophisticated viewers. Women also were among the early professional photojournalists in the United States; Frances Benjamin Johnston, who exhibited at salons and joined the Photo-Secession, was a free-lance magazine photographer of note *(see Chapter 8)*. In 1900, she collected and took abroad 142 works by 28 women photographers for exhibition in France and Russia—further evidence that as a medium without a long tradition of male-dominated academies, photography offered female

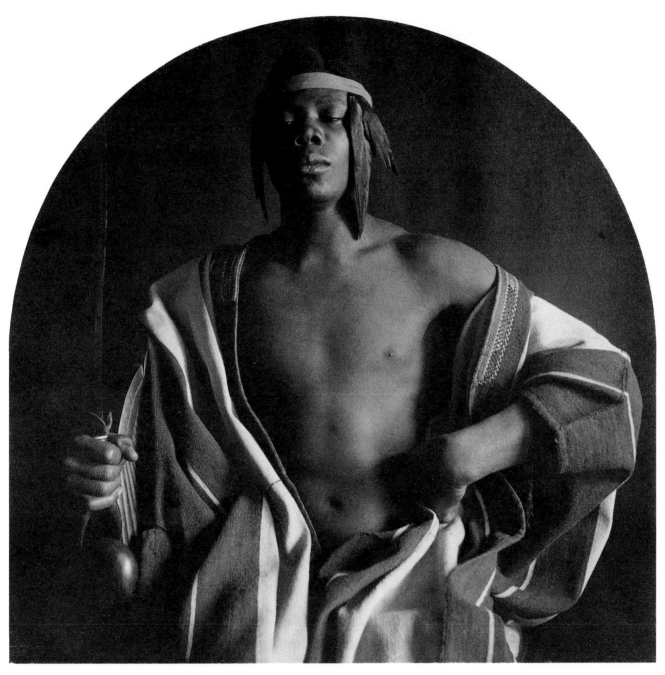

386. F. Holland Day. *An Ethiopian Chief*, c. 1896. Platinum print.
Metropolitan Museum of Art, New York; Alfred Stieglitz Collection, 1933.

participants an opportunity for self-expression denied them in the traditional visual arts.[29]

Another difference between Americans and Europeans involved attitudes toward the manipulation of prints that made photographs look like works of graphic art. Reflecting the considerable disagreement among American critics about the virtues of handwork on negatives and prints, photographers in the United States chose less frequently to work with processes that completely obscured the mechanical origin of camera images. Whether members of the Photo-Secession or not, they preferred platinum, carbon, and, less often, gum-bichromate, sometimes in combination with platinum, to bromoil and oil pigment materials. Even when availing themselves of the variety of colorations made possible with gum-bichromate, they favored, with several notable exceptions, direct printing without hand intervention on relatively smooth rather than heavily textured papers.

Traces of a wide variety of tendencies current in graphic art are to be seen in the work of American Pictorialists.

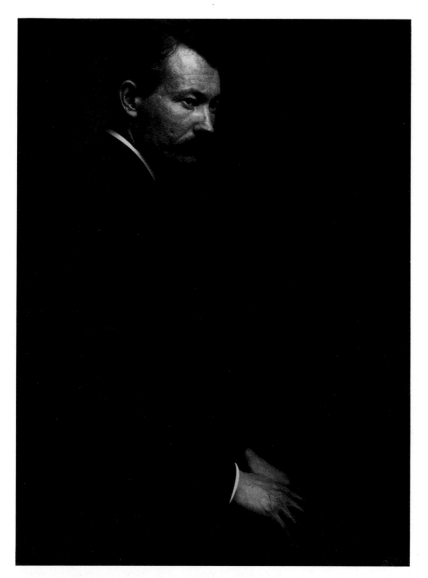

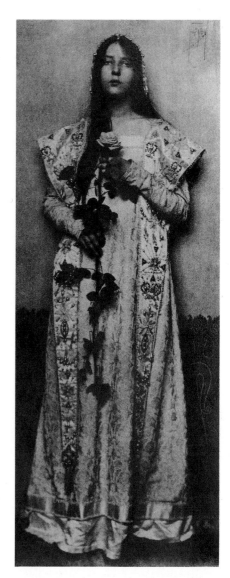

387. GERTRUDE KÄSEBIER. *Robert Henri*, c. 1908.
Silver print toned and coated to simulate gum print.
Sheldon Memorial Art Gallery, University of Nebraska,
Lincoln; F.M. Hall Collection.

388. EVA WATSON-SCHUTZE. *The Rose*,
1903 or before. Gum bichromate print.
Metropolitan Museum of Art, New York;
Alfred Stieglitz Collection, 1949.

Within the Photo-Secession and in some of the better-organized Pictorialist societies in the East, the dominant styles were derived from Tonalist and Symbolist paintings, but the influence of other movements in the arts, in particular that of the French Barbizon painters, is also visible. Toward 1900, the art of the Japanese became an especially potent influence, reaching both graphic artists and photographers in the United States in part through the writings of the eminent art teacher Arthur Wesley Dow, who translated its concepts into a system of flat tonal harmonies called *notan*. With its emphasis on subtle ungraduated tonalities, this manner of handling chiaroscuro, in concert with simplicity of composition and absence of deep spatial perspective, imparted a distinctively decorative aspect to many Pictorialist images.

Several regional Pictorialist groups were primarily concerned with landscape imagery. Many members of the Photographic Society of Philadelphia—a venerable club organized in 1862 and the first to actively promote artistic photography—drew nourishment from the earlier tradition of landscape imagery supported by *The Philadelphia Photographer (see Chapter 3)*, as well as from the Naturalistic concepts of Emerson. Individual members, among them Robert S. Redfield, Henry Troth, and Woodbridge endeavored to achieve "unity of style and harmony of effect"[30] and to subordinate description to artistic purpose in subtly modulated landscapes printed on platinum *(pl. no. 390)*. In New York State, another such group, the Buffalo Camera Club (organized 1888) also displayed a reverential attitude toward nature. Asserting the need for attention to "harmonious composition and well-managed lights and shadows,"[31] their handling of light and atmosphere, exemplified in founding member Wilbur H. Porterfield's *September Morning*, 1906, *(pl. no. 391)*, projects a melancholy mood similar to that in the tonalist paintings of Inness, Ranger, and Alexander Wyant.

Photographers in these groups and others working on their own in the same tradition often were not considered first-rate by the mentors of Pictorialism, in part because they tended to cling to outdated attitudes regarding theme and treatment. For instance, Leigh Richmond Miner, instructor of art at Virginia's Hampton Institute around the turn of the century, viewed the black farmers and fishermen living on the islands off the coast of South Carolina with reverence and cast his many images of them in a heroic mold. Other photographers of Southern rural life,

among them Clarence B. Moore, a member of the Photographic Society of Philadelphia, and Rudolf Eickemeyer, Jr., a well-known New York Pictorialist, transformed rural people into ingratiating genre types, emphasizing industriousness and nobility of character through their choices of lighting and pose. Remnants of this approach lingered into the 1930s, as can be seen in portraits made by Prentice Hall Polk, official photographer at Tuskeegee Institute *(pl. no. 392)*, and by New York portraitist Doris Ulmann, who idealized the inhabitants of the Appalachian highlands where she photographed in the late 1920s and '30s *(pl. no. 393)*.

Similar picturesque qualities characterize many of the portraits made by Arnold Genthe of the inhabitants of San Francisco's Chinese quarter *(see Chapter 6)*, except that a number of his images, though seen through the haze of a romanticizing vision, have a refreshing spontaneity that distinguishes them from more statically posed rural genre images. Genthe was a member of the California Camera Club, which was organized in 1890 in San Francisco and,

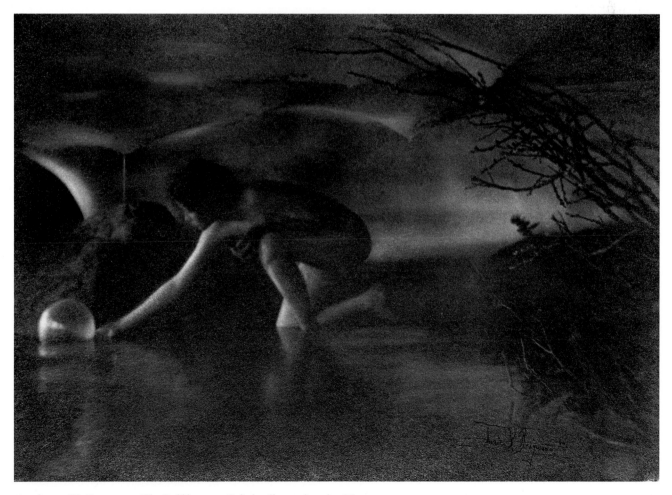

389. ANNE W. BRIGMAN. *The Bubble*, 1905. Gelatin silver print. Art Museum, Princeton University, Princeton, N.J.; gift of Mrs. Raymond C. Collins.

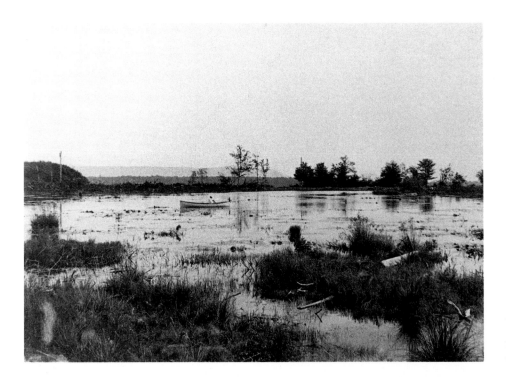

390. LOUISE DESHONG WOODBRIDGE. *Outlet on the Lake*, 1885. Platinum print, 1898. Janet Lehr, Inc., New York.

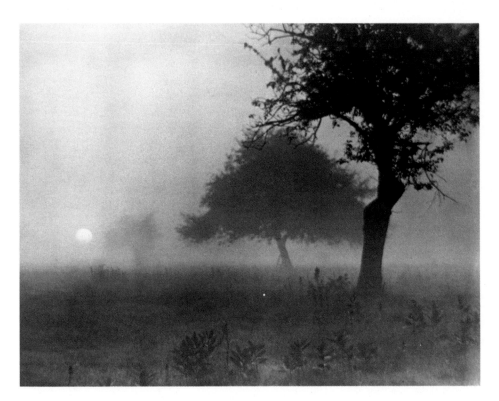

391. WILBUR H. PORTERFIELD. *September Morning*, 1906. Gelatin silver print. Buffalo and Erie County Historical Society, Buffalo, N.Y. © Cowles-Media.

with 400 or so members, was for many years the primary enclave of art photography on the West Coast. Although members of the group, including Laura Adams Armer, Anne W. Brigman, William Dassonville, and Oscar Maurer, participated in Salon exhibitions on the East Coast and in Europe, and several became members of the Photo-Secession, no cohesive style of California photography emerged.

Instead, the flat massing of tonal areas, seen in Armer's *Chinatown (pl. no. 394)* and in many other examples from this region, seems related to the pervasive interest in the arts of Japan that affected photography everywhere in the United States during the last decade of the 19th century.

Idealization was the keynote of the extensive pictorial document of American Indian life undertaken in 1899 by

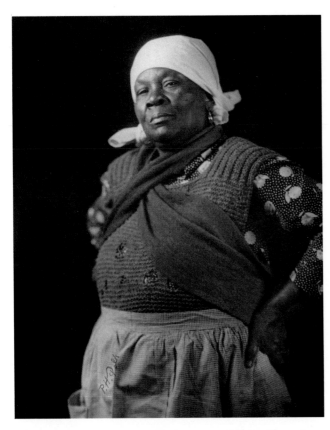

392. PRENTICE HALL POLK. *The Boss*, 1933. Gelatin silver print. Courtesy and © Prentice Hall Polk.

Edward S. Curtis. While camera studies of Indian life were being made at the time by a number of photographers, Curtis (funded in part by the financier J. P. Morgan) may be considered with the Pictorialists because he selected for his portrayal of the "vanishing race" picturesque individuals—mainly women and elders—and on occasion even provided them with appealing costumes. He composed and cropped scenes carefully and printed on platinum paper or by gravure, eventually producing 20 volumes and a like number of portfolios of text and images entitled *The North American Indian*. The photographer's endeavor to conjure up a rhapsodical vision of American Indian experience, rather than to make an ethnographically correct document, is exemplified in *The Vanishing Race (pl. no. 196)*. His work, which briefly found a market soon after the turn of the century, appealed to Americans who had begun to regard Native Americans as an "exotic spectacle" to be promoted as a tourist activity rather than as a menace to expansionist plans.

The Photo-Secession

With adherents throughout the nation who embraced a variety of approaches and a wide latitude of standards with regard to artistic photography, the Pictorialist movement was spread out and amorphous during the last years of the 19th century. Cohesiveness, direction, and exclusivity followed the formation in 1902 of the Photo-Secession. Organized by Stieglitz to compel "the serious recognition of photography as an additional medium of pictorial expression"[32] and of himself as a prime figure, it grew out of works selected and sent abroad in 1900 by Day and Stieglitz, both of whom were eager to demonstrate the high quality of aesthetic photography in the United States. Nevertheless, although Day's exhibition, "The New American School of Photography," had been exceptionally well-received in London and Paris, by 1902 he was forced to recognize that Stieglitz had emerged as leader of a vanguard movement that he baptized the Photo-Secession. Eventually numbering some 100 members, the founders included John G. Bullock, of the Photographic Society of Philadelphia, Eugene, Käsebier, Joseph Keiley—an important critic and publicist for the movement—Edward Steichen, and Clarence H. White. All were prominent in organizing and showing work in the national and international exhibitions of art photography held around 1900. While constituted as a national body, the Photo-Secession was most active in New York City, where Stieglitz served as editor of its publication, *Camera Work*, and presided over 291.

The formidable role played by Stieglitz in the establishment of this elite wing of American Pictorialism has received ample attention, but the active participation of Steichen, who found and installed the exhibition space, designed the cover and publicity for *Camera Work*, and initiated contacts with the French graphic artists whose works eventually formed an important part of Secession exhibits and publications, is less well known. Steichen's own work in photography during this early period (before he gave up painting) displayed a mastery of manipulative techniques that enabled him to use gum and pigment processes as well as platinum to suggest subtle nuances with a distinctive flair *(pl. no. 336)*. Because his later work in advertising photography had an even more signal effect on American photography, his contribution will be discussed more fully in Chapter 10.

Another of the founders, White *(see Profile)* was active in aesthetic photography *(pl. no. 395)* first in the Midwest and after 1906 in New York, where he turned to teaching both as a way of making a living and of imparting to others his profound belief in the expressive potential of the medium. Involved primarily with light and its symbolism, he used it to invest ordinary domestic scenes with subtlety, tenderness, and a genteel quality similar to that found in the work of American painters William Merritt Chase, John Singer Sargent, and James Abbott McNeill Whistler.

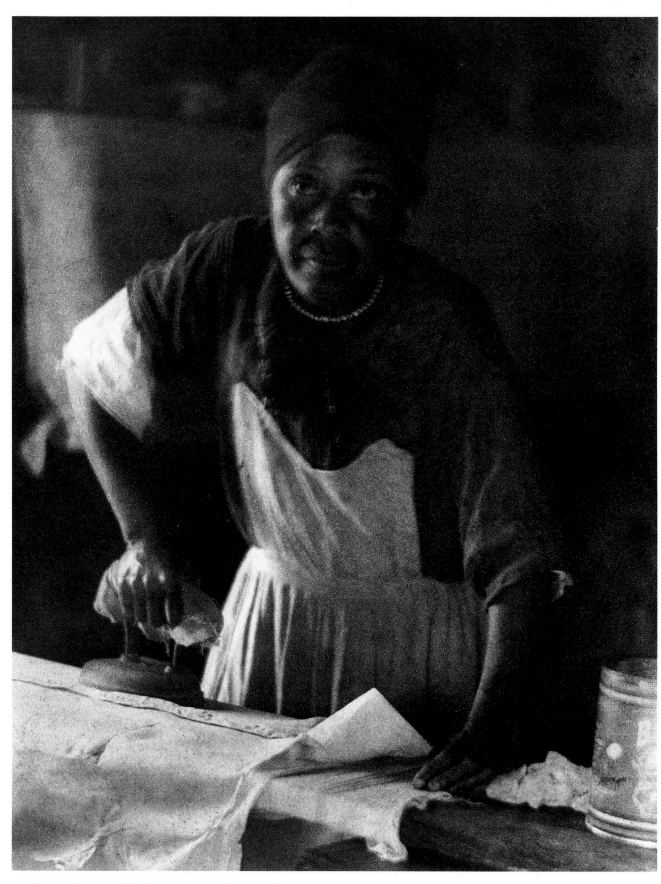

393. DORIS ULMANN. *Untitled*, c. 1925–34. Gravure print.
Museum of Modern Art, New York; gift of Mrs. John D. Rockefeller, III.

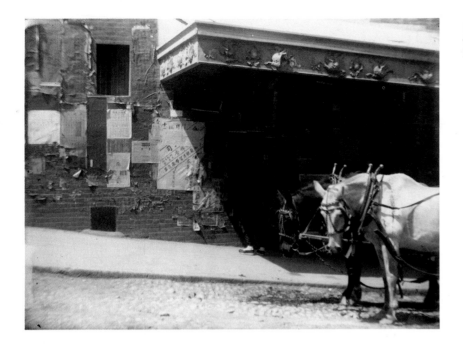

394. LAURA ADAMS ARMER. *Chinatown*, c. 1908. Gelatin silver print. California Historical Society Library, San Francisco.

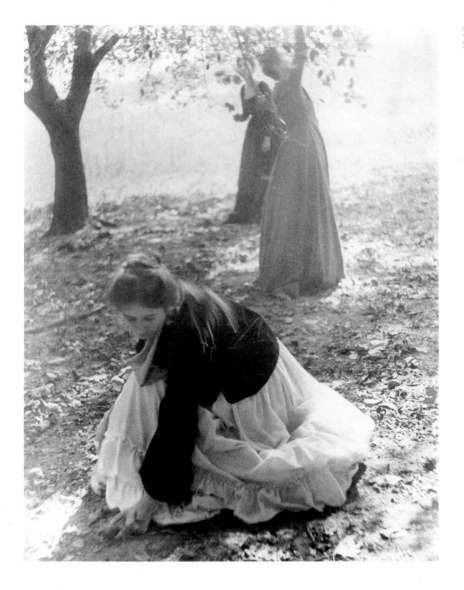

395. CLARENCE H. WHITE. *The Orchard*, 1902. Gravure print. Private Collection.

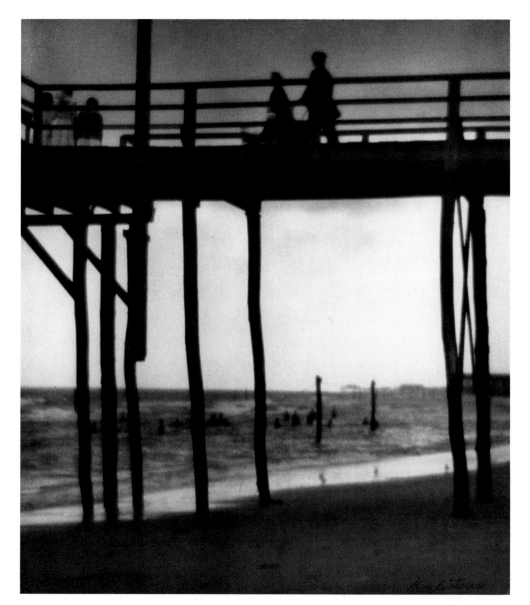

396. KARL STRUSS. *Low Tide, Arverne, New York,* 1912. Gelatin silver print. Stephen White Gallery, Beverly Hills, Cal.

RIGHT:

397. ALVIN LANGDON COBURN. *Brooklyn Bridge,* 1910–12. Gravure print. Royal Photographic Society, Bath, England.

In the main, Photo-Secession members produced landscapes, figure studies, and portraits—themes favored by Pictorialists everywhere—but a small group that included Coburn, Paul Haviland, Steichen, Stieglitz, and Karl Struss undertook to portray the city—heretofore an "untrodden field" in artistic photography.[33] In common with their contemporaries, the painters of the New York Realist school (The Eight, later known popularly as the Ashcan painters), these photographers found their subjects in the bridges, skyscrapers, and construction sites they regarded as affirmations of the vitality of urban life during the opening years of the 20th century. The Flatiron building, a looming prow-shaped structure completed in 1902, was seen as a symbol of power and culture—"a new Parthenon"—in images by Coburn, Haviland, Steichen, and Stieglitz. The harbor, with traffic that brought new work-

ers to the continent and day workers to the city, inspired Coburn, Haviland, and Stieglitz. Brooklyn Bridge and other East River crossings still under construction were photographed by Steichen, Struss *(pl. no. 396),* and Coburn *(pl. no. 397),* who actually considered these structures metaphors for the conquest of nature by human intelligence.

Coburn in particular regarded the camera as the only instrument, and photography the only medium, capable of encapsulating the constantly changing grandeur of the modern city.[34] As a younger Secessionist—he was twenty-two when he joined in 1904—his willingness to experiment with a variety of themes that included portraiture, urban views *(pl. no. 398),* and industrial scenes animated the Secession's activities during its early years despite his fairly regular travels between the United States and England. A consummate printer in platinum and gum,

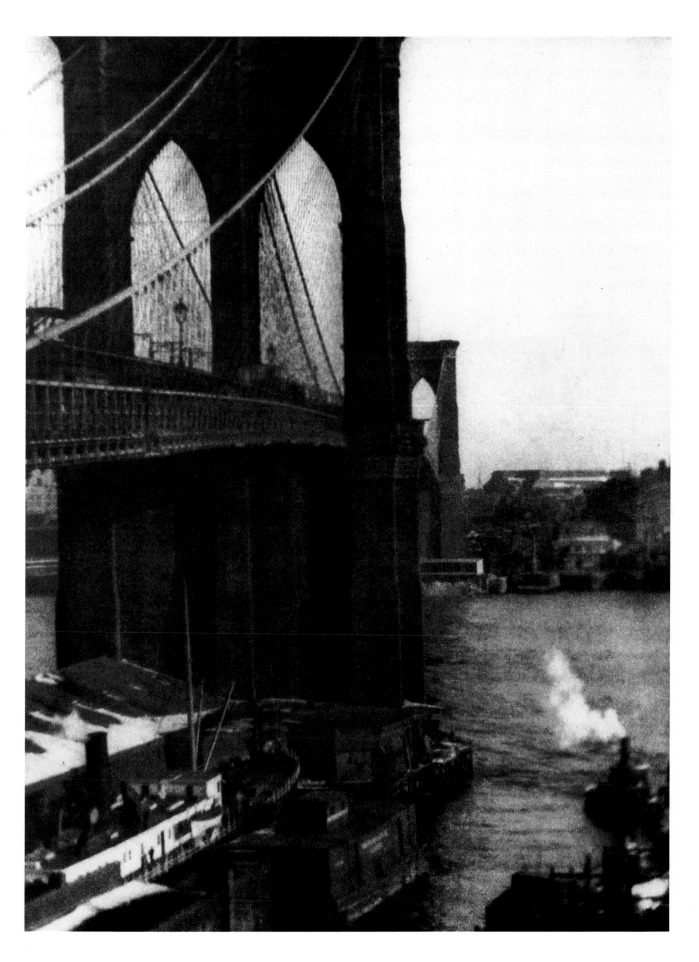

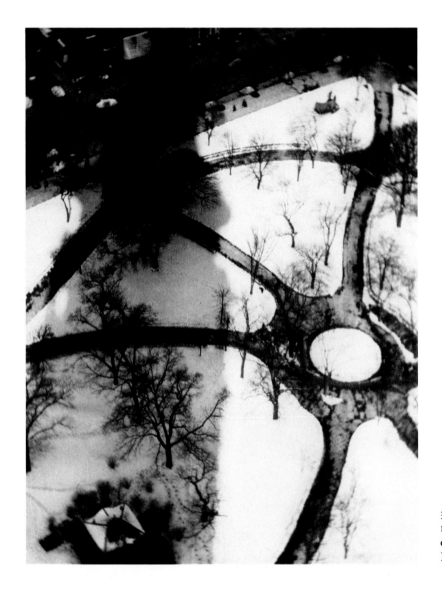

398. ALVIN LANGDON COBURN. *The Octopus*, 1912. Platinum print. International Museum of Photography at George Eastman House, Rochester, N.Y.

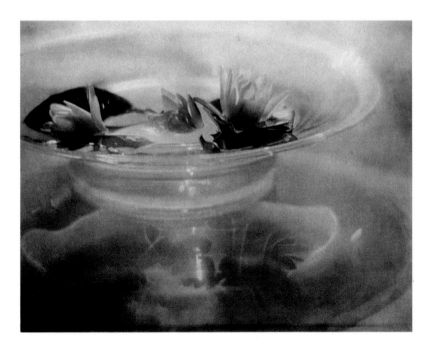

399. ADOLF DE MEYER. *Water Lilies*, 1906. Platinum print. Metropolitan Museum of Art, New York; Alfred Stieglitz Collection, 1933.

Coburn also worked in gravure, setting up his own press in London in 1909 and experimenting extensively with Autochrome. In spite of the brilliance of his early work and the avant-garde nature of the abstractions he made in 1917 *(see Chapter 9)*, after World War I he gave up serious involvement with the medium to pursue other interests.

In terms of vitality and influence, the American Pictorialist movement expired during the second decade of the 20th century despite efforts by several Pictorialists, among them White and Coburn, to keep an organization and periodical afloat.[35] The Photo-Secession had from the start planned to show other visual art along with photographs at its gallery, but, following their introduction in 1907, camera images began to play a less important role in both the exhibition schedule of 291 and in *Camera Work*, largely as a result of Stieglitz's conviction that little creative work was being produced in photography. This view was strengthened by criticism (by Hartmann and others) of the camera images shown at the Dresden Exposition of 1909 and in the Albright Gallery in Buffalo in 1910—the last large-scale exhibition of Pictorialist photography sponsored by the Secession. Between 1911 and 1916, only three photographic shows were held at 291: portraits and still lifes by Adolf de Meyer *(pl. no. 399)*, a German-born photographer who was just beginning a fashionable career in London; Stieglitz's own work, timed to coincide with the Armory Show of modern art in 1913; and the last exhibition of photographs before the gallery closed—the work of Paul Strand in 1916, which included early soft-focus landscapes as well as cityscapes. The choice of these startling "candid" portraits of New York street people and of the virtually abstract studies by Strand for the final issue of *Camera Work* signaled the shift in sensibility that was taking place on an international scale at the time.

In Europe, most of the aesthetic movement, already by 1910 a victim of organizational dissension and prewar malaise, was abruptly terminated by the first World War, which put an end to the leisurely life that had provided much of its impetus and thematic material. After 1914, individual European photographers were scattered and isolated, with artistic interchange in virtually all media difficult. Even before the hostilities, however, the new aesthetic concepts that had become visible in the other visual arts began to influence photographers. In addition to the reaction against extensive hand-manipulation of the print, which had been in the air for a number of years, some photographers, among them Stieglitz, Steichen, and Kuehn, began to introduce greater definition and to deal with form in the more abstract fashion visible in Kuehn's *Artist's Umbrella* of 1910 *(pl. no. 400)*, a work in which the view from

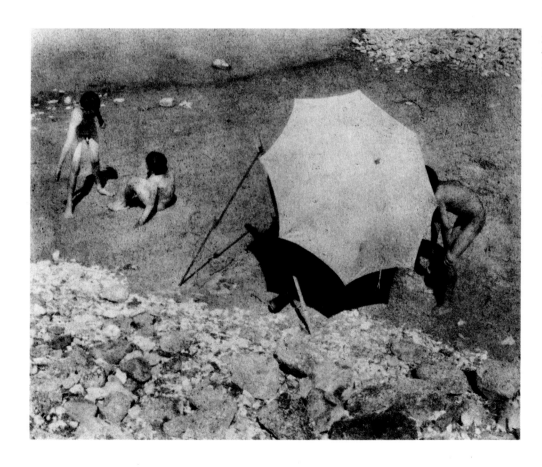

400. HEINRICH KUEHN. *Artist's Umbrella*, before 1910. Gravure print. Metropolitan Museum of Art, New York; Alfred Stieglitz Collection, 1949.

above converts the picture plane into a two-dimensional design. A new interest in realism also emerged to herald the concern with straight photography and modernist style that would engage the next generation of photographers.

Pictorialism was an instrument that enabled the aesthetic photograph to be regarded as a persuasive expression of personal temperament and choice. Despite misguided attempts to emulate traditional paintings and works of graphic art, despite disagreements about the qualities that give the photographic prints their unique character, and despite many images that now seem hackneyed and uninspired, a

body of forceful work was created under the banner of aesthetic photography. Both the seriousness of purpose and the efforts by the movement to erase the division between the way critics and the public viewed images made entirely by hand and those produced by a machine have continued to be vital concepts that still engage photographers and graphic artists alike.

Profile: Alfred Stieglitz

Alfred Stieglitz proclaimed his belief in the uniqueness of his native heritage in a credo written for an exhibition of

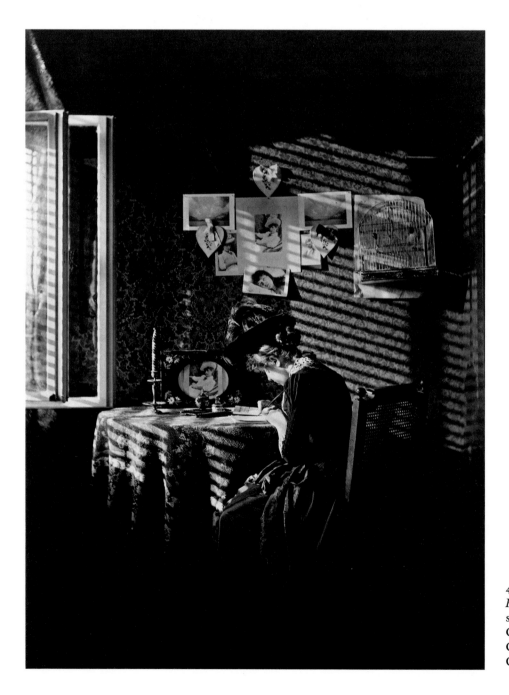

401. ALFRED STIEGLITZ. *Sun's Rays—Paula, Berlin*, 1889. Gelatin silver print. Art Institute of Chicago; Alfred Stieglitz Collection. Courtesy Georgia O'Keeffe, New Mexico.

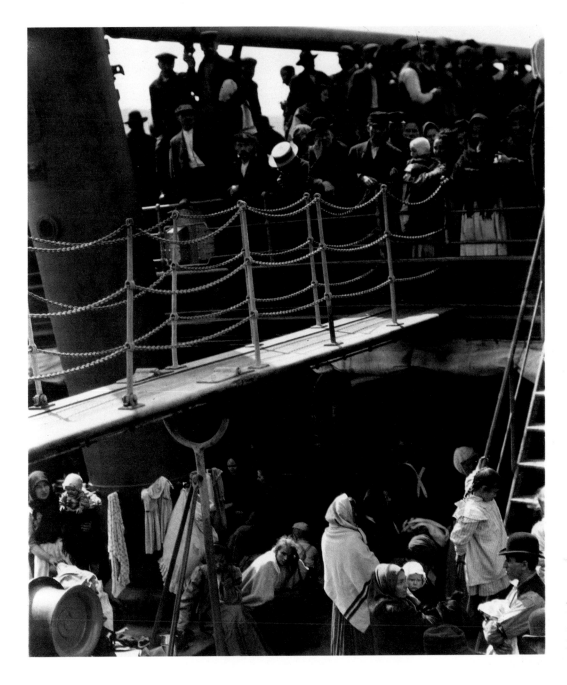

402. ALFRED STIEGLITZ.
The Steerage, 1907.
Gravure print.
Private Collection.

his work in 1921: "I was born in Hoboken. I am an American. Photography is my passion. The search for truth my obsession."[36] Nevertheless, as a body, his images suggest a complexity of influences and sources of which the American component was at first the least marked. The oldest of six children of a part-Jewish German family that had emigrated to the United States in 1849, Stieglitz spent his youth in a comfortable milieu that placed unusual emphasis on education, culture, and attainment. Taken to Germany in 1881 to complete his education, he enrolled in a course in photochemistry given by the eminent Dr. Hermann Wilhelm Vogel; from then on he was absorbed

mainly by photography and by other visual art, although he continued an interest in science, music, and literature. *Sun's Rays—Paula, Berlin (pl. no. 401)*, a study made in Berlin by Stieglitz in 1889, reveals a fascination with the role of light and with the replicative possibilities of photography, as well as an understanding of how to organize forms to express feeling.

After almost ten years abroad, during which his ability as a photographer had become recognized, Stieglitz returned to New York City in 1890 and became a partner in the Photochrome Engraving Company. He soon found himself more interested in campaigns to promote the rec-

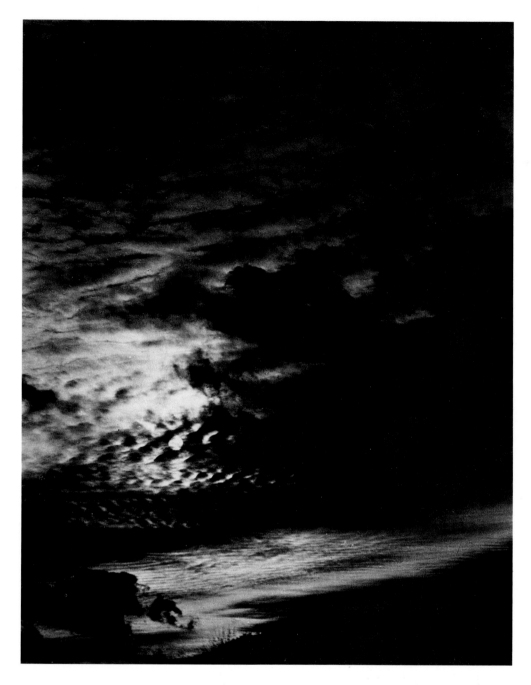

403. ALFRED STIEGLITZ. *Equivalent*, 1929. Gelatin silver print. Art Institute of Chicago; Alfred Stieglitz Collection. Courtesy Georgia O'Keeffe, New Mexico.

ognition of photography as a means of artistic expression, working at first as editor of the journal *American Amateur Photographer*, then through the Camera Club of New York and its periodical *Camera Notes*, and finally through the Photo-Secession and *Camera Work*, which he published and edited from 1903 to 1917. Besides organizing and judging national exhibitions of Pictorialist photography, Stieglitz presided, until 1917, over 291, the Photo-Secession gallery, where, along with Steichen and, later, with Paul Haviland and Marius de Zayas, he helped awaken the American public and critics to modern European movements in the visual arts. He was in contact for a brief period in 1915

with the New York Dada movement through the journal *291* and the Modern Gallery.

In his development as a photographer, Stieglitz began to draw upon the urban scene for his subjects shortly after his return to New York in 1890 *(pl. no. 312)*. At the time, his motifs were considered inappropriate for artistic treatment in photography even though Realist and Impressionist painters in Europe had been dealing with similar material for over 40 years. As his personal style evolved, the influence of German *fin-de-siècle* painting, of the Japanese woodblock, and of Symbolist and Cubist *(pl. no. 402)* currents became visibly interwoven into coherently structured and moving images that seem to embody the reality of their time. Following the closing of the gallery and journal in 1917, Stieglitz turned full attention to his own work—a many-faceted portrait of his wife-to-be the painter Georgia O'Keeffe. In the early 1920s, he undertook what he called *Equivalents (pl. no. 403)*—images of clouds and sky made to demonstrate, he claimed, that in visual art, form, and not specific subject matter, conveys emotional and psychological meaning. Another series from later years consisted of views of New York skyscrapers taken from the window of his room in the Shelton Hotel *(pl. no. 404)*, which incorporate abstract patterns of light and shadow that express the duality of feeling, the fascination and loathing he had come to feel for the city.

Feeling incomplete without a gallery or publication, between 1917 and 1925 Stieglitz used rooms at the Anderson Galleries to promote the work of a circle of American modernists in painting and photography that comprised, besides himself, Arthur Dove, Marsden Hartley, John Marin, O'Keeffe, and Strand. The Intimate Gallery opened in 1925, lasted four years, and was followed by An American Place, which endured until his death in 1946. Aside from exhibits of his own work, only four of photography were held between 1925 and 1946, suggesting that his interest in the medium had become parochial.

Stieglitz's career spanned the transition from the Victorian to the modern world, and his sensibilities reflected this amplitude of experience. His creative contribution,

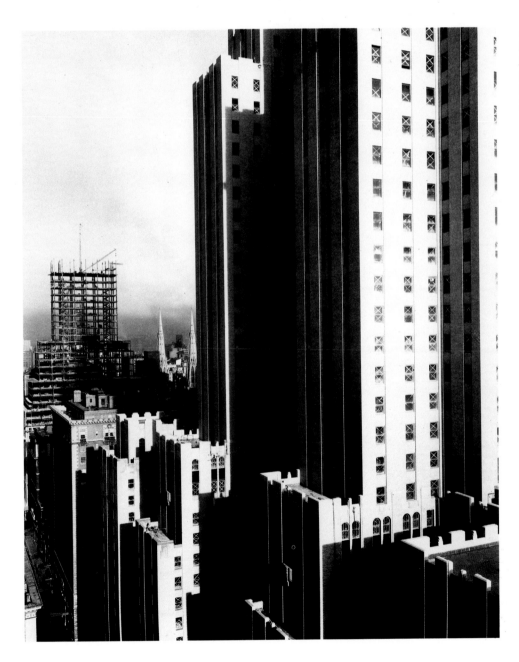

404. ALFRED STIEGLITZ. *From the Shelton Westward— New York*, 1931–32. Gelatin silver print. Philadelphia Museum of Art; lent by Dorothy Norman.

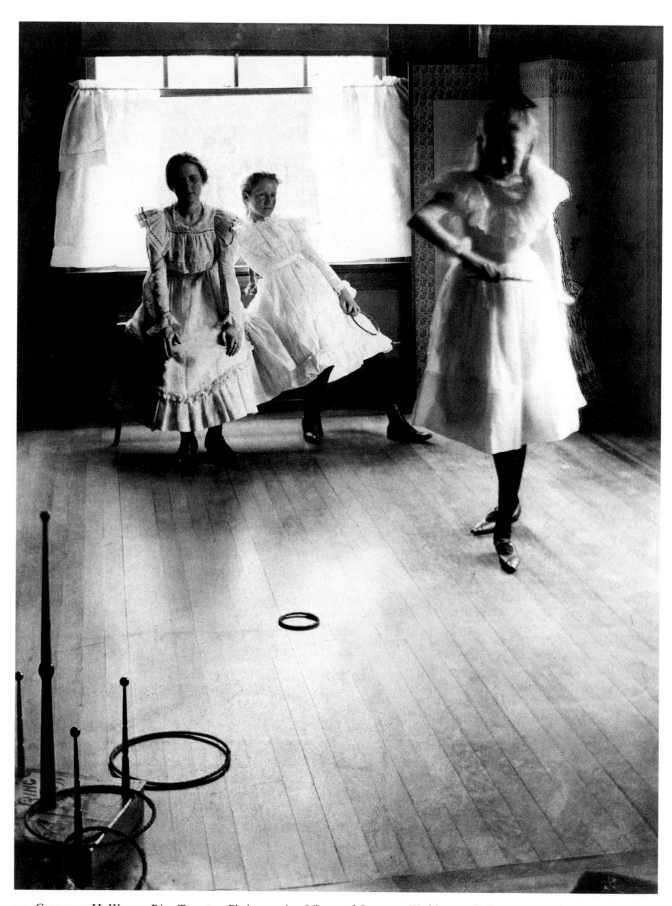

405. Clarence H. White. *Ring Toss*, 1899. Platinum print. Library of Congress, Washington, D.C.

summed up by Theodore Dreiser in 1899 as a "desire to do new things" in order to express "the sentiment and tender beauty in subjects previously thought devoid of charm,"[37] was conjoined to a great sense of mission. While not unique, his efforts to improve the way photographs were presented at exhibitions and reproduced in periodicals were notably effective in the campaign for the recognition of the photograph as an art object, while his openness to new sensibilities enabled him to introduce Americans to European modernism and to the avant-garde styles of native artists. In both roles—as expressive photographer and impresario—he probably has had a more profound influence on the course of aesthetic photography in America than any other single individual.

Profile: Clarence H. White

Clarence H. White may be considered the archetypal Pictorialist photographer of the United States. Neither flamboyant in personality nor bohemian in taste, he emerged from a background of hardworking midwestern provincialism to create works of unusual artistic sensitivity and sweet compassion, with the people and places of his intimate surroundings as subjects. His best images, among them *Ring Toss (pl. no. 405)*, reveal a perceptive appreciation of the special qualities of domesticity and feminine activi-

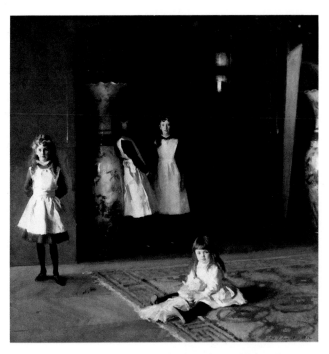

406. JOHN SINGER SARGENT. *The Daughters of Edward D. Boit*, 1882. Oil on canvas. Museum of Fine Arts, Boston; gift of Mary Louise Boit, Jane Hubbart Boit, and Julia Overing Boit, in memory of their father.

ties, themes that also attracted a number of the painters of the time, including William Merritt Chase and John Singer Sargent *(pl. no. 406)*. Despite his preference for genre and allegorical subjects, White's camera images rarely are hackneyed or sentimental. His receptivity to a variety of aesthetic influences—the art of Japan, the Pre-Raphaelites, Whistler, and *Art Nouveau*—which had reached middle America in contemporary magazine illustration, may account for the captivating freshness of his vision.

Working full-time as an accountant for a wholesale grocery firm, White still found opportunities for his own photography and time to promote Pictorialism in the Newark (Ohio) Camera Club. Shortly before 1900, he joined with Day, Käsebier, and Stieglitz in organizing and jurying the major American exhibitions of Pictorialist photography. During his lifetime, he showed work in more than 40 national and international exhibitions, frequently garnering top honors and critical acclaim. In 1906, two years after leaving his job to devote himself entirely to his medium, he moved his family to New York City in the hope that it might be more possible to earn a living in photography. A year later, White began to teach, first at Columbia University, then at the Brooklyn Institute of Arts and Sciences, and finally at his own Clarence White School of Photography, which he founded in 1914. Among his celebrated students were Margaret Bourke-White, Anton Bruehl, Laura Gilpin, Dorothea Lange, Paul Outerbridge, Ralph Steiner, and Doris Ulmann, attesting to the marked influence of this school on many photographers of the next generation.

During White's first years in New York, he and Stieglitz collaborated on a series of nude studies, exemplified by a sensuous image of *Miss Thompson (pl. no. 407)*, but on the whole, White's creativity did not flourish in the city, because of the time and energy required to pursue a teaching career and manage a school. Although his contributions to Pictorialism were recognized by Stieglitz when the latter assigned him a special gallery in the 1910 "International Exhibition of Pictorial Photography" in Buffalo, the relationship between the two started to deteriorate as Stieglitz identified White with Pictorialist themes and styles he now considered repetitive and insipid. In 1916, White joined with other disaffected Secessionists to form The Pictorial Photographers of America, hoping thereby to support aesthetic photography while keeping alive the group idea, which to his mind had been one of the appealing aspects of the Photo-Secession.

Toward the 1920s, White's images began to reflect some of the changes in outlook occasioned by American awareness of modernist trends in art, but in 1925, before he could integrate the new vision into his own refined sensibility, he died while accompanying a student expedition to

Mexico. With their concentration on light and atmosphere, their carefully realized tonal and spatial tensions, and an authentic sense of domestic grace, White's photographs embody the tonalist style in American Pictorialism.

Profile: Heinrich Kuehn

Both the career and imagery of Heinrich Kuehn may be said to personify the ideals of Pictorialism in central Europe. According to a modern critic, his "works repre-sent a clear expression of the aspirations of . . . [the] period," which were to "confirm the artistic quality of photography."[38] Kuehn's sensitivity to the expressive aspects of composition, light, and form, as well as his deep involvement with a wide variety of photographic printing processes, may seem unusual in view of his background in medicine and microscopic photography, but the 1891 exhibition in Vienna of the work of The Linked Ring appears to have redirected his interest from science to aesthetics.

On joining the *Wiener Kamera Klub* in 1894 after mov-

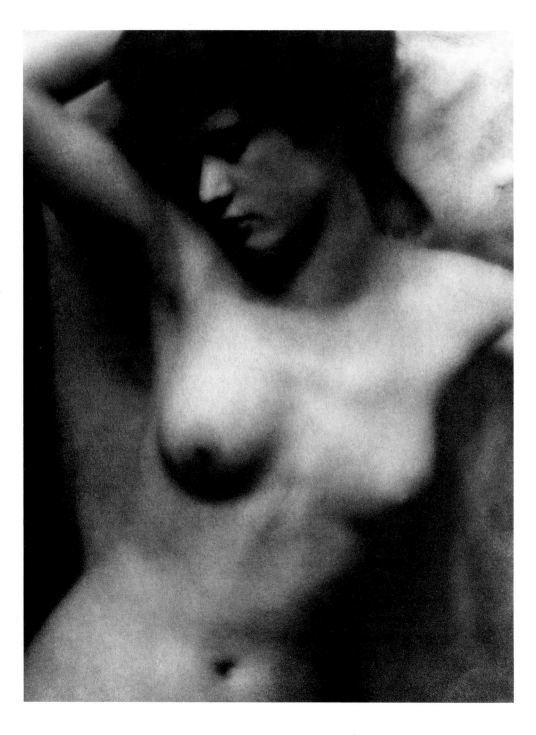

407. Clarence H. White and Alfred Stieglitz. *Miss Thompson*, 1907. Gravure print. Private Collection.

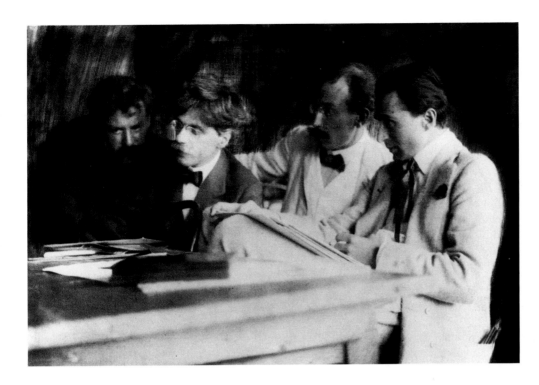

408. FRANK EUGENE.
*Frank Eugene, Alfred
Stieglitz, Heinrich Kuehn,
and Edward Steichen.* Gum
bichromate print. Royal
Photographic Society,
Bath, England.

ing to Innsbruck, Austria, from his birthplace Dresden, Kuehn formed a friendship with Hugo Henneberg, a club member who introduced him and Hans Watzek to the gum printing methods used by Demachy in Paris. From about 1898 to 1903, these three photographers worked and exhibited together, signing their images with the clover leaf monogram that invited the name *Trifolium* or *Kleeblatt*. After Watzek's death in 1902 and Henneberg's shift of interest to printmaking in 1905, Kuehn continued to organize photographic events, to work on his own experiments with gum, and to publish technical articles. His contacts with British and American Pictorialists, Stieglitz in particular, now provided the inspiration he formerly had derived from the *Kleeblatt*. A meeting in Bavaria in 1907 with Eugene, Stieglitz, and Steichen *(pl. no. 408)* led to experiments by all four photographers with the new Autochrome color plates. Around 1906, Kuehn began also to associate with members of the Vienna Secession and the founders of *Wiener Werkstätte* (Vienna Workshop), easily integrating Viennese Art Nouveau into his personal approach.

Kuehn's themes and motifs reflect a tranquil middle-class domestic existence, not entirely dissimilar from the provincial small-town life that inspired White's most moving images. In portraits of family and friends *(pl. no. 349)*, spacious interiors, and gracious still lifes, as well as in occasional genre scenes, he was profoundly concerned, as was White, with light and with decorative design. Besides the influences of Art Nouveau, one can also discern in Kuehn's photographs the impact of *fin-de-siècle* European painting, in particular that of the Germans Max Liebermann and Franz von Lenbach. A suggestion of the new concepts with which the visual arts would be concerned began to surface in Kuehn's crisper delineations of form around 1910 *(pl. no. 400)*, but on the whole his stylistic and thematic approach changed very little, and while aesthetic photography was supplanted in the 1920s and '30s by *Die Neue Sachlichkeit* (The New Objectivity), Kuehn, unlike his friend and associate Stieglitz, seems to have been unwilling or unable to embrace these new perceptions even though he continued to photograph and write on into the 1930s.

8.

DOCUMENTATION: THE SOCIAL SCENE

to 1945

The true use for the imaginative faculty of modern times is to give ultimate vivification to facts, to science and to common lives.

—Walt Whitman, 1860[1]

Documentary: That's a sophisticated and misleading word. And not really clear. . . . The term should be documentary style*. . . . You see, a document has use, whereas art is really useless.*

—Walker Evans, 1971[2]

AS AN INEXPENSIVE AND REPLICATIBLE MEANS of presenting (supposedly) truthful verifications of visual fact, camera images were bound to become important adjuncts of the campaigns waged by reformers in industrialized nations during the 19th century to improve inequitable social conditions. Nevertheless, while photography's potential for this purpose was recognized soon after the medium's inception, a characteristic form for social documentation did not emerge until the end of the century. Then, shaped by both the emergence of organized social reform movements and the invention of an inexpensive means of mechanically reproducing the photograph's halftones, social photography began to flower in the aspect that we know today.

A tandem phrase, social documentary, is sometimes used to describe works in which social themes and social goals are paramount, because the word documentary could refer to any photograph whose primary purpose is the truthful depiction of reality. Indeed before 1880, nearly all unposed and unmanipulated images were considered documentation; since then, millions of such records of people, places, and events have been made. The word social also presents problems when used to describe the intent of a photograph because many camera images have as their subject some aspect of social behavior. For instance, commercial *cartes (pl. no. 409)*, snapshots, postcards, artistic and photojournalistic images often depict social situations; that is, they deal with people, their relationships to one another and the way they live and work even though the motives of their makers have nothing to do with social commitment or programs. This said, however, it also must be emphasized that one cannot be too categorical about such distinctions, since all photographs defy attempts to define their essential nature too narrowly, and in the case of works that have social change as their prime goal the passage of time has been especially effectual in altering purpose, meaning, and resonance.

Documentary, as Evans observed, refers also to a particular style or approach. Although it began to emerge in the late 19th century, the documentary mode was not clearly defined as such until the 1930s, when American photography historian Beaumont Newhall noted that while the social documentary photographer is neither a mere recorder nor an "artist for arts sake, his reports are often brilliant technically and highly artistic"—that is, documentary

images involve imagination and art in that they imbue fact with feeling.[3] With their focus mainly on people and social conditions, images in the documentary style combine lucid pictorial organization with an often passionate commitment to humanistic values—to ideals of dignity, the right to decent conditions of living and work, to truthfulness. Lewis Hine, one of the early partisans of social documentation *(see Profile)*, explained its goals when he declared that light was required to illuminate the dark

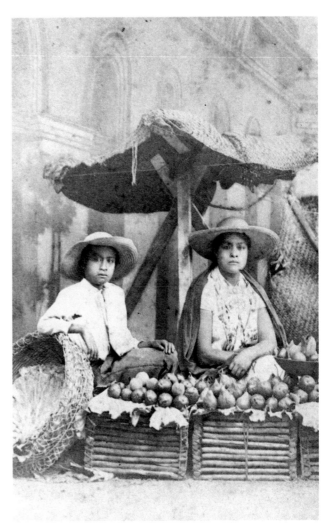

409. CRUCES AND CO. *Fruit Vendors*, 1870s. Albumen print. Bancroft Library, University of California, Berkeley.

areas of social existence, but where to shine the light and how to frame the subject in the camera are the creative decisions that have become the measure of the effectiveness of this style to both inform and move the viewer.[4]

A crucial aspect of social documentation involves the context in which the work is seen. Almost from the start, photographs meant as part of campaigns to improve social conditions were presented as groups of images rather than individually. Although they were included at times in displays at international expositions held in Europe and the United States in the late-19th and early-20th centuries, such works were not ordinarily shown in the salons and exhibitions devoted either to artistic images or snapshots. They were not sold individually in the manner of genre, landscape, and architectural scenes. Instead, socially purposive images reached viewers as lantern slides or as illustrations in pamphlets and periodicals, usually accompanied by explanatory lectures and texts. Indeed, the development of social documentary photography is so closely tied to advances in printing technology and the growth of the popular press that the flowering of the movement would be unthinkable without the capability of the halftone process printing plate to transmute silver image into inked print *(see A Short Technical History, Part II)*. In this regard, social documentation has much in common with photoreportage or photojournalism, but while this kind of camera documentation often involved social themes, the images usually were not aimed at social change.

Early Social Documentation

Few images of a socially provocative nature were made in the period directly following the 1839 announcements of the twin births of photography. The small size, reflective surfaces, and uniqueness of the daguerreotype did not suit it for this role despite attempts by some to document such events as the workers' rallies sponsored by the Chartist Movement in England in 1848 *(pl. no. 331)*. The slow exposure time and broad definition of the calotype also made it an inefficient tool for social documentation. Of greater importance, however, is the fact that the need for accurate visual documentation in support of programs for social change was a matter of ideology rather than just technology; it was not until reformers grasped the connections between poverty, living conditions, and the social behavior of the work force (and its economic consequences) that the photograph was called upon to act as a "witness" and sway public opinion.

Nevertheless, although social betterment was not initially involved, images of working people were made soon after portraiture became possible. Usually commissioned by the sitters themselves, some images straddle the line between individual portrait and genre scene, as in a daguerreotype by an unknown American depicting blacksmiths at work *(pl. no. 330)*. Its particularity of detail—it includes surroundings, tools, work garments, and individual facial characteristics—coupled with the revelation of a sense of the upright dignity of the two men pictured, reflects attitudes toward rural and artisan labor similar to those embodied in the work of the American genre painters such as William Sidney Mount.

Calotypists who favored the picturesque genre tradition generally regarded working people as types rather than individuals, and portrayed them in tableauxlike scenes such as one of hunters by the French photographer Louis Adolphe Humbert de Molard *(pl. no. 257)*. Others found more natural poses and more evocative lighting in order to place greater emphasis on individual expression and stance rather than on tools and emblems of a particular occupa-

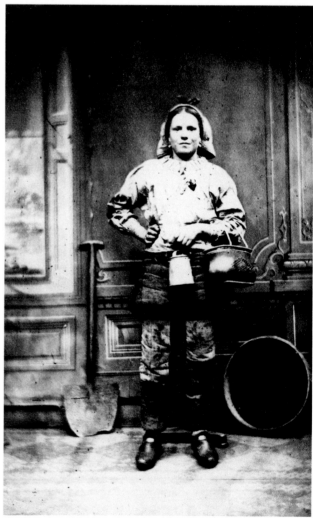

410. T. G. DUGDALE. *Pit Brown Girl, Shevington*, 1867. Albumen *carte-de-visite*. A. J. Munby Collection, Trinity College Library, Cambridge, England.

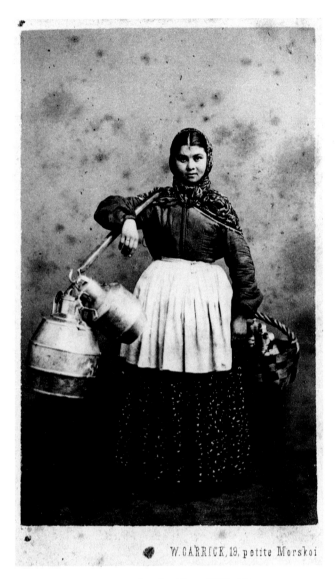

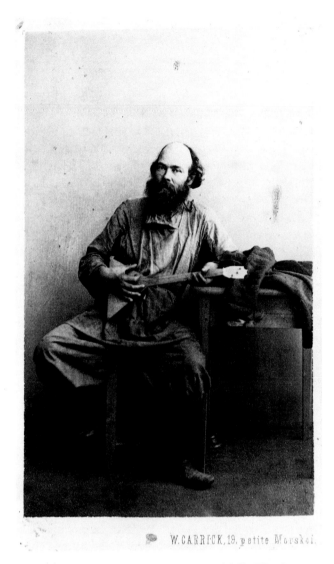

411. WILLIAM CARRICK. *Russian Types (Milkgirl)*, c. 1859.
Albumen *carte-de-visite*. Collection and © Felicity
Ashbee, London.

412. WILLIAM CARRICK. *Russian Types (Balalaika Player)*,
c. 1859. Albumen *carte-de-visite*. Collection and © Felicity
Ashbee, London.

tion or station in life. This approach, visible in images of
farm laborers made by William Henry Fox Talbot on his
estate at Lacock and of fisherfolk in Newhaven by David
Octavius Hill and Robert Adamson, may be seen as indications of the growing interest among artists and intellectuals not only in the theme of work but in working people as
individuals.

A consciously conceived effort involving the depiction
of working people was undertaken in 1845 by Hill and
Adamson. Probably the first photographic project to embrace a socially beneficial purpose, it apparently was suggested that calotypes might serve as a means of raising
funds to provide properly decked boats and better fishing
tackle that would improve the safety of the fishermen of
the village of Newhaven, Scotland. Intending to present

their subject in as favorable light as possible for cosmopolitan viewers, Hill and Adamson made beautifully composed
and lighted calotypes of individuals *(pl. no. 51)* and groups
that may be seen as especially picturesque forerunners of
the documentary style.

After the invention of the collodion negative, which
made possible the inexpensive Ambrotype, and the still
cheaper and easily replicated albumen print on paper,
working people began to be photographed more frequently, appearing on *cartes-de-visite* and other formats. With
the subjects posed in studios in front of plain backdrops,
often with the tools of their trade, these works, meant
either as mementos for the sitter or souvenir images for
travelers, ordinarily pay little attention to actual conditions
of work or to the expressive use of light and form to reveal

character. The incongruity between studio decor and occupation, for example, is obvious in an 1867 English *carte* of a female mine worker *(pl. no. 410)* who, appropriately clothed for work in clogs, trousers, and headscarf, stands squarely before a classy paneled wall with a studio prop of a shovel by her side. One exception to the generally undistinguished character of such *cartes* is the work of Danish photographer Heinrich Tönnies, who maintained a studio in the provincial town of Aalborg between 1856 and 1903.[5] In common with many such portraitists, Tönnies photographed all classes of people—carpenters, housemaids, chimney sweeps, waiters—as well as the town's more prosperous folk, but despite the anomaly of the decorated studio carpet and occasional painted backdrop, his images reveal a feeling for character that endows these working-class sitters with unusual individual presence *(pl. no. 69)*.

Similar images of working people in cultures outside of western Europe and the United States served mainly as souvenirs. To cite but two examples, William Carrick, a Scottish photographer who opened a studio in St. Petersburg, Russia, in 1859, and Eugenio Maunoury, a French national working in Peru at about the same time, each produced *cartes* of peddlers, street traders, and peasants. The distinctive quality of Carrick's *Russian Types (pl. nos. 411 and 412)*, a series of over 40 images made in Simbirsk that fall partway between portraiture and picturesque genre, probably is owed to the photographer's expressed sympathy for humble clients to whom he devoted special attention.[6] Maunoury, said to have been associated with Nadar's studio in Paris before appearing in Lima in 1861, may have been the first to introduce the genre *carte* to this part of South America, but his static studio scenes depict working-class types as glum and inert *(pl. no. 413)*.

Commercial photographers working in the Near and Far East in the latter part of the 19th century produced larger-format views in which working people, social life, native customs, and seemingly exotic dress were featured. Felix Bonfils, whose scenic views of the Near East were mentioned earlier, was a prolific producer of such socially informative views, many of which show the women of the Ottoman Empire in characteristic dress and activity but with uncharacteristic ease of pose and expression *(pl. no. 414)*. This naturalness, and the fact that in a number of instances native women posed without veils, is attributable to the pictures being taken not by Bonfils himself but by his wife, Marie Lydie Cabannis Bonfils, who worked in the family studios in Beirut, Baalbeck, and Jerusalem between 1867 and 1916. In South America, a similar engagement with the life of the lower classes can be seen in the images of field peasants by Argentinian photographer Benito Panunzi *(pl. no. 415)*.

Unquestionably, the most graceful studio portrayals of artisans, laborers, and geisha are the large-format albumen prints turned out in the Japanese commercial establishments of Félice Beato, Reteniz von Stillfried, and Kusakabe Kimbei. The subtle handling of light and the artful arrangements of props and figures create a rare tension between information—what work is done, what garments are worn—and idealization. Enhanced further at times by delicate hand-coloring or by vignetting *(pl. no. 333)*, these highly decorative images may be seen as camera equivalents of the *Ukiyo-e* woodblock prints that also often featured depictions of working people.

Social life and ways of work engrossed amateur as well as commercial photographers working or traveling in these parts of the world. During 1857, compositions by British amateur William Johnson appeared each month in the periodical *Indian Amateurs Photographic Album* under the title "Costumes and Characters of Western India" *(pl. no. 191)*. Photographs of lower-caste Hindus taken by British

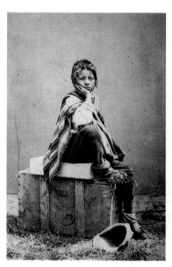 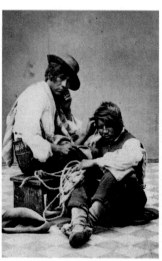 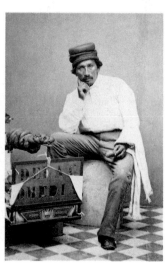

413. EUGENIO MANOURY. *Three Portraits*, c. 1863. Albumen *cartes-de-visite*. Collection H. L. Hoffenberg, New York.

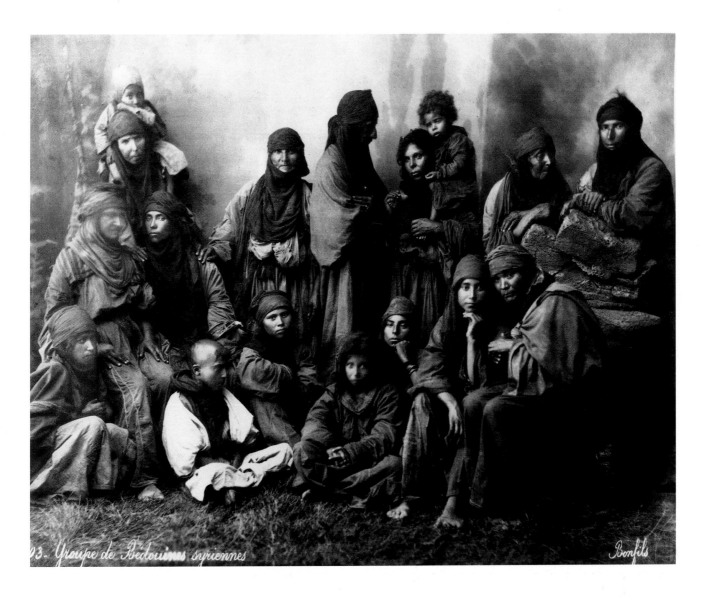

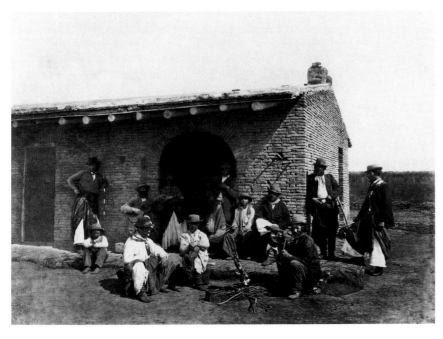

414. MARIE LYDIE CABANNIS
BONFILS. *Group of Syrian Bedouin
Women*, c. 1870. Albumen print.
Semitic Museum, Harvard University,
Cambridge, Mass.

415. BENITO PANUNZI. *Settlers in the
Countryside*, c. 1905. Albumen print.
Collection H. L. Hoffenberg,
New York.

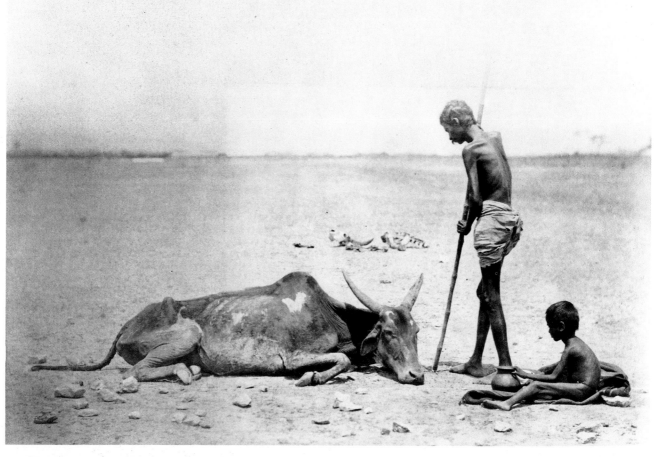

416. WILLOUGHBY WALLACE HOOPER. *The Last of the Herd, Madras Famine*, 1876–78. Albumen print. Royal Geographic Society, London.

Army Captain Willoughby Wallace Hooper are further indications of the growing interest among Westerners in the social problems of the lower classes around the world *(pl. no. 416)*. Perhaps the most completely realized result of a kind of curiosity about the way people live is a four-volume work entitled *Illustrations of China and Its People*, published by photographer John Thomson in England in 1873/74. With a lively text and 200 photographs taken during the photographer's four-year stay in China, the work attempted to make an arcane and exotic way of life understandable and acceptable to the British public by showing industrious and well-disposed natives *(pl. no. 192)* interspersed with unusual architectural and natural monuments *(pl. no. 138)*. In so doing, Thomson helped create a style and format for documentation that carried over to projects concerned with social inequities.

A somewhat different view of the non-Westerner emerged in the photographs of Native American tribesmen by cameramen attached to the geographical and geological surveys of the American West. Early images by the Canadian Humphrey Lloyd Hime, and later works by the Americans Jack Hillers, William Henry Jackson, and Timo-

thy O'Sullivan, for example, depict "native races" with a sober directness unleavened by the least sense of the picturesque. Hillers's views of the Southern Paiute and Ute tribes, made on the Powell Expedition of 1872, were especially influential in establishing a style of ethnic and social documentation that had as its goal the presentation of information in a clear fashion without either idealization or undue artistry. This approach was taken over by the Bureau of American Ethnology after 1879, and it became a cornerstone of the social documentary style that began to emerge in the late 19th century. This style also informed such sociologically oriented documents as *Report on the Men of Marwar State*, mentioned in Chapter 2 *(pl. no. 417)*.

Although the works discussed so far were sometimes published in books and albums, or were sold commercially, their impact on Western viewers is difficult to gauge. On the other hand, there is no question about the impact of the hundreds of thousands of stereograph views of similar social material published by commercial stereograph firms. From 1860 on, as capitalist nations opened up large areas of Africa, Asia, and South America for trade, exploitation, and colonization, companies such as Negretti and

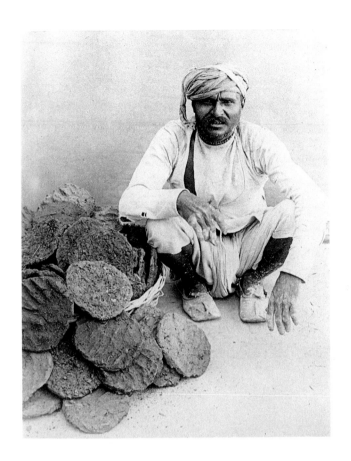

Zambra, the London Stereoscopic Company, and Underwood and Underwood sent photographers—some known, some still anonymous—to record people at work and their housing, dress, and social customs. These three-dimensional views, accepted by the public as truth that "cannot deceive or extenuate,"[7] were in fact taken from the point of view of the industrialized Westerner; but while the scenes frequently were chosen to emphasize the cultural gap between the civilized European or American and the backward non-white, it is possible that glimpses of social life, such as two stereographic views of conditions in Cuba at the turn of the century *(pl. nos. 418 and 419)*, inadvertently awakened viewers to inequities in colonized areas.

Toward the close of the 19th century, interest in social customs led some photographers to capture on glass plate and film indigenous peoples and folk customs that were in

417. UNKNOWN PHOTOGRAPHER. *1 of 1565 Aahirs; He Sells Cow Dung* (from *Report on the Men of Marwar State [Jodhpur]*, 3rd Volume), c. 1891. Albumen print. Collection American Institute of Indian Studies, Chicago. Courtesy International Center of Photography, New York ("Through Indian Eyes" Exhibition); American Institute of Indian Studies, Chicago, and Smithsonian Institution, Washington, D.C.

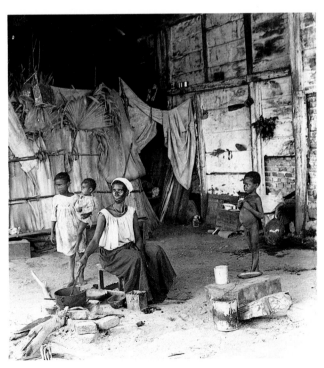

418. UNDERWOOD and UNDERWOOD (Publishers). *Wretched Poverty of a Cuban Peasant Home, Province of Santiago*, 1899. One-half of an albumen stereograph. Keystone-Mast Collection, California Museum of Photography, University of California, Riverside.

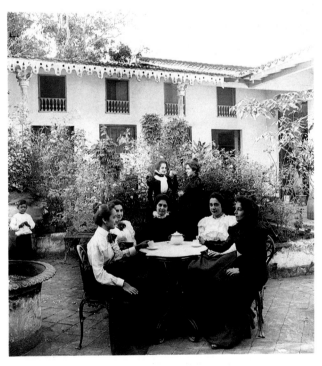

419. UNDERWOOD and UNDERWOOD (Publishers). *The Courtyard of a Typical Cuban Home, Remedios*, 1899. One-half of an albumen stereograph. Keystone-Mast Collection, California Museum of Photography, University of California, Riverside.

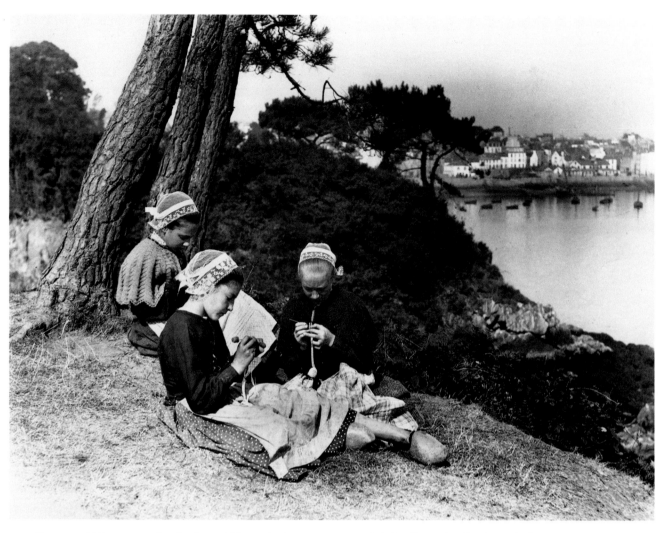

420. CHARLES L'HERMITTE. *On the Coast of Plomarc'h, Douarnenez*, 1912. Gelatin silver print. Explorer, Paris.

danger of extinction. In Europe, this role was assumed in the 1880s by Sir Benjamin Stone, a comfortably situated English manufacturer who hoped that a "record of ancient customs, which still linger in remote villages," would provide future generations with an understanding of British cultural and social history.[8] Somewhat later, José Ortíz Echagüe, a well-to-do Spanish industrialist, and Charles L'Hermitte, the son of a renowned French Salon painter, undertook similar projects, seeking out customs, costumes, and folkways in provincial byways that they believed would soon vanish with the spread of urbanization. Exemplified by L'Hermitte's photograph of lace-makers in Brittany made around 1910 *(pl. no. 420)*, such images tend toward nostalgia in that they romanticize handwork and folk mannerisms while seldom suggesting the difficulties and boredom of provincial life.

Similar attempts to use the camera to both arrest time and to make a comparative statement about past and pres-

ent can be seen also in the work of several photographers in the United States who turned their attention to native tribal life just before the turn of the century. In contrast to the earlier unnuanced records by Hillers and others of Indian dress and living arrangements, these projects, undertaken between 1895 and about 1910 by Edward S. Curtis, Karl E. Moon, Robert and Frances Flaherty, and Adam Clark Vroman, were designed to play up the positive aspects of tribal life, in particular the sense of community and the oneness of the individual Native American with nature. This attitude is especially visible in the 20-volume survey published by Curtis, which owing to its strongly Pictorialist interpretation was discussed in Chapter 7, but the handsome portraits and artfully arranged group scenes made by Moon in the Southwest, or the close-ups of cheerful and determined Inuit tribespeople of the far north *(pl. no. 197)* photographed by the Flahertys, embody a similar desire to make their subjects appear palatable to white

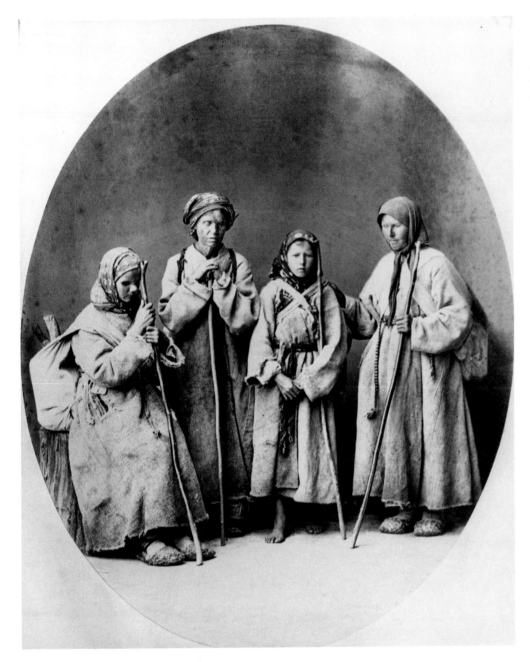

421. UNKNOWN
PHOTOGRAPHER. *Blind
Russian Beggars*, 1870.
Albumen print. Benjamin
Stone Collection,
Birmingham Central
Library, Birmingham,
England.

Americans with strong ethnocentric biases. As pioneers in the documentary film in the United States in the early 1920s, the Flahertys became known for their ability to give dramatic form to mundane events, and among the 1,500 or so still photographs they made of the Inuit there are works that seem arranged and posed to accord with a concept of their subjects as heroic and energetic peoples.

A more limited project of less grand proportions than that envisioned by Curtis occupied Adam Clark Vroman, a prosperous California businessman who also saw in photography a means to emphasize the positive virtues of American tribal life. While his images, of which *Hopi Maiden* is an example *(pl. no. 195)*, were carefully framed

to suggest the grace, dignity, and industriousness of the natives of the American Southwest, Vroman did not entirely romanticize his theme or obscure the hardships shaping Indian society of his time. In true documentary fashion, he used the photographs in slide lectures and publications in order to awaken white Americans to the plight of the Native American.

Along with an interest in making images of a social nature, collections of photographs of people at work, at home, and at recreational activities were initiated toward the end of the 19th century by individuals who believed that such reservoirs of images would enhance the study of history. Stone, for example, not only photographed vanish-

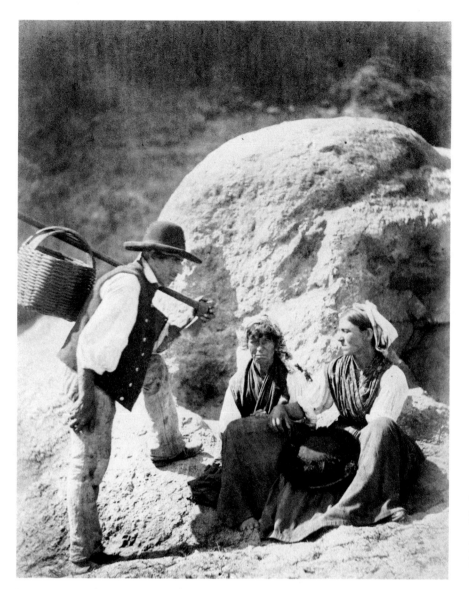

422. James Joseph Forrester.
Peasants of the Alto Douro, 1856. (From
The Photographic Album, 1857).
Albumen print. Gernsheim Collection,
Humanities Research Center,
University of Texas, Austin.

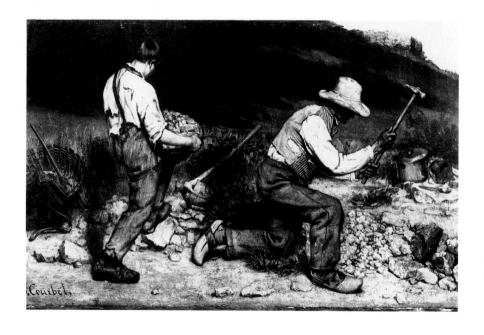

423. Gustave Courbet. *The
Stonebreakers*, 1851–52. Oil on Canvas.
Destroyed. Formerly Staatliche
Kunstsammlung, Dresden.

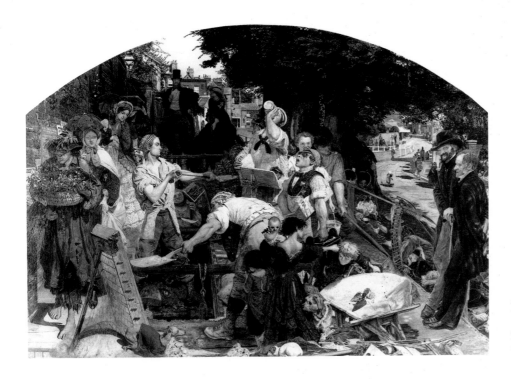

424. FORD MADDOX BROWN. *Work*, 1852. Oil on canvas. City Art Gallery, Manchester, England.

ing customs but, an inveterate traveler, he collected camera images of social experiences around the world, typified by a photograph of blind beggars in St. Petersburg by an unknown photographer *(pl. no. 421)*. He advocated the establishment of photographic surveys to be housed in local museums and libraries throughout Britain, a concept that actually was realized around the turn of the century with the establishment by Francis Greenwood Peabody, professor of social ethics at Harvard University, of a "Social Museum" that eventually comprised over 10,000 documents, including photographs, of social experience around the world.

It should be emphasized again that it is difficult to categorize many images that at first glance seem concerned with social themes such as work and living conditions, in that the goals of the makers were varied and complex. For example, should one regard views of workers on Talbot's estate at Lacock or of peasants in Portuguese vineyards owned by the family of photographer James Joseph Forrester *(pl. no. 422)* as more than a new type of picturesque genre imagery because they show us tools, dress, and relationships? *Children on a Fish Weir (pl. no. 274)* by the Venetian photographer–publisher Carlo Naya transforms the reality of working youngsters into an idyllic episode; should such commercial views be considered social documentation also? Can one really decide whether Curtis's views of tribal life in the United States are authentic documents or Pictorialist fictions?

Perhaps all of these images, no matter what their purpose, might be seen as aspects of the growing interest in problems of work and social existence on the part of Western artists and intellectuals. From the 1850s on, alongside the serious but idealized treatment of the European peasantry by Barbizon painters, realistic portrayals of less bucolic kinds of work associated with advancing industrialization had begun to appear in graphic art and literature. Exemplified by *The Stonebreakers (pl. no. 423)* of 1851/52 by French realist Gustave Courbet and by *Work (pl. no. 424)*, a grandiose composition begun in 1852 by the English Pre-Raphaelite Ford Maddox Brown, such themes signaled the mounting concern among elements of the middle class for the social and ethical consequences of rampant industrialization—a concern that helped prepare for the role of the documentary photograph in campaigns for social change.

Obviously, the complexity of ideas explored in the painting *Work*, which deals with the roles and kinds of labor necessary to the functioning of industrialized society, is difficult if not impossible to encompass in photography. Nevertheless, an effort was made by Oscar Gustave Rejlander. His composite picture *Two Ways of Life (pl. no. 253—*discussed in Chapter 5) can be seen as an attempt to deal with the moral and ethical implications of labor in a society in which the working class faces a choice between virtuous hard work or sinful ease. While Rejlander's image is derivative in style and moralistic in concept, other of his photographs embody less complex social themes and are more successful. For instance, the anxiety of unemployment is imaginatively handled in the composite image *Hard Times (pl. no. 266)* while portraits of chimney sweeps reveal an individualized grace that does not depend on social class.

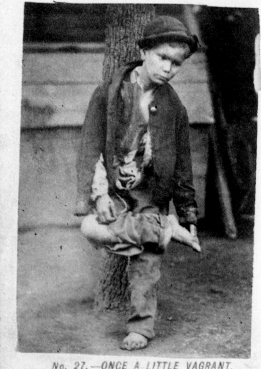

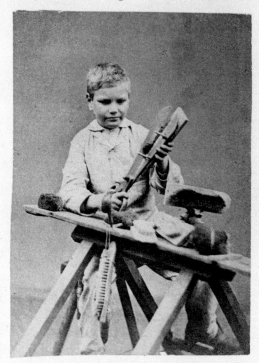

425–426. UNKNOWN PHOTOGRAPHER. *Before and After Photographs of Young Boys*, c. 1875. Albumen prints. Barnardo Photographic Archive, Ilford, England.

The Social Uses of Photographic Documentation

The concept of using camera documentation to improve social conditions could not evolve so long as poverty was regarded as a just reward for sinful behavior. Nevertheless, even before such Calvinistic religious attitudes were replaced by an understanding that improved conditions of housing and work might produce better behavior and a more efficient workforce, the photograph began to find a place in campaigns for social betterment. *Carte* portraits were turned into a quasi-sociological tool by Dr. Thomas John Barnardo, a self-appointed evangelical missionary who opened his first home for destitute boys in London in 1871 and went on to organize a network of so-called charitable institutions. To illustrate the effectiveness of his programs, Barnardo installed a photographic department to document the "before" and "after" transformations of street waifs into obedient slaveys (*pl. nos. 425 and 426*), prints of

which were kept as records and sold to raise funds. While such works have little value as expression, their production raised issues that have continued to be perceived as significant problems in social documentation. Because the transformations seen in the photographs produced under Barnardo's aegis were little more than cosmetic, effected by a good scrubbing and change of clothing, he was accused of falsifying truth for the camera, to which he responded that he was seeking typical rather than individualized truths about poverty. This attitude was considered wanting by subsequent social documentary photographers who endeavored to make absolutely authentic records while also expressing what they saw as the larger truth of a situation. Nevertheless, the "before" and "after" image became a staple of social documentation, appearing in American tracts of the 1890s and on the other side of the world in the photographs made by the firm of Raja Deen Dayal, for the nizam of Hyderabad to show the efficacy of relief programs for the starving (*pl. nos. 427 and 428*).

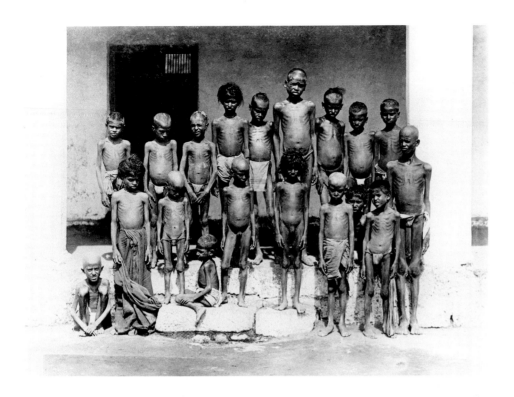

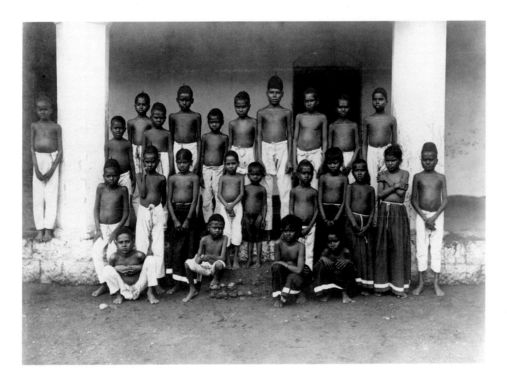

427–428. RAJA DEEN DAYAL.
Types of Emaciation, Aurangabad,
1899–1900. Gelatin silver prints.
Private Collection.

As photographs came to be accepted as evidence in campaigns to improve social conditions, it became apparent that in themselves images could not necessarily be counted on to convey specific meanings—that how they were perceived often depended on the outlook and social bias of the viewer. The *carte* images of women mineworkers mentioned earlier are a case in point; introduced before a British industrial commission as evidence that women were deprived of their feminine charms because mine work forced them to wear trousers, the same images suggested to others that hard work induced independence and good health in women.[9] Naturally, not all photographic

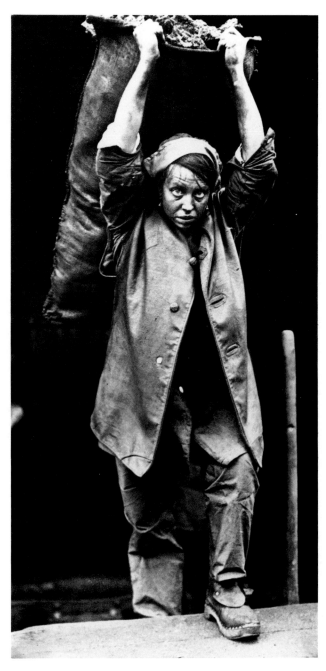

429. HORACE W. NICHOLLS. *Delivering Coal*, c. 1916. Gelatin silver print. Royal Photographic Society, Bath, England.

images can be as broadly construed as these bland *cartes* obviously were, but one of the basic tenets of the developing documentary style was that images should not only provide visual facts, they should be as unambiguous as possible in tone. For instance, in an interesting contrast to the *cartes* under discussion, an image of a young woman delivering coal *(pl. no. 429)*, taken some 50 years later by Horace Nicholls as part of a project to investigate the role of women doing "men's work" during World War I, leaves little question as to the subject's feelings.

As a social theme, mining became a subject of special

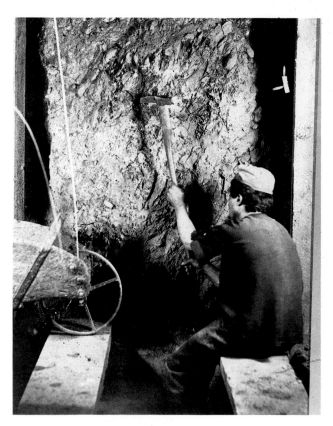

430. TIMOTHY O'SULLIVAN. *Miner at Work, Comstock Lode*, 1867. Albumen print. National Archives, Washington, D.C.

appeal to artists, writers, and photographers in the late-19th and early-20th centuries owing to its difficulties and dangers and to the perception of the mineworker as one who mixed individualism and fearlessness. One of the earliest American mine images, an 1850 daguerreotype of California goldminers *(pl. no. 431)*, presents this occupation as an open-air enterprise that seems not to entail hours of backbreaking "panning." The first underground mining pictures were made in England in 1864; some three years later, while on the Clarence King expedition, Timothy O'Sullivan documented silver miners at work in images that suggest the constriction of space and the physical difficulty of the work *(pl. no. 430)*. In the final several decades of the 19th century, mining companies themselves commissioned photographs of their operations and often displayed them at international expositions. Between 1884 and 1895, George Bretz, who pioneered subterranean photography with electric light in the United States, focused almost exclusively on mining in Pennsylvania hard-coal collieries. *Breaker Boys, Eagle Hill Colliery (pl. no. 432)* was one of a number of works acclaimed for unusual subject, technical expertise, and directness of treatment.[10] Not long afterward, Gustav Marrissiaux, a Belgian photographer commissioned by mining interests in Liège, depicted (among

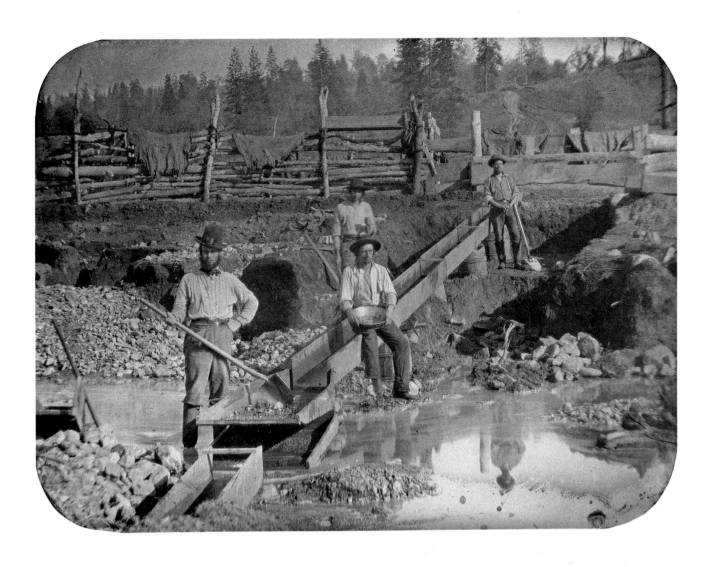

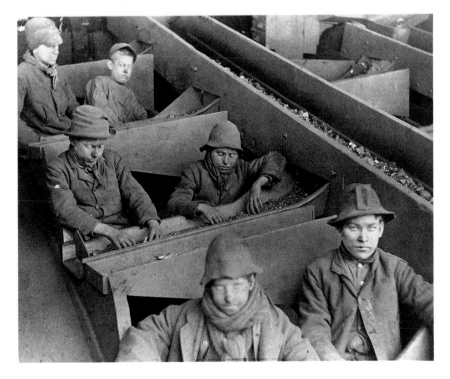

431. UNKNOWN PHOTOGRAPHER.
Goldminers, California, 1850.
Daguerreotype. International Museum of
Photography at George Eastman House,
Rochester, N.Y.

432. GEORGE BRETZ. *Breaker Boys, Eagle
Hill Colliery*, c. 1884. Gelatin silver print.
Edward L. Bafford Photography
Collection, Albin O. Kuhn Library and
Gallery, University of Maryland,
Baltimore.

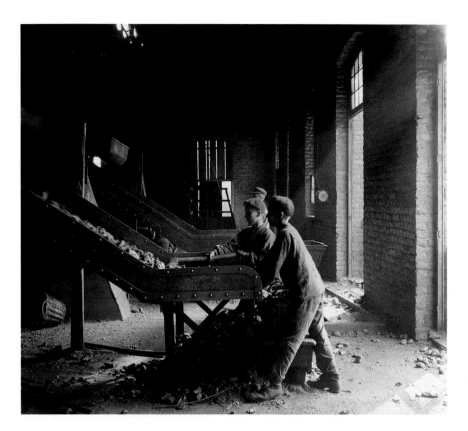

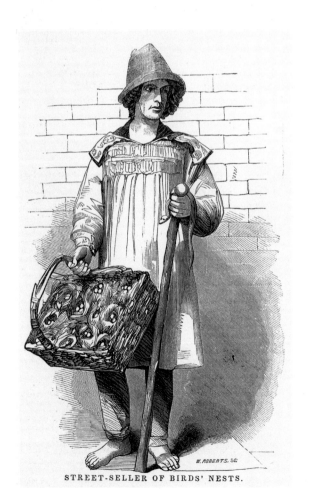

STREET-SELLER OF BIRDS' NESTS.

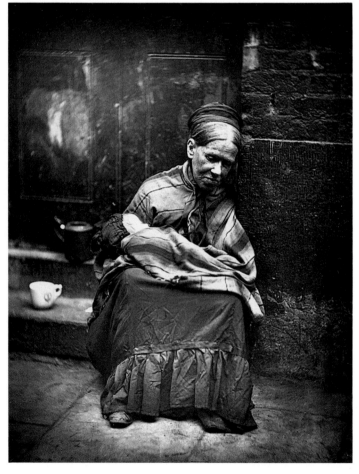

other operations) young boys similarly occupied in separating coal from slag *(pl. no. 433)*. Perhaps the most compelling images of this subject are those taken by Lewis Hine around 1910 as part of the campaign against the unconstrained use of children in heavy industry being waged by the National Child Labor Committee *(pl. no. 474)*.

The directness of style associated with social documentation emerged around 1850, the consequence of expanded camera documentations on paper and glass of historic and modern structures—buildings, railroads, bridges, and, on occasion, social facilities *(see Chapter 4)*. Commissioned mainly by government bodies, railroad lines, and publishers, the photographers involved with this work demonstrated an earnest respect for actuality and an attentive regard for the expressive properties of light. While they did not seek to obscure or mystify their subjects, they realized that the judicious management of light added an aesthetic dimension to the description of objects and events. One such documentation eloquently confirms that while actuality may be depicted without artifice, it can be made suggestive; *The Linen Room (pl. no. 436)* by Charles Nègre avoids the picturesqueness this photographer brought to his images of street types and draws one into the scene by an alternating cadence of dark and light notes that seem to imbue the scene with a mysterious silence. The series of which this is part was commissioned in 1859 by Napoleon III to demonstrate the government's benevolent concern for industrial workers injured on the job.

Social Photography in Publication

Despite the realization that photographs might be useful in campaigns for social improvement, it took a while for the medium of photography and the message of social activism to be effectively harnessed together. One early sociological venture involving camera images was Henry Mayhew's pioneering work, *London Labour and London Poor*, which first appeared toward the end of 1850. Combining illustrations based on daguerreotypes taken under the supervision of Richard Beard with "unvarnished" language in the text portions, the author sought to enliven his account of lower-class urban life, but in the translation from camera image to wood engraving the London "poor" became little more than stiffly positioned genre types *(pl. no. 434)*. Furthermore, with the backgrounds only sketchily indicated, the figures of street vendors and workers seem extracted from their environment, a visual anomaly in view of Mayhew's desire to bring the reality of working-class existence home to his readers. Curiously, the same lack of veracity characterizes his later work on English prison conditions even though by this time the engraver had access to albumen prints from collodion negatives supplied by the

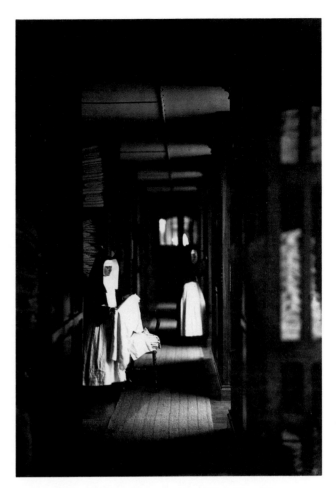

436. CHARLES NÈGRE. *Vincennes Imperial Asylum: The Linen Room*, 1859. Albumen print. Collection André Jammes, Paris; Courtesy National Gallery of Canada, Ottawa.

photographer Herbert Watkins. Even so, the format that was established—authentic language supposedly from first-hand interviews and accurate visual illustration from photographs—became the bedrock of sociological documentation—one that is still used today.

A later work, *Street Life in London*, a serial that began publication in 1877, repeated this scheme, but instead of line engravings it was illustrated with Woodburytypes made from photographs taken expressly for this project by Thomson, after his return from China. The 36 images that illustrate written vignettes supplied by author Adolphe Smith seemed to accord with the canons of the documentary style even though the text was a mixture of sensationalist reporting and moralistic opinions. The work was not a condemnation of the class system or of poverty as such, but an attempt to make the middle class more sympathetic to the plight of the poor and thus more eager to ameliorate conditions. In keeping with the tone of the writing, Thomson photographed vendors and other work-

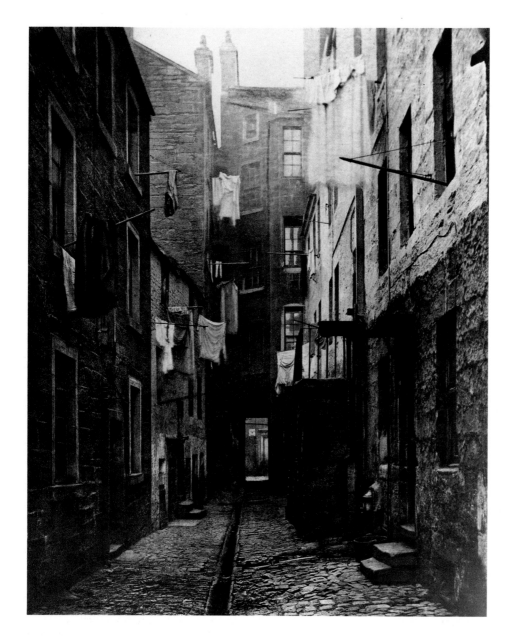

437. THOMAS ANNAN. *Close No. 75 High Street* from *Old Closes and Streets of Glasgow*, 1868. Albumen print. Edward L. Bafford Photography Collection, Albin O. Kuhn Library and Gallery, University of Maryland, Baltimore.

ing-class Londoners in an agreeable light, on the whole choosing pleasant-looking individuals and consciously arranging them in tableauxlike genre scenes. Nevertheless, at least one image—*The Crawlers (pl. no. 435)* —must have left readers with a disturbing feeling in that it depicts with considerable force and no self-consciousness an enfeebled woman seated in a scabrous doorway holding an infant. While *Street Life* may seem ambiguous in terms of purpose, one of its goals that met with eventual success was the building of an embankment to prevent the Thames River from periodically flooding the homes of the London poor.

A project that originated in the desire to make a record of slum buildings slated for demolition in central Glasgow also helped establish the documentary style even though its purpose was nostalgic rather than reformist. In 1868 and again in 1877, during a period of unsettling urban growth, the Glasgow Improvement Trust commissioned Thomas Annan, a Scottish photographer of architecture, portraits, and works of art to "record many old and interesting landmarks."[11] The results, originally printed in albumen in 1868, were reissued with later images added as carbon prints in 1878 and in two editions of gravure prints in 1900 with the title *Old Closes and Streets of Glasgow*. Because this project was not conceived in a reformist spirit, no statistical information about living conditions or comments by the inhabitants—who appear only incidentally in the images—were included. Nevertheless, Annan's images might be seen as the earliest visual record of what has come to be called the inner city slum—in this case one that excelled in "filth . . . drunkenness . . . evil smell and all that makes city poverty disgusting."[12] The vantage points selected by the photographer and the use of light to reveal the slimy and fetid dampness of the place transform scenes that might have been merely picturesque into a document that suggests the reality of life in such an environment *(pl. no. 437)*.

Whatever the initial purpose of the commission and despite their equivocal status as social documentation, many of Annan's images are surprisingly close in viewpoint to those of Jacob Riis, the first person in America to conceive of camera images as an instrument for social change. Sensitivity to the manner in which light gives form and dimension to inert objects also links Annan's work with that of French photographers Charles Marville and Eugène Atget, and supplies further evidence that the documentary style in itself is not specific to images commissioned for activist programs. This becomes even more apparent in the work of photographer Waldemar Franz Herman Titzenthaler, one of the first in his native Germany to understand that the dry plate gave the urban photographer unprecedented access to the social scene. Whether documenting urban slums, industrial enterprises, workers *(pl. no. 438)*, army cadets, or street life, Titzenthaler's images all display the same careful attention to pictorial structure and the disposition of light. Indeed, the stylistic similarities between such images and those made to realize specific social goals suggests that in addition to a particular approach on the part of the photographer, social documentation requires text and context to make its message understood.

Social Documentation in the United States

Riis was the link in the United States between older Victorian concepts and emerging Reform attitudes toward social problems. His subject was the tenement world— where the poverty-stricken half of New York's population lived. In the late 1880s, on the eve of the Reform era, millions of immigrants from Europe, largely from the eastern and southern sections, were induced by the promise of jobs to come to the United States. Needed as cheap labor for seemingly insatiable industrial appetites, those uprooted workers became the first victims of the periodic economic collapses that had occurred in the post–Civil War era, the latest of which lasted from 1882 until 1887. Disgracefully housed in tenements or actually living in the streets of major American cities, with New York by far the most over-crowded and disease-ridden, impoverished immigrants were thought by most middle-class people to be responsible for their own pauperism. Before 1890, the problems of the urban poor were completely ignored by

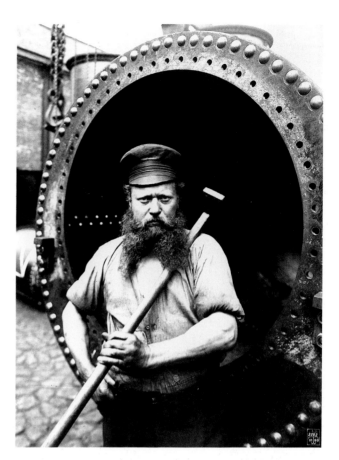

438. WALDEMAR FRANZ HERMAN TITZENTHALER. *Boiler Maker (Types of German Workers)*, c. 1900. Gold-toned printing-out paper. Carpenter Center for the Visual Arts, Harvard University, Cambridge, Mass.

public officials while private charitable organizations contented themselves with providing soup kitchens and moral uplift.

As a police reporter for *The New York Herald*, Riis, who was thrust squarely into a densely populated and malignant slum called Mulberry Bend, started to use camera images, taken by himself or under his supervision, to prove the truth of his words and to make the relationship between poverty and social behavior clear to influential people. The photographs were seen as a way to produce incontrovertible evidence of the existence of vagrant children, squalid housing, and the disgraceful lodgings provided by the police for the homeless. As lantern slides for Riis's popular lectures and as illustrations for articles and books, these pictures were significant elements of the successful campaigns to eliminate the most pestilential shanties in Mulberry Bend and to close down the police lodging houses. The first and most influential publication by Riis, *How the Other Half Lives: Studies Among the Tenements of New York*, which appeared in book form in 1890, consisted of reportage based on his personal investigation

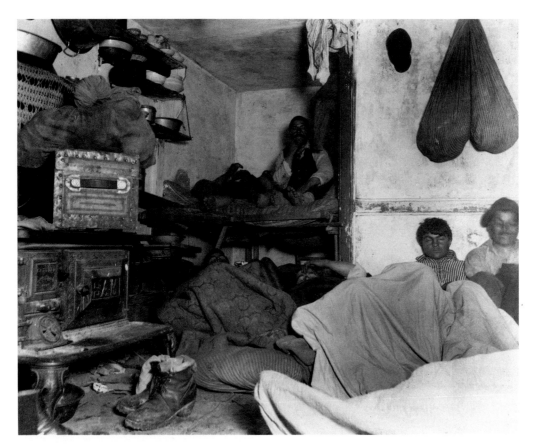

439. JACOB A. RIIS. *Five Cents Lodging, Bayard Street*, c. 1889. Gelatin silver print. Jacob A. Riis Collection, Museum of the City of New York.

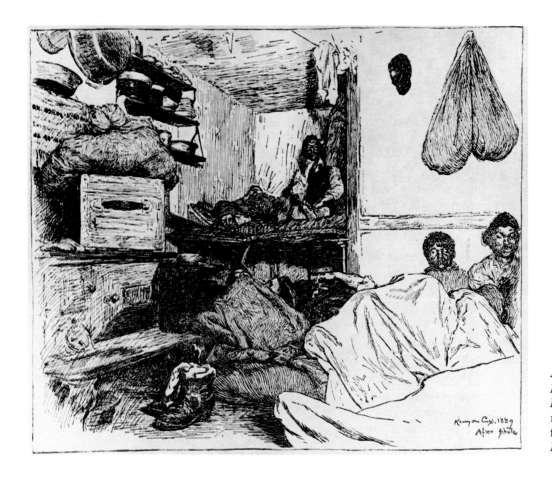

440. KENYON COX. *Lodgers in a Crowded Bayard Street Tenement*, 1890. Wood engraving from *How the Other Half Lives*. Private Collection.

and was illustrated by 40 plates, 17 of which were direct halftone reproductions of photographs.[13] Despite the poor quality of these early halftones, images such as *Five Cents Lodging, Bayard Street (pl. no. 439)* clearly are more persuasive as photographs than as line drawings *(pl. no. 440)*.

Neither their social intent nor the fact that Riis thought himself an inept photographer, uninterested in the techniques or aesthetics of printing, should blind one to the discernment with which these images were made. Fully aware of the purpose to be served, the photographer selected appropriate vantage points and ways to frame the subject, at times transcending the limitation implied in the title—that of an outsider looking at slum life from across the deep chasm separating middle- from lower-class life. While he may not have entered very deeply into the space occupied by the "other," his was not a casual view. Compare for example, the Jersey Street sheds *(pl. no. 441)* in which the figures are placed in a rigidly circumscribed patch of sunlight, hemmed in by areas of brick and shadow and so disposed that the eye must focus on them while also taking in the surrounding details, with a contemporaneous image by an unknown photographer of a London slum courtyard *(pl. no. 442)*. This scene, with its random arrangement of figures, may actually seem more authentically real to modern viewers than Riis's image, but the slice-of-life naturalism it represents did not interest social documentarians. Because social images were meant to persuade, photographers felt it necessary to communicate a belief that slum dwellers were capable of human emotions and that they were being kept from fully realizing their human qualities by their surroundings. As a result, photographs used in campaigns for social reform not only provided truthful evidence but embodied a commitment to humanistic ideals. By selecting sympathetic types and contrasting the individual's expression and gesture with the shabbiness of the physical surroundings, the photographer frequently was able to transform a mundane record of what exists into a fervent plea for what might be. This idealism became a basic tenet of the social documentary concept.

Before 1890, tracts on social problems in the United States had been largely religious in nature, stressing "redemption of the erring and sinful."[14] Such works usually were illustrated with engravings that at times acknowledged a photographic source and at others gave the artistic imagination free reign. After the appearance of *How The Other Half Lives*, however, photographic "evidence" became the rule for publications dealing with social problems even though the texts might still consider poverty to be the result of moral inadequacy rather than economic laws. In one example, *Darkness and Daylight*, an 1897 compendium of interviews, sensationalist reporting, and sermonizing, readers were assured that all the illustrations were "scenes presented to the camera's merciless and unfailing eye," notwithstanding the fact that they actually were engraved by artists using photographs.[15]

As halftone printing techniques advanced and reformist ideas took the place of religiously motivated charity, social photography became the "embodiment of progressive values,"[16] largely through the work of Hine. His career spanned 40 years, during which he enlarged on Riis's objectives and formulated new concepts and techniques. Involvement in *The Pittsburgh Survey*, a pioneering study of working and living conditions in the nation's foremost industrial city, aided Hine in developing a forceful and distinctive personal style, exemplified by the previously mentioned *Breaker Boys (pl. no. 474)*. This complex organization of informative detail and affecting expression bathed in somber light creates a miniature netherworld of intersecting triangles, a visual counterpart to Hine's characterization of child labor as "deadening in its monotony, exhausting physically, irregular," and of child workers as "condemned."[17]

The confident atmosphere engendered by the Progressive Era sustained other projects in which camera images were used to document social conditions, but few photographers were as committed to lobbying for social change as Riis and Hine. Many worked for the expanding periodical press that by 1886 had increased its use of photographs to the point where Frances Benjamin Johnston could describe herself as "making a business of photographic illustration and the writing of descriptive articles for magazines, illustrated weeklies and newspapers"[18] (at the time an unusual career for women). Her early assignments are indicative of the growing popular interest in work and workers; they include a story on coal mines, a spread on the employees in the United States Mint, one on iron workers on the Mesabi Range and on women in the mills of New England, besides news stories on the illustrious doings of celebrities. Her most fully realized commissioned documentation (as contrasted with her magazine stories) was undertaken in 1899 to publicize the educational program offered by the Hampton Institute—a school in Virginia that incorporated the Reform ideal of industrial training in a program designed to eliminate poverty among rural blacks and Indians. Johnston's highly styled arrangements, classical poses, and overall clarity of illumination—seen in *Students at Work on the Stairway (pl. no. 443)* and now so unexpected in documentary images—seem designed to suggest the temperate and disciplined approach that the school emphasized. Others who supplied imagery on social themes to the press were Arthur Hewitt, a member of the Camera Club of New York whose Pictorialist style colored his photographs of bridge-builders and longshoremen for *Everybody's Magazine*, and Jesse Tarbox Beals, whose prosaic

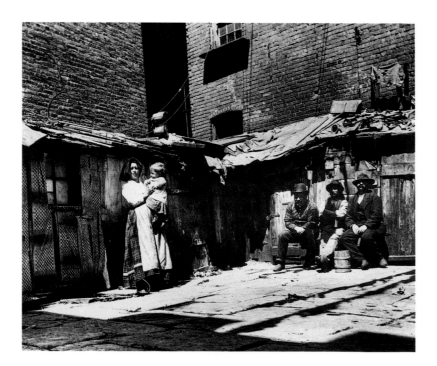

441. JACOB RIIS. *Yard, Jersey Street Tenement*, c. 1888. Gelatin silver print. Jacob A. Riis Collection, Museum of the City of New York.

442. UNKNOWN PHOTOGRAPHER. *London Slum*, c. 1889. Gelatin silver print. BBC Hulton Picture Library/Bettman Archive.

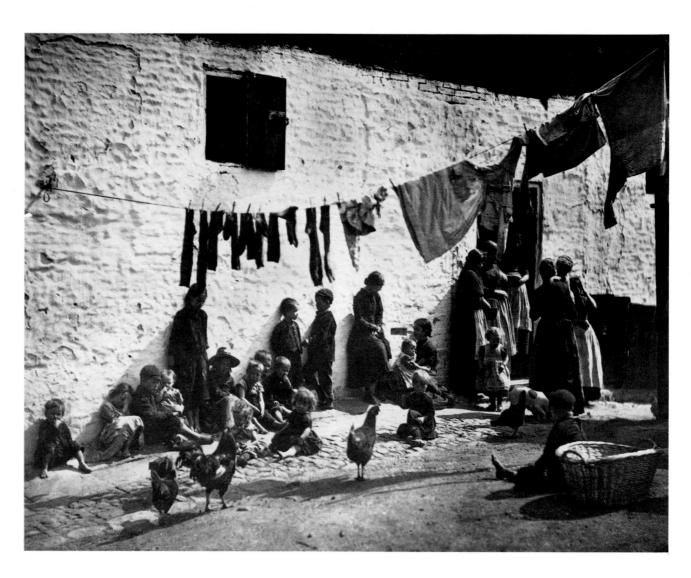

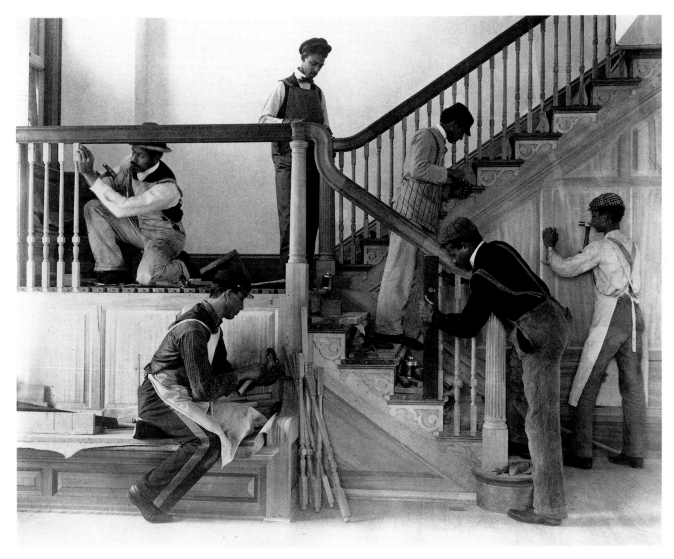

443. FRANCES BENJAMIN JOHNSTON. *Hampton Institute: Students at Work on the Stairway*, 1899–1900. Gelatin silver print. Library of Congress, Washington, D.C.

record shots of tenement life were commissioned by the charity organizations that eventually merged into the Community Services Society.

After 1915, Reformist ideals and programs withered as American energies were redirected to the crisis occasioned by the first World War. With social issues receding in importance, there was less demand for photographs that give dimension to these concerns, and at the same time fresh aesthetic winds, generated by the Armory Show of 1913, quickened interest in the European avant-garde movements in the arts. Abstraction, Expressionism, and Dadaism were some of the new styles and concepts that made Realism and the expression of human emotion and sentiment in visual art seem old-fashioned and contributed to a brief eclipse of the social documentary sensibility during the 1920s.

The Portrait as Social Document

In the United States, these changes were reflected not only in the direction taken by aesthetic photographers but in the images appearing in the periodical press, which joined with the new institution of advertising to project an image of the nation as an energetic titan ruled by rational industrial forces (*see Chapter 10*). Few photographers other than Hine regarded working people as the source of industrial wealth, and even his emphasis shifted from documenting "negative" factors such as exploitation and boredom to portraying the "positive" contributions made by individual men and women in industry. In his "Work Portraits," which appeared sporadically in industrial trade journals during the 1920s, he attempted to bring out the human component in industry through facial close-ups and by relating the

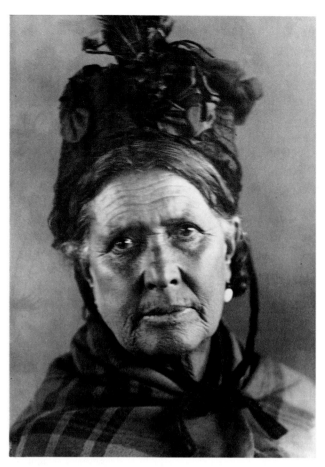

444. EMILE OTTO HOPPÉ. *Flower Seller*, 1921. Gelatin silver print. Mansell Collection Limited, London.

forms of worker and machine, an endeavor that culminated in the documentation of the construction of the Empire State Building in 1930 and 1931 *(pl. no. 481)*.

Owing to the emphasis in Europe on political action rather than social reform, European photographers during the first decades of the 20th century were not given the opportunity to produce social documentation in the manner of Riis or Hine. Nevertheless, as individuals, Emil O. Hoppé, Helmar Lerski, and August Sander *(see Profile)* sought to create, in Sander's word, an "honest" document of an age[19] through portraits that presumably would awaken the viewer to the character of different classes and occupations in society. Of the three, Hoppé, who opened a studio in London in 1907 after leaving Germany, actually was a commercial photographer of taste and discernment who undertook to photograph women workers *(pl. no. 444)* and became adept at reusing these images in a variety of contexts in publication and advertising work. Lerski, born in Strasbourg and trained as an actor, spent many years in the United States, where he became interested in photography about 1911. Theatrical lighting effects and large-scale facial close-ups that entirely fill the picture space

(pl. no. 445) characterize his attempt to create a socio-psychological portrait of people in a variety of occupations, which he published in Germany in 1931 as *Kopfe des Alltags (Ordinary Faces)*.

The towering figure in this kind of documentation through portraiture is Sander. From 1910 until he was censured by the Nazi regime in 1934, he made beautifully lighted and composed images of individuals and groups from all professions and classes in Germany *(pl. nos. 446 and 447)*. The clarity and directness with which he approached social portraiture connect his work with both 19th-century Realist painting and the New Objectivity *(Der Neue Sachlichkeit)* style that emerged in German visual art in the 1920s. Individually and as an aggregate his images are infused with an ironic dimension that suggests the entrenched role of stratified social hierarchies in the Germany of his time. Sander's project culminated in 1929 in the publication of *Antlitz der Zeit (Face of Our Time)*, in which only a small number of the more than 500 images initially envisioned for this work were reproduced. The book was later banned in part because the images showed Germans to be greatly more varied in facial characteristics and temperament than the official mythology decreed.

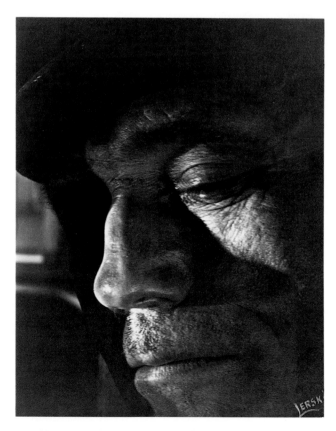

445. HELMAR LERSKI. *German Metal Worker*, 1930. Gelatin silver print. Gernsheim Collection, Humanities Research Center, University of Texas, Austin.

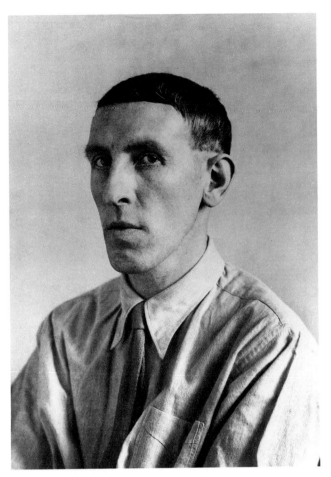

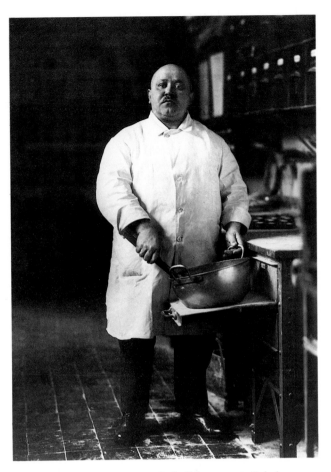

446. AUGUST SANDER. *The Painter Heinrich Hoerle, Cologne*, 1928. Gelatin silver print. Robert Miller Gallery, New York; © Estate of August Sander.

447. AUGUST SANDER. *Pastry Cook, Cologne*, 1928. Gelatin silver print. Sander Gallery, New York; © Estate of August Sander.

No American photographer of the time attempted such a vast project dealing with portraiture of all sectors of society. Of the few who were attracted to "everyday" faces, Hine limited himself to portraits of skilled industrial workers while Doris Ulmann, a sophisticated New York portraitist trained at the Clarence White School, sought to document the rural population of the Southern highlands and plains in a style that invokes pictorialist ideas as much as social documentation *(pl. no. 393)*. Inspired by the revived interest in rural customs and handicraft as a way of preserving America's pre-industrial heritage, her portraits, made in natural light with a large-format view camera and soft-focus lens, embody the photographer's conviction that simplicity and closeness to the soil were of greater moment than progress. A similar idea about the independent character of rural folk can be seen in *The Boss (pl. no. 392)*, an image by Prentice Hall Polk, photographer for Tuskegee Institute, that verges on being an idealized genre type rather than a document of social reality. Indeed, even commercial portrait photographers in the 20th century were

sometimes in a position to provide a sociological document of the people among whom they lived. One thinks of James Van Der Zee, whose images of Harlem's middle- and upper-class citizens during the 1920s *(pl. no. 322)* are poignant testimony to the aspirations of these ghetto dwellers. A similar view into the social structure of a provincial society can be seen in the work of Peruvian portraitist Martin Chambi. In the careful attention to details of dress and ambiance, his individual and group portraits made in a studio in Cuzco or in the fields in the 1930s reveal not only physical features but suggest social hierarchies *(pl. no. 448)*.

Social Photography During the Depression

The documentary movement was born afresh in the United States in the 1930s. As William Stott has pointed out in his study of the period, the motive force was the "invisible nature" of the economic and social castastrophe known as the Great Depression.[20] Lasting about ten years,

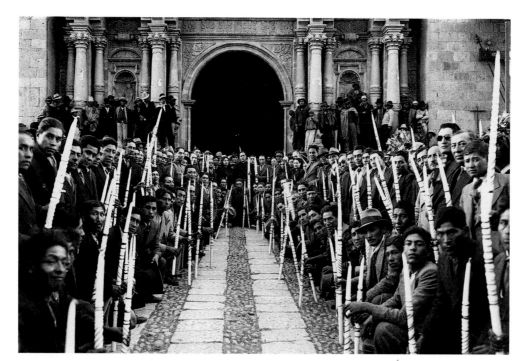

from 1931 until American entry into the second World War, the period was characterized by high unemployment, labor unrest, and agricultural disaster caused by persistent drought and misuse of the land. Pervasive rural poverty resulted in waves of internal migrations as families from the heartland made their way west in search of jobs and arable land. The upheaval, both urban and rural, moved the Federal government under President Franklin Delano Roosevelt's New Deal to relieve the suffering of "one third of a nation" by providing resettlement loans to farmers and work programs for the urban unemployed.

The most completely realized photography project of the period—one of a number sponsored by government agencies—was undertaken by the Historic Section of the Resettlement Administration, later the Farm Security Administration or F.S.A. *(see Profile)*.[21] Initially unfocused as to purpose, the project evolved first into a documentation of the conditions of work and life faced by displaced farmers who had suffered the double calamities of drought and economic depression, and eventually into a portrayal of the more positive aspects of rural life. This project should be seen in relation to other Federally sponsored cultural endeavors in that all originated from the practical necessity of providing jobs and recording the effects of relief and reconstruction programs. Besides the immediate relief they offered those on their payroll, they were influential in directing interest to the American scene and reviving a taste for realistic representation in the visual arts; as a result, in the United States the realist style enjoyed a brief period

of coexistence with more formally conceived modes of expression derived from European modernist movements.

The patronage of the R.A./F.S.A. in particular exerted an exceptionally bracing effect on social documentary photography because, unlike many other Federally sponsored projects, it embraced a structure and a purpose. This was effected through the interaction between Section Director Roy E. Stryker, a brilliant if somewhat narrowly focused propagandist *(pl. no. 449)*, and the photographers, who not only were conscious of the need for a compassionate approach but possessed a fresh eye and a high regard for their craft. Another factor in the exceptional caliber of this project, which produced some 270,000 images, was the variety of artistic approaches employed by the individual photographers.[22] For example, Ben Shahn, who worked with a 35mm camera, directed Stryker's attention to the human element as a source of emotional appeal; Dorothea Lange, who worked with a Rollei, upheld the need for the photographer to exercise control over the negatives, while Walker Evans, using an 8 x 10 inch view camera, insisted on the right to realize his own particular concept of documentation.

In common with other government agencies that embraced photographic projects, the F.S.A. supplied prints for reproduction in the daily and periodical press. In that project photographers were given shooting scripts from which to work, did not own their negatives,[23] and had no control over how the pictures might be cropped, arranged, and captioned, their position was similar to that of photo-

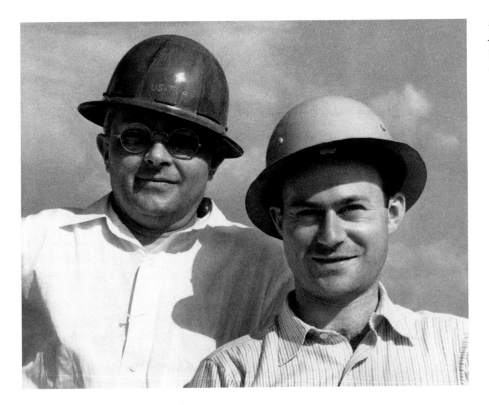

449. UNKNOWN PHOTOGRAPHER.
Arthur Rothstein and Roy Stryker,
1941. Gelatin silver print. Collection
Arthur Rothstein, New York.

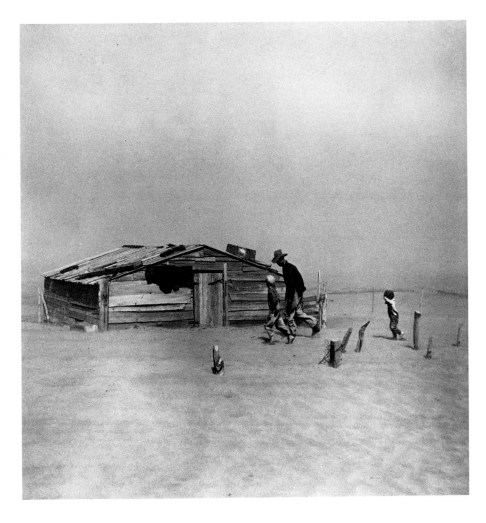

450. ARTHUR ROTHSTEIN. *Dust
Storm, Cimarron County*, 1937.
Gelatin silver print. Library of
Congress, Washington, D.C.

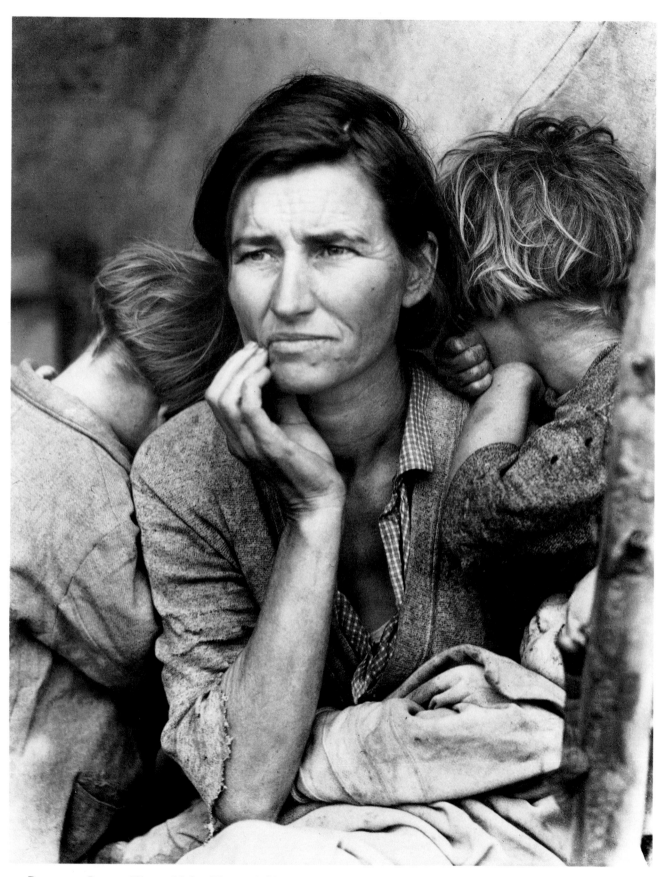

451. DOROTHEA LANGE. *Migrant Mother, Nipomo, California*, 1936.
Gelatin silver print. Library of Congress, Washington, D.C.

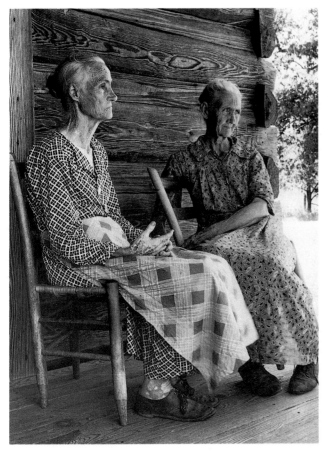

452. MARGARET BOURKE-WHITE. *Two Women, Lansdale, Arkansas*, 1936. Gelatin silver print. George Arents Research Library, Syracuse University, Syracuse, New York.

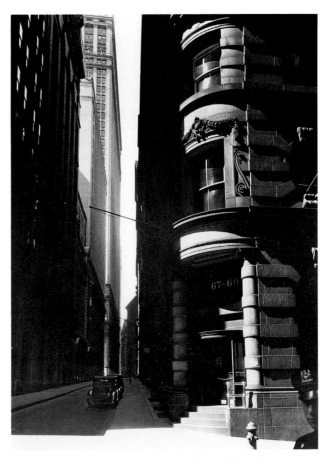

453. BERENICE ABBOTT. *Cedar Street from William Street*, New York, 1939. Gelatin silver print. Private Collection.

journalists working for the commercial press—a situation that both Evans and Lange found particularly distasteful. On the other hand, the images were transformed into photographic works of art when they were exhibited under the auspices of the Museum of Modern Art.[24] As a consequence, for the first time photographs made to document social conditions—that is, to propagandize—were accorded the kind of recognition formerly reserved for aesthetically conceived camera images.

The F.S.A. images were considered truthful expression by some viewers and socialistic propaganda by others who mistook the emphasis on social issues for socialism itself, but there is little doubt that at the time both the consciousness of those portrayed and the consciences of more affluent Americans were affected. Furthermore, the impact of the Great Depression on rural communities has been perceived by later generations on the basis of this body of work—in particular certain key images. While Arthur Rothstein's *Dust Storm, Cimarron County (pl. no. 450)* and *Migrant Mother (pl. no. 451)* by Lange are the most famous icons of the time—the latter selected by Stryker as *the*

picture to symbolize the concern of the Federal government for displaced farmers and their families—in actuality it is the sum of the images that creates the force of the document.[25]

Few other officially sanctioned projects that dealt with rural themes used photography as successfully as the F.S.A., but an individually initiated effort by writer Erskine Caldwell and industrial photographer turned photojournalist Margaret Bourke-White resulted in an influential amalgam of text and image that was issued in an inexpensive paperback format entitled *You Have Seen Their Faces*. It contained numerous dramatically lighted close-ups of Southern tenant-farm families *(pl. no. 452)*, frequently photographed from below, that were offset by a relatively reserved text based on interviews and documentation of the conditions of farm tenancy. Along with the many analogous publications that used F.S.A. images, this inexpensive paperback revivified the form established by earlier social-reform tracts and helped prepare the way for the profusion of post–World War II photographic books on a wide spectrum of social issues.

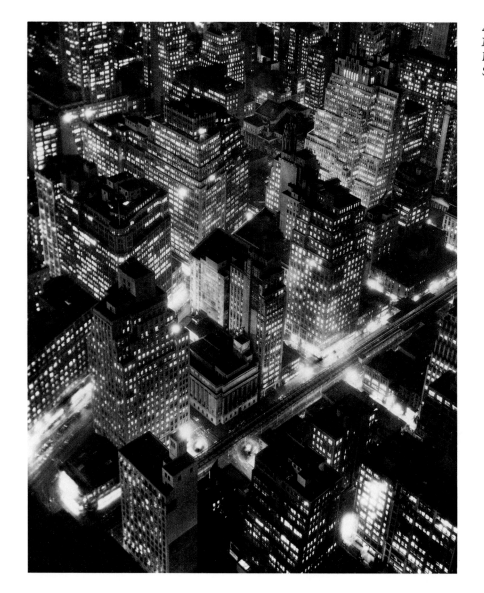

454. BERENICE ABBOTT. *New York at Night*, 1933. Gelatin silver print. Museum of Modern Art, New York; Stephen R. Currier Memorial Fund.

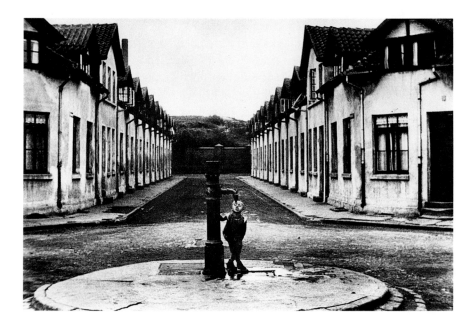

455. WALTER BALLHAUSE. *Untitled*, 1930–33. (From the series *Kinder in der Grossstadt (City Children)*. Gelatin silver print. Schirmer/Mosel, Munich. © Walter Ballhause.

The urban experience during the Depression was photographed under the banners of the Federal Art Project and the Works Progress Administration, and by a group of socially committed photographers who formed the Film and Photo League, from which the Photo League (to be discussed shortly) emerged in 1936. The most fully realized project was a documentation of New York City initiated by Berenice Abbott. On the basis of her experiences as a photographer in Paris, and inspired by the work of Atget, she conceived of the city as a theme that might reflect "life at its greatest intensity."[26] In Abbott's vision, *Changing New York*, as the project came to be called, was meant to evoke "an intuition of past, present and future,"

and to include, besides single images, series of related pictures supported by texts. With its strong contrast between the heavy geometrical curves of the buildings and the narrow shaft of light representing the sky, *Cedar Street from William Street (pl. no. 453)*, one of a number of views that suggest something of the stable commercial underpinnings of the city, is typical of the resonant clarity of the photographs she made for the project *(see also pl. no. 454)*.

Documentation of the urban scene from the point of view of the political left became an issue toward the end of the 1920s when photographers in Europe especially felt moved to deal with unemployment and the rising strength of the working class. However, the aims of those involved

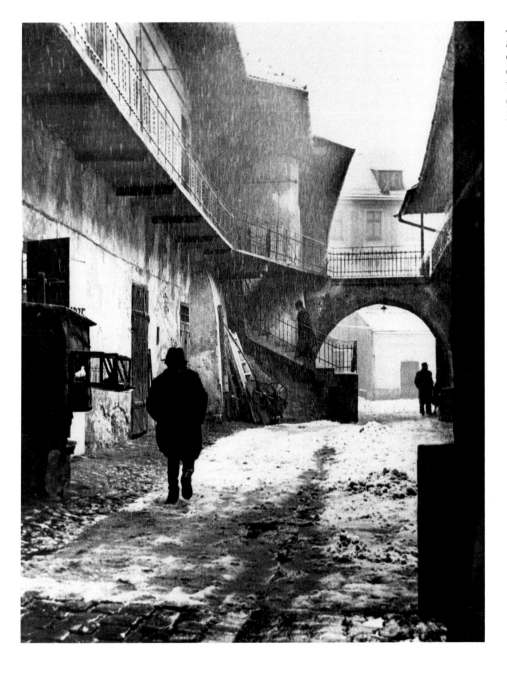

456. ROMAN VISHNIAC. *Entrance to the Ghetto, Cracow*, 1937. Gelatin silver print. International Center of Photography, New York; International Fund for Concerned Photography, Purchase. © Roman Vishniac.

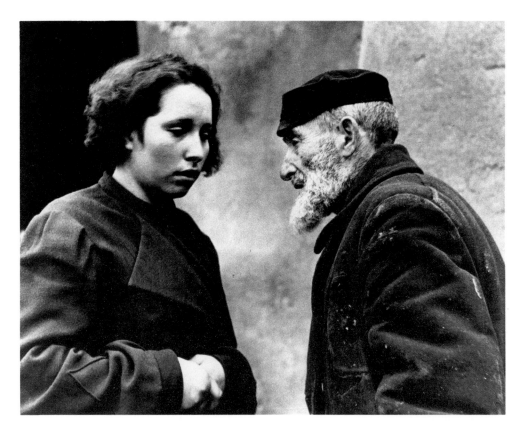

457. ROMAN VISHNIAC. *Granddaughter and Grandfather, Warsaw*, 1938. Gelatin silver print. International Center of Photography, New York; International Fund for Concerned Photography, Purchase. © Roman Vishniac.

in what came to be known as the worker–photographer movement differed significantly from the reformist goals of social documentarians like Riis and Hine. Instead of images meant to provide middle-class viewers with evidence of the need to improve conditions, photographs by participants in the worker–photographer organizations were intended to make other working people conscious of their conditions and their political strengths. European photographers of the left took their cue from social and stylistic developments in the Soviet Union *(see Chapter 9)*, exhibiting camera images in places where working people congregated and reproducing them in the leftist press. For example, *Der Arbeiter-Fotograf (The Worker-Photographer)*, a publication of the German worker–photographer movement, promoted the camera as a "weapon" in an ideological struggle, claiming that a "proletarian eye was essential for capturing a world invisible to the more privileged."[27] That this outlook did not interfere with the expression of a poetic vision can be seen in images made by Walter Ballhause, a working-class activist who used a Leica camera in the early 1930s to portray the unemployed, the elderly, and the children of the poor in Hannover *(pl. no. 455)*. In the singular gesture of the child, anchored within a symmetrical and barren urbanscape, one senses the pervading uneasiness of the time. With politically oriented photographers most active in Eastern Europe, the style of leftist imagery

was varied; indeed a Czech publication of 1934—*Sociální fotografie (Social Photography)*—specifically discussed the integration of avant-garde visual ideas and leftist political ideology. Images with strong political content were shown in two large international exhibitions held in Prague in 1933 and 1934, in which photographers from Czechoslovakia, Hungary, the Soviet Union, Belgium, Holland, and France participated.

Motivated less by political ideology than by a sense of impending catastrophe, Roman Vishniac, living in Berlin as a refugee from the Soviet Union where he had been trained in the biological sciences,[28] produced an extensive documentation of Eastern European Jews in Poland on the eve of the Holocaust. Photographed on the streets and indoors, his subjects generally were unaware of being filmed, a circumstance that lends a vitality to this document of some 5,000 images, of which *Entrance to the Ghetto, Cracow (pl. no. 456)* is one; they are made especially poignant by our knowledge today that everything—people, places, traditions—has vanished *(see also pl. no. 457)*.

The worker–photographer movement had fleeting successes in England, where concern for the problems of the under-class was prompted more by personal sympathy than by class-conscious considerations. The well-known English photographer Humphrey Spender, employed as a photographer for the *London Daily Mail*, in 1937-38 par-

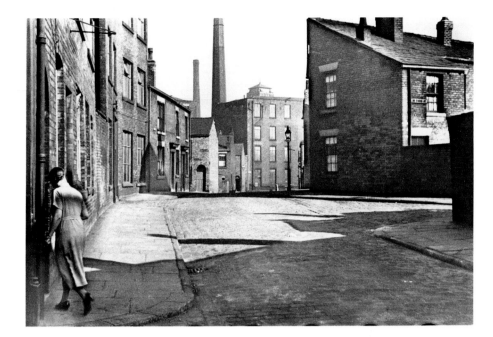

458. HUMPHREY SPENDER. *Street Scene in a Milltown*, 1937–38. (From *Mass-Observation* published as *Worktown People*, 1982). Gelatin silver print. Falling Wall Press, Bristol, England. © Humphrey Spender.

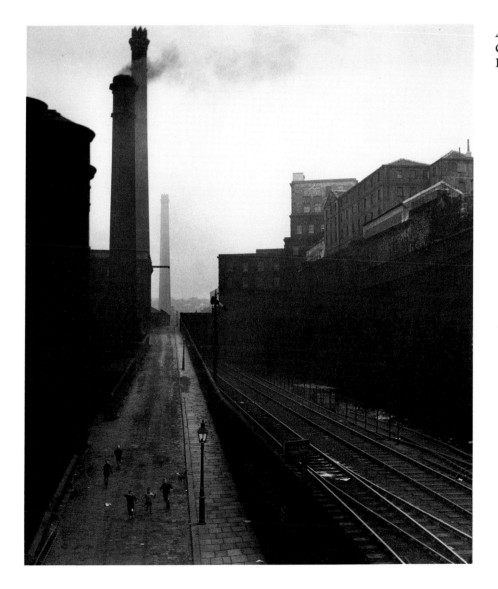

459. BILL BRANDT. *Halifax*, 1936. Gelatin silver print. © Bill Brandt/ Photo Researchers.

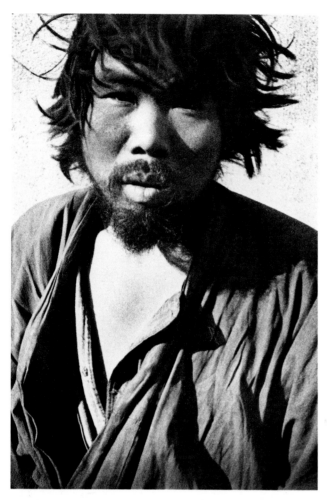

460. HORINO MASAO. *Beggar*, 1932. Gelatin silver print. Japan Photographers Society/Kurita-Bando Literary Agency, Tokyo.

ticipated in a project called "Mass-Observation," which was designed to be an absolutely "objective documentation," in the manner of an anthropological study, of life in the mill towns of the industrial north *(pl. no. 458)*. Bill Brandt, initially attracted to Surrealism, returned to his British homeland in 1931 to depict the divisions between social classes in London as well as working-class life in mining villages. The long, bleak vista and inhospitable structures that all but engulf the tiny figures in *Halifax (pl. no. 459)* seem to symbolize the enduring human spirit that is all but crushed by poverty and industrialism.

During this same period, a number of Japanese photographers, with great interest in Western attitudes toward art and photography, found in the "new photography" (to be discussed in Chapter 9) the means for a humane portrayal of the hitherto despised and unrecorded lower classes. Horino Masao, a photographer of great versatility who also was interested in montage and industrial imagery, made large close-up portraits of working men, beggars *(pl. no. 460)*, and street people. The invigorating documentary trend made possible by the greater diversity of subject and approach in Japanese photography also can be seen in vibrant street images by Kuwabara Kineo, among them *Scene at a Fair (pl. no. 461)* of 1936 and in documentations of life in the occupied territories of Manchuria by several of Japan's most notable photographers. By the 1940s, however, photographers put their cameras at the service of the government bureaucracy or they portrayed the pleasures of rural life, as in the images made by Hamaya Hiroshi between 1940 and 1944 for *Snow Country (pl. no. 462)*. The

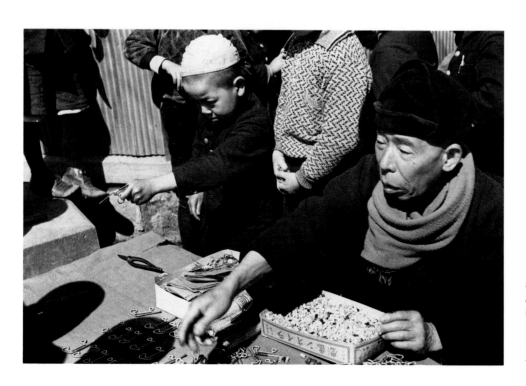

461. KUWABARA KINEO. *Scene at a Fair*, 1936. Gelatin silver print. Japan Photographers Society/ Kurita-Bando Literary Agency, Tokyo.

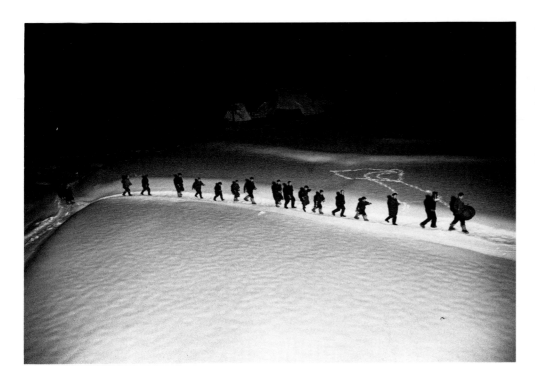

462. HAMAYA HIROSHI. *Untitled* (from *Snow Country, a Record of Folk Customs during the Lunar New Year Celebrations in Niigata Prefecture)*, 1940–44. Gelatin silver print. Japan Photographers Society/Kurita-Bando Literary Agency, Tokyo.

463. SID GROSSMAN. *Coney Island*, 1947. Gelatin silver print. National Gallery of Canada, Ottawa. © Sid Grossman.

conflict that had expanded from China to a confrontation with the United States on the Pacific islands effectively interrupted a brief but exhilarating period of expressive documentation.

In the United States, the Photo League, formed by a group of politically conscious photographers, was committed to the tradition of straight picture-making that its members traced back to Hill and Adamson, Stieglitz, and Hine. With this concept, the league eventually encompassed a broad range of styles and goals, but, as initially conceived by its photographer–founders Sid Grossman *(pl. no. 463)* and Sol Libsohn, its specific purpose was the promotion of documentary photography through a school and the establishment of "feature groups"—units organized to depict aspects of urban life in depth. Projects included the Chelsea and Pitt Street documents, with the most fully realized being the Harlem Document.[29] This was a three-year effort headed by Aaron Siskind, and including Harold Corsini, Morris Engel, and Jack Manning (all later respected professionals), that produced a searching look at life in New York's most significant black neighborhood. An image of a woman and children *(pl. no. 464)* by Engel (who became an independent filmmaker) encapsulates both the claustrophobia and the humanity of the ghetto, while Siskind's many images of street life in the same community reveal the way blacks "grasped a patch of happiness whenever and wherever they could find it."[30]

Responding to the general movement in the arts toward more personalized modes of expression, league mem-

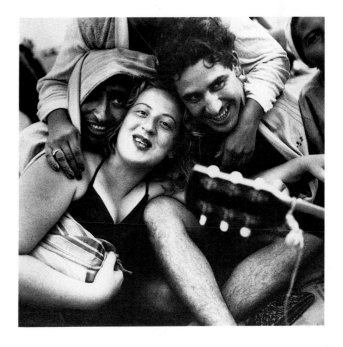

bers adopted the concept of creative photography in the late 1940s, but despite this subtle shift away from pure documentation many former members continued their commitment to humanist ideals even after the organization's politically inspired demise in 1951.[31] Former league president Walter Rosenblum, for instance, undertook a series of self-motivated projects to document life in East Harlem, in Haiti, and in the South Bronx *(pl. no. 465)*; W.

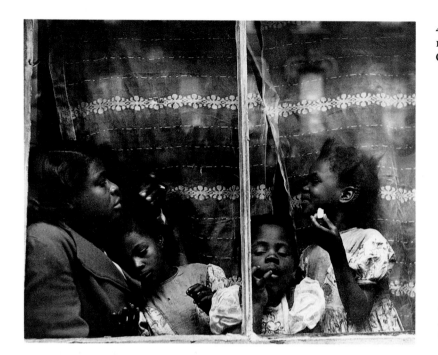

464. MORRIS ENGEL. *Rebecca, Harlem,* 1947. Gelatin silver print. Private Collection. © 1947 Morris Engel.

465. WALTER ROSENBLUM. *Mullaly Park, Bronx, New York,* 1980. Gelatin silver print. Courtesy and © Walter Rosenblum.

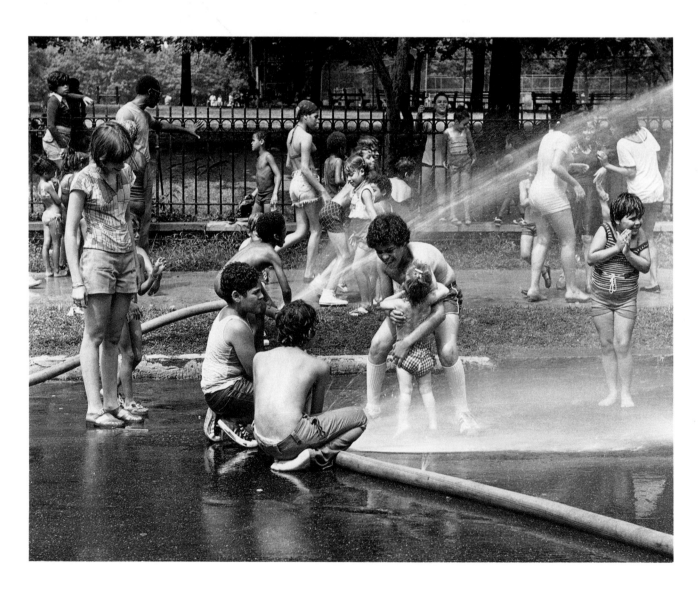

Eugene Smith, also a former president, continued his commitment to these ideals in Minamata; while others, among them Bernard Cole, Arthur Leipzig, and Dan Weiner, found a limited opportunity to treat humanistic themes in the flourishing field of postwar photojournalism (see Chapter 10).

Before the 1930s, Pictorialists and their supporters subscribed to the idea that art ought not to be utilitarian. In consequence, they were blind to the fact that genuine feeling and innovative vision might imbue camera images made for a social purpose with imagination and meaning. At the same time, those who used documentary works frequently disregarded the individual photographer and reproduced the images without credit and at times without permission. Often social documentary photographers were unknown unless their work was used in a specific context. The outstanding quality of the work done under the aegis of the F.S.A. and by Abbott for *Changing New York* were factors that helped transform this situation, demonstrating to the photographic community and to viewers at large that divisions between art and document are difficult to maintain when dealing with images of actuality. These and other works made clear that, no matter what its purpose, any camera image may transcend the mundaneness of its immediate subject and transmute matter into thought and feeling—the essential goal of all visual art. Recognizing that purposeful photographs also may enlarge vision and inspire compassion even after the specific problems they addressed have disappeared, the generation of photographers that grew to maturity after the second World War rejected the compartmentalization of photographic expression that had been the legacy of the Pictorialist movement. Instead they sought to imbue their work, no matter what its ultimate purpose, with the passion and immediacy found in social documentation at its best.

Profile: Lewis W. Hine

Lewis Hine, whose sociological horizons gave his images focus and form, was a photographer in touch with his time. When the twenty-seven-year-old Hine came east in 1900 from his birthplace in Oshkosh, Wisconsin, to teach natural sciences, he already had experienced the exploitation of the workplace that he was to spend a good part of his life documenting. His first serious photographs were made in response to a desire on the part of his principal at the Ethical Culture School in New York to use the camera as an educational tool. As an arm of the Progressive Movement, the school sought in photography a means of counteracting the rampant prejudice among many Americans against the newly arrived peoples from eastern and southern Europe, so, besides recording school activities and teaching photography, in 1904 Hine began photographing immigrants entering Ellis Island. Notwithstanding the chaos of the surroundings, his inability to communicate verbally, and his cumbersome 5 x 7 inch view camera and flash powder equipment, he succeeded in producing images that invest the individual immigrant with dignity and humanity (*pl. no. 473*), in contrast to the more common distanced view.

In 1907, after convincing a group of social welfare agencies that photographs would provide incontrovertible evidence for their reform campaigns, Hine (along with graphic artist Joseph Stella) was invited to participate in *The Pittsburgh Survey*, a pioneer sociological investigation of working and living conditions in the nation's most

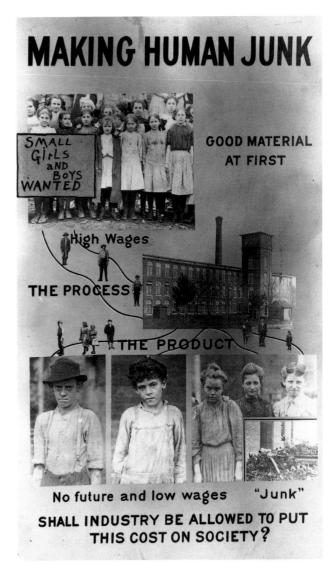

466. LEWIS HINE. *Making Human Junk*, c. 1915. Poster. Library of Congress, Washington, D.C.

industrialized city; after this experience he left teaching and set himself up as a professional "social photographer." From then until 1917, he was the staff photographer for the National Child Labor Committee, traveling more than 50,000 miles from Maine to Texas to photograph youngsters in mines, mills, canneries, fields, and working on the streets, in order to provide "photographic proof" that "no anonymous or signed denials" could contradict.[32] The images were used in pamphlets, magazines, books, slide lectures, and traveling exhibits (pl. no. 466), many of which Hine organized and designed.

Toward the end of the first World War, when the waning interest in social welfare programs became apparent, Hine went overseas as a photographer on an American Red Cross relief mission to France and the Balkans. On his return, he embarked on a project of "positive documentation," hoping to portray the "human side of the system," which he felt should be recognized by a society convinced that machines run themselves. This period started with a series of individual portraits—"Work Portraits"—which were critically acclaimed although not greatly successful financially, and culminated for Hine in his 1930 commission to photograph the construction of the Empire State Building (pl. no. 482). The photographer followed its progress floor by dizzying floor, clambering over girders and even being swung out in a cement bucket to take pictures. At the conclusion of the project, he organized a number of the images along with others from the "Work Portrait" series into Men at Work, a pioneering photographic picture book that featured good reproduction, full page bleeds, and simple modern typography.

The last decade of Hine's life coincided with the Great Depression, but while F.S.A. photographers were given the opportunity to produce a stirring document of social conditions, the photographic programs of the agencies for which Hine worked—the Rural Electrification Agency, the Tennessee Valley Authority, and the Works Progress Administration—had little creative vision concerning the use of photographs in this manner. The frustration of Hine's last years was offset to a degree by the efforts of Berenice Abbott, Elizabeth McCausland, and the Photo League to rescue his work from oblivion with a retrospective exhibition in New York in 1939.

Profile: August Sander

August Sander's dream was to create a visual document of "Man in 20th-Century Germany." He hoped that through a series of portraits, sequenced in a "sociological arc" that began with peasants, ascended through students, professional artists, and statesmen, and descended through urban labor to the unemployed, he would make viewers aware of the social and cultural dimensions as well as the stratifications of real life. After the publication of only one volume, which appeared in 1929 as Antlitz der Zeit (Face of Our Time), this ambitious project was banned as presenting a version contrary to official Nazi teachings about class and race, and Sander was forced to abandon it.

Born in 1876 in a provincial village near Cologne to a family deeply rooted in traditional peasant culture, Sander was introduced fortuitously to photography while employed as a worker in the local mines. He soon began to make straightforward, unretouched portraits of local families; this approach, along with his later apprenticeship as a photographer of architectural structures and his training in fine art at the Dresden Academy of Art, helped establish the hallmarks of his mature vision. Though for a time the portraits he turned out in a commercial studio he opened in Linz displayed his mastery of Pictorialist techniques, he preferred, as he wrote in a publicity brochure for another of his studios a few years later, "simple, natural portraits that show the subject in an environment corresponding to their own individuality."[33] This attitude soon found its fruition in the grand project that began in earnest after the end of the first World War.

A thoughtful man, well-read in classical German literature, Sander drew his ideas from the twin concepts of physiognomic harmony and truth to nature. The former (discussed in Chapter 2) held that moral character was reflected in facial type and expression, a notion that the photographer enlarged upon by introducing the effect of environment on creating social types as well as typical individuals. Sander was convinced also that universal knowledge was to be gained from the careful probing and truthful representation of every aspect of the natural world—animals, plants, earth, and heavens. To this rationalist belief he added an ironic view of German society as an almost medieval hierarchy of trades, occupations, and classes.

Sander's circle of friends in Cologne during the 1920s included intellectuals and artists, many of whom were partisans of the New Realism or New Objectivity. While the work of these artists may have influenced his ideas, it is at least as possible that the simple frontal poses, firm outlines, and undramatized illumination visible in paintings by German artists Otto Dix and Edwin Merz, for example, owe something to Sander's portraiture; that all shared a belief in the probing nature of visual art to dissect truth beneath appearances also is evident.

The suppression of Sander's work by the Nazis was followed by the harrassment of his family and the loss of many of his friends in the arts who were either in exile or had been put to death. Sander, forced to turn his camera lens to landscape and industrial scenes, sought in land-

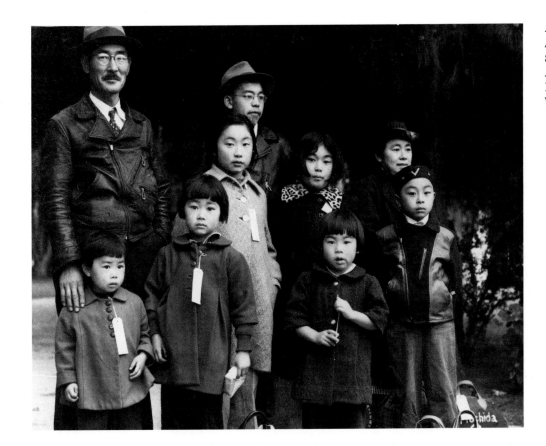

467. DOROTHEA LANGE.
Hayward, California, May
8, 1942. Gelatin silver print.
Audiovisual Division,
National Archives,
Washington, D.C.

scapes of the farming communities of his native region to insinuate a suggestion of the historical role of the human intelligence in shaping the land, while the detailed close-ups of organic forms may have been meant as symbols of his abiding faith in the rational spirit. He survived the second World War, the deaths of several family members, and the loss of his negatives in a fire, to find his work republished and himself honored by photographers throughout the world.

Profile: The Historical Section Project, F.S.A.

The photographic documentation sponsored by the U.S. government under the auspices of the Historical Section of the Farm Security Administration, known popularly as the F.S.A. project, is a paradigm of what can be accomplished when sensitive photographers working with a stubborn yet visionary director are given opportunities and financial and psychological support in their efforts to make visual statements about compelling social conditions. When Roy E. Stryker, a former teacher in the Economics Department at Columbia University, was called to Washington in 1935 to head the Historical Section, he envisaged an effort that would use photographs to record the activities of the government in helping destitute farm-

ers. Ultimately, the project demonstrated that despite insufficient funding and hostility from Congress and the press, contemporary social problems could become vivid and stirring through photography. Now regarded as a "national treasure," this documentation was the work of eleven photographers: Arthur Rothstein, Theo Jung, Ben Shahn, Walker Evans, Dorothea Lange, Carl Mydans, Russell Lee, Marion Post Walcott, Jack Delano, John Vachon, and John Collier (listed in the order in which they were hired). All of them helped shape the overall result through their discussions and their images.

Rothstein, a former Columbia University student who was the first photographer hired, set up the files and darkroom and recorded the activities of the section before being sent to the South and West. While on assignment in drought-stricken regions in 1936, where he made the famous *Dust Storm, Cimarron County (pl. no. 450)*, he also photographed a bleached steer skull in several positions; it was an experiment that precipitated a bizarre political controversy about the truthfulness of images made under government sponsorship and raised questions concerning the legitimacy of social documentation.[34] In its wake, some documentary photographers supported the photographer's right to find essential rather than literal truths in any situation, while others, notably Evans, insisted on absolute veracity, maintaining that for images to be true to both

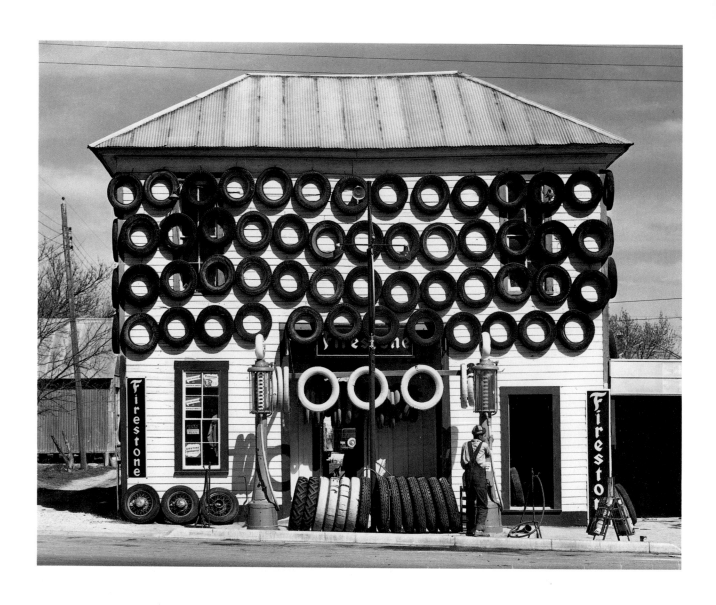

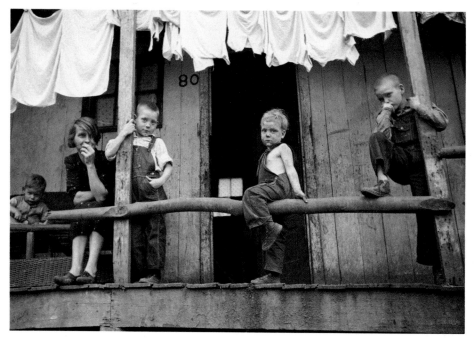

468. RUSSELL LEE. *Second Hand Tires, San Marcos, Texas*, 1940. Gelatin silver print. Library of Congress, Washington, D.C.

469. MARION POST WOLCOTT. *Family of Migrant Packinghouse Workers, Homestead, Florida*, 1939. Gelatin silver print. Library of Congress, Washington, D.C.

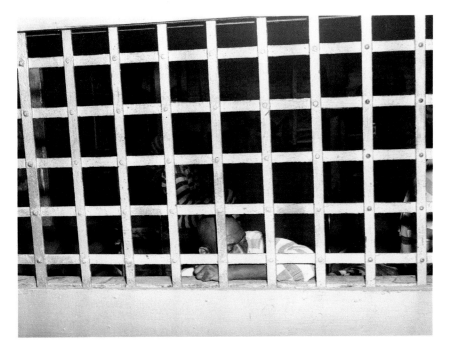

470. JACK DELANO. *In the Convict Camp, Greene County, Georgia*, 1941. Gelatin silver print. Library of Congress, Washington, D.C.

471. BEN SHAHN. *Cotton Pickers, Pulaski County, Arkansas*, 1935. Gelatin silver print. Fogg Art Museum, Harvard University, Cambridge, Massachusetts; gift of Mrs. Bernarda B. Shahn.

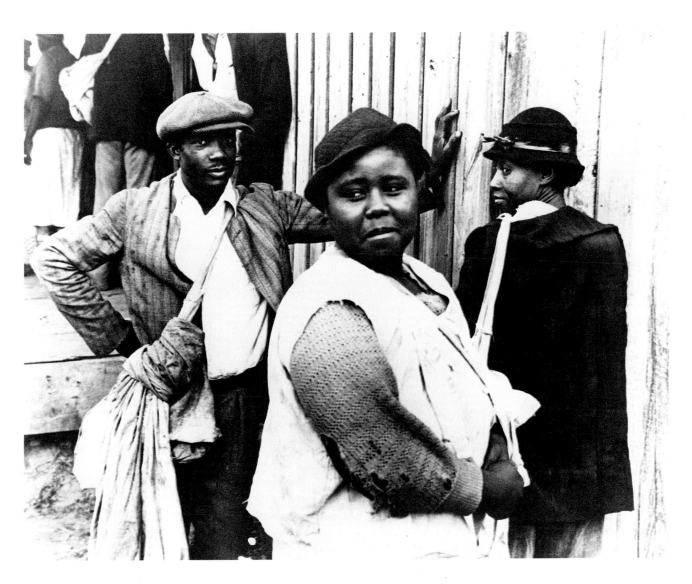

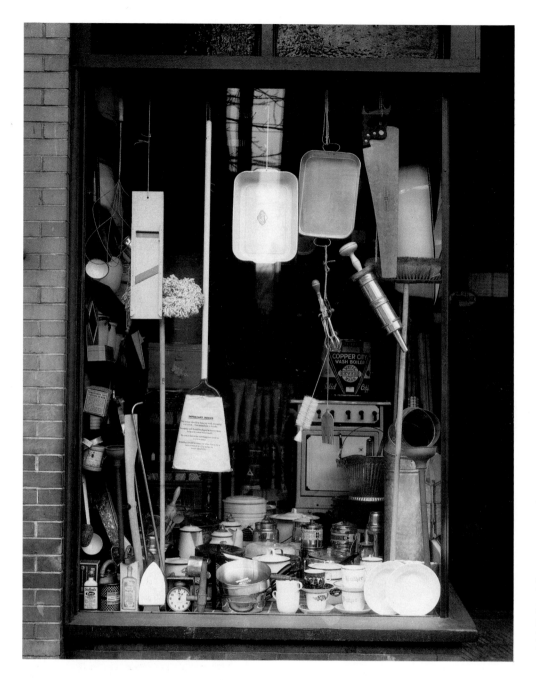

472. WALKER EVANS.
*Window Display, Bethlehem,
Pennsylvania*, Nov., 1935.
Gelatin silver print.
Library of Congress,
Washington, D.C.

medium and event, situations should be found, not re-enacted.

The painter Shahn, employed by the Special Skills Department of the Resettlement Administration, may have been the most persuasive voice in shaping attitudes and approaches on the project in that he convinced Stryker that record photographs were not sufficient to dramatize social issues, that what was needed were moving and vibrant images that captured the essence of social dislocation. Briefly instructed by Evans in the use of the Leica, Shahn had made candid exposures in New York streets for use in his graphic art. He displayed a vivid understanding of the

dimensions of documentation; his discussions with Stryker and the other photographers helped clarify the need for interesting and compassionate pictures instead of mere visual records whether they portrayed inanimate objects or people. In themselves, his images reveal a profound social awareness and a vivid sense of organization that captures the seamlessness of actuality *(pl. no. 471)*.

Although quite different, the rigorous aesthetic and craft standards maintained by Evans, who was employed by the section for about two years, also broadened Stryker's understanding of the potential of photography to do more than record surface appearances. The only photographer to consistently use the 8 x 10 inch view camera (as well as smaller formats), Evans photographed extensively in the South, engrossed by its "atmosphere . . . smell and signs."[35] His subjects were exceptionally diverse, including portraits, interiors, domestic and factory architecture, folk craft, and popular artifacts (*pl. no. 472*). Of all the section photographers, he was least in sympathy with the social implications of the project and regarded Stryker's call for file photographs and the bureaucratic restrictions of the project with indifference; therefore he was not unhappy to receive a leave in 1936 to work with writer James Agee on an article on tenant farmers for *Fortune* magazine. This experience, and the resulting publication, *Let Us Now Praise Famous Men*, convinced Evans of the need for sufficient time and freedom to define for himself the aesthetic and ideological significance of his themes.

The compassionate vision of Lange, "the supreme humanist," also influenced Stryker and the direction taken by the section, even though they were at odds over the question of printing, which the photographer preferred to do herself rather than leave to the darkroom technicians at the F.S.A. A former portraitist trained in the Pictorialist aesthetic, Lange was employed first on a California rural relief project where her innate capacity to penetrate beneath appearances was recognized. Concentrating on gesture and expression, and possessing the patience to wait for the telling moment (*pl. no. 451*), she seemed able to distill the meaning of the crisis to the individuals involved in terms that the nation at large could understand. On occasion, her pictures actually impelled authorities to take immediate steps to relieve suffering among migrant farm families. After leaving the project in 1940, Lange continued to work on her own in the same tradition, producing a memorable series of photographs of Japanese-Americans who had been unjustly interned by the Federal government during the hysteria that accompanied the opening of hostilities between Japan and the United States (*pl. no. 467*).

Of the other photographers, both Mydans and Jung worked on the project for relatively short times. Lee, called "the great cataloguer" by Lange, took over Mydan's place when the latter was asked to join the staff of the newly established *Life*, and he remained with the section the longest. Though most committed to the goals of amassing as complete a visual record as possible, his images celebrate individuality and spunk and display a wry humor (*pl. no. 468*). Post Wolcott, one of the relatively few female professional newspaper photographers of the time, was hired in 1938, when the direction of the project was being shifted toward a more positive view of the activities of the F.S.A. (*pl. no. 469*). Delano, whose W.P.A. photographs of a bootleg mining operation in Pennsylvania came to the attention of Stryker when he was looking for a replacement for Rothstein in 1940, was also expected to make positive images, but a long stay in Greene County, Georgia, where he was among the first to photograph prisons and labor camps, resulted in moving evocations of socially generated anguish and loneliness (*pl. no. 470*). Vachon, hired originally as a messenger, was responsible for the ever-growing picture file. Taught to handle a camera by both Shahn and Evans, Vachon saw his pictures begin to find their way into the file, and in 1940 he was promoted to photographer. Collier, the last hired for the Project, had barely time to work in the field before the Historical Section was transferred to the Office of War Information in 1942.[36]

The interrelationship between photographer, government agency, and public was crucial to the formation of this unique document, and owes much to Stryker's tenacity. Despite a certain narrowness with regard to the poetic resonances of camera images, and an autocratic attitude toward the use and cropping of the photographs; despite a willingness to bow to demands for superficial and positive images of the American experience, Stryker's ability to act as a buffer between photographers, bureaucrats, and press created the conditions for an exceptional achievement that found an audience in its own time. And the fact that this extensive documentation still exists is owed to his scheme to have the Library of Congress take over the collection and keep it intact, unlike the fate of some of the other Federally funded works of visual art that have disappeared or been destroyed.

Illuminating Dark Places: A Lewis W. Hine Album

Throughout his career as a social-documentary photographer, Lewis W. Hine sought not only to provide evidence of inferior living and working conditions but to portray America's immigrant working people with dignity and compassion. From his first reverential portraits of immigrants at Ellis Island, taken in 1904 and 1905, to the exciting views of the construction of the Empire State Building made between 1930 and 1931, Hine emphasized the "human element." This unwavering humanist commitment informed a style that became progressively more complex as the photographer's experience on The Pittsburgh Survey and as a staff member of the National Child Labor Committee enabled him to handle grouping, backgrounds, and lighting with greater naturalness and effect. A firm believer in the power of knowledge to vanquish evil, Hine in his photographs illuminated not only conditions but the human spirit that until then had been invisible to middle-class Americans.

473. LEWIS HINE. *Albanian Woman with Folded Head Cloth, Ellis Island*, 1905. Gelatin silver print. Private collection.

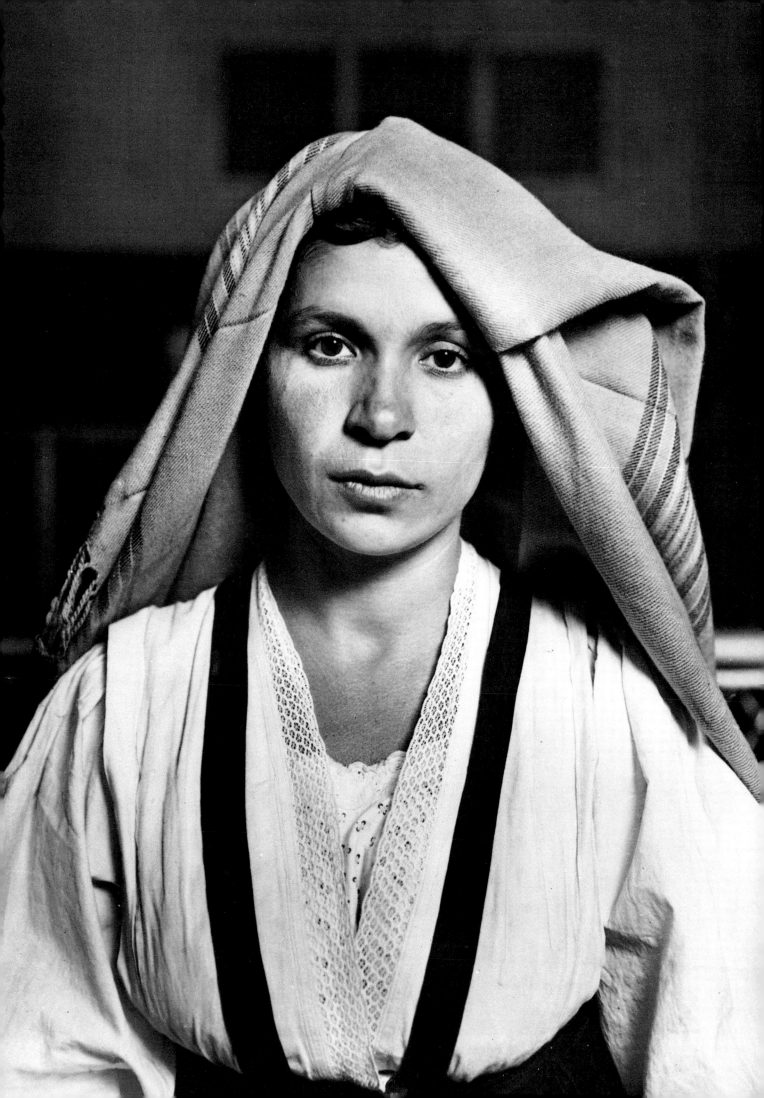

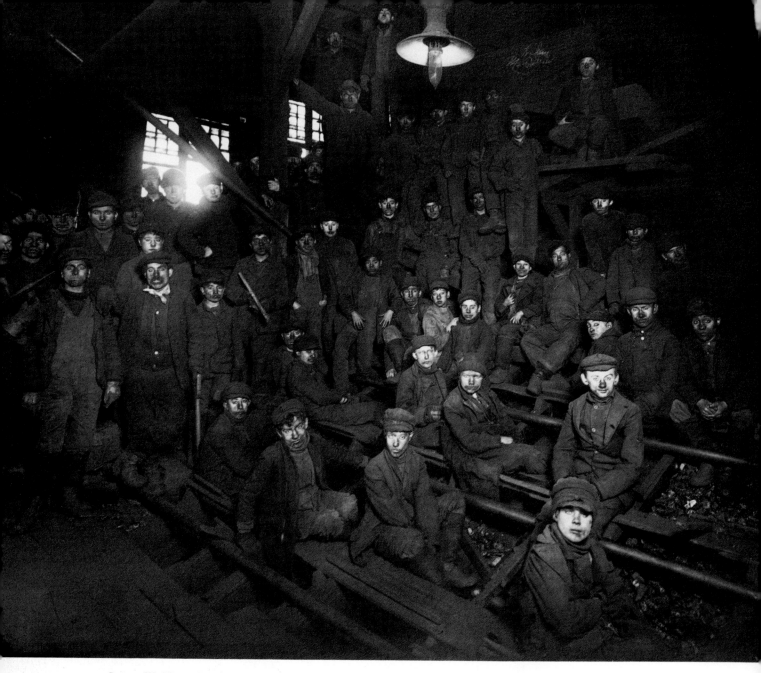

474. LEWIS W. HINE. *Breaker Boys in a Coal Mine, South Pittston, Pa.*, 1911. Gelatin silver print. Private collection.

OPPOSITE ABOVE:

475. LEWIS W. HINE. *Polish Boy, Quidnick Mill, April 16, 1909.*
Gelatin silver print. Private collection.

OPPOSITE BELOW:

476. LEWIS W. HINE. *Ten-Year-Old Spinner, North Carolina Cotton Mill,*
1908–09. Gelatin silver print. Private collection.

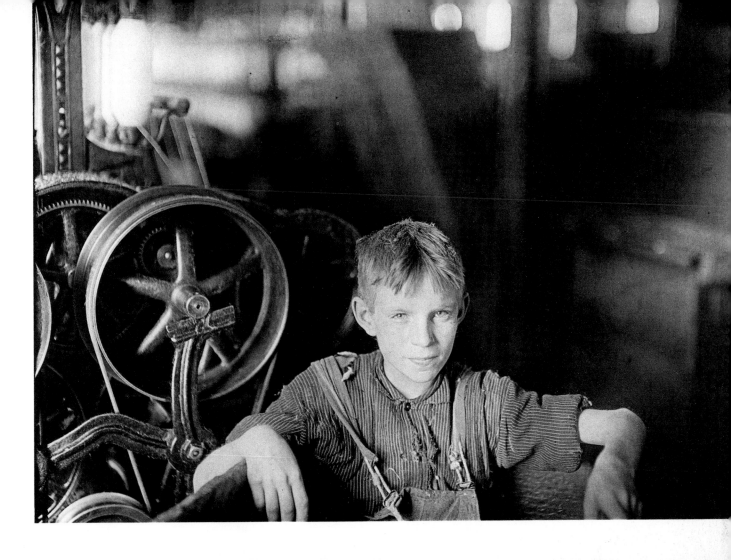
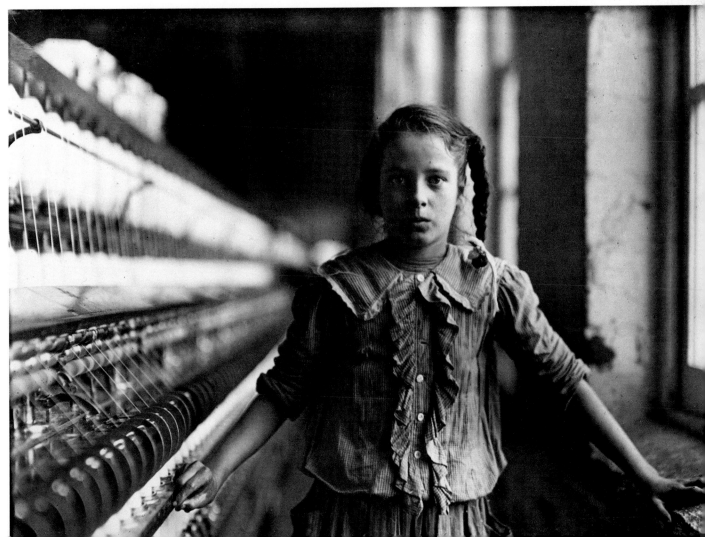

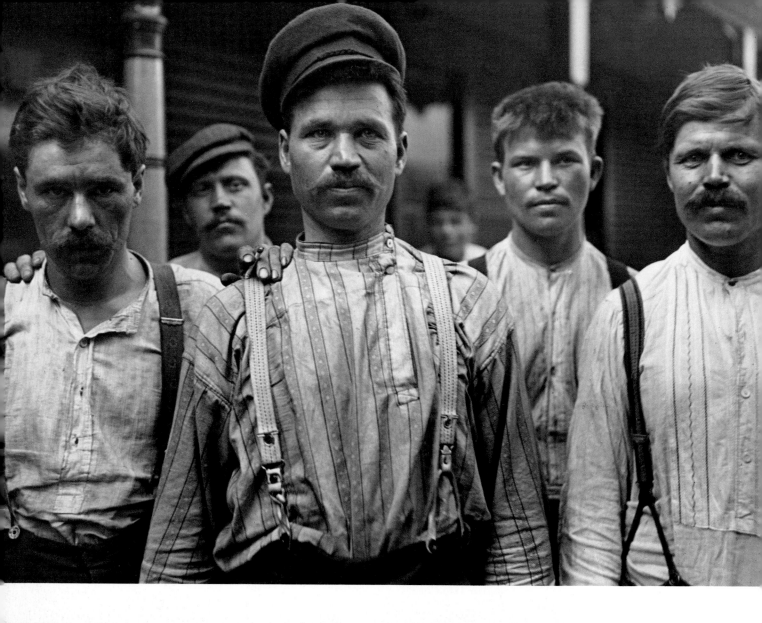

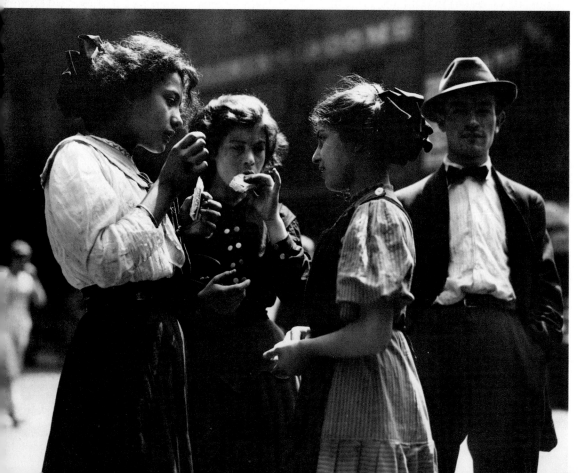

477. LEWIS W. HINE. *Steel Workers at the Russian Boarding House, Homestead, Pa.*, 1908. Gelatin silver print. Private collection.

LEFT:

478. LEWIS W. HINE. *Lunch Time, New York City*, 1915. Gelatin silver print. Private collection.

RIGHT:

479. LEWIS W. HINE. *Ellis Island Madonna*, c. 1905. Gelatin silver print. Private collection.

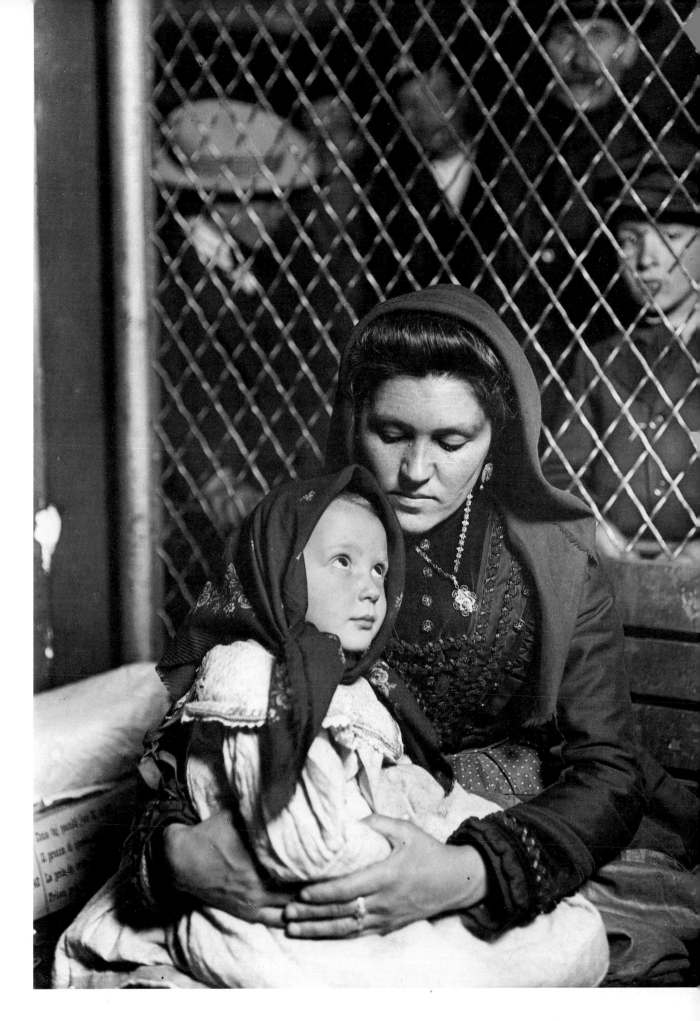

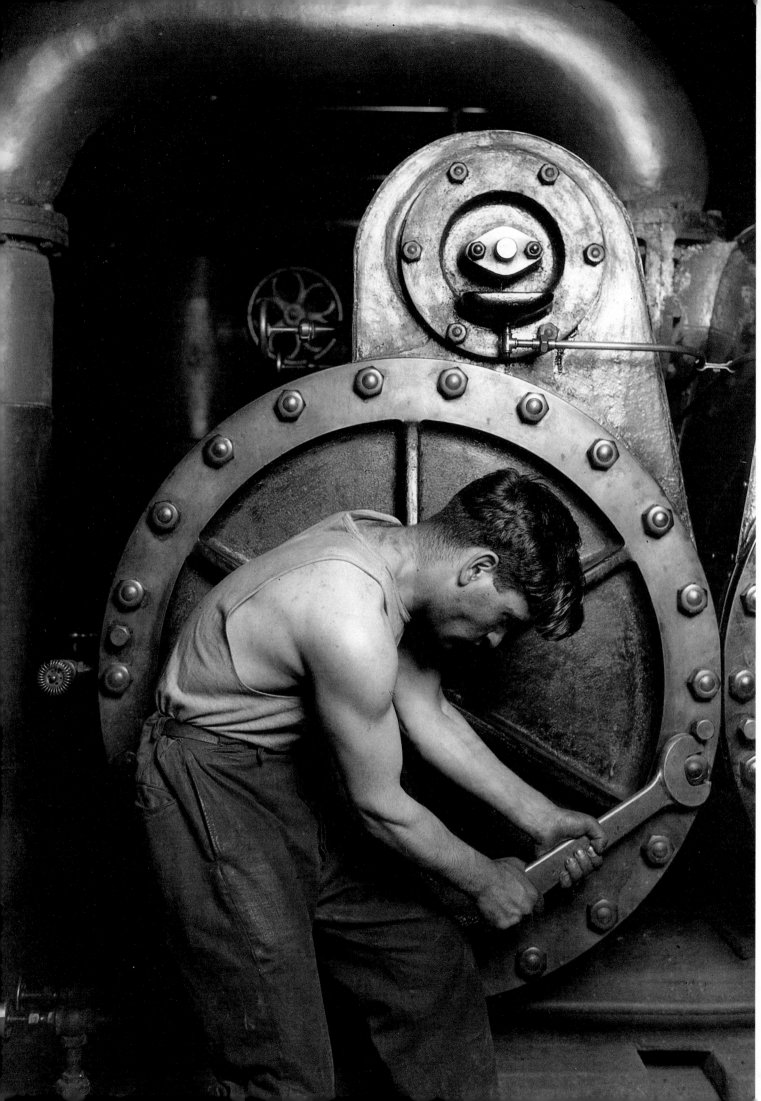

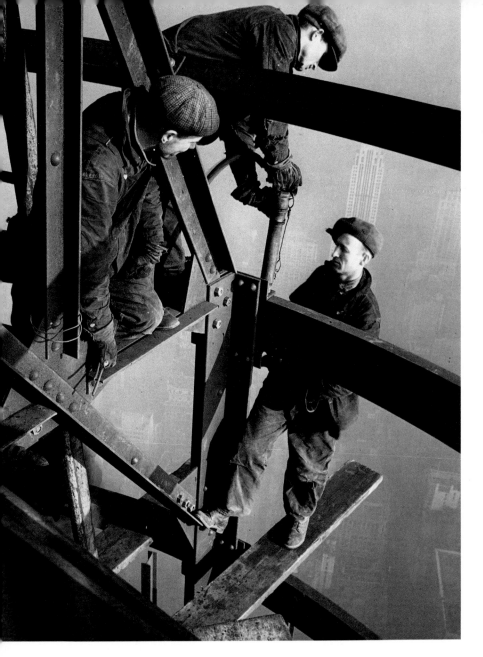

FACING PAGE:

480. LEWIS W. HINE. *Powerhouse Mechanic*, 1925. Gelatin silver print. Private collection.

481. LEWIS W. HINE. *Top of the Mooring Mast, Empire State Building*, 1931. Gelatin silver print. Private collection.

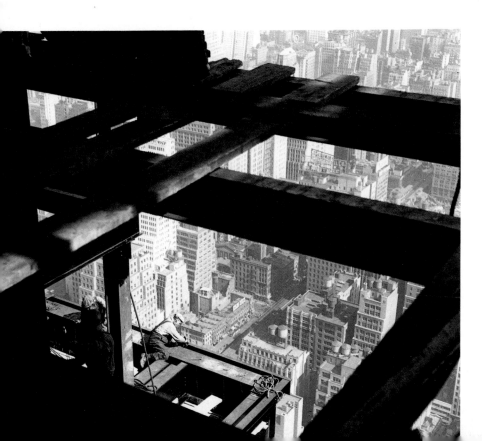

482. LEWIS W. HINE. *Construction, Empire State Building, New York City, 1930-31.* Gelatin silver print. Private collection.

9.

ART, PHOTOGRAPHY, AND MODERNISM

1920–1945

The new camera counts the stars and discovers a new planet sister to our earth, it peers down a drop of water and discovers microcosms. The camera searches out the texture of flower petals and moth wings as well as the surface of concrete. It has things to reveal about the curve of a girl's cheek and the internal structure of steel.

—Egmont Arens, 1939 [1]

IF ANY PERIOD can be said to have encompassed the full potential of photography it would have to be the era between the two World Wars. Some 80 years after the medium first appeared, photographers and their patrons discovered forms and uses for camera images that imbued them with exceptional inventiveness and immediacy. Photography was not only enriched by expanded roles in journalism, advertising, and publicity, but it was nourished also by acceptance within avant-garde movements in the graphic arts. In fact, it might with justice be claimed that except for holography all later directions were foretold during this period. The extraordinary vitality of the medium was apparent in many different localities—in England, France, Central Europe, the Soviet Union, Japan, and North America—yet photographs also retained distinctive national characteristics. This chapter will survey the range of experimentation and explore the relationship of the "new vision," as it is sometimes called, to other visual art of the time; Chapter 10 will be concerned with the flowering of the medium in journalism, advertising, and book publication.

A distinguishing feature of the photography of the 1920s was the emergence of a wide variety of techniques, styles, and approaches, all displaying unusual vigor. Responding to greater economic opportunities in the medium and involved in the intense intellectual, political, and cultural ferment that followed the first World War, many photographers became conscious of the effects of technology, urbanization, cinema, and graphic art on camera expression. In addition to the "isms" of prewar avant-garde art—especially Cubism—the aesthetic concepts associated with Constructivism, Dadaism, and Surrealism inspired a climate of experimentation, with photo-collage, montage, cameraless images, nonobjective forms, unusual angles, and extreme close-ups marking the photographic expression of the era. In common with other visual artists, photographers also took note of Freudian and related theories of the psyche and of the part that images might play in the social and political struggles of the times.

In Europe the new vision was nurtured by the complex artistic and social tendencies that emerged following the revolutionary uprisings at the end of the first World War. Embodied in Russian Constructivism, the German Bauhaus—a school of architecture and design—and the

Deutsches Werkbund (German Work Alliance), these movements and organizations viewed artistic expression as concerned with the analysis and rational reconstruction of industrial society rather than as a means of producing unique decorative objects based on personal feelings or experiences for an elite class. With art activity conceived as a way to improve the lives of ordinary people through the redesign of their physical and mental environments, the artist emerged as an individual who "remained true . . . to reality [in order] to reveal the true face of our time."[2] In the eyes of a significant number of artists, the various media were no longer regarded as discrete entities; the applied arts were considered as important as the "fine" arts of painting and sculpture; and respect for machine technology led to a high regard for both printing press and camera as the most effective visual instruments of the age.

Experimentation in Europe: Light Graphics

The developments that followed the end of the first World War had been heralded earlier in the breakdown of conventional modes of artistic expression. As the 1914–18 conflict raged in Europe, Dadaists urged that the moribund art of the past be jettisoned; that new themes and new forms be found to express the irrational nature of society. This attitude opened fertile fields for all kinds of visual experimentation, including the production of cameraless photographic images. It will be recalled that "photogenic drawing"—Talbot's name for prints made by exposing real objects placed directly on light-sensitive paper—actually had preceded photography through the use of a camera. In updating this concept, photographers of the new vision employed a variety of substances and light sources to create nonrepresentational images. The earliest examples were made in 1918 by Christian Schad, a German artist soon to become a leading exponent of the New Objectivity in painting, who exposed chance arrangements of found objects and waste materials—torn tickets, receipts, rags—on photographic film *(pl. no. 483)*; the results, baptized Schadographs by the Dada leader Tristan Tzara, expressed the Dadaist interest in making art from junk materials.

Independently, the American Man Ray (born Emmanuel Radenski), a close associate of Duchamp and Francis Picabia during their New York Dada period, undertook similar experiments that the photographer called Rayographs *(pl. no. 484)*, a designation incorporating both his name and a reference to their source in light. Made soon after Man Ray's arrival in Paris in 1921, these cameraless images were effected by arranging translucent and opaque materials on photographic paper, at times actually immersed in the developer during their exposure to moving or stationary light sources. Indifferent to conventional distinctions between "fine" and applied art, yet devoted to the expression of intuitive states of being and chance effects, Man Ray sought commercial as well as artistic outlets for his extensive visual output that, besides Rayographs, included straight photographs, paintings, collages, assemblages, and constructions.

Cameraless images also were called photograms *(pl. no. 485)*, the name given the technique worked out together by Lucia Moholy and Laszlo Moholy-Nagy. Originally from Czechoslovakia and Hungary respectively, but active after 1923 at the Bauhaus School in Germany, these two artists

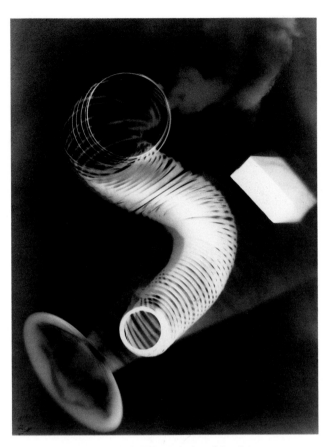

484. MAN RAY. *Untitled (Wire Spiral and Smoke)*, 1923. Gelatin silver print. Private Collection, New York, © Man Ray Estate/A.D.A.G.P.

held that, like other products produced by machine, photographic images—cameraless and other—should not deal with conventional sentiments or personal feelings, that they should be concerned with light and form. It is ironic that even though they promoted photography as the most fitting visual form for the machine age precisely because the camera image could be easily and exactly replicated, photograms are unique one-of-a-kind examples for which no matrix exists for duplication. Other Europeans who experimented with cameraless imagery—or light graphics as this aspect of photography came to be called—include Raoul Hausmann, Gyorgy Kepes, Kurt Schwitters, the Russians El Lissitzky and Alexander Rodchenko, the Czech artist Jaromir Funcke, and Curtis Moffat, English assistant to Man Ray. For reasons to be discussed presently, interest in this form of expression did not develop in the United States until after the Bauhaus relocated in Chicago in 1938 as the Institute of Design.

Collage and Montage

In Europe, an even more fertile field for experimentation involved collage and montage—techniques whose

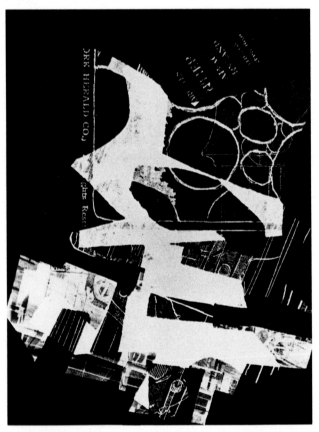

483. CHRISTIAN SCHAD. *Schadograph*, 1918. Gelatin silver print. Edward L. Bafford Photography Collection, Albin O. Kuhn Library and Gallery, University of Maryland, Baltimore. Courtesy Mrs. Christian Schad. © G. A. Richter Rottach-Egern.

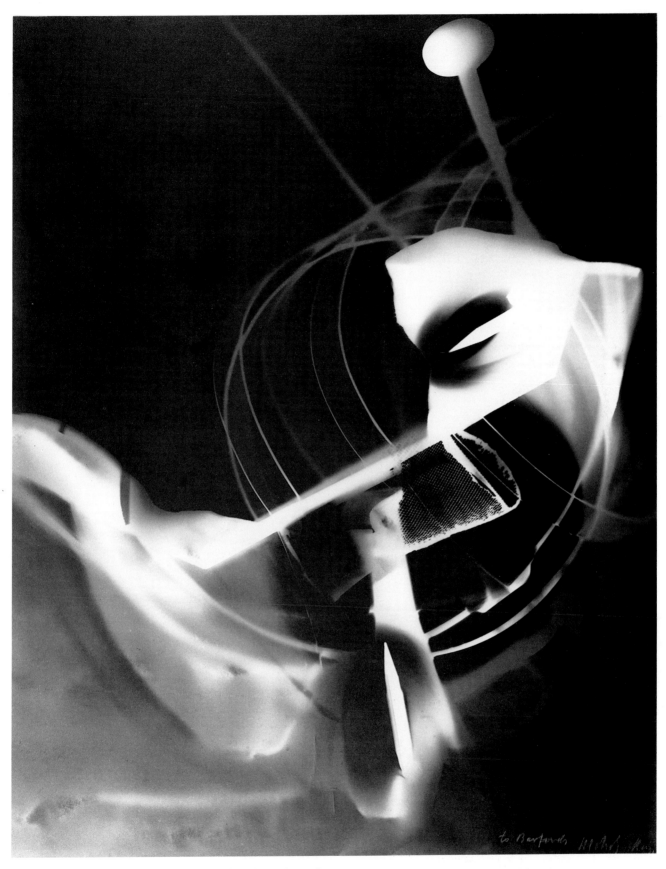

485. Laszlo Moholy-Nagy. *Photogram*, n.d. Gelatin silver print.
Art Institute of Chicago; gift of Mr. and Mrs. George Barford.

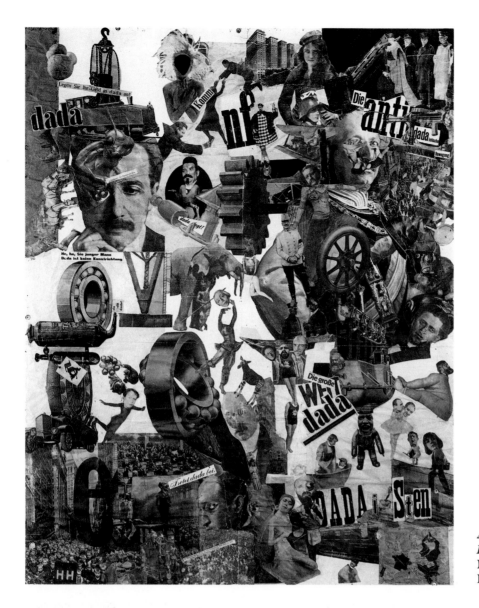

486. HANNAH HÖCH. *The Cut of the Kitchen Knife*, 1919. Montage. Nationalgalerie, Staatliche Museen Preussischer Kulturbesitz, Berlin.

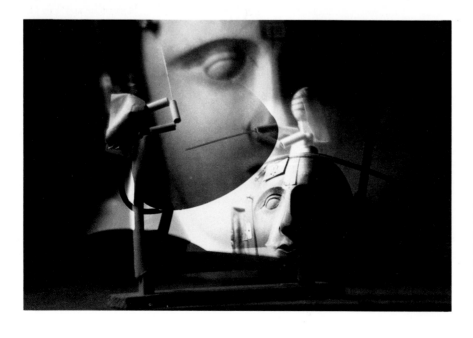

487. RAOUL HAUSMANN. *Mechanical Toys*, 1957. Gelatin silver print; double exposure of two photographs showing Hausmann's Dadaist sculpture "Mechanischer Kopf," 1919. Schirmer/Mosel, Munich.
© Association of the Friends of Raoul Hausmann, Limoges, Frances.

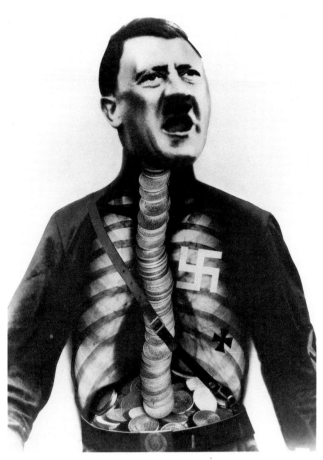

488. JOHN HEARTFIELD. *Adolph the Superman; He Eats Gold and Spews Idiocies*, 1932. Gelatin silver print. Courtesy Mrs. Gertrud Heartfield, Berlin.

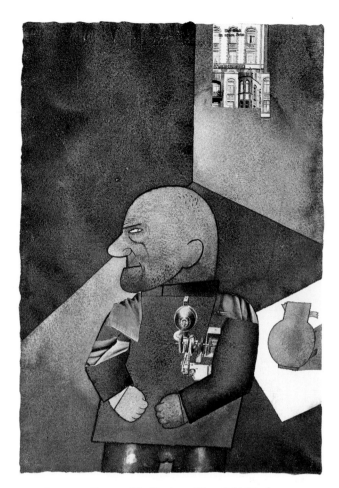

489. GEORGE GROSZ. *The Engineer Heartfield (Dada Monteur)*, 1920. Watercolor and collage of pasted postcard and halftone. Museum of Modern Art, New York; gift of A. Conger Goodyear.

terms sometimes are used interchangeably. The former (from the French *coller*, to glue) describes a recombination of already existing visual materials effected by pasting them together on a nonsensitized support and, if desired, re-photographing the result *(pl. no. 486)*. Montage refers to the combining of camera images on film or photographic paper in the darkroom *(pl. no. 487)*. The creation of a new visual entity from existing materials appealed to avant-garde artists in part because it was a technique employed by naive persons to create pictures—a folkcraft, so-to-speak—and in part because it used mass-produced images and therefore did not carry the aura of an elitist activity. These artists also felt that the juxtaposition of unlikely materials might serve to arouse feelings in the spectator that conventional photographic views no longer had the power to evoke. Besides, collage and montage promised to be extremely malleable—amenable to the expression of both political concerns and private dreams. Constructivists in the Soviet Union, who regarded the visual arts as a means

to serve revolutionary ideals, hailed collage and montage as a means to embody social and political messages in an unhackneyed way, while for artists involved with personal fantasies these techniques served to evoke witty, mysterious, or inexplicable dimensions. Still other individuals, inspired by the aesthetic elements of Cubism, used these techniques to control texture, form, and tonality to achieve nuanced formal effects.

Although a number of artists have claimed to be inventors of montage, as with cameraless photography it was an old idea whose time had come. Hausmann, painter, poet, and editor of a Dada journal, was one of its earliest partisans, realizing in the summer of 1918, as he later recalled, "that it is possible to create pictures out of cut-up photographs."[3] Needing a name for the process, he, along with artists George Grosz, Helmut Herzfelde (who later renamed himself John Heartfield), and Hannah Höch, selected photomontage as a term that implies an image "engineered" rather than "created." To these origi-

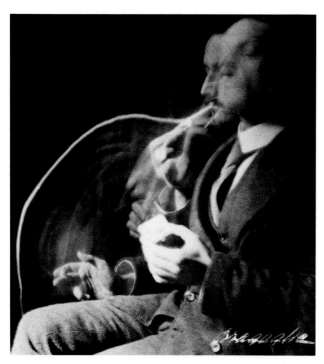

490. ANTON GIULIO and ARTURO BRAGAGLIA. *The Smoker*, 1913. Gelatin silver print. Weston Gallery, Inc., Carmel, Cal.

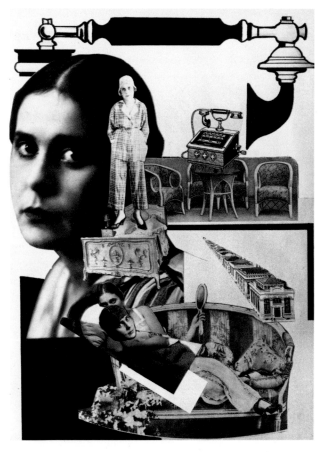

491. ALEXANDER RODCHENKO. *Montage*, c. 1923. Gelatin silver print. *Sovfoto Magazine* and VAAP, Moscow.

nators, montage seemed to reflect "the chaos of war and revolution,"[4] visible in Hausmann's preoccupation with savagery and irrationality or in Höch's expressions of disturbing private fantasies. A strong political component characterized the work of Heartfield *(pl. no. 488)*, who was initially a Dadaist and was pictured by his colleague Grosz as the quintessential photomontagist, or "*Dada Monteur*," of the era *(pl. no. 489)*.

Photographers in Italy found montage a versatile technique with which to express "spiritual dynamism," the term they used to describe their interest in urbanism, energy, and movement that had emerged in the wake of the Futurist Manifesto of 1908. Then, the brothers Anton Giulio and Arturo Bragaglia (among others) had incorporated the scientific experiments of Marey into what they called "Photodynamics," making multiple exposures on a single plate *(pl. no. 490)* to suggest a world in flux. After World War I, Italian modernists, among them Vincio Paladini and Wanda Wulz, continued in this vein, combining printed and pasted materials in two and three dimensions with multiple exposures.

Montage found favor in the Soviet Union during the 1920s as an instrument for revealing what was termed "documentary truth." Instead of relying on conventional time-consuming modes of graphic representation, Constructivists, notably Lissitzky and Rodchenko, sought to awaken working-class viewers to the meaning of contemporary socialist existence by utilizing photographs and text in visual messages *(pl. no. 491)*. Like their counterparts in Russian film (then considered the most advanced of the era), they were convinced that montage—which they called "deformation" of the photograph—and straight camera images taken from unusual angles or from extremely close to the subject might communicate new realities.[5]

Toward the end of the 1920s, true photographic montage, effected on light-sensitive materials rather than by cutting and pasting, became more commonplace and was sometimes combined with other darkroom manipulations such as solarization.[6] Owing to its flexibility, it could be structured to serve a variety of different stylistic and thematic ends—personal as well as political. To cite only a few examples, Anton Stankowski, working in Germany, explored an enigmatic psychological component in *Eye-Montage (pl. no. 492)* of 1927; Czech photographer Karel Teige embraced a similar theme in a 1937 cover for a surrealist journal *(pl. no. 493)*; and Man Ray's ironic wit is seen in the oft-reproduced *Violin d'Ingres (pl. no. 494)*. Socially oriented concerns were expressed by Alice Lex Nerlinger, one of a German husband and wife team, in *Seamstress (pl. no. 495)* of 1930. Incidentally, the themes of eye, hand, and work visible in several of these images engaged many photographers of the period whether they worked with

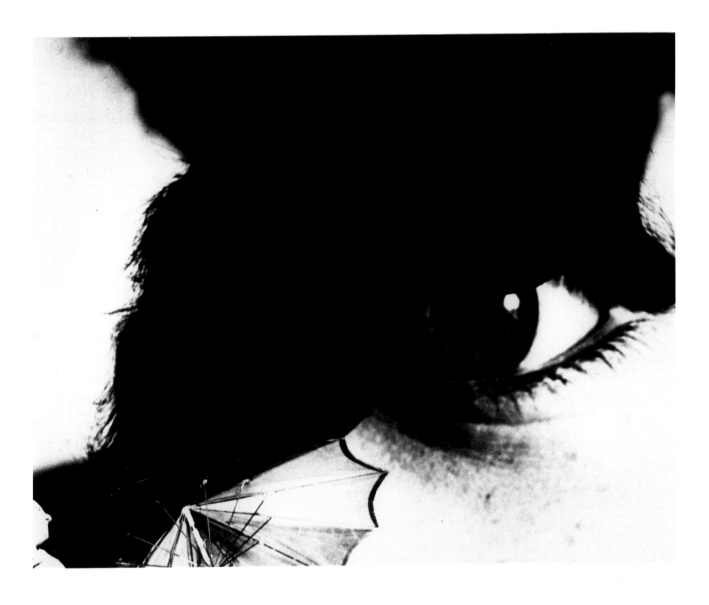

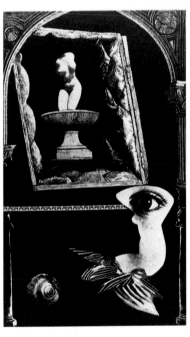

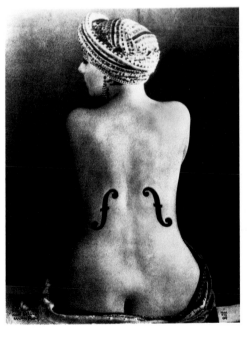

492. ANTON STANKOWSKI. *Eye-Montage*, 1927. Gelatin silver print. Prakapas Gallery, New York.

LEFT:

493. KAREL TEIGE. *Untitled*, 1937. Montage. Collection Jaroslav Andel, New York.

RIGHT:

494. MAN RAY. *Violin d'Ingres*, 1924. Gelatin silver print. Savage Collection, Princeton, N.J. © Man Ray Estate.

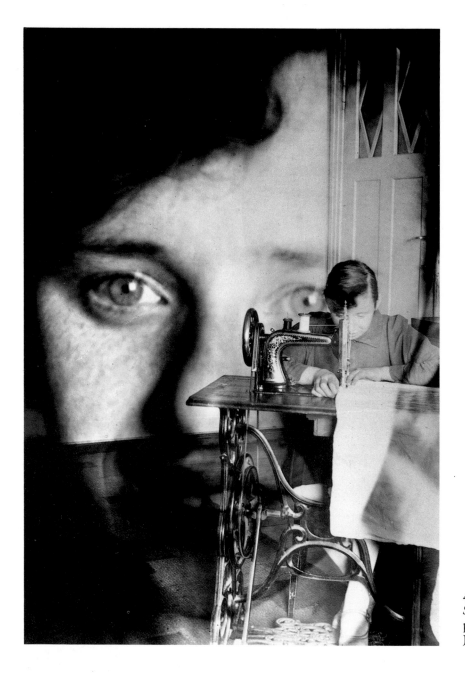

495. ALICE LEX NERLINGER.
Seamstress c. 1930. Gelatin silver
print. Art Institute of Chicago;
Julien Levy Collection.

montage or straight images. The eye obviously can be taken as a symbol for camera or photographer, while the combined emphasis on all of these elements suggest that camera work was seen as the result of both craft and vision, a concept embodied in the theories and programs of Constructivism, the Bauhaus, and the *Werkbund*.

The New Vision: Straight Photography in Europe

The new vision invigorated straight photography by presenting the known world in uncharacteristic ways. Even though polemical messages may have been more difficult to convey than in montage, photographers found that they could express social and psychological attitudes and explore aesthetic ideas through a variety of visual initiatives. These included making use of actual reflections, unusual angles, and close-ups. Inspiration for many of these experiments in seeing can be traced to the avant-garde cinema, which, in the opinion of at least one photographer of the time, saved still photography from itself.[7] Reflections, which in former times had aided photographers in composing interior scenes and landscapes, now offered them a means to explore the expressive possibilities of industrially produced refractive surfaces such as plate glass and polished metals. The overlay of natural forms and geometric patterns reflected in the shop windows of Atget's images *(pl. no. 319)* frequently evokes a dreamlike aura; in the hands of modernist photographers this stratagem served to confound one's sense of space or to introduce seemingly unrelated visual references. To select but a single example, in *Frau G. Kesting*, 1930, *(pl. no. 496)* German photographer Edmund Kesting structured an image resonant with restlessness and ambiguity from the reflections in the automobile windshield, the tense expression on his wife's face, and the tectonic elements of car and building.

Distorted reflections, effected by using special mirrors and lenses or by capturing objects refracted in spherical forms, provided a device that might serve to mimic the formal experiments of Cubist painters as well as to express disturbing personal or social realities. First seen in 1888, when Ducos du Hauron produced a series of experimental portraits *(pl. no. 497)*, the distorted image was reintroduced in the late 1920s by Hungarian photographer André Kertész

(pl. no. 498), whose interest had been aroused initially as he photographed the bodies of swimmers refracted in a pool. In 1933, using a special mirror, he produced a series of nudes similar in treatment to the deformations of the human body that engrossed Picasso at the time. The potential of this technique in social or personal comment was explored by Polish photographer Marian Dederko *(pl. no. 499)* whose work in the modernist vein is combined with old-fashioned gum printing techniques, while the distorted scene refracted in the polished headlamp of a car in *The Fierce-Eyed Building (pl. no. 500)*, by American neo-Romantic Clarence John Laughlin, seems to signify the photographer's view of modern urban life as inhumane.

Photographers especially influenced by Surrealism sought to express intuitive perceptions through found symbols as well as accidental reflections. In *Optic Parable (pl. no. 501)*, by Mexican photographer Manuel Alvarez Bravo, reflections in a shop window combine with the repetitive

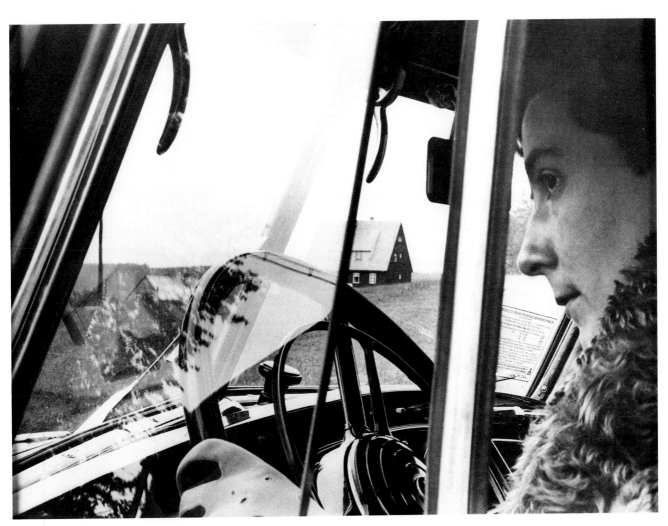

496. EDMUND KESTING. *Frau G. Kesting*, 1930. Gelatin silver print.
San Francisco Museum of Modern Art; purchase, Mrs. Ferdinand C. Smith Fund.

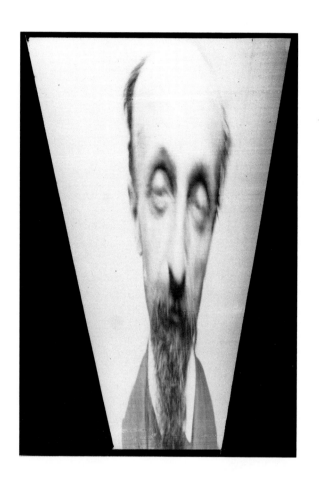

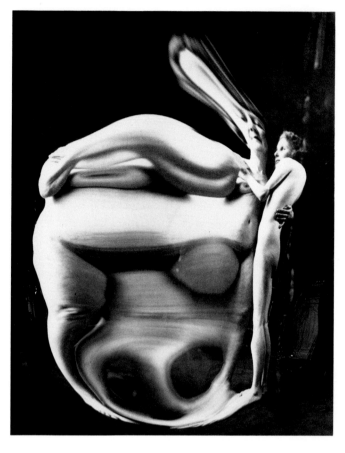

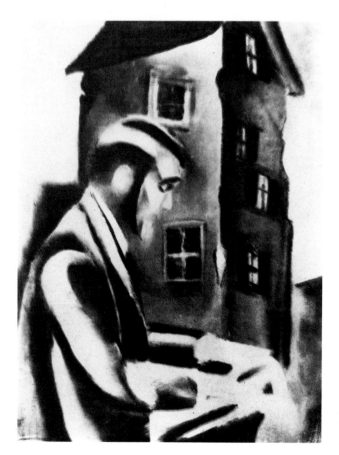

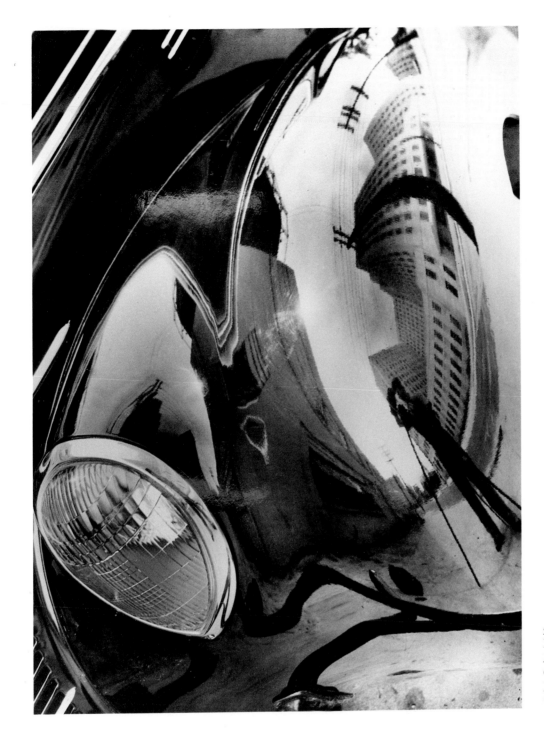

500. CLARENCE JOHN
LAUGHLIN. *The
Fierce-Eyed Building*, 1938.
Gelatin silver print. Robert
Miller Gallery, New York.
© Clarence John Laughlin.

forms of a naively painted eye-glass sign, seen in reverse as if to intimate an all-seeing but perverse presence. Bravo's style, formed during the 1930s cultural renaissance in his native land, suggests a complex amalgam of sophisticated theories of the unconscious, elements of indigenous folk culture, and commitment to the humanist ideals of the Mexican revolution.

The influence of the "isms" of art culture—Cubism, Constructivism, Surrealism, Precisionism—are visible in the work of virtually all photographers of the new vision,

but while most regarded these concepts as allowing them the freedom to fragment and restructure reality, some individuals actually included in their photographs the typical geometric furnishings of Constructivist and Cubist paintings. Cones, spheres, and overlapping transparent planes found their way into the work of European photographers Herbert Bayer and Walter Peterhans, both of the Bauhaus, as well as that of Funcke, Florence Henri, and the American Paul Outerbridge. Henri's studies at the Bauhaus and with painter Fernand Léger may account for her preference

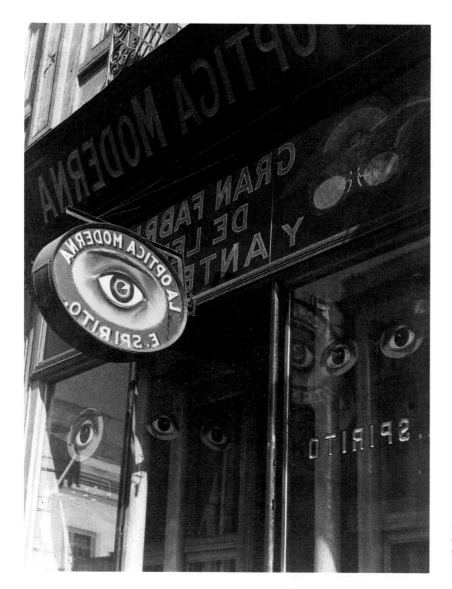

501. MANUEL ALVAREZ BRAVO. *Optic Parable*, 1931. Gelatin silver print. Museum of Modern Art, New York; gift of N. Carol Lipis. © Manuel Alvarez Bravo.

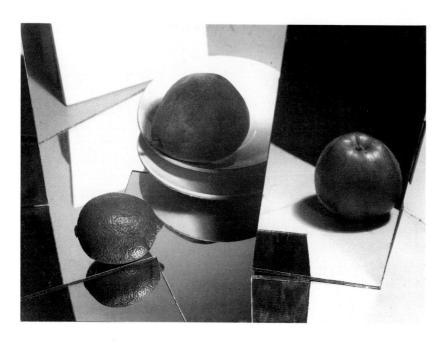

502. FLORENCE HENRI. *Abstract Composition*, 1929. Gelatin silver print. © Galerie Wilde, Cologne.

for the mirrors and spheres that appear again and again in her abstract compositions *(pl. no. 502)* and portraits; other Cubist photographers allowed themselves greater latitude in the artifacts they assembled for Cubist-like still lifes. In the same fashion, the emblems of Surrealism—endless vistas, melting clocks, and checkerboard patterns –appeared in photographs by Man Ray, the British theatrical portraitist Angus McBean, and the American theatrical and fashion photographer George Platt Lynes *(see Chapter 10)*.

Perhaps the most striking characteristic of the straight photography of this time is the predominance of unconventional vantage points. This development was forecast in the work done in the second decade of this century by American photographers Stieglitz, Coburn, Steichen, and Strand following their exposure to modern European art exhibited at 291, The Armory Show, and the Modern Gallery. Indeed, the downward view and the rigorous organization of all the tectonic elements in Stieglitz's 1907 image *The Steerage (pl. no. 402)* resulted in a complex formal structure that is said to have impelled Picasso later to remark that the two artists were working in the same avant-garde spirit. Fresh points of view, unhackneyed themes, geometry, and sharp definition were heralded by Coburn, who observed that photographers "need throw off the shackles of conventional expression."[8] His image *The Octopus (pl. no. 398)* of 1913 is a flattened arrangement

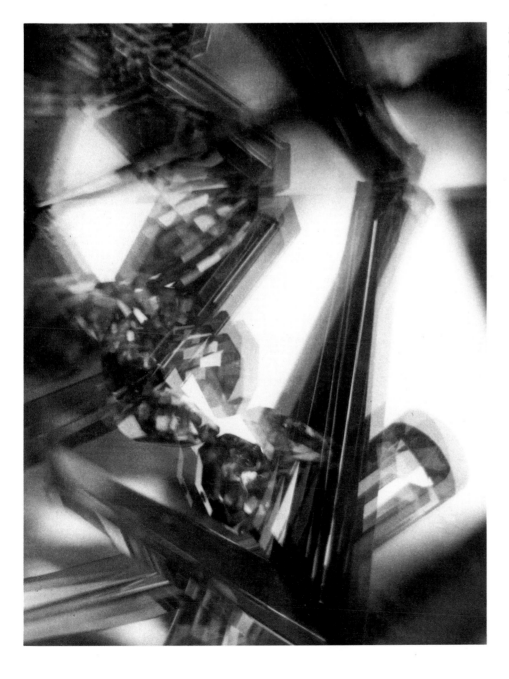

503. ALVIN LANGDON COBURN. *Vortograph No. 1*, 1917. Gelatin silver print. Museum of Modern Art, New York; gift of Alvin Langdon Coburn.

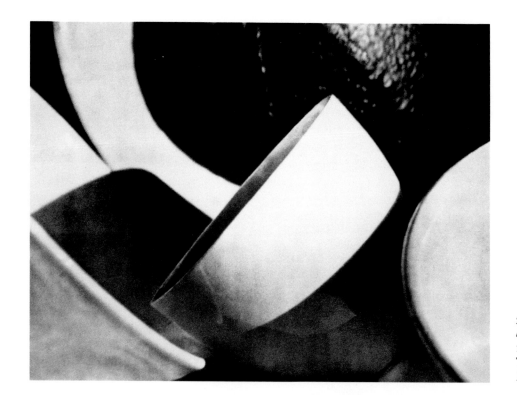

504. PAUL STRAND. *Orange and Bowls, Twin Lakes, Conn.*, 1915. Platinum print. © 1981 The Paul Strand Foundation, Millerton, N.Y.

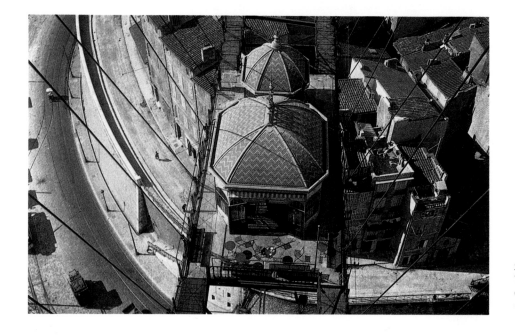

505. HERBERT BAYER. *Pont Transbordeur, over Marseilles*, 1928. Gelatin silver print. Courtesy and © Herbert Bayer.

of planes and arcs achieved by photographing downward from a position high over Madison Square Park in New York City. Three years later, Coburn's involvement in Vorticism, the English variant of Cubism, led him to photograph through a kaleidoscope-like device consisting of three mirrors; these completely abstract formations were dubbed Vortographs *(pl. no. 503)* by Wyndham Lewis, the British leader of the movement.

Around 1916, Strand created a series of near-abstractions using ordinary household objects. Exemplified by *Orange and Bowls (pl. no. 504)*, these images concentrated on form, movement, and tonality rather than on naturalistic depiction or atmospheric lighting. Although abstraction as such did not interest him for long, Strand's utilization of unconventional angles and his high regard for pictorial structure also can be seen in the downward views of New

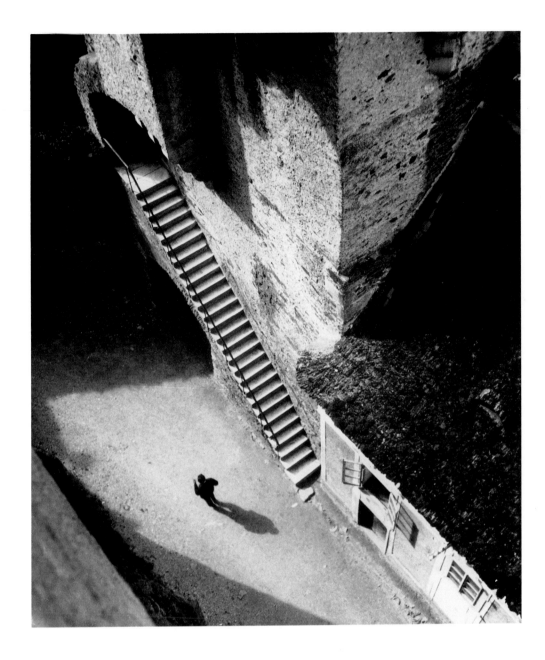

506. JAN LAUSCHMANN.
Castle Staircase, 1927.
Gelatin silver print.
© Jan Lauschmann.

York streets and the close-ups of anonymous street people and of machine and organic forms with which he was preoccupied until the end of the 1920s. No Americans besides Coburn and Strand went quite so far in experimenting with abstraction before the twenties, but some, including Stieglitz, Charles Sheeler, Morton L. Schamberg, Steichen, Karl Struss, and Paul Lewis Anderson showed themselves exceptionally sensitive to geometric elements as they appeared in reality and to formal structure in their images.

The fact that mundane scenes and ordinary objects could be revealed in a fresh light made the unconventional vantage point a favorite of those associated with Constructivism and the Bauhaus precisely because these groups were dedicated to viewing everyday society in new ways. *Pont Transbordeur (pl. no. 505)*, a view by Bayer from a bridge looking down on the streets of Marseilles, typifies the many images of the time in which the visual field is transformed into a relatively flat pattern—one that retains just enough suggestion of depth and texture to be ambiguous. Besides unusual camera angle, the absence of any reference to scale, seen in *Castle Staircase (pl. no. 506)* by Czech photographer Jan Lauschmann, can produce a work that is spatially baffling but visually authoritative. Lauschmann, a photochemist by profession, was one of the first in his country to conclude that photography should be an independent branch of art, and that straight printing was more relevant to modern concerns than the hand-manipulated gum printing techniques that lingered in Eastern Europe until the 1930s.

In another example of the downward view that is arrest-

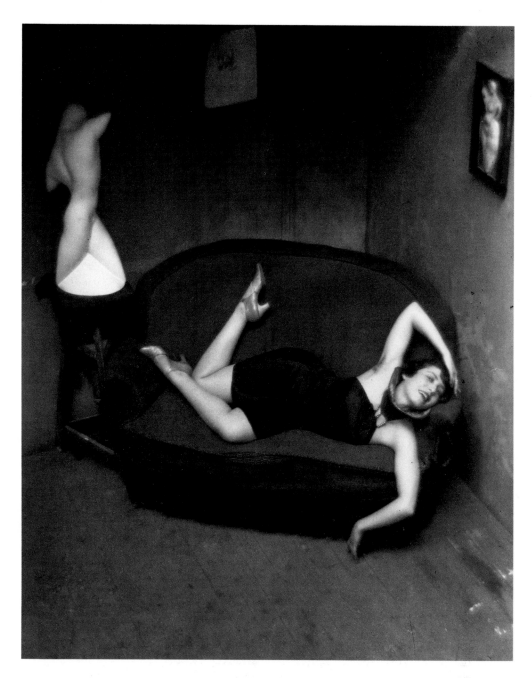

507. ANDRÉ KERTÉSZ.
Satiric Dancer, Paris, 1926.
Gelatin silver print.
Susan Harder Gallery,
New York. © André
Kertész.

ing from several positions—*Carrefour, Blois (pl. no. 508)* by Kertész—the puzzling configuration of lines and shapes of architectural elements seen from above serve as a foil for the animate forms, resulting in a refreshing vision of a scene that had been more commonly photographed from street level. Neither a Pictorialist nor yet an entirely objective photographer, Kertész supported himself as a freelance journalist soon after moving to Paris from his native Hungary in 1925; using the newly invented Leica camera *(see A Short Technical History, Part III)* he embraced the new vision as a means to extract lyrical moments from the ordinariness of daily existence. While he utilized virtually the entire vocabulary of modernism—reflections, close-ups,

and unusual vantage points—his images seem to project wit *(pl. no. 507)*, human compassion, and poetry rather than a concern with formal problems or didactic ideas.

The view from above made possible the ambiguous reading of shadow and substance visible in a work of 1929 entitled *Little Men, Long Shadows (pl. no. 509)* by Vilho Setälä, a skillful Finnish professional photographer whose visual interplay of figures and shadows suggests a typically urban experience of anonymity and mechanized existence. At times the relationship between shadow and substance in photographs taken from this viewpoint is so tenuous that the images can be viewed from any angle with equal comprehension. As a result of increased attention to camera

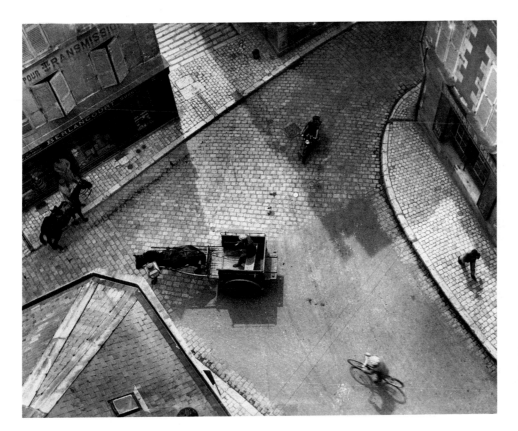

508. André Kertész. *Carrefour Blois*, 1930. Gelatin silver print. Susan Harder Gallery, New York. © André Kertész.

509. Vilho Setälä. *Little Men, Long Shadows*, 1929. Gelatin silver print. Photographic Museum of Finland, Helsinki.

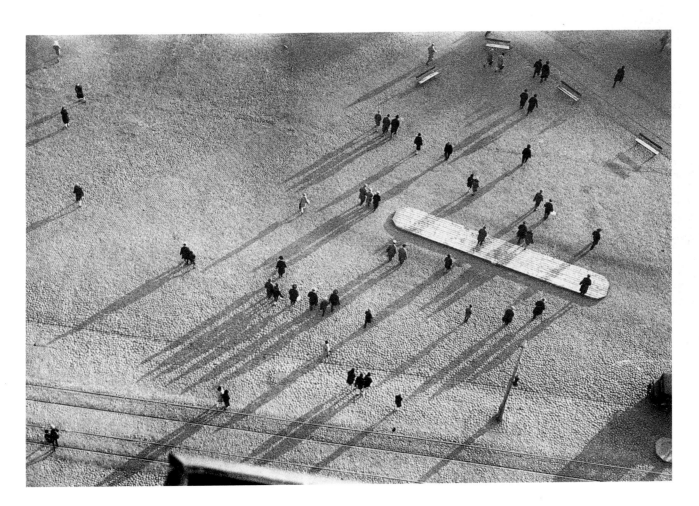

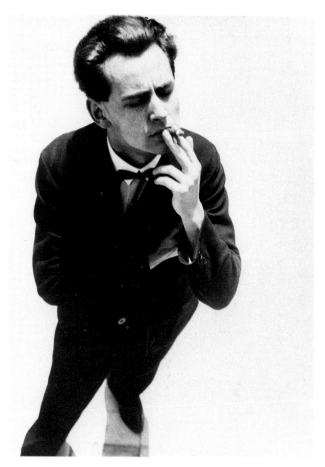

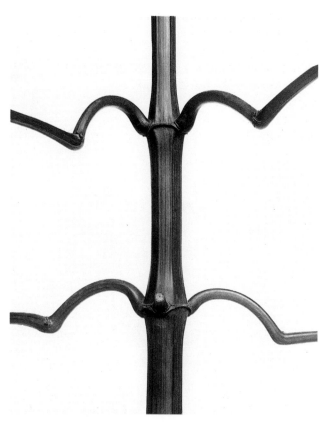

510. T. Lux Feininger. *Clemens Röseler*, c. 1920s.
Gelatin silver print. Prakapas Gallery, New York.

511. Karl Blossfeldt. *Impatiens Glandulifera,*
Balsamine, Springkraut, 1927. Gelatin silver print.
Galerie Wilde, Cologne.

angle, a portrait of Clemens Röseler *(pl. no. 510)* by T. Lux
Feininger, who was involved with the theater and dance
program at the Bauhaus, is imbued with tension and fresh
interest through the extreme foreshortening.

Another hallmark of the new vision is the close-up, a
view in which the lens acts like an enlarging device to call
attention to patterns, textures, and structures that might
ordinarily pass unnoticed. Reflecting in part the advances
in scientific photography during the 20th century, the
close-up was regarded as one means for "the objective
presentation of fact," which frees the viewer from the
confusion of individual representation.[9] This concentration on discrete objects also signified that to some photographers the camera seemed to be more suitable for
revealing specific appearances than for depicting complex
psychological or social relationships. The close-up recom-
mended itself strongly to German partisans of the New
Objectivity, among them professor of art Karl Blossfeldt
who sought through his images of plant forms to establish
a link between form in a natural world "governed by some
fixed and eternal force"[10] and in art *(pl. no. 511)*.

The New Objectivity's most renowned advocate, Albert
Renger-Patzsch, a professional photographer in Germany,
also sought to make his lens reveal analogies between natural formations and factory-produced objects, in order to
suggest the formal structures that are basic to plants,
bridges, factories and their products. Focusing his large-
format camera on intrinsic design elements and searching
out repetitive pattern, he eliminated atmosphere, chance
illuminations, and all personal subjective reactions to
achieve a transcendental level of pure decoration in images
such as *Sempervivum Percarneum*, 1922, *(pl. no. 512)*. At times
his work seemed to approach abstraction despite his expressed "aloofness to art for art's sake." A similar attentiveness to the clarity of line and form characterizes Werner
Mantz's views of German modern architecture of the 1920s
and '30s, while Hans Finsler, Swiss-born but influential as
a teacher and professional in Germany, used the camera to
make vivid the precise geometries of mass-produced machined objects *(pl. no. 513)*.

The camera close-up, especially as it served the ideals of
the New Objectivity, garnered international adherents

owing to the acclaim outside Germany for Blossfeldt's *Unformen der Kunst (Art Forms in Nature)*, published in 1928, and Renger-Patzsch's *Die Welt Ist Schön (The World Is Beautiful)*—the latter considered by the photographer "a model book of objects and things."[11] The style and its typical themes informed the work of many other Europeans, including French photographer Emmanuel Sougez and Dutch photographer Piet Zwart *(pl. no. 515)*, whose robust image of a cabbage can be compared with a similar image by Czech photographer Ladislav Berka *(pl. no. 514)*.

While the close-up opened a fresh way of viewing that most commonplace of subjects—the human face and form—it did not prevent the photographer from introducing personal feelings. Indeed, Rodchenko's *Portrait of My Mother (pl. no. 516)*, reveals the shape, texture, and forms of aging, and also expresses a tender though unsentimental compassion. Tonal contrast, outsize scale, and assymetrical placement in Lucia Moholy's *Portrait of Florence Henri (pl. no. 518)* is a striking example of the formalistic concerns of the photographer yet suggest the essence of the sitter's personality. *Eye of Lotte (pl. no. 517)*, by the influential

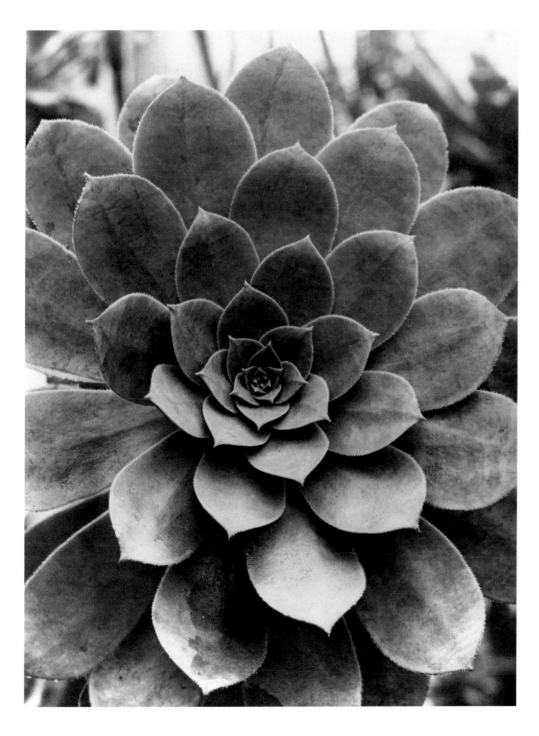

512. ALBERT RENGER-PATZSCH. *Sempervivum Percarneum*, c. 1922. Gelatin silver print. Folkwang Museum, Essen, Germany.

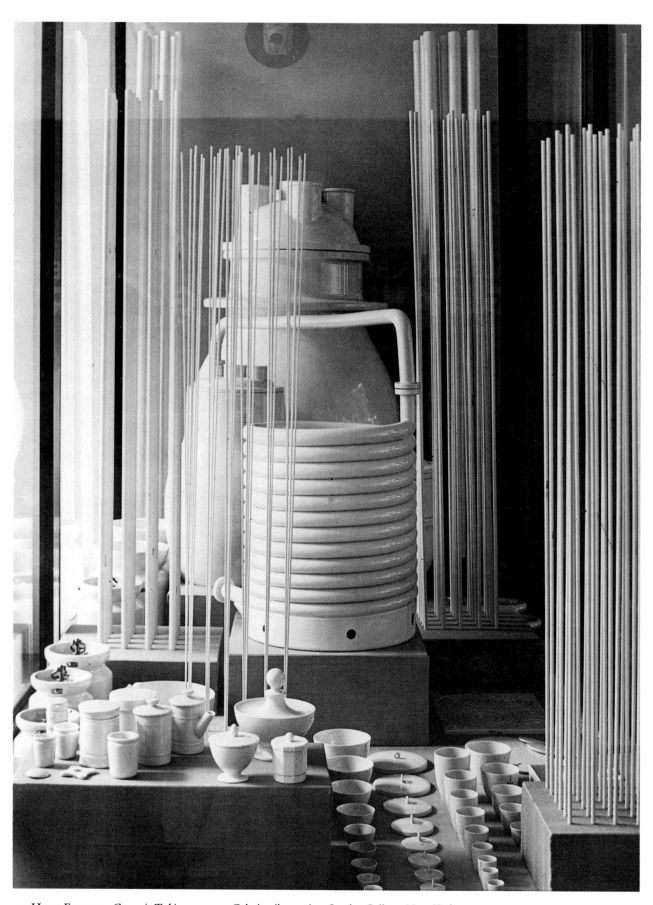

513. HANS FINSLER. *Ceramic Tubing*, c. 1930. Gelatin silver print. Sander Gallery, New York.

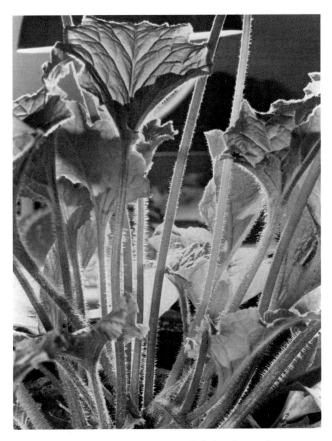

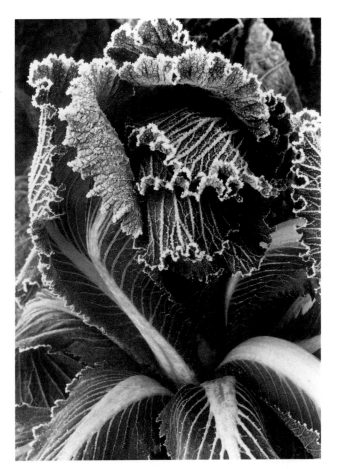

514. LADISLAV BERKA. *Leaves*, 1929. Gelatin silver print.
© Ladislav Berka.

515. PIET ZWART. *Cabbage*, 1930. Gelatin silver print.
Haags Gemeentemuseum, The Hague, Netherlands.

German teacher Max Burchartz, a work that undoubtedly was considered the "leit-motif for the modern photography movement,"[12] because it so fully embraces the stylistic devices of the era—the close-up, unusual framing, emphatic geometrical design—at the same time projects the innocence and freshness of youth. As seen in *Child's Hands (pl. no. 519)* by German photographer Aenne Biermann and the image of work-hardened hands *(pl. no. 520)* by Italian photographer Tina Modotti, the close-up view obviously can be imbued with either personal or social comment.

The New Vision in Japan

Japanese photographers were attracted to the new vision as a result of the curiosity about Western ideas in general that surfaced during the so-called "Taisho democracy" of the 1920s. Access to articles, exhibitions, and reproductions of camera images from Europe led to the expansion of photographic activity beyond the previously limited areas of portraiture and genre scenes and brought about an invigorating diversity of stylistic and thematic directions. While a late-blooming pictorialism continued to evoke a

"redundancy of misty scenes and blurry figures,"[13] many more photographers, who were engaged in documentation and portraiture (including that of the despised lower classes—see Chapter 8) or in exploring new approaches to still life and the nude, embraced the entire vocabulary of the "new photography," as it was called in Japan as well as in the West. Urged to "recognize the mechanistic nature of the medium,"[14] photographers began to use sharper lenses and to experiment with close-ups, montage, and solarization, producing during the 1930s works clearly influenced by Surrealism *(pl. no. 521)* and the New Objectivity. Images such as *Hosokawa Chikako (pl. no. 522)*, a portrait by Kozo Nojima reminiscent of the Burchartz image mentioned earlier, or the emphatically geometric *Ochanomizu Station, 1933, (pl. no. 523)*, by Yoshio Watanabe, were instrumental in bringing Japanese photography into the modern era.

The New Vision in the United States: Precisionism

Within limits, the new vision attracted all significant photographers in the United States in the 1920s, many of

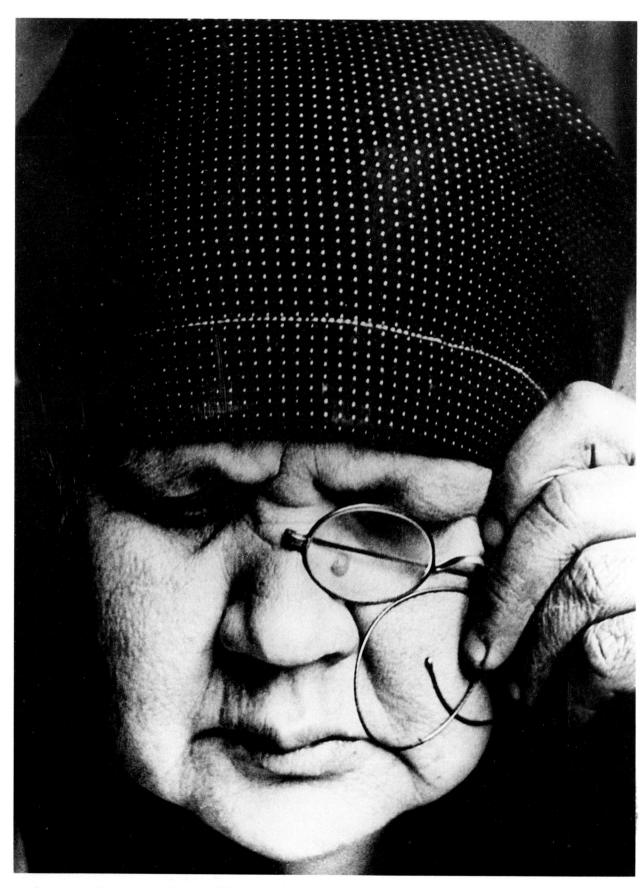

516. ALEXANDER RODCHENKO. *Portrait of My Mother*, 1924.
Gelatin silver print. Collection Alexander Lavrientiev, Moscow.

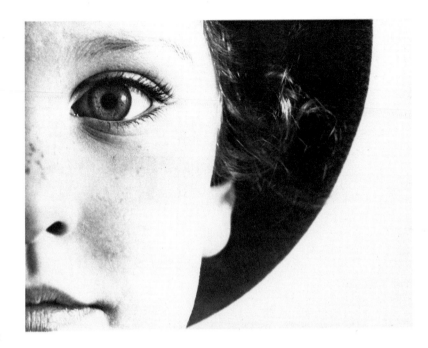

517. MAX BURCHARTZ. *Eye of Lotte*, c. 1928. Gelatin silver print. Folkwang Museum, Essen, Germany.

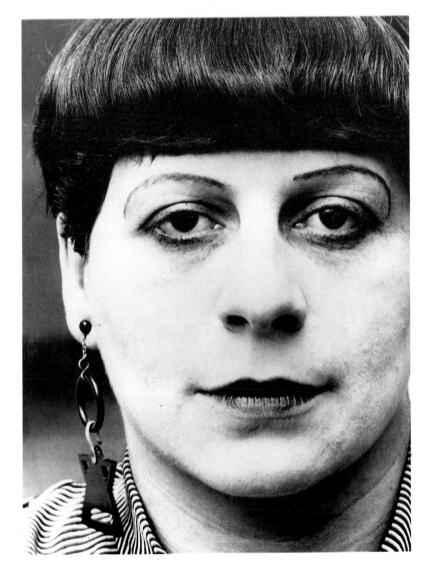

518. LUCIA MOHOLY. *Portrait of Florence Henri*, 1926–27. Gelatin silver print. Art Institute of Chicago; Julien Levy Collection.

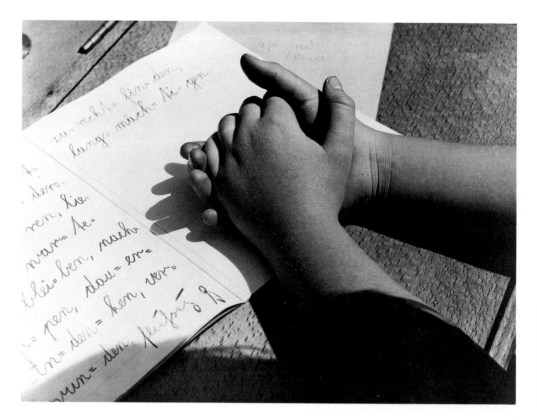

519. AENNE BIERMANN. *Child's Hands*, 1929. Gelatin silver print. Kunstbibliothek, Staatliche Museen Preussischer Kulturbesitz, Berlin.

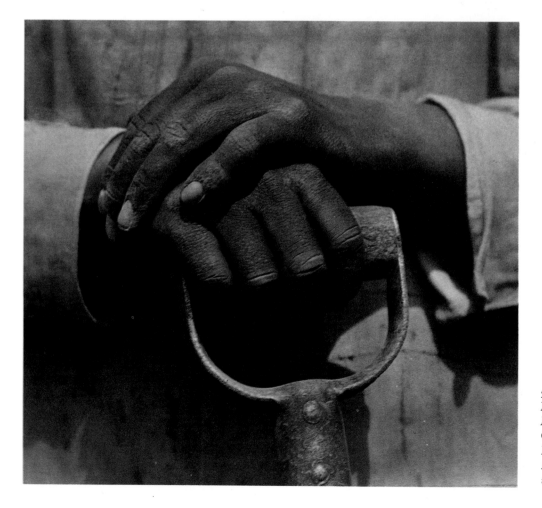

520. TINA MODOTTI. *Number 21 (Hands Resting on a Tool)*, n.d. Gelatin silver print. Museum of Modern Art, New York; anonymous gift.

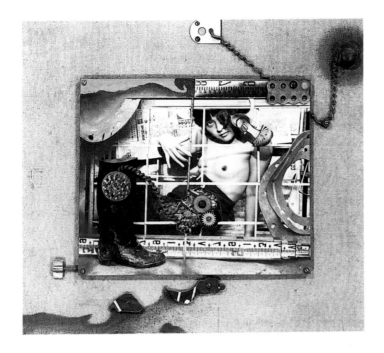

521. GINGO HANAWA. *Concept of the Machinery of the Creator*, 1931. Photocollage. Kurita-Bando Literary Agency, Tokyo.

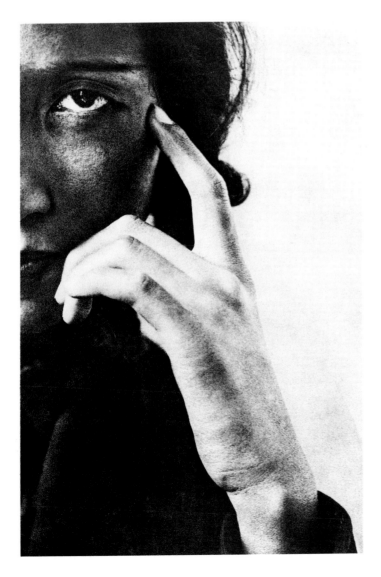

522. KOZO NOJIMA. *Hosokawa Chikako*, 1932. Gelatin silver print. Kurita-Bando Literary Agency, Tokyo.

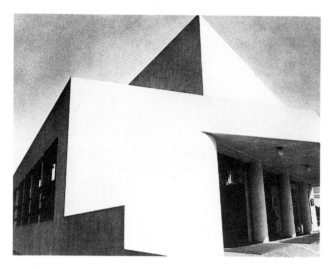

523. YOSHIO WATANABE. *Ochanomizu Station*, 1933.
Gelatin silver print. Kurita-Bando Literary Agency,
Tokyo.

whom accepted the idea that "absolute unqualified objectivity" constituted the unique property of the camera image.[15] Whether depicting nature, person, artifact, machinery, or architecture, American photographers emphasized the material properties of the real world even as they sought to embrace modern aesthetic ideas, an attitude they shared with the Precisionist painters of the period.

Of the older generation, neither Steichen nor Stieglitz, with their roots in Pictorialism, adhered strictly to the vocabulary of the New Objectivity, though both incorporated elements of the style with brilliant results. Steichen's preference for sharper definition and his interest in compositional theory in the postwar years is owed in part to his experiences in an aerial photography unit during the first World War. In 1922, a unique opportunity to become chief photographer for Condé Nast publications enabled him to fuse his extensive experience and intuitive decorative flair in a practical enterprise to be discussed in Chapter 10. As for Stieglitz, his consistent belief in the primacy of subjective feeling underlay the stylistic devices he chose to incorporate into his imagery, as the close-ups of O'Keeffe, the abstraction of the Equivalents, and the assertive geometry of the late New York scenes all affirm.

As the first World War was ending, Strand (whose role was discussed earlier) and Precisionist painter–photographers Schamberg and Sheeler emerged as the flag-bearers of the new approach. Schamberg, probably the first American to incorporate abstract machine forms in painting, used the camera for portraiture and to create complex Cubist-like juxtapositions of geometric shapes in the few urban landscapes *(pl. no. 524)* he made before his untimely death in 1918. In early images of rural architecture, Sheeler,

who began in 1912 to sustain his painting activity with commercial architectural photography, sought out the clarity of simple geometric relationships. He collaborated in 1920 with Strand on *Manhatta*, a short expressive film about New York City based on portions of Whitman's *Leaves of Grass*, and, following a stint in advertising and publicity photography, landed a coveted commission in 1927 to photograph the nation's largest automotive plant— the Ford Motor Works at River Rouge. Though Sheeler often exhibited paintings and photographs together and his work was included in the prestigious German *Film Und Foto* (Fifo) exhibition in 1929 *(see below)*, a growing ambivalence about the creative nature of photography eventually caused him to regard the camera as a tool for making studies, as in the untitled arrangement of stacks and funnels *(pl. no. 525)* that he transformed into the lucid oil *Upper Deck (pl. no. 526)*.

The Clarence White School of Photography proved to be a fountainhead of modernist ideas despite the Pictorialist outlook of its director, perhaps because in pursuing its goal of training photographers for jobs in advertising and publicity it needed to stress modern design. The successful transformation of the vocabulary of the new vision into a style of both personal expressiveness and commercial util-

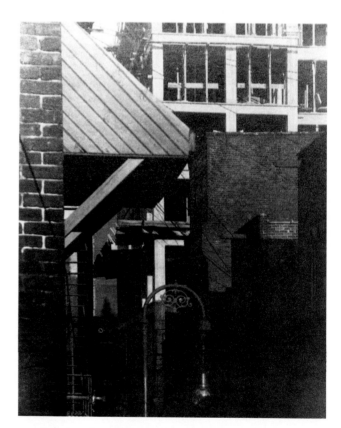

524. MORTON SCHAMBERG. *Cityscape*, 1916. Gelatin
silver print. New Orleans Museum of Art, New Orleans.

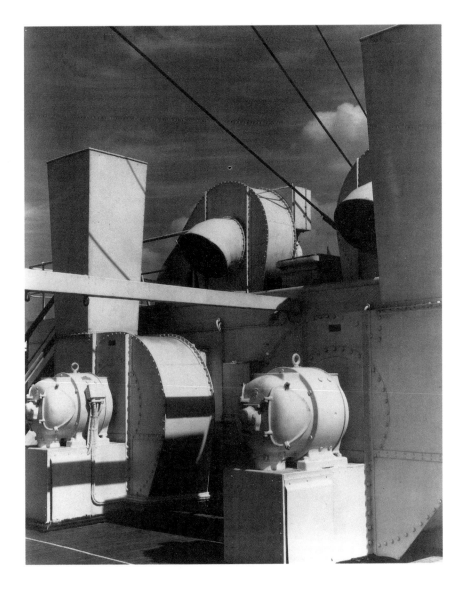

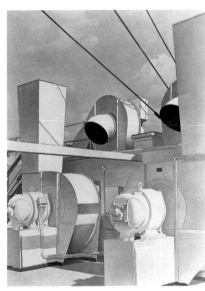

525. CHARLES SHEELER. *Untitled*, c. 1928. Gelatin silver print. Gilman Paper Company, New York.

526. CHARLES SHEELER. *Upper Deck*, 1929. Oil on canvas. Fogg Art Museum, Harvard University, Cambridge, Mass.; Louise E. Bettens Fund.

ity is visible in the work of a number of illustrious students, notably Ralph Steiner, Outerbridge, Gilpin, Bruehl, and Bourke-White (the latter two will be discussed in Chapter 10). At the outset of Steiner's long career in professional photography and documentary film, he produced *Typewriter Keys*, 1921, *(pl. no. 580)*, a close-up that in its angled view and insistent pattern predates the appearance of this approach in Europe. This image—later used in an advertising campaign for a paper company—was a harbinger of the facility with which Steiner handled the modernist idiom in both commercial and personal work. Outerbridge's restrained treatment of city architecture and machined objects is exemplified in *Marmon Crankshaft (pl. no. 527)*, a work inspired by the series of machine images made by Strand in 1921. After a brief period in attendance at the White School, Gilpin returned to her native Southwest to open a commercial portrait studio, but her handling of local architectural and landscape themes during

the 1920s reveals an interest in abstract geometrical pattern visible in the stark design of *Church of San Lorenzo, Picuris (pl. no. 529)*.

That the aesthetics of the new vision also informed the early work of photographers who eventually chose other paths can be seen in the work of Berenice Abbott and Walker Evans, both of whom were in Europe during the cultural ferment of the 1920s *(see Abbott's portrait of James Joyce, pl. no. 528)*. The high vantage point and spatial ambiguity visible in Abbott's view from the elevated tracks above Lincoln Square *(pl. no. 530)* is reminiscent of the handling of such views by European Bauhaus followers, but the image itself suggests the staccato flavor of New York. Similarly, Evans, whose brief sojourn in Europe occurred before his commitment to photography revealed itself, imbues the decided geometric pattern of *Wall and Windows (pl. no. 531)* with emphatic tonal contrast that brings to mind the rude energy of the American urban scene.

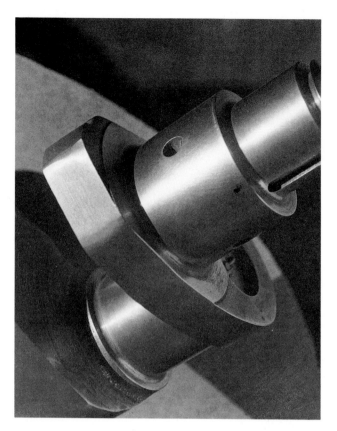

527. PAUL OUTERBRIDGE. *Marmon Crankshaft*, 1923.
Platinum print. Art Institute of Chicago, Chicago; Julien
Levy Collection. © G. Ray Hawkins Gallery, Los Angeles.

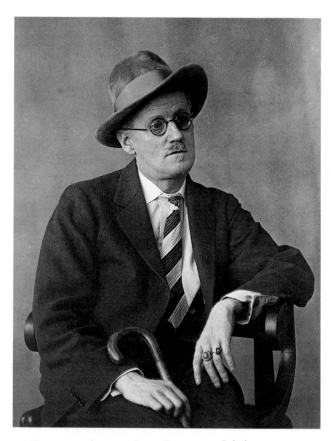

528. BERENICE ABBOTT. *James Joyce*, 1928. Gelatin
silver print. Museum of Modern Art, New York;
Stephen R. Currier Memorial Fund.
© Berenice Abbott.

Precisionist Photographers: The West Coast

The Americanization of the "New Objectivity" reached its height in the work of West Coast photographers. Through personal contact, as well as articles and reproductions in European and American periodicals, Johan Hagemeyer, Edward Weston *(see Profile)*, Margarethe Mather, Imogen Cunningham, and Ansel Adams became aware of the new photographic vision. Hagemeyer, a former horticulturist and close friend of Weston, was the first to bring the anti-Pictorialist message back from the East in 1916, but despite his newfound preference for contemporary themes and high vantage points *(pl. no. 532)*, a dreamy romanticism continued to pervade his imagery. Weston's attempts to slough off the soft-focus style that had gained him national renown were more successful; in a 1922 image of the American Rolling Mill (Armco) works *(pl. no. 584)* made in the course of a trip east, he handled the industrial theme with sharp definition and singular sensitivity to the dramatic character of stacks and conveyors. Weston described the object-oriented images on which he concen-

trated in the late 1920s as revealing "the very substance and quintessence of the thing itself";[16] at times such intense concentration on form virtually transmuted the object into an abstraction, as in *Eroded Plank from Barley Sifter*, 1931, *(pl. no. 533)*.

Mather, until 1922 Weston's associate in his California studio, transformed the misty orientalism of her early work into a style marked by sharply defined close-ups and emphasis on pattern *(pl. no. 534)* while still retaining the Eastern spirit. After Cunningham established contact with Weston and European examples of the new vision in the 1920s, her earlier penchant for fuzzy allegorical figures cavorting on wooded slopes was replaced by an interest in close-ups of plant forms *(pl. no. 535)* and other organisms, while her clean stark views of industrial structures *(pl. no. 583)* may be considered, along with Weston's, paradigms of the Precisionist style. Beginning around 1927, Brett Weston, following in his father's footsteps, also showed himself intensely concerned with form and texture in images of nature.

A deep respect for the grandeur of the landscape of the American West combined with the active promotion of the straight photograph brought world-renown to Ansel

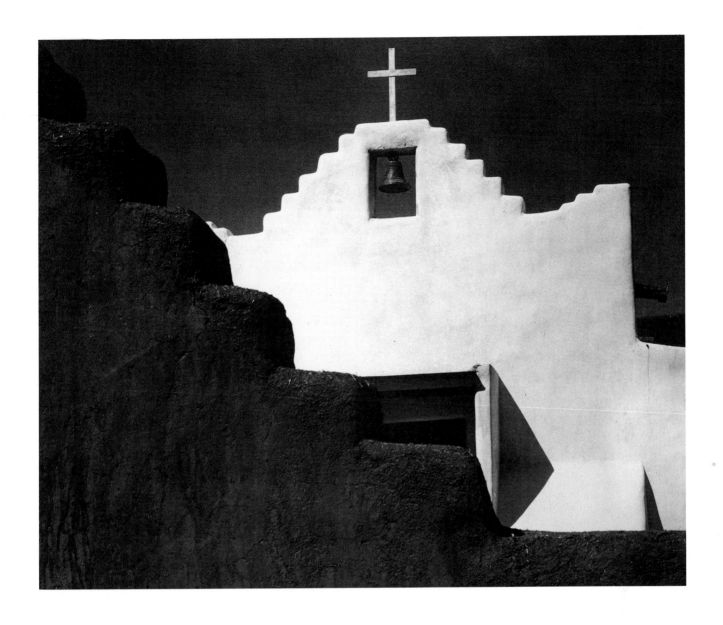

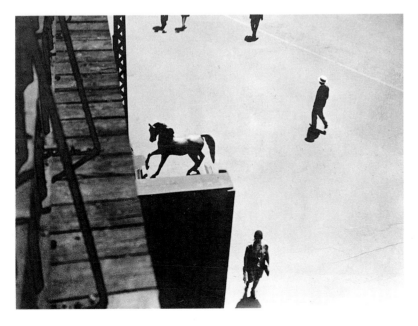

529. LAURA GILPIN. *Church of San Lorenzo Picuris, New Mexico*, 1963. Gelatin silver print. Collection Centre Canadien d'Architecture/Canadian Center for Architecture, Montréal. © 1981 Laura Gilpin Collection, Amon Carter Museum, Fort Worth, Texas.

530. BERENICE ABBOTT. *El at Columbus and Broadway, New York*, 1929. Gelatin silver print. Art Institute of Chicago. © Berenice Abbott.

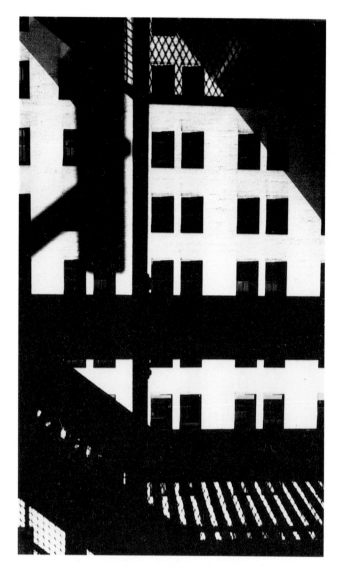

531. WALKER EVANS. *Wall and Windows*, c. 1929.
Gelatin silver print. Art Institute of Chicago.
© Walker Evans Estate.

Adams. Involved with the medium throughout the 1920s, though not completely convinced of its transcendental possibilities until about 1930, Adams's approach to his chosen theme—large-scale nature in all its pristine purity—is similar in its emphasis on form and texture to that of other Precisionist photographers, with the exception that it also embodies a technique for scientifically controlling exposure, developing, and printing. His special gifts are visible in the incisive translation of scale, detail, and texture into an organic design seen in the early *Frozen Lake and Cliffs, Sierra Nevada (pl. no. 536)*, a work that set the standard for his accomplishments in photographing the wilderness landscape for over 50 years *(see also pl. nos. 537 and 538)*.

In 1930, the "*f/64*" group, informally established in San Francisco, promoted Precisionism through its advocacy of the large-format view camera, small lens aperture (hence the name), and printing by contact rather than enlarging. Besides Adams, Cunningham, and Weston, members included Consuelo Kanaga and Willard Van Dyke—the latter a guiding light in the group's activities who went on to renown as a documentary filmmaker. Ironically, *f/64*'s optimistic celebration of technology, exemplified in the crisp forms of Van Dyke's *Funnels*, 1932, *(pl. no. 581)*, was about to be supplanted by a different sensibility as the onset of the Great Depression altered perceptions about the wonders of industrialism.

Photography and Industrialism

Between the Armistice of 1918 and the Depression of the 1930s, the remarkable expansion of industrial capacity throughout the world commanded the attention of forward-looking photographers everywhere. The widespread belief in progress through technology held by followers of the Bauhaus, by Soviet Constructivists, and by American industrialists provided inspiration and, in conjunction with the emergence of pictorial advertising, made possible unprecedented opportunities to photograph industrial sub-

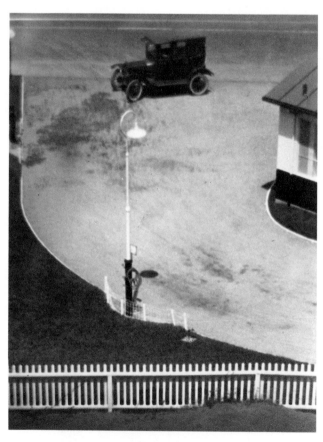

532. JOHAN HAGEMEYER. *Modern American Lyric
(Gasoline Station)*, 1924. Gelatin silver print. Art Institute
of Chicago.

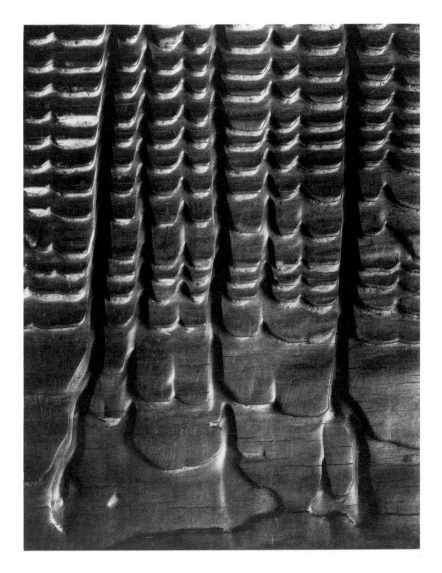

533. EDWARD WESTON. *Eroded Plank from Barley Sifter*, 1931. Gelatin silver print. © 1981 Arizona Board of Regents, Center for Creative Photography, University of Arizona, Tucson.

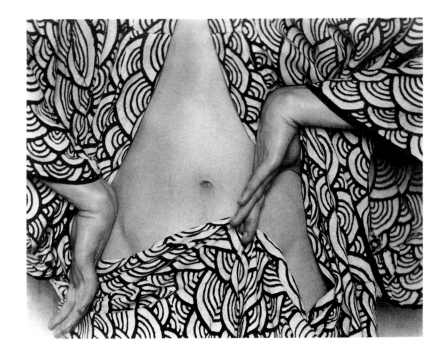

534. MARGARETHE MATHER. *Billy Justema in Man's Summer Kimono*, c. 1923. Gelatin silver print. Center for Creative Photography, University of Arizona, Tucson; Courtesy William Justema.

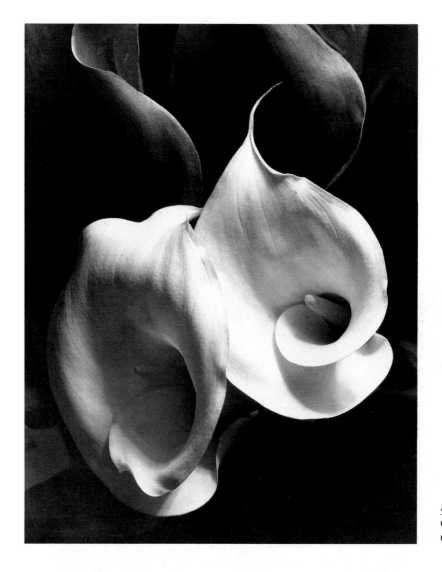

535. IMOGEN CUNNINGHAM. *Two Callas*, 1929. Gelatin silver print. © 1970 Imogen Cunningham Trust, Berkeley, Cal.

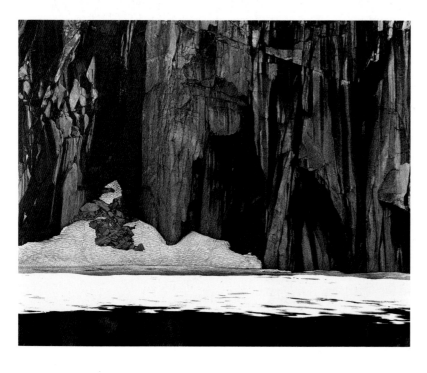

536. ANSEL ADAMS. *Frozen Lake and Cliffs, Sierra Nevada*, 1932. Gelatin silver print. Courtesy and © Ansel Adams.

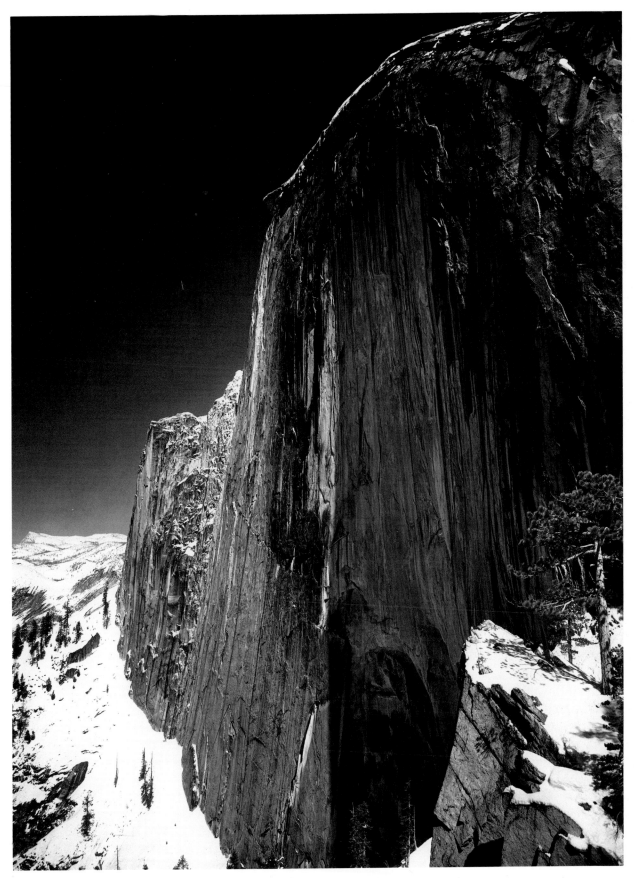

537. ANSEL ADAMS. *Monolith, The Face of Half Dome, Yosemite Valley, California*, c. 1927.
Gelatin silver print. Courtesy and © Ansel Adams.

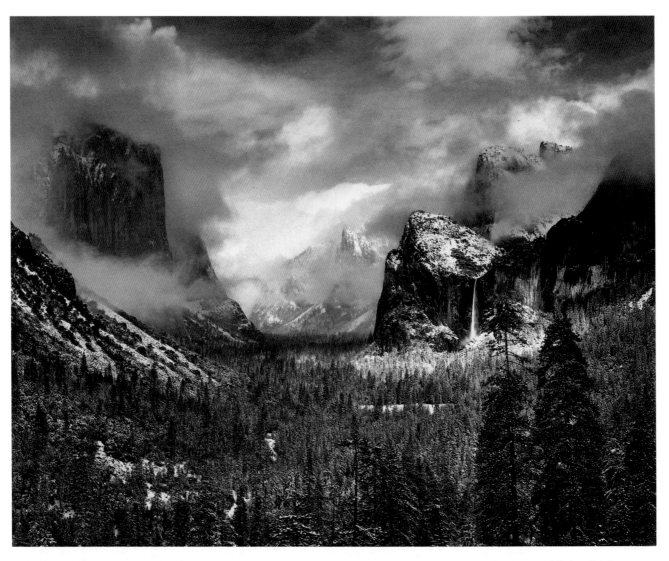

538. ANSEL ADAMS. *Clearing Winter Storm, Yosemite Valley, Caifornia*, c. 1944. Gelatin silver print. Courtesy and © Ansel Adams.

jects and sites. As might be expected, Europeans often treated these themes more experimentally than Americans. For example, Hans Finsler's *Bridge at Halle (pl. no. 539)* and the American Sherril V. Schell's *Brooklyn Bridge (pl. no. 540)* are each concerned with geometric design, but the vertiginous angle of the former is at once disorienting and stimulating in contrast to Schell's spatially more comprehensible and starkly decorative treatment. Many Europeans, among them Ilse Bing, Germaine Krull, and Eli Lotar, emphasized abstract qualities and formal relationships *(pl. no. 541)* without suggesting the utilitarian component of their industrial subject matter. In another example, the acute upward angle chosen by Russian photographer Boris Ignatowich *(pl. no. 542)* expresses the force and energy embodied in these structural beams but tells little about the size, shape, or usefulness of the objects pictured.

Not so in the United States, where machine images

achieved a balance between expressive and descriptive elements in part because they were commissioned by industrial firms for advertising and public relations. However, even the photographs of machine tools, products, and mills made by Strand *(pl. no. 578)*, Outerbridge, and Weston in the early 1920s idealize technology and suggest that it can be tamed and controlled. The emphasis on line and volume in Sheeler's treatment of the blast furnace and conveyors at the Ford River Rouge plant *(pl. no. 585)* were rightly assumed to express an "industrial mythos," a faith in industrial production as the sensible new American religion.[17] This view was shared initially by Bourke-White, whose expressive handling of modernist vocabulary can be seen in a forceful 1929 image of a bridge structure in Cleveland *(pl. no. 543)* taken before a commission for a large steel company launched her on an illustrious career as one of America's leading industrial photographers *(see also pl.*

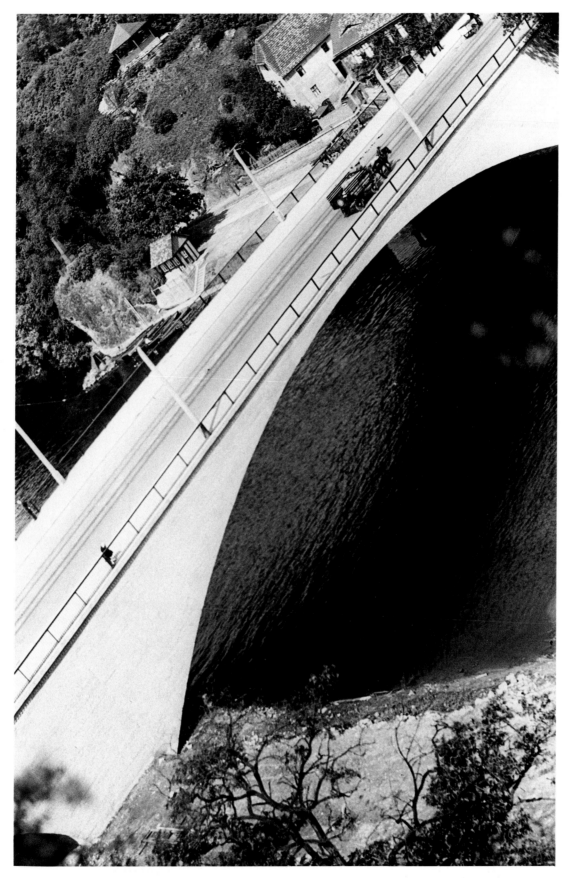

539. HANS FINSLER. *Bridge at Halle*, c. 1929. Gelatin silver print.
Kunstgewerbemuseum der Stadt, Zurich, Switzerland.

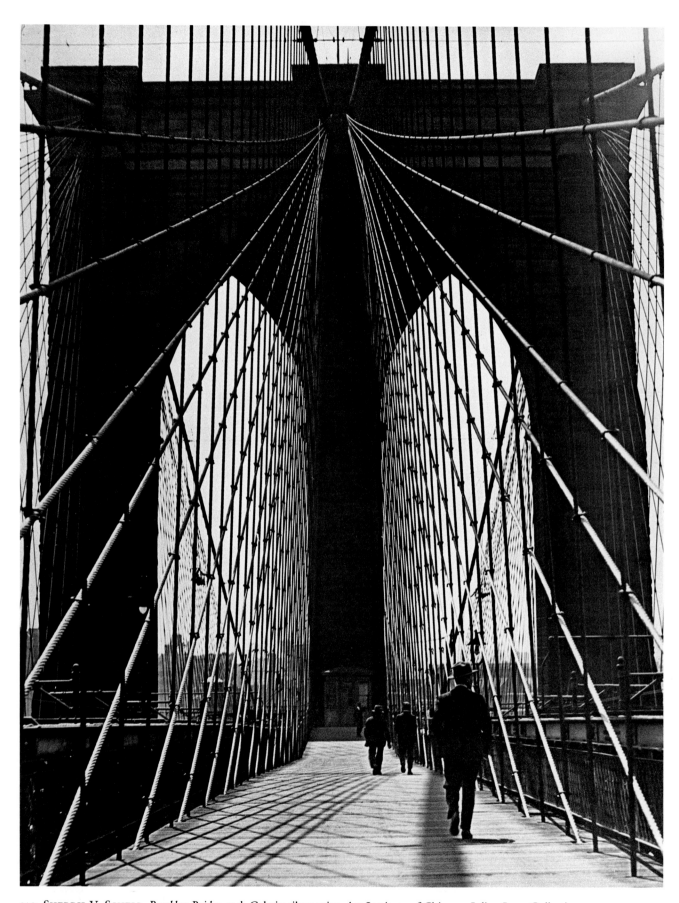

540. SHERRIL V. SCHELL. *Brooklyn Bridge*, n.d. Gelatin silver print. Art Institute of Chicago; Julien Levy Collection.

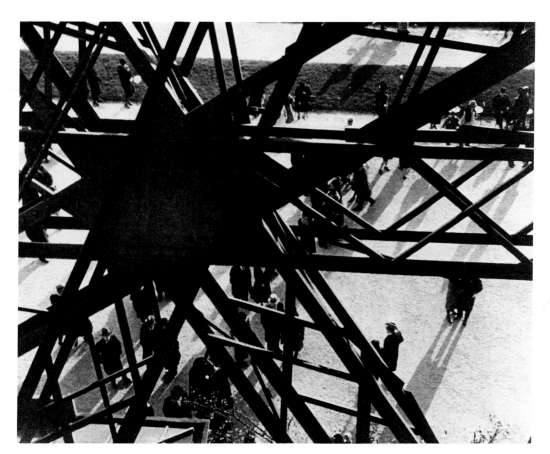

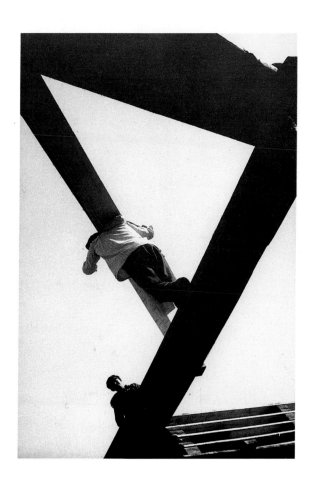

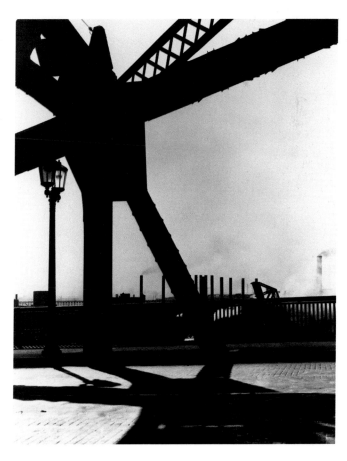

no. 582). While Sheeler and Bourke-White were the most renowned, by the mid-1930s Bruehl, John Mudd, William Rittase, and Thurman Rotan also were associated with high quality industrial photography commissioned for advertisements and articles. And although Hine was motivated by a wish to celebrate the worker behind the machine rather than by any reverence for industrial formation as such, his factory images *(pl. no. 480)* and views of the Empire State Building in construction *(pl. no. 481)* also reflect a belief that machines and technology ultimately were beneficial to mankind.

Industrial images were made mainly for advertisements and publicity in trade journals, but the interest in this theme among artists and intellectuals can be gauged by the many gallery exhibitions and articles in general publications on this theme that appeared during the 1920s and early '30s.[18] One example might suffice: of the images submitted to the Exhibition of Photographic Mural Design, held at the Museum of Modern Art in 1932, the largest number were concerned with industrial subjects. Sheeler submitted a montage triptych based on the River Rouge images *(pl. no. 585)*, while Abbott, Aubrey Bodine, Rotan, and Steichen entered works depicting skyscraper construction, smelting furnaces, and bridge structures. In the late 1920s, industrial and machine images began to appear in popular photographic journals, annuals, and Pictorialist salons also. The acceptance of "Beauty in Ugliness," as one article called it,[19] occurred almost a quarter of a century after Coburn had justly pointed out that both bridge-builder and photographer were creatures of the modern era.

The New Vision: The Nude

The nude also appealed to photographers of the new vision. A quintessentially artistic theme, it lent itself to a variety of visual experiments in Europe, figuring in montages, solarizations, oblique and close-up views by Feininger, Hausmann, Kesting, Man Ray, Moholy-Nagy, and Tabard *(pl. no. 544)*, among others. The work of Frantisek Drtikol, a Czech, can be taken as typical of the artfulness with which the theme was handled; it was unusual, too, in that Pictorialist darkroom processes, such as pigment printing, were used for avant-garde ends, creating mannered and stylized "art deco" arrangements typified by an untitled image *(pl. no. 545)* of 1927.

As a theme, the nude—male as well as female—inspired special interest among American photographers who were relieved to find the subject more acceptable in straight photography than it had been before. Besides Stieglitz, whose belief in the nude as a symbol of life-giving energy inspired his images of O'Keeffe, others who sought ways

of imbuing this subject with vitality included Cunningham, Outerbridge, Sheeler, Strand, and Weston. A 1928 work by Cunningham *(pl. no. 546)* transforms a torso into a series of irregular triangles that are affecting because the geometrical shapes still intimate the softness of flesh, and evoke a delicately sensual feeling. Weston, according to companion Charis Wilson, found in the female nude image a "lifelong challenge"[20]—an instrument to explore both the formal problems involved in the new vision and his own sexuality. *Nude (pl. no. 547)*, 1926, transforms sentient flesh into stone hardness, suggesting that "the thing itself" can be transmuted according to one's perceptions into something other. While less common, photographs of the male nude or of both sexes together, were made by a small number of photographers, among them Lynes, whose study *(pl. no. 548)* turns reality into fantasy. Through his handling of the shadows that suggest the ambiguous nature of sexuality, Lynes found a means to give photographic form to Surrealist concepts.

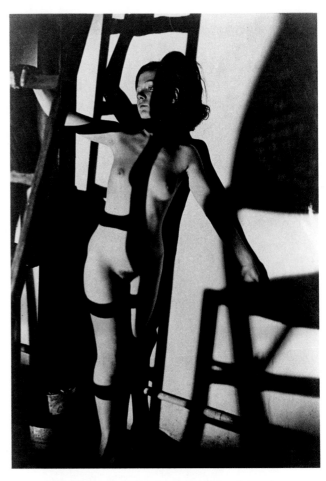

544. MAURICE TABARD. *Nude*, 1929. Gelatin silver print. New Orleans Museum of Art; Museum Purchase, 1977, Acquisition Fund Drive.

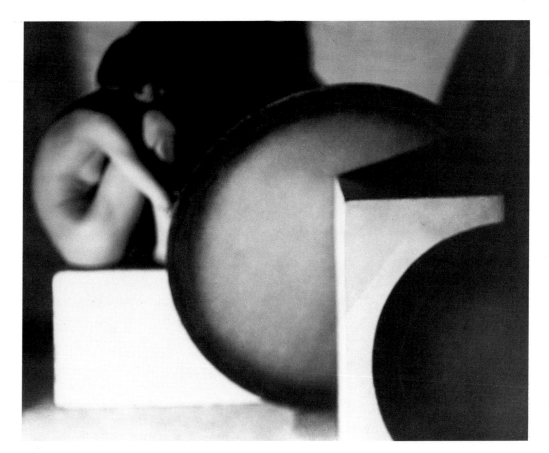

545. FRANTISEK DRTIKOL. *Untitled*, 1927. Gelatin silver or bromoil print. Private collection.

546. IMOGEN CUNNINGHAM. *Triangles*, 1928. Gelatin silver print. © 1970 Imogen Cunningham Trust, Berkeley, Cal.

In view of the affinities between movements in graphic art and photographic expression during this period, it is not surprising to find the camera used in the late 1920s to explore Surrealist ideas and vocabulary. Montage and other darkroom techniques mentioned earlier provided an obvious means to express fantasy visions, but the desire to present the subconscious as an aspect of reality impelled straight photographers to fabricate, arrange, and illuminate objects and their settings in order to create synthetic realities. Manikins and dolls often were seen as metaphors of sexuality, as in the work of the Argentinian photographer Horacio Coppola *(pl. no. 549)*, or in the bizarre creations of the German artist Hans Bellmer, who made movable *papier mâché* figures that he photographed in various postures and settings *(pl. no. 550)*. A number of photographers, including Umbo (Otto Umbehrs), utilized commercial manikins as symbols of the real/unreal conundrum explored by Surrealists *(pl. no. 551)*. Erwin Blumenfeld, born in Germany but active in fashion photography in Paris and later the United States, romanticized the Surrealist genre by draping the nude figure in wet muslin; the results *(pl. no. 552)* suggest classical sculpture given rapturous animation. As one of the few who successfully adapted Surrealism to fashion photography, his contribution will be discussed in the next chapter, along with oth-

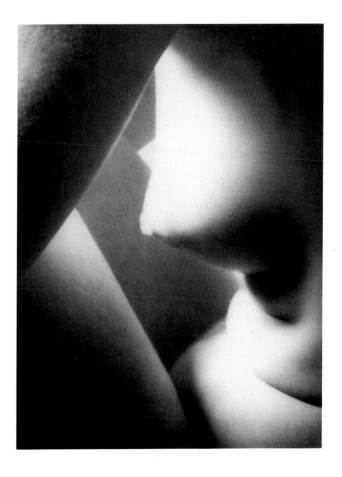

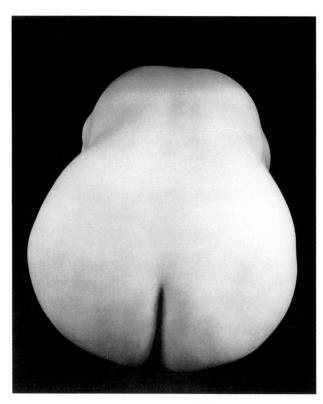

547. EDWARD WESTON. *Nude*, 1926. Gelatin silver print.
© 1981 Arizona Board of Regents, Center for Creative
Photography, University of Arizona, Tucson.

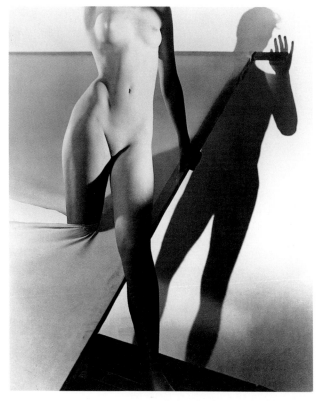

548. GEORGE PLATT LYNES. *Arthur Lee's Model*, 1940.
Gelatin silver print. Robert Miller Gallery, New York.

ers who made commercial use of the style. Still others, whose interest in enigmas, dreams, and fantasies did not begin until the late 1930s and '40s, will be treated in subsequent chapters.

Until the 1930s, light graphics, montages, solarizations, and other darkroom manipulations appealed to few American photographers besides Man Ray (who in any case lived in Paris) and Francis Bruguière, a former California member of the Photo-Secession who had gained renown as a New York theatrical photographer. Around 1926, Bruguière began to work with multiple exposures and what he called "light abstractions" *(pl. no. 553)* made by illuminating and exposing cut paper shapes. At times these works transcend the technique of their manufacture, and the flowing abstract forms express a sense of drama and mystery. Following a move to England, Bruguière continued to "create his own world,"[21] producing Surrealist photographs and abstract films, among them *Light Rhythms*.

After the Bauhaus was reincarnated in the Institute of Design in 1938, montage and cameraless photography came to the attention of a wider spectrum of Americans. Lotte Jacobi, a former Berlin portraitist resettled in New York, began to produce photogenics *(pl. no. 554)*, the term she used to describe combinations of light graphics and straight imagery. Others who started to regard photography as a way of working with light rather than solely as representing objects included Carlotta Corpron, who embarked on a series of light graphics *(pl. no. 555)* in response to the teaching of Kepes, Arthur Siegel, whose tenure at the Institute of Design prompted several generations of students to investigate experimental photography, and Barbara Morgan, a former painter open to the full range of experimentalist ideas. In a work entitled *Spring on Madison Square*, 1938, *(pl. no. 556)* Morgan invoked both montage and cameraless imagery to express the visual and kinetic energy she discerned in New York City *(see also* her photographs of dancer Martha Graham, *pl. no. 557)*.

Toward the end of the 1920s, the key concepts behind the new photography had become clearly articulated. A 1928 article entitled *"Nicht Mehr lesen, Sehen"* ("Forget Reading, See") acclaimed camera images as "the greatest of all contemporary physical, chemical, technological wonders," with the capacity to "be one of the most effective weapons against . . . the mechanization of spirit,"[22] a statement that in essence repeats the ideas expressed a decade earlier by Strand. The following year, this grand concept was embodied in both the exhibition *Film Und Foto (Fifo)* organized by the *Deutsches Werkbund* at Stuttgart, Germany, and in the publication based on it by photographer Franz Roh and graphic designer Jan Tschichold

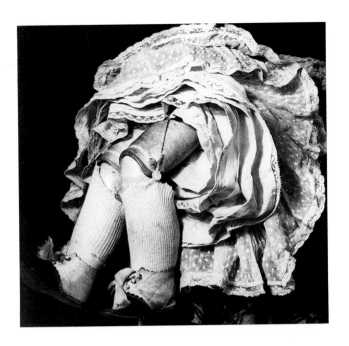

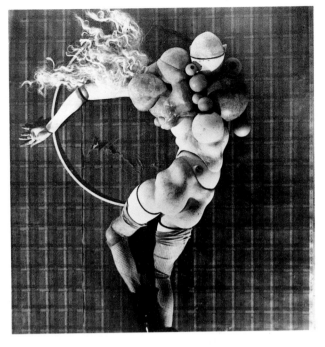

ABOVE LEFT:

549. HORACIO COPPOLA. *Grandmother's Doll* , 1932. Gelatin silver print. San Francisco Museum of Modern Art; purchase. Courtesy Sander Gallery, New York.

ABOVE RIGHT:

550. HANS BELLMER. *Les Jeux de la Poupée (Doll's Games), plate VIII*, 1936. Gelatin silver print with applied color. Robert Miller Gallery, New York.

LEFT:

551. UMBO (OTTO UMBEHRS). *Untitled (Three Mannikins)*, 1928. Gelatin silver print. Art Institute of Chicago; Julien Levy Collection.

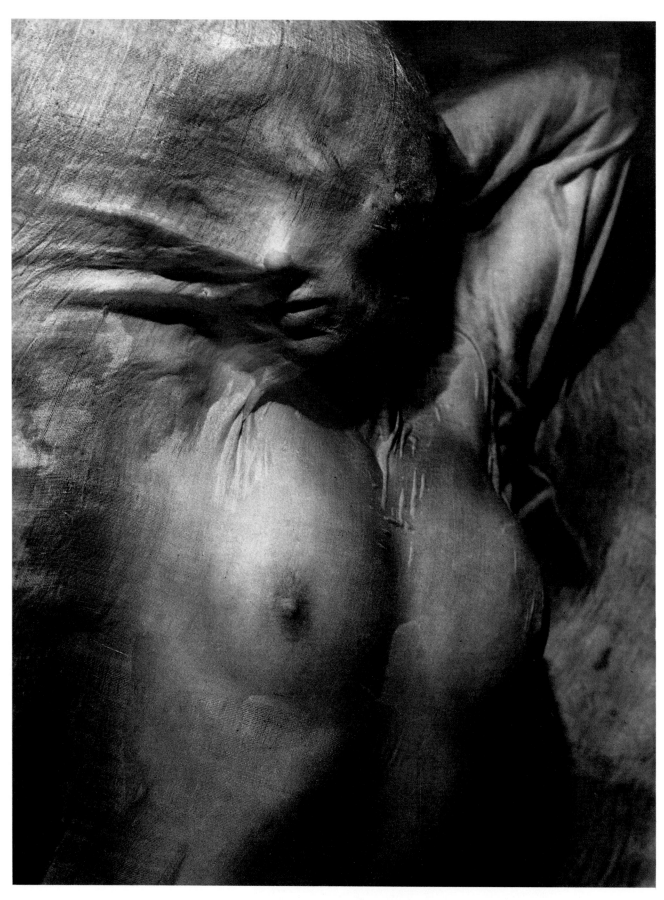

552. ERWIN BLUMENFELD. *Wet Veil, Paris*, 1937. Gelatin silver print. Witkin Gallery, New York. Courtesy Marina Schinz, New York.

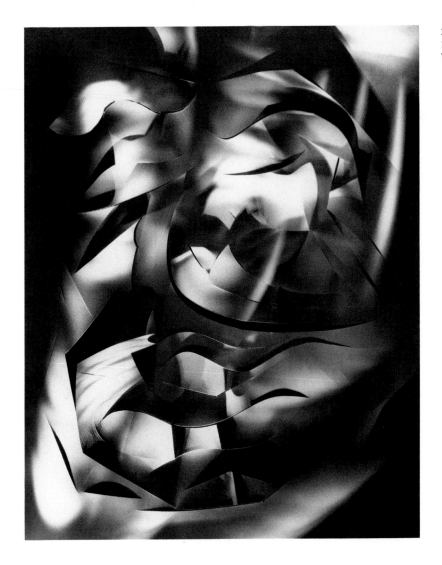

553. FRANCIS BRUGUIÈRE. *Light Abstraction*, 1920s. Gelatin silver print. Collection Sam Wagstaff, New York.

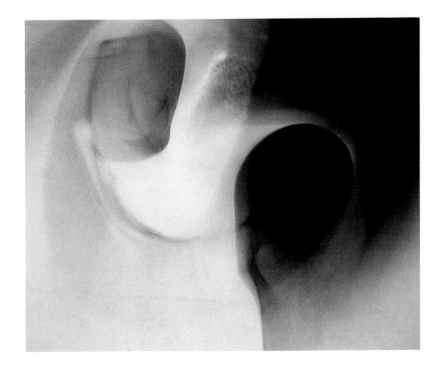

554. LOTTE JACOBI. *Photogenic*, c. 1940s–50s. Gelatin silver print. Franklin Institute Science Museum, Philadelphia, © Lotte Jacobi.

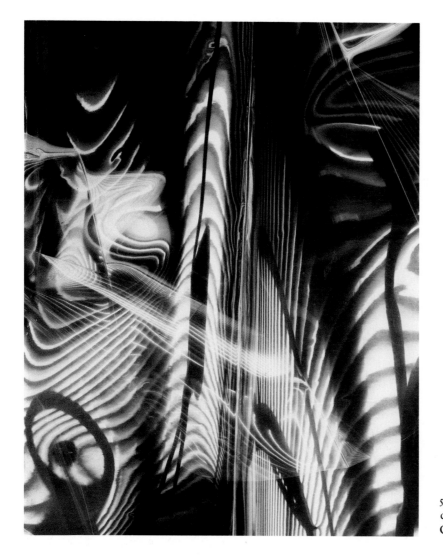

555. CARLOTTA CORPRON. *Mardi Gras*,
c. 1946. Gelatin silver print. Marcuse Pfeifer
Gallery, New York. © Carlotta Corpron.

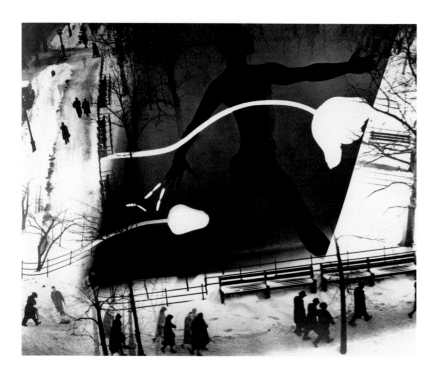

556. BARBARA MORGAN. *Spring on Madison
Square*, 1938. Gelatin silver print. Courtesy
and © 1980 Barbara Morgan.

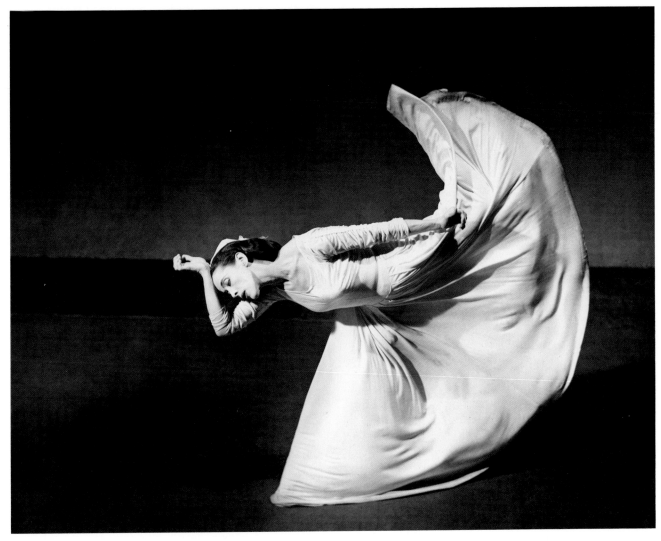

557. BARBARA MORGAN. *Martha Graham: Letter to the World (Kick)*, 1940.
Gelatin silver print. Courtesy and © 1980 Barbara Morgan.

entitled *Foto Auge/Oeil et Photo/Photo Eye*. The exhibit, its dramatic poster depicting man and camera dominating the world *(pl. no. 558)*, included photographs by Europeans and Americans, the latter, selected by Steichen and Weston.[23] Included were scientific works, publicity, advertising, and fashion photographs, collages, montages, light graphics, movie stills, and straight images made as personal expression.

This show (as well as others in various localities that both preceded and followed it) summed up the extraordinary vitality of photographic communication of the time and revealed avenues that have continued to invigorate the medium up until the present. It reflected an ardent belief that the fresh vision of reality that issued from the camera would, in common with other products of the machine, improve the quality of ordinary life and permit the creative control of technology. Curiously *Fifo* omitted photo-

journalism, a technological force that already had begun to exert a compelling (and not always beneficial) influence on the reading public's perception of events. Along with the development of advertising and publicity, the relationship of word and image in print journalism became increasingly significant factors and will be explored in the following chapter.

Profile: Lázsló Moholy-Nagy

Lázsló Moholy-Nagy, a "Renaissance" figure of the technical era, was active in a spectrum of endeavors that included painting, photography, film, and industrial and graphic design. He ignored traditional distinctions between graphic and photographic expression, between art for self-expression and for utility, and between practice and theory to work creatively in all the styles and media of his choice.

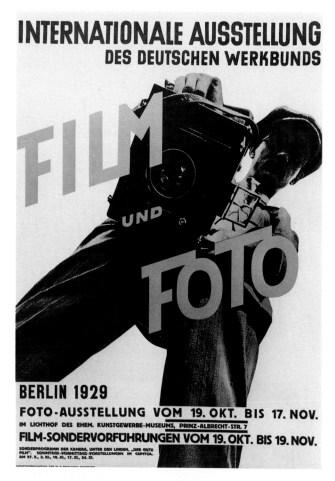

558. *Film und Foto International Exhibition*, Stuttgart, Germany, 1929. Poster. Kunstbibliothek mit Museum für Architektur, Modebild und Grafik-Design; Staatliche Museen Preussischer Kulturbesitz, Berlin.

As a writer and teacher, he explored many of the unconventional areas of visual activity that continue to engage artists, among them abstract film, light shows, constructed environments, and mixed media events.

Born in a provincial section of Hungary in 1895, Moholy-Nagy studied law while also participating in art and literary activities in his native land and in Vienna before and after his army service during World War I. He moved to Berlin in 1920, making contact with the Dadaists and soon becoming well known in avant-garde circles for his paintings, light graphics, and articles based on Constructivist theory. While serving as director of the metal workshop and later of the foundation course of the Bauhaus, Moholy-Nagy and his wife Lucia Moholy, herself a photographer, worked together to explore the potentials of light for plastic expression. As "manipulators of light," they suggested that through the technological medium of photography artists in the industrial era might arrive at individualized nonmechanical expression.

After leaving the Bauhaus in 1928, Moholy-Nagy worked on exhibitions, stage designs, and films in Berlin before being forced by events in Germany to emigrate to Amsterdam in 1935. A year later he moved to London, and in order to support himself took on commercial assignments in photography, including a commission to illustrate several books. In 1937, he was invited to head a reactivated Bauhaus being set up in the United States, which a year later was established as the School of Design (later Institute of Design) in Chicago. He died in that city in 1946.

Moholy-Nagy's photographic output spanned the entire range of ideas, processes, and techniques embraced by the concept of "the new vision," which he had helped to formulate. Included are views from above and below, close-ups, collages, montages, reflections, refractions, and cameraless images made by manipulating light through various devices. His themes embraced portraiture, landscape, the nude, architecture, the machine, organic form, and the urban street scene. While his work does not fall exclusively within any one of the distinctive styles of the period, a unifying thread is its extraordinary liveliness, reflective of the photographer's interest in actual life as well as in problems of form.

Moholy-Nagy's oft-quoted statement that "the illiterate of the future will be ignorant of camera and pen alike"[24] stems from his understanding of the camera as a modern graphic tool—a device for capturing aspects of reality that might stand by themselves or be reworked into further visual statements. In addition to the book *Malerei Fotografie Film (Painting Photography Film)*, 1925, these concepts were embodied in numerous other publications, which include in English translation, "Light—A Medium of Plastic Expression," published in the American magazine *Broom* in 1923 and *Vision in Motion*, which appeared posthumously in 1947. Though Moholy-Nagy has long been admired mainly as theorist and teacher, it is possible that in the future his photographs themselves will be regarded as the more significant expressions of his ideas.

Profile: Paul Strand

Paul Strand's debut in photography coincided with the first stirrings of modernism in the visual arts in America. Born in New York in 1890, he attended both the class and club in photography taught by Hine at the Ethical Culture School in 1908. A visit to Stieglitz's 291 gallery arranged by Hine inspired Strand to explore the expressive possibilities of the medium, which until then he had considered a hobby. Although he was active for a brief period at the Camera Club of New York, whose darkrooms he continued to use for about 20 years, his ideas derived first from the circle around Stieglitz and then from the group that evolved around the Modern Gallery in 1915, including Sheeler and Schamberg. Strand's work, which was exhibited at 291, the Modern Gallery, and the Camera Club, gained prizes at the Wanamaker Photography exhibitions and was featured in the last two issues of *Camera Work*. From about 1915 on, he explored the visual problems that were to become fundamental to the modernist aesthetic as it evolved in both Europe and the United States. During the 1920s he mainly photographed urban sites, continued with the machine forms *(pl. no. 578)* begun earlier, and turned his attention to nature, using 5 x 7 and 8 x 10 inch view cameras and making contact prints on platinum paper. In these works, acknowledged as seminal in the evolution of the New Objectivity, form and feeling are indivisible and intense. In addition, Strand's writings, beginning in 1917 with "Photography and the New God," set forth the necessity for the photographer to evolve an aesthetic based on the objective nature of reality and on the intrinsic capabilities of the large-format camera with sharp lens.

After service in the Army Medical Corps, where he was introduced to X-ray and other medical camera procedures, Strand collaborated with Sheeler on *Manhatta*, released as *New York the Magnificent* in 1921. Shortly afterward, he purchased an Akelcy movie camera and began to work as a free-lance cinematographer, a career that he followed until the early 1930s when the industry for making news and short features was transferred from New York to the West Coast. Aware of the revolutionary social ideas being tested in Mexico through his visits to the Southwest, Strand sought the opportunity to make still photographs and to produce government-sponsored documentary films; *Redes*, or *The Wave*, released in 1934, depicted the economic problems confronting a fishing village near Vera Cruz. Following a futile attempt to assist the Russian director Sergei

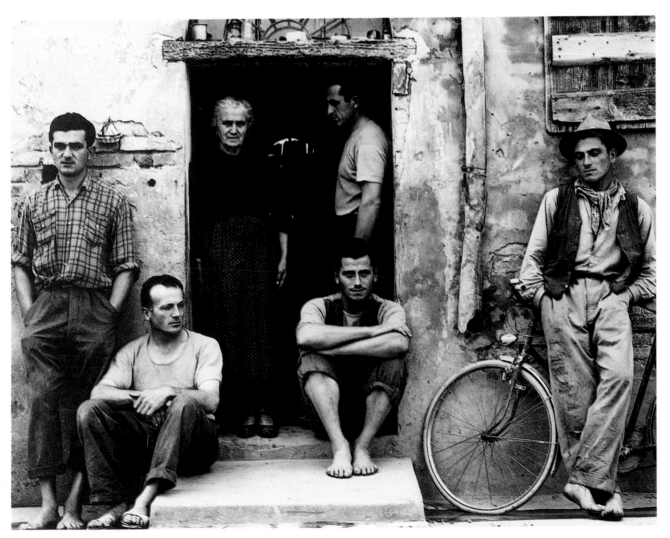

559. PAUL STRAND. *The Family, View II, Luzzara, Italy*, 1953. Gelatin silver print. © 1976, 1982 Paul Strand Foundation, as published in *Paul Strand: Sixty Years of Photography*, Aperture, Millerton, 1976.

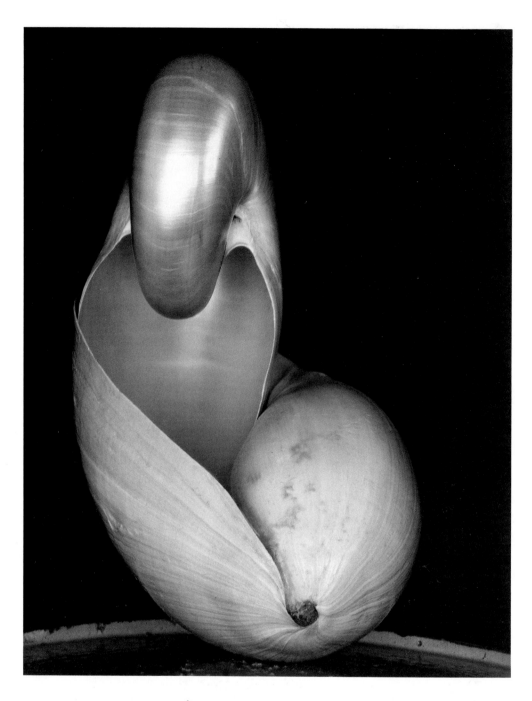

560. EDWARD WESTON. *Shells*, 1927. Gelatin silver print. Witkin Gallery, New York. © 1981 Arizona Board of Regents, Center for Creative Photography, University of Arizona, Tucson.

Eisenstein in the Soviet Union in 1935, Strand worked with Pare Lorentz on *The Plough that Broke the Plains*, following which he and other progressive filmmakers organized Frontier Films to produce a series of pro-labor and anti-Fascist movies. Their most ambitious production, *Native Land*, which evolved from a Congressional hearing into antilabor activities, was released in 1941 on the eve of the second World War, at which time its message was considered politically divisive.

Unable to finance filmmaking after World War II, Strand turned to the printed publication for a format that might integrate image and text in a matter akin to the cinema. *Time in New England*, a collaboration with Nancy Newhall, sought to evoke a sense of past and present through images of artifact and nature combined with quotations from the region's most lucid writers. Strand continued with enterprises of this nature after he moved to Europe in 1950, eventually producing *La France de profil (A Profile of France)* with Claude Roy (1952), *Un Paese (A Village)* with Cesare Zavattini (1955), and *Tir a' Mhurain* with Basil Davidson (1962), among other works. At his death in 1976, he had been photographing for nearly three-quarters of a century, gradually finding his ideal of beauty and decorum in nature and the simple life *(pl. no. 559)*.

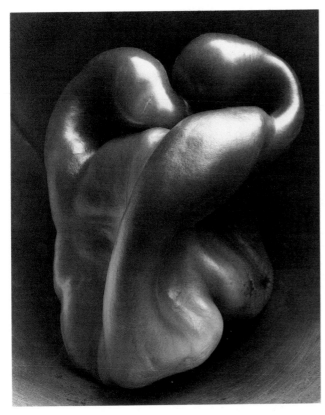

561. EDWARD WESTON. *Pepper*, 1930. Gelatin silver print. Witkin Gallery, New York. © 1981 Arizona Board of Regents, Center for Creative Photography, University of Arizona, Tucson.

Profile: Edward Weston

From an accomplished commercial photographer of Pictorialist persuasion, Edward Weston developed into the quintessential American artist/photographer of his time. Born in Illinois in 1886, he opened a portrait studio in California in 1911, finding time also to exhibit at Pictorialist salons. After his definitive break with Pictorialism, seen in the 1922 *Armco* images *(pl. no. 584)*, Weston embarked on the life of an impecunious but free artist, singlemindedly devoted to creative endeavor. Convinced at this time that "the photographer . . . can depart from the literal recording to whatever extent he chooses" as long as the methods remain "photographic,"[25] he controlled form and tone through choice of motif, exposure time, and the use of the

ground-glass focusing screen of the large-format camera. This way of working, which he called pre-visualization, was a factor in Weston's exclusion of temporal and transient effects of light, atmosphere, and movement in order to concentrate on revealing the object in its "deepest moment of perception."

Following a four year period in Mexico, during which he opened a portrait studio with Tina Modotti and became part of the revitalized Mexican artistic movement of the period, Weston returned to a simple existence in Carmel, California. In 1927, he began to photograph single objects —both organic forms and artifacts—removed from their ordinary contexts. In addition to the well-known nautilus shells *(pl. no. 560)* and green peppers *(pl. no. 561)*, he arranged and illuminated a series of household implements whose shapes seemed intrinsically beautiful, and photographed them close-up with great precision in order to reveal "an essence of what lies before the . . . lens," thus creating an "image more real and comprehensible than the actual object."[26] The nude was especially significant in Weston's work, representing, as it also did for Stieglitz, more than a convenient artistic theme. The cool and elegant forms of the more than one hundred nude studies Weston produced between 1918 and 1945 not only represent his search for formal perfection but also reflect the erotic and sexual enigmas with which he struggled for much of his life.

Freedom from financial strain, made possible by Guggenheim grants in 1937 and 1938—the first awarded to a photographer—enabled Weston to embark on a period of sustained work. In fusing the formal insights gained during the late 1920s with his intense feeling for the California landscape, Weston achieved the richest and most personally nuanced imagery of his career. A selection of these photographs appeared in *California and the West*, published in 1940, and ten years later in an elegantly printed portfolio, *My Camera at Point Lobos*. Starting in 1923 and continuing for 20 years, Weston kept a daily journal. Published in 1961, three years after his death, his *Daybooks*, edited by Nancy Newhall, detail the problems of daily existence and creative activity in the photographer's life. A unique document, it lays bare the inner resolve that impelled this photographer to transcend financial distress and emotional anxiety and create works that seem untouched by the mundane or temporal.

A Short Technical History: Part II

MATERIALS, EQUIPMENT, AND PROCESSES

The unwieldy nature of wet collodion on glass led to continued efforts to find other supports of chemical substances for negatives during the third quarter of the 19th century. Collodion dry plates, invented by French scientist Dr. J. M. Taupenot and manufactured in England in 1860, were too slow in action to replace the wet plate. In the late 1870s, experiments by English physician Dr. Richard Leach Maddox to substitute a gelatin bromide plate for collodion and refinements made in 1873 by John Burgess and Richard Kennett, and in 1878 by Charles Harper Bennet, led to a practicable dry plate. These appeared on the market in 1878 and were soon being manufactured by firms in Europe and the United States, ushering in a new era in photography. Consisting initially of a glass support coated with a silver bromide emulsion on a specially prepared gelatin ground (produced either by "ripening" or "digestion"), the fragile glass was replaced by celluloid[1] in 1883, after it had become possible to manufacture this material in standardized sheets of about .01 inch thickness.

A paper roll film (first conceived by British inventor Arthur James Melhuish in 1854—*see below*) was commercially produced by the Eastman Company in Rochester, New York, in 1888. At first, the gelatin emulsion had to be removed or "stripped" from the paper backing, transferred to glass, and then developed and printed, but with the substitution of transparent celluloid roll film in 1889,[2] and the addition in 1895 of a paper backing that enabled the film to be loaded in daylight, roll film as it is known today came into being.

The improvement of the color sensitivity of film began during the collodion era when the renowned German photochemist Hermann Wilhelm Vogel added dyes to silver bromide emulsions. This process, called optical sensitizing, in 1873 produced the first orthochromatic plates (sensitive to all but red and oversensitive to blue light) and it was applied to gelatin dry plates when they supplanted collodion. Experiments, notably by Adolphe Miethe of the German Agfa works in 1903, resulted in the development of panchromatic film sensitive to all colors but still requiring a yellow filter to cut down the sensitivity to all blue light.

Permanence and long tonal scale in printing papers were difficult problems to solve satisfactorily because of the many variables (such as atmospheric conditions, water quality, amount and thoroughness of washing) that characterized photographic printing procedures. In spite of its uneven performance, albumen paper continued to be manufactured until the end of the 19th century, but new papers were being developed to respond to the need for sharper definition and speed created by the increased use of camera images for records, documentation, and reproduction in newspapers and magazines. Two types of printing papers were produced: printing-out paper and developing-out paper. Gelatin-silver-chloride emulsion papers (marketed in the United States under the names Aristotype and Solio), which required no chemical development, became available in 1890, while developing-out papers coated with silver bromide emulsions became popular in the late 1880s even though this product had been introduced as early as 1873. Gelatin-silver-chloride paper for printing by gas light (known as Velox) also appeared around 1890. At the same time that these materials were manufactured to serve com-

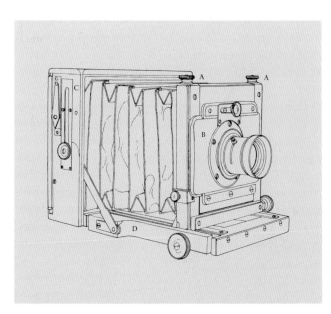

562. *Hare Camera.* On George Hare's camera of 1882, screwed rods (A) were used to secure the front panel (B), which could be moved toward the rear panel (C). When the lens was removed, the hinged baseboard (D) could be folded up.

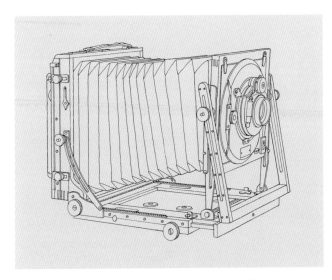

563. *Sanderson Camera*. Frederick Sanderson used two slotted stays on either side of the lens panel in his 1895 camera. This allowed a considerable degree of vertical, horizontal, and swing movement to be applied to the lens panel.

mercial needs, platinum paper, based on John Herschel's discovery of the light sensitivity of chloride of platinum, was produced in England under the trade name Platinotype. This expensive material appealed to well-to-do amateurs and serious photographers who required a printing paper of permanence with a long tonal scale.

The standardization of papers went hand-in-hand with the automation of large-scale photographic printing. Improving on the steam-driven machines that had made it possible to expose, print, and fix *carte-de-visite* portraits and stereographs during the 1860s, the new machinery installed by large photographic firms such as Automatic Photographs of New York and Loescher and Petsch in Berlin was capable, for example, of exposing 245 cabinet-size pictures a minute and turning out 147,000 prints daily on the new fast-acting bromide paper.[3]

During the first 30 years of photography, camera design was subject to continual experimentation. Instruments were made in large and small formats to accommodate plate sizes that ranged from mammoth to tiny postage size, while multiple lenses and septums were added to boxes to make *cartes de visite (pl. no. 226)* and stereographs *(pl. no. 225)*. By the 1880s, camera design needed to expand further to accommodate new negative materials—the dry plate and celluloid film. The folding-bed view cameras, introduced in England in 1882 by camera designer George Hare became the prototype for similar instruments manufactured in other parts of Europe and the United States *(pl. no. 562)*. Variations of the basic instrument incorporated the capacity to advance the rear element, change from hori-

zontal to vertical format, and fold the front element down into the base. Some models were given sliding racks that enabled the bellows to be greatly extended. As improved by British designer Frederick H. Sanderson in 1895 *(pl. no. 563)*, the view camera became an instrument of great sensitivity and precision, provided the subject was immobile.

A serious effort to make possible fast exposure, control over focus, and large image size resulted in the development of the single-lens reflex camera. Based on the use of a mirror to redirect the light rays to a horizontal ground-glass focusing surface, an early model of this type was patented in 1861 by Thomas Sutton. The most influential design was that of the Graflex, introduced by Folmer and Schwing in 1898; it assumed its inimitable shape of cubic box with bellows extension and four-sided hood on top around 1900 *(pl. no. 564)*. A mirror, usually inserted at a 45 degree angle to the axis of the lens focused the image onto a screen within the hood and dropped out of the way when the exposure was made. In the hand or on the tripod, reflex cameras (which came in a variety of sizes) were flexible enough to accommodate naturalists in the field, news and portrait photographers, and individuals looking for street subjects.

Reputable equipment with which one could almost simultaneously view the scene, make the exposure, and advance the film in ordinary daylight did not become generally available until the 1920s *(see A Short Technical His-*

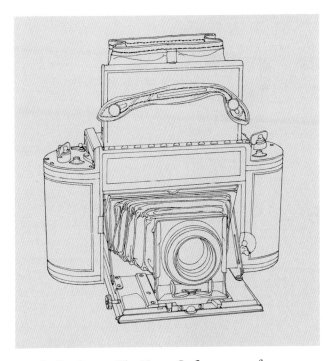

564. *Graflex Camera*. The No. 1A Graflex camera of 1910 was a single-lens reflex camera for roll-films. It was fitted with the Graflex multispeed focal plane shutter.

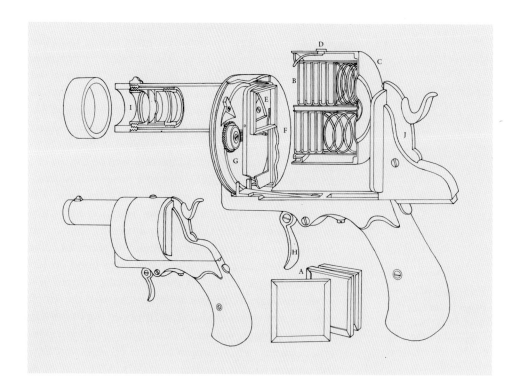

565. *Photo-Revolver de Poche*. E. Enjalbert's *Photo-Revolver de Poche* of 1882 carried small plates (A) in a compartment (B) in the chamber (C). When a catch (D) was slid, a plate moved into the exposing position (E). When the chamber was rotated through 180°, the exposed plate was transferred to a second compartment (F). The chamber was turned again to its original position for the next exposure. This movement also set the rotary shutter (G), which was released by the trigger (H). The lens (I) was mounted in the barrel. The hammer (J) held and located the plate chamber (C).

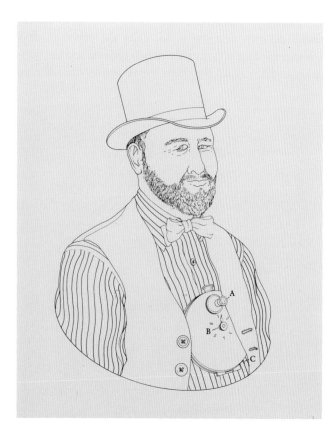

566. *Stirn Secret Camera*. The Carl P. and Rudolph Stirn Secret or Waistcoat camera of 1886 was worn under a waistcoat, the lens (A) poking through a buttonhole. The circular plate was turned and the shutter set when the pointer (B) was rotated. Exposures were made by pulling on a string (C).

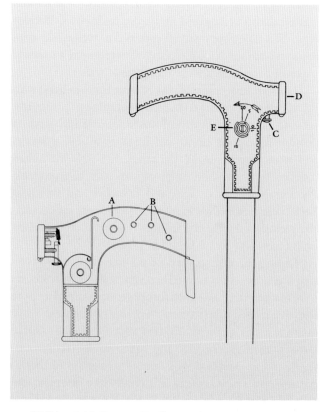

567. *Walking-Stick Camera*. Emile Kronke's walking-stick camera of 1902 took spools of roll-film (A), carried in the handle. Storage space (B) for three spare spools was provided. A shutter release knob (C) was placed underneath the front of the handle. (D) Lens panel. (E) Winding-on key.

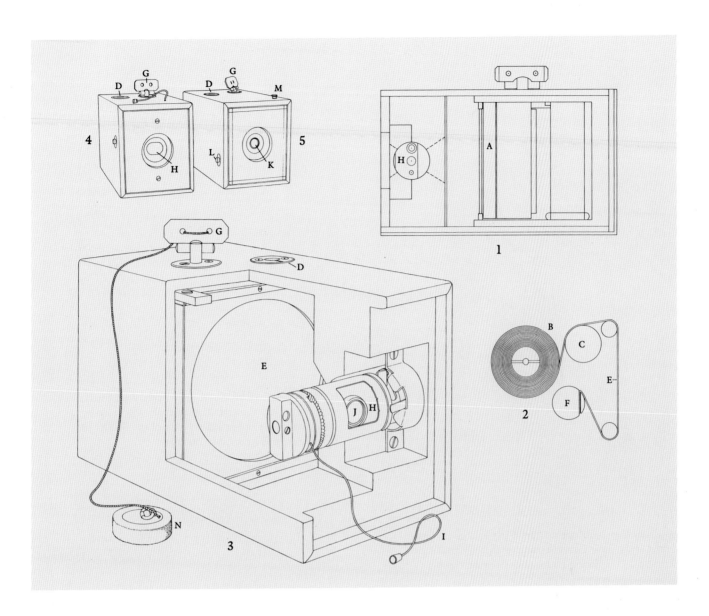

568. *Eastman's Kodak Camera of 1888*. (1) Sectional view, (2) roll-holder as seen from above, (3) cutaway view, (4) external view. The camera had an integral roll-holder (A), in which George Eastman's American Film (B) was first fed over a metering roller (C), the end of which carried a disc with an index mark visible through a window (D) on the top of the camera. The film was then fed past the circular exposing aperture (E) and onto the take-up roller (F), which was turned by a key (G). The cylindrical shutter (H) was set by pulling a string (I). The lens (J) was fitted within the shutter. (5) A new model, designated the No. 1 Kodak camera, was introduced in 1889. It differed from the 1888 version in having a sector shutter (K); the positions of the shutter release (L) and setting string (M) were also altered. Both models had lens plugs (N) for protection; the plugs also permitted time exposures to be made.

569. *Schmid Camera*. In 1883, the first popular hand-held dry plate camera was designed by William Schmid.

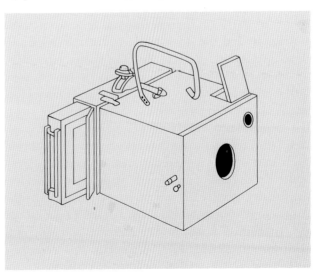

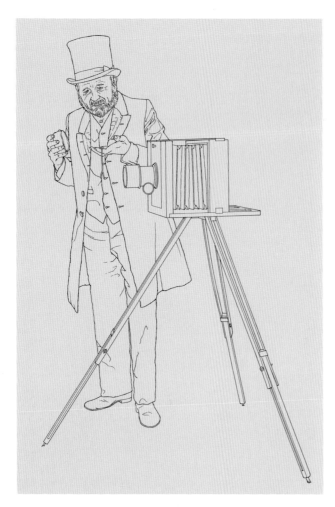

570. *Lens Cap*. Until the advent of the gelatin dry plate in the 1870s, most exposures were made by removing the lens cap and replacing it after a suitable interval of seconds—or minutes.

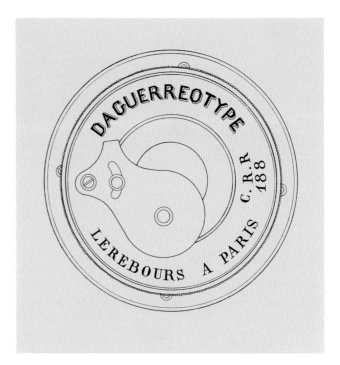

571. *Sliding cap shutter*. Some early lenses were fitted with sliding cap shutters. This example was made by N. P. Lerebours and is a close copy of the shutter on the Daguerre-Giroux camera of 1839.

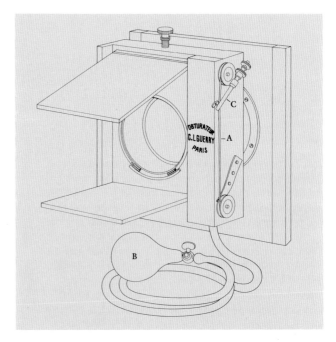

572. *Guerry's Flap Shutter*. C. I. Guerry's flap shutter of 1883 had two pivoted flaps, which were connected by a string-and-pulley system (A), set on the side. As a pneumatic release (B) was pressed, the two flaps were raised to uncover and cover the lens in turn. A screw-adjusted device (C), bearing on the string, was used to vary the period of opening by altering the relationship between the two flaps.

tory, Part III), but long before then it was possible to capture some street action using small cameras with a single short-focus lens. Other than the 1886 Gray-Stirn Vest Camera *(pl. no. 566)*, an instrument designed to be worn under a waistcoat and that took 1¾ inch diameter negatives, these instruments, made to look like books, binoculars, revolvers *(pl. no. 565)*, and walking sticks *(pl. no. 567)*, were little more than novelties. The dry-plate hand cameras that began to appear in the early 1880s were a different story; they became known as detective cameras because, though larger than the concealed cameras, they too were inconspicuous to operate and could capture spontaneous activity under certain conditions. An early, widely sold model was the Patent Detective Camera *(pl. no. 569)*, invented by the American William Schmid in 1883, but the Kodak *(pl. no. 568)*, announced in 1888 by The Eastman Company, was both easier to operate and revolutionary in that it created a completely new system and a different constituency for

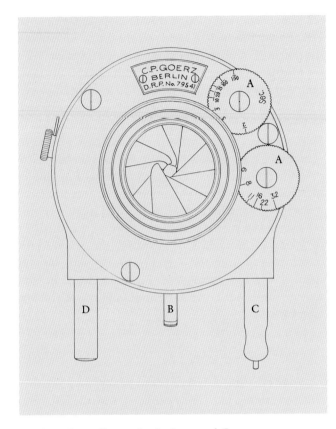

573. *Goerz Sector Shutter*. In the improved Goerz sector shutter of 1904, designed by Carl Paul Goerz, the functions of an iris diaphragm and a shutter were combined. The apertures and speeds were set on dials (A). The shutter was cocked by a lever (B) and released by a pneumatic cylinder (C). Slow speeds were provided by a pneumatic delay cylinder (D).

photography. This simple box, incorporating spools to hold roll film, a winding key to advance the film, and a string to open the shutter for the exposure, was an immediate success and prompted other manufacturers to design similar apparatus that would make use of the Kodak roll film. Actually, roll film attachments for plate cameras had been invented in 1854 by Melhuish and Joseph Blakeley Spencer, and in the following years Humbert de Molard and Camille Silvy also designed such devices. In 1875 Leon Warnerke, a Russian émigré in London, patented a practicable holder that accommodated stripping film in 100 exposure lengths, but the film itself was not sensitive enough for the camera's capabilities. This was followed by a similar holder invented in 1884 by George Eastman and William H. Walker, which also had to be attached to a plate camera. Undoubtedly it was the simplicity of a camera with integral roll-film holder, the ease of operation, and the freedom from the necessity of processing that attracted amateurs to the "smallest, lightest and simplest of all Detective cameras"[5]—the Kodak. The Eastman Company, which

from the start had been involved with both the manufacture and the processing, soon gave up the processing aspects. Like Lumière, its counterpart in France, Eastman employed many women workers as it continued to provide photographic supplies and develop new processes and equipment for a growing market.

In the early years of photography, exposure usually was effected by removing and replacing the lens cap manually *(pl. no. 570)* or by moving a simple plate that pivoted over the lens *(pl. no. 571)*. Although shutters had at times been used earlier, with the coming of the more sensitive gelatin dry films they became a necessity. They could be purchased separately to be affixed in front of the camera lens. Commonly of the flap, drop, or sliding plate construction, they were activated either by a string or a pneumatic cylinder attached to a rubber bulb *(pl. no. 572)*. In the late 1880s, sets of metal blades called diaphragm shutters were sometimes mounted within the lens barrel *(pl. no. 573)*, usually with settings of 1/100 to a full second. In about 1904, the compound shutter, designed for the Zeiss Company by Friedrich Deckel, introduced sets of blades totally enclosed within the camera that controlled both the size of the aperture and the length of time it remained open; after improvements it became standard on all better hand cameras *(pl. no. 574)*. The focal plane shutter, positioned in the camera behind the lens but in front of the plate or film, was derived from earlier roller-blind shutters that operated on the principle of a window shade. Various designs for this type were made during the 1870s and '80s, but the most famous, patented in 1888 by the German photographer Ottomar Anschütz for his instantaneous animal studies, made possible exposures at 1/1000 of a second *(pl. no. 575)*.

Improvements in glass manufacture in Jena, Germany, after 1880 made possible new designs in lenses. Besides the all-purpose rapid rectilinear lenses with which hand and view cameras initially were fitted, the German firms of Carl Zeiss and Carl Goerz began in the early 1890s to manufacture anastigmats—lenses that resolved distortion in both vertical and horizontal planes and made possible apertures up to f/4.5. The Dallmeyer firm in England and Bausch & Lomb in the United States also contributed new designs, but between 1890 and 1904 the German firms preempted the field by introducing the Zeiss Protar and Tessar and the Goerz Dagor lenses. While the wide-angle Globe lens, designed by the American Charles C. Harrison, had been used since 1860, the first telephoto lens was patented in 1891 by Thomas Rudolf Dallmeyer.

During the collodion era, exposure meters had not been necessary because wet plates were sensitized differently by different photographers, who determined the correct exposure time on the basis of experience. With the

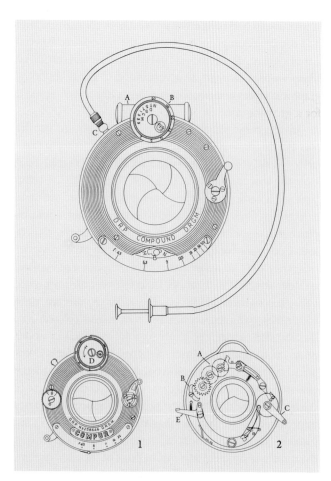

574. *Deckel's Compound Shutter.* Fredrich Deckel's improved compound shutter of 1911 had slow speeds provided by a pneumatic delay cylinder (A). Speeds were set on a dial (B). This model had a cable release socket (C); earlier models were pneumatically released.

Deckel's Compur Shutter. Deckel's compur shutter of 1912 was based on the Ilex design; (1) exterior view, (2) sectional view. Slow speeds were provided by a train of gears (A), controlled by a rocking pallet (B). A lever (C) was used to cock the shutter; the speeds were set on a dial (D). The shutter was released by another lever (E).

manufacture of standardized silver bromide plates in the late 1870s, methods of measuring the light reflected from an object and relating it to the sensitivity of the negative material became important. The first device to effectively measure and establish this relationship was a slide-rule-type exposure calculator designed and patented in 1888 by Charles Driffield and Ferdinand Hurter (*pl. no. 576*). Working in England as an engineer and a physical chemist respectively, in 1890 the two jointly published a significant work on sensitometry, having devised the mathematical equations on which to base a table of exposures. Evidence of a consistent relationship between image brightness, exposure, and emulsion sensitivity was welcomed by most

photographers even though this development prompted Peter Henry Emerson to briefly reconsider his ideas about the potential of photography for artistic expression.

Measuring the light reflected from objects was done both with chemical meters—actinometers—that employed a strip of light-sensitive paper that darkened when exposed, and optical or visual devices. The latter, first made in France around 1887, consisted of numbered gradations seen through an eyepiece in which the last number visible gave the exposure time. Design changes on this kind of meter continued to be made until 1940, but none produced a reading as accurate as that produced by a photoelectric cell meter. Making use of the light-sensitive characteristics of selenium, discovered in the 1870s, the photoelectric meter was first marketed in 1932 (*pl. no. 577*), but until the 1940s it was too expensive to be widely used. In 1938, cameras themselves began to be manufactured with built-in light meters.

Developments in Color

From the earliest days of photography, the absence of color was almost universally deplored, with the result that daguerreotypes were tinted with dry pigments and calotypes were painted with watercolors. In the wake of a patent taken out by Richard Beard in 1842 for a coloring method, instructional manuals and specialized materials appeared on the market and remained popular throughout the collodion era. However, soon after the invention of the medium, efforts by scientists to determine the sensitivity of silver salts to the colors of the spectrum had engendered the hope that photography in color would soon be possible. In these experiments, by Herschel in 1840, by Edmond Becquerel in 1848, by Niepce de Saint-Victor in the 1850s and Alphonse Poitevin in 1865, various chemicals were added to the silver compounds without conclusive results.

In 1851 a method of making daguerreotypes in color, supposedly achieved by American Levi L. Hill, also was found to be inconclusive although it is possible that Hill had stumbled upon a result that he was unable to duplicate. Positive images in color on glass were produced in 1891 by German physicist Gabriel Lippmann on the basis of the interference theory of light waves—the phenomenon one sees in oil slicks and soap bubbles—but while the results were said to be "an admirable reproduction of the colors of nature,"[5] the long exposures and difficulties in viewing the images prevented commercial exploitation.

Experimentation to achieve viable color materials was based on the researches into human vision carried out in England by Thomas Young in the early 1800s, which were later elaborated by Herman von Helmholtz in Germany.

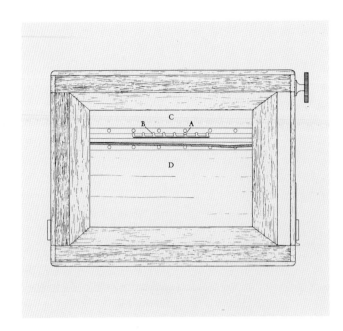

575. *Anschütz Focal Plane Shutter.* Ottomar Anschütz's focal plane shutter of 1888 was adjusted from the back of the camera. A catch (A) could be set in one of several notches (B) on the lower edge of the upper blind (C). A cord linkage, which was attached to the catch, adjusted the position of the lower blind (D), setting the width of the gap and, thus, affecting the exposure time.

These researchers held that all colors in nature are combinations of three primary colors—red, blue, green. The full range of spectral colors can be duplicated either by adding portions of the primaries together, or by subtracting them by using filters of complementary colors. In 1861, Scottish physicist James Clerk Maxwell produced a color photograph by superimposing three positive lantern slides of a striped tartan ribbon (*pl. no. 337*); both the taking and the projection were effected through liquid filters. At about the same time in France, Louis Ducos du Hauron attempted to perform similar experiments; in 1869, he and Charles Cros, working independently, published proposals for color processes based on the addition of three primary colors to represent the entire spectrum. However, until the invention of panchromatic film in the early 20th century, the plates used in these experiments were not sensitive enough to all spectral hues to make these efforts truly successful.

In his 1869 publication entitled *Les Couleurs en Photographie (Photography in Color)*, Du Hauron had proposed another method by which the additive theory might result in a color image. This comprised a screen ruled with fine lines in primary colors that, when properly blocked off by their complements, would yield all the hues in nature. In other words, the primaries were to be encompassed on one

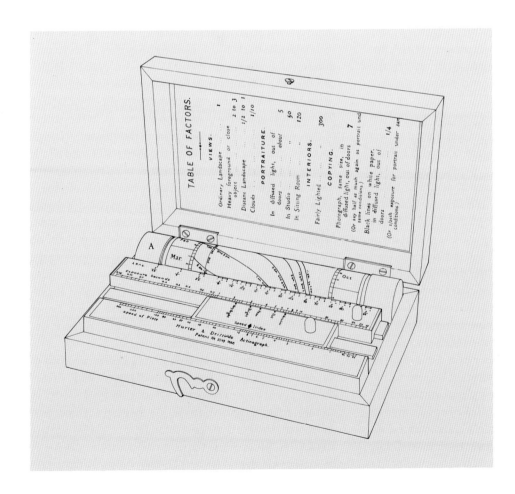

576. *Hurter and Driffield Actinograph.* The Actinograph, patented in 1888 by Ferdinand Hurter and Vero Charles Driffield, was a slide-rule form of exposure calculator. A rotary cylinder (A) was calibrated for a range of times of day and year; thirteen versions were available for different latitudes.

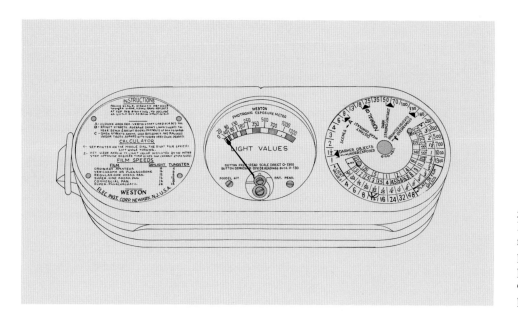

577. *Weston Exposure Meter.* In the Weston Universal 617 meter of 1932, the electric potential developed by two photoelectric cells was used to deflect the needle of a meter placed between them.

negative instead of three. Du Hauron did not actually experiment with this idea, but in 1894 John Joly in Dublin produced such a screen by ruling red, green, and blue aniline dyes on a gelatin-coated glass plate. When used in conjunction with an orthochromatic dry plate and a yellow filter, the result was a color image that was limited in accuracy by the lack of sensitivity of the plates then in use. An improved process of the same nature, patented in 1897 in Chicago, turned out to be too expensive, but Autochrome, a color plate and process invented in 1904 by the Lumière brothers in Lyon, managed to become the first commercially feasible color material.

Autochrome plates consisted of a glass selecting screen composed of minute granules of potato starch dyed in each of the three primary colors and dusted with a fine black powder to fill in the interstices that would have allowed light to pass through; this was adhered to a layer of silver-bromide panchromatic emulsion. The result was a positive transparency whose improved color sensitivity and relative ease of processing were immediately successful in spite of the high cost, long exposures, and the fact that the final result had to be seen in a viewer. Until the 1930s, the only real competition for Autochrome was plates manufactured by the French firm of Louis Dufay from about 1908 and by the German Agfa Company beginning in 1916, for which the dyes were poured and rolled on rather than ruled or dusted. Despite these improvements, researches to find an alternate color process continued since these materials all produced colors that were not thought to be natural enough, the aniline dyes were considered unstable (a problem that continues to bedevil color photography), and methods of obtaining prints from transparencies were exceedingly complicated.

Du Hauron's theories also proved to be the wellspring for experiments with subtractive color processes, which involved starting with white light (in which all spectral colors are present) and removing or absorbing those not in the scene. When three separation negatives taken by orange, green, and violet light are printed as positives on gelatin bichromate sheets of their complementary colors—cyan (blue-green), magenta, yellow—and placed in register, each color absorbs its own complement; together all three produce a full color image that Du Hauron called a Heliochrome. The advantages of subtraction include the avoidance of filters in the making of exposures, thereby enabling more light to reach the plate, with a consequent shortening of exposure time, and convenience in the viewing. Neither lines nor granules are visible in the final result, and all the light is absorbed where the primaries overlap, so that the stock on which the images are printed remains unaffected—white paper stays white. Experiments based on this theory involved the design of equipment to make three color negatives, either at one time or with repeating backs on the camera, and improved methods of superimposing the three complementary positives. In this endeavor, the contributions of Frederick E. Ives, who had invented a Kromskop camera and viewer in 1895 and produced a Tripak camera that eventually was marketed in 1914 as the Hicro Universal camera, were significant.

To produce color prints, photographers turned first to the carbon process. Following Du Hauron's early Heliochromes on tissues dyed cyan, magenta, and yellow, nearly all color printing revolved around gelatin and carbon materials, with the Pinatype process in France, the Ives-Hicro and Carbro processes in the United States, and the Jos-Pe process in Germany the best known. None of these processes survived after the middle of the 20th century, when they were replaced by methods worked out during the 1930s and popularized commercially after the second World War (*see A Short Technical History, Part III*).

Photomechanical Processes

Photomechanical reproduction developed during the late 19th century to respond to the growing demand for photographic reproductions for social documentation and, later, advertising. While excellent reproduction of camera images was achieved by the Woodburytype process (confusingly called *photoglyptie* in France)—a procedure in which no line or dot matrix is needed to break up the continuous tones into discrete ink-holding particles—these prints were not compatible with mechanical type, and in addition had to be trimmed and mounted separately in books and periodicals. Gravure printing, called photogravure, invented in 1879 by Karl Klič in Vienna, produced a subtly graduated print by transferring the photograph to a flat copperplate using a fine-line screen and etching it like an aquatint. It was not necessary to trim the print, which simplified its insertion into books, but the picture still could not be printed in the same operation as the type, and furthermore required expert handling on the part of the platemaker. The absence of a visible mechanically imposed facture in this process made it the method of choice for aesthetically oriented photographers, among them Peter Henry Emerson, Alvin Langdon Coburn, Craig Annan, and Alfred Stieglitz. In 1890, a time-saving improvement (of no interest to aesthetic printers) led to the invention of rotogravure. Using cylindrical gravure plates on a rotary press, this development made possible high-quality photographic reproduction in popular periodicals and newspapers.

Photolithography or collotype was another development of the second half of the 19th century. Based on Senefelder's 1796 discovery that the mutual repulsion of oil and water on a prepared stone could be made to yield a printed impression in greasy ink, photolithography was at first only suitable for line impressions. Success with photographic halftones followed the 1855 discovery by Poitevin that when bichromated gelatin is hardened by exposure to light, it not only causes the stone to repel water and accept ink but also produces reticulation—a fine grain that restructures continuous tonalities into barely visible dots. Poitevin received the Duc de Luynes prize for this promising discovery, and in the late 1860s refinements by Bavarian photographer Josef Albert, who called the process Albertype, and by Ernest Edwards, an English photographer who perfected it as Heliotype, made these processes economically feasible for mass production even though they, too, were not directly compatible with type.

Heliotypes were used in England in 1872 for the photographic illustrations of Charles Darwin's *Expression of the Emotions in Man and Animals*, and in 1873 for John Thomson's multivolume *Illustrations of China and Its People*. Collotype continued to be highly regarded in Europe as an optimum method for printing special editions and accurate reproductions of works of art, but though it achieved a measure of popularity in the United States in the late 1860s through the efforts of the painter and occasional photographer Albert Bierstadt, interest was brief. A modified photolithographic procedure employed by newspaperman Stephen Horgan made possible the first directly transcribed photolithographic illustration in an American newspaper, *The New York Graphic*, in 1873.

The lack of interest in collotype in the United States, ascribed by some writers at the time to the humid climate in the East that made all gelatin and carbon technologies difficult, actually was owed to the greater interest in developing a successful relief printing process. By using a screen (a method suggested by Talbot in 1852), the continuous tones of the photograph were transformed into a code of dots small enough not to interfere with the visual information in the picture. First patented in 1881 by Ives, who continued for the next 25 years to refine equipment and procedures, this invention revolutionized the delivery of photographic images to the public because illustration and type could be printed in the same operation. Experimentation with screens for the process was carried on by Georg Meisenbach in Germany and by Ives, Max Levy, and Horgan in the United States, eventually resulting in the basic halftone process called photoengraving.

This involves coating a plate with a light-sensitive emulsion, exposing it to a negative through one of a variety of fine- or coarse-lined screens, and processing the plates to make the resultant "dots" acid resistant. After etching the plate to remove the metal from around the "dots," its raised surfaces are inked with a roller (unlike gravure plates, where the etched areas receive the ink and the surface is wiped clean) and the image is transferred under pressure to paper. Whether of indifferent or excellent quality—and wide latitude is possible in photoengraving—printing with process halftone plates resulted in considerable savings of time and expense. Despite initial difficulties with paper quality and platemaking, photoengraving proved to be exactly right for large-scale pictorial illustration in periodicals and books. In the early 1890s, "visual surrogates of reality," as photographs were called, began to appear in halftone in books, magazines, pamphlets, and broadsides, to become an integral aspect of the campaigns for social reform. The development of the process halftone plate also inaugurated an era of photojournalism of a broader nature.

The Machine:
Icons of the
Industrial Ethos

This album presents a selection of images by eight leading American photographers who worked in the Precisionist style in the 1920s and '30s. During this period, photography was hailed as the visual medium most in harmony with the conditions and culture of modern life. Factories, machine tools, assembly lines, multistoried buildings, and mechanized vehicles (in short, the technology that has come to dominate existence in all industrialized societies) attracted photographers who believed that the camera was eminently suited to deal with their forms and textures. In the United States, where the industrial ethos was predominant, reverential attitudes toward machinery and its products were especially strong. Commissions from advertising agencies and publications that sought attractive images of consumer goods and industrial installations made it possible for photographers Edward Steichen and Ralph Steiner to photograph cutlery and typewriters, and for Charles Sheeler and Margaret Bourke-White to celebrate the visual possibilities of the Ford Motor plant and Fort Peck Dam. Others who may have been less convinced of the unalloyed benefits of industrialism—among them Imogen Cunningham, Paul Strand, Willard Van Dyke, and Edward Weston— were nonetheless also drawn to portray water towers, machine tools, ship funnels, and smoke stacks. Whatever the ideological positions of these photographers with regard to machinery, their images reveal a compelling respect for clarity, for clean crisp lines, and for precise geometrical volumes in the products of machine culture.

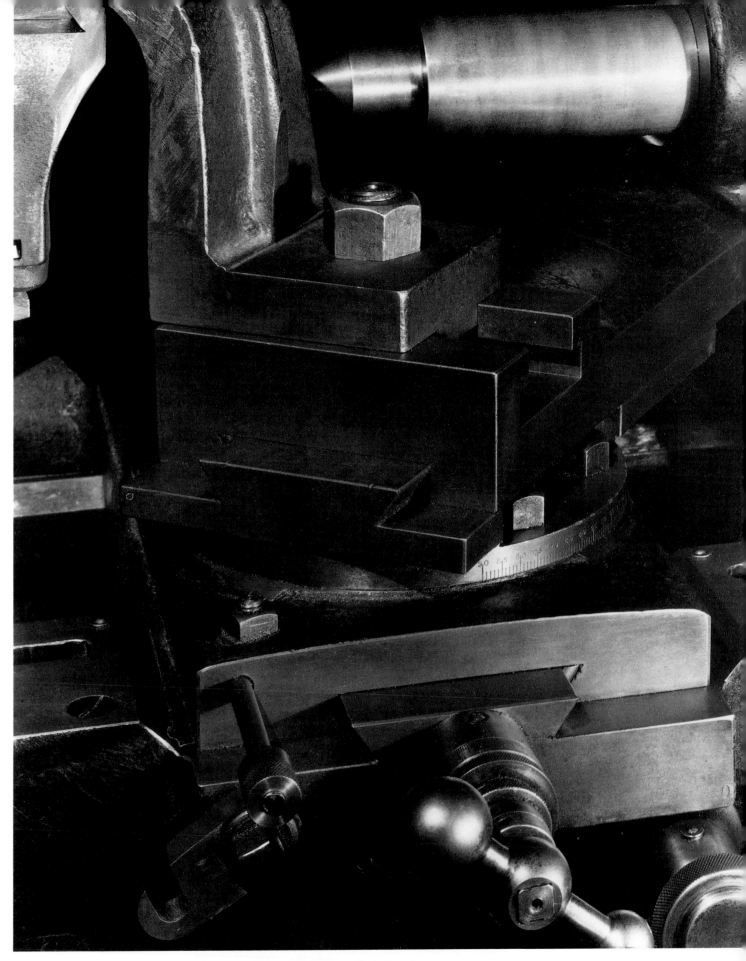

578. PAUL STRAND. *Lathe No. 3, Akeley Shop, New York*, 1923. Gelatin silver print.
© 1980 The Paul Strand Foundation, Millerton, N.Y.

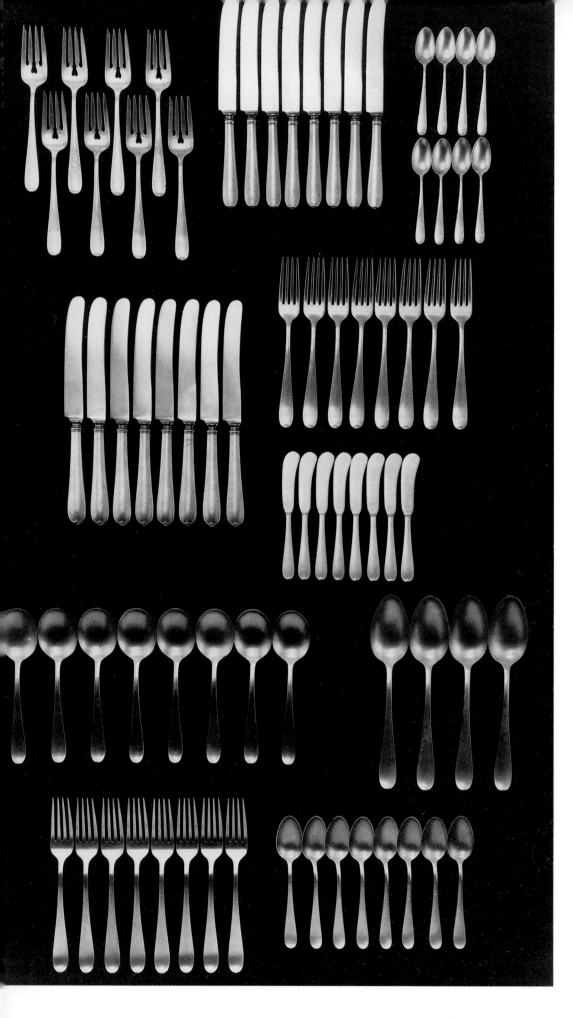

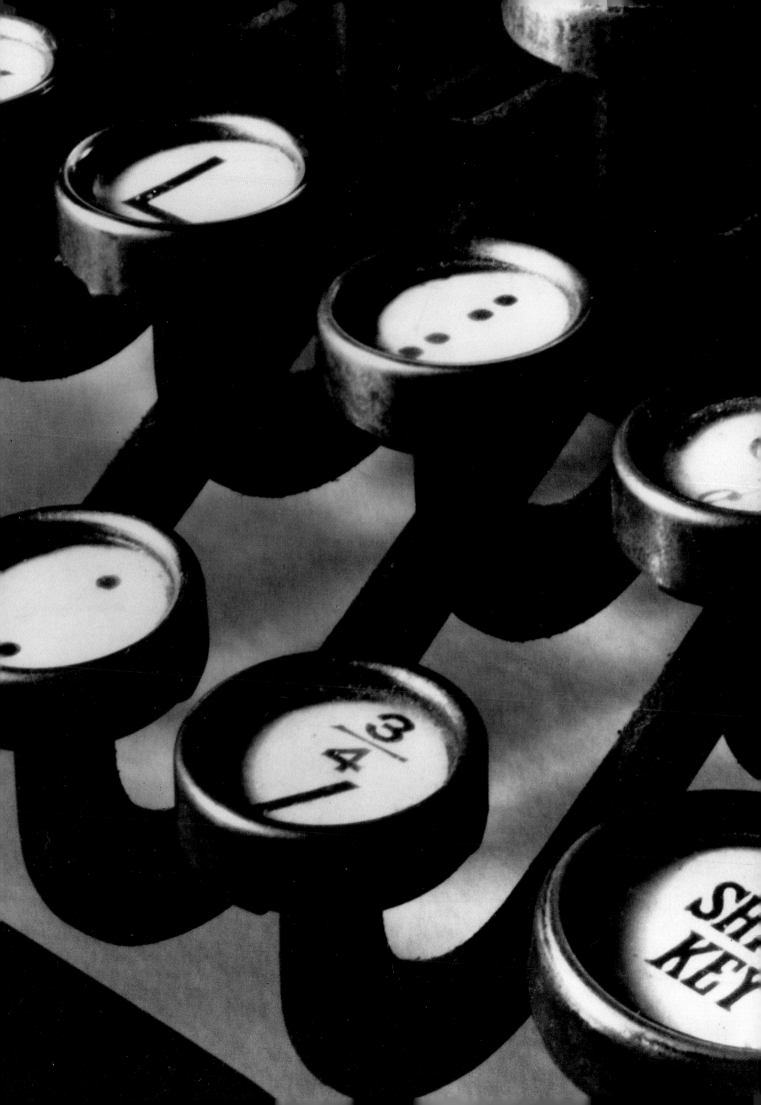

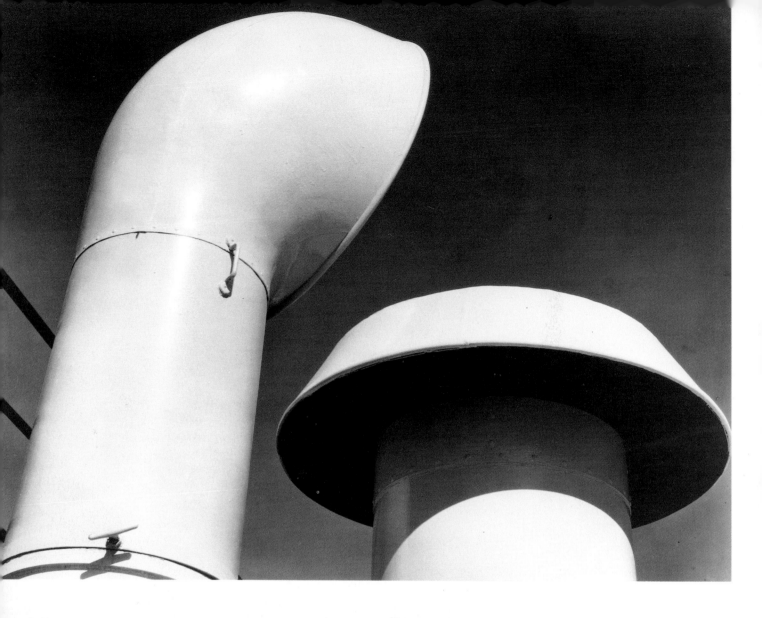

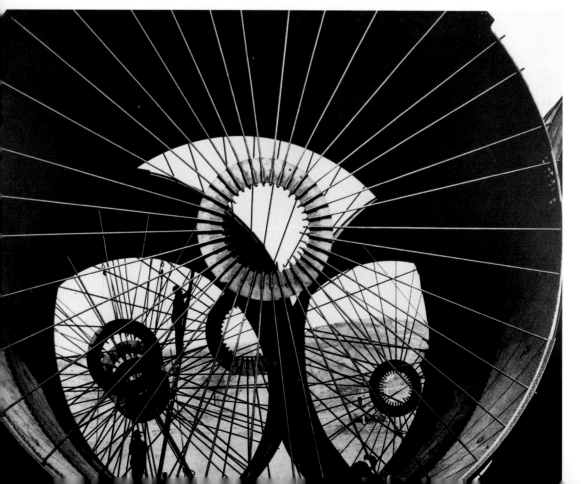

581. WILLARD VAN DYKE. *Funnels*, 1932. Gelatin silver print. Courtesy and © Willard Van Dyke.

LEFT:

582. MARGARET BOURKE-WHITE. *Construction of Giant Pipes Which Will Be Used to Divert a Section of the Missouri River During the Building of the Fort Peck Dam, Montana*, 1936. Gelatin silver print. *Life Magazine* © 1936 Time Inc.; courtesy Life Picture Service, New York.

RIGHT:

583. IMOGEN CUNNINGHAM. *Shredded Wheat Water Tower*, 1928. Gelatin silver print. © 1979 Imogen Cunningham Trust, Berkeley, Cal.

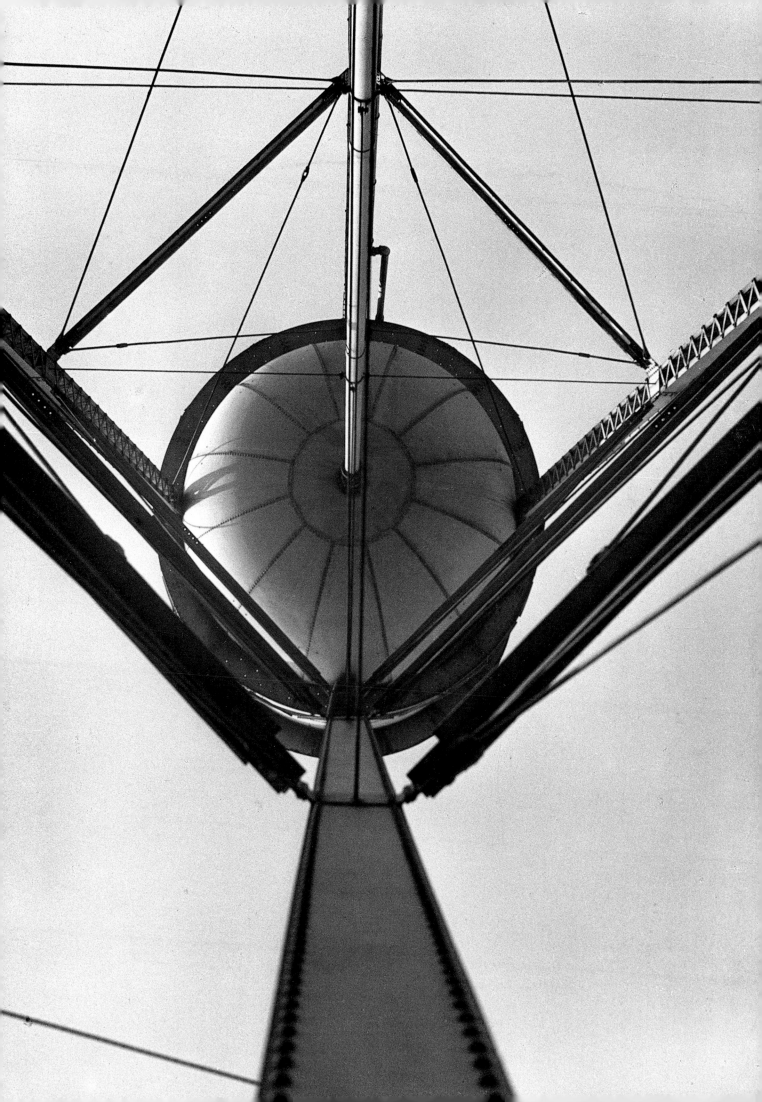

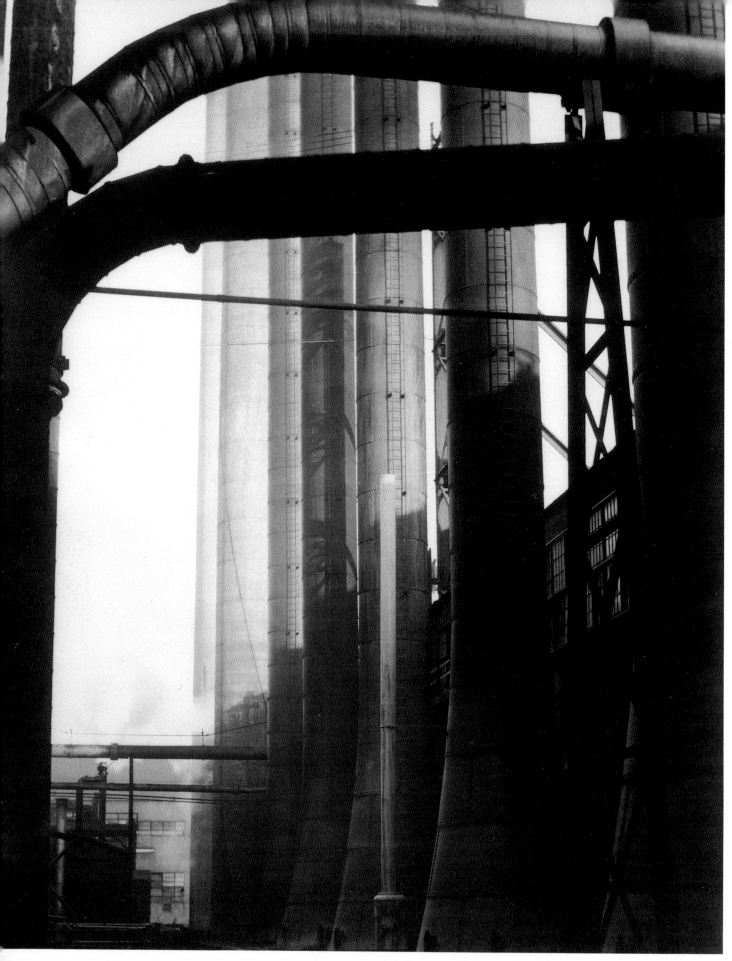

584. EDWARD WESTON. *Armco Steel, Ohio*, 1922. Gelatin silver print. © 1981 Arizona Board of Regents,
Center for Creative Photography, University of Arizona, Tucson, Ariz.

585. CHARLES SHEELER. *Industry*, 1932. (Montage, middle panel of a triptych). Gelatin silver print. Art Institute of Chicago; Julien Levy Collection.

IO.

WORDS AND PICTURES: PHOTOGRAPHS IN PRINT MEDIA

1920–1980

Every propagandist knows the value of a tendentious photograph: from advertising to political posters, a photograph if properly chosen, punches, boxes, whistles, grips the heart and conveys the one and only new truth.

—Peter Panter (Kurt Tucholsky), 1926[1]

"HERE COMES THE NEW PHOTOGRAPHER"[2] was the rallying cry of European modernists in the 1920s. This characterization embraced more than just the fresh aesthetic and conceptual viewpoints discussed in the preceding chapter; it applied equally to photoreportage. As halftone printing techniques and materials improved, new outlets for camera images were opened in journalism and advertising. Fast and portable equipment (see A Short Technical History, Part III) introduced different ways of working, which in turn changed attitudes about taking, making, and displaying photographs. Even the documentary sensibility, discussed in Chapter 8, was affected by the spread of photojournalism as magazines became the prime vehicle for picture essays. The relationship of trenchant images to carefully organized texts created an interplay of information, attitudes, and effects that, along with the related enterprises of advertising and publicity, revolutionized the role of the photographer, the nature of the image, and the manner in which the public received news and ideas.

Turn of the Century Trends in Print Media

It is difficult to pinpoint any particular time or event as the start of the new forms of photojournalistic communication, because just before the turn of the century the illustrated magazines already had taken on a different complexion, becoming less oriented toward family reading and more concerned with the needs of the literate urbanized individual. Besides providing this readership with informative and entertaining articles on political matters, cultural and sporting events, and issues of social concern, the weeklies began to recognize "the importance of the camera as a means of illustration."[3] It is true that engravings and lithographs based on photographs had enlivened magazines since the mid-1850s, but with the inauguration of halftone screen printing techniques in the 1890s (see A Short Technical History, Part II) the photograph no longer had to be redrawn or restructured by an artist to be usable in newspapers or magazines. General interest journals such as Illustrated American, Illustrated London News, Paris Moderne, and Berliner Illustrierte Zeitung, as well as other periodicals that were directed toward special issues such as social reform (including World's Work and Charities and the Commons), were among the first to recognize that the photograph was both more convincing and more efficient than the artist's sketch.

At first little imagination governed the way that pictures were incorporated into the text of articles, but soon after 1890 periodicals began to pay more attention to page layouts. The pictures were not simply spotted throughout the story; images of different sizes and shapes began to be deliberately arranged, sometimes in overlapping patterns and even occasionally crossing onto the adjacent page. Also, feature stories and articles consisting of just photographs and captions made an appearance. Along with the more arresting layouts, the work of such photographers as Roll and Vert for the French periodical press and of James H. Hare, J. C. Hemment, and Arthur Hewitt for the American weeklies helped inaugurate an interest in picture journalism; this development was a factor in the eventual success of Life, Look, Picture Post, and Paris Match in the 1930s.

The poor quality of newsprint prevented the news dailies from adopting photography as wholeheartedly as the weekly journals did, because newspaper publishers simply preferred a crisply reproduced handmade drawing to an indistinct camera image. However, even when improved paper and platemaking capabilities enabled these publications to shift to halftones soon after 1900, the daily exigencies of deadlines and layouts generally resulted in undistinguished camera images. One exception is the series by Arnold Genthe of the 1906 San Francisco earthquake and fire (pl. no. 586), reproduced in the San Francisco Examiner;[4] however, these pictures, taken by Genthe with a borrowed camera while his own studio and equipment burned, were not the result of an assignment but were made on his own to record the event and express the eerie beauty of the ruins.

Shortly before the new century began, increasing competition for readers among weekly periodicals prompted editors to feature stories of national concern, among which wars and insurrections figured prominently. Reporters and photographers, armed with field- and hand cameras that were somewhat lighter than those used during the Crimean and American Civil wars were dispatched to battlefields around the world to capture, as the Illustrated American put it, "a picturesque chronicling of contemporaneous history."[5] Continuing in the vein explored earlier in the

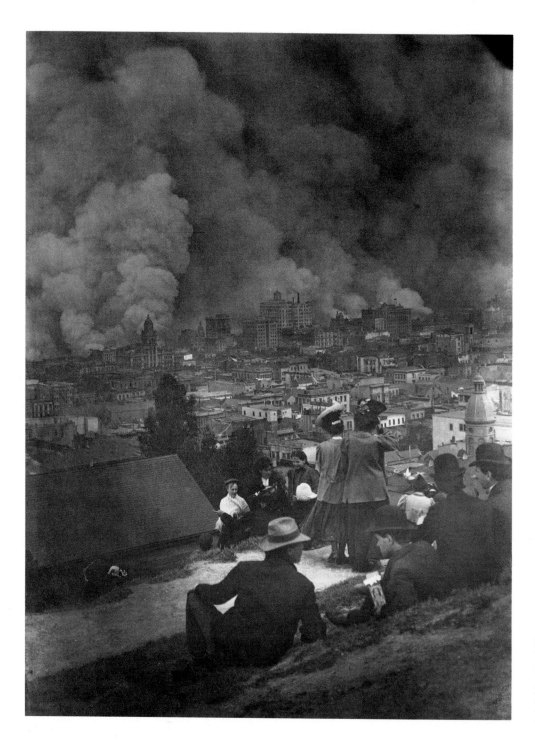

586. ARNOLD GENTHE.
The San Francisco Fire,
1906. Gelatin silver print.
Museum of Modern Art,
New York; gift of the
photographer.

century by Roger Fenton, Mathew Brady, Alexander Gardner, and George N. Barnard *(see Chapter 4)*, Luigi Barzini photographed the Boxer Rebellion and the Russo-Japanese War (and the Peking to Paris Auto Race of 1907) for the Italian journal *Corriere della Sera*; selections of these articles were later published in book form.[6] Horace W. Nicholls covered the Boer War for the British press, intending to make "truthful images" that also would "appeal to the artistic sense of the most fastidious."[7] However, verism not art was the primary aim of most news photographers, in-

cluding Hare and Agustín Víctor Casasola, both of whom photographed conflicts in the Americas around 1900. Hare, an English-born camera designer who emigrated to the United States in 1889, was sent in 1898 by *Collier's Weekly* to Cuba to cover the Spanish-American War. Using a hand camera, he regularly achieved the sense of real-life immediacy seen in *Carrying Out the Wounded During the Fighting at San Juan (pl. no. 587)*; these and similar scenes by Hare of the later Russo-Japanese War enabled *Collier's* to increase both circulation and advertising, which in turn

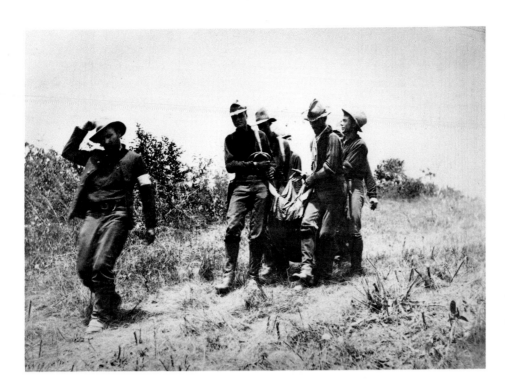

587. JIMMY HARE. *Carrying Out the Wounded During the Fighting at San Juan*, 1898. Gelatin silver print. Humanities Research Center, University of Texas, Austin.

prompted other magazines to use photographs more generously. Images of the Mexican revolution by Casasola, probably the first photographer in his country consciously to think of himself as a photojournalist, seem surprisingly modern in feeling even though made with a view camera and tripod. Unfortunately, no picture magazines, such as the later Spanish weekly *Nosotros*, were on hand to take advantage of this photographer's keen eye for dramatic expression and gesture *(pl. no. 588)*; aside from a poorly reproduced selection published as *Album Gráfico Histórico*[8] in 1920, they remained unseen by the public.

War images continued to be a staple of photoreportage, but during the first World War civilian photographers found it difficult to cover the action owing to the strict censorship directed against all civilian cameramen, including the well-regarded Hare who, sent to England and France in 1914 by *Collier's*, complained that "to so much as make a snapshot without official permission in writing means arrest."[9] Compelling visual embodiments of the tension, trauma, or courage associated with this four-year conflict with its nine million fatalities were not often published because military authorities had little conception of the public's appetite for dynamic images.[10] Nevertheless, the setback was only temporary; new attitudes toward reportorial photography that resulted in part from advances in equipment during the mid-1920s and in part from growing prominence of picture journals affected combat photography as well as all other kinds of images.

A crucial factor in this development was the invention in Germany of small, lightweight equipment—the small-plate Ermanox camera, but especially the 35mm roll-film Leica that appeared on the market in 1925. Descended from the amusing detective playthings of earlier times, in that they could be used unobserved, these cameras helped to change the way the photographic image looked and the manner in which photojournalism (and eventually much self-expressive photography) was practiced. Easy to handle, with a fast lens and rapid film-advancement mechanism, the Leica called forth intuitive rather than considered responses and permitted its users to make split-second decisions about exposure and framing, which often imbued the image with a powerful sense of being a slice-of-life excised from a seamless actuality. Other 35mm cameras that appeared in quick succession, as well as the somewhat larger twin-lens Rolleiflex in 1930, promoted this kind of naturalism in photoreportage. Owing to the ease with which exposures were made, the small size of the negative, and the pressures of publication deadlines, 35mm film often was developed and printed in professional laboratories, with either the photographer or—more likely—the picture editor selecting and cropping images for reproduction. The freedom from processing, along with the possibility of representing movement, of capturing both evanescent expression and the sometimes surreal-looking juxtapositions of unlikely elements in the visual field, soon appealed to photographers interested in personal expression as well as those engaged in photojournalistic reportage. As a consequence, a new ideological stance concerning camerawork emerged during the 1930s and grew stronger in subsequent decades. With the increasing acceptance of blurred and sometimes enigmatic shapes and grainy enlargements either in silver print or in printer's ink, this new concept of the photograph differed substantially from the earlier notion of the camera image as a pre-visualized, uniformly sharp, and finely printed artifact.

Photojournalism in Europe: the 1920s and '30s

With other aspects of photography taking on exceptional luster in Germany during the years of the Weimar Republic, it seems natural that photojournalism also should have flourished there. In addition to the well-established *Berliner Illustrierte Zeitung (BIZ)*, which had introduced halftone reproduction of photographs in the 1890s, a host of new illustrated weeklies appeared after 1918, among them the dynamic *Münchner Illustrierte Presse (MIP)*. The quest for interesting views and layouts *(pl. no. 589)* reflected the desire on the part of cosmopolitan readers for picture stories about social activities, movies, sports, and life in foreign lands. The photographer was expected to shoot sequences that might be cropped, edited, and arranged to form a narrative in pictures with only a minimum of text, making it almost possible to "forget reading" as some were to counsel.[11] The idea for this kind of picture story actually had surfaced almost 40 years earlier when Nadar staged an interview between himself and the chemist/color theorist

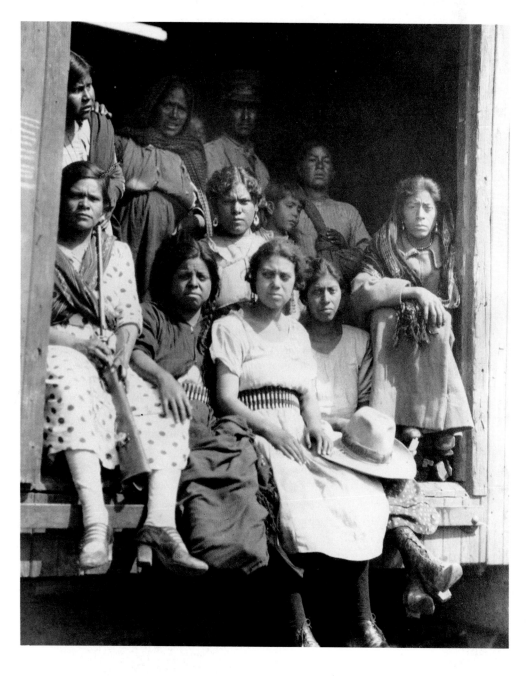

588. AGUSTÍN VÍCTOR CASASOLA. *Mexican Revolution*, c. 1912. Gelatin silver print. Private collection.

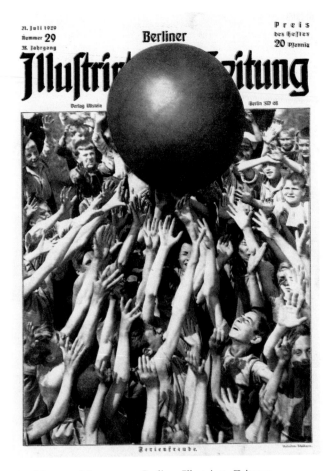

589. MARTIN MUNKACSI. *Berliner Illustrierte Zeitung (BIZ)*, July 21, 1929. Magazine cover. Private collection.

Eugène Chevreul, which his son Paul Nadar photographed using a camera with a roll-film attachment. The 27 images, eight of which appeared in *Le Journal illustré* in 1886 *(pl. nos. 590–593)*, reveal a degree of posturing; this stiffness would later be avoided with faster film, more sensitive lenses, and the easier handling of 35mm equipment.

As magazines began to use sequences of captioned images more extensively, the role of the picture editor became crucial. In Germany, the new vitality in selection, spacing, and arrangement was exemplified by Stefan Lorant, a former Hungarian film editor whose persuasive handling of pictorial material for *MIP* was guided by a keen awareness that readers wished to be entertained as well as informed. The appetite for dynamic picture images also led to a new role for the picture agency. These enterprises had evolved from companies that during the 1890s had stocked large selections of photographs, including stereographs, to meet the demands of middle-class viewers and burgeoning magazines. Agencies now concerned themselves with generating story ideas, making assignments, and collecting fees in addition to maintaining files of pic-

tures from which editors might choose suitable illustrations. In mediating between publisher and photographer, agencies such as *Photodienst*, or *Dephot* as it was known, and *Weltrundschau*, the two main sources of images for German weeklies after 1928, became almost as important to the course of photojournalism as the photographer. Almost, but not quite. The individual photographer was still the "backbone of the new journalism,"[12] as both amateurs and professionals, willing to wait hours "to catch the right moment,"[13] sought provocative and unusual points of view in order to avoid banal or merely descriptive images.

Reportage using available light first emerged in 1928 in the work of Erich Salomon, a German lawyer turned businessman turned photographer who, at age forty-two, began to photograph with the Ermanox (a plate camera of exceptional sensitivity). Well-educated and widely known in political and social circles in Berlin, Salomon, who was in a position to insinuate himself into privileged situations such as political meetings, courtrooms, and diplomatic functions, made his exposures under ordinary lighting conditions; his subjects usually were unaware of the exact instant of exposure even though a shutter speed of about 1/25th of a second and a tripod were required. Artless but full of surprises, these "candid" pictures, as they began to be called, were reproduced in pictorial weeklies in Germany, where their naturalness and psychological intensity contrasted sharply with the usual stiffly posed portraits of politicos and celebrities. Published in book form in 1931 as *Berühmte Zeitgenossen in Unbewachten Augenblicken (Famous Contemporaries in Unguarded Moments)*, Salomon's works convey a delicious sense of spying on the forbidden world of the rich and powerful *(pl. no. 594)*.

In looking back at this period, Tim Gidal, himself a participant, singled out, besides Salomon, Walter Bosshard, Alfred Eisenstaedt, André Kertész, Martin Munkacsi, Felix H. Man (Hans Baumann), Willi Ruge, and Umbo (Otto Umbehrs) as among those who had imposed a distinctive style on their materials. For instance, Munkacsi, initially a painter and sportswriter in Hungary, was exceptionally sensitive to the expressive possibilities of design in split-second reportage, as is apparent in the silhouetted forms of *Liberian Youths (pl. no. 595)*, made on assignment in Africa in 1931. Eisenstaedt, a photojournalist with the Associated Press in Germany until 1935, was more engrossed by gesture and suggestive detail *(pl. no. 596)* than by pictorial design, while Kertész celebrated the poetic quality of ordinary life *(pl. no. 508)* in pictures made for German and French periodicals. The career of Umbo exemplifies the rich and varied background of many of the photojournalists in the early years in that he was trained at the Bauhaus in painting and design and worked in film in Berlin and with the still photographer and montagist Paul Citroën. These

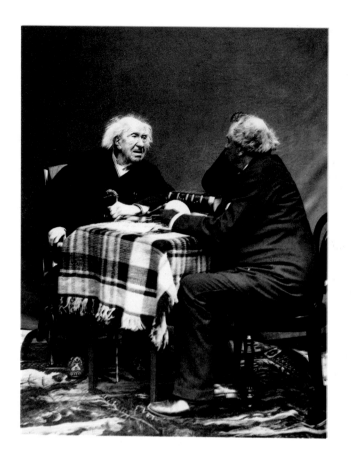
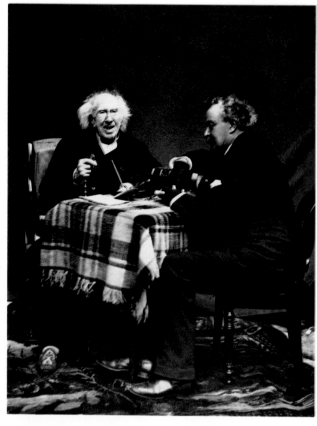
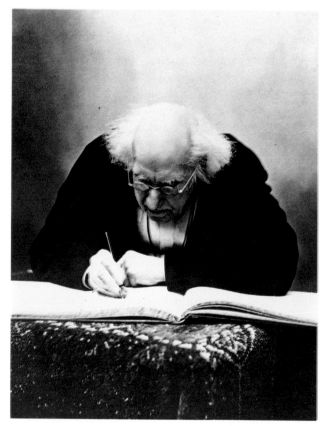
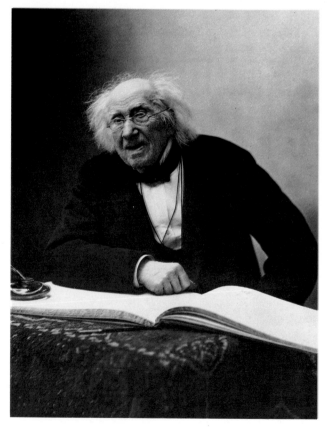

590–93. PAUL NADAR. *The Art of Living a Hundred Years; Three Interviews with Monsieur Chevreul . . .
on the Eve of his 101st Year.* From *Le Journal illustré*, September 5, 1886. Bibliothèque Nationale, Paris.

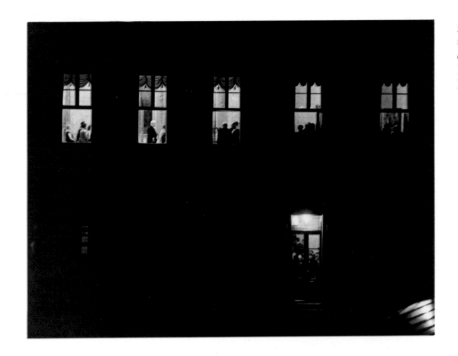

594. ERICH SALOMON. *Presidential Palace in Berlin, Reception in Honor of King Fuad of Egypt*, 1930. Gelatin silver print. Kunstbibliothek, Staatliche Museen Preussischer Kulturbesitz, Berlin.

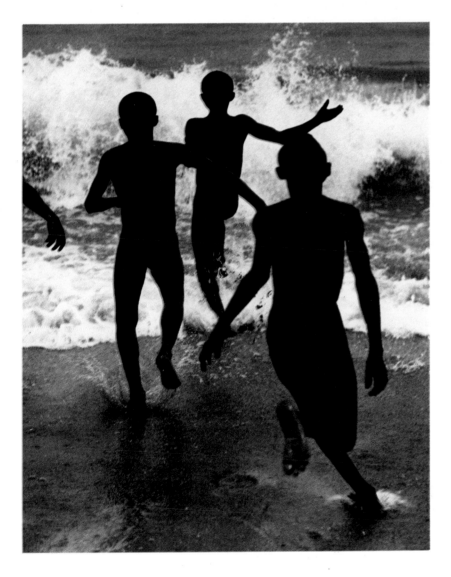

595. MARTIN MUNKACSI. *Liberian Youths*, 1931. Gelatin silver print. International Center of Photography, New York, and Joan Munkacsi, Woodstock, N.Y.

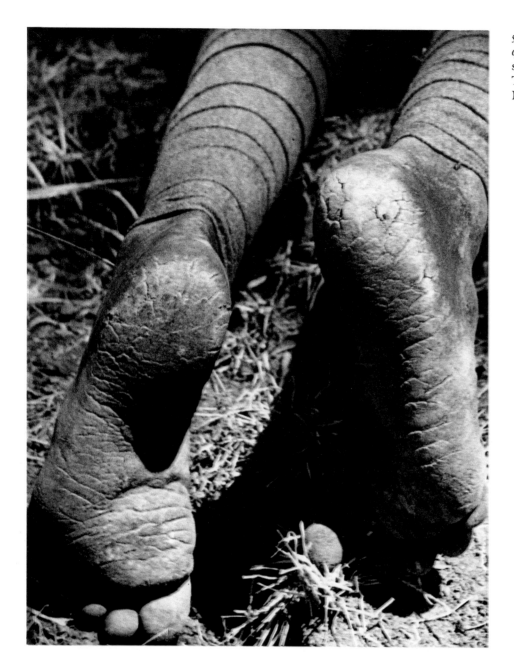

596. ALFRED EISENSTAEDT. *Feet of Ethiopian Soldier*, 1935. Gelatin silver print. *Life Magazine* © 1944 Time Inc; Life Picture Services, New York.

experiences, coupled with his feeling for the brittle and offhand quality of contemporary life in Berlin, helped produce photographs that are a kind of visual equivalent of "street slang" *(pl. no. 599)*.

The journal *Arbeiter Illustrierte Zeitung (AIZ)*, published between 1925 and 1932 in Germany and later in Czechoslovakia, was exceptional because, in addition to photoreportage, its cover pages featured montages by John Heartfield *(see Chapter 9)*, who combined Dadaist sensibility with left-wing ideology. Inspired by the example of Russian Constructivist artists who used photographic collage and montage for utilitarian ends, Heartfield (along with George Grosz) changed this form from one aimed at shocking elitist viewers out of their complacency into a

tool for clarifying social and political issues for a working-class audience. In the designs for book and magazine covers, for posters and illustrations for the Communist press and the publishing company in which he and his brother were involved, Heartfield transformed object into symbol, constructing meaning from materials clipped from newspapers, magazines, and photographic prints made especially for his purposes *(pl. no. 597)*.

Photography in the Soviet Union has been responsive to the ideological changes that have governed the role of all the visual arts, but the emphasis always has been on the camera image as a utilitarian rather than a private personal statement. From the early period around 1917, when portraits and views of Revolutionary leaders and activities by

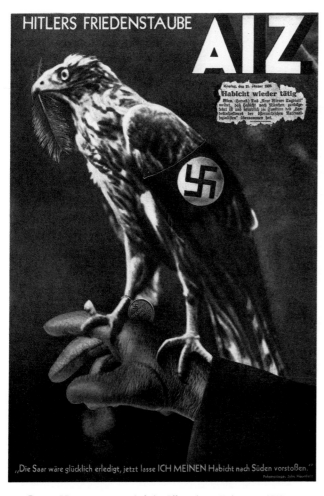

HITLERS FRIEDENSTAUBE

597. JOHN HEARTFIELD. *Arbeite Illustrierte Zeitung (AIZ)*, January 31, 1935. Magazine cover. *Hitler's Dove of Peace.* International Museum of Photography at George Eastman House, Rochester, N.Y.; courtesy Mrs. Gertrud Heartfield.

Pyotr Otsup and Jakob Steinberg convinced Soviet authorities of the medium's potential in mass communication, to the present, the camera has been conceived as a tool for projecting the constructive aspects of national life in books, magazines, and posters. This socially oriented concept gave the formal Constructivist ideas of Alexander Rodchenko their specific tension and made them acceptable because the techniques he used—montage, the close-up, and the raking view from an unusual angle—were regarded as a means of creating a fresh vision of a society building itself.

The adaptability of montage in particular led Soviet artists to consider it "a direct and successful way of achieving the mammoth task of re-educating, informing, and persuading people."[14] Rodchenko's handling of this technique in designs for book jackets, illustrations—including a series for Vladimir Mayakovsky's poem *Pro Eto* ("About This")—and especially for the magazine of the arts *LEF (Left Front of the Arts)* and *Novyi LEF (New Left) (pl. no. 598)* with which he was associated during the mid-1920s, invigorated Soviet graphic art. A compatriot, the painter El Lissitzky, also contributed photographic montages for book covers and posters that were intended to construct a fresh vision of reality through rearranging reproductions of that very reality. Rodchenko's straight photography also had a significant influence on the photojournalism of the 1920s. For example, the marked tonal contrast and the diagonal forms in an image of a construction site *(pl. no. 542)* by Boris Ignatovich (who with his sister were pupils of Rodchenko) recreate visually the dynamism of the activity itself, while symbolizing its larger meaning for society.

An opposing trend in Russian photojournalism that

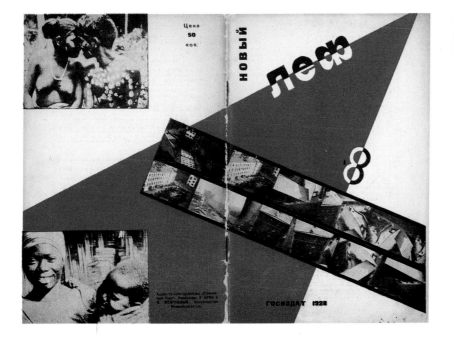

598. ALEXANDER RODCHENKO. *Novyi LEF*, August, 1928. Magazine cover. Ex Libris, New York.

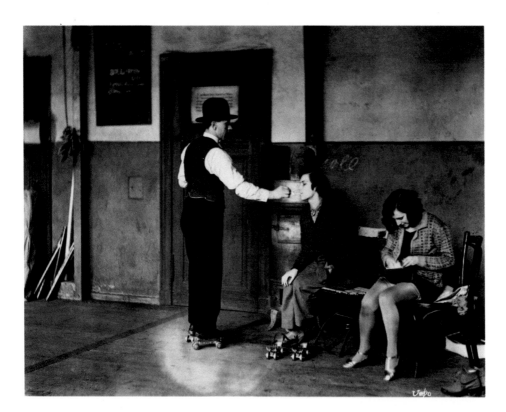

also was visible at the time, which during the mid-1930s became predominant, favored less formalistic visual means and a more humanistic approach. This attitude is embodied in the work of Arkady Shaikhet, Max Alpert, and Georgy Zelma, to cite but three of the well-regarded photojournalists of the period. Alpert, a photoreporter first for *Pravda* and then for the influential journal *The U.S.S.R. in Construction* (published in four languages), concentrated on stories about major construction projects in the provinces, seeking through the close-up and long shot to project the vastness and communal activity required by such enterprises as the building of the Fergana Grand Canal in Uzbekistan *(pl. no. 600)*. An even greater reliance on gesture and expression rather than on formal elements as visual metaphors for the dynamism of society can be seen in Zelma's 1932 image of a child being joyfully propelled forward off the ground *(pl. no. 601)*.

Combinations of words and images became a significant force in the graphic arts of other Eastern European nations. In Poland, *Kemal Pasha (pl. no. 603)*, by foremost montagist Mieczyslaw Szczuka, who referred to the form as "visual poetry,"[15] and *City, Mill of Life (pl. no. 604)* by the avant-garde painter Kazimierz Podsadecki, are two examples of book covers produced under the active influence of Constructivism. Karel Teige was the most prominent of a number of Czech photographers whose montages appeared on publicity and book jackets *(pl. no. 493)*. In these countries, montage, collage, and other modernist techniques continued to prove their vitality up to and beyond the second World War.

Soon after the start of the new small-camera journalism in Germany, its attractions were felt in other western European centers. *Vu* was introduced in Paris in 1928 by Lucien Vogel, a socially concerned individual who regarded the magazine as "at once a form of expression and a means of action."[16] More stylish and more politically committed than *BIZ*, it departed from German magazine practice by including works by non-photojournalists, reproduced at times solely to introduce a decorative, poetic, or humorous element. In this regard, *Vu* and other French picture magazines of this era reflected the fairly long tradition of piquant photojournalistic images that had been appearing in such weekly journals as *L'Illustration* and *Paris Moderne* since the 1890s. Frequently, the reportage commissioned by *Vu* (as well as by others) was neither illustration nor strictly reportorial photojournalism but, as in the case of Kertész *(pl. no. 508)*, pictures whose visual content and formal elegance might be savored without captions or written text. Under the artistic direction of Alexander Liberman (later with *Vogue*), *Vu* not only made liberal use of such photographs but also was distinguished by the inventive use of montage on its covers and in many of its feature articles.

Political events in Germany during the 1930s inadvertently aided the spread of the new journalism and popularized the 35mm camera as an expressive instrument. As

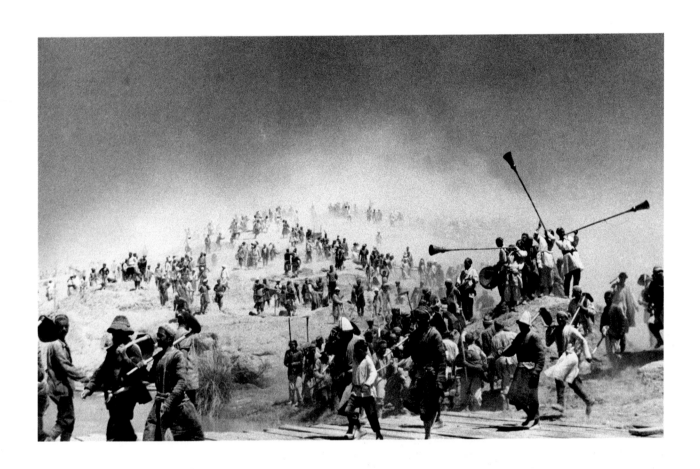

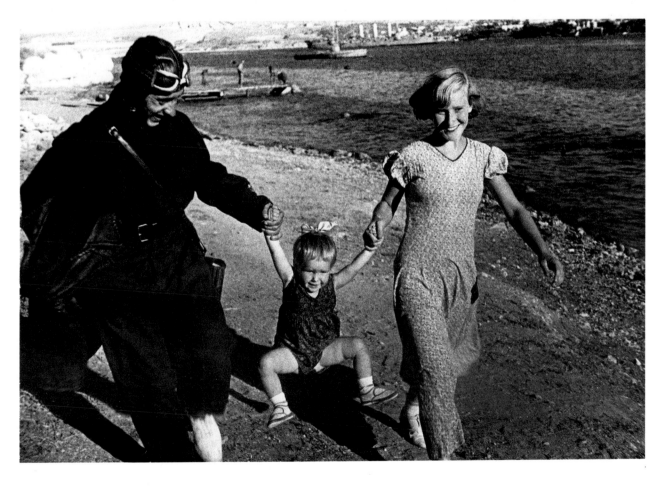

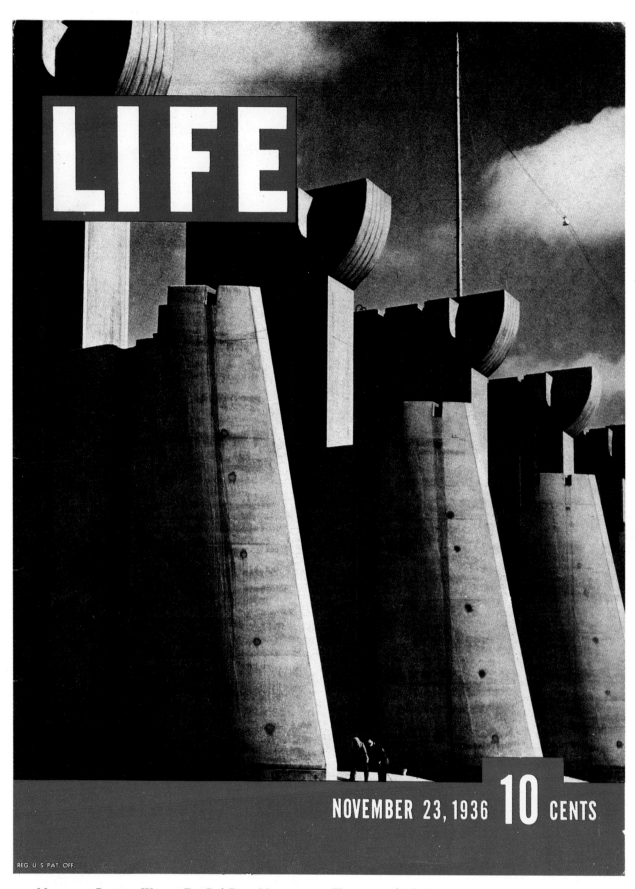

602. MARGARET BOURKE-WHITE. *Fort Peck Dam, Montana*, 1936. First cover of *Life Magazine*, November 23, 1936.
Life Magazine © 1936 Time Inc.; Life Picture Service, New York.

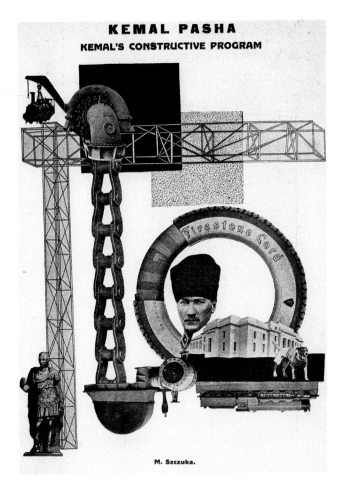

KEMAL PASHA
KEMAL'S CONSTRUCTIVE PROGRAM

M. Szczuka.

603. MIECZYSLAW SZCZUKA. *Kemal Pasha: Kemal's Constructive Program*, c. 1928. Photocollage. Museum of Fine Art, Lodz, Poland; International Center of Photography, New York.

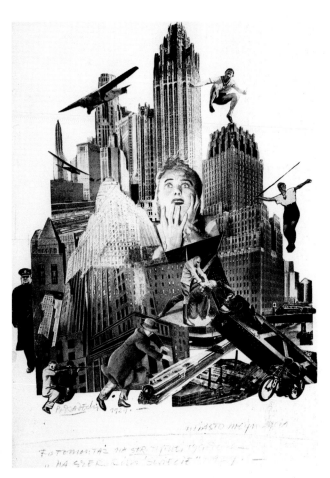

604. KAZIMIERZ PODSADECKI. *City, Mill of Life*, 1929. Photomontage. Museum of Fine Art, Lodz, Poland; International Center of Photography, New York.

illustrated magazines were converted into propaganda arms of the Nazi regime, many of the editors and photographers who had conceived of the idiom fled Germany, carrying their equipment, experiences, and outlook beyond France to England, and—when the second World War engulfed Europe—to the United States. To cite only a few examples of this rich influx of talent, Lorant's stimulating editing enlivened the pages of *Weekly Illustrated* and *Picture Post* in London during the 1930s before he came to the United States where he turned his talent with words and images to book format. After 1933, Munkacsi, working as a fashion photographer for *Harper's Bazaar*, projected a new image of informality in that field, while Eisenstaedt became one of the mainstays of *Life* magazine, which featured over a thousand of his feature stories during the next 40 years. Salomon was one of the few well-known photojournalists to have been trapped by the Nazis; in the midst of an illustrious career in the Netherlands he was arrested for being Jewish and sent to his death in Auschwitz in 1944.

Picture journalism in England during the early 1930s

reflected a variety of influences as photographers drew upon the styles associated with Russian Constructivism and the New Objectivity and on their own picturesque and genre traditions in photography. As was true generally of the picture weeklies everywhere, the competition with cinema newsreels for public attention prompted British journals such as *The Listener* and *Weekly Illustrated* to give greater consideration to lively formats and compelling images that might suggest the complexity of contemporary events. This direction continued and was reinforced with the publication in 1938 of *Picture Post*, a journal that transformed the German photojournalistic experience into an acceptably British product through the efforts of its editor Lorant and the German exile photographers Kurt Hutton (Hübschmann) and Man. Britishers Humphrey Spender and Bill Brandt gave their photojournalistic images a socially oriented direction, while Bert Hardy, who began his career on *Picture Post* in the early 1940s and eventually became known as an "all-round cameraman," established what has been called a "populist idea of Britain."[17]

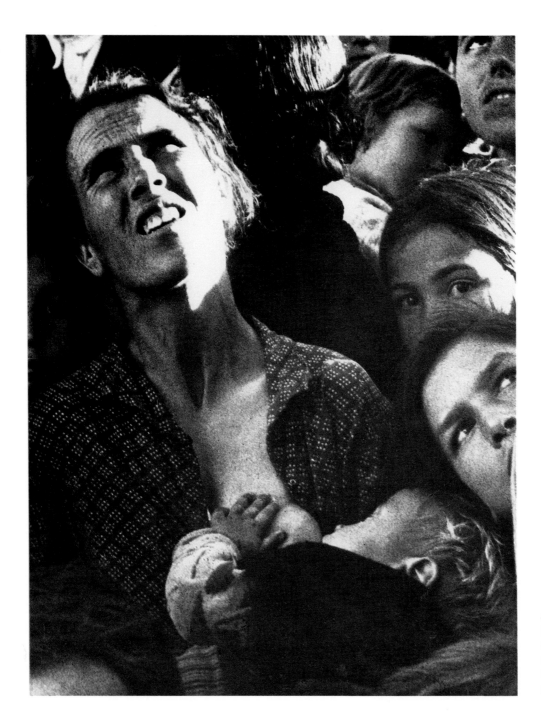

605. CHIM (DAVID
SEYMOUR). *Air Raid
Over Barcelona*, 1936.
Gelatin silver print.
© Chim (David Seymour)/
Magnum.

Photojournalism—War Reportage

In the United States in the late 1930s, *Life* magazine, which had evolved from ideas and experiences tested in Europe even though it was itself quintessentially American, came to represent a paradigm of photojournalism. For its concept, *Life*, a publication of Henry Luce, drew upon many sources. In addition to the example of the European picture weeklies, it took into account the popularity of cinema newsreels, in particular *The March of Time* with which the Luce publishing enterprise was associated. The

successes of Luce's other publications—the cryptically written *Time* and the lavishly produced *Fortune*, with its extensive use of photographic illustration to give essays on American industrialism an attractive gloss—also were factors in the decision to launch a serious picture weekly that proposed to humanize through photography the complex political and social issues of the time for a mass audience.

Following *Life*'s debut in 1936, with a handsome industrial image of the gigantic concrete structure of Fort Peck Dam by Margaret Bourke-White on its first cover *(pl. no. 602)*, the weekly demonstrated that through selection,

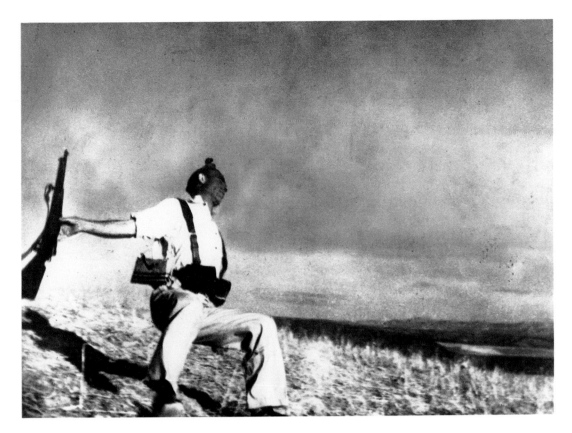

606. ROBERT CAPA. *Death of a Loyalist Soldier*, 1936. Gelatin silver print. © Robert Capa/Magnum.

607. ROBERT CAPA. *Normandy Invasion*, June 6, 1944. Gelatin silver print. © Robert Capa/Magnum.

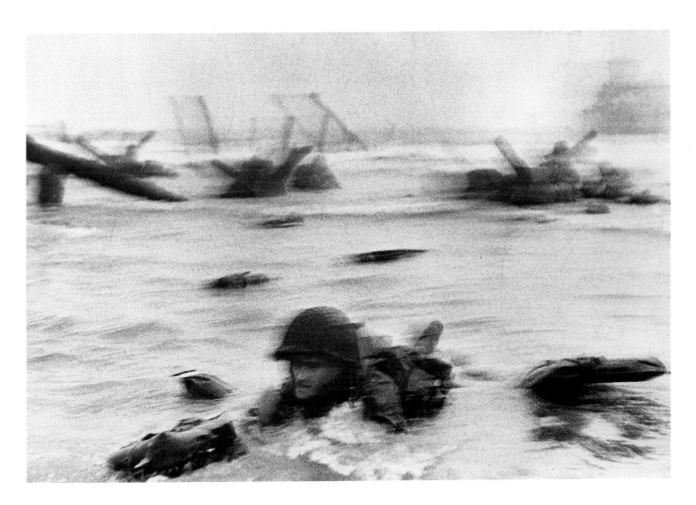

arrangement, and captioning, photographs could, in the words of its most influential picture editor Wilson Hicks, "lend themselves to something of the same manipulation as words."[18] Vivid images, well printed on large-size coated stock, attracted a readership that mounted to three million within the magazine's first three years. *Life* was followed by other weeklies with a similar approach, among them *Look* and *Holiday* in the United States, *Picture Post, Heute, Paris Match,* and *Der Spiegel* in Europe.

The first ten years of *Life* coincided with the series of conflicts in Africa, Asia, and Europe that eventually turned into the second World War. Not surprisingly, between 1936 and 1945 images of strife in Abyssinia, China, France, Italy, the Soviet Union, and remote Pacific islands filled the pages of the magazine; for the first time worldwide audiences were provided a front-row seat to the global conflict. In response to the insatiable demand for dramatic pictures and despite censorship imposed by military authorities or occasioned by the magazine's own particular editorial policy, war images displayed a definite style, thanks in part to new, efficient camera equipment. The chance to convince isolation-prone Americans of the evils of Fascism undoubtedly was a factor in the intense feeling visible in a number of the images by European photojournalists on the battlefields.

In style, these photographs were influenced by both the precise character of the New Objectivity and the spontaneity engendered by the small camera. Eisenstaedt's portrayal of an Ethiopian soldier who fought in puttees and bare feet against Mussolini's army during the Italian conquest of Abyssinia in 1935 *(pl. no. 596)* focuses in on an unusual and poignant detail to suggest the tragedy of the unprepared Abyssinians fighting a ruthless well-equipped army. *Air Raid Over Barcelona (pl. no. 605)* by Chim (David Seymour) conveys through harsh contrast and the facial expression of the woman looking upward the (then) incomprehensible act of bombing civilian populations, carried out with force for the first time during the Spanish Civil War. An even more famous image of this conflict is *Death of a Loyalist Soldier (pl. no. 606)* by Robert Capa, a Hungarian-born photojournalist whose images of the Civil War appeared in *Vu, Picture Post,* and, in 1938, in a book entitled *Death in the Making.*[19] At the time, the totality of Capa's views of civilians, soldiers, and bombed ruins seemed to sum up the shocking irrationality of war, but the photographer also established the mystique of the photojournalist's commitment to being part of the action being recorded. While Capa quipped that he preferred to "remain unemployed as a war photographer," he held that "if your pictures aren't good enough you're not close enough."[20] Eventually he found himself photographing the invasion of Normandy on D-Day *(pl. no. 607)* for *Life;* he died in 1954

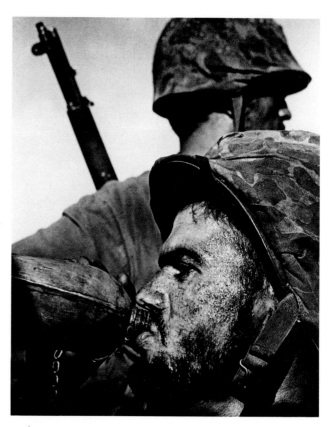

608. W. EUGENE SMITH. *Marines under Fire, Saipan,* 1943. Gelatin silver print. © W. Eugene Smith/Black Star.

on a battlefield in Indo-China where he was killed by a landmine—a fate similar to that of other photojournalists who photographed war action.

Bourke-White, Ralph Morse, Carl Mydans, George Rodger, George Silk, and W. Eugene Smith, among other American photojournalists, were active on various fronts during World War II, while photographers in the Armed Services also provided coverage. The profound empathy that impelled a few photographers to want to share as well as to photograph the day-by-day life of fighting men is embodied in the work of American photojournalist Smith *(see Profile). Marines Under Fire, Saipan (pl. no. 608),* made in 1944 during the Pacific campaign, is one of many images that express compassion for the victimized, whether participants or civilians, who are caught up in an incomprehensible set of circumstances. This attitude continued to be a leit-motif of the imagery made by Western Europeans and Americans during the second World War and its aftermath. It is visible in the work of David Douglas Duncan in Korea, Philip Jones Griffiths in Vietnam, Romano Cagnoni in Cambodia and Pakistan *(pl. no. 610),* and Donald McCullin in Vietnam, Cyprus, and Africa *(pl. no. 611),* to name only a few of the many photojournalists reporting the struggles that continued to erupt in the less-industrialized parts of the world. At times, these photographers relieved the grimness of events by concentrating on the picturesque aspects of the visual scene, exemplified in Duncan's image of the maneuvers of the Turkish cavalry in the snow *(pl. no. 609)*, in which small figures disposed over the flattened white ground bring to mind the miniature art of the Ottoman Empire rather than contemporary preparations for war.

By the way of contrast, the work of Polish and Russian photographers covering the Eastern Front during World War II, seen in Galina Sankova's frozen and dismembered German *(pl. no. 612)* and Dmitri Baltermants's *Identifying the Dead, Russian Front (pl. no. 613)*, often reveal anger or an aroused sense of nationalistic fervor; nor do images of the liberation of Paris by Albert and Jean Seeberger *(pl. no. 614)* concentrate on victimization. Both the German and Japanese photographic record of the war also emphasizes the feats of native soldiers and civilians in Europe and the Pacific, but images taken by Japanese photographers of the aftermath of the atom bombings of Hiroshima and Nagasaki by the United States Air Force are of a different dimension entirely; divested of nationality, the victims have become emblems of the nuclear tragedy that might efface humanity everywhere.

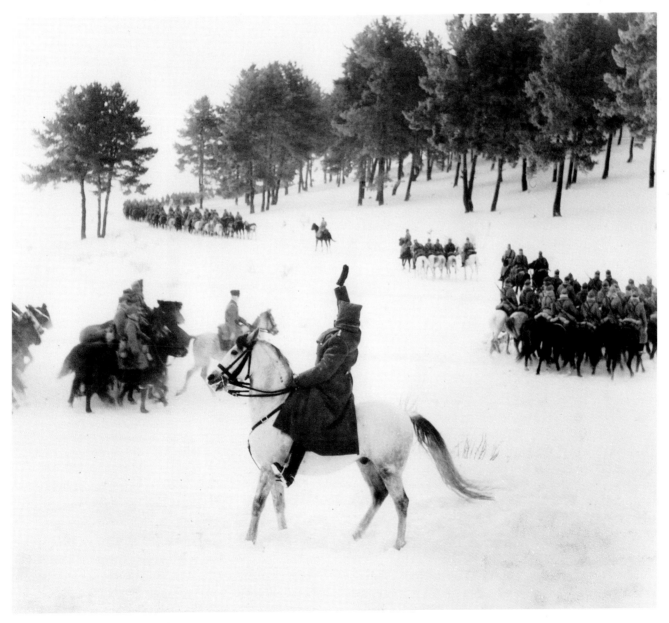

609. DAVID DOUGLAS DUNCAN. *"Black Avni" Turkish Cavalry on Maneuvers*, 1948. Gelatin silver print. Collection Nina Abrams, New York. © David Douglas Duncan.

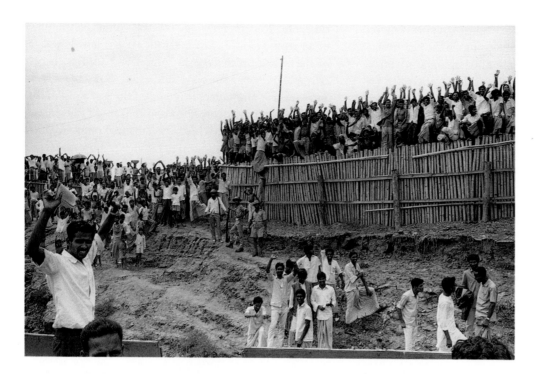

610. ROMANO CAGNONI. *East Pakistan: Villagers Welcoming Liberation Forces*, 1971. Gelatin silver print. © Romano Cagnoni/Magnum.

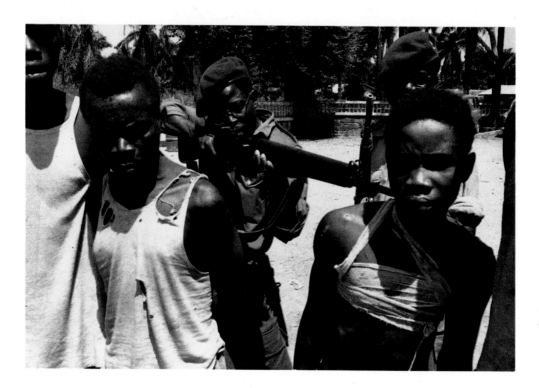

611. DONALD McCULLIN. *Congolese Soldiers Ill-Treating Prisoners Awaiting Death in Stanleyville*, 1964. Gelatin silver print. © Donald McCullin/Magnum.

Postwar Photojournalism

Photographs reproduced in *Life*, *Look*, and other picture journals from 1936 on were by no means solely concerned with war and destruction. The peripatetic photojournalist, pictured in a self-portrait by Andreas Feininger as an odd-looking creature of indeterminate sex, age, and nationality with camera lenses for eyes *(pl. no. 616)*, roamed widely during the mid-century flowering of print journalism. Through photographs, readers of picture weeklies became more conscious of the immensity of human resources and of the varied forms of social conduct in remote places of the globe, even though these cultures ordinarily were seen from the point of view of Western capitalist society.

Readers also were introduced to the immensely useful role played by photographs of the scientific aspects of animal and terrestrial life. By including the microphotographs of Roman Vishniac and Fritz Goro (both émigrés to the United States from Hitler's Germany) as well as views taken through telescopes and from airborne vehicles, the magazine enlarged knowledge of the sciences generally and provided arresting visual imagery in monochrome and color that helped pave the way for the public to accept similar visual abstractions in artistic photography.

In its efforts to encompass global happenings, *Life* included picture stories of the Soviet Union. Taken by Bourke-White, they brought American magazine readers their first glimpse of a largely unknown society; later the mysteries of existence in more remote places were revealed by an array of photographers, among them the Swiss photojournalists Werner Bischof, René Burri *(pl. no. 615)*, and Ernst Haas and the French photographers Cartier-Bresson and Marc Riboud, all of whom aimed their cameras at life in the Orient. Outstanding images of the hinterlands of South America and India were contributed by Bischof, and of sub-equatorial Africa by Cagnoni, Rodger, Lennart Nilsson, and, in the 1960s, McCullin *(pl. no. 611)*. With the need for photographic essays expanding rapidly, picture agencies became even more significant than before, leading to the establishment of new enterprises in the field, including a number of photographer's collaboratives. The best known, Magnum, was founded in 1947 by Robert Capa, Cartier-Bresson, Chim, and Rodger.

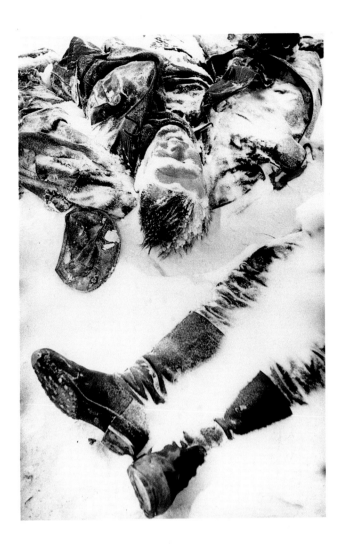

612. GALINA SANKOVA. *Fallen German Soldiers on Russian Front*, 1941. Gelatin silver print. *Sovfoto Magazine* and VAAP, Moscow.

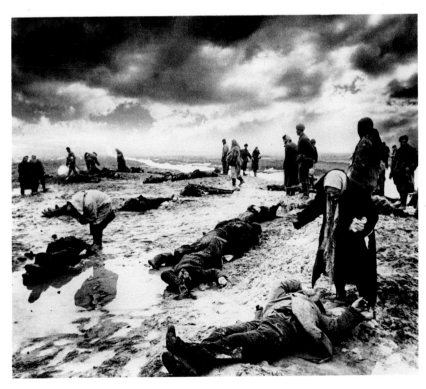

613. DMITRI BALTERMANTS. *Identifying the Dead, Russian Front*, 1942. Gelatin silver print. Courtesy Citizen Exchange Council, New York.

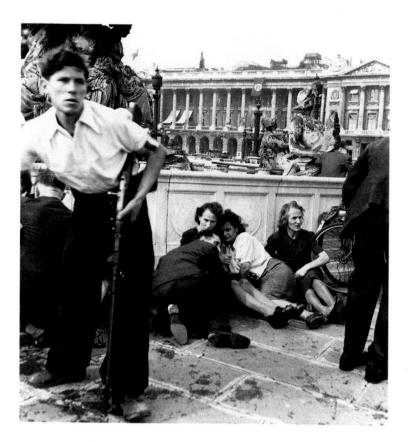

614. ALBERT and JEAN SEEBERGER. *Exchange of Fire at the Place de la Concorde*, 1944. Gelatin silver print. Zabriskie Gallery, New York.

615. RENÉ BURRI. *Tien An Men Square, Beijing*, 1965. Gelatin silver print. © René Burri/ Magnum.

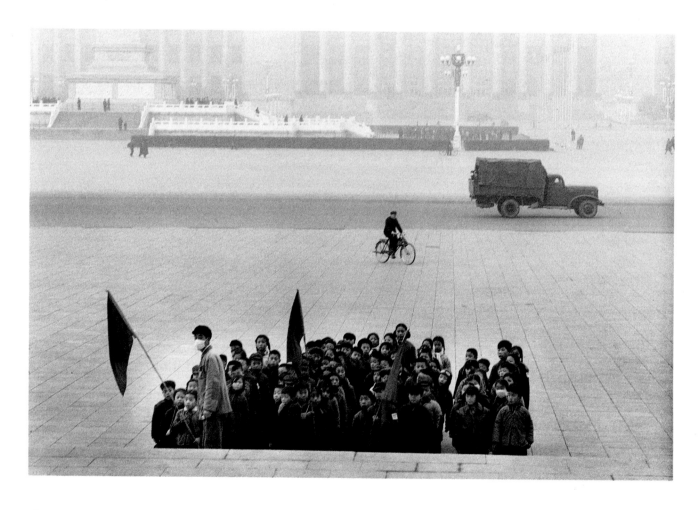

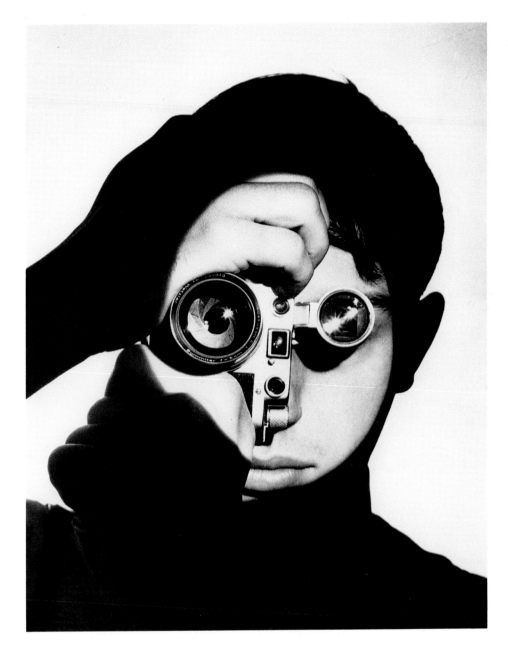

616. ANDREAS FEININGER. *The Photojournalist*, 1955. Gelatin silver print. Life Magazine © 1955 Time Inc.; Life Picture Service, New York.

Gathering bits and pieces of lively "color," these post-war photoreporters and their editors reflected the popular yearning in the West for "one world," an understandable response to the divisiveness of the war. The stability of tradition seen in Constantine Manos's image of Greek villagers pulling a boat *(pl. no. 617)* and the beneficent contrast of old and new in Bischof's *India (pl. no. 618)* are but two examples of recurrent themes and attitudes. Editors and photographers working for periodicals seemed to agree with the pronouncement that "the most important service photography can render . . ." is to record human relations and "explain man to man" and man to himself.[21] This benign idea, which ignored very real political and social antagonisms on both domestic and foreign fronts,

formed the theme of *The Family of Man*, a highly praised joint exhibition and publication consisting largely of journalistic images. Organized by Edward Steichen in 1955, shortly after he was appointed director of the Department of Photography of the Museum of Modern Art, the exhibition consisted of 508 photographs selected from 68 countries that were treated as a three-dimensional picture magazine—enlarged, reduced, and fitted into a layout designed by Steichen in collaboration with photographer Wayne Miller and architect Paul Rudolph, ostensibly to celebrate the "essential oneness of mankind throughout the world." Photographers whose work was displayed in *The Family of Man* had no control over size, quality of print (all were processed in commercial laboratories), or the context in

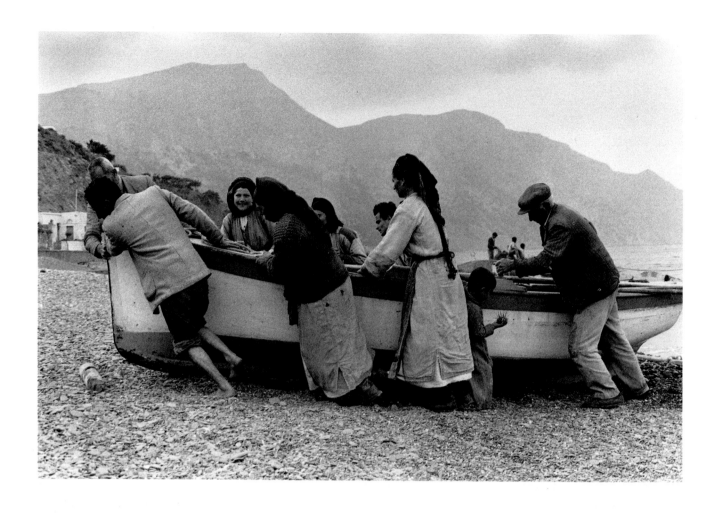

617. CONSTANTINE MANOS. *Beaching a Fishing Boat, Karpathos, Greece c.* 1963. Gelatin silver print. © Constantine Manos/ Magnum.

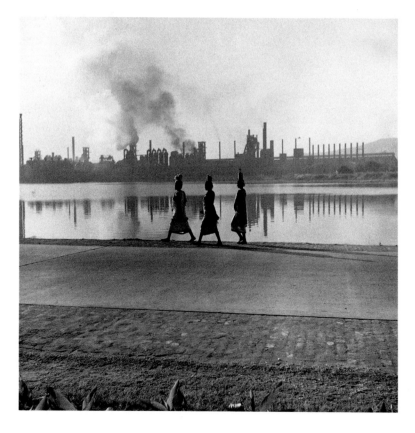

618. WERNER BISCHOF. *India: Jamshedpur Steel Factory,* 1951. Gelatin silver print. © Werner Bischoff/Magnum.

which their work was shown, conditions that were taken over from prevailing magazine practice.[22]

An essential aspect often overlooked in photojournalism has been the relationship between editorial policy and the individual photographer, especially in stories dealing with sensitive issues. Whereas underlying humanist attitudes sometimes provide a common ground between editor and photographer, the latter still has had to submit to editorial decisions regarding selection, cropping, and captioning. That the photographer's intended meaning might be neutralized or perverted by lack of sufficient time to explore less accessible facets of the situation or by editorial intervention in the sequencing and captioning is illustrated by Smith's experiences at *Life*: his numerous picture essays, of which "Spanish Village" *(pl. nos. 654–658)*, photographed in 1950 and published on April 19, 1951, is an example, gave *Life* a vivid yet compassionate dimension, but the photographer's battle for enough time and for control over the way his work was used was continual, ending in 1954 with Smith's resignation.[23]

Toward the mid-1960s, as magazines went out of business or used fewer stories, it became apparent that photojournalism in print was being supplanted by electronic pictures—by video. In 1967, the Fund for Concerned Photography (later the International Center for Photography) was founded to recognize the contributions made by humanistic journalism during the heyday of the picture weeklies. This endeavor, initiated by Cornell Capa, brother of Robert and himself a free-lance photojournalist of repute, celebrated the efforts of "concerned photographers"—initially Bischof, Robert Capa, Leonard Freed, Kertész, Chim, and Dan Weiner—to link photojournalistic images with the humanistic social documentary tradition established by Jacob Riis, Lewis Hine, and the Farm Security Administration photographers. Involving exhibitions, publications, and an archive, the center has since broadened its activities to include photographers whose humanism reveals itself through images of artifacts and nature.

Small Camera Photography in the 1930s

Initially devoted to conveying fact and psychological nuance in news events, the small camera began to appeal to European photographers as an instrument of perceptive personal expression as well. Indeed, the photographs made by Kertész and Henri Cartier-Bresson during the 1930s suggest that it is not always possible to separate self-motivated from assigned work in terms of style and treatment. Kertész saw his work exhibited as art photography at the same time that it was being reproduced in periodicals in Germany and France;[24] what is more, his unusual sensitivity to moments of intense feeling and his capacity to organize the elements of a scene into an arresting visual structure *(see Chapter 9)* inspired both Cartier-Bresson—a photojournalist—and Brassaï (Gyula Halász)—a self-motivated photographer—in their choices of theme and treatment.

Cartier-Bresson approached photography, whether for himself or made in the course of assignments for *Vu* and other periodicals, with intellectual and artistic attitudes summed up in his concept of the "decisive moment." This way of working (with the Leica) embodies an interrelationship of eye, body, and mind that intuitively recognizes the moment in time when formal and psychological elements within the visual field take on enriched meanings. For example, in *Place de l'Europe (pl. no. 619)* one recognizes the ordinary and somewhat humorous gesture of a hurrying person trying to avoid wetting his feet in a street flood, but the picture also involves a visual pun about shadow and substance, life and art. It illustrates (though it hardly exhausts) the photographer's claim that "photography is the simultaneous recognition, in a fraction of a second, of the significance of an event as well as of a precise organization of forms which give the event its proper expression."[25] *(See also pl. nos. 620 and 621.)*

Brassaï, a former painting student transplanted from Hungary to Paris in 1923, found himself mesmerized by the city at night and, on Kertész's suggestion, began to use a camera (a 6.5 x 9 cm. Voigtländer Bergheil) to capture the spectral life at bars, brothels, and on the streets. By turns piquant, satiric, and enigmatic in tone, Brassaï's images for this project display a sensitive handling of light and atmosphere, whether of fog-enshrouded avenues *(pl. no. 622)* or harshly illuminated bars *(pl. no. 623)*, and reveal the photographer's keen sense for the moment when gesture and expression add a poignant dimension to the scene.

An interesting comparison with the subtle suggestiveness of Brassaï's voyeurism, visible in *Paris de Nuit (Paris by Night)* published in 1933, are the strident images included in *Naked City*, a 1936 publication of photographs, many made at night, by American photographer Weegee (Arthur Fellig). This brash but observant free-lance newspaper photographer, who pursued sensationalist news stories with a large press camera, approached scenes of everyday life—and of violence and death—with uncommon feeling and wit; exemplified by *The Critic (pl. no. 624)*, they transcend the superficial character of most daily photoreportage.

Virtually all subsequent 35mm photography was influenced by Cartier-Bresson's formulation of the "decisive moment." In France, heirs to this concept include Robert Doisneau, Willy Ronis, Izis (Bidermanas), and Edouard Boubat—all active photojournalists during the 1940s and later, whose individual styles express their unique sensibilities. Doisneau, who gave up a career in commercial and

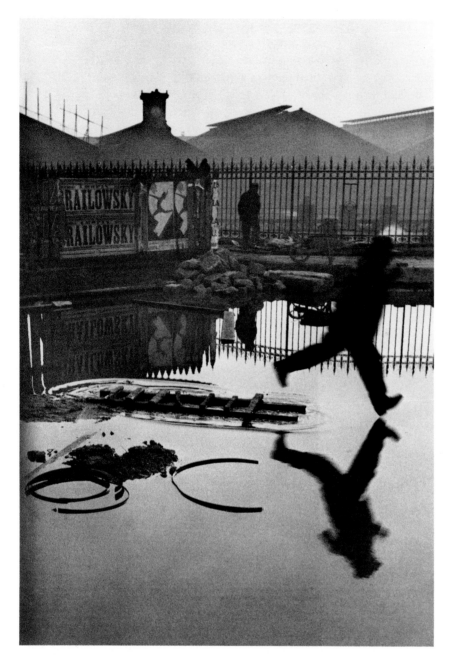

fashion photography late in 1940 to devote himself to depicting life in the street, has brought a delightful and humane humor to his goal of celebrating individuality in the face of encroaching standardization of product and behavior *(pl. no. 625)*. The work of Ronis and Izis *(pl. no. 626)* is lyrical and romantic, while Boubat's images, made during the course of numerous assignments in foreign countries for *Réalités* and *Paris Match*, are tender and touching *(pl. no. 627)*.

A change in attitude toward the photographic print as a visual artifact accompanied the developments discussed so far. Many photographers, Brandt, Brassaï, and Cartier-Bresson among them, refused to consider the photographs they produced as aesthetic objects despite the aesthetic judgments they obviously exercised in making them. The idea, promoted by individuals such as Paul Strand or Edward Weston, that the single print or small edition, sensitively crafted in the individual photographer's darkroom, constituted the paramount standard in expressive photography was challenged when these photographers began to use professional laboratories to process negatives and make prints. With the separation of the act of seeing from the craft of making, there emerged a new aesthetic posture that accepted grainy textures, limited tonal scale, and strong, often harsh contrasts as qualities intrinsic to the photographic medium. This development brought

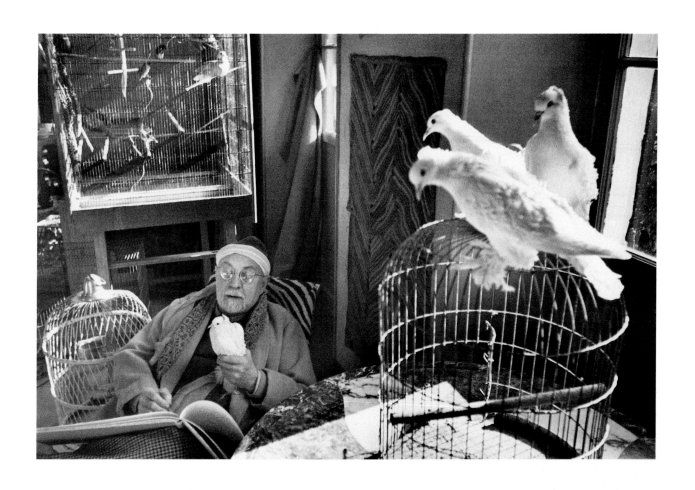

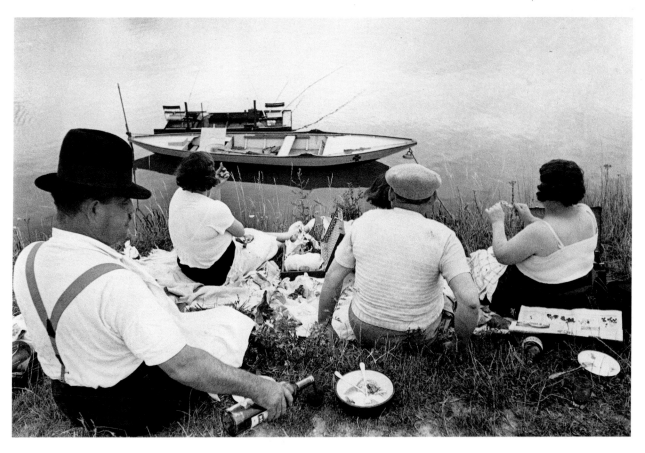

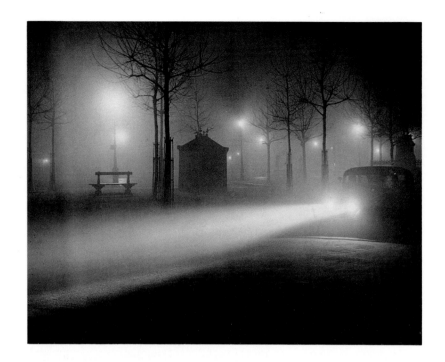

622. BRASSAÏ. *Avenue de l'Observatoire (Paris in the Fog at Night)*, 1934. Gelatin silver print. Metropolitan Museum of Art, New York; Warner Communications, Inc., Purchase Fund, 1980. © Brassaï.

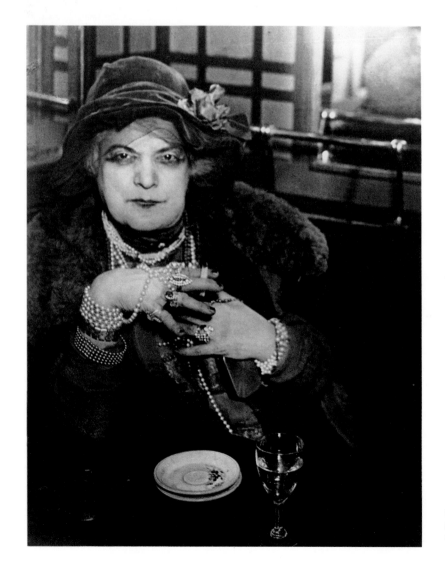

623. BRASSAÏ. *Bijou, Paris*. c. 1933. Gelatin silver print. Marlborough Gallery, New York. © Brassaï.

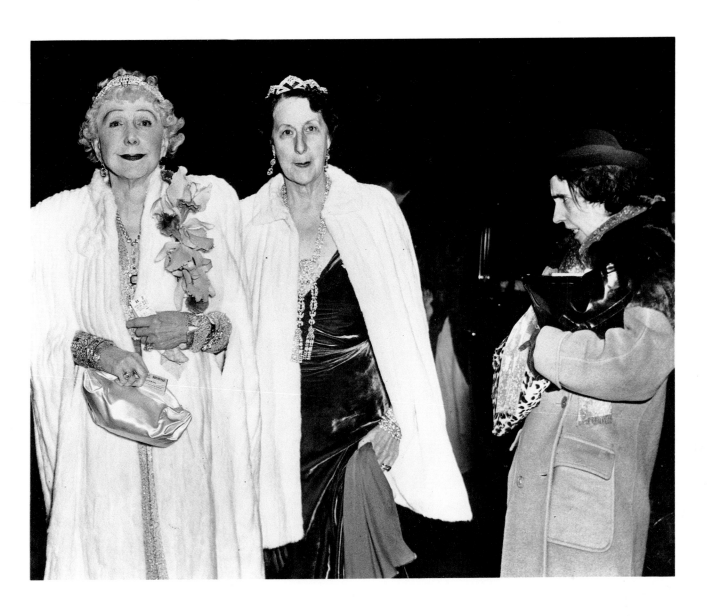

624. WEEGEE (ARTHUR FELLIG). *The Critic
(Opening Night at the Opera)*, 1943. Gelatin
silver print. Museum of Modern Art,
New York.

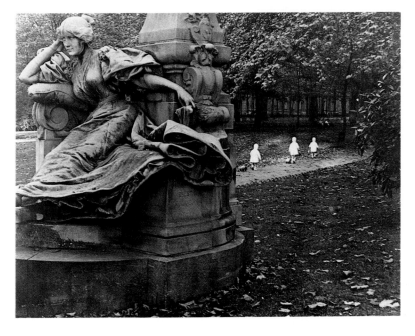

625. ROBERT DOISNEAU. *Three Children in the
Park*, 1971. Gelatin silver print. © Robert
Doisneau/Photo Researchers.

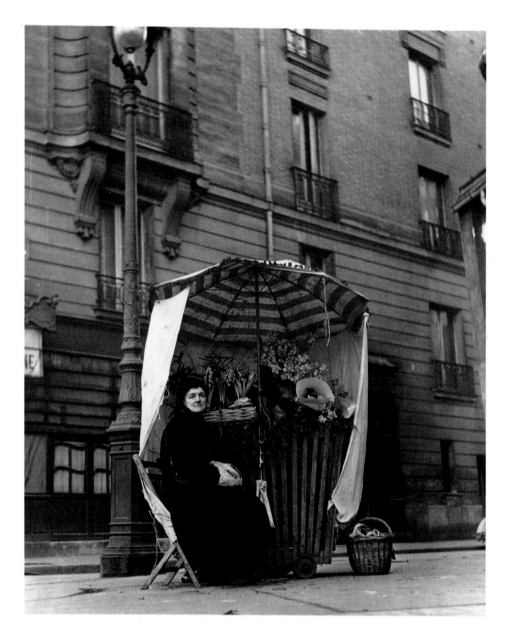

626. IZIS. *Place St. André des Arts, Paris*, 1949. Gelatin silver print. Zabriskie Gallery, New York.

RIGHT:

627. EDOUARD BOUBAT. *Portugal*, 1958. Gelatin silver print. Private collection. © Edouard Boubat.

images originally meant for reproduction in periodicals into prominence as aesthetic objects—suitable for savoring in books, hanging on walls, or collecting.

Public acceptance of photojournalism influenced the publication of full-length works combining words and pictures. Aside from the continuance of elegant and expensive books and portfolios that carried on the tradition of illustrating texts set in type with original photographs, collotypes, or Woodburytypes (discussed in earlier chapters), publishers on both sides of the Atlantic and in Japan during the 1930s and 1940s increasingly used gravure, offset lithography, and halftone plates to reproduce photographs. Such books frequently were organized around popular themes—localities, the arts, social classes and their life-styles—with image and text bearing a relationship sim-

ilar to that found in the essays in picture magazines. Starting in the 1950s, when photojournalistic as well as aesthetic photographs began to appear more frequently on gallery and museum walls and in collections, publishers seemed more willing to issue books in which the photographs were their own justification. Almost 25 years separate *The World Is Beautiful* by Albert Renger-Patzsch (1928) from Cartier-Bresson's *Images à La Sauvette (The Decisive Moment)* (1952), and apart from revealing their photographers' antithetical aesthetic ideas and ways of working, the two books represent somewhat different attitudes toward the purpose of photography books. The earlier work utilizes the photograph to point the reader toward the concordances of form in nature and industry, as the title indicates, while *The Decisive Moment* refers to the intervention of the individual

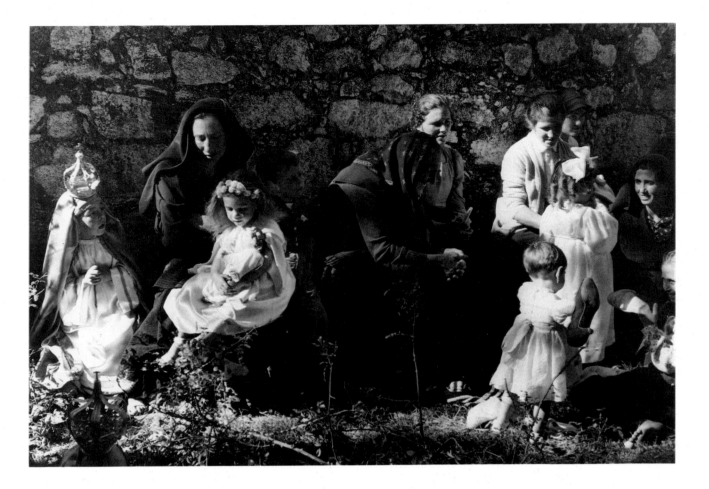

photographer's hand and eye to reveal what Cartier-Bresson called "a rhythm in the world of real things." The commercial success of *The Decisive Moment* indicated to publishers that photographers' images were marketable, and this helped encourage a large literature on and about the medium and its figures. In the 1960s and '70s many more titles in photography appeared, issued by such specialized publishers as Aperture and David R. Godine in the United States, Teriade, Delpire, and, later, Créatis and Schirmer-Mosel in Europe, several of whom also issued periodicals and works on the aesthetics of the medium.

Pictures in Print: Advertising

It would be difficult to imagine a world without advertising and ads without photographs, but the importance of camera images in this context was not widely recognized before the 1920s. The advertising field itself was young then, and the problems and expenses of halftone reproduction effectively limited the use of photographs to sell goods and services. Nor were the visual possibilities of transforming factual camera records into images of seductive suggestibility clearly foreseen. But during the early 1920s the situation began to change. The British journal *Com-*

mercial Art and Industry noted in 1923 that photography had become "so inexpensive and good" that it should be used more often in ads, and the American trade magazine *Printers Ink* pointed out the "astounding improvement in papers, presses and inks."[26] Six years later, the prestigious German printing-arts magazine *Gebrauchsgraphik* prophesied that the photograph would soon dominate advertising communication and "present an extraordinarily fruitful field to the gifted artist,"[27] because whether distorted or truthful, camera images are grounded in reality and are consequently persuasive to buyers. By 1930, advertising had become "the agent of new processes of thought and creation,"[28] and photographs would play a central role in this creative upsurge.

The new attitudes were the result of a number of factors. As indicated in the preceding chapter, public taste after World War I tended toward styles that suggested objectivity rather than sentimentality; a popular appetite for machine-made rather than handmade objects had developed; and delight in the cinema as a form of visual communication predisposed the public to accept still photographs in advertising. Most important, the realization that the camera could be both factual and persuasive and could imply authenticity while suggesting associative

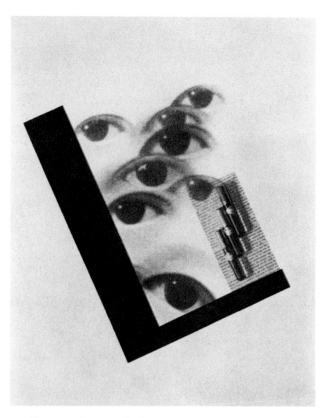

628. KIYOSHI KOISHI. *Smile Eye-Drops*, 1930. Halftone reproduction. Kurita-Bando Literary Agency, Tokyo.

qualities—manliness, femininity, luxury—made it a desirable tool in this fast-growing and competitive field. In a utopian effort to make excellence available to all by wiping out the distinctions between fine and applied art and between art and utilitarian object, Bauhaus and Constructivist artists and photographers had promoted the camera image as a means of transcending these traditional divisions. As a result many photographers in the 1920s began to ignore the division between self-expression and commercial work that Pictorialists had been at pains to erect around the turn of the century. The advertising industry in all advanced capitalist countries embraced these concepts from the art world, forecasting also that by integrating the latest modern ideas into visual communication, advertising would improve the aesthetic taste of the populace.

During the 1930s, photographers of stature produced images for commerce. Herbert Bayer, Cecil Beaton, Hans Finsler, Man Ray, Moholy-Nagy, Paul Outerbridge, Jr., Charles Sheeler, Steichen, and Maurice Tabard were among those eager to work on commission for magazines, advertising agencies, and manufacturers at the same time that they photographed for themselves and were honored as creative individuals by the critics. A number, including Laure Albin-Guillot, Bourke-White, Anton Bruehl, Victor

Keppler, Nickolas Muray, worked almost exclusively in the advertising field, convinced that they too were making a creative contribution to photography in addition to selling products. In the Far East, Japanese commercial photographers kept abreast of the modernist style, employing close-ups, angled shots, and montages, exemplified by *Smile Eye-Drops (pl. no. 628)*, a 1930 ad by Kiyoshi Koishi, third-place winner in the First Annual Advertising Photography Exhibition held in Japan in that year.

This honeymoon between photographer and commercial patron was relatively short-lived. Even though Steichen thought such patronage to be the equivalent of the Medici's support for Renaissance artists, "the purely material subject matter" with which most advertising photographers had to deal could not be considered comparable to Renaissance religion and philosophy, as Outerbridge observed.[29] Nevertheless, commercial opportunities have continued to have a substantial impact on photography, affecting not only the kinds of images produced and the taste of the public, but to some extent the materials on the market with which all photographers must work.

Sources and influences in advertising photography are difficult to sort out because from the start Americans and Europeans looked to each other for inspiration, with Europeans envious of the munificence of advertising budgets on this side of the Atlantic and Americans aware of the greater freedom in Europe for experimentation. However, no matter where they were produced, the most visually arresting images reflected the ascendant stylistic tendencies in the visual arts in general. One wellspring in the United States was the Clarence White School of Photography. While little is known of its curriculum, the significance of its contribution to the modernization of advertising photography can be seen in the roll call of faculty and students who became active in the field during the 1920s and '30s. Bruehl, Bourke-White, Outerbridge, Ralph Steiner, and Margaret Watkins translated the design precepts taught in the school into serviceable modernistic visual imagery, as can be seen in an image for an ad prepared by Watkins in 1925 for the J. Walter Thompson Agency *(pl. no. 629)*.

As might be expected, the style associated with the "New Objectivity," with its emphasis on "the thing itself," was of paramount interest. Finsler in Germany, Tabard and the Studio Deberney-Peignot in France, and Steichen in the United States all realized (as did others) that the close-up served as an excellent vehicle to concentrate attention on intrinsic material qualities and to eliminate extraneous matters. One consequence of this emphasis, as an article on advertising photography in the late 1930s noted, is that "the softness of velvet appears even richer and deeper than it actually is and iron becomes even

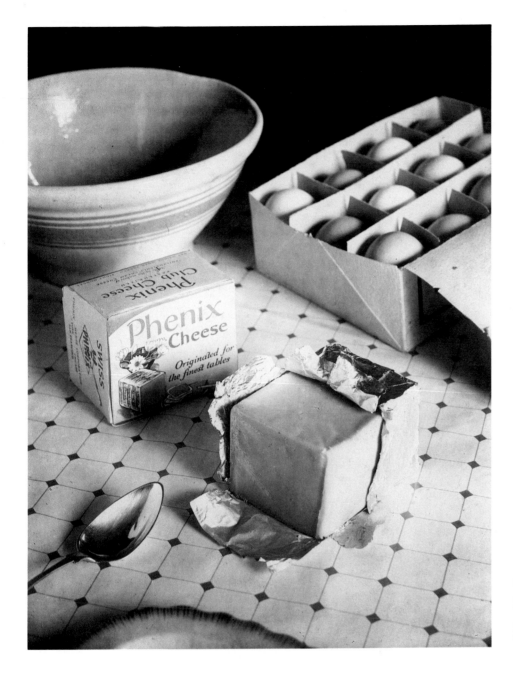

629. MARGARET WATKINS. *Phenix Cheese* (for J. Walter Thompson), 1925. Gelatin silver print. Light Gallery, New York. © Watkins Estate.

harder";[30] in addition, lighting and arrangement were further manipulated to glamorize the product. Nor were close-ups limited to inanimate still lifes or the products of machines; a view of hands engaged in the precise task of threading a needle *(pl. no. 630)*, photographed by Bruehl as part of a campaign for men's suits, was meant to suggest the care, quality, and handwork (still a sign of luxury goods) that ostensibly went into this line of men's wear.

The provocative nature of bizarre imagery for advertising also was recognized. French commercial photographer Lucien Lorelle suggested that it provided the "shock" needed to "give birth to the acquisitive desire."[31] Startling views of ordinary objects were obtained by selecting ex-

treme angles, by using abstract light patterns, and by montaging disparate objects. Just before 1930, photograms found their way into European advertising in works by Man Ray, Moholy-Nagy, and Piet Zwart, which were produced for an electrical concern, an optical manufacturer, and a radio company, respectively. Montages by Finsler and Bayer were used to sell chocolate and machinery, while distorted views of writing ink by Lissitzky for Pelikan and of automobile tires by Tabard for Michelin were considered acceptable. Americans, on the other hand, were warned away from excessive distortion. Product pictures by Bruehl, Muray *(pl. no. 631)*, Outerbridge, Steichen *(pl. no. 579)*, and Ralph Steiner *(pl. no. 580)* are essentially precise still lifes of recognizable objects. Even the dramatic angles chosen by Bourke-White to convey the sweep and power of large-scale American industrial machinery were selected with regard for the clarity of the forms being presented. Eventually, when montages and multiple images did enter American advertising vocabulary, these techniques were used for fashion and celebrity images and only after World War II for more prosaic consumer goods.

Most advertising images in the United States (and elsewhere) were not conceived in the modernist idiom by any means. Heavily retouched, banal photographic illustrations filled the mail-order catalogs issued by Sears, Roebuck and Montgomery Ward, while the advertising pages of popular magazines and trade journals were full of ordinary and often silly or sentimental concoctions. However,

some very competent work was done by individuals working in an old-fashioned vein. The highly acclaimed arrangements photographed by Lejaren à Hiller *(see Chapter 8)* required historically researched costumes and construction of sets in addition to careful attention to lighting. While technically a photograph, tableaux such as *Surgery Through the Ages (pl. no. 632)*, part of a campaign for a pharmaceutical company, are really forerunners of contemporary video advertising in that they rely on theatrical and dramatic content rather than aesthetic means to get their message across.

After the second World War, a number of photojournalists continued to be involved with an amalgam of advertising imagery and journalistic reporting that had made its initial appearance in the feature sections of *Fortune*

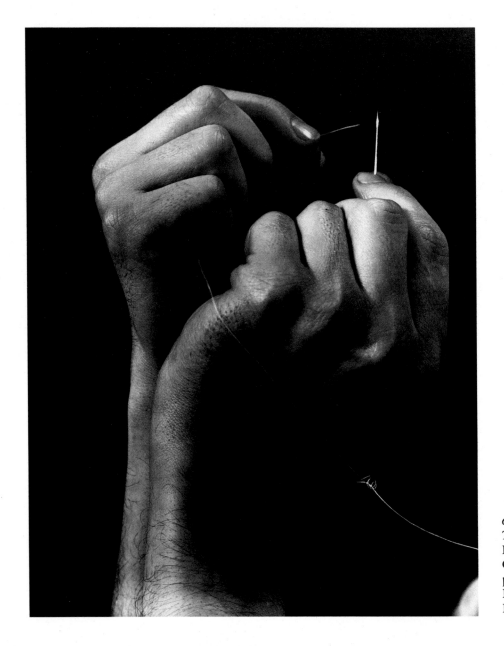

630. ANTON BRUEHL. *Hands Threading a Needle* (Weber and Heilbroner Advertising Campaign), c. 1929. Gelatin silver print. International Museum of Photography at George Eastman House, Rochester, New York.

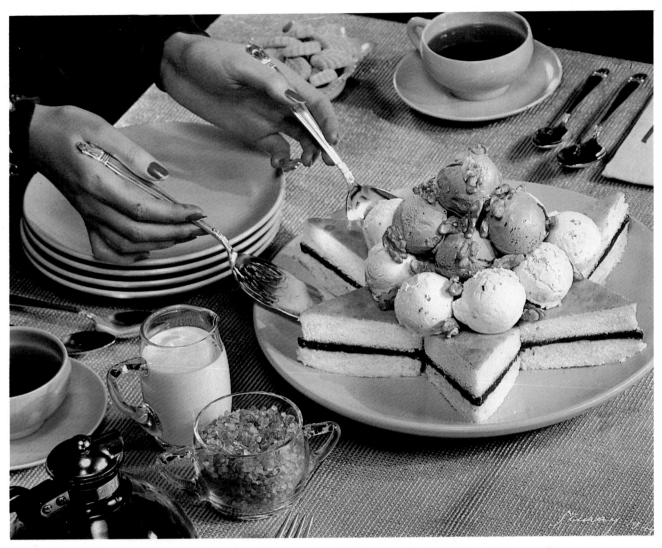

631. NICKOLAS MURAY. *Still Life*, 1943. Reproduced in *McCall's Magazine*. Carbro (assembly) print.
International Museum of Photography at George Eastman House, Rochester, N.Y.

in the 1930s. Even during the nadir of the Depression, articles illustrated with well-reproduced, stylish photographs and signed artwork "sold" the positive aspects of the American corporate structure; indeed, Bourke-White felt that "the grandeur of industry," which she pictured for *Fortune*'s pages, exerted the same appeal on manufacturer and photographer alike.[32] While she herself revised this opinion, and later photojournalists may not have been as sanguine about the benefits of large-scale industrial enterprises, photographing for the broad range of print media that emerged after the war made it necessary for photographers to present "clear, coherent and vivid" pictures of business activities. As a result, the glossy corporate image that appears in annual reports in the guise of photojournalistic reporting has come down as one of the legacies of photojournalism to advertising and an example of the difficulties in categorizing contemporary photographs.

An important aspect of the alluring quality of current advertising images is the use of color. By 1925, according to the British graphic arts magazine *Penrose's Annual*, the public had come to expect "coloured covers and illustrations [in] . . . books and magazines . . . posters . . . showcards . . . catalogues, booklets and all forms of commercial advertising."[33] Even so, the desire for such materials did not immediately produce accurate and inexpensive color images on film or printed page; it was not until the late 1930s that both amateurs and professionals obtained negatives, positive transparencies, and prints with the capacity to render a seductive range of values and colors in natural and artificial light *(See A Short Technical History, Part III)*. Even though these materials were flawed by their impermanence—as they still are—such means were acceptable because their use in print media satisfied the public craving for color.

A method commonly used to create color images in advertising during the Depression was the Trichrome/Carbro print, made from separation negatives produced in a repeating-back camera such as the Ives Kromskop. Based on the addition of dyes to gelatin carbon printing methods, Carbro printing was a highly complicated procedure involving as many as 80 different steps; but despite the expense and the special facilities required, it flourished because "the commercial aspects of color were as important as the aesthetic or technical angles"[34] in determining the kind of color work that publishers and agencies, competing for a limited market, favored. Condé Nast was one of the first publishers to print the richly hued advertising photographs of Bruehl and Fernand Bourges in *Vogue* in 1932. In the mid-1930s, the Bruehl-Bourges studio did colorwork for a range of product manufacturers reading like a veritable Who's Who of American corporations, while Will Connell, Lejaren à Hiller, Keppler, Muray, Outerbridge, Valentine Sarra, and H.i Williams also were active in working out eye-catching spectrums for ads for food *(pl. no. 631)*, fashion, and manufactured goods that appeared in *House Beautiful* and similar magazines.

There can be little argument that in modern capitalist societies the camera has proved to be an absolutely indispensible tool for the makers of consumer goods, for those

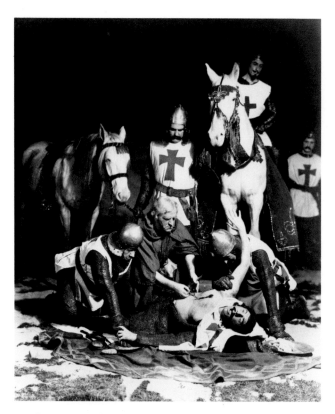

632. LEJAREN À HILLER. *Hugh of Lucca (d. 1251) from the Surgery Through the Ages Series*, (Pharmaceutical advertising campaign) 1937. Gelatin silver print. Visual Studies Workshop, Rochester, N.Y.

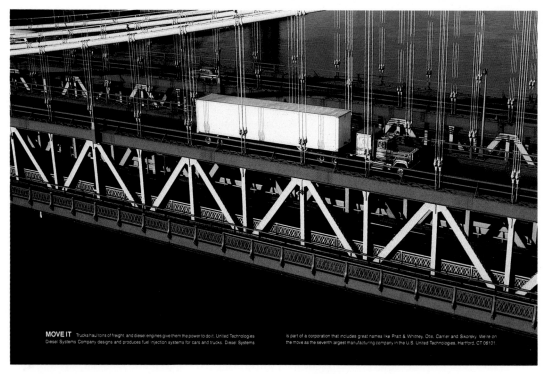

633. JAY MAISEL. *United Technologies*, 1982. Advertisement. Art Director, Gordon Bowman. Copywriters, Gordon Bowman/Christine Rothenberg. Courtesy and © 1982 United Technologies, Hartford, Conn.

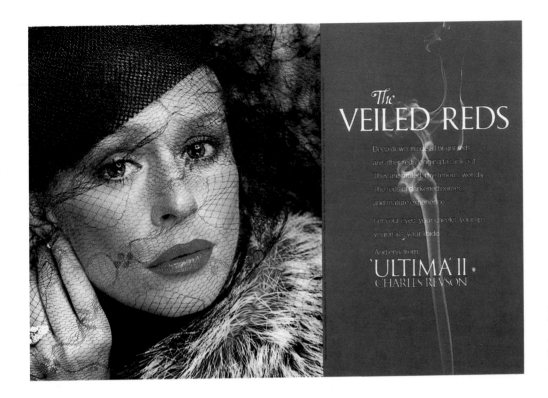

involved with public relations and those who sell ideas and services. Camera images have been able to make invented "realities" seem not at all fraudulent and have permitted viewers to suspend disbelief while remaining aware that the scene has been contrived.[35] The availability of sophisticated materials and apparatus, of good processing facilities, and the fact that large numbers of proficient photographers graduate yearly from art schools and technical institutions, combined with the generous budgets allocated for advertising, guarantee a high level of excellence in contemporary advertising images *(pl. nos. 633 and 634)*. As in the past, the photographs deemed exceptional often reflect current stylistic ideas embraced in the arts as a whole and in personally expressive photography in particular; indeed, the dividing line between styles in advertising and in personal expression can be a thin one, with a number of prominent figures working with equal facility in both areas.

The imagination that inspired early enthusiasts (such as Brodovitch) to foresee in advertising a great creative force, is less evident in contemporary advertising photography. Whether picturing industrial equipment or luxury goods, the fact is that for the most part the style and content of such images are controlled by manufacturer and ad agency, and not by individual photographer. Designed to attract the greatest number of viewers, there is little compass for personal approach, while the images that are considered exceptional tend to generate considerable emulation. The bland sameness that characterizes the field is more true of advertising imagery in the United States than in Europe, owing to the larger budgets and greater role that advertising plays in American life, but it also reflects the fact that in the past there was more leeway in Europe for visual experimentation in applied photography and graphic design.

Pictures in Print: Fashion and Celebrities

Commercial uses of photography always have included fashion and celebrity images, a specialty that is neither strictly documentation nor yet advertising. The appearance in the 1920s of specialized periodicals devoted to fashion enlarged the creative opportunities for photographers interested in these subjects. Often they were permitted a more fanciful approach than was considered suitable in ordinary product advertising or photojournalism because their goal was to create an illusion, in which artifice was a prime ingredient. Made to establish canons of taste while attracting buyers, these pictorial configurations of model, garment, pose, and decor are as much indications of changing styles in the arts as of attire. And it can be argued also that fashion imagery is significant as an index of transformations in social, cultural, and sexual mores and thus is indicative of attitudes by and toward women in society.

Fashion imagery, as might be expected, got its start in the world's fashion capital—Paris—where in the late 1800s the Reutlinger studio *(pl. no. 635)*, Bissonais et Taponnier, and Seeberger Frères, among others, provided images for

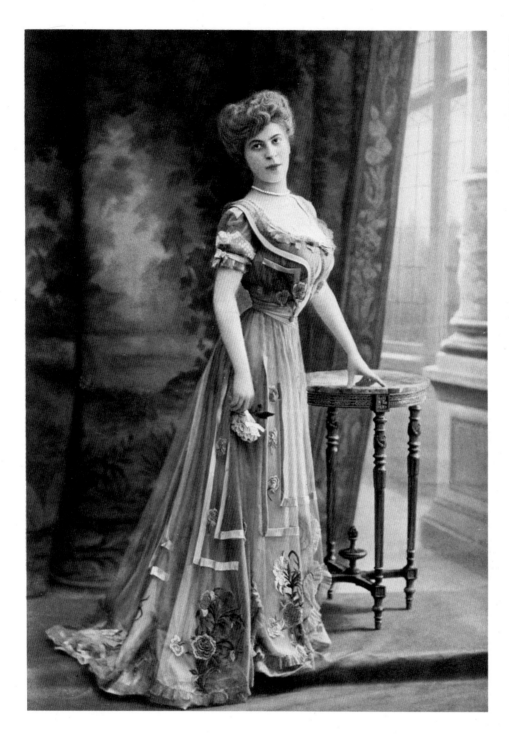

Parisian magazines. But it was the transformation of *Vogue*, late in the second decade of this century, from a society journal to a magazine devoted to presenting elegant attire for the elite that marked the real beginning of fashion photography as a genre. Published in three separate editions in London, New York, and Paris by Condé Nast, *Vogue* at first featured opulent soft-focus confections *(pl. no. 636)* exemplified by the work of Pictorialist Adolf de Meyer (known as Baron), who was replaced by Steichen in 1923, but continued to photograph in what had become an outmoded style for *Harper's Bazaar*. Steichen, in his role as chief photographer for Condé Nast publications in the United States, was the catalyst behind the "new look" in fashion photography during the 1920s; he arranged and composed individual models, groups, and properties into vividly patterned ensembles that displayed an instinctive flair for dramatic contrasts and for the decorative possibilities of geometric shapes. His work was immediately recog-

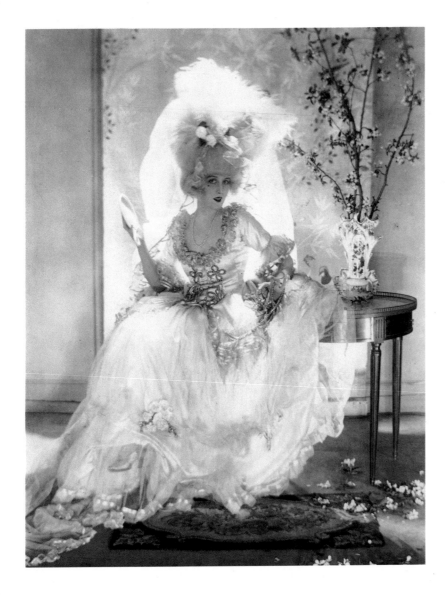

636. BARON ADOLF DE MEYER. *A Wedding Dress, Modeled by Helen Lee Worthing*, 1920. Gelatin silver print. *Vogue*, New York. © 1920 (renewed 1948) by The Condé Nast Publications, Inc., New York.

nized as stylistically consistent with other emblems of 1920s' modernism—the skyscraper, machine forms, and jazz. And toward the end of the decade, as the New Objectivity came to the fore, Steichen transformed this style into a chic yet expressive language suitable for both fashion and celebrity images, as can be seen in his close-up of actress Anna May Wong *(pl. no. 637)*, which, in addition to creating an arresting design reminiscent of Brancusi's sculptured heads, suggests characteristics of inwardness and mystery.

Steichen's influence was felt in Europe as well as in the United States. In its wake, George Hoyningen-Huené, born in Russia and active in France between 1925 and 1935, during which time he contributed regularly to Paris *Vogue*, combined his strong admiration for the statuary of classical antiquity with the clean functionalism of the New Objectivity, achieving the distinctive if somewhat bizarre style typified by his 1930 spread for bathing attire *(pl. no. 638)*. Also working in France at the time, Egidio Scaione, an

Italian photographer with a large commercial practice, handled similar themes with an icy elegance that epitomizes *le style moderne*—the French version of the New Objectivity. When inventive British photographer and stage designer Beaton turned to celebrity and fashion images in 1929, he joined his penchant for lush baroque fantasies with a modern touch, producing alluring pictures such as *Marlene Dietrich (pl. no. 639)* of 1932. The British editions of both *Vogue* and *Harper's Bazaar* provided commissions for a number of British fashion photographers, among them Dorothy and Shaw Wildman who transferred the mechanistic suavities of the objective manner to their portraits of celebrities.

Involved primarily with form—indeed the content is seldom the actual personage or garment but the "aura" created by the photographer—fashion and celebrity images were especially quick to reflect changes in aesthetic sensibility. During the Depression, the cool hermetic elegance of

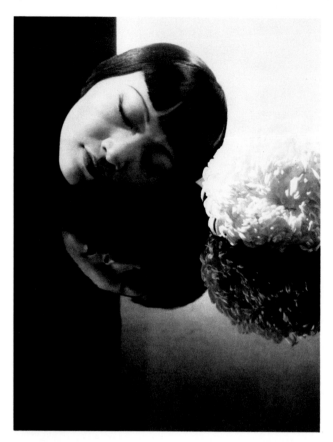

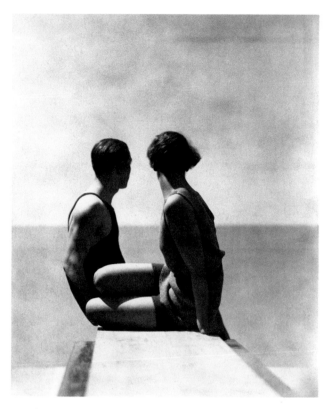

637. EDWARD STEICHEN. *Anna May Wong*, 1930. Gelatin silver print. Collection George H. Dalsheimer, Baltimore. *Vanity Fair*, New York. © 1930 (renewed 1958) by The Condé Nast Publications, Inc., New York.

638. GEORGE HOYNINGEN-HUENÉ. *Untitled*, (*Fashion Izod*), 1930. *Vogue*, New York. © 1930 (renewed 1958) by The Condé Nast Publications, Inc., New York.

the New Objectivity was challenged in the United States both by the naturalism of small-camera photojournalistic documentation and the preference for American-made products that prompted editors to avoid what they conceived as aesthetic styles imported from Europe. As a consequence of the search for a wide readership also, fashion imagery became more democratic in theme and approach. Ironically, this breath of air was imported; as noted earlier, it was the Hungarian Munkacsi who first applied candid techniques to fashion photography, snapping a bathing suit model running on a beach in 1933 *(pl. no. 640)*. These unstilted images of active, athletic models photographed in natural light, out-of-doors, established this approach as one of the two poles between which fashion imagery has continually rebounded, the other extreme being the contrived studio shot. The American Toni Frissel was one of a number of fashion photographers who also were attracted by the spontaneous look; she combined natural settings and the casual stances of photojournalism with angled shots and stark silhouettes, exemplified in a series for *Vogue* in 1939 featuring fur garments *(pl. no. 641)*.

Images that ostensibly explored the landscape of the mind and reflected the prevailing interest in psychoanalysis and the Surrealist art movement during the 1930s began to appear in fashion work. Horst Peter Horst, a former student of Purist architecture in Paris, devised montages and mirror tricks to confound reality with *trompe l'oeil* settings, while others, including Angus McBean, a London-based photographer of theatrical personalities, who ordered a Daliesque background to be constructed and painted especially for a portrait of actress Elsa Lanchester *(pl. no. 642)*, were directly inspired by Surrealist paintings. Besides the well-known Dali, painters Christian Berard, Giorgio De Chirico, and Yves Tanguy influenced fashion images by the English painter–photographer Peter Rose-Pulham and the Americans Clifford Coffin and George Platt Lynes, for example. Surrealist photographs were a natural offshoot of Beaton's preoccupation with fantasy, while Man Ray, in arranging a couturier beach robe against a backdrop of his own painting entitled *Observatory Time—The Lovers (pl. no. 644)* for a spread in *Harper's Bazaar*, came to this languid mix of luxury and desire from the even more irrational pre-

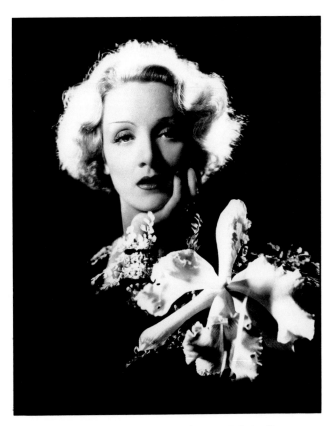

639. CECIL BEATON. *Marlene Dietrich*, 1932. Gelatin silver print. Collection Sam Wagstaff, New York. © Sotheby's Belgravia, London.

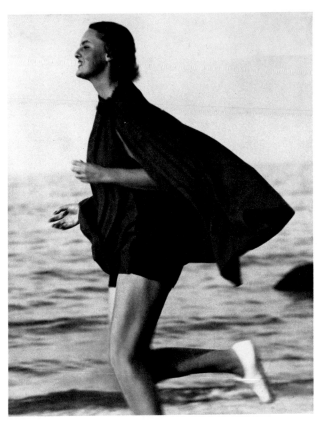

640. MARTIN MUNKACSI. *Untitled*, 1934. Reproduced in *Harper's Bazaar*, December, 1934. Gelatin silver print. Joan Munkacsi, Woodstock, N.Y.

cincts of Dadaism. Continued interest in the temporal and spatial confusions of dreams combined during the 1940s with awareness of the war in Europe to give fashion images, as conceived by Erwin Blumenfeld and the American John Rawlings, a macabre aspect. Rawlings, a former director of *Vogue's* London studio, arranged mirrors to create a sense of undefined time and place *(pl. no. 643)* suggestive of austerity and even regimentation for a *Vogue* cover that came out during the second World War in 1944. A multiple image by Blumenfeld *(pl. no. 645)*, who worked in the United States after his release from a Nazi internment camp, brings to mind the shattering experiences of war and incarceration rather than the seductive fantasies one usually finds in fashion pictures.

In the postwar years, fashion photographers were heir to a wealth of traditions that included New Objectivity, Surrealism, and the documentary mode. They sought to integrate these concepts with the revived taste for luxury, at the same time developing distinctive individual styles. Less elitist than formerly but often more opulent because fashion images were now made largely in color for a reader-

ship eager to make up for wartime austerity, the new sensibility is apparent in the work of Richard Avedon, Lillian Bassman, Louise Dahl-Wolfe, Irving Penn, and Bert Stern, and in the still lifes of Leslie Gill, to name only a small number of those active in the field after the war.

Richly patterned colors and decor were orchestrated for *Harper's Bazaar* by Dahl-Wolfe (originally a painter), who rose to prominence on the strength of an impeccable color sense combined with skill in arranging the more naturalistic decor now desired in fashion photography *(pl. no. 646)*. Her task, along with that of others in the field, was made easier by the increase in air travel that enabled photographers to drop themselves and their models virtually anywhere around the globe—on Caribbean beaches and western American deserts, in front of monuments and palaces in North Africa, India, and Europe. Penn (also a trained painter) created elegant confections that often make reference in their arrangements and color schemes to well-known paintings, as in an image featuring model Lisa Fonssagrives taken in an exotic setting in Morocco *(pl. no. 649)*. Working in similar style but with still-life objects rather

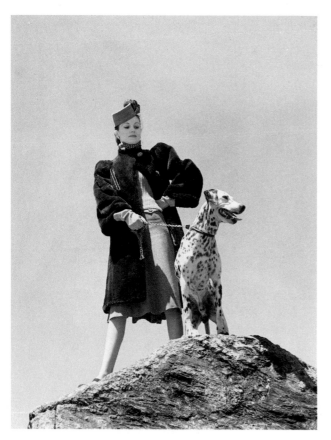

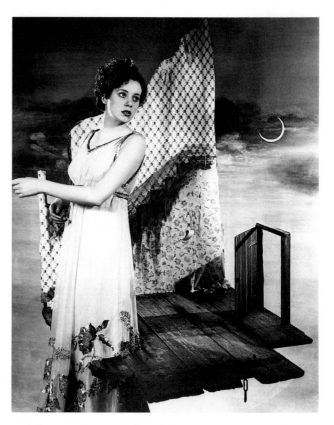

641. TONI FRISSELL. *Boom for Brown Beavers*, 1939. Reproduced in *Vogue*, August 1, 1939. Gelatin silver print. Toni Frissell Collection, Library of Congress, Washington, D.C.

642. ANGUS MCBEAN. *Elsa Lanchester*, 1938. Reproduced in *The Sketch*, June 22, 1938. Gelatin silver print. Courtesy and © Angus McBean.

than live models, Gill created numerous covers and spreads of uncluttered opulence for *Harper's Bazaar* over more than a 20-year period beginning in 1935 *(pl. no. 650)*. From the 1960s on, Avedon, whose stated desire was to "never bring the same mental attitude toward the same problem twice"[36] probably had the greatest influence on fashion photography. The style of his own work veered between an early somewhat frenetic naturalism, derived from Munkacsi, and a later taste for highly contrived lighting, pose, and camera angle, as in *Donyale Luna in Dress by Paco Rabanne (pl. no. 651)*, which appeared in *Vogue* in December, 1966. This particular treatment of female form and dress has been seen as a reflection of the decade's profound changes in sexual and social mores rather than merely as a search for novelty to attract the jaded eye. Both naturalism and mannerism continued to inspire up-and-coming fashion photographers to frame individualized approaches. Casual documentation ostensibly characterized the fashion style of Diane Arbus, William Klein, and Bob Richardson, while Stern updated the Surrealism of Blumenfeld and the mannerism of Penn with a touch of "pop" culture. In the 1970s, Hiro (born Yasuhiro Wakebayashi in Shanghai),

working in the United States for *Vogue*, achieved a distinctive amalgam combining athleticism and elegance with his own aesthetic heritage *(pl. no. 647)*.

Eclipsed by Americans during the war and immediate postwar years, the European fashion world regained its aplomb at the beginning of the 1960s with David Bailey's work in London; by the 1970s, when Paris *Vogue* featured the work of European newcomers Guy Bourdin and Helmut Newton, it reflected changing perceptions of women (by men and women themselves). Bourdin's macabre fantasies depict them as graceless, vulnerable, and frenzied while Newton shows them as sexually aggressive yet frigid. These strange visions, photographed in strident color, inspired the French photographer Sarah Moon *(pl. no. 648)* and the American Deborah Turbeville *(pl. no. 652)*, but, though still concerned with alienation and uneasiness, both have softened the vision of women as social and sexual predators, in part through the atmospheric backgrounds and muted impressionist color they favor.

One of the developments of the 1980s is the attention paid male fashion by both manufacturers and the fashion industry, but it is doubtful whether this new thrust will

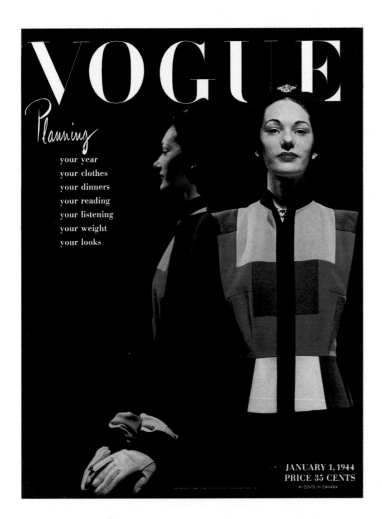

643. JOHN RAWLINGS. *Untitled*, 1944. *Vogue* cover, January 1, 1944. Halftone reproduction. Fashion Institute of Technology, New York; Edward C. Blum Design Laboratory. *Vogue*, New York. © 1944 (renewed 1972) by The Condé Nast Publications, Inc., New York.

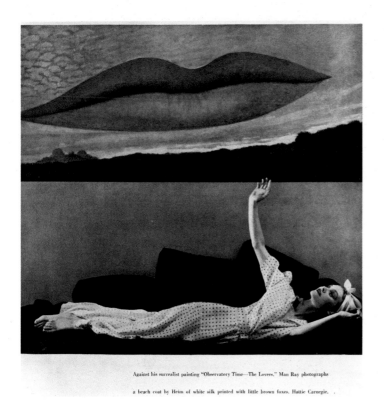

644. MAN RAY. *Untitled*, 1936. Published in *Harper's Bazaar*, November, 1936. Halftone reproduction. New York Public Library, Astor, Lenox, and Tilden Foundations.

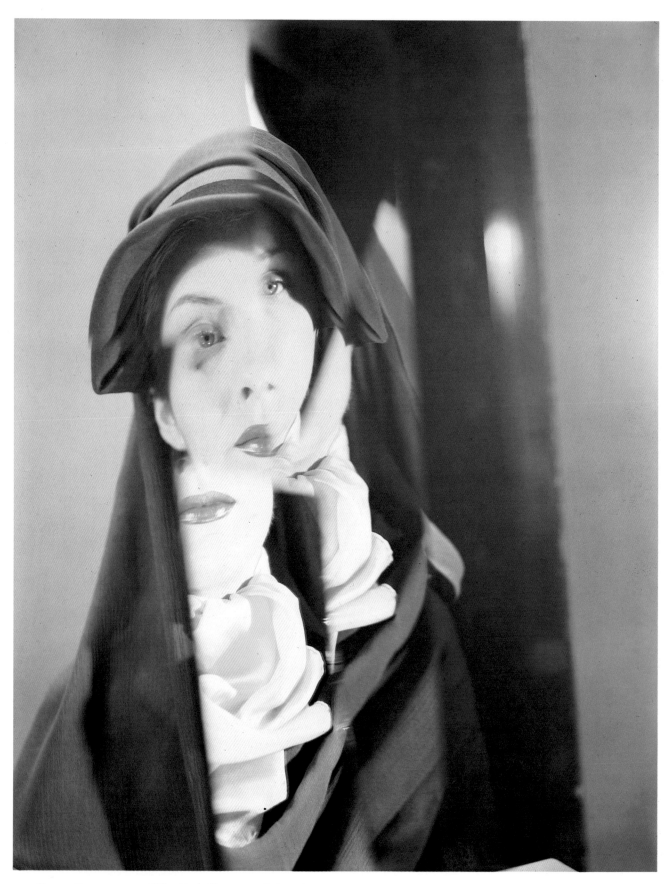

645. ERWIN BLUMENFELD. *What Looks New*, 1947. Color (chromogenic development) transparency.
Collection Marina Schinz, New York.

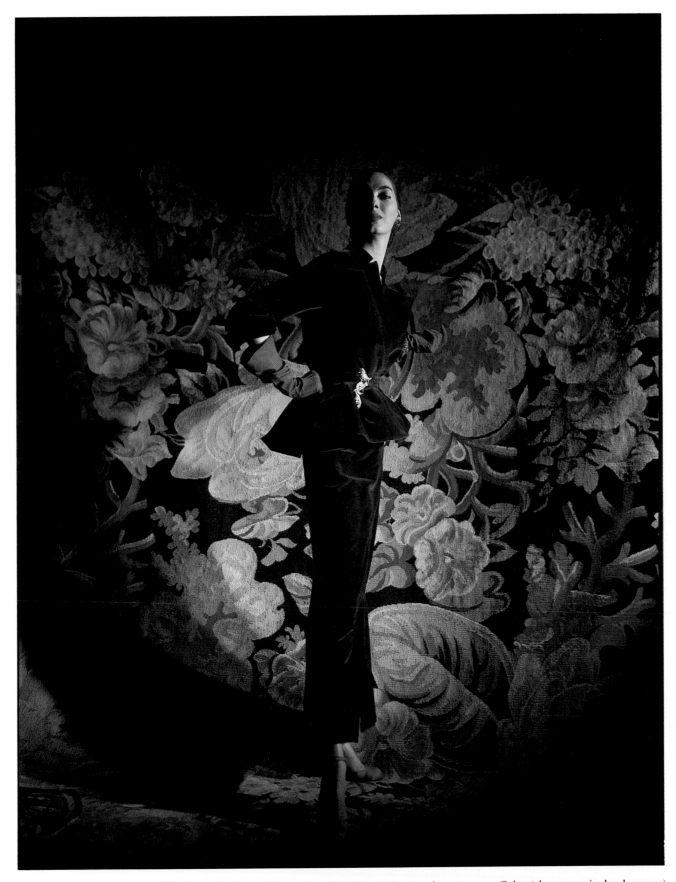

646. LOUISE DAHL-WOLFE. *The Covert Look*, 1949. Reproduced in *Harper's Bazaar*, August, 1949. Color (chromogenic development) transparency. Fashion Institute of Technology, New York; Edward C. Blum Design Laboratory.

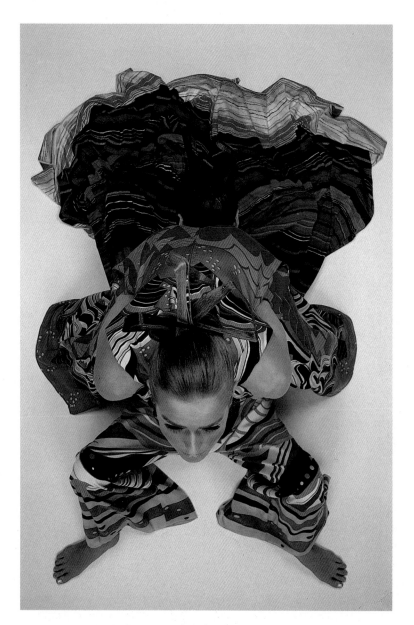

647. HIRO. *Fabric, Harper's Bazaar*, February, 1967. Color (chromogenic development) transparency. Courtesy and © 1967 Hiro.

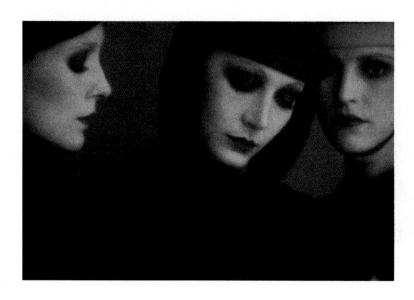

648. SARAH MOON. *Faces*, 1973. Reproduced in *French Vogue*, February, 1973. Color (chromogenic development) transparency. Courtesy the artist.

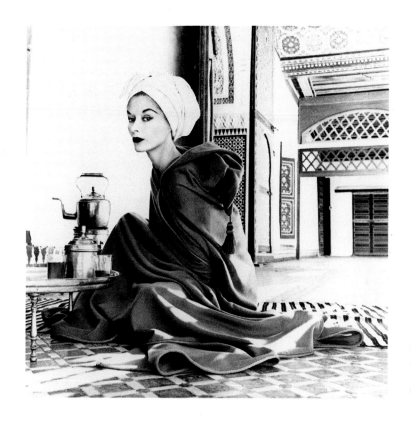

649. IRVING PENN. *Woman in Moroccan Palace (Lisa Fonssagrives), Morocco*, 1951. Gelatin silver print. *Vogue*, New York. © 1951 (renewed 1979) by The Condé Nast Publications, Inc., New York.

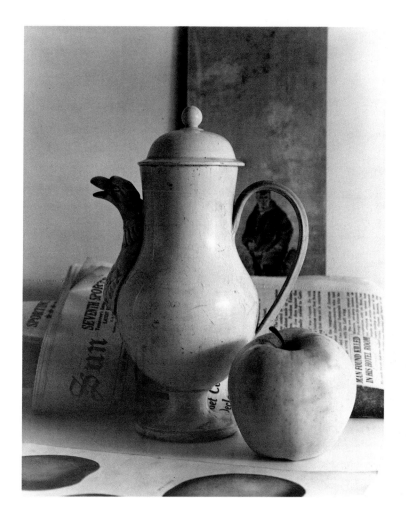

650. LESLIE GILL. *Chocolate Pot and Apples I*, 1950. Gelatin silver print. Courtesy and © 1982 Frances McLaughlin Gill, New York.

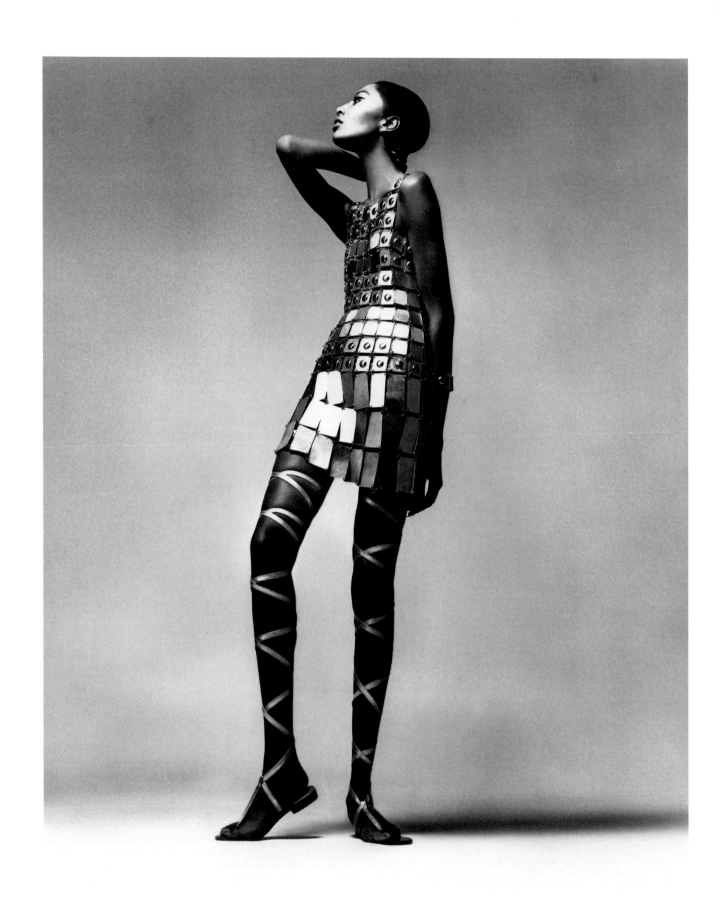

651. RICHARD AVEDON. *Donyale Luna in Dress by Paco Rabanne, New York Studio,* January, 1966. Gelatin silver print. Courtesy and © Richard Avedon.

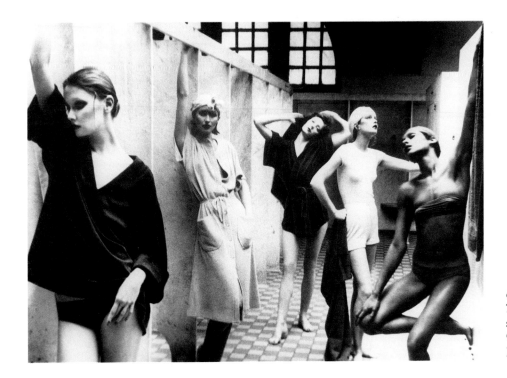

652. DEBORAH TURBEVILLE. *Terry Covering*, 1975. Gelatin silver print. *Vogue*, New York. © 1975 by The Condé Nast Publications, Inc., New York.

forestall the problems faced by arbiters of fashion as the democratization of this once elitist interest continues in Europe as well as the United States. With a broad range of styles offering a heterogeneous public many choices of how to look, prominent fashion photographers may find themselves with greater freedom to choose models, styles, decor, and ambience and even to suggest how their work be used in publication. At the same time, however, as fashion images also are collected and studied as aesthetic artifacts, photographers in this field also will be competing with a wider spectrum of image-makers for a place on gallery and museum walls and in the critical sun, as well as on the printed page.

"The transformation of everything into images" has had an unsettling effect on perception, as Roland Barthes noted in *Camera Lucida*.[37] While the omnipresent photograph may not have served to "de-realize the human world of of conflicts and desires" to the extent this author suggests, there is no question that it has affected responses to pain, suffering, and pleasure in real life, making these facets of human experience seem somehow commonplace, less intensely felt, and less urgent. Advertising photography in particular has promoted a continuous search for pictorial novelty; while this emphasis may be of value in selling products in consumer oriented societies, it is open to question as an end in itself in creative expression. The fact that commercial photographs may be seen only subliminally, with the message registered but the relationship of forms and the disposition of light unremarked, has influenced the

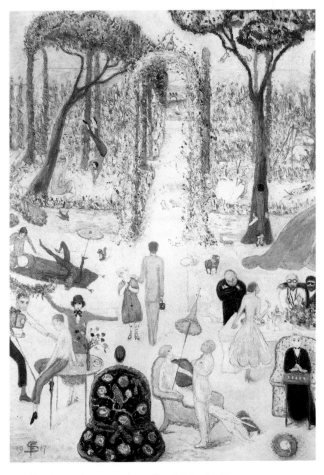

653. FLORINE STETTHEIMER. *Sunday in the Country*, 1917. Oil on canvas. Cleveland Museum of Art, Cleveland, Ohio; gift of Ettie Stettheimer.

casual way in which the public approaches expressive camera images in general. Conversely, it also is true that the prevalence of the photographic image in print, whether in advertising or journalism, has made the public more willing to accept camera images in all their guises and has led to a more sophisticated appreciation of them, providing readers for books on photography, viewers for exhibitions, and collectors for individual works.

Profile: Edward Steichen

In the range and quality of his production in the fashion and advertising fields, Edward Steichen might be said to embody the development of utilitarian photography in the 20th century. Steichen was engaged with much that was vital and new in the medium during the 20th century, from a beginning as a Pictorialist photographer through activities in the commercial sector to a position as director of the most prestigious museum photography department in the United States (at the Museum of Modern Art). As a creative individual, as a designer of exhibitions and periodicals, as a director of projects, he left an unmistakable imprint on the photographic trends of his time.

Born Eduard Steichen, in Luxembourg in 1879, he was brought to the United States as an infant. When he displayed artistic ability he was apprenticed after 1894 to a firm of lithographers in Milwaukee; he both painted and photographed, submitting to Pictorialist salons during the 1890s. Clarence H. White noticed him in 1900 and soon after brought him to the attention of Stieglitz, with whom he shortly began to collaborate on the installations for the gallery 291 and on the founding of *Camera Work*, for which he designed the first cover and the initial publicity. Still not entirely committed to photography, Steichen spent the greater part of the period before the first World War painting in France. There his knowledge of Symbolism, Expressionism, and Cubism enabled him to direct Stieglitz's attention to these significant art movements. Besides paintings (nearly all of which he later destroyed), Steichen made sensitive photographs in the Symbolist style of landscapes, genre scenes, and New York cityscapes *(pl. no. 336)* and perceptive portraits of wealthy and creative individuals in Paris and New York during this period. As part of the active New York art scene of the time, he was portrayed photographing Marcel Duchamp in *Sunday Afternoon in the Country*, a 1917 oil by Florine Stettheimer *(pl. no. 653)*. Other photographers included in the painted scene are Arnold Genthe and Baron de Meyer.

Steichen's experiences as director of aerial photography for the Allied Forces during World War I, followed by a period of several years of photographic experimentation based on his interest in the theory of dynamic symmetry,

enabled him to shed the vestiges of his Pictorialist sensibility and open himself up to modernist ideas. In his position with Condé Nast from 1922 and also as a free-lance advertising photographer, he explored the vocabulary of the New Objectivity during the 1920s in order to create ingenious advertising and fashion images in what was still a relatively fresh field. This phase of Steichen's career, which he brought to an end in 1938 when he realized that commercial work was no longer personally stimulating, prepared him to embrace a broader concept of photography and to assume a role as administrator. Although not himself involved in photoreportage or the documentary movement, by the late 1930s he was convinced that the fine quality of work produced by photographers working for the Farm Security Administration and for *Life* had effectively erased aesthetic distinctions among images made as personal expression, as photojournalism, or as social commentary.

In 1947, after serving as director of Naval Combat Photography during World War II, Steichen accepted the directorship of the Department of Photography of the Museum of Modern Art. His purpose, he said, was to make sure that what he called the "aliveness in the melting pot of American photography" and "the restless seekings, probing aspirations and experiments of younger photographers"[38] would be represented in the museum collection. During his tenure, which lasted until 1961, he organized and promoted exhibitions, wrote numerous articles, helped publish books on the medium, and was instrumental in making photographic images acceptable in a museum setting. In 1955, Steichen organized *The Family of Man* exhibition and catalog, which he considered the culmination of his career. He believed that this show promoted photography as "a tool for penetrating beneath the surface of things" and that it proved that journalistic photographs had their own aesthetic forms. Long before he died in 1972, he was recognized as one of the small group of individuals whose ideas, energy, and images had helped shape photography in the 20th century.

Profile: W. Eugene Smith

A strong sense of compassion made W. Eugene Smith a legend in his own time. Whatever the circumstances and settings of his assignments—and the range of those assignments was broad—he thought of his camera as an extension of his conscience and his images as reflections of his need to get to the heart of the matter. Following a semester as a student at the University of Notre Dame, Smith came to New York City in 1937 at a time when photoreportage was changing the nature of magazine journalism and providing unparalleled opportunities for young photographers. Immediately successful, his early work showed such skillfulness that within two years Smith, though only nineteen years old, found himself on part-time contract to *Life* magazine.

Demanding of himself as well as others, Smith at first found many assignments trivial, but he continued to cover domestic events for *Life*, and later *Collier's* and *Parade*. As the war expanded to involve the United States, he felt impelled toward the field of conflict in the South Pacific, where he went in 1943 on an assignment for *Flying* magazine. Eventually he returned to this front, sent by *Life* to cover the action on the Pacific islands. Involvement on the field of battle changed Smith's understanding of war and influenced his photographic style, moving him to compose his images as if sharing the same emotionally charged space as his subjects *(pl. no. 608)*. Compulsively driven to partake of the reality of combat, he was seriously wounded in Okinawa in 1945.

Smith's continued advocacy of the moral responsibility of the photojournalist prompted him to join the Photo League after World War II, and to accept its presidency in 1949. He also rejoined the staff of *Life* in 1946 in an effort to have his images reach as wide an audience as possible. Despite ongoing battles over deadlines, picture size, layout, and captioning, more than 50 of his essays were used between 1946 and 1952, among them the memorable "Spanish Village" *(pl. nos. 654–658)*, "Country Doctor," and "Nurse Midwife." Smith resigned permanently in 1954 when he realized that he could not alter publication policies that denied the photographer a voice in the final appearance and meaning of the published photo essay.

In the following years, Smith took on a variety of photojournalistic projects that gave him freedom to develop his craft and ideas. Although their free-lance nature meant that his income was irregular, his work of this period enabled him to explore the photo essay form more profoundly in order to "force the genre in an epic poetic mode."[39] Works that exemplify this ambitious concept include an extensive essay on Pittsburgh published in *Popular Photography Annual, 1959*, under the title "A Labyrin-

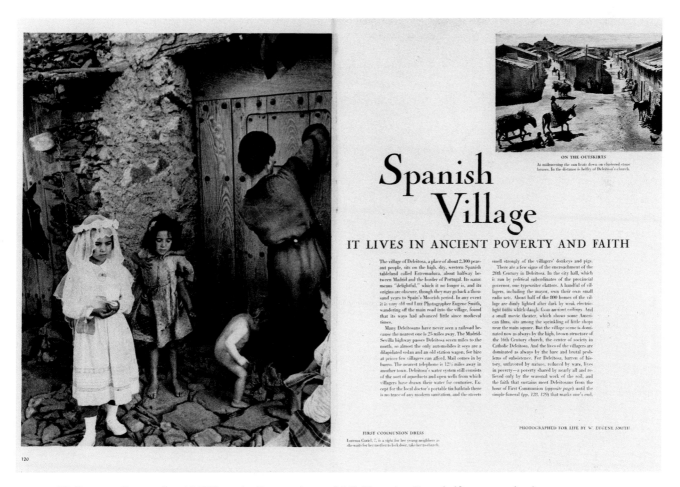

654–658. W. EUGENE SMITH. *Spanish Village*, April 9, 1951 issue of *Life Magazine*. From halftone reproductions. Designer: Bernard Quint. *Life Magazine* © 1951 Time Inc.; Courtesy Life Picture Service.

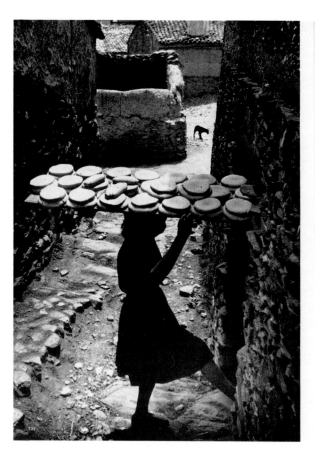

"EL MEDICO"

Dr. Joel Martin makes rounds with lantern to light patients' homes. He does minor surgery, sending serious cases to city of Cáceres, and treats much typhus.

SMALL BOY'S WORK

The youngest son in the Curiel family, 5-year-old Esteban, scoops up manure from the street outside his home. It is carefully hoarded as fertilizer, will be used on the eight small fields the family owns or rents a few miles out of town.

"SEÑOR CURA"

Out on a walk, the village priest, Don Manuel, 60, passes barred window and curtained door of a home. He has seldom meddled in politics—the village was bloodily split during the civil war—but sticks to ministry. Villages like that.

◄ YOUNG WOMAN'S WORK

Latona Curiel's big sister Bernardina, 18, kicks open door of community oven, which the village provides for public use. At least once a week she bakes 24 loaves for the family of eight. The flour comes from family grain, ground locally.

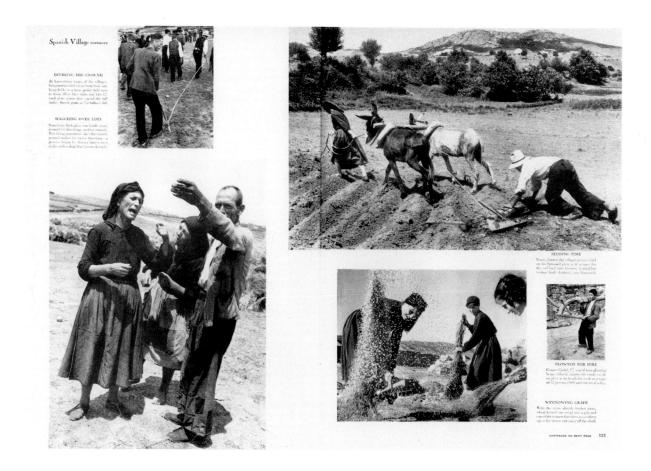

DIVIDING THE GROUND

At harvest time, all of the villagers bring methodsled wheat from their own living fields to a large public field next to town. Here they stake out like 42-yard plots where they spread the full stalks, thresh grain as forefathers did.

HAGGLING OVER LOTS

Sometimes luck gives one family stony ground for threshing, another smooth. This brings arguments, since the town's ground makes for easier threshing—a process begun by sharing barren stony stalks with a dog that frowns keenly.

SEEDING TIME

Beans planted, the villager presses hard on his flat-nosed plow as it scrapes the dry soil back into furrows. A neighbor woman leads donkeys, sows beanseed.

PLOWBOY FOR HIRE

Genaro Curiel, 17, son of town planting beans (above), carries his crude wooden plow as he heads for work as a wage earner at 12 pesetas (30¢) and one meal a day.

WINNOWING GRAIN

With the straw already broken away, wheat kernels are swept into a pile and one of the women threshes tosses them up so the breeze can carry off the chaff.

CONTINUED ON NEXT PAGE 125

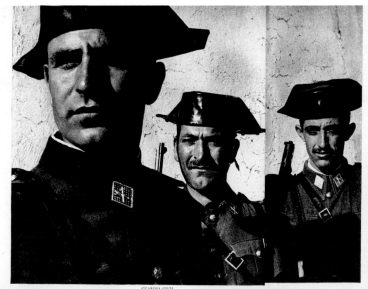

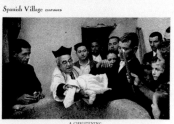

A CHRISTENING
While his godfather holds him over a font, the priest Don Manuel dries the head of month-old Buenaventura Jimenez Moreno after his baptism at village church.

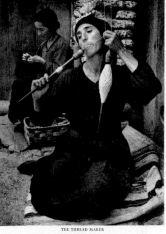

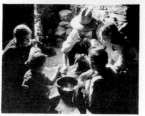

GUARDIA CIVIL
These stern men, enforcers of national law, are Franco's rural police. They patrol countryside, are feared by people in villages, which also have local police.

VILLAGE SCHOOL
Girls are taught in separate classes from the boys. Four rooms and four lay teachers handle all pupils, as many as 200 in winter, between the ages of 6 and 14.

◄ — FAMILY DINNER
The Curiel eat thick bean and potato soup from common pot on dirt floor of their kitchen. The father, mother and four children all share the one bedroom.

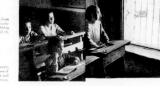

THE THREAD MAKER
A peasant woman moistens the fibers of locally grown flax as she joins them in a long strand which is spun tight by the spindle (right), then wrapped around it.

CONTINUED ON NEXT PAGE 127

126

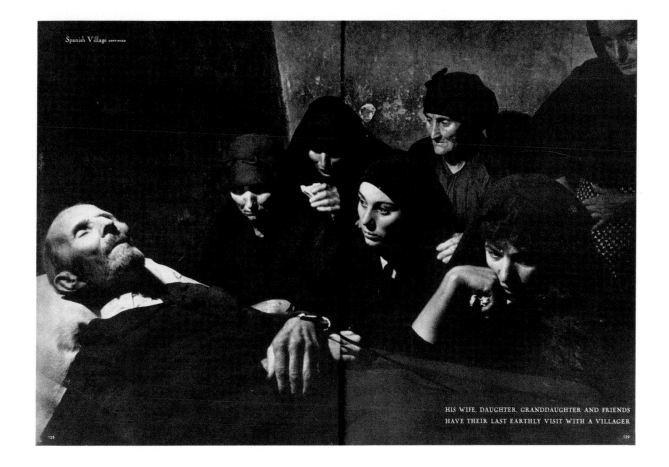

HIS WIFE, DAUGHTER, GRANDDAUGHTER AND FRIENDS
HAVE THEIR LAST EARTHLY VISIT WITH A VILLAGER

128

129

thine Walk" (part of this work also appeared in the book mentioned earlier on that city by Lorant), and a lyrical story entitled "As From My Window I Sometimes Glance," that evokes the tempo of urban life as it is affected by changing seasons, weather, atmosphere, and mood. A project undertaken by the photographer and his second wife from 1971 to 1975 in Minamata, Japan, reveals the agonizing human price of industrial pollution; it includes an image that recalls Michelangelo's *Pièta (pl. no. 659)* and represents Smith's culminating endeavor to use photography to "right what is wrong."

Profile: Henri Cartier-Bresson

Called "equivocal, ambivalent and accidental"[40] when first exhibited at the Julien Levy Gallery in New York in 1933, the work of French photographer Henri Cartier-Bresson has come to be regarded as one of the seminal visions of the 20th century. After studying painting for a number of years, including a year with André Lhote, Cartier-Bresson began to photograph with a Leica around 1930, soon revealing a remarkable ability to create images

that invest moments in time with enduring mystery or humor. Throughout a career of some 35 years, he consistently upheld the primacy of individuality and spontaneity in the photographic process; maintaining that "you have to be yourself and you have to forget yourself" in order to discover the exact instant and position from which the photographer might be able to extract a moment of meaning from ongoing existence.[41]

Commissions from *Harper's Bazaar* and *Vu* magazine in 1932 started Cartier-Bresson in photojournalism. Convinced of the constraining quality of preconception, he approached actuality with an intuitive sense for forms ripe with emblematic significance and an eye for precise visual organization. While he has often avowed that his way of working is unlearnable, he also has acknowledged the influence on his ideas of the early journalistic images of Kertész, Munkacsi, and Umbo, all of whom shared a similar capacity to give photographic form and structure to evanescent moments of human experience. For example, the disparities of scale and the seemingly irrational juxtapositions of forms in images made in Spain in 1933, among them *Arena, Valencia (pl. no. 660)*, suggest the uneasy tensions that even-

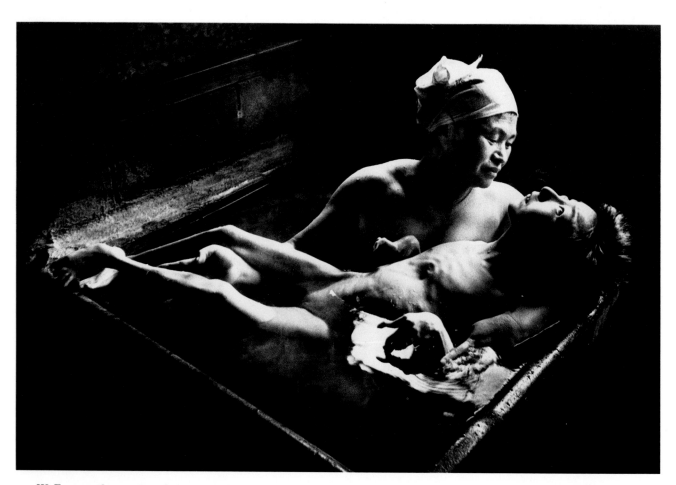

659. W. Eugene Smith. *Tomoko in Her Bath, Minamata, Japan*, 1972. Gelatin silver print. © Aileen and W. Eugene Smith/Black Star.

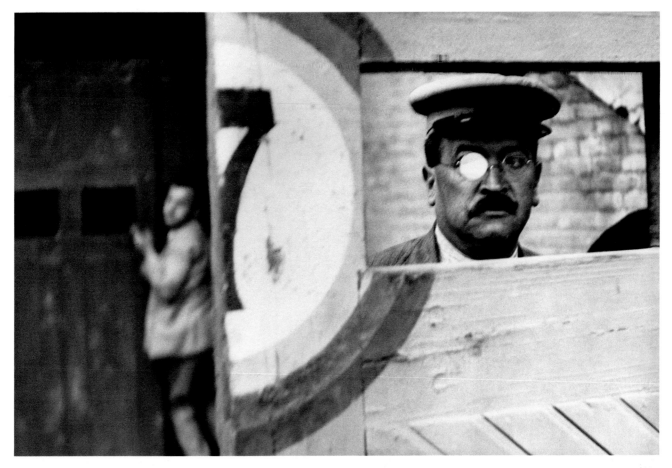

660. HENRI CARTIER-BRESSON. *Arena, Valencia, Spain*, 1933. © Henri Cartier-Bresson/Magnum.

tually erupted into civil war, even though their intent was poetic rather than political. During the 1930s, he photographed in Mexico and the United States, seeking not only the momentary action framed in the viewfinder of the camera but some essential truth about the larger society of which it was a part. Cartier-Bresson approached portraiture in the same way, contending that in the transient expressions of the many figures in the arts whom he photographed during the 1940s in the United States and France can be found the key to their individual personalities.

Cartier-Bresson also studied film technique, working with Strand in the United States and with Jean Renoir in France. In 1937, for Frontier Films, he produced *Return to Life*, a film about the delivery of medical aid to Spanish Loyalists, and in 1945, after his own escape from 36 months of captivity as a German prisoner-of-war, he made the film *Le Retour* about the return of French soldiers and prisoners to their homeland. Following a retrospective exhibi-

tion of his still photographs at the Museum of Modern Art in 1946, and the founding a year later of the collaborative agency Magnum, Cartier-Bresson embarked on indefatigable travels in Europe, Asia, and the Americas to make photographs. He published the results in scores of magazine articles and more than a dozen books, including *D'Une Chine à l'Autre (China in Transition)* (1954), *Moscou (The People of Moscow)* (1955), and *Visage d'Asie (Face of Asia)* (1972). While the photographer insists that he is not interested in documenting particular peoples and events but in evoking universal dreams and intuitions, he has drawn nourishment from the political and social contingencies of the events he has witnessed and at the same time affirmed the vitality and intensity of life everywhere. His ideas have had a profound influence on several generations of younger photographers, a number of whom have transformed his concepts into personal styles that encompass their own expressive goals.

II.

PHOTOGRAPHY SINCE 1950: THE STRAIGHT IMAGE

There is one thing the photograph must contain, the humanity of the moment. This kind of photography is realism. But realism is not enough— there has to be vision and the two together can make a good photograph. It is difficult to describe this thin line where matter ends and mind begins.

—Robert Frank, 1962[1]

IN 1850 IT WOULD HAVE BEEN UNUSUAL to find someone who had handled a camera or looked at a photograph, but 100 years later the reverse would have been true—the camera had become a ubiquitous device, its techniques manageable by even the clumsiest and least sophisticated person. By 1950, photographic images in silver, in colored dyes, and in printer's ink had penetrated to all parts of the globe, through all layers of society, and had become the daily visual diet of everyone living in urban centers of the West. Is it any wonder that in the second-half of the 20th century photography has come to be perceived as the paramount means of visual communication, that it has attracted gifted and imaginative artists as well as professionals and amateurs, and that it has infiltrated the art marketplace as a commodity while continuing to fulfill established roles in informing and advertising?

Photographs had become more visible than ever before after the second World War, owing greatly to the picture magazines, which continued to be popular during the 1970s despite the inroads made by television. With their accomplished reportage, seductive advertising, and even abstract-looking scientific pictures *(pl. no. 661)* made possible by new techniques in aerial photography and microphotography, picture journals helped prepare the way for public acceptance of a wide variety of imagery—for abstractions, sequences, visual manipulations of various kinds, and color. Furthermore, photographs as such began to be more frequently reproduced in book format, more often exhibited in galleries and museums, and were collected by private individuals and business enterprises. As a result, their history and provenance became the subjects of scholarly study; concurrently the nature of perception and the effect of photography on the quality of life became the stuff of intellectual speculation.

That photography also had become an international medium is evident from its short history, during which processes and ideas traversed national boundaries with ease, owing in part to the increasingly undifferentiated character of life in urban industrial societies and in part to the continual competition among Western nations in all scientific and industrial fields. However, after World War II, as European and Far Eastern nations struggled to rebuild shattered economies, the wellspring of visual culture shifted temporarily to the United States. In that America was physically untouched by the war and was entering upon a period of relative economic well-being, it provided the proper conditions for photography, and indeed all the visual arts, to flourish. Eventually, publications, traveling exhibitions, and peripatetic photographers on assignment acquainted Europeans with the styles of postwar camera expression originating in the United States. Following the return to stability abroad, camera activity in Europe, Latin America, and the Far East also prospered. In view of these historical circumstances, it seems logical to discuss developments in the United States first, and in somewhat greater detail, before turning to tendencies abroad.

Postwar Photographic Trends in the United States

Choosing wars as demarcations of cultural time segments may seem simplistic, but there is little question that a new sensibility made its appearance in the United States after World War II. As the nation entered upon a period that was characterized (until the late 1960s) by domestic peace, political conformism, and expansive consumerism, many in the arts began to grapple with problems of pure form, with the expression of inner visions, and with ways of representing new perceptions of social realities. Reflecting this trend, a significant group of photographers concentrated on what have been called "private realities,"[2] drawing ideas and inspiration from a variety of sources, among them Abstract Expressionist painting, psychoanalytic thought, Zen, and other systems of Eastern philosophy. Others were inspired by the photographic experimentalism implanted on the American soil by the Bauhaus as well as by the tendency among many painters to obscure the traditional line between photographic and graphic expression by involving themselves with mixed media—a development that, along with photographic color expression, will be treated in Chapter 12. The work of young photographers who continued to espouse straight photography also exhibited subtle changes, becoming colored by more subjective or ironic attitudes. Alongside these new sensibilities, traditional approaches to image-making still attracted adherents, giving the medium extraordinary range and vitality.

The explosion of photographic activity in the United

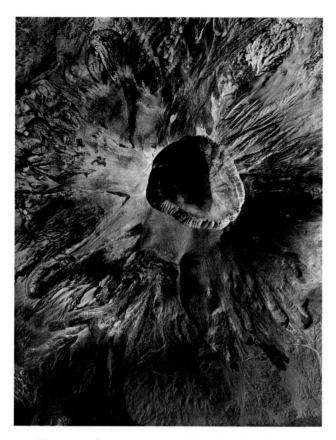

661. UNKNOWN PHOTOGRAPHER. *Mount Vesuvius, Italy, after the Eruption of 1944*, 1944. Gelatin silver print. Imperial War Museum, London.

States stemmed in part from the general economic well-being of the nation and in part from the opportunities given former members of the Armed Forces to attend art schools and colleges at government expense. This education introduced many young people to the camera as a vocational tool and as a means of contemporary personal expression. One such educational fountainhead was the Institute of Design—the American incarnation of the Bauhaus—which proposed that photographers be first and foremost concerned with the expressive manipulation of light, "free from cultural indoctrination."[3] Setting aside the social intent and utopian ideals explicit in the original Weimar and Dessau Bauhaus programs, the Institute program advocated a "new vision" that was involved primarily with finding fresh personal ways of looking at the commonplace.

Of the photographers associated with the Institute in its early days, Harry Callahan and Aaron Siskind were the most influential in terms of their own work. Reflecting the school's emphasis on experimentation, Callahan used both 35mm and 8 x 10 inch formats, worked in color, and made multiple exposures, montages, and collages. However, his straight images exemplify attempts to find a visual means

of "revealing the subject in a new way to intensify it,"[4] as in the early *Weed Against the Sky, Detroit*, 1948 *(pl. no. 664, see also pl. no. 662)*. Siskind's attraction to abstract form in nature and the built world, already visible in architectural details he photographed in Martha's Vineyard in the mid-1930s, became stronger over the next few decades as the photographer committed himself to "relaxing beliefs . . . to seeing the world clean, fresh and alive."[5] Acknowledging the influence of the accidental and spontaneous gestures favored by Abstract Expressionist painters, Siskind found in the canvases of Willem de Kooning, Franz Kline, and Jackson Pollock suggestions for the motifs he extracted from street environments *(pl. no. 663)*. While much of the experimentalism fostered by the Institute took the form of manipulative interventions *(see Chapter 12)*, a number of graduates, including Linda Connor, Art Sinsabaugh, and Geoffrey Winningham, applied the precepts to straight photography, at times using unusual formats or special lenses to embody a fresh vision of reality.

Another dimension was given to postwar photography by Minor White, a figure whose search for allusive or metaphorical meanings in the appearances of reality attracted a cult-following during the 1960s. Through extensive educational and publishing activities, White's was probably the most persuasive voice to urge that the photograph embody a mystic essence, that the camera reveal "things for what they are" and "for what else they are."[6] Unsympathetic to the idea that the medium should draw upon ideas relevant to the graphic arts by emulating either their forms or maneuvers, White sought instead to continue the directions in straight photography mapped out by Stieglitz and Weston, to approach nature with a large-format camera, a sharp lens, and an eye for the equivalencies of form and feeling. As Weston had, White obliterated clues to size, scale, atmosphere, and geographic locale, giving his images the enigmatic quality seen in *Moencopi Strata, Capitol Reef, Utah*, 1962, *(pl. no. 665)*, a work that is both a depiction of actual rock formations, an arresting visual design, and an invitation to see within it whatever the viewer desires.

Young photographers inspired by the intensity of White's credo and the force of Weston's images sought in natural phenomena of all kinds the forms that might express the oneness of the individual with the world of nature. Eroded surfaces, tangled branches, translucent petals, watery environments, and rock structures photographed close-up and with large-format cameras were favored by Walter Chapell and Paul Caponigro *(pl. no. 666)* as a means of going beyond perception to evoke the mystic divinity in all nature. The power of light to unlock "the greatest secrets of the unknown"[7] is central also to the imagery of Wynn Bullock *(pl. no. 667)*, a Californian who was close to

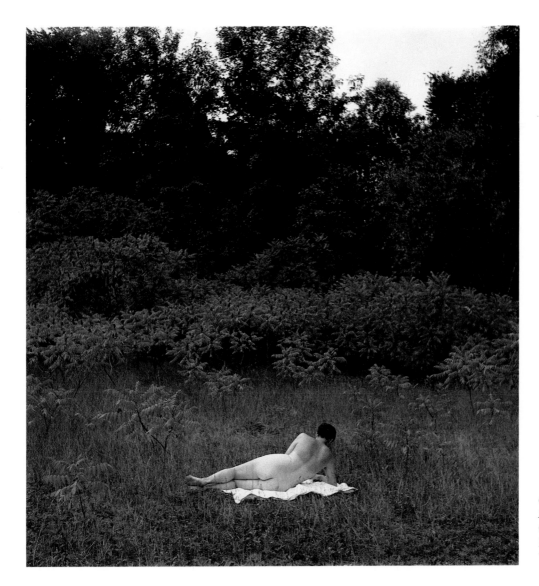

662. HARRY CALLAHAN.
Eleanor, Port Huron, 1954.
Gelatin silver print. Pace/
MacGill Gallery, New
York. © Harry Callahan.

Weston personally and ideologically. A similar attitude about the transcendent meaning of nature has inspired Connor's images of sacred trees, rocks, and waterfalls, taken in many parts of the world. Another means used to invest the landscape with fresh regard has been to view it from an unusual angle or position. William Garnett (*pl. no. 668*) and Bradford Washington both photograph from the air, transforming the shifting patterns of desert, eroded soil and farmland into elegantly structured visual abstractions through framing and the quality and direction of the light.

During the 1960s, this concept of the camera image as a lofty emblem of some universal truth was challenged by several groups—by those who believed that "the interior truth ultimately is the only truth,"[8] by those engaged by conceptual issues, and by those who responded to social realities but in a subjective fashion. The first two groups turned to manipulative and directorial interventions in the

photographic process while, for the most part, photographers of the social scene continued to favor straight photography. However, the changing character of American life coupled with the popularity of the 35mm camera and fresh ideas about photographic aesthetics produced a distinctive style and tone in straight street photography, with the prevailing tenor becoming distanced and ironic. This approach had surfaced first in street images by Walker Evans and Callahan made in the early 1940s, but its main impetus seems to have come from two former Europeans working in the United States from the 1950s on. One, Lisette Model, whose mordant views of bench sitters in Monte Carlo (*pl. no. 669*) were followed by sardonic images of New Yorkers on the streets and at play, became an influential teacher; the other, Robert Frank, a Swiss-born émigré, was even more predominant in establishing a tone and style for the next generation.

Awarded a Guggenheim grant in 1955, Frank made a

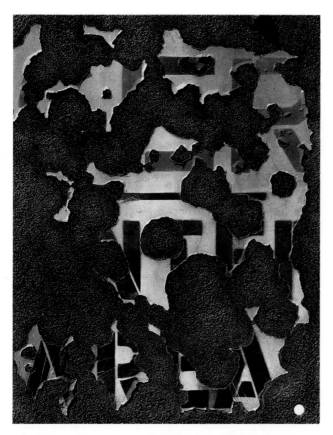

663. AARON SISKIND. *New York No. 6*, 1951. Gelatin silver print. Courtesy and © Aaron Siskind.

rapher of fashion and street views, also ignored traditional precepts about sharpness, tonal range, and print quality, as in *Garment Center*, 1954 *(pl. no. 672)*—a work that resonates with the anxieties of modern urban life. Another reaction to the pretensions of the middle class can be seen in the derisive treatment by Diane Arbus of so-called normal individuals and her compassion for those whom society considers bizarre—transvestites, homosexuals, and prostitutes, for example. Prompted by what she termed the "ceremonies of our present,"[9] Arbus, whose mentor was Model and whose model was Weegee *(see Chapter 9)*, approached such material without artifice or moral prejudgment, but when she photographed ordinary people in ordinary situations her reaction was invariably ungenerous. Whatever her subject, she usually favored direct head-on poses that often mimicked the style of the family snapshot as in *Mother Holding Her Child, New Jersey (pl. no. 673)*, one of the more alienated images of motherhood in the history of visual art *(see also pl. no. 674)*.

Indeed, one of the signal influences on straight camera images during the 1960s was the "snapshot aesthetic." The appetite for this naive form of popular camera imagery accorded with the era's taste for vernacular and "pop" culture—a taste reflected in the themes and techniques of graphic art also. Like the painters of soup cans, road signs, and comic-book characters, photographers were attracted by the omnipresent emblems of contemporary culture—by

photographic odyssey through the United States, using a 35mm Leica. His status as an outsider enabled him to regard cherished national institutions and pastimes with detached irony, while his sensitive eye transformed situations and events into metaphors for the factiousness and consumerism of American postwar society. For example, contrasts in facial expressions, the gestures of the riders, and the structural design of *Trolley, New Orleans (pl. no. 670)* encompass the psychological and emotional complexities as well as the actual divisions that characterized racial attitudes in the South without rhetoric or doctrinaire statement. *(See also pl. no. 671)* Frank's images were meant to be seen as a group rather than individually and were published in book format as *The Americans*—first in France and later in 1959 in the United States, where their irreverent, unposed, erratically framed, and sometimes blurred forms (reflective also of their maker's anti-aesthetic attitude toward print quality) adumbrated the taste of a generation that had had its fill of heroes and icons. William Klein's raw and grating views of New York in the 1950s were even less acceptable as a vision of American society, with the result that a book of just his New York images still has not been published here. Klein, an American resident of France who is a painter, designer, and filmmaker in addition to being a photog-

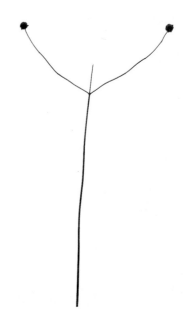

664. HARRY CALLAHAN. *Weed Against Sky, Detroit*, 1948. Gelatin silver print. Pace/MacGill Gallery, New York. © Harry Callahan.

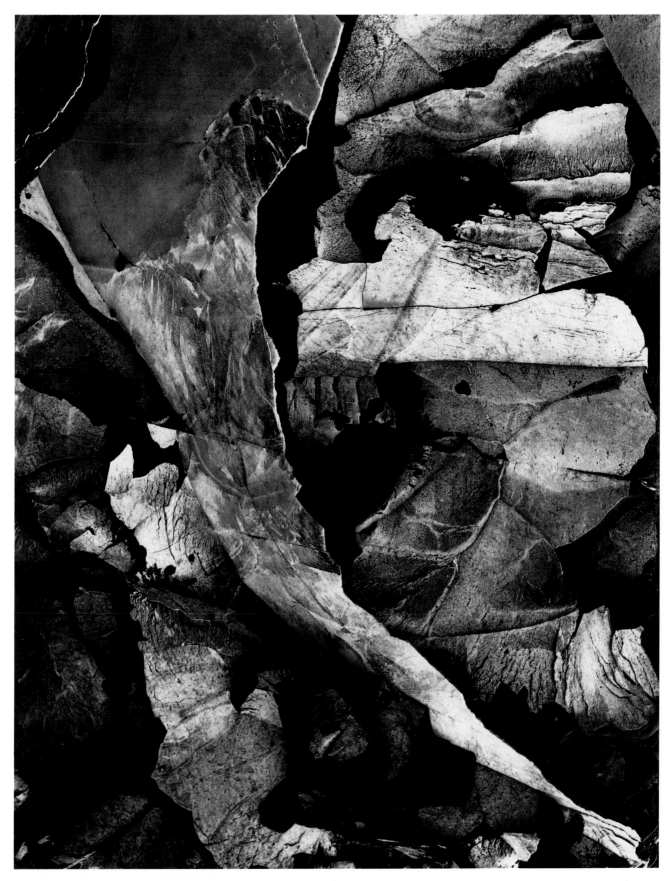

665. MINOR WHITE. *Moencopi Strata, Capitol Reef, Utah*, 1962. Gelatin silver print.
Museum of Modern Art, New York; Purchase. Courtesy and © The Minor White Archive, Princeton University, N.J.

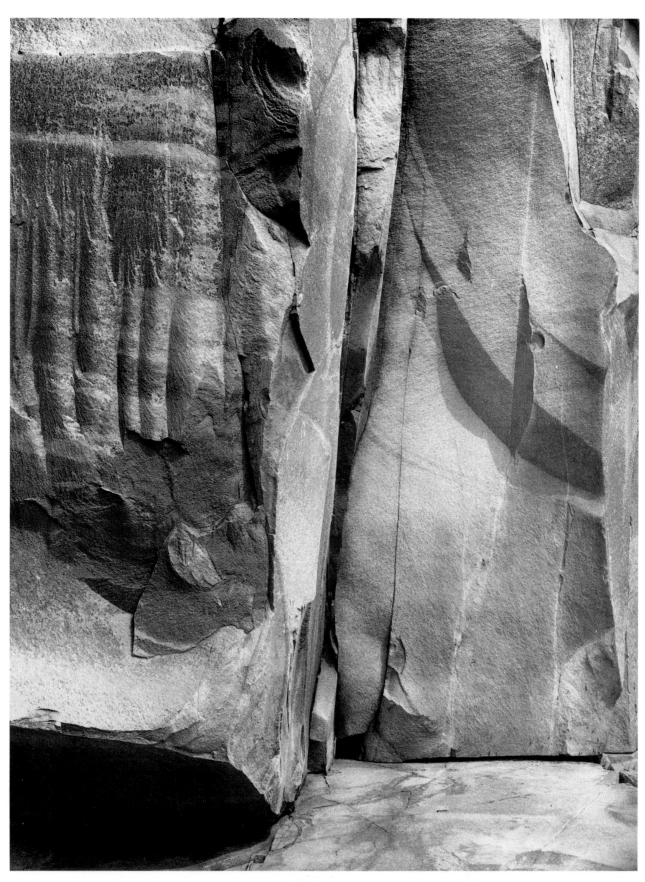

666. PAUL CAPONIGRO. *Schoodic Point, Maine,* 1960. Gelatin silver print.
International Museum of Photography at George Eastman House, Rochester, N.Y. © 1960 Paul Caponigro.

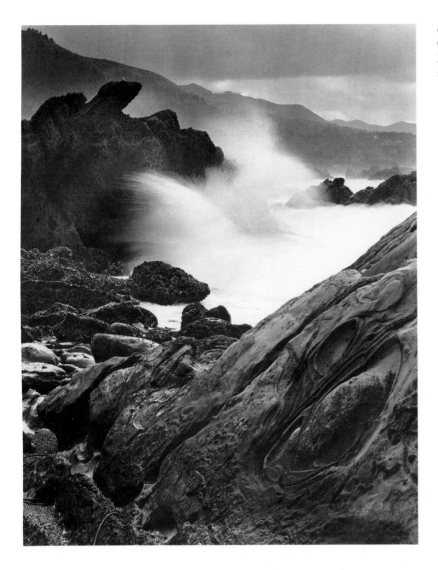

667. WYNN BULLOCK. *Point Lobos Wave*, 1958. Gelatin silver print. Collection Mr. and Mrs. Robert E. Abrams, New York. © Wynn and Edna Bullock Trust.

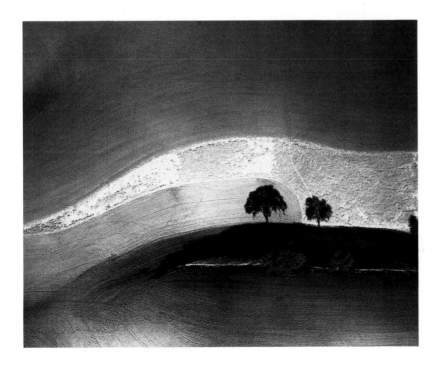

668. WILLIAM A. GARNETT. *Two Trees on a Hill with Shadows, Paso Robles, California*, 1947. Daniel Wolf, Inc., New York. © William A. Garnett.

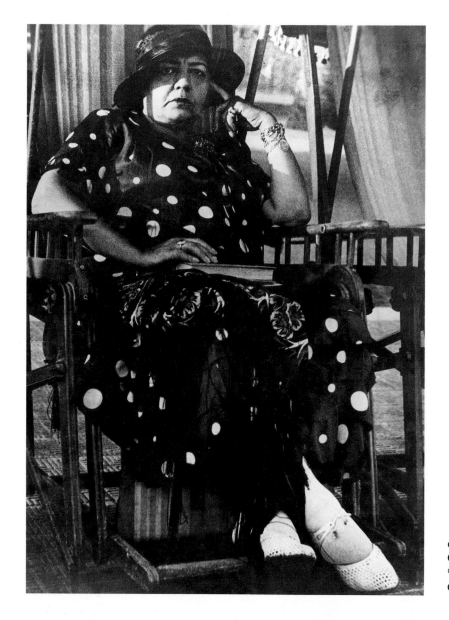

669. LISETTE MODEL. *French Riviera*, 1937. Gelatin silver print. Private Collection. © Estate of Lisette Model, Courtesy Sander Gallery, New York.

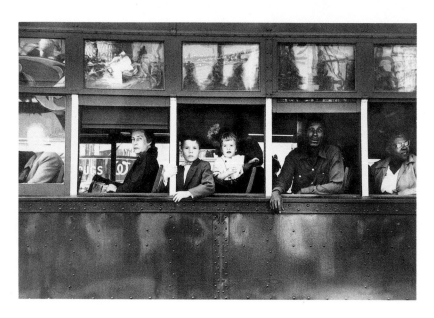

670. ROBERT FRANK. *Trolley, New Orleans*, c. 1955. Gelatin silver print. © Robert Frank/Zebra Corporation.

the automobile, advertising signs, graffiti, and provincial storefronts. What is more, they portrayed these artifacts, as well as people and situations, in a casual style that seemed to paraphrase the lack of artifice and the neutral emotional tone of most snapshots. To relate this approach to social documentation, in 1966 photographer–educator Nathan Lyons coined the phrase "social landscape"[10] as a means of expanding the vocabulary of documentation while avoiding what he and others felt to be the presumptive sentimental posture of the older documentary style. This concept appealed especially to photographers whose view of reality tended to be disjunctive and who no longer canonized artistic photography or the pre-visualized large-format, beautifully printed camera image.

To make pictures that affirmed the camera's capacity for observation evolved from interest in the snapshot and emerged as a significant impulse, nurtured from the late 1960s by John Szarkowski, director of the Department of Photography of the Museum of Modern Art. In theory, the apparent avoidance of overt psychological or ideological posture in a photograph allows the viewer to interpret the work freely, without the interference of the photographer's political or social biases. As exemplar of this mode of working, the images of Garry Winogrand, according to Szarkowski, are statements about "the uniquely prejudicial (intrinsic) qualities of photographic description"[11] and not about their ostensible subjects. Winogrand's photograph of a young woman *(pl. no. 675)* is arresting in the way it integrates and structures reflections and geometric ele-

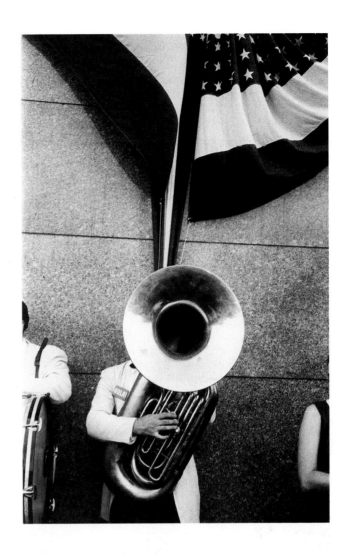

671. ROBERT FRANK.
Political Rally, Chicago,
c. 1955. Gelatin silver print.
© Robert Frank/Zebra
Corporation.

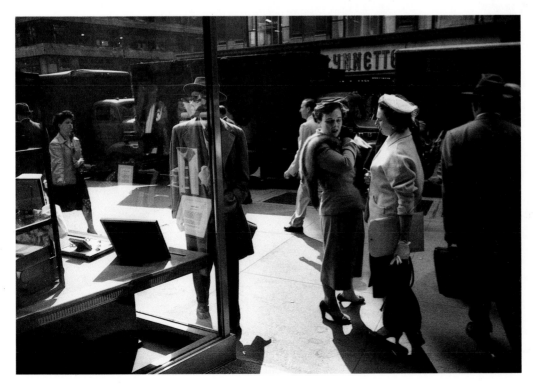

672. WILLIAM KLEIN.
Garment Center, 1954.
Gelatin silver print.
Courtesy and © William
Klein.

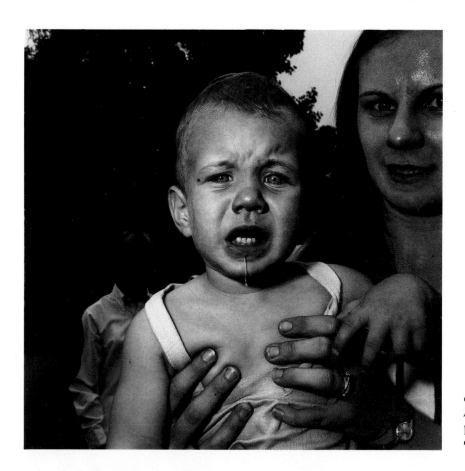

673. DIANE ARBUS. *Mother Holding Her Child, N.J.*, 1967. Gelatin silver print. Courtesy and © 1967 Estate of Diane Arbus.

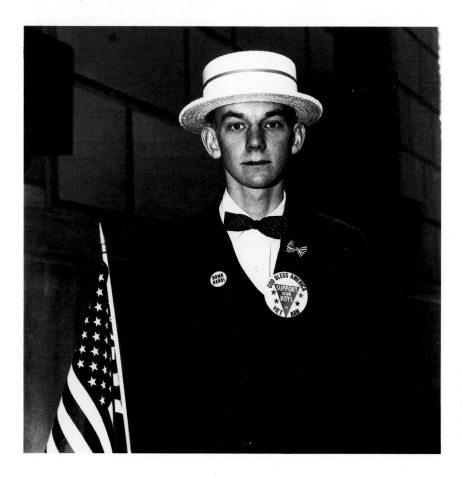

674. DIANE ARBUS. *Patriotic Boy With Straw Hat, Buttons and Flag, Waiting to March in a Pro-War Parade, New York City*, 1967. Gelatin silver print. Museum of Modern Art, New York; gift of the artist. © 1967 Estate of Diane Arbus.

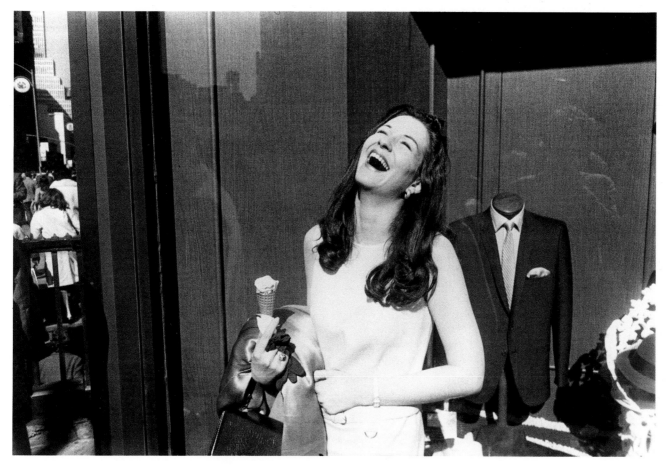

675. GARRY WINOGRAND. *Untitled*, c. 1964. Gelatin silver print. Courtesy Fraenkel Gallery, San Francisco, and the Garry Winogrand Estate.

ments, and relates the principal figure to the manikin and to the city background, but it is not a categorical statement about a situation. Sharing a similar interest in people and things, Lee Friedlander makes views of city streets that are similarly ambiguous *(pl. no. 676)* but are suggestive nevertheless of an uneasy urban tension. Along with the uninflected portrayals of ordinary people by Todd Papageorge and Larry Fink and the street views of Mark Cohen and Joel Meyerowitz—to cite but four of the numerous young photographers attracted to this style—these works project the individual photographer's reaction to the moment and permit viewers to decide for themselves whether a particular image is derisive or amusing, whether it is interesting as social or political comment, as an example of the problems of picture-making, or, like the vast majority of photographs, just momentarily intriguing.

The casual strategies of the vernacular mode had an unexpected side-effect: they prepared the way for the acceptance of humor in seriously conceived images. In the United States, pictorialists and modernists alike had been fairly earnest about photography, and until recently witty or humorous images were relegated to formats meant for advertising or popular entertainment, or to family snapshots in which clowning often was invoked. Within the diversity of photographic expression that emerged in the 1960s, humor came to be seen as a legitimate element. Elliott Erwitt and Burk Uzzle, for example, are both successful photojournalists who regard people, animals, and artifacts with disarming wit *(pl. no. 677)*. Although this vein still has not been extensively mined in the United States, other photographers, among them Winningham and Bill Owens, gently satirize obviously comical anomalies in contemporary culture, while the unvarnished selling strategies of advertising visuals inspire William Wegman's antic dog images *(pl. no. 678)* and Neal Slavin's facetiously posed group portraits *(pl. no. 763)*. Still another approach to humor can be seen in the whimsical confusions between reality and camera image explored by conceptualist photographer Kenneth Josephson *(see Chapter 12)*.

Evolving out of the concept of "social landscape," images that present the artifacts and landscapes of contemporary industrial culture without emotional shading have been given the name "new topographics."[12] Robert Adams, Lewis Baltz, Frank Gohlke, Roger Mertin, and

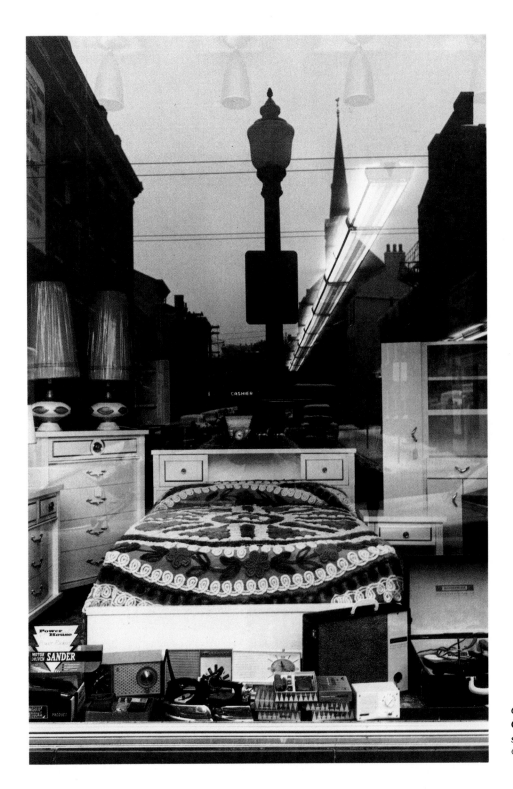

676. LEE FRIEDLANDER. *Cincinnati, Ohio*, 1963. Gelatin silver print. Courtesy and © Lee Friedlander.

Stephen Shore, among others, photograph tract housing, factory buildings, western land developments, and urban streets, depicting this despoiled landscape seemingly without rhetoric or personal comment. Adams, for example, may share with Ansel Adams (no relation) a concern for the beauty of the land from the Missouri westward, but for his photographs he selects vantage points and effects of light that show its grandeur diminished by roads, lumbering camps, and housing developments. *South Wall, Mazda Motors (pl. no. 679)*, one of a 1974 series on industrial parks by Baltz, is meant to provide "sterile information with no emotional content," according to the photographer who conceives of his vocation as a way to "describe with a camera how something looks as a photograph."[13] Nevertheless, all photographers face decisions concerning selection of motif, management of light, and organization of form; indeed, the fact that "topographical" images usually are highly structured suggests that their uneventfulness and lack of emotional commitment are in themselves emblems of a style and are no more "factual" as records of what actually exists than images that reflect more socially oriented points of view. One consequence of this approach is that such images may serve multiple purposes—some aesthetic, some informational, some propagandistic. Because "topographical" views—whether Baltz's factories or Gohlke's grain elevators—maintain a neutral stance they often are indistinguishable from similar images commissioned to illustrate annual corporate business reports.

In the period under discussion, photographers with a broadly humanist outlook, among them Roy DeCarava, Louis Faurer, Jerome Leibling, Helen Levitt, Walter Rosenblum *(pl. no. 465)*, and Max Yavno continued to work on a variety of self-motivated projects whose central theme concerned people, despite the fact that for a time museums and galleries tended to give greater support to other kinds of photographic images. Levitt's lyrical views of youngsters *(pl. no. 680)*, begun in the 1940s and continued intermittently, illuminate the toughness, grace, and humor of those growing up in New York's inner city neighborhoods. *Pepsi, New York*, 1964, *(pl. no. 681)* by DeCarava may incorporate some components of the vernacular style—consumer products, billboard ads—but the highly structured handling of light and architectonic ele-

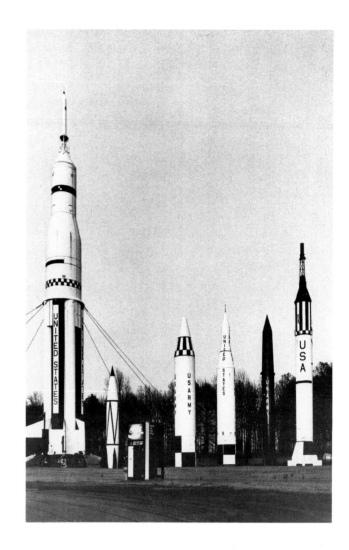

677. ELLIOT ERWITT. *Alabama*, U.S.A., 1974. Gelatin silver print. © Elliott Erwitt/Magnum.

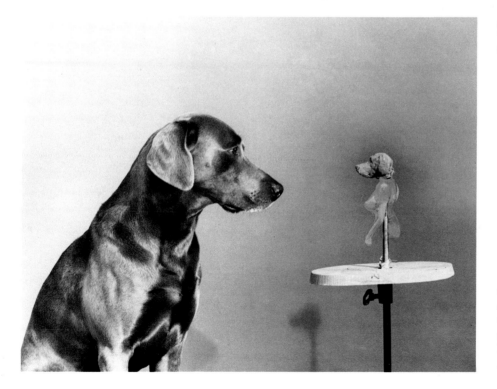

678. WILLIAM WEGMAN. *Man Ray with Sculpture*, 1978. Gelatin silver print with ink applied. Holly Solomon Gallery, New York; Collection Ludwig, Aachen. © William Wegman.

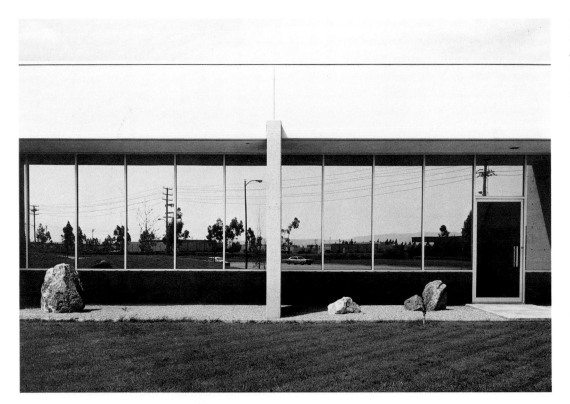

679. LEWIS BALTZ. *South Wall, Mazda Motors*, 1974. Gelatin silver print. Castelli Graphics, New York. © 1975 Lewis Baltz.

680. HELEN LEVITT. *New York*, c. 1945. Gelatin silver print. Collection Judith Mamiye, Oakhurst, N.J. © 1981 Helen Levitt.

ments serve to focus attention on the physical and psychological exhaustion of the central figure and leave no doubt as to where the photographer's interest and sympathy lie. Liebling's grasp of abstract form is apparent in the repeated arclike shapes formed by head, shoulders, and plate in *Blind Home, St. Paul*, 1963, *(pl. no. 682)*, but these elements generate a sense of the circumscribed world of the sightless. A somewhat cooler romantic sensibility can be seen in the work of George Tice, a younger photographer whose interest in the customs and physical surroundings of the Amish in Pennsylvania and of ordinary folk in the small towns of New Jersey *(pl. no. 683)* is imbued with a sense of wistfulness through careful control of tonality and pictorial structure.

In the 1960s, the still image was again seen as a vivid element of a social statement. A number of factors were responsible for this revival of interest in the traditional forms of social documentation. One was the emergence of funding agencies both in and out of government. Support from the national and state arts endowments, from private granting bodies such as the venerable John Simon Guggenheim Memorial Foundation (which from 1946 on had funded a range of photographic projects), from banks, economic assistance programs, and labor unions made possible individual and group camera studies of decaying and regenerated neighborhoods, rural communities, nuclear and other power installations, conditions of industrial and farm labor, to mention only a few of the multiplicity of projects that

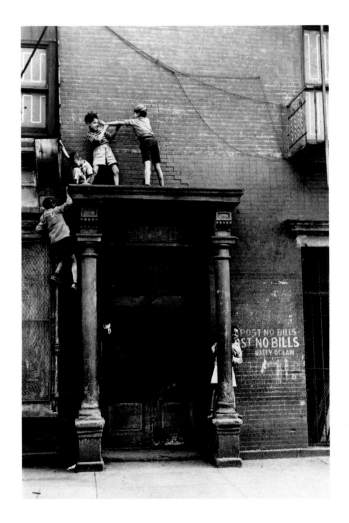

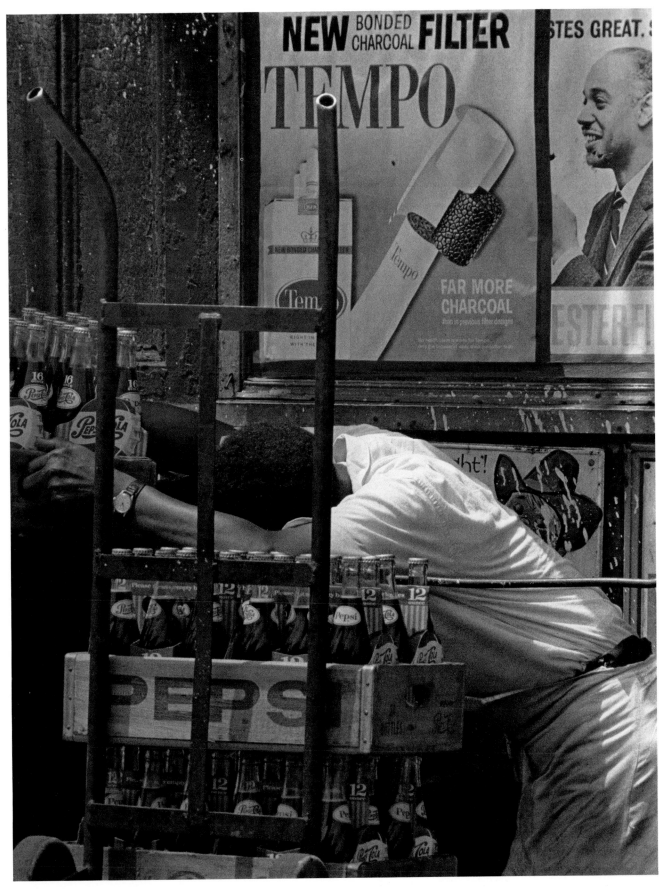

681. ROY DeCARAVA. *Pepsi, New York*, 1964. Gelatin silver print. Courtesy and © 1981 Roy DeCarava.

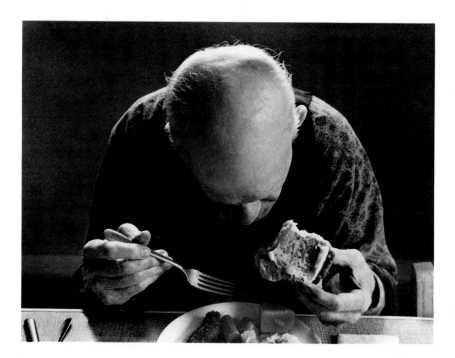

682. JEROME LIEBLING. *Blind Home, St. Paul, Minnesota*, 1963. Gelatin silver print. Courtesy and © Jerome Liebling.

683. GEORGE A. TICE. *Joe's Barbershop, Paterson, N.J.*, 1970. Gelatin silver print. Courtesy and © George A. Tice.

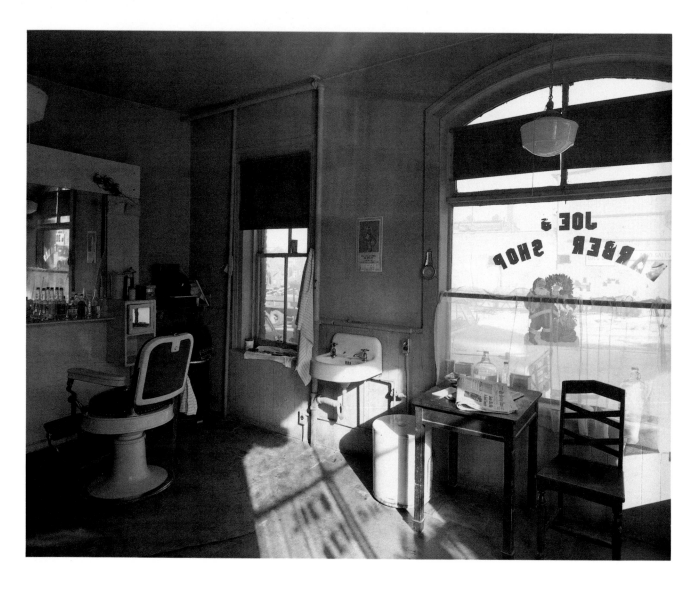

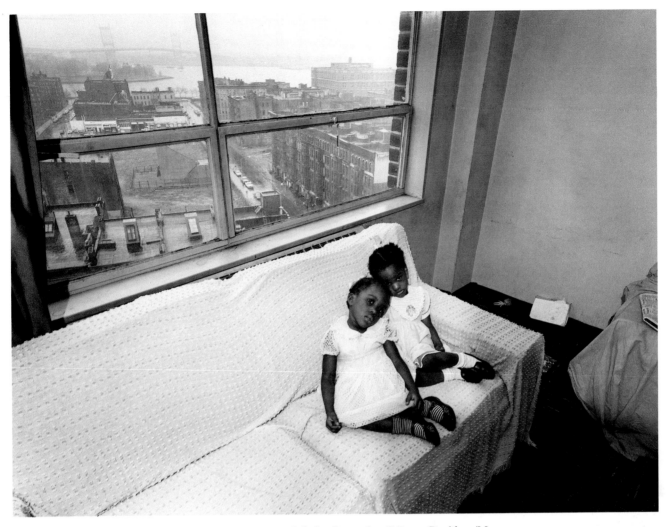

684. BRUCE DAVIDSON. *Untitled, East 100th Street*, 1966. Gelatin silver print. © Bruce Davidson/Magnum.

made use of images in connection with words in slide talks, exhibitions, and publications.

Another factor was the involvement of photojournalists in the increasingly volatile social events in America. For instance, Bob Adelman, Bruce Davidson, Leonard Freed, Danny Lyon, and Mary Ellen Mark were among the photojournalists who covered the Civil Rights struggles of the 1960s for the press and continued afterward to confront social issues and conditions on their own, approaching their themes with greater penetration than was possible for magazine deadlines. When Davidson undertook subsequent photographic projects in East Harlem *(pl. no. 684)* and on the New York subways, he was able to move away from the somewhat equivocal tone of his very early work toward more traditional humanist concerns, even though he claims that the evidences of fear, affection, and hopelessness he captured in these images serve to help him "to discover who the person was who took the picture."[14] In the wake of experiences with the Civil Rights movement in the

South, Lyon, whose initial work had included an evocative picture essay on the Hell's Angels bike riders, depicted life in Texas State prisons; *Conversations with the Dead*, the book that resulted from this project, vividly communicates the photographer's sense of the "unmitigated sorrow"[15] of this form of social estrangement *(pl. no. 685)*. A similar intent to illuminate the psychological consequences of inhumane circumstances inspires many photographers to depict not only, or even primarily, the squalor of the environment but to seek moments that sum up the effect of life's experiences on the individual. In one such example Eugene Richards, who photographs in the poverty-stricken slum neighborhoods of Boston, evokes a moment of frenzied joy—a brief respite from reality *(pl. no. 686)*—while Jill Freedmen's picture stories involving poor people and street cops celebrate their humor and compassion.

The documentation of life in America's black communities, the emergence of a substantial number of Afro-American professional photographers, and the flowering

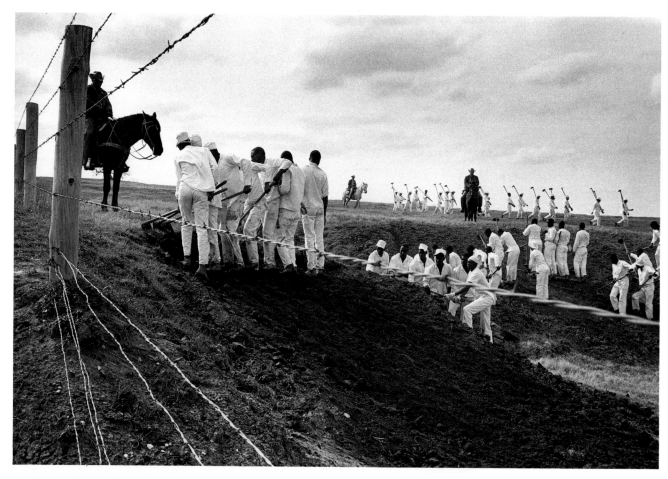

685. DANNY LYON. *The Line*, 1968. Gelatin silver print. © Danny Lyon/Magnum.

among them of photography as personal expression also owes something to the socially oriented climate of the late 1960s. Roland L. Freeman, for example, began to use a camera while working for the Poor People's Campaign and went on to produce a touching visual document of the Baltimore neighborhood of his youth *(pl. no. 687)*. In 1973, the first *Black Photographer's Annual* appeared; in this and subsequent issues, Afro-American photographers show themselves to be fully aware of the range of contemporary trends even as they focused their camera lenses on the way American black life is lived. Among those who were enabled to enter the ranks of photojournalism at this time, Chester Higgins, Anthony Barboza, and Beuford Smith have evolved distinctive individual styles.

The work of photographers commissioned by labor unions and government agencies during the 1960s and '70s may be said to be situated firmly in the tradition of social documentation because the images are intended to make visible, in the manner of Riis and Hine, conditions that need changing. Like that of earlier documentarians, their goal involves more than just producing a record of working and living environments; it is to make poignant to viewers

the effect of conditions on the individual. The human consequences of social conditions in the workplace are illuminated in photographs by Richard Bermack made for agricultural unions in California; by John Kouns taken for the automobile workers' union; and by Earl Dotter for mining unions and Federal regulatory agencies such as the Occupational Safety and Health Administration. As is true of all lasting social documentation, Dotter's image of a mine disaster in Scotia, West Virginia, *(pl. no. 688)* can stand on its own as an evocation of grief, but its forcefulness is increased by seeing it in concert with other images of the aftermath of the fire and explosion in this mining community.

Contemporary Straight Photography Elsewhere

The numerous directions explored in America after the second World War soon attracted photographers in other parts of the world. They were tempted to varying degrees by abstraction, conceptualism, and symbolism, but perhaps most by the forceful irony of Frank's subjective approach

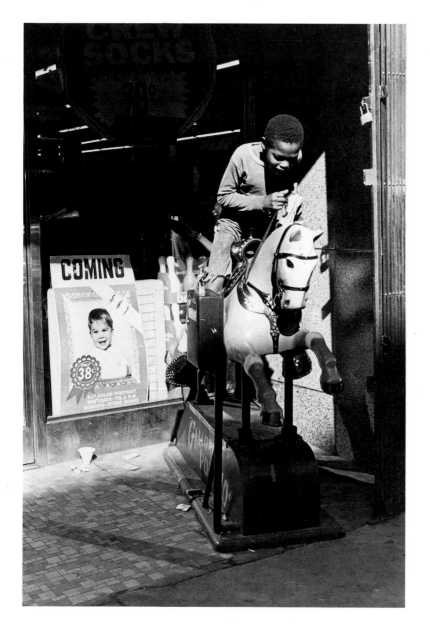

686. EUGENE RICHARDS. *Street Horse,
Dorchester Days*, 1970s. Gelatin silver print.
Private collection. © Eugene Richards/
Magnum.

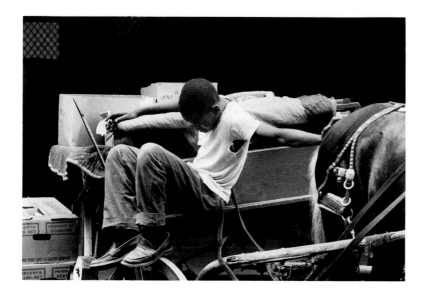

687. ROLAND L. FREEMAN. *Araber's Helper,
June*, 1969. Gelatin silver print. © Roland L.
Freeman/Magnum.

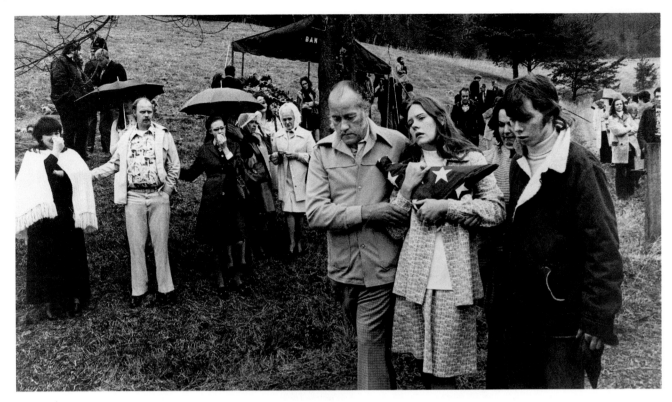

688. EARL DOTTER. *Scotia Mine Disaster*, 1976. Gelatin silver print. Private collection. © Earl Dotter.

to documentation, or by "subjective realism," as German photographer Otto Steinert called "humanized and individualized photography."[16] Camerawork also became more frequently exhibited, collected, and reproduced in Europe, and the quickening of interest in contemporary photographic expression prompted the establishment of workshops, conferences, and foundations for the support of the medium. Even though the photographs still are less esteemed by intellectuals and artists than in the United States, these developments have been accompanied by increased concern for the rich treasuries of images housed in national and private archives and by a consequent attentiveness to historic scholarship and preservation. The leading European figures in this endeavor have included photographers Fritz Kempe, director of the Staatliche Landesbildstelle in Hamburg; Steinert, associated with the Folkwang Museum in Essen; Samuel Morozov in the Soviet Union; Jean-Claude Lemagny in France; and Petr Tausk in Czechoslovakia; while in Canada James Borcoman of the National Gallery has been prominent in organizing a national collection of photography.

Canada and Latin America

Like many of their counterparts below the border, Canadian photographers have turned away from viewing camera images as basically descriptive information. They now are engaged by more personal concepts, initiated by the ideas of Frank and the social landscapists of the 1960s. Sharing this sensibility, Lynn Cohen, Charles Gagnon, and Gabor Szilasi are among those who have transformed the uningratiating forms of urban environments into deliberately structured visual entities. Street photography that integrates the common totems of the style—urban setting, automobile, reflections, and perplexing incident—is exemplified in the lucidly organized *St. Joseph de Beauce, Quebec (pl. no. 689)* by Szilasi, a Hungarian-born photographer whose aim is to allow people "to gain awareness of the environments they live in."[17] In a contrasting tendency, Robert Bourdeau represents a topographic approach and works with a large-format camera in the tradition (at times on the actual locations) of grand landscape, communicating a fresh appreciation of a theme easily productive of banality or heroics *(pl. no. 690)*.

For Latin American photographers, the year 1977 signaled the end of "the utter obstinacy which persisted in denying photography its quality as art,"[18] as a hemispheric conference held in Mexico City revealed the vigor and diversity as well as the geographic and ethnic differences that characterized camera expression throughout the region. In terms of direction, photographers in Argentina, Brazil, Cuba, Guatemala, Panama, Peru, Mexico, and Venezuela

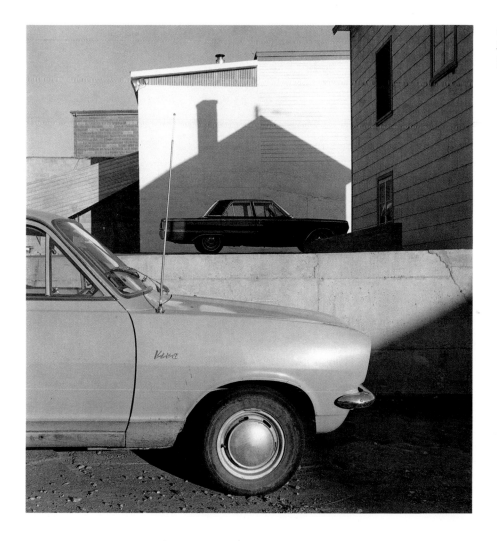

689. GABOR SZILASI. *St. Joseph de Beauce, Quebec*, 1973. Gelatin silver print. Courtesy and © Gabor Szilasi.

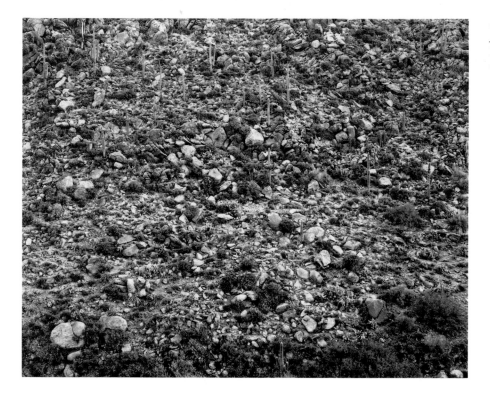

690. ROBERT BOURDEAU. *Arizona*, 1973. Gelatin silver print. National Gallery of Canada, Ottawa. © Robert Bourdeau.

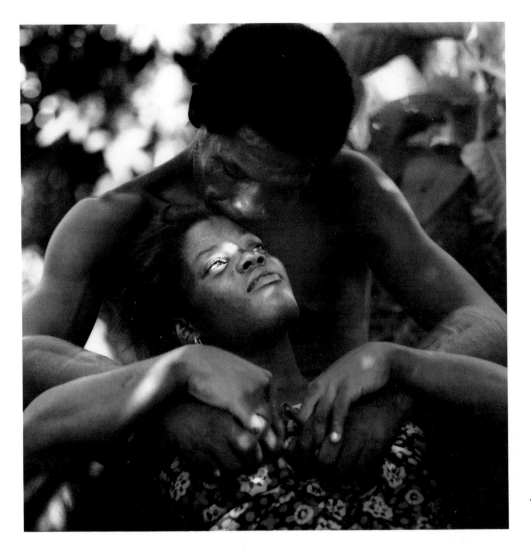

691. SANDRA ELETA. *Lovers from Portobelo*, 1977. Gelatin silver print. Courtesy and © Sandra Eleta.

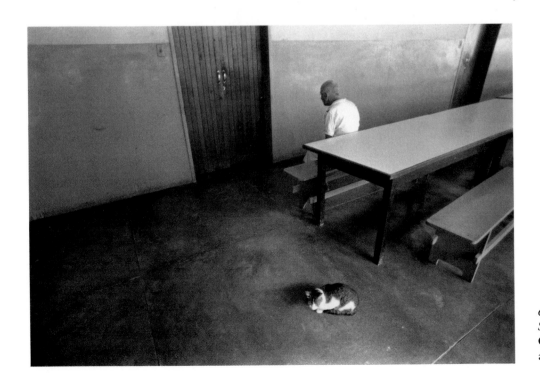

692. ROBERTO FONTANA. *Scene in an Asylum*, 1980. Gelatin silver print. Courtesy and © Roberto Fontana.

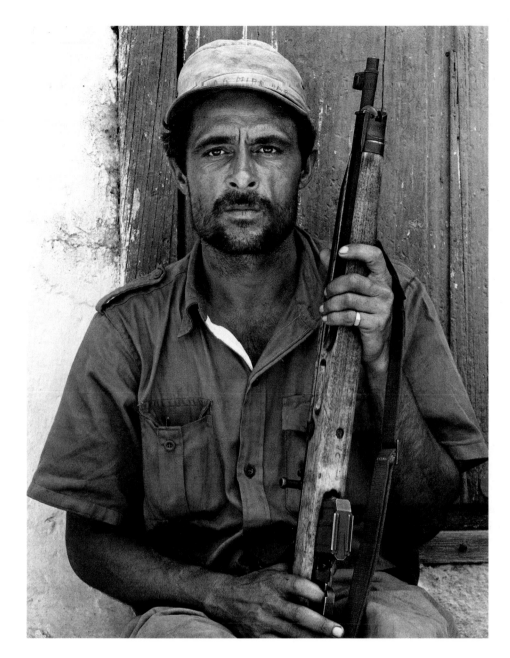

693. PAOLO GASPARINI. *Cuba, Militiaman*, 1961. Gelatin silver print. Courtesy and © Paolo Gasparini.

seem most interested in using the 35mm camera to explore the effects of rapid social and economic change on the traditional character of their respective societies; they are considerably less involved with transcendent landscape imagery, aesthetic experimentation for its own sake, or with the picturization of personal and private realities.

A range of attitudes characterizes these portrayals of urban and provincial street life, which for the most part are seen by the public in books and periodicals rather than on gallery walls. The strength of the humanist tradition is exemplified in the spirited images of ordinary working people *(pl. no. 691)* by Panamanian photographer Sandra Eleta. Infused with grace, these works transcend the momentary and convey a feeling of the vibrancy of intimate

human relationships. A similar intensity transforms studies of the Yanomani and Xingu tribesmen by Brazilian photographers Claudia Andujar and Maureen Bisilliat from routine anthropological documentation to inspired interpretation. Another direction in social documentation can be seen in the work of Roberto Fontana *(pl. no. 692)* of Venezuela, and Argentinian photographers Alicia D'Amico and Grete Stern, all of whom use the small camera to express the condition of those alienated by sickness or poverty from contemporary society.

An opposing concept of documentation is embraced by Paolo Gasparini *(pl. no. 693)*, working in Venezuela. His aim is to fashion a statement, usually involving word and image, that clarifies the social and economic consequences

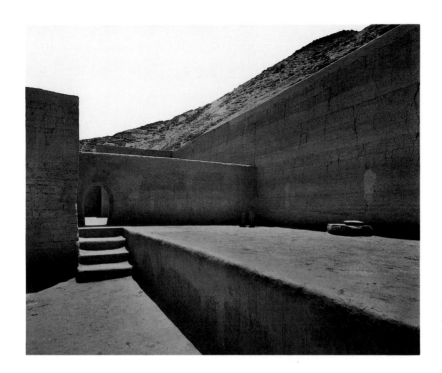

694. JOSÉ GIMENO CASALS. *Puruchuco*, 1979–80. Gelatin silver print. Courtesy and © José Gimeno Casals.

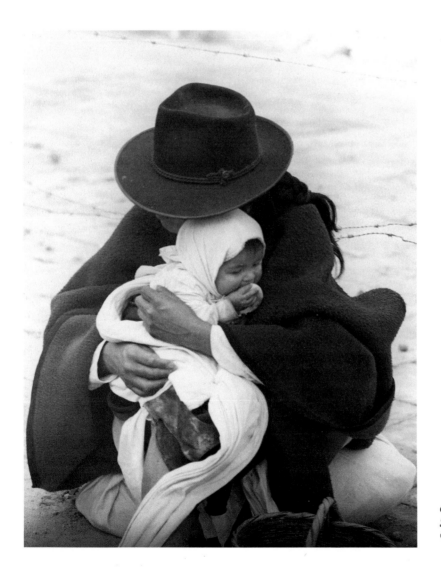

695. ENRIQUE BOSTELMANN. *Father and Son*, 1983. Gelatin silver print. Courtesy and © Enrique Bostelmann.

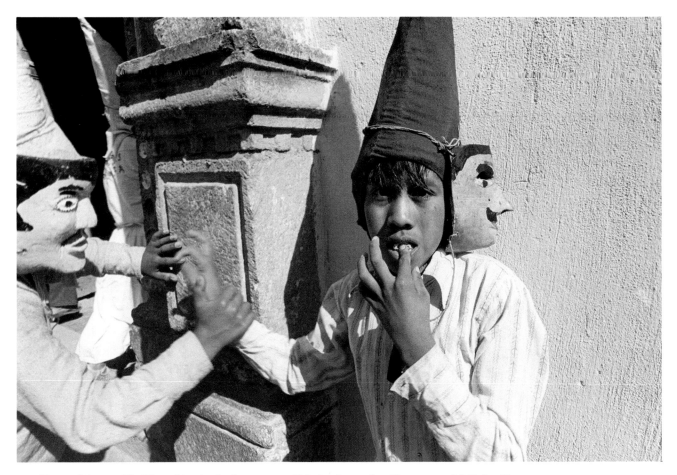

696. PEDRO MEYER. *The Unmasking in the Square*, 1981. Gelatin silver print. Courtesy and © Pedro Meyer.

of the intrusion of foreign capital and culture into Latin American life. Ironically, this view of the didactic role of social documentation (which has its origins in Soviet Constructivism and the German political climate of the 1920s) is not shared by photographers working in Cuba. Instead they are influenced by the multiform directions pursued in the United States, and their work includes sequential photographs, manipulations of various kinds, and subjective documentation. A buoyant humor, visible in the work of Cuban photographers Raul Corrales, Maria Eugenia Haya, and Mario Garcia Joya, is another aspect that is unusual in Latin American photography as a whole. While the predominant interest is in people and their condition, notable landscapes, still lifes, and architectural views have been made by Christian Alckmin Mascaro of Brazil and José Gimeno Casals of Peru. In a view of Pre-Columbian ruins at Puruchuco *(pl. no. 694)*, the solid silent forms suggest the ancient cultures of the region.

Owing in part to the favorable cultural climate engendered by the Mexican government during the 1920s and '30s and in part to the presence in Mexico of Tina Modotti, Paul Strand, Edward Weston, and other foreign photog-

raphers, Mexican photographers have been aware since then of the need to personalize the medium's intrinsic formal means. As the nation's foremost native-born photographer, Manuel Alvarez Bravo *(see Chapter 9)* found it possible to embrace the mythic implications of his own culture while at the same time acknowledging cultural ideas imported from Europe and the United States *(pl. no. 501)*. This trend has continued but the means have changed. The work of Enrique Bostelmann, made with a 35mm camera, shows a concern for formal structure, a sensitivity to placement, contrast, and silhouette, especially in a series taken in Ecuador in 1969 *(pl. no. 695)* that generates a tender yet distinctive sense of parental love. Images by Pedro Meyer, born in Spain but active in Mexico since 1962, suggest the mysterious nature of indigenous folk ritual through harsh tonal contrasts, ambiguous gesture, and the intensity of facial expression, as, for example, in *The Unmasking (pl. no. 696)*. Other contemporary Mexican photographers whose work seems to have been inspired by subjective realism are Graciela Iturbide, Pablo Ortiz Monasterio, José Angel Rodriguez *(pl. no. 697)*, Jesús Sanchez Uribe, and José Luis Neyra.

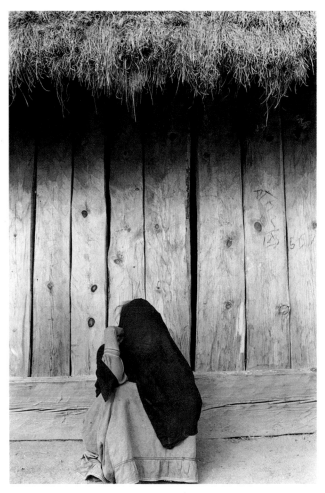

697. JOSÉ ANGEL RODRIGUEZ. *Campesina (Peasant)*, 1977. Gelatin silver print. Collection Jain and George W. Kelly, New York. © José Angel Rodriguez.

Straight Photography in Europe

In Europe, the second World War, lasting from 1939 to 1945, disrupted cultural life but did not entirely wipe out photographic activity. August Sander, for example, was prevented from pursuing his documentation of German life but made landscapes of his native region. In Czechoslovakia, Josef Sudek, whose photographic ideas had been nurtured by both Pictorialism and the New Objectivity, continued to produce lyrical tabletop still lifes *(pl. no. 698)* as well as neo-Romantic garden scenes. By the mid-1960s, Europeans had recovered sufficiently from the dislocations of the war to welcome a range of fresh ideas about photography. Even though support for the photograph as an art commodity was still insignificant compared to that in the United States, and photographers had mainly to contend for photojournalistic assignments, a variety of modes began to flourish as equipment and materials, including Polaroid and color film, became available and less

expensive. Besides embracing photojournalistic ways of depicting actuality, some younger Europeans looked across the Atlantic to the subjective and conceptual approaches popular in the United States. Other photographers became aware of their own experimentalist past and elected to work with collage, montage, and sequential statements. Like their American counterparts, they sometimes obscured the divisions between analytic and synthetic processes, between the actions of light and of pigment, fusing the means and methods of photographic and graphic art *(see Chapter 12)*.

Of the Europeans, British photographers seem to have been somewhat less attracted to extensive experimentalism and subjectivity. The narrative tendency remained strong, prompted by long experience with documentation. Curiously, the focus on informational content in England was reinforced by Moholy-Nagy; during a brief sojourn in London in 1936 this catalyst of experimentalism in the United States promoted the camera image as a way to observe "a fragment of present day reality from a social and economic point of view."[19] Traditional documentation was carried on and modified after the war by photojournalists Bert Hardy, George Rodger, Philip Jones Griffiths, and Don McCullin, among others. It was transformed in the 1960s by the ironic and charitable humor of Tony Ray-Jones, whose *Glyndebourne*, 1967, *(pl. no. 699)* displays a witty view of upper-class pleasures that suggests Brandt's themes, Doisneau's whimsicality, and Frank's irony. Recently, Roger Mayne has sought to give documentary themes a somewhat more consciously aesthetic and equivocal dimension.

Brandt, Britain's best-known photographer, presents a unique phenomenon. Involved with Surrealism through his association with Man Ray in the 1920s, he turned to the documentation of contrasts among the classes in the 1930s, and collected a number of such images in his first publication, *The English at Home* of 1936; his later portraits, landscapes, and nude studies encompass a variety of different approaches. In the search for what he termed "something beyond the real,"[20] Brandt found that optic distortions *(pl. no. 700)*—the result of using an extremely wide-angle lens and a very small aperture—produce a curious yet poetic landscape in which human form and nature imperceptibly merge. While this particular pathway has attracted relatively few followers in his native country, Brandt's emphasis on inner realities and their expression through the imaginative use of light inspire the work of Paul Hill, whose affinity to the mysticism of Minor White, also, is apparent in *Ashbourne Car Park (pl. no. 701)*.

The revitalization of photography on the Continent after the war was reflected in several developments. One was the establishment of a movement to encourage artistic photography. In the south of France, members of the

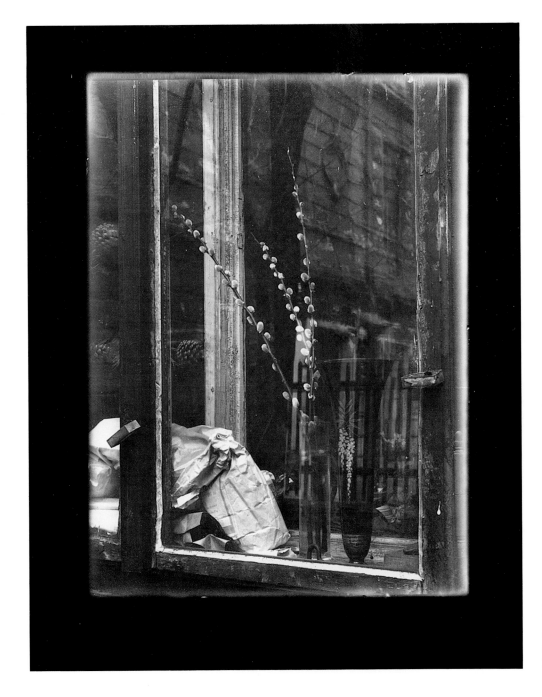

698. JOSEF SUDEK.
Window in the Rain, 1944.
Gelatin silver print.
Collection Jaroslav Andel,
New York.

Expression Libre (Free Expression) group, founded in 1964, sought to enhance the status of photography by urging among other measures that it be introduced into university curricula. In their own productions, however, the photographers—Denis Brihat, Lucien Clergue, among them—intervened in the photographic process by directing the model, establishing the settings, or manipulating negative and print *(see Chapter 12)*. The work of Bernard Plossu (now living in the United States) represents the direction known as "subjective realism"; while his themes may appear to be of a social nature, the photographer claims to

be concerned mainly with "a personal vibration . . . an autobiographical sign."[21]

In Italy in the 1960s, photographers emerged from what has been called a "peripheral ghetto"[22]—the result of more than 20 years of cultural isolation and indifference to the camera as an expressive tool. With increased opportunities for exhibition and publication, they embraced a full array of contemporary modes. Within this ferment of ideas and styles, Italian landscape and photojournalistic images seem to display the greatest formal resolution. The beauty of the land, made even more poignant by increasing indus-

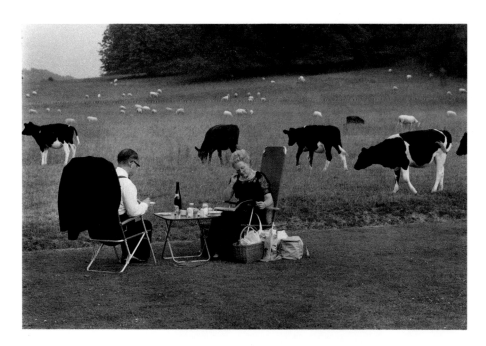

699. TONY RAY-JONES.
Glyndebourne, 1967. Gelatin silver
print. Courtesy and © Anna Ray-
Jones, New York.

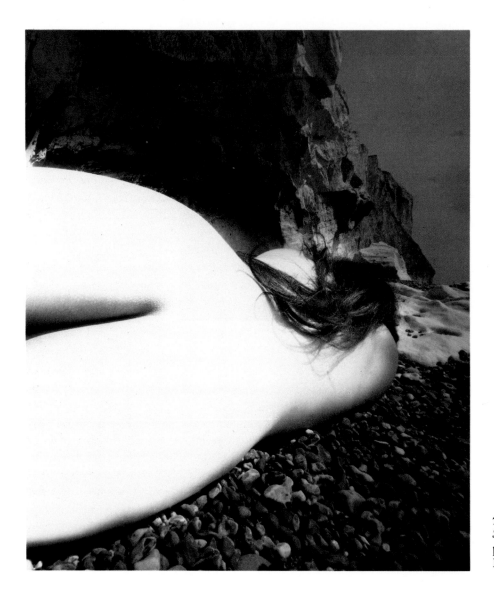

700. BILL BRANDT. *Nude, East
Sussex Coast*, 1953. Gelatin silver
print. © Bill Brandt/Photo
Researchers.

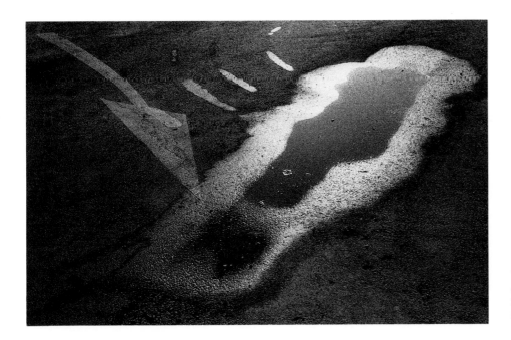

701. PAUL HILL. *Arrow and Puddle, Ashbourne Car Park*, 1974. Gelatin silver print. Courtesy and © Paul Hill.

trialization, has prompted Gianni Berengo, Franco Fontana, Mario Giacomelli, and Georgio Lotti—all photojournalists—to produce views of nature that are romantic in tenor and transcendent in effect. Exemplified by an early work of Giacomelli *(pl. no. 702)*, these images sustain interest because they mediate between the world as it is and as it is photographed, without calling undue attention to the aesthetic or conceptual aspects of the medium. For instance, the marked tonal contrast in this image of a harvest in the Marche region creates a clearly defined abstract pattern but it also evokes the calm abundant beauty of the Italian countryside.

Photojournalism

Photojournalism continued to provide an outlet for the skills of numerous photographers who contributed to the vitality of both European and American picture journals during the 1960s and '70s. Even though photo essays had become more or less predictable in style and superficial in content, individual photographers were at times able to transcend these limitations. One example is the work of Peter Magubane, South Africa's leading photojournalist. His images of the struggles of black South Africans, among them a photograph of a momentary gesture that seems to symbolize the sorrow and anger of their situation *(pl. no. 703)*, undoubtedly are so strong because the photographer himself suffered imprisonment under the Apartheid rules of his native country.

Photojournalists outside the United States were unable to count on the kind of foundation support enjoyed by some of their American counterparts, but they were interested nevertheless in in-depth photographic documentation of social classes and circumstances. In consequence, a number of them structured their own projects. For instance, Swedish photographer Anders Petersen photographed the habituées of a cafe in Hamburg's working class district over a period of several years; they were published in 1978 as *Cafe Lehmnitz*. Petersen acknowledges the influence of Davidson's work on his own, but looks upon his pictures not as a means of personal salvation but as a way to clarify something for others. Rune Hassner, one of Sweden's most active photographers, has brought a lyric dimension to photoreportage and through extensive researches and publishing activities has given form to the history of photojournalism and social documentation.

Czech photographer Josef Koudelka has followed a similar path in his documentation of European gypsy life. Eventually a member of Magnum, he initially was prompted by a profound empathy to photograph gypsies in Rumania, Spain, France, and the British Isles throughout much of the 1960s. His work probes the varied aspects of their particular nomadic existence—familial affection, pride in animals *(pl. no. 704)*, love of the dramatic gesture, isolation. Like many others of his generation who work with 35mm equipment, Koudelka finds in lens distortions, blurs, and tipped horizons an expressive means to evoke essential feelings.

During the 1970s, a number of European photojournalists turned to collectives such as Saftra in Sweden and Viva in France in order to carry out progressive social documentation that they felt was not welcomed by the established agencies and journals. French photographer Martine Franck, one of the founders of Viva, applied a rigorous

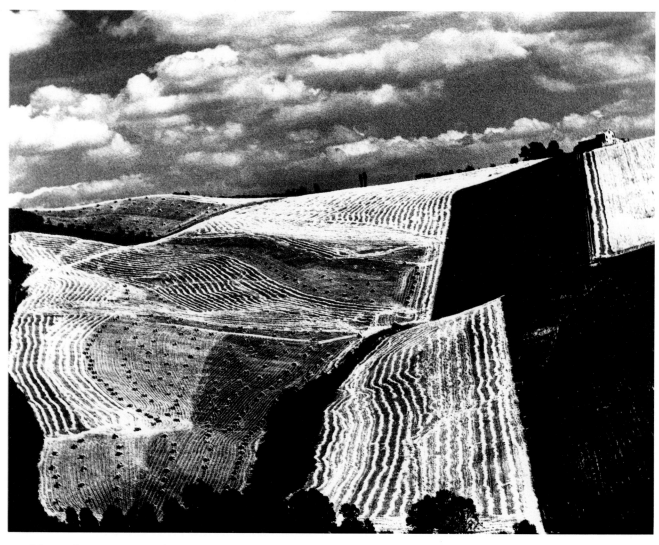

702. MARIO GIACOMELLI. *Landscape #289*, 1958. Gelatin silver print.
Bristol Workshops in Photography, Bristol, R.I. © Mario Giacomelli.

formal structure to her documentations of the effects of middle-class culture on the individual. The angular shapes, stacatto tonal contrasts, and spatially isolated figures seen in *Provence (pl. no. 705)* seem to suggest the dehumanization and oppressiveness of affluence. This approach to social issues characterizes the work of Jean-Philippe Charbonnier and Gilles Peress also, except that Charbonnier's attitude seems more distanced, his structuring less obvious, and his message more ambiguous. Peress imbues his photoreportage with a distinctive personal dimension, at times viewing the situations he confronts with ironic detachment, and at others creating through the structure and forms of the picture a powerful sense of alienation. In still another approach to documentation, Italian photographer–anthropologist Marialba Russo photographs the stages of ritual observances in a style that neither heightens nor dramatizes the visual experience but presents it as though the viewer

were a participant in the event who does not necessarily understand its significance. Heinrich Riebesehl, of West Germany, is similarly committed to the documentation of the rituals, objects, and artifacts of his native land, at times in serial format.

Photojournalism continues to be the predominant concern of photographers in the Soviet Union. With few exceptions *(see Chapter 12)*, little attention is given to photography as a counterfoil for texts with didactic messages, or as a personal means of artistic expression. Nevertheless, many of the younger photographers who came of age during the 1960s and '70s have embraced the same techniques used in both subjective and photojournalistic imagery in the West, including the distortion of spatial perspective, the blurring of part of the visual field, and the incorporation of lens reflections in the images. To cite but two examples from among this generation of photojournal-

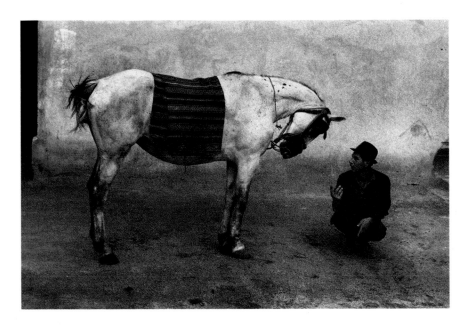

703. PETER MAGUBANE. *Fenced in Child, Vrederdorp*, 1967. Gelatin silver print. Courtesy and © Peter Magubane.

704. JOSEF KOUDELKA. *Rumania*, 1968. Gelatin silver print. © Josef Koudelka/Magnum.

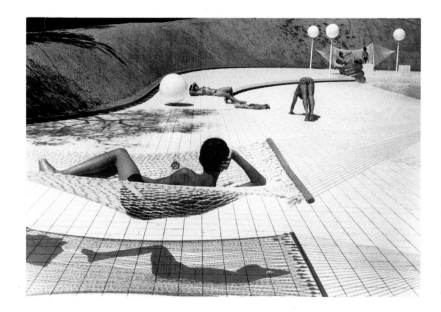

705. MARTINE FRANCK. *Provence*, 1976. Gelatin silver print. © Martine Franck/ Magnum.

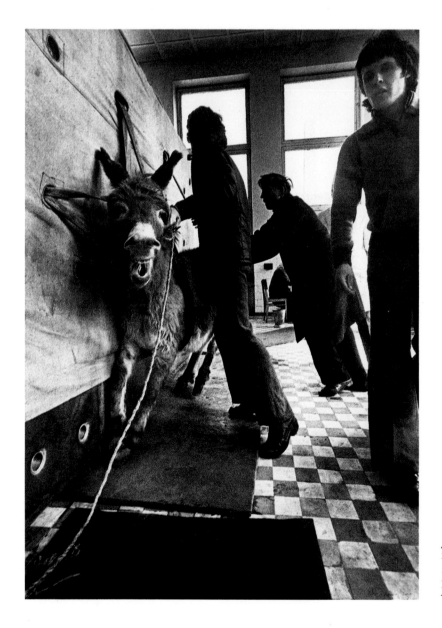

706. ALEKSANDRAS MACIJAUSKAS. *In the Veterinary Clinic*, 1977. Gelatin silver print. Private collection. © Aleksandras Macijauskas.

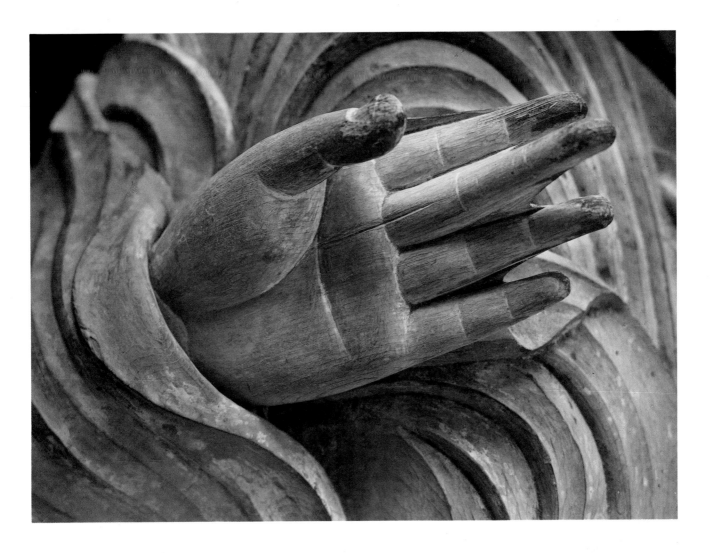

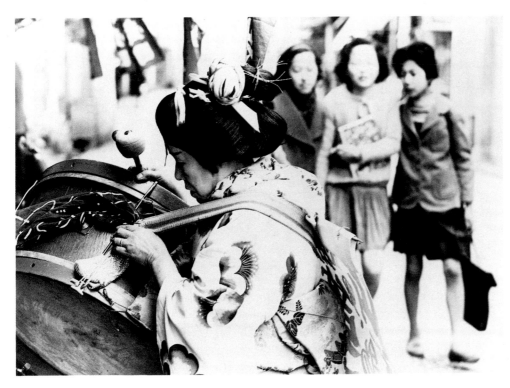

707. KEN DOMON.
Detail (Left Hand of the
Sitting Image of Buddha
Shakamuni in the Hall
of Miroku, the Muro-ji),
c. 1960s. Gelatin silver
print. © Ken Domon/
Pacific Press Service.

708. SHOMEI
TOMATSU. *Sandwich*
Man, Tokyo, 1962.
Gelatin silver print.
Museum of Modern
Art; gift of the artist.
© Shomei Tomatsu.

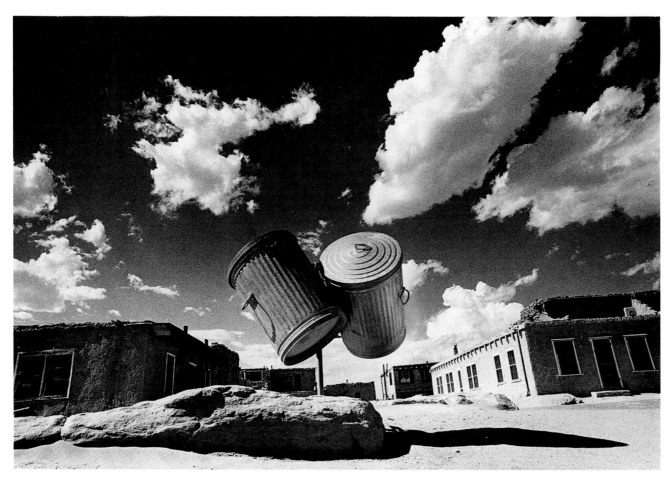

709. Ικκο. *Two Garbage Cans, Indian Village, New Mexico, U.S.A.*, 1972. Gelatin silver print. Courtesy and © 1983 Ikko.

ists, Mikola Gnisyuk, a Ukrainian photojournalist working in Moscow, uses a wide-angle lens to invest his portraits of screen personalities with a somewhat surrealistic playfulness that stops just short of being bizarre, while Lithuanian photographer Aleksandras Macijauskas employs the same means to heighten the viewer's sense of the emotional drama *(pl. no. 706)* in ordinary activities such as in a veterinary hospital.

The Far East

In view of the homogenization of contemporary global culture, one would expect to find Japanese photographers responding to the same influences as Americans and Europeans, but while developments in Japan have indeed reflected the influences of the West they have unfolded under unique conditions. Just before the second World War, after a short period of modernist creativity, expressive photography in Japan parroted painting or soft-focus Pictorialism; with the exception of the exquisite documentations of traditional Japanese art objects by Ken Domon, *(pl. no. 707)* made between 1940 and 1954, straight photog-

raphy as aesthetic expression seemed of little interest. However, American ideas on photography were implanted in postwar Japan by Yasuhiro Ishimoto when he returned to his homeland in 1953 after studying at the Institute of Design, although with different structures and apparatus for disseminating photographs; instead of the museum and marketplace activities that had emerged in the West, Japanese photographers found themselves working mainly for publication, emphasizing sequenced images rather than the single print. As a consequence, there is not the same interest as in the West in the fine print or in experimentation with processes and techniques to create a singular artistic object. The goal of contemporary photographers, according to critic Shoji Yamagishi, is to "demonstrate that photography is a kind of consciousness that can be shared by everyone in his daily life, rather than simply an expression of one's own personality or identity."[23]

This concept is central to the work of Shomei Tomatsu, a former photojournalist and author of eight photographic books (including one on the Hiroshima–Nagasaki bombing done in collaboration with Domon). *Sandwich Man, Tokyo*, 1962, (from the book *Nippon, pl. no. 708*) is a forceful

711. Liu Ban Nong.
Construction, early 1930s.
Gravure. Courtesy Zhang
Suicheng, Beijing.

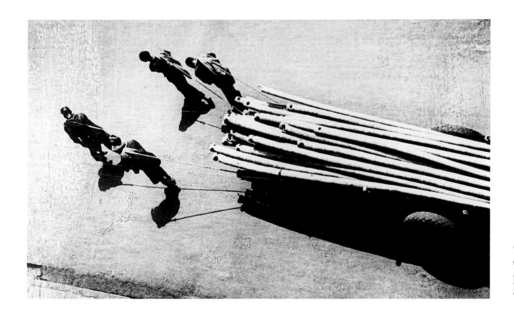

711. Zhang Yin Quan.
Cart Pullers, 1935. Gelatin silver
print. Courtesy Zhang
Suicheng, Beijing.

but enigmatic image that takes as its subject a tradition on the verge of obliteration due to the radical changes in contemporary Japanese life—a social theme that has engaged this photographer since the 1960s. The socially oriented images of Daidoh Moriyama, among them a series called *Nippon Theater*, involve ideas similar to Tomatsu's and in a similar manner share with the work of many Westerners a preference for close-ups, graininess, blurs, and

stark tonal contrasts to heighten the emotional texture of the situations they depict.

Ikko (born Ikko Narahara) probably is, along with Eikoh Hosoe *(see Chapter 12)*, the Japanese photographer best known internationally. Though a straight image in terms of its technique, his *Two Garbage Cans, Indian Village, New Mexico (pl. no. 709)*, part of a series entitled *Where Time Has Vanished*, is surreal in effect, suggesting in its

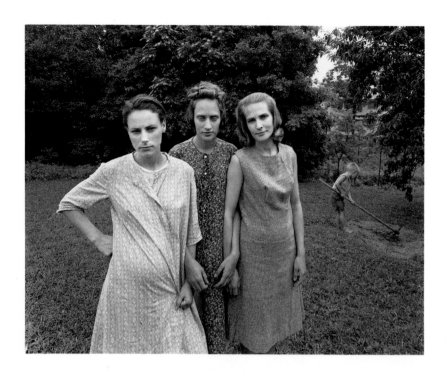

712. EMMET GOWIN. *Edith, Ruth and Mae, Danville, Virginia*, 1967. Gelatin silver print. Light Gallery, New York. © Emmet Gowin.

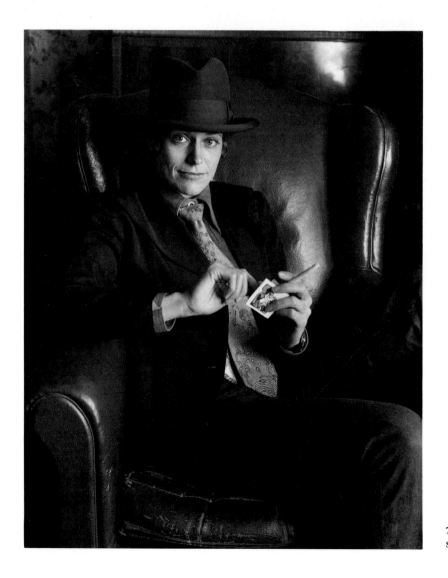

713. JUDY DATER. *Laura Mae*, 1973. Gelatin silver print. Courtesy and © Judy Dater.

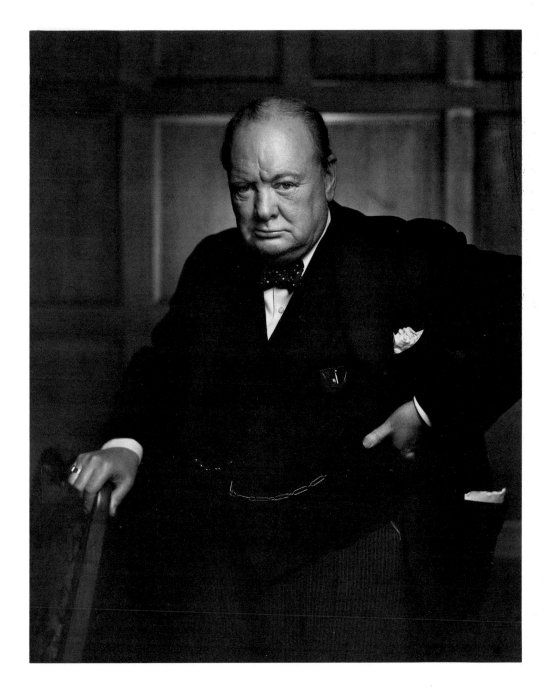

714. YOUSUF KARSH.
Winston Churchill, 1941.
Gelatin silver print.
International Center of
Photography. © 1941
Karsh, Ottawa.

razor sharpness and the strange juxtaposition of organic forms and mechanically produced objects the photographer's reaction to the perplexing timelessness of the culture of the American West. No such philosophical preoccupations characterize the work of Kishin Shinoyama, possibly the most highly recognized photographer in his own country. In addition to themes relating to the traditions and customs of Japan, as in a series devoted to portraits of individuals who have been ritualistically tatooed, Shinoyama produces polished images of nudes and landscapes that seem stylistically and thematically to fit comfortably into the tradition of *Ukiyo-e* woodblock art, and at the same time satisfy the modern demand for photographic representations.

Photography in China in the 20th century offers a contrast to developments elsewhere. While camera expression has been seen for some 80 years almost entirely in the light of its contribution to the political struggles that have consumed the nation, isolation from Europe and the United States, and relative underdevelopment, have deprived photographers of access to the rich creative ideas of Constructivism, or the tradition of Western social-documentation. In the wake of the revolutionary ferment during the first decade of the century, picture-news journals

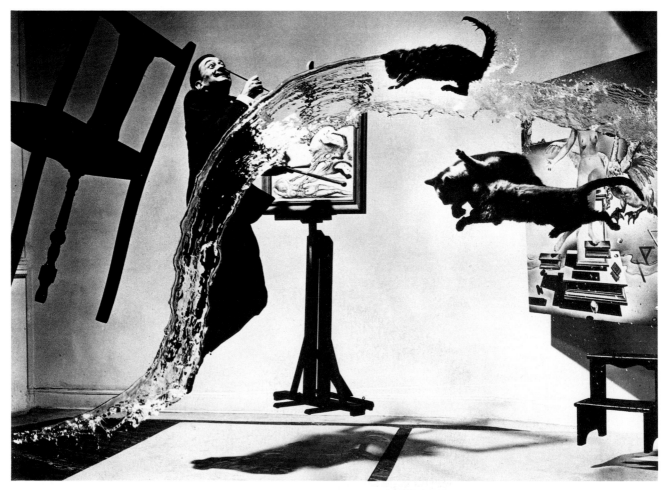

715. PHILLIPPE HALSMAN. *Dali Atomicus*, 1948. Gelatin silver print. Neikrug Gallery, New York. © Phillippe Halsman Estate.

emerged to promote photoreportage as a means to preserve the facts of life while symbolizing the country's political and economic advances. For instance, *Le Monde* (edited in Paris and published in Shanghai), which was started in 1907 as the first Chinese language picture journal, reproduced between 100 and 200 images per issue. Following the outbreak of the war with Japan in 1937, photoreportage on the Communist side especially became difficult because of the lack of materials, and therefore was almost exclusively concerned with presenting information about the hostilities and the activities of the Eighth Route Army in the remote areas of northwestern China.

With the appearance of picture magazines such as *China Pictorial* and *China Reconstructs* after the establishment of the People's Republic in 1949, the demand for photojournalistic images increased but the style of the images became less factual and more frankly propagandistic, a role they continued to play during the Cultural Revolution. Somewhat less proscribed as to theme since then, photographers nevertheless continue to portray industrial workers, peasants, and indeed all sectors of the populace in a confident and picturesque fashion, and the images, though technically proficient, seldom probe beyond superficial appearances or investigate problematical aspects of life.

Understandably, during this historical epoch, photography as artistic expression has not received the same support as photoreportage. Books of scenic views emphasizing the beauty of the countryside were published in Shanghai in the early part of the century, and in the 1930s the Pictorialist style attracted a small following among amateurs and professionals who sent works to the international salons and competitions—among them Wu Yinbo, the most consciously artistic of professionals who later became a photojournalist for *China Pictorial*. The emulation of the themes, compositions, and treatment of scroll painting that characterized Chinese Pictorialist photography continues into the present, with calligraphed characters sometimes applied directly to the print. An effort was made during the 1930s to adapt this style to working-class themes, as in *Construction (pl. no. 710)* by Liu Ban Nong, and in another approach *(pl. no. 711)* photographer Zang Yin

Quan tried to fuse the ideas of the new vision with socially significant subjects; both these attempts appear to have been short-lived. On the whole, while there are fine photographers at work, such as the veteran photojournalist Zhang Suicheng, Chinese photography is circumscribed by a number of factors: by the high cost of materials and of photographic reproduction in a relatively poor nation, by the strong hold of traditionalism on all visual expression, and by the limited view among officialdom of the medium's potential to create images that transcend utilitarian needs.

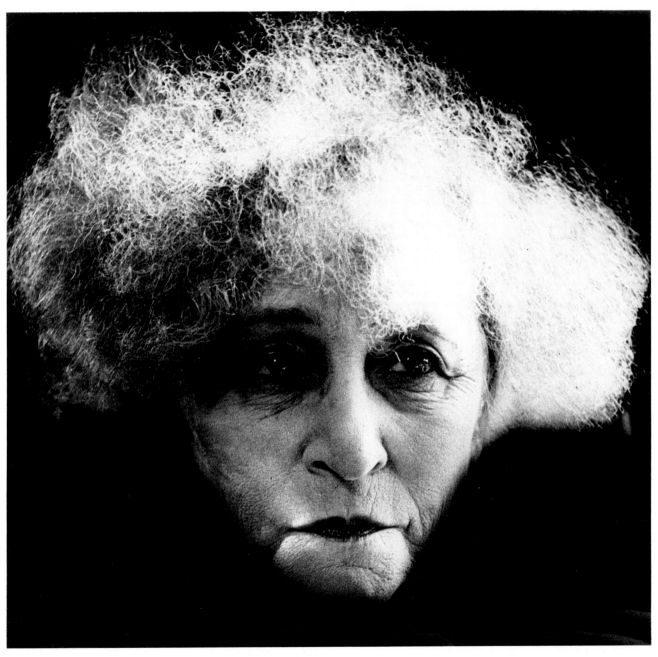

716. MADAME D'ORA (DORA KALLMUS). *The Writer Colette*, c. 1953. Gelatin silver print. Museum für Kunst und Gewerbe, Hamburg.

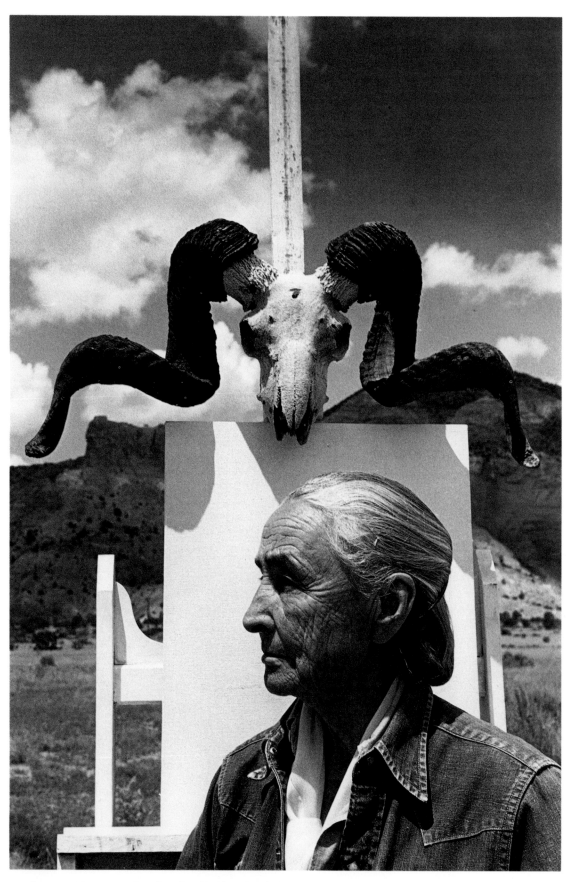

717. ARNOLD NEWMAN. *Georgia O'Keeffe, Ghost Ranch, New Mexico*, 1968.
Gelatin silver print. Courtesy and © Arnold Newman.

Contemporary Portraiture

Formal portraiture—an area of photographic activity that still engages photographers everywhere—has been less influenced by changes in aesthetic theory in the postwar years. In general, the treatment of the human face links the modern era with the period of the medium's infancy as expression, gesture, lighting, and decor continue to be seen as keys to the revelation of class, vocational interest, and psychological complexion. This traditional outlook is encouraged in part by the undiminished curiosity among people for images of the famous, which in turn prompts editors and publishers to reproduce such images in magazines and book format. There are notable photographers, among them Yousuf Karsh of Canada *(pl. no. 714)*, Arnold Newman *(pl. no. 717)* and Phillipe Halsman *(pl. no. 715)* of the United States, who devote themselves exclusively to this pursuit. Working in both color and black and white, Newman, for instance, incorporates stylistic and/or iconographical emblems into richly orchestrated representations, exemplified by *Georgia O'Keeffe*, in which the treatment of space and props are meant to bring to mind the sitter's own preoccupations. Other notable portraitists, who have worked either on commission or from personal choice, among them Gisèle Freund and Madame d'Ora in France, Brandt in England, Chargesheimer and Kempe in Germany, Anatole Sanderman in Argentina (again only a few of many), suggest personality by discovering a moment of characteristic expression and by the management of lighting, as in the d'Ora portrait of Colette *(pl. no. 716)*.

Uncommissioned portraits of uncelebrated people, often unknown to the photographer, are largely a 20th-century phenomenon made possible by the acceptance of the camera as a commonplace instrument. Frequently such images have a dual purpose; they may capture appealing facial expression and gestures, and may also serve as a vehicle for aesthetic and ideological statements or subjective feelings. Portraiture as a channel for personal feelings can be seen in the dour portraits of family members by Emmet Gowin *(pl. no. 712)*. A conceptual idea is embodied in portraits by California photographer Judy Dater, who worked during the 1970s (with Jack Welpott) on a series entitled *Women and Other Visions*; they are emblematic of the photographer's interest in the role of women in American society. The sitters, taken in their own homes and given a degree of freedom in the choice of pose and costume, reflect a distinctive sense of self, as in *Laura Mae (pl. no. 713)*, but they also seem to have responded to their perception of Dater's involvement in the emerging feminist movement. In contrast to these directorial techniques, many photographers view candid street portraiture as a way of effecting a seamless interplay of fact, feeling, and ideology, a means of allowing feelings about the individual and society to surface through the fortuitous interrelationship of expression, gesture, and ambiance.

The foregoing discussion has shown that individualized expression in straight photography has expanded considerably in the past several decades. Photographers and the public have come to accept the camera image as a metaphor, as the expression of private experience, as a subjective document, and as a conceptual statement of the potential and limitations of photography. In addition, the camera has continued its role in journalism. Owing to the fact that photographs (original and in reproduction) are relatively inexpensive and that, like materials, equipment, and techniques they are readily exportable, concepts and styles formulated in one place have become part of an international mainstream. In effect, camera expression has become a language with more or less a common vocabulary in the industrialized nations of the world. When one adds the possibilities offered by manipulations of all sorts, and by color—both to be discussed shortly—this language will be seen to be one of invigorating richness.

12.

PHOTOGRAPHY SINCE 1950: MANIPULATIONS AND COLOR

The camera . . . on the one hand extends our comprehension of the necessities that rule our lives; on the other, it manages to assure us of an immense and unexpected field of action.

—*Walter Benjamin, 1930*[1]

IN THE RECENT PAST there has been an exceptional interest among photographers in the manipulation of subject and process as a means of creating a unique personal statement. Light-sensitized images that are achieved by altering and combining negatives or prints, or by joining graphic and photographic procedures, or that bypass the camera entirely reflect the experimentalist attitudes and the variety of stylistic ideas found within contemporary visual art expression as a whole. This involvement with means suggests that photographers today have become familiar with the medium's history. They have become especially aware also that for the past 50 or so years manipulation has been a common practice not just in personally expressive photography but in the creation of advertising images. The fragmented and reconstituted "realities" visible on magazine pages and billboards (and eventually on video screens), for which staging scenes, directing models, cropping, retouching, and combining photographs have become a matter of course, have served consciously or otherwise as a pattern book of possibilities. An additional spur to the interest in photographic experimentalism has been the role of art directors and photographers who have been in a position, as influential teachers, to promote the techniques and ideas used in advertising among a wide spectrum of students. In concert with the experimentalist curriculum at the Institute of Design in Chicago *(see Chapter 11)*, these developments have insured that manipulative concepts in creative photography would reach and attract far greater numbers than at any previous time.

As a result of the general experimentalism in art culture in the United States after the second World War, artists working with unconventional materials (industrial paint, welded steel, plastics) and trying out unusual techniques (splattering, dripping, extruding) tended also to ignore time-honored distinctions between the various categories of visual expression. Mixed media events (part theatrical, part graphic, part photographic) and assemblages (agglomerations of seemingly unrelated artifacts) made it clear that it was no longer relevant to the art culture of the period to continue to regard painting, sculpture, printmaking, and photography as discrete entities. Photographers, in common with the numbers of graphic artists who were questioning traditional beliefs, subjects, and materials during the 1960s, began to evaluate the assumptions of pure and documentary photography, to extend the medium so that camera images might avail themselves of a range of means in order to express subjective feelings and public and private realities. These extensions ran a gamut from the pairing and sequencing of straight camera images of the found environment, to the arrangement of scenes and the disposition of models for the camera, to actual interventions in the production of images either by manually reassembling portions of photographs or by interfering in optical and chemical procedures.

Conceptualizing the Photograph

The presentation of photographs in paired and sequenced arrangements is perhaps the simplest maneuver undertaken to alter the way photographs are experienced. This ordering in a preselected format not only reflects the way in which photographs commonly are presented in picture journals or in advertising, it also serves to underline the point of view that in photography, as in all visual art, the reality that is framed is contingent upon both the inherent potentials of the medium and the stance of the photographer. Camera documentation, these photographers seem to be saying, is what the light reveals, the lens embraces, and the chemical substances make visible from where the photographer chooses to be positioned, and has little to do with ultimate or demonstrable truths; change the angle and position of the camera, and another "truth" will reveal itself. For instance, in presenting two paired views of the same event *(pl. no. 718)* or arrangement of objects, photographer Eve Sonneman seems to suggest that with the passage of time or a shift of vantage point the same situation will take on a different appearance, both equally truthful.

This approach to image-making also embraces the notion that photographs are in essence uninflected information, descriptions rather than emotionally nuanced experiences. In arranging a sequence of images of parking lots in a book entitled *Thirty-four Parking Lots in Los Angeles*—exemplified by the single frame shown *(pl. no. 719)*—California painter–photographer Edward Ruscha claims to be providing "a catalog of neutral objective facts."[2] His purpose may be ironic and the images themselves suggestive of the attitudes implicit in the New Topo-

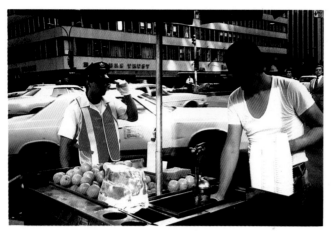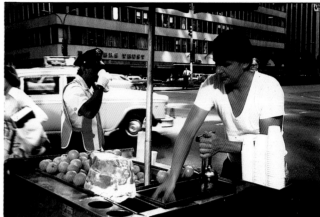

718. EVE SONNEMAN. *Oranges, Manhattan*, 1978. Cibachrome (silver-dye bleach) print. Castelli Graphics, New York. © Eve Sonneman.

graphics *(see Chapter 11)*, but both his words and pictures bring to mind techniques used in advertising photography to emphasize the abundance of material goods, and in fact may be taken as a comment on the consumerist aspects of American life. Aside from their stated goals, such images also are appealing for the architectonic qualities that relate them to the work of both the Minimalist and Pop artists who were engaged in geometric serializations during the 1960s.

Conceptual ideas do not always presuppose that the photographer will work with multiple images. In staging scenes that show a photograph within a photograph, Kenneth Josephson of the United States exemplifies those who make a wry comment, in terms of size, spatial position, and incident, on the supposed reality that the camera captures, which, in some cases, is still another camera picture *(pl. no. 720)*. The relation of image to reality to the medium that has become the central theme in such works has its antecedents in the 1889 image *Sun Rays—Paula, Berlin (pl. no. 401)*. In this seemingly descriptive scene the characteristics and potentials of the medium also are suggested by the inclusion of a variety of camera pictures of the sitter made at other times and in different positions.

The relationship between image and reality also engages photographers who embrace the photographic sequence, at times adding texts of their own devising, as a way of revealing subjective experience. In common with a significant number who are involved with enigmatic visual occurrences that express "private realities," Duane Michals uses himself as model or directs others in staged, preconceived sequences such as *Chance Meeting*, 1969 *(pl. no. 721)*—six visually unexceptional shots that transform the narrative means commonly used in photojournalism and advertising to private expressive ends. Inspired by Surrealist ideas, in particular those of painter René Magritte and by the cool

irony of Robert Frank's imagery, Michals's emphasis on the primacy of subjective vision and his embrace of the sequential format have struck a sympathetic chord among many young photographers in the United States and Europe.

Like their counterparts in America, Europeans have demonstrated an interest in conceptual problems and have used series, sequences, and grid formats to embody them. One example can be seen in the work of Bernd and Hilla Becher, German photographers who are content with size, shape, materials, date, and area in topographical photographs of the cooling towers and other industrial structures they have tracked down in England, France, and the United States as well as their native land *(pl. no. 722)*. These images, printed in formats that include from three to eight photographs and at times measure some six feet, are more about similarities than distinctions, according to the photographers, and are meant to demonstrate that the camera image can provide the kind of visual detail that the human eye might be able to take in only over a long period of familiarity with the object.[3]

While the makers of such informational images, whether they be parking lots or cooling towers, disavow aesthetic intentions, the appeal of these works undoubtedly is due to factors other than their completeness as information; indeed it is doubtful whether any two-dimensional translation of the complex interaction of space, volume, and atmosphere (much less a photograph) can be accepted as an accurate documentation of any or all of the "facts" involved. This problem persists with regard to all photographic depictions of architectural and structural entities, whether they be public or private buildings, factories, cooling towers, living spaces, or gardens. Despite the fact that specialists in architectural photography, notably Ezra Stoller, take such views from various angles and in differ-

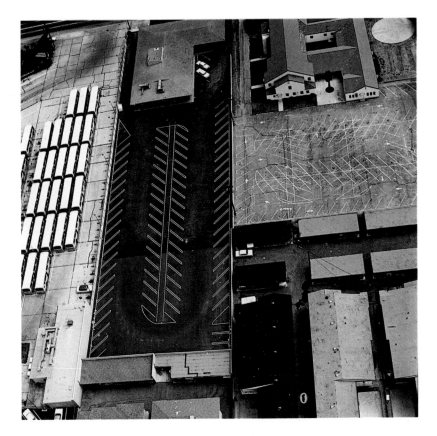

719. EDWARD RUSCHA. *State Board of Equalization, 14601 Sherman Way, Van Nuys, California*, c. 1967. (One of a series: *Thirty-four Parking Lots in Los Angeles*: Los Angeles, 1967.) Gelatin silver print. Leo Castelli Gallery, New York. © 1967 Edward Ruscha.

720. KENNETH JOSEPHSON. *Drottningholm, Sweden*, 1967. Gelatin silver print. Courtesy and © Kenneth Josephson.

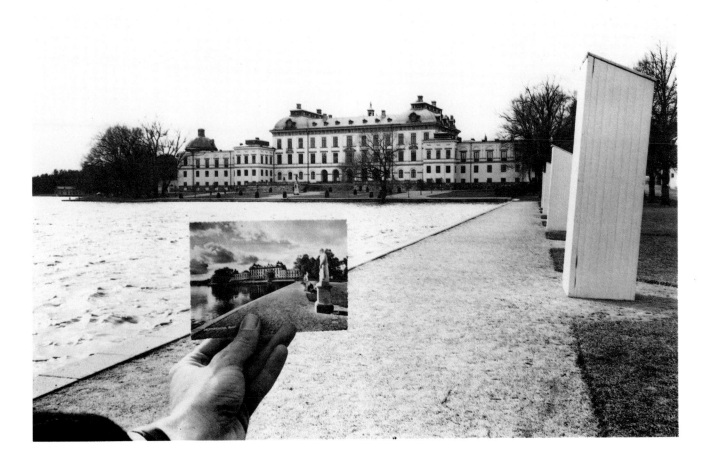

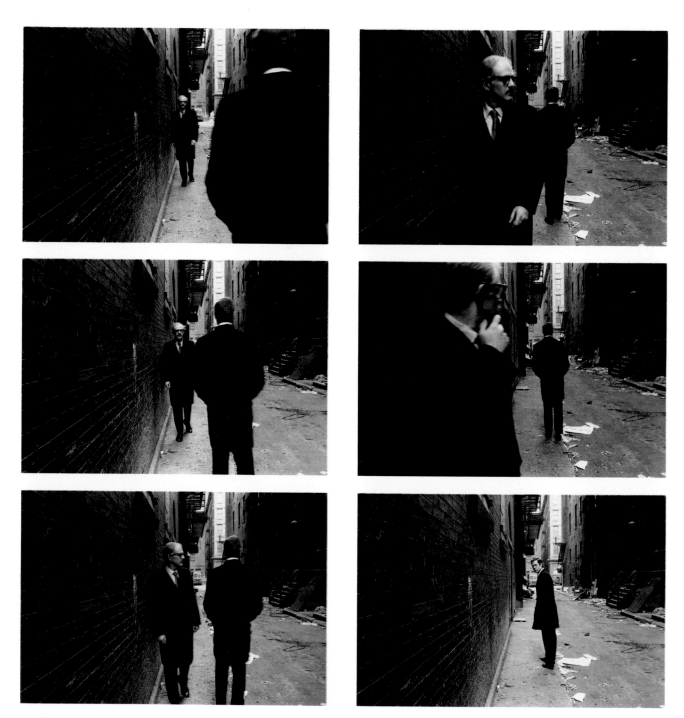

721. DUANE MICHALS. *Chance Meeting*, 1969. Gelatin silver prints. Courtesy and © Duane Michals.

ent light conditions in order to recreate a sense of the actual space, the physical and psychological significances of the architectural experience cannot be fully apprehended through the photograph.

Other examples of the use of series, sequences, and grids to embrace conceptual ideas are the repetitions and mirrored reflections of forms in the work of Italian photographers Guiseppe Penone and Michelangelo Pistoletto; the sequential arrangements of figures favored by German photographers Floris M. Neusüs, Klaus Rinke, and Manfred Willman; the photographic grids assembled from landscape images by Dutch graphic artist Ger Dekkers. That those concepts attract artists in eastern Europe as well can be seen in the work *Myself As . . . (pl. no. 723)* by Polish photographer Andrzej Lachowicz. An assemblage in grid format of 36 slightly different images of his own cast shadow, this work suggests not only the equivocal nature of the image but of the artist-photographer as well.

More recently, a concept of photography known as Postmodernism has evolved from the conceptualist ideas of the previous decade. In part, this development represents an effort to counter the transformation of the photograph from document into aesthetic commodity; at the same time, it seeks to formulate a new relationship between the camera image and social realities. Postmodernists claim that as representations of reality camera images cannot claim uniqueness, in that (unlike one-of-a-kind handmade images) they appropriate and duplicate something that already exists. Furthermore, they propose that since neither photographer nor viewer can reach beyond the shared cultural patterns of their time to invest the camera image with aesthetic or personal aura, the photograph should endeavor instead to provoke thought about social relationships and phenomena.[4]

Individuals involved with this approach have devised a number of different courses through which to express ironic attitudes toward cultural stereotypes in general and toward the particular claims of the photograph as aesthetic experience. Some among them are photographing already well-known photographic images, mimicking high-gloss advertising photographs but omitting the texts, and arranging scenes in which live models or dolls imitate photographic illustrations in consumer magazines or impersonate real-life situations. Another approach, which recalls the idea of deformation of the image prevalent during the 1920s, endeavors to "deconstruct" the myths of contemporary society by using found photographs and attaching texts that make the viewer aware of attitudes implicit in advertising. For example, British artist Victor Burgin appends his own messages, set in type, to photographs of common scenes (*pl. no. 724*), which he then rephotographs. All of these photographic maneuvers are meant to reposition such imagery in the viewer's awareness, bringing to light underlying consumerist and sexist messages, rather than to appeal to feelings or a sense of beauty.

Interventions and Manipulations

Actual intervention in the creation of camera images has assumed a variety of different forms, all of which have as their central principle the freedom of the photographer to be as spontaneous and inventive as the graphic artist while

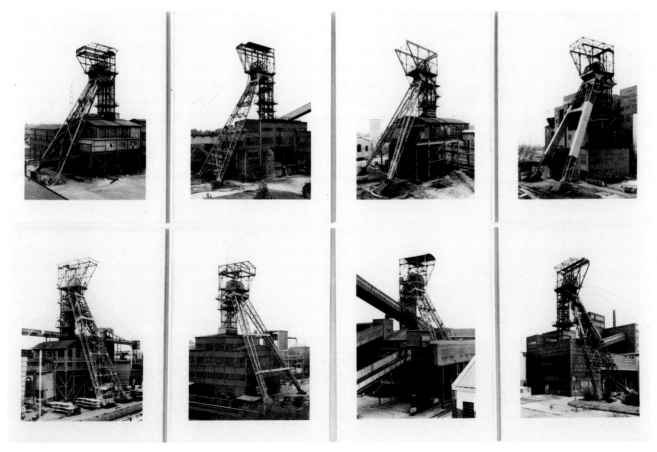

722. BERND and HILLA BECHER. *Winding Towers* (1976–82), 1983. Gelatin silver prints. Sonnabend Gallery, New York. © Bernd and Hilla Becher.

still preserving the specific tactile qualities and replicative aspects of the medium. Such interventions embrace images produced without a camera, which have come to be called light graphics; they include collage and montage, in which photographs are cropped and recombined in an infinite number of ways either by gluing together or reforming them in the enlarger. Images for which distorting lenses are used, or settings and action created and directed, whether of live models, dolls, or paper cutouts, constitute examples of other methods of asserting the nonmechanical aspects of the medium—of emphasizing the centrality of the individual imagination in the creation of camera images. In view of the experimentalism implicit in these approaches to photography, it is not surprising to find that nearly all of these techniques were embodied in the avant-garde curriculum of the 1920s Bauhaus.

The photogram—a unique cameraless image that results either from playing a beam of light across a sensitized

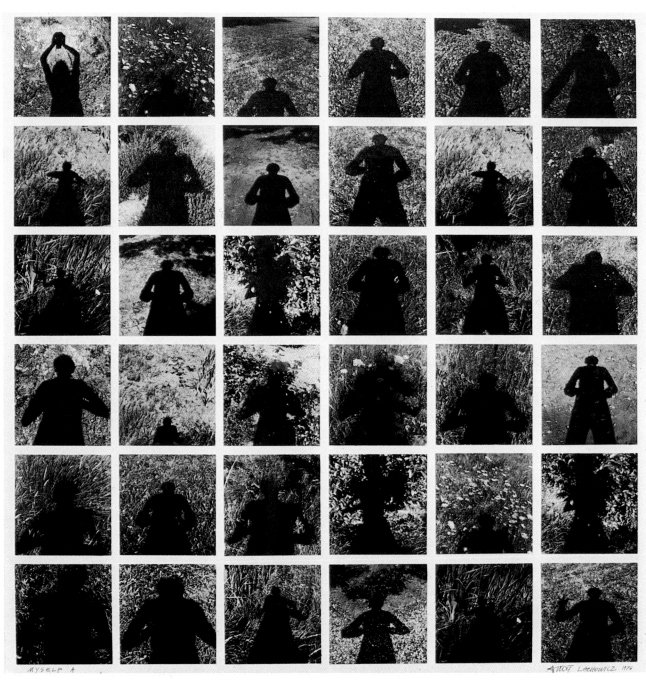

723. ANDRZEJ LACHOWICZ. *Myself As . . .* , 1976. Color (chromogenic development) transparency. International Center of Photography, New York.

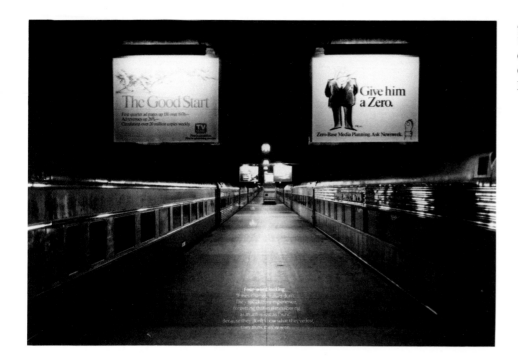

724. VICTOR BURGIN. *Four Word Looking* from *U.S. 77*, 1977. Gelatin silver print. John Weber Gallery, New York. © Victor Burgin.

paper surface or from exposing to a fixed or moving light source a variety of translucent and opaque objects arranged on photographic paper—is an early 19th-century discovery that was updated during the 1920s *(see Chapter 9)* and more recently in the 1940s when it was sometimes combined with other procedures. In the United States, Carlotta Corpron, Lotte Jacobi, and Nathan Lerner were among those who involved themselves with free-form procedures, as can be seen in the lyrical abstractions called "photogenics" by Jacobi *(pl. no. 554)*. Barbara Morgan, who frequently combined light drawing, photograms, and montage in the same image *(pl. no. 557)*, began her initial experiments with these techniques in 1939 by photographing the moving light patterns made by a dancer holding a flashlight. During the 1950s, several Europeans, among them Herbert W. Franke in Austria, Peter Keetman in Germany, and Jaroslav Rajzik in Czechoslovakia, using oscilloscopes and prisms produced lucid geometric abstractions, a number of which bring to mind the work of Constructivist sculptors Naum Gabo and Antoine Pevsner.

A type of cameraless imagery that attracted attention in the 1950s combined photogram techniques with a modern version of *cliché verre*. Achieved by the random patterns formed on glass by such substances as viscous liquids and crystals, this process provided a negative for printing on sensitized paper. Henry Holmes Smith, one of the first Americans to involve himself with this procedure, worked with a syrupy mixture on glass plates to create nonobjective variations that he printed on both monochromatic silver and multichrome dye-transfer materials. In its bold forms

and strong colors, *Small Poster for a Heavenly Circus* by Smith *(pl. no. 727)* proclaims its connections with the Abstract Expressionist painting style of the era. Smith's onetime student Jaromir Stephany continues to explore this direction using ink on film in both 4 x 5 and 35mm formats to create visionary images that suggest galactic events. The great flexibility of *cliché verre* appealed to photographer–artist Frederick Sommer, who began to work with glass and cellophane in the 1950s, painting on or fuming these materials with smoke to create nonobjective shapes. Sommer, a complex personality as fascinated by putrescence as by living beauty, also makes montages, assemblages *(pl. no. 726)*, and straight photographs, seeking in all to give visible form to the mysteries he has discovered in both the real and imaginary worlds, which he regards as one and the same.

Somewhat later in the same decade, French photographer Jean Dieuzaide, whose photographic interests embrace aerial views and close-ups of forms and textures in nature also, began experimenting with pitch (a coal byproduct) to produce sensual abstractions *(pl. no. 725)*, while Jean Pierre Sudre explored the aesthetic and metaphorical possibilities offered by random arrangements of chemical salts on glass—a technique he calls "crystallography." Heinz Hajek-Halke, who began to work with both optical and chemical means after a quarter of a century as a successful press and scientific cameraman in Germany, creates "luminograms" with moving beams of light, and what he calls "lightgraphics" by exposing granular and liquid substances on film to directed light sources. Such chemical interven-

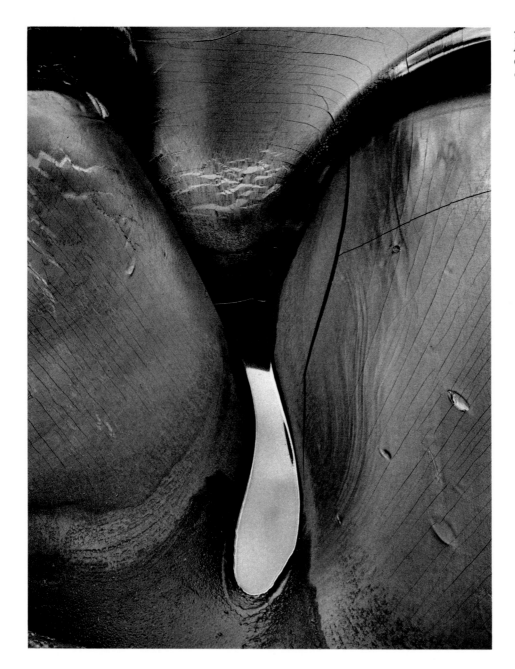

tion is paramount also in the "chemigrams" of Pierre Cordier produced by manipulating light while the printing paper is being chemically processed.

Collage attracted a number of photographers in the United States as a means of generating fresh visions of commonplace experiences; many were associated with the Institute of Design in the 1950s and '60s. Unlike the work of Sommer, who followed the example of earlier Dadaists in using not only photographs but other found objects—torn as well as cut, dimensional as well as flat—these collages generally are created from photographs only and explore the possibilities of cropping, repeating, and rearranging segments to form a freshly synthesized but purely

photographic statement. While pleasing in pattern, *Arches*, 1967 *(pl. no. 729)*, a typical work by Ray K. Metzker that exemplifies this interest, is not meant as a decorative object but as an expression in new form of the emotional texture of the generating experience—in this case the excitement of street life in downtown Chicago.

Collage as a means of dealing with conceptual ideas began to appeal to photographers in Europe during the 1960s. In their efforts to extend visual experience beyond that based on a single image taken from one position and one point in time and then exhibited or reproduced as an emblem of reality, Rinke, Willman, and Italian photographer Franco Vaccari, among others, combine complete or partial photographs of the same object, place, or individual, taken from different vantage points and at different times. Their aim is to suggest the "incomplete, unstable and unending forms that reality assumes,"[5] and to provide such images with a horizontal dimension and scale that requires the viewer to include time as an element in their perception.

Both collage and montage—the restructuring and combining of negatives in the enlarger—were seen by the postwar generation as an especially fruitful method of projecting private visions, of dealing with the possibility that, as American photographer Jerry N. Uelsmann has written, "the mind knows more than the eye and camera can see."[6] Indeed, already in the early 1930s, printing multiple images on the same photographic support had enabled some American photographers to explore mystical realms that seemed impossible to evoke through straight photographs. At that time, William Mortensen, whose "medieval sensibility"[7] led him to imagine scenes that seemed at once bizarre and amusing to many contemporaries, resorted to montage to create his visions of wickedness and lust *(pl. no. 730)*. In the same decades, Edmund Teske combined chemical manipulation with montage techniques to make poignant his sense of the melancholy eroticism of small-town American life; and in the following years, Clarence John Laughlin, bemused by the "unreality of the real and the reality of the unreal," worked not only with montage but created settings, costumed models, and directed action to formalize his conviction that "the physical object is merely a stepping stone to an

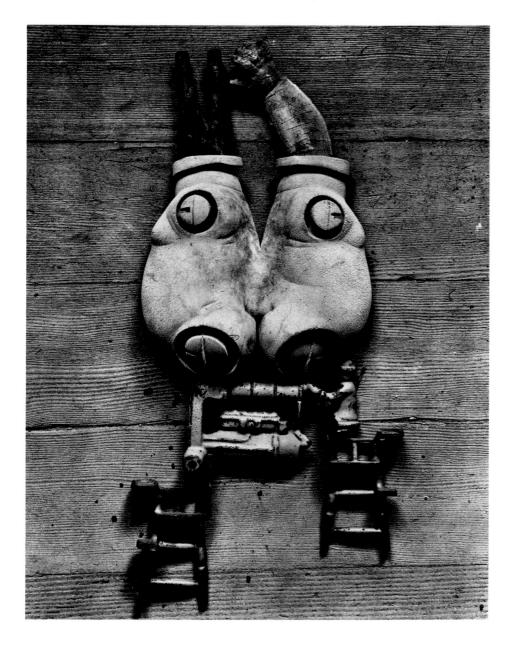

726. FREDERICK SOMMER. *The Giant*, 1946. Gelatin silver print. Collection Crocker Art Museum, Sacramento, Cal. Light Gallery, New York. © Frederick Sommer.

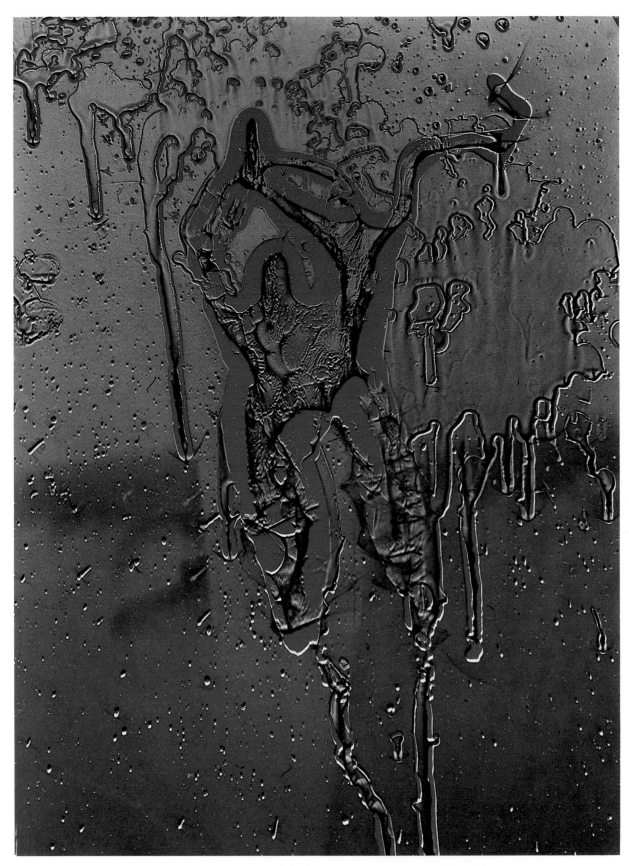

727. HENRY HOLMES SMITH. *Small Poster for a Heavenly Circus*, 1974–75. Dye transfer (dye imbibition) print from 1974 monochrome refraction drawing in the Henry Holmes Smith Archive, Art Museum, Indiana University. Collection Ted R. Smith. © 1975 Henry Holmes Smith.

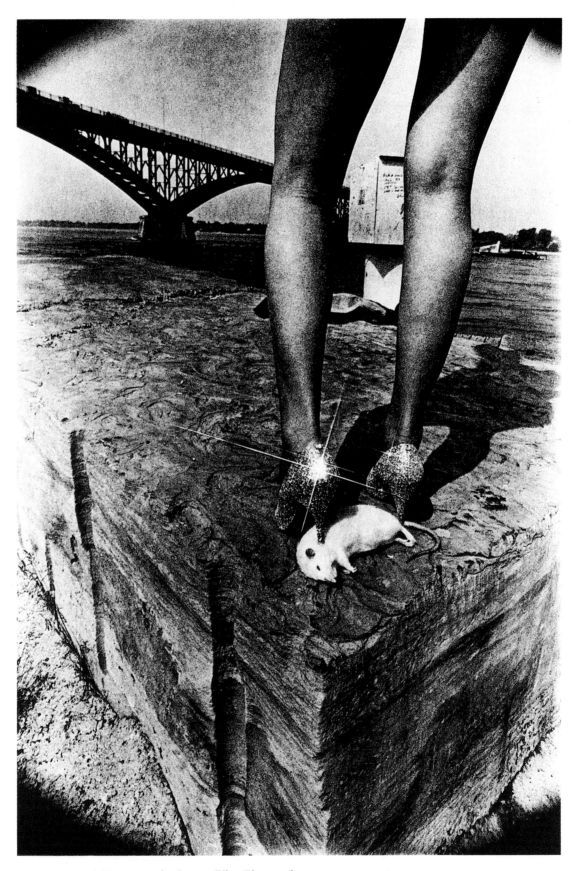

728. LES KRIMS. *Homage to the Crosstar Filter Photograph*, 1971.
Gelatin silver print on Kodalith paper. Courtesy and © Les Krims.

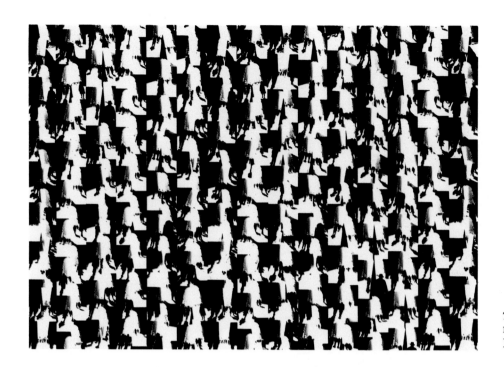

729. RAY K. METZKER. *Arches*, 1967. Gelatin silver print. © 1967 Ray K. Metzker.

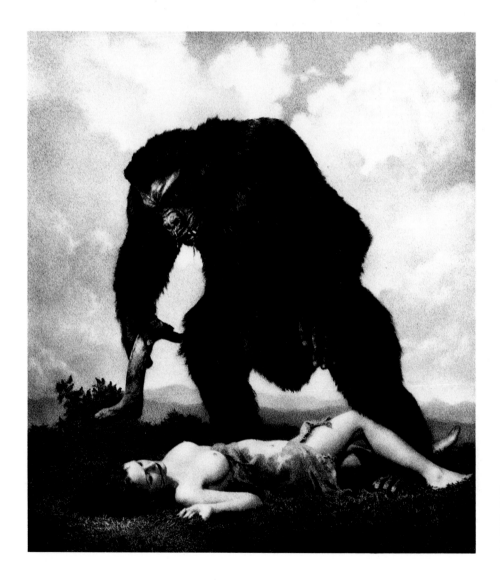

730. WILLIAM MORTENSEN. *L'Amour*, c. 1936. Gelatin silver print with textured screen. Courtesy and © 1980 Mortensen Estate.

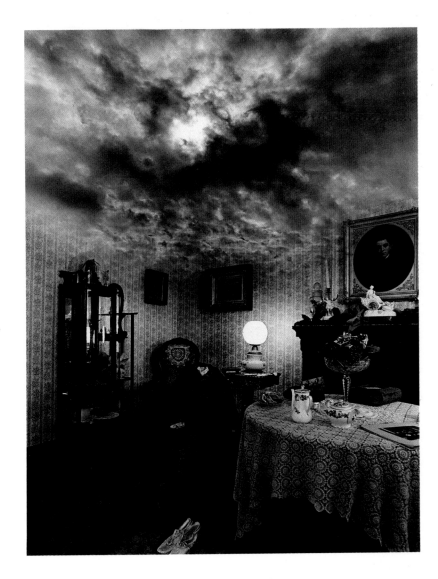

731. JERRY N. UELSMANN. *Untitled (Cloud Room)*, 1975. Toned gelatin silver print. Collection Jain and George W. Kelly, New York. © 1975 Jerry N. Uelsmann.

inner world."[8] More recently, Vilem Kriz in California and Allen A. Dutton in the Midwest have fabricated images to create an imaginative symbolism in the work of Kriz and a believable spatial continuum for the "outlandish dream-scapes"[9] of Dutton, while Les Krims draws on the iconography of both Surrealism and Pop Art in his sardonic and at times horrifying statements about middle-class life style in modern American society *(pl. no. 728)*.

Uelsmann is one of a group of photographers who since the 1960s has consistently used montage as a means to create poetic fantasies. Pieced together from an array of his own negatives, his work achieves a seamless transition between real and imagined spaces and events. While his early images manifest a lucid if not markedly original perception of women as fertility figures from whom all life radiates, later montages, among them an untitled interior with clouds *(pl. no. 731)*, seem concerned with less bromidic ideas despite their obvious relationship to the paintings of Magritte. The lyrical montages of Eikoh Hosoe, a

Japanese photographer of international renown, project a more somber note *(pl. no. 732)*. In contrast to these works, montages by California printmaker and photographer Robert F. Heinecken are full of gritty allusions to the rampant and often violent sexism visible on magazine pages, billboards, and video screens. Working with commercial printing materials and transfer techniques *(see below)* and at times on a scale that reinforces the affinity between these images and commercial advertising, Heinecken's productions seem to embody confusing elements of wish-fulfillment as well as of condemnation *(pl. no. 733)*.

In view of the wide acceptance of collage and montage by Surrealist artists in Europe before World War II, it is not surprising to find that a later generation of European photographers engaged by similar psychoanalytical concepts have turned to these means. Joan Fontcuberto in Spain, Italian-born Lorenzo Merlo, and Czech photographers Martin Hruska and Jan Saudek are among those who create dreamlike visions and erotic statements both

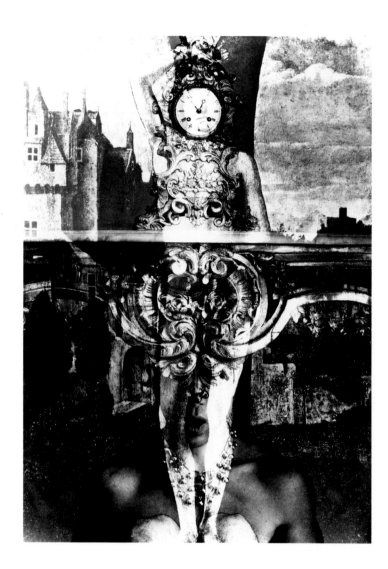

732. EIKOH HOSOE. *Ordeal by Roses #29*, 1961–62. Gelatin silver print. Light Gallery, New York. © Eikoh Hosoe.

733. ROBERT HEINECKEN. *Le Voyeur/Robbe-Grillet #1*, 1972. Photographic emulsion on canvas; bleached; pastel chalk. International Museum of Photography at George Eastman House, Rochester, N.Y. Light Gallery, New York. © Robert Heinecken.

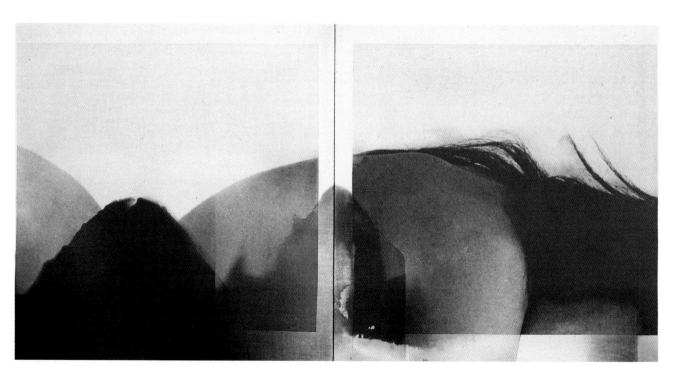

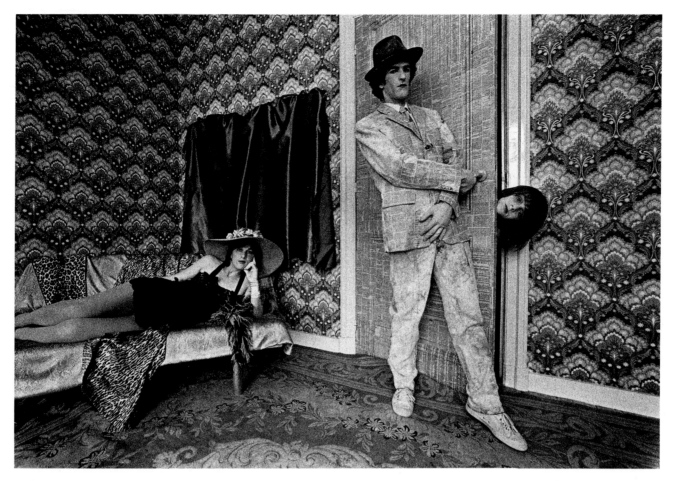

734. PAUL DE NOOIJER. *Menno's Head*, 1976. Gelatin silver print. Courtesy and © 1976 Paul de Nooijer.

by staging scenes and combining images in the enlarger. While the work of individuals concerned with the psyche on occasion recalls the specific spatial configurations and symbols invented by painters Salvador Dali and Giorgio De Chirico, concepts and iconography drawn from postwar cultural phenomena such as advertising imagery, popular entertainments, and video productions also inform their images. For example, Paul de Nooijer (*pl. no. 734*), like Krims, addresses the excesses of consumerist culture by staging and montaging outrageous parodies of bourgeois fetishes and by printing his images in a grainy style that mimics cheap print reproduction.

The fabrication of settings and the direction of models as a means of suggesting the irrational content of dreams and visions has been mentioned in connection with montage, but for a number of photographers the ordering of the pictured environment provides an end in itself. In common with the montagists, these photographers also draw upon ideas that surfaced earlier in the century in graphic art and still- and motion-picture photography, to which they too add elements of postwar popular culture in the construction of their own realities for the camera lens.

Some alter settings only slightly while others stage complete fictions, with sets, models, costumes, and action directed entirely by the photographer. As an example of the former, Ralph Eugene Meatyard photographed family and friends (*pl. no. 735*) posed in unpretentious settings, but took advantage of the suggestive shapes and forms of shadows and of the blurs caused by movement to intimate a ghostly presence—an invisible dimension of psychological nuance. In other of his photographs, his subjects wear Halloween masks while seemingly engaged in the most ordinary activities—a contrast that imbues these images with a discomfiting sensation. At the other exteme, the fantasies created by a large number of photographers, including M. Richard Kirstel (*pl. no. 736*), Krims, Kriz, and Arthur Tress (*pl. no. 737*) in the United States, by De Nooijer, Bernard Faucon, Fontcuberto, and Merlo in Europe, by Boris Kossoy in Brazil—the list is extensive—are at times entirely fabricated. Faucon, for example, devotes considerable time to creating actual backgrounds, fabricating figures, and managing lighting effects for works that draw upon popular entertainments for their whimsicality. Whether they deal with classical psychoanalytic sym-

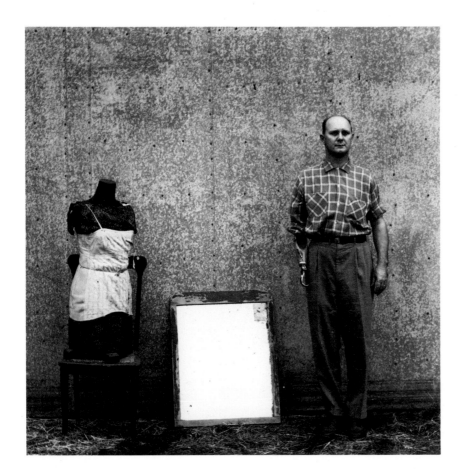

bolism, or with idiosyncratic and bizarre combinations of objects and figures, and however the elements are arranged and lighted, the resulting images in all cases depend for their effects on whether the individual viewer is convinced that what appears in a photograph must to some degree be truthful.

The camera lens itself can provide photographers with an expressive tool, either by lending actual scenes a sense of unreality through subtle distortion, or by dramatically enhancing expression and gesture. In the 1950s, following earlier experiments by Kertész and others, Berenice Abbott and Weegee—both advocates until then of straight photography—were drawn to make distortions of figures and objects for which they used special lenses, but their images were on the whole tentative. One consistently resolved body of work to emerge from the exploration of extremely wide-angle lens capabilities has been that of Bill Brandt (discussed in Chapter 11), but others work in a style more closely related to classical Surrealism; the distortions of Christian Vogt, a successful Swiss photojournalist, incorporate notations from the camera images of Erwin Blumenfeld and the paintings of De Chirico *(pl. no. 738)*. French photographer Claude Nori employs a wide-angle lens to invest both ordinary scenes and his staged enactments

with an unnerving sense of endless depth, while Emmet Gowin's fish-eye lens alters reality only slightly. That distortion accidentally caused by the lens also can be used to dramatize gesture and expression in real situations where no fantastic or conceptual statements are intended can be seen in many examples from straight photography and photojournalism, among them Otto Steinert's *Children's Carnival (pl. no. 739)*.

It is obvious from the foregoing discussion that the various methods and procedures used in the pursuit of the imaginary landscape can overlap; in choosing manipulative modes over straight photography, individuals are apt to experiment with a wide range of creative possibilities. Collage and montage images at times include negative and positive versions of the same or different photographs; portions may consist of optical distortions and solarizations—the latter a technique for partially reversing the tonality of the negative by exposing it to light during development. Photographers using these techniques often modify the chemical aspects of the photographic process to achieve fogginess or grain, or they add tone to the image. In resorting to these combinations of means, the individual is asserting a right to make imaginative or conceptual as well as realistic statements with the camera, an

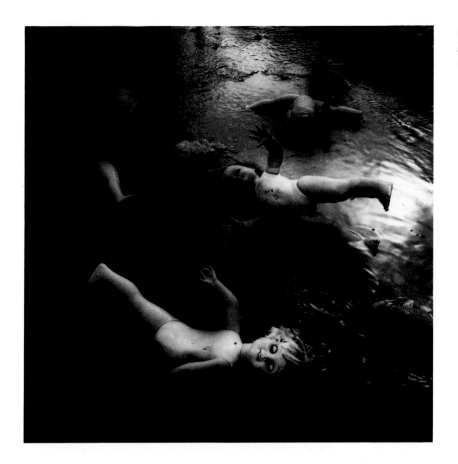

736. M. RICHARD KIRSTEL. From *Water Babies*, 1976. Gelatin silver print. Courtesy and © M. Richard Kirstel.

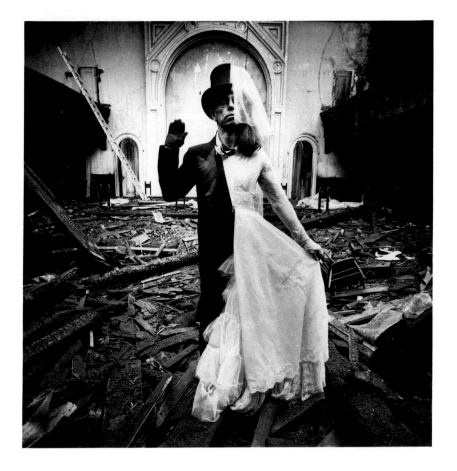

737. ARTHUR TRESS. *The Actor*, 1973. Gelatin silver print. Courtesy and © 1973 Arthur Tress.

attitude toward the medium that can be traced back to the work of Oscar Gustave Rejlander and Henry Peach Robinson in the 19th century.

Of course, staging events does not result invariably in conceptual, grotesque, or even surreal imagery, as photographs of both still life and of the nude prove. Denis Brihat, one of the founders of *Expression Libre*, brings out concordances between organic forms and nature. In *William Pear (pl. no. 740)*, for instance, the fruit has been isolated and lighted to suggest a human torso and its flesh has become stonelike through special chemical intervention in the processing. Lucien Clergue, a founder of *Expression Libre*, stages his scenes, posing nude models in a landscape of sea and sand for close-up views that ostensibly are evocations of mythic earth goddesses *(pl. no. 741)*.

Photography and Mechanical and Electronic Printing

Over the past 30 years or so, photographers in highly technological societies have displayed a signal interest not only in expanding their control over the processes of photography, but in combining camera images with mechanical and electronic printing procedures. This development, too, is an outgrowth of 20th-century stylistic movements in the arts, in particular Pop Art, which celebrated the effects of post World War II industrial technology on consumer goods. The involvement with "process

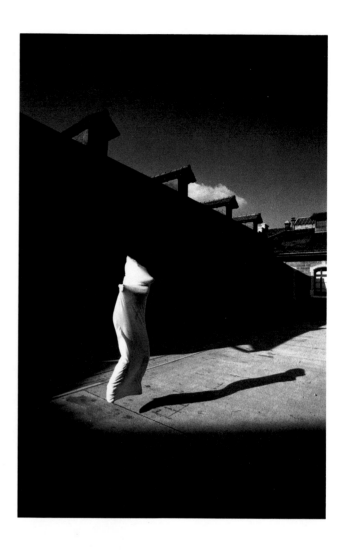

738. CHRISTIAN VOGT. *Untitled (Metaphysical Scene)*, 1972. Toned gelatin silver print. Courtesy and © Christian Vogt.

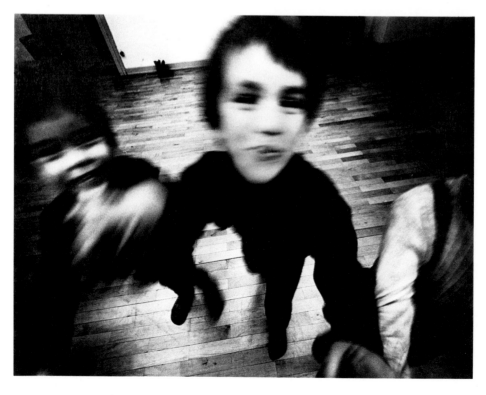

739. OTTO STEINERT. *Children's Carnival*, 1971. Gelatin silver print. Folkwang Museum, Essen, Germany. Courtesy Mrs. Marlie Steinert.

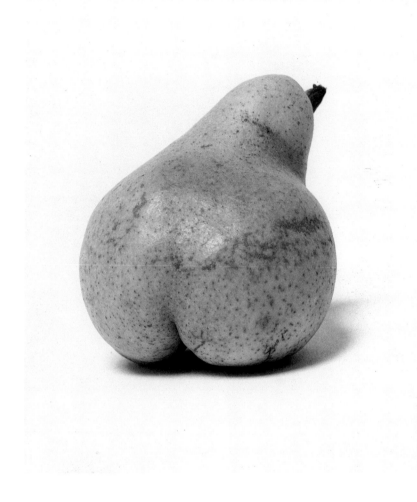

740. DENIS BRIHAT. *William Pear*, 1972. Gelatin silver print. Courtesy and © Denis Brihat.

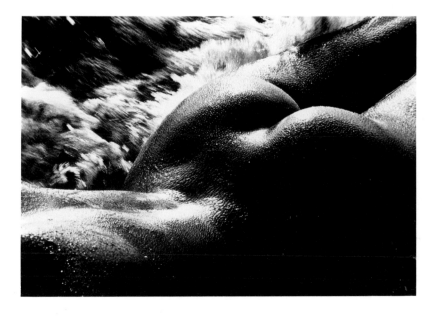

741. LUCIEN CLERGUE. *Nude*, 1962. Gelatin silver print. Worcester Art Museum, Worcester, Mass. © Lucien Clergue.

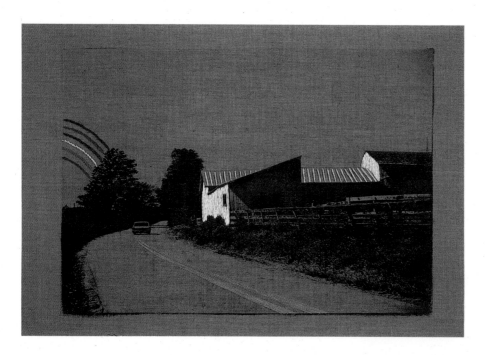

742. BETTY HAHN. *Road and Rainbow*, 1971. Gum bichromate on cotton with stitching. Courtesy and © 1971 Betty Hahn.

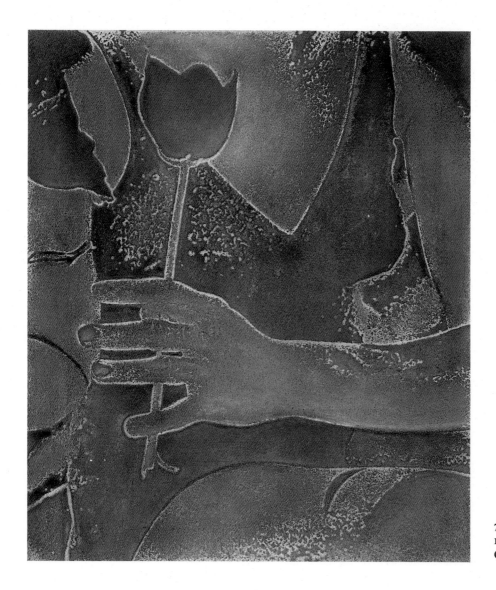

743. NAOMI SAVAGE. *Pressed Flower*, 1969–80. Photo/intaglio with pastel. Courtesy and © Naomi Savage.

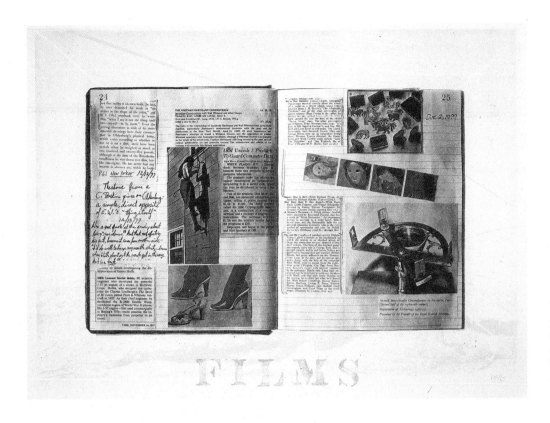

744. THOMAS BARROW.
Films, 1978.
Photolithographic print.
Art Museum, University
of New Mexico,
Albuquerque, N. M.
© Thomas Barrow.

as medium," as this interest has been called, embraces the combining of images with various unlikely materials and their transformation through procedures that are not intrinsic to photography. It can be viewed also as an aspect of a new Pictorialism in that the images produced are not meant either as utilitarian objects—that is, advertising or political posters—or as windows into exterior or private realities, but primarily as unique aesthetic artifacts.

Neither darkroom manipulations nor the use of mechanical printing modes are new to photography; in fact the conjoining of the photographic image and mechanical printing processes was contemplated and pressed from the medium's inception and, with the development of photogravure, Woodburytype, heliotype, and the process halftone plate, became an accomplished fact. With the later addition of silkscreen and, more recently, electronic duplicating methods, and with the involvement since the 1920s of photographers in advertising and journalism, it is obvious that the reproduced photograph has become part of a vast network of utilitarian images that practically everyone in urban industrial societies takes for granted. It also should be recalled that printing photographs on materials other than sensitized paper was a common practice during the latter part of the 19th century, when camera images appeared on glass, porcelain, tile, leather, and fabric artifacts as memorializations and decorations.

What is new, however, is the conjunction of personal expression with technology. Today, print media are regarded by photographers as a means of creating unique objects that depend for their aesthetic interest primarily on the processes used in their production rather than as techniques to duplicate images. In some cases, the authors of these works seem to be making conceptual statements, to be suggesting that valid camera expression need not be limited to straight silver images. One example of this concept is Betty Hahn's work; this photographer translates camera negative into gum-bichromate positive on muslin with embroidery added *(pl. no. 742)*, or uses cyanotype (blueprinting) in conjunction with handwork to suggest that mechanically produced images can be aesthetically linked with age-old handcraft, and, further, that photographers might look to the history of their own medium for viable artistic techniques.

The ease with which established mechanical printing processes lend themselves to manipulative concept can be seen in the work of numbers of photographers who have explored etching, engraving, lithography, and silkscreen. Photoetching generally has long been recognized by both photographers and graphic artists for its capacity to retain an aura of reality while avoiding verisimilitude, but Naomi Savage, who works with this technique, is interested in the inked and intaglio relief print *(pl. no. 743)* as a means to vary color; she considers the matrix itself a relief image with an aesthetic character of its own. Since the 1960s, Thomas Barrow, Scott Hyde, William Larsen, Joan Lyons, Bea Nettles, Robert Rauschenberg, Todd Walker, and Andy Warhol, among numbers of Americans, have been involved with photolithography and silkscreen—processes that are as amenable to reproducing straight photographs, collages, and montages on a variety of materials; furthermore, such images can be additionally manipulated by folding, stitching, quilting, or forming, to achieve unusual effects. For instance, whereas Barrow *(pl. no. 744)* and Nettles employ a fairly direct method of offset lithography to print their images, Rauschenberg at times combines this process with photosilkscreen, adds handwork, and laminates the results to handmade papers *(pl. no. 745)*, in effect merging procedures traditionally associated with the fine and the mechanical arts. In the case of Hyde, photolithography offers an opportunity to work in color without working with color film; he photographs in black and white, transfers the negative images onto litho film and prints them in color from the aluminum plates used in photo-offset lithography, a method that enables him to consider each work an original in that he does not allow the results of this process to be reproduced again *(pl. no. 747)*. In working with silkscreen, photographers also avoid the problems of archival instability that bedevil dye-color films and prints, and at the same time produce images that proclaim their identity as artistic productions. Photolithography and silkscreen both enable Walker, for example, to translate the infinite gradations of the silver

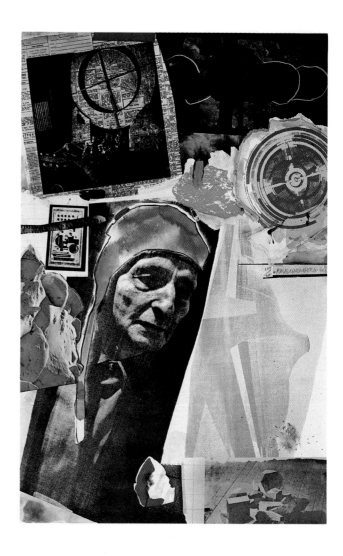

745. ROBERT RAUSCHENBERG. *Kiesler*, 1966. Offset lithograph. Museum of Modern Art, New York; John B. Turner Fund.

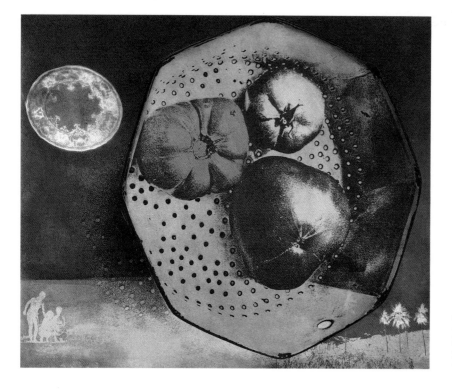

746. BEA NETTLES. *Tomato Fantasy*, 1976. Kwikprint. International Museum of Photography at George Eastman House, Rochester, N.Y. © 1976 Bea Nettles.

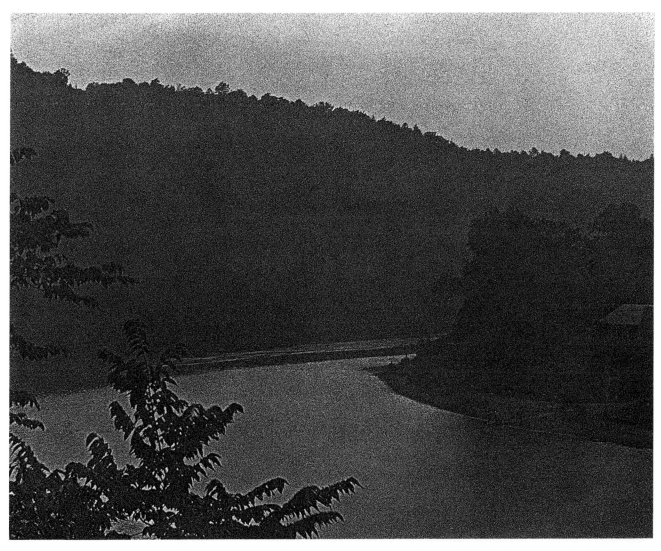

747. SCOTT HYDE. *Delaware Water Gap*, 1979. Original offset lithograph. Courtesy and © 1984 Scott Hyde.

print into disjunctured areas that are further formalized by the color and texture of the screen paint.

Electronically produced images—xerography, Kwik-printing *(pl. no. 746)*, and Verifaxing—are the results of more modern replicative technologies and actually are more accessible to photographers than offset lithography in that they do not require entree to printing plants or to the etching and lithography presses in artist's studios. Though no paint or ink obtrudes on the surface, the grain structure of electronic copy prints, whether in black and white or color, introduces an element of distance between reality and the image. Barrow, who works both with photo-lithography and electronic printing techniques and has been one of the first to recognize and take advantage of this disjuncture, found Verifax copying a suitable process for his goal of connecting "the encyclopedic aspects of photography with the overwhelming materialism of our times."[11] With endless possibilities owing to the fact that

almost any image, whether photographic or hand-drawn, in black and white and in color, from virtually any private or public source, can be combined and recombined with itself—and with substances such as hair, papers of various textures, petals, leaves, waste materials, and so forth—electronic duplication does indeed offer the visual artist an encyclopedic array of choices.

Holography

Giving images formed by light rays another dimension has been the literal aim of holography. This process produces pictures that appear to exist in space by using split laser beams that interact with each other and then are recorded on photographic emulsions, thereby enabling the viewer to see a three-dimensional reflection of an object. Perfected in both the Soviet Union and the United States in the early 1960s, holography presents scientists with precise methods of recording artifacts and their surroundings. For example, not only the size and shape of objects found in archeological excavations, but also their relationship to the other objects and their spatial position in the stratum in which they are discovered can be revealed through holography. The process also has been used imaginatively to create images, among them space-odyssey landscapes and aesthetic and conceptual montages. Curiously, creative holography appears to have attracted few photographers; many of those working with the process in Canada, France, the Soviet Union, the United Kingdom, and the United States are trained in the fine arts, and often they regard this technology as a means of creative research.

The New Era of Color Photography

Perhaps the single most significant catalyst in the transformation of camera imagery during the past several decades has been the interest shown by creative photographers in working with dye-color materials. It will be recalled that, from the beginning years on down, the absence of color was regretted; hand-coloring was considered not just acceptable but necessary to enliven the

pallid tonalities of daguerreotype and paper portraits, and sometimes of scenic views as well. Efforts to find workable color processes occupied individuals throughout the later part of the 19th century, and in 1904 when the Lumières came out with Autochrome, it was immediately successful because both photographers and the public believed that images in color would be both more artistic and more natural-looking.

The chromatic effects achieved by Autochrome transparencies were the result of adding starch granules stained with colored dyes to the silver emulsion on glass. While further experiments to improve and simplify color photography were based on a different color theory—on subtractive rather than additive principles *(see A Short Technical History, Part III)*—these, too, involved the incorporation of dyes with silver. However, by the time a practicable dye-color film appeared on the market (Kodachrome in 1935, Agfacolor Neu in 1935, followed by Ektachrome in 1942), aesthetic concepts relating to photography had changed perceptibly. Most creative photographers of the time, having discarded the manipulative ideas and symbolist themes of Pictorialism in favor of straight images of objective reality, found the opulent colors of the dyes

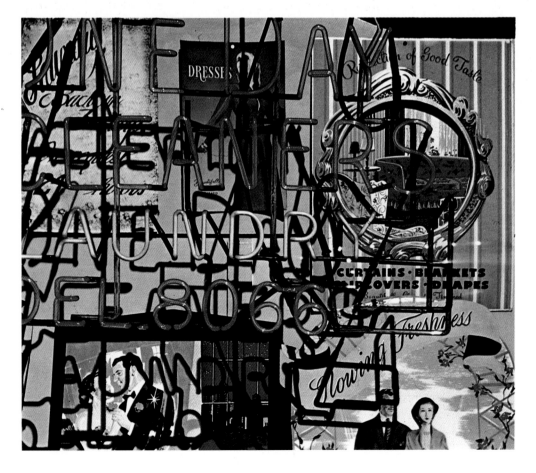

748. ARTHUR SIEGEL. *Untitled (Drycleaners)*, 1946. Color (chromogenic development) transparency. Courtesy Edwynne Houk Gallery, Chicago. © The Siegel Estate.

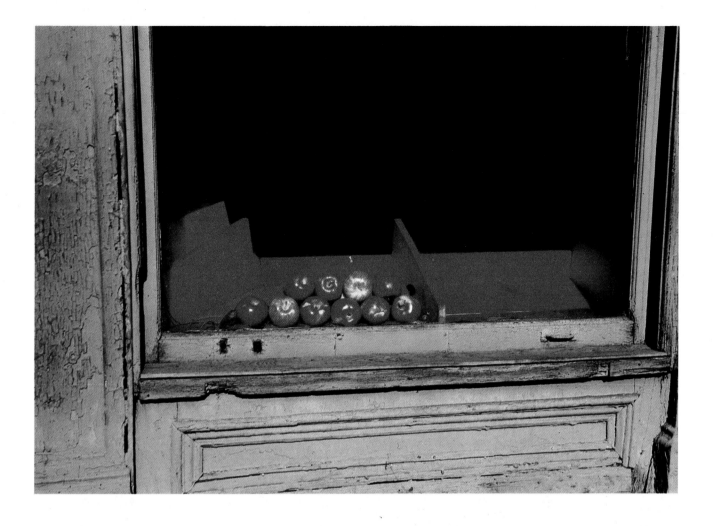

749. HARRY CALLAHAN. *Chicago*, 1951.
Dye transfer (dye imbibition) print.
Pace/MacGill Gallery, New York.
© Harry Callahan.

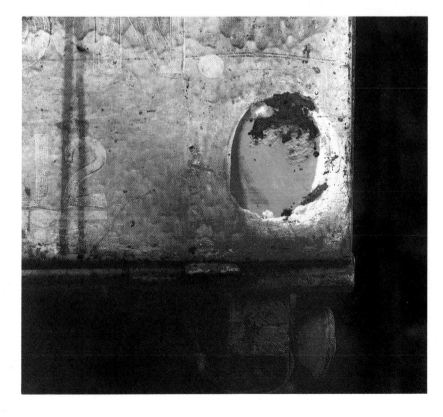

750. SYL LABROT. *Untitled*, c. 1957.
Carbro (assembly) print. Visual Studies
Workshop Collection, Rochester, N.Y.
© Barbara Wilson Labrot.

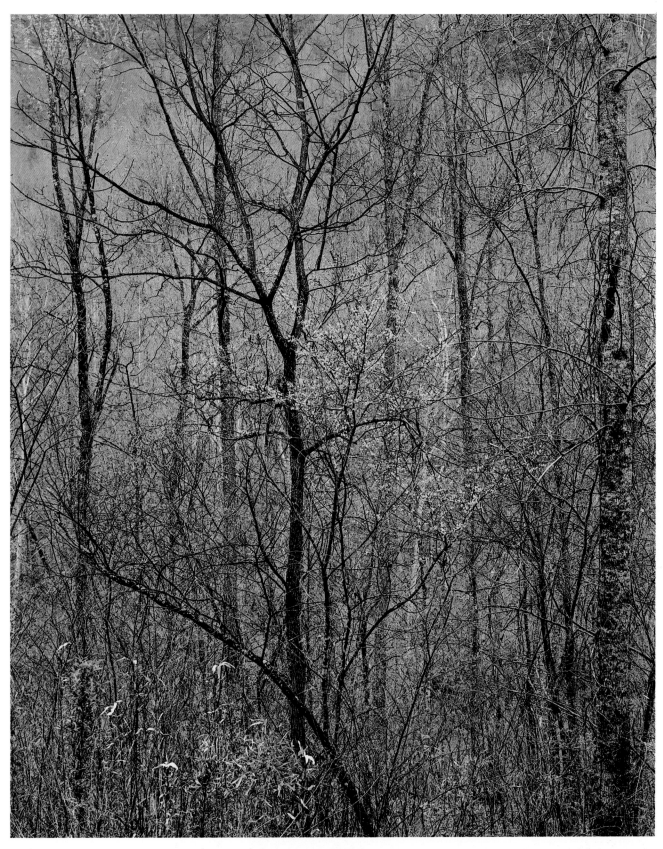

751. ELIOT PORTER. *Red Osier, New Great Barrington, Massachusetts*, 1957.
Dye transfer (dye imbibition) print. Daniel Wolf, Inc., New York. © Eliot Porter.

used in film unsuitable either for the depiction of reality, the evocation of subjective feelings, or the documentation of social conditions. The result was that in its early period color film was left to amateurs and advertising photographers, who became its greatest users.

However, while most documentarians and aesthetic photographers ignored color photography and snapshot amateurs seemed content with the cheery colors during the 1940s and '50s, the advertising community was determined to explore the potentialities of color for "making the implausible plausible."[12] Because it had arrived on the scene during the severe economic depression of the 1930s, color film was regarded as a way to glamorize images of products and people. By coupling real and unreal, by creating abstractions and surreal statements, by giving consumer goods an attractive gloss, these early enthusiasts of color helped establish the guidelines within which modern color photography has developed. Within the past 15 or so years, these developments have invited the attention of photographers primarily concerned with self-expression. More recently still, photojournalists, who for the most part had shunned the brilliant dyes of color film as too seductive for expressing the stark realities of poverty or war, have started to use this material in social documentation.

In view of the emphasis on abstraction in American visual art of the immediate postwar period it is not surprising that of the few noncommercial photographers who did experiment with color film in these years, several were intrigued most by its formal possibilities. In a 1946 abstraction based on window signs (pl. no. 748), Arthur Siegel treated the red neon tubing as an element in an allover linear pattern, as a visual metaphor of nervous energy that not only evokes the tensions of modern urban life but suggests the calligraphic style of several of the Abstract Expressionist painters. Seemingly more illusionistic in terms of its depiction of space, a color image that plays off blocks of intense blue-green, black, and reds in a mundane street still life taken by Harry Callahan in the early 1950s (pl. no. 749) affords pleasure for its geometric simplicity and its color contrasts. The broad areas of color in Syl Labrot's image (pl. no. 750) underscore the interest among photographers in surface texture, nonrepresentational form, and color for color's sake during this period.

The natural landscape rather than the built environment provided Eliot Porter and Charles Pratt with opportunities to create formally satisfying statements and at the same time recreate the wondrous range of colors found in rocks and foliage under varying conditions of light. Porter, who began his career as a naturalist photographer of bird life, often emphasizes the delicate tracery of patterns and colors in foliage and grasses (pl. no. 751), while in a view of Maine rocks (pl. no. 752) Pratt achieved an engaging balance

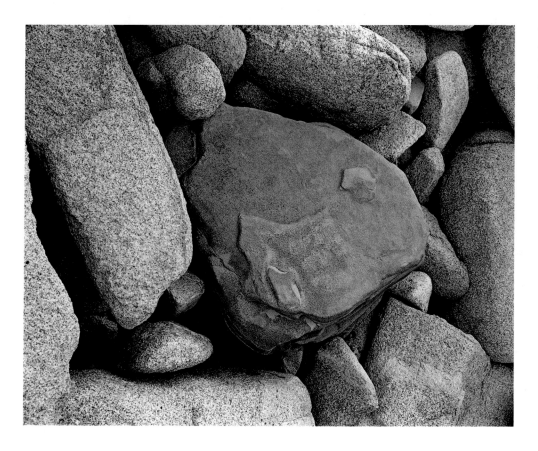

752. CHARLES PRATT. *Maine*, 1968. Dye transfer (dye imbibition) print. Sander Gallery, New York. © Estate of Charles Pratt.

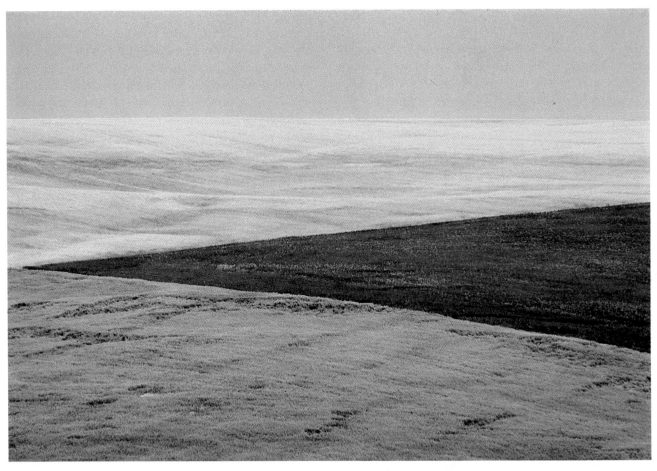

753. FRANCO FONTANA. *Landscape*, 1975. Color (chromogenic development) transparency. Courtesy and © Franco Fontana.

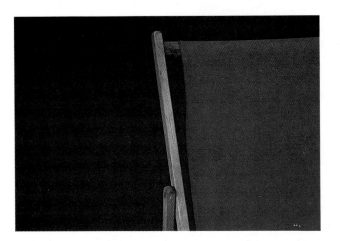 

754. JOHN BATHO. *Deauville*, 1977. Color (chromogenic development) transparencies. Courtesy and © John Batho.

between actuality—the weightiness and texture of the stones—and formal resolution—the abstract design and subtle modulation of the color.

The strong interest among European and Far Eastern photographers in abstraction also was moderated by an attachment to the real world and a desire to reveal its

wonders in a fresh way. Landscapes by Italian photographer Franco Fontana *(pl. no. 753)* that on first glance appear to be geometric triangles of subtle coloration, on closer inspection reveal these shapes as demarcating fields of wheat, flowers, and up-turned soil, lending his images a dimension beyond the purely aesthetic. The irregular blocks of color in the work of French photographer John Batho maintain a satisfying tension between real objects and structured design *(pl. no. 754)*. And on the other side of the world, Hiroshi Hamaya of Japan and Grant Mudford of Australia exemplify photographers who handle color as an element of both nature and art, seeking moments when the character of light creates extraordinary chromatic happenings *(pl. no. 755)*. Within the last decade or so, the preoccupation with the aesthetic nature of color has continued, even though the styles within which such works are conceived reflect the general shift toward less formalistic concerns, as in David Hockney's *Henry Avoiding the Sun (pl. no. 756)*. Nevertheless, Jan Groover, who arranges tabletop still lifes of common kitchen implements, or pieces together fragments of architectural notations to form mellow harmonies, has proclaimed that for her, "formalism is everything."[13] Her finely tuned color sense and tasteful handling of form reveal the possibilities of a purely aesthetic approach *(pl. no. 757)*.

In the wake of the interest in Pop culture during the 1970s, many other photographers have turned to the consumerist emblems of American middle-class life—to automobiles, eating places, swimming pools, advertising, and street signage—for their themes. Among them, William Eggleston, singled out by John Szarkowski as the individual responsible for "inventing color photography,"[14] has used color film to reveal the deserted streets, waste products, and abandoned cars in his home environment in the South *(pl. no. 758)*. These works have been seen both as vivid embodiments of the banality and uneasiness of small-town life, and as aesthetically contrived chromatic exercises. Other Americans who, like Eggleston, produce what at first glance may seem to be a color catalog of visual facts of the American scene include Joel Meyerowitz and Stephen Shore. In switching from 35mm to large-format equipment, and from spontaneous views of street life to considered compositions of the built and natural environment, Meyerowitz also transformed his handling of color, renouncing the jazzy dissonance of the earlier works for the deep harmonies evident in the Cape Cod series *(pl. no. 759)*. Along with a rigorous sense of architectonic structure, the cool and crystalline colors in Shore's images have the effect of

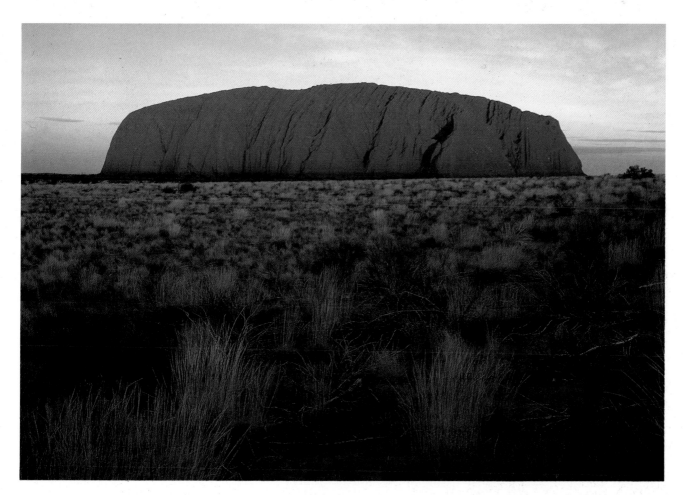

755. GRANT MUDFORD. *Ayers Rock*, 1973. Color (chromogenic development) transparency. Courtesy and © 1973 Grant Mudford.

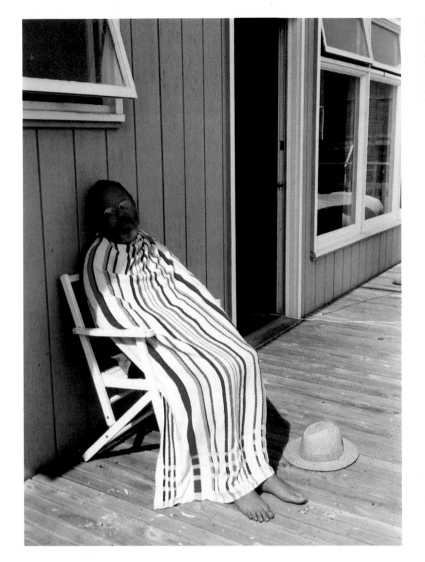

756. DAVID HOCKNEY. *Henry Avoiding the Sun*, 1976. (From the portfolio *20 Photographic Pictures*, published by Sonnabend Press, 1976.) Ektacolor (chromogenic development) print. Sonnabend Gallery, New York. © David Hockney.

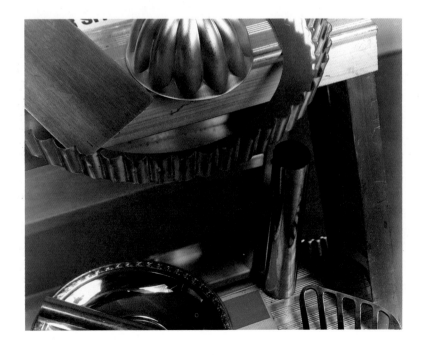

757. JAN GROOVER. *Untitled*, 1979. Type-C (chromogenic development) print. Blum Helman Gallery, New York. © Jan Groover.

laundering banal vistas; a street view made in Los Angeles *(pl. no. 760)* transforms a chaotic jumble of gas stations and signage into an aesthetically gratifying object.

The tendency of dye-color materials to cast a rosy tint over landscape and urban views can be seen in images concerned with actuality, among them works by Mitch Epstein, Len Jenshel, Ruth Orkin, and Joel Sternfeld. Contrasting the muted grays and browns of the terrain and buildings with brilliantly colored patches of clothing, or with a pyramid set aglow by the setting sun, Epstein views the landscape of India as a stage setting for exotic effects *(pl. no. 761)*, thus continuing in color a tradition established in black and white in the 1850s of photographing in the Near East and the Orient. In the same sense, the tasteful colorations of the interiors taken by Kishin Shinoyama, Japan's foremost color photographer, seem to exude a glossily romantic aura *(pl. no. 762)*. Owing to the color, these works, along with such images as Meyerowitz's Cape Cod and St. Louis Arch series, invite comparison with the glossy ads and color pages in travel magazines.

A somewhat different approach to color can be seen in the work of a number of photographers who play up stri-

dent effects and unpleasing contrasts. Mark Cohen, for example, photographs street life in urban centers, pushing saturated reds, blues, and yellows in order to emphasize the raucous energy he perceives in these environments, while interiors by Roger Mertin indicate that this photographer adjusts exposure, processing methods, and lighting in order to change colorations and drain them of their lush subtleties. In portraying such "sociological" artifacts as rooms decorated for Christmas, Mertin's acid colors create aesthetic visual experiences designed to obvert the habitual sentimental response to such themes.

Portraiture and still life clearly lend themselves to the individualized treatment of form and color in that the photographer can control all the elements of the work—the objects themselves, their arrangements, chroma, and lighting. The illustrative settings and highly saturated hues that characterize Neal Slavin's group portraits of from two to 2,000 figures lend a sprightly note to works that parody both commercial portraiture of the past and the bogus fabrications of current magazine and television advertising *(pl. no. 763)*. In still lifes by Marie Cosindas, both the objects themselves—old lace, brocades, dolls, flowers—and the

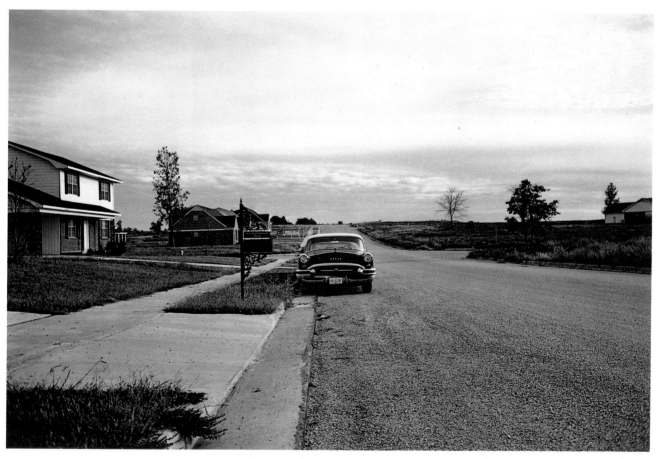

758. WILLIAM EGGLESTON. *Memphis, Tennessee*, 1971. Dye transfer (dye imbibition) print. Middendorf Gallery, Washington, D.C. © William Eggleston.

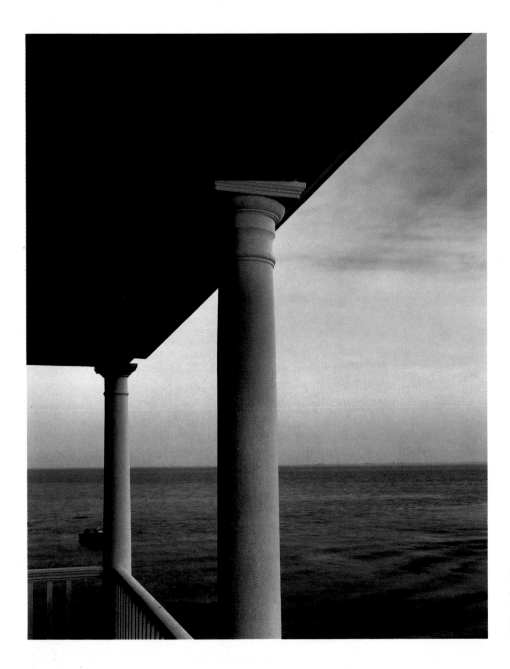

759. Joel Meyerowitz. *Porch, Provincetown*, 1977. Ektacolor (chromogenic development) print. Courtesy and © Joel Meyerowitz.

muted yet harmonious colors are designed to project an unabashedly romantic view *(pl. no. 764)*, whereas the lively color contrasts and geometrical arrangements of printed papers and reproductions of art arranged by Victor Schrager have a similar function but reveal a different sensibility. By way of contrast, the jumble of artifacts amassed by Lucas Samaras *(pl. no. 765)* and the lurid colors in which they are bathed suggest an uneasy schism between the rational and illogical, between the culture of the past and the excesses of the present. Samaras, who works with one-step color processes *(see A Short Technical History, Part III)*, finds that the instant feedback of seeing the color almost immediately after the exposure allows him to adjust and vary these creations and, in smaller versions known as

sx-70 film, to intervene in the actual chemical processing to create his Photo-Transformations—self-portraits that embrace bizarre changes in the artist's own physiognomy through changes in the process.

As has been suggested in the first part of this chapter, there exists a pronounced compatibility between color and photographic manipulations; indeed, the color, whether achieved by using dye-color films and prints for collage and montage, or by employing such processes as Fresson (a complicated gum process), gum bichromate, and cyanotype, or by hand-coloring images, usually enhances the aesthetic and affective dimensions of these creations, as can be seen in a wide range of contemporary examples. To cite only a few: collages in color produced by Joyce Niemanas

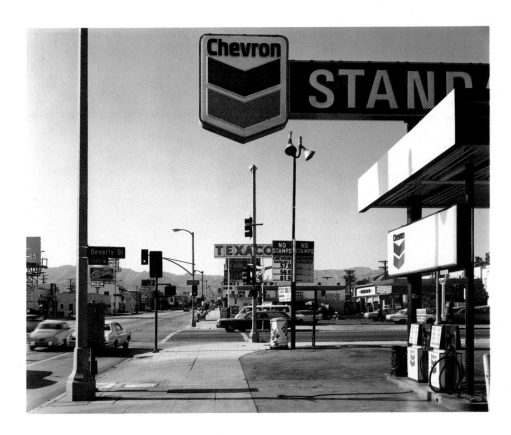

760. STEPHEN SHORE.
Beverly Boulevard and LaBrea Avenue, Los Angeles, California, June 21, 1975.
Ektacolor (chromogenic development) print.
Courtesy and © Stephen Shore.

761. MITCH EPSTEIN.
Pushkar Camel Fair, Rajasthan, India, 1978.
Ektacolor (chromogenic development) print.
Courtesy and © Mitch Epstein.

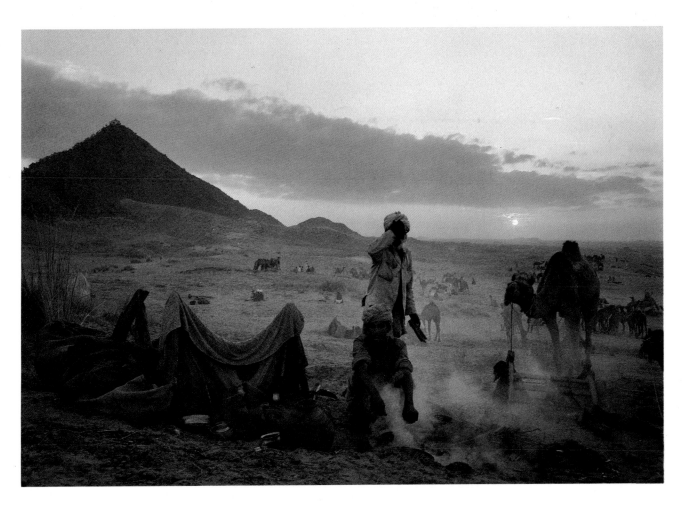

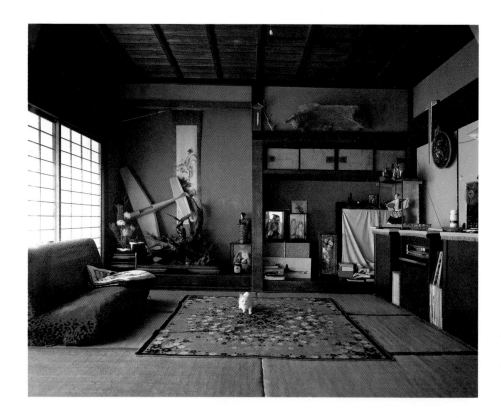

762. KISHIN SHINOYAMA. *House*, 1975. Color (chromogenic development) transparency. © Kishin Shinoyama/Pacific Press Service.

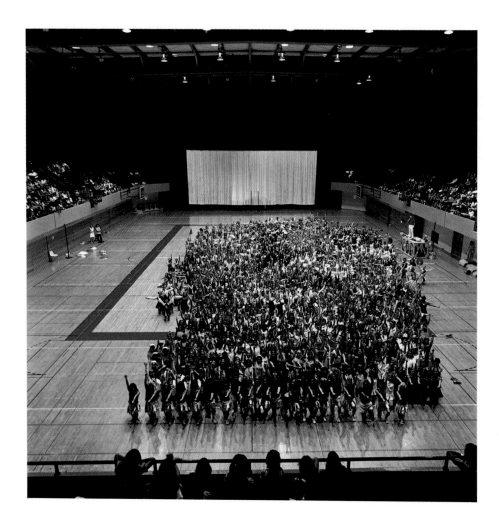

763. NEAL SLAVIN. *National Cheerleaders Association*, 1974. Ektacolor (chromogenic development) print. Courtesy and © Neal Slavin.

metamorphosis of animal and human forms owes as much to the eerie colors as to the strange visual shapes *(pl. no. 768)* created by montage.

The revival of historic processes has enabled some contemporary photographers to use color while bypassing problems associated with dye-color films and prints. Hand-tinting, whether subtle as in the work of Nina Raginsky, a Canadian-born photographer who tints snapshot-like portraits to make them seem old, or strongly chromatic, as in an image by Alice Steinhardt that maintains a tenuous balance between painting and photography *(pl. no. 769)*, is one method of transforming the mechanically produced photograph into a unique object, of moving it from realism to art. This approach can be combined with the projection of one or more images onto canvas and, in the procedures favored by Heinecken, the use of bleaching agents, pastels, or tinting colors to make the viewer aware of an equilibrium between the mechanically defined and the manually asserted. Turn-of-the-century processes that provided Pictorialists of that time with a means to avoid "mechanicalization" also have been revived. Fresson printing is preferred by French photographer Bernard Plossu and American Sheila Metzner, while Hahn has turned to gum bichromate in combination with other interventions. In noting that "Art is an attitude that produces an object by using media,"[15] Neimanas is asserting the right recognized by all these photographers to employ whatever means are necessary, including color, to create imaginative works.

Obviously, in the hands of creative photographers color may have many dimensions. It may be romantically nuanced, bellicose, eerie, or chic and sensuous, but it rarely is real-looking. In fact, in the past, photographs of real situations in color have invited a sense of ambiguity, an element of distrust on the part of viewers, perhaps because the saturated dyes of color film seem to have an equivocal relationship to the harsher realities of social conditions. For instance, color images taken by several of the Farm Security Administration photographers were not felt to be evocative enough (in contrast to their work in black and

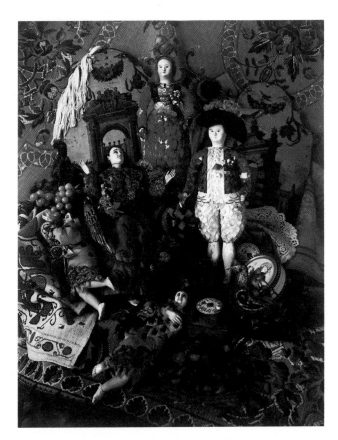

764. MARIE COSINDAS. *Conger Metcalf Still Life*, 1976. Polaroid (internal dye-diffusion transfer) print. Courtesy the artist. © Polacolor.

involve positioning sx-70 prints to destroy the ordinary camera depiction of space and make the viewer aware of the work as an individualized aesthetic statement *(pl. no. 766)*. Olivia Parker and Rosamond W. Purcell are among those who combine color with montage to invent a personal iconography; in Parker's still life, the addition of bright red cords affords an unsettling contrast with the decaying overripe fruit *(pl. no. 767)* and continues the kind of intervention initiated by American Pop artists; in Purcell's work the sense of uneasiness emanating from the

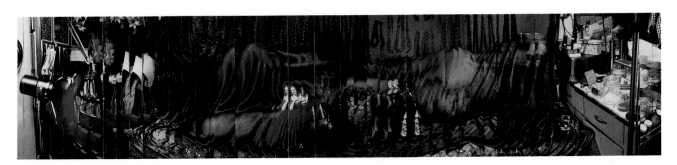

765. LUCAS SAMARAS. *March 19, 1983*, 1983. Polaroid (internal dye-diffusion transfer) prints. Pace Gallery, New York. © Lucas Samaras.

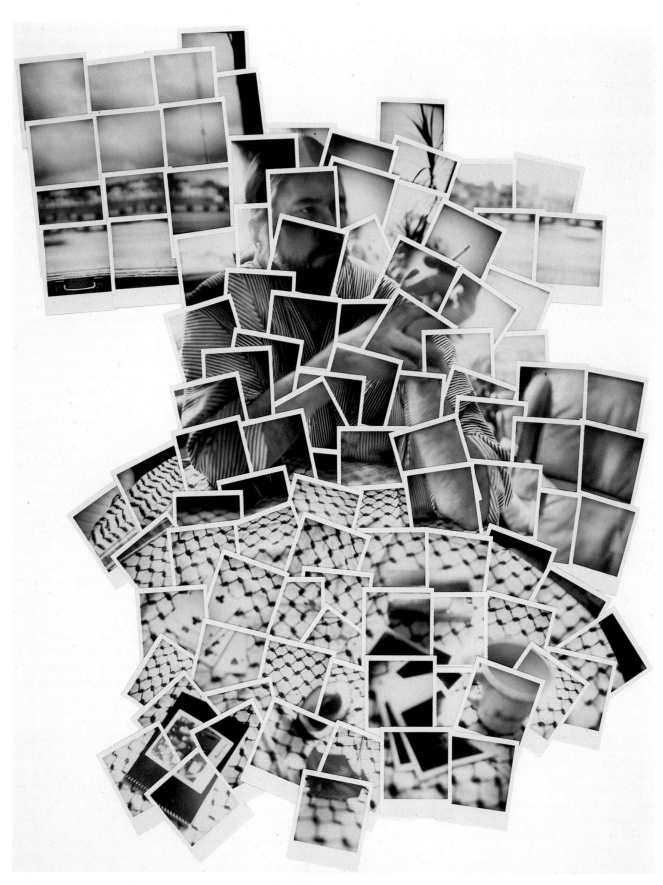

766. JOYCE NEIMANAS. *Untitled*, 1981. SX-70 (internal dye-diffusion transfer) prints.
Courtesy and © 1981 Joyce Neimanas.

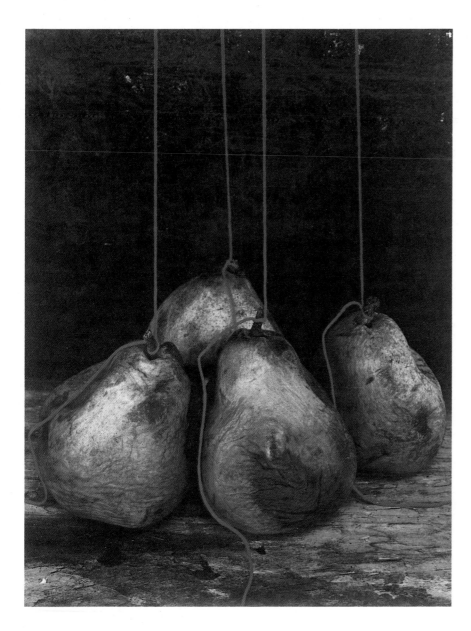

767. OLIVIA PARKER. *Four Pears*, 1979. Polacolor (internal dye-diffusion transfer) print. Marcuse Pfeifer Gallery, New York. © Olivia Parker.

white) to warrant the expense of reproduction in print media. Recent changes in taste, however, have made both socially oriented and photojournalistic images in color more acceptable. Among the street photographers of the 1970s who used color film to encapsulate their perceptions of urban social conditions are Bruce Davidson, Jerome Liebling, Helen Levitt, and Danny Lyon. Levitt, one of the first to find color film sympathetic to this pursuit, captures dissonances and harmonies, contrasting the drabness of tenement backgrounds with the lively colors of the clothing worn by her subjects. The hues in Davidson's large-format subway pictures are sometimes lurid and sometimes pretty, lending an uncertain aura to the intensity of gesture and expression revealed by these bored and discontented riders of New York's appalling underground. With viewers more willing to accept the nature of dye

colors, there is little question that other socially concerned photographers will seek ways to make this material expressive of their feelings about actual conditions.

That color has become acceptable to photographers who document social realities is in part owed to the great increase in color images in picture journals. During the 1950s, the dye-color films perfected just before the second World War made it possible for photojournalists to work in color, while improved printing methods enabled the journals to print their stories. This is not to suggest that magazines had not printed photographs in color before this time. In fact, in an earlier period, some magazines, notably *National Geographic*, had regularly featured color reproductions from Autochrome plates, but in general color processes and the methods of making engraved or lithographic color plates for periodicals were time-consuming

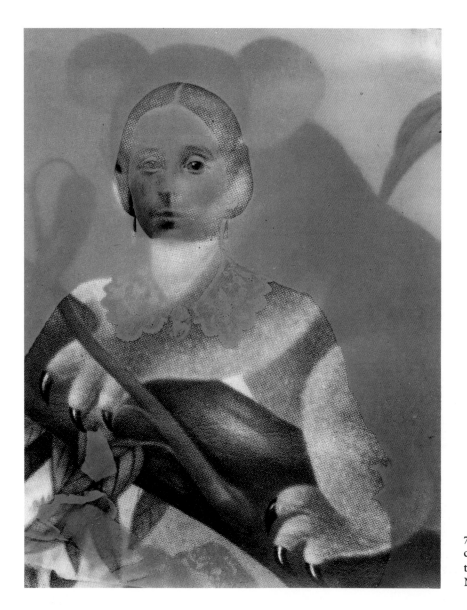

768. ROSAMOND W. PURCELL. *Untitled*, c. 1978. Polaroid (internal dye-diffusion transfer) print. Marcuse Pfeifer Gallery, New York. © Rosamond W. Purcell.

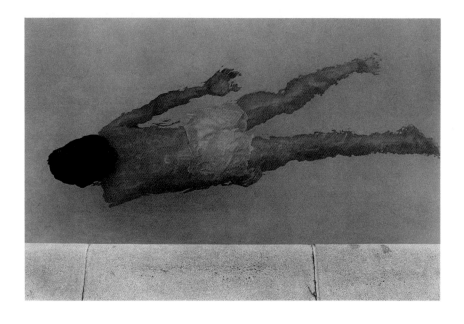

769. ALICE STEINHARDT. *The Swimmer*, 1978. Oil color on gelatin silver print. Courtesy and © 1978 Alice Steinhardt.

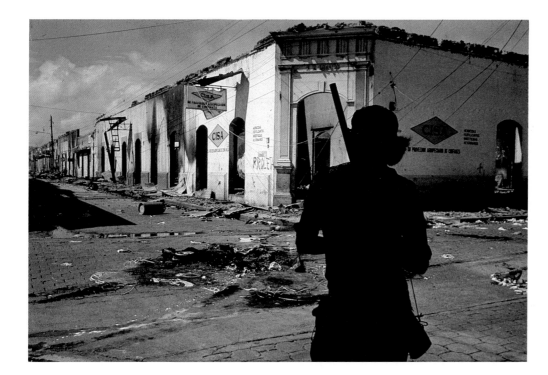

and too expensive for popular journals. When the Depression created keen competition among periodicals for readers (and among manufacturers for customers), a diligent search for less complicated means of making color images on film ensued *(see A Short Technical History, Part III)*. In 1952, *Life* reproduced its first picture story in color—a series of views of New York by Ernst Haas that proved that color was capable of imbuing reality with an appetizing gloss. Haas, a former painter, found color film to be an inspiring tool for "transforming an object from what it is to what you want it to be,"[16] but later photojournalists, especially those working in areas of conflict during the 1970s, have used color materials to express a wide range of perceptions about the actualities framed by their viewfinders. For instance, the color in Larry Burrow's images of Viet Nam adds a realistic dimension; it augments the poignancy of Susan Meiselas's photographs of the Sandinista uprising in Nicaragua *(pl. no. 770)*; it enhances the dissolute sensuality of Rio Branco's story of the Maciel district of the Brazilian city of Salvador *(pl. no. 771)*; it bathes a contemporary scene of peasant labor in China by Zeng Yue in a picturesque glow *(pl. no. 772)*.

Painting and Photography

By now it has become apparent that painting and photography have existed in symbiotic relationship since the earliest days of the younger medium. Both Realist and Romantic painters (whether or not they acknowledged it) used camera images for information about how to depict the model's pose, the fall of drapery, the shape of rock, tree, and built structures, with the result that many lesser artists were afforded a surer grasp of line and form in less time. In the second half of the century, when the camera, at times in conjunction with the microscope and telescope, became a sophisticated tool capable of describing movement too swift and substances too small for the unaided eye to see, or too far away to comprehend, its products still supplied painters with "facts."

But beyond making factual information available, camera images helped transform artistic vision in other respects, as French critic Ernest Chesneau acknowledged in 1859. When he wrote that "the majority of painters today use photography as their most precious aid," Chesneau referred specifically to the "general toning down of the color range"[17] in paintings, but new ideas in the treatment and organization of form and space were of equal importance. Already in the 19th century, photographs made in the street with short focal-length cameras and lenses revealed actuality as seamless and casually organized rather than discrete and hieratically composed. When the rectangular frame of the photographic plate sliced through figures, structures, and events, with little respect for the canons of pictorial organization, graphic artists became more aware of new ways to depict the life around them. They represented scenes from unusual angles, included portions of figures cut off by the edge of the canvas and paper, reproduced events as though the participants had been surprised in the midst of activity, employing strategies that gave their work a naturalistic vivacity. They also

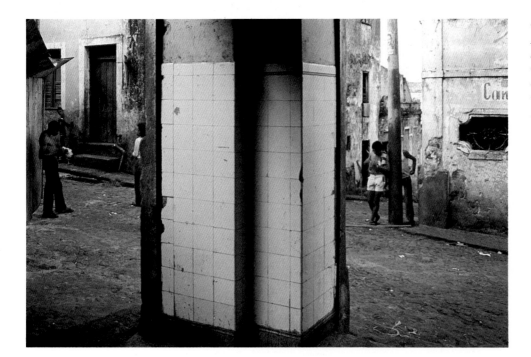

771. RIO BRANCO. *Prostitutes of Maciel, Salvador, Brazil,* 1976. Color (chromogenic development) transparency. © Rio Branco/Magnum.

depicted objects and figures with less attention to their three-dimensional actuality, at times flattening and compressing them into a shallow pictorial space. As has been pointed out by a number of authorities, this treatment of form was in part the result of the avid interest among French, British, and, later, American graphic artists in a similar handling of figure and ground in the Japanese woodblock prints that had arrived in Europe starting in the 1860s, but the influence also of the photographic image cannot be denied. Together, photograph and *Ukiyo-e* woodblock exerted a telling influence on Realist and Impressionist painters who created an intriguing tension between naturalism and decoration in images of urban life.

During the early part of the 20th century, this intimate if not readily acknowledged relationship between the two visual media continued and actually became more cordial in some respects. Although some graphic artists still adamantly denied the aesthetic potentials of the medium, American painters as precise in style as Charles Sheeler and as tonally oriented as Edward Steichen worked in both media with equal sensitivity, with the former eventually elevating painting, and the latter photography, to a favored position. In Europe during the 1910s and '20s, Dadaists, Futurists, and Constructivists went even further, transforming scientific camera images such as the stop-motion studies of Marey and Muybridge into statements expressive of the tempo and energy of modern life. Some artists incorporated graphic and photographic material in the same works and called for an end to art terminology and concepts based upon traditional divisions among media.

For about 25 years during the mid-century flowering of Regionalism, Social Realism, and, later, Abstract Expressionism, these ideas were more or less dormant, but they reasserted themselves again in the 1960s in a number of contexts. Photographs, the most ubiquitous emblem of mass culture, found an obvious place in Pop Art, and were embraced by those intent on repudiating the preciosity of action painting. To cite only a few examples, Larry Rivers and Robert Rauschenberg—the latter a photographer of sensitivity as well as a painter—employed silkscreen techniques and incorporated snapshots and news photos along with an array of junk materials to suggest the gritty texture of contemporary urban life *(pl. no. 745)*. James Rosenquist, Andy Warhol, and Tom Wesselmann in the United States and Richard Hamilton in England were among those who mined (and mimed) billboard and other photographic advertising imagery, in particular publicity posters for mass-entertainment celebrities. Enlarged, repeated, and juxtaposed, these works were meant to suggest the replicative aspects of all mass-consumer items, whether the phenomenon was wearable, edible, or cultural *(pl. no. 773)*.

Almost in tandem with the Pop Art style, sharp-focus realism—sometimes called Photorealism—emerged as a distinctive style in American painting of the late 1960s. A sort of Precisionism revisited, it too derived its energizing ideas from the artifacts, consumer goods, and built environments so prominently featured in visual advertising. Photorealist painters, like their forerunners in the 1920s (and in common with many photographers), usually are interested more in the abstract appearance of reality than in "realism"

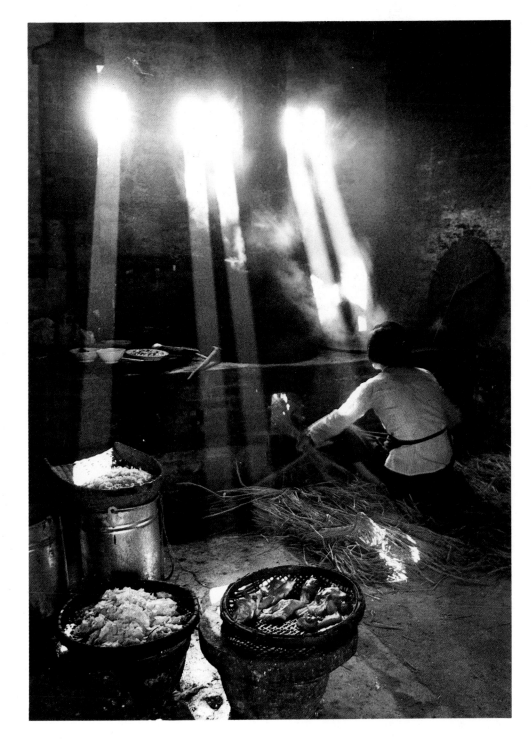

772. ZENG YUE. *The New Rice*, 1981 (from *China Reconstructs Magazine*, Oct., 1982). Ektacolor (chromogenic development) print. Xin Hua News Agency, Beijing. Courtesy Zhang Suicheng, Beijing.

itself, finding the formal configurations of actuality "far more exciting than most abstract painting."[18] The quest for the meticulous representation of the real world—in particular of the machine-made portion of reality—prompted this generation of painters to look to the camera for aid in translating spatial dimension onto a flat surface *(pl. no. 774)*; indeed many painters employed projection techniques perfected earlier as methods for advertising illustration.

The distinguishing feature of Photorealist painting,

however, is that the photograph is more than just a preparatory device or an aid to verisimilitude as it usually is in illustration. Photographs help the painter objectify the subject, theoretically bypassing choice and subjective feelings and substituting a neutral facture for the artist's hand. These paintings mimic the visual appearance of photographs, portraying space in the specific manner of certain lens capabilities or from the vantage point peculiar to camera images, as in Lowell Nesbitt's enlarged close-ups of

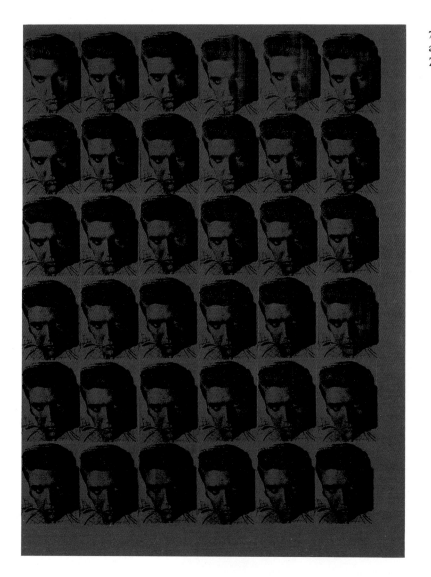

773. ANDY WARHOL. *Red Elvis*, 1962. Acrylic and silkscreen on linen. Galerie Bischofberger, Zurich.

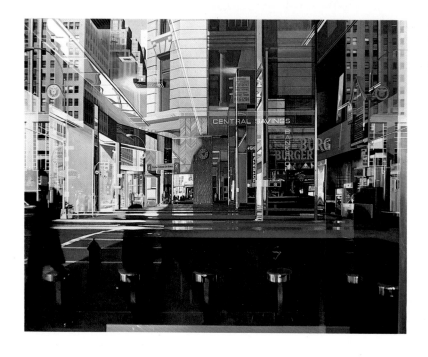

774. RICHARD ESTES. *Central Savings*, 1975. Oil on canvas. Allan Stone Gallery, New York. Collection Nelson-Atkins Museum of Art, Kansas City, Mo.

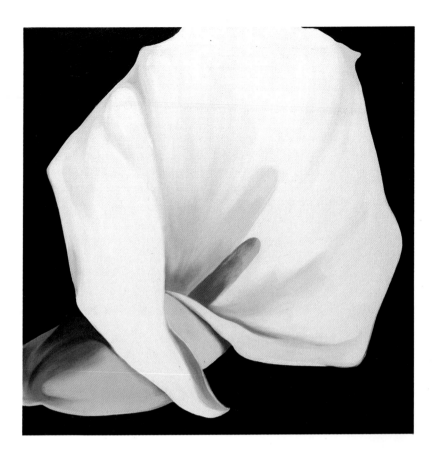

775. LOWELL NESBITT. *White Calla Lily*, 1978. Oil on canvas. Andrew Crispo Gallery, New York.

776. FRANZ GERTSCH. *Irene*, 1980. Acrylic on unprepared cotton. Collection Susan Pear and Louis K. Meisel, New York.

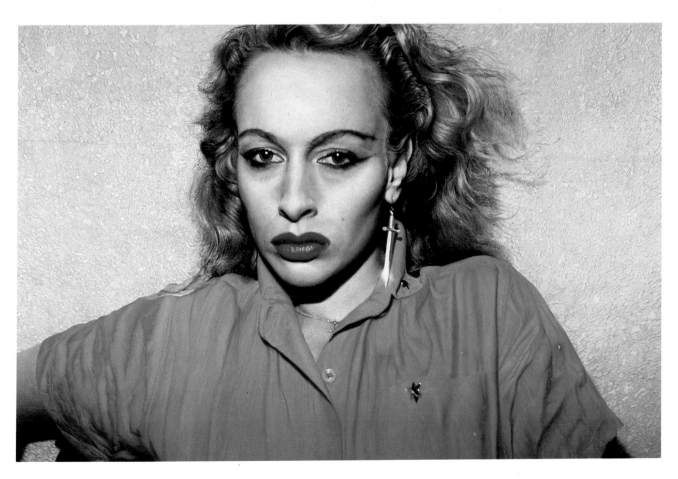

flowers *(pl. no. 775)*. Synthesized at times from a number of camera images rather than projected, as is true of the work of Estes and Frank Gertsch, Europe's best-known Photorealist, such paintings paraphrase the high-gloss surface emulsions of photographic papers, or emulate photographic dye materials, as in paintings by Gertsch *(pl. no. 776)* and John Baeder. In a series of Kodachrome-like scenes of diners *(pl. no. 778)*, which he has chosen to "document" as a theme of disappearing Americana, Baeder has adopted an approach usually thought to be the province of photography. In another example, Chuck Close paints portraits using the age-old technique of squaring off photograph and canvas, and transferring each sector from the smaller to the larger surface, but the finished paintings emulate enlarged photographic portraits in scale, surface treatment, and monochromatism *(pl. no. 777)*.

At the opposite end of the ideological spectrum, photographs also have played a conspicuous role in the conceptual styles that rose to prominence in the late 1960s, even though a connection between these least and most abstract visual forms may seem curious. But as Sol Lewitt noted, "when the artist uses a conceptual form of art . . . the idea becomes a machine that makes art," and the camera is the machine that records the idea. In Lewitt's work, for example, photographs of metal street grids are emblems of the artist's concept rather than communications with aesthetic, personal, or social content. Without the photographic records of such concepts as Yves Klein's body art, Robert Smithson's earthworks, and Christo's wrappings, productions that were meant to be created and then destroyed would have no permanent form; indeed it is difficult to imagine that they would have been conceived if they could not have been photographed.

In themselves, camera images also may be regarded by

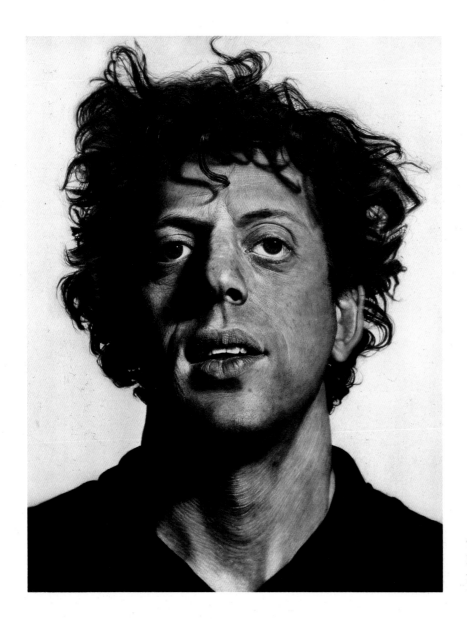

777. CHUCK CLOSE. *Phil*, 1969. Synthetic polymer on canvas. Whitney Museum of American Art, New York; gift of Mrs. Robert M. Benjamin.

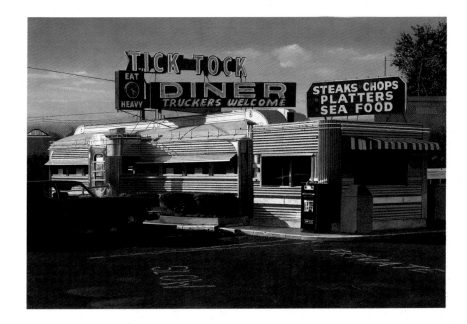

778. JOHN BAEDER. *Tick Tock Diner, Clifton, N.J.*, 1983. Oil on canvas. O. K. Harris Works of Art, New York. © 1983 John Baeder.

painters as found objects, to be assembled as testament to individual taste or to a sense of irony—contemporary analogues of Marcel Duchamp's "ready-mades." They may form the basis of egocentric statements, supplying such painters as Samaras and Joseph Beuys in Germany with the means to investigate political and social ideas and to integrate their discoveries with concepts of self. In sum, as difficult as it would be to conceive of contemporary photography without taking into account developments in the graphic arts, it is even less possible to visualize contemporary painting without its alter-ego, the photograph.

As the foregoing discussion has indicated, photography's potential for personal expression has expanded radically in the past several decades. Camera images have be-

come transformed: besides the traditional two-dimensional monochromatic entity in shades of black and white—more often than not dealing with some facet of reality—the medium now embraces objects conceived in a variety of shapes, colors, and sizes, concerned with providing information, selling ideas and products, moving people, making formal and analytical statements. New technologies, new aesthetic theories, in concert with the enhanced role of the photograph as a marketable commodity, have influenced the way the medium currently is being used and perceived. To show that the current expanded state of the medium is the result of a rich history in which the photograph flourished all the more for being so closely related to developments in technology, in the arts, and in the social sphere, has been the purpose of this work.

A Short Technical History: Part III

DEVELOPMENTS SINCE 1910

Cameras and Equipment

In the early years of the 20th century, refinements in camera equipment were made in response to the increased demand for different kinds of images for advertising, documentation, and photojournalism. Two flexible-plate cameras, incorporating features from earlier cameras, were introduced around 1910—the Linhof *(pl. no. 779)*, designed by Valentin Linhof in Germany, and the Speed Graphic *(pl. no. 780)*, patented by William Folmer of the Folmer and Schwing Division of the Eastman Kodak Company in Rochester, New York; both remained relatively unchanged in design into the 1950s. The movement characteristics of these hand and stand cameras also were integral to modern view and studio cameras.

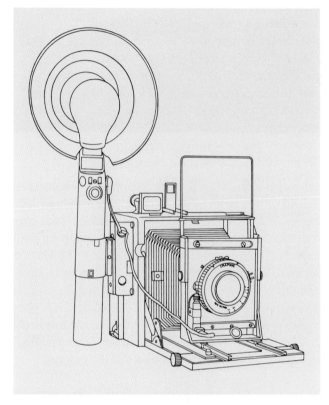

780. *Speed Graphic Camera.* A favorite with American press photographers in the 1940s, Speed Graphic is here shown (in a later model) with a flash-gun, which is connected to an electromagnetic release on the between-the-lens shutter. The shutter thus opened as the flash-gun was fired.

Single-lens reflex cameras were improved by being made smaller and lighter. Suggestions that such cameras be equipped with a pentaprism in order to make eye-level viewing possible eventually led to the East German Zeiss-Ikon Company's introduction in 1949 of the Contax S—the first camera produced with this mechanism built in *(pl. no. 785)*. The modern twin-lens reflex camera evolved from apparatus developed in the 19th century in which the image received in the upper viewing lens was reflected by a mirror onto a ground glass at the top of the camera in order to facilitate focusing. Several different models were introduced between 1889 and 1928, but it was not until the

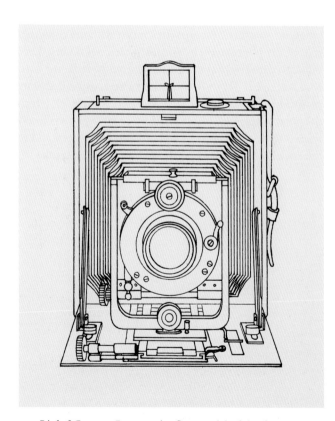

779. *Linhof Camera.* In 1910, the first model of the famous and versatile Linhof press and professional camera appeared. It had a full range of movements and adjustments.

appearance of the Rolleiflex *(pl. no. 783)* in that year that this type of camera achieved wide public acceptance.

The most significant development in professional equipment in the 20th century was the invention of a small, lightweight 35mm roll-film camera. The Leica *(pl. no. 784)*, introduced in 1925 (but based on a 1913 model devised by Oskar Barnack of the Leitz Company to make use of leftover movie film), became the first commercially successful instrument to incorporate instantaneous exposure, fast film advance, and a high level of image definition under a variety of lighting conditions. Even though the earlier Ermanox *(pl. no. 786)*, a small-plate camera with an exceptionally fast lens, had performed well in low-light situations, the Leica demonstrated that it was better suited to make repeated exposures and to stop action without attracting the attention of the subject. This camera and the other 35mm instruments that quickly followed changed the tenor of photojournalistic reportage in that the images they produced were sharp enough to be enlarged and when reproduced could be arranged in sequences that paralleled the action they depicted. Eventually 35mm apparatus inspired new aesthetic standards in personal photographic expression, too. Recent improvements to 35mm equipment have been the motor drives that automatically advance the film and prepare the shutter for the next exposure.

Camera equipment designed for amateur use also underwent significant improvement during the 20th century. The fixed-focus Eastman Brownie camera *(pl. no.*

789)*, introduced in 1900 as the cheapest and simplest camera on the market, was revised over the years until by 1963 it had evolved into the Kodak Instamatic *(pl. no. 790)*—a lightweight eye-level instrument that accepted film cassettes; by 1972 it had become small enough to be called a pocket Instamatic, accepting 16mm film.

The outstanding event in the amateur field was the introduction in 1948 of a camera and film that made instant one-step photography possible. The Polaroid camera *(pl. no. 782)*, designed by Edwin H. Land, was based on an idea virtually as old as photography itself—that of sensitizing and processing the film inside the camera. A number of 19th- and early-20th-century inventions, exemplified by the Dubroni *(pl. no. 781)*, had incorporated this concept, but the Polaroid was the first instant-print camera, requiring in its original version just a minute after exposure to produce a monochromatic positive print by means of a sealed pod of developer-fixer and a complicated image receiver (positive). In that this system also provided a simple means to make test shots to previsualize arrangement, lighting, and decor in advertising and fashion work, Polaroid film was adapted for use in professional studio and field cameras; there are now a wide range of instant-print professional Polaroid films, including Polacolor film, which was intro-

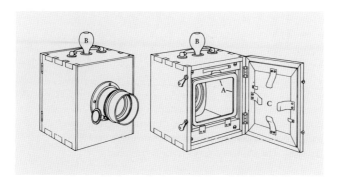

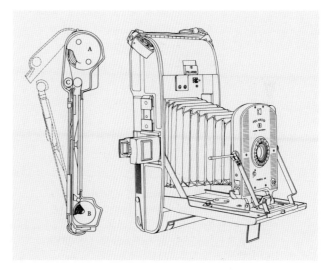

781. *Dubroni Camera.* The Dubroni camera of 1864 took a collodion-coated plate, which was held firmly against the flat-ground edges (A) of a ceramic or glass container, forming the inside of the camera. The sensitizing silver nitrate solution was introduced through a hole in the top of the camera by means of a pipette (B) and was made to flow over the plate when the camera was tilted onto its back. After exposure had taken place, the sensitizing solution was sucked out of the camera and processing chemicals were introduced into it, again by using the pipette. A yellow glass (C) in the rear door allowed the progress of development to be inspected.

782. *Polaroid Land Camera.* The first instant-print camera was the Polaroid Land 95 camera of 1948. A large roll of print paper (A) and a smaller roll of negative paper (B), connected by a leader, fitted into the top and bottom of the camera back. By means of the leader, the negative paper and the print paper were brought together and drawn between a pair of rollers (C), which broke a pod of processing chemicals, carried on the print strip, and spread its contents evenly between the two strips. After one minute, the finished print could be removed from the camera through a flap in the back.

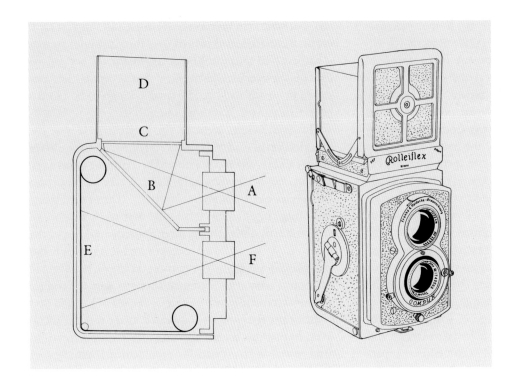

783. *Rolleiflex Camera*. The principle of the twin-lens reflex camera: Light, passing through the upper lens (A), is reflected from a mirror (B) onto a ground-glass focusing screen (C), which is viewed through a hood (D). The film (E) is exposed through the lower lens (F). The Rolleiflex camera of 1928 was the first of the modern twin-lens reflex cameras.

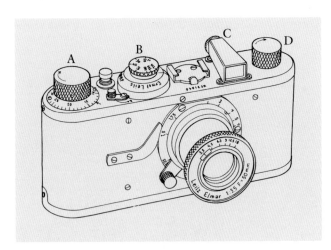

784. *Leica Camera*. The Leica camera of 1925: the film winding knob (A) also set the shutter, the six speeds of which were set on a dial (B). A direct-vision, optical viewfinder (C) was fitted near the film rewind knob (D). The noninterchangeable lens was set in a helically focused, telescoping mount.

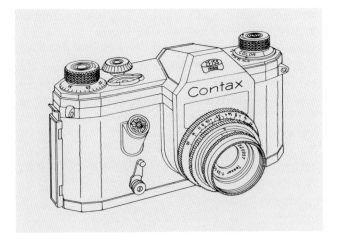

785. *Contax S Camera*. The Contax S camera of 1949 was the first 35mm single-lens reflex camera to be equipped with a built-in pentaprism; it was set in the viewfinder housing. The camera's specification included a delayed-action shutter mechanism and screw-mounted, interchangeable lenses.

duced in 1962. The apparatus has been continually improved, with the sx-70 system, introduced in 1972, recently supplanted by a 600 system that features automatic focus and electronic flash, with the batteries incorporated in the high-speed instant-color film pack. Besides Polaroid, Eastman Kodak and Fuji now manufacture instant print materials.

One fresh innovation in photographic technology is the use of standard color negative film in specially designed 35mm cameras to produce three-dimensional images in color that can be viewed in the hand without a special viewer. Another involves a camera and film system based on a disk (rather than a roll of film) that can be inserted in a camera the size of a cigarette box. Whether or not they are ultimately successful, both developments are geared to the mass photography market, where, it has been esti-

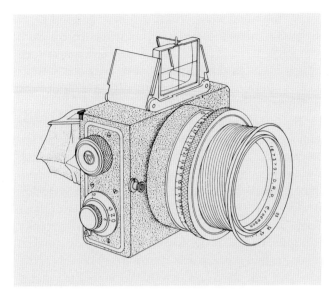

786. *Ermanox Camera*. The Ernemann Ermanox camera of 1924 carried its f/2 Ernostar lens in a helical focusing mount. A folding, optical frame viewfinder was fitted, and the focal plane shutter gave speeds from 1/20 to 1/1,000 second.

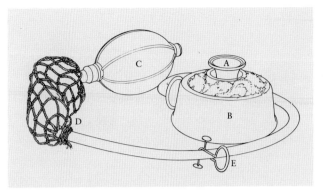

787. *Ceramic Magnesium Lamp*. A ceramic magnesium lamp, typical of the powder flash lamps made in the 1890s. A charge of magnesium powder was placed in the funnel (A), which was surrounded by a circular tray (B). When lit, the spirit-soaked cotton wool in this tray gave a circular flame. A rubber bulb (C) was squeezed to inflate a thin-walled rubber bag (D), connected to the lamp by a clamped (E) tube. When the clamp was released, the puff of air propelled the magnesium powder through the flame.

mated, amateur photographers have taken over 10 billion pictures a year since 1980.[1]

A development of great service to both amateur and professional photographers was that of electric flash illumination. Magnesium, in wire, ribbon, and powder form, had been ignited by several methods from the 1860s on *(pl. no. 787)*, but most uses became obsolete after the introduction in 1925 of the flashbulb, invented in Germany by Dr. Paul Vierkötter. By encasing the magnesium wire in glass, artificial illumination was made safer, smoke-free, and produced less contrast. Foil-filled lamps appeared in 1929; like the wire bulbs, they were set off by batteries *(pl. no. 788)* and eventually could be triggered by the exposure mechanism of the camera. After the second World War, flash synchronization became a standard built-in feature of virtually all cameras *(pl. no. 790)*; a modern mini-version is the flash cube. After 1950, the development of dry-cell battery-powered circuitry and transistors made possible even lighter units. High-speed electric flash, known since Talbot's 1852 experiments, with flash duration of about 1/100,000 of a second, required laboratory facilities and was mainly available for special projects such as those carried on by Ernst Mach in Czechoslovakia in 1887 and Harold Edgerton in the United States starting in 1940. Heavy-duty electric flash systems for studio use were introduced by Kodak in the 1940s and were followed by gradually lighter and more portable electronic flash (stroboscopic) equipment, among which a unit designed in 1939 by Edward Rolke Farber, an American newscameraman, was probably the first.

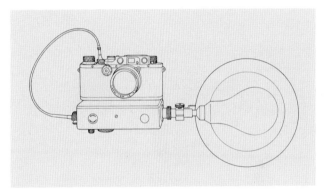

788. *Burvin Synchronizer*. The Burvin Synchronizer of 1934 was designed for miniature cameras, notably the Leica. It was fitted to the underside of the camera and was coupled to the shutter by means of a cable release. The synchronizer could be precisely adjusted so that the flash was fired when the shutter was fully open.

Materials and Processes

According to film manufacturers, black and white film speeds have increased 23 million times since the beginning of photography.[2] Both black and white and color film differ in sensitivity according to the size of the silver halide crystals suspended in the gelatin emulsion. Black and white and color films are rated from slow (ASA/ISO 25) to fast (ASA/ISO 1000 or more), with the larger crystals in the faster film more sensitive to light, thereby enabling faster shutter speeds to be used in making the exposure. However, the larger crystals in high-speed film ordinarily result

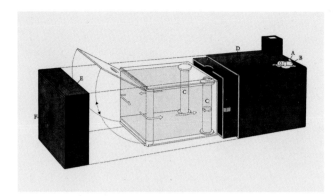

789. *Eastman's Brownie Camera*. The original Brownie camera of 1900 had the shutter release (A) and the film winding key (B) on the top; the film rolls (C) were placed vertically. To help in aiming the camera, V-lines (D) were marked on it. The first Brownie models had a push-on back (E) with a red window (F), but an improved back, hinged at the bottom and with a sliding catch at the top, was soon introduced.

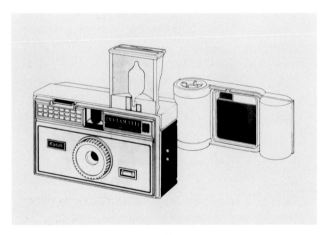

790. *Kodak Instamatic Camera*. The Kodak Instamatic cameras were introduced in 1963. They took a drop-in cartridge that greatly simplified the loading of the cameras. Like most of the Instamatic cameras, the model 100 had a built-in, pop-up flash gun, released by a button.

in grainier and less tonally defined images (especially in enlargement). In general, color film has less latitude for inaccurate exposure than black and white film, but in recent years both black and white and color positive and negative films have been vastly improved in terms of speed and resolution. For use in scientific documentation and for penetrating haze conditions, infrared film, sensitive to light that is not visible to the human eye, is being used. Recently both Agfa and Ilford have marketed a film of extremely wide latitude in which the final monochromatic (black and white) image is formed by dye-couplers in addition to silver crystals.

For black and white prints, two basic kinds of paper are available: resin-coated (RC) and fiber-based. Both have a gelatin coating over the light-sensitive emulsion on a paper base, but the RC papers carry extra plastic layers on the bottom and beneath the emulsion layer. Both come in different grades of contrast.

The most significant development in the 20th century with regard to materials and processing has been the improvement of color. The color materials that appeared following the invention of Autochrome plates (Dufay Dioptichrome, Fenske's Aurora, Szezepanik-Hollborn Veracolor, Whitfield's Paget Colour Plates, Dawson's Leto Colour Plates, and Agfacolor) were all based on additive color principles. By 1925, as the demand for color grew stronger, efforts to find a practicable system based on subtractive principles redoubled and were further stimulated during the Great Depression by competition for limited markets.

The possibility of adapting subtractive color theory to the production of color film was suggested early in the century by Karl Schinzel of Austria and Rudolph Fischer of Germany. They envisaged the formation of a triple-layer emulsion containing dye-couplers in primary colors that would block out their complements, which was realized some 25 years later in Kodachrome. Invented by American amateur chemists and musicians Leopold Godowsky and Leopold Mannes in collaboration with Kodak Research Laboratory personnel, it became the first tripak film to be released first in 1935 as movie film and as sheet film in 1938, and as a negative Kodacolor roll film in 1941. The German Agfa Company, which introduced a color plate that rivaled Autochrome in 1916 and had been experimenting with tripak systems based on subtractive theory, in 1936 announced Agfacolor Neu, a three-layer film in which the color couplers were incorporated in the layers and released during development; this enabled the film to be processed in individual darkrooms. In 1942, the American firm Ansco announced an almost identical product.

Initially, Kodak color products were returned to the company for processing and were received back by customers in the form of positive transparencies rather than color prints. In consequence, the use of 35mm color film gave rise to renewed interest among amateurs in slides and slide projection during the late 1940s. Color positive films (transparencies) still are preferred by many professionals because they have a finer grain and are therefore sharper than corresponding color negative film, with the result that the projection of images is no longer just an amateur pastime but has become of interest again to educational institutions and corporations who have discovered in color slides and sophisticated multiple imaging systems successful teaching and sales tools.

Starting with Ducos du Hauron, color prints were made by using a variant of the carbon process that is now called assembly printing. This procedure was transformed into Ozobrome, invented in 1905 by Thomas Manley in England, from which Carbro (or Trichrome Carbro) evolved during the early 1920s and remained popular for some ten years. The Eastman Wash-Off Relief process, introduced in 1935, was similar to the Carbro process except that greater control was possible to insure that there were fewer variations from print to print. In 1934, Eastman introduced a substitute—the Kodak Dye-Transfer (or imbibition) system—whereby three separation negatives were used to produce three gelatin relief images that were dyed yellow, magenta, and cyan; eventually the three images were made directly from a tripak negative film by exposing it through filters. For the print, the three dyed reliefs were transferred in exact register to gelatin-coated paper.

At present, negative and positive color images are created by one of two methods: the chromogenic system in which dyes are created during the processing, and the dye-destruction (or dye-bleach) system in which a complete set of dyes is present at the start and the ones not needed to form the image are subsequently removed by bleaching. The latter method, which evolved from experiments undertaken in Hungary in 1930 by Bela Gaspar, is basic to Cibachrome. Within the chromogenic system, two methods are used: the dye-injection system mentioned above in connection with Kodachrome, and the dye-incorporated method. In the last-named procedure, used in the manufacture of nearly all well-known color films and color printing papers, the chemicals that will form the dyes are included in each layer of the emulsion and are activated during the processing.

Holography

Holography is an entirely new idea in image-making that has developed within the last 35 or so years. A hologram (from the Greek *holos*—whole—and *gramma*—message) is a three-dimensional image that appears on a film or glass that has been coated with photographic emulsion and exposed to laser light reflected from an object. In order to produce a hologram, the laser beam must be split into two parts by a beam splitter (partial mirror). A full mirror directs one beam to the object while the other, known as the reference beam, is directed by another mirror to the emulsion surface on which the image will be recorded. In the area where the light from the reference beam and the light from the object meet, they expose a pattern of lines (interference fringes) that will form the image after the emulsion is photographically processed. The hologram becomes visible when it is illuminated from

the same direction as the original reference beam. There are two main kinds of holograms, called transmission and reflection. Transmission holograms are illuminated from either laser or white light sources located behind or below the emulsion surface, whereas reflection holograms become visible when white light bounces off the surface of the emulsion.

Holography is based on experiments in the reconstruction of optical phenomena conducted by Hungarian scientist Dennis Gabor in 1947 (for which he was awarded a Nobel Prize in 1971), and on the discovery in 1960 of a new source of light known as laser. In 1962, Emmett Leith and Juris Upatnieks in the United States and Yuri Denisyuk in the Soviet Union independently invented techniques for recording on photographic plates the image of objects illuminated by laser beams. Recent additions to the perfecting of holographic techniques have included methods of making full color holograms discovered by Stephen Benton and Professor Denisyuk. Holograms have found a practical use in operations requiring scanning and recognition, in advertising display, in scientific and optical measurements, and in the creation of three-dimensional models of industrial objects, buildings, and human cells. They are being proposed for efficient data storage and for the creation of three-dimensional movies and television images. Holograms have been embraced by artists in the United States, the Soviet Union, Japan, England, and Australia as a means of personal artistic expression.

Conservation

As greater numbers of serious photographers began to work in color during the 1970s, questions regarding the stability of the images became more pressing. Central to the problem is the fact that yellow, magenta, and cyan dyes change and fade at differing rates when exposed to regular light and to ultraviolet radiation. Also, color materials are affected to an even greater degree than monochromatic silver crystals by humidity, heat, and chemicals in the surrounding environment. With both color and black and white images being collected by individuals and museums, knowledge about the conservation of photographic materials has prompted efforts on the part of manufacturers to produce more stable products. Specialists in conservation have devised ways to print, store, and display all photographs to minimize deterioration. At the same time, interest in restoring works that already have deteriorated has grown. These developments reflect the fact that the photograph has become an artistic commodity with market value, but they also offer a promise that the images themselves will continue to exist no matter what their original purpose may have been.

New Ways
of Seeing:
Images in
Aid of Science

Beyond what the unaided human eye can see lies a universe of hidden forms
and processes; photography—alone and in alliance with sensing tools that
extend time and space—has made these visible. In concert with microscope
and telescope, the camera has magnified infinitesmal organisms and structures
and reduced the vastness of space. Affixed to satellites and helium balloons,
it has made visual documents of the earth's surface from one hundred miles up
and has taken pictures of the atmosphere. Attached to tiny probes, it has
entered and recorded events within the human body, as in the growth of a
fetus. Coupled with stroboscopic illumination (pioneered by Harold Edgerton
in the 1930s), the camera has frozen time segments of up to millionths
of a second. Portions of the invisible electromagnetic spectrum (X-rays,
infrared, ultraviolet, gamma, and sonic rays) have been used to penetrate solid
bodies in order to portray internal structures. Through electro- or Kirlian
photography (named after the Soviet scientists who were pioneers in
the field), the aura or corona of substances undergoing a high-voltage charge
can be seen.

Cameras, sensors, and computers are integral to a relatively new technology
called image processing. These instruments, which process pictorial
information for use in medical diagnostics, satellite surveillance, astronomy,
agriculture, and industry, make it possible to construct an enhanced version
of an original picture, or to transform pictorial information into numeric
data or graphic formats. Enhancement may be in terms of linear, tonal, and
coloristic values; in the case of the latter, the computer adds arbitrary colors to
the image (not natural to the object depicted) to take advantage of the fact
that the eye discriminates more readily between a large number of colors than
between tonal differences in the gray scale.

All the examples in this album of scientific photographs, whether straight
or processed, have been selected for their intrinsic visual interest and

because they suggest the range of techniques and uses in contemporary images of complex physical and chemical phenomena. They include straight photographs, several made with electron microscopes, and images that are achieved by a combination of cameras, scanning sensors, and digital computers. Among the latter are computerized tomography and color-enhanced X-rays used in medicine to reveal normal and abnormal cellular activity, and thermographs that make use of colors to portray in pictorial form heat losses in organic and inorganic bodies. In other examples of computer-enhanced images, color is used to denote the density of helium gas in flares erupting on the surface of the sun and to clarify the position and extent of mineral deposits in the terrestrial land mass of the earth.

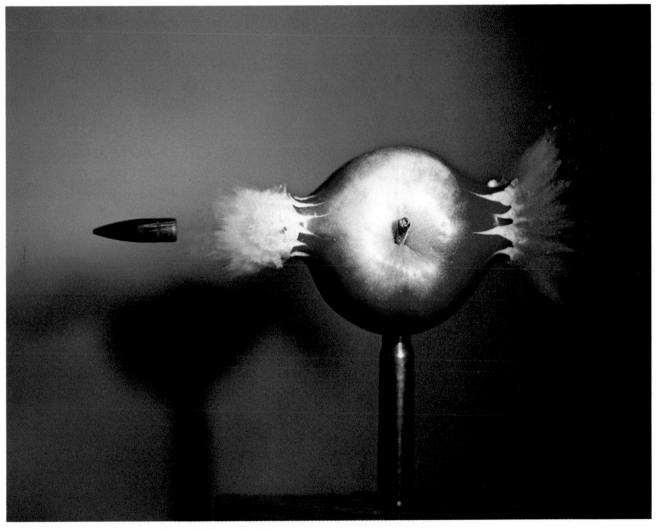

791. HAROLD EDGERTON. *An Apple Shot with a Bullet Traveling at 900 Meters Per Second*, 1964.
Stroboscopic photograph made with a microflash at an exposure of one-third of a micro-second.
Dye transfer (dye imbibition) print. Palm Press, Inc., Littleton, Mass. © Harold Edgerton.

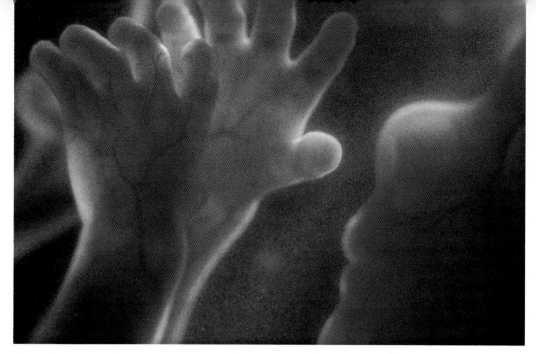

792. CLAUDE EDELMANN. *Human Fetus*, c. 1980. Hands developing near the fifth month.
© Claude Edelmann/Black Star.

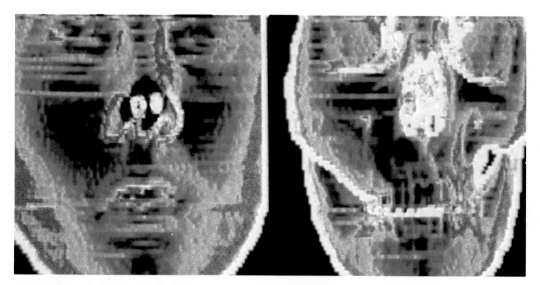

793. MICHAEL VANNIER, Mallinckrodt, Washington University Medical School, St. Louis, Mo.
Skull and Tissue, 1983. Color-enhanced image of skull and facial soft tissue, reassembled by computer to create 3-D models, used in plastic surgery applications. Courtesy Gould Inc. Imaging and Graphics Division, San Jose, Cal.

FACING PAGE ABOVE:

794. MANFRED KAGE. *Compound Eye of Fruit Fly*, c. 1980. Scanning Electron micrograph.
© Manfred Kage/Peter Arnold, Inc.

FACING PAGE BELOW:

795. NATIONAL AERONAUTICS and SPACE ADMINISTRATION (NASA), Ames Research Center, Moffett Field, Cal. *Arizona Silver Mine*, 1982. LANDSAT photograph pseudo-colored to show silver-bearing rocks in dark purple (upper right). The original image was made with a high-resolution film camera. Courtesy Gould Inc. Imaging and Graphics Division, San Jose, Cal.

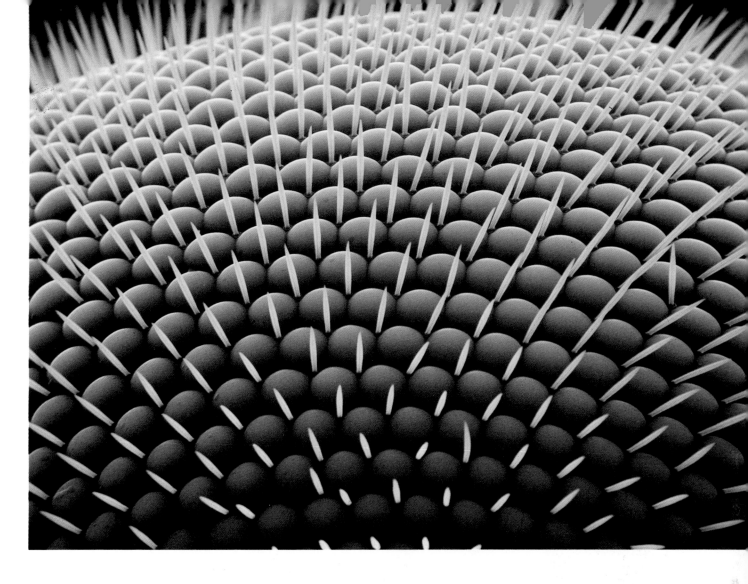
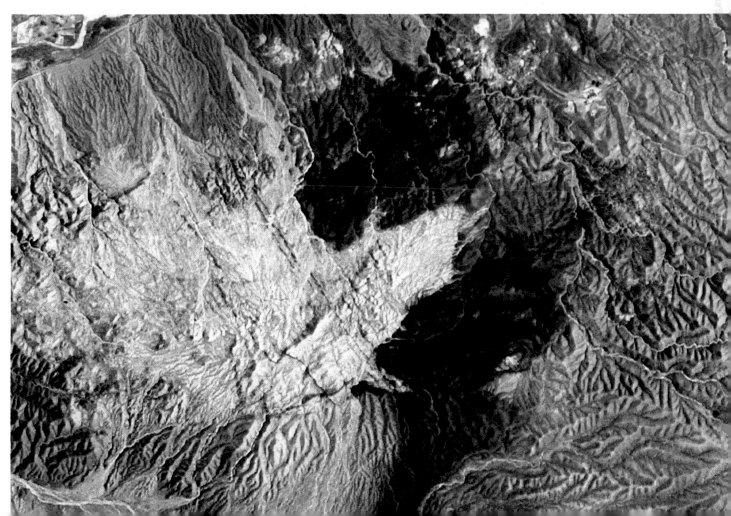

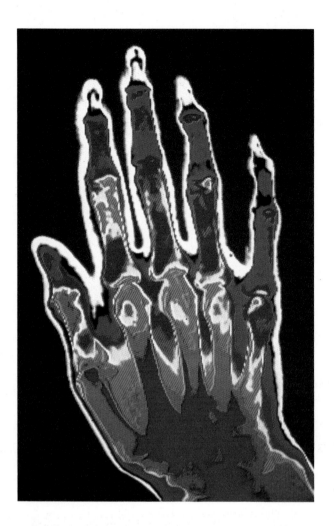

796. HOWARD SOCHUREK. *Hand*, 1981. Computer-enhanced color-code tomography (focused X-ray). Tomography highlights disfigured fingers, indicating that this hand is arthritic; specific colors connote different densities. © Howard Sochurek.

797. MANFRED KAGE. *Begonia Leaf*, c. 1975. Electrophotography (Kirlian). Pioneered by Semyon and Valentina Kirlian, Soviet scientists, electrophotography is only partially understood and is now undergoing serious examination as a possible diagnostic tool. To make a Kirlian photograph, an object is placed on a sheet of unexposed film, which receives a burst of electricity from a metal plate beneath it. The developed film reveals a corona. © Manfred Kage/Peter Arnold, Inc.

798. MARK COCO. *Meteor and Star Trails, Mt. Pinos, Cal.*, August, 1980. Astrophotograph made with 35mm Nikon EM camera with a 50mm lens at f/1.7, with 15 minute exposure. Original color (chromogenic development) transparency.

799. NATIONAL AERONAUTICS and SPACE ADMINISTRATION (NASA), Washington, D.C. *Erupting Volcano on Io*, 1979. Computerized color-enhanced image made by Voyager I, from a range of half-a-million kilometers, showing an eruption region on the horizon. This method of color analysis allows scientists to combine data from four pictures, taken in ultraviolet, blue, green, and orange light, to study the amount of gas and dust in the eruption.

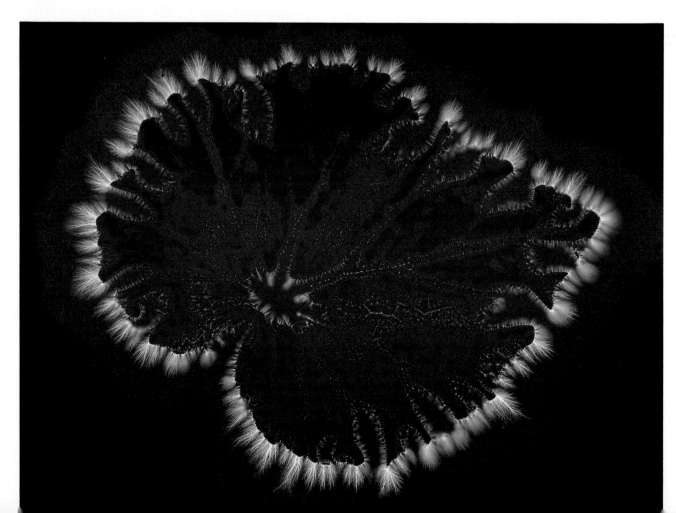

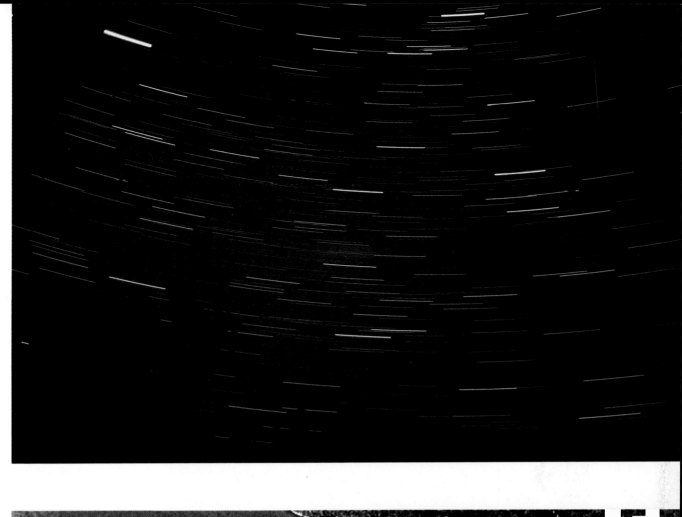

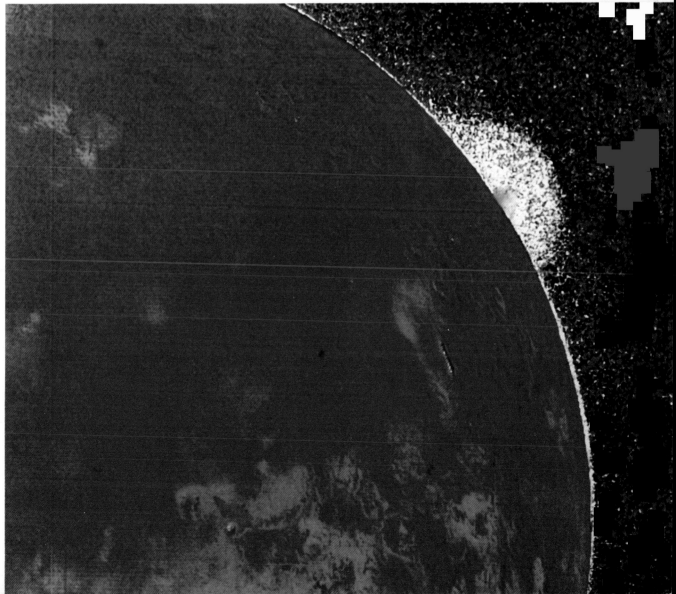

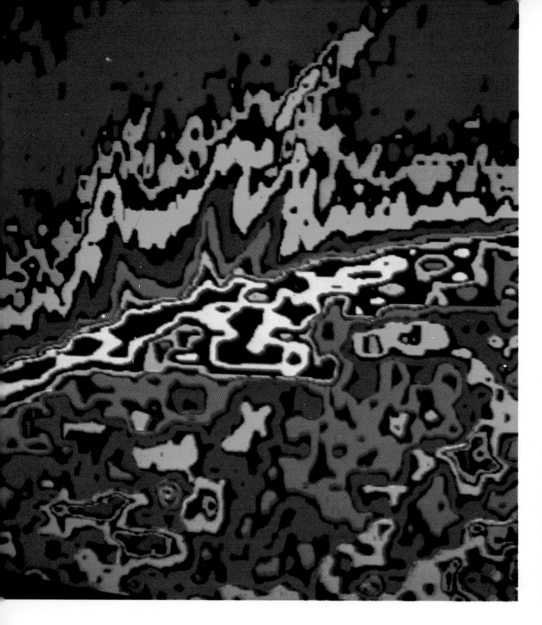

800. NATIONAL AERONAUTICS and
SPACE ADMINISTRATION (NASA),
Washington, D.C. *The Sun*, 1974.
Computerized color-enhanced image
made by solar telescope on Skylab, the
first full-scale manned astronomical
observatory in space. The original black-
and-white images were color enhanced to
facilitate interpretation of ultraviolet
solar data, highlighting subtle but
important brightness differences.

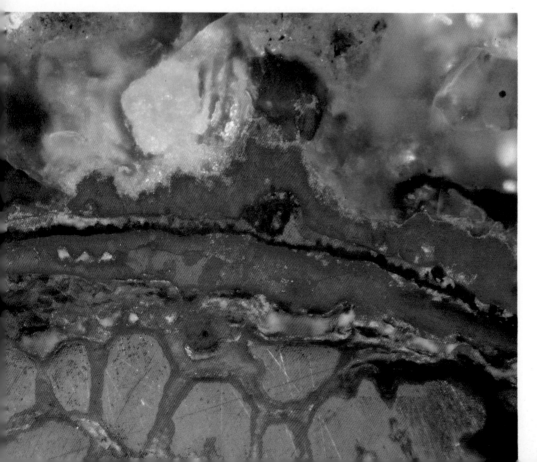

801. WILLIAM MARIN, JR., Brookhaven
National Laboratory, Upton, N.Y.
Ancient Bronze Specimen, 1975.
Photomicrograph of ancient bronze
specimen from Thailand showing
interface between metal and corrosion
layers, viewed with polarized illumination
at 400X. Originally photographed with
4 x 5 color negative (chromogenic
development) material.

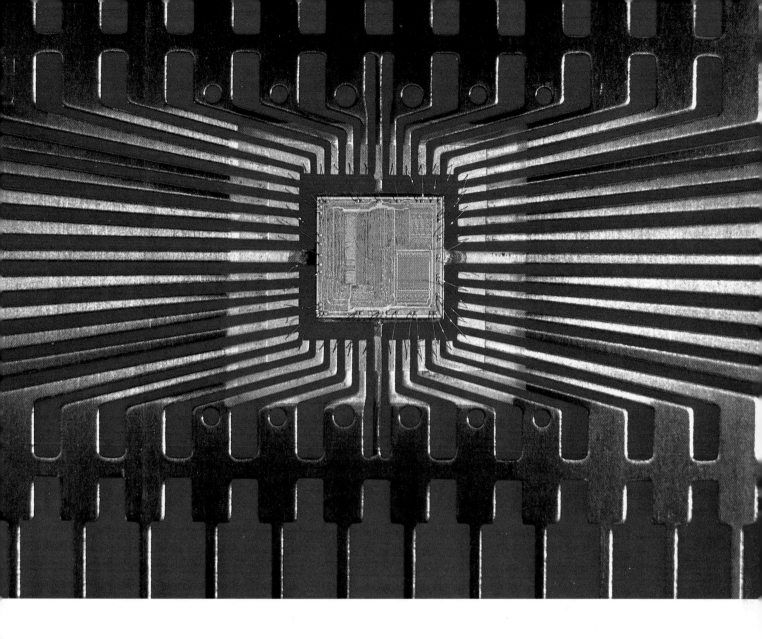

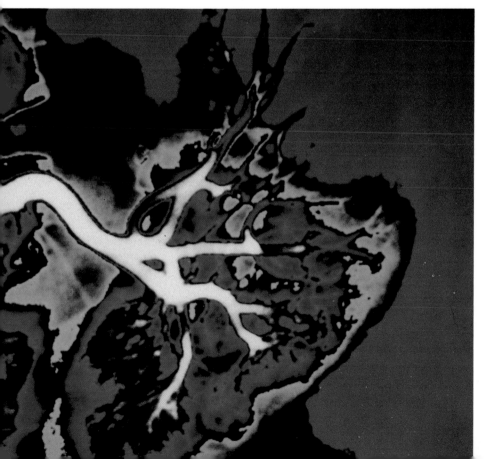

802. DAN McCoy. *Xilog Computer Circuit with Chip*, c. 1983. 35mm photograph made with 60mm macro lens. © Dan McCoy/Rainbow.

803. CURTIS FUKUDA. *Kidney*, 1983. Enhanced X-ray photograph, pseudo-colored to show circulation. Photographed from a display monitor (video screen). Courtesy Gould Inc. Imaging and Graphics Division, San Jose, Cal.

Notes

CHAPTER 1: THE EARLY YEARS

1. Unsigned article, *Journal of the Franklin Institute*, April 23, 1839, p. 263.

2. C. R. Leslie, *Memoirs of the Life of John Constable Composed Chiefly of His Letters* (1845), reprint edition, London, 1951, p. 323.

3. See Note 5, *A Short Technical History, Part I*.

4. An annuity of 6,000 francs for Daguerre and 4,000 for Isidore Niépce, with whom Daguerre had renegotiated the contract after the death of Isidore's father, was paid by the French government; see Helmut and Alison Gernsheim, *L. J. M. Daguerre: The History of the Diorama and the Daguerreotype*, reprint edition, New York, 1968, pp. 92-93 for text of the contract between the parties.

5. Josef Maria Eder, *History of Photography*, reprint of 3rd edition, New York, 1978, p. 246.

6. S. D. Humphrey, "On the Daguerreotype," *Humphrey's Journal*, 20, 10, February 15, 1859, p. 307.

7. Oliver Wendell Holmes, "The Stereoscope and the Stereograph," *Atlantic Monthly*, 8, June, 1859, p. 739; Holmes was himself an amateur photographer; see Carol Schloss, "Oliver Wendell Holmes as an amateur photographer," *History of Photography*, 5, 2, April, 1981, pp. 119-24.

8. This definition obviously is inadequate in view of the possibilities of producing direct positive prints, combination prints with both positive and negative images, one-step images, and one-of-a-kind light graphics without a camera. It might be restated as any process by which images are rendered by the action of light on a photosensitive surface.

9. Letter dated May 9, 1839, from John W. Herschel to William Henry Fox Talbot, The Science Museum, London, in which Herschel praises the fine detail of the daguerreotype.

10. See Weston J. Naef, "Hercules Florence, 'Inventor do Photographia,'" *Artforum*, February, 1976, p. 58; the information about Florence was first brought to light by Brazilians Alfred Santos Pressaco in 1965 and Boris Kossoy in 1973. Maedler's use of the word photography is mentioned in Erich Stenger, "The Word Photography," *British Journal of Photography*, 3777, LXXIX, September 23, 1932, pp. 578-79.

11. Talbot took out four patents on photographic processes—in 1841, 1843, 1849 (with Thomas Malone), and 1851.

12. H. J. P. Arnold, *William Henry Fox Talbot: Pioneer of Photography and Man of Science*, London, 1977, p. 211.

13. From an article in *The Economist*, July 26, 1851, p. 812, cited in Arnold, pp. 177, 341 n5.

14. *Atheneum*, March, 1845, cited in Arnold, p. 155.

15. Bayard received 600 francs to improve equipment and subsidize further experiments, with a request to defer publication of his process; see H. and A. Gernsheim, *L. J. M. Daguerre*, p. 88.

16. Talbot was involved in only one court case against an unfranchised user of the calotype process, but in 1854 he brought suits against James Henderson and Martin Laroche for the unlicensed use of sensitized collodion. The Laroche case came to trial first and was decided against him.

17. Holmes, "The Stereoscope and the Stereograph," p. 728.

18. See Edward W. Earle, ed., *Points of View: The Stereograph in America—A Cultural History*, Rochester, N.Y., 1979. While interest in stereograph photography and viewing was somewhat cyclical in the 19th century, it did not seriously decline until the improvement in magazine printing, which was made possible by the invention of the process halftone plate toward the end of the century.

19. H. and A. Gernsheim, *L. J. M. Daguerre*, pp. 192-94.

20. *The Literary Gazette*, February 5, 1841, cited in Gail Buckland, *Fox Talbot and The Invention of Photography*, Boston, 1980, p. 62.

CHAPTER 2: A PLENITUDE OF PORTRAITS

1. Charles Baudelaire, "The Modern Public and Photography," 1859; translated and reprinted in Alan Trachtenberg, ed., *Classic Essays on Photography*, New Haven, Conn., 1980, pp. 86-87.

2. Albert S. Southworth, "An Address to the National Photographic Association of the United States;" reprinted in the *Philadelphia Photographer*, VIII, October, 1871, p. 320.

3. Johann Kaspar Lavater, *Essays on Physiognomy* (1789), quoted in Elizabeth Anne McCauley, *Likenesses: Portrait Photography in Europe, 1850-1870*, Albuquerque, N.M., 1980, p. 3.

4. According to Helmut and Alison Gernsheim, *L. J. M. Daguerre: The History of the Diorama and the Daguerreotype*, reprint edition, New York, 1968, p. 116, up to 2,000 prints could be made from a physionotrace plate, but unless the copper plates were refaced and re-etched, this seems unlikely.

5. Baudelaire, "The Modern Public and Photography," in Trachtenberg, ed., *Classic Essays on Photography*, p. 87.

6. Antoine Claudet, "Progress and Present State of the Daguerreotype Art," *Journal of the Franklin Institute*, 10, Third Series, July, 1845, p. 45.

7. Stuart Bennett, "Jabez Hogg Daguerreotype," *History of Photography*, 1, 4, October, 1977, p. 318. The sitter is thought to be William Johnson, father of John Johnson, inventor with Wolcott of the mirror camera.

8. Unsigned article, *The Bath and Cheltenham Gazette*, April 5, 1842, p. 4. Daguerreotypes also were likened to "fried whiting glued to a silver plate" by Francis Wey, eminent French essayist and author of *"Theorie du Portrait,"* a series that appeared in the photographic journal *La Lumière*; see Part II, May, 1851, p. 511.

9. Fritz Kempe, *Daguerreotype im Deutschland: Vom Charme der frühen Fotografie*, Seebruck am Chiernsee, 1979, p. 26.

10. Branibor Debeljković, "Early Serbian Photography," *History of Photography*, 3, 3, July, 1979, p. 234.

11. Nathaniel Hawthorne, *The House of the Seven Gables*, paperback edition, New York, 1967, p. 153.

12. Unknown author, "Reporting by Photography," *Humphrey's Journal*, 1, 6, April 15, 1854, p. 15. Brady signed his name with a middle initial B although no name has come to light. For a discussion of the photographer's relationships with the political and commercial figures of the time, see Roy Meredith, *Mathew Brady's Portrait of an Era*, New York and London, 1982, pp. 30, 47. See also Josephine Cobb, "Mathew B. Brady's Photographic Gallery in Washington," *Records of the Columbia Historical Society of Washington, D.C.*, 1959, pp. 28-67.

13. Southworth, "An Address to the National Photographic Association," see Note 2.

14. Unknown author, "Daguerreotypes, Etc.," *Ballou's Pictorial Drawing-Room Companion*, IX, 8, August 25, 1855, p. 125.

15. N. G. Burgess, "The Value of Daguerreotype Likenesses," *Photographic and Fine Art Journal*, VIII, 1, January, 1855, p. 19.

16. Walt Whitman, quoted in Justin Kaplan, *Walt Whitman: A Life*, New York, 1980, p. 112.

17. Richard Rudisill, *Mirror Image: The Influence of the Daguerreotype on American Society*, Albuquerque, N.M., 1971, p. 238.

18. David Octavius Hill, quoted in *The Hill/Adamson Albums*, London, 1973, unpaged.

19. Hamilton L. Smith invented the process. The patent was taken over by William and Peter Neff, who called the product a melainotype, and by Victor M. Griswold, who called it a ferrotype; later it became known as a tintype. See Beaumont Newhall, *The History of Photography*, completely revised and enlarged edition, New York, 1982, p. 63.

20. Anthony Trollope, *Barchester Towers*, paperback edition, New York, 1963, p. 181.

21. Originally ascribed to Adolphe Braun; re-ascribed by Jan Coppens to Louis Pierson, who joined the firm of Ad. Braun et Cie. in 1878; see J. Coppens, "La Castiglione," *Foto*, 29, December, 1974, pp. 36-39; *"Mayer en Pierson portretfotografen onder het tweede keizerrijk,"* *Foto*, 30, February, 1975, pp. 26-27.

22. Quoted in Nigel Gosling, *Nadar*, New York, 1976, p. 37.

23. Philippe Burty, "Nadar's Portraits at the Exhibition of the French Society of Photography" (1859); translated and reprinted in Beaumont Newhall, *Essays and Images*, New York, 1980, p. 109.

24. This portrait is one of a series of stereographic portraits taken by Gardner sometime between early February and the second week in April, 1865; see James Mellon, *The Face of Lincoln*, New York, 1979, pp. 184-85, 201. Stefan Lorant, *Lincoln, Picture Story of His Life*, revised edition, New York, 1957, p. 258, dates it to April 10, 1865, as the last portrait made of Lincoln.

25. William Henry Shelton, "Artist Life in New York in the Days of Oliver Horn," *The Critic*, XLIII, 1903, quoted in Ben L. Bassham, *The Theatrical Photographs of Napoleon Sarony*, Kent, Ohio, 1978, p. 13.

26. Unknown author, "How the Camera Came to Japan," *The East*, XVI, 5/6, June, 1980, p. 32; see also John Dower, ed., *A Century of Japanese Photography*, New York, 1980, p. 3.

27. Judith Mara Gutman, *Through Indian Eyes: 19th and Early 20th Century Photography From India*, New York, 1982, pp. 15-16 ff; that native photographers photographed differently from Westerners is the thesis of this work.

28. Quoted in Brian Hill, *Julia Margaret Cameron: A Victorian Family Portrait*, London, 1973, p. 127.

29. Unknown author, "Report of the Exhibition Committee," *The Photographic Journal*, 162, October 16, 1865, p. 161.

30. Mrs. George Frederick Watts, quoted in Charles-Harvey Gibbs-Smith, "Mrs. Julia Margaret Cameron, Victorian Photographer," *One Hundred Years of Photographic History*, Van Deren Coke, ed., Albuquerque, N.M., 1975, p. 71.

31. Gosling, *Nadar*, p. 27.

CHAPTER 3: LANDSCAPE AND ARCHITECTURE

1. Marcus Aurelius Root, *The Camera and the Pencil*, New York, 1864, p. XVI.

2. Oliver Wendell Holmes, "The Stereoscope and the Stereograph," *Atlantic Monthly*, 8, June, 1859, pp. 747-48.

3. Quoted in André Jammes and Robert Sobieszek, *French Primitive Photography*, New York, 1970, unpaged.

4. Patrick Connor, *Savage Ruskin*, Detroit, Mich., 1979, p. 49.

5. Richard Rudisill, *Mirror Image: The Influence of the Daguerreotype on American Society*, Albuquerque, N.M., 1971, p. 12.

6. Rudisill, *Mirror Image*, pp. 142-49.

7. Unknown author, "The Application of the Talbotype," *The Art Union*, July, 1846, p. 195.

8. See André Jammes and Eugenia Parry Janis, *The Art of the French Calotype*, Princeton, N.J., 1983, pp. 55-56, for a discussion of this question.

9. Quoted in Robert Hershkowitz, *The British Photographer Abroad*, London, 1980, p. 82.

10. Francis Steegmuller, ed., *Flaubert in Egypt: A Sensibility on Tour*, Boston, 1972, pp. 23-24; Du Camp used Blanquart-Evrard's improved damp calotype process.

11. First commercially published album in France to be illustrated with photographs, issued by Gide and Baudry in 1852 with images from negatives made by Du Camp; see Isabelle Jammes, *Blanquart-Evrard et les origines de l'edition photographiques Français*, Geneva, 1981, p. 81. According to Nissan Perez, "Aimé Rochas, Daguerreotypist," *Image*, June, 1970, p. 11, three photographs in this album were by Aimé Rochas, a French daguerreo-

typist traveling in the Near East at the same time. The metal plates were rephotographed on albumen-coated glass from which prints were made.

12. James Borcoman, *The Painter as Photographer*, Vancouver, 1978, unpaged.

13. Unsigned article [Lady Elizabeth Eastlake], "Photography," *Quarterly Review*, CI, 1857, p. 462, see Note 1, Chapter 5.

14. Another version exists in oval format according to Mark Haworth-Booth, "Landscape in Amber: Camille Silvy's River Scene," *Mid-19th Century Photography: Images on Paper*, Edinburgh, 1979, pp. 6-7. Silvy's work was praised by an unknown author in *The Photographic Journal*, 78, February 5, 1859, p. 179.

15. For a discussion of Le Gray's seascapes, see Nils Walter Ramstedt, *The Photographs of Gustave Le Gray*, Ph.D. dissertation, University of California at Santa Barbara, 1977, pp. 147-76.

16. Quoted in Ian Jeffrey, "British Photography from Fox Talbot to E. O. Hoppé," *The Real Thing*, London, 1975, p. 16.

17. This point was expressed by Holmes in "The Stereoscope and the Stereograph," p. 747, as "Form is henceforth divorced from matter. In fact, matter as a visible object is of no great use any longer. . . ."

18. John Hannavy, *Roger Fenton of Crimble Hall,*, Boston, 1976, p. 180.

19. See Rolf S. Schutze, *Victorian Books with Original Photographs*, London, 1962. Julia Van Haaften, Curator of photographically illustrated books at The New York Public Library estimates the number of books illustrated with photographs issued between 1855 and 1915 as closer to 4,000 (Conversation with the author, May, 1984).

20. Gerda Peterich, "G.W.W.," *Image*, March, 1956, p. 22.

21. Robert Sobieszek, "Vedute Della Camera," *Image*, March, 1979, p. 1.

22. From *The (London) Times*, 1857, quoted in Helmut and Alison Gernsheim, *The History of Photography*, New York, 1969, p. 286.

23. Quoted in Bill Jay, *Victorian Cameraman: Francis Frith's Views of Rural England, 1850-1898*, Newton Abbot, England, 1973, p. 22.

24. First of eleven volumes and three sets of stereographs illustrated with Frith images; published by J. S. Virtue, London, 1858. Included among other Frith publications is *The Holy Bible: Containing the Old and New Testaments . . . Illustrated with Photographs by Frith*, Glasgow, 1862/63.

25. Alexander Hunter, *Madras Exhibition of Raw Products and Manufactures of South India*, quoted in G. Thomas, "Linnaeus Tripe in Madras Presidency," *History of Photography*, 5, 3, October, 1981, p. 330.

26. For example, Walter Woodbury, "Photography in Java," *The Photographic News*, 129, February 22, 1861, notes the "twenty-seven coolies" who carried apparatus and provisions. Adolphe Braun required the services of 15 porters to make five exposures when he ascended the Stralhorn in the Alps; see William Culp Darrah, *A History of Stereographs in America and Their Collection*, Gettysburg, Pa., 1964, p. 56.

27. Clark Worswick and Ainslee Embree, *The Last Empire: Photography in British India, 1855-1911*, Millerton, N.Y., 1964, p. 56.

28. John Thomson, *The Straits of Malacca, Indo-China & China*, New York, 1875, pp. 188-89.

29. See Keith F. Davis, *Désiré Charnay: Expeditionary Photographer*, Albuquerque, N.M., 1981, pp. 104-107, for mention of other photographers who documented archaeological sites in Central America.

30. Diary entry, September 14, 1872; reprinted in Don D. Fowler, ed., *Photographed All The Best Scenery: Jack Hiller's Diary of the Powell Expedition, 1871-1875*, Salt Lake City, Ut., 1972, p. 143.

31. William Goetzmann, *Exploration and Empire: The Explorer and the Scientist in the Winning of the American West*, New York, p. 479, notes that "throughout the seventies the various surveys vied with one another in these lavish photographic productions for propaganda purposes."

32. Richard J. Huyda, *H. L. Hime, Photographer, 1858: Camera in the Interior*, Toronto, 1975, pp. 19-20.

33. Samuel Bourne, "A Photographic Journey Through the Higher Himalayas," *British Journal of Photography*, XVII, 515, March 18, 1870, pp. 28-29.

34. This was a judgment about Frith's work. See unknown author, "Photographic Contributions to Knowledge," *British Journal of Photography*, VII, 111, February 1, 1860, p. 32.

35. Weston J. Naef and James N. Wood, *Era of Exploration: The Rise of Landscape Photography in the American West, 1860-1885*, Buffalo and New York, 1975, pp. 129-30.

CHAPTER 4: OBJECTS AND EVENTS

1. Oliver Wendell Holmes, "Doings of the Sunbeam," *Atlantic Monthly*, 12, July, 1863, p. 11.

2. Oliver Wendell Holmes, "The Stereoscope and the Stereograph," *Atlantic Monthly*, 8, June, 1859, p. 744.

3. William M. Ivins, Jr., *Prints and Visual Communication*, Cambridge, Mass., 1953, p. 94.

4. Four volumes with 155 photographic prints issued in 1852 in an edition of 140; see Nancy B. Keller, "Illustrating the 'Reports by the Juries' of the Great Exhibition of 1851: Talbot, Henneman and Their Failed Commission," *History of Photography*, 6, 3, July, 1982, pp. 257-72.

5. John Szarkowski, *Looking at Photographs*, New York, 1973, p. 18.

6. F. Jack Hurley, ed., *Industry and the Photographic Image*, New York, 1980, p. 3.

7. John Thomson, *Illustrations of China and Its People*, London, 1873; reprint edition, New York, 1982, unpaged.

8. For a discussion of Curtis's attitude toward his subject, see Christopher M. Lyman, *The Vanishing Race and Other Illusions: Photographs of Indians by Edward S. Curtis*, New York, 1982, pp. 17-23.

9. Unsigned article, "On the Application of Photography to Printing," *Harper's New Monthly Magazine*, LXXVI, 13, September, 1856, p. 433.

10. Alison Gernsheim, "Medical Photography in the Nineteenth Century," Part I, *Medical and Biological Illustration*, XI, 2, April, 1961, p. 87; Part II appeared in July, 1961, pp. 147-55.

11. Alex J. Macfarlan, "On the Application of Photography to the Delineation of Disease with remarks on Stereo-micro-photography," *The Photographic Journal*, 116, December 16, 1861, pp. 326-29.

12. For a full discussion, see George S. Layne, "Kirkbride-Langenheim Collection: Early Use of Photography in Psychiatric Treatment in Philadelphia," *The Pennsylvania Magazine of History and Biography*, CV, 2, April, 1981, pp. 182-202.

13. Others who photographed during the Crimean War were Carol (Charles) Popp de Szathmari, photographer to the Rumanian court, and French Army Colonel Jean Charles Langlois. See Constantin Savulescu, "First Photographic War Reportage," *Image*, March, 1973, pp. 13-16.

14. Helmut and Alison Gernsheim, *Roger Fenton, Photographer of the Crimean War*, 1954; reprint edition, New York, 1973, p. 22, indicates that the entire collection consisted of 360 photographs. Weston J. Naef, "From Illusion to Truth and Back Again," in Weston J. Naef and Lucien Goldschmidt, *The Truthful Lens: A Survey of the Photographically Illustrated Book, 1844-1914*, New York, 1980, p. 27, notes that 660 negatives were made by Fenton.

15. Roger Fenton to William Agnew, May 18 and May 20, 1855; reprinted in H. and A. Gernsheim, *Roger Fenton*, p. 75.

16. Roger Fenton to William Agnew, April 19, 1855; reprinted in H. and A. Gernsheim, *Roger Fenton*, p. 62.

17. Unknown author, "Photographs from Sebastopol," *Art Journal*, October 1, 1855, p. 285.

18. Jorge Lewinski, *The Camera at War*, New York, 1978, p. 43.

19. Donald E. English, *Political Uses of Photography in the Third French Republic, 1871-1914*, Ann Arbor, Mich., 1981, pp. 33-46.

20. William J. Hoppin, *U.S. Army and Navy Journal* (1863-64), p. 350, quoted in *The Civil War: A Centennial Exhibition of Eyewitness Drawings*, Washington, D.C., 1961, p. 22. The viewpoint that Civil War photographs lacked "the beauty of finish and fidelity which distinguishes the better European artists" was expressed by the unknown author of "American Photographs," *The Photographic Times*, I, 22, September 15, 1862, pp. 184-85.

21. Joel Snyder and Doug Manson, *The Documentary Photograph as a Work of Art: American Photographs, 1860-1876*, Chicago, 1976, p. 22.

22. According to Philip Kunhardt, Jr., "Images of which history was made bore the Mathew Brady label," *Smithsonian Magazine*, 8, 4, July, 1977, p. 33, Gardner claimed that the idea for a photographic documentation of the Civil War originated with him.

23. Alexander Gardner, "A Harvest of Death," *Gardner's Photographic Sketchbook of the Civil War*, reprint edition, New York, 1959, pl. no. 36.

24. Unknown author, "Photographic Views of Sherman's Campaign by George N. Barnard," *Harper's Weekly*, X, 519, December 8, 1866, p. 771.

25. See Note 24, Chapter 2.

26. Linda Nochlin, *Realism*, Middlesex, Hammondsworth, England, 1971, p. 31.

27. For a discussion of Fenton's attitude toward this development, see John Hannavy, *Roger Fenton of Crimble Hall*, Boston, 1976, pp. 95-98.

TECHNICAL HISTORY: PART I

1. See Arthur K. Wheelock, Jr., "Constantijn Huygens and Early Attitudes Towards the Camera Obscura," *History of Photography*, I, 2, April, 1977, pp. 93-103; also Kathleen Kissick, "Count Algarotti on the Camera Obscura," *History of Photography*, 3, 3, July, 1979, pp. 193-94.

2. Actinic rays are those capable of the radiant energy needed to produce chemical changes, as in photography.

3. John A. Hammond, *The Camera Obscura: A Chronicle*, Bristol, 1981, pp. 58-60.

4. "An Account of a Method of Copying Paintings on Glass and Making Profiles by the Agency of Light upon Silver Nitrate Invented by T. Wedgwood with Observations by H. Davy," *Journal of the Royal Institute*, London, I, 1802.

5. According to Pierre G. Harmant, "Paleophotographic Studies: Was Photography Born in the 18th Century?" *History of Photography*, 4, 1, January, 1980, pp. 39-45, the Niépce brothers may have experimented with an image-making process as early as 1798.

6. Gail Buckland, *Fox Talbot and the Invention of Photography*, Boston, 1980, p. 62.

7. See Chapter 1, Note 10; Naef states that Florence first used the term photography in 1832.

8. See Chapter 1, Note 5.

9. Guncotton was discovered in 1846 by Swiss chemist C. F. Schonbein; in the following year a method of dissolving the substance in alcohol was discovered. Called collodion, its initial use was as a medical dressing for wounds.

10. Fred Beyrich, "Concerning the Use of Albumenized Paper," *Humphrey's Journal*, December 1, 1864, p. 236.

11. Unknown author, "The Solar Camera," *The Photographic News*, July 29, 1859, p. 244.

CHAPTER 5: PHOTOGRAPHY AND ART

1. Unsigned article [Lady Elizabeth Eastlake], "Photography," *Quarterly Review*, April, 1857, p. 461. Elizabeth Rigby was the most frequent female sitter for David Octavius Hill and Robert Adamson, appearing in 16 portraits and three group scenes. In 1849, she married Charles Eastlake, who was knighted in 1850 and became director of the Royal Academy in 1855. Lady Eastlake published art criticism and travel journals.

2. Unknown author, "Photography and Chromolithography: Their Influence on Art and Culture," *The Philadelphia Photographer*, 5, 52, April, 1868, p. 115.

3. François Arago, *Comptes Rendus des Scéances de l'Academie des Sciences*, IX, August 19, 1839, p. 260; see also Helmut and Alison Gernsheim, *The History of Photography from the Camera Obscura to the Beginning of the Modern Era*, New York, 1969, p. 70; Gisèle Freund, *Photography and Society*, Boston, 1980, p. 26.

4. William Hauptman, "Ingres and Photographic Vision," *History of Photography*, 1, 2, April, 1977, pp. 117-28; Aaron Scharf, *Art and Photography*, Baltimore, 1969, p. 27.

5. Ernest Lacan, "*Esquisses Photographiques—La Physiologie du Photographe*," *La Lumière* (1852); reprinted in André Jammes, "*Histoire*," *Terre d'Images*, 2, 1964, p. 231; see also Aaron Sheon, "French Art and Science in the Mid-Nineteenth Century: Some Points of Contact," *Art Quarterly*, Winter, 1971, p. 434.

6. Francis Wey, "*De l'influence de l'Héliographie sur les Beaux Arts*," *La Lumière* (1851); reprinted in Heinz Buddemeier, *Panorama, Diorama, Photographie*, Munich, 1970, p. 262.

7. Charles Baudelaire, "*Le Public Moderne et la Photographie*" (1859); reprinted in Alan Trachtenberg, ed., *Classic Essays on Photography*, New Haven, Conn., 1980, p. 88.

8. Quoted in François Boucher, "Introduction," A. d'Eugny and R. Coursaget, *Au temps de Baudelaire, Guys et Nadar*, Paris, 1945, p. 12.

9. Eugène Delacroix, journal entry, May 21, 1853, *The Journal of Eugène Delacroix*, translated from the French by Walter Pach, New York, 1948, p. 314. In 1865, when Philippe Burty, critic for the *Gazette des Beaux Arts*, purchased an album of 32 photographs by Eugène Durieu from the Delacroix estate sale, he noted: "He often used them as reference material"; see Scharf, *Art and Photography*, pp. 89-94, 267-68.

10. Robert Hunt, *A Popular Treatise on Photography*, 1841; facsimile edition, Athens, Ohio, 1973, p. 92.

11. Philip Gilbert Hamerton, "The Relationship between Photography and Painting," *Thoughts About Art*, Boston, 1874, p. 52; this essay was written in 1860.

12. Ruskin's changing viewpoint about photography is discussed in R. N. Watson, "Art Photography and John Ruskin," *British Journal of Photography*, XCI, 1944, Part I, March 10, pp. 82-83; Part II, March 24, pp. 100-101; Part III, April 7, pp. 118-19.

13. Scharf, *Art and Photography*, p. 79.

14. Unknown author, "Photography in its relation to the Fine Arts," *The Photographic Journal*, 117, January 15, 1862, p. 359.

15. Louis Figuier, *La Photographie au Salon de 1859*, Paris, 1860, p. 14.

16. The process involves drawing with a sharp tool on a glass plate that has been coated with either fogged collodion or etching ground and then exposing the plate against a sheet of sensitized paper to sunlight. A less common technique, used by Corot, involves painting in various degrees of opacity on the glass plate before exposing it against the sensitized paper.

17. See Elizabeth Glassman, "Cliché-verre in the 19th Century," *Cliché-verre: Hand-drawn, Light-printed*, Detroit, 1980, p. 30.

18. G. Sadoul, "*Peinture et Photographie*," *Arts de France*, 19/20, 1948, pp. 5-23; Van Deren Coke, *The Painter and the Photograph*, Albuquerque, 1964; Scharf, *Art and Photography*. For a different interpretation, see Kirk Varnedoe, "The Artifice of Candor: Impressionism and Photography Reconsidered," *Art in America*, January, 1980, pp. 66-78, and "The Ideology of Time: Degas and Photography," *Art in America*, Summer, 1980, pp. 96-110.

19. In the mid-19th century, articles on photographic copyright laws began to appear in the British press; toward the end of the 1860s a Fine Art Copyright Bill, relating to photography, was introduced in Parliament. Painters and graphic artists have continued to use photographs without acknowledging their authorship despite suits filed by photographers to protect their work. See Marianne Goodwin, "Artists Pressure Agencies to Heed Their Rights," *Adweek*, April 4, 1983, pp. 28, 30, for a recent discussion.

20. Unknown author, "Review of The Sunbeam," *Photographic Notes*, 11, November 15, 1856, p. 83.

21. See Edgar Yoxall Jones, *Father of Art Photography: O. G. Rejlander, 1813-1875*, Greenwich, Conn., 1973, p. 74. Nigel Gosling, *Nadar*, New York, 1976, p. 68, suggests that an 1855 Nadar nude study of Christine Roux may have inspired Ingres in his painting *La Source*; however, that work was begun in 1820 and finished in 1856.

22. Gordon Hendricks, *The Photographs of Thomas Eakins*, New York, 1972, p. 6, states that these photographs "are not connected in any direct way with Eakins's plans for a painting," but details of landscape and figures accord with the camera images. Despite the painter's discrete handling, Edward Horner Coates, who had commissioned the work, exchanged it for a painting without nudity.

23. Quoted in *After Daguerre: Masterworks of French Photography (1848-1900) from the Bibliothèque Nationale*, New York, 1981, unpaged, pl. no. 6.

24. Alfred Frankenstein, *After The Hunt*, Berkeley and Los Angeles, 1969, p. 66, suggests that William Harnett, the American painter of *trompe l'oeil* still lifes, may have been directly inspired by these images.

25. Jones, *Father of Art Photography*, p. 18.

26. Unknown author, "Fifth Annual Photographic Exhibition," *Art Journal*, April 1, 1858, pp. 120-21.

27. O. G. Rejlander, "Photographic Criticism Addressed to An Art-Critic," *British Journal of Photography Almanac*, 1870, p. 148.

28. Henry Peach Robinson, "Paradoxes of Art, Science, and Photography," *The Photo-American*, III, 7, May, 1892, p. 179.

29. Henry Peach Robinson, "Some Remarks on Composition in Landscape Photography," *The Eye*, August 28, 1886, p. 5.

30. Antonio Errera, "*Storia e Statistica delle industrie venete*," 1870; quoted in Italo Zannier, *Venice, the Naya Collection*, Venice, 1981, p. 38.

31. Rev. Henry J. Morton, "The Sister Art," *The Philadelphia Photographer*, 3, 27, March, 1866, p. 71.

32. Quoted in Samuel I. Prime, *The Life of Samuel F. B. Morse*, New York, 1875, p. 404.

33. Elizabeth L. Cock, *The Influence of Photography on American Landscape Painting*, Ph.D. dissertation, New York University,

1967; see also Cock, "Frederick Church's Stereographic Vision," *Art in America*, September/October, 1973, pp. 71-77. Van Deren Coke, *The Painter and the Photographer*, p. 200, notes that a stereograph view of the Parthenon by D. Constantin, found in the painter's studio at Olana, New York, served as a guide for the 1871 painting, *The Parthenon*. See also David C. Huntington, *Landscapes of Frederick Edwin Church*, New York.

34. Grant B. Romer, "Gabriel Harrison, the Poetic Daguerrian," *Image*, September, 1979, p. 8.

35. Douglas G. Severson, "Oliver Wendell Holmes: Poet of Realism," *History of Photography*, 2, 3, July, 1978, p. 235.

36. Unknown author, "Composition Photographs," *The Philadelphia Photographer*, 4, 39, March, 1867, p. 79.

37. These characteristics of photographic expression were discussed throughout P. H. Emerson, *Naturalistic Photography*. See, for example, 3rd. edition, New York, 1899, pp. 30, 174-75.

38. *Naturalistic Photography*, pp. 31-32.

39. Naomi Rosenblum, "Adolphe Braun: a 19th-Century Career in Photography," *History of Photography*, 3, 4, October, 1979, pp. 365, 371 n36.

40. This problem is discussed by James Marston Fitch, "Physical and Metaphysical in Architectural Criticism," *Architectural Record*, July, 1982, pp. 114-19, in which the author states that while "a work of art is designed only to be seen . . . perceiving [buildings] visually is only one component of [a] complex experience."

41. Felix Roubaud, "*Revue scientifique*," *L'Illustration*, 619, January, 1855, quoted in James Borcormon, *Charles Nègre, 1820-1880*, Ottawa, 1976, p. 42.

42. Emerson's emphasis on "truthful pictures" was meant to contradict "the antiquated notions and book" of H. P. Robinson; see Nancy Newhall, *P. H. Emerson: The Fight for Photography as a Fine Art*, Millerton, N.Y., 1975, p. 67.

43. *Naturalistic Photography*, p. 58.

CHAPTER 6: NEW TECHNOLOGY

1. William M. Ivins, Jr., *Prints and Visual Communication*, Cambridge, Mass., 1953, p. 134.

2. Oliver Wendell Holmes, "Doings of the Sunbeam," *Atlantic Monthly*, 12, July, 1863, p. 12.

3. See Beaumont Newhall, *Airborne Camera: The World from the Air and Outer Space*, New York, 1969, p. 27.

4. Invented in 1855 by German chemist Robert Wilhelm Bunsen, who later worked with British scientist Henry Roscoe on the use of actinometers to measure sunlight.

5. From the *Literary Gazette*, June 28, 1851, p. 443, quoted in H. J. P. Arnold, *William Henry Fox Talbot, Pioneer of Photography and Man of Science*, London, 1977, p. 172.

6. Following his exoneration in the shooting death of his wife's lover, Muybridge traveled to Central America and did not resume his experiments with stop-motion photography until 1877, when he again was associated with Leland Stanford. In 1882, Stanford agreed to the publication of *The Horse in Motion* with J. D. Stillman rather than Muybridge as author, contending in a deposition following a suit by the photographer that the success of the venture was the result of following his (Stanford's) directives and suggestions.

7. The first discussion of the erroneous representation of the horse in art appeared in Emile Duhousset, *Le Cheval*, Paris, 1874; see Françoise Forster-Hahn, "Marey, Muybridge and Meissonier, The Study of Movement in Science and Art," *Eadweard Muybridge: The Stanford Years 1872-1882*, Palo Alto, Cal., 1972, p. 87.

8. Robert Bartlett Haas, *Muybridge, Man in Motion*, Berkeley, Los Angeles, London, 1976, p. 155.

9. In 1878, Muybridge copyrighted and published *The Horse in Motion*—a set of six views of horses running and trotting; these were sold in Europe and the United States for $2.50; see *Eadweard Muybridge: The Stanford Years*, p. 66.

10. *E. J. Marey: 1830/1904, La Photographie du Mouvement*, Paris, 1977, pp. 30-31.

11. Motion pictures are dependent on a phenomenon called the persistence of vision. The reconstitution of motion using instantaneous photographs was discussed in Etienne Jules Marey, *Animal Mechanism*, New York, 1874, p. 137. See also M. Langlois, "The Kinescope," *Photographic News*, XIII, 552, April 2, 1869, p. 165.

12. Quoted in Haas, *Muybridge: Man in Motion*, 120. See also William I. Homer and J. Talbot, "Eakins, Muybridge and the Motion Picture Process," *Art Quarterly*, 2, Summer, 1963, pp. 18-35.

13. Aaron Scharf, *Art and Photography*, Baltimore, 1969, pp. 255-68. See also Forster-Hahn, "Marey, Muybridge and Meissonier, The Study of Movement in Science and Art," *Eadweard Muybridge: The Stanford Years*, p. 103.

14. Unknown author (untitled article), *Photographic News*, 84, October, 1859, pp. 239-40; see also Gerda Peterich, "G.W.W.," *Image*, December, 1956, p. 21, in which George Washington Wilson is quoted as stating: "My aim is to secure some fleeting effect, which could only be caught if caught quickly."

15. Scharf, *Art and Photography*, p. 179. See also Kirk Varnedoe, "The Artifice of Candor: Impressionism and Photography Reconsidered," *Art in America*, January, 1980, pp. 66-78, and "The Ideology of Time: Degas and Photography," *Art in America*, Summer, 1980, pp. 96-110.

16. Brian Coe and Paul Gates, *The Snapshot Photograph*, London, 1977, p. 14. Regarding the number of snapshots, see unknown author, "From the British Side," *American Amateur Photographer*, IX, 12, December, 1897, p. 549, in which it is noted that 25,000 entries were received in a Kodak competition held in London and later sent to New York; see also *The Critic*, 29, January, 1898, p. 31.

17. Alfred Stieglitz, "The Hand Camera—Its Present Importance," *The American Annual of Photography*, 1897, p. 19.

18. John A. Tennant, "Street Photography," *The Photo-Miniature*, II, 14, May, 1900, p. 50.

19. Wm. Geo. Oppenheim, "The Law of Privacy," *American Amateur Photographer*, IX, 1, January, 1897, p. 5.

20. Roy Flukinger, Larry Schaaf, and Standish Meacham, *Paul Martin: Victorian Photographer*, Austin, Tex. and London, 1977, p. 47.

21. Paul Martin, *Victorian Snapshots*, New York, 1939, p. 18.

22. Sadakichi Hartmann, "A Plea for the Picturesqueness of New York," *Camera Notes*, 4, 2, October, 1900, pp. 91-97.

23. Stieglitz, "The Hand Camera," p. 22.

24. Arnold Genthe, *As I Remember*, New York, 1936, p. 32.

25. See, for instance, John Szarkowski, ed., *E. J. Bellocq: Storyville Portraits: Photographs from the New Orleans Red-Light District, Circa 1912*, New York, 1970.

26. Until after the first World War, not many women were involved in the major commercial enterprises or camera associations in Europe.

27. H. C. Price, *How to Make Pictures: Easy Lessons for Amateur Photographers*, New York, 1882.

28. Georges Herscher, "Conversations with J. H. Lartigue," *The Autochromes of J. H. Lartigue*, New York, 1980, unpaged.

29. R. W. Buss, "On the Uses of Photography to Artists," *Journal of the Photographic Society*, June 21, 1853, p. 75.

30. John Szarkowski and Maria Morris Hambourg, *The Work of Atget* in four volumes: Vol. I. *Old France*, New York, 1981; Vol. II. *The Art of Old Paris*, New York, 1982; Vol. III. *The Ancien Regime*, 1984; and Vol. IV. *Modern Times* (to be published).

CHAPTER 7: ART PHOTOGRAPHY

1. William Howe Downes, "Massachusetts Photographer's Work," *Photo Era*, 4, 3, March, 1900, p. 69.

2. Antony Guest, *Art and The Camera*, London, 1907, p. 25.

3. Alfred Stieglitz, "Pictorial Photography," *Scribner's Magazine*, 26, 5, November, 1899, p. 528; the same phrase was used much earlier, see "Correspondence," *Photographic Notes*, IX, December 1, 1864, p. 69.

4. Hector E. Murchison, "The Photography of the Future," *British Journal of Photography*, XLII, 1860, December 27, 1895, p. 823.

5. Andrew Pringle, "The Naissance of Art in Photography," *The Studio*, 1, 3, June, 1893; reprinted in Peter Bunnell, ed., *A Photographic Vision: Pictorial Photography 1889-1923*, Salt Lake City, Ut., 1980, p. 21.

6. Joseph Pennell, "Is Photography Among the Fine Arts?", *The Contemporary Review*, 72, December, 1897; reprinted in Bunnell, *A Photographic Vision*, p. 51.

7. Today, dichromate is the preferred term for this chemical compound containing two chromium atoms per anion (negatively charged ion).

8. Samuel Morozov, "Early Photography in Eastern Europe—Russia," *History of Photography*, 1, 4, October, 1977, p. 345.

9. J. Craig Annan, "Photography as a Means of Artistic Expression," *Photographic Journal*, 46, 1899, p. 319.

10. Stieglitz's choice of subject was influenced by where he found himself; between 1890 and 1907, on trips to Europe he photographed rural peasantry; while in New York City during the same years he favored street genre scenes. In both cases he saw the particular scene as symbolic; see Ian Jeffrey, *Photography: A Concise History*, New York and Toronto, 1981, p. 101.

11. John LaFarge, *Higher Life in Art*, New York, 1908; quoted in Peter Bermingham, *American Art in the Barbizon Mood*, Washington, D.C., 1975, p. 96.

12. Gleeson White, "The Nude in Photography," *The Photographic Times*, XXIX, 5, May, 1897, p. 210.

13. White, "The Nude in Photography," p. 209. For a discussion of changing attitudes toward photographing the nude, see Robert Sobieszek, "Addressing The Erotic: Reflections on the Nude Photograph," and Ben Maddow, "Nude in a Social Landscape," Constance Sullivan, ed., *Nude Photographs 1850-1980*, New York, 1980, pp. 167-79, 181-96.

14. J. M. B. W., "A Note on Some Open-air Nude Studies," *The Amateur Photographer and Photographic News*, July 5, 1910, pp. 20-21.

15. Unknown author, "The Nude in Photography, with some studies taken in the open air," *The Studio*, 1, 1898, p. 108.

16. Marmaduke Humphrey, "Triumph in Amateur Photography," *Godey's Magazine*, January, 1898; quoted in Estelle Jussim, *Slave to Beauty: The Eccentric Life and Career of F. Holland Day*, Boston, 1981, p. 119.

17. Charles H. Caffin, "Philadelphia Photographic Salon," *Harper's Weekly*, November 5, 1898, p. 1118.

18. J. J. Vezey, Letter to the editors, *British Journal of Photography*, November 9, 1900; quoted in Jussim, *Slave to Beauty*, p. 135.

19. For a discussion of the reception of Autochrome color photography, see J. Nilsen Laurvik, "The New Color-Photography," *The Century Magazine*, 75, 3, January, 1908, pp. 323-30; see also Charles Holme, ed., *Colour Photography & Other Recent Developments of the Art of the Camera*, London, Paris, New York, 1908.

20. Roland Rood, "The Three Factors in American Pictorial Photography," *American Amateur Photographer*, 16, August, 1904; quoted in Harry W. Lawton and George Know, eds., *The Valiant Knights of Daguerre: Selected Critical Essays on Photography and Profiles of Photographic Pioneers by Sadakichi Hartmann*, Berkeley, Los Angeles, London, 1978, p. 4.

21, 22. See Margaret Harker, *The Linked Ring: the Secession Movement in Photography in Britain, 1892-1910*, London, 1979, p. ix.

23. In 1883 the firm of T. & R. Annan, owned by J. Craig's father, purchased the sole rights in Great Britain to the Karl Klič photogravure process; in consequence, J. Craig Annan became outstanding in gravure printing.

24. E. J. Constant Puyo, "La Photographie Synthétique," ("Synthetic Photography"), *La Revue de Photographie*, 2, April 15, May 15, June 15, 1904; reprinted in Bunnell, *A Photographic Vision*, p. 168.

25. José Ortíz Echagüe, *España: Tipos y Trajes, España: Pueblos y Paisajes, España Mística*, and *España: Castillos y Alcazares*. Ten editions were published in Madrid between 1937 and 1957.

26. Adam Sobota, "Art Photography in Poland," *History of Photography*, 4, 1, January, 1980, p. 25.

27. Unknown author, "The Work of the Year," *Photograms of the Year*, London, 1900, p. 66.

28. Unknown author, "The Käsebier Exhibit," *Photo Era*, 4, 4, April, 1900, p. 128, in which Harvard art professor Denman Ross is quoted; see also R. A. Cram, "Mrs. Käsebier's Work," *Photo Era*, 4, 5, May, 1900, p. 131.

29. Toby Quitsland, *Frances Benjamin Johnston and Her Feminine Colleagues* (exhibition catalog), New York, 1979, unpaged.

30. For a discussion of the conflict between Pictorialist attitudes in New York and Philadelphia, see Mary Panzer, *Philadelphia Naturalist Photography 1865-1900*, New Haven, Conn., 1982.

31. Elizabeth Flint Wade, "Artistic Pictures, Suggestions How to Make Them," *American Amateur Photographer*, V, 10, October, 1893, p. 441.

32. Alfred Stieglitz, "The Photo Secession," *Bausch and Lomb Lens Souvenir*, 1903; reprinted in Sarah Greenough and Juan Hamilton, *Alfred Stieglitz: Photographs and Writings*, Washington, D.C., and New York, 1983, p. 190.

33. Sadakichi Hartmann, "A Plea for the Picturesqueness of New York," *Camera Notes*, 4, 2, October, 1900, p. 97.

34. Stieglitz's reference to the "new Parthenon" is mentioned in Dorothy Norman, *Alfred Stieglitz: An American Seer*, New York, 1973, p. 76; Coburn's attitude toward modern structures is cited in J. J. Firebaugh, "Coburn, Henry James's Photographer," *American Quarterly*, 2, 1955, p. 224.

35. Coburn, Käsebier, and White launched *Platinum Print* in 1913 and established the Pictorial Photographers of America in 1915.

36. Alfred Stieglitz, *Catalogue of an Exhibition of Photographs*, Anderson Gallery, New York, 1921.

37. Theodore Dreiser, "The Camera Club of New York," *Ainslee's*, 4, 3, October, 1899, p. 328.

38. Odette M. Appel-Heyne, *Heinrich Kühn*, Cologne, 1981, p. 63.

CHAPTER 8: THE SOCIAL SCENE

1. Quoted in William Stott, *Documentary Photography and Thirties America*, New York, 1973, p. *vii*.

2. Leslie Katz, "Interview with Walker Evans," *Art in America*, March/April, 1971, p. 87.

3. Beaumont Newhall, "Documentary Approach to Photography," *Parnassus*, 10, March, 1938, p. 5.

4. Stott, *Documentary Photography and Thirties America*, p. 12 *ff*, suggests that there are two tendencies in documentation—one informative and the other expressive.

5. The work of Tönnies was rediscovered by Alexander Alland, Sr., during researches into the background of Jacob Riis; see Alexander Alland, Sr., *Heinrich Tönnies: Cartes-de-Visite Photographer Extraordinaire*, New York, 1978.

6. See Felicity Ashbee, "William Carrick, A Scots Photographer in St. Petersburg," *History of Photography*, 2, 3, July, 1978, pp. 207-22.

7. Unknown author, "America in the Stereoscope," *Art Journal*, 1860; quoted in Edward W. Earle, ed., *Points of View: The Stereograph in America—A Cultural History*, Rochester, N.Y., 1979, p. 32.

8. Sir Benjamin Stone, quoted in Bill Jay, *Customs and Faces—Photographs by Sir Benjamin Stone, 1838-1914*, London, 1972, unpaged.

9. See Michael Hiley, *Victorian Working Women: Portraits from Life*, London, 1979, pp. 36-80.

10. See Tom Beck, and George M. Bretz, *Photographer in the Mines*, Baltimore, 1977, pp. 10-13.

11. Anita Ventura Mozley, "Introduction," *Thomas Annan: Photographs of the Old Closes and Streets of Glasgow, 1868-1877*, New York, 1977, p. *v*.

12. Nathaniel Hawthorne, American consul in Liverpool, visited Glasgow during the mid-1850s; quoted in Mozley, *Thomas Annan: Old Closes*, p. *vi*.

13. Alexander Alland, Sr., *Jacob A. Riis: Photographer and Citizen*, Millerton, N.Y., 1974, p. 30, notes that *How The Other Half Lives* (1890) was one of the first full-length publications in the United States to use halftone reproduction of photographs for many of its illustrations. Through Alland's efforts, Riis's negatives were found and donated to the Museum of the City of New York.

14. Mrs. Helen E. Campbell, Col. Thomas W. Knox, and Superintendent Thomas Byrnes, *Darkness and Daylight, or Lights and Shadows of New York Life*, Hartford, Conn., 1897, p. 41.

15. Preface to *Darkness and Daylight*, p. *x*; the publishers claimed also that "the modern camera is the basis for every illustration in the volume. . . . every illustration is from a photograph made from life."

16. Alan Trachtenberg, "Essay," Walter and Naomi Rosenblum and Alan Trachtenberg, *America and Lewis Hine; Photographs 1904-1940*, Millerton, N.Y., 1977, p. 122.

17. Lewis Hine, "Baltimore to Biloxi and Back," *The Survey*, 30, May 3, 1913, p. 167.

18. Quoted in Pete Daniel and Raymond Smock, *A Talent for Detail: The Photographs of Miss Frances Benjamin Johnston, 1889-1910*, New York, 1974, p. 23.

19. "Therefore let me speak the truth in all honesty about our age and the people of our age," quoted in Robert Kramer, "Historical Commentary," *August Sander: Photographs of an Epoch*, Millerton, N.Y., 1980, p. 27.

20. Stott, *Documentary Expression*, p. 67.

21. Photographic projects were undertaken by a number of Federal agencies, including the Rural Electrification Administration, the Tennessee Valley Authority, and the Works Progress Administration, but despite the excellent photographers employed, the images were not used in the same fashion as those made for the F.S.A.

22. This figure is given by Grace M. Mayer in Edward Steichen, ed., *The Bitter Years, 1935-1941*, New York, 1962, p. *iv*. Hank O'Neal, *A Vision Shared*, New York, 1976, p. 300, mentions 200,000 unprinted negatives in the Library of Congress F.S.A. Collection. *America 1935-1945*, a circular announcing the availability of these images on microfiche, notes that there are 87,000 captioned images in the F.S.A. and O.W.I. (Office of War Information) collections.

23. See F. Jack Hurley, *Portrait of a Decade: Roy Stryker and the Development of Documentary Photography in the Thirties*, Baton Rouge, La., 1972, pp. 56-58, 128, 130.

24. Seventy prints were exhibited in the International Photographic Exhibition at the Grand Central Palace in New York in 1938 and subsequently traveled throughout the United States under the auspices of the Museum of Modern Art; see Hurley, *Portrait of a Decade*, p. 134; Walker Evans's F.S.A. work was included in his exhibition, *American Photographs*, at the Museum of Modern Art in 1938.

25. During the period in which the F.S.A. functioned, it sent out prepackaged exhibition panels to local communities and state fairs. Selections of the photographs were published in some 15 books, among them James Agee and Walker Evans, *Let Us Now Praise Famous Men*, 1941; Sherwood Anderson, *Home Town: The Face of America*, 1940; Dorothea Lange and Paul Schuster Taylor, *An American Exodus: A Record of Human Erosion*, 1939; Archibald MacLeish, *Land of the Free*, 1938. *Life*, *Look*, *Survey Graphic*, and *U.S. Camera* magazines used F.S.A. photographs in picture stories while newspapers used mainly individual images.

26. Both this and the following quotations are from Michael G. Sundell, *Berenice Abbott: Documentary Photographs of the 1930s*, Cleveland, Ohio, 1980, pp. 6, 7.

27. Edwin Hoernle, "The Working Man's Eye," *Der Arbeiter-Fotograf*; reprinted in David Mellor, ed., *Germany: The New Photography, 1927-1933*, London, 1978, p. 48.

28. Roman Vishniac, who has advanced degrees in both medicine and zoology, is renowned for his photomicrographs, especially of insect and marine life.

29. See Anne Tucker, "The Photo League," *OVO Magazine*, 10, 40/41, 1981, pp. 3-9; this article is based on a book in progress.

30. Gordon Parks, "Foreword," Ann Banks and Charles Traub, eds., *Harlem Document: Photographs 1932-1940: Aaron Siskind*, Providence, R.I., 1981, p. 5.

31. The Photo League was placed on the Attorney General's list of "subversive" organizations in 1950; during the ensuing period of political conservatism, it found itself unable to battle against this designation and in 1952 went out of existence.

32. O. R. Lovejoy, *Report to the Board of the National Child Labor Committee*, Samuel McCune Lindsay Papers, Rare Book and Manuscript Library, Columbia University, New York.

33. Quoted in Kramer, "Historical Commentary," *August Sander*, p. 17.

34. In moving a bleached steer skull, found in North Dakota, from its original location to another nearby in order to photograph it in several ways, Rothstein provided political opponents of the New Deal, who objected to the employment of artists and photographers on Federal projects, with an opportunity to claim that documentary photographs were being "faked"; see Hurley, *Portrait of a Decade*, pp. 86-90.

CHAPTER 9: PHOTOGRAPHY AND MODERNISM

1. Egmont Arens, American social critic and magazine editor, quoted in W. G. Briggs, *The Camera in Advertising and Industry*, London, 1939, p. 5.

2. Gustav Hartlaub, quoted in Peter Selz, "The Artist as Social Critic," *German Realism of the Twenties*, Minneapolis, Minn., 1980, p. 32.

3. Dawn Ades, *Photomontage*, New York, 1976, p. 10.

4. Raoul Hausmann, quoted in Jean A. Keim, "Photomontage After World War I," Van Deren Coke, ed., *One Hundred Years of Photographic History*, Albuquerque, N.M., 1976, p. 86.

5. See Ades, *Photomontage*, pp. 15-16.

6. Although initially somewhat different in meaning, solarization is now used to refer to a partial reversal of image tone caused by exposing the image to light during development. Another term for this phenomenon is Sabattier effect, after Armand Sabattier, who first described it in 1862.

7. The interrelationship between still and motion picture photography and its effect on the new vision is discussed in John Willett, "The Camera Eye, new photography, Russian and avant-garde films," *Art and Politics in the Weimar Period: The New Sobriety, 1917-1933*, New York, 1978, pp. 139-49.

8. Alvin Langdon Coburn, "The Future of Pictorial Photography," *Photograms of the Year*, 12, 1916; reprinted in Peter Bunnell, ed., *A Photographic Vision: Pictorial Photography, 1889-1923*, Salt Lake City, Ut., 1980, p. 194.

9. Andreas Haus, *Moholy-Nagy: Photographs and Photograms*, New York, 1980, p. 20.

10. Karl Nierendorf, "Preface," *Urformen der Kunst*, 1928; translated and reprinted in David Mellor, ed., *Germany: The New Photography, 1927-33*, London, 1978, p. 17.

11. The title, *Die Welt Ist Schön*, was chosen by the publisher in place of Renger-Patzsch's original title, *Die Dinge (Things or Objects)*; see Herbert Molderings, "Urbanism and Technological Utopianism: Thoughts on the Photography of Neue Sachlichkeit and The Bauhaus," Mellor, ed., *Germany: The New Photography*, p. 91. See also Fritz Kempfe, "The World is Beautiful: A Model Book of Objects and Things," *Albert Renger-Patzsch*, Cologne and Paris, 1979, p. 7.

12. Van Deren Coke, "Introduction," *Avant-Garde Photographs in Germany, 1919-1939*, San Francisco, 1980, p. 13.

13. John W. Dower, "Introduction," *A Century of Japanese Photography*, New York, 1980, p. 16.

14. Nobuo Ina, "Return to Photography," 1932; quoted in Dower, *A Century of Japanese Photography*, p. 17.

15. Paul Strand, "Photography," *The Seven Arts*, 2, August, 1917, p. 524.

16. Edward Weston, "Photography—Not Pictorial," *Camera Craft*, 37, 7, 1930; reprinted in Nathan Lyons, ed., *Photographers on Photography*, Englewood Cliffs, N.J., and Rochester, N.Y., 1966, p. 155.

17. Charles Sheeler, manuscript autobiography (1937), Archives of American Art, Smithsonian Institution, Washington, D.C.; see also Susan Fillin Yeh, "Charles Sheeler's Upper Deck," *Arts Magazine*, 55, 5, January, 1979, p. 90, and Martin Friedman, *Charles Sheeler*, New York, 1975, p. 65.

18. Among the exhibitions held in the late 1920s and early '30s in the United States were *The Art Center and Industry*, New York, 1926; *The Machine Age Exposition*, New York, 1927; *Art and Industry*, Chicago, 1933; *Machine Art*, New York, 1934. For a discussion of the attitude among artists and intellectuals toward machine

imagery, see R. F. B. [Richard F. Bach], "Machanalia," *Magazine of Art*, 22, 2, February, 1931, pp. 101-102, and Dickran Tasjian, *Skyscraper Primitives: Dada and the American Avant-Garde, 1910–1925*, Middletown, Conn., 1975, pp. 204-26.

19. Edward D. Wilson, "Beauty in Ugliness," *Photo Era*, 64, June, 1930, pp. 303-304.

20. Charis Wilson, "Remembrance," *Edward Weston: Nudes*, Millerton, N.Y., 1977, unpaged.

21. Francis Bruguière, "Creative Photography," *Modern Photography Annual*, 1935/36; reprinted in Lyons, *Photographers on Photography*, p. 34.

22. Johannes Molzahn, "Nicht mehr lesen, Sehen," *Das Kunstblatt*, 1928; quoted in Ute Eskildsen, "Photography and the Neue Sachlichkeit Movement," *German Realism of the Twenties*, London, 1978, p. 91.

23. Weston was asked by architect Richard Neutra to select a representative group of American photographs and to write a catalog foreword; see Nancy Newhall, ed., *The Daybooks of Edward Weston: California*, New York and Rochester, 1966, p. 103.

24. Laszlo Moholy-Nagy, "From Pigment to Light," *Telehor*, 1, 2, 1936; translated and reprinted in Lyons, *Photographers on Photography*, p. 80.

25. Edward Weston, "Seeing Photographically," *The Complete Photographer*, 9, 49, 1943; reprinted in Lyons, *Photographers on Photography*, p. 159.

26. Weston, "Seeing Photographically," p. 163.

TECHNICAL HISTORY: PART II

1. Celluloid was invented in 1861 by Alexander Parkes. In 1888, when it could be rolled thin enough, it became practicable as a base for photographic emulsion. John Carbutt was the first on the market with a celluloid dry plate film; see William Welling, *Photography in America: The Formative Years 1839-1900*, New York, 1978, p. 324.

2. Reverend Hannibal Goodwin applied for a patent for celluloid roll film in 1887, but, lacking funds, did not produce a product. A patent was granted to Henry A. Reichenbach for a flexible film for the Kodak camera in 1889. After Goodwin's death, his patent was acquired by the Anthony Company, which sued the Eastman Dry Plate and Film Company, claiming that the Eastman product was essentially the same as the product covered by the Goodwin patent. After 12 years of litigation, the suit was settled in favor of the Anthony Company, which by that time had merged with the Scovill Company to become Ansco.

3. Made possible by machinery invented in 1894 and used by the Automatic Photograph Company; see Welling, *Photography in America*, pp. 362-63.

4. Eaton S. Lothrop, Jr., *A Century of Cameras from the Collection of the International Museum of Photography at George Eastman House*, Dobbs Ferry and Rochester, 1973, p. 37.

5. In 1888, Vero Charles Driffield and Ferdinand Hurter patented an actinograph—a slide rule arrangement that enabled the user to equate variables governing exposure. In 1890, they jointly published *Photochemical Investigations and a New Method of Determining the Sensitiveness of Photographic Plates*.

6. Quoted in Brian Coe, *Colour Photography: The First Hundred Years 1840-1940*, London, 1978, p. 21.

CHAPTER 10: WORDS AND PICTURES

1. Peter Panter (pseud. Kurt Tucholsky), "*Ein Bild saght mehr als 1000 worte*" ("A Picture is worth more than 1,000 words"), *UHU*, 3, 2, 1926/27, p. 83. Besides the pseudonym Peter Panter, Tucholsky, a well-known satirist and social critic in Germany during the Weimar years, used the names Theobold Tiger, Ignaz Wrobel, and Kaspar Hauser. In 1929, he collaborated with John Heartfield on a book with satirical text and montage entitled *Deutschland, Deutschland Über Alles*, Berlin, 1929. Facsimile edition in English translation, Amherst, Mass., 1972.

2. Werner Gräff, *Es Kommt der neue Fotograf!* (*Here Comes the New Photographer!*), Berlin, 1929; a plea to photographers to transcend the limitations of verisimilitude.

3. A. Lee Snelling, "Photographic Illustration," *The International Annual of Anthony's Photographic Bulletin*, VI, New York, 1893, p. 184.

4. On finding his own camera damaged by falling debris in his studio, Genthe borrowed a 3A Kodak Special from a camera shop and for several weeks used this equipment to record the disaster; see Arnold Genthe, *As I Remember*, New York, 1936, p. 89.

5. Unknown author, "As a News Magazine—The Illustrated American," *Illustrated American*, 1, March 1, 1890, p. 48.

6. Luigi Barzini, *La Battaglia di Mukden (The Battle of Mukden)*, 1907, is cited in Jorge Lewinski, *The Camera at War*, New York, 1978, pp. 59, 236.

7. Lewinski, *The Camera at War*, p. 56.

8. Águstin Víctor Casasola began an extensive archive called the File of the Mexican Revolution that was continued by his sons, both of whom also were photojournalists; see Carlos Monsiváis, "The Continuity of Images," *Artes Visuales*, 2, October/December, 1976, pp. 37-38.

9. Lewis L. Gould and Richard Greffe, *Photojournalist: The Career of Jimmy Hare*, Austin, Tex., 1977, p. 123.

10. According to Lewinski, *The Camera at War*, p. 63, "the public saw very few pictures of the war, only those of the most innocuous kind." Since thousands upon thousands of photographs of the conflict were made by press and official armed forces photographers, censorship must have played a decisive role in deciding what images the public would see.

11. Johannes Molzahn, "*Nicht mehr lesen, Sehen*" ("Forget Reading, See"), Das Kunstblatt, 12, 1928, p. 79.

12. Tim N. Gidal, *Modern Photojournalism, Origin and Evolution, 1910-1933*, New York, 1972, p. 19.

13. Umbo (Otto Umbehrs), quoted in Wilhelm Marckwardt, *Die Illustrierten der Weimar Zeit (The Illustrated Weeklies of the Weimar Period)*, Munich, 1980, p. 128.

14. Dawn Ades, *Photomontage*, New York, 1976, p. 16.

15. Urszula Czartoryska, "Twentieth Century Experimentation," *Fotografia Polska*, New York, 1979, p. 16.

16. Sandra S. Phillips, "The French Magazine *Vu*," *Picture Magazines Before Life*, Woodstock, N.Y., 1982, unpaged.

17. See David Mellor, "Patterns of Naturalism, Hoppé to Hardy," *The Real Thing*, London, 1975, p. 35, and Tom Hopkinson, "Introduction," *Bert Hardy*, London, 1975.

18. Wilson Hicks, *Words and Pictures*, New York, 1952, p. 42.

19. Questions raised by O. D. Gallagher and cited in Lewinski, *The Camera at War*, p. 88, concerning the authenticity of this image (which was used on the dust wrapper for Robert Capa, *Death in The Making*, New York, 1938) appear to be without foundation according to Richard Whalen, whose biography of Robert Capa is forthcoming in 1985.

20. Quoted in *The Concerned Photographer*, New York, 1968, unpaged.

21. Edward Steichen, "Introduction," *The Family of Man*, New York, 1955, pp. 3-4.

22. According to Steichen, some two million photographs were submitted; they were narrowed down by Steichen and his staff to 10,000, and then to 503; see *The Family of Man*, p. 4, and Edward Steichen, *A Life in Photography*, Garden City, N.Y., 1963, unpaged.

23. See essays by William Johnson and John Morris in "W. Eugene Smith: Early Work," *Center for Creative Photography Bulletin* (Tucson, Ariz.), 12, July, 1980, pp. 5-20, 21-26.

24. Kertész's first exhibition in 1927 at the gallery Le Sacre de Printemps was the first one-man show of photography held in Paris; see Carol DiGrappa, "The Diarist," *Camera Arts*, 1, 1, January/February, 1981. At the time, Kertész's photographs appeared in *UHU*, the *Berlin Illustrierte*, and *Vu* magazines, among others.

25. Quoted in Beaumont Newhall, "The Instant Vision of Henri Cartier-Bresson," *Camera*, October, 1955, p. 485.

26. Unknown author, "Help from the Camera," *Commercial Art and Industry* (London), November, 1923, p. 311; see also Herman Blauvelt, "When the Modernist Invades Advertising," *Printer's Ink Monthly*, May, 1925, p. 65.

27. R. L. Dupuy, "Advertising Photo in France," *Gebrauchsgraphik*, 6, 8, August, 1929, p. 17.

28. Pierre Mac Orlan, "*Graphismes*," *Arts et Métiers Graphiques*, 11, May/June, 1929, unpaged; drawings and layout by Alexey Brodovitch.

29. Paul Outerbridge, Jr., *Photographing in Color*, New York, 1940, p. 55; for Steichen's attitude see Carl Sandburg, *Steichen the Photographer*, New York, 1929, p. 53.

30. Ansel Adams, quoted in Jacob Deschin, "Photography in the 'Ads,'" *Scientific American*, 152, April, 1935, p. 175.

31. Lucien Lorelle and D. Langelaan, "La Photographie Publicitaire," Paris, 1949, unpaged.

32. Margaret Bourke-White, "Photographing This World," *The Nation*, 142, 3685, February 19, 1936; quoted in Theodore M. Brown, *Margaret Bourke-White: Photojournalist*, Ithaca, N.Y., 1972, p. 43.

33. Quoted in Louis Walton Sipley, *A Half-Century of Color*, New York, 1951, pp. 66-67.

34. Sipley, *A Half-Century of Color*, p. 86.

35. See Sally A. Stein, "The Composite Photographic Image and the Composition of Consumer Ideology," *Art Journal*, 41, 1, Spring, 1981, pp. 39-45.

36. Quoted in Nancy Hall-Duncan, *The History of Fashion Photography*, New York, 1979, p. 142.

37. Roland Barthes, *Camera Lucida: Reflections on Photography*, New York, 1981, p. 118.

38. Press Release, Museum of Modern Art, 1947.

39. William Johnson, *W. Eugene Smith: Master of the Photographic Essay*, Millerton, N.Y., 1981, pp. 41, 46.

40. Sheila Turner Sheed, "Henri Cartier-Bresson" (interview), *Popular Photography*, May, 1974, p. 142.

41. B. Newhall, "The Instant Vision of Henri Cartier-Bresson," p. 485.

CHAPTER II: THE STRAIGHT IMAGE

1. Quoted in Ben Maddow, *Faces: A Narrative History of the Portrait in Photography*, Boston, 1979, p. 527.

2. The name given an exhibition and catalog of photographs concerned with the expression of subjective visions; see Clifford S. Ackley, *Private Realities*, Boston, 1974.

3. Henry Hope Smith, quoted in Charles A. Traub and John Grimes, *The New Vision: Forty Years of Photography at the Institute of Design*, Millerton, N.Y., 1982, p. 30.

4. Harry Callahan, quoted in John Szarkowski, ed., *Callahan*, Millerton, N.Y., 1976, p. 14; see also Traub and Grimes, *The New Vision*, p. 27.

5. Aaron Siskind, quoted in Carl Chiarenza, "Aaron Siskind and His Critics," *Center for Creative Photography Bulletin* (Tucson, Ariz.), 7/8, September, 1978, p. 5.

6. Minor White, *mirrors messages manifestations*, Millerton, N.Y., 1969, p. 106.

7. Wynn Bullock, quoted in *Wynn Bullock*, Millerton, N.Y., 1976, p. 5.

8. Duane Michals, quoted in Barbaralee Diamonstein, *Visions and Images: American Photographers on Photography*, New York, 1981, p. 118.

9. From Diane Arbus's application for a Guggenheim grant in 1963; cited in *Diane Arbus: A Monograph of Seventeen Photographs*, Los Angeles, 1980, unpaged.

10. Nathan Lyons, ed., *Contemporary Photographers Towards a Social Landscape*, New York and Rochester, 1966.

11. John Szarkowski, *Mirrors and Windows*, New York, 1978, pp. 23-24.

12. *New Topographics: Photographs of a Man-Altered Landscape*, Rochester, 1975.

13. Quoted in Lee D. Witkin and Barbara London, *The Photo-

graph Collector's Guide, New York, 1979, 78; see also Jonathan Green, *American Photography: A Critical History 1945 to the Present*, New York, 1984, p. 166.

14. Quoted in Witkin and London, *The Photograph Collector's Guide*, p. 120.

15. Danny Lyon, *Conversations with the Dead*, New York, Chicago, San Francisco, 1969, p. 12.

16. Allan Porter, "Otto Steinert," *Contemporary Photographers*, New York, 1983, p. 723.

17. Gabor Szilasi, "Gabor Szilasi," *Contemporary Photographers*, p. 747.

18. Diego Rivera, quoted in Raquel Tibol, "Hecho en Latino America," *Venezia 79*, New York, 1979, p. 248.

19. Laszlo Moholy-Nagy, "Introduction," *Street Markets of London* (1936), quoted in David Mellor, "Patterns of Naturalism, Hoppé to Hardy," *The Real Thing*, London, 1975, p. 33.

20. Aaron Scharf, "The Shadowy World of Bill Brandt," *Bill Brandt, Photographs*, London, 1970, p. 18.

21. Claude Nori, "Bernard Plossu," *Contemporary Photographers*, p. 602.

22. Italo Zannier, "Contemporary Italian Photography," *Venezia 79*, p. 280.

23. Shoji Yamagishi, "Introduction," *New Japanese Photography*, New York, 1974, p. 12.

CHAPTER 12: MANIPULATIONS AND COLOR

1. Walter Benjamin, "The Work of Art in the Age of Mechanical Illustration," *Zeitschrift für Socialforschung*, V, 1, 1936; translated and reprinted in Hannah Arendt, ed., *Illuminations: Walter Benjamin*, New York, 1969, p. 236.

2. This concept of photography as documentation without style or emotion has been called "Scientific Realism"; see Jonathan Green, *American Photography: A Critical History, 1945 to the Present*, New York, 1984, pp. 220-21.

3. Klaus Honnef, "Bernd and Hilla Becher," *Contemporary Photographers*, New York, 1983, pp. 53-54; see also William Jenkins, "Introduction," *New Topographics: Photographs of a Man-Altered Landscape*, Rochester, N.Y., 1975, p. 7.

4. See Abigail Solomon Godeau, "Winning the Game When the Rules have been Changed: Art Photography and Post-Modernism," and Christopher Burnett, "Photography, Postmodernism, Contradictions," *New Mexico Studies in the Fine Arts*, VIII, 1983, pp. 5-13, 21-27. See also Michael Starenko, "Postmodernism as Bricolage: Or, can Cindy Sherman act?" *Exposure*, 21, 2, 1983, pp. 20-23.

5. Michael Badura, quoted in Jean Luc Daval, *Photography, History of an Art*, New York, 1982, p. 244.

6. William E. Parker, "Uelsmann's Unitary Reality," *Aperture*, 13, 3, 1967, unpaged.

7. A. D. Coleman, *The Grotesque in Photography*, New York, 1977, p. 150.

8. Clarence J. Laughlin, "A Statement by the Photographer," *Clarence John Laughlin*, Millerton, N.Y., pp. 13, 14.

9. Coleman, *The Grotesque in Photography*, p. 150.

10. See Rosanne T. Livingston, "Introduction," *Photographic Process As Medium*, New Brunswick, N.J., 1975, p. 5.

11. "Thomas Barrow," *Contemporary Photographers*, p. 45.

12. Aline B. Louchheim, "Introduction," *The Art and Technique of Color Photography*, Alexander Liberman, ed., New York, 1951, p. *xiv*.

13. Quoted in Renato Danese, ed., *American Images*, New York, 1979, p. 140.

14. Quoted in Douglas Davis, "A Call to the Colors," *Newsweek*, November 23, 1981, p. 115; see also Max Kozloff, "Photography: the coming to age of color," *Artforum*, 13, January, 1975, pp. 30-35, and A. D. Coleman, "Is Criticism of Color Photography Possible?" *Camera Lucida*, 5, 1982, pp. 23-29.

15. Joyce Neimanas, "Statement—Recent Color," *The Archive*, 14, December, 1981, p. 7.

16. Ernst Haas, quoted in *Color*, A Time-Life Book, New York, 1970, p. 166.

17. Quoted in Aaron Scharf, *Art and Photography*, Baltimore, 1969, p. 108.

18. Richard Estes, quoted in John Canaday and John Arthur, *Richard Estes: The Urban Landscape*, Boston, 1978, cited in John Arthur, *Realism Photorealism*, Tulsa, Okla., 1980, p. 67.

TECHNICAL HISTORY: PART III

1. "The Photographic Industry, 1980-81," *The Wolfman Report on the Photographic Industry in the United States*, 1981-82, p. 24.

2. Unknown author, "Kodak Research Today," *Kodak Studio Light*, Centennial Issue, 1980, p. 69.

Glossary

ADDITIVE COLOR: The principle by which all colors of light can be mixed optically by combining in different proportions the three primary colors of the spectrum—red, green, and blue. White light is a mixture of all three.

ALBERTYPE—*see* COLLOTYPE

ALBUMEN (*also spelled* ALBUMIN): Eggwhite. Used on glass as a medium for light-sensitive emulsions to make finely detailed negatives. Albumen positive prints are made on paper coated with eggwhite and salt solution and sensitized with silver nitrate solution. The print is made by exposure to sunlight through a negative.

AMBROTYPE: The name for a glass collodion positive process patented in 1854 in the United States by James Ambrose Cutting.

APERTURE: The size of the adjustable opening in a lens that determines the amount of light that will pass through. Relative aperture is expressed as an f/number, which represents the focal length of the lens divided by the diameter of the aperture.

ARCHIVAL PROCESSING: Processing designed to preserve a print or negative for as long as possible by protecting it against deterioration due to chemical reactions.

AUTOCHROME: A screen-plate color process in which starch grains dyed to the primary colors—red, green, and blue—are mixed and sifted onto a glass plate covered with a sticky substance. The plate is then coated with black powder, varnished, coated with a sensitized emulsion, and exposed in the camera. After development the image formed is a positive transparency.

AUTOTYPE (*see also* CARBON PROCESS): The name for a carbon print made by the Autotype Printing and Publishing Company, founded in London is 1868.

BICHROMATE (*also called* DICHROMATE PROCESS)—*see* GUM BICHROMATE

BLUEPRINT—*see* CYANOTYPE

BROMOIL: A process by which a gelatin silver-bromide contact print or enlargement is treated with a potassium bichromate solution that simultaneously bleaches the dark silver image and bichromates the gelatin so that it selectively hardens to absorb more or less oil pigment. The pigment is usually applied by hand and may be in a variety of colors.

CALOTYPE (*also called* TALBOTYPE): A process patented in 1841 by William Henry Fox Talbot by which a latent image produced by exposing paper sensitized with potassium iodide and silver nitrate solutions in a camera is then developed in gallic acid and silver nitrate. Positives are subsequently made by contact-printing these paper negatives in daylight onto salted paper, which has been treated with silver nitrate and salt. The first successful negative/positive process.

CAMERA: The instrument with which photographs are taken. Basically, it consists of a lighttight box with an aperture that generally contains a lens to admit and focus the light, as well as a holder for film.

CAMERA LENS: Usually a composite of optically ground glass or plastic disks aligned on an axis to transmit a focused image at a specific distance.

CAMERA LUCIDA: An instrument consisting of a prism and lens supported by a telescoping stand set over drawing paper. Used for copying drawings and sketching views of nature.

CAMERA OBSCURA: Forerunner of the photographic camera. Originally a room in which observers could view images of outside subjects projected onto a wall through a pinpoint light source. Later this evolved into a portable box with an aperture, lens, and a viewing screen.

CARBON PROCESS: A nonsilver process in which a positive print is produced by exposing a negative against a pigmented gelatin tissue sensitized with potassium bichromate, which hardens in relation to the amount of light it receives. The gelatin that remains soft and soluble is then washed off, leaving the image. The first truly practical method for printing in permanent pigment.

CARBRO PROCESS (*also called* OZOBROME): A method of making a carbon print from a silver bromide print by pressing the silver print against a bichromated gelatin tissue to which a silver bleaching agent is added. The gelatin hardens on contact and is then processed like a carbon print.

CARTE-DE-VISITE: A 4½ by 2½ inch mounted photographic print popular in the late 19th century, usually a portrait and generally made as one of a number of images on a single photographic plate.

COLLAGE: An image made from combinations of photographs, graphics, type, and/or other two-dimensional materials pasted onto a backing sheet.

COLLODION PROCESS: A wet-plate process in which a negative is made possible by coating a sheet of glass with a light-sensitive emulsion of collodion—gun cotton dissolved in alcohol and ether

—to which potassium iodide and potassium bromide have been added. The plate is inserted into the camera and exposed while wet.

COLLOTYPE: The name for a group of related processes that use metal or glass plates coated with bichromated gelatin to produce a printing surface. After exposure through a negative, the plate is washed and treated with glycerin. The gelatin surface becomes selectively absorbent, and greasy ink adheres most easily to the parts of the image containing the least water. Variants of the process are called albertype, heliotype, *phototypie*, and *lichtdruck*.

COLOR SEPARATION: The method of recording on separate sheets of black and white film, through filters, each of the three primary color components of a photographic subject, for the purpose of printing that subject in color.

COMBINATION PRINTING: The technique of printing more than one negative, or multiple exposures of a single negative, on one sheet of sensitized paper.

CYANOTYPE: A low-cost permanent print made by exposing a matrix in contact with paper impregnated with iron salts and potassium ferricyanide, which darkens when exposed to light. The image usually is white on a blue ground.

DAGUERREOTYPE: The first practical photographic process, in which an image is formed on a copper plate coated with highly polished silver that is sensitized by fumes of iodine to form silver iodide. Following exposure the latent image is developed in mercury vapor, resulting in a unique image on metal that cannot be used as a negative for replication.

DETECTIVE CAMERA: Early name for small hand-held cameras, many of which were designed to be concealed in clothing or parcels or made to look like books, walking sticks, or other articles.

DEVELOPMENT: The process by which exposed film or photographic paper is chemically treated to produce a visible and relatively permanent image. Also the step in which film or photographic paper is bathed in a chemical that produces the silver image.

DRY PLATE: A negative made by exposing a glass plate coated with silver halides suspended in gelatin. Called dry to distinguish it from wet collodion plates.

DYE COUPLERS: Substances activated during development that help form dye colors in relation to the amount of reduced silver being formed.

DYE TRANSFER: A process by which a subject is photographed through filters on three separate gelatin negatives that are dyed cyan, magenta, and yellow; these are contact printed in register onto a single sheet of sensitized paper to form a positive color image.

EMULSION: Any light-sensitive coating applied to photographic film, paper, or other material. Commonly contains silver halide crystals suspended in gelatin.

EXPOSURE: The act of allowing light to fall on a photosensitive material. Also, the amount of light allowed to reach the material.

F/NUMBER—*see* APERTURE

FERROTYPE (*also called* TINTYPE and MELAINOTYPE): A positive image formed by exposing a thin varnished sheet of iron coated with sensitized collodion in a camera. Used almost exclusively for inexpensive portraiture.

FILM: Most commonly the transparent, flexible acetate or plastic material that supports a layer of light-sensitive emulsion.

FIXING BATH (*also called* HYPO): A chemical solution—usually sodium thiosulfate or ammonium thiosulfate—that makes a photograph insensitive to further exposure to light by dissolving unaffected silver halides.

FOCAL LENGTH: Commonly used to mean the distance from the lens to the plane on which the image is focused (focal plane) when the lens is set on infinity. Wide-angle lenses have a short focal length, and telephoto lenses have a long focal length.

GELATIN: A colloidal protein obtained from animal tissue and hooves. Used as a binder to hold silver halide crystals in suspension in modern photographic emulsions, and in nonsilver light-sensitive reproduction techniques.

GLASS COLLODION POSITIVE: A positive made by the collodion process in which an underexposed negative image, produced on glass coated with light-sensitive collodion, is mounted in front of a dark background or backed with opaque varnish to make the image become visible as a positive.

GUM BICHROMATE (*also called* GUM DICHROMATE): A procedure by which an image is formed by exposing a negative to a surface coated with an emulsion of gum arabic, potassium bichromate, and pigment. The emulsion hardens in relation to the amount of light it receives through the negative. Unexposed emulsion is washed away with water to leave the hardened, pigmented image.

HALFTONE SCREENED ENGRAVING: An image made by re-photographing a picture (photographic or other) through a screen in order to break up the continuous tones into a code of regular dots. Dark areas of the image appear as large, closely spaced dots, while the dots forming light areas appear smaller and farther apart.

HAND CAMERA: Any camera that can be carried and used without a tripod.

HELIOTYPE—*see* COLLOTYPE

HOLOGRAPHY: A method of creating an illusion of a three-dimensional image. A laser beam is split into two parts; one part is reflected from an object and interferes with the other part, which comes directly from the laser. The interference pattern created when the two beams merge is recorded on a photographic plate, which, when illuminated by laser or white light, produces a three-dimensional image.

HYPO (*see also* FIXING BATH): Sodium thiosulfate—the active ingredient in most fixers.

IMAGE: In photography, the two-dimensional representation of a subject formed as a result of exposing and processing a light-sensitive emulsion.

INFRARED: The band of the electromagnetic spectrum that includes radiation of wavelengths longer than that of visible red light but shorter than radio waves. Some films are sensitive to infrared light.

INSTANTANEOUS PHOTOGRAPHY: A term used loosely in the early days of photography for exposures of less than one second.

LATENT IMAGE: The invisible image produced on sensitized material by exposure to light, which is converted to a visible image by chemical development.

MACROPHOTOGRAPHY: The process of making greatly enlarged photographic images of a subject—life-size or larger.

MAGNESIUM FLASH: An early method of artificial illumination; a device that made indoor or night photography possible. Light is produced by igniting magnesium powder or wire.

MATRIX: In photography, an image from which prints can be made; specifically, in dye-transfer printing the three dyed gelatin reliefs used to make a print on gelatin-coated paper.

MICROPHOTOGRAPHY: Photography done through a compound microscope, resulting in the enlargement of extremely small objects or forms.

NEGATIVE: Any photographic image in which the tones are the reverse of those in the original subject. Also the film, plate, or paper exposed to light in a camera and processed to make the negative image.

ONE-STEP PHOTOGRAPHY: A process that produces a positive print within seconds after exposure by rolling a sandwich of a negative, a positive, and development chemicals through the mechanism.

ORTHOCHROMATIC: A film, plate, or emulsion that is sensitive only to blue and green light. Renders all colors except red in tones of grey, reflecting the relative brilliance of these colors in the subject.

PANCHROMATIC: A film, plate, or emulsion that is sensitive to blue and green light and also to some or all of the red portion of the spectrum. Renders the colors in tones of grey, reflecting their relative brilliance in the subject.

PANORAMIC CAMERA: A camera designed to permit photographs to be taken with a greatly enlarged lateral field of view.

PHOTOGENIC DRAWING: An early process for producing paper negatives, in which objects placed on paper sensitizd with salt and silver nitrate were exposed. The paper darkened in propor-

tion to the amount of light it received, resulting in a negative image that was fixed with a salt solution.

PHOTOGRAM (*also called* SCHADOGRAPH, RAYOGRAM, LIGHT GRAPHICS): A photographic image made without a camera, either by placing objects on a sensitized surface—paper or film—that is exposed to a moving or stationary source of light, or simply by directing light onto the material.

PHOTOGRAVURE (*also called* GRAIN GRAVURE): A printing process for reproducing the appearance of the continuous range of tones in a photograph. A copper plate covered with resin dust and bichromated gelatin tissue is exposed to a negative and etched so that dark areas of the image will hold more ink than do light areas.

PHOTOMONTAGE: A composite image made by joining together portions (or all) of more than one photograph to synthesize an image not found in reality.

PINHOLE: A tiny aperture in a camera without a lens. Light passing through it forms an image on film that is less sharp than one produced through a lens.

PLATE: Usually a glass or metal sheet coated with light-sensitive emulsion that is intended to receive the image through the aperture when it is inserted in a camera.

PLATINUM PRINT (*also called* PLATINOTYPE *after its British trade name*): A print formed by exposing a negative in contact with paper that has been sensitizd with iron salts and a platinum compound and then developing it in potassium oxalate. Considered highly permanent.

POSITIVE: A photographic image on any support or material in which the tonalities and colors accord with those of the subject portrayed. At times used interchangeably with print.

PRIMARY COLORS: Red, green, and blue light. When mixed in different proportions these colors produce all others; together, they produce white light. In pigment, the primary colors are magenta, cyan, and yellow.

PRINT: Generally, an image on paper formed by photographic means; usually but not necessarily a positive.

PRINTING-OUT PAPER: Photographic paper that produces a visible image without need for chemical development when exposed to light.

REFLEX CAMERA: A camera with a built-in mirror that reflects the image in the lens onto a glass viewing screen.

SABBATIER EFFECT (*also called* SOLARIZATION): A partial reversal of tones in an image, caused by reexposing the film or paper to light during development. Named after Armand Sabbatier, who discovered the phenomenon in 1862.

SALTED PAPER: A printing-out paper made by soaking writing paper in a weak salt solution and then brushing it with a silver nitrate solution to form silver chloride that permeates the paper fibers.

SHUTTER: A device that controls, by opening and closing, the amount of light that enters the camera and strikes the film or plate.

SILVER HALIDES: Silver chloride, silver bromide, and silver iodide; the light-sensitive component in photographic emulsions.

SOLARIZATION—*see* SABBATIER EFFECT

SPECTRUM: The band of visible wavelengths perceived as color. Consists of a continuous range of tones from deep violet through blue, green, yellow, orange, and red. Visible when white light is viewed through a prism.

STEREOGRAPH: A pair of photographic views taken side by side from very slightly different angles and mounted side by side. Though viewed separately by each eye in a stereoscope viewer, the two images appear to combine to produce the illusion of three dimensions.

STEREOSCOPE: A device for viewing stereographs, consisting of a set of eyepieces and a holder for one or more stereographs.

SUBTRACTIVE COLOR SYSTEM: A method of color photography in which the colors are produced by filtering out their complements from white light. Colors result when dyes containing varying amounts of the three pigment primary colors, cyan, magenta, and yellow, subtract their colors from white light, leaving a color made of the combination of light from the rest of the spectrum.

TINTYPE—*see* FERROTYPE

TONING: A process that changes the color of a silver print either during or after development by changing the chemical makeup of the image or by coating it with a chemical compound.

ULTRAVIOLET: The band of the electromagnetic spectrum that includes radiation of wavelengths shorter than that of visible violet light but longer than that of most X-rays.

VIEW CAMERA: A type of camera in which the lens forms the image on a glass screen directly at the plane of the film. The image viewed is exactly the same as the image on the film, which replaces the viewing screen during exposure.

WAXED PAPER PROCESS: A variation of the calotype process in which the paper is treated with wax before sensitizing, making it more transparent, more sensitive to detail, and improving its keeping properties.

WET PLATE—*see* COLLODION PROCESS

WOODBURYTYPE: A photomechanical printing process that produces continuous tone reproductions by exposing a negative to bichromated gelatin to create a relief mold, which is then embedded in lead for the printing. Pigmented gelatin is poured on the mold and is transfered to paper under pressure, resulting in an image in which the deepest parts of the mold produce the darkest areas of the print. Obsolete.

XEROGRAPHY: A process for copying graphic or photographic material in which light acts on an electrically charged photoconductive insulating plate. The latent image is developed with a resinous powder and heat.

Bibliography

The following books include those mentioned in the text as well as others selected from the extensive literature on photography to provide a comprehensive introduction to all aspects of this field. These works are mainly in English, except where the importance of a publication in another language merited inclusion. In addition to the full-length volumes listed below, the reader should be aware of the English language periodical *History of Photography*, published since 1977, and the French journal *Photographies*, published since 1983, both of which are devoted exclusively to the history of the medium.

GENERAL HISTORIES

Braive, Michel F. *The Photograph: a Social History*. New York: McGraw-Hill, 1966.

Daval, Jean-Luc. *Photography: History of an Art*. New York: Rizzoli International Publications, Inc., 1982.

Eder, Josef Maria. *History of Photography*. Translated by Edward Epstean. New York: Columbia University Press, 1945, 1972; Reprint edition, Dover Publications, Inc., 1978.

Freund, Gisèle. *Photography and Society*. Boston: David R. Godine, Publisher, 1980.

Gernsheim, Helmut and Alison. *The History of Photography: from the Camera Obscura to the Beginning of the Modern Era*. New York, St. Louis, San Francisco: McGraw-Hill Book Company, 1969.

Jeffrey, Ian. *Photography: A Concise History*. New York and Toronto: Oxford University Press, 1981.

Moholy, Lucia. *100 Years of Photography: 1839–1939*. Hammondsworth, Middlesex: Penguin Books, Ltd., 1939.

Newhall, Beaumont. *The History of Photography: from 1839 to the Present*. New York: Museum of Modern Art, Completely revised and enlarged edition, 1982.

Pollack, Peter. *Picture History of Photography*. New York: Harry N. Abrams, Inc., 1969.

Stenger, Erich. *The History of Photography*. Easton, Pa.: Mack Printing Company, 1939.

Taft, Robert. *Photography and the American Scene: A Social History, 1839–1889*. (1938). Reprint ed., New York: Dover Publications, Inc., 1964.

Tausk, Peter. *Photography in the 20th Century*. London: Focal Press, 1980.

Welling, William. *Photography in America: The Formative Years, 1839–1900*. New York: Thomas Y. Crowell Company, 1978.

AESTHETICS, CRITICISM, AND INTERVIEWS.

Adams, Robert. *Beauty in Photography: Essays in Defense of Traditional Values*. Millerton, N.Y.: Aperture, 1981.

Artscanada: An Inquiry into the Aesthetics of Photography. Toronto: Society for Art Publications, 1974.

Barthes, Roland. *Camera Lucida, Reflections on Photography*. New York: Hill and Wang/A Division of Farrar, Straus, Giroux, 1981.

Benjamin, Walter. "The Work of Art in the Age of Mechanical Reproduction," *Illuminations*, Hannah Arendt, ed. New York: Schocken Books, 1969.

Bunnell, Peter, ed. *A Photographic Vision: Pictorial Photography, 1889–1923*. Salt Lake City, Ut.: Peregrine Smith, 1980.

Caffin, Charles H. *Photography as a Fine Art*. Hastings-on-Hudson, N.Y.: Morgan & Morgan, Inc., 1971 (facsimile edition).

Diamondstein, Barbaralee. *Visions and Images: American Photographers on Photography*. New York: Rizzoli International Publications, 1981.

Goldberg, Vickie. *Photography in Print: Writings from 1916 to the Present*. New York: Simon and Schuster, 1981.

Hartmann, Sadakichi. *The Valiant Knights of Daguerre: Selected Critical Essays on Photography and Profiles of Photographic Pioneers*, edited by Harry W. Lawton and George Knox. Berkeley: University of California Press, 1978.

Hill, Paul, and Thomas Cooper, eds. *Dialogue with Photography*. New York: Farrar/Straus/Giroux, 1979.

Kozloff, Max. *Photography & Fascination*. Danbury, N.H.: Addison House, 1979.

Lyons, Nathan, ed. *Photographers on Photography: A Critical Anthology*. Englewood Cliffs, N.J.: Prentice-Hall, 1956.

Newhall, Beaumont, ed. *Photography: Essays & Images*. New York: The Museum of Modern Art, 1980.

Petruck, Peninah, ed. *The Camera Viewed: Writings on Twentieth Century Photography*, 2 vols. New York: E. P. Dutton, 1979.

Sontag, Susan. *On Photography*. New York: Farrar, Straus and Giroux, 1973.

Szarkowski, John. *The Photographer's Eye*. New York: The Museum of Modern Art and Doubleday & Co., 1966.

Thomas, Alan. *Time in A Frame—Photography and the 19th Century Mind*. New York: Schocken Books, 1977.

Trachtenberg, Alan, ed. *Classic Essays on Photography*. New Haven, Conn.: Leete's Island Books, 1980.

THE ART OF PHOTOGRAPHY;
ART AND PHOTOGRAPHY.

Ades, Dawn. *Photomontage*. New York: Pantheon Books, 1976.

Avant-Garde Photography in Germany, 1919–1939. Van Deren Coke, intro. San Francisco, Cal.: San Francisco Museum of Modern Art, 1980.

Bannon, Anthony. *The Photo-Pictorialists of Buffalo*. Buffalo, N.Y.: Media Sudy, 1981.

Camera Work, A Photographic Quarterly, Edited and Published by Alfred Stieglitz, 1903–1917. New York: Kraus Reprints, 1969 (reprint edition).

Coke, Van Deren. *The Painter and The Photographer, From Delacroix to Warhol*. Albuquerque: University of New Mexico Press, 1964; revised and enlarged edition, 1972.

Coleman, A. D. *The Grotesque in Photography*. New York: Ridge Press/Summit Books, 1977.

Emerson, Peter Henry. *Naturalistic Photography for Students of the Art* (1889. 3rd. ed. 1899). Reprint edition, New York: Arno Press, 1973.

Glassman, Elizabeth, and Marilyn F. Symmes. *Cliché-verre: Hand-Drawn, Light-Printed, A Survey of the Medium from 1839 to the Present*. Detroit: The Detroit Institute of Arts, 1980.

Fantastic Photographs, Text by Attilio Colombo. Photographs selected by Lorenzo Merlo and Claude Nori. New York: Pantheon Books, 1979.

Fotografica Pittorica, 1889–1911. Venice and Florence: Electa Editrice and Edizioni Alinari, 1979.

Galassi, Peter. *Before Photography: Painting and the Invention of Photography*. New York: The Museum of Modern Art, 1981.

Gräff, Werner. *Es Kommt der Neue Fotograf!* Berlin: H. Reckendorf, 1929.

Green, Jonathan, ed. *Camera Work: A Critical Anthology*, Millerton, N.Y.: Aperture, 1973.

Harker, Margaret. *The Linked Ring: The Secession Movement in Photography in Britain, 1892–1910*. London: Heineman, 1979.

Homer, William Innes. *Alfred Stieglitz and the American Avant-Garde*. Boston: New York Graphic Society, 1977.

Homer, William Innes. *Alfred Stieglitz and the Photo-Secession*. Boston: A New York Graphic Society Book, Little, Brown and Company, 1983.

Margolis, Marianne Fulton, ed. *Camera Work: A Pictorial Guide*. New York: Dover Publications, 1978.

Mann, Margery. *California Pictorialism*. San Francisco, Cal.: the San Francisco Museum of Modern Art, 1977.

Mellor, David, ed. *Germany: the New Photography, 1927–33*. London: Arts Council of Great Britain, 1978.

Naef, Weston. *Fifty Pioneers of Modern Photography: the Collection of Alfred Stieglitz*. New York: The Metropolitan Museum of Art and Viking Press, 1978.

Neue Sachlichkeit and German Realism of the Twenties. London: Arts Council of Great Britain, 1978.

Panzer, Mary. *Philadelphia Naturalistic Photography, 1865–1906*. New Haven, Conn.: Yale University Art Gallery, 1982.

Photographie Futuriste, Italienne—1911–1939. Paris: Musée d'Art Moderne de la Ville de Paris, 1982.

Pictorial Photography in Britain 1900–1920. London: Arts Council of Great Britain, 1978.

Pictorialism in America: The Minneapolis Salon of Photography, 1932–1946. Minneapolis, Minn.: The Minneapolis Institute of Arts, 1983.

Pultz, John, and Catherine B. Scallen. *Cubism and American Photography, 1910–1930*. Williamstown, Mass.: Sterling and Francine Clark Art Institute, 1981.

Roh, Franz, and Jan Tschichold. *Foto-Auge/oeil et Photo/Photo-Eye*. Tübingen: Ernst Wasmuth Verlag, 1929. Reprint ed., New York: Arno Press, 1978.

Rotzler, Willy. *Photography as Artistic Experiment: From Fox Talbot to Moholy-Nagy*. Garden City, N.Y.: Amphoto, 1976.

Scharf, Aaron. *Art and Photography*. London and Baltimore: Allen Lane, The Penguin Press, 1968, 1969.

Sullivan, Constance, ed. *Nude Photographs: 1850–1980*. New York: Harper and Row, Publishers, 1980.

Szarkowski, John. *Mirrors and Windows: American Photography since 1960*. New York: The Museum of Modern Art, 1978.

Thornton, Gene. *Masters of the Camera: Stieglitz, Steichen and Their Successors*. New York: A Ridge Press Book/Holt, Rinehart, Winston, 1976.

Tucker, Jean S. *Light Abstractions*. St. Louis: University of Missouri, 1980.

COLOR

Coe, Brian. *Colour Photography: the first hundred years, 1840–1940*. London: Ash & Grant, 1978.

Eauclaire, Sally. *The New Color Photography*. New York: Abbeville Press, Inc., 1981.

Friedman, Joseph S. *The History of Colour Photography*. London and New York: Focal Press, 1968.

Géhard, Paul, and André Barret. *Lumière: les premières photographies en couleurs*. Paris: André Barret, 1974.

Holme, Charles, ed. *Colour Photography and other Recent Developments in the Art of the Camera*. London, Paris, New York: The Studio, 1908.

Alexander Liberman, ed. *The Art and Technique of Color Photography*. New York: Simon & Schuster, 1951.

Rathbone, Belinda. *One of a Kind: Recent Polaroid Color Photography*. Boston: David R. Godine, Publisher, n.d. [1979].

Sipley, Louis Walton. *A Half Century of Color*. New York: The Macmillan Company, 1951.

Wall, E. J. *The History of Three Color Photography*. American Photographic Publishing Company, 1925.

DOCUMENTATION: TRAVEL, SOCIAL CONDITIONS, AND WAR.

1910–1916 Antarctic Photographs Herbert Ponting & Frank Hurley: Scott, Mawson and Shackleton Expeditions. South Melbourne: The Macmillan Company of Australia, 1979.

Blom, Benjamin. *People Mostly: New York in Photographs 1900–1950*. New York: The Amaryllis Press, 1983.

Bull, Deborah, and Donald Lorimer. *Up the Nile, A Photographic Excursion: Egypt 1839–1898*. New York: Clarkson N. Potter, Inc., 1979.

Buckland, Gail. *Reality Recorded: Early Documentary Photography*. Greenwich, Conn.: New York Graphic Society, 1974.

Fabian, Rainer, and Hans-Christian Adam. *Masters of Early Travel Photography*. New York: Vendome Press, 1983.

Goetzmann, William. *Exploration and Empire: The Explorer and the Scientist in the Winning of the American West*. New York: Alfred A. Knopf, 1966.

Goodrich, L. Carrington, and Nigel Cameron. *The Face of China As Seen by Photographers & Travelers, 1860–1912*. Millerton, N.Y.: Aperture, 1978.

Hales, Peter Bacon. *Silver Cities: The Photography of American Urbanization, 1839–1915*. Philadelphia: Temple University Press, 1984.

Herskowitz, Robert. *The British Photographer Abroad: The First Thirty Years*. London: Robert Herskowitz, Ltd., 1980.

Hodgson, Pat. *Early War Photographs*. Boston: New York Graphic Society, 1974.

Hurley, F. Jack. *Portrait of a Decade: Roy Stryker and the Development of Documentary Photography in the Thirties*. Baton Rouge: Louisiana State University Press, 1972.

Lewinski, Jorge. *The Camera at War*. New York: Simon and Schuster, 1978.

Lloyd, Valerie. *The Camera and Dr. Barnardo*. Hertford, England: Barnardo School of Printing, n.d.

Lyons, Nathan, ed. *Contemporary Photographers: Toward a Social Landscape*. Rochester: Horizon Press in collaboration with George Eastman House, 1966.

Naef, Weston J., and James N. Wood. *Era of Exploration: The Rise of Landscape Photography in the American West, 1860–1885*. Buffalo, N.Y.: Albright-Knox Art Gallery and New York: The Metropolitan Museum of Art, 1975.

New Topographics: Photographs of a Man-altered Landscape. William Jenkins, intro. Rochester: International Museum of Photography at George Eastman House, 1975.

O'Neal, Hank. *A Vision Shared: A Classic Portrait of America and its People, 1935–1943*. New York: St. Martin's Press, 1976.

Snyder, Joel, and Doug Munson. *The Documentary Photograph as a Work of Art: American Photographs, 1860–1876*. Chicago: The David and Alfred Smart Gallery, The University of Chicago, 1976.

Stott, William. *Documentary Expression and Thirties America*. New York: Oxford University Press, 1973.

Stryker, Roy, and Nancy Wood. *In this Proud Land: America 1935–1943 as Seen in FSA Photographs*. Greenwich, Conn.: New York Graphic Society, 1913.

Vaczek, Louis, and Gail Buckland. *Travelers in Ancient Lands: A Portrait of the Middle East, 1839–1919*. Boston: New York Graphic Society, 1981.

Wolf, Daniel, ed. *The American Space; Meaning in Nineteenth Century Landscape Photography*. Middletown, Conn.: Wesleyan University Press, 1983.

Worswick, Clark, and Ainslee Embree. *The Last Empire: Photography in British India, 1855–1911*. Millerton, N.Y.: Aperture, 1976.

Worswick, Clark, and Jonathan Spence. *Imperial China: Photographs 1850–1912*. Millerton, N.Y.: Aperture, 1976.

ADVERTISING, FASHION, AND PHOTOJOURNALISM.

The Concerned Photographer. New York: Grossman Publishers in cooperation with The International Fund for Concerned Photography, Vol. 1, 1968; vol. 2, 1972.

Devlin, Polly. *Vogue Book of Fashion Photography, 1919–1979*. New York: Simon and Schuster, 1979.

Gidal, Tim N. *Modern Photojournalism: Origin and Evolution, 1910–1933*. New York: Collier Books, A Division of Macmillan Publishing Co., Inc., 1972.

Hall-Duncan, Nancy. *The History of Fashion Photography*. New York: A Chanticleer Press Edition, Alpine Book Co., 1977.

Hassner, Rune. *Bilder för miljoner (Pictures for the Millions)*. Stockholm: Swedish Radio/Rabén & Sjögren, 1977.

Hicks, Wilson. *Words and Pictures: An Introduction to Photojournalism* (1952). Reprint edition, New York: Arno Press, 1973.

Pinney, Roy. *Advertising Photography*. New York: Hastings House Publishers, 1962.

Rothstein, Arthur. *Photojournalism: Pictures for Magazines and Newspapers*. New York: American Photographic Book Publishing Co., Inc., 1965.

GENERAL TOPICS

After Daguerre: Masterworks of French Photography (1848–1900) from the Bibliothèque Nationale. New York: The Metropolitan Museum of Art in association with Berger-Levrault, Paris, 1980.

Bensusan, Arthur D. *Silver Images: A History of Photography in Africa*. Cape Town: H. Timmins, 1966.

Bernard, Bruce. *Photodiscovery: Masterworks of Photography 1840–1940*. New York: Harry N. Abrams, 1980.

Bertell, Richard, with Roy Flukinger, Nancy Keeler and Sydney Kilgore. *Paper and Light: The Calotype in Great Britain and France, 1839–1870*. Boston: David R. Godine, 1984.

The Black Photographers Annual, 4 vols., 1973–1976. Brooklyn, N.Y.: Black Photographers Annual, Inc.

Brewster, Sir David. *The Stereoscope, Its History, Theory and Construction*. Facsimile ed. Dobbs Ferry, N.Y.: Morgan & Morgan, 1971.

Buerger, Janet E. *The Era of the French Calotype*. Rochester: International Museum of Photography at George Eastman House, 1982.

Cato, Jack. *The Story of the Camera in Australia*. Melbourne: Georgetown House, Ltd., 1955.

A Century of Japanese Photography. John Dower, intro. New York: Pantheon Press, 1980.

Coe, Brian, and Paul Gates. *The Snapshot Photograph*. London: Ash and Grant, 1977.

Coke, Van Deren, ed. *One Hundred Years of Photographic History: Essays in Honor of Beaumont Newhall*. Albuquerque: University of New Mexico Press, 1975.

Darrah, William Culp. *Stereo Views: A History of Stereographs in America and Their Collection*. Gettysburg, Pa.: Times and News Publishing Co., 1964.

Dugan, Thomas. *Photography Between Covers*. Rochester: Light Impressions, 1979.

Earle, Edward W., ed. *Points of View: The Stereograph in America —A Cultural History*. Rochester, N.Y.: The Visual Studies Workshop Press in collaboration with the Gallery Association of New York State, 1979.

Farwell, Beatrice. *The Cult of Images: Baudelaire and the 19th-century Media Explosion*. Santa Barbara: University of California, 1977.

Ferrez, Gilberto, and Weston J. Naef. *Pioneer Photographers of Brazil*. New York: Center for Inter-American Relations, 1976.

Film und Foto der zwanziger Jahre: Eine Betrachtung der Internationalen Werkbundaustellung "Film und Foto" 1929. Stuttgart: Verlag Gerd Hatje, 1979.

Fontanella, Lee. *La Historia de la Fotografía en España desde sus orígenes hasta 1900*. Madrid: Ediciones El Viso S. A., 1981.

Fotografia Polska, 1839–1945. New York: International Center of Photography, 1979.

Fotografie Lateinamerika von 1860 bis heute. Zurich: Kunst haus, 1981.

"From today painting is dead": The Beginnings of Photography. London: Arts Council of Great Britain, 1972.

The Frozen Image: Scandinavian Photography. Minneapolis, Minn.: Walker Art Center and New York: Abbeville Press, 1982.

Gee, Helen. *Photography of the Fifties: An American Perspective*. Tucson: Center for Creative Photography, 1980.

Goldschmidt, Lucien, and Weston J. Naef. *The Truthful Lens: A Survey of the Photographically Illustrated Book, 1844–1914*. New York: The Grolier Club, 1980.

Green, Jonathan, ed. *The Snapshot*. Millerton, N.Y.: Aperture, 1974.

Greenhill, Ralph, and Andrew Birrell. *Canadian Photography, 1839–1920*. Toronto: The Coach House Press, 1979.

Group f.64. St. Louis: University of Missouri—St. Louis, 1978.

Gruber, Renate, and L. Fritz. *The Imaginary Photo Museum*, with texts by Helmut Gernsheim, L. Fritz Gruber, Beaumont Newhall, and Jeane von Oppenheim. New York: Harmony Books, 1981.

Gutman, Judith Mara. *Through Indian Eyes: 19th and Early 20th Century Photography from India*. New York: Oxford University Press and International Center for Photography, 1982.

Heyert, Elizabeth. *The Glass-House Years: Victorian Portrait Photography 1839–1870*. Montclair and London: Allanheld & Schram/George Prior, 1979.

Hillier, Bevis. *Victorian Studio Photographs*. London: Ash and Grant, 1975.

Hopkinson, Tom. *Treasures of the Royal Photographic Society, 1839–1919*. London: Focal Press, Inc., 1980.

Hurley, F. Jack. *Industry and the Photographic Image: 153 Great Prints from 1850 to the Present*. New York: Dover Publications, Inc., in association with George Eastman House, Rochester, 1980.

"In unnachahmlicher Treve" Photographie im 19. Jahrhundertihre Geschichte in den deutschsprachigen Ländern. Cologne: State Museum, 1979.

Une Invention du XIXᵉ siècle: la photographie; collections de la société française de photographie. Paris: Bibliothèque Nationale, 1976.

Jammes, André, and Robert Sobieszek. *French Primitive Photography*. Millerton, N.Y.: Aperture, 1970.

Jammes, André, and Eugenia Parry Janis. *The Art of French Calotype*. Princeton: Princeton University Press, 1983.

Jammes, Isabelle. *Blanquart-Evrard et les origines de l'édition photographique française: catalogue rausonné des albums photographiques édités, 1851–1855*. Geneva and Paris: Librarie Droz, 1981.

Japanese Photography Today and its Origin. Bologna: Gratis Edizioni d'arte, 1979.

Kahmen, Volker. *Art History of Photography*. New York: A Studio Book, The Viking Press, 1974.

Katzman, Louise. *Photography in California, 1945–1980*. New York: Hudson Hills Press, in association with the San Francisco Museum of Modern Art, 1984.

Kempe, Fritz. *Daguerreotypie in Deutschland*. Seebruck am Chiemsee: Heering Verlag, 1979.

Loke, Margaret. *The world as it was: Photographic Portrait, 1865–1921*. New York: Summit Books, 1980.

Lucie-Smith, Edward. *The Invented Eye: Masterpieces of Photography, 1839–1914*. New York and London: Paddington Press Ltd., 1975.

Maddow, Ben. *Faces: A Narrative History of the Portrait in Photography*. Boston: New York Graphic Society, 1977.

Magelhaes, Claude, and Laurent Roosens. *Photographic Art in Belgium 1839–1940*. Antwerp: Het Sterckshof Museum, 1970.

Mathews, Oliver. *The Album of Carte-de-visite and Cabinet Portrait Photographs 1854-1914*. London: Reedminster Publications Ltd., 1974.

McCauley, Elizabeth Anne. *Likenesses: Portrait Photography in Europe 1850-1870*. Albuquerque: Art Museum, University of New Mexico, 1980.

Morgan, Hal, and Andreas Brown. *Prairie Fires and Paper Moons, the American Photographic Postcard: 1900-1920*. Boston: David R. Godine, 1981.

Newhall, Beaumont. *Airborne Camera: The World from the Air and Outer Space*. New York: Hastings House, Publishers, 1969.

Newhall, Beaumont. *The Daguerreotype in America*, 3rd revised edition. New York: Dover Publications, Inc., 1976.

Newhall, Beaumont. *Latent Image: The Discovery of Photography*. Garden City, N.Y.: Anchor Books, Doubleday & Co., Inc., 1967.

Pfister, Harold Francis. *Facing the Light: Historic American Portrait Daguerreotypes*. Washington, D.C.: Smithsonian Institution Press for the National Portrait Gallery, 1978.

Photography Rediscovered: American Photographs, 1900-1930. Essay by David Travis. New York: Whitney Museum of American Art, 1979.

Photography in Switzerland: 1840 to today. New York: Visual Communications Books, Hastings House, Publishers, 1974.

The Real Thing: An Anthology of British Photographs, 1840-1950. Essays by Ian Jeffrey and David Mellor. London: Arts Council of Great Britain, 1975.

Rinhart, Floyd and Marion. *The American Daguerreotype*. Athens: University of Georgia Press, 1981.

Robinson, William F. *A Certain Slant of Light: The First Hundred Years of New England Photography*. Boston: New York Graphic Society, 1980.

Rudisill, Richard. *Mirror Image: The Influence of the Daguerreotype on American Society*. Albuquerque: University of New Mexico Press, 1971.

Scharf, Aaron. *Pioneers of Photography*. New York: Harry N. Abrams, Inc., 1975.

Un siècle de photographie de Niépce à Man Ray. Paris: Musée des arts décoratifs, 1965.

Shudakov, Grigory, Olga Suslova, and Lilya Ukhtomskaya. *Pioneers of Soviet Photography*. London: Thames and Hudson, 1983.

Szarkowski, John. *New Japanese Photography*. New York: Museum of Modern Art, 1974.

Tucker, Ann, ed. *The Woman's Eye*. New York: Alfred A. Knopf, 1973.

Watson, Wendy M. *Images of Italy: Photography in the Nineteenth Century*. South Hadley, Mass.: Mount Holyoke College Art Museum, 1980.

Women of Photography: An Historical Survey. San Francisco, Cal.: San Francisco Museum of Art, 1975.

MONOGRAPHS

BERENICE ABBOTT

O'Neal, Hank. *Berenice Abbott, American Photographer*. New York: McGraw-Hill Book Company, An Artpress Book, 1982.

Abbott, Berenice. *New York in the Thirties*. Reprint edition of *Changing New York*, text by Elizabeth McCausland (1939). New York: Dover Publications, 1973.

ANSEL ADAMS

Ansel Adams: Images 1923-1974, Boston: New York Graphic Society, 1974.

Newhall, Nancy. *Ansel Adams: The Eloquent Light*. San Francisco: Sierra Club, 1963.

Adams, Ansel. *Photographs of the Southwest*. Boston: New York Graphic Society, 1976.

ALINARI BROTHERS (company)

Zevi, Filippo. *Alinari—Photographers of Florence, 1852-1920*. Edinburgh and Florence: Idea Editions and Edizioni Alinari in association with the Scottish Arts Council, 1978.

THOMAS ANNAN

Annan, Thomas. *Photographs of the Old Closes and Streets of Glasgow, 1868-1877*. Anita Ventura Mozeley, intro. Reprint edition: New York: Dover Publications, Inc., 1977.

DIANE ARBUS

Diane Arbus. Millerton, N.Y.: Aperture, 1972.

Bosworth, Patricia. *Diane Arbus: A Biography*. New York: Alfred A. Knopf, 1984.

EUGÈNE ATGET

Abbott, Berenice. *The World of Atget*. New York: Paragon Books, G. P. Putnam's Sons, 1979.

Szarkowski, John, and Maria Morris Hambourg. *The Work of Atget*, Vol. I: *Old France*; Vol. II: *The Art of Old Paris*; Vol. III: *The Ancien Regime*; Vol. IV: *Modern Times* (to be published). New York: Museum of Modern Art, 1981, 1982, 1984.

A Vision of Paris; The Photographs of Eugène Atget; The Words of Marcel Proust. Arthur D. Trottenberg, ed. New York: The Macmillan Company, 1963.

ALICE AUSTEN

Novotny, Ann. *Alice's World: The Life and Photography of an American Original*. Old Greenwich, Conn.: Chatham Press, 1976.

GEORGE N. BARNARD

Barnard, George N. *Photographic Views of Sherman's Campaign*. Preface by Beaumont Newhall, New York: Dover Publications, Inc., 1977.

HIPPOLYTE BAYARD

Lo Duca, [Joseph-Marie]. *Bayard*. (1943). New York: Arno Press reprint, 1979.

HERBERT BAYER

Herbert Bayer: Photographic Works. Essay by Beaumont Newhall. Los Angeles: Arco Center for Visual Art, 1977.

F. J. BELLOCQ

Bellocq, E.J. *Storyville Portraits*. John Szarkowski, ed.; preface by Lee Friedlander. New York: The Museum of Modern Art, 1970.

KARL BLOSSFELDT

Blossfeldt, Karl. *Urformen der Kunst*. Tübingen: Ernst Wasmuth Verlag, 1928.

ERWIN BLUMENFELD

Blumenfeld: My One Hundred Best Photographs. Hendel Teicher, ed. New York: Rizzoli, 1981.

MARGARET BOURKE-WHITE

The Photographs of Margaret Bourke-White. Sean Callahan, ed. Boston: New York Graphic Society, 1972.

Silverman, Jonathan. *For the World to See: The Life of Margaret Bourke-White*. New York: A Studio Book, The Viking Press, 1983.

Bourke-White, Margaret, and Erskine Caldwell. *You Have Seen Their Faces*. New York: Modern Age Books, 1937. Reprint edition: New York: Dover Publications, Inc., 1975.

SAMUEL BOURNE

Bourne, Samel. *Images of India*. Carmel: The Friends of Photography, 1983.

MATHEW BRADY

Meredith, Roy. *Mathew Brady's Portrait of an Era*. New York & London: W. W. Norton & Company, 1982.

BILL BRANDT

The Shadow of Light: A collection of Photographs from 1931 to the Present. Cyril Connolly, intro. London: Bodley Head, 1966.

BRASSAÏ

Brassaï. Lawrence Durrell, intro. New York: Museum of Modern Art, 1968.

Brassaï (Gyula Halász). *Paris de Nuit*. Paris: Arts et Metiers Graphiques, 1933.

Brassaï (Gyula Halász). *The Secret Paris of the 1930s*. (Published in Paris as *Le Paris secret des années 30*). New York: Random House, Pantheon Books, 1976.

M. ALVAREZ BRAVO

Livingston, Jane. *M. Alvarez Bravo*. Boston and Washington, D.C.: David R. Godine, Publisher, and The Corcoran Gallery, 1978.

FRANCIS BRUGUIÈRE

Enyeart, James. *Bruguière: His Photographs and His Life*. New York: Alfred A. Knopf, 1977.

WYNN BULLOCK

Wynn Bullock, Photography: A Way of Life. Liliane de Cock, ed. Dobbs Ferry, N.Y.: Morgan & Morgan, 1973.

HARRY CALLAHAN

Callahan. John Szarkowski, ed. New York and Millerton, N.Y.: Museum of Modern Art and Aperture, 1976.

Harry Callahan: Photographs. Keith F. Davis, ed. Kansas City, Mo.: Hallmark Cards, Inc., 1981.

JULIA MARGARET CAMERON

Ford, Colin. *The Cameron Collection, An Album of Photographs by Julia Margaret Cameron Presented to Sir John Herschel*. New York: Van Nostrand Reinhold and London: The National Portrait Gallery, 1975.

Victorian Photographs of Famous Men and Fair Women. Intro. by Virginia Woolf and Roger Fry. Preface and notes by Tristram Powell. Boston: David R. Godine, 1973.

Gernsheim, Helmut. *Julia Margaret Cameron: Pioneer of Photography*. London: Fountain Press, 1948; 2nd edition, Millerton, N.Y.: Aperture, 1975.

ROBERT CAPA

Capa, Robert. *Death in the Making: Photographs by Robert Capa and Gerda Taro*. Arrangement by André Kertész. New York: Covici Friede, 1938.

PAUL CAPONIGRO

Paul Caponigro, Millerton, N.Y.: Aperture, 1967.

LEWIS CARROLL

Gernsheim, Helmut. *Lewis Carroll, Photographer*. (1949). Revised ed. New York: Dover Publications, Inc., 1979.

HENRI CARTIER-BRESSON

Henri Cartier-Bresson: Photographer. Boston: New York Graphic Society, 1979.

Cartier-Bresson, Henri. *The World of Henri Cartier-Bresson*. New York: Viking, 1968.

Cartier-Bresson, Henri. *The Decisive Moment*. New York: Simon and Schuster, 1952.

DÉSIRÉ CHARNAY

Davis, Keith F. *Désiré Charnay—Expeditionary Photographer*. Albuquerque: University of New Mexico Press, 1981.

ALVIN LANGDON COBURN

Alvin Langdon Coburn: Photographer—An Autobiography. Helmut and Alison Gernsheim, eds. (1968). Revised ed. New York: Dover Publications, Inc., 1978.

IMOGEN CUNNINGHAM

Imogen Cunningham: Photographs. Margery Mann, intro. Seattle: University of Washington Press, 1970.

EDWARD S. CURTIS

The North American Indians: A Selection of Photographs by Edward S. Curtis. Joseph Epes Brown, intro. New York: Aperture, 1972.

Graybill, Florence Curtis, and Victor Boesen. *Edward Sheriff Curtis: Visions of a Vanishing Race.* New York: American Legacy Press, 1976.

Lyman, Christopher M. *The Vanishing Race and Other Illusions: Photographs of Indians by Edward S. Curtis.* New York: Pantheon Books, 1982.

LOUIS JACQUES MANDÉ DAGUERRE

Daguerre, Louis Jacques Mandé. *An Historical and Descriptive Account of the Various Processes of the Daguerreotype and the Diorama* (1839). Reprint ed. with intro. by Beaumont Newhall. New York: Winter House, Ltd., 1971.

Gernsheim, Helmut and Alison. *L.J.M. Daguerre: The History of the Diorama and the Daguerreotype.* Reprint ed. New York: Dover Publications, Inc., 1968.

BRUCE DAVIDSON

Davidson, Bruce. *East 100th Street.* Cambridge, Mass.: Harvard University Press, 1970.

F. HOLLAND DAY

Jussim, Estelle. *Slave to Beauty: The Eccentric Life and Controversial Career of F. Holland Day.* Boston: David R. Godine, 1981.

ROY DECARAVA

Roy DeCarava, Photographs. James Alinder, ed., intro. by Sherry Turner DeCarava. Carmel: Friends of Photography, 1981.

DeCarava, Roy, and Langston Hughes. *The Sweet Flypaper of Life.* New York: Simon and Schuster, 1955.

RAJA LALA DEEN DAYAL

Worswick, Clark. *Princely India: Photographs by Raja Lala Deen Dayal, Court Photographer (1884-1910) to the Premier Prince of India.* New York: A Pennwick/Agrinde Book Published with Alfred A. Knopf, 1980.

ROBERT DEMACHY

Jay, Bill. *Robert Demachy; 1859-1936: Photographs and Essays.* London: Academy Editions, 1974.

ADOLPHE DE MEYER

De Meyer. Robert Brandau, ed.; essay by Philippe Jullian. New York: Alfred A. Knopf, 1976.

ROBERT DOISNEAU

Le Paris de Robert Doisneau et Max Pol Fouchet. Paris: Les Éditeurs Français Réunis, n.d.

Three Seconds From Eternity: Photographs by Robert Doisneau. Boston: New York Graphic Society, 1979.

THOMAS EAKINS

Hendricks, Gordon. *The Photographs of Thomas Eakins.* New York: Grossman Publishers, 1972.

ALFRED EISENSTAEDT

Eisenstaedt, Alfred. *Witness to Our Time.* Foreword by Henry R. Luce. New York: Viking Press, 1966; revised ed., 1980.

P. H. EMERSON

Newhall, Nancy. *P. H. Emerson: The Fight for Photography as a Fine Art.* Millerton, N.Y.: Aperture, 1975.

Turner, Peter, and Richard Wood. *P. H. Emerson: Photographer of Norfolk.* Boston: David R. Godine, 1974.

FREDERICK H. EVANS

Newhall, Beaumont. *Frederick H. Evans: Photographer of the majesty, light and space of the medieval cathedrals of England and France.* Millerton, N.Y.: Aperture, 1973.

WALKER EVANS

Walker Evans. John Szarkowski, intro. New York: Museum of Modern Art, 1971.

Walker Evans, First and Last. New York: Harper and Row, 1978.

Walker Evans, Photographs from the Farm Security Administration, 1935-1938. Jerald C. Maddox, intro. New York: Da Capo Press, 1975.

Agee, James, and Walker Evans. *Let Us Now Praise Famous Men.* Boston: Houghton Mifflin Company, The Riverside Press, Cambridge, 1960.

ROGER FENTON

Gernsheim, Helmut and Alison. *Roger Fenton, Photographer of the Crimean War.* (1954). Reprint ed. New York: Arno Press, 1973.

Hannavy, John. *Roger Fenton of Crimble Hall.* Boston: David R. Godine, Publisher, 1975.

ROBERT FRANK

Frank, Robert. *Les Américains.* Paris: Delpire, 1958. Published in English as *The Americans.* Intro. by Jack Keroac. New York: Grove Press, 1959. Revised editions: Millerton, N.Y.: Aperture, 1969, 1978.

FRANCIS FRITH

Jay, Bill. *Victorian Cameraman: Francis Frith's View of Rural England, 1850-1898.* Newton Abbot: David and Charles, 1973.

Frith, Francis. *Egypt and the Holy Land in Historic Photographs.* New York: Dover Publications, Inc. Reprint ed., 1980.

ALEXANDER GARDNER

Gardner, Alexander. *Gardner's Photographic Sketchbook of the Civil War.* New York: Dover Publications, Inc., 1959.

ARNOLD GENTHE

Genthe, Arnold. *As I Remember.* New York: Reynal & Hitchcock, 1936. Arno Press: reprint edition, 1979.

JIMMY HARE

Gould, Lewis L., and Richard Greffe. *Photojournalist: The Career of Jimmy Hare*. Austin and London: University of Texas Press, 1977.

RAOUL HAUSMANN

Hausmann, Raoul. *Photographies 1927–1957*. Paris: Éditions Créatis, 1979.

LADY HAWARDEN

Clementina, Lady Hawarden. Graham Ovenden, ed. London: Academy Editions and New York: St. Martin's Press, 1974.

JOHN HEARTFIELD

Herzeflde, Wieland. *John Heartfield: Leben und Werke*. Dresden: VEB Verlag der Kunst, 1970.

Heartfield, John. *Photomontages of the Nazi Period*. New York: Universe Books, 1977.

Tucholsky, Kurt. *Deutschland, Deutschland Über Alles*, with montages by John Heartfield. Amherst: University of Massachusetts Press, 1972.

DAVID OCTAVIUS HILL AND ROBERT ADAMSON

An Early Victorian Album: The Photographic Masterpieces (1843–47) of David Octavius Hill and Robert Adamson. Ed. and intro. by Colin Ford; essay by Roy Strong. New York: Alfred A. Knopf, 1976.

Schwarz, Heinrich. *David Octavius Hill: Master of Photography*. London: George C. Harrap & Co., 1932.

LEWIS W. HINE

Gutman, Judith Mara. *Lewis W. Hine and the American Social Conscience*. New York: Walker and Co., 1967.

Rosenblum, Walter and Naomi, and Alan Trachtenberg. *America and Lewis Hine*. Millerton, N.Y.: Aperture, 1977.

Hine, Lewis W. *Men at Work*. New York: The Macmillan Company. (1932). Reprint edition, Dover Publications, Inc., 1977.

WILLIAM HENRY JACKSON

Jackson, Clarence S. *Picture Maker of the Old West, William Henry Jackson*. New York: Charles Scribner's Sons, 1947.

Newhall, Beaumont, and Diana E. Edkins. *William H. Jackson*. Ft. Worth, Tex.: Amon Carter Museum and Dobbs Ferry, N.Y.: Morgan and Morgan, 1974.

FRANCES B. JOHNSTON

Daniel, Pete, and Raymond Smock. *A Talent for Detail: The Photographs of Frances Benjamin Johnston, 1889–1910*. New York: Harmony Books, 1974.

Johnston, Frances Benjamin. *The Hampton Album*. New York: The Museum of Modern Art, 1966.

GERTRUDE KÄSEBIER

Homer, William Innes. *A Pictorial Heritage: The Photographs of Gertrude Käsebier*. Wilmington: Delaware Art Museum, 1979.

ANDRÉ KERTÉSZ

André Kertész: Sixty Years of Photography, 1912–1972. Nicholas Ducrot, ed. New York: Grossman Publishers, 1972.

Kertész, André. *J'Aime Paris*. New York: Grossman Publishers, A Division of Viking Press, 1974.

Kertész, André. *On Reading*. New York: Grossman Publishers, 1971.

WILLIAM KLEIN

William Klein: Photographs. Profile by John Heilpern. Millerton, N.Y.: Aperture, 1981.

JOSEF KOUDELKA

Koudelka, Josef. *Gypsies*. Millerton, N.Y.: Aperture, 1975.

DOROTHEA LANGE

Dorothea Lange: Photographs of a Lifetime. Millerton, N.Y.: Aperture, 1982.

Elliot, George P. *Dorothea Lange*. New York: Museum of Modern Art, 1966.

Meltzer, Milton. *Dorothea Lange, A Photographer's Life*. New York: Farrar, Straus, Giroux, 1978.

Lange, Dorothea, and Paul S. Taylor. *An American Exodus*. Oakland, Cal.: Oakland Museum and New Haven: Yale University Press, 1969.

JACQUES HENRI LARTIGUE

Lartigue, Jacques Henri. *Boyhood Photos of J. H. Lartique: The Family Album of a Gilded Age*. Lausanne: Ami Guichard, 1966.

Lartigue, Jacques Henri. *Instants de Ma Vie*. Paris: Éditions du Chêne, 1970.

CLARENCE JAY LAUGHLIN

Laughlin, Clarence John. *Ghosts Along the Mississippi*. New York: Bonanza Books, 1961.

RUSSELL LEE

Hurley, F. Jack. *Russell Lee, Photographer*. Dobbs Ferry, N.Y.: Morgan & Morgan, 1978.

HELMAR LERSKI

Lerski, Helmar. *Kopfe des Alltags*. Berlin: Hermann Reckendorf Verlag, 1931.

HELEN LEVITT

A Way of Seeing. Essay by James Agee. New York: Museum of Modern Art, 1965.

DANNY LYON

Lyon, Danny. *Conversations with the Dead*. New York: Rinehart and Winston, 1971.

PETER MAGUBENE

Magubene, Peter. *Magubene's South Africa*. New York: Alfred A. Knopf, 1978.

MAN RAY

Penrose, Roland. *Man Ray*. Boston: New York Graphic Society, 1975.

Man Ray. *Self-Portrait*. Boston: Little, Brown and Company, 1963.

E. J. MAREY

E. J. Marey: 1830–1904, La Photographie du Movement. Paris: Centre Georges Pompidou, 1977.

PAUL MARTIN

Flukinger, Roy, Larry Schaaf, and Standish Meacham. *Paul Martin: Victorian Photographer*. Austin: University of Texas Press, 1977.

RALPH EUGENE MEATYARD

Ralph Eugene Meatyard. James Baker Hall, ed. Millerton, N.Y.: Aperture, 1974.

JOEL MEYROWITZ

Meyrowitz, Joel. *St. Louis & the Arch*. Preface by James N. Wood. Boston: New York Graphic Society in association with the St. Louis Art Museum, 1980.

LISETTE MODEL

Lisette Model. Preface by Berenice Abbott. Millerton, N.Y.: Aperture, 1979.

TINA MODOTTI

Constantine, Mildred. *Tina Modotti: A Fragile Life*. New York and London: Paddington Press Ltd., 1975.

LÁSZLÓ MOHOLY-NAGY

Haus, Andreas. *Moholy-Nagy: Photographs and Photograms*. New York: Pantheon Books, 1980.

Moholy-Nagy, László. *Malerei Photographie Film* Bauhausbook 8. Munich: Albert Langen Verlag, 1925, revised 1927. English edition, *Painting Photography Film*. Cambridge, Mass.: The M.I.T. Press, 1969.

Moholy-Nagy, László. *Vision in Motion*. Chicago: Paul Theobold and Co., 1947.

BARBARA MORGAN

Barbara Morgan: Photomontage, Dobbs Ferry, N.Y.: Morgan & Morgan, 1980.

Morgan, Barbara. *Martha Graham: Sixteen Dances in Photographs*. New York: Duell, Sloan & Pearce. (1941). Reprint edition, Dobbs Ferry, N.Y.: Morgan & Morgan, 1980.

WRIGHT MORRIS

Wright Morris: Photographs and Words. James Alinder, ed. Carmel: The Friends of Photography, 1982.

MARTIN MUNKACSI

White, Nancy, and John Esten. *Style in Motion: Munkacsi Photographs '20s, '30s, '40s*. New York: Clarkson N. Potter, Inc., Publishers, 1979.

EADWEARD MUYBRIDGE

Haas, Robert Bartlett. *Muybridge: Man in Motion*. Berkeley, Los Angeles, London: University of California Press, 1976.

Hendricks, Gordon. *Eadweard Muybridge—The Father of the Motion Picture*. New York: Grossman Publishers, A Division of Viking Press, 1975.

Eadweard Muybridge: The Stanford Years, 1872–1882. Anita Ventura Mozley, intro. Palo Alto: Stanford University Museum of Art, 1972.

Muybridge's Complete Human and Animal Locomotion. Anita Ventura Mozley, intro. 3 vols., New York: Dover Publications, Inc., 1979.

NADAR

Gosling, Nigel. *Nadar*. New York: Alfred A. Knopf, 1976.

Prinet, Jean, and Antoinette Dilasser. *Nadar*. Paris: Armand Colin, 1966.

Nadar. *Quand j'étais photographe*. Preface by Leon Daudet. (1900). New York: Arno Press reprint, 1979.

NAYA (company)

Zannier, Italo. *Venice, The Naya Collection*. Venice: O. Böhm, Publishers, 1981.

CHARLES NÉGRE

Borcorman, James. *Charles Nègre*. Ottawa: The National Galleries of Canada, 1976.

ARNOLD NEWMAN

One Mind's Eye: The Portraits and Other Photographs of Arnold Newman. Boston: David R. Godine, Publisher, 1974.

WILLIAM NOTMAN

Harper, J. R., and S. Triggs. *William Notman: Portrait of a Period*. Montreal: McGill University Press, 1975.

TIMOTHY O'SULLIVAN

Snyder, Joel. *American Frontiers: The Photographs of Timothy H. O'Sullivan, 1867–1874*. Millerton, N.Y.: Aperture, 1981.

PAUL OUTERBRIDGE, JR.

Paul Outerbridge, Jr.: Photographs. Graham Howe and G. Ray Hawkins, eds. New York: Rizzoli, 1980.

IRVING PENN

Penn, Irving. *Worlds in a Small Room*. New York: Grossman/Viking Press, 1974.

ELIOT PORTER

Intimate Landscapes: Photographs by Eliot Porter. Essay by Weston J. Naef. New York: The Metropolitan Museum of Art/E. P. Dutton, 1979.

GIUSEPPE PRIMOLI

Vitali, Lamberto. *Un Fotografo fin-de-siècle: Il Conte Primoli*. Turin: Einaudi, 1968.

SERGEI MIKHAILOVICH PROKUDIN-GORSKII

Photographs for the Tsar: the Pioneering Color Photography of Sergei Mikhailovich Prokudin-Gorskii. Robert H. Allhouse, ed. New York: The Dial Press, 1980.

OSCAR GUSTAVE REJLANDER

Jones, Edgar Yoxall. *Father of Art Photography, O.G. Rejlander 1813–1875*. Greenwich, Conn.: New York Graphic Society, 1973.

ALBERT RENGER-PATZSCH

Albert Renger-Patzsch, 100 Photographs, 1928. Essays in English, German and French. Cologne and Boston: Schürman & Kicken Books and Paris: Créatis, 1979.

Renger-Patzsch, Albert. *Die Welt ist Schön: Einhundert Photographische Aufnahme*. Published in English as *The World is Beautiful*. Munich: Kurt Wolff Verlag, 1928.

JACOB A. RIIS

Alland, Alexander, Sr. *Jacob A. Riis, Photographer and Citizen*. Millerton, N.Y.: Aperture, 1974.

Riis, Jacob A. *How the Other Half Lives: Studies Among the Tenements of New York*. New York: Charles Scribner's Sons, 1890. Reprint edition with added photographs, New York: Dover Publications, Inc., 1971.

HENRY PEACH ROBINSON

Robinson, Henry Peach. *Pictorial Effect in Photography*. Intro. by Robert Sobieszek. Reprint edition, Pawlet, Vermont: Helios, 1972.

ALEXANDER RODCHENKO

Alexander Rodchenko: 1891–1956. David Elliot, ed. Oxford: Museum of Modern Art, 1979.

Karginov, German. *Rodchenko*. London: Thames and Hudson, Ltd., 1979.

ARTHUR ROTHSTEIN

Rothstein, Arthur. *The Depression Years as Photographed by Arthur Rothstein*. New York: Dover Publications, Inc., 1978.

ERICH SALOMON

Hunter-Salomon, Peter. *Erich Salomon: Portrait of An Age*. New York: The Macmillan Co., 1967.

Salomon, Erich. *Porträt Einer Epoch*. Frankfurt/M-Berlin: Verlag Ullstein GmbH, 1963. Published in English as *Portrait of an Age*. New York: The Macmillan Company, 1967.

AUGUST SANDER

August Sander: Photographs of an Epoch, 1904–1959. Preface by Beaumont Newhall; historical commentary by Robert Kramer. Millerton, N.Y.: Aperture, 1980.

Sander, August. *Antlitz der Zeit*. Munich: Kurt Wolff/Transmare Verlag, 1929.

Sander, August. *Men Without Masks: Faces of Germany, 1910–1938*. Greenwich, Conn.: New York Graphic Society, 1971.

BEN SHAHN

The Photographic Eye of Ben Shahn. Davis Pratt, ed. Cambridge: Harvard University Press, 1975.

CHARLES SHEELER

Millard, Charles W., III. "Charles Sheeler, American Photographer," *Contemporary Photographer*, vol. 6, no. 1 (1967) entire issue.

AARON SISKIND

Aaron Siskind Photographer. Nathan Lyons, ed. Rochester, N.Y.: George Eastman House, 1965.

Siskind, Aaron. *Places: Aaron Siskind Photographs*. New York: Light Gallery and Farrar, Straus, Giroux, 1976.

W. EUGENE SMITH

W. Eugene Smith: His Photographs and Notes. Millerton, N.Y.: Aperture, 1969.

W. Eugene Smith: Master of the Photographic Essay. William S. Johnson, ed. Millerton, N.Y.: Aperture, 1981.

Smith, W. Eugene and Aileen M. *Minamata*. New York: Holt, Rinehart and Winston, 1975.

FREDERICK SOMMER

Venus, Jupiter and Mars: Frederick Sommer. John Weiss, ed. Wilmington: Delaware Art Museum, 1980.

ALBERT SANDS SOUTHWORTH AND JOSIAH JOHNSON HAWES

Sobieszek, Robert, and Odette M. Appel. *The Spirit of Fact: the Daguerreotypes of Southworth and Hawes*. Boston and Rochester: David R. Godine and The International Museum of Photography, 1976.

EDWARD STEICHEN

Longwell, Dennis. *Steichen, the Master Prints, 1895–1914*. New York: Museum of Modern Art and Boston: New York Graphic Society, 1978.

Steichen, Edward. *A Life in Photography*. Garden City, N.Y.: Doubleday, 1963.

RALPH STEINER

Steiner, Ralph. *A Point of View*. Middletown, Conn.: Wesleyan University Press, 1978.

ALFRED STIEGLITZ

Greenough, Sarah, and Juan Hamilton. *Alfred Stieglitz, Photographs & Writings*. Washington: National Gallery of Art and New York: Callaway Editions, 1983.

Homer, William Innes. *Alfred Stieglitz and the Photo-Secession*. Boston: A New York Graphic Society Book, Little, Brown and Company, 1983.

Norman, Dorothy. *Alfred Stieglitz: An American Seer*. Millerton, N.Y.: Aperture and New York: Random House, 1973.

Waldo, Frank, et al. *America and Alfred Stieglitz: A Collective Portrait*. (1934). New rev. ed., Millerton, N.Y.: Aperture, 1979.

BENJAMIN STONE

Jay, Bill. *Customs & Faces: Photographs by Sir Benjamin Stone, 1838–1914*. London: Academy Editions and New York: St. Martin's Press, 1972.

PAUL STRAND

Paul Strand: Sixty Years of Photographs. Profile by Calvin Tompkins. Millerton, N.Y.: Aperture, 1976.

Paul Strand: A Retrospective Monograph, the Years 1915–1968, 2 vols. Millerton, N.Y.: Aperture, 1971.

Strand, Paul, and Nancy Newhall. *Time in New England*. New York: Oxford University Press, 1950; Reprint Edition, revised, Millerton, N.Y.: Aperture, 1982.

Strand, Paul, and Claude Roy. *La France de Profile*, Lausanne: Editions Clairefontaine, 1952.

Strand, Paul, and Cesare Zavattini. *Un Paese*. Turin: Einaudi, 1955.

KARL STRUSS

Harvith, Susan and John. *Karl Struss: Man With a Camera*. Bloomfield Hills: Cranbrook Academy of Art Museum, 1976.

JOSEF SUDEK

Bullaty, Sonja, *Sudek*. New York: Clarkson N. Potter, Inc., 1978.

FRANK SUTCLIFFE

Hiley, Michael. *Frank Sutcliffe*. Boston: David R. Godine, Publisher, 1974.

WILLIAM HENRY FOX TALBOT

Arnold, H. J. P. *William Henry Fox Talbot: Pioneer of Photography and Man of Science*. London: Hutchinson Benham Ltd., 1977.

Buckland, Gail. *Fox Talbot and the Invention of Photography*. Boston: David R. Godine, Publisher, 1980.

Talbot, William Henry Fox. *The Pencil of Nature*. Facsimile edition. New York: Da Capo Press, 1961.

JOHN THOMSON

Thomson, John. *China and its People in Early Photographs; An unabridged reprint of the classic 1873/74 work*. New York: Dover Publications, Inc., 1982.

Thompson [sic], John, and Adolphe Smith. *Street Life in London*. Bronx, N.Y.: Bernard Blom, Inc., 1969 (facsimile edition).

HEINRICH TÖNNIES

Alland, Alexander, Sr. *Heinrich Tönnies: Carte-de-visite Photographer Extraordinaire*. New York: Camera Graphic Press, 1978.

JERRY N. UELSMANN

Jerry N. Uelsmann. Essay by Peter Bunnell. Millerton, N.Y.: Aperture, 1970.

Uelsmann, Jerry N. *Silver Meditations*. Dobbs Ferry, N.Y.: Morgan & Morgan, 1975.

DORIS ULMANN

The Darkness and the Light: Photographs by Doris Ulmann. Millerton, N.Y.: Aperture, 1974.

JAMES VAN DER ZEE

James Van Der Zee, Dobbs Ferry, N.Y.: Morgan & Morgan, 1973.

ROMAN VISHNIAC

Roman Vishniac, New York: Grossman Publishers, A Division of Viking Press, 1974.

ADAM CLARK VROMAN

Webb, William, and Robert A. Weinstein. *Dwellers at the Source: Southwestern Indian Photographs by A. C. Vroman, 1895–1904*. New York: Grossman Publishers, 1973.

CARLETON WATKINS

Palmquist, Peter E. *Carleton E. Watkins: Photographer of the American West*. Albuquerque: University of New Mexico Press, 1983.

WEEGEE (ARTHUR FELLIG)

Weegee. Louis Stettner, ed. New York: Alfred A. Knopf, 1977.

Weegee. *Naked City*. New York: Essential Books, 1946.

BRETT WESTON

Brett Weston: Voyage of the Eye, Millerton, N.Y.: Aperture, 1975.

EDWARD WESTON

Edward Weston Nudes. Millerton, N.Y.: Aperture, 1977.

Maddow, Ben. *Edward Weston: Fifty Years*. Millerton, N.Y.: Aperture, 1973.

The Daybooks of Edward Weston, 2 vols. Nancy Newhall, ed. Millerton, N.Y.: Aperture, 1973.

Weston, Edward. *My Camera at Point Lobos*. Yosemite National Park: Virginia Adams and Boston: Houghton Mifflin Co., 1950.

Wilson, Charis, and Edward Weston. *California and the West.* (1940). Reprint ed., Millerton, N.Y.: Aperture, 1978.

CLARENCE H. WHITE

Homer, William Innes. *Symbolism of Light: The Photographs of Clarence H. White.* Wilmington: Delaware Art Museum, 1977.

MINOR WHITE

Minor White: Rites and Passages. His Photographs Accompanied by Excerpts from His Diaries and Letters. Millerton, N.Y.: Aperture, 1978.

GEORGE WASHINGTON WILSON

Taylor, Roger. *George Washington Wilson: Artist and Photographer 1823-93.* Aberdeen: Aberdeen University Press, 1981.

GARRY WINOGRAND

Winogrand, Garry. *Women Are Beautiful.* New York: Farrar, Straus & Giroux, 1975.

HEINRICH ZILLE

Ranke, Winfried. *Heinrich Zille: Photographien Berlin, 1890-1910.* Munich: Schirmer-Mosel, 1975.

PHOTOGRAPHIC TECHNOLOGY
PRINTING TECHNOLOGY, AND CONSERVATION.

Aver, Michel. *The Illustrated History of the Camera, from 1839 to the Present.* Boston: New York Graphic Society, [1975].

Coe, Brian. *Cameras: From Daguerreotypes to Instant Pictures.* New York: Crown Publishers, Inc., 1978.

Coe, Brian, ed. *Techniques of the World's Great Photographers.* Secaucus, N.J.: Chartwell Books, Inc., 1981.

Crawford, William. *The Keepers of the Light—A History and Working Guide to Early Photographic Processes.* Dobbs Ferry, N.Y.: Morgan & Morgan, 1979.

Edgerton, Harold E., and James R. Killian, Jr. *Moments of Vision: The Stroboscopic Revolution in Photography.* Cambridge, Mass.: MIT Press, 1979.

Goldsmith, Arthur. *The Camera and Its Images.* New York: A Ridge Press book/Newsweek Books, 1979.

Hammond, John H. *The Camera Obscura: A Chronicle.* Bristol: Adam Hilger Ltd., 1981.

Jenkins, Reese V. *Images and Enterprises: Technology and the American Photographic Industry, 1839-1925.* Baltimore and London: The Johns Hopkins University Press, 1975.

Jussim, Estelle. *Visual Communication and the Graphic Arts: Photographic Technologies in the Nineteenth Century.* New York: R. R. Bowker Company, 1974.

Keefe, Laurence E., Jr., and Dennis Inch. *The Life of a Photograph.* Boston and London: The Focal Press, 1983.

Land, Edwin H., Howard G. Rogers, and Vivian K. Walworth. *One-Step Photography.* New York: Van Nostrand Reinhold Company. Reprint ed., 1977.

Lothrop, Eaton S., Jr. *A Century of Cameras from the Collection of the International Museum at George Eastman House.* Dobbs Ferry, N.Y.: Morgan & Morgan, 1973.

Mees, C. E. Kenneth. *From Dry Plates to Ektachrome Film.* New York: Ziff-Davis, 1961.

Pirenne, M. H. *Optics, Painting & Photography.* Cambridge: Cambridge University Press, 1970.

Time-Life Books. *Caring for Photographs: Display, Storage, Restoration.* New York: Time-Life, Inc., 1972.

Willsberger, Johann. *The History of Photography: Cameras, Pictures, Photographers.* Leverkusen: Agfa-Gevaert Foto-Historama, 1977.

Wilson, Edward L. *Wilson's Photographics: A Series of Lessons . . . on All Processes Which Are Needful in the Art of Photography.* (1881). New York: Arno Press. Reprint edition, 1973.

REFERENCE WORKS

Beaton, Cecil and Gail Buckland. *The Magic Image: The Genius of Photography from 1839 to the Present Day.* Boston, Toronto: Little, Brown and Company, 1975.

The Encyclopedia of Photography. Willard D. Morgan, ed., 20 vols. New York: Greystone Press, 1963-64.

The Focal Encyclopedia of Photography, Desk Edition. London and New York: Focal Press, 1965.

Jones, Bernard E., ed. *Encyclopedia of Photography.* Reprint ed., Cassell's *Cyclopedia of Photography.* (1911). New York: Arno Press, 1973.

Life Library of Photography, 17 vols. New York: Time-Life Books, 1970-72.

Walsh, George, Colin Naylor, and Michael Held, eds. *Contemporary Photographers.* New York: St. Martin's Press, 1983.

Weinstein, Robert A., and Larry Booth. *Collection, Use, and Care of Historical Photographs.* Nashville, Tenn.: American Association for State and Local History, 1977.

Witkin, Lee D. and Barbara London. *The Photograph Collector's Guide.* Boston: New York Graphic Society, 1979.

Identification of Photographic Processes

With these charts it is possible to identify by process almost any monochrome photograph. A series of simple sequential decisions can be followed that will lead to the name and approximate time span of the process.

The first decision to be made is whether the image is indeed a photograph. Examination with a magnifying glass will show whether the image is continuous in its halftones (and thus photographic) or is broken up by a line, dot, or grain structure (the product of a printing process). Inspection of a few known printed images—newspapers, magazines, etc.—will clarify this.

The next decision is whether the photograph is a negative or a positive. In a negative the natural tones of light and shade are reversed: skies appear dark and shadows appear light. If a negative is in question, follow the chart headed Negative Image. For photographs in which the tones appear in their natural values, follow the chart headed Positive Image. Normally a positive is made by exposing a light-sensitive surface behind a negative, thus making a "print." An exception to this is a reversal process in which chemical treatment of an original exposure converts the image directly to a positive.

EXAMPLE: To demonstrate the use of the chart, suppose the image being considered is an ordinary black and white photograph taken on your last vacation. This is the series of decisions that will identify the process: 1. A positive. 2. On paper. 3. Coated paper. 4. Thick coating, high gloss, black and white: GELATIN PAPER PRINT, 1880 on.

This convenient method of recognizing photographic processes was comissioned by the Sub-Committee on the Conservation of Photographs, Technical Committee, Society of Archivists. The charts are the work of Brian Coe, Curator, Kodak Museum; Tom J. Collings, Senior Lecturer in Applied Science on Photographic Conservation, Camberwell School of Arts and Crafts; Arthur T. Gill of the Royal Photographic Society. The charts were first published by the Historical Group of the Royal Photographic Society in November, 1976.

There are several photographic pigment processes (see Glossary), produced by brushing oil pigment on a brichromated surface, that are not included in these charts.

(For Positive Image charts, see pages 646 and 647.)

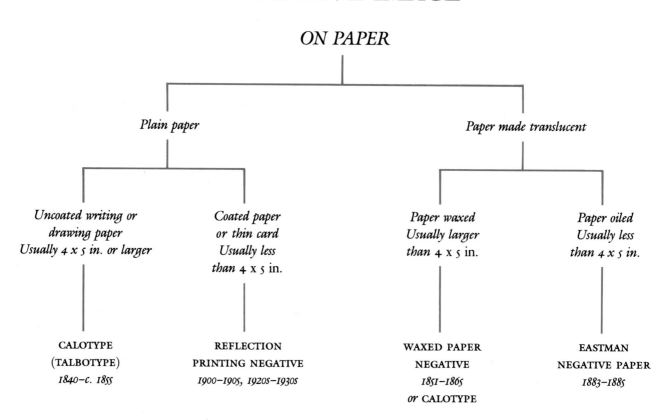

NEGATIVE IMAGE

ON PAPER

Plain paper

Uncoated writing or drawing paper
Usually 4 x 5 in. or larger

**CALOTYPE
(TALBOTYPE)**
1840–c. 1855

Coated paper
or thin card
Usually less
than 4 x 5 in.

**REFLECTION
PRINTING NEGATIVE**
1900–1905, 1920s–1930s

Paper made translucent

Paper waxed
Usually larger
than 4 x 5 in.

**WAXED PAPER
NEGATIVE**
1851–1865
or CALOTYPE

Paper oiled
Usually less
than 4 x 5 in.

**EASTMAN
NEGATIVE PAPER**
1883–1885

NEGATIVE IMAGE

ON TRANSPARENT MATERIAL

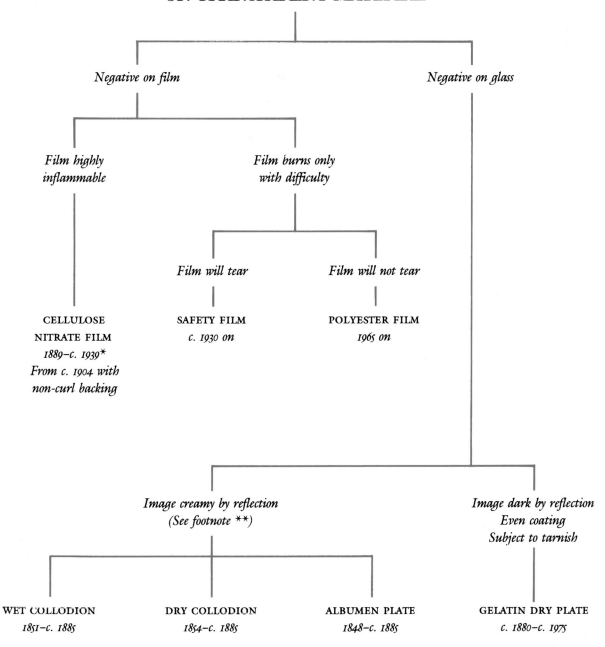

Negative on film

Negative on glass

Film highly inflammable

Film burns only with difficulty

Film will tear

Film will not tear

CELLULOSE NITRATE FILM
1889–c. 1939*
From c. 1904 with non-curl backing

SAFETY FILM
c. 1930 on

POLYESTER FILM
1965 on

Image creamy by reflection (See footnote **)

Image dark by reflection Even coating Subject to tarnish

WET COLLODION
1851–c. 1885

DRY COLLODION
1854–c. 1885

ALBUMEN PLATE
1848–c. 1885

GELATIN DRY PLATE
c. 1880–c. 1975

---

*Film negatives for Frena cameras have square notched edges, 1890–c. 1910. Autographic films—written information photographically on film, 1914-1934.

**Distinct differentiation between these processes is uncertain. Differences in formulation and treatment of the process could produce variations as wide as the different processes.

Wet collodion process is the most common. Coating was uneven, particularly at the edges; often one corner (where it had been held) is uncoated. Wet collodion dark-slides have silver wire across or near the corners; sometimes this shows on the plates. However, it would show as well on dry processes used in the same apparatus.

Dry collodion processes. There were very many variations, and they probably were coated with less haste than wet collodion, with a more even result. Albumen plates are probably darker and can be differentiated by testing edge scrapings of the coating in acetone. Albumen is less soluble than collodion.

Collodion-albumen process cannot be identified this way.

POSITIVE IMAGE

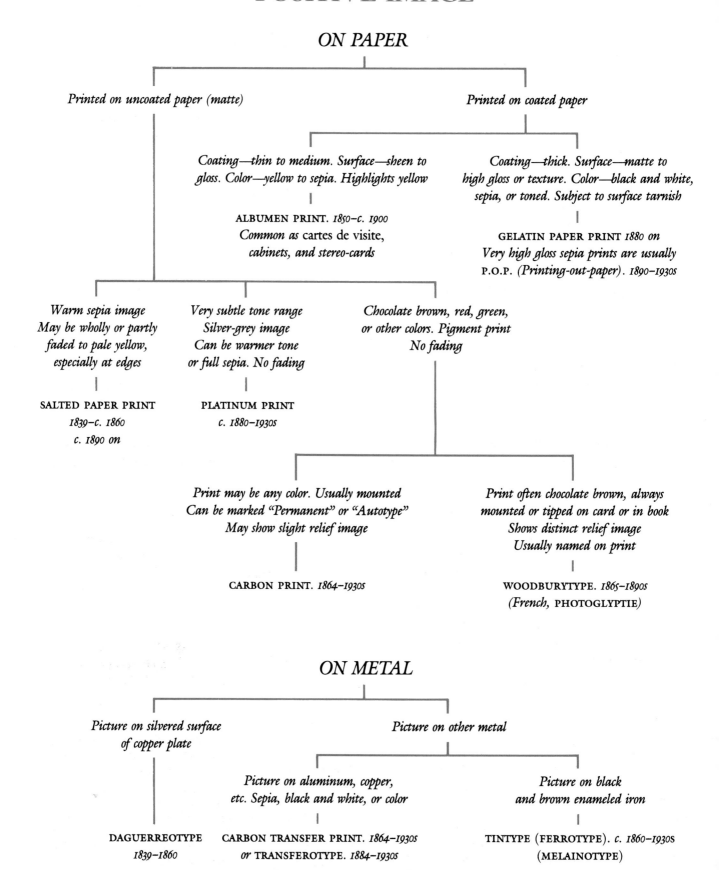

ON PAPER

Printed on uncoated paper (matte)

Printed on coated paper

Coating—thin to medium. Surface—sheen to gloss. Color—yellow to sepia. Highlights yellow

ALBUMEN PRINT. *1850–c. 1900*
Common as cartes de visite, *cabinets, and stereo-cards*

Coating—thick. Surface—matte to high gloss or texture. Color—black and white, sepia, or toned. Subject to surface tarnish

GELATIN PAPER PRINT *1880 on*
Very high gloss sepia prints are usually
P.O.P. *(Printing-out-paper). 1890–1930s*

*Warm sepia image
May be wholly or partly faded to pale yellow, especially at edges*

SALTED PAPER PRINT
1839–c. 1860
c. 1890 on

*Very subtle tone range
Silver-grey image
Can be warmer tone
or full sepia. No fading*

PLATINUM PRINT
c. 1880–1930s

*Chocolate brown, red, green, or other colors. Pigment print
No fading*

*Print may be any color. Usually mounted
Can be marked "Permanent" or "Autotype"
May show slight relief image*

CARBON PRINT. *1864–1930s*

*Print often chocolate brown, always mounted or tipped on card or in book
Shows distinct relief image
Usually named on print*

WOODBURYTYPE. *1865–1890s*
(French, PHOTOGLYPTIE*)*

ON METAL

Picture on silvered surface of copper plate

Picture on other metal

Picture on aluminum, copper, etc. Sepia, black and white, or color

Picture on black and brown enameled iron

DAGUERREOTYPE
1839–1860

CARBON TRANSFER PRINT. *1864–1930s*
or TRANSFEROTYPE. *1884–1930s*

TINTYPE (FERROTYPE). *c. 1860–1930s*
(MELAINOTYPE)

POSITIVE IMAGE

ON TRANSPARENT MATERIAL

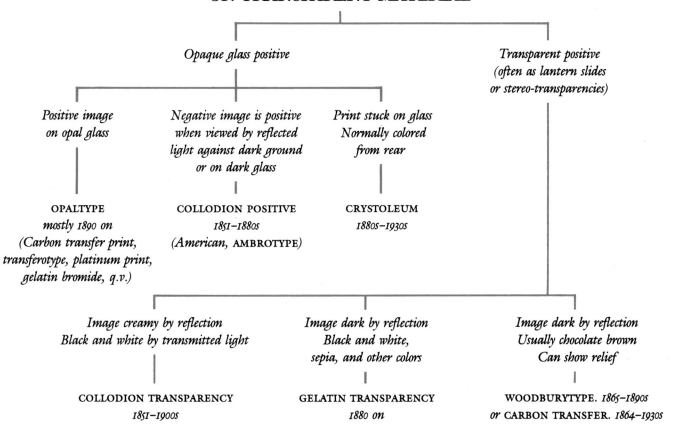

Opaque glass positive

Transparent positive
(often as lantern slides
or stereo-transparencies)

Positive image
on opal glass

Negative image is positive
when viewed by reflected
light against dark ground
or on dark glass

Print stuck on glass
Normally colored
from rear

OPALTYPE
mostly 1890 on
(Carbon transfer print,
transferotype, platinum print,
gelatin bromide, q.v.)

COLLODION POSITIVE
1851–1880s
(American, AMBROTYPE)

CRYSTOLEUM
1880s–1930s

Image creamy by reflection
Black and white by transmitted light

Image dark by reflection
Black and white,
sepia, and other colors

Image dark by reflection
Usually chocolate brown
Can show relief

COLLODION TRANSPARENCY
1851–1900s

GELATIN TRANSPARENCY
1880 on

WOODBURYTYPE. *1865–1890s*
or CARBON TRANSFER. *1864–1930s*

ON OTHER MATERIAL

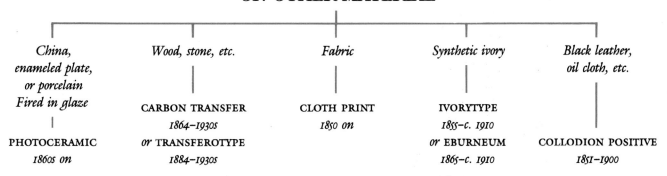

China,
enameled plate,
or porcelain
Fired in glaze

Wood, stone, etc.

Fabric

Synthetic ivory

Black leather,
oil cloth, etc.

PHOTOCERAMIC
1860s on

CARBON TRANSFER
1864–1930s
or TRANSFEROTYPE
1884–1930s

CLOTH PRINT
1850 on

IVORYTYPE
1855–c. 1910
or EBURNEUM
1865–c. 1910

COLLODION POSITIVE
1851–1900

NOTES

COLORS: Black and white includes all intermediate shades of grey— "halftones." Brownish-black is termed "warm"; bluish-black, "cold." Photographically, *sepia* is rather warmer (more reddish) than the artist's pigment. Chocolate brown is the color of plain chocolate.

Photographs may be toned chemically. The image appears in the range of tints of the color.

Paper may be colored. Early in this century, in pastel tints; now, metallic and fluorescent color papers are also available.

TEXTURE: Paper without surface shine is called "matte," with high reflection, "glossy." Intermediate terms are "luster" and "sheen." "Rayon," "linen," and "velvet" textures are self-explanatory.

FADING: Many photographic images are subject to fading due to the action of light, chemical reaction within the photographic substance or its support, or the adhesive, or between any of these and atmospheric pollution. The effect on the photograph may be partial or allover; the image tones are lightened and there may be a change of color, usually toward yellow, brown, or the color of the mount.

Index